D0818555

LAROUSSE

Dictionary of

TWENTIETH CENTURY HISTORY

LAROUSSE

Dictionary of TWENTIETH CENTURY HISTORY

Editor
Min Lee

LAROUSSE
Larousse plc
43–45 Annandale Street, Edinburgh EH7 4AZ
Larousse Kingfisher Chambers Inc.
95 Madison Avenue, New York, New York 10016

First published by Larousse plc 1994

10 9 8 7 6 5 4 3 2 1

Copyright © Larousse plc 1994

All rights reserved

British Library Cataloguing in Publication Data
for this book is available from the British Library

Library of Congress Cataloging in Publication Data
for this book is available from The Library of Congress

ISBN 0-7523-0003-2

Cover design: Paul Wilkinson, Larousse plc

Typeset from author-generated disks by BPC Digital Data Ltd
Printed in Great Britain by Clays Ltd, St Ives plc

Preface

This book provides a concise overview of the history of the 20th century. It is based on the work compiled by the extensive team of contributors and consultants for the *Dictionary of World History*, and has been updated and added to where appropriate. Like that work, it concentrates on the main diplomatic, military and political, rather than the cultural and social, landmarks. The selection of events and people has been made on the basis of the influence which they have exerted in the 20th century. Thus some people are included who lived most of their lives in the 19th century.

Reference to the information contained here will be swift and easy, because all articles follow a strict alphabetical order. Within an article, the highlighting of a word or phrase in bold type indicates that a full reference to it can be found elsewhere in the book. The presence of additional information on any topic is indicated by the symbol ▷ at the end of each entry.

The strength of a small book such as this lies both in the accuracy and relevance of each short entry, and in its careful and accurate cross referencing. For the first strength I thank the contributors, and for the second the two editors, Angela Cran and Alison Jones, who have endlessly searched the editorial database.

Min Lee
June 1994

Acknowledgements

Grateful acknowledgements are due to all contributors and consultants to *Dictionary of World History* and especially to Bruce Lenman the Consultant Editor and Katharine Boyd the Managing Editor of that title.

A

Abalkin, Leonid Ivanovich (1930–)
Soviet economist. He was for a time Director of the Institute of Economics of the USSR Academy of Sciences and a member of the Supreme Soviet of the USSR, with special responsibility for economic affairs. His published works centre on the theoretical problems of political economy under socialism. Under Mikhail **Gorbachev** he was one of the major advocates of rapid economic reform.

Abbas, Ferhat (1899–1955)
Algerian nationalist leader. He founded a Muslim Students' Association in 1924, before becoming a chemist. He served as a volunteer in the French army in 1939, but after France's defeat he produced in 1942 a 'Manifesto of the Algerian People'. In 1955 he joined the Front de Libération Nationale (**FLN**), the main Algerian resistance organization, and worked with **Ben Bella** in Cairo, before founding in 1958 a 'Provisional Government of the Algerian Republic' in Tunis. After independence in 1962, he was appointed President of the National Constituent Assembly but he fell out favour and was exiled. He was rehabilitated shortly before his death. ▷ **Algerian War of Independence**

'Abbas II (1874–1943)
Khedive of Egypt (1892/1914). He succeeded his father, Tewfik Pasha, and attempted to rule independently of British influence. At the outbreak of **World War I** in 1914 he sided with Turkey and was deposed when the British made Egypt a protectorate.

Abboud, Ibrahim (1900–83)
Sudanese soldier. Commander-in-Chief of the Sudanese army from the time of attainment of independence (1956), he was the leader of the military regime in the Sudan which obtained power when Abdullah Khalil surrendered the reins of government to the army in 1958. Abboud's regime was unable either politically or economically to maintain effective rule over the country, and was overthrown in 1964. Abboud himself resigned and retired into private life.

Abd al-Hadi, Awni (1889–1970)
Palestinian politician. He was involved in Arab nationalist activity directed against the Turks prior to **World War I**, and helped to organize

the 1st Arab Congress in Paris in 1913. A member of King Abdullah of Transjordan's staff after the so-called 'liberation' of Palestine in the latter years of the war, Abd al-Hadi subsequently became involved in the pan-Arab movement, was a member of the Arab Higher Committee in 1936 and was also behind the Arab 'Rebellion' of the same year. Exiled by the British from 1937 until 1941, he was subsequently involved in the formation of the Arab League in 1944. He was Jordanian Ambassador to Britain (1951–5) and, despite holding government posts in Jordan, spent the later years of his life in Egypt. ▷ **Alexandria Protocol**

Abd al-Krim, Muhammad (1882–1963)
Berber chief. Born at Ajdir, Morocco, he led revolts in 1921 and 1924 against Spain and France, but surrendered before their combined forces in 1926. He was exiled to the Island of Réunion, and later amnestied (1947). He then went to Egypt, where he formed the North African Liberation Committee. He died in Cairo.

Abdul Rahman, Tunka Putra (1903–90)
Malaysian politician. The son of the Sultan of Kedah, he trained as a lawyer and joined the Civil Service in Kedah in 1931, becoming a public prosecutor in 1949. In 1952 he was nominated to the Executive and Legislative Councils of the Federation of Malaya, becoming Chief Minister in 1955 and Prime Minister, on independence, in 1957. He negotiated the formation of the Federation of Malaysia, to embrace Sabah, Sarawak and Singapore (1961–2) and remained Prime Minister of that enlarged entity when it came into being in 1963. After the outbreak of violent Malay–Chinese riots in Kuala Lumpur (May 1969), he withdrew from active politics. In his later years, he became an outspoken newspaper columnist.

Abdullah, Sheikh Muhammad (1905–82)
Kashmiri politician. Known as the 'Lion of Kashmir', he was a leading figure in the struggle for India's independence and the fight for the rights of Kashmir. He participated actively in the Muslim struggle to overthrow the Hindu maharajah and substitute constitional government, for which he was imprisoned several times. He was the founder of the Kashmir Muslim (later, National) Conference, and then the Quit Kashmir movement in 1946, when he was again detained. A year later, he was released by the emergency administration and in 1948 he was appointed Prime Minister of Kashmir. However, for his championing of the cause of an independent Kashmir, and his subsequent treasonable refusal to pledge his loyalty to India, he was again imprisoned for most of the period 1953–68. He contested the 1972 elections at the head of his Plebiscite Front, but lost to the Congress Party. As Chief Minister of Jammu and Kashmir from 1975 until his death, he was instrumental in persuading

the Indian Prime Minister, Indira **Gandhi**, to grant Kashmir a degree of autonomy, making him a central figure in the fight for Kashmiri national rights.

Abdullah ibn Husayn (1882–1951)
King of Jordan (1946/51). Born in Mecca, he was the second son of **Husayn ibn 'Ali**, and the grandfather of King Husayn. He was made the ruler of the British-mandated territory of Transjordan in 1921, and became the first King of Jordan when the mandate ended in 1946. He was assassinated in Jerusalem.

Abernathy, Ralph (1926–90)
US civil rights leader. A Baptist minister, he became chief aide to Martin Luther **King**, Jr, and helped organize the boycott of buses by the black community in Montgomery in 1955. He assumed the presidency of the **SCLC** (Southern Christian Leadership Conference) after King was assassinated in 1968 and continued in that post until his resignation in 1977. ▷ **civil rights movement; Parks, Rosa Lee**

Abgrenzung
A German term meaning 'delimitation'. Following the success of Federal (West) Germany's **Ostpolitik** in the early 1970s, the East German authorities feared that increased personal contact between East and West Germans might undermine the GDR's legitimacy. They therefore stressed the differences between 'socialist' and 'capitalist' Germany, which were deemed more significant than a common German nationhood. ▷ **Germany, East; Germany, West**

Aboriginals
The native inhabitants of Australia, who reached the country some 40 000 years ago. By 1788, there were c.600 territorially defined groups, with a population of 300 000–1 million. Numbers fell dramatically thereafter, partly through conflict with Europeans, but mainly through epidemics of European diseases such as smallpox, and by 1933 the population was only c.66 000. Most Aboriginals were confined to government or mission reserves, which offered little protection against the demands for land from pastoral and, later, mining interests, or from the government's own policies such as closer settlement. Defying European theory, the Aboriginal population rose from the nadir of the 1930s to reach 145 000 in 1981. Aboriginal confidence also grew: a day of mourning was planned to mark the 150th anniversary of the European invasion in 1838 and Aboriginal stockmen went on strike for better wages, with the Arbitration Commission awarding them equal pay in 1965. In 1967 a referendum gave the federal government powers to legislate for Aboriginals, making aid available. Aboriginal Land Trusts, to which remaining reserves were

transferred, were set up in most states from the mid-1960s, but the European doctrine of erra nullius, reaffirmed by the courts, left the Aboriginals with little or no claim to the land in law. Aboriginal activism, however, kept the issue alive. The **Whitlam** government set up the Aboriginal Land Fund and the Aboriginal Land Rights (Northern Territory) Act (1976) to enable land transfers. In 1981, land for Aboriginal use amounted to some nine per cent of the total land area, but much of this was in the desert centre. Since then, the momentum has slowed, with growing opposition from commercial interests and economic difficulties reducing the scope for positive government action. Although Aboriginals have gradually been appointed in the Department of Aboriginal Affairs, they remain the most deprived section of the population.

Abu Nidal (Sabri Khalil al-Banna) (1937–)
Palestinian terrorist. Having joined Yasser **Arafat**'s Fatah guerrilla group in the late 1950s, he grew impatient with its relatively 'moderate' stance and established his own group, the 'Revolutionary Council of Fatah' (often simply called the 'Abu Nidal Group'), in 1973. Sentenced to death for his extremism by the 'mainstream' **PLO** the following year, Abu Nidal went on to head a group which gained notoriety for its brutal activities. The group has targeted Arabs viewed as traitors to the Palestinian cause, and its attacks have included the killing of 'moderate' PLO member Issam Sartawi in 1983 and that of the Israeli-appointed Mayor of Nablus in 1986. It also killed passengers at Rome and Vienna airports. Bowing to pressure from Arab states and the PLO, in 1988 Abu Nidal reportedly agreed to abide by the latter's ban on terrorism.

Abyssinia, Conquest of (1935)
The bellicose venture by **Mussolini** aimed at winning popular support at home, an increase in Italian prestige and strategic gains to pressurize the British in the Eastern Mediterranean. The invasion began in Oct 1935, against the advice of **Victor Emmanuel III** and most of his generals. Victory was achieved by General **Badoglio** in May 1936 and the King was declared Emperor. However, the campaign was not a success: Italy had to commit over 650 000 men to subduing an ill-equipped and badly organized army and won the profound enmity of the British government. Limited economic sanctions were also imposed by the **League of Nations**.
▷ **autarchia; De Bono, Emilio**

Acheampong, Ignatius Katu (1931–79)
Ghanaian soldier and politician. He taught in commercial colleges before joining the army in 1953. Trained in the UK and USA, he served with the **UN** in the Congo (Zaire) and, following the 1966 military overthrow of **Nkrumah**, was Chairman of the Western Region's administration for the National Liberation Council. Acting head of the 1st Brigade when

he led the coup overthrowing Kofi **Busia** (13 Jan 1972), he became Chairman of the National Redemption Council and then Chairman of the Supreme Military Council and head of state (1972–8), until he was deposed and later executed.

Acheson, Dean Gooderham (1893–1971)
US lawyer and politician. Educated at Yale and Harvard, he was Under-Secretary (1945–7) and then Secretary of State (1949–53) in the Truman administration. He developed US policy for the containment of **communism**, helped to formulate the **Marshall Plan** (1947–8) and participated in the establishment of **NATO** (1949).

Achille Lauro Hijacking (7–9 Oct 1985)
The Italian cruise liner hijacked, when sailing between Alexandria and Port Said, by four members of the Tunis-based faction of the Palestine Liberation Front (PLF), part of the **PLO** (Palestine Liberation Organization). The hijackers demanded the release of 50 Palestinians being held in Israel and threatened to kill the ship's 180 passengers if their demands were not met. However, after negotiations with Egyptian and Italian intermediaries and PLO officials, the terrorists surrendered. Despite the hijackers' claims that no-one had been harmed, after their surrender it transpired that a US Jewish passenger, Leon Klinghoffer, had been shot dead and thrown overboard. The hijackers and an alleged Syrian accomplice were tried on charges of illegal possession of arms and explosives in Genoa the following month; all were convicted and sentenced to between four and nine years' imprisonment.

Achimota College
A college founded in the Gold Coast by the Governor Sir Gordon Guggisberg in 1924 with the intention of developing an educated African elite capable of taking over a large proportion of the administrative tasks in the colony. By 1938 it was offering degree courses to a small number of students.

Acker, Achille Henry van (1898–1975)
Belgian politician. A socialist, he began his career in trade unions after **World War I** and was MP for his home town of Bruges (1927–74). He was appointed Cabinet Minister for Labour and Social Affairs in 1944, and thereafter became Prime Minister on four occasions. He is remembered for his role in the education debate, in the controversy leading to the King's abdication, and in social legislation. After 1958 he took less controversial political roles, first as a minister of state, and then as chairman of the House of Representatives until 1974. ▷ **Belgian Socialist Party**

Adams, Sir Grantley Herbert (1898–1971)
Barbadian politician. After studying classics at Oxford, he was called to the English Bar in 1924 and returned to the West Indies to practise. He was a prominent figure in Caribbean politics and became Premier of Barbados (1954–8) before being elected the first Prime Minister of the short-lived Federation of the **West Indies** (1958–62), which would have united seven former British colonies into a single state.

Adams, Gerry (Gerald) (1948–)
Northern Irish politician, born in Belfast. He became politically active at an early age, joining the Irish nationalist party, **Sinn Féin**, the political wing of the **IRA**. During the 1970s he was successively interned and then released because of his connections with the IRA, and in 1978 was elected vice-president of Sinn Féin and later president. In 1982 he was elected to the Northern Ireland Assembly and in the following year to the UK parliament as member for Belfast West, but has declined to take up his seat at Westminster. He has been frequently criticized for his association with the IRA, and the UK government protested when he was granted a visa to visit the USA in 1994.

Addams, Jane (1860–1935)
US social reformer. She founded the first US settlement house, Hull House in Chicago, dedicated to settlement work among the immigrant poor, where she made her home. Addams worked to secure social justice by sponsoring legislation relating to housing, factory inspection, female suffrage, and the cause of pacifism. She also campaigned for the abolition of child labour and the recognition of labour unions. Many of these reforms were adopted by the Progressive Party as part of its platform in 1912; Addams seconded Theodore **Roosevelt**'s nomination for President and was an active campaigner on his behalf. In 1931 she shared the Nobel Peace Prize, awarded in recognition of her efforts to end hostilities in **World War I**.

Adenauer, Konrad (1876–1967)
German politician. He studied at Freiburg, Munich, and Bonn, before practising law in Cologne, where he became Lord Mayor (1917). He was President of the Prussian State Council (1920–33). In 1933 the Nazis dismissed him from all his offices, and imprisoned him in 1934, and again in 1944. In 1945, under Allied occupation, he helped to found the Christian Democratic Union (**CDU**) and served briefly again as Lord Mayor of Cologne. As the first Chancellor of the Federal Republic of Germany (1949–63), he established closer links with the French, and aimed to rebuild West **Germany** on a basis of partnership with other West European nations through **NATO** and the **EEC**. Although relations

were restored with the USSR, relations with other countries in Eastern Europe remained frigid.

ADGB (*Allgemeiner Deutscher Gewerkschaftsbund*, 'General German Trade Union Federation')
The predominant, socialist-inclined German trade-union organization in the **Weimar Republic**. Founded in 1919, the ADGB strove to unite all employees in a single federation and to gain recognition from the employers as the legitimate representative of German labour. Initial successes were undermined by a vigorous employers' counter-offensive, but the ADGB remained a significant organization with a membership of around 4 to 5 million. On 2 May 1933 it was banned by the National Socialist government. ▷ **Nazi Party**

affirmative action
The name given to US policies requiring businesses and other institutions to enact employment practices concerning minorities ranging from the employment and promotion of ethnic minorities and women, to the setting of employment quotas. Such policies were established in the early 1970s to counteract discrimination in the past, but have been challenged in recent times as 'reverse discrimination'.

Afghan Wars (1838–42, 1878–80 and 1919)
A series of wars between Britain and Afghanistan, prompted by the British desire to extend control in the region to prevent the advance of Russian influence towards India. The treaties which followed the third Afghan War (1919) reinforced the country's independent political status.

Afghanistan
Republic in South Asia. Britain saw Afghanistan as a valuable bridge between India and the Middle East but failed to gain control during a series of Afghan Wars (the last in 1919). The feudal monarchy survived until after World War II, when the constitution became more liberal under several Soviet-influenced five-year economic plans. The king was deposed in 1973, and a republic was formed. A new constitution was adopted in 1977, but a coup in 1978 installed a new government under the communist leader, Nur Mohammad Taraki. A further coup in 1979, which brought to power Hafizullah Amin, led to invasion by Soviet forces. The troops effected their final withdrawal in 1989 but faction fighting continued.

AFL–CIO (American Federation of Labor and Congress of Industrial Organizations)
A federation of labour unions in the US, Canada, Mexico, Panama and US dependencies, formed in 1955 from the merger of the AFL (mainly

craft unions, founded in 1886) with the CIO (mainly industrial workers' unions, founded in 1935). Its aims include educational campaigns on behalf of the labour movement, the settlement of disputes among affiliates and political support for beneficial legislation. ▷ **Lewis, John L; United Automobile Workers**

Aflaq, Michel (1912–89)
Syrian politician. A schoolteacher and then journalist in Damascus, he was, with Salah al-Din **Bitar**, the founder of the Ba'ath Party. The ideology behind the party was essentially socialist, with an emphasis on Arab unity. It was also anti-Zionist and instrumental in the foundation with Gamal Abd al-**Nasser** of the **United Arab Republic** (1958–61). Ousted from Syria in 1966, his own political influence declined, but even today (hostile) Arab presses are inclined to refer to the Ba'ath Party as being Aflaqi.

African Development Bank
Established in 1963 in the same year as the **Organization of African Unity** and based in Abidjan, it began operations in 1966. Its funds come from both individual countries and multilateral sources and loans are made, on preferential rates, for development schemes.

African National Council
A Zimbabwean political organization founded in 1972 on the roots of the Zimbabwe African People's Union (**ZAPU**) to express to the Pierce Commission black opposition to a proposed constitutional arrangement agreed between Ian **Smith** and British Prime Minister Sir Alec Douglas-Home. Its leader was Bishop Abel **Muzorewa** who developed it into a political party. Its success in the late 1970s depended upon the continued banning of its forerunners and its strength rapidly reduced after independence in 1980. ▷ **Home of the Hirsel, Baron**

Afrifa, Akwasi A (1936–79)
Ghanaian soldier and politician. Educated at Adisadel College, he joined the colonial army in 1956, trained at Sandhurst and twice served with the **UN** in the Congo (Zaire). He was one of the group which overthrew **Nkrumah** in 1966 and became a member, later chairman, of the National Liberation Council. He handed power over to civilians in 1969, but, when the military intervened again in 1972, he was for a while detained. When civilian rule returned, he was tried and executed for corrupt practices.

Afrika Corps
German expeditionary force of two divisions under the command of **Rommel**, sent to North Africa (Mar 1941) to reinforce Italian troops there. It had been given special desert training in Germany, and proved

highly effective in desert warfare between 1941 and 1943. ▷ **North African Campaign; World War II**

Afrikaners

An early 18c term to describe those Europeans who had been born in the Dutch colony at the Cape and were therefore 'Africans', also known as **Boers** (in Dutch, 'farmers'). They emerged as a separate people derived from an admixture of Dutch, German, French, and non-White. During the 18c they penetrated the interior of the Cape as pastoral farmers. After 1835, groups left Cape Colony and established independent republics in the interior, which later coalesced into the Orange Free State and the South African Republic. After the Boer War (1899–1902) the British hoped to encourage emigration to South Africa, transforming the Afrikaners into a minority. Such large-scale emigration failed to materialize, and after the Union of South Africa in 1910 the Afrikaners became the dominant force in White South African politics. Never a monolithic force, they have produced repeated political fission in the search for security against the African majority. ▷ **apartheid; Boer Wars; Smuts, Jan**

Aga Khan

The title of the hereditary head of the Nizari Ismailian sect of Muslims, notably Aga Khan III (1877–1957), in full Aga Sultan Sir Mohammed Shah, born at Karachi, who succeeded to the title in 1885. He worked for the British cause in both World Wars, and in 1937 was president of the **League of Nations**. He owned several Derby winners. He died at Versoix, Switzerland, and was succeeded as 49th Imam by his grandson, Aga Khan IV (1936–), Karim, the son of Aly Khan. ▷ **World War I; World War II**

Agadir

A port on the Atlantic coast of Morocco which was visited in July 1911 by the German gunboat Panther, supposedly to protect German interests in Morocco threatened by the French, whom **Kiderlen-Wächter** had accused of acting contrary to the agreements reached at the 1906 Conference of **Algeciras**. It was the British government, however, who were the more alarmed by the presence of the Panther in a port relatively close to Gibraltar. They suspected the Germans of seeking to establish a naval presence in Agadir, thereby posing a threat to British trade routes. The 'Second Moroccan Crisis' came close to precipitating hostilities. These were, however, averted.

Aganbegyan, Abel Gazevich (1932–)

Soviet economist. Part-Armenian, part-Hungarian, he was born in Tbilisi in Georgia, studied economics in Moscow and made his name in the Institute of Industrial Production in Novosibirsk, eventually as Director

(1967–85). He met Mikhail **Gorbachev** through **Zaslavskaya** and was initially one of the main contributors to his reform programme. An early influence on Gorbachev's **perestroika**, although he transferred to Moscow, he fell into the background in the late 1980s.

Agitprop

An abbreviation for the Department of Agitation and Propaganda, established in 1920 as a section of the Central Committee Secretariat of the Soviet Communist Party. Its role was to ensure the compatibility of activities within society with Communist Party ideology. The term later came to be widely used in an artistic or literary context for works which adopted an ideological stance. ▷ **communism**

Agnew, Spiro Theodore (1918–)

US politician. The son of a Greek immigrant, after service in **World War II** he studied law at the University of Maryland. In 1966 he was elected Governor of Maryland on a liberal platform, supporting anti-discrimination and anti-poverty legislation, but by 1968, he had become considerably more conservative. As a compromise figure acceptable to many in the Republican party, he became Richard **Nixon**'s running mate in the 1968 election, and took office as Vice-President in 1969. He resigned in 1973 after charges of corruption during his years in Maryland politics were brought against him. ▷ **Republican Party**

Agrarian Reform Law (1950)

One of the first measures implemented by the Chinese People's Republic established in 1949. It aimed to complete the process, begun in the late 1940s in areas under communist control, to redistribute land amongst landless and poor peasants. In contrast to previous measures, however, agrarian reform in 1950 was to be relatively moderate, in line with the prevailing view that there was to be a gradual transition towards socialism and collectivization. Although the land and property of landlords (who made up about four per cent of the population and owned 30 per cent of the cultivated land) were to be confiscated and redistributed, dispossessed landlords could still be given a share. Moreover, land worked by rich peasants was protected and they could even rent land to tenant farmers, providing it did not exceed the amount of land they cultivated themselves. Nevertheless, agrarian reform, completed in 1952, produced a large class of individual peasant owner-cultivators. Socially and politically, the influence of the landlord class was eliminated; many landlords were subject to denunciation and even execution by communist-organized peasant associations.

Aguinaldo, Emilio (1870–1964)
Filipino revolutionary. He was a central figure in the rising against Spain (1896–8), and against the USA (1899–1901). After capture by the Americans in 1901, he took the oath of allegiance to the USA, the new colonial power.

Aguirre, José Antonio (1904–60)
Basque politician. Born into a middle-class, Carlist family, he became leader of the conservative Basque Nationalist Party (**PNV**), the main Basque party of the 1930s. He was elected as the first President (or Lendakari) of the Basque country (or Euzkadi) after the Republic passed the Autonomy Statute in Oct 1936. After the fall of Bilbao in June 1937, Aguirre took the government into exile in France. Following the outbreak of **World War II**, he was denied passage to England, and so undertook an extraordinary journey via Nazi Germany (complete with artificial moustache and glasses), Sweden, and Brazil to Uruguay. After the war, he headed the government in exile in France. ▷ **Basque Autonomy Statutes**

Aguiyi-Ironsi, Johnson (1925–66)
Nigerian soldier and politician. He joined the colonial army in 1942 and was trained in the UK before commanding the Nigerian contingent in the **UN** involvement in the Congo (Zaire). Appointed Commander-in-Chief in 1965, he assumed power following the officers' coup of Jan 1966, but was killed in the counter-coup, led by **Gowon** (July 1966).

Ahidjo, Ahmadou (1924–89)
Cameroonian politician. Educated at the Ecole Supérieure d'Administration, Yaounde, he was a radio operator in the post office before entering politics in 1947, being elected to the Territorial Assembly. He represented Cameroon in the Assembly of French Union 1953–7. From 1957 to 1960 he held senior positions in the Territorial Assembly of Cameroon. In 1960, when most of the British Cameroons was amalgamated with the French Cameroons, he became President and was re-elected to that post in 1972, 1975 and 1980. He resigned in 1982 and went into voluntary exile in France. His one-party state, although severe on the rival, but outlawed, *Union des Populations Camerounaises* (UPC), was relatively successful economically and less repressive than many West African states.

Ahmadzai Najibullah (1947–)
Afghan communist leader. A Pusthtun (Pathan), he was educated at Kabul University and trained as a doctor. He joined the Communist People's Democratic Party of Afghanistan (PDPA) in 1965, allying with its gradualist Parcham (banner) faction, and was twice imprisoned for anti-government political activities during the 1960s and 1970s. After the

Soviet invasion of Dec 1979 he was appointed head of KHAD, the State Information Service (secret police), and, inducted into the PDPA's Politburo (1981). In May 1986 he replaced Babrak Karmal as Party, and thus national, leader and was formally elected State President in Oct 1987. He sought to broaden support for the PDPA regime, encouraging non-communist politicians to join the government and promulgating a non-Marxist constitution which enshrined a multi-party system, mixed economy and dominant position for Islam. However, his hold over power became imperilled following the withdrawal of Soviet military forces in Feb 1989.

Akali Movement (and Akali Dal)
Primary Sikh political organization in Punjab. The original Akalis were 17c Sikh zealots who became censors for the community. During the Independence movement, the Akalis cooperated with Congress but tended to promote Sikh communal concerns. They were especially concerned with the control of Sikh shrines. Following Muslim agitation for the creation of Pakistan, the Akalis agitated for an independent Sikh state within the Punjab, but settled for a greater language-based autonomy in 1966. In recent years the Akali Dal has once again become active in the Sikh independence cause.

Akhromeyev, Sergei Fedorovich (1923–91)
Soviet commander in **World War II**. He joined the **Red Army** in 1940 and was in command of a tank battalion by 1945. He then rose steadily to be first Deputy-Chief of the General Staff by 1979 and Marshal by 1981. Opposed to escalating military expenditure, he was called in to replace **Ogarkov** as Chief of the General Staff in 1984 and aided Mikhail **Gorbachev** in his post-1985 arms control talks. He tried, but failed, to accommodate fully to the Gorbachev era, and resigned in 1988 in disgust at Gorbachev's unilateral troop cuts. He committed suicide in the aftermath of the attempted coup in 1991, in apparent dismay at the results of **perestroika**. ▷ **August Coup**

Akihito (1933–)
Emperor of Japan (1989/). The eldest son of Emperor **Hirohito**, he was born and educated in Tokyo, where he studied politics and economics. Invested as Crown Prince in 1952, he became the first Crown Prince to marry a commoner, Michiko Shoda, in 1959.

Alanbrooke (of Brookeborough), Alan Francis Brooke, 1st Viscount (1883–1963)
British field marshal and leading strategist of **World War II**. He joined the Royal Field Artillery in 1902, and fought in **World War I**. He commanded the 2nd Corps of the **British Expeditionary Force** in France

(1940), and later was Commander-in-Chief Home Forces. Chief of the Imperial General Staff 1941–6, he was Winston **Churchill**'s principal strategic adviser at the conferences with **Roosevelt** and **Stalin**. He was created baron (1945) and viscount (1946).

Alawi

An alternative name for Nusayri Shiites, who currently hold power in Syria. The Syrian leader Hafez al-**Asad** is an Alawi (Alawite). ▷ **Shiites**

Albania

Republic in the west part of the Balkan Peninsula. Albania's independence followed the end of Turkish rule in 1912, but Italian forces occupied the country from 1914 until 1920. It became a republic in 1925 and a monarchy in 1928, under King Zog I. Occupied by Germany and Italy in World War II, Albania became a new republic in 1946. It was involved in a dispute with the Soviet Union in 1961, and withdrew from the Warsaw Pact in 1968. The Socialist People's Republic was instituted in 1976 and the first free elections were held in 1991 as the country began to move towards democratic reform and westernization.

Albert I (1875–1934)

King of the Belgians (1909/34). The younger son of Philip, Count of Flanders, he succeeded his uncle, Leopold II. At the outbreak of **World War I** he refused a German demand for the free passage of their troops, and after a heroic resistance led the Belgian Army in retreat to Flanders. He commanded the Belgian and French Army in the final offensive on the Belgian coast in 1918, and re-entered Brussels in triumph on 22 Nov. After the war he took an active part in the industrial reconstruction of the country; the Albert Canal, linking Liège with Antwerp, is named after him. He was killed in a climbing accident in the Ardennes, and was succeeded by his son, **Leopold III**.

Alcalá Zamora, Niceto (1877–1949)

Spanish politician. A lawyer and landowner from Andalucia, he was Liberal Minister of Development in 1917 and Minister of War in 1922. In opposing the dictatorship of **Primo de Rivera**, he joined the Republican cause and, with the establishment of the Republic, headed both the provisional government and the Constituent Cortes's first administration. He resigned in Oct 1931 over the new constitution's anticlerical clauses, but accepted the presidency in Dec of the same year. A florid orator, he proved a highly conscientious if conservative and interventionist president, finally being removed in Apr 1936 after a decisive vote of the Cortes (238–5) against him. He died in exile in Buenos Aires.

Alessandri (Palma), Arturo (1868–1950)
Chilean politician. He became a member of the Chamber of Deputies (1897–1915), Senator (1915–18 and 1944–50) and Minister of the Interior (1918–20). Elected President on a reform platform in 1920, he was ousted, but was soon recalled by the armed forces (1924–5). In 1932–8 he served a second, more conservative, term.

Alexander (1893–1920)
King of Greece (1917/20). The second son of **Constantine I** and Queen Sophia, he became King in June 1917 after his father, under pressure from Eleuthérios **Venizélos** and the Allies to enter **World War I**, was obliged to abdicate. Greece then entered the war on the side of the Allies and Venizélos returned as Prime Minister. Alexander's death in Oct 1920, after being bitten by a pet monkey, precipitated a constitutional crisis which led to the election defeat of Venizélos and the triumphant return of his father as king.

Alexander I Karageorgević (1888–1934)
King of the Kingdom of Serbs, Croats and Slovenes (1921/9) and King of Yugoslavia (1929/34). The second son of **Peter I Karageorgević** of Serbia), he was Commander-in-Chief of the Serbian Army during **World War I** while acting as Prince-Regent of Serbia (1914/21). A Serbian nationalist, he aimed to create a centralized state governed from Belgrade and roused the resistance of other non-Serb national groups in the kingdom. In 1929, after the collapse of the constitutional system hastened by the murder of the Croatian leader Stjepan **Radić**, he imposed a royal dictatorship, dissolving the assembly, abolishing the political parties and imprisoning many of their leaders. Supported by the **Little Entente** and France, in 1934 he was assassinated while on a state visit to Marseilles by a Macedonian terrorist linked to the Italian-backed Croatian **Ustaša**. ▷ **Korošec, Anton; Maček, Vladko; Pavelić, Ante; Pribićević, Svetozar; Trumbić, Ante; VMRO**

Alexander (of Tunis), Harold Rupert Leofric George, 1st Earl (1891–1969)
British field marshal. In **World War I** he commanded a brigade on the Western Front, and in 1940 was the last officer out of Dunkirk. He served in Burma, and in 1942–3 was Commander-in-Chief, Middle East, his **North African Campaign** being one of the most complete victories in military history. Appointed field marshal on the capture of Rome in June 1944, he became Supreme Allied Commander, Mediterranean Theatre, for the rest of the war. He later became Governor-General of Canada (1946–52) and Minister of Defence (1952–4), and was created Viscount (1946) and Earl (1952). ▷ **World War II**

Alexandra Feodorovna (1872–1918)

Empress of Russia. A princess of Hesse-Darmstadt, and granddaughter of Queen Victoria, she became Empress upon her marriage to **Nicholas II** in 1894. Alexandra came under the influence of **Rasputin**, and meddled disastrously in politics, being eventually imprisoned and shot by Bolshevik revolutionaries, along with her husband and children, at Ekaterinburg. ▷ **Bolsheviks; February Revolution** (Russia)

Alexandria Protocol (1944)

This agreement was the outcome of a conference of Arab states convened in Alexandria by the Egyptian Prime Minister Mustafa al-**Nahhas**. His aim was to determine the form that future Arab unity should take. Al-Nahhas, backed on this issue by King Farouk, wished to obtain agreement to the formation of a 'League of Arab States' consisting of the sovereign states in the Arab world, and this was embodied in the Alexandria Protocol.

Alexei (Sergei Vladimirovich Simansky) (1877–1970)

Russian Orthodox ecclesiastic. He accommodated to the Soviet regime to save Orthodoxy. First elected to a bishopric in 1913, he was made Metropolitan of Leningrad in 1933 and, despite one spell of exile, he was able to survive to earn a reputation for his courage during the Siege of **Leningrad**. He was then elected Patriarch of Moscow and All Russia in 1944, in succession to Patriarch **Sergei**, and generally supported Soviet attitudes to the world at large in order to protect his Christian flock at home, in which he was certainly not unsuccessful.

Alfonsín (Foulkes), Raúl (1927–)

Argentine politician. Educated at military and law schools, he joined the Radical Union Party (UCR) in 1945. He later served in local government (1951–62), but was imprisoned by the **Perón** government for his political activities in 1953. During two brief periods of civilian rule, between 1963 and 1976, he was a member of the Chamber of Deputies, at other times practising as a lawyer. When constitutional government returned in 1983, he was elected President. He ensured that several leading military figures were brought to trial for human rights abuses and in 1986 was joint winner of the Council of Europe's human rights prize. His conduct of economic policy remained equivocal: an initial success, the Plao Austral, failed to dampen inflation, and he proved unable to open up the economy to international investment. The failure of economic policy under the UCR resulted in the election in 1989 of Carlos **Menem**, of the Peronist Party, as President.

Alfonso XIII (1886–1941)

King of Spain (1886/1931). A member of the Spanish House of Bourbon, he was the posthumous son of Alfonso XII. Until 1902, his mother, María Cristina of Austria, acted as regent on his behalf. At 16 he assumed his majority, thereafter frequently attempting to influence politics, and showing marked sympathy for the Spanish army. In 1923 he allowed General Miguel **Primo de Rivera** to destroy the parliamentary system and establish a dictatorship: the dictator's fall in 1930 left Alfonso discredited and, in 1931, after sweeping Republican gains in local elections, he left Spain, never to return. In 1941, shortly before his death in Rome, he 'abdicated' in favour of his third son, Don Juan.

Algeciras, Conference of (1906)

This conference was called to defuse the differences between France and Germany which derived from the **First Moroccan Crisis**. The conference resulted in the acceptance by Germany, outmanoeuvred diplomatically by the French and particularly by the British, of the Act of Algeciras. The Germans had hoped both to curb the growth of French influence in Morocco and to harm the developing cordiality in relations between France and Britain. They were, however, constrained under the Act to accept provisions whereby, with due respect to the authority of the Sultan of Morocco, France and Spain were authorized to 'police' Morocco under the supervision of a Swiss Inspector-General.

Algerian War of Independence (1954–62)

Growing resentment against French colonial rule in Algeria, fuelled by Arab nationalism (which had been gathering strength since **World War II**) and ignited by the **FLN** (*Front de Libération Nationale*), first expressed itself on the night of 1 Nov 1954, when Algerian nationalists attacked French military and civilian targets. By 1956, guerrilla warfare was widespread in rural areas; by the late 1950s, between 60 000 and 100 000 nationalists, with Tunisian support, were actively involved in the fight for independence. The 400 000–500 000-strong French army under General Jacques Massu, responded, but its harsh methods led to widespread criticism, and public opinion in France began to turn. In May 1958 there was a revolt in Algiers by French officers under Massu, who suspected that the **Mendès-France** government might enter negotiations with the FLN. This came close to triggering civil war in France, and brought about the fall of the government. This led to the inauguration of the Fifth Republic of General de **Gaulle** (1 June 1958) who, later that year, promised self-determination to Algeria. Despite subsequent attempts by right-wing French colonists, the army general, Raoul **Salan**, and the **OAS** (*Organisation Armée Secrète*), to prevent the attainment of Algerian independence, peace talks began at Evian-les-Bains in France (Mar 1962), and a cease-fire was agreed. Algeria was declared independent on 3 July

1962, with Ahmed **Ben Bella** as Premier of the new Algerian government.
▷ **Evian Agreements; Republic, Fifth** (France)

Algiers Agreement (1975)
This agreement, negotiated between the government of the Shah of Iran and Saddam **Hussein** of Iraq, granted a considerable area of border territory north of the Shatt al-Arab waterway to Iran, coupled with the recognition of the waterway itself as constituting the border between the two states (as opposed to the low-water mark on the Iranian side), in return for a cessation of military assistance by Iran to the Kurds in the north of Iraq. The abrogation of this agreement by Saddam Hussein may be regarded as effectively provoking the 1980–8 Iran–Iraq War.

Ali, (Chaudri) Muhammad (1905–80)
Pakistani politician. He was educated at Punjab University and, in 1947, on the partition of India, became the first Secretary-General of the Pakistani government. In 1951 he became Finance Minister, and in 1955 Prime Minister. He resigned a year later because of lack of support from members of his own party, the **Muslim League**.

Ali, Maulana Muhammad (1878–1931) and **Ali, Maulana Shaukat** (1873–1938)
Muslim Indian political activists and leaders of the **Khilafat Movement**. Muhammad 'Ali was closely associated with the states of Rampur and Baroda, and in the internal politics of Aligarh College prior to **World War I**. In 1911 he founded *Comrade*, an English-language weekly paper espousing pan-Islamic views. Shortly thereafter he moved the paper to the new seat of government, Delhi, and also bought an Urdu paper, *Hamdard*, which he used to set forth his political views. Shaukat Ali was also prominent in Aligarh College politics and in 1913 organized *Anjuman-i-Khuddam-i-Kaaba* to provide Indian support of Muslim causes in the Middle East. The continued activities of this movement after the outbreak of World War I resulted in the detention of both brothers between 1915 and 1919. On their release, they joined the Khilafat Conference, of which Muhammad soon became the leader. Because of M K **Gandhi**'s support of the Khilafat Movement, the brothers allied with the **Indian National Congress** and Muhammad convinced the Khilafat Conference to adopt M K Gandhi's **Satyagraha** strategy. As a result of a Khilafat Conference resolution calling upon Muslims to refuse to serve in the Indian army, the brothers were again arrested in 1921. In 1923, Muhammad Ali was elected President of the Congress. Mustafa Kemal's 1924 abolition of the Caliphate undermined the Khilafat movement, which continued on with dwindling support and influence. During the late 1920s both brothers broke with Congress over the issue of safeguards for Muslims in an autonomous India. Following this, they concentrated

on affairs solely concerning the Muslim community, although they remained highly influential national political leaders. ▷ **Atatürk, Kemal**

Ali Salim Rubay (1934–78)
Yemeni politician. He was the president of the People's Democratic Republic of Yemen during the period of left-wing socialist rule there and was overthrown and executed in 1978.

Alia, Ramiz (1925–)
Albanian communist leader. Born of poor Muslim peasants, during **World War II** he fought in the Army of National Liberation, attaining in 1945 the rank of Lieutenant Colonel and receiving a Yugoslav military decoration. In 1949 he became a member of the Central Committee of the Albanian Workers Party, was Minister for Education and Culture (1955–8) and member of the Agitation and Propaganda Department (1958). He was made an alternate member of the Politburo in 1966, becoming a full member and Secretary of the People's Assembly in 1982. As Chairman of the Presidium of the People's Assembly in 1982 he became nominal head of state. On the death of Enver **Hoxha** (1985), he took over as First Secretary of the Albanian Workers Party Central Committee, thus becoming the national leader.

Aliev, Geidar Alievich (1923–)
Azerbaijani secret police officer. He moved to politics and survived from Leonid **Brezhnev**'s to Mikhail **Gorbachev**'s time. His move to the Central Committee came in 1971 and to the Supreme Soviet in 1974. Yuri **Andropov** made him a full member of the **Politburo** in 1982 as someone from a non-Russian republic, and in this respect he was useful to Gorbachev, too. The latter, however, pushed him out in 1987 for his lack of enthusiasm for reform, and on account of allegations of corruption. ▷ **perestroika**

Aliyah
The name given to the Jewish migrations from Europe to Palestine, which started in 1882, and laid the foundations of the modern state of Israel. The ideals of the second Aliyah (1904–14) were redemption of the soil, and personal labour as a means of salvation. It pioneered the cooperative settlement which was to develop into the modern kibbutz. The third Aliyah was associated with a search for a National Home, while the fourth (1925) reflected Jewish persecution in Eastern Europe, mainly Poland. The fifth Aliyah (1932) represented flight from early Nazi Persecution. ▷ **Zionism**

All-India Muslim League ▷ **Muslim League**

Allenby, Edmund Henry Hynman, 1st Viscount (1861–1936)
British field marshal. As Commander of the 3rd Army during the Battle of Arras (1917), he came close to breaching the German line. He then took command of the Egyptian Expeditionary Force, and conducted a masterly campaign against the Turks in Palestine and Syria, capturing Jerusalem (1917), Damascus and Aleppo (1918), and securing an armistice. He was made a viscount in 1919. ▷ **World War I**

Allende (Gossens), Salvador (1908–73)
Chilean politician. A medical doctor who helped found the Chilean Socialist Party (1933), he was a member of the Chamber of Deputies (1937–9), Minister of Health (1939–41), and Senator (1945–70). Unsuccessfully standing for the presidency in 1952, 1958 and 1964, he was finally elected in 1970 as leader of the left-wing **Unidad Popular** ('Popular Unity') coalition, which promised a 'transition to socialism'. Undermined by US policy under Richard **Nixon** and Henry **Kissinger**, he was overthrown in 1973 by the army under General Augusto **Pinochet** and gunned down in the Casa Rosada, the presidential palace.

Alliance for Progress
A 10-year programme (1961–71) of modernization and reform for 22 countries in Latin America, sponsored by the US government in reaction to the advent of Fidel **Castro**'s Cuba and **Kubitschek (de Oliveira)**'s abortive 'Operation Pan American' initiative. However, it fell foul of the Kennedy administration's **Cold War** impulse and its partiality for orthodox economic policies, and few of its aims were achieved. ▷ **Kennedy, John F**

Alliance of Free Democrats (1989)
The most immediately successful of the new non-communist parties in Hungary after the **Democratic Forum**. Events in 1989 intensified public interest in reform and many new groupings emerged. The Alliance showed greater concern for marketization and, in coalition with the Democratic Forum following the 1990 elections, it moved policy in this direction. However, there was already a Federation of Young Democrats in position to press for more radical restructuring still.

Allied Intervention in Russia (1918–22)
The term refers to the intervention of foreign troops in Russian affairs following the Bolshevik **October Revolution** (1917). France, Britain, Japan and the USA were initially concerned to stiffen resistance to Germany by landing contingents in the north and the south of Russia and in eastern Siberia. Before these could become effective, **Lenin** had con-

cluded the separate Treaty of **Brest-Litovsk** (Mar 1918), and they got drawn instead into the **Russian Civil War** on the side of his opponents. This did nothing to help defeat Germany and soured Western-Soviet relations for years to come. Most of the troops had been withdrawn by 1920, but it was Oct 1922 before the Japanese left Vladivostok. ▷ **Bolsheviks**

Allon, Yigal (1918–)
Israeli military commander and politician. After Israeli independence in 1948, he attended university in Jerusalem and Oxford. Under the **British Mandate**, Allon was prominent in the **Haganah** and Palmach, involved both in the allied occupation of Syria and Lebanon and in military activities against the British administration in Palestine. Having played a vital role in the War of Independence, Allon turned to academia and politics during the 1950s and 1960s. He became Deputy Prime Minister in 1968, having helped to shape Israeli strategy in the **Six-Day War**, and became Foreign Minister in 1974. ▷ **Israel, State of**

Amal
A Lebanese Shiite movement established by the Imam Musa Sadr in the early 1970s. After Sadr's disappearance in 1978 during a trip to Libya, Nabih Berri assumed the leadership of the organization. Amal has a fighting force of over 4 000 men. ▷ **Shiites**

Amanullah Khan (1892–1960)
Amir and King of Afghanistan (1919/29). He established Afghan independence (1922) after a war with Britain. His push for internal reforms provoked opposition, and led to his abdication. He spent the rest of his life in exile, and died in Zurich, Switzerland.

Ambedkar, Bhimrao Ranji (1893–1956)
Indian politician. A champion of the depressed castes, he was born in a Ratnagiri village, Bombay. Educated in Bombay, New York and London, he became a London barrister, later a member of the Bombay Legislative Assembly and leader of 60 000 000 Untouchables. Appointed Minister of Law in 1947, he took a leading part in framing the Indian Constitution. With thousands of his followers, he publicly embraced the Buddhist faith not long before his death, in New Delhi. ▷ **India, Partition of**

Amendola, Giovanni (1882–1926)
Italian journalist, politician and philosopher. He was elected to parliament in 1919 and was made Under-Secretary for Finances in the **Nitti** government (1920) and Minister for Colonies under **Facta** (1922). He vehemently opposed the fascist seizure of power and led the **Aventine**

Secession. Attacked several times by fascist thugs, he fled to France after a particularly savage beating, dying shortly afterwards of his injuries. ▷ **fascism**

Amer, Abd al-Hakim (d.1967)
Egyptian politician. He was one of the nine officers who, meeting in the aftermath of the disastrous 1948 war, formed the original constituent committee of the **Free Officers** movement in 1949. In 1950 Gamal Abd al-**Nasser** was elected Chairman of this committee and, when he became Prime Minister in 1954, it was Amer (by this time a general) who took over the War Ministry. In 1967, following the **Six-Day War**, Amer (now field marshal), disillusioned by what he saw as Nasser's betrayal of the army, allegedly took part in a conspiracy against him. Arrested for his supposed part in this plot, Amer was arrested and subjected to a campaign of vilification by the press. He committed suicide while in custody.

America First Committee
Political organization (1940–41) in the USA opposing US involvement on behalf of the Allies in **World War II**. The committee attracted support from many conservatives fearing costly military commitment as well as pro-Nazi sympathizers, and the renowned aviator Charles **Lindbergh** was a chief spokesman. It campaigned unsuccessfully against the **Lend-Lease Agreement** and the repeal of the **Neutrality Acts**, but its propaganda was undoubtedly effective in the early years of the war. After the Japanese attack on **Pearl Harbor** (7 Dec 1941), however, the committee ended its activities, urging its members to support the war effort.

American Legion
In the USA, an association for former members of the armed forces (veterans) of **World War I** and **World War II**, the **Korean War** and the **Vietnam War**. It is the largest such organization in the world. Incorporated in 1919, its aims are to rehabilitate veterans, promote child welfare, ensure a strong national defence, and encourage patriotism.

Amin (Dada), Idi (c.1925–)
Ugandan soldier and President. He joined the King's African Rifles in 1946, fought with the British army in the Kenyan **Mau Mau** uprising and was heavyweight boxing champion of Uganda. He benefited from the rapid Africanization of the army after Uganda's independence in 1961 and was promoted to major-general in 1968. He seized power from President **Obote** in Jan 1971, dissolved parliament and was proclaimed President. During his presidency, there was widespread violence in Uganda, a mass expulsion of British Asians and the massacre of opponents, especially from the Langi and Acholi peoples. Deposed by exiled Ugandans with the help of the Tanzanian army in 1979, he fled to

Libya and thence he went to Saudi Arabia (1980–8). After a brief sojourn in Zaire, he returned to the Arab world.

Amnesty International

A British-based pressure group, founded in London in 1961, that campaigns for the release of any person detained for their political or religious beliefs or who has been unjustly imprisoned for any other reason.

Amritsar Massacre (13 Apr 1919)

On 10 Apr 1919 riots broke out in Amritsar in the Punjab in the course of an agitation for Indian self-rule. A gathering assembled three days later at Jallianwalla Bagh, a public park, on the festive occasion of Baisakhi. While they were being addressed, General Dyer, the local British commander, marched in. With barely a warning to the assembly and leaving no adequate means for the crowd to disperse, he ordered his troops to fire on the unarmed crowd, which included women and children, killing 379 Indians and wounding nearly 1 200. A government commission of inquiry severely censured Dyer and he had to resign his commission. Back in England, however, the House of Lords passed a motion approving of his actions and Dyer was widely acclaimed as 'the man who saved India' (the *Morning Post* launched a fund for him, raising £26 000 towards his retirement). The long-term effect of the massacre was the reverse of what Dyer had intended: many Indians were driven into supporting the **Indian National Congress**, and M K **Gandhi** himself became convinced of the impossibility of just rule under the British and the necessity for Indian independence.

anarchism

A generic term for political ideas and movements that reject the state and other forms of authority and coercion, in favour of a society based exclusively upon voluntary cooperation between individuals. To anarchists the state, whether democratic or not, is always seen as a means of supporting a ruling class or elite, and as an encumbrance to social relations. However, they differ in their view of the nature of their future society, their proposals ranging from a communist society based on mutual aid to one based on essentially self-interested voluntary exchange. They reject involvement in political institutions, and support civil disobedience action against the state, and on occasions political violence. Anarchist movements were most prevalent in Europe in the second half of the 19c and early 20c, but virtually died out apart from fringe groups after the **Spanish Civil War**.

Anastasia (Grand Duchess Anastasia Nikolaievna Romanova) (1901–19)

Daughter of Tsar **Nicholas II**. She is thought to have died when the Romanov family were executed by the **Bolsheviks** in Ekaterinburg (19

July 1918). Several women claimed to be Anastasia, notably Anna Anderson, from the Black Forest (d.1984). Conflicting opinions by members of the Romanov family and others failed to establish the truth, and her claim was finally rejected by a Hamburg court in May 1961. The mystery has been the theme of books, plays, and films and has not been resolved by further evidence produced following the collapse of the USSR. ▷ **Romanov Dynasty; Russian Revolution**

ANC (African National Congress)

The most important of the South African nationalist organizations opposed to white minority rule. It began life in 1912 as the South African Native National Congress and, under the influence of M K **Gandhi**, organized passive resistance to white power. Led by members of a growing black middle class, it steadily extended its support both into the urban black community and also into some liberal white quarters. Its central policy document, the **Freedom Charter**, was issued in 1956 and is social democratic, believing in non-racialism rather than the racial exclusivity of its rival **Pan-Africanist Congress**. When the party was declared an unlawful organization (Apr 1960), it began a campaign of industrial and economic sabotage through its military wing (**Umkhonto we Sizwe**), but essentially followed a two-track policy of direct action within South Africa and diplomacy abroad. It was generally recognized as the dominant voice of Black protest, by the **National Party** inside South Africa as well as the international community, and was unbanned in Feb 1990. It suspended its armed struggle in Aug 1990 and its leaders, notably Nelson **Mandela,** Walter **Sisulu** and Cyril **Ramaphosa** were involved in talks about a transition to a democratic South Africa; Nelson Mandela became president following the first all-race elections in 1994.

Anders, Wladyslaw (1892–1970)

Polish general. He was Commander-in-Chief of the Polish forces in the Middle East and Italy in **World War II**. After the war, deprived of his nationality by the Polish communist government (1946), he became Inspector-General of the Polish forces in exile, and a leading figure in the 140 000-strong Free Polish community in Britain. He died in London.

Andrada Family

Arguably one of the most impressive political dynasties of Latin America, founded by three brothers, José Bonifácio de Andrada e Silva, Antônio Carlos de Andrada e Silva and Martim Francisco Ribeiro de Andrada. All educated at Coimbra University, Portugal, they played major roles in the making of the Brazilian empire between 1815 and 1826. Their descendants often achieved powerful positions as councillors to Pedro II, and as senators or deputies, generally for São Paulo and Minas Gerais; they were often lawyers and drawn from families holding landed property in the most prosperous regions of those provinces. The more conservative, Minas, branch of the family played a leading role in support of Getúlio **Vargas**'s 1930 'revolution' as Governor of Minas and during his subsequent vice-presidency. José Bonifácio de Andrada e Silva served as President of the Chamber under the Costa e Silva government (1967–9).

Andreev, Andrei Andreevich (1895–)
Russian government minister and long-serving apparatchik. He joined the Communist Party in 1914 and was active in the Petrograd metal workers union in the period 1917–19. He was a member of the Central Committee by 1935 and a secretary by 1938. In 1946 he moved on to be Deputy Chairman of the Ministerial Council and, as such, had special responsibility for improving agriculture. Pressure did little to increase yields, though, and in the early 1950s Nikita **Khrushchev** took on the job and began enlarging collectives instead. However, this did very little good either, and agriculture became institutionalized as the major economic problem.

Andropov, Yuri (1914–84)
Soviet politician. The son of a railwayman, he became head of the **KGB** (1967–82), and in 1973 was made a member of the **Politburo**. On the death of Leonid **Brezhnev** (1982), he became General-Secretary of the Soviet Communist Party, consolidating his power (June 1983) with the presidency. He fell ill later that year, and died soon after, in Moscow. ▷ **communism; Hungarian Uprising**

Anglo-Egyptian Treaty (1936)
In 1922 the British government had issued a declaration which recognized Egypt as an 'independent sovereign state', but retained for Britain control of the Suez Canal, the right to keep troops in the Canal Zone and the condominium in the Sudan. The 1936 treaty gave more of the substance of independence to Egypt. British residents in Egypt lost their legal and financial privileges, the British occupation was formally ended and Egypt gained control of her armed forces for the first time since 1882. In wartime, the British had the right to reoccupy the country, a right they exercised in 1939.

Anglo-Iraqi Treaty (1930)
This treaty prepared the way for ending Britain's mandate in Iraq. The two countries formed a 25-year alliance in which they agreed to consult each other where they had common interests in foreign policy. Britain would retain the use of some air bases in Iraq and would train the Iraqi army. In 1932 Iraq became independent and joined the **League of Nations**.

Anglo-Irish Agreement (1985)
A joint agreement allowing the Irish Republic to contribute to policy in Northern Ireland for the first time since 1922, signed (15 Nov 1985) by the British and Irish Prime Ministers, Margaret **Thatcher** and Garrett **Fitzgerald**. It established an intergovernmental conference to discuss political, security, and legal matters affecting Northern Ireland; early meetings focused on border cooperation. Both governments pledged not to change the status of Northern Ireland without the consent of the majority. The agreement was opposed by the Irish Republic's opposition party, **Fianna Fáil**; in Northern Ireland, Unionist leaders withdrew cooperation with ministers and boycotted official bodies.

Anglo-Japanese Alliance (1902)
The first modern alliance between a Western and Asian power, which lasted until 1921. It reflected the anxiety both countries felt at increasing Russian encroachment in **Manchuria**. The alliance took account of each country's interests in China, as well as Japan's interests in Korea, and provided for joint action in the event that either of the signatories was involved in war with more than one power in East Asia. Each signatory would remain neutral if the other fought only one power. The alliance was renewed twice (1905 and 1911), extending its scope to the protection of Britain's interests in India and recognizing Japan's annexation of Korea in 1910. Although the alliance brought benefits to both countries, the irrelevance of Russia as a threat in East Asia after 1918 and persistent US hostility led to its replacement in 1921 at the Washington Conference by a much looser consultative Four-Power Pact (USA, Britain, France and Japan).

Anglo-Russian Entente (1907)
A crucial settling of differences between Russia and Britain which in the event almost amounted to an alliance. The Russian and British empires had been rivals in the Near, Middle and Far East for at least a century. However, they were gradually brought together by mutual distrust of an aggressive Germany and mutual interest in friendship with a worried France, with which Russia had had an alliance since 1894 and Britain an entente since 1904. Neither was prepared to sink their differences so far as to conclude a treaty. However, agreeing their respective spheres of influence, particularly in Persia, enabled them to operate as a diplomatic bloc that went to war in 1914.

Anglo-Tibetan Agreement (1904)
The agreement reached in Lhasa between Tibetan officials and a British expeditionary force (under Sir Francis Younghusband) fearful of potential Russian influence. Tibet recognized British overlordship of Sikkim and agreed to open relations with India. Trade marts were also to be

opened in Gyantse and Gartok (western Tibet), where British officials and troops could be stationed. This agreement was virtually repudiated by the British government when it signed a convention with China in 1906 reaffirming China's position in Tibet and promising not to interfere in Tibetan affairs, in return for China's guarantee to keep Tibet free from encroachment by a third power.

Angola, formerly (until 1992) **People's Republic of Angola**
Republic in south-west Africa. A Portuguese colony since the 15c, it became an Overseas Province of Portugal in 1951. In 1975 independence was followed by civil war with three internal factions: the Marxist MPLA (Popular Movement for the Liberation of Angola), the UNITA (the National Union for the Total Independence of Angola), and the FNLA (National Front for the Liberation of Angola). The USA supplied arms to the FNLA and UNITA in 1975–6. Cuban combat troops arrived from 1976 at the request of MPLA. South African forces occupied an area along the Angola–Namibia frontier in 1975–6, and were active again in support of UNITA in 1981–4. Angola gave refuge to the Namibian independence movement SWAPO (South West Africa Peoples' Organization), who launched attacks on Namibia from Angolan territory. At the end of 1988, the Geneva agreement linked arrangements for the independence of Namibia with the withdrawal of Cuban troops, the cessation of South African attacks, and support for UNITA. A peace agreement between UNITA and the government in 1991 was followed by multiparty elections but the first results were not accepted by UNITA and fighting resumed.

Angry Brigade
A left-wing group with anarchist sympathies, active in Britain in the 1960s and early 1970s, which took sporadic violent action against representatives of the establishment in the name of the working class. Its leaders were tried and imprisoned for a bomb attack on the home of Robert Carr, Secretary of State for Employment, in 1971. ▷ **anarchism**

Annam
A French protectorate, occupying the central part of Vietnam. The name was originally a T'ang Chinese term for Vietnam (literally, 'the pacified south'), but was then revived by the French. In 1887, Annam was brought together with the French colony of **Cochin-China** and the Cambodia and Tonkin protectorates to form the *Union Indochinoise*. Economic conditions in parts of Annam were notably harsh. This was an important element in the fierceness of the local opposition to French rule, as demonstrated in the uprisings in Nghe-An and Ha-Tinh at the beginning of the 1930s. The imperial capital of Vietnam, Hue, was situated in Annam.

Anschluss

The concept of union between **Austria** and Germany, expressly forbidden by the Treaties of **Versailles** and **St Germain** (1919), but with widespread support, especially in Austria, after the collapse of the Habsburg Empire. A proposed customs union (1931) was vetoed by France and Czechoslovakia. **Hitler** pursued the idea once in power, and in 1938, after the forced resignation of the Austrian Chancellor von **Schuschnigg**, the Germans occupied Austria. The union of Austria and Germany was formally proclaimed on 13 Mar 1938.

Antall, Jozsef (1932–93)

Hungarian historian and reforming politician. After working as an academic in Budapest, he came to politics in 1956 when he led one of the revolutionary committees. Active in the Smallholders Party, he was arrested in 1957 and banned from practising his profession until 1963. He did not enter politics again until the late 1980s, when he became President of the Democratic Forum in 1989. He entered parliament in 1990 and was chosen Prime Minister later the same year, with the difficult task of presiding over a coalition government.

Anti-Comintern Pact

An agreement between Germany and Japan, concluded in 1936, which outlined both countries' hostility to international **communism**. The pact was also signed by Italy in 1937. In addition to being specifically aimed against Soviet Russia, it also recognized Japanese rule in Manchuria. ▷ **Comintern**

Anti-Confucian Campaign (1973–4)

An ideological campaign launched by the Chinese Communist Party on the eve of its Tenth Congress (Aug 1973). It was apparently the inspiration of **Mao Zedong**'s radical supporters who used the campaign, ostensibly to condemn the persistence of traditional ideas, as a veiled attack on the policies of Premier **Zhou Enlai**. Just as Confucius and his followers attempted to restore feudal society and practices, so Zhou was seen as trying to roll back **Cultural Revolution** innovations (in such areas as education) and rehabilitate purged party officials. After the Congress, however, the campaign was specifically linked to a denunciation of **Lin Biao**, Mao's former deputy, who was identified with the excesses of the Cultural Revolution, suggesting that the campaign had been taken over by Zhou and his more moderate allies.

Anti-Party Plot (1957)

The name given by Nikita **Khrushchev** to the attempt made by senior opponents to oust him from his position as First Secretary of the Communist Party. Ever since **Stalin**'s death he had been strengthening his position and, in the process, introducing changes to existing policies. He had therefore incurred the hostility of hardliners and opponents of reform such as **Malenkov**, **Molotov**, **Kaganovich** and **Shepilov**, who succeeded in defeating his decentralization proposals at a meeting of the Party Presidium. However, Khrushchev managed with great skill to convene a meeting of the Central Committee, where he commanded a majority, and had the Presidium vote overturned and the plotters expelled. In a similar situation in 1964, he was unable to repeat his success since many of his reforms had proved useless.

Anti-Revolutionary Party (*Anti-Revolutionaire Partij*, ARP)
Dutch political party founded in 1878 by Abraham **Kuyper** on principles of Calvinist opposition to the Enlightenment and the **French Revolution** (hence 'anti-revolutionary'). Its programme was for limited social and political reform, together with a Calvinist approach to all things including politics: thus it was an early Christian–Democrat party. Since 1888 the ARP has regularly taken part in Dutch government coalitions, usually with the Catholics. Kuyper's successor, **Colijn**, led the country during the 1930s, and in 1973 the ARP joined the other Dutch confessional political parties in the **Christian Democratic Appeal**. As a result of this merger, the ARP ceased to exist in Sep 1980.

Anti-Spiritual Pollution Campaign (1983)
Ideological campaign promoted by the Chinese Communist Party and initially encouraged by **Deng Xiaoping**. At a time of economic reform, which aimed to dismantle state controls, and increasing contacts with the West, 'spiritual pollution' referred to pernicious Western influences in the realm of political thought and culture that were seen to encourage excessive individualism and hedonism. Intellectuals were criticized for their espousal of humanism and the notion that alienation could exist in a socialist society, while Western trends in dress and music were condemned as decadent.

Antonescu, Ion (1882–1946)
Romanian general and politician. He was military attaché in Rome and London and served as Minister of War from 1934 to 1938. Right-wing and nationalistic, while out of office he maintained links with the **Iron Guard**. In 1940 he established a dictatorship with the trappings of fascism, taking the title *conducător* (leader) and assuring **Hitler** of his support. In Jan 1941, to maintain the internal stability essential for German interests, he crushed an uprising of the Iron Guard with the Romanian army backed by German forces. He was executed as a war criminal. ▷ **Codreanu, Corneliu Zelea; Michael** of Romania

ANZAC (Australia and New Zealand Army Corps)
A unit in which troops from both countries fought during **World War I** in the Middle East and on the Western Front. Anzac Day (25 Apr) commemorates the Gallipoli landing in 1915; the fighting lasted until Jan 1916, during which time 7 600 were killed and 19 500 wounded. ▷ **Gallipoli Campaign**

Anzio Landing (22–3 Jan 1944)
Landing by 50 000 US and British troops during **World War II** at a small port 60 miles behind the German defences of the so-called Gustav Line. Although the Germans were taken by surprise, they were able to confine the Allied troops and prevent them from using Anzio as a bridgehead. In late May the forces at Anzio eventually made contact with the advancing troops of General Alexander who had overrun the Gustav Line.

ANZUS (1951)
An acronym for the treaty concluded between Australia, New Zealand, and the United States for mutual security in the Pacific against armed attack. The treaty encompasses not only the metropolitan territories of the three, but also island territories under their jurisdiction, their armed forces, and their aircraft and shipping. New Zealand participation lapsed in 1985, following that country's refusal to admit US nuclear-powered warships to its waters.

apartheid (Afrikaans 'apartness')
The policy of separate racial development in the Republic of South Africa, supported traditionally by the Nationalist Party, and more recently by other right-wing parties. The ideology has several roots: Boer concepts of racial, cultural, and religious separation arising out of their sense of national uniqueness; British liberal notions of indirect rule; the need to preserve African traditional life while promoting gradualism in their Christianization and westernization; and the concern for job protection, promoted by White workers to maintain their status in the face of a large and cheaper Black proletariat. Under the policy, different races were given different rights. In practice, the system was one of White supremacy, Blacks having no representation in the central state parliament. Many of the provisions of apartheid regarding labour, land segregation (reserves, Homelands, Bantustans), municipal segregation, social and educational separation, and a virtually exclusive White franchise, were in place before the Nationalist victory of 1948, but after that date it was erected into a complete political, social, and economic system, down to the provisions of 'petty apartheid' relating to transport, beaches, lavatories, park benches, etc. Its principal architect, Hendrik **Verwoerd**, was assassinated in 1966. The commitment of the de Klerk government to universal suffrage and the dismantling of apartheid culminated in all-

race elections in 1994, although the process of change was vehemently opposed by certain extremist whites and also by some blacks. ▷ **Afrikaners; Black Consciousness Movement; indirect rule; Sharpeville Massacre**

Apartheid Laws

A body of legislation in South Africa passed by the Nationalist government after its victory in 1948. Earlier laws such as the Natives Land Act of 1913 and the Natives (Urban Areas) Act of 1923 created a foundation for the more extreme form of separation promoted by the Nationalists. The laws included the Prohibition of Mixed Marriages Act and the Population Registration Act (both 1949), the Immorality Act and the Group Areas Act of 1950, the Prevention of Illegal Squatting Act (1951), the Bantu Authorities Act and the Bantu Education Act (1953). Most of these laws were repealed after F W **De Klerk** became President of South Africa in 1989 and announced the abandonment of the apartheid programme.

Apis ▷ **Dimitrijević, Dragutin**

APO (*Ausser parlamentarische Opposition*, 'Extra-parliamentary Opposition')

After the formation of an **SPD–CDU** coalition in Federal Germany in 1966, there was no effective opposition in the **Bundestag**. Radical, student-dominated, groups therefore took their opposition to the political system into the streets, declaring the Federal Republic to be a parliamentary dictatorship. The formation of an SPD–**FDP** coalition in 1969 (leaving the CDU/**CSU** as a credible opposition) defused much of the criticism, but the **Baader–Meinhof Group** had roots in the APO.

Apollo-Soyuz Project

A landmark joint space mission conducted by the USA and USSR in July 1975, following an agreement signed by President Richard **Nixon** and Premier Alexei **Kosygin** in May 1972. A project of the period of US–Soviet **détente**, Apollo-Soyuz also demonstrated the capability for joint operations between the major space powers and, as such, the potential for on-orbit emergency rescue missions. The rendezvous (17 July 1975) lasted nearly two days. The crews (T Stafford, V Brand, D Slayton and A Leonov, V Kubasov) conducted a series of joint experiments. A special adaptor docking module was constructed for the mission.

appeasement

A foreign policy based on conciliation of the grievances of rival states by negotiation and concession to avoid war. The term is most often applied to the unsuccessful British and French attempts before **World War II** to satisfy **Hitler**'s demands over German grievances arising out of the Treaty of **Versailles**. As a result, Hitler remilitarized the **Rhineland**, secured **Anschluss** with **Austria**, and gained the **Sudetenland** from Czechoslovakia. ▷ **Chamberlain, Neville**

April Theses
A programme of revolutionary action announced by **Lenin** in Apr 1917 shortly after the **February Revolution** and his return to Russia. In it he advocated the transformation of the Russian 'bourgeois-democratic' revolution into a 'proletarian-socialist' revolution under the slogan of 'All power to the Soviets'. ▷ **Bolsheviks; July Days; October Revolution; Russian Revolution**

Aquino, Benigno ('Ninoy') (1932–83)
Filipino politician. Born into a political family, he rose rapidly through provincial politics to become a senator at the age of 35. He was the principal opposition leader during the period of martial law, declared by President Ferdinand **Marcos** in 1972; it is generally accepted that if martial law had not been declared then, and the 1973 presidential election thereby abandoned, Aquino would have succeeded Marcos as President. However, Aquino was arrested and sentenced to death on charges of murder and subversion (Nov 1977). In 1980, suffering from a heart condition, he was allowed to leave for the USA for surgery (and exile). On his return to the Philippines (21 Aug 1983), he was assassinated at Manila airport; this, it was widely believed, on the orders of the established regime. His death unleashed mass demonstrations against the Marcos order, which were to lead, in Feb 1986, to the collapse of the Marcos presidency and the succession of Benigno's widow, Corazon **Aquino**.

Aquino, Corazón ('Cory') (1933–)
Filipino politician. In 1956 she married Benigno **Aquino**, and after his imprisonment in 1972 by President **Marcos** kept him in touch with the outside world. She lived in exile with Benigno in the USA until 1983, when he returned to the Philippines and was assassinated at Manila airport. She took up her husband's cause, and with widespread support claimed victory in the 1986 presidential elections, accusing President Marcos of ballot-rigging. The non-violent 'people's power' movement which followed brought the overthrow of Marcos and Aquino's installation as President. Her presidency was, however, much troubled by internal opposition; in 1989 the sixth, and most serious, attempted coup against her was resisted with assistance from the USA.

Arab Cooperation Council (ACC)
The ACC was founded by Egypt in 1989 in cooperation with Iraq, Jordan and Yemen when Saddam **Hussein** appeared to have been excluded from

the Gulf Cooperation Council (GCC). Its establishment had as its formal aim, economic cooperation between the member states, but the underlying objective was to establish a consultative assembly whereby the more extravagant policies of Iraq might be subjected to at least some form of control. The ACC ceased to function as an effective body when Saddam Hussein annexed Kuwait (Aug 1990).

Arab League

A League of Arab States, founded (Mar 1945) with the aim of encouraging Arab unity. The League's headquarters was established in Egypt, but moved to Tunis after the signing of Egypt's peace treaty with Israel in 1979. Today the Arab League has 22 member states including Palestine, which is represented by the **PLO** (Palestine Liberation Organization).

Arab Legion (1921)

Established in the state of Transjordan in 1921, initially as a police force, command of the force passed in 1939 to Major John Bagot Glubb (later known as Glubb Pasha), under whose training it developed into a military force of the highest discipline and quality. Making a considerable contribution to the **World War II** effort in the Middle East, the legion was also instrumental in the 1948 struggle with Israel in retaining East Jerusalem and the West Bank for the Arabs. This provided the basis of additional territory, which enabled King Abdullah to proclaim his Hashimite Kingdom of Jordan which consisted of the former Transjordan and the territories won by the legion. Glubb Pasha (now Colonel Sir John Glubb), resigned in 1956, at which time the legion became part of the regular Jordanian army.

Arab Revolt (1916)

The result of British negotiations with Sharif **Husayn ibn 'Ali** of Mecca, in part at least encouraged by the **Husayn–McMahon Correspondence**, the revolt was led by the Sharif's son, Faysal. Attached to the Arab forces during the revolt was T E **Lawrence** ('Lawrence of Arabia'). Amongst the achievements of the revolt was the destruction of the **Hijaz Railway** between Ma'an and Medina, and the capture of Aqaba. Essentially a revolt against Turkish occupation, the Arabs were also under the impression that a greater Arab nation had been promised them by the British. The revolt cleared the way for British troops under **Allenby** to advance northwards into Syria, where the capture of Damascus effectively brought Turkish hegemony to a close. Unsurprisingly, the Arabs felt aggrieved, if not betrayed, by the provisions of the subsequent **Balfour Declaration** (providing for a national home for the Jews in Palestine) and by the provisions for British and French 'spheres of influence', initially negotiated by Sykes and Picot and confirmed after **World War I** by the **League of Nations**. ▷ **Faysal I; Sykes–Picot Agreement**

Arab–Israeli Wars
Four wars (1948, 1956, 1967 and 1973) fought between Israel and the Arab states over the existence of the state of Israel and the rights of the Palestinians. The June 1967 war is known by supporters of Israel as the '**Six-Day War**' and by others as 'The June War.' The 1973 war is called the '**Yom Kippur War**' by Israelis, the 'Ramadan War' by Arabs, and the '**October War**' by others. ▷ **Zionism**

Arafat, Yasser or **Yasir,** originally **Mohammed Abed Ar'ouf Arafat** (1929–)
Palestinian resistance leader, born in Cairo of Palestinian parents. He co-founded the Fatah resistance group in 1956, which gained control of the Palestinian Liberation Organization (**PLO**) in 1964. Acknowledged as the PLO leader, he gradually gained world acceptance for the organization. In 1983, however, his policies lost majority PLO support, and he was forced to leave Lebanon with his remaining followers. He then based himself at the PLO headquarters in Tunis. The *Intifada* (uprising) in the **West Bank** in 1988 paved the way for his dramatic recognition of Israel and renunciation of terrorism in Dec 1988. In 1993 he and the Prime Minister of Israel, Yitzhak **Rabin**, negotiated a peace agreement at the White House (signed in Cairo in 1994), by which Israel agreed to withdraw from Jericho and the **Gaza Strip**.

Arbatov, Georgi Arkadevich (1923–)
Soviet journalist, academic, party official and adviser to Mikhail **Gorbachev**. A Russian born in the Ukraine, he graduated in international relations, was a contributor to serious periodicals and got his first academic posting in 1962. His first Communist Party appointment came in 1964 and his major breakthrough was in 1967, becoming Director of the Institute for American Studies. This made him chief Soviet interpreter of US policies, a role that acquired a new importance with Gorbachev's rise to power. He clearly influenced the Gorbachev–**Reagan** link that ended the **Cold War**. In the late 1980s, however, the need for his talents declined.

Aref, Abd al-Salam (1921–66)
Iraqi politician. He took over as Ba'ath socialist President of Iraq from Abd al-Krim **Qassim** in 1963. Amongst his achievements were improved relations with Gamal Abd al-**Nasser**'s Egypt and the nationalization of the oil industry. Under Ba'athist ideological influences, he moved further towards the establishment of Iraq as a secular state, but his rule ended suddenly with his death in a helicopter crash. He was succeeded by his brother, Abd al-Rahman Aref, until he was toppled in the Ba'ath coup of July 1968 and replaced as President by Hasan al-**Bakr**, who ruled in concert with the Ba'ath leader, Saddam **Hussein**.

Arens, Moshe (1925–)
Israeli politician, born in Lithuania. Educated at Massachusetts and California Institutes of Technology, he lectured in aeronautical engineering at the Israel Institute of Technology, Haifa, and was Deputy Director of Israel Aircraft Industries before entering the Knesset in 1973. He served as Ambassador to the USA (1982–3), and was then a Minister without portfolio until 1987, when he was appointed Foreign Minister.
▷ **Likud**

Arias Navarro, Carlos (1908–)
Spanish politician. Notorious as the 'Butcher of Malaga' for being state prosecutor there during the Nationalists' savage repression during the **Spanish Civil War**, between 1957 and 1965 he was the Director-General of Security and from 1965 to 1973 the Mayor of Madrid. Named Minister of the Interior (June 1973), he became Prime Minister after the assassination of **Carrero Blanco** in Dec 1973. Following **Franco**'s death, he was confirmed as the first Prime Minister of the monarchy. He resigned in July 1976, having proven too hardline to effect the transition to democracy.

Arias Sanchez, Oscar (1940–)
Costa Rican politician. He was educated in the UK, then returned to Costa Rica, where he started a law practice. He entered politics, joining the left-wing National Liberation Party (PLN) and eventually becoming its Secretary-General. Elected President of Costa Rica in 1986, on a neutralist platform, Arias Sanchez was the major author of a Central American Peace Agreement aimed at securing peace in the region, and particularly in Nicaragua.

Armenia, Independence of (1991)
One of the 14 non-Russian Republics that gained their independence with the disintegration of the USSR. The Armenians had a history going back to the Roman period and including years of relative independence. Those who were not retained under Turkish control were taken over by the Russians in 1828. Christians, galvanized by earlier Turkish massacres and encouraged by **Lenin**, they declared their independence in 1918; however, they lost it again on his orders in 1920 for allegedly consorting with Soviet enemies. In 1991 they emerged not only with a distaste for Russia, but in an armed dispute with **Azerbaijan** over the Armenian enclave trapped across the border in the autonomous region that **Stalin** had set up in Nagorno-Karabakh.

Armenian Massacres (19–20c)
These killings resulted from the persecution of Armenians in the **Ottoman Empire** by Sultan **Abd ul-Hamid II** in 1894–6 and by the Young Turk government in 1915. By the late 1880s there were, in the Ottoman Empire,

two and a half million Armenians who, encouraged by Russia, sought autonomy. When they refused to pay vastly increased taxes in 1894, Turkish troops killed thousands and burnt their villages. Two years later, Armenians seized the Ottoman Bank in Istanbul to draw European attention to their plight: this sparked off riots in which over 50 000 Armenians were killed. In **World War I** the secret recruitment of Turkish Armenians to fight on the side of Russia led the Turkish government to deport the Armenian population to Syria and Palestine, during which a million died of starvation or were killed.

Army, (British) Indian (1748–1947)

British-controlled and officered military force in India in which the rank and file were recruited from the native populace, although some purely European regiments existed until 1860. The main functions of the Army between 1858 and 1914 were guarding the North-West Frontier and maintenance of order, although it was designed to be used in emergencies between Suez and Hong Kong. In 1895, the armies of the three Presidencies were amalgamated into one British Indian Army. In 1903 Lord Kitchener administratively combined the Staff and Troops, and renamed the force the Indian Army. Because of their performance during **World War I** and the changing political climate, Indians became eligible for the King's Commission in 1917. In 1922 the army was again reorganized and 'Indianization' of the officer corps was accelerated. By 1924 there were 8 wholly Indian units and in 1934 an Indian Military Academy for the training of officers was opened at Dehra Dun. In **World War II** units of the Indian Army were employed throughout the world in the Allied cause, although the bulk of the force fought in Burma and remained in India to maintain order. With Indian independence in 1947, the British Indian Army ceased to exist, its resources having been divided equally between India and Pakistan.

Arnhem, Battle of (Sep 1944)

Major confict in occupied Dutch territory towards the end of **World War II**, in which the German forces thwarted Allied attempts to break through. Operation 'Market Garden' was designed by Field Marshal **Montgomery**, and involved the largest airlift operation of the war, parachuting 10 000 troops on 17 Sep 1944 into the Dutch rivers area, to take key bridges over the Rhine, Maas and Waal. Allied forces advanced to Nijmegen, but at Arnhem met the 9th and 10th German Panzer divisions, which successfully resisted attack and eventually forced an Allied withdrawal on 25 Sep to behind the Rhine River.

Arrow Cross (1938–45)

Hungarian right-wing fascist-type party. Like similar parties in other East European countries, it emerged from a combination of nationalist dissatisfaction, anti-**communism** and anti-Semitism that was rooted in the failure of successive Hungarian governments to reverse the defeat marked by the Treaty of **Trianon** in 1920 or to overcome the 1929 depression. These feelings were strengthened by the successes of **Mussolini** and **Hitler**, and leaders were found in malcontents such as **Szalasi**, a former officer who became Prime Minister in 1944.

Artyukhina, Alexandra Vasilevna (1889–1969)
Soviet politician. An early champion of Soviet women's rights, she failed in the face of traditional male chauvinism. A textile worker, she was active in the union movement in the pre-revolutionary period and was arrested several times. She held various government jobs after the **Russian Revolution**, but in 1927 she was appointed head of *zhenotdel*, the women's section of the **Communist Party of the Soviet Union**. In this she did much good work until it was shut down in 1930. Thereafter, her jobs were more honorific than real, but at least she survived **Stalin**.

Arusha Declaration (29 Jan 1967)
Although strictly only Part IV, the Arusha Declaration usually refers to all of an important document, written under President Julius **Nyerere**'s direction and accepted by **TANU**'s National Executive Committee in Arusha on 29 Jan 1967. It set out the assumptions underlying Tanzania's version of African Socialism, emphasizing the dignity and equality of people, the primacy of rural production, self-reliance, the importance of hard work and the role of the party. Later documents ('Education for Self-Reliance', 'Socialism and Rural Development' and 'After the Arusha Declaration') developed Nyerere's ideas of creating a uniquely African and egalitarian socialism in Africa, but it proved economically disastrous although, for the most part, politically popular.

Asad, Hafez al- (1928–)
Syrian general and politician. He was Minister of Defence and Commander of the Air Force (1966–70), instigated a coup in 1970 and became Prime Minister and then President (1971–). He belongs to the minority **Alawi** sect of Islam. After the 1973 Arab–Israeli War, he negotiated a partial withdrawal of Israeli troops from Syria. In 1976 he sent Syrian troops into Lebanon, and did so again in early 1987. By 1989 he had imposed Syrian control over the greater part of Lebanon. He has long enjoyed Soviet support, and was one of the few Arab leaders to support Iran in its war with Iraq. He also supports the Palestinian radicals against **Arafat**'s mainstream **PLO** (Palestine Liberation Organization). ▷ **Iran–Iraq War**

Asanuma Inejiro (1898–1960)
Japanese politician. Initially he was a member of the **Japanese Communist Party** and in 1924 was imprisoned for participating in anti-government demonstrations. In 1936 he was elected to the Diet as a member of the Social Masses Party (Shakai Taishuto), one of many pre-**World War II** socialist parties. After 1945 he helped found the **Japan Socialist Party**, becoming its Secretary-General. He acquired notoriety in 1959 on a visit to Beijing when he declared that US imperialism was the common enemy of China and Japan. In 1960 he was assassinated by a right-wing fanatic while attending a televised political rally.

Ashanti (Asante)
A Kwa-speaking Akan people of southern Ghana and adjacent areas of Togo and Ivory Coast. They form a confederacy of chiefdoms, founded by the ruler Osei Tutu in the late 17c; the paramount chief was established at Kumasi, and the Golden Stool was the symbol of Ashanti unity. The independent Ashanti state was at the height of its powers in the early 19c, and became a major threat to British trade on the coast, until defeated (1873) by a force under Sir Garnet **Wolseley**. The state was annexed by the British in 1902 after a further campaign in which the Golden Stool was seized and removed to London. Traditional culture and religion still flourish, with rich ceremonial and internationally famous art.

Ashdown, Jeremy John Durham (Paddy) (1941–)
British politician. After a career in the Royal Marines (1959–71) and the diplomatic service (1971–6) he entered politics, becoming Liberal MP for Yeovil (1983). He was Liberal spokesman on trade and industry (1983–6) and succeeded David **Steel** as leader of the Social and Liberal Democrats (1988). ▷ **Liberal Party** (UK)

Ashida Hitoshi (1887–1959)
Japanese politician. Formerly a Finance Ministry bureaucrat, he was first elected to the Diet in 1932. In the first post-**World War II** cabinet (Oct 1945) he was Minister of Health and Welfare. In 1947 he helped to organize the Democratic Party (Nihon Minshuto), one of the two principal conservative parties at the time. In June 1947 he joined a coalition cabinet headed by the socialist **Katayama** Tetsu and became Prime Minister when the coalition collapsed (Mar 1948). Ashida was a vigorous advocate of Japanese rearmament. In Oct 1948 he was forced to resign following alleged involvement in the Showa Denko Scandal.

Asquith, H(erbert) H(enry), 1st Earl of Oxford and Asquith (1852–1928)
British Liberal politician and Prime Minister. He was called to the Bar (1876), and became a QC (1890) and MP (1886), Home Secretary

(1892–5), Chancellor of the Exchequer (1905–8), and Premier (1908–16). His regime was notable for the upholding of free trade, the introduction of old-age pensions, payment for MPs, the Parliament Act of 1911, Welsh disestablishment, suffragette troubles, the declaration of war (1914), the coalition ministry (1915), and the **Sinn Féin** rebellion (1916). His replacement as Premier by Lloyd George provoked lasting bitterness; in 1918 he led the Independent Liberals who rejected Lloyd George's continuing coalition with the Conservatives. He was created an earl in 1925. ▷ **Liberal Party** (UK); **suffragettes**

Assize Court

A legal system in England and Wales, dating from the time of Henry II of England, which was abolished by the Courts Act, 1971. Assize courts were presided over by High Court judges, who travelled on circuit to hear criminal and civil cases. The functions of Assize courts continue to be exercised by High Court judges sitting in Crown Courts throughout England and Wales.

Association of South-East Asian Nations (ASEAN)

An association formed in 1967 to promote economic cooperation between Indonesia, Malaysia, the Philippines, Singapore, and Thailand; Brunei joined in 1984. It has become an important political force, particularly with respect to the Vietnamese incursion into Cambodia in 1978.

Astor, Nancy Witcher Langhorne, Viscountess (1879–1964)

British politician. The first woman MP to sit in the House of Commons (1919–45), she succeeded her husband as MP for Plymouth in 1919, and became known for her interest in women's rights and social problems, especially temperance.

Astrid (1905–35)

Queen of the Belgians (1934/5). The daughter of Prince Charles of Sweden and Princess Ingeborg of Denmark, on 4 Nov 1926 she married **Leopold III**, Crown Prince of Belgium, who succeeded to the throne on 23 Feb 1934, with Astrid as Queen. The mother of three children, Josephine-Charlotte, **Baudouin I** (later king), and Albert, she was killed in a car accident near Küssnacht in Switzerland.

Asturias, Principality of

A former principality of northern Spain, co-extensive with the modern province of Oviedo. It was the centre of Christian resistance to Muslim invasion during the 8–9c and became part of the Kingdom of Leon in 911. In the 20c it was the scene of an unsuccessful left-wing revolution in 1934.

Atatürk, Kemal (Mustafa Kemal) (1881–1938)
Turkish army officer and politician. During **World War I** he fought against the British in the Dardanelles and earned the title pasha. He drove the Greeks from Anatolia (1919–22), raising a nationalist rebellion in protest against the post-war division of Turkey. In 1921 he established a provisional government in Ankara. The following year the Ottoman Sultanate was formally abolished, and Turkey was declared a secular republic, with Kemal as President (1923–38). The focus of a strong personality cult, he launched a programme of revolutionary social and political reform intended to transform Turkey from a feudal absolute monarchy into a modern republic. His reforms included the political emancipation of women (1934) and the introduction of the Latin alphabet to replace Arabic script, as well as increased educational opportunities and the suppression of traditional Islamic loyalties in favour of a secular Turkish nationalism. In 1934, upon the introduction of surnames into Turkey, he took the name Atatürk ('Father of the Turks'). ▷ **Graeco-Turkish War; Lausanne, Treaty of**

Atlantic, Battle of the (1940–3)
The conflict arising out of German attacks on shipping in the Atlantic during **World War II**. The German strategy was to cut off Britain's supplies of food and munitions by submarine action. Only at the end of 1943 were the attacks countered, and the threat brought under control.

Atlantic Charter (Aug 1941)
A declaration of principles to govern the national policies issued by US President Franklin D **Roosevelt** and British Prime Minister Winston **Churchill** after a secret meeting off the Newfoundland coast. Echoing Woodrow **Wilson**'s **Fourteen Points**, and the **Four Freedoms** of Roosevelt's Jan 1941 State of the Union Address, the charter called for the rights of self-determination, self-government and free speech for all peoples, promised a more equitable international economic system, and called for the abandonment of the use of force, pending the establishment of a system of general security. After the entry of the USA into the war, the charter was endorsed internationally by the inclusion of its provisions in the Declaration of the United Nations signed by the USA, Great Britain, the USSR and China, on 1 Jan 1942, and by 22 other states on the following day. It served as an ideological basis for Allied cooperation during the war. ▷ **World War II**

Attlee (of Walthamstow), Clement (Richard), 1st Earl (1883–1967)
British politician. Early converted to **socialism**, he became the first Labour Mayor of Stepney (1919–20), an MP (1922), Deputy Leader of the Opposition (1931–5), and then Leader (1935). He was Dominions Secretary (1942–3) and Deputy Prime Minister (1942–5) in Winston

Churchill's war cabinet. As Prime Minister (1945–51), he carried through a vigorous programme of nationalization and social welfare, including the introduction of the National Health Service (1948). His government granted independence to India (1947) and Burma (1948). He was Leader of the Opposition again (1951–5) until he resigned and accepted an earldom.

Auchinleck, Sir Claude (John Eyre) (1884–1981)
British field marshal. He joined the 62nd Punjabis in 1904, and served in Egypt and Mesopotamia. In **World War II**, he commanded in northern Norway and India, and then moved to the Middle East (1941). He made a successful advance into Cyrenaica, but was later thrown back by **Rommel**. His regrouping of the 8th Army on **El Alamein** is now recognized as a successful defensive operation, but at the time he was made a scapegoat for the retreat, and replaced (1942). In 1943 he returned to India, serving subsequently as Supreme Commander India and Pakistan (1947). ▷ **North African Campaign**

August Coup (1991)
The conservative attempt to reverse the process of reform in the USSR, which ended in failure. Communist opponents of Mikhail **Gorbachev**'s policies had been able to slow down, but not to stop, the reforms. The coup's leaders included **Yanaev**, the Vice-President, and **Yazov**, Defence Minister. The military in particular were split, and the planning left Boris **Yeltsin** free to act in full view of the world. The plotters achieved the very opposite of what they wanted: Yeltsin took over from Gorbachev and accelerated the reforms. Those behind the coup succeeded, however, in undermining the USSR; the **CIS**, its emasculated successor, may yet give them another opportunity.

Aung San (1915–47)
Burmese nationalist. He was the dominant figure in the nationalist movement during and after the Pacific War. At the beginning of the 1940s, Aung San, working with Japanese agents, formed the anti-British Burma Independence Army, which entered Burma with the invading Japanese in Jan 1942. He rapidly became disillusioned with the Japanese, however, and, as a leading figure in the Anti-Fascist People's Freedom League (AFPFL), turned his troops against them (Mar 1945). In the immediate post-war period he became President of the AFPFL and, in 1946, was effectively Prime Minister in the Governor's Executive Council. In Jan 1947 he travelled to London to negotiate, with success, Burma's independence. On 19 July, however, he was assassinated by a political rival. His death removed the one figure who might have held together Burma's warring political interests as the country achieved independence (4 Jan 1948).

Auriol, Vincent (1884–1966)

French politician. A socialist, he studied law, and was a Deputy (1914–40 and 1945–7), Minister of Finance in the **Popular Front** government (1936–7) and Minister of Justice (1937–8). He opposed the granting of power to **Pétain** in 1940, and joined the French Resistance, escaping to Algeria in 1943, where he became President of the Foreign Affairs Committee of the Consultative Assembly. He represented France at the first meeting of the **UN**, was elected President of the Constituent Assembly in 1946, and was first President of the Fourth Republic (1947–53). ▷ **Republic, Fourth** (France); **Resistance Movement** (France)

Aurora (1917)

The Russian warship that went over to the **Bolsheviks** in Oct 1917, and thus tipped the balance in their favour. Although ordered by the **Russian Provisional Government** to put to sea, it stayed in the River Neva across from the **Winter Palace**, fired a blank shell that frightened away many of the government's supporters and eventually fired some live shells to help overcome its defenders. Its action was, however, essentially symbolic, indicating that the authorities had lost a major source of power.

Auschwitz

The largest Nazi **concentration camp**, founded in 1941, on the outskirts of Oświecim, south-west Poland, where 3–4 million people, mainly Jews and Poles, were murdered between 1940 and 1945. Gas chambers, watch towers, and prison huts are preserved at the camp, part of which is now a museum. ▷ **Holocaust**

Australian Council of Trade Unions (ACTU)

Australia's national trade-union organization, formed in 1927. Its prestige has come from representing the unions' case before the Australian Conciliation and Arbitration Commission, and in helping to settle industrial disputes. By 1986 162 unions were affiliated, with a claimed total membership of 2.6 million. In 1983 the ACTU and the **Australian Labor Party** (ALP) signed an accord on economic policy, which was put into effect when the ALP came to power. ▷ **Australian Workers' Union (AWU)**

Australian Labor Party (ALP)

Australia's oldest political party, founded in 1891 in New South Wales. It formed the world's first labour government in Queensland in 1899 for one week. It has always been a social democratic party, committed to evolutionary not revolutionary change. Despite a commitment to '**socialism**', it has generally been moderate and pragmatic when in government. Three major splits in the ALP occurred: in 1916–17 over conscription, in 1931 over economic policy to combat the Depression and in 1955 over attitudes to **communism**. ALP has had only some success in winning federal government (1908–9, 1910–13, 1914–15, 1929–32, 1941–9, 1972–5 and 1983–), but has done better at state level. Its most important national figures have been Prime Ministers W M **Hughes** (1915–16), James Scullin (1929–32), John **Curtin** (1941–5), Ben **Chifley** (1945–9), Gough **Whitlam** (1972–5), R J L ('Bob') **Hawke** (1983–91), and Paul **Keating** (1991–). The party has always had fewer members than its main rival, the **Liberal Party of Australia**. Although initially unpopular, Keating gained widespread approval for his willingness to tackle difficult issues, such as the land rights of **Aboriginals**, and his commitment to making Australia a republic by the end of the century. ▷ **Democratic Labor Party; Petrov Affair**

Australian Workers' Union (AWU)

The largest Australian trade union from the early 1900s to 1970, and still one of the largest, with over 120 000 members in 1985. It was formed in 1894 by the merging of the Amalgamated Shearers' Union (formed 1886) and the General Labourers' Union (formed 1890), and has traditionally recruited lesser paid workers. It has always been a conservative force in trade union and labour politics. ▷ **Australian Council of Trade Unions**

Austria, Republic of

Following the collapse of Austria-Hungary at the end of **World War I**, those German-speaking lands of the Habsburg Empire not annexed by other successor states constituted themselves on 12 Nov 1918 as 'German Austria', renamed Austria on the insistence of the victor powers. Between the wars the republic led an uneasy existence, with most of the public and most politicians seeking union with Germany. Union with **Hitler**'s Germany, which occurred in Mar 1938 (**Anschluss**), was more controversial. After **World War II**, Austria was reconstituted as a distinct territory by the Allies and in 1955 became an independent, neutral state. Since its declaration of neutrality, Austria has been a haven for many refugees. ▷ **Austrian State Treaty**

Austrian State Treaty (May 1955)

The agreement between **Austria** and the four Allied victor powers under which Austria regained its independence as a federal republic in return for restrictions on armaments and curbs on close relations with Germany. In Oct 1955 this was supplemented by an Austrian declaration of permanent neutrality.

autarchia

The Italian word ('autarchy' or 'self-sufficiency') used to describe the policy of economic self-sufficiency pursued by the fascist regime in Italy. Originally it was largely limited to a drive for greater grain production, the so-called 'battle for wheat'. However, when limited economic sanctions were imposed in response to Italy's invasion of Abyssinia in 1935, an increased effort was made to replace imports with ersatz goods. ▷ **Abyssinia, Conquest of; fascism**

Autumn Harvest Uprisings (1927)
A series of attempted peasant insurrections launched by the Chinese Communist Party in the provinces of Hunan and Hubei following the collapse of the United Front (June 1927). An emergency party conference in Aug 1927 called for communist-led attacks on major cities in the hope of igniting urban revolution. **Mao Zedong** led one such uprising, but following its defeat he led the remnants of his ragtag force to the mountains of **Jinggangshan** where he began to create a rural base area. By the end of 1927, all other insurrections had collapsed.

Aventine Secession (June 1924)
In protest at fascist vote-rigging and the murder of **Matteotti**, the deputies of the main Italian opposition parties staged a walk-out from parliament. Designed to register protest and deny legitimacy to **Mussolini**'s regime, the actual consequence was to hand the fascists dominance of the Italian Chamber. The measure was further undermined by the reluctance of **Giolitti** and other leading liberals to support what they felt to be a useless boycott. Those deputies who joined the walk-out were said to have 'gone to the Aventine hill'.

AVNOJ (*Antifašističko Veče Narodnog Oslobodjenja Jugoslavije*, 'Anti-Fascist Council for the National Liberation of Yugoslavia')
Organized by the partisan leader, **Tito**, the council first met at Bihać in Bosnia to establish a central government for Yugoslavia (Nov 1942). Communist-dominated, it challenged the authority of the royalist government-in-exile in London. In Nov 1943 it met at Jajce and declared itself the true representative government of Yugoslavia. Its political programme included the reorganization of the country on a federal basis and the establishment of a republic. At the end of **World War II**, it had created an effective administrative structure throughout the country and became the national provisional assembly until the Nov 1945 elections. That Yugoslavia alone of the Balkan countries was under communist control at the end of the war was due to the successful organization of AVNOJ. ▷ **Djilas, Milovan; Kardelj, Edvard; Stojadinović, Milan**

Awami League
East Pakistani (later Bangladeshi) political party founded initially to promote East Pakistani autonomy, and later Bangladeshi independence. The Awami League rose to political prominence in the late 1960s when, under the leadership of Sheikh Mujibur Rahman, it protested against the fact that profits from jute, produced in highly populated East Pakistan,

were being kept in relatively sparsely populated West Pakistan. The Awami League's second cause was for parliamentary representation by population. As the government of General **Ayub Khan** became increasingly unstable in 1968, Sheikh Mujib and the Awami League publicized a six-point programme to limit the powers of the central government in East Pakistan. The central government responded by imprisoning all opposition leaders. The following year Ayub Khan resigned and was replaced by General Yahya Khan who proceeded with a policy of political militarization while preparing to return parliamentary democracy. Although representation by population was part of Yahya Khan's plan, dissatisfaction in East Pakistan grew and popular feeling began to call for independence. In the election of 7 Dec 1970, the Awami League won 160 of 162 seats in East Pakistan. In Mar 1971 Sheikh Mujib set forth full internal autonomy as his condition for the Awami League's participation in the National Assembly. He was arrested shortly thereafter and the Awami League was outlawed. These actions on the part of the central government led directly to the bloody 1971 Pakistani civil war, which saw the emergence of the new state of Bangladesh following India's military invasion in support of the Awami League. While the League managed to retain democratic control of Bangladesh through the nation's first independent election in 1973, it was overthrown by a coup in 1975. Since then, the Awami League has remained a major political party in Bangladesh.

AWB (*Afrikaanse Weestand Beweging*, 'Afrikaner Resistance Movement')
A paramilitary group founded in 1973, and led by Eugene Terr'Blanche, it is prepared to support its aim of preserving white control of South Africa by force.

Awolowo, Chief Obafemi (1909–87)
Nigerian politician. Educated in Protestant schools, he was a teacher, trader, trade union organizer and journalist, before being an external student of law at London University and becoming a solicitor and advocate of the Nigerian Supreme Court. He helped found and then led the Action Group, a party based on the Yoruba of Western Nigeria, 1951–66 (when the party was banned). He was Premier of the Western Region (1954–9) and then leader of the opposition in the federal parliament from 1960 to 1962, when he was imprisoned. Released after the 1966 coup, he was Federal Commissioner for Finance and Vice-President, Federal Executive Council of Nigeria (1967–71), when he returned to private practice. But he returned to politics in 1979 as the unsuccessful presidential candidate for the Unity Party of Nigeria.

Axis Powers
The name given to the co-operation of Nazi Germany and Fascist Italy (1936–45), first used **by Mussolini**. In May 1939 the two countries signed

a formal treaty, the 'Pact of Steel'. In Sep 1940, Germany, Italy and Japan signed a tripartite agreement, after which all three were referred to as Axis Powers. ▷ **Nazi Party; World War II**

Ayub Khan, Mohammed (1907–74)
Pakistani soldier and politician. Educated at Aligarh Moslem University and Sandhurst, he served in **World War II**, became first commander-in-chief of Pakistan's army in 1951 and field marshal in 1959. He became President of Pakistan in 1958 after a bloodless army coup, and established a stable economy and political autocracy. In Mar 1969, after widespread civil disorder and violent opposition from both right and left wings, Ayub Khan relinquished power and martial law was re-established.

Azad, Abu'l-Kalam (1888–1958)
Muslim Indian politician and leader of the **Indian National Congress**. His pan-Islamic articles in his newspaper, Al-Hilal, resulted in detention in 1915, after release from which he became active in the **Khilafat Movement**. In 1923 Azad presided over a special session of the Indian National Congress, and in 1940 he was elected President — a position which he held until 1946. While President of Congress he conducted important negotiations with Sir Stafford Cripps and Field Marshal Lord **Wavell**. He was interned throughout most of the war. Following Indian independence, Azad became India's Education Minister, a post he held until his death.

Azaña (y Díaz), Manuel (1880–1940)
Spanish politician and intellectual. He qualified as a lawyer, served as a bureaucrat, but became eminent in the literary and political world. In 1925 he founded a political party, Acción Republicana. With the advent of the Second Republic (1931), he became Minister of War and then Prime Minister (1931–3) of a reforming government. An outstanding orator and thinker, he himself was closely identified with army reform and anticlericalism. In opposition from Sep 1933 to Feb 1936, he was the chief architect of the Popular Front coalition which triumphed in the general election of Feb 1936. He resumed the premiership then, and was elevated to the presidency in May 1936. He remained President during the **Spanish Civil War** until Feb 1939, then went into exile in France, where he died. Azaña was the leading politician of the Second Republic and the greatest embodiment of its liberal, reformist vision. ▷ **Republic, Second** (Spain)

Azcona del Hoyo, José Simon (1927–)
Honduran politician. He trained as a civil engineer in Honduras and Mexico and developed a particular interest in urban development and low-cost housing. As a student he became interested in politics and fought

the 1963 general election as a candidate for the Liberal Party of Honduras (PLH) but his career was interrupted by a series of military coups. He served in the governments of Roberto Suazo and Walter Lopez (1982–6), which were ostensibly civilian administrations but, in reality, controlled by the army commander-in-chief, General Gustavo Alvarez. The latter was removed by junior officers in 1984 and in 1986 Azcona narrowly won the presidential election.

Azerbaijan, Independence of (1991)
One of the non-Russian Republics that gained their independence with the disintegration of the USSR. The Azeris had a long history, mainly of subjection to the neighbouring empires. A Turkish people converted to Islam, they came under Tsarist Russian rule in 1813. The development of the oil industry in and around Baku produced leaders who, encouraged by **Lenin**, declared for independence in 1918. However, in 1920 they were reconquered on his instructions for allegedly siding with Soviet enemies. Before re-emerging in 1991, Azerbaijan became locked in a struggle with **Armenia** over the autonomous region that **Stalin** had set up for the latter's co-nationals in Nagorno-Karabakh.

Azhari, Ismail al- (1900–69)
Sudanese politician. He was the leader of the Sudanese Unionist Party which, to the surprise and indeed disappointment of the British, was the victor of the first Sudanese parliamentary elections in 1953. Al-Azhari formed the first government in 1954. Opposed by the Mahdists, he was nonetheless able to guide the Sudan towards independence, which was achieved on 1 Jan 1956. After the deposition of Ibrahim **Abboud** in 1964, al-Azhari became President of the Supreme Council of the Sudan. However, a military coup in 1969 resulted in his being placed under house arrest and he died during this confinement.

Azikiwe, Nnamdi (1904–)
Nigerian journalist and politician. He spent four years as a government clerk before going to the USA, where he studied at Storer College, Lincoln University and Howard University. He then taught at Lincoln, where he obtained two further degrees. He returned to Africa in 1934 and edited the *African Morning Post* in Accra before going back to Nigeria to take up the editorship of the *West African Pilot* in 1937. He was a member of the executive of the Nigerian Youth Movement (1934–41) and helped found the National Council of Nigeria and the Cameroons (**NCNC**) of which he was Secretary (1944–6) and President (1946–60). A member of the Nigerian Legco in 1947–51, he became Premier of the Eastern Region in 1954 after two years as Leader of the Opposition. He was appointed the first black Governor-General of Nigeria in 1960 and was President of the first Nigerian Republic in 1963–6. He was in Britain

at the time of the 1966 military coup, but returned as a private citizen to Nigeria soon afterwards. He returned to politics in 1979 as leader of, and successful candidate for, the Nigerian People's Party. He was a member of the Council of State 1979–83.

B

Ba'ath Socialist Party
The political manifestation of Ba'athism, an Islamic ideology of the 1930s. Founded by Michel **Aflaq** and Salah al-Din **Bitar**, the party's ideology faced problems in coping with combining a Marxist social analysis with an Islamic religious basis, but eventually became the ruling party in both Syria and Iraq. However, rather than closening relations between the two countries, the term became divorced from its ideological bases and has in no way served to reduce the rancour which has existed between the two countries over the ages.

Baader–Meinhof Group
The popular name for *Rote Armee Fraktion* (RAF), after its leaders, Andreas Baader (1943–77) and Ulrike Meinhof (1934–76). A left-wing German revolutionary, terrorist group, which recruited largely from the middle-class, younger generation, it carried out political bombings in Germany in the early 1970s. Baader, Meinhof, and 18 other members were arrested in 1972. On a much smaller scale RAF continued into the 1980s.

Babangida, Ibrahim (1941–)
Nigerian soldier and politician. Educated at military schools in Nigeria and later in India, UK and USA, he was commissioned in 1963 and became an instructor at the Nigerian Defence Academy. During the Nigerian Civil War, he commanded an infantry battalion, then became an instructor at the Nigerian Defence Academy (1970–2) and later commander of the Armoured Corps (1975–81). Involved in the military overthrow of President **Shagari** in 1983, he became a member of the Supreme Military Council and Chief of Staff in 1985 and was himself the leader of the coup which overthrew **Buhari** in 1985. He was mainly responsible for the cautious and controlled way Nigeria returned to civilian rule, imposing a two-party system and staged elections on the country.

Babi Yar
A huge ravine near Kiev in the Ukraine into which over 30 000 Jews were herded and massacred by Nazi German troops in 1941. It is also the title of a poem by Yevegeny Yevtushenko (1961) and a novel by Anatoly Kuznetsov (1966) dedicated to the victims. ▷ **Holocaust; Nazi Party**

Baden-Powell, Robert (Stephenson Smyth), 1st Baron (1857–1941)
British general. Educated at Charterhouse, he joined the army, served in India and Afghanistan, was on the staff in Ashanti and Matabeleland, and won fame as the defender of Mafeking in the second Boer War. He founded the Boy Scout movement (1908) and, with his sister Agnes (1858–1945), the Girl Guides (1910). ▷ **Boer Wars; Mafeking, Siege of**

Badoglio, Pietro (1871–1956)
Italian general. Governor of Libya (1929–34), by 1932 he had achieved the pacification of the Sanusi tribesmen. In 1935 he replaced **De Bono** at the head of the Conquest of **Abyssinia** where he conducted a campaign of extreme brutality; he became Viceroy of the new colony in May 1936. At the outbreak of **World War II** he initially favoured neutrality but rapidly dropped his opposition to intervention and in June 1940 was made Commander-in-Chief. Humiliating defeats suffered by the Italian Army in Greece and Albania prompted Badoglio's resignation (Dec 1940). In 1943 he was asked by **Victor Emmanuel III** to form an anti-fascist government after the arrest of **Mussolini**. On 25 Sep Badoglio signed an armistice with the Allies at Malta and in mid-Oct declared war on Germany. Apr 1944 saw the formation of a broad coalition government under Badoglio's leadership (including **Togliatti**, **Croce** and Carlo **Sforza**), but after the liberation of Rome in June he was obliged to stand down under pressure from the Americans and politicians with better anti-fascist credentials. He was replaced by Ivanoe **Bonomi**.

Bagaza, Jean-Baptiste (1946–)
Burundian politician and soldier. After attending military schools in Belgium he returned to Burundi and became assistant to the head of the armed forces, with the rank of lieutenant-colonel. In 1976 he led a coup to overthrow President Micombero and was appointed President by a Supreme Revolutionary Council. In 1984 the post of prime minister was abolished and Bagaza was elected Head of State and Government. In 1987 he was himself ousted in a coup led by Major Pierre Buyoya.

Baghdad Pact
Originally a treaty between Turkey and Iraq (1955) aimed at mutual cooperation against militants of the left. Britain, Pakistan and Iran joined later in 1955 but there was general opposition in Jordan when King Hussein proposed becoming a signatory. The Suez Crisis compromised Britain's position in 1956 and after the withdrawal of Iraq in 1958 (after the murder of the royal family) the pact ceased to exist as such and was supplanted by the Central Treaty Organization (CENTO).

Bakatin, Vadim Viktorovich (1937–)
Russian politician. Educated as an engineer in Novosibirsk, he worked in the construction industry before being selected for political work in the Communist Party of the USSR. With further training in social sciences he worked his way up from First Secretary in Kirov (1985–7) and in Kemerovo (1987–8) to the Central Secretariat in Moscow. In search of new blood, Mikhail **Gorbachev** appointed him Minister of the Interior in 1988 but dismissed him under right-wing pressure (Dec 1990) as too liberal, particularly on the nationalities question. In June 1991 he ran against Boris **Yeltsin** and others for election as President of the Russian Federation, allegedly as Gorbachev's candidate, but he came bottom of the poll. After the failure of the **August Coup** of the same year, Gorbachev appointed him head of the **KGB** with instructions to convert it to a normal police force as he struggled to retain Soviet power.

Baker, James Addison (1930–)
US public official. He was educated at Princeton and the University of Texas. Baker served President Ford as Under-Secretary of Commerce, and President **Reagan** as White House Chief of Staff (1981–5) and Secretary of the Treasury (1985–8) before resigning to manage George **Bush**'s campaign for the presidency. After winning the election, Bush made him Secretary of State.

Baker v Carr (1962)
The US Supreme Court decision that state electoral districts must contain approximately the same voting population, bringing to an end the long-standing rural domination of state legislatures.

Bakhtiyaris
A nomad tribe from the south of what is now Iran. In early 20c Persia they supported the nationalist cause which had been given impetus by gaining the agreement, albeit reluctant, of the Qajar Shah Muzaffar al-Din to the formation of a national assembly. Muzaffar al-Din was succeeded by his son Muhammad Ali who was just as reluctant to have his powers circumscribed as his father had been and, after a bomb attack in an attempt to assassinate him, he called upon Russian-officered Cossack brigades to crush the nationalists in Tehran and Tabriz. Against this background, the Bakhtiyaris, under their leader Sirdari Asad, moved first against Isfahan where they put an end to the autocratic rule of the local governor, and then led a combined nationalist combat force against Tehran. The nationalists succeeded in seizing the capital and deposing the Shah. The Bakhtiyaris were thus instrumental in assisting the Persian nationalists to a triumph albeit short lived as a result of Great Power (in this case Russia and Britain) involvement in the politics of the country.

Bakr, Hasan al- (1914–82)

President of Iraq. He succeeded Abd al-Rahman Aref as President in 1968, following the Ba'ath coup of July 1968. A leader of the socialist Ba'ath Renaissance Party, he held power with Saddam **Hussein**, the Ba'ath leader. Because of his border claims against Iran, al-Bakr was involved in conflict with the Kurds in the north of Iraq, a problem he eventually resolved through an agreement reached in 1975. On the economic front, he developed the modernization of both agriculture and industry, the former particularly as a result of irrigation financed by oil revenues. Politically, he made an alliance with the USSR, supported the **PLO** (Palestine Liberation Organization) and was an ally of Syria and Egypt in the 1973 Yom Kippur War. He was succeeded by Saddam Hussein in 1979.

Balaguer, Joaquim (1907–)

Dominican Republic politician. He was Professor of Law at Santo Domingo University from 1938 and Ambassador to Colombia and Mexico in the 1940s before entering politics. He served in the dictatorial regime of Rafael **Trujillo**, after whose assassination in 1961 he fled to the USA in 1962, returning in 1965 to win the presidency in 1966 as leader of the Christian Social Reform Party (PRSC). He was re-elected in 1970 and 1974. The failure of the economic policies of the Dominican Revolutionary Party (PRD) brought the PRSC and Balaguer back to power in 1986, at the age of 79.

Balbo, Italo (1896–1940)

Italian politician. An early supporter of Italian intervention in **World War I**, Balbo served from 1915 as an officer in the Alpini. From 1920 he played a key part in the fascist movement: he was one of the most energetic **ras** and a Quadrumvir in the **March on Rome**. During 1923–4 he was commander of the **MVSN** and in 1926 became Secretary of State for Aviation. In Jan 1934 he was made Governor of Libya but was killed when his plane was accidentally brought down by Italian anti-aircraft fire in 1940. He was one of several fascist leaders who disliked **Mussolini**'s move towards **Hitler** and who spoke out in defence of the Jews.

Balczerowicz, Leszek (1947–)

Polish economist and politician. A talented economic researcher at the Central School of Planning in Warsaw, he was also a strong supporter and adviser of **Solidarity**. In 1989 he was appointed Finance Minister after the **Wałesa** revolution and achieved something of an economic miracle in stabilizing the currency and introducing the first stage of marketization. Following the 1991 elections, Wałesa judged his economic stringency too unpopular and engineered his dismissal in 1992. His achievement, nonetheless, won wide international praise.

Baldwin (of Bewdley), Stanley, 1st Earl (1867–1947)
British politician. He worked in his family business before becoming a Conservative MP in 1908. He was President of the Board of Trade (1921–2) and Chancellor of the Exchequer (1922–3), and then unexpectedly succeeded Bonar **Law** as Prime Minister. His periods of office (1923–4, 1924–9 and 1935–7) included the **General Strike** (1926) and was interrupted by the two minority Labour governments of 1924 and 1929–31. During the **MacDonald** coalition (1931–5), he served as Lord President of the Council. He played a leading role in arranging the abdication of **Edward VIII** in 1936. He resigned from politics in 1937, when he was made an earl. ▷ **Conservative Party** (UK)

Balewa, Sir Abubakar Tafawa (1912–66)
Nigerian politician. After a career as a teacher and education officer, he entered the Nigerian Legco and was a founder member of the Northern People's Congress. He entered the Federal Assembly in 1947 and was appointed consecutively Federal Minister of Works (1952–4), Minister of Trade (1954–7), Chief Minister (1957–9) and Prime Minister (1959–66). Essentially sympathetic to Western priorities, he was seen within Nigeria as a supporter of northern interests in the first years of independence. He was overthrown and assassinated in the 1966 coup.

Balfour, Arthur James, 1st Earl (1848–1930)
British politician. He entered parliament in 1874, becoming Secretary for Scotland (1886) and Chief Secretary for Ireland (1887–91), where his policy of suppression earned him the name of 'Bloody Balfour'. A Conservative, he was Prime Minister (1902–5) and First Lord of the Admiralty (1915–16). As Foreign Secretary (1916–19), he was responsible for the **Balfour Declaration** (1917), which promised Zionists a national home in Palestine. He resigned in 1922, was created an earl, but served again as Lord President (1925–9). ▷ **Zionism**

Balfour Declaration (2 Nov 1917)
A short communication from the British Foreign Secretary, A J Balfour, to Lord Rothschild, expressing the British government's disposition towards a Jewish national home in Palestine. The central portion reads: 'His Majesty's Government view with favour the establishment in Palestine of a national home for the Jewish people ... it being clearly understood that nothing shall be done which may prejudice the civil and religious rights of existing non-Jewish communities'. Britain having received the Mandate for Palestine in 1920, the vagueness of the Balfour Declaration was clarified in 1923: Jewish immigration was to be encouraged; an appropriate Jewish body formed to that end; the rights of non-Jews were to be protected; and English, Hebrew and Arabic were to be given equal status. However, the ensuing two decades showed Britain to

be either unwilling or unable to deliver its promise to the Jews, especially in view of increasing Arab hostility to Jewish immigration. ▷ **Haganah; Irgun; Jewish National Fund; Zionism**

Balilla

The umbrella term for the youth movement founded by the **Fascist Party** in 1926. Its official name, the *Opera nazionale Balilla*, was altered to *Gioventù Italiana del Littorio* in 1937. The organization had many branches for boys and girls of different age groups and aimed at fascist indoctrination and the cultivation of patriotic fervour; it also provided youth clubs, sports facilities and rudimentary military training. Its success in attracting members can be largely attributed to the fascist abolition of the Catholic Boy Scouts Movement in 1928.

Balkan Entente (1930)

A cultural and political alliance formed between Greece, Yugoslavia, Romania and Turkey after the first Balkan Conference held in Athens. It became in effect a defensive alliance against revisionist Bulgaria, which sought to regain territory lost to Greece and Yugoslavia by the Treaty of **Neuilly** (1919). In 1934 the member states signed a pact of mutual security and consultation, but cooperation was limited and the Entente could not counteract great power interference in the Balkans. During the 1930s, with the establishment of authoritarian regimes in all the Balkan states, the whole region moved closer to the German and Italian camp.

Balkan Wars (1912–13)

A series of military campaigns fought in the Balkans. In 1912 Bulgaria, Serbia, Greece and Montenegro attacked Turkey, securing swift victories. A preliminary peace was drawn up by the Great Powers in May 1913, in which Turkey surrendered most of her European territories and the new state of Albania was created. Disputes between the Balkan allies over the spoils of war led to a second war, in which Bulgaria attacked her former allies, and was defeated. As a result of the two wars, Turkish territory in Europe was reduced to an area around Adrianople and Constantinople, Albania was established, Macedonia was partitioned, Serbia and Montenegro almost doubled in size, and tension among the Great Powers in Europe was considerably increased.

Balli Kombëtar

The National Front Albanian resistance movement during **World War II**. Formed in Oct 1942 under Ali Klissura and Midhat Frashëri, it was nationalistic and liberal, favouring the establishment of a republic and an extensive programme of domestic reform. Relations with the communist-led resistance were vexed by the issue of **Kosovo**, which since 1941 had been included within Albania by the Italians: while Balli Kombëtar wanted to retain Kosovo, the Albanian communists, under pressure from their Yugoslav masters, did not. In 1943, under Allied pressure, the two resistance groups joined to form the Committee for the Salvation of Albania, but at the end of the war many members of Balli Kombëtar fell victim to Enver **Hoxha**'s drive to destroy all internal opposition to communist rule. ▷ **Albanians**

Baltic states

The countries of Estonia, Latvia and Lithuania on the east shore of the Baltic Sea. They were formed in 1918 from the Russian Baltic provinces or governments of Estonia, Livonia and Courland, and parts of the governments of Pskov, Vitebsk, Kovno, Vilna and Suvalki. The states were independent until 1940, when they were annexed by the USSR. They reclaimed their independence in 1991.

Banda, Hastings Kamuzu (officially 1905, probably 1898–)

Doctor and politician. He left Malawi by foot for South Africa, from where he travelled to the USA and Britain to obtain medical qualifications. He set up practice first in Liverpool and then on Tyneside before moving to London, where he became deeply involved in opposition to the Central African Federation, but, after a scandal involving his liaison with a white woman, he went to Ghana, from where he was persuaded to return to Malawi to lead the Nyasaland African National Congress there. He was jailed in 1959 but was soon released and was appointed Minister of National Resources and Local Government (1961–3), Prime Minister of Nyasaland (1963–4) and then of independent Malawi (1964–6). When the country became a republic, he was its first President and Life President from 1971. He retained many portfolios, notably Defence, throughout his period as President. He made himself Life President of the only political party, the **Malawi Congress Party**. Depending on a unique mix of populism, a functioning political party and ruthless use of his security apparatus, he has survived as the dominant figure in Malawi for over 30 years.

Bandaranaike, Sirimavo (1916–)

Sri Lankan politician. The widow of S W R D **Bandaranaike**, who was assassinated in 1959, she became the first woman prime minister in the world when she was elected in 1960. She held office from 1960 to 1965, and again from 1970 to 1977. Her second term was especially turbulent, with the 1971 **JVP** (People's Liberation Front) insurrection followed by the introduction of a new republican constitution in 1972 and a period of severe economic shortages. The **UNP** (United National Party) government of J R **Jayawardene** stripped her of her civil rights in 1980, forcing her to relinquish temporarily the leadership of the **SLFP** (Sri Lanka Freedom Party) to her son, Anura.

Bandaranaike, S(olomon) W(est) R(idgeway) D(ias) (1899–1959)
Ceylonese (Sri Lankan) politician. Educated in Colombo and Oxford, he was called to the Bar in 1925. He became President of the Ceylon National Congress, and helped to found the **UNP** (United National Party). He was Leader of the House in Ceylon's first parliament, and Minister of Health. In 1951 he resigned from the government and organized the **SLFP** (Sri Lanka Freedom Party). In 1956 he was the main partner in a populist coalition which defeated the UNP in an election dominated by the issue of national language and the spirit of Buddhist revivalism. Bandaranaike's Sinhala-only proposals were opposed by representatives of the Tamil minority and swiftly followed by outbreaks of Sinhala–Tamil violence. In 1959 he was assassinated by a Buddhist monk. ▷ **Bandaranaike, Sirimavo**

Bandung Conference (Apr 1955)
A meeting in Bandung, Indonesia, of 29 newly-independent Afro-Asian countries, anxious to distance themselves from the superpower rivalry between the USA and the USSR. Representatives included **Zhou Enlai** (China), **Nehru** (India), **Sihanouk** (Cambodia), U **Nu** (Burma) and Gamal Abd al-**Nasser** (Egypt). Communist China's participation, which signalled its emergence as an actor on the world stage, indicated Beijing's determination to pursue a foreign policy independent of that of Moscow and the desire to deal amicably with those governments (such as that of India) hitherto deemed 'lackeys' of US imperialism. Zhou Enlai expressed this new conciliatory policy with his Five Principles of Peaceful Co-Existence (first enunciated in 1954), which looked forward to peaceful relations with all countries (including the USA) on the basis of mutual respect for each other's territorial integrity, non-interference in each other's affairs, and non-aggression. Thus, the conference sought to establish the non-aligned, newly-emerging nations as a major force in world politics, free from the shabby self-interest and manipulative interventions practised by the established blocs. It was a major triumph, domestically and internationally, for the Indonesian president, **Sukarno**.

Bangladesh War (1971)
The suspension of democracy following a sweeping electoral victory by the **Awami League** in East Pakistan (1970), the devastation of this province of Pakistan by a cyclone in the same year, and the Dacca government's ineffectual response to the disaster—which claimed 220 000 lives and countless homes and crops—triggered fighting, which developed into a full-scale border war in 1971. Pakistan surrendered the territory only months later, following a popular uprising and military intervention by India, which had accepted huge numbers of Bangladeshi refugees, and the independent republic of Bangladesh was created. It joined the Commonwealth a year later.

Bangladesh formerly **East Pakistan**

Bangladesh was part of the State of Bengal until Muslim East Bengal was created in 1905, separate from Hindu West Bengal. They were reunited in 1911, partitioned again in 1947, with West Bengal remaining in India and East Bengal forming East Pakistan. Disparity in investment and development between East and West Pakistan (separated by over 1 000miles/1 600km), coupled with language differences, caused East Pakistan to seek autonomy. Rebellion in 1971 led to independence, helped by India. The constitution was suspended in 1975, following political unrest, and the first president, Sheikh Mujib, was assassinated. There were further coups in 1975, 1977 and 1982, but the constitution was restored in 1986. The nation came to a standstill during strikes in 1992 and there were many deaths and injuries.

Bani-Sadr, Abolhassan (1935–)

Iranian politician. He studied economics and sociology at the Sorbonne in Paris, having fled there in 1963 after being imprisoned in Iran for involvement in riots against the Shah's regime. He was an important figure in the Iranian Revolution of 1978–9, a member of the Revolutionary Council, and was elected first President of the Islamic Republic of Iran in 1980. From the start, however, he was threatened by a deepening conflict with the fundamentalist Muslim clergy; he was eventually criticised by Ayatollah **Khomeini**, and dismissed (mid-1981). He fled to France, where he was granted political asylum.

Banna, Hasan al- (1906–49)

Islamic fundamentalist. Born at Mahmudiya, near Cairo, he was the founder in Egypt in 1928 of the Society of Muslim Brothers (better known as the **Muslim Brotherhood** or Brethren), which preached a return to the purity of early Islam. In 1948 the Egyptian Prime Minister, Nuqrashi Pasha, was killed by a Brotherhood member, and the following year al-Banna was himself murdered, although he had condemned the assassination. His movement has had considerable influence on contemporary Islamic fundamentalism.

Bao Dai (1913–)

Indo-Chinese ruler. He succeeded his father in 1925, ascending the throne in 1932. He collaborated with the Japanese during **World War II** and, after the Japanese surrender, found very brief favour with **Ho Chi Minh**. He abdicated in 1945, but returned to Saigon in 1949 (having renounced his hereditary title), as Chief of the State of Vietnam within the French Union. In 1955 he was deposed by **Ngo Dinh Diem** and South Vietnam became a republic.

Bar–Lev Line

The chain of fortifications established after the **Six-Day War** on the east of the Suez Canal by Chaim Bar Lev, Israeli Chief of Staff. This was in response to continued Egyptian attacks under Gamal Abd al-**Nasser**, despite cease-fire agreements. In the **Yom Kippur War** of 1973, however, the Bar–Lev Line was not able to withstand the initial onslaught of Egyptian forces. ▷ **Arab–Israeli Wars**

Bardoli

A town in Surat district, near Bombay, it was the scene of a very successful tax reduction campaign lasting from 12 Feb to 4 Aug 1928. Led by Sardar **Patel**, using M K **Gandhi**'s **Satyagraha** technique, the protest called for an impartial review of an apparently arbitrary increase in local land revenue forecast used for tax assessments. In Mar 1929 an appointed committee reported that the increase was excessive by 15.75 per cent, and the rate was lowered.

Barre, Raymond (1924–)

French conservative politician. He made his reputation as an influential neo-liberal economist at the Sorbonne and as Vice-President of the European Commission (1967–72). He was Minister of Foreign Trade under President **Giscard d'Estaing** and was appointed Prime Minister (1976–81) after the resignation of Jacques **Chirac** in 1976. Holding concurrently the Finance Ministry portfolio, he concentrated on economic affairs, gaining a reputation as a determined budget-cutter. With unemployment mounting between 1976 and 1981, he became deeply unpopular, but his term as Prime Minister was later favourably reassessed after the failure of the 1981–3 socialist administration's reflationary experiment. During the 1980s he built up a firm political base in the Lyons region, representing the centre-right Union for French Democracy (UDF). He contested the 1988 presidential election but was eliminated in the first ballot.

Barre, Mohamed Siad (1919–)

Somali soldier and politician. Educated locally and at an Italian military academy, he was a police officer in Somaliland, under both Italian and British Trusteeship, before joining the Somali army in 1960. He led a successful coup in 1969. Using a **KGB**-trained secret service and manipulating the clan divisions of the Somalis, he was backed first by the USSR and then by the USA. When uprisings took place in 1989, his use of the air force and army to stamp out the opposition proved unavailing and he was forced to leave Mogadishu (Jan 1991), leaving behind an impoverished country divided into competing warring factions.

Barrow, Errol Walton (1920–87)
Barbadian politician. Born in Barbados, he flew with the Royal Air Force (1940–7) and then studied at London University and Lincoln's Inn. Returning to Barbados, he became active in the Barbados Labour Party (BLP) and was elected to the House of Assembly in 1951. In 1955 he left the BLP and co-founded the **Democratic Labour Party (DLP)**, becoming its Chairman in 1958. In the elections following independence in 1961 the DLP was victorious and Barrow became the first Prime Minister. His unbroken tenure was ended in 1976 by the BLP, led by 'Tom' Adams. In 1986, a year after Adams's death, Barrow returned to power with a decisive majority but he died in the following year and was succeeded by Erskine Lloyd Sandiford.

Barthou, Jean Louis (1862–1934)
French politician. He practised law, and was a member of parliament from 1889 until his death. From 1894 onwards he frequently held ministerial office, becoming Prime Minister in 1913, when he introduced three-year conscription. He was briefly Foreign Minister in 1917 and criticized the Treaty of **Versailles** (1919) for not providing enough security for France. After **World War I** he was almost continually in office, as Minister of War (1921–2, 1930–1), Minister of Justice (1922–4, 1926–9) and Foreign Minister (1934). He presided over the French delegation at the Genoa Conference (1922), and was President of the Reparations Committee. As part of his attempt to strengthen French links with the states of Eastern Europe against the threat from Germany (an 'Eastern Locarno Treaty'), he invited King Alexander I of Yugoslavia to France; he was assassinated with him by Croatian terrorists in Marseilles.

Baruch, Bernard Mannes (1870–1965)
US financier. In 1918 he was appointed by President Woodrow **Wilson** to head the War Industries Board, with sweeping powers to establish priorities and increase production. His appointment symbolized a new alliance between a Democratic administration which had previously acted against the excesses of big business, and industry which now wished to combine patriotism with its own interests. A conservative Democrat and supporter of Al **Smith**, Baruch was one of the few speculators who anticipated the **Wall Street Crash** and so preserved his fortune. Often critical of the more radical aspects of the **New Deal**, he nevertheless frequently advised President Franklin D **Roosevelt**. In 1946 he presented the US plan for atomic energy control to the UN.

Barzani, Mustafa al- (1904–79)
Kurdish military leader and mullah. He commanded the peshmerga guerrillas and negotiated a promise of autonomy for the Kurds in northern Iraq in 1970. However, President **Bakr**'s failure to honour his pledge

led to further Iraqi-Kurdish conflict, resulting in the defeat of the peshmerga by Saddam **Hussein**, who took over the presidency in 1979.

Basic Law (*Grundgesetz*)

The Basic Law forms a major component within the Federal German constitutional order. In the period 1949–90, the Basic Law accepted the western Allied provision that Federal Germany have a market-oriented economy (although it did not exclude alternative options in the future) and that in political matters ultimate sovereignty lay with the (non-functioning) Allied Control Commission. With German reunification these limitations on sovereignty have lapsed. In its content the Basic Law represents a summation of previous German constitutional experience which learns from previous successes and failures. It establishes the principle of constitutional democracy with ultimate sovereignty lying with the people and it defines the rights of the **Bund** and *Länder*. The Basic Law has been amended dozens of times by act of parliament and although previously regarded as a provisional creation, pending eventual reunification, it has survived in slightly amended form in a reunited Germany. ▷ **Land**

Basic Treaty (*Grundvertrag*) (8 Nov 1972)

The treaty signed between Federal (West) and East **Germany** under which each promised to respect the other's independence and sovereignty. East **Germany** claimed that the agreement finalized Germany's division, the West maintained in a note delivered to East Berlin that it did not preclude the possibility of unification in a future, more peaceful Europe. The treaty marked a key success in Willy **Brandt**'s policy of **Ostpolitik**, not least because it allowed the resumption of personal contacts between East and West Germans. ▷ **Berlin, Partition of**

Basque Autonomy Statutes (1936 and 1979)

One of the oldest peoples in Europe, the Basques first formed a political entity with their unification under the Kingdom of Navarre in the 10c and 11c. With the decline of Navarre, the Basque provinces became integrated into the Kingdom of Castile by the 16c. The Basques retained their feudal laws and privileges until these were steadily abolished during the 19c. The Second Republic (1931–6) created an autonomous regime through the Statute of Oct 1936, but this was rescinded at the end of the **Spanish Civil War** by General **Franco**. Franco's dictatorship (1939–75) tried to suppress all aspects of Basque independence and culture. In 1979 a new Basque Autonomy Statute was passed, although it did not include Navarre, which obtained its own autonomous arrangement in 1982. The 1979 Autonomy Statute provided for the Basque country's own parliament, police force, tax authority, and control of the means vital to the survival of Basque culture, such as Basque schools and television in

Euskera (the Basque language). The fight for outright independence is maintained by **ETA**. ▷ **Republic, Second** (Spain)

Basque Nationalist Party ▷ **PNV**

Basques

A people of uncertain origin living in north-west Spain and neighbouring areas in France. They are physically similar to their neighbours, and are Roman Catholics, but their language, Basque, spoken by c.500 000, does not relate to any other European language, and is thought to be a remnant of the languages spoken in Western Europe before the advent of the Indo-European family. Despite extensive cultural and linguistic assimilation, urbanized Basques retain strong ethnic identity, and their main city, Bilbao, is a centre of Basque nationalism. Most Basques supported the Spanish Republic, which granted an autonomy statute in Oct 1936, during the **Spanish Civil War**. After the fall of Bilbao (June 1937), many went into exile. Since the death of **Franco** (1975), the new liberal Spanish monarchy has granted Basques some local autonomy (1978–9), but the more militant continue to agitate for a separate Basque state through the terrorist organization, **ETA**.

Batista (y Zaldívar), Fulgencio (1901–73)

Cuban dictator. In 1933 he organized a military coup (the 'Sergeants' Revolt'), consolidated his power, and became President (1940–4). In 1952 he overthrew President Prio Socorras, and ruled as dictator until his overthrow by Fidel **Castro** (Jan 1959), when he found refuge in the Dominican Republic.

Baudouin I (1930–93)

King of the Belgians (1951/93). The elder son of **Leopold III** and his first wife, Queen **Astrid**, he succeeded to the throne on the abdication of his father over the controversy of the latter's conduct during **World War II**. In 1960 he married the Spanish Fabiola de Mora y Aragon.

Bauer, Gustav (1870–1944)

German politician. A senior trade unionist before **World War I**, Bauer became an **SPD** member of the **Reichstag** in 1912. In Oct 1918 he was appointed a Junior Minister of Labour and became Minister of Labour in Feb 1919. He succeeded **Scheidemann** as Chancellor and on 26 June 1919 headed the government which signed the Treaty of **Versailles** under protest. He resigned as Chancellor during the **Kapp Putsch** (Mar 1920) and, after holding various further ministerial posts, eventually resigned from parliament in 1928 on becoming involved in a corruption trial.

Bay of Pigs (Apr 1961)
The failed invasion of Cuba by anti-**Castro** Cuban exiles sponsored by the USA. The invasion force of 1 500 men landed at Bahía de Cochinos ('Bay of Pigs') on the southern coast, but failed to win local support and was rapidly overwhelmed and defeated by Cuban troops. The episode was an embarrassment to John F **Kennedy**'s administration.

Beatrix (Wilhelmina Armgard) (1938–)
Queen of the Netherlands (1980/). The eldest daughter of Queen **Juliana** and Prince Bernhard zur Lippe-Biesterfeld, she acceded to the throne on the abdication of her mother. In 1966 she married West German diplomat Claus-Georg Wilhelm Otto Friedrich Gerd von Amsberg, causing much controversy in the Netherlands; there were hostile demonstrations at her wedding and her coronation. Their son, Prince Willem-Alexander Claus George Ferdinand, is the first male heir to the Dutch throne in over a century. There are two other sons: Johan Friso Bernhard Christiaan David and Constantijn Christof Frederik Aschwin.

Beatty, David Beatty, 1st Earl (1871–1936)
British admiral. He served in the Sudan (1896–8), and as battleship commander took part in the China War (1900). At the outbreak of **World War I** he steamed into Heligoland Bight, and destroyed three German cruisers. He later sank the *Blücher* (Jan 1915), and took part in the Battle of **Jutland** (May 1916). He became Commander-in-Chief of the Grand Fleet in 1916 and First Sea Lord in 1919, when he was created an earl.

Beck, Jozef (1894–1944)
Polish colonel. He helped Marshal **Piłsudski** to seize control in his 1926 coup, became Deputy Foreign Minister in 1930 and was finally Foreign Minister from 1932 to 1939. Following **Hitler**'s rise to power, he tried to maintain first an equilibrium between Nazi Germany and the USSR and then a policy of partial cooperation with Hitler to expand and defend his country. He assisted in the dismemberment of Czechoslovakia (Sep 1938) and defeated the Anglo-French bid to form an alliance with the USSR (May 1939). In Aug of the same year, he had to face the consequences when Hitler invaded a Poland that was virtually defenceless. Beck escaped abroad.

Begin, Menachem (1913–92)
Israeli politician. Born and educated in Brest-Litovsk, Poland (now Russia), he studied law at Warsaw University. An active Zionist, he became head of the Polish Zionist movement in 1931. He fled to Russia in 1939, enlisted in the Free Polish Army (1941), and was sent to British-mandated Palestine. In 1943 he commanded the **Irgun** Zvai Leumi resistance group in Israel, and in 1948 founded the Herut Freedom Movement,

becoming Chairman of the Herut Party. In 1973 three parties combined to form the nationalist **Likud** Front with Begin as its leader, and in the 1977 elections he became Prime Minister at the head of a coalition government. In the late 1970s he attended peace conferences in Jerusalem (Dec 1977) and at Camp David (Sep 1978) at the invitation of President **Carter**. In 1978 he and President Anwar **Sadat** of Egypt were jointly awarded the Nobel Peace Prize. He resigned the premiership in 1983.

Beiyang (Pei-yang) Army

China's first modern army dating from 1899. Under the command of **Yuan Shikai**, the Beiyang army grew in size during the last decade of the **Qing Dynasty**. Many of its officers were either trained in Japan or in new military academies in China. After 1911 the army was the basis of Yuan Shikai's power in his struggle with the **Guomindang**. Many of Yuan's generals later went on to become influential militarists (warlords) in their own right.

Belaúnde, Terry Fernando (1913–)

Peruvian politician. He was an architect before entering politics, leading the Popular Action Party (AP) in 1956. He campaigned for the presidency in 1956 and 1962, eventually winning it in 1963, but was deposed by the army in a bloodless coup in 1968. He fled to the USA where he lectured at Harvard. He returned to Peru two years later but was deported and did not re-establish himself until 1976. He won the presidency again in 1980, and was the first civilian to hand over to another constitutionally elected civilian (1985).

Belgian Socialist Party (*Parti Socialiste Belge*; *Belgische Socialistische Partij*)

The principal left-wing political party in Belgium, formed in 1940 after the German invasion had caused the abolition of its predecessor, the Belgian Workers' Party (founded in 1885). The party first gained important political influence after the constitutional revision of 1893 had introduced universal suffrage, and gave the socialists 27 MPs. After **World War I** the party dropped its Marxist and revolutionary attitude, and became a regular coalition partner in Belgian governments, often leading them in the 1950s and 1960s. After years of dispute between the French-speaking and Flemish-speaking sections of the party, they formally broke apart in 1978, with their own leaders, programmes and policies. Since the mid-1950s, when the socialists had 37 per cent of the vote, their popularity has declined, but they remain a major force in Belgian politics. Principal leaders have been E **Vandervelde**, H de **Man**, P H **Spaak**, A van **Acker**, and C **Huysmans**.

Belgium
Kingdom in north-west Europe. In recent decades, political tension between Walloons and Flemings has caused the collapse of several governments. In 1980 Wallonia and Flanders were given regional 'sub-governments'. A new federal constitution of 1989 divided Belgium into the autonomous regions of Flanders, Wallonia and Brussels. Constitutional amendments in 1993 were designed to continue the trend of devolving power to the regions.

Belize formerly (until 1973) **British Honduras**
Independent state in Central America. Once a British Colony, Belize began a ministerial system of government in 1961 and in 1964 internal self-government was achieved. Its name was changed from British Honduras to Belize in 1973 and it gained full independence in 1981. Guatemalan claims over Belize territory led to a British military presence. In the early 1990s Guatemala established diplomatic relations with Belize and almost all of the British presence has been withdrawn.

Bello, Sir Ahmadu (1910–66)
Nigerian politician. Educated at Katsina College, he started his career as a teacher but became a major political figure following his appointment as Saudana of Sokoto (1938). He led the Northern People's Congress from 1951, reaching the post of Prime Minister in 1954. He was a major figure in national politics, exercising his power through the NPC from his base in the Hause-dominated north of the country and was assassinated in the coup of Jan 1966.

Belorussia, Independence of (1991)
One of the 14 non-Russian Republics that gained their independence with the disintegration of the USSR. The Belorussians were one of the original Slav tribes, like the Russians themselves. They remained slightly distinct because they lived in the exposed western border area and were subject to long periods of foreign, particularly Polish rule. Under Tsarist control from 1795, they eventually developed a national movement that declared independence in 1917. However, a feeble Belorussia had a troubled existence and was incorporated into the USSR in 1921. In 1945 its territory was expanded at the expense of Poland and, for Soviet political reasons, it was given separate membership of the **UN**. Yet its sense of national identity remained comparatively undeveloped until its chance came in 1991.

Ben Ali, Zine el Abidine (1936–)
Tunisian politician. After studying electronics at military schools in France and the USA, he began a career in military security, rising to the position of Director-General of National Security. He became Minister

of the Interior and then Prime Minister under 'President-for-life' Habib **Bourguiba**, who had been in power since 1956. In 1987 he forced Bourguiba to retire and assumed the presidency and immediately embarked on constitutional reforms, promising a greater degree of democracy.

Ben Bella, Ahmed (1918–)
Algerian politician. A key figure in the **Algerian War of Independence** against France, he fought with the Free French in **World War II**, and in 1949 became head of the *Organisation Spéciale* ('Special Organization'), the paramilitary wing of the Algerian nationalist *Parti du Peuple Algérien* (Party of the Algerian People'). In 1952 he escaped from a French-Algerian prison to Cairo, where he became a key member of the **FLN** (*Front de Libération Nationale*). Captured by the French in 1956, he spent the remainder of the war in a French prison. Following independence in 1962, he became Algeria's first Prime Minister (1962–3), and President (1963–5). His deposition in 1965 was followed by 15 years of imprisonment, from which he was released in 1980.

Ben-Gurion, David (1886–1973)
Israeli politician. Born in Poland, he emigrated to Palestine in 1906. Expelled by the Turks during **World War I**, he recruited Jews to the British Army in North America. In Palestine in 1919 he founded a socialist party and became Secretary to the **Histadrut** in 1921. He led the **Mapai Party** from its formation in 1930 and headed the **Jewish Agency** in 1935. Ben-Gurion moulded the Mapai into the main party of the **Yishuv** during British rule and became Prime Minister after independence (1948–53), when he was responsible for Israel absorbing large numbers of refugees from Europe and Arab countries. He was Prime Minister again from 1955 to 1963. ▷ **Jewish Labour Movement in Palestine**

Benelux
An economic union between Belgium, the Netherlands, and Luxembourg. It began as a customs union which came into existence in 1948 as the result of a convention concluded in London in 1944. Despite the difficulties of achieving economic integration and the exclusion of agriculture from the union, mutual trade between the three countries expanded. A treaty established a more ambitious economic union between the three in 1958.

Beneš, Edvard (1884–1948)
Czechoslovak politician. He was Professor of Sociology at Prague, then as an émigré during **World War I** worked in Paris with Masaryk for Czech independence, becoming Foreign Minister of the new state (1918–35), and for a while Premier (1921–2). In 1935 he succeeded Masaryk as President, but resigned in 1938 following the Munich Agreement. He

then left the country, setting up a government in exile, first in France, then in Britain. Beneš returned to Czechoslovakia in 1945 and was re-elected President the following year, but resigned after the Communist takeover in 1948.

Bengal, Partition of (1905)
The division of Bengal for administrative purposes, conceived and carried out by Lord Curzon while he was Viceroy. Because of Bengal's combination with Orissa and Bihar for administrative purposes, the provincial population was enormous, and administration had become unwieldy. Largely because of this and poor communications to the east of Calcutta, East Bengal had been neglected in favour of West Bengal, Orissa and Bihar. Curzon decided to combine East Bengal with Assam, making Dacca the capital, and to leave Calcutta as the capital of West Bengal and India. Because the partition created an East Bengal with a large Muslim majority, Hindus felt that they would be marginalized in that region. Many Bengalis believed that the partition was an attempt to destroy nationalism, which was more highly developed in Bengal than elsewhere. The public outcry was manifested in rural agitation, mass meetings, boycott of foreign goods and even terrorism. Although the partition took place, East and West Bengal were reunited in 1911, with Assam and Orissa-Bihar becoming two new administrative districts. The outrage of nationalists and Bengali Hindus over the partition was largely responsible for both Curzon's early removal from the Viceroyalty, and the transformation of the **Indian National Congress** from a middle-class pressure group to a popular nationwide political party.

Benn, Tony (Anthony (Neil) Wedgwood Benn) (1925–)
British politician. The son of Viscount Stansgate, he became a Labour MP in 1950 but was debarred from the Commons on succeeding to his father's title. He renounced his title, and was re-elected in a by-election in 1963. He held various government posts under Harold **Wilson** and James **Callaghan**, notably Minister of Technology (1966–70), Secretary for Industry (1974–5) and Secretary for Energy (1975–9). He was the main focus for the left-wing challenge to the Labour leadership in the late 1970s and 1980s which ultimately failed but which persuaded some on the right to leave the party and form the **Social Democratic Party**. ▷ **Foot, Michael; Kinnock, Neil; Labour Party**

Bennett, Richard Bedford, 1st Viscount (1870–1947)
Canadian politician. Educated in Nova Scotia, he trained as a lawyer, and entered politics in 1897. He was Conservative leader from 1927, and while Prime Minister (1930–5) convened the Imperial Economic Conference in Ottawa (1932), from which emerged a system of empire

trade preference. He retired to England in 1938 and was made a peer in 1941. ▷ **New Deal** (Canada); **Price Spreads Commission**

Beran, Josef (1888–1969)
Czech Catholic priest and archbishop. Imprisoned in **Dachau** concentration camp in **World War II**, he became Archbishop of Prague in 1946. Although the Catholic Church was anxious to avoid too close an involvement in politics, he spoke out in favour of democracy during the communist seizure of power in Feb 1948. Within a year the Church was persecuted, and Beran and most churchmen were cut off from contact with Rome. It was 1965 before the situation eased sufficiently for him to leave for Rome, where he was appointed cardinal.

Beran, Rudolf (1887–1954)
Czechoslovak politician. He became Secretary-General of the powerful right-wing Agrarian Party in 1918 and its President in 1935. Torn between dislike of **Hitler** and hatred for **Stalin**, he quickly opted for a policy of appeasing Germany in the hope of securing local concessions. His behaviour in 1938 was close to treasonable as he negotiated behind President **Beneš**'s back. His reward was to become Prime Minister for a time after the **Munich Agreement**, but in 1946 he was imprisoned as a collaborator. He undoubtedly undermined the Czechoslovak position in the face of Hitler.

Berdyaev, Nikolai (1874–1948)
Russian religious philosopher. Born into an aristocratic family in Kiev, he developed strong revolutionary sympathies as a student and supported the **Russian Revolution** of 1917. He secured a professorship at Moscow but his unorthodox spiritual and libertarian ideals led to his dismissal in 1922. He moved to found in Berlin an Academy of the Philosophy of Religion which he later transferred to Clamart, near Paris, where he died. He described himself as a 'believing freethinker' and his fierce commitment to freedom and individualism brought him into conflict with both ecclesiastical and political powers.

Berggrav, Eivind (1884–1959)
Norwegian Lutheran bishop. After some years as a teacher, pastor and prison chaplain, he became Bishop of Troms and then Bishop of Oslo and Primate of the Norwegian Church (1937–50). Following the Nazi occupation of 1940, he led the Church's opposition to the **Quisling** government, refusing to endorse the war against Russia as a fight against atheism, and opposing Nazi attempts to monopolize the education of young people. For this he was imprisoned (1941–5). He wrote some 30 books and was a strong supporter of the ecumenical movement, becoming a president of the World Council of Churches (1950–4).

Beria, Lavrenti Pavlovich (1899–1953)
Soviet secret police chief. After holding local positions in his native Georgia, he became Soviet Commissar for Internal Affairs in 1938. During **World War II** he was Vice-President of the State Committee for Defence, and was active in purging **Stalin**'s opponents. After **Stalin**'s death (1953), he belonged briefly with Giorgiy **Malenkov** and Molotov to the collective leadership. Accused by his colleagues of conspiracy, he was shot after a mock 'treason' trial.

Berlin
The capital of Germany. The city was divided into eastern and western sectors in 1945. In 1949 West Berlin became a province of the Federal Republic of Germany, and East Berlin became the capital and a county of the German Democratic Republic. The two halves of the city were separated by a wall built in 1961 by the East German government to prevent citizens moving from East to West. In 1989 contact between East and West Berlin was restored, following government changes in East Germany and the dismantling of the Berlin Wall. A unified Berlin became the capital of the unified Germany in 1990.

Berlin, Battle of (Apr–May 1945)
On 25 Apr 1945 advancing Soviet troops surrounded Berlin. **Hitler** had ordered the 9th and 11th Armies to relieve Berlin on 24 Apr, but they were unable to break through the Soviet lines. There followed a Soviet offensive on the city which resulted in days of bitter street fighting. On 30 Apr, Hitler committed suicide and on 2 May the German Commander in Berlin, General Weidling, surrendered to the Soviet commander, Marshall **Zhukov**.

Berlin, Partition of
Founded in the 13c, Berlin became the residence of the **Hohenzollern Dynasty** and the capital of Brandenburg. Later it was the capital of **Prussia**, becoming an industrial and commercial centre in the 18c. As the capital of Germany, it was partitioned during the late 1940s into East Berlin and West Berlin. In 1949, West Berlin became associated with the Federal Republic of Germany (although under Four Power control) and East Berlin became, *de facto*, a county of the German Democratic Republic. The two halves of the city were separated by a wall built around West Berlin in 1961 to prevent the movement of citizens from East to West. Contact between the two halves of the city was restored in Nov 1989, following the **Revolution of 1989** in East Germany, and it was made the capital of unified Germany in 1990. ▷ **Berlin Wall; Germany, East**

Berlin Airlift (1948–9)

A massive airlift of essential supplies flown in to **Cold War** Berlin by British and US aircraft in round-the-clock missions. It was carried out in response to the action of the Soviet military authorities in Berlin, who had attempted to isolate the city from the West by severing all overland communication routes (June 1948). **Stalin** lifted the blockade in May 1949.

Berlin blockade (1948–9)

An attempt by **Stalin** to weaken US preparedness to remain in Europe indefinitely following **World War II**, and also to secure his control over Eastern Europe by strengthening his hold on the east of Germany. Specifically, the idea was to prevent supplies getting through to the western zones of Berlin, in the hope that the Allies would withdraw. In the event, the Allies flew in food and fuel for almost 11 months until Stalin had to back down. It was after this that the **Cold War** intensified, with the establishment of **NATO** and **Comecon** in 1949.

Berlin Wall

A concrete wall built by the East German government in 1961 to seal off East Berlin from the part of the city occupied by the three main Western powers. Built largely to prevent mass illegal emigration to the West, which was threatening the East German economy, the wall was the scene of the shooting of many East Germans who tried to escape from the eastern sector. The wall, seen by many as a major symbol of the denial of human rights in Eastern Europe, was unexpectedly opened in Nov 1989, following revolutionary upheaval in East **Germany**. Following reunification, most of the wall has now been taken down. ▷ **Berlin, Partition of; Revolution of 1989**

Berlinguer, Enrico (1922–84)

Italian politician. Born into a wealthy Sardinian landowning family, from 1943 he was a member of the Italian Communist Party (PCI) and played an active role in the resistance. Secretary-General of the Federation of Young Communists (1949–56), he was elected to parliament in 1968 and became Vice-Secretary of the party in 1969; he was made Secretary-General in 1972. In Sep 1973 he proposed the 'historic compromise' with the **Christian Democrat Party**: in return for social reforms and an increased say on policy formation, the PCI agreed to respect the Church and constitutional institutions and discourage labour militancy. Shortly afterwards, he also endorsed **NATO** and, in Dec 1977, PCI deputies voted in favour of Italy's foreign and defence policies. Under Berlinguer's influence, Italian communism flourished in the 1970s: in the 1976 elections, the PCI received 34.4 per cent of votes, rivalling the 38.7 per cent polled by the DC, and by Mar 1978 the PCI had entered the government's parliamentary majority. However, traditional DC suspicion of the left, the openly anti-communist stance of Pope **John Paul II** (elected Oct 1978) and the anti-Soviet feeling generated by the invasion of Afghanistan undermined the coalition. So too did the more militant wing of the PCI which never welcomed cooperation with the DC. Berlinguer was consequently forced to jettison his conciliatory position and by 1979 was once again in opposition. During the remaining years of his life, he continued to pursue his vision of 'Eurocommunism' which rejected the rigid Stalinist doctrines of the USSR. However, support for the PCI never again reached its peak of the late 1970s.

Bernadotte, Count Folke (1895–1948)
Swedish diplomat. He was the nephew of King **Gustav V** of Sweden. He acted as a mediator in **World War I** and, as Vice-President of the Swedish Red Cross, negotiated with **Himmler** in the spring of 1945 for the liberation of Scandinavian prisoners from German concentration camps. Appointed by the **UN** to try to reach a settlement of the Palestine question, he produced a plan of partition but was assassinated by the **Stern Gang** in Jerusalem.

Bernhard Leopold (1911–)
Prince of the Netherlands. The son of Prince Bernhard Casimir of Lippe and Armgard von Cramm, in 1937 he married **Juliana**, the only daughter of **Wilhelmina**, Queen of the Netherlands. During **World War II** he commanded the Netherlands Forces of the Interior (1944–5). In 1976 he was involved in a bribery scandal, in which he was found to have received money for promoting the Dutch purchase of aircraft from the Lockheed Aircraft Corporation.

Bernstein, Eduard (1850–1932)
German socialist leader. An associate of Engels, he played a major part in unifying the German socialist movement in 1875. As a leading intellectual in the Social Democratic Party (**SPD**), he was prominent in establishing its Marxist ideology. Later he was an advocate of revisionism, an evolutionary form of **Marxism**, and a member of the **Reichstag** periodically (1902–28). He was exiled for his beliefs (1888–1901), during which time he lived in London, where he influenced, and was in turn influenced by, the British Fabians and other socialists. ▷ **Fabian Society**

Bernstorff, Johan Heinrich, Count (1862–1939)
German diplomat. After a varied diplomatic career, Bernstorff became German ambassador to the USA in 1908. During **World War I** he sought unsuccessfully to dissuade his government from waging submarine warfare, the latter bringing the USA into the war. He then became German Ambassador to the **Ottoman Empire** before serving as a member of the **Reichstag** for the liberal **DDP** during the Weimar era and as German delegate on the League of Nations Disarmament Commission.

In 1933 he sought exile in Switzerland where he pursued his publishing interests. ▷ **Weimar Republic**

Berri, Nabih (1939–)

Lebanese politician and soldier. Born in Freetown, Sierra Leone, he was the son of an expatriate Lebanese merchant. He studied law at Beirut University and practised as a lawyer for a time. In 1978 he became leader of Amal ('Hope'), a branch of the Shi'ite nationalist movement founded by Iman Musa Sadr. Backed by Syria, he became the main Shi'ite military force in West Beirut and Southern Lebanon during the country's civil wars, but in 1988 its Beirut branch was heavily defeated by the Iranian-backed Hezbollah ('Party of God') and was disbanded. Berri joined the Lebanese government in 1984 as Minister of Justice.

Bessarabia

The region between the Prut and Dniester Rivers, the Black Sea and Danube delta. Settled by the Slavs (6c), then the Mongols (13c), at the end of the 14c it became part of Wallachia and was named after the ruling Wallachian Dynasty. In the 15c it passed to Moldavia and from the 16c was subject to the Ottomans until 1812 when, by the Treaty of **Bucharest**, together with half of Moldavia, it passed to Russia. In 1918 it declared itself independent, voted to join Romania and under the Treaty of **Paris** (1920) was awarded to Romania. In the **German–Soviet Pact** (1939) the USSR was promised Bessarabia with northern **Bukovina** and in 1940, with part of the Ukraine, it became part of the Soviet Socialist Republic of Moldavia. Although occupied by the Romanian Army during **World War II**, it was returned to the USSR in 1947, after which its control was disputed by the Soviet and Romanian governments.

Betancourt, Rómulo (1908–81)

Venezuelan politician and reformer. One of the founders of the *Partido Democrático Nacional* (National Democratic Party) in 1936, he held power from 1945 to 1947. On the fall of the Pérez Jiménez dictatorship (1950–8), he was elected President (1959–64) of the new Venezuelan democracy. He chose a moderate course, adopting an agrarian law in Mar 1960, and ambitious economic development plans which provided for a transition from the dictatorship.

Bethlen, István (Stephen), Count (1874–1947)

Hungarian politician. He was a leader of the counter-revolutionary movement after **World War I**, and as Prime Minister from 1921 to 1931 promoted Hungary's economic reconstruction.

Bethune, Mary McLeod (1875–1955)
US educator and administrator. She was founder and President of the National Council of Negro Women and of Bethune-Cookman College. Serving as adviser to President Franklin D **Roosevelt**'s **New Deal** administration, she worked to expand awareness of minority issues within government agencies. She was director of the division of Negro Affairs within the National Youth Administration at a time when 40 per cent of black youths were suffering unemployment. As such she was quietly insistent that the number of blacks enrolled in the programme be increased despite the reluctance of state administrators. Black college students also benefited from the Special Negro Fund which she administered. In 1945 she was accredited by the State Department to attend the San Francisco Conference to establish the **UN**.

Bevan, Aneurin (1897–1960)
British politician. One of 13 children, he worked in the pits on leaving school at 13, and led the Welsh miners in the 1926 **General Strike**. He entered parliament for the **Independent Labour Party** in 1929, joining the **Labour Party** in 1931. He established a reputation as a brilliant, irreverent, and often tempestuous orator. As Minister of Health (1945–51), he introduced the National Health Service (1948). He became Minister of Labour in 1951, but resigned in the same year over the National Health charges proposed in the Budget. From this period dated 'Bevanism', a left-wing movement to make the Labour Party more socialist and less 'reformist'. He married Jennie **Lee** in 1934, and died while still an MP. ▷ **socialism**

Beveridge, William Henry Beveridge, 1st Baron (1879–1963)
British economist, administrator, and social reformer. He entered the Board of Trade (1908) and became Director of Labour Exchanges (1909–16). He was Director of the London School of Economics (1919–37) and Master of University College, Oxford (1937–45). He is best known as the author of the *Report on Social Insurance and Allied Services* (The Beveridge Report, 1942), which provided a blueprint for the creation of the welfare state. He was knighted in 1919, became a Liberal MP (1944–6), and was made a baron in 1946. ▷ **Liberal Party** (UK)

Bevin, Ernest (1881–1951)
British politician. Orphaned by the age of seven, and self-taught, he early came under the influence of trade unionism and the Baptists, and was for a time a lay preacher. A paid official of the dockers' union, he gained a national reputation in 1920 when he won most of his union's claims against an eminent barrister, earning the title of 'the dockers' KC'. He built up the National Transport and General Workers' Union, and became its General-Secretary (1921–40). In 1940 he became a Labour

MP, Minister of Labour and National Service in Winston **Churchill**'s coalition government, and was Foreign Secretary in the Labour governments (1945–51). ▷ **Labour Party** (UK)

Bhattari, Krishna Prasad (1925–)
Nepalese politician. As an opponent of absolute monarchy, he was in hiding for 12 years until 1990, when, as Leader of the centrist Nepali Congress Party, he became Prime Minister in the wake of the revolution that year, which ended the uncontested rule of King **Birendra**. However, in May 1991, in Nepal's first multi-party elections in three decades, he offered his resignation to the King after losing his own seat in the 205-member House of Representatives to the Marxist leader of the United Communist Party, Madan Bhandari.

Bhave, Vinoba (1895–1982)
Indian social and land reformer. M K **Gandhi** took him under his care as a young scholar, an event which changed his life. Distressed in 1951 by the land hunger riots in Telengana, Hyderabad, Bhave began a walking mission throughout India to persuade landlords to give land to the peasants and thus founded the **Bhoodan** movement. A barefoot, ascetic saint, his silent revolution led to 4 000 000 acres of land being redistributed in four years. He was claimed to be the most notable spiritual figure in India after the death of Gandhi, whose ardent disciple he was.

Bhindranwale, Sant Jarnail Singh (1947–84)
Indian politician and former Sikh extremist leader. Born into a poor Punjabi Jat farming family, he trained at the orthodox Damdani Taksal Sikh missionary school, becoming its head priest in 1971 and assuming the name Bhindranwale. Initially encouraged by Sanjay Gandhi (1946–80), the son and political adviser of Indira **Gandhi**, who sought to divide the Sikh Akali Dal movement, he campaigned violently against the heretical activities of Nirankari Sikhs during the later 1970s. His campaign broadened into a demand for a separate state of 'Khalistan' during the early 1980s, precipitating a bloody Hindu-Sikh conflict in Punjab. After taking refuge in the Golden Temple complex at Amritsar and building up an arms cache for terrorist activities, with about 500 devoted followers, he died at the hands of the Indian Security Forces who stormed the temple in 'Operation Blue Star'. ▷ **Akali Movement**

Bhoodan (Bhudan)
Literally 'land-giving' in Hindi, Bhoodan is a late 20c agrarian Indian social movement, which encouraged the donation of land to the landless peasantry. Bhoodan was conceived and led by Vinoba **Bhave**.

Bhumibol Adulyadej (1927–)
King of Thailand (1946/). The second son of Prince Mahidol of Songkhola and grandson of King Chulalongkorn, he was educated in Bangkok and Switzerland and became monarch, as King Rama IX, after the death, in controversial circumstances, of his elder brother, King Ananda Mahidol. He married Queen Sirikit in 1950 and has one son and three daughters. As king, he has been a stabilizing influence in a country noted for its political turbulence, and was active, with popular support, in helping to overthrow the military government of Field Marshal Thanom Kittikachorn in 1973. He is a highly respected figure, viewed in some quarters as semi-divine, and wields considerable political influence behind the scenes.

Bhutto, Benazir (1953–)
Pakistani politician. After an education at Oxford University, she returned to Pakistan and was placed under house arrest between 1977 and 1984 by General **Zia ul-Haq**, who had executed her father Zulfikar Ali **Bhutto**, following the 1977 coup against him. During her subsequent exile in England with her mother, she formed the Pakistan People's Party, returning to Pakistan with the lifting of martial law in 1986 and beginning her campaign for open elections. She married in 1987, and, following General Zia's death the same year, she was elected Prime Minister in 1988, taking Pakistan back into the Commonwealth in 1989. Increasing friction between her Administration and the conservative presidency led to her Government being dismissed in Aug 1990, and soon after corruption charges were made against her; her husband was placed in custody on related alleged criminal offences. At the start of 1991, she began a lecture tour of America and Europe, but she dismissed speculation that she was choosing self-exile in return for her husband's release.

Bhutto, Zulfikar Ali (1928–79)
Pakistani politician. A graduate of the Universities of California and Oxford, he began a career in law. He joined the Pakistani Cabinet in 1958 as Minister of Commerce, and became Foreign Minister in 1963. Dropped from the Cabinet, he founded the Pakistan People's Party (PPP) in 1967. After the secession of East Pakistan (now Bangladesh) in 1971, he became President (1971–3) and Prime Minister (1973–7). He introduced social and economic reforms, but opposition to his policies, especially from right-wing Islamic parties, led to the army under General **Zia ul-Haq** seizing control after the 1977 elections. Tried for corruption and murder, he was sentenced to death in 1978. In spite of worldwide appeals for clemency, the sentence was carried out in 1979.

Biafra
The south-eastern province of Nigeria, inhabited by the **Igbo** people. Under the leadership of Colonel Ojukwu, it attempted to break away

from the federation, thus precipitating the civil war of 1967–70. After the war, Nigeria was reorganized into a new provincial structure in an attempt to avert continuing instability.

Biafran War (1967–70)

Two military coups in 1966 left Nigeria racked by ethnic divisions and on 26 May 1967 Lt-Col Chukuvemoka **Ojukwu** was mandated by the Ibo consultative assembly to declare the Eastern Region of Nigeria independent as the state of Biafra. Civil war then broke out as the Federal government, led by **Gowon**, sought to keep Nigeria one. It was not until Jan 1970 that the federal forces prevailed and, with Ojukwu's exile, peace was restored.

Bibó, István (1911–)

Hungarian political writer and, briefly, revolutionary politician. A supporter of the so-called Smallholders Party, he held middle-of-the-road views and had a difficult time practising as a writer in the early 1950s. However, in 1956, between the two Soviet interventions, he was chosen to be a member of Imre **Nagy**'s cabinet and tried to exert a calming influence. He was subsequently condemned to death by the **Kádár** government and was only saved by protests from the West. It was not until 1963 that he was released from prison as a sign that reform was on the way.

Bidault, Georges (1899–1982)

French politician. He became a professor of history, served in both world wars, and was a member of the French Resistance. He became leader of the MRP (*Mouvement républicain populaire*), and apart from his periods as Premier (1946 and 1949–50), was Deputy Prime Minister (1950 and 1951), and Foreign Minister (1944, 1947 and 1953–4). After 1958 he opposed de **Gaulle** over the **Algerian War**, was charged with plotting against the security of the state, and went into exile (1962–8). ▷ **Resistance Movement**

Bierut, Bolesław (1892–1956)

Polish Communist Party functionary. In the interwar period he was in and out of prison and of Poland; then and later he spent formative periods in Moscow. In 1946 he was appointed Interim President, and the following year he was elected President. In 1948 he took over from **Gomułka** as Secretary of the party, and then from 1952 to 1954 he was Prime Minister. His main claim to fame was following the Stalinist line and doing much damage to his country and colleagues in the process.

Big-Character Poster (*Dazibao/Ta-tzu pao*)

A form of wall-poster in China that has served as a unique means of public expression free of government or party control. Often anonymous, and handwritten, these posters have appeared on walls or billboards erected in public places. The first wallposter to gain notoriety was the one displayed by the Philosophy Department of Beijing University on 25 May 1966, criticizing university authorities for stifling political debate. In Aug 1966 **Mao Zedong** himself wrote a wallposter which denounced revisionism. Although the right to erect wallposters expressing one's opinions was guaranteed in the 1975 and 1978 Constitutions, such a privilege was withdrawn in 1980 following a protest movement the previous year calling for greater democracy.

Biko, Steve (Stephen) (1947–77)

South African black activist. He studied medicine at Natal University from where he became President of the all-black South African Students Organization (1969) and Honorary President of the Black People's Convention (1972). He was the major figure in the **Black Consciousness Movement** and his challenge to **apartheid**, expressed in his organization of the Black Community Programme, led to his being banned and then detained. He died in police custody as a result of beatings received.

Bil'ak, Vasil (1917–)

Czechoslovak politician. He had a fairly undistinguished career in the Communist Party until 1968 when, as a Slovak, he succeeded Alexander **Dubček** as Secretary of the Central Committee of the Slovak Section. It was at this point that Dubček moved up to the secretaryship of the whole party and initiated the **Prague Spring**. Bil'ak was a reluctant reformer and in July and Aug of 1968 turned against Dubček, eventually welcoming the Soviet invasion. He was subsequently too unpopular to achieve high office but he remained a member of the party presidium, resisting any change, for two decades.

Bilingualism and Biculturalism, Royal Commission on (1963–71)

Canadian governmental inquiry. Instituted by the Pearson administration, it was a response to the increasing separatist pressure in Quebec. Its aims were to research the origins of the crisis and to propose measures which would lead to a more equitable relationship between francophones and anglophones. Joint presidents of the commission were André Laurendeau, editor of the newspaper *Le Devoir*, and A Davidson Dunton, President of Ottawa's Carleton University. The final report revealed the extent to which French-Canadians were disadvantaged, both economically and culturally by their origins. It recommended the adoption of both French and English as official languages throughout the federal bureaucracy and in business. Whilst the report refused to advocate separate nationhood for Quebec, it did propose the concept of a two-nation federation, and the establishment of a ministry for multiculturalism, which was enacted in 1972.

bill of rights

A list of citizens' rights set out in constitutional documents. Usually accompanying the document is an elaboration of the institutional means and powers by which such rights may be enforced. The best-known example is the one adopted in 1791 as the first 10 amendments to the **US Constitution**. The American Bill of Rights protects the liberties of private citizens in relation to the federal and state governments in such matters as freedom of speech, religion, the press and assembly, and legal procedure.

Bird, Vere Cornwall (1910–)

Antiguan politician. In 1939 he was a founder-member of the Antigua Trades and Labour Union and then leader of the Antigua Labour Party (ALP). In the pre-independence period he was elected to the Legislative Council and became Chief Minister (1960–7) and Premier (1967–71 and 1976–81). When total independence, as Antigua and Barbuda, was achieved in 1981 he became Prime Minister; he and his party were re-elected in 1984, and again in 1989.

Birdwood, William Riddell, 1st Baron Birdwood of Anjac and Totnes (1865–1951)

Australian military leader, he served in the Indian Army, became Secretary of the Indian Army Department and a member of the Viceroy's legislative council (1912). In 1914 he was put in command of the Australian and New Zealand Army contingents, and planned the landing at Gallipoli, on Anzac Cove as it was subsequently known. Upon evacuation from the Peninsula, he took his troops to the Western Front, through the Battles of the Somme and Ypres in 1916 and 1917. After **World War I** he returned to India to command the Northern Army, becoming Commander-in-Chief in 1925, and retiring in 1930. ▷ **Gallipoli Campaign; Somme, Battle of the**

Birendra, Bir Bikram Shah Dev (1945–)

King of Nepal (1972/). Educated at St Joseph's College, Darjeeling, Eton, and Tokyo and Harvard Universities, he married Queen Aishwarya Rajya Laxmi Devi Rana in 1970, and has two sons and one daughter. Appointed Grand Master and Colonel-in-Chief of the Royal Nepalese Army in 1964, he became King on the death of his father, King Mahendra. During his reign, there has been gradual progress towards political reform, but Nepal remained essentially an absolute monarchy, with political activity banned, until 1990, when Birendra was forced to concede much of his power.

Birkenhead, Frederick Edwin Smith, 1st Earl of (1872–1930)
British politician and lawyer. A Conservative, he entered parliament in 1906, where he became known as a brilliant orator. In the Irish crisis (1914) he supported resistance to **Home Rule**, but later helped to negotiate the Irish settlement of 1921. He became Attorney-General (1915–19) and Lord Chancellor (1919–22) and was made an earl in 1922. His conduct as Secretary of State for India (1924–8) caused much criticism, and he resigned to devote himself to a commercial career. ▷ **Conservative Party (UK)**

Birla, G D (1894–1983)
Indian industrialist. Until recently, he was India's biggest paper magnate, in charge of the huge Oriental Paper empire. He was also a large-scale philanthropist, contributing to the causes of scientific and medical research. Most famous for his close friendship with M K **Gandhi** and his strong support for the **Indian National Congress** in the 1920s, 1930s and 1940s. He was himself elected to the Indian Central Legislative Assembly in 1926. In 1944 he compiled the so-called Bombay Plan, along with two other businessmen, Thakurdas and J R D Tata, which set the pattern of state and private investment that was characteristic of India's five-year plans after Independence.

Biryukova, Alexandra Pavlovna (1929–)
Soviet politician. She was trained as a textile engineer and continued until as late as 1968 with her professional job in a factory. However, she had earlier taken official jobs, and in 1968 she became Secretary of the Trade Union Presidium and in 1985 Deputy Chairman. In 1986 Mikhail **Gorbachev** selected her for the Secretariat of the Central Committee of the Communist Party and in 1988 appointed her Deputy Prime Minister responsible for Social Development. She was also made a candidate member of the **Politburo**, the first woman since **Furtseva** to achieve this distinction. One of the few Soviet women to reach positions of political importance, in the turmoil of 1990–1, she was, however, pushed aside.

Bishop, Maurice (1946–83)
Grenadian politician. He was the leader of the New Jewel Movement which overthrew the government of Eric **Gairy** in 1979 and set up a Marxist People's Revolutionary Government. Disagreements over policy led to Bishop's overthrow and murder by his deputy, Bernard Coard, and the Commander of the Armed Forces, General Austin (Oct 1983), and the creation of a Revolutionary Military Council (RMC). The USA and moderate Caribbean governments, shocked by the bloody coup and fearful of imagined Cuban influence, instigated military intervention to depose the RMC and arrest the coup leaders. Coard, Austin and 12

others were sentenced to death, but these sentences were commuted to life imprisonment in 1991.

Bitar, Salah al-Din

Syrian politician. Co-founder in 1943 with Michel **Aflaq** of the **Ba'ath Socialist Party**, he played a considerable part in the founding of the short-lived **United Arab Republic** (UAR), a union of Egypt and Syria established in 1958, from which Syria seceded in 1961. Despite a broad influence through its essentially socialist and pan-Arab ideology, the failure of the UAR dealt a considerable blow to the Ba'ath as originally conceived by Bitar and Aflaq, and paved the way for the separate development of one-party Ba'athist rule in Syria and Iraq.

Biya, Paul (1933–)

Cameroonian politician. He graduated with a law degree from Paris University and entered politics under the aegis of **Ahidjo**. He was a junior minister in 1962, a minister of state in 1968 and Prime Minister in 1975. When Ahidjo unexpectedly retired in 1982, he became President and reconstituted the government with his own supporters. He survived a coup attempt in Apr 1984 (almost certainly instigated by Ahidjo) and was re-elected President in 1988 with more than 98 per cent of the vote.

Bjelke-Petersen, Sir Jo(hannes) (1911–)

New Zealand-born Australian politician, of Danish parents. In 1913 the family moved to Kingaroy, Queensland. He entered state politics in 1947 as a Country Party (later National Party) member of the Legislative Assembly, becoming a minister in 1963. In 1968, as a result of his firm stand on law and order, he was made Police Minister, then Deputy Leader and, following the sudden death of Jack Pizzey, became Premier of Queensland. A vocal supporter of states' rights against federal intervention, he controlled a strongly right-wing government, first in coalition with the **Liberal Party of Australia** and after 1983 in his own right. He was knighted in 1982 and retired from the premiership in 1987. ▷ **National Party of Australia**

Björnsson, Sveinn (1881–1952)

Icelandic diplomat and politician. Born in Copenhagen, he was the son of an Icelandic newspaper editor. He studied law in Copenhagen and was elected a member of the Icelandic parliament in 1914–16 and 1920. During **World War I** he was envoy to the USA and Britain, and was ambassador to Denmark in 1920–4 and 1926–41. During the German occupation of Denmark he was elected regent of Iceland and, when Iceland declared its independence of Denmark in 1944, he was elected the new republic's first President. Re-elected in 1948, he died in office.

Black, Hugo Lafayette (1886–1971)
US jurist. He practised law in his home state of Alabama and became a police court judge. In 1927 he entered the US Senate and as a liberal leader promoted the Tennessee Valley Authority as well as legislation that would set minimum wages and impose limits on working hours. In 1937 he was appointed to the US Supreme Court, where he served until his death. Black, a libertarian, opposed undue economic regulation by the states or the federal government. Central to his philosophy was the conviction that the Fourteenth Amendment made the Bill of Rights generally applicable to the states and that the First Amendment's guarantees of freedoms were absolute. Late in his career he supported civil rights legislation.

Black and Tans
Additional members of the Royal Irish Constabulary, recruited by the British government to cope with Irish nationalist unrest in 1920. The shortage of regulation uniforms led to the recruits being issued with khaki tunics and trousers and very dark green caps, hence their name. Terrorist activities provoked severe and brutal reprisals by the Black and Tans, which caused an outcry in Britain and the USA.

Black Consciousness Movement (South Africa)
A loose movement formed by Steve **Biko** in 1969, when he led African students out of the multi-racial National Union of South African Students and founded the South African Students Organization. From this emerged the Black People's Convention in 1972 which sought to create cooperation in social and cultural fields among all non-white peoples. Banned in 1976, most of its leaders were imprisoned in 1977 and Biko himself died in police custody soon afterwards.

Black Dragon Society (*Kokuryukai*)
A Japanese ultra-nationalist conspiratorial organization founded in 1901 by Uchida Ryohei and Toyama Mitsuru. Strongly influenced by the concept of Pan-Asianism, the society sought to enhance Japan's influence on the Asian mainland, initially in Manchuria (and thereby eliminate Russian influence) and then throughout China. It maintained ties with a number of government officials, Diet politicians, and military officers, continually pressing for an assertive foreign policy to combat Western influence in Asia, an aim that was often linked with domestic renovation. The society also carried out espionage work on the Asian mainland. As with other ultra-nationalist organizations, the Black Dragon Society was disbanded in 1945 following Japan's defeat in **World War II**.

Black Hand

The common name for the secret organization 'Unification or Death' (*Ujedinjenje ili Smrt*) formed by Serbian nationalist army officers in 1911. Led by Colonel Dragutin **Dimitrijević**, alias Apis, its objective was the political unification of all the Serbs. It lay behind the assassination by the Bosnian Serb Gavrilo **Princip** of **Francis Ferdinand,** Archduke of Austria, in Sarajevo (June 1914), an event which led directly to the outbreak of **World War I**. ▷ **Mlada Bosna**

Black Hundreds (post-1905)

The name given to the right-wing terrorists opposed to the reforms conceded by **Nicholas II** during the Russian **Revolution of 1905**. Operating under fine-sounding names such as Union of the Russian People, Union of the Russian Land, or Russian Orthodox Committee, they were well-to-do and well connected. Often with official connivance, they resorted to violence against individuals or groups supporting democratic reform and helped to discredit such representative institutions as were tolerated.

Black Muslims

A black religious movement in the USA, also known as the Nation of Islam, founded in 1930 by Wali Farad (Wallace D Fard), who proclaimed that black Americans are descended from an ancient Muslim tribe. Followers adopted Muslim names and believed Farad to be an incarnation of God. Following Farad's mysterious disappearance in 1934, Elijah **Muhammad** became leader of the movement until his death in 1975. Muhammad urged his followers to avoid contact with whites and demanded a separate state for blacks as well as reparation for past injustices. **Malcolm X** was one of the movement's most inspiring preachers, while the boxer Muhammad Ali was one of its most famous members. After Elijah Muhammad's son, Warith Dean (Wallace D), assumed leadership, the organization adopted orthodox Muslim beliefs. There were some, however, who continued to hold to the original tenets of the movement, including its separatist stance. Louis Farrakhan emerged as that faction's spokesman and has continued in that role.

Black Panthers Party

US militant black political party, founded by Huey P **Newton** and Bobby Seale in 1966, promoting the use of physical force and armed confrontation for black liberation. The party was active in the 1960s, but was split by rival groups in the 1970s and diminished in importance.

Black Power

The slogan used by black activists in the USA from the mid-1960s to reflect the aspiration of increased black political power. It formed part of the more radical wing of the **civil rights** movement, was against integrationist policies, and rejected non-violence. Some political results were achieved in terms of registering black voters, together with much wider attitudinal change. ▷ **Black Panthers Party; Congress of Racial Equality (CORE)**

Black Saturday (26 Jan 1952)
After guerrilla attacks on their bases in Egypt, the British acted against suspects, including the Egyptian police. British forces surrounded police headquarters at Ismailia and called on the police to surrender; they refused and 50 were killed in the attack on their headquarters. The next day — Black Saturday — Egyptian crowds, led by the Muslim Brotherhood, burnt down British and foreign shops and restaurants in the centre of Cairo. Egyptian troops did not intervene to bring the situation under control until evening. King Farouk and the government blamed each other for the delay and there began a period of ministerial instability, as governments followed one another rapidly. This led the Free Officers to bring forward the coup they were planning for 1954 or 1955 to July 1952, when army units seized key points in the capital and Farouk was forced into exile.

Black September (Sep 1970)
This refers to the month when Fedayeen and the **PLO** (Palestine Liberation Organization) resisted an attempt by the Jordanian government to establish control over them and their guerrillas who were carrying out operations against Israel. A civil war resulted and King Hussein was saved by the loyalty of his Bedouin regiments.

Black Thursday (24 Oct 1929)
The date of the crash of the New York stock market that marked the onset of the **Great Depression**.

Blackshirts
The colloquial name for members of Oswald **Mosley**'s British Union of Fascists (BUF), formed in Oct 1932. It derived from the colour of the uniforms worn at mass rallies and demonstrations organized by the BUF on the model of European fascist parties. After clashes and disturbances in Jewish areas of London (1936), the Public Order Act prohibited the wearing of uniforms by political groups. ▷ **Union Movement**

Blaize, Herbert Augustus (1918–89)
Grenadian politician. After qualifying and practising as a solicitor, he entered politics and helped to found the centrist Grenada National Party (GNP), being elected to parliament in 1957. He held ministerial posts before becoming Premier in 1967. After full independence, in 1974, he led the official opposition and then went into hiding (1979–83) following

the left-wing coup by Maurice **Bishop**. After the US invasion of 1983, when normal political activity resumed, he returned to lead a reconstituted New National Party (NNP) and win the 1984 general election.

Blamey, Sir Thomas (1884–1951)
Australian soldier. He joined the regular army in 1906 and attended Staff College at Quetta. He saw service on the north-west frontier of India, and in **World War I** played an important part in the evacuation of Gallipoli. He became Chief of Staff of the Australian Corps in 1918 and between 1925 and 1936 was Chief Commissioner of Police in Victoria. At the outbreak of **World War II** he was given command of the Australian Imperial Forces in the Middle East. He had command of Commonwealth operations in Greece (1941) and served as Deputy Commander-in-Chief to Wavell. On the establishment of the south-west Pacific command he became Commander-in-Chief of Allied land forces (1942) and received the Japanese surrender in 1945. In 1950 he was made a field marshal, the first Australian soldier to hold this rank. ▷ **Gallipoli Campaign**

Blasco Ibáñez, Vicente (1867–1928)
Spanish politician and writer. A federalist Republican leader of revolutionary leanings, he was first elected to parliament in 1898. His populist appeal laid the foundations for the PURA (Party of Republican Autonomist Union), otherwise known as the 'Blasquist' movement, which became the dominant political force in Valencia until the **Spanish Civil War**. At the same time as the Barcelona leader Alejandro **Lerroux** (an ally), Blasco Ibáñez formed the first modern political party in Spain. Although Blasco abandoned politics for writing in 1907, his political pronouncements made a greater impact than ever. During **World War I** he backed the Allies, most notably through his novel *The Four Horsemen of the Apocalypse*. His broadsides against the monarchy and **Primo de Rivera**'s dictatorship (1923–30) were highly effective. During the early part of the 20c he was probably the most famous living Spanish writer in the world. He died in exile in France.

blitz
The colloquial name for the series of air raids on British cities by the German Air Force (Sep 1940–May 1941). The purpose of the raids was to weaken British resistance to projected invasion. The cities of London and Coventry were particularly badly affected. ▷ **Blitzkrieg; Luftwaffe; World War II**

Blitzkrieg
A term (literally, 'lightning war') coined, in Sep 1939, to describe the German armed forces' use of fast-moving tanks and deep-ranging aircraft in techniques which involve bypassing resistance and aiming the focus of

effort at the enemy's rear areas rather than making frontal attacks. *Blitzkrieg* tactics were used with great success by the Germans from 1939 to 1941 to achieve rapid and conclusive victories. ▷ **World War II**

Bloc national (1919)

A French electoral coalition which won the 1919 elections, producing a Chamber of Deputies with a conservative majority, called the 'blue horizon' Chamber, so named after the colour of French Army uniforms. It was defeated by the **Cartel des gauches** ('Left-wing Cartel') in 1924. The term 'bloc' in this context had been coined by **Clemenceau** in 1891, in a famous phrase describing the French Revolution, and first applied to the *Bloc de Défense républicaine* ('Republican Defence') at the time of the **Dreyfus** Affair (1899–1902).

Bloc Populaire

Quebecois nationalist political party. It was formed in 1942 by liberals who opposed Canadian participation in **World War II** and the introduction of conscription, and by Catholic radicals like André Laurendeau who wished to base industrial relations on papal encyclicals and to forbid the entry of foreign capital. After winning four seats in the provincial elections of 1944, the party fragmented, with the **Union Nationale** having benefited considerably from its extremism.

Bloody Sunday (9 Jan 1905)

Political opposition to Tsarist autocracy had intensified in 1904 as Russia suffered defeats in its war with Japan. In the new year, on this day, Father **Gapon** led a group of workers to the **Winter Palace** in St Petersburg to present a petition to **Nicholas II**. They were joined by a large but peaceful crowd. Troops opened fire, killing over 100 people and wounding several hundred more. This marked the beginning of the Russian **Revolution of 1905** and, symbolically, made something like the **February Revolution** (1917) more or less inevitable.

Bloody Sunday (30 Jan 1972)

The name given, especially by Republicans in Northern Ireland, to events occurring during a Catholic civil rights protest march in Londonderry. The British Army opened fire, killing 14, mainly young, demonstrators. This action led to increased support for the **IRA** and to many more deaths from political violence. Indirectly, it led to the ending of the **Stormont** parliament and the reimposition of direct rule by the British government over Northern Ireland.

Blueshirts

The pejorative term coined by the Japanese to refer to a Chinese elite revolutionary corps set up within the **Guomindang** (Nationalist Party).

Founded in 1932 by close associates of **Chiang Kai-shek**, it sought to root out corruption within the Guomindang, promote state-sponsored industrial development, and create a militarized and disciplined society. Admirers of European fascism, the Blueshirts also wished to see Chiang Kai-shek elevated to the position of supreme leader, around whom national unity would be forged. They made little headway amongst the entrenched interests and factions within the Guomindang, however, and were disbanded in 1938.

Blum, Léon (1872–1950)
French politician. He trained in the law and was elected a Deputy in 1919, becoming the leader of the Parliamentary Group of Socialists, and an influential writer in the party newspaper. He was Prime Minister of the **Popular Front** governments (1936–7 and 1938). He opposed the **Vichy** regime, and was arrested and put on trial at Riom as one of those responsible for the defeat of 1940. The trial was abandoned, but he remained in prison, and was deported to Germany. He returned to France in 1944 and resumed his position as leader of the **Socialist Party**, becoming Prime Minister of a brief caretaker government (1946–7), before retiring from active politics. ▷ **Riom Trial**

Blundell, Sir Michael (1907–93)
Kenyan farmer and politician, born in London. He emigrated to Kenya in 1925 to farm, and served throughout **World War II**. He then involved himself in settler politics, being a member of Legco (1948–63) and leader of the European members in 1952–4 and then Minister of Agriculture (1955–9 and 1961–3). He broke with the dominant white group to espouse political change involving black Kenyans in national politics and was much vilified for this. However, he was an essential bridge between the white-dominated colonial years and the black majority rule of independent Kenya.

Blunt, Anthony (Frederick) (1907–83)
British double agent. An art historian, he became a Fellow at Trinity College, Cambridge (1932), where he shared in the left-wing communist-respecting tendencies of the time, and first met **Burgess**, **Philby** and **Maclean**. Influenced by Burgess, he acted as a 'talent-spotter', supplying to him the names of likely recruits to the Soviet communist cause, and during his war-service in British Intelligence, was in a position to pass on information to the Soviet government. Although his spying activities appear to have ceased after the war, he was still able to assist the defection of Burgess and Maclean in 1951, although suspected by British Intelligence. In 1964, after the defection of Philby, a confession was obtained from Blunt in return for his immunity, and he continued as Surveyor of the Queen's Pictures until 1972. His full involvement in espionage was

made public only in 1979, and his knighthood (awarded 1956) was annulled.

Blyukher, Vasili Konstantinovich (1890–1938)
Russian soldier. A **Red Army** hero in the **Russian Civil War**, he ended up commanding the forces that expelled the Japanese from the Soviet Far East. In 1924–7 he was military adviser to **Chiang Kai-shek**'s **Guomindang**. In 1929 he was put in command of Soviet troops in the Far East and fought successfully with the Chinese that year and with the Japanese in 1938. However, he proved too successful for **Stalin** who had him arrested, tried and executed; this, among other things, left the USSR particularly powerless against Japan.

boat people
Vietnamese who fled Vietnam by boat after the communist victory in 1975, travelling to Australia, Hong Kong, Japan, and several other parts of South-East Asia. Many died on the long voyages, or were killed by pirates. Voluntary repatriation schemes gained momentum in 1989, and the first involuntary repatriation operation from Hong Kong was carried out in Dec 1989.

Boer Wars (1880–1 and 1899–1902)
Two wars fought by the British and the Boers for the mastery of southern Africa. The first Boer War ended with the defeat of the British at Majuba Hill, and the signing of the Pretoria and London Conventions of 1881 and 1884. The second Boer War can be divided into three phases: (1) (Oct 1899–Jan 1900) a series of Boer successes, including the sieges of **Ladysmith**, **Kimberley**, and **Mafeking**, as well as victories at Stormberg, Modder River, Magersfontein, Colenso, and Moderspruit; (2) (Feb–Aug 1900) counter-offensives by Lord **Roberts**, including the raising of the sieges, the victory at Paardeberg, and the capture of Pretoria; (3) (Sep 1900–May 1902) a period of guerrilla warfare when **Kitchener** attempted to prevent Boer commando raids on isolated British units and lines of communication. The Boers effectively won the peace. They maintained control of 'native affairs', won back representative government in 1907, and federated South Africa on their terms in 1910. On the other hand, British interests in South Africa were protected and, despite internal strains, the Union of South Africa entered both **World War I** and **World War II** on the British side. ▷ **Vereeniging, Peace of**

Boers ▷ **Afrikaners**

Bogomolov, Alexei Yefremovich (1900–)
Soviet soldier, diplomat and lecturer. He served in the **Red Army** from 1919 to 1930 and spent the period 1930–8 teaching. His career changed

again in 1939 when he became a deputy, and in 1941 when he became an ambassador. He served two years in the UK, helping to get the British government accustomed to the idea of a **Czechoslovak–Soviet Alliance**. Later, he spent the years 1954–7 in Prague, as Czechoslovakia escaped from some of the less happy consequences of the 1943 treaty.

Bogomolov, Oleg Timofeevich (1927–)
Soviet economist and official. He was educated at the Moscow Institute of Foreign Trade and moved, after a short spell at the Soviet Ministry of Foreign Trade, to a long spell at **Comecon**. He then served on the State Planning Commission and the Communist Party Central Committee, before becoming Director of the Institute of the Economics of the World Socialist System in 1969. There he was involved in attempts to improve Comecon output in Leonid **Brezhnev**'s time, and he became a reformist adviser to both Yuri **Andropov** and Mikhail **Gorbachev**. In 1990 he was elected to the Soviet Congress of Deputies, but his influence appeared to decline as more radical ideas came to the fore.

bogotazo (9 Apr 1948)
A serious urban riot in Bogota, Colombia, arising from the assassination of the popular liberal and nationalist politician, Jorge Eliécer Gaitán. A turning-point in the history of modern Colombia, it resulted in hundreds of deaths and much material damage. The mob violence was inspired by both the ultra-right followers of Laureano Gómez and Gaitáns's leftists; this in turn sparked off sporadic revolts in the countryside and the spread of martial law under moderate conservative Mariano Ospina Pérez. Gómez, an admirer of **Hitler** and **Franco**, was elected President in 1950.

Bohemia
Historic province of western Czechoslovakia, bounded to the east by Moravia, west and south by Germany and Austria and north by Poland. Part of the Moravian Empire in the 9c, it was at its peak in the early Middle Ages, especially in the 14c under Charles I. Bohemia came under Habsburg rule in the early 16c and became a province of Czechoslovakia in 1918. It became part of the Czech Socialist Republic of western Czechoslovakia in 1968.

Bohemian Protectorate (1939–45)
The form of government **Hitler** used to control Bohemia and Moravia following the destruction of Czechoslovakia in Mar 1939. Officially, there was a Czech president, **Hácha**, and a ruling cabinet, but they were instruments of the German protector, particularly after the murder of **Heydrich** in 1942. However, while terror was used, Hitler was careful not to push the Czechs too far since their agricultural and industrial

production was essential for his war effort. In the end, though, he faced resistance there as well as elsewhere in Europe.

Bokassa, Jean Bedel (1921–)
Central African soldier and politician. He was educated in mission schools before joining the French army in 1929. He rose through the ranks and, after independence, was made Army Commander-in-Chief, with the rank of colonel. On 1 Jan 1966 he led the coup which overthrew President **Dacko** and steadily entrenched his own power, first making himself Life President; then in 1976, modelling himself on Napoleon, he crowned himself Emperor of the renamed Central African Empire. His rule was noted for its gratuitous violence and in Sep 1979 he was driven from the country and went into exile, first in the Ivory Coast and then France, being sentenced to death in absentia. However, in 1986 he was returned for trial and found guilty of murder and other crimes, being sentenced to life imprisonment.

Bolgikh, Vladimir Ivanovich (1924–)
Soviet politician and engineer. Born in the Krasnoyarsk region and educated in Irkutsk, he worked in engineering for 20 years before being drawn into the party machine in 1969. He climbed the political ladder quickly in **Brezhnev**'s command economy and in 1972 became a secretary in the Central Committee, and in 1982 a candidate member of the **Politburo**. He appeared to be in line for further promotion, but in 1988 Mikhail **Gorbachev** dismissed him and closed down the heavy industry section of the party secretariat as no longer relevant to a marketizing economy.

Bolsheviks
From the Russian meaning 'majority-ites', the term describes members of the hard-line faction of the Marxist Russian Social Democratic Labour Party, formed by **Lenin** when he split the party at its second congress in London in 1903 and won a spurious majority; the forerunner of the modern **Communist Party of the Soviet Union**. In Oct 1917 the Bolsheviks led the revolution in Petrograd which established the first Soviet government. ▷ **April Theses; Cheka; July Days; Mensheviks; October Revolution; Russian Revolution**

Bongo, El Hadj Omar (Albert-Bernard) (1935–)
Gabonese politician. Educated in Brazzaville, he joined the French civil service in 1957, becoming Head of the Ministry of Information and Tourism (1963), and then Minister of National Defence (1964–5). He was made Vice-President in 1967. When President **M'ba** died in 1967, he took over the interlocking posts of President, Prime Minister and Secretary-General of the *Parti Democratique Gabonais*, establishing a one-

party state in 1968. Converting to Islam in 1973, he has presided over the exploitation of Gabon's rich mineral resources (it has the highest per capita income of any African country) without notably diminishing inequalities. In 1986 he was re-elected for the third time.

Bonner, Yelena (1923–)
Soviet civil rights campaigner. After the arrest of her parents in **Stalin**'s 'great purge' of 1937, and the subsequent execution of her father and imprisonment of her mother, Bonner was brought up in Leningrad by her grandmother. During **World War II** she served in the army, becoming a lieutenant, but suffered serious eye injuries. After the war she married and worked as a doctor. On separating from her husband (1965), she joined the CPSU, but became disillusioned after the Soviet invasion of Czechoslovakia (1968) and drifted into 'dissident' activities. She married Andrei **Sakharov** in 1971 and resigned from the CPSU a year later. During the next 14 years she and her husband led the Soviet dissident movement. Following a **KGB** crackdown, Sakharov was banished to internal exile in Gorky in 1980 and Bonner suffered a similar fate in 1984. After hunger strikes, she was given permission to travel to Italy for specialist eye treatment in 1981 and 1984. The couple were finally released from Gorky in 1986, as part of a new 'liberalization' policy under Mikhail **Gorbachev**'s administration, and remained prominent campaigners for greater democratization.

Bonomi, Ivanoe (1873–1952)
Italian politician. A graduate in natural sciences and law, Bonomi took up journalism in 1898, writing for *Avanti!* and *Critica socialista*. In 1909 he was elected to parliament. Expelled from the Italian Socialist Party in 1912, he founded a reformist socialist movement. In 1916–21 he was a minister on a number of occasions, serving under **Orlando**, **Nitti** and **Giolitti**, and was briefly Premier himself (1921–2). He opposed **Mussolini**'s seizure of power but left politics in 1924. From 1942, he was a leading figure in the anti-fascist struggle, replacing **Badoglio** as Prime Minister (June 1944) and establishing a broad, anti-fascist coalition government. In 1945 he was forced to resign in favour of the more radical **Parri**; he became President of the Senate in 1948.

Bonus Army (June 1932)
A US protest march of some 20 000 unemployed ex-servicemen on Washington DC, demanding Congressional passage of a bill authorizing the immediate payment of a bonus due to **World War I** veterans. When the bill was defeated in the Senate, some veterans refused to return home. At the end of July, on the orders of President Herbert **Hoover**, General **MacArthur** evicted the marchers but incurred great odium by doing so with violence and cruelty.

Borah, William Edgar (1865–1940)
US politician. He was elected as a Republican senator for Idaho in 1907. An advocate of disarmament and a leading isolationist, Borah was instrumental in blocking the USA's entry into the **League of Nations** in 1919.

Borden, Sir Robert Laird (1854–1937)
Canadian politician. He practised as a barrister, and became leader of the Conservative Party in 1901. As Conservative Prime Minister (1911–20), he led Canada through **World War I**, the Conscription crisis, and the introduction of income tax. At the Imperial War Conference of 1917, he called for greater recognition of the dominions' autonomy, a step towards the building of a Commonwealth. ▷ **Compulsory Service Act; Lapointe, Ernest; War Measures Act**

Boris III (1894–1943)
King of Bulgaria (1918/43). He was the son of **Ferdinand I** and Maria Luisa Bourbon-Parma. After his father's abdication, he became king, the numeral III implying his succession to the great medieval Bulgarian emperors. After a series of military coups, in 1935 he established an authoritarian regime, securing the removal of Colonel Kimon Georgiev, abolishing the **Zveno**-backed Military League and returning the country to civilian control. Married to the daughter of the King of Italy and an admirer of German culture, he maintained good terms with Benito **Mussolini** and **Hitler**. Although formally neutral at the outbreak of **World War II**, Bulgaria through Boris's diplomacy was firmly in the Axis camp. He died suddenly, shortly after a stormy visit to Hitler, and recent research has lent credence to the rumour that he was poisoned. He was succeeded by his son, **Simeon II**.

Bormann, Martin (1900–45)
German Nazi politician. One of **Hitler**'s closest advisers, he became *Reichs-minister* (1941) after **Hess**'s flight to Scotland, and was with Hitler to the last. His own fate was uncertain, but he is now known to have committed suicide by a poison capsule during the breakout by Hitler's staff from the Chancellory (1 May 1945). He was sentenced to death in his absence by the Nuremberg Court (1946). ▷ **Nuremberg Trials; World War II**

Borodin, Mikhail (1884–1951)
Russian adviser in China from 1923 to 1927. Born Mikhail Markovich Grusenberg, Borodin participated in the Jewish worker movement in his native Russia and met **Lenin** in 1904. After 1905 he lived in exile in Britain and the USA. When the **United Front** was formed between the **Guomindang** and the Chinese Communist Party in 1923 Borodin, as the

representative of both the **Comintern** and the Soviet Communist Party, became a personal adviser to **Sun Yat-sen**. He helped transform the Guomindang into a disciplined and centrally-controlled revolutionary party, as well as convincing Sun of the necessity of creating mass-based organizations. When the United Front broke down in 1927 Borodin was compelled to leave China. Made the scapegoat for the failure of **Stalin**'s policy in China, Borodin was henceforth given only minor posts. He died in a Siberian prison camp.

Bosch, Juan (1909–)
Dominican Republic politician and writer. The founder of the Dominican Revolutionary Party, Bosch lived in exile in Cuba and Costa Rica during the **Trujillo** dictatorship. He became President in 1963 but his reformist government lasted only six months before it was overthrown by the army (Sep 1963) and he was again exiled. He has been the losing candidate in every presidential election since 1966 and, although by 1990 he had moderated his **Marxism**, his Dominican Liberation Party again lost the election of that year, despite having appeared to be the front runner.

Bose, Subhas Chandra (1897–1945)
Indian nationalist leader. A successful candidate for the Indian Civil Service in 1920, he did not take up his appointment, returning instead to Calcutta to work in the **Non-Cooperation Movement** and the **Swaraj** Party. He also managed the Calcutta newspaper, *Forward*, and became Chief Executive Officer of the Calcutta Corporation when Congress won its control in 1924. He spent the years 1925–7 under detention in Mandalay. In 1928 Bose formed an Independence League with Jawaharlal **Nehru** in opposition to Congress's objective of dominion status. During the 1930s Bose took part in the **civil disobedience** movement, but became increasingly dissatisfied with the non-violent methods of M K **Gandhi** and increasingly radical in his beliefs. Bose felt that a disciplined mass revolutionary movement, espousing a combination of Fascism and communism was the fastest and best path toward Indian statehood. He was twice in succession President of the **Indian National Congress** (1938). Having resigned from the organization (1939), he formed Forward Bloc, a militant nationalist party. With the outbreak of **World War II**, he supported the Axis Powers. Escaping from detention, he fled to Nazi Germany, then (1943) sailed to Singapore to take command of the Indian National Army (INA), a force formed of prisoners of war of the Japanese army. This force fought against the British in Burma and participated in the disastrous Japanese attempt to invade India from Burma. In Oct 1943 he announced the formation of the Provisional Government of Free India. He was reported killed in an aircrash in Taiwan. For many years, however, his most devoted followers

still refused to believe that he was dead, and many still cherish his ideas, attitudes and beliefs.

Bosnia and Herzegovina, Republic of

After a series of peasant revolts culminating between 1875 and 1878 in mass uprisings against the Ottomans (the medieval state of Bosnia had fallen to the Turks in 1463, the Duchy of Herzegovina in 1482), Bosnia and Herzegovina became an Austrian protectorate (1879); the two provinces were then annexed by Austria in 1908; in 1914 it was at Sarajevo, the capital of Bosnia, that a Bosnian Serb nationalist assassinated the Austrian Archduke Francis Ferdinand, prompting Austria to declare war on Serbia and thus precipitating **World War I**. In 1918 Bosnia and Herzegovina became part of the Kingdom of Serbs, Croats and Slovenes (later Yugoslavia). In **World War II** it was the scene of some of the heaviest fighting between the occupying forces and **Tito**'s partisans who held the first and second meetings of **AVNOJ** at Bihać and Jajce. In 1945 Bosnia-Herzegovina was established as one of the six republics within the Socialist Federal People's Republic of Yugoslavia. In Mar 1992 under its elected president, Alia Izetbegović, it followed the Republics of Slovenia and Croatia in declaring its independence from Yugoslavia. Civil war broke out among nationalist elements of Bosnians, Croats and Serbs and engulfed the civilian population until all civil order dissolved.

▷ **Andrić, Ivo; Mlada Bosna**

Botha, P(ieter) W(illem) (1916–)

South African politician. The son of an internee in the Anglo-Boer War, he was steeped in politics. His early life lacked success (he dropped out of university), but he found his metier as a party organizer. With his confidence and courage, he was a formidable operator. An advocate of **apartheid** before the **National Party** gained power, he entered Parliament in 1948 and became Deputy Minister of the Interior (1958–61), Minister of Community Development, Public Works and Coloured Affairs (1961–6), Minister of Defence (1966–78) and Prime Minister (1978–89). He led the Cape section of the National Party, and in 1966 was chosen as leader of the Party on **Vorster**'s resignation on the second ballot only because the Transvaal Nationalists were divided. He thus became Prime Minister. Having built up the defence forces and supported the invasion of Angola in 1975, he now sought constitutional changes, but his ideas, although too progressive for some of his Party (some members defected in 1982 to form the **Conservative Party**), were too cautious to appeal to the Black opposition. He suffered a stroke in 1989 and resigned later that year.

Bottai, Giuseppe (1895–1959)

Italian politician. One of the founders of the **Fascist Party**, Bottai took an active part in the **March on Rome**. He was one of the **Fascist Grand**

Council members who demanded **Mussolini**'s resignation in July 1943. Sentenced to death by the Republic of **Salò** and to life imprisonment by the Italian authorities after **World War II**, he escaped and joined the French Foreign Legion. He returned to Italy on being amnestied.

Boumédienne, Houari (Mohammed Bou Kharrouba) (1925–78)
Algerian soldier and statesman. Educated at Constantine and El Azhar University in Cairo, he became a teacher. In 1954 he joined the **FLN** for whom for eight years he conducted guerrilla operations against the French, serving as chief of staff (1960–62) with the rank of colonel. When Algeria gained independence in 1962, he became minister of national defence. In 1965 he led a military coup against President **Ben Bella** and established an Islamic socialist government, presiding over the Council of Revolution as effective head of state until he formally accepted election as president in 1976. In home affairs, he directed a four-year plan which increased industrial output and revolutionized agricultural production. Not long before his death, he was seeking to establish a North African socialist federation.

Bourassa, Henri (Joseph-Napoléon-Henri) (1868–1952)
Canadian politician and journalist (as a founder and editor of *Le Devoir*). A grandson of Louis Joseph Papineau, he was a French-Canadian nationalist who consistently opposed French Canada's forced participation in British wars. He resigned his independent Liberal seat in the federal House of Commons when **Laurier** sent Canadian troops to the Boer War, but, since most French-Canadians felt the same way, he was returned by acclamation. Bourassa was also the focal point for French-Canadian outrage at the Naval Act of 1910, using *Le Devoir* to advocate his views and making an important contribution to the **Liberal Party** defeat in the election of 1911. He was also a vigorous opponent of Canadian involvement in **World War I**. An advocate of European liberal Catholic thinking, he was opposed to industrial capitalism and emerged as a social reformer in the 1920s and 1930s. ▷ **Boer Wars**

Bourassa, Robert (1933–)
Canadian politician. Leader of the Quebec Liberal Party when it won an emphatic election victory in 1970, despite the nationalist unrest of the period. By refusing to give prominence to the constitutional and language controversies and promising to help the unemployment crisis by generating 100 000 jobs, his party won 41.8 per cent of the vote and 72 seats. During the **October Crisis** Bourassa was accused of being too ready to hand over power to Ottawa by those who suspected that he hoped to undermine his nationalist and left-wing opponents. Bourassa responded by reinforcing his demands for a special status for Quebec within the Confederation. He resigned as party leader when the Liberals lost the

1976 provincial elections to the **Péquistes**, but he was re-elected in 1983 and led the party to victory in 1986, this time with a huge hydro-electric project as the electoral promise.

Bourguiba, Habib ibn Ali (1903–)

Tunisian politician. He studied law in Paris and became a radical Tunisian nationalist in 1934. Over the next 20 years he served three prison sentences imposed by the French authorities. In 1956, however, the French government of **Mendès-France** in Paris recognized that, in contrast to other Arab leaders, Bourguiba was moderate in his demands and he was accepted as Tunisia's first prime minister, becoming president in 1957. By 1962 he had secured the withdrawal of the French from their Tunisian military bases; thereafter he was able to improve trading contacts with the former imperial power. In 1975 he was declared president for life. His authority, however, was threatened by riots instigated by Islamic fundamentalists in 1983 and 1984, and subsequently he exercised little influence on policy. In 1987 he was deposed by his prime minister, General **Ben Ali**, on the grounds of senility.

Bourj al-Barajneh

Palestinian refugee camp on the outskirts of Beirut, Lebanon. It was created following the evacuation of Palestinians from the city after Israeli attacks on Palestinians and Syrians (June 1982). The camp was the scene of a prolonged siege in 1987.

Boxer Rising (1898–1900)

An anti-foreign uprising in China (in Chinese, *Yi He Tuan*). Its popular name derives from the secret society to which the rebels belonged, the 'Righteous Harmonious Fists', whose members adopted boxing and ritual forms of combat, in the belief that foreign weapons would thus not harm them. The movement originated in Shandong, where it destroyed churches and expelled missionaries. It also defeated the Qing forces dispatched to suppress it. It spread across north China, invading Beijing and Tianjin. The foreign powers sent a combined force to rescue their envoys in Beijing, occupying the capital, and the rising was suppressed. By the International Protocol of 1901, the Qing court agreed to pay a massive indemnity, and a foreign garrison was established in the Legation Quarter of Beijing. ▷ **Qing Dynasty**

bracero

The term used to describe seasonal labour from Central and Southern Mexico, working on large-scale agro-industrial enterprises in California and Texas. Often 'wetbacks', who had illegally entered the USA by crossing the Rio Grande, they did not benefit from minimum wage and employee-protection legislation in either California, Texas or New

Mexico. They had often been used as 'scab' or strike-breaking labour in both states, so were not easily accepted into US trade unions. Drives to unionize them began in the mid-1960s, thanks to the activities of leaders such as Cesar Chavez; against heavy opposition from both the **AFL–CIO** and local employers, they were supported by the Republican Governor, Ronald **Reagan**. The influx of *braceros* increased during the 1980s, in the wake of the Mexican debt crisis and the endemic civil wars of Central America.

Bradley, Omar Nelson (1893–1981)

US soldier. He entered the army in 1915 and served in World War I. A brigadier general from 1941, he commanded II Corps in Tunisia and Sicily in 1943. He commanded the US First Army at the Normandy invasion in 1944, and later the US 12th Army Group in Europe until the end of World War II. He became the first permanent chairman of the US Joint Chiefs of Staff (1949–53), and in 1950 was promoted to a five-star general of the army. He retired in 1953.

Bradshaw, Robert (1916–78)

St Kitts-Nevis politician. Bradshaw took St Kitts-Nevis to associated statehood in 1967. The founder and leader of the St Kitts-Nevis Labour Party (1940) and Federal Minister of Finance (1958–62), he briefly made the world press in 1969, when his dispute with Anguilla forced that island to declare its independence of St Kitts; this action resulted in a farcical British military intervention.

Brady bill

Legislation passed by the US Congress in Nov 1993, imposing a mandatory five-day waiting period for anyone buying a handgun to allow for police checks on the purchaser. The restriction was limited to five years, during which time additional funds would be made available to update police computer records to permit instant background checks. The bill, the most significant gun-control statute in recent years, was named after James Brady, the press secretary of Ronald **Reagan**, who was permanently disabled by gunfire during the assassination attempt on the president in 1981.

Brandeis, Louis Dembitz (1856–1941)

US judge. He was educated in the USA and in Europe and, after graduating from Harvard Law School, he practised law in Boston. He conducted many labour arbitrations, and was frequently involved in cases challenging the power of monopolies and cartels, as well as others that dealt with the constitutionality of maximum hours and minimum wages legislation. He formulated the economic doctrine of the New Freedom adopted by **Woodrow Wilson** for his 1912 presidential campaign.

Appointed to the US Supreme Court in 1916, he favoured governmental intervention to control the economy where public interest required it, but was also a strong defender of the principle of private property. Brandeis, who supported most of **Roosevelt**'s New Deal legislation, is remembered as one of the most perceptive and thoughtful Supreme Court judges.

Brandt, Willy (1913–92)

West German politician. Born Karl Herbert Frahm, he was an anti-Nazi who fled in 1933 to Norway. There he changed his name, adopted Norwegian nationality and worked as a journalist, until the occupation of Norway (1940) forced him to move to Sweden. In 1945 he returned to Germany, and was a member of the **Bundestag** (1949–57). A pro-Western leader, he was Mayor of West Berlin (1957–66), and chairman of the Social Democratic Party (1964). In 1966 he led his party into a coalition government with the **Christian Democrats**, and in 1969 was elected Chancellor in a coalition government with the Free Democrats. Dedicated to restoring relations with Eastern Europe and especially East Germany, his success brought him the 1971 Nobel Peace Prize. He resigned as Chancellor in 1974, and later chaired a commission on the world economy (the Brandt Commission Report, 1980). ▷ **Ostpolitik**

Branting, Karl Hjalmar (1860–1925)

Swedish politician. He was co-founder of the **Social Democratic Party** of Sweden in 1889 and was its first parliamentary representative in 1896. He became Chairman of the party in 1907 and helped to lead it away from revolutionary Marxism towards a more moderate 'revisionist' programme. He was Prime Minister in 1920, 1921–3 and 1924–5. In 1921 he shared the Nobel Peace Prize and was Sweden's first representative at the **League of Nations** in 1922–5.

Brătianu, Constantine (1866–?1948)

Romanian politician. He became the leader of the Liberal Party after the assassination of the Liberal Prime Minister, Ion Duca (Dec 1933). Opposed to the dictatorship of **Charles II**, he operated part of the 'tolerated opposition' under Ion **Antonescu**. He advocated Romania's withdrawal from the war after the winning back of **Bessarabia** and **Bukovina**. In 1944 he was involved in the anti-fascist coup against Antonescu and became a minister without portfolio in the new government. He refused to hold office in the communist regime of Petru **Groza** and was arrested and imprisoned without trial. The year of his death, in prison, is not known, but is generally held to be between 1948 and 1952.

Braun, Otto (1872–1955)

German politician. After an early career in political journalism and in municipal and Prussian state politics as a member of the **SPD**, Braun became a member of the German National (Constituent) Assembly in 1919 and a member of the **Reichstag** in 1920. His main role, however, was as SPD Minister-President of **Prussia** from 1920 to 1932, where he carried out important welfare and Civil Service reforms which earned his government the hostility of the political right. The unsuccessful SPD candidate for the German presidency in 1925, he sought exile in Switzerland in 1933.

Brazil

Republic in east and central South America. Large numbers of European immigrants arrived in the early 20c to what was then a republic. A revolution, headed by Getúlio Vargas, established a dictatorship (1930–45), and a liberal republic was restored in 1946. Another coup in 1964 led to a military-backed presidential regime. A military junta was established in 1969. In 1979 a process of liberalization began, allowing the return of political exiles to stand for state and federal offices. New elections ending military rule took place in 1985. Elected governments face a particularly difficult economic situation.

Brazzaville Conference (30 Jan 1944)

French colonial governors and delegates of the French Consultative Assembly met at Brazzaville, the capital of French Equatorial Africa, in the presence of de **Gaulle** to lay down the principles which were to govern relations between France and her colonies in the **French Union**, created by the constitution of 1946. They envisaged assimilation and integration, rather than independence or even autonomy.

Brennan, William Joseph Jr (1906–)

US jurist. He was educated at the University of Pennsylvania and Harvard, and after practising law he rose in the New Jersey court system to the state Supreme Court. Named to the US Supreme Court in 1956, he took an active role in the liberal decisions handed down under Chief Justice Earl **Warren**. He retired from the Court in 1990.

Brest-Litovsk, Treaty of (Mar 1918)

A bilateral treaty signed at Brest-Litovsk between the new Soviet state and the **Central Powers**. Under its terms, Russia withdrew from **World War I**, hostilities ceased on Germany's Eastern front, and the new Soviet state ceded vast areas of territory and economic resources to Germany and her newly-created protectorates. **Lenin** argued against his opponents that Russia must 'sacrifice space in order to gain time'.

Bretton Woods Conference

An international conference held at Bretton Woods, New Hampshire, USA, in 1944, which led to the establishment of the International Monetary System, including the International Monetary Fund (IMF) and the World Bank (International Bank for Reconstruction and Development). The agreement, signed by the USA, UK and 43 other nations, aimed at controlling exchange rates, which were fixed for members in terms of gold and the dollar. The system was used until 1973, when floating exchange rates were introduced.

Brezhnev, Leonid Ilich (1906–82)

Russian politician. Born in the Ukraine, he trained as a metallurgist and became a political commissar in the **Red Army** in **World War II**. After the war, he was a party official in the Ukraine and Moldavia, becoming a member (1952–7) and then Chairman (1960–4) of the Presidium of the Supreme Soviet. He succeeded Nikita **Khrushchev** as General-Secretary of the **Communist Party of the Soviet Union** (1964–82), and gradually emerged as the most powerful figure in the USSR, the first to hold simultaneously the position of General-Secretary and President of the Supreme Soviet (1977–82). He was largely responsible for the enormous military machine and ailing economy that Mikhail **Gorbachev** inherited.

▷ **Brezhnev Doctrine**

Brezhnev Doctrine

The term applied to the policies of Leonid **Brezhnev**, General-Secretary of the Soviet Communist Party (1964–82), which, while combining strict political control internally with peaceful co-existence and détente abroad, specifically justified intervention (including military) in the internal affairs of other socialist states, as in Czechoslovakia (1968).

Briand, Aristide (1862–1932)

French politician. He began his political career on the extreme left, advocating a revolutionary general strike, but soon moved to the centre as a 'republican socialist', refusing to join the United Socialist Party (SFIO), which did not allow its members to join 'bourgeois' governments. He held ministerial office almost continuously from 1906, being a cabinet minister 25 times, and Prime Minister 11 times. Apart from his periods as Prime Minister (1909–11, 1913, 1915–17, 1921–2, 1925–6 and 1929), his most important offices were as Minister of Public Instruction and of Religion (1906–8), during which he implemented the **Separation of Church and State** (voted 1905), and as Foreign Minister (1925–32), when he became known as the 'apostle of peace'. He was a fervent advocate of the **League of Nations**, and of Franco-German reconciliation. He shared the Nobel Peace Prize in 1926, concluded the **Kellogg–Briand Pact** outlawing war (1928), and launched the idea of a United States of Europe (1929). ▷ **Socialist Party** (France)

brinkmanship
A tactic in international relations of deliberately allowing a potential crisis situation to escalate until the threat of war seems imminent. This high-risk strategy is intended to put the other side under pressure, and to force concessions out of them. The term was first coined by US strategic analyst, Thomas Crombie Schelling (1921–), drawing on a remark of John Foster **Dulles** in 1957 about going 'to the brink' of war.

Britain, Battle of (1940)
The name given to the air war campaign of late summer 1940 in which the German **Luftwaffe** attempted to destroy the Royal Air Force (RAF) as a prelude to the invasion of Great Britain. The aerial offensive began in Aug, the German bomber aircraft and fighter escorts concentrating on wiping out the RAF both by combat in the air and by bombing their vital airfields in the south of the country. British resistance proved stubborn, with the Spitfires and Hurricanes of RAF Fighter Command being directed by radar onto the incoming bomber streams. Badly mauled, the *Luftwaffe* switched their offensive from attacks on airfields to attacks on British cities (the '**blitz**'), losing their opportunity to gain true air superiority. Between 1 July and 31 Oct the *Luftwaffe* lost 2 848 aircraft to the RAF's 1 446. ▷ **World War II**

British Empire
There were in fact several British Empires: the empire of commerce and settlement in the Caribbean and North America, founded in the 17c and partly lost when the 13 colonies declared their independence in 1776; the empire in the East, founded in the 17c but developed through the extensive conquest of India (1757–1857) and the acquisition of islands, trading posts, and strategic positions from Aden to Hong Kong; the empire of white settlement in Canada, Australia, New Zealand and the Cape in South Africa, each of which had been federated as 'dominions' by 1910; and the 'dependent territories' in Africa and elsewhere acquired during the 'New Imperialism' of the last few decades of the 19c. To this must be added the British 'informal empire': territories which the Empire did not rule directly, but which fell under its influence because of its industrial and commercial power. These included parts of South America, the Middle East, the Persian Gulf and China. In 1919 the Empire reached its fullest extent through the acquisition of mandates over German and Ottoman territories in Africa and the Middle East. It was this diversity which gave rise to such famous phrases as 'the empire on which the sun never sets'. By the late 19c the empire was bonded together not only by industrial strength, but by Britain's vast merchant marine and powerful

navy. After **World War I** it was apparent that Britain could not control such an extensive empire: the dominions secured effective independence in 1931; the Middle Eastern mandates were virtually lost by **World War II**; India gained her independence in 1947, and the other Asian colonies soon followed; while most of the rest of the Empire was decolonized in the 1960s. Many of the countries of the Empire remained in the British **Commonwealth of Nations**.

British Expeditionary Force (BEF)

An army, first established in 1906, sent to France (Aug 1914 and Sep 1939) to support the left wing of the French armies against German attack. In **World War II** its total strength was 394 000, of whom 224 000 were safely evacuated, mainly from Dunkirk, in May–June 1940. ▷ **French, John; Haig, Douglas; Marne, Battle of the; World War I**

British South Africa Company

A company, formed by Cecil **Rhodes**, which used a series of concessions from King Lobengula and other Central African chiefs to secure a Royal Charter from the British government in 1889. Mashonaland was invaded in 1890 and by 1900 the Company ruled much of Central Africa despite considerable African resistance. In 1923–4 its territories were divided into Northern Rhodesia (Zambia after 1964) and Southern Rhodesia (Zimbabwe after 1980). It retained extensive mineral rights.

British–Iraqi Treaty (1930)

This treaty carried, amongst others, clauses providing for mutual assistance between Iraq and Britain in time of war and special rights for Britain in respect of 'essential communications' through Iraq and was, in effect, the treaty which brought to a close the British mandate in Iraq. It also granted Britain two air bases on the condition that these were not in any way to be regarded as constituting an occupation; nor were they to be seen as interfering with the principle of Iraqi sovereignty. The treaty, therefore, although ending the mandate and securing full independence for Iraq, bound Iraq to Britain in what was de facto a military alliance, due under the treaty to last for 25 years.

Brizola, Leonel de Moura (1922–)

Brazilian politician. He became a state deputy in 1947 on a **Vargas** ticket, and went on to become leader of the *Partido Trabalhista Brasileiro* (PTB, 'Brazilian Workers' Party') a decade later. As Governor of Rio Grande do Sul, his support for his brother-in-law, João **Goulart**, Getúlio Vargas's heir, was crucial in Aug 1961, when he enabled Goulart to assume office as President and in Mar 1964 when, as Popular Deputy for Guanabara, he urged the Left to take to the streets in defence of the President. Exiled in 1964, he advocated armed opposition to the new regime, and by the

1970s had become the standard-bearer of the exiled Social Democrats. Amnestied in 1979, he founded the *Partido Democratico Trabalhista* ('Democratic Workers' Party'), a grouping based on his personal appeal, but limited to his personal following in Rio and Rio Grande do Sul. He became Governor of Rio de Janeiro in the first direct elections in 1982 and led the successful campaign in 1985 which ended the military government. Narrowly defeated by **Lula** in 1989 for the left-wing candidacy for the presidency, he was elected Governor of Rio de Janeiro in 1990; he is viewed as the éminence grise of the nationalists.

Broederbond
A secret Afrikaner organization founded in 1918. Membership, limited to male Afrikaners, is by invitation only and was intended to integrate potential leaders across the country first to promote Afrikaner political ambitions and then to protect them. Since the early 1980s, it has become somewhat more open as it split between its reformist (or verligte) and its reactionary (*verkrampte*) wings.

Brookeborough, Basil Stanlake Brooke, 1st Viscount (1888–1973)
Irish politician. He was elected to the Northern Ireland parliament in 1929, became Minister of Agriculture (1933), Commerce (1941–5), and then Prime Minister (1943–63). A staunch supporter of union with Great Britain, he was created viscount in 1952, and retired from politics in 1968.

Brown v Board of Education of Topeka, Kansas (1954)
US Supreme Court case in which Chief Justice Earl **Warren**, speaking for a unanimous bench declared that separate educational facilities were inherently unequal and inhumane. With this decision the court overturned **Plessy v Ferguson** (1896), which had supported 'separate but equal' facilities, and undermined the major principle upon which **Jim Crow Laws** depended. Critics contended that it encroached on **states' rights**, and that it represented judicial legislation rather than interpretation. In 'Brown II' (1955) the Supreme Court acknowledged the problems faced by school boards in implementing the earlier decision; they ordered district courts therefore to integrate schools 'with all deliberate speed'. ▷ **segregation**

Bruce, Stanley Melbourne, 1st Viscount Bruce of Melbourne (1883–1967)
Australian politician. Bruce attended Trinity Hall, Cambridge (1902–5), and spent much time in England because of business interests. After service in **World War I** with a British regiment, he entered Australian federal politics in 1918, representing Australia at the **League of Nations** in 1921 (and again 1932–9). He became treasurer in 1921 and Prime Minister and Minister for External Affairs (1923–9) in a coalition with

Page's Country Party. Bruce's primary concern was Australian economic development within the framework of the British Empire, to which end he encouraged immigration, overseas investment and imperial preference. Attacks on the arbitration system and the trade-union movement led to the fall of his government in 1929. He led the Australian delegation at the **Ottawa Conference** in 1932 and was High Commissioner in London (1933–45). He became Viscount Bruce in 1947 and was the first Chancellor of the Australian National University (1951–61). ▷ **National Party of Australia**

Brundtland, Gro Harlem (1939–)
Norwegian politician. She studied medicine at Oslo and Harvard, qualifying as a physician. She married (1960) a leader of the opposition Conservative Party, Arne Olav, and worked in public medicine services in Oslo until, in 1969, she joined the Labour Party and entered politics. She was appointed Environment Minister (1974–9) and then, as leader of the Labour Party group, became (1981) Prime Minister of Norway, the first woman to hold the post. She was Prime Minister again in 1986, and in 1987 chaired the World Commission on Environment and Development which produced the report *Our Common Future*. In 1988 she was awarded the Third World Foundation prize for leadership in environmental issues.

Brüning, Heinrich (1885–1970)
German politician. He studied in Bonn and at the London School of Economics, and during the **Weimar Republic** became (1929) leader of the predominantly Catholic *Zentrum* (**Centre Party**) and then Chancellor (1930–2). Faced with the problems of economic depression, he attempted to rule by decree, but was eventually forced out of office, to make way for the more conservative Franz von **Papen**. In 1934 he left Germany, spending most of the rest of his life in US universities.

Brusilov, Alexei (1856–1926)
Russian soldier. He served in the war against Turkey (1877). In **World War I** he led the invasion of Galicia (1914) and the Carpathians. From 1916 he distinguished himself on the eastern front, notably in command of the South Western Army Group in the only partly successful 'Brusilov Offensive' against the Austrians in 1916. He became Chief of Staff in 1917, but the second 'Brusilov Offensive' was frustrated, many of his troops mutinied and added to the unrest that produced the Bolshevik Revolution. ▷ **Brusilov Offensives**

Brusilov Offensives (1916 and 1917)
Two crucial Russian actions during **World War I**. In June 1916 General **Brusilov** launched a massive offensive against Austria at the request of

the Western powers. He advanced into Galicia, relieved the Italians and encouraged the Romanians to enter the war. This helped eventually to destroy the Austrian Empire, but the cost in men and materials damaged Russian morale and weakened the Russian economy. The second offensive in July 1917, intended to strengthen the **Russian Provisional Government** that followed the **February Revolution**, was an abysmal failure and contributed to the worsening social and political unrest that the **Bolsheviks** then exploited in Oct of the same year.

Bubnov, Andrei Sergeevich (1883–1940)
Russian politician. He was a typical middle-ranking Bolshevik who suffered for the cause and was then consumed by it. Expelled from the Agricultural Institute in Moscow for political activity, he was quickly drawn into organizing and making propaganda for **Lenin** and his colleagues. He was arrested many times before 1917 and became a **Politburo** member in that year. Between 1918 and 1924 he was associated with **Trotsky**, but he broke clear and was entrusted with political education in the Russian Republic in 1929. That, however, did not save him from **Stalin**'s vengeance in 1937 and he died in prison three years later.

Buchan, John, 1st Baron Tweedsmuir (1875–1940)
British author and politician. During **World War I** he served on HQ staff (1916–17), when he became Director of Information. He was MP for the Scottish Universities (1927–35), when he was made a baron, and became Governor-General of Canada until 1940. In 1937 he was made a Privy Councillor and chancellor of Edinburgh University. Despite his busy public life, Buchan wrote over 50 books, especially fast-moving adventure stories, such as *Prester John* (1910) and *The Thirty-Nine Steps* (1915).

Bucharest, Treaties of (1812 and 1913)
Two treaties, marking important stages in the achievement of Balkan nationhood. The 1812 Russo-Turkish treaty, concluding the Serbian revolt which had begun in 1804, granted Serbia autonomy within the **Ottoman Empire** and launched her on the path to outright independence in 1878. The treaty of Aug 1913 ended the second Balkan War between Bulgaria and Greece, Serbia and Romania, her recent allies against Turkey in the first of the **Balkan Wars** (1912–13). Its terms, involving Bulgaria's surrender of north Macedonia to Serbia, south Macedonia to Greece, and the south Dobrudja to Romania, finally extinguished any prospect of a 'Greater Bulgaria'.

Buchenwald
German concentration camp. Established near Weimar in Aug 1937, it became a major part of the **SS**'s economic empire during **World War II**. Among its 239 000 internees (of whom 56 000 died) were many Soviet

and Polish prisoners of war as well as German political detainees. Many major firms, as well as the SS's own Earth and Stone Co Ltd, exploited its inmates as forced labour. Liberated by the US Army in Apr 1945, Buchenwald subsequently passed under Soviet control and served as an internment camp until 1950. ▷ **Holocaust**

Budenny, Simeon Mikhailovich (1883–1973)
Russian soldier. The son of a Cossack farmer, he fought as a Cossack private in the **Russo-Japanese War** (1904–5) and as an NCO in **World War I**. After the revolution he became a Bolshevik and raised a Cossack unit to fight the White forces on the Don, and defeated the Whites in the battles of Tsaritsyn (1918–19). He served in the war against Poland (1920), and was made a marshal in 1935. In 1941 he commanded the south-west sector against the German invasion, but was relieved by **Timoshenko** after a disaster at Kiev. ▷ **Bolsheviks; Russian Revolution**

Budi Utomo
The first and most important of the ethnic-based organizations formed in the Dutch East Indies just before **World War I**. Founded in 1908, it drew in younger members of the Dutch-educated Javanese aristocracy who, in seeking to create a modernized Javanese culture, wished to establish for themselves a greater influence in the colonial world. Moderate in tone and unable to decide whether to pursue a purely cultural programme or whether to take up political ambitions, it was soon overshadowed by overtly political indigenous movements, although it remained in existence until the mid-1930s.

Buhari, Muhammadu (1942–)
Nigerian soldier and politician. Educated locally and then at military academies in Nigeria, England and India, he was military governor of North-Eastern State (1975–6), of Bornu State (1976), and then Federal Commissioner for Petroleum Resources (1976–8) and Chairman of the Nigerian National Petroleum Corporation (1976–9). He returned to army duties (July 1976) but led the military coup which ousted Shehu **Shagari** (31 Dec 1983), when he became President. He was himself removed in a coup led by Ibrahim **Babangida** on 27 Aug 1985.

Bukharin, Nikolai Ivanovich (1888–1938)
Russian Marxist revolutionary and political theorist. Dubbed by **Lenin** 'the darling of the Party', he was active in the Bolshevik underground (1905–17), and after the **February Revolution** returned to Russia, playing a leading role in the organization of the **October Revolution** in Moscow. He was a considerable theorist. As a member of the **Politburo** he came round to supporting Lenin's **New Economic Policy**, but had an ambivalent attitude to **Stalin**'s collectivization campaign. In 1937 he was arrested

in Stalin's Great Purge, expelled from the Party, tried on trumped-up charges, and shot. In 1987 he was officially rehabilitated by a board of judicial inquiry, and posthumously readmitted to the Party in 1988. ▷ **Bolsheviks; Brest-Litovsk, Treaty of**

Bukovina

The region lying in the north-east of the Carpathian Mountains, which was settled by Ruthenians and Moldavians, and became part of Moldavia in the 14c. It was ceded to Austria by the Turks (1775) and governed by a mainly Polish administration as part of Galicia, first as a duchy and then as a crown land (1786–1849). During 1848, demands were made for separation and in 1853 it received its own diet and a separate administration. Romania, after gaining full independence (1879), sought Bukovina, occupied it during **World War I** and received it by the Treaty of **Trianon** (1920). The Romanian government then began to impose a Romanian cultural identity in the region. In **World War II** Soviet troops seized northern Bukovina and in 1947 incorporated it into the Ukrainian Soviet Socialist Republic, while the southern part around Suceava remained within Romania. Populated by Ukrainians, Romanians, Germans, Jews, Poles and Hungarians, under **Ceaușescu** its rule was disputed with the USSR.

Bulganin, Nikolai Alexandrovich (1895–1975)

Soviet politician. An early member of the Communist Party, he was Mayor of Moscow (1931–7), a member of the Military Council in **World War II**, and held various defence appointments after the war. Following **Stalin**'s death he became Vice-Premier in Malenkov's government, and was Premier after Giorgiy **Malenkov** resigned (1955–8), with Nikita **Khrushchev** wielding real power. 'B and K' travelled extensively abroad for propaganda purposes. Bulganin was dismissed in 1958, and retired into obscurity.

Bulgaria

Republic in the east of the Balkan Peninsula. Under Turkish rule until 1878, it achieved full independence in 1908. Bulgaria was a kingdom from 1908 to 1946, when it was proclaimed a Socialist People's Republic. It had aligned with Germany in the World Wars and in 1944 had been occupied by the USSR. In the early 1990s a multiparty government introduced political and economic reforms.

Bulge, Battle of the (1944)

The last desperate German armoured counter-offensive through the Ardennes in **World War II** (beginning 16 Dec), to prevent the Allied invasion of Germany. It achieved early success, but ground to a halt, and the

Germans were then pushed to retreat by the Allies by the end of Jan 1945.

Bunau-Varilla, Philippe Jean (1859–1940)
French engineer. The chief organizer of the Panama Canal project, he was instrumental in getting the waterway routed through Panama instead of Nicaragua. He incited the Panama revolution (1903), was made Panamanian minister to the USA and negotiated the Hay-Bunau-Varilla Treaty (1903) giving the USA control of the Canal Zone.

Bunche, Ralph (Johnson) (1904–71)
US diplomat. He studied at Harvard and the University of California, then taught political science at Howard University, Washington (1928–50). In 1944 he assisted the Swedish Nobel prize winner Gunnar Myrdal in the creation of *An American Dilemma*, a study on American blacks. He directed the **UN** Trusteeship department (1946–54), and became UN mediator in Palestine, where he arranged for a ceasefire. Awarded the Nobel Peace Prize (1950), he became a UN undersecretary for Special Political Affairs from 1957 to his death.

Bund
Literally 'federation', this is the name given to the German federal level of government and its competences, as against those of the states (*Länder*) and of local government. The *Bund* shares sovereignty with the Länder. ▷ **Basic Law; Germany, West; Land**

Bundesrat (1949–)
The upper house of the current German parliament. Its members are appointed by the state (**Land**) governments and scrutinize all federal legislation. A two-thirds majority can block legislation proposed by the lower, elected house (**Bundestag**). The *Bundesrat* also serves to represent state interests at federal level. ▷ **Basic Law**

Bundestag
The lower house of parliament of the Federal Republic of Germany, elections for which are held every four years in the autumn. It is possible for the *Bundestag* to be dissolved and elections held before the end of the fixed term, as in 1972 and 1983 when the government actually lost, or contrived to lose, its majority. In addition to legislating, the Bundestag selects the Chancellor and supports his government.

Bundeswehr (Federal German Armed Forces)
Following Federal German entry into **NATO** on 9 May 1955, the *Bundeswehr* accepted 101 volunteers on 12 Nov. This ended the period of disarmament following capitulation in May 1945. In contrast to earlier

German armed forces, the Bundeswehr was unequivocally subordinated to parliament and its conscripts perceived as 'citizens in uniform'. Virtually entirely within the NATO command structure, the Bundeswehr became the largest element in NATO with 340 000 soldiers and 8 600 tanks, 104 000 airmen and 400 front-line aircraft and 37 500 sailors. Following reunification, the Bundeswehr absorbed the surviving elements of the East German armed forces.

Buraimi Dispute (1952)
Buraimi, a group of oases on the borders of Abu Dhabi (now one of the United Arab Emirates) and Oman, was the subject of a territorial claim voiced by Saudi Arabia in 1949. A small armed force from Saudi Arabia occupied Buraimi in 1952, but was expelled on behalf of the rulers of Abu Dhabi and Oman by the Trucial Oman Scouts, a local force with British officers. There seems little doubt that the motivation behind the original claims and the occupation of Buraimi was the oil-bearing potential of the area recognized by the American oil concerns operating in Saudi Arabia; also that the **CIA** was involved in the organization of the attempted military seizure of the oasis.

Burger, Warren Earl (1907–)
US jurist. Educated at the University of Minnesota, he taught and practised law in St Paul from 1931 before he became Assistant Attorney-General of the USA (1953) and US Court of Appeals judge for the District of Columbia in 1955. Richard **Nixon** appointed him Chief Justice of the US Supreme Court in 1969. Burger, whose philosophy inclined toward judicial restraint and caution toward change, reined in the liberal tendencies the Court had shown in previous years. He resigned from the Court in 1986.

Burgess, Guy (Francis de Moncy) (1910–63)
British double agent. Recruited as a Soviet agent in the 1930s, he worked with the BBC (1936–9), wrote war propaganda (1939–41), and again joined the BBC (1941–4) while working for MI5. Thereafter, he was a member of the Foreign Office, and second secretary under **Philby** in Washington in 1950. Recalled in 1951 for 'serious misconduct', he and **Maclean** disappeared, reemerging in the USSR in 1956. He died in Moscow. ▷ **Blunt, Anthony**

Burgos, Carmen (1879–1932)
Spanish feminist. Born in the remote province of Almeria, she married young but moved to Madrid after being abandoned by her husband. Having become a teacher, Burgos was elected to the presidency of the International League of Iberian and Hispanoamerican Women. She was an outstanding advocate of women's rights, above all through her writ-

ing. She published not only a vast quantity of journalism both in Spain and Latin America (being the first Spanish female war correspondent in 1909), but also many books on women's issues under the pseudonym 'Colombine'.

Burlatsky, Fedor Mikhailovich (1927–)
Soviet intellectual. Born in Kiev, he studied law and philosophy in Tashkent and Moscow and went on to be an academic, journalist and political consultant in the 1950s and 1960s. Under a slight cloud in the 1970s, he transferred first to the Institute of State and Law and then to the Institute of Social Sciences, where his work in political science and sociology prepared some of the ground for the 1980s. As a journalist and politician in Mikhail **Gorbachev**'s time, he did much to propagate constitutional practices and to increase concern for Soviet human rights. He played a critical ideological role within the establishment from Nikita **Khrushchev** to Gorbachev.

Burma (Myanma) formerly **The Socialist Republic of the Union of Burma**
Republic in south-east Asia. Separated from India in 1937, it was occupied by the Japanese in World War II. Independence was proclaimed as the Union of Burma under Prime Minister U Nu in 1948. U Ne Win led a military coup in 1962, and Burma became a single-party socialist republic in 1974. In 1988 there was another military coup. The National League for Democracy opposes the military government.

Burma Road
A road linking the Burmese railhead at Lashio with Kunming, 700 miles distant in Yunnan province, China. Completed by the Chinese in 1938, it was of great strategic importance to the Allies during **World War II**.

Burnham, Forbes (1923–85)
Guyanese politician. British-educated, Burnham represented the African element in the Guyanese population and was co-leader with **Jagan** of the multiracial People's Progressive Party until 1955. In that year he split with Jagan over the latter's support for international **communism** and set up a rival African-based party, the **People's National Congress** (PNC). The PNC slowly gained adherents in Jagan's troubled years after 1961 and in 1964 Burnham became Prime Minister. He negotiated an independence constitution in 1966 and in 1970 established Guyana as a 'cooperative socialist republic', remaining its President until his death.

Bush, George (Herbert Walker) (1924–)
Politician and 41st US President. He served in the US Navy (1942–5) and after the war received a degree in economics from Yale and established an

oil-drilling business in Texas. In 1966 he devoted himself to politics, and was elected to the House of Representatives. Unsuccessful in his bid for the Senate in 1970, he became US ambassador to the **UN**. During the **Watergate** scandal he was chairman of the Republican National Committee. Under President **Ford** he served as US envoy to China, and then became Director of the **CIA**. In 1980 he sought the Republican presidential nomination, but lost to Ronald **Reagan**, later becoming his Vice-President. He became President in 1988, defeating the Democratic candidate, Governor Michael Dukakis of Massachusetts. As President, he focused on US foreign policy, which was changed most dramatically by the dissolution of the USSR, and he presided over the USA-led UN coalition to defeat Iraq in the **Gulf War**. In 1992 he failed to be re-elected, perhaps because of the perception that he had ignored US domestic issues. ▷ **Republican Party**

bushido

The Japanese notion of 'way of the warrior'. The samurai code until 1868, which taught personal loyalty to a master, death rather than capture/surrender, and stoic indifference to material goods. The bushido tradition continued into modern times, eg Japanese officers carried swords in **World War II**.

Busia, Kofi (1913–78)

Ghanaian academic and politician. Educated in Kumasi and at Achimota College, he then obtained an external BA degree from London and a DPhil from Oxford. He was one of the first Africans to be appointed an administrative officer in the Gold Coast (Ghana). He resigned that position to become a lecturer, and later Professor of Sociology, at the University College of Ghana. Elected to Legco (1951), he became a leader of the National Liberation Movement (1954–9) in opposition to **Nkrumah** and went into exile (1959–66), taking up the chair of sociology at Leiden University. After the 1966 coup, he returned as adviser to the National Liberation Council and then founded, and led, the Progress Party which won the 1969 election. He was Prime Minister (1969–72) before being overthrown in another coup, going into exile again in 1972. He held various academic posts and died in Oxford.

Bustamante, (William) Alexander, originally **William Alexander Clarke** (1884–1977)

Jamaican politician. The son of an Irish planter, he was adopted at the age of 15 by a Spanish seaman called Bustamante and spent an adventurous youth abroad before returning in 1932 to become a trade-union leader. In 1943 he founded the **Jamaica Labour Party (JLP)** as the political wing of his union and in 1962, the year Jamaica achieved independence, became its first Prime Minister. He was knighted in 1955.

Buthelezi, Chief Mangosuthu Gatsha (1928–)

South African politician and Zulu leader. Expelled from Fort Hare University College in 1950, where he was a member of the **ANC** (African National Congress), he was a government interpreter in the Native Affairs Department (1951–7). Officially appointed as Chief of the Buthelezi tribe in 1957, he was also assistant to the Zulu King, Cyprian (1953/68), before being elected leader of the Zulu Territorial Authority in 1970 and Chief Minister of KwaZulu in 1976, with the ANC's approval. He was sympathetic to the ANC's opposition to **apartheid** and he rejected the South African plan to turn Zululand into a 'bantustan' or 'homeland', but increasingly his readiness to work within the system and his Zulu nationalism distanced him from the radical forces of South Africa's opposition. He founded, and remains President of, the **Inkatha Freedom Party**; the Party at first boycotted the 1994 elections, but its eventual participation allowed them to proceed peacefully. In May 1994 he became Minister of Home Affairs in the South African government formed by Nelson Mandela.

Butler, R(ichard) A(usten), Baron (1902–82)

British politician. He became Conservative MP for Saffron Walden in 1929. After a series of junior ministerial appointments, he became Minister of Education (1941–5), introducing the forward-looking Education Act of 1944, and then Minister of Labour (1945). He became Chancellor of the Exchequer (1951), Lord Privy Seal (1955), Leader of the House of Commons (1955), Home Secretary (1957), First Secretary of State and Deputy Prime Minister (1962). He narrowly lost the premiership to Douglas-Home in 1963, and became Foreign Secretary (1963–4). He was appointed Master of Trinity College, Cambridge (1965–78), and was made a life peer. ▷ **Butskellism; Conservative Party** (UK)**; Home of the Hirsel, Baron**

Butler, Uriah 'Buzz' (1897–1977)

Grenadian-born politician and labour leader. In 1921 he emigrated to Trinidad to work in the oilfields. An industrial accident in 1929 led him towards the Moravian Baptist Church and organized labour and in 1935 he broke with **Cipriani**'s Trinidad Labour Party (TLP) and set up the British Empire and Citizens' Home Rule and Workers' Party. In 1937 his fiery oratory whipped up agitation in the oilfields, and an attempt to arrest him at Fyzabad led to rioting and several deaths at Port Fortin. Interned for sedition in **World War II**, he returned to politics in 1945, but by then was a spent force.

Byng (of Vimy), Julian Hedworth George, 1st Viscount (1862–1935) British general. He commanded the 9th Army Corps in the **Gallipoli Campaign** (1915), the Canadian Army Corps (1916–17), and the 3rd Army (1917–18). After **World War I** he became Governor-General of Canada (1921–6) and Commissioner of the Metropolitan Police (1928–31), and was made a viscount in 1928 and a field marshal in 1932.

C

Cabral, Amilcar (1924–73)

Guinean nationalist leader. Educated at Lisbon University, he worked as an agronomist and agricultural engineer for the colonial authorities. He founded the PAIGC in 1956 and, after abortive constitutional discussions with the Portuguese government, initiated a revolutionary war in 1963. Noted for his commitment to politicizing the peasantry and establishing alternative institutions in liberated territories, he presided over a successful war which forced the Portuguese to concede independence. He was murdered in 1973 just as his aim was being achieved.

Cabral, Luiz (1931–)

Guinean nationalist leader. The brother of Amilcar **Cabral**, he was educated in Portuguese Guinea and became a clerk and a trade union organizer. As a member of the PAIGC, he went into exile in 1960 and took part in the guerrilla struggle to win independence for Guinea Bissau. Success made him President of the new Republic (1974–80), but he was then overthrown in a coup.

Cadorna, Luigi (1850–1928)

Italian general. Commander-in-Chief of the Italian Army from 1914, he held the Austrian forces successfully from the outbreak of war in Mar 1915 until the the disastrous defeat of the Battle of **Caporetto**, after which he was replaced by the more flexible **Diaz**.

Caetano, Marcelo (1906–80)

Portuguese politician and academic. The son of a schoolteacher, Caetano had a meteoric rise during the counter-revolution following the First Republic. He played a key judicial role in the establishment of the **Estado Novo**. From 1944 to 1947 he was Minister of the Colonies, and from 1955 until 1958 Deputy Prime Minister. Extrovert, ambitious and less submissive than other ministers, in 1951 Caetano had attempted to replace **Salazar** as Prime Minister. Yet in 1968 he was chosen as Salazar's successor as one of the most notable figures in Estado Novo politics. From 1969 to 1971 he liberalized the country in certain respects, but there was no promise of a liberal democracy; he was simply too closely identified with the authoritarian regime to execute authentic liberalization. Enormous discontent within the army over the costly and militarily unsuccessful 13-year war waged in Portuguese Africa against

independence movements led to the bloodless coup of 25 Apr 1974 which, in its turn, resulted in the revolution of 1974–5. He died in exile in Brazil.
▷ **Republic, First** (Portugal)

Cai Chang (Ts'ai Ch'ang) (1900–90)
Chinese revolutionary and women's leader. The younger sister of Cai Hesen (1890–1931), friend and colleague of **Mao Zedong**, she went to France in 1919 on a work-study scheme. She returned to China in 1924 after further study in Moscow. During 1924–6 she helped organize women textile workers in Shanghai and was Head of the Women's Department in Mao Zedong's **Jiangxi Soviet** from 1931 to 1934. At the Seventh National Congress of the Chinese Communist Party in 1945, Cai Chang was the sole woman elected to full membership of the Central Committee. With the establishment of the People's Republic in 1949 Cai Chang founded and led the All-China Federation of Democratic Women.

Cai Yuanpei (Ts'ai Yuan-p'ei) (1868–1940)
Chinese educator, scholar and politician. One of the youngest candidates ever to obtain the highest degree in the classical **civil service examination system**, Cai taught in various schools and colleges in his home province of Zhejiang and in Shanghai. He joined **Sun Yat-sen**'s anti-Manchu republican movement and in 1911 became the first Minister of Education of the new Chinese Republic, presiding over the creation of a new school system. Although he resigned in 1912, Cai continued to be active in educational affairs, helping to promote a work-study programme for Chinese students in France and assuming the chancellorship of Beijing University in 1916. He encouraged free debate and scholarship at the university, transforming it into one of the country's foremost intellectual centres. He later became a member of the **Guomindang**, but became increasingly critical of the party's suppression of free speech. He died in Hong Kong.

Caillaux, Joseph (1863–1944)
French radical politician. He was several times Finance Minister (1899–1902, 1906–9, 1911, 1913–14 and 1925), unsuccessfully advocating a progressive income tax. As Prime Minister (1911–12), he negotiated the treaty with Germany, following the Agadir Incident, by which France was given a free hand to subjugate Morocco, and to turn it into a protectorate. He was attacked for being too ready to conciliate Germany, and was arrested in 1918 on a charge of contacting the enemy. Tried by the Senate, acting as a special High Court, he was sentenced in 1920 to three years' imprisonment, and to loss of political rights. Amnestied in 1925, he resumed his political career in the influential post of President of the Finance Committee of the Senate, and as one of the leading elder statesmen of the **Radical Party**. In 1914 his second wife shot and killed

Gaston Calmette, editor of *Le Figaro*, who had published letters written to her by Caillaux while he was married to his first wife; she was acquitted after a sensational trial.

Cairo Conference (1921)
Convened by Winston **Churchill**, this conference had as its objective the consideration of the many problems afflicting the Middle East, particularly those thrown up by **World War I**. Discussions covered such questions as defence in the area and the treatment of the Iraqi Kurds (on which no decision was reached), but perhaps the most important result (if not actual decision) of the conference was the emergence of two Hashimite rulers: the King of Iraq and the Amir of Transjordan. The latter subsequently became King of Jordan after the creation of the state of Israel and the addition to the former Transjordan of the West Bank and the Old City of Jerusalem.

Cairo Conference (1943)
A meeting held between Winston **Churchill** and **Roosevelt** which was attended by **Chiang Kai-shek**. Chiang was anxious that the allies continue to support the war effort in China at a time when they were considering inviting **Stalin** to bring the USSR into the Pacific War and whether to concentrate on capturing the Pacific Islands (from where Japan might be bombed rather than from Chinese airfields). Both developments would render the China Theatre marginal. Chiang was handicapped by both Anglo-American differences over strategy and by Roosevelt's increasing hostility to Chiang's regime, which was seen as hopelessly corrupt. The Cairo Conference was a significant turning-point in Washington's policy towards Chiang Kai-shek, hitherto considered a crucial actor in the war against Japan. Chiang did not receive the assurances he desired, while later in the same year Stalin pledged to enter the war in return for privileges in Manchuria.

Callaghan, (Leonard) James ('Jim') (1912–)
British politician. After a secondary education, he joined the Civil Service (1929), and in 1945 was elected Labour MP for South Cardiff. As Chancellor of the Exchequer under **Wilson** (1964–7), he introduced the controversial corporation and selective employment taxes. He was Home Secretary (1967–70) and Foreign Secretary (1974–6), and became Prime Minister (1976–9) on Wilson's resignation. He resigned as Leader of the Opposition in 1980. ▷ **Labour Party** (UK)

Calles, Plutarco Elías (1877–1945)
Mexican politician. An ex-schoolmaster, he became Governor of Sonora (1917), and President of Mexico (1924–8). Anticlerical, he challenged the pretensions of the Church, implementing the 1917 constitution and

provoking the **Cristero Revolt**; he dominated the presidency until 1934, enhancing the power of the state, creating the PNR but limiting agrarian reform. Defeated by his protégé, **Cárdenas**, he was exiled to the USA, but was allowed to return in 1941.

Calvo Sotelo, José (1893–1936)
Spanish politician. Under the dictator **Primo de Rivera**, he was made the Director-General of Local Government, introducing the stillborn Municipal Statute in 1924. He was also a controversial Minister of Finance, attempting to overhaul the tax system (only to be thwarted by the banks) and creating state monopolies, in particular the petroleum company, CAMPSA. His much-criticized monetary policies contributed to the regime's fall. He went into exile on the advent of the Second Republic in 1931, returning with the amnesty of 1934. Having founded the totalitarian National Bloc, he soon became the most powerful civilian figure on the extreme Right. His assassination on 13 July 1936 triggered off the military rising that led to the **Spanish Civil War**. ▷ **Republic, Second** (Spain)

Camacho, Marcelino (1918–)
Spanish trade union leader. He joined the Communist Party in 1934 and fought for the Republicans in the **Spanish Civil War**. Jailed by the Nationalists, he escaped to French Morocco and then Algeria, where he earned his living as a millwright (1944–57). An amnesty in 1957 allowed him to return to Spain and during the 1960s he rose within the clandestine Workers' Commissions (CCOO), becoming the leading trade union leader in Spain by the early 1970s. For most of the period 1967–75 he was in jail. He was a Communist Party Deputy (1977–82) as well as being a member of the Party's Central Committee. Following the Communists' dismal showing in 1982, he was one of those who pressed **Carrillo** to resign. In 1987 he retired as Secretary-General of the CCOO, but remained its Honorary President. ▷ **CCOO (Comisiones Obreras)**

Cambó, Francesc (1876–1947)
Catalan politician. The leader of conservative Catalan nationalists, he was a businessman and banker, who founded with Enric **Prat de la Riba** the *Lliga Regionalista* in 1901. As a middleman for foreign companies, he became the most prominent self-made businessman of that period. His overriding political objective was to establish the Catalan bourgeoisie as the ruling class in Spain. To this end, he attempted to organize a nationwide movement for political reform, but the general strike of 1917 led him to change course. From this time on, he was closely allied to the central ruling oligarchy, joining the 'National Government' of Antonio **Maura** in 1918 as Minister of Economic Development and remaining in government until Mar 1922. During the Second Republic he relaunched

the **Lliga** (as the *Lliga Catalana*), but his oligarchical nationalism was overshadowed throughout by the Catalan Left. He spent the **Spanish Civil War** in Italy, thereafter living in Argentina until his death. ▷ **Republic, Second** (Spain)

Cambodia formerly **Kampuchea** (1975–89) and **Khmer Republic** (1970–5)
Republic in south Indo-China, South-East Asia. Part of Indo-China since 1887, it gained independence from France in 1953, with Prince Sihanouk as Prime Minister. Sihanouk was deposed in 1970 and a right-wing government was formed. The country was renamed the Khmer Republic. Fighting throughout the country involved troops from North and South Vietnam and the USA. In 1975 Phnom Penh surrendered to the **Khmer Rouge**, a Communist guerrilla force which opposed the government, and the country became known as Kampuchea. An attempt to reform the economy on co-operative lines by **Pol Pot** in 1975–8 caused the deaths of an estimated one million people, and there was further fighting in 1977–8. Phnom Penh was captured by the Vietnamese in 1979, causing the Khmer Rouge to flee. In 1981 a constitution established a seven-member Council of State and a 16-member Council of Ministers. The Paris conference in 1988–9 between the Phnom Penh regime, the opposition coalition led by Prince Sihanouk and the Khmer Rouge ended with no agreement. The name of Cambodia was restored in 1989, the year that Vietnamese troops completed their withdrawal from Cambodia. A UN peace plan was agreed in 1991. In 1992 a UN Transitional Authority in Cambodia was planned but the Khmer Rouge refused to comply and UN trade sanctions were imposed in 1993. A new constitution was adopted in 1993.

Cameroon
Republic in West Africa. The division of the German protectorate of Kamerun into French and British Cameroon in 1919 was confirmed by the League of Nations mandate in 1922. The **UN** turned these mandates into trusteeships in 1946. French Cameroon acquired independence as the Republic of Cameroon in 1960. The north sector of British Cameroon voted to become part of Nigeria, and the southern sector part of Cameroon. The Federal Republic of Cameroon was established, with separate parliaments, in 1961. The federal system was abolished in 1972, and its name changed to the United Republic of Cameroon. The word 'United' was dropped from the name after a constitutional amendment in 1984.

Camp David Accords (1978)
Documents signed by Anwar **Sadat**, President of Egypt, and Menachem **Begin**, Prime Minister of Israel, and witnessed by US President Jimmy **Carter** at Camp David, Maryland, USA, in Sep 1978. Regarded by many

as a triumph of US diplomacy, they were preliminary to the signing of the formal peace treaty (1979) between the two countries, which gave Egypt back the Sinai Desert, captured in the 1967 War. ▷ **Arab–Israeli Wars; PLO**

Campbell-Bannerman, Sir Henry (1836–1908)
British politician. He became a Liberal MP in 1868, was Chief Secretary for Ireland (1884), War Secretary (1886 and 1892–5), Liberal leader (1899), and Prime Minister (1905–8). A 'pro-Boer', he granted the ex-republics responsible government, and his popularity helped to reunite a divided **Liberal Party**. He supported the Lib–Lab pact of 1903, which played a part in the Liberal landslide of 1906. ▷ **Boer Wars**

Campoamor, Clara (1888–1972)
Spanish politician and feminist. Of working-class origin, she graduated in law in 1924, and from then onwards agitated widely on behalf of women's issues. In 1931 she was elected to the Constituent Cortes of the Second Republic as a deputy for the **Radical Republican Party**. She was responsible more than anyone else for the inclusion of women's suffrage in the Constitution of 1931. During the legislature of 1931–3 she was Vice-President of the Labour Commission and participated in the reform of the Civil Code. In addition, she represented Spain at the **League of Nations** and founded the Republican Feminine Union. In 1933–4 she was also the Director-General of Charity. During the 1930s she wrote extensively on women's rights and aspirations. In 1938 she chose exile in Buenos Aires, moving in 1955 to Lausanne, where she died. She was one of the principal figures of the 20c in the struggle for women's rights in Spain. ▷ **Republic, Second** (Spain)

Campos, Roberto de Oliveira (1926–)
Brazilian political economist and diplomat. A Jesuit-trained economist, he served as a diplomat on the US-Brazil Economic Commission in the 1950s, and was later Director of the National Economic Development Bank (BNDE) under **Kubitschek (de Oliveira)**. Associated with attempts to achieve an 'orthodox' economic policy by the nationalist press, he was the natural choice for Planning Minister under **Castelo Branco**. He co-authored the 'Government Economic Action Programme, 1964–6' (PAEG), with Otávio Gouveia de Bulhões: this introduced modern fiscal and monetary policy instruments, as well as indexation and the centralization of expenditure, while encouraging 'corporate' management of the economy, drawing on the heritage of the **Vargas** era. He espoused the trickle-down theory of economic growth and the encouragement of foreign investment.

Campos Salles, Manuel Ferraz de (1841–1913)
Brazilian politician. The 'Political Architect of the Republic', he was a slave-owner, *fazendeiro* and lawyer in Campinas, then the centre of the coffee-growing region of Brazil. He became a Republican in the 1870s and was Minister of Justice in the Provisional Government of the Republic (1889–91), when he was responsible for the separation of Church and State and the introduction of civil marriage. He was Governor of São Paulo in 1896–8, and then became President (1898–1902). Charged with radical financial reform, designed to protect the country from foreign intervention, and pledged to a 'privatization' programme, he emasculated a nationalist Congress by agreeing a pact with incumbent governors: the President would protect them from federal intervention if they, in their turn, pledged their support for him in Congress. This system, known as the 'Politics of the Governors', led to one-party state administrations and provided the basis for political management until 1930; vestiges of it remain to this day.

Canaris, Wilhelm (1887–1945)
German naval commander. He entered the Imperial German Navy in 1905, and served in the *Dresden* at the Battles of Coronel and the Falklands in **World War I**. He escaped from internment in Chile and made his way back to Germany, and served in U-boats in the Mediterranean. He retired with the rank of rear-admiral in 1934. Though disapproving of aspects of the Nazi regime, he rose under **Hitler** to become admiral of the German Navy and chief of the *Abwehr*, the military intelligence service of the High Command of the armed forces. Involved in the anti-Nazi resistance and associated with the 1944 bomb plot against Hitler, he was arrested, imprisoned and hanged in Apr 1945, just before the entry of the Soviet Army into **Berlin**. ▷ **Nazi Party**

cangaço
The golden age of the *cangaço*, the rural banditry in north-eastern Brazil, occurred between 1860 and 1930. The great droughts of 1877–9 and 1888–90, and the demise of slavery coincided with the decline of the region's importance in national politics and a long boom in cotton production. The result was to intensify feuding between powerful local landowners, whose ancient prerogative of *homísio* (personal protection to any individual seeking it) protected bandits. *Cangaceiros* were recruited from, and formed part of, the irregular forces which *coroneis* retained in order to preserve their local hegemonies, and their forces were enlisted by both federal and state authorities during the 1920s. Bandit leaders such as Antônio Silvino and **Lampião**, who led large and well-equipped bands in the sertão capitalized on the notion of the 'good thief', but were liquidated by the centralized federal government after the 1930

revolution. Their defiance of authority has made them popular heroes to this day.

Cao Dai/Hoa Hao

Two major religious movements, established in **Cochin-China** (southern Vietnam) from the final decades of French rule. The Cao Dai religion, officially founded in 1926, claimed to be heir to all the religions of the world. It preached the virtues of spiritualism, Confucian piety and vegetarianism. Hoa Hao Buddhism, founded in 1939 by a charismatic faith-healer, Huynh Phu So, was extremely puritanical. It sought to eliminate idol worship and elaborate ritual. In the late 1940s the attractiveness of Cao Dai and Hoa Hao were a major obstacle to the advance of the **Viet Minh** in the rural south. The Hoa Hao was strongly hostile to the communists, to the extent that it was allied with the French against them. In 1947 the communists seized, tried and executed Huynh Phu So. The power of the sects in the politics of post-war southern Vietnam, reinforced over a number of years by French subventions, was sharply curbed by **Ngo Dinh Diem** in 1955.

capitalism

The chief economic system of the West, also known as the free market or free enterprise economy. It is based on the principles of private ownership of production processes and the supply and demand of goods as the determiner of the market, rather than government intervention. Although capitalist societies have existed since classical times, the system was most fully adopted after the Industrial Revolution of the 18c and 19c. The tenets of free enterprise that underlie classical capitalism are most famously put forward in Adam Smith's *Inquiry into the Nature and Causes of the Wealth of Nations* (1776). In practice, most capitalist systems involve some degree of government control, for poverty relief, to steady an unstable economy (a lesson learned after the **Great Depression** particularly) and to limit abuse of the system, such as financial fraud and monopolies. With the retreat of **communism**, capitalism has become more prevalent across the world, often co-existing (as in China) as private enterprise within a largely government-controlled system.

Capitalist Encirclement (1928–53)

An excuse used by **Stalin** to justify his dictatorship. In his attitude to the outside world, Stalin moved from advocating **World Revolution** to accepting **peaceful co-existence**. However, in order to maintain his control over the Communist Party and the people, he exaggerated the hostility of surrounding states, especially Britain, Germany, Japan and the USA, by raising the spectre of a terrible capitalist encirclement.

Capone, Al(phonse) (1899–1947)

US gangster. He achieved worldwide notoriety as a racketeer during the prohibition era in Chicago. Such was his power that no evidence sufficient to support a charge against him was forthcoming until 1931, when he was sentenced to 10 years' imprisonment for tax evasion. Released on health grounds in 1939, he retired to his estate in Florida, where he died.

Caporetto, Battle of (24 Oct–4 Nov 1917)

The disastrous defeat for the Italian Army under **Cadorna** by the Austro-German forces of General Belov. The battle broke the stalemate which had characterized the first two years of the war in Italy. The Italians lost 300 000 men and were forced back to the River Piave, where, with the assistance of French and British divisions, they managed to establish a defensive line. The defeat led to Cadorna's replacement by **Diaz**.

Cárdenas (del Río), Lázaro (1895–1970)

Mexican general and politician. His presidency (1934–40) shaped modern Mexico. He promoted the return of the **ejido** in the south and the extension of the rancho (small property) principally in the north. His presidency also witnessed the creation of **PEMEX** from nationalized foreign (mainly British) companies, and the PRM (*Partido de la Revolución Mexicana*, Mexican Revolutionary Party), precursor of the **PRI**. Left-wing in his sympathies, he introduced many social reforms and reorganized the ruling party.

Cardozo, Benjamin (1870–1938)

US jurist. He sat on the bench of the New York Court of Appeals from 1913 to 1932, during which time the court became internationally famous. Appointed to the US Supreme Court by President Herbert Hoover, he succeeded Oliver Wendell Holmes, serving for six years, 1932–8. Although he served for such a relatively brief time, and although many of his opinions dissented from the majority, he was remarkably influential because of his eloquence and learnedness. He was generally liberal and believed that the courts could effect social change.

Caribbean Community (CARICOM)

An association of former British colonies in the Caribbean, some of which (Barbados, Jamaica, and the Leeward Islands) existed as the Caribbean Federation, with the aim of full self-government, until the establishment of the Federation of the **West Indies** (1958–63). When Jamaica became independent in 1962, the Federation was dissolved. In 1969 certain of the remaining islands in the Windward and Leeward Islands were offered associated status within the **Commonwealth of Nations**, and in 1969 the West Indies Associated States was formed. In 1968 many of the islands agreed to the establishment of the Caribbean Free Trade Area (CARIFTA).

Carinthia (Kärnten)

A federal state in southern Austria bordered by Styria, Italy and Slovenia. At the end of **World War I**, though it remained within Austria, parts were ceded to Italy and the Kingdom of Serbs, Croats and Slovenes (later Yugoslavia). During the **Anschluss** it became part of the Reichsgau Kärnten (1938–45) and since 1945 has been a federal state within Austria. It is populated mainly by Germans but has a large Slovene minority.

Carl XVI Gustaf (1946–)

King of Sweden (1973/). As his father had died in an air accident in 1947, he became Crown Prince from the time of the accession of his grandfather, King **Gustav VI Adolf**, in 1950. A new constitution, which reduced the king to a purely ceremonial head of state, was approved by the Swedish Parliament just before his accession. In 1976 he married Silvia Sommerlath, the daughter of a West German businessman. They had two daughters, Victoria and Madeleine, and a son, Carl Philip.

Carlism

A Spanish dynastic cause and political movement, officially born in 1833, but with its origins in the 1820s. Against the claim to the Spanish throne by Isabella II, daughter of Ferdinand VII, Carlists supported the claim of the latter's brother, Don **Carlos**. In the 19c, Carlism attracted widespread popular support chiefly in conservative, Catholic districts of rural northern Spain. After 1876, Carlism ceased to be a vehicle for widespread anti-capitalist protest and became a narrower movement espousing ultra-rightist, 'traditionalist' principles. It took the Nationalist side in the **Spanish Civil War**, providing c.100 000 volunteers. Since 1939, both during and after the **Franco** regime, the cause has suffered division and serious decline, although small Carlist groups persist.

Carlsson, Ingvar Costa (1934–)

Swedish politician. Educated at Lund (Sweden) and North Western (USA) universities, he was secretary in the prime minister's office (1958–60) before entering active party politics. He became president of the youth league of the Social Democratic Labour party (SAP) in 1961, and in 1964 was elected to the Riksdag (parliament). After holding a number of junior posts (1967–76), he became deputy to Olof **Palme** in 1982 and succeeded him as prime minister and SAP leader after Palme's assassination in 1986.

Carmona, António (1869–1951)

Portuguese politician and soldier. Having entered the army in 1888, he was made a general in 1922 and briefly served under the First Republic as Minister of War (1923). Following the coup d'état of 28 May 1926 against the Republic, Carmona emerged as de facto Prime Minister (from July 1926) and as President (from Nov 1926). Although he lacked a political programme, he was able to consolidate his position by balancing the various factions within the armed forces. As military dictator for six years (1926–32), he adopted a low profile, partly because he was an uncharismatic bureaucratic officer and partly because the regime was headed by a coalition of officers. Carmona oversaw the rise of **Salazar** and the **Estado Novo**, protecting him against opposition, especially during the major cabinet crises of 1929 and 1930. On the other hand, Salazar's success ensured Carmona's own future. Once Salazar was established as dictator, Carmona was content to act as a figurehead president. Although by 1945 he had become disillusioned with Salazar, his control over national affairs was by now negligible. He died as President, bitter at his political impotence. ▷ **Republic, First** (Portugal)

Carniola (Krain)

A part of Roman Pannonia, it was settled by the Slavs (6c), emerging as a distinct district in the 10c. During the 19c it was the centre of the Slovene national awakening; in 1848, nationalists tried to form an autonomous Slovene kingdom within the Habsburg Monarchy but in 1849 Carniola was again organized as a crown land. In 1918 it became part of the Kingdom of Serbs, Croats and Slovenes (later Yugoslavia) and after 1947 was absorbed, in its entirety, within Slovenia.

Carranza, Venustiano (1859–1920)

Mexican politician. A senator under Porfirio **Díaz** and a supporter of **Madero**, he emerged as the leader of Constitutionalist forces against the dictator, Victoriano Huerta, in 1914. A fervent protagonist of Liberal aims, he was forced to accept the radical constitution of 1917, but limited agrarian reform to military measures, destroying **Zapata** and **Villa** in the process. He was assassinated when attempting to retain the presidency.

Carrero Blanco, Luis (1903–73)

Spanish politician and naval officer. Director of Naval Operations in 1939, he later rose to the rank of admiral (1966). In 1941 he became an under-secretary to the presidency, and for the next 32 years he was effectively **Franco**'s right-hand man. He became a minister in 1951, Vice-Premier in 1967 and, in 1973, the first prime minister other than Franco since 1939. He was the politicial alter ego of Franco, not only because of his absolute loyalty, but also because he shared the same ultra-reactionary outlook, hating 'communists', 'freemasons', and 'liberals', although his visceral anti-Semitism set him apart. The key figure of the regime after Franco and the embodiment of continuity, his assassination by **ETA** (Dec 1973) was a grave blow to the regime.

Carrillo, Santiago (1915–)
Spanish political leader. He became Secretary-General of the Socialist Youth at only 19. Jailed for participation in the Asturian rising of Oct 1934, he was a key figure in the merger of the Socialist Youth with the Communists before the **Spanish Civil War**. He has been widely held responsible for the massacre of Nationalist prisoners at Paracuellos de Jarama in Nov 1936. Having become General-Secretary of the exiled **PCE** in 1960, he took the party from its neo-Stalinism to, in the 1970s, Eurocommunism. He returned to Spain in 1976. Although the PCE won 23 seats in the 1979 general election, it plummeted to a mere four in 1982. He resigned to found his own communist party, finally entering the **PSOE** in 1991. ▷ **Stalinism**

Carrington, Peter (Alexander Rupert), 6th Baron (1919–)
British politician. A Conservative, he held several junior posts in government (1951–6), before becoming High Commissioner to Australia (1956–9). He then served as First Lord of the Admiralty (1959–63) and Leader of the House of Lords (1963–4). He was Secretary of State for Defence (1970–4) and briefly for Energy (1974), and also Chairman of the Conservative Party organization (1972–4). Upon the Conservative return to office he was Foreign Secretary (1979–82), until he and his ministerial team resigned over the Argentinian invasion of the Falkland Islands. He later became Secretary-General of **NATO** (1984–8), and **EC** mediator during the crisis in Yugoslavia (1991–2). ▷ **Conservative Party** (UK)

Carson, Edward Henry, Baron (1854–1935)
Irish politician and barrister. He became known in 1895 for his successful prosecution of Oscar Wilde. He was Solicitor-General for Ireland (1892) and for England (1900–6), Attorney-General (1915), First Lord of the Admiralty (1916–17), and Lord of Appeal (1921–9). Strongly opposed to **Home Rule**, he organized the Ulster Volunteers. ▷ **Conservative Party** (UK)

Cartel des gauches (1924)
Literally 'left-wing cartel', this term describes an electoral coalition in France of the radical, socialist and other left-wing parties which defeated the **Bloc national**.

Carter, Jimmy (James Earl) (1924–)
US politician and 39th President. Educated at the US Naval Academy, he served in the US Navy until 1953, when he took over the family peanut

business and other enterprises. As Governor of Georgia (1971–5), he showed sensitivity towards the rights of blacks and women. In the aftermath of the **Watergate** crisis he won the Democratic presidential nomination in 1976, and went on to win a narrow victory over Gerald **Ford**. As president (1977–81), he arranged the peace treaty between Egypt and Israel (1979), known as the **Camp David Accords**, and was concerned with human rights both at home and abroad. His administration ended in difficulties over the **Iran Hostage Crisis**, and the Soviet invasion of Afghanistan, and he was defeated by Ronald **Reagan** in the 1980 election.

Carton de Wiart, Count Henri (1869–1951)
Belgian politician, writer and historian. A Catholic, he founded the Christian-Democratic newspaper *L'Avenir Social* in 1891, and represented Brussels in the Belgian parliament. From 1911 to 1950 he was frequently a cabinet minister, holding at various times the portfolios of Justice, Home Affairs, Social Services and Public Health; in 1920–1 he was also Prime Minister.

casa del pueblo
Spanish grass-roots political institution. Literally 'House of the People', the term describes a meeting-place and educational, social and welfare centre for political activists. Based on a Belgian socialist model, the *casa del pueblo* was introduced into Spain in 1906 by the Republican populist Alejandro **Lerroux**. The first casa del pueblo opened in Barcelona with a clinic, theatre and a consumer cooperative, which provided insurance and pension schemes as well as legal aid. It was designed to replace the traditional and more exclusive Republican casinos, thereby helping to create a truly mass party by forging a new basis for collaboration between workers and the Republicans. The casas compensated for some of the glaring deficencies of the state's welfare provisions and became best-known as an important focus of support for the Socialist Party and its trade union movement, the **UGT**.

Casablanca Conference (Jan 1943)
A meeting in North Africa between Franklin D **Roosevelt** and Winston **Churchill** during **World War II**, at which it was decided to insist on the eventual 'unconditional surrender' of Germany and Japan. Attempts to overcome friction between Roosevelt and the Free French under de **Gaulle** had only limited success. The combined Chiefs of Staff settled strategic differences over the projected invasion of Sicily and Italy.

Casey, Richard Gardiner, Baron Casey (1890–1976)
Australian politician. He was elected to the House of Representatives in 1931. He became first Australian Minister to the USA in 1940, Minister

of State in the Middle East (a war-cabinet rank) in 1942, and Minister for External Affairs in 1951. A life peerage was conferred on him in 1960.

Cassin, René (1887–1976)
French jurist and politician. During **World War II** he joined General de **Gaulle** in London. He was principal legal adviser in negotiations with the British government and, in the later years of the war, held important posts in the French government in exile in London and Algiers, and subsequently in the Council of State (of which he was President, 1944–60) in liberated France. He was the principal author of the Universal Declaration of the Rights of Man (1948) and played a leading part in the establishment of UNESCO. He was a member of the European Court of Human Rights from 1959, and its President (1965–8). In 1968 he was awarded the Nobel Prize for Peace.

caste
A system of inequality, most prevalent in Hindu Indian society, in which status is determined by the membership of a particular lineage and associated occupational group into which a person is born. The groups are ordered according to a notion of religious purity or spirituality thus, the Brahmin or priest caste, as the most spiritual of occupations, claims highest status. Contact between castes is held to be polluting, and must be avoided. Caste was officially abolished in the Constitution of Independent India in 1951. However, controversy has erupted in the 1980s and 1990s over the extension of 'reservations' — a policy of positive discrimination in the allocation of government posts and student places in universities — intended to remove the disadvantages of, and prejudices against, the lower castes created by the caste system. ▷ **Mandal Commissions**

Castelo Branco, Humberto de Alencar (1900–67)
Brazilian politician. He was educated at the Pôrto Alegre Military Academy in Rio Grande do Sul and at France's École Supérieure de Guerre, as well as the General Command course at Fort Leavenworth, USA. He went on to fight with the Brazilian army in Italy, and coordinated the anti-**Goulart** military conspiracy of 1964. Linked to other veteran officers in the Escola Superior da Guerra, founded in the 1940s in Rio de Janeiro, his foreign policy was anti-communist, and he believed that short-term arbitary technocratic measures should be taken to create the conditions for democracy. As President from 1964 to 1967, although the economy had been stabilized, the financial system reorganized and foreign debt renegotiated, his government failed to alter traditional patterns of authority and prevent the emergence of hard-line factions amongst the military, which established the 'tutelary regime' which survived until 1985.

Castle, Barbara Anne (1911–)
British politician. She became Labour MP for Blackburn (1945–87) and was Chairman of the Labour Party (1958–9), Minister of Overseas Development (1964–5), and a controversial Minister of Transport (1965–8), introducing a 70 mph speed limit and the 'breathalyser' test for drunken drivers. She became Secretary of State for Employment and Productivity (1968–70) and Minister of Health and Social Security (1974–8). She then returned to the backbenches, but became Vice-Chairman of the Socialist Group in the European Parliament in 1979, when she became an elected member of that body, a post she held until 1985. ▷ **Labour Party** (UK); **socialism**

Castro (Ruz), Fidel (1927–)
Cuban revolutionary. He studied law in Havana and in 1953 was imprisoned after an unsuccessful rising against **Batista**, but released under an amnesty. He fled to the USA and Mexico, then in 1956 landed in Cuba with a small band of insurgents. In 1958 he mounted a full-scale attack and Batista was forced to flee. He became Prime Minister (1959–), later proclaimed a 'Marxist-Leninist programme', and set about far-reaching reforms. His overthrow of US economic dominance, and the routing of the US-connived émigré invasion at the **Bay of Pigs** (1961) was balanced by his dependence on Soviet aid. Castro became President in 1976. Although Cubans gained substantially in terms of general social provision, by the late 1980s the economic experiment had failed, and the collapse of the USSR isolated his regime.

Catalan Autonomy Statutes (1932 and 1979)
Catalonia (the 'land of castles') has always been distinguished from the rest of Spain by its culture, language and geography. The dynastic union of Ferdinand of Aragon (which included Catalonia) and Isabella of Castile in 1469 allowed Catalonia to retain its laws and privileges until the end of the War of the Spanish Succession in 1714. Philip V of Spain thereupon abolished the *fueros* (medieval laws and customs) and the **Generalitat**, a parliament of medieval origin. During the late 19c a Catalan nationalist movement developed which eventually led to the establishment of a limited form of self-government in the shape of the Mancomunitat in 1913. This was abolished by the dictatorship of General **Primo de Rivera** in 1923, but the Second Republic (1931–6) provided Catalonia with an autonomy statute in Sep 1932. This restored the Generalitat, proclaimed Catalan as the official language, and gave the Catalans control over most regional issues, although the period of self-government was cut short by **Franco**'s victory in the **Spanish Civil War**. In 1977 the Generalitat was revived and in 1979 Catalonia regained its autonomy with a substantial measure of home rule. ▷ **Republic, Second** (Spain)

Cataví Massacre (21 Dec 1941)

An attack on striking Bolivian tin-miners and their families by Bolivian soldiers at the Cataví mining camp, in which several hundred people were killed. The incident brought about the emergence of the powerful silver miners' union, culminating in the upheaval of Dec 1943, which brought the MNR (*Movimiento Nacionalista Revolucionario*) to power, with Víctor **Paz Estenssoro** as mentor. Cataví was chosen as the ceremonial site for the nationalization of Bolivia's tin mines in Oct 1952, under Estenssoro's presidency.

Catholic People's Party (*Katholieke Volkspartij*, KVP)

Dutch political party, founded in 1945 as a continuation of the Roman Catholic National Party (RKSP, founded 1922). Traditionally the Catholic Party in the Netherlands polled about a third of the votes; in the 1960s that percentage began to drop radically, due to general secularization and the departure of various Catholic splinter groups. As a result the KVP decided in 1973 to join the Dutch Protestant parties in an interconfessional grouping, the **Christian Democratic Appeal** (CDA), and in 1980 the KVP ceased to exist as a separate party. As a centre party the KVP was regularly in government, and it (or the CDA) has taken part in all Dutch cabinets since **World War II**.

Catt, Carrie Clinton Chapman (1859–1947)

US suffragist. In 1887 she joined the Iowa Woman Suffrage Association and quickly climbed the ranks of the national movement. Succeeding Susan B Anthony as president of the **National American Woman Suffrage Association** in 1900, her strategy of working on both state and national levels and through both political parties led to the ratification of the 19th Amendment in 1920 and secured the suffrage for women. She organized the Women's Peace Party during **World War I**.

Cavaco Silva, Anibal (1939–)

Portuguese politician. After studying economics in Britain and the USA, he became a university teacher and then a research director in the Bank of Portugal. With the gradual re-establishment of constitutional government after 1976, he was persuaded by colleagues to enter politics and was Minister of Finance (1980–1). In 1985 he became leader of the Social Democratic Party (PSD) and Prime Minister. Under his cautious, conservative leadership, Portugal joined the European Community (EC) in 1985 and the Western European Union (WEU) in 1988.

CCF (Cooperative Commonwealth Federation)

Canadian socialist political party. Founded in Calgary in 1932, it was led by J S **Woodsworth** and held its first meeting at Regina in 1933, with representatives of intellectual groups, organized labour, socialists and farmers. The 'Regina Manifesto' included economic planning, central financial control and price stabilization, the extension of public ownership in communications and natural resources, the creation of a welfare state and an emergency relief programme. By 1934 the party had become the official opposition in Saskatchewan and in British Columbia, and hundreds of CCF clubs had sprung up throughout the country (except in the Maritimes Provinces and Quebec). The party avoided the fate of the US **Socialist Party** because of its strong adherence to parliamentary principles and the support it was given by both trade unionists and intellectuals, although it was damaged severely by **Duplessis**'s **Padlock Act**. In Ontario the CCF became the official opposition in 1943, while in the following year it was elected into government in Saskatchewan. Its challenge forced the Liberals into a far stronger emphasis on social reforms, and such federal legislation as the 1944 Families Allowances Act led to a decrease in support for CCF during the election of 1945. The continuation of this trend in **Liberal Party** policies eventually led the CCF to drop the most doctrinaire elements from its manifesto in 1956. In 1961 the party evolved into the **New Democratic Party** with 'Tommy' **Douglas**, the CCF Premier of Saskatchewan, as its leader.

CCM (Chama Cha Mapinduzi)

Sometimes referred to as the Revolutionary Party of Tanzania, this party was formed in 1977 by the merger of **TANU** and the Afro-Shirazi Party. It is the only legal party in Tanzania, but is relatively pluralist with active women's, youth, and local branches.

CCOO (Comisiones Obreras)

Spanish trade union organization (literally, 'Workers' Commissions'). Its origins lay in the spontaneous rank and file committees set up in the late 1950s in the Asturian coalfields and the Basque country to organize strike action. By the mid-1960s, it had established a parallel organization to the official syndicate; thereby it became the first democratic broadly-based union organization in Spain since the **Spanish Civil War**. By the late 1960s it was firmly under Communist control, being severely repressed after the major demonstration of 1967 until **Franco**'s death in 1975. It is now one of the two main trade union forces in Spain.

CDU (*Christlich Demokratische Union*, 'Christian Democratic Union')

German political party. An ideologically heterogeneous collection of regional organizations gradually coalesced between 1947 and 1950 to form the main party of government in post-war Federal Germany. The CDU has roots in the pre-1933 **Centre Party**, but functions as a multi-denominational, 'people's' party committed to social progress within a **social market economy**. Its membership is socially diverse, but with a definite middle-class flavour; initially more within the independent middle classes, now among salaried and professional groups. It dominated government under the leadership of Konrad **Adenauer** (1949–63) and presided over Germany's great economic miracle (**Wirtschaftswunder**), but in 1966 was forced into coalition with the **SPD** and in 1969 went into opposition. Under Helmut **Kohl** the CDU regained power in 1982 with its customary ally, the **CSU**, and with the **FDP**. This coalition oversaw the reunification of Germany during 1989 and 1990.

Ceauşescu, Nicolae (1918–89)

Romanian politician. Born into a peasant family, he joined the Communist Party in 1936 and was imprisoned for anti-government activities (1936–8). He became a member of the Central Committee of the Romanian Communist Party (RCP) in 1952 and of the Politburo in 1955. In 1965 he succeeded **Gheorgiu-Dej** as *de facto* party leader, becoming General-Secretary of the RCP in 1965 and its first President in 1967. Under his leadership, Romania became increasingly independent of the USSR and pursued its own foreign policy, for which Ceauşescu was decorated by many Western governments. In internal affairs he extended the rigid programme of his Stalinist predecessor, instituting a strong personality cult and filling offices with his family. He manipulated Romanian nationalism and ruthlessly forced national minorities to adopt Romanian culture. His policy of 'systematization' in the countryside, uprooting traditional villages, roused an international outcry in the late 1980s. In 1989 he was deposed when elements in the army joined a popular revolt. Following a trial by military tribunal, he and his wife, Elena, who had been second only to him in political influence, were shot.

CEDA (*Confederación Española de Derechas Autónomas*, 'Spanish Confederation of Autonomous Rightist Groups')

Spanish political party. The CEDA, founded in Feb 1933, was the principal non-Republican conservative force under the Second Republic. Ultimately, the proto-fascist CEDA aimed to replace the Republic by an authoritarian, corporatist state: many of its goals were assumed by **Franco**. The CEDA dominated the governments of 1933–5 through an alliance with the **Radical Republican Party**, demolishing the reforms of 1931–3 and preparing the army for a rising. Its legalistic strategy for power was thwarted by the collapse of the Radicals, the President's refusal to allow the CEDA to head an administration and, finally, its failure to win the general election of Feb 1936. The party not only provided funds for the rising of July 1936, but the vast majority of its members joined the Nationalists. However, there was no place for the CEDA in Nationalist Spain, so it was dissolved in Apr 1937. ▷ **Republic, Second** (Spain)

Ceka

The gang of hired thugs, often recruited from the criminal classes, employed by **Mussolini** to intimidate his political opponents. Their attacks were responsible for the death of **Matteotti** and for the flight from Italy of, among others, **Nitti** and **Amendola**. They were also used to harass **fuorusciti**.

CENTO (Central Treaty Organization)

A political-military alliance signed in 1955 between Iran (which withdrew after the fall of the Shah), Turkey, Pakistan, Iraq (which withdrew in 1958) and the UK, as a defence against the USSR.

Central African Federation (1953–63)

A federal territory established by the British Government to bring together the administrations of Northern and Southern Rhodesia and Nyasaland (now Zambia, Zimbabwe and Malawi). It was designed to act as a counterweight to South Africa, which had been dominated by the Afrikaans Nationalists since the election of 1948, and to encourage investment in the region. Theoretically its society and government were to be developed on the basis of racial partnership, but in reality it became a means for the extension of white settler power. It stimulated African nationalist resistance and an emergency was declared after disturbances broke out in Nyasaland in 1959, together with strikes and political activism in Northern Rhodesia. After the Devlin and Monckton Commission reports the Federation was wound up, leading to the independence of Zambia and Malawi and the unilateral declaration of independence in Rhodesia.

Central American Common Market (CACM)

An economic association initiated in 1960 between Guatemala, Honduras, El Salvador, Nicaragua, and (from 1963) Costa Rica. Its early apparent success was offset by growing political crisis in the late 1970s. ▷ **EEC**

Central Powers

Initially, the members of the Triple Alliance (Germany, Austria-Hungary, Italy) created by Bismarck in 1882. As Italy remained neutral in 1914, the term was later used to describe Germany, Austria-Hungary, their ally Turkey, and later Bulgaria in **World War I**. ▷ **Alliance, Triple**

Centre Party (Germany; *Zentrum*)

German political party. This interest-group party was founded (1870–1) after the creation of the German **Reich**, to defend the rights and identity of the Catholic Church and the Catholic minority (33 per cent of the population) within the country. By the turn of the century, the Centre

Party had long escaped the Kulturkampf, or political persecution it initially suffered under Bismarck and from 1918 onward played a key role in the creation and governance of the **Weimar Republic**. It contained politicians and supporters right across the social spectrum, whose politics were only accommodated with difficulty during the 20c. A staunch opponent of **Hitler** at the end of Weimar, the Centre Party then supported his enabling legislation in Mar 1933 in return for guarantees on the rights of Catholics. The Centre dissolved itself in July 1933.

Centre Party (Sweden)
The name adopted in 1958 by the Agrarian Party, which had been formed in 1921 by the union of a number of farmers' groups. It supported the Social Democrats between 1932 and the later 1950s and indeed joined them in coalition governments in 1936–45 and 1951–7. After this, the party moved away from its former allies. It took up the environmentalist and anti-nuclear cause and succeeded in broadening its electoral base. In 1976–82 the leader of the party, Torbjörn Fälldin, headed non-socialist coalition governments.

Cerezo Arevalo, Mario Vinicio (1942–)
Guatemalan politician. Educated at San Carlos University, Guatemala, he joined the Christian Democratic Party (PDCG), founded in 1968. From 1974 there was widespread political violence and democratic government was virtually suspended. With the adoption of a new constitution in 1985, the PDCG won the congressional elections and Cerezo became the first civilian president for 20 years.

Černík, Oldřich (1921–)
Czechoslovak politician. A man of reasonable ability, he worked his way up through the official hierarchy to become Chairman of the State Planning Commission in 1963. As such, he favoured moderate change to make the economy more efficient. However, in Jan 1968, when Alexander **Dubček** became General-Secretary, Černík became Prime Minister and followed a more far-reaching reform policy. In July and Aug of the same year he tried to restrain the more radical supporters of the **Prague Spring**, and after the Soviet invasion he struggled to try to retain something of its achievements. But within two years, like Dubček, he was removed from the party and the government.

Černý, Jan (1874–1959)
Czechoslovak official and politician. Partly as a result of its proportional representation system, interwar Czechoslovakia had, on occasions, difficulty in finding a coalition government. In two such periods (1920–1 and 1926), President **Masaryk** employed the device of appointing a cabinet of officials. In both of these, Černý acted as Prime Minister and did

an efficient job. His experience as an official in the Ministry of the Interior stood him in good stead, although it added to his unpopularity among the social democrats in particular. He subsequently served brief periods as Minister of the Interior, including just before and after the **Munich Agreement**.

CGT (*Confédération générale du travail*, 'General Confederation of Labour')
French trade-union organization, formed in 1895, which today claims a membership of c.2 million, mainly production and blue-collar workers. It is now closely linked to the **Communist Party**, but originally adopted by the Charter of Amiens (1906) a policy of avoiding all links with political parties and espousing the doctrines of revolutionary syndicalism (according to which the trade union movement should destroy capitalist society through strike action, and create a new society run by the workers' unions, as opposed to State socialism). By 1921 it had evolved to a moderate position, which led to a schism, and the founding of the CGTU (*Confédération génerale du travail unitaire*), which soon came to be controlled by the Communist Party. The CGT and CGTU were reunited in 1936, under the CGT banner; after being banned during **World War II**, the CGT emerged under communist control, which led to a new schism in 1948, with the formation of the CGT *Force ouvrière*, ('Workers' Force'), close at that time to the **Socialist Party** and consisting mainly of civil servants and clerical workers. There are several other trade-union federations, of which the most important are the *Confédération française démocratique du travail* (CFDT, 'French Democratic Confederation of Labour') formed in 1964, out of the *Confédération française des travailleurs chrétiens* (CFTC, 'French Confederation of Christian Workers'), a Catholic federation originally established in 1920, which however also continued to exist. There is also the *Confédération générale des cadres* (CGC) founded in 1944, consisting mainly of white-collar workers. One of the largest unionized workforces, the schoolteachers, have their own *Fédération de l'éducation nationale* (FEN) independent of all the general federations. The main characteristics of French trade-unionism are its fragmentation and weakness; a much smaller proportion of workers are members of any trade union than in comparable economies.

Chaco War (1932–5)
A territorial struggle between Bolivia and Paraguay in the disputed Northern Chaco area. Owing to the brilliant tactics of Colonel José Félix **Estigarribia**, Paraguay won most of the area, and a peace treaty was signed in 1938. Around 50 000 Bolivians and 35 000 Paraguayans died in the war. The outcome of the war decisively shaped the history of the decades which followed, defeat ultimately contributing to the formation of the MNR (*Movimiento Nacionalista Revolucionario*) in Bolivia, and

victory to a succession of dictatorships in Paraguay, culminating in that of Alfredo **Stroessner** in 1954.

Chadli, Benjadid (1929–)

Algerian politician and soldier. In 1955 he joined the guerrillas (*maquisards*) who were fighting for independence as part of the **FLN**. Under Houari **Boumédienne**, Defence Minister in **Ben Bella**'s government, he was military commander of Algiers, and then when Boumédienne overthrew Ben Bella in 1965 he joined the Revolutionary Council. He succeeded Boumédienne as Secretary-General of the FLN and President of Algeria in 1979.

Chak(k)ri Dynasty

A Siamese dynasty founded in 1782 by General P'raya Chakri, who as Rama I (1782/1809) established his capital at Bangkok, and instituted a period of stability and prosperity in Siam; also known as the 'Bangkok Dynasty'. His successors, especially Rama III (1824/51), Rama IV (1851/68), and Rama V (1868/1910), opened the country to foreign trade and championed modernization. The dynasty still reigns under the constitutional monarchy established after a bloodless revolution in 1932.

Chamberlain, (Arthur) Neville (1869–1940)

British politician. He was the son of Joseph **Chamberlain** by his second marriage. He was Mayor of Birmingham (1915–16), a Conservative MP from 1918, Chancellor of the Exchequer (1923–4 and 1931–7), and three times Minister for Health (1923, 1924–9 and 1931), where he effected notable social reforms. He played a leading part in the formation of the National Government (1931). As Prime Minister (1937–40), he advocated '**appeasement**' of Italy and Germany, returning from Munich with his claim to have found 'peace in our time' (1938). Criticism of his war leadership and initial military reverses led to his resignation as Prime Minister (1940), and his appointment as Lord President of the Council. ▷ **Conservative Party** (UK); **Munich Agreement; World War II**

Chamberlain, Sir (Joseph) Austen (1863–1937)

British politician. The eldest son of Joseph **Chamberlain**, he was elected a Liberal Unionist MP in 1892, and sat as a Conservative MP until his death in 1937. He was Chancellor of the Exchequer (1903–6 and 1919–21), Secretary for India (1915–17), Unionist leader (1921–2), Foreign Secretary (1924–9), and First Lord of the Admiralty (1931). He received the 1925 Nobel Peace Prize for negotiating the Locarno Pact. ▷ **Conservative Party** (UK)

Chamoun, Camille (1900–87)
Lebanese politician. The curious constitutional provisions of Lebanon after its independence provided for a Muslim Prime Minister and a (Maronite) Christian President. Camille Chamoun held the presidency from 1952 until 1958. A pro-USA Maronite, his reluctance to surrender the presidency to Fuad Chehab, a Maronite more acceptable to Lebanese Muslims, led to the outbreak of civil war. His policy aimed at peaceful coexistence between Christians and Muslims, but his support for France and Britain during the Suez Crisis seriously undermined the credibility of his regime. His position was only saved during the civil war by the intervention, in 1958, of US Marines (who caused a stir by coming ashore on the bathing beaches of the Lebanese coast). Although he did not seek re-election, he continued in politics and in 1980 his National Liberal Party split from the Phalangists. He survived an assassination attempt in 1987, but died later the same year.

Chapultepec, Act of (1945)
Signed in Mexico, this act established that American states should aid each other in the event of aggression from any source whatsoever. It also met the need to coordinate, by a single instrument, the various measures calling for the peaceful settlement of disputes in the Inter-American system. It was designed as a regional counterpoise to the **UN**. Its corollary was the Inter-American Treaty of Mutual Assistance (TIAR), subsequently signed in Rio de Janeiro, and the Organization of American States (OAS), drawn up in Bogotá in 1948, as well as the Inter-American Treaty on Pacific Settlement (Pact of Bogotá) outlining procedures for the peaceful settlement of Inter-American disputes. Subsequent amendments have strengthened the economic and social functions of the OAS.

Charles, (Mary) Eugenia (1919–)
Dominican politician. After qualifying in London as a barrister, she returned to the West Indies to practise in the Windward and Leeward Islands. She entered politics in 1968 and two years later became co-founder and first leader of the centrist Dominica Freedom Party (DFP). She became an MP in 1975. Two years after independence, the DFP won the 1980 general election and she became the Caribbean's first female Prime Minister. She was re-elected Prime Minister in 1985 and again in 1990.

Charles (Philip Arthur George), Prince of Wales (1948–)
Eldest son of HM Queen **Elizabeth II** and HRH Prince Philip, Duke of **Edinburgh**, and heir apparent to the throne of Great Britain. Duke of Cornwall as the eldest son of the monarch, he was given the title of Prince of Wales in 1958, and invested at Caernarvon (1969). He served in the RAF and the Royal Navy (1971–6), and in 1981 married Lady Diana

Frances, younger daughter of the 8th Earl Spencer, from whom he separated in 1992. They have two sons, Prince William Arthur Philip Louis and Prince Henry Charles Albert David. In the 1980s he made a number of controversial statements about public issues, including architecture and educational standards.

Charles I (1887–1922)

Last ruler of the Austro-Hungarian monarchy (1916/18). He succeeded his grand-uncle, Francis Joseph, in 1916, having become heir presumptive on the assassination at Sarajevo (1914) of his uncle, Archduke Francis Ferdinand. In Nov 1918 he was compelled to abdicate upon the collapse of Austria-Hungary. Two attempts at restoration in Hungary (1921) failed, and he died in exile in Madeira.

Charles II (1893–1953)

King of Romania (1930/40). Involved in a scandalous affair with Magda Lupescu, he renounced his right of succession (1925) and went to live in Paris. In 1930 he returned to Romania as King and succeeded in concentrating political power in his own hands during the subsequent rapid changes of ministry. In 1938 he established a royal dictatorship, gaining full powers through a new constitution, organizing his own political party, the Front of National Rebirth, and adopting many of the themes of the fascist-style **Iron Guard**. In 1940, after agreeing to the Vienna Award, which gave part of Transylvania to Hungary, he became so unpopular that he was obliged to abdicate in favour of his son, **Michael**.

Charter 77 (post-1977)

An informal association of individuals devoted to the assertion of lost human rights in Czechoslovakia. The '**normalization**' following the Soviet invasion of Czechoslovakia in 1968 suppressed many civil rights, including that to free expression of views. However, in 1976 the Czechoslovak government signed the international convention on human rights confirmed in the **Helsinki Final Act**. This gave the opposition the opportunity to protest and publish its 'charter' on 1 Jan 1977. The founders included the Foreign Minister from 1968, Jiří **Hajek**, and the President since Dec 1989, Václav **Havel**. Charter 77 suffered much harassment, but it attracted international condemnation of the communists and eventually contributed to their downfall in 1989.

Chartered companies

A series of companies chartered to rule colonies in late Victorian times, designed to produce imperialism on the cheap. The idea for these companies was based upon the monopolistic ventures of the mercantilist period, like the East India Company of 1599 and the Hudson's Bay

Company of 1670, whose charters had been abrogated in the 19c. The British North Borneo Company was chartered in 1882 and survived until the Japanese invasion of 1941. The Royal Niger Company ruled in Nigeria between 1886 and 1898; the Imperial British East Africa Company was chartered to run British East Africa (Kenya and Uganda) from 1888 to 1893; and the British South Africa Company received a charter to rule in Southern and Northern Rhodesia between 1889 and 1923.

Chatila
Palestinian refugee camp on the outskirts of Beirut in Lebanon. It was created following the evacuation of Palestinians from the city after Israeli attacks on Palestinians and Syrians (June 1982). The camp was the scene of a massacre by Christian Phalangists (Sep 1983).

Chautauqua Movement
A late 19c and early 20c US adult education movement, organized at Lake Chautauqua, New York, under Methodist auspices by Lewis Miller (1829–99) and Bishop John H Vincent (1832–1920), with home reading programmes and lectures in the arts, sciences, and humanities. At its peak it attracted up to 60 000 participants annually to regional centres in the USA and elsewhere.

Chavez, Cesar Estrada (1927–)
US union official. A farm worker, he organized the National Farm Workers Association (NFWA) in 1962, which in 1966 merged with an agricultural group of **AFL–CIO** to form the United Farm Workers Organizing Committee (UFWOC). This later became the United Farm Workers of America (UFW), and Chavez was appointed as its president. Originally a migrant himself, he has consistently worked to improve conditions for migrant agrarian workers by means of strikes, boycotts, marches and public support.

Chebrikov, Viktor Mikhailovich (1923–)
Soviet **KGB** operative. A Russian, he served in the army in **World War II** and afterwards qualified in metallurgy in Dnepropetrovsk in the Ukraine. Having transferred to party work, he came into contact with Leonid **Brezhnev** who, in 1967, appointed him to the KGB to keep an eye on Yuri **Andropov**. He eventually switched his loyalty, and in 1982 Andropov made him chairman of the KGB. In 1985 he cast his vital note for Mikhail **Gorbachev**, who made him a full member of the **Politburo**. As he began to take fright at the implications of Gorbachev's reforms and veered towards Yegor **Ligachev**; he was carefully but firmly removed from all his posts in 1988–9.

Chehab, Fuad (1902–73)
Lebanese politician and soldier. From a Maronite Christian family who had settled initially in the Chouf Mountains of Lebanon in Ottoman times, he came to prominence when he was appointed to command the new Lebanese army in 1945. He rose to become Minister of Defence in Camille **Chamoun**'s government, formed in the aftermath of the Suez affair in 1956. During the insurrection and disturbances following the declaration of the **United Arab Republic** of Egypt and Syria in 1958, Chehab refused to use the Lebanese army to crush the rebellion. This, coupled with the call by the rebels for the resignation of Chamoun, won Chehab the respect of the Muslim section of the community; and in July 1958 Chehab, who had by this time resigned command of the army, was elected President, to succeed Chamoun when the latter demitted office. Despite initial problems, he succeeded in restoring stability to Lebanon. His six-year term of office saw an attempt to establish a social policy aimed at improving the lot of the common people. That this was unsuccessful may be seen, to some extent, as a contributing factor to the disastrous currents which were to overwhelm Lebanon a decade later.

Cheka
An acronym from Russian letters **che+ka**, for the All-Russian Extraordinary Commission for Combating Counter-Revolution and Sabotage, established in 1917. It was in effect a political police force whose duties were to investigate and punish anti-Bolshevik activities. During the **Russian Civil War** it was responsible for executing thousands of political opponents in what came to be called the 'Red Terror'. ▷ **Bolsheviks; communism**

Chen, Eugene (Ch'en Yu-jen) (1878–1944)
Chinese lawyer and politician. Born in Trinidad he had a Catholic education and trained to be a lawyer. After the creation of the Chinese republic in 1912, Chen was appointed legal adviser to the Ministry of Communications. He became particularly close to **Sun Yat-sen** and served as his foreign affairs adviser. Chen was identified with the left wing of the **Guomindang**, which established its own government in Wuhan in early 1927 in opposition to **Chiang Kai-shek**. As Foreign Minister in the Wuhan government he pursued a vigorous anti-imperialist policy, negotiating the return of the British concessions of Hankou and Jiujiang. After 1927, when the Wuhan government was dissolved, Chen was briefly associated with anti-Chiang Kai-shek separatist movements.

Chen Boda (Ch'en Po-ta) (1905–)
Chinese political propagandist and interpreter of **Mao Zedong**'s thought. He joined the Chinese Communist Party (CCP) in 1927 and studied in Moscow until 1930. After teaching in Beijing, Chen went to the com-

munist base at Yan'an (Yenan) in 1937. He became Mao Zedong's personal secretary and helped popularize Mao's concept of the 'Sinification of Marxism' (adapting Marxism to Chinese conditions). After 1949 he continued to be influential in the party's propaganda department, becoming chief editor of the party organ, *Hongqi* (Red Flag), in 1958. During the **Cultural Revolution** Chen became associated with the radicals and in 1969 reached the apogee of his influence when he was appointed to the Politbureau. In the campaign against leftist excesses the following year, however, Chen was arrested and expelled from the CCP. In 1980–1 he was put on public trial along with the **Gang of Four** and sentenced to 18 years in prison. ▷ **Chinese Communist Party**

Chen Duxiu (Ch'en Tu-hsiu) (1879–1942)
Chinese revolutionary and publicist. In 1915 Chen founded the journal 'New Youth' (*Xin Qingnian*), which heralded the beginnings of a new cultural movement calling for a rejection of the Confucian tradition and the promotion of democracy and science. In 1917 he became Dean of the College of Letters at Beijing University, where he attracted a large student following. By 1920, disillusioned with the prospects of cultural change, he had become attracted to Marxism and established a communist cell in Shanghai. Although Chen was in Canton when the Chinese Communist Party (CCP) was formally created in Shanghai (July 1921), he was a founder member and was elected its first Secretary-General. With **Comintern** prodding, he led the CCP into the first United Front with the **Guomindang** in 1923 and oversaw a considerable expansion of the party's membership. When the Guomindang turned on its erstwhile communist allies in 1927, which resulted in the near total annihilation of the party, Chen was made a scapegoat for the disaster and replaced as Secretary-General.

Chen Yi (1901–72)
Chinese communist leader. He studied in France, and joined the Chinese Communist Party on his return. He supported **Mao Zedong** in the struggle with the **Guomindang**, and the Japanese (1934). Chen Yi formed the 4th Route Army in Jiangxi (1940), commanded the East China Liberation Army (1946) and restyled the 3rd (East China) Army (1948). He prepared an amphibious operation against Taiwan, but failed to capture Quemoy Island in 1949. Created Marshal of the People's Republic in 1955, he became Foreign Minister in 1958, but was dropped from the Politburo during the **Cultural Revolution** in 1969.

Chen Yong'gui (Ch'en Yung-kuei) (1915–86)
Chinese 'model' peasant and politician. During the **Cultural Revolution** Chen, an illiterate peasant, was hailed as a model worker in the Dazhai Production Brigade in the north-western province of Shanxi. As leader

of the brigade and supporter of Maoist policies, Chen was elected to the Central Committee in 1969 and elevated to the Politbureau in 1973. After **Mao Zedong**'s death in 1976, amidst a general reversal of Maoist policies, doubts were raised about Dazhai's claim as the successful embodiment of self-reliance and egalitarianism. Chen increasingly lost influence and he was dropped from the Politbureau in 1981. ▷ **Maoism**

Chen Yün (Ch'en Yun) (1905–)
Chinese communist leader and economic planner. Chen joined the Chinese Communist Party in 1924 and became a labour organizer in Shanghai. By 1940 he was a member of the Politbureau. As Minister of Heavy Industry (1949–50) and a member of the State Planning Commission (1952–4), Chen was an important economic planner in the new communist government, helping to formulate the first Five-Year Plan. As an advocate of central planning and the need to maintain production, he clashed with **Mao Zedong** over the **Great Leap Forward** campaign in 1958, which led to his official eclipse until after Mao's death. In 1978 he was reinstated as party Vice-Chairman and appointed a vice-premier in 1979, overseeing economic policies. He has been a consistent critic of the post-Mao leadership's attempt to introduce elements of a market economy, arguing for the need to maintain the dominant role of the state sector. Chen retired from party posts in 1987.

Cherikov, V (1900–)
Soviet marshal and typical post-**Russian Revolution** commander. A Russian peasant, he joined the **Red Army** in 1918 and the Communist Party in 1919. He became a regimental commander in the **Russian Civil War** and graduated from the Frunze Military Academy in 1925. During **World War II** his activities included serving as adviser to **Chiang Kai-shek** and then participating in the Battle of **Stalingrad** (1943) and the final assault on Berlin in 1945. He was Deputy Commander (1946–53), then Commander-in-Chief of Soviet forces in Germany, and Deputy Minister of Defence (1960–5).

Chernenko, Konstantin Ustinovich (1911–85)
Soviet politician. He joined the Communist Party in 1931, and held several local posts. An associate of Leonid **Brezhnev** for many years, he became a member of the **Politburo** in 1978, and the Party's chief ideologist after the death of Mikhail **Suslov** (1982). Regarded as a conservative, Chernenko was a rival of Yuri **Andropov** in the Party leadership contest of 1982, and became Party General-Secretary and Head of State after Andropov's death in 1984. He suffered from ill health, and died soon after in Moscow, to be succeeded by Mikhail **Gorbachev**.

Chernobyl

A city in central Ukraine, situated north of Kiev, near the junction of the Pripyat and Ushk rivers. In 1986 one of the reactors at the Chernobyl Nuclear Power Station emitted unprecedentedly large amounts of radioactivity into the atmosphere. Traces of radiation were reported in Western Europe (including Scandinavia and the UK) and in areas of North America. More than 30 people died in the incident and c.300 people were treated in hospital. Residents in the surrounding contaminated areas were evacuated, although some chose to return later.

Chernov, Viktor Mikhailovich (1876–1952)

Russian peasant politician. Although the peasants were not fully emancipated until 1905, individuals and groups participated increasingly in the opposition to **Nicholas II**. Chernov was originally a populist but, influenced by Marxism, he helped to found the **Socialist Revolutionaries** in 1901, a party oscillating between terrorism and peaceful advocacy of far-reaching land reform. Half-way through the Provisional Government's life in 1917, he joined it as Minister of Agriculture and supported the peasants' seizure of all available land. This divided it in the face of the Bolshevik threat. His party gained a majority in the **Russian Constituent Assembly** elected in Nov 1917 and convened in Jan 1918 under his chairmanship. But power lay not with the peasants and their representatives, but with the **Bolsheviks** and their soldiers. Within two days, **Lenin** dissolved the assembly and consigned it and Chernov to history.

Cherry Blossom Society (*Sakurakai*)

The secret society formed by young Japanese army officers in 1930 under the leadership of Lieutenant-Colonel Hashimoto Kingoro of the Army General Staff. Violating the ban on army involvement in politics, the society met to discuss the renovation of the state, reflecting increasing army dissatisfaction with civilian government run by political parties. It was involved in two abortive coups in 1931, in alliance with ultranationalist civilians, to set up a military cabinet. The society was dissolved shortly afterwards.

Chervenkov, Vulko (1900–80)

Bulgarian politician. He joined the Bulgarian Communist Party (BCP) in 1919 and went to the USSR where he studied at the Moscow Military Academy and Lenin International School and acted as secretary to Georgi **Dimitrov**. Returning to Bulgaria in 1944, he held a series of appointments within the BCP: Secretary for AgitProp (1949–50), Deputy Prime Minister (1949–50), General-Secretary (1950–61), Prime Minister (1950–6) and Deputy Prime Minister (1956–61). Known as Bulgaria's 'Little **Stalin**', he fell victim to Nikita **Khrushchev**'s anti-Stalinist campaign in the early 1960s. In 1962 he was expelled from the party and replaced by Todor **Zhivkov** who had denounced him at the 1961 and 1962 party conferences. Later he was rehabilitated (1969) and awarded a state pension.

Chetniks (*Četnici*)
Bands of royalist Serbian guerrilla fighters active in Yugoslavia during **World War II**. Anti-communist and anti-Croat, they were organized by Colonel Draža **Mihailović** and a small group of Serbian officers after the collapse of the Yugoslav Army (1941). They fought **Tito**'s communist partisans rather than the Axis occupiers and so forfeited Allied support in 1944.

Chiang Ching-kuo (1910–88)
Taiwanese politician. The son of **Chiang Kai-shek**, he studied in the USSR during the early 1930s, returning to China with a Russian wife in 1937 at the time of the Japanese invasion. After the defeat of Japan in 1945 he held a number of government posts before fleeing with his father and the defeated **Guomindang** forces to Taiwan in 1949. He became Defence Minister (1965–72), and was Prime Minister from 1972 to 1978. He succeeded to the post of Guomindang leader on his father's death (1975) and became state President in 1978. Under his stewardship, Taiwan's post-war 'economic miracle' continued, but in the political sphere there was repression. During the closing years of his life, with his health failing, he instituted a progressive programme of political liberalization and democratization, which was continued by his successor, **Lee Teng-hui**.

Chiang Kai-shek (Jiang Jieshi) (1887–1975)
Chinese revolutionary leader. He was the effective head of the Nationalist Republic (1928–49), and head thereafter of the émigré Nationalist Party regime in Taiwan. Born into a merchant family in Zhejiang, he interrupted his military education in Japan to return to China and join the Nationalist revolution. In 1918 he joined the separatist revolutionary government of **Sun Yat-sen** in Canton, where he was appointed Commandant of the new Whampoa Military Academy. After Sun's death (1925), he launched an expedition against the **warlords** and the Beijing government, entering Beijing in 1928, but fixed the Nationalist capital at Nanjing (Nanking). During the ensuing decade the Nationalist Party steadily lost support to the Communists. When Japan launched a campaign to conquer China (1937), Nationalist resistance was weak. Defeated by the Communist forces, he was forced to retreat to Taiwan (1949), where he presided over the beginnings of Taiwan's 'economic miracle'. His son, **Jiang Jingguo**, became Prime Minister in 1971 and President in 1978.

Chicherin, Grigoriy Vasilevich (1872–1936)
Russian revolutionary, politician, and diplomat. He joined the Russian Social Democratic Labour Party in 1905 and engaged in party work in Germany, France and England. At first he sided with the **Mensheviks**, but after the **October Revolution** he supported the **Bolsheviks** and was arrested for subversive activities in Britain. He was later exchanged for the ex-British ambassador in Russia. In 1918 he helped negotiate the Treaty of **Brest-Litovsk**, and became People's Commissar for Foreign Affairs. During the 1920s he represented the USSR at many international conferences. In 1930, ill health and differences with **Stalin** over his conduct of foreign affairs led to his being relieved of his post, and he lived in retirement until his death.

Chidzero, Bernard Thomas G (1927–)
Zimbabwean politician and **UN** administrator. Educated in Southern Rhodesia and Marianhill in South Africa, he went to Pius XII Catholic College Lesotho, Ottawa University and then Nuffield Colege, Oxford, from where he graduated with a DPhil in 1960. He was successively assistant research officer Economic Commission for Africa in Addis Ababa (1961–3), representative of UN Technical Assistance Board in Kenya (1963–6), Resident Representative UNDP, Kenya (1966–8), Director Commodities Division UNCTAD (1968–77) and Deputy President General (1977–80). Elected to the Zimbabwe Senate (1980), he has been Minister of Economic Planning and Development since then. Although not a member of the Politburo, he has been the chief architect of Zimbabwe's economic policy and the leading figure among reformists who prevailed over the radicals' wish for a more socialist and Leninist state.

Chifley, Joseph Benedict (1885–1951)
Australian politician and Labor Prime Minister (1945–9). In early life an engine driver, he entered parliament in 1928, and became Defence Minister in 1931. Defeated in the 1931 election, he returned to parliament in 1940, becoming Treasurer in 1941, a post he combined with that of Minister for Post-War Reconstruction (1942–5), and Prime Minister on **Curtin**'s death in 1945. As Prime Minister, he expanded social services and reformed the banking system, although his attempt to nationalize the banks failed. He continued as leader of the **Australian Labor Party** until his death.

Childers, (Robert) Erskine (1870–1922)
Irish nationalist and writer. He fought in the **Boer Wars** and **World War I**, and wrote a popular spy story, *The Riddle of the Sands* (1903), and several works of nonfiction. After the creation of the **Irish Free State**, he joined the IRA, and was active in the civil war. He was captured

and executed at Dublin. His son, Erskine Childers (1905–74) was President of Ireland in 1973–4.

Chile

Republic in south-west South America. It declared independence from Spanish rule in 1810, although Spain continued to fight until 1818. Economic unrest in the late 1920s led to a military dictatorship until 1931. The Marxist coalition government was ousted in 1973 and was replaced by a military junta, banning all political activity, and resulting in considerable political opposition, both at home and abroad. A constitution providing for an eventual return to democracy came into effect in 1981. After 1988 there were limited political reforms, with a schedule for further elections. A National Congress was restored in 1990.

China

Socialist state in Central and East Asia. The Manchus overthrew the Ming Dynasty in 1644 and ruled until 1911, enlarging the empire to include Manchuria, Mongolia, Tibet, Taiwan and parts of Turkestan. The **Boxer Rising** in 1900 was the last attempt to oppose foreign influence. The Republic of China was founded by Sun Yatsen in 1912. Unification took place under Jiang Jieshi (**Chiang Kai-shek**), who made Nanjing the capital in 1928. Conflict between Nationalists and Communists led to the **Long March** in 1934–5, with Communists moving to north-west China under **Mao Zedong** (Mao Tse-tung). The Nationalists were defeated and withdrew to Taiwan in 1950. The People's Republic of China was proclaimed in 1949, with its capital at Beijing (Peking). The first Five-Year Plan (1953–7) was a period of nationalization and collectivization. The **Great Leap Forward** (1958–9) emphasized local authority and the establishment of rural communes; the **Cultural Revolution** was initiated by Mao Zedong in 1966. Many policies were reversed after Mao's death in 1976, and there was a drive towards rapid industrialization and wider trade relations with the West. The killing of student-led pro-democracy protesters in **Tiananmen Square**, Beijing in 1989 provoked international outrage and the introduction of economic sanctions, relaxed after 1990. Tough economic controls were imposed in 1993.

China Democratic League

A political group formed in 1944 in response to **Chiang Kai-shek**'s attempt to ease controls on minority party activity and thereby enhance the credibility of the **Guomindang** government. Calling for constitutional guarantees and the creation of a coalition government, the league's criticism of Chiang's intransigence towards the Chinese Communist Party (CCP) and its condemnation of the renewed civil war in 1946 aroused the hostility of the authorities. Outlawed in 1947, the league was resuscitated after 1949 by the new communist regime and its leaders allowed to participate in government. In 1957, following general criticism of the CCP during the **Hundred Flowers Campaign**, the leaders of the league were accused of being rightists and were purged from official life.

Chinese Civil War (1946–9)

After Japan's **World War II** defeat (Aug 1945), civil war broke out again in China between the communists and the **Guomindang** (Nationalist) forces under **Chiang Kai-shek**. A truce (14 Jan 1946), mediated by US envoy General George Marshall, broke down and US supplies to the Guomindang were stopped (July 1946). Nonetheless, the better-equipped Guomindang took the communist capital, Yan'an, on 19 Mar 1947. The communists, meanwhile, stepped up their campaign from rural-based guerrilla warfare to full-scale battles, recapturing the city a year later. The communists' strategy of focusing on rural rather than urban areas had succeeded in isolating the Guomindang and severely taxing their resources. They followed up their advantage in late 1948 and early 1949 with the so-called Battle of **Huai-Hai**, the series of decisive engagements in the civil war, in which the Guomindang lost more than half a million men. The communists went on, in 1949, to capture Beijing and Tianjin (Jan), Nanjing (Apr) and Shanghai (May) and Canton (Oct). The People's Republic of China was formally proclaimed by **Mao Zedong** on 1 Oct 1949; the Nationalists withdrew to Taiwan (Formosa) on 7 Dec of the same year.

Chinese Communist Party (CCP)

Formally created in July 1921 by 14 delegates (including **Mao Zedong**), the party represented six communist cells established the previous year. **Comintern** representatives from Moscow persuaded **Chen Duxiu**, the party's first Secretary-General, to join with the more powerful **Guomindang** (Nationalist Party) in a United Front to combat imperialism and restore national unity, the long term aim being to take over leadership 'from within'. During this period of cooperation (1923–7) the CCP increased its membership to 6 000 and gained significant influence over mass organizations. The party's urban base was destroyed after 1927 when the Guomindang turned on its erstwhile communist allies. Henceforth, Mao Zedong's strategy of protracted rural revolution, emphasizing the creation of base areas and reliance on a peasant Red Army, came to be accepted by the CCP leadership. Membership of the party again increased substantially during the war with Japan (1937–45) and totalled 1.2 million by 1945. With Mao confirmed as Leader at the Party's Seventh Congress (1945), the CCP emerged victorious from the civil war with the nationalists (1946–9) and established the People's Republic in 1949. By the time of the party's Eighth Congress (1956), membership totalled 10.5 million. Party authority was undermined during the **Cultural Revolution** (1966–9) but at the party's Ninth Congress (1969) the policy of rebuilding and reasserting party control was confirmed. Since Mao's death in 1976,

Deng Xiaoping has sought to rejuvenate and reform the party, but this has not prevented it gradually losing credibility amongst the population during the 1980s. ▷ **communism**

Chinese Eastern Railway (CER)

The railroad in north Manchuria, covering a distance of 1 073 miles. In 1896 China granted Tsarist Russia the concession of building the railway as an extension of the Trans-Siberian railroad begun in 1891; Russia also obtained the right of policing the line. The 1896 agreement stipulated that the line would either be redeemed by China after 36 years for 700 million roubles or would pass to Chinese control without compensation after 80 years. Although the new Bolshevik government in 1920 promised to abolish all Tsarist Russia's privileges in China, the CER remained under Soviet control until 1935, when it was sold to Japan. In 1945 the CER came under joint Sino-Russian control as part of the price paid for Soviet entry into the war against Japan. The CER was not restored to full Chinese control until 1954.

Chinese Labour (Canada)

The reputation of the Chinese for hard work meant they were in great demand, especially by the railway interests for the building of the British Columbian sections of the Canadian Pacific Railway. Their rate of immigration into British Columbia was such that the province attempted to restrict their entry with the introduction of a 'head tax'. This rose from $50 in 1885 to $100 in 1900; by 1903 it had risen to $500, but still did not put off those seeking fortune in the 'Land of the Golden Mountains'. Anti-Chinese sentiment was pronounced among the trade unions who feared that the labour movement would be undermined, while throughout the province there were fears that society would be destabilized. In 1902 the **Laurier** government set up a royal commission and as a result Chinese immigration was severely restricted. In response companies, led by the Canadian Pacific, began to bring in East Indians and Japanese in their stead. The unions became even more alarmed by the arrival of the Japanese, for they were considered more competitive and were supported by a government whom neither the Canadian nor the British governments wished to displease. With the formation of the Asiatic Exclusion League and after the violent riots of 1907, the Laurier government introduced severe restrictions on the entry of all Oriental immigrants. ▷ **Immigration Legislation (USA)**

Chinese Revolution (1911)

The events relating to the overthrow of the Manchu **Qing Dynasty** and the subsequent creation of a republic in China. It broke out in Wuchang, Hubei province (central China) on 10 Oct 1911 with a mutiny in one of the new army units created by the Qing as part of its reform programme designed to strengthen the dynasty. Officers in these army units, while studying in Japan, had been influenced by the republicanism of **Sun Yat-sen** and his followers, who attributed China's weakness to the corruption of the Qing monarchy and its subservience to the foreign powers. The anti-Qing uprising quickly spread to other central and southern provinces, where mutinous army units were joined by provincial gentry elites disillusioned with the Qing government's half-hearted attempts at constitutional reform and its failure to prevent foreign encroachment in China, particularly with regard to railway concessions. By 1 Jan 1912 delegates from 16 provinces had elected Sun Yat-sen provisional president of a Chinese republic. Aware of the weakness of his own military forces and fearful that the foreign powers might intervene to protect their economic interests, Sun offered the presidency to **Yuan Shikai**, commander of the Qing forces, on the condition he abide by a republican constitution. On 12 Feb 1912 the court announced the abdication of the boy-emperor, **Puyi**, and Yuan Shikai became President of a unified republic. The 1911 Revolution can be viewed as a nationalist revolution, but in other respects it was an ambivalent one. Spearheaded by traditional elites, who were its principal beneficiaries (rather than Sun Yat-sen's republican revolutionaries), the revolution brought no significant social change in its wake, while the new president had been an important official of the *ancien régime* who, as events were to show, had scant respect for constitutional government.

Chirac, Jacques (René) (1932–)
French politician. A Gaullist, he was first elected to the National Assembly in 1967, and gained extensive governmental experience before being appointed Prime Minister by **Giscard d'Estaing**. In office from 1974 to 1976, he resigned over differences with Giscard and broke away to lead the Gaullist Party. Mayor of Paris since 1977, he was an unsuccessful candidate in the 1981 and 1988 presidential elections. ▷ **Gaulle, Charles de; Gaullists**

Chisholm, Shirley (1924–)
US politician. She was elected to the New York State Assembly in 1964, and was the first black woman to become a member of the House of Representatives when elected as a Democrat in 1968. In the 1972 Democratic Convention she won a 10 per cent vote for the presidential nomination. ▷ **Democratic Party**

Chissano, Joaquim (1939–)
Mozambique politician. He graduated from high school in Maputo and went to Portugal to study medicine, where he became involved in political activity. He was a founder member of **Frelimo** and was in charge of its Department of Security and Defence. A close confidant of Samora

Machel, he became Foreign Minister after independence in 1975, being responsible for negotiating the **Nkomati Accord** with South Africa. He succeded Machel in 1986 and began the process of change inside Mozambique.

Choibalsan (d.1952)
Mongolian revolutionary leader. Originally trained as a lamaist monk, he went to Siberia, where he made contact with Russian revolutionaries. He founded his first revolutionary organization in 1919 and joined up with Sukhe Bator in 1921 to establish the Mongolian People's Revolutionary Party. When Soviet **Red Army** units entered Urga, the capital of Outer Mongolia (which had broken free of Chinese control in 1912) in 1921 and sponsored the creation of a pro-Soviet government, Choibalsan became a deputy War Minister. In succeeding years he became the dominant leader of the Mongolian People's Republic (formally established in 1924) and had eliminated all his rivals by 1940. His policies were modelled on those of **Stalin**, including the cultivation of a personality cult and harsh treatment of landowners. He was also responsible for the execution of thousands of lamaist monks.

Chrêtien, Joseph-Jacques-Jean (1934–)
Canadian politician. As Chancellor in Pierre **Trudeau**'s administration he introduced two budgets in 1978 in an attempt to encourage industrial growth and fight inflation, but he failed in the latter since he also introduced tax cuts. In 1980 as Minister of Justice he fought against the concept of an independent Quebec, organizing the campaign leading up to the referendum. After Trudeau's resignation in 1984, the **Liberal Party**'s tradition of alternating francophone and anglophone leaders meant that it was John Turner who took over the leadership of the party rather than Chrêtien.

Christian Democrat Party (*Democrazia Cristiana*, DC)
The most powerful of Italian parties in the post-fascist era and invariably the chief component in the coalition governments which are the basis of modern Italian politics. Emerging in 1942 as a clandestine anti-fascist group that was Catholic, but formally secular and non-confessional, it was the ideological heir of the **Popolari** from which its early leaders (eg **Gronchi** and **De Gasperi**) were drawn. Although embracing quite a wide range of views, the Christian Democrat Party is essentially one of moderate conservatives of clerical sympathies.

Christian Democratic Appeal (*Christen-Democratisch Appèl*, CDA)
Dutch political party, founded in 1973 as an amalgamation of the three main confessional parties: the **Catholic People's Party**, the **Anti-Revolutionary Party**, and the **Christian Historical Union**. The CDA was

formed as a common defence against falling electoral support for the three member parties in the 1960s and 1970s, which was a result of general secularization. At first the CDA was a loose federation, but in 1976 it campaigned on a single electoral list, and in 1980 the member parties dissolved themselves as separate entities. The CDA is the party of Ruud **Lubbers**, the Dutch Prime Minister since 1982.

Christian Democrats
Members of Christian Democratic political parties, most of which were formed in Western Europe after 1945, and which have since become a major political force. The Christian Democratic philosophy is based upon strong links with the Catholic Church and its notions of social and economic justice. It emphasizes the traditional conservative values of the family and church, but also more progressive, liberal values such as state intervention in the economy and significant social welfare provision. Christian Democrat parties emerged to fill the vacuum created by the general disillusionment with parties of the right and left after **World War II**, a major exception being the UK, which has no such party. Electorally, the most successful example is the West German Christian Democratic Union (**CDU**) which, in alliance with its Bavarian sister party, the **CSU**, polled nearly 50 per cent of the votes in 1983. ▷ **Bundestag**

Christian Historical Union (*Christelijk Historische Unie*, CHU)
Dutch Calvinist political party founded in 1908 as an extension of the Free **Anti-Revolutionary Party** (ARP, founded 1895). At the end of the 19c some Dutch Calvinist politicians, members of the Anti-Revolutionary Party (ARP), expressed their doubts about the democratic and religiously schismatic tendencies of the ARP leader, Abraham **Kuyper**. These more conservative and perhaps more patrician Christian Democrats eventually gathered in the CHU, led by A F de **Savornin Lohman**. The CHU has been a regular party of government, combining with other Christian Democrat parties. In the late 1960s increasing secularization began to reduce the CHU's support, to less than 5 per cent in 1972. In 1976 it joined the **Christian Democratic Appeal**, and in 1980 the CHU ceased to exist as a separate party.

Christian People's Party (*Parti Social Chrétien*, PSC; *Christelijke Volkspartij*, CVP)
Belgian Roman Catholic political party founded in 1945 as a renewal of the previous Catholic Block (founded 1936). The first modern Catholic Party in Belgium was formed in 1884, which then dominated politics until 1914. Between the world wars it underwent changes of structure and name (1921, Belgian Catholic Union), and as the largest party in the country, the CVP/PSC has participated in all Belgian coalitions since 1950, with the exception of 1954–8. In 1968 the French and Dutch-

speaking wings of the party split apart over the Leuven University language affair, although they still vote together except on language-related issues. As a broad party, it has seen some friction between the representatives of employers and Catholic trade unions.

Christian X (1870–1947)
King of Denmark (1912/47) and of Iceland (1888/1944). The son of **Frederick VIII**, he was revered as a symbol of resistance during the German occupation in **World War II**. In 1915 he signed a new constitution granting the vote to women, and in 1918 signed the Act of Union with Iceland which granted Iceland full independence in personal union with the Danish sovereign (this ended in 1944). During World War II he elected to stay on in Denmark; he would ride on horseback through the streets as a defiant reminder of his presence, until he was put under house arrest by the Germans (1943–5). He married Alexandrine, Duchess of Mecklenburg-Schwerin, and was succeeded by their son, **Frederick IX**.

Christopher, Warren M (1925–)
US lawyer and government official. After training as a lawyer and practising in Los Angeles, he became deputy attorney general under Andrew **Johnson** and served in the State Department during the **Carter** presidency. He was instrumental in the passing of the 1968 Civil Rights bill. As a stalwart Democrat, he was selected by Bill **Clinton** after his electoral victory to oversee the transitionary team, and subsequently became Secretary of State under the new administration.

Christophersen, Henning (1939–)
Danish politician. A member of the Danish parliament **(Folketinget)** from 1971 to 1984, he led the Danish Liberal Party (*Venstre*) from 1978 to 1984. In 1978–9 he was Minister of Foreign Affairs and in 1982–4 was Minister of Finance and Deputy Prime Minister. He has been a member of the EC Commission since 1984 and is a vice-president, in charge of economic and monetary cooperation.

Chu Minyi (Ch'u Min-i) (1884–1946)
Chinese politician and educator. He studied medicine at the University of Strasbourg (1915–21) and subsequently became Vice-President of the Institut Franco-Chinois attached to Lyons University. In 1925 he joined the **Guomindang** and was closely associated with **Wang Jingwei**, leader of the party's left wing. Following their invasion of China in 1937, the Japanese sponsored a separate Chinese nationalist regime under Wang Jingwei in 1940 and Chu accepted the position of Foreign Minister in the new government. The regime gained little international support and crumbled with Japan's defeat in **World War II**. Chu was executed in 1946 for collaborating with the Japanese.

Chun Doo-hwan (1931–)
South Korean soldier and politician. He trained at the Korean Military Academy and was commissioned as a second lieutenant in the South Korean army in 1955. After further training at the US Army Infantry School, in 1960 he worked with the Special Airborne Forces group and in military intelligence. After President **Park**'s assassination (Oct 1979), he took charge of the Korean Central Intelligence Agency (KCIA) and led the investigation into Park's murder. He assumed control of the army and the government after a coup in 1979. In 1981 he was appointed President and retired from the army to head the newly formed Democratic Justice Party (DJP). Under his rule, the country's 'economic miracle' continued, but popular opposition to the authoritarian nature of the regime mounted, which eventually forced his retirement in 1988.

Churchill, Sir Winston (Leonard Spencer) (1874–1965)
British politician and author. The eldest son of Randolph **Churchill**, he was gazetted to the 4th Hussars in 1895, and his army career included fighting at Omdurman during the 1898 Nile Expeditionary Force. During the second Boer War he acted as a London newspaper correspondent. Initially a Conservative MP (1900), he joined the Liberals in 1904, and was Colonial Under-Secretary (1905), President of the Board of Trade (1908), Home Secretary (1910), and First Lord of the Admiralty (1911). In 1915 he was made the scapegoat for the Dardanelles disaster, but in 1917 became Minister of Munitions. After **World War I** he was Secretary of State for War and Air (1919–21), and (as a 'Constitutionalist' supporter of the Conservatives) Chancellor of the Exchequer (1924–9). In 1929 he returned to the Conservative fold, but remained out of step with the leadership until **World War II**, when he returned to the Admiralty; then, on Neville **Chamberlain**'s defeat (May 1940) formed a coalition government, and, holding both the premiership (1940–5) and the defence portfolio, led Britain through the war against Germany and Italy with steely resolution. Defeated in the July 1945 election, he became a pugnacious Leader of the Opposition. In 1951 he became Prime Minister again, though he was less effective after a stroke (1953) which was concealed from the public. From 1955 until his resignation in 1964, he remained a venerated backbencher. He achieved a world reputation not only as a great strategist and inspiring war leader, but as a classic orator with a supreme command of English, a talented painter and a writer with a great breadth of mind and a profound sense of history. He was knighted in 1953, and won the Nobel Prize for Literature the same year. ▷ **Boer Wars; Conservative Party** (UK); **Liberal Party** (UK)

Chvalkovský, František (1885–1944)
Czechoslovak politician. He was Foreign Minister in the unhappy post-Munich period. A career diplomat, he served as Ambassador to Rome, endeavouring to win strong Italian support for Czechoslovakia against

Germany. As this became impossible, he veered towards cooperation with the Axis powers, which made him a natural choice for his post-Munich post. However, in 1939 he was bullied into accepting **Hitler**'s demands and, with President **Hácha**, acceding to the division and domination of Czechoslovakia in Mar. He had the dubious privilege of proving that **appeasement** backfires.

CIA (Central Intelligence Agency)

The official US intelligence gathering organization responsible for external security, established under the National Security Act (1947) and reporting directly to the President. The CIA was conceived as the co-ordinator of foreign intelligence and counter-intelligence, but it has also engaged in domestic operations. As a result of abuses of power in both the domestic (notably in the **Watergate** affair) and foreign arenas, the CIA must now co-ordinate domestic activities with the FBI and report on covert activities to Congress.

Ciano, Galeazzo, di Galeazzo, Count (1903–44)

Italian politician and diplomat. Son of an admiral, he took part in the **March on Rome** and had a successful diplomatic career from 1925 to 1930, when, after marrying **Mussolini**'s daughter, he was rapidly promoted to Under-Secretary for Press and Propaganda and a seat on the **Fascist Grand Council**. In June 1936 he became Foreign Minister. He negotiated the Axis Agreement with Germany and supported the Italian invasion of Albania (1939) and the Balkans (1940–1), but was unenthusiastic about the invasion of France, especially after **Hitler**'s unilateral and early declaration of war. Dismissed as Foreign Minister (Feb 1943), Ciano was one of those who called for the **Duce**'s resignation in July 1943. He fled to Germany after his father-in-law's arrest but was blamed by Hitler and **Ribbentrop** for Mussolini's defeat and was executed.

científicos

The pejorative term (literally, 'scientists') used to describe the intellectual supporters of Mexico's President Porfirio **Díaz** from 1876 to 1911. *Científicos* were generally Positivists, who championed the application of practical scientific (especially social sciences') methods to the solution of national problems such as industrialization and education, arguing that 'individual absolute right is worth as much as absolute monarchy'. They were pre-eminent in the period 1876–1906, arguing that the government's duty was to assure landowners of their rights. They also believed that 'scientific-technical progress' decreed the demise of the Indian, the end to customary law which protected him, and the integration of Mexico into the international economy and European society.

Cipriani, Arthur 'Tattoo' (1875–1945)
Trinidadian white labour leader. Cipriani represented the working man in the Trinidad legislature in the 1920s and 1930s. Of French-Corsican origin, he served as an officer in **World War I** and on his return set up the Trinidad Workingmen's Association (1922). Once elected to the Legislative Council, he championed the cause of the 'barefoot man' and, in 1932, founded the moderate Trinidad Labour Party which campaigned for a strong trade-union movement, racial harmony and constitutional change. His failure to effect substantial socio-political progress in part led to the **Disturbances** (1935–7), and the conversion of labour to the more militant policies of Uriah **Butler**.

CIS (Commonwealth of Independent States)
A grouping (1991) of 11 independent states out of the 15 republics that formerly made up the Soviet Union, which was formally dissolved in Dec 1991. They are: Armenia, Azerbaijan, Belorussia, Kazakhstan, Kirghizia, Moldavia, Russia, Tajikistan, Turkmenistan, Ukraine, and Uzbekistan. In Oct 1993, ten of the states (including Russia) signed an agreement on monetary union in an attempt to stabilize the rouble and to co-ordinate economic policy.

Civic Forum (1989)
The broad-based alliance of anti-communist groups in Czechoslovakia that came together to force the resignation of the communist government in Nov. This was subsequently christened the **Velvet Revolution**, since the toppling of the government was achieved without serious bloodshed. The moving force had for long been **Charter 77** led by Václav **Havel** who subsequently became President. Civic Forum won 51 per cent of the votes in the June 1990 election but split into two rival groups in Jan 1991.

civil disobedience
A political strategy adopted by M K **Gandhi** and his followers in India in 1930, in opposition to Britain's imperial rule: launched by a march to the coast in order to break the law symbolically by making salt (on which tax was payable), it was a non-violent, mass, illegal protest, intended to discredit the authority of the state. The movement was banned, and many were arrested, including Gandhi; but a pact was reached in 1931, and Gandhi then participated in the second of the **Round Table Conferences**. The strategy was later used by Martin Luther King Jr to good effect, and is a path sometimes advocated by opponents of nuclear weapons.

Civil Guard

Founded in Spain as a militarized police force in 1844 to keep down banditry, the Civil Guard was organized like an army, led by a general and officers with military rank. Its brutal vigilance of the countryside in defence of the status quo led the ruling classes to regard it as the *Benemérita* (the 'well-deserving'), while for the lower classes its distinctive three-cornered hat, green uniforms, and great cloaks made it one of the most hated symbols of the *ancien régime*. Most of the Civil Guard sided with the Nationalists in the **Spanish Civil War**, though it played a leading role in holding places such as Madrid and Barcelona for the Republic. Under **Franco** the Civil Guard's dominance of the countryside was consolidated. In 1986 the first civilian appointee was made its Director General. Today it numbers 60 000, with its energies divided between controlling the traffic on the highways, patrolling the countryside, guarding foreign embassies, and combating terrorism.

civil rights

The rights guaranteed by certain states to its citizens. Fundamental to the concept of civil rights is the premise that a government should not arbitrarily act to infringe upon these rights, and that individuals and groups, through political action, have a legitimate role in determining and influencing what constitutes them. Historically, civil rights in England have been protected by the Magna Carta and in the USA by the **Constitution** and **Bill of Rights**. In common usage, the term often refers to the rights of groups, particularly ethnic and racial minorities, as well as to the rights of the individual.

Civil Rights Acts

US legislation which prohibits the states from discriminating against any citizen on the grounds of race or colour. The act of 1866 included blacks within its definition of US citizenship. President Andrew Johnson's veto so angered Republican moderates in Congress that radicals were able to override the veto, and incorporated its provisions in the Fourteenth Amendment. However the act was undermined by the Supreme Court in the Slaughterhouse Cases (1873) and US v Cruikshank (1875). The act of 1875, passed as a memorial to Charles Sumner, upheld the equal rights of blacks in the use of inns, theatres and public transport (though education was specifically excluded), but was declared unconstitutional in the Civil Rights Cases of 1883. By the 1950s only about a quarter of those Southern blacks who were qualified to vote could actually do so because state officials were adept at preventing them from registration. The Act of 1957 therefore established the Civil Rights Commission to examine such cases. It was backed up by a new Civil Rights Division in the Justice Department which could seek injunctions to prevent denial of the right to vote. Even when bolstered in 1960 the Act did not prove very effective. By the Act of 1964 the Attorney General was authorized to institute proceedings directly when voting rights were abused, and empowered to accelerate the desegregation of schools. Agencies which practised racial discrimination were liable to lose federal funding, and an Equal Opportunities Commission was set up to end job discrimination on the grounds of race, religion or sex. Discrimination was also prohibited in hotels and public transport. This legislation, together with the establishment of the Community Relations Service, indicated the federal government's awareness of the difficulties in dismantling the structures of white supremacy and was more effective than any previous **civil rights** legislation.

civil rights movement

A movement in the USA, especially 1954-68, aimed at securing through legal means the enforcement of the guarantees of racial equality contained in the Civil War Amendments to the **US Constitution**, namely, the Thirteenth, Fourteenth, and Fifteenth Amendments, and by civil rights acts of the 1860s and 1870s. These guarantees were severely curtailed by later legislation. In particular, the Supreme Court rulings of 1883, which declared the Civil Rights Act of 1875 unconstitutional because Congress had no right to trespass on the states' internal powers of economic regulation, opened the way to racial segregation. The civil rights movement began as an attack on specific forms of segregation in the South, then broadened into a massive challenge to all forms of racial discrimination. It made considerable gains, especially at the level of legal and juridicial reform, culminating in the Supreme Court case of **Brown v Board of Education of Topeka, Kansas** (1954), in which Thurgood **Marshall** successfully argued against school segregation. The first major challenge was the Montgomery bus boycott of 1955, which was sparked by an incident in which a black woman, Rosa **Parks**, refused to give up her seat to a white man. As a result of the boycott, the buses were desegregated and Martin Luther **King**, Jr, emerged as the movement's leader. King was a major force in establishing the **SCLC** (Southern Christian Leadership Conference). Forming a coalition with the **NAACP** and other organizations such as the **Urban League**, the **Congress of Racial Equality (CORE)** and the Student Non-Violent Coordinating Committee (SNCC), he led a campaign aimed at desegregating all public facilities, including schools, restaurants, stores, and transportation, by non-violent means, and at winning for blacks the unrestricted right to vote and to hold public office. Major actions included the first big clash over school desegregation (1957), which took place in Little Rock, Arkansas; the efforts of the 'freedom riders', groups of blacks and whites who challenged segregation in interstate transport (1961); the national March on Washington (1963), in which over 200 000 blacks and whites participated; and the voter registration drive in Alabama, which culminated in the march from Selma to Montgomery (1965). As white resistance grew, many participants in the marches and demonstrations were arrested, many were beaten, and some lost their lives. But by the late 1960s most of the original goals had been achieved as a result of Court decisions, major legislation and the actions of Presidents **Eisenhower**, **Kennedy** and especially Lyndon **Johnson** in enforcing the law. The Civil Rights Act of 1964 barred discrimination in public accommodations and employment; the Voting Rights Act (1965) ensured blacks' right to vote in places where it had hitherto been denied; and the Civil Rights Act of 1968 prohibited discrimination in the sale or rental of housing. One result of the '60s legislation was the increased participation of blacks in political life, even in Southern communities that were once bastions of segregation. But by the mid-60s, different problems were arising in the black ghettos of the Northern cities when blacks began rioting to protest their poverty, high unemployment and poor living conditions. Both King, who turned his attention northward in the last three years of his life, and more militant black leaders such as **Malcolm X**, recognized that the struggle for equality was moving into the economic sphere. So did Jesse **Jackson**, an associate of King's, who focused on the importance of creating jobs by investment in black businesses. But, unlike King, Malcolm X and his followers were advocating black separatism rather than integration, and the use of force to reach their goals. Significantly, widespread rioting followed King's assassination in 1968. In the decades since his death, although the economic condition of US blacks improved, the large gap between blacks and whites remained, and has led to racial tensions that have yet to be resolved.

Cixi (Tz'u Hsi) (1835–1908)
Chinese consort of the Xianfeng Emperor (1851/62). She rose to dominate China by manipulating the succession to the throne and bore the Xianfeng Emperor his only son, who succeeded at the age of five as the Tongzhi Emperor. Cixi (whose personal name was Yehenala), however, kept control even after his majority in 1873. After his death (1875), she flouted the succession laws of the Imperial clan to ensure the succession of Zai Tian, another minor, as the Guangxu (Kuang-hsu) Emperor, and continued to assert control even when the new Emperor reached maturity. In 1900 she took China into war against the combined treaty powers in support of the Boxer movement. Only after her death in Beijing was it possible to begin reforms. ▷ **Boxer Rising; Qing Dynasty**

Clark, Joe (Charles Joseph) (1939–)
Canadian politician. At first a journalist and then Professor of Political Science, he was elected to the Federal Parliament in 1972, becoming leader of the Progressive Conservative Party (1976) and of the Opposition (1980–83). In 1979 he became Canada's youngest-ever Prime Minister. His minority government lost the general election the following year, and

he was deposed as party leader in 1983. In 1984 he became Canada's Secretary of State for External Affairs.

Clark, Mark Wayne (1896–1984)
US army officer. Chosen by Dwight D **Eisenhower** to plan the 1943 Allied invasion of North Africa, he became commander of the Allied armies in Italy in 1944. In 1945, after **World War II**, he headed the US forces occupation in Austria. During the **Korean War** he served as commander of the **UN** forces, participated in the lengthy peace talks of 1952–3, and signed the armistice.

CLC (Canadian Labour Congress)
Canadian labour organization. It was established in 1956 with the merger of the Trades and Labor Congress (associated with the US AFL) and the Canadian Congress of Labour (similarly associated with the US CIO). Unlike the US labour movement, the CLC was ready to take direct political action and in 1961 it united with the **CCF** (Cooperative Commonwealth Federation) to form the **New Democratic Party**. ▷ **AFL–CIO**

Clemenceau, Georges Eugène Benjamin (1841–1929)
French politician. He studied medicine and visited the USA (1865–9), where he married an American. A leader of the radicals (on the extreme Left), he was also a leader of the campaign for the rehabilitation of **Dreyfus**, which allowed his return to parliament as a Senator in 1903. Clemenceau was Prime Minister in 1906–9 and 1917–20, when his determination spurred France to make the effort to pursue victory in **World War I**. He presided at the **Paris Peace Conference** (1919), where he sought unsuccessfully to obtain in the Treaty of **Versailles** a settlement that would preserve France from another German attack. Nicknamed 'the Tiger' for the ferocity of his oratorical attacks on his political opponents, he was equally renowned for his journalism, in *'Aurore*, at the time of the Dreyfus Affair, and in his own newspaper, *'Homme libre* (renamed *'Homme enchainé* after a quarrel with the censor) during the war.

Clementis, Vladimír (1902–52)
Slovak politician. He became a Czechoslovak communist MP in 1935 but criticized the Nazi–Soviet Pact in 1939 and spent **World War II** in London. In 1945 he became Vice-Minister of Foreign Affairs in the first postwar government. One of the organizers of the 1948 coup, he succeeded Jan **Masaryk** as Foreign Minister, but was forced to resign in 1950 as a 'deviationist'. During the Stalinist purges, he was hanged along with Rudolf **Slánský**. ▷ **German–Soviet Pact**

Clinton, William ('Bill') (1946–)

US politician and 42nd President. Educated at Georgetown University and Yale Law School, and a Rhodes scholar at Oxford, he taught law at the University of Arkansas (1973–6) before being elected state attorney general in 1976. In 1978, at the age of 32, he was elected Governor of Arkansas, the youngest person ever to hold that office, and served for five terms (1979–81 and 1983–92). In 1992 he was elected President, campaigning on a platform of hope and change in a climate of economic recession and voter disillusionment and ending a 12-year Republican hold on the office.

Clinton, Hillary Rodham (1947–)

US lawyer, known particularly for her advocacy of children's rights, and wife of President Bill **Clinton**. As an attorney in Little Rock, Arkansas, she became head of the state Rural Health Advisory Committee and later of the Children's Defense Fund (1986–92). Barred from paid office by anti-nepotism laws, she was appointed chief of a White House task force on National Health Reform, commissioned to prepare proposals on legislative reforms to restructure the health care system of the United States. The new blueprint was unveiled to Congress in Sep 1993.

CMEA–EEC Agreement (1988)

The mutual recognition and trade agreement between **Comecon**, based in Moscow, and the Brussels-based **EEC**. Their hostility was linked with the continuance of the **Cold War** and with a specific disagreement concerning how trade should be conducted. Mikhail **Gorbachev**'s emergence helped calm tension and a compromise was found according to which individual CMEA members made comprehensive deals with the EEC as a whole. This further reduced tension and contributed to the dissolution of CMEA in 1990.

CNCA (*Confederación Nacional Católico-Agraria*, 'National Catholic-Agrarian Confederation') (1917–42)

Spanish agrarian organization. Organized and funded by large landowners, the CNCA built up a large following among smallholders of north and central Spain through its propaganda and services. It claimed 500 000 members by 1919. Conservative and religious in outlook, its aim was to combat the rising power of the urban and rural working class by mobilizing middle-class support for the ruling classes. In this respect it was similar to the ACNP (National Catholic Association of Propagandists). It was an important source of support for the Right during the Second Republic, especially for the **CEDA**. In 1942 it was transformed into the National Union of Rural Cooperatives (UNCC), more recently the UNACO. ▷ **Republic, Second** (Spain)

CND (Campaign for Nuclear Disarmament)

An organization formed in 1958 to oppose Britain's development of a nuclear weapons programme. It organized annual Aldermaston marches and briefly persuaded the Labour Party to declare a policy of unilateral disarmament in 1960, only to see it effectively reverse that decision a year later. An effective pressure group in the 1960s, its popularity and influence had already begun to decline before the signing of nuclear non-proliferation pacts in the 1980s, although supporters agreed that as part of a European movement it played a part in halting the arms race.

CNT (*Confederación Nacional de Trabajo*, 'National Confederation of Labour')

Spanish anarcho-syndicalist movement. The emergence of the CNT in 1911 provided Spanish anarcho-syndicalism with its first national framework. It was based on already existing trade unions, most of them in Catalonia, which were sympathetic to anarchism. Centred on Barcelona, Saragossa, and rural Andalucia, the CNT became the largest trade union movement in Spain during the social crisis sparked by **World War I**. The CNT's influence in Catalonia was at its greatest from 1918 to 1923, but it met with the brutal resistance of the employers. The CNT was severely repressed under the **Primo de Rivera** dictatorship of 1923–30. Under the Second Republic, against a background of continuing if lesser repression, it spurned electoral politics (though many CNT members voted for the Left in 1931 and 1936), split over the issue of revolutionary confrontation with the Republic, and pursued a series of largely fruitless strikes and risings, most notably those of Jan and Dec 1933. However, it also extended its influence in Madrid and other areas as the voice of the marginalized sections of the working class. While the anarchist rural and industrial collectives during the **Spanish Civil War** often proved both a social and an economic success, the failure of the anarchist militia undoubtedly undermined the Republican war effort. The CNT's revolutionary conception of the war clashed with that of most other Republican forces. Nonetheless in Nov 1936 four anarchists joined the government — the only occasion in the history of anarchism. The Communist assault on the CNT in May 1937 lost it the political initiative, and it declined thereafter. Anarchist opposition to **Franco** was ineffectual, its revival after his death being unimpressive. ▷ **Republic, Second** (Spain)

Coastal Command

A separate functional Command within the British Royal Air Force (1936–69). Moves to transfer it to the Royal Navy caused a political storm in 1958–9. During **World War II**, the Command destroyed 184 German U-boats and 470 000 tonnes of enemy shipping, and played a decisive role in winning the Battle of the **Atlantic**.

Cochin-China

A French colony, occupying the southern part of Vietnam. The colony was established in 1862 when three eastern provinces were ceded to the French. Three western provinces were added in 1867. In 1887, Cochin-China was brought together with the French protectorates of **Annam**, Tonkin and Cambodia to form the *Union Indochinoise*. During the period of French administration, Cochin-China emerged as an important rice-exporting region. In the 1930s it became a key focus of rural unrest. In 1949 as the French sought to establish a Vietnamese alternative to **Ho Chi Minh** in the north, Cochin-China became part of the Associated State of Vietnam within the French Union.

Codreanu, Corneliu Zelea (1899–1938)

Romanian political leader. From a peasant family of Ukrainian or Polish ancestry, in 1927 he organized the Legion of the Archangel Michael, the quasi-religious and nationalist organization of which the **Iron Guard** formed the military wing. In 1938 he was tried for treason and sentenced to 10 years in prison; later that year, he and a group of followers were shot, apparently while trying to escape. ▷ **Antonescu, Ion; Charles II** of Romania

Cold War

A state of tension or hostility between states that stops short of military action or a 'hot' war. The term is most frequently used to describe the relationship between the USSR and the major Western powers — especially the USA — following **World War II**. Tension was particularly high in the 1960s when the nuclear 'arms race' intensified. The process of détente, begun in the late 1960s, led through two decades of arms reduction and control negotiations to the 'end' of the Cold War in 1990, mainly as a result of a dramatic change in the Soviet attitude under Mikhail **Gorbachev**.

Colijn, Hendrikus (1869–1944)

Dutch politician. His first career was in the Dutch colonial army (1892–1909); then he became a member of the Dutch parliament for the Calvinist **Anti-Revolutionary Party**, of which he was the leader from 1920 on. He also had business interests (as Director of the Batavian Oil Company) and was chief editor of the Calvinist daily newspaper *The Standard* from 1922. He first took cabinet office as Minister of War (1911–13) and then as Minister of Finance (1923–5). From 1925 to 1939 he was Prime Minister of no less than six cabinets, and was the figurehead of the tough deflationary Dutch government policies of the 1930s. When the Germans invaded his country in 1940 he toyed with accepting the New Order; he soon rejected this, and was interned in 1941. He died in Ilmenau in Germany.

collaboration (France) (1940–4)
The act of collaborating with the Germans during their occupation of France in **World War II**. It could take various forms: economic, literary, journalistic and political. The latter applies especially to political figures who remained in Paris, rather than following the French government to **Vichy**, although the distinction became blurred in 1943–4. The most extreme collaborators fought on the Eastern Front: LGF (*Légion des volontaires français contre le bolchévisme*, 'French Legion of Volunteers against Bolshevism') or in the auxiliary police force (*Milice*) within France, which committed appalling atrocities. ▷ **French State**

Collective Leadership (post-1956)
In the USSR, the term used, with occasional justification, to differentiate between the leadership methods of **Stalin**, who was accused of the **Cult of Personality**, and those of his successors. But as general-secretaries of the Communist Party both Nikita **Khrushchev** and Leonid **Brezhnev** reverted to virtual single-handed rule in the later years of their tenure. Mikhail **Gorbachev** amended the party's rules in 1986 to include collective leadership but had himself appointed President as well as General-Secretary in 1990.

Collectivization (post-1929)
The process, initiated by **Stalin** in the USSR, of forcing peasants into large communal farms where in theory they worked for one another and not for themselves or their own families. Stalin's aims were to solve the food crisis through large-scale farming, by the same means to accumulate capital and secure spare labour for industrial development, and to create a revolutionary peasantry to maintain and intensify the spirit of revolution. Despite fierce resistance and pauses to gather breath, the main aims were achieved; casualties were, however, very high. Productivity also remained remarkably low, and agriculture became one of the weak points of the economy, leading to the collapse of Soviet socialism in recent years. The extension of collectivization to much of Eastern Europe after **World War II** led to very similar results.

Collins, Michael (1890–1922)
Irish politician and **Sinn Féin** leader. He was an MP (1918–22), and organized the nationalist intelligence system against the British. With Arthur **Griffith**, he was largely responsible for the negotiation of the treaty with Great Britain in 1921. Commander-General of the government forces in the civil war, he was killed in an ambush between Bandon and Macroom.

Collor de Mello, Fernando (1950–)
Brazilian politician. Born into a family in the north-eastern state of Alagoas, he grew up in Rio de Janeiro. He made use of his family's extensive media holdings to lever himself into the Prefecture of Maceió (1979–82) and then become Governor of Alagoas (1986). A political conservative, he leapt to prominence as a critic of 'corruption', achieving a leading position, at the head of his National Renovation Party, in the race for the presidency in Nov 1989. His ability to project the image of a young and dynamic 'messias', professing a modern social democratic approach, caught the traditional PMDB and radical PT off guard. Once in office (Mar 1990), he embarked on a bold programme of economic reform, before he built up a significant base within Congress. Control over Congress lay in the hands of groups which had benefited from the 1988 Constitution, which protected special interests directly affected by the presidential programme. He resigned in Dec 1992 as his impeachment, on charges of corruption, began in the Senate.

Colonial and Imperial Conferences
A series of conferences at which representatives of the British colonies and dominions discussed matters of common imperial concern; usually held in London. The first Colonial Conference was held in 1887, and this was followed by others in 1894, 1897, 1902 and 1907. They were particularly concerned with defence, although they also dealt with issues of trade and communications. The first Imperial Conference was held in 1911, the change of name implying a new status for the colonies, and was followed by others in 1921, 1923, 1926, 1930 and 1937, mainly concerned with constitutional changes and economic matters. After **World War II** they were replaced by the Conferences of Commonwealth Prime Ministers, now by the Commonwealth Heads of Government meetings. ▷ **British Empire; Commonwealth of Nations**

Colonial Development and Welfare Acts (1929, 1940, 1945, 1949 and 1950)
A series of acts designed to offer funds for the development of British colonies. They represented a departure from the notion that colonies should be self-supporting and a recognition that development might serve to combine colonial idealism with British economic self-interest. The 1929 act made available £1 million; the 1940 act was partly a response to riots in the West Indies and partly designed to encourage sympathy and loyalty during **World War II**. £20 million was set aside, but only £3 million was spent in the first four years. The principle was extended in the post-war climate of trusteeship when £120 million was invested under the three acts introduced by Clement **Attlee**'s Labour government.

colonialism
A form of imperial domination of one country (the colonial power) over others (its colonies) for political, economic, or strategic purposes. The

main period of colonial rule was 1870–1960, when Western European powers 'scrambled' to gain control over territories in Africa, Asia and the Far East. The French and British had the largest colonial empires. Colonialism is said by some to have established a system of 'dependency' in the colony, whose economy and political administration served primarily not its own needs but those of the colonial power. This has made it difficult for the colony to develop on its own terms and in its own direction. This situation is said to prevail even after the granting of 'independence', and these dependent countries make up the 'underdeveloped' Third World.

Combes, Emile (1835–1921)
French politician. Originally intended for the Church, after education in a seminary, he studied medicine and practised as a doctor. He was elected to the Senate (1885), and became Prime Minister (1902–4). He used the law on Associations (1901), first presented as little more than a tidying-up of administrative regulations, but turned by strained interpretation into a measure to dissolve nearly all religious orders and confiscate their property. This opened a conflict with the papacy that led, perhaps against his own intentions, to the **Separation of Church and State** (1905).

Combined Operations Command
A British force established in 1940 when Winston **Churchill** appointed Admiral of the Fleet Lord Keyes to coordinate British commando raids against German-occupied Europe. Keyes's successor Lord **Mountbatten** (1941–3) directed larger operations involving all three Services, and prepared for the eventual Allied invasion of France, in which Combined Operations techniques were to play a crucial role. ▷ **D-Day; World War II**

COMECON (Council for Mutual Economic Assistance)
A body founded in 1949 by **Stalin**, dominated by the USSR, but frequently thwarted by other member states. Its purpose was ostensibly the economic integration of the Eastern bloc as a means of counteracting the economic power and political influence of the West. The 10 member states were eventually the USSR, Bulgaria, Cuba, Czechoslovakia, Hungary, Poland, Romania, East Germany, Mongolia, and Vietnam. With the overthrow of **communism** in Eastern Europe in 1989–90 and the weakening of the USSR, COMECON was disbanded in 1991.

Cominform (Communist Information Bureau)
An organization founded by **Stalin** in 1947 as a successor to the **Comintern**, which had been established in 1943. Its purpose was the coordination of the propoganda and politics of the communist parties of Bulgaria, Czechoslovakia, France, Hungary, Italy, Poland, Romania, the USSR, and Yugoslavia. Its headquarters were moved from Belgrade to

Bucharest following the break between Stalin and **Tito** which culminated in Yugoslavia's expulsion in 1948. Cominform became an instrument in the **Cold War**, expressing hostility towards capitalism, and was also used by Stalin as an additional means of dominating Eastern Europe. After the rapprochement between the USSR and Yugoslavia in 1956, the Cominform was dissolved.

Comintern

An abbreviation for the Third or Communist International, founded in Moscow in Mar 1919 at the behest of the Soviet Communist Party, its purpose being to promote the expected international proletarian revolution by rallying communists and left-wing socialists. It adopted Leninist principles in its policies, rejecting reformism in favour of revolutionary action, which it encouraged against capitalist governments. It gradually became an instrument of **Stalin**'s foreign policy and was ultimately little used. It was disbanded in May 1943 when Stalin was anxious to strengthen his **World War II** friendship with **Roosevelt** and Winston **Churchill**. ▷ **Cominform; Marxism-Leninism**

Committee for the Liberation of Upper Italy (*Comitato di Liberazione nazionale Alta Italia*, CLNAI)

The organization established (Jan 1944) to coordinate the activities of anti-German and anti-fascist partisans, often already grouped within local **Committees of National Liberation** (CLNs). Originally the CLNAI asserted its claims to power not only against the Germans and fascists but also against the Allies and the anti-fascist government in Rome. In Dec 1944, CLNAI delegates agreed to the so-called 'Protocols of Rome' by which, in exchange for a subsidy from the Allies, they promised to hand over all authority after liberation to the Allied Military Government. During the last months of **World War II** the CLNAI burgeoned, assisted by a remarkable degree of political collaboration among the leaders of all the main anti-fascist parties. By late Apr 1945 most of the north had fallen to the CLNAI, which established its own *de facto* administration before the arrival of the Allies. Although the CLNAI laid down its weapons, it retained a strong bargaining position which its leaders used to win much greater representation in Rome, forcing the resignation of **Bonomi** and the appointment of **Parri** as Prime Minister. The new CLNAI-dominated government carried out widespread purges against anyone associated with the former fascist regime, alienating a good deal of public opinion in the process. Blamed for the prevailing dire economic conditions and high unemployment, as well as for the anti-fascist witch-hunts, the Parri government fell from office (Dec 1945); it was replaced by the **De Gasperi** government.

Committee of National Liberation (Algeria)
The committee set up by Charles de **Gaulle** on 3 June 1943, through which the Algerians were promised a full voice in the running of their country. The failure to fulfil this promise was, more than any other single factor, responsible for the hardening of native Algerian resistance to the presumptions of the French in Algeria, which eventually resulted in the **Algerian War of Independence**.

Committees of National Liberation (*Comitati di Liberazione nazionale*, CLNs)
The first CLN emerged in the autumn of 1943 from the 'United Freedom Front' set up by Ivanoe **Bonomi** in Apr of that year. Bonomi's organization was aimed at coordinating the efforts of the main anti-fascists, whether Catholic, communist or socialist. However, as the Allies advanced through Italy, autonomous CLNs were established throughout Italy to organize partisan activity; these usually had no affiliation to Bonomi's central organization. In German-occupied northern Italy especially, the CLNs often became a *de facto* government in areas where the anti-fascist resistance was victorious, and in Jan 1944 the **Committee for the Liberation of Upper Italy** was established to coordinate their efforts. ▷ **Parri, Ferruccio; Party of Action**

Common Agricultural Policy (CAP)
The most important of the common policies of the European Community, which accounts for about 65 per cent of **EC** expenditure. Its basic principles are free trade for agricultural commodities within the Community, Community preference for domestic production, control of imports from the rest of the world, and common prices and subsidization. The main objectives are increased agricultural productivity, a fair standard of living for farmers, reasonable market prices for the consumer, stability of markets, and secure food supplies. Most of these objectives have been met through the use of subsidies on certain types of farming or certain crops, which in turn have generated surpluses of most major commodities, such as the 'butter mountain' and 'wine lake'. An important additional objective for the CAP is to contain these surpluses and limit the huge cost associated with their disposal. Radical reforms involving the reduction of target prices for cereals, beef, and dairy produce were introduced in May 1992.

Commonwealth of Nations
A voluntary organization of autonomous states which had been imperial possessions of Britain. Its head is the reigning British monarch. It was formally established by the Statute of Westminster (1931) and meets

frequently to discuss matters of mutual interest and concern. While most states, on independence, chose to become members of the Commonwealth, three have left (Irish Republic, 1949; Pakistan, 1972; Fiji, 1987). South Africa also left the Commonwealth in 1961, but rejoined in 1994.

communalism

The term used in India to characterize the use of religion for political ends, particularly by Muslims and Hindus. Early expressions of communalism arose within the Cow Protection Societies formed by Hindus, to whom the cow is sacred; these often came into conflict with Muslims, to whom the slaughter of animals is required during some religious festivals. Conflict also arose over holy sites used by both Hindus and Muslims for worship. British intervention in such disputes often only exacerbated them: nationalists have argued that this was a conscious policy, part of the colonial tactic of 'divide and rule'. Certainly, from an early stage the British colonial government treated Hindus and Muslims (as well as tribals) as entirely separate communities, making cooperation between them very difficult to achieve. Despite this, there was a considerable degree of cooperation between Hindu and Muslim politicians in the Indian independence movement, particularly in 1915–22 when both Mohammed Ali **Jinnah** (the leader of the **Muslim League**) and M K **Gandhi** (by 1917 the leader of the **Indian National Congress**) strove to forge a united front against the British during the Khilafat, Rowlatt and Non-Cooperation campaigns. This unity collapsed, however, in 1922 after the suspension of the **Non-Cooperation Movement** by Gandhi. Conflict between the two communities increased markedly during the Great Depression, in the late 1930s when Congress provincial governments were formed, and during **World War II**, when the League supported the British and the Congress was banned in the wake of the **Quit India** Campaign of 1942. Jinnah's demands for Muslims to have their own separate nation led ultimately to the partition of India into separate Hindu and Muslim nations (India and Pakistan) in 1947. Three wars between India and Pakistan have subsequently fuelled the conflict, and within India itself the 110 million-strong Muslim population remains the focus of fierce political dispute. A secular constitution and a secular majority amongst Indian politicians has tended to curb serious conflict, but at times of social and economic crisis the threat of 'communalism' has always re-emerged.

Communes, People's

The basic unit of government in the Chinese countryside, first created in 1958 as part of the **Great Leap Forward** campaign. Originating in 1957 with the large-scale mobilization of rural labour for irrigation and water conservancy projects, the communes amalgamated previously-existing collectives and combined administrative, economic and social functions. **Mao Zedong** hailed the communes as a symbol of China's transition to

communism that would boost rural productivity and enhance collective life. By the end of 1958 740 000 collectives had been amalgamated into 26 000 communes; private plots were abolished, communal mess-halls and nurseries created, and rural industrialization promoted. Disastrous economic results and widespread peasant opposition forced the leadership after 1959 to modify the extreme forms of collectivism and devolve some of the communes' functions to the production brigade (the former collective). During the 1980s the communes were virtually dismantled as the individual peasant household became the unit of agricultural production.

communism

A political ideology which has as its central principle the communal ownership of all property, and thereby the abolition of private property. Although examples of early social and religious groupings based upon communal sharing of property have been cited, modern communism is specifically associated with the theories of Karl Marx. Marx saw the emergence of a communist society as being the final stage in a historical process that was rooted in human material needs, preceded by feudalism, capitalism, and (a transitional stage) socialism. Communism, according to Marx, would abolish class distinctions and end the exploitation of the masses inherent in the capitalist system. The working class, or proletariat, would be the instrument of a revolution that would overthrow the capitalist system and liberate human potential. A fully developed communist system would operate according to the principle of 'from each according to his ability, to each according to his need', and as there would be no cause for the state to regulate society, it would 'wither away'. Marx's writings provided a powerful ideological basis for communist and many socialist parties and governments, which legitimized the implementation of their policies by reference to them. The **Communist Party of the Soviet Union** (CPSU), first of all under **Lenin**'s leadership and then under **Stalin**'s, reinterpreted Marxist ideology as Marxism–Leninism–Stalinism, a major feature of which came to be democratic centralism. Unlike the spontaneous, decentralized organization envisaged by Marx, the CPSU was a highly centralized, monolithic, and secretive organization. Under Stalin's leadership it became an instrument in the development of a totalitarian dictatorship. The CPSU provided the ideological lead for European communist parties; indeed, at the creation of the Third **International** or **Comintern** in 1919, it was clear that only those socialist parties which accepted the discipline, leadership, and organizational structure of the Soviet Communist Party would be allowed to join. Much the same was true of the **Cominform** established in 1947. Increasingly from the 1960s onwards, however, the compulsory leadership of the CPSU was questioned and challenged, partly because of the economic difficulties resulting from the rigidities of democratic centralism in industrial states, where decentralization and flexibility were required. Nonetheless, Yugoslavia had been the only country to challenge Soviet dominance successfully (it was expelled from the Cominform in 1948); other countries such as Hungary (1956), Czechoslovakia (1968), and Poland (1980–1) were prevented by military force from breaking away from the Soviet model. But in 1989–90, the establishment of a non-communist government in Poland and popular uprisings elsewhere in Eastern Europe, followed by reasonably free elections, saw the almost total eclipse of communism there. The uprisings were political and economic, and one reason for their success was the changing nature of Soviet communism under Mikhail **Gorbachev**'s reforming leadership and the growing demand in the USSR for the same kind of changes as Eastern Europe wanted. Within a year of the failed coup against Gorbachev in Aug 1991, the Soviet Communist Party was declared illegal and much of the mechanism of communist rule was dismantled. There remains the possibility of some kind of communist recovery in the USSR as well as in Eastern Europe. But faith in communism worldwide has been seriously weakened, at least in its manifestations hitherto. And even Chinese communism, which was never slavishly Soviet in its ideology and practices, is changing quite noticeably.

Communist Party (Cuba)
The only political party in existence in Cuba since 1959. Originally named the Popular Socialist Party and then the United Party of the Socialist Revolution (when **Castro** was not yet a hard-line Marxist), it became the Communist Party of Cuba in 1965. Castro has always sought to maintain the ideological purity of the party, enunciating policy in the party newspaper, *Granma*, resisting Mikhail **Gorbachev**'s call for **perestroika** and purging the state of undesirables (no matter how high), such as General Ochao (a member of the Central Committee of the Party and a Hero of the Revolution, who was executed in 1989 for drug offences). ▷ **communism**

Communist Party (Finland)
Founded in Moscow (Aug 1918) by members of the Finnish Red Army and **Social Democratic Party** who had been defeated by the Finnish Whites and their German allies in the civil war earlier in the year, its most prominent leader was Otto **Kuusinen**. In 1919 it joined the **Comintern** and was declared illegal in Finland the same year. Suppressed by the Finnish authorities, it worked underground and, although it failed to win the allegiance of the majority of the working class, who were loyal to the Social Democrats, it nevertheless gained significant footholds in working-class organizations through a front organization, the Socialist Workers' Party. However, its organizations in Finland were effectively smashed by anti-communist legislation introduced in 1930 under pressure from the **Lapua Movement**. The party remained largely inactive until it

was legalized in 1944, following Finland's defeat in the **Continuation War** of 1941–4. Despite its widespread perception as a tool of Moscow, the party was able to draw on solid support among both industrial workers in the south and the small farmers of northern and eastern Finland. Through its front organization, the Finnish People's Democratic League (SKDL), the party did well in the immediate post-war period. Following electoral success in 1945, they were represented in government from 1945 to 1948, and in 1958 gained their best ever result, with 25 per cent of the vote, becoming the largest party in parliament. They were, however, kept from office for many years by the other parties' refusal to cooperate with them. From 1966 onwards the Communist Party was weakened by conflicts between Moscow loyalists and those advocating a reformist, Eurocommunist line, but it was a regular participant in government. Ultimately, the party split, with the reformist minority breaking away to form the Democratic Alternative. At the same time, the party's electoral support declined, falling to 13 per cent in 1983. ▷ **communism**

Communist Party (France)

Founded in 1920 when a majority of members of the **Socialist Party** (SFIO) voted to join the Third International and to become the Communist Party, officially known until 1943 as SFIC (*Section française de l'Internationale communiste*, 'French Section of the Communist International'). The 1924 elections showed that few voters were prepared to support the new party, and by 1932 it had only 11 Deputies. It was saved by the **Popular Front**, and emerged after **World War II** as a major political force with over a quarter of the vote and representation in a coalition cabinet (1945–7). In spite of retaining substantial electoral support (usually around 20 per cent of the vote), it never again held office until the victory of the left in the election of 1981, when it joined in a coalition with the socialists until 1984. This apparent success coincided with a rapid decline in voting support, to under 10 per cent in 1986. ▷ **communism**

Communist Party of Great Britain

Formed in 1920 through the merger of various leftist groups, it acknowledged from its inception the authority of Moscow. Its fortunes improved with Soviet intervention in **World War II**, but it never won more than four seats in parliament, and the 1956 **Hungarian Uprising** saw many defections. Unlike many European parties, its influence was minimal long before the collapse of the USSR (1990–1). ▷ **communism**

Communist Party of India (Marxist)

The split between the USSR and China caused a split within the ranks of the Communist Party of India, the splinter group becoming the CPI (M) or CPM (where 'M' stands for 'Marxist') in 1964, a party which has since opposed the dominant political party, the Indian National

Congress, in national and state elections. Its greatest success has been in Bengal, where it has been the party in power for much of the time since first forming a coalition government in 1967. The first government though lasted only briefly after another faction split from the party, calling itself the CPM–L (where 'M–L' stands for 'Marxist–Leninist'), and attempted to raise a general revolt by undertaking direct action against class enemies, beginning in the district of Naxalbari, from which they derived the name 'Naxalites'. Having committed themselves, like the CPI, to the parliamentary route to socialism, violent confrontations between the CPM supporters and the CPM–L resulted, leading to intervention by the central government. After a period of Congress rule and Indira Gandhi's Emergency in 1975–7, the CPM again returned to office with a huge majority in 1977, with Jyoti Basu as Chief Minister, and it has remained there ever since, as the leading party in a Left coalition, its popularity based on its successful land reform and rural development programmes and its pragmatic, secular, social policies, which have made Bengal, despite its poverty, the only Indian state with a considerable Muslim population in recent years to have largely escaped the threat of communal violence. ▷ **communism; Communist Party of India; Indian National Congress**

Communist Party of India (CPI)

Founded in Dec 1926, it was an expatriate Bengali, M N Roy, who recruited and trained the first party members in the USSR. Early attempts to link up with radicals in India were frustrated by the Kanpur and Meerut conspiracy trials (1923 and 1929), but the communists, although persecuted and effectively illegal, were able to establish a network of members and supporters, infiltrating not only the **Indian National Congress** and trade union movements, but also setting up workers' and peasants' societies, with a view to mobilizing the masses in the struggle against colonialism. Relations with the Gandhian Congress were not always easy, although members of the Congress Socialist Party and Congress leaders such as Jawaharlal **Nehru** were sympathetic. This was due not only to disagreements over tactics, particularly the use of violence, but also because the **Comintern** policy between 1929 and 1935 was to reject cooperation with bourgeois–democratic movements. Before and after these dates, however, CPI members occupied prominent positions in the Indian National Congress. Increasingly active in the late 1930s, after the collapse of Gandhi's **civil disobedience** movement, and despite the fact that officially the CPI supported the British government in the struggle against fascism during **World War II**, local level members of the Workers' and Peasants' Parties played a prominent part in the violent Quit India agitation of 1942. In 1946 the CPI contested elections held by the British to the provincial and central assemblies and won a considerable number of votes, though a limited number of seats, as the runner-up to the Congress in most constituencies. Despite this, the CPI was not consulted by the British in the negotiations over Independence, and party members organized strikes and agitations, particularly in the independent princely states, which threatened to break away from the Indian Union and set up their own autocratic regimes. Of greatest importance was the **Telengana Disturbances** in Hyderabad. After Independence, CPI members continued to contest elections and gained a number of seats in parliament. However, they were closely allied with the Congress Party (at least until 1974) and therefore generally supported the government. ▷ **Bengal, Partition of; communalism; Ghadr Party and Movement; India, Partition of; Indian National Congress; Quit India Movement**

Communist Party of the Soviet Union (CPSU)

The party which controlled political, economic, and social life in the USSR from the Bolshevik Revolution in 1917 until its abolition in 1991. It was the only party with the right to put forward candidates in elections, and most of the country's important jobs were filled by selected party members. Membership comprised only c.10 per cent of the population, and the party itself was highly undemocratic, being run by the small **Politburo** or the slightly larger Central Committee. ▷ **communism**

Compact Theory of Confederation

Canadian constitutional theory. An interpretation of the British North America Act which argued that confederation meant the entrusting of certain powers to Ottawa while the provinces still retained their autonomy. As a compact, the agreement could not be altered without the acceptance of the signatories and could even be nullified if they so wished. The theory was supported in the 1880s by Quebeckers such as Honoré Mercier and by English-speaking provincial leaders like Mowat in Ontario and Norquay in Manitoba. The federal power which provincial governments most wanted to remove was that of disallowing provincial legislation, because, along with a policy of economic centralization, it would result in the severe limitation of provincial rights. At the 1927 Dominion-Provincial Conference the compact theory was proclaimed the true interpretation of confederation by both the Liberal Premier of Quebec and the Tory Premier of Ontario and during the 1930s it was used to place the Prime Minister, Richard **Bennett**, under political pressure. The theory actually disintegrates under examination because the original signatories comprised only three provinces.

Compaore, Blaise (1940–)

Burkino Faso soldier and politician. Educated locally and in military academies in Senegal and France, including St Cyr, he joined the army in 1958 rising to command the Artillery Group (1975–6). In 1980 he was appointed Minister of Rural Development and was second in command to Thomas **Sankara** (1983–7), when he overthrew his colleague on 15 Oct 1987 and became Chairman of the Popular Front of Burkino Faso and

Head of Government. Originally a very close friend and confrere of Sankara's, he came to reject what he felt was the overly egalitarian thrust of Sankara's policies.

Compton, John George Melvin (1926–)

St Lucian politician. He graduated at the London School of Economics and was called to the English Bar. In 1951 he established a law practice in St Lucia and three years later joined the St Lucia Labour Party (SLP), becoming its Deputy Leader. He left in 1961 to form the United Workers' Party (UWP) and, on independence in 1979, was St Lucia's first Prime Minister. He was defeated in the same year by the Labour Party but returned in 1982, and was narrowly re-elected in 1987.

Compulsory Service Act (1917)

Canadian conscription legislation. It was introduced because Canada's voluntary militia had been unable to fulfil the commitment to provide four full divisions on the Western Front. **Borden**'s Minister for Militia, Sir Sam Hughes, had deterred many French-Canadians from volunteering by his Ulster Protestant prejudices. The Act was particularly unpopular in Quebec, where many believed they were being asked to fight for the empire, while being denied equal rights at home. With **World War II** the government tried to maintain a policy of 'no conscription' to ensure national unity, despite continuous pressure from the English-speaking provinces, especially after the fall of France. In response **King** held a referendum which showed that although 80 per cent of the English-speaking population wished to free the government from its pledge, 72 per cent of French-Canadians were against doing so. King therefore retained the policy and sacked his Defence Minister when he was advised that there were not enough volunteers to maintain the Canadian commitment after the Normandy landings in 1944. But with the failure of the policy to enlist home defence draftees, King was forced to reintroduce conscription. Protest from French-Canadians, both among civilians and in the forces, was fierce, while one French-Canadian minister resigned from the government and 34 Quebec Liberals voted against it in a vote of confidence. Even so, King managed to survive the election of 1945, albeit with a reduced majority.

concentration camp

A detention centre for political prisoners; known primarily from the camps established in Germany soon after the Nazi seizure of power, which soon came under **SS** control and were administered with extreme cruelty. The coming of war swelled the camp population with millions of Jews, Gypsies, slave workers, Soviet prisoners of war, and other 'enemies of the state' whom the SS regarded as an economic unit of resource. Following the Wannsee Conference (Jan 1942), which plotted the destruction of European Jewry, the concentration camps established in Poland, such as **Auschwitz** and Treblinka, became purpose-made extermination centres in which over 6 million Jews died. ▷ **Holocaust; Nazi Party**

Condominium (Anglo/Egyptian Sudan)
After the defeat of the Mahdist forces by **Kitchener**, the area of the Upper Nile was linked with Egypt, named the Anglo/Egyptian Sudan and controlled nominally by Britain and Egypt as a 'condominium'. In practice, though, real power lay in British hands as Britain was, at the time, in effective control of Egypt. The period of the condominium, initially both economically and socially advantageous to the Sudan, led (through the development of an educated class) to a desire for independence. Some progress was made and in 1948 Britain recognized the validity of these aspirations. However, the movement of the Sudanese towards independence received a setback when, in 1951, King Farouk of Egypt proclaimed himself also King of the Sudan. Farouk's subsequent fall led to Egypt's recognition, in principle, of the Sudanese right to independence, and full independence was declared in 1955.

Confessing Church
A Church formed in Germany by Evangelical Christians opposed to Nazism and the Nazi-supported 'German Christian Church Movement'. Its Synod of Barmen published the *Barmen Declaration* (1934), which became influential in Germany and beyond as a basis for resistance to oppressive civil authorities, It was succeeded in 1948 by the 'Evangelical Church in Germany'. ▷ **Nazi Party**

confino
The practice of internal exile or banishment to remote provinces and islands; it was used extensively against critics of **Mussolini**'s government after Nov 1926.

Congo formerly **People's Republic of Congo**
West central African republic. Part of French Equatorial Africa, known as the 'Middle Congo' from 1908 until 1958, it gained independence as the Republic of the Congo in 1960. A military coup created the first Marxist state in Africa, and the country was renamed the People's Republic of the Congo in 1968. Marxism was renounced in 1990 and opposition parties were permitted. Fighting between ethnic and political groups followed the disputed election results of 1993.

Congress (USA)
The national, or federal, legislature of the USA, consisting of two elected chambers: the Senate and the House of Representatives. The Senate contains two members from each state (irrespective of size), serving six-

year terms, with a third of the terms expiring every two years. Representation in the House is for a two-year term, and is calculated on the basis of population. Congress initiates legislation, and significantly amends or rejects presidential legislative proposals. The **US Constitution** endows it with the 'power of the purse', and all revenue bills must originate in the House. For a bill to become law it must be passed in identical form by both chambers and signed by the President. A presidential veto may be overturned by a two-thirds majority in each chamber. Legislation receives detailed consideration in the powerful Congressional committees. Although the chambers are organized along party lines, party discipline is weak. The majority party leader of the House occupies the influential position of Speaker.

Congress of Racial Equality (CORE)

US **civil rights** organization founded in 1942. In the 1960s CORE sponsored sit-in demonstrations, the freedom riders' challenge to segregation in interstate public buses, and registration of black voters in the South.

conscription

The practice of compelling young men of eligible age and fitness to serve by statute in the armed forces of a nation. To meet the huge manpower needs of **World War I**, conscription was introduced in Great Britain in early 1916. Conscription was again enforced in Britain from 1939 to 1945, continuing in peacetime as National Service, which was finally abolished in 1962.

Conservative Party (UK)

One of the two major political parties in the UK, its full name being the Conservative and Unionist Party. It developed from the Tory Party during the 19c and pursued policies, first under Peel and then Disraeli, designed to broaden its appeal beyond the English landowners and supporters of the Church of England. It has largely succeeded in this, having been in power either solely or as the dominant element in coalitions for approximately two-thirds of the period since Disraeli's election victory of 1874. Its main support, however, has remained English rather than British and the party is stronger in rural than in urban areas. ▷ **Tories**

Conservative Party of South Africa

A South African party formed in 1982 by reactionary (*verkrampte*) members of the **National Party** who had been expelled from Parliament. It was led by Andries **Treurnicht** and, after the 1987 general election, became the chief opposition party in the white parliament and opposed the liberalization measures of President **De Klerk**.

Constantine I (1868–1923)
King of Greece (1913/17 and 1920/2). He was the son and successor of George I. As a military commander he was unsuccessful in the Turkish War of 1897, but led the Greeks to victory in the **Balkan Wars** (1912–13). As the brother-in-law of Kaiser **William II** of Germany, he insisted on Greek neutrality in **World War I**, but was forced to retire in favour of his son, Alexander, by the rival government of Eleuthérios **Venizélos** and the Allies in 1917. In 1920 he was restored to the throne by plebiscite, but after a military revolt in 1922, abdicated again in favour of his son, **George II**.

Constantine II (1940–)
King of Greece (1964/73). The son and successor of **Paul I** of Greece, soon after his accession he married Princess Anne-Marie, younger daughter of **Frederick IX** of Denmark and sister of Queen **Margrethe** of Denmark. In Apr 1967 the 'Colonels' seized power in a military coup; Constantine made an abortive attempt to regain power, then fled into exile in Rome (Dec 1967). He was formally deposed in June 1973, and the monarchy was abolished by national referendum in 1974. His heir is Crown Prince Paul (1967–).

Constantinople Agreements (Mar–Apr 1915)
Britain and France feared that Russia would make a separate peace with Germany unless she was offered significant territorial gains. They secretly agreed, therefore, that after **World War I** Russia should receive Constantinople (Istanbul) and land along the Straits. This was a remarkable change in British policy particularly, as throughout the 19c Britain had opposed Russia gaining control of the Straits. After the **October Revolution**, however, the **Bolsheviks** rejected all agreements made by the Tsarist government.

Constitution Act of 1982
The statute which 'patriated' the constitution of Canada, adding a Charter of Rights and Freedoms, and a general amendment procedure. It was the result of 18 months of hectic negotiation following the 1980 Quebec referendum on independence during which the federal government had promised a national settlement of constitutional issues. Through the summer of 1980 a series of very public discussions explored the items of a prepared agenda for a First Ministers' conference in Sep. After this broke down in acrimony, the federal government announced a unilateral approach to the British parliament, a resolution whose validity was finally accepted by the Supreme Court in Sep 1981 as allowable though objectionable. 'Constitutional convention plus constitutional law equal the total constitution of the country,' it said in a judgement that was used to support the arguments of both sides. At a final conference in

Nov 1981, the so-called Kitchen Meeting paved the way for compromise, which, however was rejected by Quebec. ▷ **Meech Lake Accords**

Conte, Lansana (c.1945–)
Guinean soldier and politician. Military commander of the Boke Region, he led a bloodless coup on the death of Sekou **Toure** (Mar 1984) and set up the Military Committee for National Recovery with himself as President. He relaxed the centralizing policies of Toure and successfully encouraged many exiles to return. An attempted coup was thwarted by loyal troups in 1985 and the process of reintegrating into the Western world was continued.

Continuation War (1941–4)
Known also as the Soviet–Finnish War, Finland's attack on the USSR (June 1941) in partnership with Nazi Germany was intended to reverse the verdict of the **Russo-Finnish War** of 1939–40. After initial success, the Finnish front was stabilized until the great Russian offensive of June 1944. However, the Finnish government had decided as early as Feb 1943 that it must seek peace. With the assistance of Swedish mediation, an armistice was signed (Sep 1944) and the war was formally ended by the Treaty of Paris (Feb 1947). ▷ **Tanner, Väinö; World War II**

Convention People's Party (CPP)
Formed in 1949 by Nkwame **Nkrumah** as a breakaway from the **United Gold Coast Convention** (UGCC), the CPP appealed to a mass, especially urban, following and was instrumental in propelling Ghana to independence in 1957 and Nkrumah to the premiership. It became the only legal party in 1964 (with the slogan 'the CPP is Ghana and Ghana the CPP') and lost popular support quickly, putting up no defence for Nkrumah when he was ousted in a coup in 1966. Nevertheless, later parties were built upon CPP foundations.

Cook, Sir Joseph (1860–1947)
British-born Australian politician. A miner, he emigrated to Australia in 1885 and was elected to the New South Wales Assembly in 1891 as a Labor member. He left the **Australian Labor Party** (1894) and joined G H **Reid**'s Liberal ministry. He entered federal politics in 1901, supporting Reid's opposition free-trade group of which he became Deputy Leader in 1905 and leader in 1908. By now anti-socialist, he formed a coalition government with **Deakin** in 1909, serving as Minister of Defence. He was Prime Minister (1913–14), Deputy Prime Minister in **Hughes**'s Nationalist government (1917), Treasurer (1920–1) and Australian High Commissioner in London (1921–7).

Coolidge, (John) Calvin (1872–1933)
US politician and 30th President. He became a lawyer, and was Governor of Massachusetts (1919–20) when he gained national attention for his firm handling of the Boston police strike. Elected Vice-President in 1921, he became President on the death of Warren G Harding (1923). A strong supporter of US business interests, he was triumphantly re-elected in 1924, but refused renomination in 1928. Coolidge's policies were successful while he was in office, but were partly responsible for the great depression that followed.

Cooperative Party (UK)
A British political party which grew out of the ideas of voluntary mutual economic assistance developed in the 19c by Robert Owen (1771–1858). Established in 1917, one candidate, who joined with the parliamentary **Labour Party**, was elected to the House of Commons in 1918. Thereafter it became closely integrated with the Labour Party.

Cordobazo (May 1969)
The name given to a period of major unrest in Córdoba, Argentina, during which trade unionists and students briefly took control of the city in protest against the military dictatorship of Juan Carlos Onganía. The event indicated the potential for an alliance between left-wing **Peronism** and student activists inspired by more traditional (ie European) left-wing ideologies. It also revealed the structural weaknesses of the military regime.

Corfu, Declaration of (20 July 1917)
During **World War I**, in anticipation of the break-up of the Austro-Hungarian monarchy, the government of Serbia (then in exile on the island of Corfu), together with the **Yugoslav Committee**, agreed to work together to create a South Slav or Yugoslav state. This was to be a 'constitutional, democratic and parliamentary monarchy' under the Serbian Karageorgević Dynasty. The declaration, although it had no legal force, marked an important stage in the creation of the Kingdom of Serbs, Croats and Slovenes (later Yugoslavia).

Corfu Incident (Aug 1923)
When an Italian general and four members of his staff were shot while on a mission determining the Greek–Albanian frontier, **Mussolini** saw it as an insult to national pride and an opportunity to test Italian strength. The Greek island of Corfu was bombarded and occupied. A Greek appeal to the **League of Nations** was successful in getting the Italians to evacuate the island, but the Greeks were also ordered to pay Italy a large indemnity. After the Corfu incident, Mussolini adopted a more conciliatory position in international relations for a number of years.

coronelismo

The Spanish term denoting the unfettered rule of a proprietor (frequently a trader) over a community, which was a natural result of the settlement of the vast interior of Brazil. Such men were often heads of extended families (*parentelas*) and were frequently nominated to public office, especially the National Guard, in recognition of their rule. Their position was vastly strengthened under **Campos Salles**, who encouraged the creation of one-party government in the states. Though many never held formal office in the Guard, the title *coronel* implied the ability to muster a substantial vote from local tenants and clients, and to produce *agregados* as personal militia in support of a state governor. The golden age of *coronelismo* ended with the Estado Novo in 1937. ▷ **parentela**

Corporations

Fascist labour organizations in **Mussolini**'s Italy. They were first established in 1926 to replace the old socialist-dominated unions and were to include both employers and employees. They were supposed to minimize industrial conflict and maximize efficiency. In practice, while not a disaster, the bargaining power of workers was greatly decreased, while grateful industrialists continued to do much as they pleased. In 1930 the National Council of Corporations was set up to act as a consultative body on the economy; in reality, its views were rarely canvassed and it was most important as a means of providing jobs for loyal party members.

Cosgrave, William Thomas (1880–1965)

Irish politician. He joined the **Sinn Féin** movement at an early age, and took part in the **Easter Rising** (1916). He was elected a Sinn Féin MP (1918–22) and, after holding office as first President of the **Irish Free State** (1922–32), became Leader of the Opposition (1932–44). His son, Liam, was Leader of the **Fine Gael** Party (1965–7) and Prime Minister (1973–7).

Costa, Manuel Pinto da (1937–)

Sao Tome politician. In 1972 he founded the Movement for the Liberation of Sao Tome and Principe (MLSTP) in Gabon and in 1974, taking advantage of a military coup in Portugal, returned and persuaded the new government in Lisbon to recognize the MLSTP as the sole representative of the people and to grant independence a year later. He became president in 1975 and set his country on a politically non-aligned course.

Costa, Afonso (1871–1937)

Portuguese politician. Born in the clerical Beira Baixa province, as Minister of Justice under the First Republic he led a vigorous anticlerical campaign culminating in the separation of church and state in 1911.

Between Jan 1913 and Feb 1914 Costa, a capable and energetic administrator, headed the most popular Portuguese Republican Party (PRP) government of the Republican era, being the only government to balance the budget. Costa's PRP was the vehicle of the urban lower middle classes, disenfranchizing much of the working class by reducing the electorate by more than half to 400 000. The Costa government fell in 1914 partly through the internal divisions of the PRP and partly because it had alienated various interests, above all the army. Premier again (1916–17), Costa took Portugal into **World War I** on the side of the Allies out of fear for its colonies in the post-war settlement. But the economic impact of the war and bad military losses paved the way for a coup (Dec 1917). Disenchantment with the Republic led Costa to go into exile in Paris in 1919. ▷ **Republic, First** (Portugal)

Coty, René (1882–1962)
French politician. A barrister, he was elected a Deputy in 1923, entered the Senate in 1935 and was Minister of Reconstruction in 1947. The last President of the French Fourth Republic (1953–9), after the constitutional crisis precipitated by the generals in Algeria (May 1958), he assisted the return to power of General de **Gaulle** and the consequent birth of the Fifth Republic (Jan 1959), with de Gaulle as his successor. ▷ **Republic, Fifth** (France); **Republic, Fourth** (France)

Cox, Percy (1864–1937)
British diplomat. After receiving his military training, he served in India. During his time there, he left the army to work in the Indian political service in the Persian Gulf area; he was subsequently made Foreign Secretary in India but his major work was in Iraq, where he moved in 1914. He attended the Cairo Conference of 1921 which resulted, on his returning to Iraq, in his supervision of the emergence by resolution of the Council of Ministers of the Amir Faysal, second son of Sharif **Husayn ibn 'Ali** of Mecca, as King of Iraq (as **Faysal I**), a resolution which was ratified by a referendum upon which Cox insisted. Given his military background, he was also tasked with supervising the creation of an army for the country, and with looking after its constitutional arrangements. His last act in Iraq was his signature on behalf of the British of a Protocol to the 1922 Anglo-Iraqi Treaty which, amongst other things, reduced the effective period of the Treaty to four years, a provision which was welcomed by the King and a majority of the politicians.

Craig, James, 1st Viscount Craigavon (1871–1940)
Ulster politician. His early career was as a stockbroker. He was MP in the UK parliament (1906–21) where he vigorously campaigned to preserve the Act of Union against the Irish Nationalists. After Northern Ireland refused to join the South in 1921, he worked as its first Prime

Minister (1921–40) to maintain order in the Province and then to develop social and educational services under powers devolved to **Stormont**. His Unionist beliefs ensured that the interests of the Protestant majority in Northern Ireland would be paramount. While still in office, he died suddenly. ▷ **Carson, Edward**

Craxi, Bettino (1934–)
Italian politician. After being active in the Socialist Youth Movement, he became a member of the Central Committee of the Italian Socialist Party (PSI) in 1957, a member of the National Executive (1965) and a Deputy Secretary (1970–6). In 1976 he became General-Secretary, and after the July 1983 election he became Italy's first socialist Prime Minister, successfully leading a broad-based coalition until 1987.

Créditistes
French-Canadian partner of the **Social Credit Party**. After a revival in their fortunes the party gained 26 seats in the 1962 federal elections but declined to 24 seats in 1963 when the Quebec representatives set up their own organization. Since then the party's popularity declined with the size of the rural population and by 1980 it was eliminated.

Crerar, Thomas Alexander (1876–1975)
Canadian politician. Founder of the **Progressive Party** when he bolted from the Liberals in protest against their high tariff budget of 1920, he led the party to second place in the 1921 elections with 65 seats. Preferring to hold the balance of power, he left official opposition to the Conservatives. Within a year he resigned as leader, at least in part because he insisted on conventional principles of party organization and representation in conflict with those of his Alberta and Ontario membership. He re-entered politics, becoming Minister of Railways and Canals in Mackenzie **King**'s administration in 1929. Although he lost his seat in 1930, he won again with the Liberals in 1933, and served in the government as Minister of Mines and Resources. In 1945 he became a Senator and resigned in 1966.

Cripps, (Richard) Stafford (1889–1952)
British politician. He made a fortune in patent and compensation cases. In 1930 he was appointed Solicitor-General in the second Labour government, and became an MP in 1931. During the 1930s he was associated with several extreme left-wing movements, and was expelled from the **Labour Party** in 1939 for his 'popular front' opposing Neville **Chamberlain**'s policy of **appeasement**. He sat as an independent MP during **World War II**, was Ambassador to the USSR (1940–2), and in 1942 became Lord Privy Seal, and later Minister of Aircraft Production. In the 1945 Labour government, he was readmitted to the party and appointed Presi-

dent of the Board of Trade (1942–5). In 1947 he became Minister of Economic Affairs and then Chancellor of the Exchequer, introducing a successful austerity policy. He resigned due to illness in 1950.

Cristero Revolt (1927–9)
Rural guerrilla warfare against the Mexican government. Confined to the states of Guadalajara, Morelos, Colima, Jalisco, and Michoacán, the rebels fought under the banner 'Viva Christo Rey!'. Unlike their predecessors, they did not merely seek to restore the traditional preeminence of the Church in Mexico, but also to carry through social reforms; they thus presented a fundamental challenge to the revolutionary governments led by **Calles** and Obregón. By the end of 1927, Church and State were at stalemate: the Church suspended public worship and the State persecuted the clergy. In June 1929 the Vatican and US Ambassador Dwight Morrow achieved a compromise by which Church property was returned to the clergy and religious instruction was permitted in the Churches.

Critchlow, Hubert (1884–1958)
Guyanese trade unionist. In 1906, as an employee of Booker Brothers, he led an unofficial dockers' strike and became the mouthpiece of Guyanese labour. In Jan 1917 another 13-day strike resulted in a nine-hour day and increased wages for waterfront workers, and two years later Critchlow founded the British Guiana Labour Union, the first registered trade union in the British West Indies (1921) when unions were legalized. Although Critchlow and the BGLU lost some of their dynamism in the 1930s (when the sugar workers Manpower Citizens' Association became the dominant force in Guyanese labour), as 'father' of Guyanese unionism, he was honoured with the Secretaryship of the British Guiana Trades Union Congress in 1941.

Croatia, Independent State of (1941–5)
During **World War II**, after the disintegration of Yugoslavia, part of Croatia and Bosnia Herzegovina formed the Independent State of Croatia, a satellite state of the Axis powers. Benito **Mussolini** chose Prince Aimone of Saxony, the Duke of Spoleto, to be King, but the Prince never took over his kingdom. The state was, instead, subject to the brutal regime of Ante Pavelić, the leader of the **Ustaša** fascist movement. In 1945 Croatia became one of the constituent republics of the Socialist Federal Republic of Yugoslavia. The Croatian President Franjo **Tudjman** declared Croatia's independence from the Yugoslav federation in 1991.

Croats
Slav settlers in the Balkans, the Croats migrated (6–7c) from White Croatia in the Ukraine to the old Roman provinces of Pannonia and

Dalmatia. The Croats established their own kingdom and were ruled by Croatian kings until 1102, when the Croatian crown passed to the Árpád house of Hungary. In the 15–16c the Croats became divided between three empires: the Croats in Dalmatia were subject to Venice; those in Croatia and Slavonia to the Habsburgs; and those in Bosnia and Herzegovina to the Ottomans. Following the fall of the Venetian Republic (1797) and the disbandment of the Illyrian Provinces (1809–13), the Dalmatian Croats were subject to direct rule from Vienna. The Ausgleich (1867) divided the Croats of the Habsburg Empire between the governments at Budapest and Vienna, while those in Bosnia-Herzegovina, having revolted against Ottoman rule, found themselves within an Austrian protectorate (1879). Not until 1918 and the creation of the Kingdom of Serbs, Croats and Slovenes (later Yugoslavia) were the Croats all subject to one government. The Croatian national revival began in the 1830s under the leadership of Ljudevit Gaj. ▷ **Dubrovnik; South Slavs; Ustaša; Yugoslav Committee; Yugoslavs**

Croce, Benedetto (1866–1952)
Italian philosopher, historian, literary critic and politician. Although best remembered as a scholar, Croce had an active political life. Under the last **Giolitti** ministry he was Education Minister (1920–1) while, as a Senator following the fascist seizure of power, he profited from the virtual immunity afforded by his enormous reputation to criticize the fascist regime constantly. In 1943 he played a prominent part in organizing the anti-fascists, and was a minister in both the **Badoglio** and **Bonomi** governments of 1944. He became President of the Italian Liberal Party in 1947 and a member of the Constituent Assembly; he became a Senator again in 1948.

Croix de Feu, Ligue des
A French political movement (1927–36), which was originally an organization of veteran soldiers of **World War I**, under the leadership of Colonel de **La Rocque**. It developed into a mass movement with a membership of about 250 000, campaigning for political change in a fashion which suggested that it could be a French version of **fascism**. That this was not really the case was shown when, uniformed leagues having been prohibited in 1936, it transformed itself into a legal political party, the PSF (*Parti social français*, 'French Social Party').

Crosland, Tony (Charles Anthony Raven) (1918–77)
British politician. He taught in Oxford after serving in **World War II**. Elected as a Labour MP in 1950, he became Secretary for Education and Science (1965–7), President of the Board of Trade (1967–9), Secretary for Local Government and Regional Planning (1969–70), Environment Secretary (1974–6), and Foreign Secretary (1976–7). A strong supporter

of Hugh **Gaitskell**, he was a key member of the revisionist wing of the **Labour Party** aiming to modernize socialist ideology, and wrote one of its seminal texts, *The Future of Socialism* (1956). ▷ **socialism**

Crossman, Richard (Howard Stafford) (1907–74)
British politician. He became a philosophy tutor at Oxford, and leader of the Labour group on Oxford City Council (1934–40). In 1938 he joined the staff of the *New Statesman*. In 1945 he became a Labour MP, and under **Wilson** was Minister of Housing and Local Government (1964–6), then Secretary of State for Social Services and head of the Department of Health (1968–70). He was editor of the *New Statesman* (1970–2). His best-known work is his series of political diaries, begun in 1952, keeping a detailed, and frequently indiscreet, record of the day-to-day workings of government and political life. They were published in four volumes (1975–81), despite attempts to suppress them. ▷ **Labour Party** (UK)

CSU (*Christlich-Soziale Union*, 'Christian Social Union')
Bavarian political party. The successor to the pre-1933 Bavarian People's Party, the CSU functions as the Christian Democratic Party of Bavaria (within which the **CDU** does not organize). Founded in Jan 1946 it dominates Bavarian state politics by virtue of its absolute majority in the **Landtag** obtained in 1962 and operates in coalition with the CDU in the **Bundestag**. Somewhat to the right of the CDU, it is a staunch exponent both of Bavarian particularist, and all-German interests (with a European democratic federation as a long-term aim). Its membership is socially diverse, but is dominated by independent and salaried members of the middle classes. While leader of the CSU, the late Franz-Josef **Strauss** was a prominent advocate of right-wing Christian Democracy within Bavaria and Germany as a whole.

cuartelazo
A Spanish pejorative term meaning 'barrack room coup': one which puts first the interests of the military, narrowly defined as the motivation for the coup. Such coups have often occurred when the incumbent government was judged to have accorded a high priority to health and education, rather than military expenditure. Rulers in the 20c who owed their pre-eminence to *cuartelazos* include Chaves (Paraguay), Onganía and Videla (Argentina), Torrijos and Robles (Panama), Tinoco (Costa Rica) and Perez Jimenez (Venezuela).

Cuba
An island republic in the Caribbean Sea. It was a Spanish colony until 1898, when Spain relinquished its rights over Cuba following a revolution under José Martí, with the support of the USA. Independence was gained in 1902, with the USA retaining naval bases, and reserving the right of

intervention in domestic affairs. The struggle against the dictatorship of General **Batista** led by **Castro**, unsuccessful in 1953, was finally successful in 1959, and a Communist state was established. An invasion by Cuban exiles with US support was defeated at the **Bay of Pigs** in 1961. A US naval blockade took place after Soviet installation of missile bases in 1962. After emigration was permitted (1980) many Cubans settled in Florida. Agreement was reached in 1992 for the withdrawal of Russian troops.

Cuban Missile Crisis (Oct 1962)
A period of acute international tension and potential military confrontation between the USA and USSR, following the USA's discovery of Soviet nuclear missile sites in Cuba. President John F **Kennedy** demanded the dismantling of the base and the return of the missiles, and threw a naval blockade around the island. The crisis ended on 28 Oct, when Soviet leader **Khrushchev** agreed to Kennedy's demands, in return for the withdrawal of US missiles from Turkey.

Cult of Personality (1956)
The formula used to condemn Joseph **Stalin** and his dictatorship at the Twentieth Congress of the Communist Party of the USSR. It took some time after Stalin's death in 1953 for Nikita **Khrushchev** to establish himself and to build a suable case against him. Many of Stalin's crimes were made known, but they were attributed to his being led astray, and not to the system that allowed him to act dictatorially. Khrushchev and his successors could, therefore, still be communists and run their country autocratically, so long as they steered clear of Stalin's excesses.

Cultural Revolution (1966–76)
An abbreviation for the Great Proletarian Cultural Revolution, a radical Maoist mass movement in China initiated as a rectification campaign in 1966, which ended only with the death of **Mao Zedong** and the arrest of the **Gang of Four** in the autumn of 1976. To prevent the Chinese revolution from stagnating and to avoid 'revisionism', Mao aimed at replacing the old guard, including Liu Shaoqi (died in prison in 1969), Peng Zhen, and **Deng Xiaoping** (both disgraced in 1966), with a new generation of fervent revolutionaries. He appealed directly to the masses, in particular to young students, the **Red Guards**, who with the support of the **People's Liberation Army** overthrew not only party leaders but all so-called 'bourgeois reactionaries' and 'capitalist-roaders' in authority in schools, universities, factories, and the administration. The 10 years of social and political turmoil saw the closure of schools and universities, factories at a standstill, and millions of people sent to undertake manual labour in the countryside as re-education. ▷ **Maoism**

Cuno, Wilhelm (1876–1933)
German politician. After an early career in the senior civil service and commerce (from 1918 Director-General of the Hamburg–America Shipping Line, Hapag), Cuno served as an economic adviser to the German government at the Treaty of **Versailles** negotiations and at the subsequent **reparations** talks. In Nov 1922 he became Chancellor of Germany, despite belonging to no party, at the head of a pro-business government. His foreign and economic policies collapsed as a result of the crisis precipitated by the French occupation of the Ruhr in 1923, leading to his resignation on 12 Aug, after which he returned to the business world.

Curtin, John (Joseph) (1885–1945)
Australian politician. He was active in trade-union work, and edited a Perth newspaper. In 1928 he entered parliament, and became leader of the **Australian Labor Party** in 1935. As Prime Minister (1941–5), he appealed for support from the US and organized national mobilization during the war against Japan. He died in office.

Curzon Line
A line of territorial demarcation between Russia and Poland proposed in 1920 by the British Foreign Secretary, Lord Curzon. Poland rejected the proposal, subsequently gaining larger territories. In Sep 1939 a boundary similar to the Curzon Line became the border between German- and Soviet-occupied Poland, and in 1945 was recognized as the frontier between Poland and the USSR. ▷ **Yalta Conference**

Cvetković, Dragiša (1893–1969)
Serbian politician. After studying law at Subotica, he entered politics as a member of the Serbian Radical Party and held a series of minor government posts until 1939 when he succeeded **Stojadinović** as Prime Minister. Supported by Prince Paul Karageorgević, he negotiated the **Sporazum** with Vladko **Maček** which led to a measure of cooperation between the Croats and the Yugoslav government. In Mar 1941 he and Cincar-Marković signed an agreement with the Axis powers in which they pledged Yugoslavia's neutrality. A few days later, his government was overthrown in a coup led by General Dušan Simović. He went abroad in 1943, and eventually settled in France.

Cyprus
An island republic in the Mediterranean Sea, lying about 50 miles (80 kilometres) south of Turkey. With a recorded history of 4 000 years, its rulers have included the Greeks, Ptolemies, Persians, Romans, Byzantines, Arabs, Franks, Venetians, Turks and British. It became a British Crown Colony in 1925. Greek Cypriot demands for union with Greece (*enosis*) led to guerrilla warfare against the British administration, under

Grivas and **Makarios**, and a four-year state of emergency (1955–9). Cyprus achieved independence in 1960, with Britain retaining sovereignty over the military bases at Akrotiri and Dhekelia. There was Greek–Turkish fighting throughout the 1960s, with a UN peacekeeping force sent in 1964. Further terrorist activity took place in 1971. The 1974 Turkish invasion led to occupation of over one third of the island, with displacement of over 160 000 Greek Cypriots. The island was divided into two parts by the Attila Line, from the north-west coast above Pomos to Famagusta in the east, cutting through Nicosia where it is called the Green Line. Peace talks on reunification were inconclusive in both 1990 and 1992. Cyprus and Greece agreed upon a common defence policy in 1993 and Turkey affirmed its commitment to a political agreement with Cyprus.

Cyrankiewicz, Jozef (1911–89)
Polish politician. He became Secretary of the Socialist Party in Kraków in 1935. Taken prisoner by the Germans (1939), he escaped and organized resistance, but was sent to **Auschwitz** in 1941. He became Secretary-General of the Socialist Party in 1945, and after two periods as Premier (1947–52 and 1954–70) became Chairman of the Council of State (1970–2) and of the All-Poland Peace Committee (1973).

Czechoslovakia
The former federal state which consisted of the Czech Republic and the Slovak Republic. Formerly ruled by Austrian Habsburgs, the Czech lands united with Slovakia to form the separate state of Czechoslovakia in 1918. Germany occupied the Sudetenland region in 1938, and then the whole country. The government was in exile in London during **World War II**. Czechoslovakia achieved independence with the loss of some territory to the USSR in 1946. The 1948 coup was followed by communist rule. An attempt at liberalization by **Dubček** was terminated in 1968 by the intervention of **Warsaw Pact** troops. A strong protest movement continued, culminating in the fall from power of the Communist Party in 1989. The Czech and Slovak republics were granted increasing autonomy, and in 1993 separate states were created.

Czechoslovak Independence, Declaration of (1918)
The moment when the Czechs and Slovaks declared themselves free of Austria-Hungary and came together in a united state. Significantly, the declaration came out simultaneously in Geneva and Prague on 28 Oct, and on 30 Oct in Slovakia. Exiled politicians such as Tomáš **Masaryk** and Edvard **Beneš** played at least as great a role as those at home; and the Slovaks trailed behind the Czechs in their nationalist activities as in their economic development. Indeed it was the Czechs abroad who pressed the case for union, with support from the Allied Powers. And

this caused the union to be questioned at least twice (once following **Munich**, and the second time after the so-called **Velvet Revolution**), before it was dissolved in 1993.

Czechoslovak Legion
A corps of 30 000–40 000 Czech and Slovak volunteers and ex-prisoners of war in Russia, who fought briefly on the Eastern front and became embroiled with the **Bolsheviks** (May 1918) while being transported home along the Trans-Siberian railway. They seized many towns along the railway and for a time controlled much of Siberia. Their activities intensified the **Russian Civil War**, but also helped Tomáš **Masaryk** to gain recognition from the Allied powers for a provisional Czechoslovak government abroad.

Czechoslovak–Soviet Alliance (1935)
The treaty linking the two countries against the growing threat from Germany. Relations had been strained since 1917 and the involvement of the **Czechoslovak Legion** in the **Russian Civil War**. It was 1934 before Czechoslovakia recognized the USSR *de jure*. However, things changed in 1935 when **Hitler** announced the reintroduction of conscription and the Franco-Soviet alliance was signed. But **Beneš** only agreed to the new treaty on condition that its operation would depend on the previous functioning of the Franco-Soviet alliance. This was to ensure that he would not be left to fight Hitler with **Stalin** as his sole ally. During the Munich crisis France reneged on its international obligations and Benes did not attempt to activate his Soviet pact.

Czechoslovak–Soviet Alliance (1943)
Treaty linking the two countries against the proven threat from Germany. Relations had been strained since the **Munich Agreement** and the **German–Soviet Pact** but improved following the German invasion of the USSR in 1941. **Beneš** was anxious to liberate his country and prevent another Munich. **Stalin** wanted all possible allies to win the war and negotiate a satisfactory peace. So in 1943 a new treaty replaced that of 1935. This time it was a direct alliance, not dependent upon a third party. In return, the USSR promised non-interference in Czechoslovakia's internal affairs. Unfortunately, similar treaties signed with Poland and other states were abused along with this one. The Soviet government did not interfere; but the Communist Party did. However, in 1989 all that was reversed with the collapse of Soviet power in Eastern Europe.

D

D'Annunzio, Gabriele (1863–1938)

Italian writer. One of Italy's most important literary figures of the late 19c and early 20c. He was a fervent supporter of the **Tripolitanian War** and an active advocate of Italian intervention in **World War I**, during which he saw action as an airman. In Sep 1919 he occupied the disputed port of **Fiume** with a force of volunteer 'legionaries', where he introduced a constitution drafted by his syndicalist friend, Alceste **De Ambris**. Expelled from Fiume by the Italian navy in Jan 1921, D'Annunzio then flirted with the fascist movement and in Aug 1921 was actually invited by Dino **Grandi** and Italo **Balbo** to take over its leadership. Although D'Annunzio refused to usurp **Mussolini**'s position, the latter both admired him and considered him a threat to his dominance of the **Fascist Party** especially in the aftermath of the **Matteotti** crisis. Such fears were unfounded, as D'Annunzio never sought to challenge Mussolini for power.

D-Day (6 June 1944)

The day when the Allies launched the greatest amphibious operation in history (codenamed 'Overlord'), and invaded German-occupied Europe. By the end of D-Day, 130 000 troops had been landed on five beach-heads along an 80km/50ml stretch of the coast of Normandy, at a cost of 10 000 casualties. ▷ **Normandy Campaign; World War II**

Dachau

German concentration camp. Founded on **Himmler**'s orders on 20 Mar 1933 to accommodate political detainees under brutal conditions, Dachau was expanded during **World War II** to hold detainees from throughout Europe. By the time it was liberated by US troops in Apr 1945 about 30 000 people had died there. ▷ **Holocaust**

Dacko, David (1930–)

Central African politician. Educated at a teachers' training college in Mouyoundzi, he was a teacher and trade unionist before being elected to the territorial assembly in 1957, becoming successively Minister of Agriculture (1957–8), Minister of Administrative Affairs (1958), Minister of the Interior (1958–9) and Prime Minister (1959–60). He became the first President of the Central African Republic (1960) but was deposed in a coup, led by **Bokassa**, in 1966 and was imprisoned until 1976, when he was appointed one of Bokassa's advisers. With the help of the French, he was responsible for removing Bokassa in 1979, becoming President, a post to which he was re-elected in 1981, but was then removed from office by a military coup led by Andre-Dieudonné **Kolingba**.

Dáil Eireann

The lower house of the parliament of the Irish Republic. Unlike the upper house, the Senate (*Seanad Eireann*), which is appointed, the Dáil is elected by universal suffrage by proportional representation for a period of five years. It nominates the Prime Minister for appointment by the President. There are 144 members, who are called *Teatcha Dala*.

Daladier, Edouard (1884–1970)

French politician. In 1927 he became a leader of the **Radical Party**, and in 1933 Minister of War and Prime Minister of a short-lived government, a pattern which was repeated in 1934. In 1936 he was Minister of War in the **Popular Front** cabinet, and as Premier (1938–40) supported appeasement policies and signed the **Munich Agreement**. On 20 Mar 1940 he resigned as Prime Minister, becoming successively War and Foreign Minister in **Reynaud**'s cabinet, and on the fall of France was arrested and interned until 1945. He was one of the defendants in the **Riom Trial** (1942) of Third Republic leaders. After the war he continued in politics until 1958. ▷ **Republic, Third** (France)

Daley, Richard J (1902–76)

US politician. As Democratic mayor of Chicago (1955–76) and city boss, his political machine was so powerful that Democratic candidates at both the state and national level sought his backing. He became notorious during the 1968 Democratic Convention in Chicago, when the city's police force clubbed and gassed demonstrators protesting against the **Vietnam War**. By 1972 his influence had waned as a result of reforms which increased the representation of women, blacks and other minorities in the Democratic Party.

Dalmatia

The name given since antiquity to the narrow strip of land and over 1 000 islands along the eastern Adriatic coast from the south end of Pag to Cavtat, south of **Dubrovnik**. Occupied by **Napoleon I**'s army and included in the Illyrian Provinces (1809–13), following the Congress of Vienna (1814–15), Dalmatia was governed by Austria until 1918 when it became part of the Kingdom of Serbs, Croats and Slovenes, later Yugoslavia. Annexed by **Mussolini**'s Italy in **World War II**, in 1943 it was handed over to the **Ustaša** regime of Ante **Pavelić**. In 1945 Dalmatia became part of the Republic of Croatia within the Socialist Federal Republic of Yugoslavia.

Dalton, (Edward) Hugh (John Neale), Baron (1887–1962)
British politician. First elected as a Labour MP in 1924, he held the posts of Minister of Economic Warfare (1940–2) and then President of the Board of Trade (1942–5). In the post-war Labour government he was Chancellor of the Exchequer (1945–7), Chancellor of the Duchy of Lancaster (1948–50), Minister of Town and Country Planning (1950–1), and, briefly, Minister of Local Government (1951). He was elevated to the peerage in 1960. ▷ **Labour Party** (UK)

Damaskinos, Demetrios Papandreou (1891–1949)
Greek archbishop and regent of Greece. After serving in the army during the **Balkan Wars**, he was ordained priest (1917) and elected Bishop of Corinth (1922) and Archbishop of Athens (1938), but was exiled because of his opposition to **Metaxas**. Returning to Greece in 1941, he was able to give secret assistance to the British during the German occupation. After the withdrawal from Greece of German troops, Winston **Churchill**, eager to establish peace between the warring factions and to settle the constitutional crisis, agreed to Damaskinos' appointment as regent until a plebiscite could be held over the issue of the monarchy (Dec 1944). When the Greeks voted for the return of their king, Damaskinos resigned as regent (Sep 1946) and continued his work as archbishop. ▷ **Plastiras, Nikolaos**

Danish West Indies, Sale of (1917)
The result of an agreement reached in Jan 1916 between the governments of Denmark and the USA concerning the Danish West Indian colonies, the main islands being St Croix, St Jan and St Thomas, acquired in the 18c. The agreement stipulated that the US government would pay the Danish government $25 million for the islands, which the US considered part of its sphere of influence and of strategic importance after the opening of the Panama Canal. To the agreement was annexed a declaration in which the US government recognized the sovereignty of Denmark over the whole of Greenland. On 14 Dec 1916 a referendum about the agreement was held in Denmark with 64.3 per cent of the votes in favour of the sale and 35.7 per cent, a surprisingly high proportion, against. On 1 Apr 1917 — five days before the US declared war on Germany — the islands were handed over by the Danish government to the USA and renamed the 'Virgin Islands of the US'.

Danquah, Joseph Boakye (1895–1965)
Ghanaian nationalist and politician. After pursuing his studies in London, where he qualified as a lawyer, he returned to Ghana and founded the Times of West Africa in 1931. He was a leader of the **UGCC**, which campaigned for independence, but he fell out with its successor,

the **Convention People's Party (CPP)**, and became leader of the opposition. He was imprisoned in 1961–2 and 1964–5 and died in prison.

Dardanelles or **Hellespont**

Narrow strait in north-west Turkey, connecting the Aegean Sea and the Sea of Marmara, part of the important waterway linking the Mediterranean and the Black Sea. It was the scene of an unsuccessful Allied campaign in World War I. Intending to overcome the Turks and come to the aid of Russia, the British War Council approved a naval expedition to capture Constantinople by forcing a route up the Dardanelles. Many of the Anglo-French battleships were destroyed during the attempted passage, and efforts were subsequently concentrated on the land attack at **Gallipoli**.

Darlan, Jean (Louis Xavier) François (1881–1942)

French admiral. He passed through the Ecole Navale in 1899, became captain in 1918, and navy Commander-in-Chief in 1939. He served in the **Vichy** government as Minister of the Navy and Mercantile Marine, Vice-President of the Council of Ministers, and Secretary of State for Foreign Affairs and the Navy. He then commanded French forces in North Africa (1942), where he concluded an armistice with the Allies. He was killed by an anti-Vichy assassin in Algiers. ▷ **World War II**

Darnand, Joseph (1897–1945)

French politician. A militant in extreme-right movements, he was involved in the 1938 *Cagoule* ('hooded men') conspiracy, all financed by **Mussolini**, to murder left-wing Italian exiles in France. He collaborated with the Germans in **World War II**, organizing the *Milice*, an auxiliary police force responsible for many atrocities. He fled to Germany, was captured, tried and executed. ▷ **Vichy**

Das, Chittaranjan (1870–1925)

Bengali patriot and politician. Called to the Bar in 1894, he soon acquired a reputation for skilfully representing nationalists, such as Aurobindo Ghose (1908), accused of terrorism by the British colonial government in India. He participated in the campaign against the partition of Bengal, chaired Bengal Provincial Congress (1917) and the **Indian National Congress** (1918), and renounced his legal practice and all his property to join M K **Gandhi**'s **Non-Cooperation Movement** (1920). Imprisoned in 1921, he emerged (1922) to help form the **Swaraj** Party to contest district and provincial council elections (then boycotted by the Indian National Congress). Opposed to Hindu **communalism**, he was popular with both Muslim and Hindu communities in Bengal and with Congressmen in Bengal, the Swarajists winning a majority of seats in the Bengal Council elections of 1923–4, and Das being elected Mayor of Calcutta City Corporation in 1924. Soon after, he came to an agreement with Gandhi which allowed both Swarajists and Gandhians to campaign from the Congress platform. Although he himself rejected violence, many of his followers were either involved in terrorism or openly advocated the use of violence in opposition to colonial rule. A strong supporter of the trade union movement, Das campaigned on behalf of railway workers and labourers on the Assam tea plantations; he and his followers were thus a powerful force for radicalism within the Indian Nationalist movement, a radicalism that grew in the years following his death. Sadly, his achievements in forging unity between Hindus and Muslims in Bengal survived his death by only a few years: factionalism and violence led ultimately to the partition of the province on independence in 1947. ▷ **Bengal, Partition of; Bose, Subhas Chandra**

Daudet, Léon (1867–1942)
French writer and political activist, son of Alphonse Daudet. He studied medicine but turned to journalism, and in 1904 began to associate with the right-wing royalist *Ligue de l'action française* ('League of French Action'), whose newspaper, *Action française*, he edited from 1908 (jointly with Charles Maurras after 1917). He sat in the Chamber of Deputies as a leader of the extreme right from 1919 to 1924. He wrote several novels, but is best remembered for his numerous memoirs and critical works, especially *Le Stupide XIXe Siècle* (1922).

Davies, Clement (Edward) (1884–1962)
British politician. Elected MP for Montgomeryshire in 1929, he held his seat until his death. Although offered a post as Education Secretary in Winston **Churchill**'s 1951–5 government, he declined, and thus helped to preserve the independent existence of the **Liberal Party**, which he led from 1945 to 1956.

Dawes Plan
A report on Germany's economic problems issued in 1924 by a committee presided over by US banker Charles G Dawes. The plan laid down a schedule of annual German payments of **reparations**, outlined the reorganization of the German Reichsbank, and recommended a large foreign loan for Germany. A further report was drawn up in 1929 by an international commission chaired by US Corporation official Owen Young (1874–1962).

Dayan, Moshe (1915–81)
Israeli general and politician. During the 1930s he joined the illegal Jewish defence organization, the **Haganah**, and was imprisoned by the British (1939–41), then released to fight with the Allies in **World War II** (when he lost his left eye, thereafter wearing his distinctive black eye-patch). He

became Chief-of-Staff (1953–8), joined the Knesset as a Labour member in 1959, but left the Labour Party in 1966 to set up the Rafi Party with David **Ben-Gurion**. He won international acclaim as Defence Minister in 1967 when his heavily-outnumbered forces triumphed over Egypt, Jordan, and Syria in the **Six-Day War**, and he himself became a symbol of Israeli dash and courage. As Foreign Minister, he helped to secure the historic peace treaty with Egypt (1977). He resigned from the **Begin** government in 1979, and launched a new centre party in 1981, but died the same year.

Dazhai

A production brigade in the Chinese province of Shanxi that was personally hailed by **Mao Zedong** in 1964 as a national model for agricultural development, embodying the ideals of self-help, egalitarianism and ideological correctness. Peasants in Dazhai were said to have transformed the barren hillsides into fertile terraced fields. After Mao's death in 1976, the achievements of Dazhai were increasingly called into question and its production figures were said to have been falsified.

DDP (*Deutsche Demokratische Partei*, 'German Democratic Party')

German political party. The DDP was founded on 20 Nov 1918 from left-liberal elements who supported the transformation of post-**World War I** Germany from a semi-absolutist monarchy to a parliamentary democracy. Until its dissolution in 1930, the DDP participated actively in Weimar coalition governments, particularly with the **SPD** and the **Centre Party**. Its middle-class supporters, however, became increasingly disenchanted with the republic and abandoned the DDP in large numbers. On 9 Nov 1930 the party was wound up and its remnants integrated in the small DSP (German State Party). ▷ **Weimar Republic**

De Ambris, Alceste (1874–1934)

Italian politician and trade unionist. After leading a long strike in the Parma region in 1908, he was forced into political exile, but in 1913 was elected to the Italian parliament. He campaigned for intervention in **World War I** in the hope that it would trigger a revolution and in 1919 he joined Gabriele **D'Annunzio** in **Fiume** where he was responsible for drafting a bizarre, guild-based constitution which was later to inspire the fascist **Corporations**. He left Italy in 1922 after **Mussolini**'s seizure of power.

De Bono, Emilio (1866–1944)

Italian soldier and politician. Present at the humiliating defeat of the Battle of Adowa in 1896, De Bono commanded a corps in **World War I**. After the war, he rallied to **fascism** and took part in the **March on Rome**. He was Director of Police and then Governor of Tripolitania from 1925.

In 1935 he was placed in charge of the forces to invade Ethiopia but was quickly replaced by **Badoglio**. As early as 1940 De Bono began to have doubts over **Mussolini**'s fitness to lead Italy in a war, worried by the latter's desire to control all policy personally. He was present at the meeting of the **Fascist Grand Council** of 25 July 1943 which toppled Mussolini and was later put on trial and executed by the Republic of **Salò**.

De Gasperi, Alcide (1881–1954)
Italian politician. An Austrian subject until the end of **World War I**, he was elected to the Austrian parliament in 1911 as a deputy for the Trentino and became known as an ardent defender of the interests of the Italian minority. In 1919 after Italian annexation of his native region, he attended the first congress of the **Popolari** at Bologna and in 1921 was elected to the Italian parliament. Although he originally backed **Mussolini**'s government, he soon withdrew his support and was arrested while trying to flee the country with false papers; he was sentenced to four years in prison but served only six months. On his release, he became Vatican Librarian, a post he held until the liberation of Rome. Made Secretary-General of the **Christian Democrat Party (DC)**, he was Minister without Portfolio in the first **Bonomi** ministry, while **Parri** made him Foreign Minister. In June 1946 he became Prime Minister, successfully supporting Italy's transition from monarchy to republic and signing the peace treaty with the Allies (Feb 1947). In Jan 1947 he formed a government with the support of both socialists and communists but he soon jettisoned this alliance, excluding them from his government in May 1947. Foremost among his reasons for ending a policy of cooperation with the left was the heightening tension between the USA (on which Italy was heavily dependent for investment and aid) and the USSR and increasing pressure from Pope Pius XII, who had made it clear as early as June 1946 that he saw it as his 'main aim to fight communism'. Despite a narrower basis for his government, De Gasperi remained Prime Minister until July 1953, providing continuity even though he presided over eight separate governments. He remained Secretary-General of the DC until his death.

De Klerk, F(rederik) W(illem) (1936–)
South African politician. Born into a prominent Nationalist family (his father was a cabinet minister and President of the Senate, his uncle the Prime Minister Johannes **Strijdom**), he graduated from Potchestroom University and established a legal practice in Vereeniging, which he represented as a **National Party** member in the South African parliament from 1972. He served in the cabinets of both B J **Vorster** and P W **Botha**, but never in major positions. Elected National Party leader for the Transvaal in 1982, when **Treurnicht** left to form the Conservative Party, he used that position as the political base from which to replace

Botha on his retirement in 1989. He was chiefly responsible for the public policy of ending **apartheid**, successfully winning elections in Sep 1989 (but with a reduced majority), and a referendum supporting negotiations with the **ANC**, which he had unbanned in Feb 1990. He sanctioned the release from imprisonment of Nelson **Mandela**, with whom in 1993 he was jointly awarded the Nobel Peace Prize. By 1994 apartheid had been abolished, and in the first all-race elections in South Africa the National Party was defeated by the ANC; De Klerk was appointed vice-president under Mandela.

De Priest, Oscar Stanton (1871–1951)
US politician. Born in Alabama, he ran away from home to Chicago where he was the first black to be elected to the City Council (as a Republican in 1915). He became an alderman in 1927, and the first black congressman from the North in 1928. Holding office until 1934, when he was defeated by a black Democrat, he secured passage for a bill to reduce discrimination in the Civilian Conservation Corps.

De Valera, Eamon (1882–1975)
Irish politician. Brought up on a farm in County Limerick, he became a teacher in Dublin, and was active in various republican movements. A commandant of the Irish Volunteers in the **Easter Rising** (1916), he was arrested and narrowly escaped the firing squad. He became an MP in 1917 and was Leader of **Sinn Féin** from 1917 to 1926. He was elected President of **Dáil Eireann**, and in 1926 became Leader of **Fianna Fáil**, his newly-formed republican opposition party, which won the 1932 elections. As Prime Minister (1932–48, 1951–4 and 1957–9), he instituted social, industrial and agricultural reforms and was instrumental in framing the constitution of 1937, which established the **Irish Free State** as **Eire**. He was President of Ireland from 1959 to 1973.

Deakin, Alfred (1856–1919)
Australian politician. Out of office after 1890, his political interests increasingly centred on **federation**. He was a member of the committees which drew up draft constitutions at both the National Australasian Convention in 1891 and the Federal Convention of 1897–8, and went to Britain with Barton's delegation to present the draft constitution to the British parliament in 1900. He became Attorney-General in Barton's first federal government and was largely responsible for the immigration legislation that created the **White Australia Policy** and the Judiciary Act which established the High Court. He became Prime Minister on Barton's retirement (1903), and held the office again in 1905–8 with the support of Labor. His second ministry created much of the distinctive structure of Australian government, including 'New Protection' which attempted to link wage rates to the new protective tariff. Although a lifelong social

reformer, Deakin was wary of trade union power and the strict party discipline of Labor, and his third ministry (1909–10) was in coalition with Sir Joseph **Cook**'s anti-socialists, marking a fundamental realignment in Australian politics. A nationalist, Deakin sought greater Australian influence in imperial affairs, criticizing the naval subsidy to Britain and promoting an Australian navy and compulsory military service. Yet he was also an imperialist, so effective as an advocate of imperial preference and closer union at the 1907 Imperial Conference that some British imperialists considered inviting him to lead an imperial party in Britain. Failing health forced his political retirement in 1913.

Déat, Marcel (1894–1955)
French socialist politician. He left the SFIO in 1933 as co-founder of the 'neo-socialist' *Parti socialiste de France* ('Socialist Party of France') which did not long survive. A visceral hatred of war led him from appeasement to **collaboration**. In 1941 he created the RNP (*Rassemblement national populaire*, 'National Popular Assembly') in the zone of German occupation. In Mar 1944 German pressure forced **Laval** to accept him as Minister of Labour in the **Vichy** government; he fled to Germany, was sentenced to death *in absentia*, but evaded arrest until his death in Italy. ▷ **Socialist Party**

Debray, Regis (1941–)
French Marxist theorist. Educated at the Ecole Normale Supérieure, he gained international fame through his association with the Marxist revolutionary Ernesto Che **Guevara** in Latin America during the 1960s. His most influential writings have been *Strategy for Revolution* (1970) and *The Power of the Intellectual in France* (1979), the latter a broadside against the growing influence of 'mediacrats'.

Debré, Michel (1912–)
French politician. After taking part in the **Resistance Movement**, he helped to set up of the *Ecole Nationale d'Administration* (ENA, 'National School of Administration') in 1945, the training ground for France's governing élites in politics, industry and the Civil Service in subsequent years. He was elected to parliament as a member of the Gaullist Party (RPF) in 1948, and violently attacked the constitution of the Fourth Republic. In 1958 de **Gaulle** charged him with the task of producing the new constitution of the Fifth Republic, and made him its first Prime Minister (1959–62). ▷ **Gaullists; Republic, Fifth** (France); **Republic, Fourth** (France)

Debs, Eugene Victor (1855–1926)
US politician. He worked as a locomotive fireman, and in 1893 was founder and first President of the American Railway Union, in 1894

leading the Pullman Strike for higher wages. He helped to establish the Socialist Party of America, was imprisoned for labour agitation, and between 1900 and 1920 stood five times as socialist candidate for President. His indictment for violation of Espionage Act brought him imprisonment (1918–21).

December Ninth Movement (1935)
A massive student demonstration in the Chinese capital of Beijing to protest against Japanese military incursions in north China and to call upon the Chinese government of **Chiang Kai-shek** to lead a campaign of national resistance. Although the demonstration was brutally suppressed, the movement provided many supporters for the **Chinese Communist Party**, increasingly perceived as the genuine representative of Chinese nationalism because of its call for an anti-Japanese war.

Defence of the Realm Act ('DORA') (Nov 1914)
A British Act introduced to give the government greater controls over the activities of its citizens. The most important control related to restrictions on press reporting and other forms of censorship. The restrictions were increased as **World War I** progressed.

Degrelle, Léon (1906–94)
Belgian politician. From French-speaking Belgium, he founded the fascist **Rexism** movement in the 1930s, and achieved considerable support in the elections of 1936. During **World War II** he collaborated with the German forces, commanding the Walloon (French-speaking Belgian) regiment on the Russian front, and was briefly put in charge of German-occupied Belgium towards the end of the war. He escaped in 1945 to Spain, and was condemned to death in his absence. In 1974 he was declared an undesirable alien in Belgium.

Delfim Neto, Antônio (1929–)
Brazilian economist and politician. The son of Italian immigrants, he is widely viewed as the typical technocrat, an econometrician who believed in rapid GDP growth and centralization as an antidote to the social problems of Brazil. He was Economic Secretary to São Paulo State (1966) and Planning Minister under Costa e Silva, becoming 'economic Tsar' under his successor, Emílio **Médici**. Heavily reliant upon repression to curb the labour unions, he became the darling of the propertied class as the author of the 'Economic Miracle' of 1968–73 and was recalled to office (Aug 1979–Mar 1985). He attempted to sustain GDP and export growth as antidotes to soaring international oil prices, interest rates and a deteriorating balance of payments.

Delgado, Humberto (1906–65)
Portuguese general and politician. Born into a modest military family, in the 1920s he keenly supported the counter-revolution as a junior officer. His vertiginous rise through the military ranks led him to become, at 46, the youngest general in the Portuguese armed forces. However, **Salazar** never entirely trusted Delgado, considering him too independent. Delgado's democratic experience abroad, especially in the USA (1953–7), caused him to reject the Salazar regime and in Apr 1958 Delgado scandalized the dictatorship by standing against the official presidential candidate. His charismatic appeal led to huge demonstrations of support in Lisbon and Oporto, but a heavily-rigged vote ensured his defeat. The humiliated Salazar soon got rid of direct presidential elections, restrictive as they had been. Delgado tried to stage three coup attempts in 1958, but failed on each occasion for lack of support. He left Portugal in 1959 and attempted unsuccessfully to win over the armed forces from abroad. He was murdered in Spain, near the Portuguese border, by the **PIDE** in mysterious circumstances.

Delors, Jacques (1925–)
French politician. He served as social affairs adviser to Prime Minister Jacques Chaban-Delmas (1969–72). He joined the **Socialist Party** in 1973 and served as Minister of Economy and Finance in the administration of President **Mitterrand** (1981–4), overseeing a programme of austerity (*rigueur*). He became President of the European Commission in 1985 and was elected to a second four-year term as President in 1988. As Commission President he oversaw significant budgetary reforms and the move towards the removal of all internal barriers in the EC in 1992, with increased powers residing in Brussels.

Delta Works
Series of public works in the Netherlands to protect the coastline against storms, designed after the disastrous floods of Feb 1953. The Delta Plan (5 Nov 1957) laid down projects to strengthen the water defences by building new or improved dams, bridges and surge barriers in the southwest of the country, effectively closing off the sea-arms between Rotterdam and Antwerp. The project has cost enormous sums of public money, has opened up the Dutch province of Zeeland to economic development, has been generally successful in achieving its aims, and was officially completed in 1986.

Demirel, Süleyman (1924–)
Turkish politician. He qualified as an engineer at Istanbul Technical University and worked on hydro-electric schemes in the USA and Turkey before making the transition from public service to politics. In 1964 he became President of the centrist Justice Party (JP), now subsumed in the

True Path Party (TPP). He served three terms as Prime Minister from 1965, until a military coup in 1980 resulted in a three-year ban on political activity. He was placed in detention but released in 1983.

Democracy Wall Movement (1978–9)

A protest movement in China against the excesses of the **Cultural Revolution**, the corruption of the Chinese Communist Party, and infringement of human rights. Ironically, the movement initially may well have been unofficially encouraged by **Deng Xiaoping**, who was at the time intent on reducing the influence of his Maoist opponents. At the Third Party Plenum (Dec 1978) Deng succeeded in gaining approval for his economic reforms. Wall-posters started to appear in the centre of the city during the Third Plenum, which not only criticized **Mao Zedong** and the Cultural Revolution, but also called into question the socialist system itself. Magazines were also published advocating greater democratic and artistic freedom. Many of the people involved were young urbanites, including workers, students, and former **Red Guards** disillusioned with the party. In Mar 1979 Deng Xiaoping, fearing that the protests had gone too far, ordered a clampdown and a number of dissidents were arrested. By the end of 1979 the movement had virtually come to an end; a limited number of wall-posters were allowed only to be displayed in a park far from the city centre. ▷ **Maoism**

Democratic Centralism (post-1906)

The term used by **Lenin** in 1906 to describe the operating principles that would govern the Communist Party and the Soviet state. Elections and accountability were mandatory, but it was also ordained that lower bodies must implement the decisions of higher bodies. This was used to eliminate whatever democracy the revolutionaries of 1917 might have envisaged and to institute dictatorship. It was implicit in the 1936 constitution, explicit in that of 1977. It continued as a party rule to the end and helps to explain why **communism** was doomed as soon as open debate was allowed after 1985.

Democratic Labor Party (DLP)

Australian political party, formed in 1957 from anti-communist groups which had formerly been part of the **Australian Labor Party** (ALP). The DLP was largely centred in Victoria, and drew most of its support from parts of the Catholic section of Australian society. At its height, in the late 1950s and through the 1960s, its importance lay in its ability to prevent the ALP from winning national government. Its policies were strongly anti-communist and pro-defence, and incorporated elements of Catholic teaching on social matters. No DLP representative has been elected to the national parliament since 1974.

Democratic Labour Party (DLP)
One of the two political parties which has shared power in Barbados since 1938. From that date, Grantley **Adams**'s Barbados Labour Party dominated politics until 1961 when the DLP, led by Errol **Barrow**, took a majority of seats in the legislature. The DLP was ousted in the 1976 election by the BLP, led by 'Tom' Adams but with Adams's death in 1985, the DLP returned to power (under Barrow) later in 1986. Barrow's death that year saw the leadership of the party pass into the hands of Erskine Sandiford, and Sandiford and the DLP were again victorious in the 1991 election.

Democratic Party
US political party. Losing its mass appeal following the American Civil War, it returned to a majority position in 1932, with Franklin D **Roosevelt**'s '**New Deal**', and added large urban areas and ethnic, racial, and religious support to its conservative Southern base. It also became associated with a more liberal stance on social reform and minority rights, especially in the 1960s. It retains the preference of the majority of Americans, reflected in the Democrat-dominated House and Senate, but since the early 1960s it has had great difficulty winning the presidency, with the exception of Jimmy **Carter** (1977–81) and Bill **Clinton** (1993–).

Democratic Unionist Party
The political party formed in Northern Ireland in 1971 under the leadership of Rev Ian **Paisley** after a split in the Unionist Party over Protestant reaction to demands both by Catholics in the Province and from Westminster for greater social and political equality. It has had strong appeal to many working-class Protestants and during the 1980s attracted about one-third of the Unionist vote. Frequently suspicious in the 1970s and early 1980s that the official Unionists were less zealous in their support for Protestantism, the two Unionist parties agreed on concerted opposition to the **Anglo-Irish Agreement** (1985) and agreed in the 1987 general election not to nominate candidates against one another, thus avoiding a split in the Unionist vote.

Democrats 66 (*Democraten 66*, **'D66'**)
Dutch political party formed in 1966 on a programme of radical constitutional reform. It wished to break the mould of 'compromise politics' and Verzuiling in the Netherlands by introducing a directly elected President, and by changing pure proportional representation to a more district-based system. In other matters D66 is generally left-of-centre.

Deng Xiaoping (Teng Hsiao-p'ing) (1902–)
Chinese politician. Leader of the Chinese Communist Party, since 1978 he has been the dominant figure in Chinese politics. Educated in France,

where he joined the Communist Party, and in the USSR, he became associated with **Mao Zedong** during the period of the **Jiangxi Soviet** (1928–34). In 1954 he became Secretary-General of the Chinese Communist Party, but reacted strongly against the excesses of the **Great Leap Forward** (1958–9). When Mao launched the **Cultural Revolution** (1966), Deng was criticized and purged along with **Liu Shaoqi**, but retained the confidence of Premier **Zhou Enlai** and was restored to power in 1974. Again dismissed in 1976, after the death of Mao he was restored once more to power, and since 1978 has taken China through a rapid course of pragmatic reforms.

Denikin, Anton Ivanovich (1872–1947)
Russian soldier. He entered the army at the age of 15, and rose to lieutenant general in **World War I**. After the **Russian Revolution** of 1917 he led the White Army in the south against the **Bolsheviks** (1918–20). He won the Ukraine, but was defeated by the **Red Army** at Orel (1919), and in 1920 resigned his command and escaped to Constantinople. Thereafter he lived in exile in France (1926–45) and the USA (1945–7), and wrote books on his military experiences.

Denmark, German Invasion of (8–9 Apr 1940)
An adjunct to the German invasion of Norway which met with little or no resistance on the part of the Danish armed forces and government. The latter continued in office until dismissed by the German occupying authorities in 1943. ▷ **Norway, German Invasion of; World War II**

Department of Regional Economic Expansion (DREE)
Canadian Federal Department. In 1969 it became responsible for the administration of the Agricultural Rehabilitation and Development Act (ARDA) and the Fund for Rural Economic Development (FRED). Parliament gave the department extraordinary powers under the Regional Development Incentives Act. The choice of regions or firms which qualified for capital assistance grants was made by the minister appointed by Pierre **Trudeau**, Pierre Marchand. Up to $12 million could be allotted to the projects of his choice and soon the department was involved in many different federal/provincial development schemes, so that by 1979 the department's expenditure had grown to half a billion dollars per year.

Dergue
The name, meaning 'committee', given to the Provisional Administrative Council in Ethiopia after the military's overthrow of Emperor **Haile Selassie** in 1974 and chaired by Heile Mariam **Mengistu**. Operating like a politburo, its members increasingly also came to fill governmental

positions and it was responsible for organizing the creation of the Worker's Revolutionary Party to advance its radical socialist policies.

Desai, Morarji (Ranchhodji) (1896–)
Indian politician. Educated at Bombay University, he became a civil servant, entering politics in 1930. After various ministerial posts, he became a candidate for the premiership in 1964 and 1966, but was defeated by Indira **Gandhi**. He became Deputy Prime Minister but led a breakaway faction of Congress, the Congress (S), following the party's split in 1969. Detained during the state of emergency (1975–7), he was then appointed leader of the newly-formed Janata Party, and elected Premier (1977–9). The Janata government was, however, characterized by internal strife and he was forced to resign in 1979.

Desert Rats
Members of the 7th British Armoured Division, which in 1940 took as its badge the jerboa or desert rat, noted for remarkable leaps. The media applied the name generally to all British servicemen in the **North Africa Campaign**, and it was readily adopted by those not entitled to wear the jerboa shoulder flash. ▷ **World War II**

détente
An attempt to lower the tension between states as a means of reducing the possibility of war and of achieving peaceful coexistence between different social and political systems. A prominent feature of relations between the USA and USSR in the 1970s, it led to several agreements over arms (SALT) and security and cooperation (Helsinki). In the early 1980s, there was a cooling towards détente on the part of the USA, on the grounds that too many concessions had been made and that the USSR did not adhere to the spirit of such agreements; but there was a considerable improvement in relations in the later part of the decade. ▷ **Cold War; Helsinki Conference**

DGB (*Deutscher Gewerkschaftsbund*, 'German Trade Union Federation')
Founded in the western zones of Germany in 1949, the DGB was the successor to **Weimar Republic**'s **ADGB** as well as its liberal and Christian trade unions. It embraces 16 individual unions, each representing a major sector of the economy, and by the 1970s had organized over 7 million employees. It is closely involved in most areas of economic and social policymaking and formulates its pay policy (*Tarifpolitik*) in the light of official assessments of Germany's economic health. Consensus rather than confrontation characterizes its actions.

Dharmapala, Anagarika (1864–1930)
Sri Lankan nationalist and religious reformer. He was born Don David Hewavitarana and took the name Anagarika Dharmapala as a result of his activities with the Buddhist Theosophical Society. He wrote and spoke as the champion of Buddhist reformism and the interests of the **Sinhala** people, but never formed or led any significant political grouping. Instead he devoted his attention in his later years to campaigning for the return into Buddhist hands of Buddhist sacred sites in North India.

Díaz, Armando, Duke (1861–1928)
Italian soldier. Wounded in Tripoli in 1913, he was promoted major-general in 1914. He replaced **Cadorna** after the disaster of **Caporetto** (Nov 1917) and led the Italian Army to victory at **Vittorio Veneto**. He served as War Minister in **Mussolini**'s first cabinet (1922–4) and was made a marshal in 1927.

Díaz, (José de la Cruz) Porfirio (1830–1915)
Mexican politician, who fought against the conservatives and Emperor Maximilian's French-imposed rule in 1864–7. He seized power in 1876 and was President until 1880, returning in 1884 to remain in office until 1911, when he was ousted by Francisco **Madero**. His long period of office saw the impact of the changes brought about by the laws of La Reforma, including the emergence of a wage-earning rural populace, the rise of a powerful northern economy, export-led economic growth stimulated by the railroad and extensive foreign investment. Though a master manipulator, his regime became a gerentocracy, and his patronage of the **científicos**' attempt to 'whiten the nation' left him open to the accusation of having betrayed Mexico to foreign, mainly Anglo-American, interests. Nonetheless, his regime (known as the Porfiriato) did much to stimulate material progress in Mexico. He died in Paris, in the midst of a revolution whose outcome was influenced by the changes he had fomented.

Dictation Test
A method used by Australian governments (1902–58) to exclude certain classes of intending immigrants. Based on the example of Natal (1897), under the Immigration Act of 1901, immigrants received a test in a European language. Non-Europeans were the main target, but it was also used with those considered politically undesirable; the most celebrated case was the anti-fascist, Egon Kisch (1885–1948), who was tested in Scottish Gaelic (1934). Kisch was eventually admitted when the High Court decided that this was not a European language. ▷ **White Australia Policy**

dictatorship of the proletariat

A term used by Marx to describe the period of transition from **capitalism** to socialism, when the working class has seized political power either through revolution or through the use of democratic political institutions. Under the influence of **Lenin**, the term was transformed from its original use to that of a dictatorship imposed on behalf of, and ultimately on, the revolutionaries. ▷ **Marxism-Leninism**

Diefenbaker, John George (1895–1979)

Canadian politician. In 1940 he entered the Canadian Federal House of Commons, becoming leader of the Progressive Conservatives (1956) and Prime Minister (1957–63) after 22 years of **Liberal Party** rule. His government introduced important agricultural reforms, and extended the federal franchise to Canada's Amerindian peoples. He remained active in national politics until his death in Ottawa.

Dien Bien Phu

A district capital in north-west Vietnam, some 10 miles from the border with Laos, and the site of the major battle which brought an end to the French colonial presence in Vietnam. Dien Bien Phu is situated in a wide valley, surrounded by steep hills. In late 1953, it was reoccupied by French military forces, who intended to use it as a major base to disrupt **Viet Minh** operations. The Vietnam People's Army, under Vo Nguyen Giap, surrounded the base with heavy artillery, dragged up into the hills by human and animal carriers — an extraordinary feat of endurance. The Vietnamese assault began on 13 Mar 1954 and on 7 May the French base was overrun, with over 10 000 prisoners being taken. It was a humiliating defeat for the French.

Diktat

The name given to the Treaty of **Versailles** (1919) by its critics in Germany. Adolf **Hitler** and the **Nazi Party** in particular lambasted the republican parties for signing the *Diktat* which had, undoubtedly, triggered resentment and outrage across the political spectrum. The republicans, however, felt they had had no realistic choice but to sign under protest.

Dimitrijević, Dragutin (alias, **Apis**) (1876–1917)

Serbian army officer. The son of a craftsman, he rose swiftly through the army to become a member of the Serbian General Staff (1901), Head of Intelligence (1913) and a colonel (1916). His reputation rests on his near prodigious enthusiasm for conspiracy: he took part in the assassination of King Alexander Obrenović (1903); he founded the secret society the **Black Hand** (1911); he plotted at various times against the kings of Bulgaria and of Greece and Emperor **Franz Josef**; and he seems to have had a part in the fateful assassination of **Franz Ferdinand,** Archduke of

Austria, at Sarajevo (1914). Finally he was executed on a charge, probably trumped up by Nikola **Pašić**, of conspiracy against the Regent, Alexander **Karageorgević** (1917).

Dimitrov, Gemeto (1903–72)
Bulgarian politician. After studying medicine in Belgrade and Sofia, he began to take an active part in left-wing politics as a member of the Pladne Group of the Agrarian Union. Like many others during the dictatorship of **Boris III**, he was arrested and tortured (1935). After the outbreak of **World War II**, he organized opposition to the Tripartite Pact and had to flee to Turkey. He returned to Bulgaria in 1944 and began to reorganize the Agrarian Party. Placed under house arrest, with US assistance he escaped to the USA, where he founded the Bulgarian National Committee and the newspaper, *Free and Independent Bulgaria.*

Dimitrov, Georgi Mikhailovich (1882–1949)
Bulgarian politician. A leading figure in the Bulgarian Socialist Party before **World War I**, he helped to found the Bulgarian Communist Party in 1919. After visiting Moscow, he returned to Bulgaria and led an uprising which earned him a death sentence (1923). He fled to Yugoslavia, then lived in Vienna and Berlin and worked for **Comintern**. One of the communist leaders accused of setting fire to the **Reichstag**, he conducted a brilliant defence against the charges engineered by the Nazi prosecution and was acquitted. He then went to Moscow and served as Secretary-General of the Executive Committee of Comintern (1935–43). Returning to Bulgaria in 1945, he was elected President of the Central Committee of the **Fatherland Front** and became Prime Minister after the elections in Oct 1946 which established communist rule. ▷ **Kostov, Traicho; Velchev, Damian**

Ding Ling (Ting Ling) (1902–86)
Chinese feminist writer and Communist Party activist. From a landowning family, she went to Shanghai University in 1923–4 and published her first short story in 1927. She became increasingly politicized and joined the Chinese Communist Party in 1932, becoming active in the League of Left-Wing Writers. Arrested and placed under house arrest by the **Guomindang** authorities (1933–6), she succeeded in escaping to the communist stronghold in the north-west. In 1942 Ding Ling was censured in a rectification campaign for a series of stories and essays expressing disillusion with the failure of communist ideals to be put into practice. One essay, in particular, criticized male party attitudes towards women. After 1949 she once again became a member of the literary establishment but in the 1957 anti-rightist campaign she again fell foul of party authorities. She was expelled from the Party and Writers' Union, sent to

prison and then to a labour reform camp. She was finally rehabilitated in 1979.

Diori, Hamani (1916–87)
Niger politician. He was educated in Dahomey and then at the William Ponty School in Dakar. A teacher and then instructor in the language school for colonial administrators (1938–46), he helped form the **Rassemblement Democratique Africain** in 1946 and represented Niger in the French National Assembly (1946–51 and 1956–7). In 1956 he became Prime Minister of Niger and in 1960, at independence, its first President. Building on close relations with France, he ran one of the most stable countries in West Africa, being re-elected in 1965 and 1970, but opposition within his party (the Niger Progressive Party) led to his overthrow in Apr 1974 through a military coup. He was placed under house arrest for 13 years, before he left for Morocco, where he died.

Diouf, Abdu (1935–)
Senegalese politician. He studied at Dakar and Paris Universities before graduating with a law degree and returning to Senegal to work as a civil servant. After holding a number of posts, including that of Secretary-General to President **Senghor**, he became Prime Minister in 1970 and succeeded Senghor on the latter's retirement (1 Jan 1981). He was re-elected President of Senegal in 1983 and 1988.

disarmament
Arms control which seeks to promote international security by a reduction in armed forces and/or weapons. The levels are set by agreement, and then opened up for inspection and enforcement by the other side or an independent inspectorate. General (ie applies to all countries) and comprehensive (ie applies to all categories of forces and weapons) disarmament was first attempted in 1927 and 1934 by the **League of Nations**, and by the United Nations in the 1950s, but such moves have not been successful. Disarmament is therefore limited to agreements between two or a few countries, and restricted to particular classes of weapons and troop levels. Problems arise in determining equivalences between different types of weapons held by different countries, and in verifying arms reduction treaties, especially in respect of nuclear weapons, largely because weapons can be re-assembled. There is also the possibility of nuclear disarmament involving no agreement with other countries, used as a means of encouraging others to follow. Such unilateral action may also be taken for moral reasons and as a means of diminishing the chances of being attacked, particularly as regards nuclear and chemical weapons.

Disturbances (1935–8)
A series of strikes and riots which took place in the British West Indies, sometimes known as 'The Troubles'. These had their roots in post-1918 socio-economic deprivation and this was exacerbated by the **Great Depression** after 1929 and the lack of political representation in the Crown Colonies. Discontent surfaced first in Belize and Jamaica (1934), spread to the sugar workers in St Kitts and Guyana (1935) and culminated in serious disorder in Trinidad, Jamaica and Barbados (1937–8). In Trinidad **Butler**'s oratory provoked the oilfield workers, in Barbados Clement Payne's deportation led to the deaths of 14 people and in Jamaica the Jamaica Worker's Union of **Bustamante** brought rioting to the sugar estates and docks and the arrest of 700 people. Stung into action by the degree of unrest, the imperial government set up the **Moyne Commission**.

Djilas, Milovan (1911–)
Yugoslav politician and writer. Born in Montenegro, he was active in the outlawed Yugoslav Communist Party in the 1930s and was subsequently imprisoned (1933–6). He was, with **Tito**, a remarkable partisan leader during **World War II**. In the post-war government, he was Vice-President of Yugoslavia but concern for doctrine led him to criticize the communist system practised in Yugoslavia. Expelled from the party in 1954 and imprisoned (1956–61 and 1962–6), he was released under amnesty. He was formally rehabilitated by the Yugoslav authorities in 1989.

DNVP (*Deutsch nationale Volks partei*, 'German National People's Party')
German political party. Founded in late Nov 1918 by a coalition of conservative politicians, the DNVP came to represent much of the old, German imperial élite. It never accepted the legitimacy of the **Weimar Republic**, cooperated sporadically and unwillingly in coalition governments, and pursued particularly virulent campaigns against any compromise agreements between Germany and her erstwhile enemies. In Jan 1933 the DNVP entered a coalition with the **Nazi Party** which paved the way for **Hitler**'s overthrow of the republic, before dissolving itself in the middle of that year.

Dobi, Istvan (1898–1968)
Hungarian politician. He spent the earlier part of his life as a day labourer on various characteristically large estates. He had a brief experience as a soldier in the Hungarian Red Army in 1919, but it was not until 1935 that he joined the Independent Smallholders Party. During and after **World War II** he rose within its ranks and, as leader of its left wing, became Prime Minister within the predominantly communist government of 1949. He remained in office until 1952 during the worst of the Stalinist

purges, and was president of the state council through to 1967, including during the **Hungarian Uprising** of 1956.

Dobrynin, Anatoly Fedorovich (1919–)
Soviet diplomat and politician. He worked as an engineer at an aircraft plant during **World War II**, then joined the diplomatic service in 1946. He served as Counsellor at the Soviet Embassy in Washington (1952–5), assistant to the Minister for Foreign Affairs (1955–7), Under-Secretary at the **UN** (1957–9) and head of the USSR's American Department (1960–1), before being appointed the Soviet ambassador to Washington (1962–86). Dobrynin played an important part in resolving the **Cuban Missile Crisis** in 1962 and was influential in promoting Soviet–US entente. A member of the Communist Party (CPSU) from 1945, he became a full member of its Central Committee in 1971. In 1986, the new Soviet leader, Mikhail **Gorbachev**, appointed him Secretary for Foreign Affairs and head of the International Department. He retired in 1988.

Doctors' Plot (1952–3)
Alleged plot by nine doctors, seven of them Jewish and all paid by the USA, to get rid of several Soviet politicians. It was a fabrication by the secret police and was intended to prepare the ground for a public trial that would herald a new round of **Stalin**'s purges. Anti-Semitism and anti-Americanism were judged to be good bases on which to win support for removing Stalin's opponents. Fortunately Stalin died, and Nikita **Khrushchev** subsequently used this and other evidence to condemn his entire behaviour.

Dodecanese
A group of 12 islands including Cos, Patmos and Rhodes and several islets in the south-east Aegean, off the coast of Turkey and since antiquity inhabited by **Greeks**. In 1911, while still subject to the Ottoman Porte, the islands were occupied by Italy. The Treaties of **London** (1915) allowed Italy to keep the islands and they remained an Italian possession until the end of **World War II** when they were ceded to Greece.

Doe, Samuel Kenyon (1951–90)
Liberian soldier and politician. He joined the army as a private in 1969, reaching the rank of sergeant in 1975. In Apr 1980 he led a coup of junior officers in which President **Tolbert** was killed. In 1981 he made himself general and army Commander-in-Chief and established a party (the National Democratic Party of Liberia) in 1984 under whose aegis he narrowly won the 1985 presidential election. Widespread dissatisfaction with his rule generated several opposition groups and a virtual civil war erupted in 1989, which the **Economic Community of West African States**

(ECOWAS) attempted to mediate. Doe was killed in the ensuing internal struggle for power.

Doi Takako (1929–)
Japanese politician. After lecturing on the Japanese constitution at Doshisha University, she entered the Diet in 1969 and since 1986 has been the leader of the Japanese Socialist Party, the first woman party leader in Japan. In 1989, she became the Leader of the Upper House.

Doihara Kenji (1883–1948)
Japanese army general. He served in China (1913–20) and in 1931 became Director of Military Intelligence at Mukden in Manchuria. Doihara was a key participant in the Japanese military's plans to overrun Manchuria, which culminated in the creation of the Japanese puppet-state of **Manzhuguo** in 1933. He then became involved in a relentless campaign to expand Japan's influence in north China, a campaign that was ultimately to lead to full-scale war with China in 1937. In 1948 Doihara was executed as a Class A war criminal.

Dole, Elizabeth Hanford (1936–)
US government official and charity administrator, the wife of Robert J **Dole**. She became a lawyer and worked in various posts in Washington, DC, including that of Deputy Director of the Office of Consumer Affairs in the White House (1971–3). She was secretary of the US Department of Transport under **Reagan** (1983–7), and of the US Department of Labor (1989–90) in the **Bush** administration. In 1991 she resigned to take up the presidency of the American Red Cross.

Dole, Robert J (1923–)
US Senator. He trained as a lawyer, entered the US House of Representatives as a Republican (1961–9), and became member of the US Senate from Kansas in 1969. In 1976 he stood as a Republican vice-presidential candidate alongside **Ford**. Between 1984 and 1986 he was majority leader of the Senate, and later minority leader, and in 1993 became senior Republican representative in Washington. He ran unsuccessfully for presidential nomination in 1980 and 1988. He is married to Elizabeth Hanford **Dole**.

Dollfuss, Engelbert (1892–1934)
Austrian politician. He studied in Vienna and Berlin, and became leader of the Christian Socialist Party. As Chancellor (1932–4), he suspended parliamentary government, drove the socialists into revolt and militarily crushed them (Feb 1934). In July 1934 an attempted Nazi putsch in Vienna culminated in his assassination. ▷ **Nazi Party**

DOM-TOM (*Départements d'outre-mer* and *Territoires d'outre-mer*, 'Overseas Departments and Territories')

French colonial possessions which are now treated as being an integral part of French metropolitan territory, electing representatives to the French National Assembly, etc. They were part of the **French Union** (*Union française*), established in 1946, renamed the *Communauté* ('Community') in 1958, and are all that remained when the other colonies and associated states (protectorates) became independent.

Domela Nieuwenhuis, Ferdinand (1846–1919)

Dutch socialist and anarchist leader. Elected to parliament in 1888–91, he subsequently rejected the parliamentary way, and became an anarchist, co-founding the National Labour Secretariat in 1893 as a socialist trade-union federation. Often ridiculed for his extreme views, he was nonetheless one of the founders of the modern Dutch socialist labour movement. He had numerous international socialist contacts, and the widespread emotional support he enjoyed amongst working people was shown at his funeral when tens of thousands poured into Amsterdam for the occasion.

domino theory

A strategic theory first used by President **Eisenhower** in 1954, reflecting the view that, as neighbouring states are so interdependent, the collapse of one will spread to the others. Originally referring to the belief that if one country became Communist, others would follow, the theory relates to military collapse, as well as insurgence, and has been used to justify intervention in a country not immediately threatened, but whose neighbour is. It was an important element in the US policy of intervention in South-East Asia in the 1960s and 1970s, and in Central America in the 1980s. ▷ **Vietnam War**

Dönitz, Karl (1891–1980)

German Nazi politician and naval commander. He entered the submarine service of the German Navy in 1916, and became a staunch advocate of **U-boat** warfare. He planned **Hitler**'s U-boat fleet, was made its commander in 1936, and in 1943 became Commander-in-Chief of the German Navy. Becoming *Führer* on the death of Hitler, he was responsible for the final surrender to the Allies, and in 1946 was sentenced to 10 years' imprisonment for war crimes. ▷ **World War II**

Donoughmore Commission

A committee sent by the British government to Ceylon in 1927 to examine the Ceylonese constitution and recommend reforms. These recommendations were reluctantly accepted by Ceylonese political leaders and served as the basis for the new constitution of 1931. The reforms replaced communal electorates by territorial constituencies and extended the franchise to all resident adults. An assembly or state council with legislative and executive powers was also established under the recommendations of the Donoughmore Commission. The new constitution was in effect until 1946.

Dopolavoro (*Opera Nazionale Dopolavoro*)
In Italy, the national network of clubs and other recreational and welfare centres established by the fascists in 1925. The membership of the *Dopolavoro* (literally, 'after work') expanded massively to include 4 million by 1939. The Dopolavoro provided bars, sports facilities, libraries, dances and concerts as well as organizing holidays and was undoubtedly one of the most successful and popular innovations of the fascist state. ▷ **Balilla; fascism; Fascist Party**

Doriot, Jacques (1898–1945)
French politician. A metalworker, communist Deputy (1924) and Mayor of St Denis, a working-class suburb of Paris, he was excluded from the **Communist Party** in 1934 for advocating a **Popular Front** before it was adopted as party policy. He then co-founded the *Parti populaire français* ('French People's Party'), regarded as the only fascist-type party in France to have much popular support. However, it had already entered a period of crisis in 1938. During **World War II** he collaborated with the Germans, organizing the LVF (*Légion des voluntaires français contre le bolchévisme*, 'League of French Volunteers against Bolshevism') to fight on the Eastern Front. At the liberation he fled to Germany, where he was killed in an Allied air raid. ▷ **collaboration** (France)

Dos Santos, Jose Eduardo (1942–)
Angolan nationalist and politician. He joined the **MPLA** in 1961 and was forced into exile in Zaire, where he founded the MPLA Youth League. In 1963 he went to the USSR to study petroleum engineering and telecommunications and then to Lisbon to study medicine. He returned to Angola in 1970 to participate in the war of liberation, being responsible for the MPLA's medical services. A close confident of Agostinho **Neto**, he became Foreign Minister on independence and First Deputy Prime Minister, Planning Minister and head of the National Planning Commission. When Neto died in 1979, he succeeded to the presidency and, conscious that the cost of fighting **UNITA** with its South African backers was destroying Angola, negotiated the withdrawal of Cuban and South African forces in 1989 and then a ceasefire between MPLA and UNITA.

Douglas, William Orville (1898–1980)
US judge. Educated at Whitman College and Columbia University, he was a law professor at Yale, then a member (1936) and chairman (1937–39) of the Securities and Exchange Commission. A strong supporter of the New Deal legislation, he was appointed to the Supreme Court in 1939 to replace Louis **Brandeis**. As a justice he strongly supported civil rights and liberties, and guarantees of freedom of speech. He wrote *We the Judges* (1956), *A Living Bill of Rights* (1961) and autobiographical works and many books on his travels.

Doumer, Paul (1857–1932)
French politician. He was a working jeweller, journalist, Deputy (1888), and then Governor-General of French **Indochina** from 1897 to 1902 (where he is credited with the creation of the modern French colonial state). Doumer was President of the Chamber (1905–6), of the Senate (1927–31), and of the Third Republic (1931–2). He was shot by a Russian émigré, Gorgalov. ▷ **Republic, Third** (France)

Doumergue, Gaston (1863–1937)
French politician and first Protestant President of the French Republic (1924–31). He was Prime Minister in 1913–14 and 1934 (when he failed to carry constitutional changes); and President of the Senate 1923–4. ▷ **Republic, Third** (France)

Dowding, Hugh (Caswell Tremenheere), 1st Baron (1882–1970)
British air chief marshal. He served in the Royal Artillery and the Royal Flying Corps in **World War I**. As Commander-in-Chief of Fighter Command (1936–40), he organized the air defence of Britain during **World War II**, which resulted in the victorious Battle of **Britain** (1940). He retired in 1942 and was created a peer in 1943.

Draft
US conscription. It was introduced first in 1777 when the number of volunteers failed to meet the quotas demanded by the **Continental Congress**. It was introduced for **World War I** with the passage of the Selective Service Act of 1917, and again in 1940 in anticipation of the United States' entry into **World War II**, and again in various crises such as the invasion of Korea, the **Berlin Airlift**, and the **Cuban Missile Crisis**. Much of the opposition to the **Vietnam War**, especially the student protest, centred on the draft. Eventually offenders numbered 570 000, so that under President Richard **Nixon** a fairer lottery system was introduced in 1969, with the draft itself being ended in 1973.

Drapeau, Jean (1916–)

Canadian politician. He became Mayor of Montreal in 1954, backed both by those wanting improved municipal services and those who demanded the elimination of gambling and prostitution. Drapeau sought more autonomy for the city and when he was thwarted by **Duplessis** he became a strong critic of the provincial Premier. When the **October Crisis** occurred in 1970 Drapeau, along with the Montreal chief of police and Robert **Bourassa**, asked the federal government to implement the **War Measures Act**. When Pierre Laporte's body was found, Montreal public opinion was so hardened that Drapeau was given 92 per cent of the votes in the following city elections. His administration backed Expo 67 (when General de **Gaulle** delivered his notorious 'Vive le Québec libre' speech), and Montreal's successful bid to hold the 1976 Olympic Games, and although the financial entanglements were still being unravelled in 1980, the increase in jobs certainly benefited the working population.

Dravida Munnetra Kazhagam (DMK)

A Tamil regional nationalist party and now one of the two main political parties in the southern Indian state of Tamil Nadu. The DMK traces its origins to the Dravidian movement of the 19c, as well as to the Non-Brahmin movement of the 20c. It stands primarily for the promotion of Tamil regional cultural identity. After the death of its leader C N Annadurai in 1969, the DMK split into its two present offshoots, the DMK and the AIADMK. The AIADMK ruled Tamil Nadu from 1977 to 1987. The DMK was then briefly returned to power with Karunanidhi as Chief Minister, but lost heavily in the 1991 elections.

Drees, Willem (1886–1988)

Dutch politician. After a short period working in a bank, he moved to the Hague as a government stenographer and then entered politics, joining the Socialist Democratic Workers' Party and becoming its chairman in 1911. He sat in the Second Chamber from 1933 until the German invasion of 1940, after which he played an important part in the resistance movement. In 1947, as Minister of Social Affairs, he introduced the state pension and then became Prime Minister (1948–58). A modest, puritanical man, he became one of the most durable figures in Dutch politics.

Drees, Willem (1922–)

Dutch economist and politician. The son of Willem **Drees** (1886–1988), after graduating at the Netherlands School of Economics, Rotterdam, he joined the International Monetary Fund (IMF) in Washington (1947–50), and then worked in the Dutch embassy in Jakarta (1950–5). He returned to the Netherlands as Director of the Budget in the Ministry of Finance, as well as being Professor of Public Finance at Rotterdam.

Dreyfus, Alfred (1859–1935)
French Jewish army officer. An artillery captain on the General Staff, in 1893–4 he was falsely charged with delivering defence secrets to the Germans. He was court-martialled and transported to Devil's Island, French Guiana. The efforts of his wife and friends to prove him innocent provoked a vigorous response from militarists and anti-Semites, and deeply divided the French intellectual and political world. After the case was tried again (1899), he was found guilty but pardoned, and in 1906 the verdict was reversed. Proof of his innocence came when German military documents were uncovered in 1930.

Du Bois, William Edward Burghardt (1868–1963)
US civil rights activist, historian and sociologist. He studied at Fisk, Harvard, and Berlin, and in his writings explored the history and lives of black Americans. In politics he campaigned for full equality, opposing the tactics of Booker T **Washington**. He helped found the National Association for the Advancement of Colored People (**NAACP**), and in his later years lived in Ghana, where he died.

Duan Qirui (Tuan Ch'i-jui) (1865–1926)
Chinese politician. He took up a military career, rising to prominence as a protégé of **Yuan Shikai**, becoming his Prime Minister and remaining in office after his death (1916). His aim was to reunite the country, but his resort to force and his increasing dependence on Japan proved highly unpopular in China, and the Northern generals facing the Southern Nationalist regime refused to fight. His decision to force them to obey plunged China into the successive civil wars of its 'period of warlordism' (1916–25), in which four groups fought for control. Defeated, he retired from politics in 1920, except for a brief return in 1924. ▷ **warlords**

Duarte, José Napoléon (1925–90)
El Salvador politician. Trained as a civil engineer in the USA, he founded the Christian Democratic Party (PDC) in 1960. After serving as Mayor of El Salvador (1964–70), he was elected President in 1972 but was soon impeached and exiled for seven years in Venezuela. He returned and in 1980 regained the presidency with US backing. He lost the 1982 election and for two years witnessed a fierce struggle between right- and left-wing elements. He returned as President in 1984 but in 1988, stricken by terminal cancer, was forced to resign.

Dubček, Alexander (1921–92)
Czechoslovak politician. After living with his parents in the USSR from 1925 to 1938, he returned home and joined the Communist Party in 1939, worked underground during **World War II** and took part in the Slovak uprising in 1944. He rose through various Party and parliamentary offices

to become a full member of the Presidium in 1963 and, on the forced resignation of Antonín Novotný, First Secretary in Jan 1968. He began to introduce a series of far-reaching reforms, including the abolition of censorship and increased freedom of speech. His political liberalization policy during the **Prague Spring** provoked Soviet hostility to what he called **Socialism with a Human Face** and led to the occupation of Czechoslovakia by **Warsaw Pact** forces (Aug 1968). In 1969 he was replaced as First Secretary by Gustav Husák. He became President of the Federal Assembly for a few months in 1969, but was then expelled from the Presidium and deprived of Party membership in 1970. In 1989, following the popular uprising and the resignation of the communist government, he became Chairman of the new Federal Assembly. Not quite as radical as the post-1989 reformers, he did not play a prominent political role and, before he could develop one, he died as the result of a car accident.

Dubrovnik, Republic of

A wealthy independent city state after 1358, when it ceased to acknowledge Venetian suzerainty, Dubrovnik was governed by an oligarchy of noble families. The Congress of Vienna (1814–15) granted the republic to Austria and, as part of the province of Dalmatia, it remained subject to Vienna until 1918, when it became part of the Kingdom of Serbs, Croats and Slovenes (later Yugoslavia).

Dulles, John Foster (1888–1959)

US politician. Educated at Princeton and the Sorbonne, he became a lawyer. During **World War II** he advocated a world governmental organization, and in 1945 advised at the Charter Conference of the **UN**, thereafter becoming US delegate to the General Assembly. In 1953 he became US Secretary of State, and was known chiefly for his aggresssive anticommunist rhetoric and his policy of **brinkmanship**.

Duma

The name given to various forms of political assembly in prerevolutionary Russia, such as the medieval 'Boyars' Council'. Municipal *dumas* (town councils) similar to the rural *zemstvos* were introduced as part of local government reforms in 1870. After the Russian **Revolution of 1905**, the State Duma, a quasi-parliamentary body, was established with progressively limited constitutional powers. Four State Dumas were elected between 1906 and the 1917 revolution, when the institution was abolished. ▷ **Russian Revolution**

Dunkirk, Evacuation of (27 May–3 June 1940)

The evacuation of the **British Expeditionary Force** and other Allied troops from the port of Dunkirk in northern France, isolated after the capitulation of the Belgian army to the north and the advance of German tanks and troops to the south. The evacuation, in which approximately 200 000 British and some 140 000 French troops were safely conveyed to England, was effected with the use of hundreds of naval vessels and small civilian craft, and aided by cover from British air fighter patrols and an unruffled English Channel.

Duplessis, Maurice le Noblet (1890–1959)
Canadian politician. He led the **Union Nationale** to power in Quebec in 1936, gaining power through a methodical exploitation of *nationalisme* and fear of anglicization; yet he encouraged further encroachments by US corporations on Quebec's economic life. His campaign against radical reformers gained him the support of the Catholic Church, which he retained almost throughout his political career. His attitude towards labour was expressed in the notorious **Padlock Act** (1937) which crippled the **CCF**, but it was his antagonistic attitude towards federal government (which he claimed was invading provincial rights through the **War Measures Act**) which contributed most to his defeat in 1939, when Ernest **Lapointe** and other French-Canadian ministers threatened to resign if he was returned to office. He did regain power in 1944, defeating both the incumbent Liberals under Adélard **Godbout** and the extremist **Bloc Populaire**, and maintained his pre-war policies. An alliance between labour, professionals, academics and even some churchmen, eventually succeeded in demonstrating the scale of corruption in his government and although Duplessis himself died suddenly in 1959, the *Union Nationale* was defeated by the Liberals in 1960.

Durcansky, Ferdinand (1906–74)
Slovak Populist Party politician. Upset by the union of Czechs and Slovaks in a single state in 1918, he was active in the 1930s in trying to negotiate Slovak independence. After the **Munich Agreement** he visited **Goering** and others in Berlin and was encouraged to make trouble for the rump Czechoslovak government in Prague. Eventually **Hitler** virtually ordered him and his superior, **Tiso**, to declare independence: this was the signal for the Nazis to sweep into Prague in Mar 1939 and establish the **Bohemian Protectorate**. Durcansky was immediately made Slovak Foreign Minister, although about a year later he was dismissed as insufficiently compliant. He was condemned to death *in absentia* in 1947, and spent the remainder of his life abroad.

Durruti, Buenaventura (1896–1936)
Spanish revolutionary anarchist. He was the most prominent violent activist to emerge from the ferocious urban guerrilla warfare of 1919–23 in Barcelona between the employers (backed by the state) and the **CNT**. Exiled in Europe and South America during the period 1923–31, Durruti was the principal leader of the revolutionary **FAI**. During the Second

Republic, he agitated for an immediate revolution from below, and was frequently jailed. He led the anarchist militia in the **Spanish Civil War** until he was shot dead in Nov 1936 in mysterious circumstances, probably by a Nationalist sniper. His funeral procession in Barcelona was the last great demonstration of strength by the anarchist movement. ▷ **Republic, Second** (Spain)

Dutch East Indies

A name applied to Indonesia until 1945, when **Sukarno** declared independence: the area included the islands of Java, Sumatra, the Celebes, most of Borneo, the Moluccas, and Bali. The Dutch recognized Indonesia's independence in 1949.

Duvalier, Jean-Claude ('Baby Doc') (1951–)

Haitian politician, son of François ('Papa Doc') **Duvalier**. After studying law at the University of Haiti, he followed his father into politics. At the age of 20 he became President for life, ruling, as had his father, through a private army. In 1986 he was deposed in a military coup led by General Henri Namphrey and went into exile in Grasse, in the south of France.

Duvalier, François ('Papa Doc') (1907–71)

Haitian politician. He held power from 1957 until his death, ruling in an increasingly arbitrary fashion. His regime saw the creation of the civilian militia known as the Tonton Macoute, and the exile of many people. He became President for life in 1964, and was succeeded in this post by his son, Jean-Claude ('Baby Doc') **Duvalier**, whose regime lasted until 1986.

DVP (*Deutsche Volks partei*, 'German People's Party')

German political party. Founded in Dec 1918, the DVP represented the interests of right-wing liberalism and heavy industry in the **Weimar Republic**. Although its attitude to Weimar was equivocal, its leader, **Stresemann**, served continuously as German Foreign Minister from 1923 until his death in Oct 1929 in which post he did much to revise the more onerous provisions of the Treaty of **Versailles**. During the early 1930s, the DVP lost most of its electoral support and on 4 July 1933 the party was wound up.

Dzerzhinsky, Felix Edmundovich (1877–1926)

Russian revolutionary, of Polish descent. In 1897 he was exiled to Siberia for political agitation, fought in the Russian **Revolution of 1905**, and in 1917, as one of the organizers of the coup d'état, became chairman of the secret police and a member of the Bolshevik Central Committee until his death. After 1921 he also reorganized the railway system, and was chairman of the Supreme Economic Council (1924–6), trying to combine industrialization with good relations with the peasantry.

E

EAM (*Ethnikón Apeleftherotikón Métopon*, 'National Liberation Front')
A coalition of left-wing parties in Greece during **World War II**, it was founded and dominated by the **KKE** (Communist Party of Greece) which hoped to take power upon liberation. EAM organized a military wing, **ELAS**, established a system of government, education, health care and justice in the areas it liberated, and in Mar 1944 created the Political Committee of National Liberation (PEEA) which challenged the Greek government-in-exile. By the end of the war, the EAM enjoyed support throughout Greece and, bitterly opposed to the return of **George II**, it continued to demand a plebiscite to decide the future constitution of Greece. By 1945, dissension among its various left-wing members weakened EAM and its role was superseded by the KKE, which remained the strongest party on the Left. With armed bands at their command, the communists, royalists and republicans embarked on civil war, which lasted until 1949. ▷ **Aris Veloukhiotis; EDES; EKKA; Greek Civil War; Plastiras, Nikolaos; Vafiadis, Markos; Zachariadis, Nikos; Zervas, Napoleon**

Eanes, António Ramalho dos Santos (1935–)
Portuguese general and politician. For his role in quashing the Far Left at the end of the Revolution of Apr 1974–Nov 1975, he was promoted from an unknown colonel to Chief of Staff. With his remote, austere and humourless manner, and his dark glasses, he often appeared to be a hangover from the **Salazar** regime. In 1976 he was elected President as the principal non-communist candidate. During his 10-year presidency, the laconic and enigmatic Eanes did much to uphold the new democratic regime amidst the debilitating squabbles of the political parties, and his essential honesty won him wide popular support. Politically, he proved to be left-of-centre (though he drifted rightwards), and was distrusted by the Right. From 1986 to 1987 he was leader of the Portuguese Democratic Renewal Party.

Easter Rising (24–9 Apr 1916)
A rebellion of Irish nationalists in Dublin, organized by two revolutionary groups, the Irish Republican Brotherhood led by Patrick **Pearse** (1879–1916), and **Sinn Féin** under James Connolly (1870–1916). The focal point of the rebellion was the seizing of the General Post Office. The rising was put down and several leaders were executed. The extent of the reprisals increased support for the nationalist cause in Ireland.

Eastern Question
A complex set of diplomatic problems affecting 18c, 19c and early 20c Europe. It was created by the slowly declining power of the **Ottoman Empire**, the emergence of the Balkan nations and nationalism, and the ambitions in south-east Europe of the Great Powers, especially Russia and Austria (later Austria-Hungary).

Eban, Abba (1915–)
Israeli diplomat and politician. Born in South Africa, he was educated in England and taught oriental languages at Cambridge before serving as a liaison officer at Allied HQ during **World War II**. In 1944 he worked in the Middle East Arab Centre in Jerusalem and in 1948 was Israeli **UN** representative in New York, then ambassador in Washington (1950–9). He returned to Israel where he won a seat in the Knesset and joined David **Ben-Gurion**'s government. Between 1959 and 1974 he held several posts, under various prime ministers, and was Foreign Minister from 1966 to 1974. In the 1989 general election he was unexpectedly defeated by the opposition leader, George Price. ▷ **Mapai Party**

Ebert, Friedrich (1871–1925)
German politician. He started life as a saddler, then became a journalist on a Social Democratic newspaper and **Reichstag** member (1912). Chairman of his party (1913), he was a leader in the **Revolution of 1918**–19; his firm line against groups on the far left and deals with the old order to achieve this have provoked much controversy. He was the first President of the German Republic (1919–25).

EC (European Community)
A community of 12 states in Western Europe created for the purpose of achieving economic and political integration. It comprises three communities. The first of these was the European Steel and Coal Community, established in 1952 under the Treaty of Paris by France, West Germany, Italy, Belgium, the Netherlands, and Luxembourg. It created common institutions for regulating the coal and steel industries under a common framework of law and institutions, thereby producing the first breach in the principle of national sovereignty. In the early 1950s, unsuccessful attempts were made to establish a European Defence Community and a European Political Community. In 1958, under the Treaty of Rome, the six states established the European Economic Community and the European Atomic Energy Community, which provided for collaboration in the civilian sector of nuclear power. Six members have been added to the original six: Denmark, Ireland, and the UK (1973); Greece (1981); and Portugal and Spain (1986). Turkey is seeking to become a member. To develop and oversee the policies of economic and political integration there are a number of supranational community institutions: the

Commission, the Council, the European Parliament, and the European Court of Justice. While the Community has grown in the 1970s and 1980s and continues to progress towards economic integration, a political union seems still a distant possibility. ▷ **EEC; EU**

Ecevit, Bülent (1925–)
Turkish politician. After working as a government official and a journalist, he became an MP for the centre-left Republican People's Party in 1957. He was Minister of Labour, then in 1966 became Secretary-General of his party and subsequently (1972) Chairman. He headed a coalition government in 1974 and during office ordered the invasion of Cyprus. He was Prime Minister again in 1977 and in 1978–9, when he imposed martial law on Turkey. After the military coup of 1980, he was imprisoned twice for criticizing the military regime.

Economic Community of West African States (ECOWAS)
An organization formed (May 1975) by 15 West African states through the Treaty of Lagos: Benin, the Gambia, Ghana, Guinea, Guinea-Bissau, Ivory Coast (Cote d'Ivoire), Liberia, Mali, Mauritania, Niger, Nigeria, Senegal, Sierra Leone, Togo, and Upper Volta (now Burkina Faso). Cape Verde joined in 1977. It is based in Abuja, Nigeria. Its principle objectives are the ending of restrictions on trade between the signatories, the establishment of a common customs tariff, the harmonization of economic and industrial policies, and equalization of the levels of development of member states. In 1990 it set up a Standing Mediation Committee to mediate disputes between member states. It has also supported the free movement of peoples and has overseen a collaborative military involvement in Liberia.

Eda Saburo (1907–77)
Japanese politician. Active in the pre-war Farmers' Movement, Eda joined the Japan Socialist Party (JSP) in 1946 and was elected to the House of Councillors (upper house) in 1950. During the 1960s he served as Secretary-General of the JSP, when he incurred the wrath of the party's dominant left wing for suggesting a shift in the party's approach of confrontation with the existing capitalist system to one of promoting gradual change within the system.

Edde, Emile (1886–1949)
Lebanese nationalist and lawyer. A Maronite, he spent **World War I** in France, having been sentenced to death *in absentia* by the Turks. After the war he was adviser to Picot's deputy, Robert Coulondre, thereby acquiring considerable prestige in the eyes of the Lebanese. Disagreement between the two meant, however, that this arrangement did not last long. Edde, though, was destined to play a leading part in Lebanese politics.

In 1924 he was elected President of the Representative Council of Greater Lebanon, which was dissolved by the French High-Commissioner early the following year. By 1927 a rival to Edde's position had emerged in Bishara al-Khouri: where Edde was more at home with the French language and culture, al-Khouri, although a French-speaker, had excellent Arabic; where Edde was outspoken, al-Khouri tended to be reserved. Both politicians, however, regarded Lebanon as more a part of the Mediterranean culture than of a greater Arab world. Elected to the presidency again in 1936, Edde managed to survive, relying heavily on French support, until 1941; at this point, however, wartime shortages became too much for his already weak regime, and he was forced to resign. Edde was again active in public life from 1942, establishing his Francophile following as the National Bloc. However, despite some sympathy amongst the Christian element of the population, Edde's stance made him out of touch with the country as a whole.

Eden (of Avon), Sir (Robert) Anthony, 1st Earl (1897–1977)
British politician. He became a Conservative MP in 1923, and was Foreign Under-Secretary (1931), Lord Privy Seal (1933), and Foreign Secretary (1935), resigning in 1938 over differences with Neville **Chamberlain**. In **World War II** he was first Dominions Secretary, then Secretary of State for War, and Foreign Secretary (1940–5). Again Foreign Secretary (1951–5), he was involved with the negotiations in Korea and Indo-China, and the 1954 Geneva Summit Conference. He succeeded Winston **Churchill** as Prime Minister (1955–7), and in 1956 ordered British forces (in collaboration with the French and Israelis) to occupy the Suez Canal Zone. His action was condemned by the **UN** and caused a bitter controversy in Britain which did not subside when he ordered a withdrawal. In failing health, he resigned abruptly in 1957. He was created an earl in 1961. ▷ **Conservative Party** (UK)

EDES (*Ellinikos Dimokratikos Ethnikos Stratos*, 'National Republican Greek League')
One of the three major Greek resistance groups operating after the German invasion of Greece (6 Apr 1941). Formed during the winter 1941–2, its leader in Greece was the republican Napoleon **Zervas**. It rivalled **EAM/ELAS** in power and influence, and was favoured by the British government as a counterweight to the communists. It cooperated with Special Operations Executive and EAM/ELAS in Sep 1942, cutting German supply lines over the Gorgopotamos viaduct and, following the National Bands Agreement (summer 1943), it took part in Operation Animals. With the withdrawal of the Axis forces, conflict between the rival resistance groups grew and EDES was forced from the field by EAM/ELAS. ▷ **EKKA; Plastiras, Nikolaos; Vafiadis, Markos; Zachariadis, Nikos**

Edinburgh, Prince Philip, Duke of (1921–)
The husband of Queen Elizabeth II, the son of Prince Andrew of Greece and Princess Alice of Battenberg, born at Corfu. He became a naturalized British subject in 1947, when he was married to the Princess Elizabeth (20 Nov). In 1956 he began the Duke of Edinburgh Award Scheme to foster the leisure activities of young people. ▷ **Elizabeth II**

Edward VII (1841–1910)
King of the UK (1901/10). The eldest son of Queen **Victoria**, in 1863 he married Alexandra, the eldest daughter of Christian IX of Denmark. They had three sons and three daughters: Albert Victor, Duke of Clarence; George; Louise, Princess Royal; Victoria; Maud, who married **Haakon VII** of Norway; and Alexander. As Prince of Wales, his behaviour led him into several social scandals, and the Queen excluded him from affairs of state. As King, he carried out several visits to Continental capitals which strove to allay international animosities. ▷ **George V**

Edward VIII (1894–1972)
King of the UK (Jan/Dec 1936), and the eldest son of King **George V**. He joined the navy and, during **World War I**, the army, travelled much, and achieved considerable popularity. He succeeded his father in Jan 1936, but abdicated (11 Dec) in the face of opposition to his proposed marriage to Mrs Ernest Simpson, a commoner who had been twice divorced. He was then given the title of Duke of Windsor, and the marriage took place in France in 1937. The Duke and Duchess of Windsor lived in Paris, apart from a period in the Bahamas (1940–5), where Edward was Governor.

EEC (European Economic Community)
An association within the European Community, established in 1958 after the Treaties of Rome (1957), often referred to as the Common Market. It is essentially a customs union, with a common external tariff and a common market with the removal of barriers to trade among the members. In addition it has a number of common policies, the most important of which is the **Common Agricultural Policy**, providing for external tariffs to protect domestic agriculture and mechanisms for price support. The cost of support to agriculture takes up about 70 per cent of the European Community's budget and has shown an alarming propensity to grow. Reform of agricultural policy has been on the agenda for a number of years, but many member governments are reluctant to entertain the wrath of the farming vote which remains sizable in their countries. There are common policies for fisheries, regional development, industrial intervention, and economic and social affairs. There is also a European Monetary System, which regulates exchange rate movements among the member states' currencies in an attempt to achieve monetary

stability. In 1986 the Single European Act was passed, allowing for the completion of the process of creating a common market within the community by the beginning of 1993. ▷ **EC (European Community)**

EFTA (European Free Trade Association)

An association originally of seven Western European states who were not members of the European Economic Community (**EEC**), intended as a counter to the EEC; it was established in 1959 under the Stockholm Convention. The members (Austria, Denmark, Norway, Portugal, Sweden, Switzerland, and the UK) agreed to eliminate over a period of time trade restrictions between them, without having to bring into line individual tariffs and trade policies with other countries. Agriculture was excluded from the agreement, although individual arrangements were permitted. Both the UK (1973) and Portugal (1986) left to join the EEC, but there has been a free trade agreement between the remaining EFTA countries and the European Community, and considerable trade between the two groupings. Finland joined in 1985. ▷ **EC (European Community)**

Egypt

A republic in north-east Africa, a British protectorate from 1914, which declared its independence in 1922. It was used as a base for Allied forces during **World War II**. King Farouk was deposed by Nasser in 1952, and the following year Egypt was declared a republic. An attack on Israel, followed by Israeli invasion in 1967, resulted in the loss of the Sinai Peninsula and of control over part of the Suez Canal (regained following negotiations in the 1970s). In 1981 **Sadat** was assassinated. Relations with Arab nations were strained as a result of the agreement with Israel but improved throughout the 1980s. The government announced in 1992 that it had uncovered an Islamic fundamentalist plot to found an Islamic State, and there were violent attacks and clashes between Muslims and Coptic Christians in the early 1990s.

Ehrenburg, Ilya Grigorevich (1891–1967)

Soviet novelist and journalist. Born in Kiev, he was in exile in Paris before 1917 and returned to fight against the communists. Yet he was allowed back again in 1923 and wrote novels in praise of the system that were accepted abroad. In the **Khrushchev** period he wrote in favour of an East–West thaw and managed to open the eyes of the Soviet public to some genuine truths about the West.

Eichmann, Karl Adolf (1906–62)

Austrian **SS** officer. A fanatical Nazi and anti-Semite, he became a member of the SS in 1932 and organized anti-Jewish activities, particularly their deportation to concentration camps. Captured by US forces in 1945, he escaped from prison some months later, having kept his identity hidden, and in 1950 reached Argentina. He was traced by Israeli agents and in 1960, seized, taken to Israel, condemned for 'crimes against humanity' and executed.

Eighth Route Army
The Chinese 'Red Army', formed by the communists in 1927. It was given this name in 1937 when it entered into an uneasy alliance with the Nationalist Army of **Chiang Kai-shek** against the Japanese invaders of China.

Einaudi, Luigi (1874–1961)
Italian politician. Professor of Public Finance in Turin (1902–49), he was a Senator (1915–45) and President of Italy (1948–55). His most important role was as Budget Minister (a post specially created for him in 1947 by **De Gasperi**): he devised a rigorous deflationary policy of tight monetary control and high interest rates which was not abandoned until 1950. While this arguably slowed Italy's post-war industrial recovery and certainly contributed to high unemployment, it also helped to revive confidence in the lira and to lay the foundation for growth in the post-1950 era.

Eire
Name superseding '**Irish Free State**' under the Irish constitution of 1937 which declared the country a sovereign, independent and democratic state with a directly elected President, a restored but weakened Senate and a **Dáil Eireann** elected by proportional representation. ▷ **De Valera, Eamon; Irish Republic**

Eisenhower, Dwight David ('Ike') (1890–1969)
US general and 34th President. He graduated from the US Military Academy at West Point, and by 1939 had become chief military assistant to General Douglas **MacArthur** in the Philippines. In 1942 he commanded Allied forces for the amphibious descent on French North Africa. His ability to coordinate the Allied forces and staff led to his selection as Supreme Commander of the Allied Expeditionary Force which spearheaded the 1944 invasion of Europe. In 1950 he was made Supreme Commander of the NATO forces in Europe.In 1952 the popularity that he had gained as a war hero swept him to victory in the US presidential election, in which he ran as a Republican; he was re-elected in 1956. During his administration (1953–61) he negotiated a truce in the **Korean War** (1953) and continued US efforts to contain **communism**. During his second term the administration became more active in civil rights issues, sending troops to Little Rock, Arkansas to enforce a school desegregation order. ▷ **Republican Party; World War II**

Eisenhower Doctrine (1957)
The US declaration to protect the Middle East against communist aggression, intended to reassure the Western allies after the Suez Crisis. Addressing Congress, President **Eisenhower** stated that the USA regarded the Middle East as vital to its security and that it should give economic and military aid to any country in the region that requested it.

ejido
A traditional form of communal landholding in Mexico: *ejido* lands existed in the Valley of Mexico at the time of the conquest and were areas claimed as common or cabildo properties outside the settlement or village, which were to be protected from alienation to private holders. The idea of the ejido as a communal property was revived by the followers of Emiliano **Zapata**, who believed that title to lands should be vested in the village. Communal ejidos were created under Lázaro **Cárdenas**, who expropriated large integrated haciendas created under Porfirio **Díaz**, as a means of forming loyal peasant communities immune to pressure from the Cristeros and supporting the PRM (*Partido de la Revolución Mexicana*). Some 16.8 million hectares were distributed.

EKKA (*Ethnike Kai Koinonike Apeleutherosis*, 'National and Social Liberation')
The smallest of the three major resistance groups in Greece during **World War II**. Led by Colonel Dimitrios Psarros, its politics were liberal and republican. It took an active part in the resistance from summer 1943 onwards, but was forced from the field when its leader was murdered by **ELAS** (Apr 1944). ▷ **EAM; EDES**

El Alamein, Battle of (23 Oct–4 Nov 1943)
A battle in **World War II**, named after a village on Egypt's Mediterranean coast, which ended in the victory of the British Eighth Army commanded by **Montgomery** over **Rommel**'s Afrika Corps. It proved to be a turning point in the war in the war in Africa. ▷ **North African Campaign**

El Salvador
The smallest of the Central American republics, which gained independence in 1841. A dictatorship followed political unrest in the mid-20c. El Salvador warred with Honduras in 1965 and 1969, and there was considerable political unrest in the 1970s, with guerrilla activity directed against the US-supported government. The Archbishop of San Salvador, Oscar Romero, was assassinated in 1980. Civil war followed in which 75 000 died. A peace agreement was signed in 1992. A state of emergency was declared in 1993 as a result of an outbreak of cholera.

ELAS (*Ethnikós Laïkós Apeleftherotikós Strátos*, 'National Popular Liberation Army')

The Greek resistance army founded in Dec 1941 as the military wing of the communist-dominated **EAM**. In the field from summer 1942, while fighting to liberate Greece from the Axis forces, its ultimate goal was the establishment of communist rule at the end of the war. It worked to eliminate rival resistance bands, cooperating with **EDES** only under the auspices of the British **Special Operations Executive (SOE)**. At the end of the war, with c.70 000 men, it controlled most of Greece and refused to cooperate with the British-backed government of George **Papandreou**. Although it agreed to disarm in Feb 1945, the fighting between communists, republicans and royalists continued, erupting into the **Greek Civil War** of 1946–9.

Elizabeth II (1926–   )

Queen of the UK (1952/   ) and Head of the **Commonwealth of Nations**. The elder daughter of King **George VI**, she was proclaimed Queen on 6 Feb 1952, and crowned on 2 June 1953. Her husband was created Duke of Edinburgh on the eve of their wedding (20 Nov 1947), and styled Prince Philip in 1957. They have three sons, Prince **Charles**, Prince Andrew, and Prince Edward, and a daughter, Princess Anne.

Ellis Island

An island in Upper New York Bay. Formerly a fort and arsenal, from 1892 until 1943 it was the main US centre for the control of immigration. It has been part of the Statue of Liberty National Monument since 1965. After restoration to the main buildings during the 1980s the Ellis Island Immigration Museum was opened in 1990.

Englandspiel (1942–4)

The codename given to a highly successful German counter-espionage operation in the Netherlands during **World War II**. The occupying German forces obtained the codes used by the Dutch resistance in radio contact with Britain, and by impersonating the resistance the Germans were able to capture 57 agents sent in from England, and to arrest hundreds of resistance personnel. Several English bombers were also brought down by them. ▷ **Resistance Movement** (Netherlands)

enosis

The Greek term for the policy of seeking union with Greece, first applied in the 1840s to the Cretans' agitation for union with the Kingdom of Greece. In Cyprus in the 1950s, demands for independence from Britain and enosis became insistent, giving rise to the underground movement **EOKA**. There followed a serious and long-running conflict amounting to civil war between the island's Greek and Turkish inhabitants, with the latter bitterly opposed to enosis. ▷ **Makarios III; Grivas, Georgeios; Karamanlis, Constantine**

Entebbe
A town in south Uganda on the north shore of Lake Victoria. Founded in 1893, it was the capital of Uganda from 1894 until 1962. It was the scene in 1976 of a dramatic rescue by Israeli forces of a group of Israelis whose plane had been hijacked by a group of terrorists.

Entente Cordiale
A term first used in the 1840s to describe a close relationship between the UK and France; then given to a series of agreements in 1904 between the two countries, dealing with a range of issues, in particular establishing the predominant role of the UK in Egypt, and France's interests in Morocco.

Enver Pasha (1881–1922)
Turkish soldier and politician. A leader in the 1908 revolution of **Young Turks**, in Aug 1914 as the pro-German Minister of War he steered the Turkish government into a secret alliance with Germany directed against Russia. After the Turkish surrender in 1918 at the end of **World War I**, he fled to Russia and was killed in an insurrection in Turkestan.

EOKA (*Ethniki Organosis Kipriakou Agono*, 'National Organization of Cypriot Struggle')
A Greek-Cypriot underground movement which sought to end British rule and achieve **enosis** (union with Greece). Founded in 1955 by a Greek army officer, Colonel Georgeios **Grivas**, and supported by Archbishop **Makarios III**, it pursued a campaign of anti-British violence which came to a climax in 1956–7. EOKA declined and was disbanded after Makarios's acceptance in 1958 of independence for Cyprus rather than enosis. The organization was resurrected unsuccessfully as EOKA B during the period 1971–4. ▷ **Karamanlis, Constantine**

Equal Rights Amendment
Proposed amendment to the US Constitution stating that equal rights shall not be denied on account of sex. First introduced in 1923, it was not approved by Congress until 1972. Although the adoption deadline was extended from 1979 to 1982, the amendment fell just short of ratification by the required 38 states.

Erhard, Ludwig (1897–1977)
German economist and politician. Professor of Economics at Munich, he was appointed by the Americans as Economic Director of the Bizone

in 1948. In the following year he was elected to the Federal Parliament in Bonn and made Economics Minister in the **Adenauer** administration. He was a leading architect of the **social market economy**, a key element of the West German 'economic miracle' of recovery from wartime devastation. He succeeded Adenauer as Chancellor (1963–6), but economic difficulties forced his resignation. ▷ **Christian Democrats**

Eritrea

A country in north-east Africa, on the Red Sea. It was taken by Italy in 1882, and a colony was established in 1890. Used as a base for the Italian invasion of Abyssinia in 1935, it became part of Italian East Africa in 1936. It was taken by the British in 1941. Federated as part of **Ethiopia** in 1952, it was made a province of Ethiopia in 1962, which led to political unrest. There was civil war in the 1970s, with separatists making major gains. Soviet- and Cuban-backed government forces regained most areas after a 1978 offensive. Conflict continued into the 1980s. Following the collapse of the Ethiopian government in 1991, Eritrea became an autonomous region with the Eritrean People's Liberation Front (EPLF) establishing a provisional government. Independence was declared in 1993.

Eritrea Liberation Front (ELF)

A movement seeking independence from Ethiopia, founded in 1958. Eritrea, controlled by Italy from 1882, was federated with Ethiopia at the request of the **UN** in 1952 and then incorporated as a province in 1962. This galvanized the Front into action and, despite some divisions, it managed, through support from the Eastern bloc and some Arab countries, to prevent its destruction both while **Haile Selassie** was Emperor and when **Mengistu** was President. The collapse of the **Dergue** in 1991 advanced its position.

Erlander, Tage Fritiof (1901–85)

Swedish politician. He became active in the Social Democratic Party while he was studying at the University of Lund and was elected to parliament in 1933. He was minister without portfolio in the wartime coalition government from 1944, and was Minister for Ecclesiastical Affairs when chosen to succeed Per Albin **Hansson** as party leader and Prime Minister in 1946. He made way for the younger Sven Olof **Palme** in 1969. A moderate, his brand of consensual government was dubbed 'Harpsund democracy' after his country estate, where he consulted with leaders in all walks of society.

Ershad, Hussain Muhammad (1929–)

Bangladesh soldier and chief martial law administrator. Appointed army Chief-of-Staff by President **Ziaur Rahman** in 1978, he repeatedly demanded that the armed forces should be involved in the country's administration. In 1982 he led a bloodless military coup, becoming President the following year.

Erzberger, Matthias (1875–1921)
German politician. He became controversial when, as a leading member of the Centre Party, he began to advocate peace without annexations as early as 1917 and again (1918–19) when, as a member of the armistice delegation, he advocated acceptance, despite some fierce German opposition, of the terms of the Treaty of **Versailles**. Finance Minister and Vice-Premier in 1919, he drastically reformed the tax system and nationalized the German railways. Unsuccessful in a libel action against an unscrupulous political opponent, he resigned in Feb 1921 and was assassinated in Aug of the same year by members of an extremist group (*Organisation Consul*) in the Black Forest.

Eshkol, Levi (1895–1969)
Israeli politician. Born in the Ukraine to parents of traditional Jewish piety, he settled in Palestine as an agricultural worker in 1914. After Israeli independence in 1948, he supervised the founding of several hundred new villages to absorb immigrants. A member of the **Mapai Party**, Eshkol served as Minister of Finance (1952–63) and as Prime Minister and Defence Minister (1963–9), transferring the latter post to Moshe **Dayan** during the **Six-Day War** of 1967. Eshkol established diplomatic relations with West Germany and was also the first Israeli leader to visit the USA. Despite internal political difficulties in 1964–5, he remained Prime Minister until his death. ▷ **Restitution Agreement**

Estado Novo (Brazil)
Literally 'New State', this was the name given by President Getúlio **Vargas** to his authoritarian regime in Brazil (1937–45). The term was copied from the Estado Novo established in **Salazar**'s Portugal. The Estado Novo had a profound influence on the party political structure of Brazil until 1965. The political leadership of the various states imposed by Vargas in 1937 formed the backbone of the **PSD**, while the labour unions formed the 'nationalist' PTB (*Partido Trabalhista Brasileiro*). Francisco Campos and Carlos Medeiros Silva, architects of the Estado Novo, were brought back to reshape the constitution of 1946 in an authoritarian mould. ▷ **Estado Novo** (Portugal)

Estado Novo (Portugal)
The authoritarian political system (literally, 'New State') under **Salazar** which ruled Portugal from the early 1930s to 1969. This entailed the abolition of political parties and trade unions, total censorship, the vesting of power in an all-powerful executive, and the glorification of the

values of 'God, Country, and Family'. Despite its fascist trappings and corporatist aspirations, the aim of the Estado Novo was mass depoliticization rather than mobilization within a single party totally identified with the state. The heavily centralized and authoritarian Estado Novo effectively allowed the old elite to retain political and social control.

Estigarribia, José Félix (1888–1940)
Paraguayan general and war hero. He won fame as a brilliant commander in the **Chaco War** (1932–5), on the strength of which he became President (1939–40). He died in a plane crash near Asunción.

Estonia
A republic in eastern Europe, which achieved independence from Russia in 1918. A Soviet Socialist Republic from 1940, it was occupied by Germany during **World War II**. There was a resurgence of the nationalist movement in the 1980s. Independence was declared in 1991.

ETA (*Euskadi Ta Askatasuna*, 'Basque Homeland and Freedom')
The extremist Basque nationalist organization set up in 1959 to secure the independence of the Basque country. It was later influenced by Third World nationalism, Marxism, and the use of violence, all of which led to much inner feuding and divisions. ETA initiated a campaign of armed struggle in 1968, which has led to over 400 assassinations. Its killing of Admiral **Carrero Blanco** in 1973 undoubtedly altered the course of the post-Francoist transition. The organization's political front, *Herri Batasuna* ('Popular Unity'), generally wins about 12 per cent of the vote in the Basque country, and elected seven deputies to the Cortes in the 1986 election.

Ethiopia formerly **Abyssinia**
A state in north-east Africa. Abyssinian independence was recognized by the League of Nations in 1923. Italy invaded in 1935, and Ethiopia was annexed as Italian East Africa from 1936 to 1941, the year **Haile Selassie** returned from exile. A military coup took place, with the formation of the Provisional Military Administrative Council (PMAC) in 1974. Opposition by left-wing civilian groups was countered by mass arrests and executions in 1977–8. There was ongoing conflict with **Somalia** over Ogaden region, and internal conflict with regional separatist Eritrean and Tigrean forces. A government offensive was successful in 1978, but received setbacks in the early 1980s. The country suffered severe famine in the 1980s. The PMAC was dissolved in 1987, with the transfer of power to the People's Democratic Republic. In 1989 a coup was attempted, and in 1991 the government collapsed. There was famine again in 1992. In 1993 **Eritrea** achieved independence.

EU (European Union)
An association of 12 European countries, heralded by the Single European Act (1986) and created by the Treaty of Maastricht (in effect from 1 Nov 1993), forming the political and economic infrastructure that enables the free movement of people, goods and services between member countries. One of its main aims is monetary union, a project handled by the **EC**, which is a component part of the EU. Two other pillars of the Union that require inter-governmental cooperation are the areas of foreign and security policy and justice and home affairs.

Evatt, Herbert Vere (1894–1965)
Australian jurist and politician. He served in the state Assembly (1925–30), and was justice of the High Court of Australia (1930–40), when he entered federal politics. As Minister of External Affairs (1941–9), he was a prominent figure in the United Nations Organization and President of the General Assembly (1948–9). He was leader of the **Australian Labor Party** in opposition (1951–60) to Britain and delegate at international conferences. He represented Australia in Winston **Churchill's** war cabinet, and was Leader of the Opposition in the federal parliament (1951–60), when he became Chief Justice of New South Wales until his retirement in 1962.

Evers, Medgar (1925–63)
US **civil rights** activist. Field Secretary of the **NAACP** with responsibility for registering black voters and organizing boycotts of establishments which practised racial discrimination, he was shot dead outside his home in Jackson, Mississippi. His murder illustrated the dangers faced by black civil rights activists working in the South. A white man, Byron de la Beckwith, boasted of and was indicted for his murder, but was freed after two trials ended in hung juries.

Evian Agreements (1962)
These agreements were the result of secret talks held at Evian, on the French shore of Lake Geneva, to end the war in Algeria. The government of General de **Gaulle** and representatives of the provisional government of Algeria, led by Ben Bella, agreed to a cease-fire and to the establishment of an independent Algeria after a referendum. The agreements were given massive support in referenda in both France and Algeria, in spite of the attempts of the **OAS** (*Organisation Armée Secrète*) to undermine them.
▷ **Algerian War of Independence**

Extensive Development (post-1928)
The term used by Soviet-style economists to describe the massive, planned build-up of basic industries in backward societies like the early USSR. The emphasis was on production, not on producers or on consumers.

The twin objectives were the creation of a national capital and the expansion of the working class. The technique was imposed on the states of Eastern Europe after **World War II**, irrespective of their level of development. By the 1960s, the cry went up for intensive development, the establishment of consumer industries and the employment of new technologies. The fact that too little came too late seriously undermined Soviet-style **communism** in the 1980s.

Eyadema, (Etienne) Gnassingbe (1937–)
Togolese soldier and politician. He joined the French army in 1953, serving outside Africa for many years, and became Army Chief of Staff in 1965. He led a bloodless military coup in 1967, deposing President Grunitsky. He banned all political parties until 1969, when he founded a new organization, the *Rassemblement du Peuple Togolais*, as a vehicle for the organization of support for the government. Despite opposition, he has survived and responded by a degree of democratization.

Eyskens, Gaston (1905–)
Belgian economist and politician. After studying in Leuven and the USA, he became Professor of Economics at Leuven (1934–75). In 1939 he was elected MP for the **Christian People's Party (Belgium)**, and in 1965 became a Senator in the Upper House. He was Minister of Finance in 1945 and in 1947–9, and from 1949 to 1950 was Prime Minister for the first time. In the mid-1950s he was Minister for Economic Affairs, and led the government again in 1958–61. Appointed Minister for Finance (1965–6), he became Prime Minister twice more (1968–72 and 1972–3). He led coalitions with both left and right, and was one of the pivotal figures of post-war Belgian politics, playing a central role in the negotiations surrounding the abdication of King **Leopold III**, the debate on education funding, and the decolonization of the Congo.

F

Fabian Society

A socialist group established in 1884 which took its name from the Roman general, Fabius Maximus *Cunctator* ('the Delayer'), noted for his cautious military tactics. It adopts a gradualist approach to social reform, and sometimes 'Fabian' is applied to people who are not members of the society but who believe in reformist **socialism**. The society has remained a small select group, but has a close association with the British **Labour Party**, and has been a source of socialist ideas and arguments.

Fabius, Laurent (1946–)

French socialist politician. He had a brilliant academic career and became economic adviser to the **Socialist Party** (PS) leader, François **Mitterrand**, in 1976. Elected to the National Assembly in 1978, he was appointed Budget Minister when the PS gained power in 1981, and Minister for Research and Industry in 1983. In 1984 he was appointed Prime Minister and introduced a more free-market economic programme, which had some success, but resigned following his party's electoral defeat in Mar 1986. A popular and moderate social democrat, he heads an influential faction within the PS.

Facta, Luigi (1861–1930)

Italian politician. As Prime Minister in Mar 1922, after the collapse of the **Bonomi** ministry, he made no real effort to resist the fascist seizure of power, even given the refusal of **Victor Emmanuel III** to declare a state of emergency. His government collapsed (28 Oct 1922) and was replaced by that of **Mussolini**. ▷ **March on Rome**

Fahd (ibn Abd al-Aziz al-Saud) (1923–)

King of Saudi Arabia (1982/). As effective ruler since the assassination of his older half-brother, Faysal, in 1975, he became King on the death of his other half-brother, Khalid. A great promoter of the modernization of his country, he was also a central figure in the shaping of Saudi Arabia's foreign policy in the 1970s and 1980s, countering Soviet influence through financial assistance to moderate Arab states such as Egypt. He opposed the **Camp David Accords** and demanded a **jihad** against Israel after its annexation in 1980 of East Jerusalem. Despite this, in 1981 he produced a plan for a Middle Eastern peace settlement, apparently recognizing

Israel's right to secure boundaries. This plan, however, was never endorsed.

FAI (*Federación Anarquista Ibérica*, 'Iberian Anarchist Federation')
A semi-secret group of activists established in Spain in 1927 to preserve the purist and revolutionary anarchist tradition in reaction against the increasing syndicalism of the **CNT**. Though loosely organized, the FAI came to exercise great influence within the CNT during the Second Republic, being the major force in its split of 1932. The FAI also promoted the disastrous revolutionary risings of Jan and Dec 1933. During the **Spanish Civil War**, the FAI became a bureaucracy within the CNT, playing an important role not only in the successful agrarian and industrial collectives, but also in the often ineffective anarchist militia. ▷ **Second Republic,** (Spain)

Fair Deal
The name adopted by US President Harry S **Truman** for his post-**World War II** liberal and pro-labour domestic policies. ▷ **New Deal**

Fair Employment Practices Committee (FEPC)
Established (1941) by President Franklin D **Roosevelt**, the FEPC was created to eliminate racial discrimination in the war production industries and in government employment. President Harry S **Truman**'s efforts to establish permanent status for the committee were met with rejection by the Senate in 1946. In 1964 the Fair Employment Opportunity Commission was established to prevent discrimination in employment. ▷ **Randolph, A Philip**

Falange Española
Principal fascist movement (literally, 'Spanish Falange') of 20c Spain. Founded (Oct 1933) by José Antonio **Primo de Rivera**, the son of the military dictator of the 1920s, the Falange remained a small if vocal and violent movement during its first two years. In the general election of Feb 1936 it won a mere 0.7 per cent of the vote. Following the triumph of the Popular Front, the Falange grew rapidly as disillusioned middle-class youth deserted the mainstream right-wing parties. Party activists played a key role in the street-fighting that helped polarize the political climate in the spring and summer of 1936. The Falange also assisted in the military rebellion of July 1936 against the Republic. During the **Spanish Civil War** the Falange became the dominant political movement in the Nationalist zone and controlled the press and propaganda. But the mass influx into the Falange and the loss of its leadership (especially José Antonio, executed in Alicante jail in Nov 1936) diluted its radical spirit. The political fate of the Falange was sealed in Apr 1937 when General **Franco**, as the Nationalists' head of state and military leader,

forcibly united it with the Carlists to become the *Falange Española Tradicionalista y de las JONS*. Under the Franco dictatorship of 1939–75 the Falange adopted a subordinate role, serving as the regime's dependent and clientelist administrative arm. It organized the labour force through the 'vertical syndicates', helped control the middle classes, and acted as the political cheerleader of the dictator.

Falin, Valentin Mikhailovich (1926–)
Soviet specialist in international relations. Born in Leningrad and educated in Moscow, he held a range of Communist Party and Foreign Ministry postings from 1950 onwards. In 1968–71 he was head of the German department of the Foreign Ministry and in 1971–8 Ambassador to West Germany, the period when relations were 'normalized'. In the 1980s he was for a time influential in journalism, and in 1988 he succeeded **Dobrynin** as head of the international department of the party, but its days were numbered.

Falkland Islands or **Malvinas**
A British Crown Colony in the southern Atlantic Ocean. Britain asserted possession in 1833 and formal annexation took place in 1908 and 1917. Argentina's claims to sovereignty over the whole area resulted in invasion by Argentine military forces in Apr 1982. The dispatch of the British Task Force led to the return of the islands to British rule in June 1982.

Falklands War (Apr–June 1982)
A war between Britain and Argentina, precipitated by the Argentine invasion of the **Falkland Islands** (known to Argentinians as the Malvinas). Britain had ruled the islands continuously since 1833, but Argentina claimed them by inheritance from the Spanish Empire and through their proximity to her shores. The British had been conducting talks with Argentina on sovereignty over the Falklands, involving either a leaseback arrangement or a joint administration. When these talks broke down, the government of General **Galtieri** issued a warning to the British. The British government announced the withdrawal of HMS *Endurance* from the South Atlantic, and on 19 Mar scrap merchants landed on South Georgia, ostensibly to demolish a whaling station, but they also raised the Argentine flag. On the night of 1–2 Apr the full-scale invasion of the Falklands began. The 70 Royal Marines on the islands were overwhelmed, and the Governor was deported to Uruguay. The British immediately fitted out a task force to retake the islands, and the Foreign Office team, including Lord Carrington, resigned. The task force consisted of almost 70 ships, including some 40 requisitioned merchantmen and some well-known passenger vessels such as the *Queen Elizabeth 2*. A 200-mile maritime exclusion zone was declared around the Falklands, and on 2 May the Argentine cruiser, *General Belgrano*, was sunk by

the nuclear submarine, HMS *Conqueror*. This brought to an end peace initiatives conducted by the US Secretary of State, Alexander Haig, and the Peruvian government. South Georgia was retaken (25 Apr); the destroyer HMS *Sheffield* was sunk by an Exocet missile (4 May); 5 000 British troops were landed at Port San Carlos (21 May); and more troops were landed at Bluff Cove (6–8 June), an operation attended by much loss of life when the Argentine air force attacked the *Sir Tristram* and *Sir Galahad*. The British forces took Darwin and Goose Green on 28 May, and after the recapture of the capital, Port Stanley, the Argentinians surrendered (14 June). The war cost the British £700 million; 254 British and 750 Argentine lives were lost; and some political commentators claim that it did much to save the declining fortunes of the government of Margaret **Thatcher**.

Fanfani, Amintore (1908–)

Italian politician. A professor of political economy, he was elected as a Christian Democrat deputy in 1946 and held a number of ministerial posts until 1954 when he was elected General-Secretary of the DC. He has been Foreign Minister three times (1958–9, 1960–3 and 1965–8), a post which he has twice combined with his five periods as Prime Minister (1954, 1958–9, twice in 1960–3, and 1982–3). Nominated a life Senator in 1972, he was President of the Italian Senate in 1968–73 and 1976–82.

▷ **Christian Democrat Party**

Fang Lizhi (Fang Li-chih) (1936–)

Chinese astrophysicist and dissident. During the 1957 anti-rightist campaign he was dismissed from the **Chinese Communist Party**, but was rehabilitated during the late 1970s at a time of relative cultural freedom. As Vice-President of the University of Science and Technology in Hefei (Anhui province), he called for greater democracy and condemned party corruption. He supported student demonstrations in Dec 1986 and was once again expelled from the party for his advocacy of 'bourgeois liberalism'. In the wake of the brutal suppression of the democracy movement in 1989, Fang Lizhi was accused of being one of the ringleaders. He sought refuge in the US Embassy and was eventually allowed to leave for the West.

Fanon, Frantz (1925–61)

Martinique-born doctor and revolutionary. His study of the Algerian revolution, *The Wretched of the Earth* (1961), became the inspiration and manifesto for liberation struggles throughout the Third World. Educated as a psychiatrist in France and sent to Algeria, Fanon changed sides and joined the rebels, but died of leukaemia before seeing the achievement of independence for Algeria.

Farinacci, Roberto (1892–1945)
Italian politician. One of the founding members of Italian **fascism** and perhaps the most intransigent **ras**. He was a deputy (1921–2), Secretary-General of the **Fascist Party** (1925–6), a member of the **Fascist Grand Council** (from 1935) and a Minister of State (1938). An ardent anti-Semite, he was ideologically much closer to Nazism than most other **gerarchi**. In the famous meeting of the **Fascist Grand Council** (25 July 1943), he was one of the minority who voted for total loyalty to the alliance with Germany. At the end of the war he was captured and executed on the same day and by the same partisans as **Mussolini**.

fascism
A term applied generically, and often inaccurately, to a variety of extremely nationalistic and authoritarian, populist movements that reached their pinnacle in the inter-war years. The movement originated in Italy, centred on **Mussolini**. It is hard to define the central tenets of fascism even in Italy, where it began as a republican, anti-capitalist, anticlerical movement with a strong syndicalist influence and yet quickly switched to supporting the free market, the monarchy and the Church. However, all fascist movements (Oswald **Mosley**'s **Blackshirts** in Britain, the **Iron Guard** in Romania, the **Croix de Feu** in France or any other of its legion manifestations across Europe) shared common features: an aggressive and unquestioning nationalism; a disrespect for democratic and liberal institutions which did not, however, preclude using them to attain power; a profound hatred for socialism; an emphasis on a single charismatic leader; a strong association with militarism. There are many similarities between fascism and Nazism, the latter often being described as simply an extreme manifestation of the former. However, it should be stressed that, although xenophobic, there was nothing intrinsically anti-Semitic about Italian fascism, at least in its early stages. After the end of **World War II**, fascism was largely discredited, although groups such as the **Italian Social Movement** and the British and French National Fronts show many similarities.

Fascist Grand Council (*Gran Consiglio di Fascismo*)
Established in 1923 as a parallel fascist cabinet alongside the constitutional one, the *Gran Consiglio* did relatively little. Instead, **Mussolini** created it primarily to provide apparently prestigious posts to occupy potentially dangerous **ras**. By 1928, it had become in theory the most powerful organ of both party and state, composed almost entirely of ministers. In practice, its powers were extremely limited: it was purely advisory and could only convene on the orders of Mussolini: he did not summon it at all between 1939 and July 1943. Despite his attempts to keep the Council as no more than a forum for careerists, nonentities and sycophants, it did eventually assert itself in the famous meeting of 25 July 1943 when it voted by a majority of 17 to 7 in favour of Dino

Grandi's motion to remove the **Duce** from office: Mussolini was dismissed by King **Umberto III** and arrested the following day.

Fascist Party (*Partito Nazionale Fascista*, PNF)
The fascist movement was founded by **Mussolini** at a meeting in Milan in Mar 1919. Originally it was no more than a fringe movement, associated with the 'futurists' and anticlerical, anti-capitalist and republican in philosophy. It contested elections in 1919 disastrously and was not put on a formal party footing until Oct 1921, when the PNF was established. Its remarkable growth, both in membership and electoral support, has much to do with the chaotic political climate of the post-war years, the weakness of liberal institutions and widespread fear of **communism**, but the PNF's ideology also changed, Mussolini realizing that if it were to appeal broadly it could not continue to be anticlerical, against the free market or hostile to the monarchy. By Oct 1922 it was already the most significant political force in Italy and by 1929 had effectively become the sole Italian political party, dominating an essentially totalitarian regime. However, the nature of the party also altered: largely as a result of purges undertaken by the **Duce** it lost its revolutionary edge and became increasingly bureaucratic. By the 1930s membership was seen more as a prerequisite for advancement than a sign of genuine commitment to the ideals of **fascism**.

Fatah, al-
The popular name (in Arabic, 'Victory') for the Palestine National Liberation Movement (PNLM), created in 1957 and headed by Yasser **Arafat**. It is the single biggest Palestinian movement, and operates under the umbrella of the **PLO** (Palestine Liberation Organization).

Fateh Singh, Sant (1911–72)
Sikh religious leader. A campaigner for Sikh rights, he was involved in religious and educational activity in Rajasthan, founding many schools and colleges there. In 1942 he joined the **Quit India Movement**, and was imprisoned for his political activities. During the 1950s he agitated for a Punjabi-speaking state, which was achieved once Haryana was created as a separate state in 1966.

Fatherland Front
The popular front organized by the communists in Bulgaria during **World War II**. Formed (June 1942) from a combination of Social Democrats, **Zveno** and the left-wing Pladne Agrarians, it was from the first dominated by its communist members. In Sep 1944 it organized strikes and prepared to take over the government. Through the Front, the communists held key positions in the pro-Western government of the right-wing Agrarian Kosta Muraviev. It attacked its opponents, organized a 'people's militia',

and tried and executed members of the past governments and the regents. In Mar 1945 Georgi **Dimitrov** was elected President of the Central Committee and in Nov of the same year the Front won a majority in the elections through fraud. Its activities ensured that Bulgaria was completely under communist control by Nov 1947.

Faure, Edgar (Jean) (1908–88)
French politician. He entered politics as a radical, before becoming a Gaullist. He was Minister of Finance and Economic Affairs several times in the 1950s, and was Premier for two short periods (1952 and 1955–6). He was later Minister of Agriculture (1966), Education (1968), and Social Affairs (1969), and President of the National Assembly (1973–8). He became a Member of the European Parliament in 1979.

Faysal I (1885–1933)
King of Iraq (1921/33). He was the son of **Husayn ibn 'Ali**, King of the Hijaz. He played a major role in the **Arab Revolt** of 1916, and was for a short while King of Syria after **World War I**. Installed as King of Iraq by the British, he became a leader of Arab nationalism. He died in Berne, Switzerland.

Faysal ibn 'Abd al-'Aziz (1904–75)
King of Saudi Arabia (1964/75). Appointed Viceroy of the Hijaz in 1926, he became Minister for Foreign Affairs in 1930, Crown Prince in 1953, and succeeded his half-brother, Sa'ud, as King. He was assassinated in the royal palace in Riyadh by his nephew, Faysal ibn Musayd.

Faysal II (1935–58)
King of Iraq (1939/58). He was the great-grandson of **Husayn ibn 'Ali**, King of the Hijaz. He succeeded his father, King **Ghazi**, who was killed in an accident, and after an education at Harrow was installed as king. In Feb 1958 he concluded with his cousin, King **Hussein** of Jordan, a federation of the two countries in opposition to the **United Arab Republic** of Egypt and Syria. In July 1958, he and his entire household were assassinated during a military coup, and Iraq became a republic.

Fazl al-Haq (1873–1962)
Bengali Muslim leader. Formerly a lawyer, teacher and journalist in Calcutta, the reunification of Bengal in 1912 saw Haq become a political leader of the Muslims. He became Secretary and then President of the **Muslim League** and was chiefly concerned with the political organization of rural interest groups. Haq was Chief Minister of Bengal from 1937 to 1943. After breaking with the Muslim League in 1941, Haq reconstructed his ministry with the help of Hindus. In Pakistan, Haq was first Advocate-

General of East Pakistan and then its Chief Minister, before being appointed Governor (1956–8).

Fazl-i Husain (1877–1936)

Punjabi Muslim political leader. He participated in both Congress and **Muslim League** activities in Punjab. Husain saw the 1919 reforms as advantageous to the Punjabi Muslims, for these would give the Muslims a Legislative Council majority. Thus, he opposed the non-cooperation boycott of the legislatures and was elected to the Punjab council. He served afterwards in various high offices in the Punjab government and in the government of India, handling education and revenue. Husain was a strong supporter of separate Muslim electorates and intervened successfully to prevent his fellow-Muslims from surrendering these during negotiations in 1930–1. ▷ **Non-Cooperation Movement**

FBI (Federal Bureau of Investigation)

The US organization mainly concerned with internal security or counter-intelligence operations, although it also has responsibility for investigating violations of federal law not remitted by the federal government to any other organization. The FBI is a branch of the Department of Justice. ▷ **Hoover, J Edgar**

FDP (*Freie Demokratische Partei*, 'Free Democratic Party')

German political party. Founded in the Federal Republic in Dec 1948, the FDP was the successor to previous German liberal parties. Initially a centre-right party with close links to business, the FDP adopted a centre-left slant in its Freiburg Theses (1971) which included support for economic democracy (**Mitbestimmung**), equal opportunity in education and the fostering of individual political responsibility. The FDP has always been a minority party, typically gaining 10 per cent of the vote (and therefore 10 per cent of seats in the **Bundestag**). However, this has enabled it to hold the balance of power for most of the period since 1949, thereby modifying the programmes and policies of both **CDU/CSU** and **SPD** governments. FDP politicians such as Hans-Dietrich **Genscher** have played a major role in German government.

FEB (*Fôrça Expedicionária Brasileira*)

The only Latin American troops to serve in the European theatre in **World War II**, the 25 000-strong FEB ('Brazilian Expeditionary Force') fought alongside the US Fifth Army in Italy in 1944–5 under the command of General Mascarenhas de Moraes. Trained in US bases, combat in Italy forged a group of officers who were strongly anti-communist and committed to democracy; they were also convinced that, in the short run, arbitrary government might be necessary. Veteran FEB officers formed key groups within both the high command and the Escola Superior da

Guerra. They became a diehard opposition to Getúlio **Vargas** in 1945 and **Goulart** in 1961–4, and formed the backbone of the 1964–7 **Castelo Branco** government.

February Revolution (Russia) (Feb–Mar 1917)
Popular demonstrations, strikes and military mutinies in Petrograd, Russia, resulting from pre-war misgovernment and wartime privation, which led to the abdication of Tsar **Nicholas II** and the collapse of the tsarist government. The old regime was succeeded by a series of provisional governments composed of ostensibly liberal and moderate socialist ministers, and simultaneously by the establishment of the Soviet ('Council') of Workers' and Soldiers' Deputies. This 'dual power' prevented the emergence of decisive government and provided the opportunity for the **Bolsheviks** to prepare for their revolution, which materialized in Oct/Nov of the same year. ▷ **April Theses; July Days; Mensheviks; October Revolution**

February Revolution (Czechoslovakia) (1948)
The name given by the communists to their assumption of power in Czechoslovakia. The National Front government was divided down the middle in the approach to fresh elections due in Apr or May 1948, with communists and non-communists exchanging accusations of impropriety. East–West tension was also growing. The communists resorted to extra-parliamentary tactics, whereupon the non-communists resigned to try to force an earlier election; however, it was a minority resignation. The communists called out their militia, leaving President **Beneš** with little alternative but to ask Klement **Gottwald** to take power. However, it was hardly a revolution, and the communists soon changed their monopoly position.

Federal Reserve System (FRS)
The US central banking system, set up in 1913. Under the system, the USA is divided into 12 districts, each with its own Federal Reserve Bank. The system is supervised by a central board of governors called the Federal Reserve Board. Its responsibilities include maintaining credit and monetary conditions as well as monitoring member banks. Less than half of the 14 000 banks in the USA are members of the 'Fed'.

federation (Australia)
In Australian history, the events leading up to the political union of the colonies (1 Jan 1901). The eastern states of Australia gained self-government in the 1850s, and Western Australia in 1890. By the 1880s, colonial development raised the issue of intercolonial trade and internal tariff barriers, while the extension of European imperialism into the Pacific raised that of defence. A Federal Council was established in 1883

which New South Wales refused to join. The rivalry between free-trade New South Wales and protectionist Victoria was the greatest of the problems federationists had to overcome. Negotiations began in earnest after Sir Henry **Parkes**'s speech at Tenterfield (1889), arguing that federation was essential to Australian defence, led to the Australasian Federation Conference (1890) and the National Australasian Convention (1891). Agreement was reached on the US model of federation which protected state rights, with a lower house based on population, a senate representing the states, and a high court to adjudicate on constitutional disputes. Discussions continued through the 1890s, culminating in the Federal Convention of 1897–8 which amended the constitution drafted in 1891. Anti-federalist interests remained powerful, and it required two referendums and further amendments before the constitution was accepted by all states.

Feng Yuxiang (Feng Yu-hsiang) (1882–1948)
Chinese warlord. Known as the 'Christian General', he rose through the ranks to command an independent force. In 1924 he took Beijing, and set up a government which included members of the Nationalist Party. He supported the Nationalist government in 1927, but became apprehensive of the growing personal power of **Chiang Kai-shek**, and joined in two successive revolts, both of which failed. He left China in 1947 to visit the USA, and died in a ship fire on his return journey. ▷ **Guomindang; warlords**

Ferdinand (1865–1927)
King of Romania (1914/27). The nephew of King **Charles I** of Romania, he was named as heir to the throne in 1880. He married Princess Marie of Edinburgh, granddaughter of Queen Victoria and Tsar Alexander II. He succeeded his uncle in Oct 1914 and led Romania into **World War I** on the side of the Allies. Romania almost doubled in size at the end of the war and in 1922 he was crowned King of Greater Romania at Alba Iulia. Distrusting his son, the future **Charles II** of Romania, he named his grandson, **Michael**, as his successor.

Ferdinand I (1861–1948)
Prince and first King of modern Bulgaria (1887/1918). On the abdication of Prince Alexander of Battenberg, he accepted the crown, as Prince, in 1887. Dominated at first by the Premier Stephan Stambolov, he later took increasing control of the government. After proclaiming Bulgaria independent of the Ottoman Porte in 1908, he took the title Tsar. In 1912 he joined the Balkan League against Turkey. Allying himself with the **Central Powers**, he invaded Serbia in 1915. His armies routed, he abdicated in 1918, to be succeeded by his son, **Boris III**. ▷ **Balkan Wars**

Ferraro, Geraldine Anne (1935–)

US Democrat politician. The daughter of Italian Roman Catholic immigrants, she was educated at Marymount College, Fordham University and New York Law School and, after marrying wealthy businessman John Zaccaro in 1960, established a successful law practice (1961–74). She served as assistant district attorney for the Queens district of New York between 1974 and 1978 and worked at the Supreme Court from 1978, heading a special bureau for victims of violent crime, before being elected to the House of Representatives in 1981. In Congress, she gained a reputation as an effective, liberal-minded politician and was selected in 1984 by Walter Mondale to be the first female vice-presidential candidate of a major party, in an effort to add sparkle to the Democrat ticket. After the Democrats' convincing defeat, she returned to private law practice and in 1992 unsuccessfully sought the New York Democratic nomination for US Senator.

FFI (*Forces français de l'intérieur*, 'French Interior Forces')

The armed forces of the French Resistance within France, as distinct from the **Free French** fighting overseas; they played an important part in the battle for the liberation of France, and were incorporated into the regular army in Nov 1944. ▷ **Resistance Movement; World War II**

Fianna Fáil

Irish political party founded in 1926 by those opposed to the 1921 Anglo-Irish Treaty. It first came to power under **De Valera** in 1932, and has been the governing party for most of the period since. In the 1930s it emphasized separation from the British, and has consistently supported the unification of Ireland. In domestic issues its approach is more pragmatic than ideological.

Fierlinger, Zdenek (1891–1976)

Czechoslovak diplomat and politician. He was appointed Ambassador in Moscow in 1937 and therefore played an important role in maintaining a liaison between Edvard **Beneš** and **Stalin** before, during and after the **Munich Agreement** and again following the Soviet entry into **World War II**. A social democrat by persuasion, he inclined increasingly to the communist point of view, was Prime Minister in the interim post-war government 1945–6, and then Minister of Industry in Klement **Gottwald**'s coalition government between 1946 and 1948. In Feb 1948 he played a crucial role in persuading most of the social democrats to join the communists in taking over power and putting an end to traditional Czechoslovak democracy for more than 40 years. His influence declined particularly after Gottwald's death in 1953, but he remained useful for propaganda purposes.

fifth column

A popular expression from the early days of **World War II** to describe enemy sympathizers who might provide active help to an invader. The name originally described the rebel sympathizers in Madrid in 1936 during the **Spanish Civil War**, when four rebel columns were advancing on the city.

Figueres (Ferrer), José (Don Pepe) (1906–90)

Costa Rican politician. In May 1948 he led a civilian rising against an attempt to annul the legal election of Otilio Ulate. Figueres headed a junta for 18 months, during which he carried through fundamental reforms of a social democratic nature: abolishing the armed forces; nationalizing the banking system; creating an electoral law and another law promoting rural cooperatives; and the modernization of the educational and social security systems. The constitution of 1949 embodied these reforms. He was President twice (1953–8 and 1970–4), and is commonly known as the person who created a regime which was strong enough to survive the buffeting of civil war in neighbouring Nicaragua and El Salvador.

Fiji

A Melanesian island group in the south-west Pacific Ocean. It gained independence within the Commonwealth in 1970. The 1987 election brought to power an Indian-dominated coalition, which led to military coups in May and Sep, and the proclamation of a republic outside the Commonwealth. A civilian government was restored in Dec, and a new constitution upholding ethnic Melanesian political power was effected in 1990.

Fine Gael

Irish political party created out of the pro-Anglo-Irish Treaty (1921) wing of **Sinn Féin**. It was known as *Cumann na nGaedheal* from 1923 until it changed its name in 1933. The first government of the **Irish Free State**, it has largely been in opposition since the 1930s, and has never held power on its own. It supports an Irish confederation, and is largely pragmatic in domestic matters.

Finland

A republic in northern Europe which in the 19c was an autonomous Grand Duchy of the Russian tsar. A nationalist movement led to independence from 1917. The parliamentary system was created in 1928. Finland was invaded by Soviets in 1939 and 1940, and lost territory to the USSR after 1944.

Finlandization

Supposedly the policy of influencing the internal politics and foreign policy of a small neighbouring country by bringing pressure to bear on it. The notion refers specifically to the Soviet trade and diplomatic sanctions applied to Finland in 1958, because the Finnish government formed after the elections did not contain any communist members, although they had won a quarter of the seats. The sanctions were effective; a number of ministers resigned and a government more acceptable to the USSR was formed. But, in general, Finland retained a great freedom of action in return for unimportant concessions.

Finnbogadóttir, Vígdis (1930–)

Icelandic politician. Born in Reykjavík, she studied French language and literature in France and returned to Iceland to teach French in secondary school and French drama at the University of Iceland in Reykjavík. The first woman to be elected head of any state, she was first elected President against three male candidates (1980), was returned unopposed in 1984 and re-elected in 1988.

Fisher, Andrew (1862–1928)

British-born Australian politician. A coalminer from the age of 12, he emigrated to Queensland in 1885. From mining, he gradually moved into trade-union activity and politics, entering the Queensland state assembly in 1893 and the first federal parliament in 1901. He became **Australian Labor Party** (ALP) leader in 1907 and then Prime Minister (1908–09, 1910–13 and 1914–15). At the start of **World War I** he made the dramatic promise to support the war effort 'to the last man and the last shilling'. He was Australian High Commissioner in London (1916–21).

Fitzgerald, Garrett (Michael) (1926–)

Irish politician. He became a barrister and a lecturer in political economy (1959–73) and in 1969 he was elected **Fine Gael** member of the Irish parliament for Dublin South-East. He became Minister for Foreign Affairs (1973–7), Prime Minister (1981–2 and 1982–7) and Leader of the Fine Gael Party (1977–87).

Fiume (Rijeka)

Port in Croatia of mixed Slav and Italian population. Although not included in the areas promised to Italy by the Treaty of **London** (1915), Fiume was claimed by the Italian delegation at the Paris Peace Conference. Italian claims were rejected and the port was afforded free city status, but in Sep 1919 it was seized by the Italian poet Gabriele **D'Annunzio** and a band of nationalist 'legionaries' who ran it as an independent 'Italian producers' republic'. By the Treaty of **Rapallo** (12 Nov 1920), Yugoslavia and Italy agreed that Fiume should regain free city status and in Jan 1921 D'Annunzio was ejected by the Italian navy. Free city status was, however, never restored, the terms of Rapallo being abandoned on **Mussolini**'s seizure of power. In Jan 1924 Yugoslavia recognized Fiume as Italian, although the adjoining harbour of Susak remained under Yugoslavian control. At the end of **World War II**, it became part of the Republic of Croatia within the Socialist Federal Republic of Yugoslavia.

Five-Year Plans

Independent India adapted this model (initiated in the USSR under **Stalin** in 1928) for organizing the economy during the 1950s. The Indian Planning Commission was set up in 1950 to enable the government to supervise economic development. The commission was asked to assess development resources, formulate a national five-year plan, and assess progress, and the first plan was implemented during the period 1951–6. The plans covered the activities of both central and state governments, although states controlled their own plans.

Flandin, Pierre Etienne (1889–1958)

French politician. From 1914 to 1940 he was President of the *Alliance démocratique* ('Democratic Alliance') a moderate republican group. He frequently held cabinet office, notably as Finance Minister (1931–2); as Prime Minister (1934–5) he vainly tried to solve the economic crisis by deflation, and to counter-balance the German threat by joining with Italy in the Stresa front. He supported appeasement, and voted for **Pétain** in 1940. He was briefly in office under **Vichy** (14 Dec 1941) which ended his active political career.

Flemish Movement

A cultural and political emancipation movement in Belgium, aimed at the recognition of the rights of the Dutch-speaking inhabitants of the northern part of the country (Flanders) as opposed to the interests of the French-speaking inhabitants of southern Belgium (Wallonia) and increasingly of the capital Brussels. When the suffrage was widened in 1893 beyond the Francophone bourgeoisie, the movement gained political power and achieved an 'Equality Law' in 1898, giving the two languages equal status. There followed a long dispute over the University in Ghent, which the movement wanted as a Dutch-language institution: this was finally agreed in 1930. During both world wars elements of the Flemish Movement chose to work with the German authorities in the hope of achieving their aims: this brought the movement into some temporary disrepute. Since the war the Flemish Movement has ridden on the rising economic power of coastal Flanders, and has contributed to the political federalization of Belgium, which is now almost complete.

FLN (*Front de Libération Nationale*)

An organization founded in the early 1950s, which campaigned and fought for Algerian independence from France, under the leadership of Mohammed **Ben Bella**. The war with the FLN led to the collapse of the French Fourth Republic in 1958, and the return to power of de **Gaulle**. France's inability to defeat the FLN led to the Evian conference in 1962, and complete Algerian independence. ▷ **OAS; Republic, Fourth** (France)

FNLA (*Frente Nacional de Libertação de Angola*)

Formed in 1962, the FNLA established a government in exile under Holden Roberto in Zaire and, with US assistance, was active in northern Angola, especially after the Portuguese left the country. Poor leadership and reduced US support weakened its effectiveness and it ceased operations in the early 1980s.

Foch, Ferdinand (1851–1929)

French marshal. He taught at the Ecole de Guerre, proved himself a great strategist at the Battle of the **Marne** (1914), Ypres, and other **World War I** battles, and became Allied Commander-in-Chief in Mar 1918. He quarelled with the Prime Minister, **Clemenceau**, about the peace settlement, regarding it as not providing adequately for French security.

Folketinget

Literally 'the People's Thing', the parliament of Denmark located at Christiansborg Palace in Copenhagen. It has 179 members of whom two are elected in the Faroe Islands and two in Greenland, both self-governing regions of the Kingdom of Denmark. The members of the *Folketinget* are elected for periods of four years by universal adult suffrage. The system of voting is proportional representation. Folketinget was established by the Danish constitution of 5 June 1849 as a result of popular pressure for democratic reforms following the February Revolution in France and the death of the absolute monarch, King **Christian VIII** in 1848. In 1901, a Danish political consensus was reached to the effect that a government could not continue if a majority of the members of the Folketinget was against it, thus giving priority to the more democratically elected of the parliament's two chambers. In 1915, female suffrage was introduced in Denmark. On 5 June 1953, as part of a revision of the Danish constitution, the upper chamber of the *Rigsdagen* was abolished and the name Folketinget was carried on as the name of the Danish parliament as such.

Foot, Michael (Mackintosh) (1913–)

British Labour politician. He joined the staff of the *Tribune* in 1937, becoming editor (1948–52 and 1955–60). He was also acting editor of the *Evening Standard* (1942–4) and a political columnist on the *Daily Herald*

(1944–64). He became an MP in 1945, serving until 1992, and was Secretary of State for Employment (1974–6), Deputy Leader (1976–80) then Leader (1980–3) of the **Labour Party**, resigning after his party's heavy defeat in the general election. A prominent figure on the party's left and a pacifist, he has long been a supporter of the Campaign for Nuclear Disarmament (**CND**). A prolific writer, his best-known work is his biography of Aneurin **Bevan**.

Football War (July 1969)

A lightning war fought over several days between Honduras and El Salvador, which was rapidly halted by international pressure. It was provoked by the wave of migration from overpopulated Salvador to the unoccupied territories of Western Honduras, and was so named because recriminations between the two Central American states came to a head during the qualifying matches for the 1970 World Cup.

forced labour camp

A prison camp where those regarded as politically undesirable or of an unwanted nationality are deported to carry out forced labour on behalf of the state. In the modern world they date back to 1918 in Soviet Russia, where millions of citizens regarded with suspicion by the authorities were sent for 'correction' in the 1920s, 30s and 50s. The camps were used more as a means of punishment and social control than of political correction, and most inmates died in the camps. It is estimated that at its peak there were between 12 and 15 million people in Soviet camps. **Hitler** also established forced labour camps. The camps in what was the USSR have largely disappeared since Mikhail **Gorbachev**'s time.

Ford, Gerald Rudolph (1913–)

US politician and 38th President. Educated at the Universities of Michigan and Yale, he served in the US Navy during **World War II**. He became a Republican member of the House of Representatives (1949–73), and on the resignation of Spiro **Agnew** in 1973 became the first appointed Vice-President. He became President (1974–6) when Richard **Nixon** resigned because of the **Watergate** scandal. The full pardon he granted to Nixon the same year, combined with an economic recession and inflation, made him unpopular, and he was defeated in the 1976 presidential election by Jimmy **Carter**. ▷ **Republican Party**

Four Freedoms (1941)

Four basic human rights proclaimed in an annual message to Congress by President Franklin D **Roosevelt** as basic human rights. They included freedom of speech and worship, and freedom from want and fear.

Four Modernizations, The

This refers to the long-term policy aim of the **Chinese Communist Party** to achieve advanced development in the fields of agriculture, industry, science and technology, and national defence. Coined by Premier **Zhou Enlai** at the Third National People's Congress (1964), the phrase was downplayed during the **Cultural Revolution** when ideological correctness took precedence over strictly economic development. After **Mao Zedong**'s death in 1976 the term was revived by **Deng Xiaoping**, and at the Third Plenum of the Party's Eleventh Central Committee (Dec 1978) priority was given to the implementation of the Four Modernizations. Although ambitious targets set in 1978 had to be modified subsequently, the policy has led to free market reforms in the countryside, more autonomy being granted to urban enterprises, increasing professionalization of the army, and encouragement of foreign investment and more extensive trade with the West.

Fourteen Points

A peace programme outlined by US President Woodrow **Wilson** in a message to Congress in 1918, at the end of **World War I**. The programme offered the possibility of an acceptable peace to the Central Powers, and as a result Wilson came to be perceived as a moral leader. It was largely instrumental in bringing about the surrender of Germany and the beginning of peace talks. Several of the points, however, were compromised or defeated in the actual treaty.

Fraga Iribarne, Manuel (1922–)

Spanish politician and academic. As Minister of Information and Tourism under **Franco** (1962–9) he liberalized the regime, above all through the Press Law of 1966. By contrast, he was a hardline Minister of the Interior in 1975–6. In Sep 1976 he founded *Alianza Popular*, which became the main opposition party to the **PSOE** in 1982 and was renamed the **PP** in 1988. A conservative of authoritarian temperament, he was a dynamic, if abrasive, leader of *Alianza* in 1979–86 and was elected again in 1989. In 1990 Fraga was elected President of the regional government of Galicia, his home region.

France

A republic in western Europe. France's 20c history begins in the Third Republic, which lasted from 1870 to 1940. There was great political instability between the World Wars, with several governments holding office for short periods. The country was occupied by Germany from 1940 until 1944, with the pro-German government at Vichy and the Free French in London under Charles de Gaulle. The Fourth Republic began in 1946. There was war with Indo-China (1946–54) and conflict in Algeria (1954–62). The Fifth Republic began in 1958.

Franchet d'Esperey, Louis Félix Marie François (1856–1942)
French soldier. He was made commanding general of the French 5th Army in 1914, gaining success at the Battle of the **Marne**. In 1918 he was appointed Commander-in-Chief of Allied armies in Macedonia, where from Salonica he overthrew Bulgaria and advanced as far as Budapest; only the end of the war prevented his dash for Berlin. He was made Marshal of France in 1922. He had some links to the French extreme right but refused to support **Pétain** in 1940. ▷ **World War I; World War II**

Francis Ferdinand (1863–1914)
Archduke of Austria, nephew and heir-apparent (from 1896) to the Emperor **Francis Joseph**. On a visit to Sarajevo (in modern Yugoslavia) in June 1914 he and his wife, Sophie, were assassinated by the **Black Hand**, a group of young Serbian nationalists, among whom was the perpetrator, Gavrilo **Princip**. Austria, encouraged by Germany, used the incident as a pretext for attacking **Serbia**, which precipitated **World War I**.

Francis Joseph (1830–1916)
Emperor of Austria (1848/1916) and King of Hungary (1867/1916). He was the grandson of Emperor Francis I. During his reign the aspirations of the various nationalities of the empire were rigorously suppressed. He was defeated by the Prussians in 1866, and established the Dual Monarchy of Austria-Hungary in 1867. His annexation of Bosnia-Herzegovina in 1908 agitated Europe and especially Russia, and his government's attack on **Serbia** in 1914 precipitated **World War I**.

Franco (Bahamonde), Francisco (1892–1975)
Spanish general and dictator. He graduated from Toledo military academy in 1910, rising rapidly through the ranks in Spanish Morocco, to become Europe's youngest general in 1926. He oversaw the repression of the Asturias miners' revolt (1934), and during 1935 served as Chief of Staff. In 1936 he joined, at the last moment, the conspiracy against the Popular Front government (elected Feb 1936) which was launched on 17–18 July; the rebellion led to the **Spanish Civil War**. Franco's leadership of the vital Army of Africa, and his close relations with the rebels' Italian and German allies, led to his becoming (Sep 1936) *generalíssimo* of the rebel forces and chief of the Nationalist state. Between Oct 1936 and Apr 1939, he led the Nationalists to victory, and presided over the construction of an authoritarian regime that endured until his death. During **World War II**, he wanted to join Germany and Italy, but **Hitler** was not prepared to pay his price of France's north African territories, at Hendaye (Oct 1940). Franco therefore kept Spain out of the war, but sent the Blue Division to fight in the USSR, and provided the Germans with logistical and intelligence support. During the 1950s, his anti-communism made

possible a rapprochement with the Western powers, the Bases Agreement of 1953 with the USA providing Franco with his breakthrough. The greatest paradox of Franco was that he oversaw the modernization of the Spanish economy in the 1950s and 60s which undermined the political foundations of his police state and prepared it for the transition to democracy. In 1969 he announced that upon his death the monarchy would return in the person of **Juan Carlos**, grandson of Spain's last ruling king. Franco died in Madrid, and within two years almost every vestige of his dictatorship had disappeared.

Franco-German Treaty of Cooperation (Jan 1963)
The treaty signed by President de **Gaulle** and Chancellor **Adenauer** signalling a rapprochement and the ending of centuries of conflict. It made provisions for regular summit meetings, and cooperation and consultation in foreign, economic, and cultural affairs. A symbol of the new, post-war order in Europe, the treaty also underpinned the **EEC**.

Franjiyeh, Suleyman (1910–92)
Lebanese politician. President of Lebanon (and thus a Maronite) from 1970 to 1976, he presided over Lebanon at a particularly tense time in that Palestinian guerrillas ejected from Jordan in 1970–1 began conducting their operations from Palestinian refugee camps in Lebanon. He was President when the civil war broke out in 1975 and demitted office in 1976, the year of the Syrian invasion. He was, however, still active in Maronite politics in 1978 when, as a result of his pro-Syrian stance (which lasted until 1984), a split occurred in Maronite ranks and Phalangist militiamen murdered his son, Tony Franjieh, and other members of his family.

Frank, Anne (1929–45)
Dutch Jewish girl. Her family went into hiding in Amsterdam to evade capture by the occupying German forces during **World War II**. The diary she kept of her life during this period (1942–4) was published in 1947 and is probably the most moving single testament against oppression and persecution. The family was betrayed, and Anne died in a German **concentration camp** in 1945. ▷ **Holocaust**

Frankfurter, Felix (1882–1965)
Austrian-born US law teacher and judge. Educated at the College of the City of New York and at Harvard, he taught at the Harvard Law School (1914–39) and served as an associate justice of the US Supreme Court (1939–62). He was a noted supporter of civil liberties and helped found the American Civil Liberties Union, although in court he advocated judicial restraint in opposing both legislative and executive policy. In

constitutional cases he claimed that judges should consider whether legislators could reasonably have enacted such a law.

Franz Joseph ▷ **Francis Joseph**

Fraser, (John) Malcolm (1930–)
Australian politician. In 1955 he became the youngest MP in the House of Representatives. He was Minister for the Army (1966–8), Defence (1969–71), and Education and Science (1968–9, 1971–2). He became leader of the **Liberal Party of Australia** in 1975, and was Prime Minister in a Liberal–National Country coalition from the same year, retiring from politics after his government's defeat in 1983.

Fraser, Peter (1884–1950)
British-born New Zealand politician. In 1910 he emigrated to New Zealand, and became involved in trade union organization. A founder member of the New Zealand Labour Party (1916), he was imprisoned during **World War I** for opposing conscription. He entered parliament in 1918, became Deputy Party Leader in 1933, and Leader and Prime Minister in 1940, holding office until 1949, when his government was defeated.

Frederick VIII (1843–1912)
King of Denmark (1906/12). He was the son and successor of Christian IX, and brother of Queen Alexandra of Britain. In 1907 he made a state visit to Iceland to celebrate the granting of home rule there (1904). He married Princess Louise of Sweden, and was well-liked for his simple lifestyle. His second son, Prince Carl, became King **Haakon VII** of Norway. He was succeeded by his eldest son, **Christian X**.

Frederick IX (1899–1972)
King of Denmark (1947/72). The son and successor of **Christian X**, he trained as a naval officer (rising to rear-admiral in 1946), and was Crown Prince from 1912. During **World War II** he assisted his father in resistance to the German occupation, and was held under house arrest (1943–5). He granted home rule to the Faroes in 1948, and in 1953 a new constitution provided for female succession to the throne. In 1935 he had married Ingrid, daughter of King **Gustav VI Adolf** of Sweden; their eldest daughter now became crown princess and succeeded him as Queen **Margrethe II** in 1972. Their youngest daughter, Anne-Marie, married King **Constantine II** of Greece, who was later dethroned.

Free French
Frenchmen who answered General de **Gaulle**'s appeal, broadcast from London (18 June 1940), to reject the impending armistice between France

and Germany, and join him in fighting on. He became leader of the Free French forces, and the 2nd French Armoured Division helped to liberate Paris (25 Aug 1944). ▷ **Resistance Movement** (France); **World War II**

Free Officers

In Egypt, a small group of army officers formed after the fiasco of the 1948 war, who were bent on the expulsion of the British from Egypt and the removal of the politicians in power at the time. In the aftermath of the riots of **Black Saturday** (Jan 1952), the Free Officers, fearing that King Farouk might be about to have them arrested, rose and forced Farouk into abdication (July 1952). The Free Officers (with Neguib nominally at their head, but actually led by Gamal Abd al-**Nasser**) took control of the country; Nasser went on to run the country until his death in 1969. The Free Officers played a leading role in Egypt throughout the period until the June War of 1967 when, with the growing rift between Abd al-Hakim **Amer** and Nasser and the former's subsequent suicide, the solidarity of the Free Officers was broken.

Free Officers' Movement (Libya)

Libya became an independent country in 1951 with the Sanusi leader, Amir Idris, as King. His regime was, however, soon condemned by students and young army officers as corrupt and for being dependent on foreign support. Inspired by the pan-Arab and socialist doctrines of Gamal Abd al-**Nasser** and the Ba'ath Party, the Free Officers' Movement, consisting of middle-ranking officers and NCOs and led by Muammar al-**Gaddafi**, seized power. They set up a Revolutionary Command Council and established a military dictatorship. Foreign banks and businesses were nationalized and politcal parties and trade unions were outlawed.

Freedom Charter

The policy document adopted by the Congress Alliance (June 1955), when 3 000 opposition delegates from all regions of South Africa met to coordinate policies, and which was issued by the **ANC** (African National Congress) itself in 1956, setting out its non-racial policy for South Africa, emphasizing its Fabian principles as well as its commitment to racial equality.

Frei (Montalva), Eduardo (1911–82)

Chilean politician. He became one of the leaders of the Social-Christian Falange Party in the late 1930s, and of the new Christian Democratic Party after 1957. His presidency (1964–70) saw an ambitious programme of social reform, which brought Chile substantial international support. His initial scepticism of the **Pinochet** regime turned into outright opposition. By the time of his death, he was widely seen as the father of opposition to the dictatorship.

Freikorps

German paramilitary organizations. Formed in late 1918 and 1919 by military officers who recruited demobilized soldiers, sailors, students and members of the unemployed, the *Freikorps* (literally, 'volunteer corps') played an equivocal and often violent role in the early history of the **Weimar Republic**. Sanctioned by the Social Democratic Army Minister, Noske, their initial purpose was to suppress extreme left-wing insurgency and subsequently to defend Germany's eastern frontier, particularly in Upper Silesia, against Polish irregular forces. But they were strongly anti-republican in spirit and engaged in a campaign of terror and assassination against prominent republican figures as well as attempting to topple the republic in the **Kapp Putsch** of 1920. Despite their official dissolution in 1920, the Freikorps maintained a clandestine existence and were involved in **Hitler**'s failed 1923 putsch. Subsequently quiescent, many Freikorps officers later resurfaced as leaders of the **SA** of the **Nazi Party**.

Frelimo (*Frente de Libertação de Moçambique*, 'Mozambique Liberation Front')

Founded in 1962, it was led by Eduardo **Mondlane** and was based in Dar es Salaam. When Mondlane was assassinated, the leadership passed to Samora **Machel** and Frelimo waged a successful guerrilla war against the Portuguese, establishing liberated zones in which rudimentary governmental structures were established. At independence in 1975, it became the only legal party in Mozambique.

French, John (Denton Pinkstone), Earl of Ypres (1852–1925)

British field marshal. He joined the navy (1866), then the army (1874), and distinguished himself in the Sudan (1884–5) and South Africa (1899–1901). Chief of Imperial General Staff (1911–14), he held supreme command of the British Expeditionary Force in France (1914–15), but was criticized for indecision, and resigned. He was made a viscount (1915) and earl (1921), and was Lord-Lieutenant of Ireland (1918–21). ▷ **World War I**

French Community

A grouping of some former French colonies which under the constitution of the Fifth Republic (1958) opted to stay closely associated with France. The member states had full internal autonomy, but many matters, including currency, defence, and foreign affairs remained the responsibility of the Community, which in effect meant France. Some 12 overseas territories opted to join. Pressures for full independence continued to build up, and in 1960 it became possible to be fully independent within the Community, thus rendering it of no practical relevance. ▷ **French Union; Republic, Fifth** (France)

French State (*Etat français*) (1940–4)

The name given to the regime established after the French defeat in 1940, in which all power was placed in the hands of **Pétain**, to emphasize the break made with the Third Republic; Pétain was given power to promulgate a new constitution, but one was never drawn up. The French State is also known unofficially as the **Vichy** regime, from its capital in the zone not originally occupied by the German Army; it was abolished upon the liberation of occupied France, by an ordinance of Aug 1944. ▷ **collaboration,** (France); **Republic, Third** (France); **World War II**

French Union (*Union française*)

A term for the French Empire introduced by the constitution of the Fourth Republic in 1946. Former colonies were reclassified as departments of France or overseas territories; trust territories became overseas territories; and former protectorates became associated states. The latter had all become independent when the Union was renamed the *Communauté* ('community') in 1958; the former colonies rapidly gained their independence also, leaving only a few small overseas departments and territories (**DOM-TOM**). ▷ **Republic, Fourth** (France)

Frihedsråd

Literally 'Freedom Council', a coordinating body established in Denmark (Sep 1943) in order to regulate and escalate the country's resistance against the Nazi occupation (1940–5). The formation of the *Frihedsråd* came in response to the dismissal of the Danish government by the German occupation force (29 Aug 1943), following extensive strike action and several acts of sabotage in Danish towns and cities. The Frihedsråd gathered all factions of the Danish resistance movement, from Communists to Conservatives. By definition, the organization carried no official authority, but it played a vital role in organizing the growing sabotage campaign and in the formation and command of a Danish underground army numbering 43 000 men at the time of the German capitulation. The Frihedsråd was supported by the Allied nations, particularly the UK, and its activities contributed greatly to the recognition of Demnark as an Allied nation after **World War II**. During the war, the Frihedsråd was also involved in formulating the broadly democratic political direction that peacetime Denmark was to follow. Several of its members took office in the first Danish post-war government, formed in May 1945 immediately after the liberation of Denmark by Allied forces. ▷ **Denmark, German Invasion of**

Frolov, Ivan Timofeevich (1929–)

Soviet philosopher, ideologist and journalist. He had a long education in Moscow before turning to journalism in the 1960s and 1970s when he had two spells on the *World Marxist Review* in Prague divided by a turn as editor of *Problems of Philosophy* in Moscow. In the latter case he had some disagreements with orthodox views that made him a target for Mikhail **Gorbachev**'s recruiting policy. In 1986 he was appointed editor of *Communist*, in 1989 editor-in-chief of *Pravda*, and in 1990 a member of the **Politburo**. However, Gorbachev's role was all but past.

Front de Libération de Québec (FLQ)

Canadian terrorist organization. On the extreme left wing and anti-capitalist, it targeted the prosperous English-speaking sector of Quebec society. The FLQ had little formal organization, although arrangements were made for its members to train with the **PLO**. It gave the impression of being a much larger conspiracy than it actually was, for its name was simply appropriated by small independent groups to indicate responsibility for terrorist attacks. The arrest of Pierre Vallière and Charles Gagnon, two of the movement's theorists, set off its most active period which culminated in the **October Crisis** of 1970.

Frunze, Mikhail Vasilevich (1885–1925)

Russian revolutionary and professional soldier. Frunze exercised profound influence upon Soviet military doctrine. A Bolshevik from 1904, active in both the 1905 and 1917 events, he rose to prominence in the **Russian Civil War** with successful commands on the eastern and southern fronts. But he was soon engaged in debate with **Trotsky**, commissar for War, about creating a **Red Army** fit for the future. In 1925 he displaced him but died during an operation, often claimed to have been a medical murder. But his concept of unified command and policy won through.

▷ **Bolsheviks**

Fuad I (1868–1936)

King of Egypt (1922/36). The son of Khedive Ismail Pasha, he was Sultan of Egypt from 1917, and became King when the British protectorate was ended. His position in Egypt was not helped by the fact that his father had been responsible for the sale (at a farcically low price) of Egyptian Suez Canal shares to Britain, and his brother Tawfiq's incapacity as a ruler, which had led to the British occupation of 1883. The Egyptian nationalists of the Wafd Party despised his dispensation, and his acquisition and flaunting of conspicuous wealth, along with his corrupt entourage of hangers-on, provoked adverse comment. In an attempt to control the party, he suspended the constitution in 1931, but was forced to restore it in 1935. He was succeeded by his son, Farouk I, who was to be the last King of Egypt.

Fukuda Takeo (1905–)

Japanese politician and financier. He worked at the Ministry of Finance (1929–50) and was Deputy Vice-Minister (1945–6), Director of the Banking Bureau (1946–7), and Director of the Budget Bureau (1947–50). A member of the House of Representatives since 1952, he served as Minister of Finance (1965–6, 1968–71 and 1973–4). In 1974 he became deputy Prime Minister and Director of the Economic Planning Agency, until his appointment as Prime Minister (1976–8). He was President of the **Liberal Democratic Party** in 1966–8 and 1976–8.

Fulbright, James William (1905–)

US politician. Educated at the University of Arkansas, and George Washington University Law School, he was a Rhodes scholar at Oxford, and taught law in Washington and Arkansas. He was elected to the US House of Representatives as a Democrat in 1942 and to the Senate in 1944. He sponsored the Fulbright Act (1946), which established an exchange scholarship system for students and teachers between the USA and other countries. As Chairman of the Senate Foreign Relations Committee, he became a major critic of the escalation of the **Vietnam War**. He lost his Senate seat in 1974. ▷ **Democratic Party**

fuorusciti

The Italian word (literally, 'exile', 'outlaw', 'émigré') often applied to political opponents of the fascist regime who fled, or were forced to leave, Italy during the 1920s and 1930s. Many served in the republican armies in the **Spanish Civil War** and consequently fought against Italian troops sent by **Mussolini** to assist **Franco**. They achieved a famous victory over Italian fascist 'volunteers' at the Battle of Guadalajara (Mar 1937). ▷ **fascism**

Furtseva, Yekaterina Alexeevna (1910–74)

The first woman member of the Soviet Communist Party's **Politburo**. After a technical education, she became a party worker and rose to be district secretary in Moscow in 1942 and a member of the Central Committee in 1956. A supporter of Nikita **Khrushchev**, she was brought into the Politburo in 1957 in the aftermath of the **Anti-Party Plot**. Hardly a major political figure, she was pushed out in 1961. However, from 1960 until her death she was Minister of Culture and apparently had no difficulty in insisting on ever greater conformity.

G

Gaddafi, Muammar (1942–)

Libyan political and military leader. He abandoned his university studies in favour of military training in 1963, and went on to form the **Free Officers Movement** which overthrew King Idris in 1969. He became Chairman of the Revolutionary Command Council, promoted himself to colonel (the highest rank in the revolutionary army) and became Commander-in-Chief of the Libyan Armed Forces. As de facto head of state, he set about eradicating colonialism by expelling foreigners and closing down British and US bases. He also encouraged a religious revival and return to the fundamental principles of Islam. A somewhat unpredictable figure, Gaddafi has openly supported violent revolutionaries in other parts of the world while ruthlessly pursuing Libyan dissidents both at home and abroad. He has waged a war in Chad, threatened other neighbours, and in the 1980s saw his territory bombed and aircraft shot down by the Americans.

Gairy, Eric Matthew (1922–)

Grenadian politician. In 1950 he founded the country's first political party, the left-of-centre Grenada United Labour Party (GULP) and was soon a dominant figure in Caribbean politics. He held the posts of Chief Minister in the Federation of the **West Indies** (1957–62), Premier of Grenada (1967–74) and, on independence in 1974, Prime Minister. He was ousted by the left-wing leader, Maurice **Bishop**, in 1979 and GULP was defeated in the 1990 election by the National Democratic Congress of Nicholas Braithwaite. ▷ **West Indies, Federation of the**

Gaitskell, Hugh (Todd Naylor) (1906–63)

British politician. He became a socialist during the 1926 **General Strike**. He became an MP in 1945, was Minister of Fuel and Power (1947) and of Economic Affairs (1950), and Chancellor of the Exchequer (1950–1). In 1955 he was elected Leader of the Opposition by a large majority over **Bevan**. He bitterly opposed **Eden**'s Suez action (1956), and refused to accept a narrow conference vote for unilateral disarmament (1960). This caused a crisis of leadership in which he was challenged by Harold **Wilson** (1960) and Arthur Greenwood (1961), but he retained the loyalty of most Labour MPs. ▷ **Labour Party** (UK); **Suez Crisis**

Gallipoli Campaign (1915–16)
A major campaign of **World War I**. With stalemate on the Western Front, the British War Council advocated operations against the Turks to secure the Dardanelles and aid Russia. The land campaign began with amphibious assaults on the Gallipoli Peninsula (Apr 1915). Australian and New Zealand forces were heavily involved: the beach where they landed is still known as Anzac Cove. Allied casualties were 250 000 out of 480 000 engaged. The operation was abandoned as a costly failure, with successful evacuations of all remaining troops in Jan 1916. ▷ **Dardanelles**

Galtieri, Leopoldo Fortunato (1926–)
Argentine soldier and politician. After training at the National Military College, he was commissioned in 1945 and progressed steadily to the rank of lieutenant-general in 1979, when he joined the junta which had been in power since the military coup which ousted Isabelita **Perón** in 1976. In 1981 the leader of the junta, General Viola, died and Galtieri succeeded him as President. The state of the Argentine economy declined and, to offset mounting domestic criticism, in Apr 1982 Galtieri ordered the invasion of the long-disputed Malvinas (Falkland) Islands. Their recovery by Britain, after a brief and humiliating war, brought about his downfall. He was court-martialled in 1983 and sentenced to 12 years' imprisonment for negligence in starting and losing the **Falklands War**.

Gamelin, Maurice Gustave (1872–1958)
French soldier. He attained lieutenant-colonel's rank in 1914, but no divisional command until 1925. In 1935 seniority brought him the post of Chief of Staff of the army and membership of the *Conseil supérieur de la guerre* ('Supreme War Council') (1930); but his unfitness for overall command was exposed in his pronouncement that 'To attack is to lose'. In 1940 he refused to rethink his outmoded defensive strategy of 'solid fronts', which crumbled under the German **Blitzkrieg**. He was hurriedly replaced by General **Weygand**, tried, and imprisoned (1943–5). ▷ **Riom Trial**

Gandhi, Indira (Priyadarshini) (1917–84)
Indian politician. The daughter of Jawaharlal Nehru, she was educated at Visva-Bharati University (Bengal) and Oxford, and in 1942 married Feroze Gandhi (d.1960). She became President of the Indian Congress Party (1959–60), Minister of Information (1964) and Prime Minister (1966–77) after the death of Shastri. After her conviction for election malpractices, she declared a state of emergency (1975–7), was defeated in elections by the Janata Party, and was Premier again (1980–4). She achieved a considerable reputation through her work as a leader of the developing nations, but was unable to stem sectarian violence at home.

She was assassinated in New Delhi by Sikh extremists who were members of her bodyguard, and succeeded by her elder son, Rajiv **Gandhi.** ▷ **Indian National Congress**

Gandhi, M(ohandas) K(aramchand), 'Mahatma' (1869–1948)
Indian nationalist leader. He studied law in London, but in 1893 went to South Africa, where he spent 21 years opposing discriminatory legislation against Indians. In 1914 he returned to India, where he supported the Home Rule movement, and became leader of the **Indian National Congress**, advocating a policy of non-violent non-cooperation to achieve independence. Following his first major non-cooperation and **civil disobedience** campaign (1919–22), he was jailed for conspiracy (1922–4). In 1930 he led a 200-mile march to the sea to collect salt in symbolic defiance of the government monopoly; this marked the beginning of the second major campaign of civil disobedience. On his release from prison (1931), he attended the London Round Table Conference on Indian constitutional reform. In 1946 he negotiated with the Cabinet Mission which recommended the new constitutional structure. After independence (1947), he tried to stop the Hindu/Muslim conflict in Bengal, a policy which led to his assassination in Delhi by Nathuram Godse, a Hindu fanatic. ▷ **Non-Cooperation Movement; Round Table Conferences; Swaraj**

Gandhi, Rajiv (1944–91)
Indian politician. As the eldest son of Indira **Gandhi** and the grandson of **Nehru**, he was born into a Kashmiri-Brahmin family which had governed India for all but four years since 1947. He was educated at Doon School (Dehra Dun) and Cambridge University, where he failed his engineering degree. In contrast to his younger brother, Sanjay (1946–80), he exhibited little interest in politics and became a pilot with Indian Airlines. Following Sanjay's death in an air crash, he assumed the family's political mantle, being elected to his brother's Amethi parliamentary seat (1981) and appointed a General-Secretary of the Congress (I) Party (1983). After his mother's assassination in 1984, he became Prime Minister and secured a record majority in the parliamentary elections later that year. He attempted to cleanse and rejuvenate the Congress (I), inducting new technocrats, and introducing a freer market economic programme. Congress (I), however, suffered heavy losses under his leadership in the 1989 general election, and he was forced to resign as Premier after his party was defeated in the general election of Nov 1989. He was assassinated by Tamil terrorists during a subsequent election campaign in May 1991.

Gang of Four
A description given by **Mao Zedong** to the Shanghai-based hard-core radicals of the Chinese **Cultural Revolution**: Zhang Chunqiao, Yao Wen-

yuan, Wang Hongwen, and Jiang Qing. Zhang and Yao were veterans of the Shanghai party machine. Wang emerged as a workers' leader in the Shanghai 'January Revolution' of 1967. Jiang, Mao's wife, enjoyed his trust and was the acknowledged leader of the Gang. All were members of the politburo when they were arrested and disgraced in 1976.

Gao Gang (Kao Kang) (c.1902–55)
Chinese political leader. In the mid-1930s he was in charge of a small independent communist area at Baoan, Shaanxi, where the **Long March** led by **Mao Zedong** ended. Mao and Gao Gang became close political allies, and he later became Chief Party Secretary of Manchuria (1949). He set the national pace in economic development, but in 1955 was accused of attempting to set up a 'separate kingdom'. He apparently committed suicide. ▷ **Chinese Communist Party**

Gapon, Georgei Apollonovich (1870–1906)
Ukrainian priest and reformer. In 1902 he became leader of the so-called Union of Russian Factory Workers. Without his knowledge, this seems to have been financed by the Tsarist police as a means of penetrating and controlling the working-class movement. However, with deteriorating economic conditions, its numbers grew; and in Jan 1905 Gapon was quite happy to lead them in a procession to the Winter Palace in the sincere belief that the Tsar **Nicholas II** would accede to their demands. The result was **Bloody Sunday**. Thereafter, idealists like Gapon could exercise less and less influence on Russian developments.

Garang, Colonel John (1943–)
Sudanese soldier. After studying agricultural economics in the USA, he returned to Sudan, where he joined the army. Another period in the USA, for military training, was followed by a post at the Military Research Centre in Khartoum. In 1983 he formed the Sudanese People's Liberation Movement in the southern Sudan. Backed by Marxists in Ethiopia, the movement grew out of Garang's belief that the resources of southern Sudan were being exploited by the country's northerners. Waging a relentless guerrilla campaign, the organization has posed a considerable threat to the stability of the Sudan. Involving conflict with the regular Sudanese army, the movement's activities have done much to increase the sufferings of the people in a country already racked by famine.

García, Perez Alan (1949–)
Peruvian politician. After studying law in Lima, he continued his education in Guatemala, Spain and France. He returned to Peru in 1978 and was elected to the National Congress, for the moderate, left-wing APRA

Party, which he had joined as a youth. Four years later he became Secretary-General of the party and in 1985 succeeded Fernando **Belaúnde** as President, becoming the first civilian to do so in democratic elections. He inherited an ailing economy which forced him to trim his socialist programme. By 1991 the economy was in tatters, and García was a prisoner of the deepening struggle between the **Sendero Luminoso** and the armed forces in the Andes and a conservative Congress in Lima. He was succeeded by the conservative Alberto Fujimori.

Garvey, Marcus (1887–1940)
Advocate of black nationalism. Born and brought up in poverty in Jamaica, he promoted self-help for blacks and black pride and in 1914 founded the Universal Negro Improvement Association. Two years later, he left Jamaica for New York, his arrival in New York coinciding with the wave of black migration into Harlem. Despite little formal education, he proved to be a gifted writer and speaker. It was in the ghettos of the northern cities that he found his greatest following, reaching blacks through his weekly *Negro World* and greatly expanding his Association, a forerunner of the black nationalist movement. However, his call for a return to Africa attracted little interest. He founded such enterprises as the Black Factories Corporation and the Black Star Line, a steamship line owned and operated by blacks, which, however, collapsed in 1921 due to mismanagement. In 1923 he was convicted of mail fraud, imprisoned, and later deported. After he left the country, his black nationalist movement went into decline. He died in obscurity in London.

Gastarbeiter
A German term for the foreign, usually Mediterranean, workers who have been employed in large numbers in the Federal German economy since the 1960s. The term (literally 'guest workers') belies the fact that many of these migrants have settled in Germany with their families and that their presence is indispensable to the German economy. However, only a few have become German citizens and many return to their country of origin after completing a predetermined period of employment.

Gau
A National Socialist administrative district created initially to organize the **Nazi Party** during the **Weimar Republic** and coordinate electoral and other work. The *Gau* became a form of administration parallel to the traditional one in Nazi Germany. The *Gaue* were retained after **Hitler**'s takeover, each headed by a *Gauleiter* who was a party official answerable to Hitler, not the civil authorities. In this way, the Nazis created a regional administrative structure which operated parallel to the traditional one and allowed the party to bypass the civil service when it so desired.

Needless to say, conflict developed between the party and civil authorities over their precise areas of competence.

Gaulle, Charles (André Joseph Marie) de (1898–1970)
French general and politician. Born into a devout Catholic and conservative family, he was educated by the Jesuits and at Saint-Cyr military college, and fought with distinction in **World War I**. Only a colonel in 1940, he was known as the author of several books on military and historical topics, especially one advocating mechanized warfare. He was promoted temporary General of Brigade (1 June 1940), and four days later entered the government as Under-Secretary at the Ministry of National Defence. Refusing to accept the armistice, he fled to England, where (18 June 1940) he appealed to the French people to continue the struggle. As the leader of the **Free French**, he fought many diplomatic battles against President **Roosevelt** to ensure that France was treated as a co-belligerent, thus emerging in 1944 as head of the Provisional Government. He organized the election of an assembly to draw up a new constitution, but resigned in protest at the trend of its deliberations (Jan 1946), thus consigning himself to the political sidelines until 1958 when the Algerian crisis led to his recall to power as the last Prime Minister of the Fourth Republic. He used this position to draw up a new constitution for the Fifth Republic, which embodied the presidential system he had wanted in 1946. It was approved by a referendum (Sep 1958) and he became its first President (1959–69). He defeated two attempted coups, launched by supporters of a French Algeria, and negotiated Algerian independence (1962). France's colonies were also granted independence, while he concentrated on winning France a leading place in Europe by excluding Britain from the **EC** (European Community) and by signing an historic reconciliation treaty with Germany (both 1963). He developed a French nuclear deterrent, and removed France from its military obligations under **NATO** (1965). His supporters won by a big majority in the elections following the 'events' of 1968, but he lost a referendum on constitutional reform in 1969, and resigned. ▷ **Republic, Fifth** (France); **Republic, Fourth** (France)

Gaullists
Supporters of General de **Gaulle**, more specifically members of political parties which followed him in his lifetime, and claimed to embody his legacy after his death. Their names have changed frequently. The principal ones are RPF (*Rassemblement du peuple français*, 'Assembly of the French People') (1947–54), UNR, later UNR-UDT (*Union pour la nouvelle république*, 'Union for the New Republic') (1958–67), UDR (*Union des démocrates pour la Vᵉ République*, 'Union of Democrats for the Fifth Republic') (1967–76); and RPR (*Rassemblement pour la République*, 'Assembly for the Republic') since 1976. Gaullists emphasize the need

for a strong foreign policy, and have become one of the two main constituents of the right wing. ▷ **Independent Republican Party**

Gaylani, Rashid Ali al- (1892–1965)
Iraqi politician, the Prime Minister of Iraq in 1933, 1936–8 and 1940–1. An opponent of Nuri al-**Sa'id** and a fervent nationalist, he eventually fell in with the prevailing Iraqi opinion, which resented the British presence in the country; after initially permitting British reinforcement in Iraq, he was later implicated in supporting Iraqi armed resistance to the British and was expelled after the surrender of the Iraqi army. He returned to Iraq but, accused of plotting against Abd al-Krim **Qassim**, fled and died in exile.

Gaza Strip
An Israeli-occupied Mediterranean coastal area under military administration from 1967 to 1994. It was formerly part of Egyptian Sinai (1949–67). There has been considerable tension in the area since the beginning of the Palestinian uprising (*Intifada*) in 1988. In 1993 and 1994 peace agreements between **Israel** and the **PLO** were signed, setting out plans for limited Palestinian self-rule in the **West Bank** and the Gaza Strip.

Gdańsk formerly **German Danzig**
The capital of Gdańsk vovoidship, north Poland. Held by Prussia (1793–1919), it became a free city within the Polish tariff area in 1919. Its annexation by Germany in 1939 precipitated **World War II**, and it returned to Poland in 1945. In the 1980s the Lenin shipyard was the scene of much labour unrest in support of **Solidarity**.

Gdlyan, Telman Khorenovich (1940–)
Soviet lawyer. Of Armenian extraction, he, along with **Ivanov**, exposed misdemeanours in Uzbekistan involving the late Leonid **Brezhnev**'s son-in-law, he then proceeded to attack other figures such as Yegor **Ligachev** but encountered hostility even among Mikhail **Gorbachev**'s supporters. Both Gdlyan and Ivanov were very popular with the general public, and they certainly undermined communist credibility.

Geisel, Ernesto (1908–)
Brazilian general and dictator. Prominent in both the **Quadros** and **Castelo Branco** administrations, his ascendancy in 1973–4, largely a result of his brother Orlando's control of the military, marked the re-emergence of Golberi de Couto e Silva, nemesis of the hardliners, such as Air Force Minister Sousa e Melo and Navy Minister Rademakr, who believed in an uncompromising dictatorship. During Geisel's presidency (1974–9), he and Golberi successfully masterminded a return to a regime in which the military acted in their traditional role as a moderating power. Geisel's

imperial style allowed him subsequently to play a discrete role in politics. His support for Tancredo **Neves** in early 1985 was decisive in persuading the army to acquiesce in a return to civilian rule.

Gemayel, Amin (1942–)
Lebanese politician. The son of Pierre **Gemayel**, he trained as a lawyer and supported his brother, Bashir **Gemayel**, in the 1975–6 civil war, becoming President (1982–) after the latter's assassination. Politically more moderate, his policies initially proved no more successful in determining a peaceful settlement of the problems of Lebanese government.

Gemayel, Bashir (1947–82)
Lebanese army officer and politician. The youngest son of Pierre **Gemayel**, he joined the militia of his father's Phalangist Party and came to be the party's Political Director in the Ashrefieh sector of East Beirut, where he was an active leader of the Christian militia in the civil war of 1975–6. By the systematic elimination of rivals, he came to command the military forces of East Beirut. He distanced his party from Israeli support, and aimed to expel all foreign influence from Lebanese affairs. Having twice escaped assassination, he was killed in a bomb explosion while president-elect, ten days before he was due to take office. His brother, Amin **Gemayel**, was elected President in his stead, one week later.

Gemayel, Pierre (1905–)
Lebanese politician. A member of the Maronite Christian community of Lebanon, he was educated in Beirut and Paris and trained as a pharmacist. In 1936 he founded the Kataeb or Phalangist Party, modelled on the Spanish and German fascist organizations, and in 1937 became its leader. He was twice imprisoned (1937 and 1943), held various ministerial posts (1960–7), and led the Phalangist Militia in the 1975–6 civil war. ▷ **Gemayel, Amin; Gemayel, Bashir**

General Strike (4–12 May 1926)
A national strike in Britain, organized by the Trades Union Congress (TUC) in support of an existing miners' strike to resist wage cuts. The government organized special constables and volunteers to counter the most serious effects of the strike, and issued an anti-strike propaganda journal, *The British Gazette*. The TUC called off the strike, though the miners' strike continued fruitlessly for three more months.

Generalitat
The Catalan autonomous government; an institution of medieval origin restored under the Second Republic of 1931–6 by the Catalan Autonomy Statute of Sep 1932. Dominated by the Catalan Left, it clashed repeatedly with the right-wing administration in Madrid. In Oct 1934 it joined the

left-wing rising against the central government by declaring a Catalan Republic within a Federal Republic of Spain. Following its defeat, the Generalitat was suspended until the victory of the Popular Front in Feb 1936. At the beginning of the **Spanish Civil War**, it shared power with the **CNT**-dominated Anti-Fascist Militia Committee, but lost a great deal of power to the central government after the CNT and **POUM** had been crushed in the May Days of 1937. Dissolved under **Franco**, the Generalitat was re-established after his death. ▷ **Catalan Autonomy Statutes; Republic, Second** (Spain)

Geneva Peace Conference (1973)

The conference, arranged by Henry Kissinger under the auspices of the **UN**, to discuss the disengagement of Israeli and Arab forces and to achieve a peace settlement after the **October War**. Despite its failure to achieve substantial results, the conference (convened 21 Dec 1973), was remarkable for its efforts towards getting Egypt, Jordan and Israel together. The USA and USSR attended in what was really an observational capacity, but the actual ceasefire arrangements were achieved by Kissinger in his so-called 'shuttle' diplomacy.

Genoa, Economic Conference of (Apr–May 1922)

Conference of 34 states hosted by Italy to promote European economic reconstruction and to discuss the restoration of economic and diplomatic relations with the USSR. Presided over by Luigi **Facta**, the conference achieved little on either front. Instead, it served to bring together Soviet and German delegates who took the opportunity to arrange closer military collaboration, signing the Treaty of **Rapallo** (16 Apr 1922).

Genscher, Hans-Dietrich (1927–)

German politician. He trained as a lawyer, studying at Leipzig before he moved to West **Germany** in 1952. He became Secretary-General of the Free Democratic Party (**FDP**) in 1959, and was Minister of the Interior for five years before becoming, in 1974, Vice-Chancellor and Foreign Minister in **Schmidt**'s coalition government. In the same year, he became Chairman of the FDP, a post to which he was re-elected in 1982. He retained his cabinet post after 1982 in the coalition between the FDP and the **Christian Democrats**. He played a crucial role in the maintenance and furtherance of the **Ostpolitik** after the fall of the Social Democratic Party (**SPD**).

Gentile, Giovanni (1875–1944)

Italian philosopher and politician. Unlike his friend Benedetto **Croce**, Gentile became a firm supporter of **fascism**, being chosen by **Mussolini** to serve as Education Minister in 1922. He twice served as a member of the **Fascist Grand Council** (1923–4 and 1925–9) and rallied to the **Duce** in the autumn of 1943 when he established the fascist Republic of **Salò**. He was killed in Florence by anti-fascist partisans.

Gentlemen's Agreement (1907)
An informal pact between the USA and Japan under which Japan agreed to limit Japanese migration to the USA in return for a promise by President Theodore **Roosevelt** not to discriminate against the Japanese.

Genyosha
A Japanese ultra-nationalist organization (literally, 'Black Ocean Society') created by ex-**samurai** from Fukuoka prefecture in 1881. Dissatisfied with their lot and critical of the new Meiji state, these ex-samurai promoted conservative values at home and vigorous expansion abroad. The *Genyosha* was responsible in the 1880s for several terrorist attacks on government ministers thought to be 'soft' in their dealings with the West, and engaged in conspiratorial activity in Korea and Manchuria. While some members of the Genyosha sought genuine cooperation with Asian revolutionaries, most supported the aggressive actions of the Japanese military during the 1930s. The Genyosha was forcibly disbanded in 1945.

George II (1890–1947)
King of Greece (1922/3 and 1935/47). The son of **Constantine I** and grandson of George I of Greece, he succeeded to the throne on his father's second abdication in 1922, but was deposed the following year by a military junta. Restored to the throne by plebiscite in 1935, he worked closely with his dictatorial Prime Minister, Ioannis **Metaxas**. When Greece was overrun by the Germans, after the country had successfully resisted the Italian invasion of 1940–1, he withdrew to Crete and then England. In 1946 he was restored to the throne, again by plebiscite. He was succeeded by his brother, **Paul I**.

George V (1865–1936)
King of the United Kingdom (1910/36). He was the second son of **Edward VII**. He served in the navy, travelled in many parts of the Empire, and was created Prince of Wales in 1901. His reign saw the creation of the Union of South Africa (1910), **World War I**, the **Irish Free State** settlement (1922), and the **General Strike** (1926). His consort, Mary (1867–1953), married him in 1893; she organized women's war work (1914–18), and continued with many public and philanthropic activities after the death of her husband. They had five sons and one daughter.

George VI (1895–1952)
King of the United Kingdom (1936/52). The second son of **George V**, he served in the Grand Fleet at the Battle of Jutland (1916). In 1920 he was

created Duke of York, and married in 1923. He played at Wimbledon in the All-England tennis championships in 1926. He ascended the throne on the abdication of his elder brother, **Edward VIII**. During **World War II** he continued to reside in bomb-damaged Buckingham Palace, visited all theatres of war, and delivered many broadcasts, for which task he mastered a speech impediment. He and his wife, Elizabeth, (*née* Elizabeth Bowes-Lyon), had two children, Princess Elizabeth (later Queen **Elizabeth II**) and Princess Margaret.

gerarchi

The Italian word (literally, 'hierarch') applied by **Mussolini** to the leading figures of the **Fascist Party**; hence the name of the party periodical, *Gerarchia*.

Gerhardsen, Einar (1897–)

Norwegian politician. Of working-class origin, he rose to prominence in the Norwegian Labour Party between the wars but was not a member of the Labour government which was in power when the German invasion of Norway took place in 1940. This, together with his active participation in the Resistance, made him well qualified to lead the first post-war government in Norway. He was Prime Minister (1945–51 and 1955–65), leading Norway into membership of **NATO** in 1949 and presiding over a long period of economic growth and social welfare legislation. ▷ **Norway, German Invasion of**

German–Soviet Pact (Hitler–Stalin Pact) (23 Aug 1939)

Following Germany's failure to gain British support for, or even toleration of, her expansionist plans after 1938 and following difficulties surrounding the conclusion of a British-French-Soviet pact of mutual assistance directed against Germany, the German and Soviet governments moved swiftly to settle their differences. The respective Foreign Ministers, **Ribbentrop** and **Molotov**, signed an agreement which defined territorial interests in Eastern Europe (effectively partitioning the region between them) renounced the use of force against one another, guaranteed friendly relations and allowed extensive economic relations to develop. The fate of Poland was thereby sealed, but **Hitler**'s attack on the USSR in June 1941 ended what was always an opportunistic and cynical agreement.

Germany, East (*Deutsche Demokratische Republik*, 'German Democratic Republic')

Former socialist republic of north central Europe, divided into 14 counties, with East Berlin as its capital. Administered by the USSR after the 1945 partition of Germany, a Soviet model of government was established, with the Socialist Unity Party (**SED**) guaranteed a pre-eminent role, in 1949. Anti-Soviet demonstrations were put down in 1953, and East Germany was recognized by the USSR as an independent republic the following year. The flow of refugees to West Germany continued until 1961, but was largely stopped by the building of the **Berlin Wall.** East Germany was governed by the People's Chamber, a single-chamber parliament (*Volkskammer*) of 500 Deputies, which elected a 29-member Council of State (*Staatsrat*), a Council of Ministers (*Ministerrat*), and a National Defence Council. The movement for democratic reform, as well as mounting economic crisis, culminated (Nov 1989) in the opening of the **Berlin Wall** and other border crossings to the West, and a more open government policy. Free elections (Mar 1990) paved the way for a currency union with West Germany (July) and full political unification (Oct). ▷ **Germany, West**

Germany, West (*Deutschland* or *Deutsches Reich*; *Bundesrepublik Deutschland*, 'Federal Republic of Germany')

Former Central European state, divided into 15 states (*Länder*), with Berlin as federal capital and Bonn as seat of government. Location of the union of the ancient Germanic tribes within the Frankish Empire of Charlemagne in the 8c and of an elective monarchy after 918 under Otto I, with the Holy Roman Empire divided into several hundred states. Many reforms and territorial changes took place during the Napoleonic era, and after the Congress of Vienna (1814–15) a German Confederation of 39 states under **Austria** was formed. Under Bismarck, **Prussia** succeeded Austria as the leading German power and excluded her from the North German Confederation. The union of Germany and foundation of the Second **Reich** (1871), with the King of Prussia as hereditary German Emperor, gave rise, from around 1900, to an aggressive foreign policy which eventually led to **World War I**. After the German defeat, the Second *Reich* was replaced by the democratic **Weimar Republic** and, in 1933, political power passed to the **Nazi Party**. **Hitler**'s acts of aggression as Chancellor and Leader (*Führer*) of the totalitarian Third *Reich*, eventually led to **World War II** and a second defeat for Germany, with the collapse of the German political regime. The area of Germany was subsequently reduced, and occupied by the UK, USA, France, USSR and Poland whose zone is now recognized as sovereign Polish territory. This Western occupation softened with the creation of the Federal Republic of Germany (1949) out of the three western zones. Its federal system of government, built around 10 states (*Länder*) with considerable powers, has since absorbed East Germany (Oct 1990) as five additional states. A leading industrial and trading nation, following major reconstruction after World War II, Germany is now a dominant force in the European Monetary System. ▷ **Land**

Gestapo

An abbreviation of *Geheime Staatspolizei*, the political police of the German Third **Reich**, founded in 1933 by **Goering** on the basis of the

Prussian political police. It soon extended throughout Germany, and from 1936 came under the control of **Himmler**, as head of the **SS**. ▷ **Nazi Party**

Geyl, Pieter (1887–1966)
Dutch historian and patriot. He was educated in The Hague, at Leiden and in Italy. After serving as London correspondent of the *Nieuwe Rotterdamsche Courant* (1913–19), he was appointed the first Professor of Dutch Studies at London University (1919–36) and Professor of Modern History at Utrecht (1936–58). During **World War II**, he was imprisoned in **Buchenwald** and other Nazi concentration camps. He was a believer in a 'greater Netherlands', always mourning the loss of Dutch-speaking Flanders and Brabant during the Eighty Years Wars in the late 16c. As a historian, however, he was a climatologist and environmentalist, arguing that the outcome of the Dutch revolt against Habsburg Spain was dictated by movements of rivers and water-currents rather than religion or economics. His multi-volume history of the Eighty Years War and its sequels were published in the 1930s, translated into English as *The Revolt of the Netherlands* and *The Netherlands Divided*, while his struggle against Hitlerian domination of Europe is reflected in his *Napoleon, For and Against* (1944). He was also a poet and essayist, debating with numerous living and dead historians, and was the leading interpreter of the Dutch past to his country and the world.

Ghadr Party and Movement
Originally an organization of Indian migrants, especially Punjabis, settled in British Columbia and on the West Coast of the USA, it derived its name from the title of its journal, *Ghadr* (Urdu, 'revolution'). Influenced by the activities of Irish radicals and Russian revolutionaries, a highly-organized conspiracy was hatched at the start of **World War I**, the Indian–Berlin Committee of the 'Hindustan Ghadr Party' offering money and arms to help raise a revolt against the British in India. Accordingly, large numbers of Ghadrites returned to the subcontinent. Many were arrested, but by late 1914 a substantial body of party members and supporters was established in the Punjab. Led by men such as Rashbehari Bose and Sachin Sayal, attempts were made to foster mutiny in the Indian army; bombs were manufactured, robberies committed and arsenals raided in order to raise arms and supplies for a general uprising. However, the British pre-empted this plan, arresting large numbers of Ghadrites in Punjab, Bengal, Singapore and elsewhere. A series of trials, including the 1915 Lahore Conspiracy Case, resulted, in which Ghadrites and others accused of revolutionary activities were prosecuted under the Defence of India Act; 46 people were hanged and 194 were imprisoned. A total of 145 revolutionaries were hanged or killed by the police, and some 306 sentenced to transportation. Later, further trials of Ghadrites were held in the USA, whilst in India those revolutionary cells still active were riven

by factionalism. Attempts to revive the Ghadr Movement in India after 1919 failed due to the growing popularity and success of the Gandhian Congress, although in the 1930s and 1940s returning Ghadrites, having served out their term in prison, often became activists once again in the Indian Communist movement.

Ghaffar Khan, Abd al- (1891–1988)
Muslim Indian politician. He was from North-West Frontier Province, where in 1921 he formed *Khudai Khidmatgar* ('Servants of God') to act as an agent of social welfare and peaceful political change in the mostly Muslim province. Because of his close links with the **Indian National Congress** and his strict adherence to M K **Gandhi**'s technique of **Satyagraha** he became popularly known as the 'Frontier Gandhi'. Due to the close cooperation of Khudai Khidmatgar and the Congress, North-West Frontier province became the only one with a Muslim majority to be controlled by the Congress after the 1937 national election. Abd al-Ghaffar boycotted the July 1947 referendum on the issue of North-West Frontier province's accession to Pakistan, and this led to his political decline and that of his party. His later demands for an independent Pathan state resulted in repeated imprisonment in Pakistan and eventual exile in Afghanistan.

Ghana
A modern state created by the union of two former British territories, British Gold Coast (a Crown Colony in 1874) and British Togoland in 1957. The first British colony in Africa to achieve independence, it became an independent republic within the Commonwealth in 1960. A multiparty constitution was approved in 1992.

Ghazi (1912–39)
King of Iraq (1933/9). The son of King **Faysal I**, he proved not to be of his father's calibre and was seen as inadequate when faced with the duties required of the King of Iraq. Despite, or possibly because of, his popularity with Iraqi army officers (educated, as he himself had been, in the UK), his reign saw a general increase in anti-British sentiment throughout his country.

Gheorgiu-Dej, Gheorghe (1901–65)
Romanian politician. A railway worker, he joined the Romanian Communist Party (RCP) in 1930 and was imprisoned in 1933 for his role in the Griviţa railway strike. On his release in 1944, he became Secretary-General of the RCP and Minister of Communications (1944–6) and in 1945 was instrumental in the ousting of the coalition government of Nicolae Radescu (1874–1953) and the establishment of a communist regime. He then served in a variety of economic posts (1946–52) and as

Prime Minister (1952–5), before becoming state President in 1961. A Stalinist, he nonetheless retained the support of Nikita **Khrushchev**'s Moscow, while developing increasingly independent policies during the 1950s and 1960s. ▷ **Ceauşescu, Nicolae**

Ghosh (Ghose), Aurobindo (1872–1950)
Bengali nationalist and poet. He started the philosophy of cosmic salvation through spiritual evolution. Educated in Christian convents in India and at Cambridge, he took administrative and professorial posts in India, and then turned to the study of Indian culture. A teacher in Baroda, Ghosh showed only a passing interest in nationalist politics through the writing of a few articles prior to 1905. Coincident with the partition of Bengal, however, he returned to Calcutta to become Principal of the National College, and became prominent in the **Swadeshi** movement. Taking editorial control of the newspaper, *Bande Mataram*, he wrote and published articles which greatly increased Hindu nationalist fervour in the Bengali contingent of Congress. Acquitted of a charge of sedition in 1908, he became an acknowledged leader of the so-called 'extremist' group within the Bengal Congress. He started a new journal, *Karmayogin*, in 1910 but fled Bengal soon afterward to escape government surveillance. He went to the French colony of Pondicherry near Madras, where he founded Auroville, an international centre for spiritual development. ▷ **Bengal, Partition of**

Giap, Vo Nguyen (1912–)
Vietnamese military leader. He studied law at Hanoi University, joined the Vietnamese Communist Party, and trained in China. He led the **Viet Minh** against the French after 1945, and planned and executed the decisive defeat of their garrison at **Dien Bien Phu** in 1954. As Vice-Premier and Defence Minister of North Vietnam, he masterminded the military strategy that forced US forces to leave South Vietnam (1973) and led to the reunification of Vietnam in 1975. He was a member of the politburo from 1976 to 1982. He wrote *People's War, People's Army* (1961), which became a textbook for revolutionaries. ▷ **Vietnam War**

Gibraltar
The narrow peninsula rising steeply from the low-lying coast of southwest Spain at the eastern end of the Strait of Gibraltar, which is an important strategic point of control for the western Mediterranean. Settled by the Moors in 711, Gibraltar was taken by Spain in 1462, and ceded to Britain in 1713, becoming a British Crown Colony in 1830. As a Crown Colony, it played a key role in Allied naval operations during both World Wars. A proposal to end British rule was defeated by a referendum in 1967. The frontier with Spain was closed from 1969 until 1985, and Spain continues to claim sovereignty.

Gierek, Edward (1913–)
Polish politician. He lived in France (1923–34) during the **Piłsudski** dictatorship, and joined the French Communist party in 1931. He was deported to Poland in 1934, but moved to Belgium (1937–48), becoming a member of the Belgian resistance. On his return to Poland in 1948, he joined the ruling Polish United Workers' Party (PUWP), being inducted into its Politburo in 1956 and appointed party boss of Silesia. He became First Secretary and leader of the PUWP in 1970 when **Gomułka** resigned after strikes and riots in Gdansk, Gdynia and Szczecin. Head of the party's 'technocrat faction', he embarked on an ambitious industrialization programme which, with foreign loans, also involved high consumer spending. This plunged the country heavily into debt and, following a wave of strikes in Warsaw and Gdansk, spearheaded by the **Solidarity** free trade union movement, he was forced to resign in 1980.

Gil Robles, José María (1898–1980)
Spanish politician and academic. As a young and pugnacious leader of the **CEDA**, he was the principal figure of the Right during the Second Republic. Effectively dominating the governments of Nov 1933–Dec 1935, as Minister of War he prepared the army for the rising of July 1936. Exiled as a member of the monarchist opposition to the **Franco** regime (1936–53 and 1962–5), he was the founder and first President of the Popular Democratic Federation, and also created the Christian Social Democratic Party. However, in the 1977 general election his party was annihilated. ▷ **Republic, Second** (Spain)

Giolitti, Giovanni (1842–1928)
Italian politician. An astute and unprincipled parliamentary manager, Giolitti entered parliament in 1882 as a liberal. Prime Minister from 1892 to 1893, he was brought down by a banking scandal. He returned to politics as Interior Minister under Giuseppe Zanardelli in 1901, becoming Prime Minister again from 1903 to 1909, except for a brief spell out of office in 1905–6. As Prime Minister, he sought to combat leftist strikes and disorders through economic policy rather than confrontation; in foreign policy he strengthened Italy's ties with Austria and Germany. During his fourth spell as Prime Minister (1911–14), he brought Italy into the **Tripolitanian War**, gaining Libya, Rhodes and the Dodecanese. However, the war resulted in unpopular tax increases. A general strike forced him from office in 1914. In opposition, he urged neutrality in 1915. His fifth ministry (1920–1) failed to cope with post-war disorder or the violence of the **squadristi**, and he was unable to block **Mussolini**'s ascent to power.

Giraud, Henri Honoré (1879–1949)
French soldier. Commander of the 7th and 9th Armies in 1940, he was captured by the Germans, but escaped. Reaching North Africa in 1942,

he joined the Allied cause, and was imposed by the USA as joint chairman with de **Gaulle** of the Committee of National Liberation. Rapidly outmanoeuvred by the latter, he resigned and played no further political role of any consequence. ▷ **World War II**

Giscard d'Estaing, Valéry (1926–)

French politician. He entered the Ministry of Finance as a civil servant and was appointed Finance Minister in 1962. He led that faction of the **Independents** who remained loyal to de **Gaulle** after Algerian independence, and turned them into a new political party, the **Independent Republican Party**. He returned to the Finance Ministry in 1969, defeated **Mitterrand** and the Gaullist candidate to become President in 1974, and was then beaten by Mitterrand in 1981. ▷ **Gaullists**

glasnost

A Russian term, usually translated as 'openness', describing the changes in attitude on the part of leaders of the USSR following Mikhail **Gorbachev**'s rise to power in 1985, which have brought about a wider and franker dissemination of information and the opportunity for genuine debate both within Soviet society and in Soviet relations with foreign powers. ▷ **perestroika**

Glemp, Jozef (1929–)

Polish ecclesiastic. He became Bishop of Warmia in 1979 and succeeded Cardinal Stefan Wyszinski as Archbishop of Gniezno and Warsaw and Primate of Poland after the latter's death in 1981. A specialist in civil and canonical law, Glemp was a prominent figure during Poland's internal political unrest, attempting with some success to moderate hardline communist attitudes. He was made a cardinal in 1983.

Gleneagles Agreement (1977)

An undertaking entered into by Commonwealth Heads of Government, meeting at Gleneagles in Scotland, to discourage sporting links with South Africa as a symbol of disapproval of **apartheid**.

Glistrup, Mogens (1926–)

Danish politician. From 1956 to 1963 he was a member of the Faculty of Law at Copenhagen University. In 1972 he founded the anti-tax Progress Party (*Fremskridtspartiet*), which after the general election in 1973 became a right-wing force in Danish politics. Since 1973 he has been a member of the Danish parliament (**Folketinget**).

Glubb, John Bagot (Glubb Pasha) (1897–1986)

British soldier. Educated in Cheltenham and the Royal Military Academy, Woolwich, he served in **World War I**, and became the first organizer of the native police force in the new state of Iraq (1920). In 1930 he was transferred to British-mandated Transjordan, organizing the Arab Legion's Desert Patrol, and becoming Legion Commandant (1939). He had immense prestige among the Bedouin, but was dismissed from his post in 1956 following Arab criticism. Knighted in 1956, he then became a writer and lecturer.

Godbout, Adélard (1892–1956)

Canadian politician. He became Liberal Premier of Quebec in 1939, defeating Maurice **Duplessis** and the **Union Nationale**. In 1944 his administration placed the Montreal Light, Heat and Power Company in public ownership, the first move in breaking free from the English-speaking community's hold on the economy of Quebec. ▷ **Liberal Party** (Canada)

Goebbels, (Paul) Joseph (1897–1945)

German Nazi politician. A deformed foot absolved him from military service, and he attended several universities, obtaining his doctorate at Heidelberg. He became **Hitler**'s enthusiastic supporter, led the **Nazi Party** in Berlin from 1926 and was appointed head of the Ministry of Public Enlightenment and Propaganda in 1933. A political radical and bitter anti-Semite, his gift of mob oratory made him a powerful exponent of Nazi philosophy. Wartime conditions greatly expanded his role as a propagandist, and from 1943 Goebbels did much to squeeze every last effort from the population and economy. He retained Hitler's confidence to the last, being appointed Plenipotentiary for the Pursuit of Total War in July 1944. In the Berlin bunker, he and his wife committed suicide, after taking the lives of their six children. His diaries now constitute a major historical source. ▷ **World War II**

Goerdeler, Carl (1884–1945)

German politician. He served under **Hitler** as Commissar for Price Control (1934), but resigned from his mayoralty of Leipzig in 1937 and became one of the leaders who opposed Hitler. This opposition culminated in **Stauffenberg**'s unsuccessful bomb plot of 20 July 1944, for which Goerdeler was executed together with a number of generals.

Goering, Hermann (Wilhelm) (1893–1946)

German Nazi politician. In **World War I** he fought on the Western Front, then transferred to the Air Force, and commanded the famous 'von Richthofen Squadron'. In 1922 he joined the **Nazi Party** and was given command of **Hitler**'s stormtroopers (**SA**) until the unsuccessful 1923 putsch. In exile until 1927, he became President of the **Reichstag** in 1932, and joined the Nazi government in 1933 with responsibility for **Prussia** and air travel. He founded the **Gestapo**, and set up the concentration camps for political, racial, and religious suspects. In 1935 he took charge of the reconstituted **Luftwaffe** and in 1936 became director of the Four Year Plan, renewed in 1940, to prepare the economy for war. He played a major part in the **Anschluss** with **Austria** (1938) and in the annexation of the **Sudetenland** (1938). In 1940 he was made Marshal of the **Reich**, the first and only holder of the rank, but his political influence and personal drive declined as his wish for aggressive diplomacy was superseded by open warfare. As **World War II** went against Germany and the *Luftwaffe* failed to meet expectations, his prestige waned further. In 1945 he attempted a palace revolution, was condemned to death, but escaped, to be captured by US troops. In 1946 he was sentenced to death at the **Nuremberg Trials**, but before his execution could take place he committed suicide.

Gökalp, Ziya (Mehmet Ziya) (c.1875–1924)
Turkish thinker. He owed his education, in the major Islamic languages (Arabic and Persian in addition to his native Turkish) and in the sciences both religious and secular, to his uncle. His career was spent in an intellectual attempt to contain the contrasting and not infrequently conflicting influences of orthodox religion, mysticism and modern science with which he had come into contact. Initially a thorn in the flesh of the authorities in Istanbul with his liberal and revolutionary views, he was arraigned in 1897 and in due course exiled to his native Diyarbakir. By 1908, he was recognized as a prominent liberal writer and lecturer in his home province and in course of time returned to Istanbul where he lived from 1912 to 1919. During this period he emerged as the propounder of a nationalist ideology for the Turks, which involved a reorientation of Turkish leanings emphasizing a Western approach. Exiled to Malta by the British after **World War I**, he occasioned no surprise when, after his release in 1921, he associated himself with Mustafa Kemal (**Ataturk**) and his national movement. Gökalp died with a reputation throughout his country as a thinker who had prepared the ground for the emergence of modern Turkey.

Goldman, Emma (1869–1940)
US anarchist, feminist and birth-control advocate. Her Jewish family left Russia for Germany to avoid persecution and, in 1885, she migrated to the USA, where she began her anarchist career. Imprisoned during **World War I** for opposing government policy, she was deported to the USSR and eventually settled in France.

Goldwater, Barry Morris (1909–)
US politician. Educated at the University of Arizona, he became a US Senator for that state in 1952. In 1964 he gave up his Senate seat to become Republican nominee for the presidency, but was overwhelmingly defeated by Lyndon B **Johnson**. He returned to the Senate in 1968, serving

until 1987, and was one of the architects of the conservative revival within the **Republican Party**.

Gombos, Gyula (1886–1936)
Hungarian politician. An army officer during **World War I**, he found himself fighting Béla **Kun**'s Soviet Republic alongside Admiral **Horthy** in 1919. Following Hungary's reduction in size and status in the post-war settlement, he drifted further to the right. He became Minister of Defence (1929) and was Prime Minister (1932–6). He strengthened the totalitarian tendencies in Hungarian politics; and in foreign policy he flirted with Italy and Germany. In 1933 he was one of the first foreign statesmen to visit **Hitler** and congratulate him on his coming to power.

Gomes, Albert (1911–78)
Trinidadian politician, trade unionist and novelist. He edited an anti-establishment periodical, *The Beacon*, and founded (1937) the Federated Workers Union. As a member of the Port of Spain city council, he attacked the colonial government and maintained this criticism when elected to the Legislative Council in 1946. However, on becoming Minister of Labour (1950), with a policy of 'industrialization by invitation', he lost his earlier radicalism and quickly became less influential after the nationalist upsurge of 1956. Gomes was Deputy Leader of the Democratic Labour Party in the federation elections of 1958.

Gómez, Juan Vicente (1857–1935)
Venezuelan dictator. A rancher with no formal education, he became Vice-President under Cipriano Castro in 1899. He deposed Castro in 1908 and his dictatorial rule (1908–35) witnessed the dramatic expansion of the oil industry, mainly Standard Oil and Anglo-Dutch Shell, in the Maracaibo region. He played off the major multinationals and the army benefited accordingly.

Gomulka, Wladyslaw (1905–82)
Polish political leader. A professional trade unionist, in 1943 he became Secretary of the outlawed Communist Party. He was Vice-President of the first postwar Polish government (1945–8), but his criticism of the USSR led to his expulsion from the party in 1949 and his imprisonment from 1951 to 1954. He returned to power as Party First Secretary in 1956. In 1970, following a political crisis, he resigned office, and spent his remaining years largely in retirement.

González, Felipe (1942–)
Spanish politician. He practised as a lawyer, and in 1962 joined the Spanish Socialist Workers' Party (**PSOE**), then an illegal organization. The Party regained legal status in 1977, three years after he became

Secretary-General. He persuaded the PSOE to adopt a more moderate policy, and in the 1982 elections they won a substantial majority. González then became Prime Minister in the first left-wing administration since 1939.

Gorbachev, Mikhail Sergeevich (1931–)
Soviet politician. Educated at the Law Faculty of Moscow State University and Stavropol Agricultural Institute, he began work as a machine operator (1946), and joined the Communist Party in 1952. He held a variety of senior posts in the Stavropol city and district Komsomol and Party organizations (1956–70), and was elected a deputy to the USSR Supreme Soviet (1970) and a member of the Party Central Committee (1971). He became Central Committee Secretary for Agriculture (1979–85); candidate member of the **Politburo** (1979–80) and full member (1980–91) of the Central Committee (1979–80); and, on the death of **Chernenko**, General-Secretary of the Party (1985–91). In 1988 he also became Chairman of the Presidium of the Supreme Soviet, ie head of state, and in 1990, the first executive President of the USSR. On becoming General-Secretary he launched a radical programme of reform and restructuring (**perestroika**) of the Soviet economic and political system. A greater degree of political participation, civil liberty, public debate, and journalistic and cultural freedom were allowed under the policy of **glasnost** (openness). In defence and foreign affairs he reduced military expenditure and pursued a policy of détente, disarmament and arms control with the West. He ended the Soviet military occupation of Afghanistan (1989) and accepted the break-up of Comecon and the **Warsaw Pact**, the withdrawal of Soviet troops from Eastern Europe and the reunification of Germany. But he failed to fulfil his promise to reform the economy and improve the living standards of the Soviet people, and proved unable to cope with the rising tide of nationalism. Following the unsuccesssful coup against him in Aug 1991, he lost power to Boris **Yeltsin** despite accepting the demise of the Communist Party. In Dec 1991 he felt obliged to resign from the presidency as the USSR itself collapsed into 15 separate republics.

Gorbacheva, Raisa Maximova (1932–)
Wife of Mikhail **Gorbachev**, and the first ever wife of a Soviet leader to play a public role. Born of a railway family in the Altai region, she graduated from Moscow University and pursued a career in sociological research and lecturing. A woman of considerable intelligence and obvious charm, she had standing in her own right before 1985 when, as the General-Secretary's wife, she began to appear with him on important occasions, including overseas tours. In an unsettled society she attracted criticism, but abroad she added to her husband's political and popular prestige and did a great deal to make a success of East–West arms talks.

Gore, 'Al' (Albert) Jr (1948–)
US politician. He was educated at Harvard, and at Vanderbilt University, where he studied law and divinity. He worked as an investigative reporter for *The Tennessean* (1971–6) and in 1976 was elected as a Democrat from Tennessee to the US House of Representatives, a position he held for eight years. He became a US Senator in 1984. Four years later he mounted an unsuccessful campaign for President but in 1992 made a successful bid for vice-president on the Democratic ticket with Bill **Clinton**. An ardent environmentalist, he is the author of *Earth in the Balance* (1992).

Gorky, Maxim (1868–1936)
Russian and Soviet writer and revolutionary. Born in Nizhni Novgorod, subsequently rechristened after him, he had little formal education and learned most from his frequent wanderings. From the turn of the century his inclinations were revolutionary and in 1905 he officially joined the **Bolsheviks**. However, he was in and out of friendship with **Lenin** and disapproved of what the Bolsheviks did in the years 1917–18, but he was on good and influential terms in years 1918–21 before going abroad for his health. But he returned in 1931 to preside over the new Writers' Union and sing the praises of much of what **Stalin** was doing. This was in the spirit of the socialist realist philosophy he helped create. He died less happy in 1936; and in 1991 his birthplace took back its old name.

Gorshkov, Sergei Georgievich (1910–88)
Soviet admiral. He joined the navy in 1927 and, after graduating from the Frunze Naval Academy in 1931, he served in the Black Sea and in the Far East. From 1940 to 1955 he served mostly in the Black Sea fleet. His wartime exploits won him great fame and by 1951 he commanded the fleet. He was appointed commander-in-chief of the entire Soviet navy by Nikita **Khrushchev** in 1956, with the brief to cut back expenditure. However, after the **Cuban Missile Crisis** in 1962 and Khrushchev's ousting in 1964, the new Soviet leader, Leonid **Brezhnev**, pressed for naval expansion to enable the USSR to project itself globally. Gorshkov supported this view and oversaw a massive naval build-up, both surface and underwater, creating a force capable of challenging the West's by the 1970s. He remained in command of the navy until his death, although his influence declined rapidly after Mikhail **Gorbachev** came to power in 1985.

Gorton, Sir John Grey (1911–)
Australian politician. He was a Liberal Senator for Victoria (1949–68) and a member of the House of Representatives (1968–75). He served in the governments of Sir Robert **Menzies** and Harold **Holt** and succeeded Holt as Prime Minister in 1967. In 1971 he was defeated on a vote of

confidence and resigned in favour of William McMahon. ▷ **Liberal Party** (Australia)

Gosplan

The State Planning Commission in the former USSR. Established in 1921, it had overall responsibility for state and regional planning, translating general economic objectives into specific blueprints. Its responsibilities varied over the years, but in the end it proved to be a liability as its bureaucratic functions prevented the Soviet economy from responding to new needs.

Gottwald, Klement (1896–1953)

Czechoslovak politician. In **World War I** he fought with the Austro-Hungarian army. A Marxist, he helped to establish the Communist Party in 1921 and became its Secretary-General in 1929. He opposed the Munich Agreement of 1938 and later went to Moscow, where he was prepared by the Party for eventual office. In 1945 he became Vice-Premier in the Czechoslovak provisional coalition government. Prime Minister following elections in 1946, he pursued a pro-Soviet line and in Feb 1948 took advantage of his opponents' divisions to stage a coup d'état which averted a defeat for the Party at the polls; in June 1948 he became President. Strong in his support for **Stalin**, whose line he followed closely, he established a complete dictatorship that eliminated many of his Communist colleagues. Ironically, he died of an illness contracted while he was attending Stalin's funeral.

Gouin, Sir (Jean) Lomer (1861–1929)

Canadian politician. The Liberal Premier of Quebec from 1905 to 1920, many considered him to be dominated by the English-speaking business community who controlled the hydro-electric power, transport and manufacturing industries. He became federal Minister of Justice in the administration of Mackenzie **King**. ▷ **Liberal Party** (Canada)

Goulart, João (Belquior Marques) (1918–76)

Brazilian politician. Born in Rio Grande do Sul, he became the wealthy landowning neighbour of Getúlio **Vargas**. He was linked with the PTB in the late 1940s and, as Vargas' protégé, became Minister of Labour in 1954. He became leader of the PTB in 1960 and, having been accused by the army of nurturing pro-communist sympathies, was elected Vice-President against military hostility; the army reluctantly agreed to allow him to become President of a parliamentary regime in 1961. A weak and vacillating leader in 1963–4, he alienated moderate opinion by flirting with nationalist and left-wing groups. Goulart was ejected by a coup (Mar 1964) engineered by the army and supported by powerful conservative politicians in the UDN. The coup was precipitated by his insistence on recruiting support among non-commissioned officers in the army and navy.

Gouled Aptidon, Hassan (1916–)
Djiboutian politician. While serving as a representative of French Somaliland in France, he became increasingly active in the independence movement and in 1967 founded the African People's League for Independence (APLI). Djibouti achieved self-government in 1977 and he became the country's first President, later merging the APLI with other groups to form the country's only political party, the People's Progress Party. His policy of neutralism in a war-torn region of the continent ensured his continuing popularity and in 1987 he was re-elected for a final six-year term.

Government of India Acts
Measures passed by the British Parliament to regulate the government of India (1883–1935). They included the 1858 Act which transferred British East India Company powers to the British Crown, and the 1919 and 1935 Acts which introduced limited constitutional change. Motivated in part by the need for retrenchment and increased taxation in the wake of India's involvement in **World War I**, the 1919 Act attempted to seduce moderate Indian politicians into cooperating with the colonial regime by offering a say in local and provincial government to a small proportion of the population from among the wealthier and more influential sections of society. The 1935 Act went further, although it still fell well short of a universal franchise, and led to the establishment of elected Congress ministries in most of the Indian provinces. Although these provincial governments had no say in matters of security, and the British governors retained a right of veto over both candidates and legislation, they were nonetheless a successful experiment in self-government, persuading some colonial officials that they could perhaps live with democracy. Unfortunately, representatives of minority political parties were largely excluded from the Congress governments, fuelling communal divisions in the country, whilst many officials merely saw provincial government as an undesirable concession, forced upon them by M K **Gandhi**'s civil disobedience movement of 1930–2. The ministries resigned en masse in 1939, following the Viceroy, Linlithgow's, declaration of war with Germany without prior consultation with Indian politicians. ▷ **communalism; Montagu–Chelmsford Reforms; Scheduled Castes and Tribes**

Gowon, Yakubu (1934–)
Nigerian soldier and politician. A Christian in a Muslim area, he was educated at a CMS missionary school and then Government College Zaria. His military training began in Ghana and continued in the UK where he attended the Royal Military Academy, Sandhurst, among other

institutions. He was commissioned into the Nigerian army in 1956, serving with the **UN** force in the Congo (Zaire) in 1960–1. He became Adjutant-General in 1963 and Chief of Staff in 1966. The ethnic conflicts in the country precipitated a coup on 15 Jan 1966, led by Ibo officers, and Gowon headed a counter-coup (July 1966). He then became head of the Federal Military Government and Commander-in-Chief. Unable to prevent a civil war, he fought to retain **Biafra** (the Eastern Region) within a single Nigeria, while acceding to ethnic concerns by increasing the number of states; with the assistance of both the USA and the USSR, he prevailed. However, his retarded return to democracy encouraged another military coup; he was deposed in 1975 and went into exile.

Graaf, Sir de Villiers, Bt (1913–79)
South African politician. Educated in South Africa, the UK and Netherlands, he saw military service in **World War II**. Elected a United Party MP in 1948, he became party leader in 1956, remaining so until 1977, when he transferred his allegiance to the New Republic Party. The political heir to Jan Smuts, his opposition to the **National Party** was too gentlemanly to challenge its hegemony and too conservative to build a new coalition across the race divide. He epitomized the failure of well-meaning liberalism in these years.

Graeco-Turkish War (1921–2)
This war was ostensibly provoked by Greek fears for the safety of the Greeks in the Izmir region of Anatolia in the face of growing Turkish nationalism. By the Treaty of Sèvres (1920), Greece had received the right to administer Izmir and its hinterlands for five years. When, in Dec 1920, **Constantine I** returned to Greece, he determined to bolster his position by championing the cause of the Anatolian Greeks. In July 1921 the government ordered 100 000 troops into Anatolia to attack Kemal **Atatürk**'s men. The Turks withdrew and the Greeks foolishly advanced with the intention of taking Ankara, but became bogged down in Sep 1921. No attempt was made to evacuate the Greek troops and, in Aug 1922, they were defeated by the Turks, who entered Izmir and destroyed the town. By the Treaty of **Lausanne**, Greece lost the major gains made after **World War I** and some 1.3 million Greeks were forced to leave Anatolia, while 380 000 Turks were expelled from Greece. Utterly discredited, Constantine I abdicated and was succeeded by **George II**.

Gramsci, Antonio (1891–1937)
Italian journalist, politician and political thinker. Born in Sardinia of a humble family, he was educated at Turin University, where he was drawn into political activity in the Socialist Party. A founder member of the **PCI** (Italian Communist Party) in 1921, he was Italian delegate at the Third International in Moscow (1922). In 1924 he became leader of

the communists in parliament. He was one of a number of outspoken communist critics of the fascist regime to be arrested in 1928 and was sentenced to 20 years' imprisonment; he died a prisoner. His reputation rests primarily on his *Prison Notebooks*, a collection of thoughts and reflections written while in confinement and published posthumously.

Grandi, Dino, Count (1895–1988)
Italian politician. A powerful **ras** who in 1921, disillusioned with **Mussolini**, unsuccessfully offered the leadership of the fascist movement to Gabriele **D'Annunzio**. He was a quadrumvir in the **March on Rome**. Foreign Minister (1929–32) and Ambassador to London (1932–9), he became extremely anglophile and warned Mussolini about the likely hostile reaction of the British to his proposed Conquest of **Ethiopia**. Minister of Justice and President of the 'Chamber of Fasces and Corporations' (1939–43), he grew increasingly worried about the **Duce**'s enslavement to **Hitler**'s policies and moved the motion in the **Fascist Grand Council** (25 July 1943) that full constitutional powers be restored to **Victor Emmanuel III**. In 1944 he was sentenced to death in absentia by the Republic of **Salò**. After liberation, he retired from politics and spent most of the rest of his life in Brazil.

Graziani, Rodolfo, Marquis of Neghelli (1882–1955)
Italian soldier. He served in Libya in 1913 and on the Italian front during **World War I**. In 1930 he became Vice-Governor of Cyrenaica and in 1936 was given command of the Italian forces on the Somalian front during the Conquest of **Abyssinia**. He succeeded **Badoglio** as Viceroy of Ethiopia. In July 1940 he was placed in charge of the Italian forces in North Africa but was replaced (Mar 1941) after a series of defeats. In Sep 1943 he accepted **Mussolini**'s invitation to become Defence Minister of the Republic of **Salò**. He was captured at the end of the war and put on trial for war crimes (Oct 1948). In 1950 he was sentenced to 25 years, but was released the same year. He was active in the **Italian Social Movement** until his death.

Great Depression
The worldwide slump in output and prices, and the greatly increased levels of unemployment, which developed between 1929 and 1934. It was precipitated by the collapse of the US stock market (the Wall Street crash) in Oct 1929. This ended US loans to Europe and greatly reduced business confidence worldwide. A major Austrian bank also collapsed, producing destabilization in much of Central and Eastern Europe.

Great Leap Forward
A movement in China, initiated in 1958, which aimed at accelerating both industrial and agricultural progress, 'walking on two legs'. Abandoning

Russian models, it planned the creation of 'communes' in a true collective system. It failed miserably.

Great Patriotic War (1941–5)
The name given by **Stalin** to the war against **Hitler**. His communist ideology had allowed him to make the 1939 **German–Soviet Pact**, but what he faced after 1941 was Hitler's determination to destroy the USSR and its Slav peoples. What he also discovered was that these peoples made incredible efforts to defend their country, not the system that **communism** had impressed on it. He therefore encouraged all forms of patriotic feelings: even the Patriarchate of Moscow was reinstated. However, after 1945 it was more or less back to Soviet communism. ▷ **World War II**

Great Society
The name given to a legislative programme called for by US President Lyndon B **Johnson** ('LBJ') on 19 Jan 1965, which committed his administration to vigorous action on health insurance, education, housing and urban renewal. The opportunity and mandate for federal initiatives in what had previously been local responsibilities came from the extraordinary 1964 election results, which returned LBJ as President in his own right with a larger percentage of the popular vote (61 per cent) than ever before achieved, together with a two-thirds Democratic majority in both houses of Congress.

Greater East Asia Co-Prosperity Sphere
The term applied to Japan's empire in East and South-East Asia after 1942. It implied the creation of a politically and economically integrated Asia under Japanese leadership and free of Western colonial domination. The concept had originated in 1938 with Japan's proclamation of a New Order in East Asia following her invasion of China in 1937. The New Order was designed to create an autarchic bloc comprising Japan, China and Manchuria that would be free of Anglo-Saxon liberalism and Soviet **communism**. Japan's rapid conquest of South-East Asia in 1942 meant that no detailed preparation had been carried out on the future of the Greater East Asia Co-Prosperity Sphere. Even its geographical boundaries remained vague (with some Japanese leaders including India and/or Australia). Although a Greater East Asia Ministry was created in 1943, it had little centralized control over the separate Japanese military administrations in South-East Asia. Long-term policy was sacrificed to the immediate needs of Japan's war economy, ultimately alienating Asian opinion which had initially welcomed the Japanese as liberators. Despite the granting, or promise, of independence to some South-East Asian countries (Burma, Philippines, Indonesia), the Sphere ended in ignominy with Japan's defeat in 1945.

Grechko, Andrei Antonovich (1903–76)
Soviet marshal and politician. He fought in the cavalry during the **Russian Civil War** and held several cavalry commands in the first half of **World War II**. As Commander-in-Chief in East Germany in 1953 he helped put down the Berlin rising, and he was Commander-in-Chief of the **Warsaw Pact** when the **Berlin Wall** was erected in 1961. He became Minister of Defence in 1967 and a **Politburo** member in 1973. In the debate about East–West détente he was regarded as a hardliner.

Greece
A country in south-east Europe which occupies the southern part of the Balkan Peninsula and numerous islands. The Greek Republic was established in 1924 and the monarchy restored in 1935. German occupation in World War II was followed by civil war (1944–9). A military coup in 1967 led to a series of military governments. The monarchy was abolished in 1969, and in 1974 democracy was restored. Greece became a member of the EEC in 1981.

Greek Civil War (1944–9)
Rooted in the struggle between communist and monarchist partisans for control of Greece, the conflict erupted as the Axis forces retreated at the end of **World War II**. Britain sent troops to back the monarchist forces, while the USSR supported the communists. With US financial aid, the British were able to remain in Greece after 1945, and helped to re-establish the monarchy. The rupture between Yugoslavia and Russia in 1948 also helped to weaken communist resistance and an end to hostilities was declared in Oct 1949.

Greek Colonels (1967–74)
The name given to the right-wing military regime established in Greece after the coup led by Colonel George Papadopoulos, Colonel Nikolaos Makarezos and Brigadier Stylianos Pattakos (21 Apr 1967). Militantly anti-communist, the regime imprisoned its political opponents, frequently on island camps, where torture was widely used. Strikes were forbidden during this period, and there was strict censorship of the arts and media. In 1973, Papadopoulos declared the monarchy abolished and had himself elected President for eight years. He was ousted in a counter-coup (Nov 1973) but the new regime under General Dimitrios Ioannidis was yet more conservative, and no attempt was made to restore constitutional rule. In July 1974 the regime backed an attempt to depose Archbishop **Makarios III** in Cyprus and to declare **enosis**; Greece was on the brink of war with Turkey. Another military coup followed, in which Ioannidis was ousted and **Karamanlis** was brought back from exile. Leading members of the 'Colonels'' regime were put on trial and imprisoned for life.

Greeks

In the 8c–6c BC the Greeks settled throughout the eastern Mediterranean, establishing colonies along the shores of Asia Minor and the adjoining islands. In the southern part of the Balkan Peninsula, a distinctive Greek culture has persisted unbroken since antiquity; the Slav and Avar invaders who arrived in waves in the 6c and later settled in the southern part of the Balkan Peninsula were hellenized and assimilated into the original population. After the sack of Constantinople (1204), the Balkan Greeks fell prey to the ambitions of the Franks and Venetians and finally to the Turks who occupied Greece from 1460 to 1830. The Greek national revival began in the late 18c, and after a long war against the Turks which wrecked much of Greece (1821–8), the Greeks gained formal recognition of their independence from the Ottoman Porte in 1832. In the 20c the Greeks were at war from 1912 to 1922: first the **Balkan Wars**, then **World War I**, both of which brought substantial territorial gains, and then the disastrous war against the Turks in Anatolia (1919–22) during which c.30 000 Christians were killed in Izmir (Smyrna) in Sep 1922, and over a million Greeks were forced to leave Asia Minor where their ancestors had lived for centuries. The Greeks were again at war continuously between 1940 and 1949; during **World War II**, they organized resistance against the occupying Axis forces but rivalries between resistance groups had played upon existing divisions in Greek society and erupted in a brutal and bloody civil war (1944–9). After a tentative period of democracy, the Greeks were subject to the right-wing dictatorship of the Colonels (1967–74). Only since 1974 have the Greeks enjoyed a period of relative peace and stability. ▷ **EAM; EDES; EKKA; ELAS; enosis; EOKA; Greek Civil War; Lausanne, Treaty of; PASOK**

Green Gang (*Qingbang*)

A Chinese underworld organization active in Shanghai during the 1920s, with its headquarters in the French Concession area. Green Gang leaders were often businessmen or had links with financial circles and were involved in prostitution, gambling and opium rackets. The Nationalist leader, **Chiang Kai-shek**, also formed close ties with the Green Gang, and after he gained control of Shanghai (Mar 1927) during the **Northern Expedition**, he used it to attack communist-led labour unions in the city, often with the connivance of foreign concession authorities and the National Revolutionary Army. Ironically, following the brutal suppression of the labour unions, Chiang then turned against the very bourgeoisie who had supported the suppression: Green Gang members launched a campaign of terror against wealthy businessmen, forcing them to buy government bonds and extend loans to Chiang's regime.

Greens, The (*Die Grünen*)
German political party. This coalition of ecologist, pacifist, anti-nuclear and other special interest groups was established as a federal party in 1980 and dominates environmental politics in Germany. It has held seats in various **Land** (state) parliaments and has been represented in the **Bundestag** since 1983 and in the European parliament since 1984. Internally it is divided between *Realos* ('Realists') prepared to work with conventional parties (especially the **SPD**) and *Fundis* ('Fundamentalists') who are not.

Grenada
The most southerly of the Windward Islands in the eastern Caribbean Sea. A British Crown Colony since 1877, it gained independence in 1974. A popular people's revolution was successfully mounted in 1979. Prime Minister Maurice Bishop was killed during a further uprising in 1983. A group of Caribbean countries requested US involvement, and troops invaded the island in Oct 1983 to restore stable government.

Griffith, Arthur (1872–1922)
Irish nationalist politician. He worked as a compositor, then as a miner and journalist in South Africa (1896–8), before editing *The United Irishman* (1899). In 1905 he founded the newspaper, *Sinn Féin*, editing it until 1914, was twice imprisoned (1916–17 and 1920–1), and became an MP (1918–22). He headed the delegation which signed the Anglo-Irish Treaty (Dec 1921) and was President of **Dáil Eireann** (1922). ▷ **Sinn Féin**

Grishin, Viktor Vasilevich (1914–92)
Soviet politician. He was a supporter of Leonid **Brezhnev**, whom he expected to succeed. A genuine railwayman, he only took up party work during **World War II**. From 1956 to 1967 he was head of the Soviet trade unions and managed to keep them firmly in line. In 1967 he became First Secretary of the Moscow party and succeeded in making it toe the line for 18 years. In 1985 Mikhail **Gorbachev** replaced him almost immediately and put Boris **Yeltsin** in his place, an obvious sign of reform.

Grivas, Georgeios (Theodoros) (1898–1974)
Greek-Cypriot nationalist leader. He commanded a Greek army division in the Albanian campaign of 1940–1, and led a secret ultra right-wing organization called 'X' (Khi) during the German occupation of Greece. An ardent nationalist, in 1955 he became head of the underground campaign against British rule in Cyprus; as founder and leader of **EOKA**, he began to call himself 'Digenis Akritas' after a legendary Greek hero. In 1959, after the Cyprus settlement, he left Cyprus and was promoted general in the Greek army. In 1971 he returned secretly to Cyprus and, as leader of EOKA-B, directed a terrorist campaign for **enosis** (union

with Greece) until his death, at Limassol. He was accorded a hero's funeral.

Groener, Wilhelm (1867–1939)
German military commander and politician. A prominent member of the German General Staff during **World War I**, General Groener led army negotiations with the Social Democratic government in Nov 1918 to guarantee the old army's survival in the republic. Successful in this, he later held various ministerial posts in Weimar governments, serving as Army Minister and as Interior Minister under **Brüning**. His failure to sustain a ban on the **SA** of the **Nazi Party** coupled with the fall of Brüning's government ended his political career in May 1932. ▷ **Weimar Republic**

Gromyko, Andrei Andreevich (1909–89)
Soviet politician and diplomat. He studied agriculture and economics, and became a research economist at the Soviet Academy of Sciences. In 1939 he joined the staff of the Russian Embassy in Washington, becoming Ambassador in 1943; after **World War II** he was permanent delegate to the **UN** Security Council (1946–8) and then Deputy Foreign Minister for most of the period 1949–57. As longest-serving Foreign Minister (1957–85), he was responsible for conducting Soviet relations with the West during the **Cold War**, presenting an austere and humourless public demeanour for which he became notorious in diplomatic circles. Mikhail **Gorbachev** promoted him to the largely honorific and mainly domestic post of President in 1985, but he retired from office following the 19th Party Conference in 1988, when he was replaced in a much stronger presidency by Gorbachev himself.

Gronchi, Giovanni (1888–1978)
Italian politician and President. One of the founders of the **Popolari**, he entered **Mussolini**'s first government as Under-Secretary of State for Industry and Commerce, but in 1923 he moved into the opposition and led his party in the **Aventine Secession**. He took part in the resistance and was elected to the post-war Constituent Assembly as a Christian Democrat. He was President of Italy from 1955 to 1962. ▷ **Christian Democrat Party**

Grósz, Károly (1930–)
Hungarian politician. The son of a steel worker, he began his career in 1946 as a printer and rose to be a newspaper editor in 1958–61. Having joined the ruling Hungarian Socialist Workers' Party in 1945, he moved to Budapest in 1961 to work in the agitprop department, becoming its deputy head in 1968 and its head in 1974. Grósz served as Budapest Party chief (1984–7) and was inducted into the Politburo in 1985. He

became Prime Minister in 1987 and succeeded János **Kádár** as Party leader in 1988, giving up his position as Prime Minister six months later. He moved pragmatically with the times and, following the lead given by Mikhail **Gorbachev** in Moscow, became an apparently committed and frank-speaking reformer in both the economic and political spheres, seeking to establish in Hungary a new system of 'socialist pluralism'. However, when, in Oct 1989, the Party reconstituted itself as the new Hungarian Socialist Party, he was replaced as leader by Rezsö Nyers, a more radical ex-Communist.

Groulx, Abbé Lionel (1878–1967)
French-Canadian nationalist historian and novelist. In reaction to the more moderate interpretations of the early 20c, he depicted French-Canadian history as an unremitting struggle against English domination, and in such works as *Notre maître le passé* (1944) he celebrated the clerical and agrarian elements of that past, although he never explicitly advocated separatism.

Groza, Petru (1884–1958)
Romanian politician. During the 1930s he led the Ploughmen's Front which drew its support from the Transylvanian peasantry. When Romania entered **World War II** in 1944, he joined the communist front organization, the National Democratic Front (FND). In Nov 1944 together with his fellow 'home Communist' **Gheorgiu-Dej** he represented the FND in the government of Sănătescu. In Feb 1945 **Stalin** approved his appointment as presiding minister in the FND government, a post he held until 1952 when he became President of the Presidium of the Romanian Communist Party.

Gruppi d'Azione Patriottica
Anti-German and anti-fascist urban guerrillas during **World War II**. Usually attached to the communists, the so-called *Gappisti* were especially active in the closing stages of the war, where their daring and ruthless actions often elicited brutal German reprisals.

Guadalcanal, Battle of (1942)
A battle in the South Pacific in **World War II**. Following the attacks on **Pearl Harbor** and Singapore (7–8 Dec 1941), Japan advanced into the South Pacific, reaching Guadalcanal in the Solomon Islands in May 1942. US forces reinvaded and after six months of bitter fighting, in one of the crucial actions of the war, they halted the Japanese advance.

Guandong (Kwantung) Army
The Japanese military force that protected the leasehold territory on the Liaodong Peninsula (southern Manchuria) and the South Manchuria

Railway, acquired by Japan in 1905 as a result of the **Russo-Japanese War**. During the 1920s, at a time when China was in turmoil, the Guandong Army began to act independently of the civilian government in Tokyo in pursuit of Japanese interests in the region, a situation helped by the fact that the Army's commander reported directly to the General Staff rather than to the Prime Minister. In 1931 the Guandong Army exploited a sabotage incident on the South Manchuria railway to justify a full-scale offensive in Manchuria, and by 1932 had created the puppet state of **Manzhuguo**. The Guandong Army henceforth exercised dominant political control in Manchuria, calling for a mobilization of all resources to counter the USSR, which it perceived as Japan's main threat. Tokyo's decision in 1941 to advance towards South-East Asia, however, precluded any decision to go to war with the USSR. Six days after the USSR itself declared war on Japan (9 Aug 1945), the Guandong Army had to surrender to Soviet forces. Thousands were sent to labour camps in the USSR, and the survivors were not repatriated until the mid-1950s.

Guchkov, Alexander I (1862–1936)
Russian politician. From a business family he believed in gradual constitutional change and helped to found the Octobrist Party, which based itself on the representation promised in **Nicholas II**'s 1905 **October Manifesto**. But he became disillusioned with a powerless **Duma** and eventually with Nicholas, who would not prosecute the 1914 war seriously. In 1917, although he regretted the passing of the **Romanov Dynasty** with Nicholas's abdication, he became Minister of War in the **Russian Provisional Government** in the hope of promoting moderate change. But his advocacy of continuing the war and his opposition to far-reaching land-reform undermined his position and he was forced out of office in May, even before the main assault by the **Bolsheviks** in Oct 1917.

Guderian, Heinz (Wilhelm) (1888–1953)
German general and creator of the German Panzer (armoured) forces. He was a career soldier from his first commission in 1908. After serving in **World War I**, he stayed in the small army allowed to Germany by the Treaty of **Versailles**, and was an ardent pioneer of mechanized warfare. Created general of Panzer troops in 1938, he advocated the idea of fast-moving '**Blitzkrieg**' warfare which he later put into brilliant effect, commanding forces in France and the USSR. He had a stormy relationship with **Hitler**, being dismissed and reinstated several times. ▷ **World War II**

Guernica
A Basque town in north-east Spain. German planes bombed the town in 1937 during the Spanish Civil War. This event was recalled in a famous painting by Picasso (now in Madrid).

Guerra, Alfonso (1940–)
Spanish politician. A close friend of Felipe **González** from the early 1960s, Guerra was largely responsible for the transformation of the **PSOE** in the 1970s into a major political organization. He has complemented the charismatic appeal of González well through his outstanding administrative abilities, though his control of the party machine has been heavily personalized and intolerant of dissent. A deputy in every election since 1977, he was Deputy Prime Minister from 1982 until his major split with González in 1991. A ruthless, sarcastic and demagogic politician, who specializes in inflammatory attacks on opponents, he has made many enemies both inside and outside the Socialist Party.

Guesde, Jules (Bazile) (1845–1922)
French politician. A supporter of the Paris Commune uprising in 1871, he was sentenced *in absentia*, and fled abroad, where he was converted to Marxism. On his return to France (1876) he was a leading figure in the first attempts to create a workers' movement. In 1882 he founded his own party, the POF (*parti ouvrier français*, 'French Workers' Party'), which he led until it was incorporated in the United Socialist Party (SFIO) in 1905. The united party accepted Guesde's rigid Marxism in theory, but in practice **Jaurès**'s parliamentary tactics had greater influence. Guesde was a Deputy (1893–8 and 1906–22), and accepted office during **World War I**. He did not join the **Communist Party** in 1920. ▷ **Socialist Party**

Guevara, Che (Ernesto Guevara (de la Serna)) (1928–67)
Argentine revolutionary leader. He trained as a doctor (1953), and played an important part in the Cuban revolution (1956–9), after which he held government posts under Fidel **Castro**. He left Cuba in 1965 to become a guerrilla leader in South America, and was captured and executed in Bolivia. His career was important as an inspiration to a variety of left-wing groups throughout the continent, and his failure to stimulate peasant revolt in Bolivia indicated that the Cuban experience of revolution could not be repeated elsewhere.

Gulag
The acronym of *Glavnoye Upravleniye Ispravitelno-Trudovykh Lagerey* ('Main Administration of Corrective Labour Camps'). From 1930 this was the Soviet secret police department that administered the system of forced labour camps for those found guilty of what were known as crimes against the state (and which were very broadly defined). Many Soviet dissidents were 'punished' in this way and many innocent victims died. The system was exposed by Alexander Solzhenitsyn in his *Gulag Archipelago*, which was finally published in 1973.

Gulf Co-Operation Council (GCC)
An organization which provides for co-operation between the states surrounding the Persian Gulf. It was established in 1981 by Bahrain, Kuwait, Oman, Qatar, Saudi Arabia, and the United Arab Emirates.

Gulf of Tonkin Resolution (1964)
The US constitutional authorization to escalate the **Vietnam War**, passed at the request of President Lyndon **Johnson** by an overwhelming majority in Congress, after two US destroyers had reportedly been attacked by North Vietnamese torpedo boats. Its repeal in 1970, the result of mounting opposition to the war and doubts as to the wisdom of giving such discretion to the President, was unopposed by President Richard **Nixon**, who believed that he had the necessary authority to achieve US aims in the war by virtue of his powers as Commander-in-Chief.

Gulf War (16 Jan–27 Feb 1991)
A war which followed the invasion of Kuwait by Iraq in Aug 1990. A rapid air and land campaign, codenamed 'Desert Storm', was mounted by a US-led international coalition based in Saudi Arabia on the authority of George **Bush**, after Iraq failed to withdraw from Kuwait by the **UN** deadline. The Bush administration gained its highest popular approval ratings during the crisis, largely due to the president's impassioned attacks on the Iraqi leader, Saddam **Hussein**. Iraqi forces were expelled from Kuwait and a large part of Iraq's military resources was destroyed. US casualties were set at 79 killed, 213 wounded, 45 missing and 9 captured. Casualty figures for Iraq are unavailable, although they have been estimated at 35 000 killed, 175 000 captured.

Guomindang (Kuomintang, KMT)
The Chinese Nationalist Party, founded by **Sun Yat-sen** in 1919 and later led by **Chiang Kai-shek**. It ruled China from Nanjing (Nanking) 1927–37 and 1945–9, and from Chonqing during the war with Japan (1937–45). It retreated to Taiwan in 1949.

Gursel, Cemal (1895–1966)
Turkish general. He emerged as leader of the rebel grouping, the 1960 revolution, against the Menderes government, ending the period of control by the Democratic Party by arresting Menderes himself (who was later executed) and other members of his cabinet. Gursel and a group of officers formed a National Unity Committee and assumed control of the country. A new constitution was drawn up by a national constituent assembly and this was ratifed by popular vote in 1961. Gursel was President of the Turkish Republic from 1961 until his death.

Gush Emmunim

An Israeli pressure group set up after the 1973 elections, dedicated to an active settlement policy in territories such as the West Bank, occupied by the Israelis after the 1967 war. The name is Hebrew, meaning 'Bloc of the faithful'. ▷ **Arab–Israeli Wars**

Gustav V (1858–1950)

King of Sweden (1907/50). The son and successor of **Oscar II**, he was the longest-reigning king in Swedish history. Shy and reserved by nature, he disliked pomp and spectacle and refused a coronation ceremony, thus becoming the first 'uncrowned king' on the Swedish throne. Nevertheless, he sought to assert the personal power of the monarchy and, in 1914, in his famous 'Courtyard Speech' to a farmers' rally, challenged the Liberal government with a call for greater spending on defence. The government resigned in protest, but demands for his abdication were stilled by the outbreak of **World War I**, when Sweden mobilized but remained neutral. Thereafter he reigned as a popular constitutional monarch, and in **World War II** came to symbolize the unity of the nation. He continued, however, to exercise political influence, and his threat to abdicate in 1941 was a factor in persuading the Swedish government to give way to German demands. He married Princess Viktoria, daughter of the Grand Duke of Baden and great-granddaughter of Gustav IV Adolf, thus uniting the reigning house of Bernadotte with the former royal house of Vasa. His nephew was Count Folke **Bernadotte**. He was succeeded by his son, **Gustav VI Adolf**.

Gustav VI Adolf (1882–1973)

King of Sweden (1950/73). The son and successor of **Gustav V**, he was a respected scholar and archaeologist, and an authority on Chinese art. In 1905 he married Princess Margaret (the grand-daughter of Queen Victoria), by whom he had four sons and a daughter. In 1923 he married Lady Louise Mountbatten, the sister of Earl **Mountbatten** of Burma. His eldest son, Gustav Adolf, having been killed in an air-crash (1947), he was succeeded by his grandson, **Karl XVI Gustaf**.

H

Haakon VII (1872–1957)
King of Norway (1905/57). Born Prince Carl of Denmark, the second son of King **Frederick VIII**, he was elected King of Norway when the country voted for independence from Sweden. In 1896 he married Princess Maud, youngest daughter of King **Edward VII** of Britain. Known as the 'people's king', he dispensed with much of the pomp of royalty. When Germany invaded Norway in 1940 he refused to abdicate, and when further armed resistance was impossible, carried on the resistance from England, returning in triumph in 1945. He was succeeded by his son, **Olav V**. ▷ **Norway, German Invasion of**

Habash, George (192?–)
Palestinian guerrilla leader. A radical, it was his Damascus-based Popular Front for the Liberation of Palestine (PFLP), created in 1967, which carried out the first Middle East airliner hijackings. Attacks carried out by the PFLP have included the May 1972 incident at Lod Airport (Tel Aviv), when 27 civilians were killed by Japanese Red Army gunmen who opened fire in the terminal building, and the June 1976 hijacking of an Air France airliner to Entebbe Airport in Uganda (which resulted in a successful Israeli commando rescue raid during which four civilians died). A brief furore was caused in early 1992 when Habash was flown from Tunis to Paris for emergency brain surgery following a stroke. He is now presumed back in Tunisia.

Habre, Hissene (c.1930–)
Chadian nationalist and politician. The son of a desert shepherd, he worked as a clerk for the French army before becoming an administrator. He joined the FAN guerrillas in the early 1970s but, having made his peace with President Malloum in 1978, he was appointed Prime Minister. When Goukouni seized power in 1979, he became Defence Minister. However, supported by the CIA, he fought against Goukouni and took power himself in 1982. With French military assistance and support from African Heads of State, he forced Libya to withdraw from northern Chad and, although uneasily, retained power.

Habyarimana, Juvenal (1937–)
Rwandan soldier and politician. He was educated at a military school, joined the National Guard and rose rapidly to the rank of major-general,

and head of the Guard, by 1973. In the same year, as fighting between the Hutu and Tutsi tribes restarted, he led a bloodless coup against President Gregoire Kayibanda and established a military regime. He founded the National Revolutionary Development Movement (MRND) as the only legal party and promised an eventual return to constitutional government.

Hácha, Emil (1872–1945)

Czechoslovak lawyer and politician. He became President of Czechoslovakia in Oct 1938 on **Beneš**'s resignation following the German annexation of Sudetenland; under duress, he made over the state to **Hitler** in Mar 1939. He was puppet president of the subsequent German protectorate of Bohemia and Moravia. Arrested after liberation in 1945, he died in prison.

Haganah

The Jewish underground militia in Palestine, founded in the 1920s during the period of the **British Mandate** in response to nationalist Arab attacks on Jewish settlements. Banned by the British authorities, the *Haganah* ('self-defence') maintained a policy of restraint, opposing the terrorism of the **Irgun** and others. However, this changed when the British sought to limit Jewish immigration after **World War II**. The Haganah comprised a part-time membership, but 1941 saw the creation of a full-time striking force, the *Palmach*. After the War of Independence in 1948, in which it played a central role, the Haganah became the Israel Defence Force, the official Israeli army. ▷ **Jewish Agency; Israel, State of; Likud; Stern Gang**

Hague Peace Conferences

Two conferences at The Hague, Netherlands, in 1899 and 1907. The first met on the initiative of Count Muravyov, the Russian Foreign Minister, to discuss the limitation of armaments, but the 26 countries represented made little progress. A permanent court of arbitration was set up for states in dispute wishing to use its services. The second met on the initiative of President Theodore **Roosevelt**, sat under the chairmanship of Tsar **Nicholas II** and, with 44 countries represented, produced a series of conventions to try to limit the horrors of war.

Haig, Alexander Meigs (1924–)

US general and administrator. Educated at the US Military Academy at West Point and at Georgetown, he held a number of staff and field positions, serving in the **Vietnam War**. A full general by 1973, he then retired from the army to become White House Chief-of-Staff during the last days of Richard **Nixon**'s presidency. Returning to active duty, he became supreme NATO commander before returning again to civilian life. He served President Ronald **Reagan** as Secretary of State in 1981–2, and sought the Republican nomination for the presidency in 1988.

Haig, Douglas, 1st Earl Haig of Bemersyde (1861–1928)
British field marshal. He obtained a commission in the 7th Hussars, and served in Egypt, South Africa and India. In 1914 he led the 1st Army Corps in France, and in 1915 became commander of the **British Expeditionary Force**. He waged a costly and exhausting war of attrition, for which he was much criticized, but led the final successful offensive in front of Amiens (Aug 1918). In post-war years he devoted himself to the care of ex-servicemen, organizing the Royal British Legion. His earldom was awarded in 1919. ▷ **World War I**

Haile Selassie I (Prince Ras Tafari Makonnen) (1892–1975)
Emperor of Ethiopia (1930/6 and 1941/74). He led the revolution in 1916 against Lij Eyasu and became regent and heir to the throne, becoming Emperor in 1930. He set about westernizing the institutions of his country, but was driven out when the Italians occupied Ethiopia in 1935 and settled in England. Restored in 1941 by the British, he became a father-figure of African nationalism and was central to the establishment of the **Organization of African Unity**, whose headquarters were established in Addis Ababa. His authoritarian rule, however, built up centres of opposition, both among the elite and among non-Amharic peoples. He survived an attempted coup in 1971, but the famine of 1973 led to economic crisis, industrial strikes and ultimately a mutiny in the army and he was deposed (12 Sep 1974). He died a year later at army headquarters.

Hailsham, Quintin (McGarel) Hogg, 2nd Viscount (1907–)
British politician. He became a Conservative MP in 1938 and succeeded to his title in 1950. He was First Lord of the Admiralty (1956–7), Minister of Education (1957), Lord President of the Council (1957–9 and 1960–4), Chairman of the **Conservative Party** (1957–9), Minister for Science and Technology (1959–64), and Secretary of State for Education and Science (1964). In 1963 he renounced his peerage and re-entered the House of Commons in an unsuccessful bid to become Leader of the Conservative Party. In 1970 he was created a life peer (Baron Hailsham of Saint Marylebone) and was Lord Chancellor (1970–4), a post he held again from 1979 until his retirement in 1987.

Hajek, Jiri (1913–)
Czechoslovak academic, diplomat, politician and dissident. A political scientist and social democrat, he was imprisoned in a **concentration camp** for much of **World War II**. On the left wing of his party, he joined with the communists in 1948 and soon began to rise: ambassador in London (1955–8); Deputy Foreign Minister (1958–62); Ambassador to the **UN**

(1962–5); and Minister of Education (1965–8). In 1968 Alexander **Dubček** appointed him Foreign Minister, in which post he tried to act as broker between the USSR and the West and, after the Soviet invasion in Aug, tried to condemn the Soviet action by flying to the UN in New York. But he was summoned home and soon deprived of all his positions and privileges. In 1977 he was one of the founders of **Charter 77** and was frequently harassed thereafter. Thoroughly disillusioned by the communist subversion of socialism, he had the satisfaction of witnessing the so-called **Velvet Revolution** in 1989.

Halifax, Edward Frederick Lindley Wood, 1st Earl of (2nd creation) (1881–1959)

British politician. He became a Conservative MP (1910–25), and held a range of political posts before becoming (as Baron Irwin, 1925) Viceroy of India (1926–31). He was Foreign Secretary (1938–40) under Neville **Chamberlain**, whose '**appeasement**' policy he implemented, and Ambassador to the USA (1941–6). He was created an earl in 1944. ▷ **Conservative Party** (UK)

Hallstein Doctrine

Federal German foreign policy stance, named after the State Secretary for Foreign Affairs, Dr Walter Hallstein. Following **Adenauer**'s visit to Moscow in 1955, which saw the opening of diplomatic relations between the USSR and the Federal Republic of Germany, the West German government declared that it would not maintain diplomatic relations with any state (other than the USSR) which maintained relations with East Germany. Relations were accordingly severed with Yugoslavia in 1957, but the Hallstein Doctrine fell into abeyance during the late 1960s and more particularly in the early 1970s with the inception of **Ostpolitik**. ▷ **Germany, East; Germany, West**

Halsey, William F(rederick), Jr, known as **'Bull Halsey'** (1882–1959)

US naval officer. He held destroyer commands in World War I and thereafter (1919–25). He qualified as a naval pilot in 1934, and commanded the Carrier Division as rear admiral (1938) and vice-admiral (1940). During the Pacific War (1941–5) he distinguished himself in carrier battles and amphibious operations, latterly as commander of the 3rd Fleet in the battles for the Caroline and Philippine islands, and in the air strikes on the Japanese mainland. In October 1944 he led the defeat of the Japanese at the Battle of **Leyte Gulf**. He was made admiral of the fleet in 1945.

Hamaguchi Osachi (1870–1931)

Japanese politician. He began his career as a Finance Minister bureaucrat and was elected to the lower house of the Diet in 1915. In 1927 he assumed the presidency of the Minseito, one of the two main political parties of the time, and became Prime Minister of a Minseito government in 1929. Renowned for his incorruptibility and dogged determination, he adopted a policy of domestic financial austerity and better relations with the USA and UK. He aroused the bitter hostility of the navy when, in 1930, he pushed through the Diet ratification of the London Naval Treaty, which placed restrictions on Japan's naval development. In assuming sole responsibility for the ratification of the treaty and ignoring the opinions of the navy, Hamaguchi was accused by both the military and ultra-nationalists of infringing the Emperor's prerogative of supreme command. In Nov 1930 he was shot by a right-wing fanatic and died the following year.

Hammarskjöld, Dag Hjalmar Agne Carl (1905–61)
Swedish politician. He was the son of Hjalmar Hammarskjöld, Conservative Prime Minister of Sweden during the early years of **World War I**. He became in 1933 an assistant professor at the University of Stockholm, in 1935 State Secretary of Finance and from 1941 to 1948 was Chairman of the Bank of Sweden. He was a cabinet minister from 1951 to 1953, when he became Secretary-General of the **UN**. Hammarskjöld, who once described himself as 'the curator of the secrets of 82 nations', played a leading part in the setting up of the UN Emergency Force in Sinai and Gaza in 1956, in conciliatory moves aimed at securing peace and stability in the Middle East in 1957–8 and in sending observers to Lebanon in 1958. He was awarded the Nobel Peace Prize in 1961, after his death in an air crash near Ndola in Zambia while he was attempting to resolve the Congo crisis.

Hammer, Armand (1898–1991)
US financier and philanthropist. Using his Russian origins and business contacts, he became an intermediary between five Soviet general-secretaries and US presidents from Franklin **Roosevelt** to Richard **Nixon**. With **Stalin**'s accession to power, Hammer left Russia, taking with him many Russian paintings which he used to found the Hammer Galleries in New York City. Retiring to Los Angeles after building a second fortune, in 1961 he bought Occidental Petroleum, a company near bankruptcy and by 1965 had made it a major force in the oil industry. Convicted of making illegal contributions to Nixon's re-election fund, he was put on a year's probation and fined US$3 000. President **Bush** pardoned him in 1989.

Hansson, Per Albin (1885–1946)
Swedish politician. He rose to prominence in the Social Democratic youth movement and was elected to parliament in 1918. He served as Minister of Defence in Social Democrat administrations in 1918–25

under Hjalmar **Branting**, whom he succeeded as leader of the party (1925). Hansson became Prime Minister of a minority Social Democrat government in 1932, but secured the support of the Agrarians in the so-called 'cow deal' the following year and, apart for a brief period in 1936, was in office from then until his death. He presided over the foundation of the modern welfare state in Sweden and guided his country's successful policy of neutrality during **World War II**.

Hara Kei (1856–1921)
Japanese politician. From a **samurai** family, he worked as a newspaper editor before joining the Ministry of Foreign Affairs (1882). He resigned from government service to join the **Seiyukai**, a political party formed in 1900, and shortly afterwards gained a seat in the lower Diet. As Home Minister in various non-party cabinets (1906–8, 1911–12 and 1913–14) and Leader of the *Seiyukai*, Hara was able to advance the party's interests by appointing pro-Seiyukai provincial governors and promoting regional economic development. As the head of the majority party in the Diet, he became Prime Minister in 1918 and presided over the first party cabinet since the establishment of the **Meiji Constitution**. He proved to be a conservative premier, however, moving cautiously on political and social reform. Although he expanded the electorate by lowering tax qualifications, he did not endorse the principle of universal manhood suffrage. He was assassinated by an ultra-nationalist fanatic.

Hardie, (James) Keir (1856–1915)
British politician. He worked in the mines between the ages of seven and 24, and was victimized as the miners' champion. He became a journalist and the first Labour MP, entering parliament for East Ham in 1892. He founded and edited *The Labour Leader*, and was Chairman of the **Independent Labour Party** (founded 1893). Instrumental in the establishment of the Labour Representation Committee, Hardie served as Chairman of the **Labour Party** (1906–8). His strong pacifism led to his becoming isolated within the party, particularly once **World War I** had broken out.

Harding, Warren G(amaliel) (1865–1923)
US politician and 29th President. A successful journalist, he gained a seat in the Ohio State Senate (1899) and the lieutenant-governorship (1902), after which he returned to journalism until 1914, when he was elected to the US Senate. Emerging as a power in the **Republican Party**, he won its nomination. As President (1921–3), he campaigned against US membership of the **League of Nations**. ▷ **Prohibition; Teapot Dome Scandal**

Harriman, William Averell (1891–1986)
US politician and diplomat. Educated at Yale, he became Ambassador to the USSR (1943) and Britain (1946), Secretary of Commerce (1946–8), and special assistant to President **Truman** (1950–1), helping to organize **NATO**. He was Director of the Mutual Security Agency (1951–3), Governor of New York (1955–9), ambassador-at-large (1961 and 1965–8) and US representative at the Vietnam peace talks in Paris (1968). He negotiated the partial Nuclear Test Ban Treaty between the USA and USSR in 1963, and continued to visit the USSR on behalf of the government, making his last visit there at the age of 91. ▷ **Vietnam War**

Hartling, Poul (1914–)
Danish politician. He represented the Liberal Party (*Venstre*) and was Danish Foreign Minister (1968–71) and Prime Minister (1973–5). From 1978 to 1985 he was the UN High Commissioner for Refugees.

Harvester Judgement (1907)
A landmark decision of the Australian Conciliation and Arbitration Court made by Justice H B **Higgins** under the Excise Tariff Act (1906) which allowed firms paying fair wages to claim exemption from excise duty. Giving judgement on the claim of the harvester manufacturer, H V Mackay, Higgins calculated the fair wage for an unskilled labourer on the basis of need, establishing the principle of the minimum or family wage tied to the cost of living. It remained a central feature of the Australian industrial system until the end of the 1960s.

Haryana
The northern Indian state carved out of the erstwhile state of Punjab in 1966. Haryana's population is largely Hindi-speaking. There remain disputes between Punjab and Haryana over the transfer of Chandigarh, their joint capital, to Punjab, and the transfer, in return, of Hindi-speaking areas to Haryana. Haryana, like Punjab, is a predominantly agricultural state, though industries have come up in the last few years. It has sites like Kurukshetra and Panipat where historic battles have been fought. Politics in Haryana is dominated dualistically by the Congress Party and the opposition **Lok Dal** which, under various guises, allies from time to time with the BJP and Congress fragments.

Hasluck, Sir Paul Meernaa Caedwalla (1905–93)
Australian politician and historian. A journalist on the *West Australian* (1922–38), he was lecturer in history at the University of Western Australia (1939–40). Seconded during **World War II** to the Australian Department of External Affairs, he became head of the Australian mission to the United Nations, returning to the university in 1948. He entered federal politics in 1949, and was successively Minister for Territories

(1951–63), for Defence (1963–4), and for External Affairs (1964–9). He was Governor-General of Australia (1969–74).

Hassan II (1929–)
King of Morocco (1961–). Educated in France, Crown Prince Hassan served his father as head of the army and, on his accession as King in 1961, also became Prime Minister. He suspended parliament and established a royal dictatorship in 1965 after riots in Casablanca. Despite constitutional reforms in 1970 and 1972, he retained supreme religious and political authority. His forces occupied Spanish (Western) Sahara in 1957. He mobilized a large army to check the incursion of **Polisario** guerrillas across his western Saharan frontier from 1976 to 1988. Unrest in the larger towns led Hassan to appoint a coalition 'government of national unity' under a civilian prime minister in 1984.

Hatoyama Ichiro (1883–1959)
Japanese politician. He was first elected to the Diet in 1915 and became a prominent leader of the **Seiyukai** in the 1930s. As Education Minister (1931–4), he clamped down hard on liberal university teachers who questioned the nature of the Japanese state. In 1946 he organized the conservative Japan Liberal Party (*Nihon Jiyuto*), which gained a victory in the elections of that year. On the verge of becoming Prime Minister, he was purged from official life by the US occupation authorities for his role in supporting the military cabinets of the 1930s. Although he was rehabilitated in 1951, he found that leadership of the Liberal Party was now firmly in the hands of **Yoshida** Shigeru. He formed a new conservative party, the Japan Democratic Party (*Nihon Minshuto*), which successfully ousted Yoshida from power (Dec 1954), when Hatoyama became Premier. During Hatoyama's premiership (1954–6), relations with the USSR were normalized, thus paving the way for Japan's entry into the **UN** in 1956, and the two conservative parties were merged to form the **Liberal Democratic Party** (LDP).

Haughey, Charles (James) (1925–)
Irish politician. He became a **Fianna Fáil** MP in 1957. From 1961 he held posts in the Ministries of Justice, Agriculture, and Finance, but he was dismissed in 1970 after a quarrel with the Prime Minister, Jack **Lynch**. He was subsequently tried and acquitted on a charge of conspiracy to import arms illegally. After two years as Minister of Health and Social Welfare, he succeeded Lynch as Premier (1979–81), was in power again for a nine-month period in 1982, and again from 1987 to 1992, after defeating Garrett **Fitzgerald** in the 1987 elections. He resigned after allegations of illegal telephone-tapping led his Progressive Democrat coalition allies to withdraw their support.

Havel, Václav (1936–)
Czechoslovak dramatist and reluctant but distinguished politician. Educated at the Academy of Dramatic Art in his native Prague, he began work in the theatre as a stagehand and became resident writer for the Prague 'Theatre on the Balustrade' (1960–9). Having been chairman of the Writers' Union during the **Prague Spring**, his work was then judged subversive. He was one of the founders of Charter 77 in 1977 and was subsequently imprisoned several times, his plays only being performed abroad. During the so-called **Velvet Revolution** in Dec 1989, which ended **communism** in Czechoslovakia, he was elected President by direct popular vote. Although he subsequently opposed the division of Czechoslovakia into two separate states, he nevertheless was elected President of the Czech Republic in Jan 1993.

Hawke, 'Bob' (Robert James Lee) (1929–)
Australian politician. He worked for the **Australian Council of Trade Unions** for over 20 years, before becoming an MP in 1980. His **Australian Labor Party** defeated the **Liberal Party of Australia** in the 1983 election, only one month after adopting him as leader. The most successful Labor Prime Minister in Australian history, he won his fourth general election in 1990, but was replaced in Dec 1991 by Paul **Keating**.

Hay–Bunau-Varilla Treaty (1903)
An agreement between the USA and Panama creating the Panama Canal Zone under US sovereignty, and giving the USA the right to build and operate the Canal, in return for a US$10 000 000 fee and US$250 000 annual rent. The chief parties involved were US Secretary of State John Hay, and Philippe Bunau-Varilla, representing Panama.

Hay–Herrán Treaty (1903)
An agreement between the USA and Colombia giving the USA the right to build a canal across the isthmus of Panama, then part of Colombia. Its rejection by the Colombian Senate led to the Panamanian revolt for independence, with US sponsorship. The parties involved were US Secretary of State John Hay, and Tomás Herrán, Colombian chargé d'affaires based in Washington. ▷ **Hay–Bunau-Varilla Treaty**

Haya de la Torre, Víctor Raúl (1895–1979)
Peruvian politician and political thinker. Educated in Lima, he was the founder (1924) of APRA (*Alianza Popular Revolucionaria Americana*), known as the Aprista Party, the voice of radical dissent in Peru. Imprisoned (1931–3) after standing against Colonel Luis Sánchez Cerro, he was released on the latter's assassination (1933), and went into hiding (1934–45). The Aprista Party changed its name to the *Partido del Pueblo* (People's Party) in 1945, and supported the successful candidate, José

Luis Bustamante; control of the government, however, lay in Haya's hands. On Bustamante's overthrow (1948), Haya sought refuge in the Colombian embassy in Lima and later (1954) left for Mexico. He returned to Peru when constitutional government was restored (1957) and fought the bitter 1962 election campaign which, after army intervention, he lost to Terry Fernando **Belaúnde**. Haya was instrumental in drafting the constitution of 1979 restoring parliamentary democracy, but died before the People's Party finally gained power in 1985 under Perez Alan **Garciá**.

Hayden, Bill (William George) (1933–)
Australian politician. He entered the federal parliament in 1961, serving under Gough **Whitlam** whom he replaced as **Australian Labor Party** leader in 1977. In 1983 he surrendered the leadership to the more charismatic Bob **Hawke** and was Foreign Minister in his government (1983–8). In 1989 he became Governor-General of Australia.

Haykal, Muhammad Hasanayn (1924–)
Egyptian journalist and author. Early in his career he covered the 1948 War and the **Korean War**. He had contacts with the **Free Officers** before the 1952 coup, and his subsequent career has spanned the period from Gamal Abd al-**Nasser**'s presidency to the period in office of Hosni **Mubarak**. The most influential journalist of his generation, Haykal became editor of the respected Cairo newspaper *al-Ahram* in 1957, writing, on subjects such as Nasser's relations with world leaders such as Nikita **Khrushchev** and Lyndon B **Johnson**, in addition to other Arab heads of state. He also had contacts with guerrilla leaders, including Che **Guevara**. Removed from the editorship of *al-Ahram* in 1974 following his criticism of Anwar **Sadat**'s conduct of the **October War**, Haykal was briefly held under arrest in 1981 when Sadat, ostensibly to deal with the religious extremism of the **Muslim Brotherhood**, extended his purge to include journalists and opposition party leaders.

Haywood, William Dudley ('Big Bill') (1869–1928)
US labor leader. After working as a miner, homesteader, and cowboy, he joined the Western Federation of Miners in 1896, and quickly achieved prominence. In 1905 he helped to found the Industrial Workers of the World (**IWW**), which was committed to revolutionary labour politics and to the organization of all workers in one big union. An active socialist, he was convicted of sedition in 1917 for his opposition to **World War I**. He fled from the USA in 1921, and took refuge in the USSR, dying in Moscow.

He Long (Ho Lung) (1896–1977)
Chinese Red Army general. The son of a lowly army officer and with little formal education, he was active as a bandit during the 1910s in his

home province of Hunan, before enrolling in the provincial army. He Long joined the **Guomindang** in 1926 and became a commander in the National Revolutionary Army. He was a participant in the Nanchang army uprising against the Guomindang on 1 Aug 1927, a date that is now considered by the Chinese Communist Party to mark the birth of the Red Army. During the **Sino-Japanese War** (1937–45) he became a divisional commander in the communist **Eighth Route Army** and was elected a member of the party's Central Committee in 1945. Always a firm believer in party control of the army, he was made Marshal of the People's Republic of China (1955) and elected to the Politburo in 1956.

He Xiangning (Ho Hsiang-ning) (1880–1972)
Chinese revolutionary and feminist. Educated in Hong Kong and Japan, she married fellow revolutionary **Liao Zhongkai** in 1905 and was an active advocate of links with the communists and Russia. Her husband was assassinated in 1925, and when two years later **Chiang Kai-shek** broke with the communists, she returned to Hong Kong and was an outspoken critic of his leadership. She returned to Beijing in 1949 as head of the overseas commission. Ho Hsiang-ning was one of the first Chinese women to cut her hair short and publicly to advocate nationalism, revolution and female emancipation.

Heath, Edward (Richard George), ('Ted') (1916–)
British politician. He served in **World War II**, and became a Conservative MP in 1950. Following a career in the Whips' office (1951–9), he was Minister of Labour (1959–60), then Lord Privy Seal (1960–3) and the chief negotiator for Britain's entry into the European Common Market (**EEC**). He became the **Conservative Party**'s first elected leader in 1965, and remained Leader of the Opposition until the 1970 election, when he became Prime Minister (1970–4). After a confrontation with the miners' union in 1973, he narrowly lost the two elections of 1974, and in 1975 was replaced as leader by Margaret **Thatcher**. He has continued to play an active part in politics, being particularly critical of his successor's policies.

Heimwehren
Austrian volunteer defence leagues. These were organized after **World War I** to protect Austria's southern (Yugoslav) frontier. By the late 1920s the *Heimwehren* were explicitly anti-socialist and anti-republican, receiving financial aid and encouragement from right-wing Austrian governments and from fascist Italy. Involved both in the crushing of the Austrian socialists (Feb 1934) and of the Austrian Nazis (July 1934), the Heimwehren were subsequently disbanded by the **Schuschnigg** government in 1936. ▷ **Austria, Republic of; Nazi Party**

Heinemann, Gustav (1899–1976)
West German politician. He practised as an advocate from 1926 and lectured on law at Cologne (1933–9). After the war he was a founder of the Christian Democratic Union (**CDU**), and was Minister of the Interior in **Adenauer**'s government (1949–50), resigning over a fundamental difference over defence policy; being a pacifist, he opposed Germany's rearmament. He formed his own neutralist party, but later joined the Social Democratic Party (**SPD**), was elected to the **Bundestag** (1957) and was Minister of Justice in **Kiesinger**'s 'Grand Coalition' government from 1966. In 1969 he was elected President but resigned in 1974.

Hekmatyar, Gulbuddin (1949–)
Afghan guerrilla leader. Formerly an engineer, in the 1970s he opposed the republican government of General Mohammad Daud Khan, and rose to prominence during the 1980s in the fight to oust the Soviet-installed communist regime in Afghanistan. As leader of one of the two factions of the Hizb-i Islami (Islamic Party), he was seen as the most intransigently fundamentalist, refusing to join an interim 'national unity' government with Afghan communists as the USSR began to wind down its military commitment. He was injured in a car bomb attack on his group's headquarters in Peshawar in 1987, and in 1988 briefly served as President of the seven-party mujahadin alliance.

Helsinki Conference (1975)
A conference on security and co-operation in Europe, attended by the heads of 35 states, including the USA and USSR, with the objective of forwarding the process of détente through agreements on economic and technological co-operation, security, disarmament and human rights. These were set out in the Final Act within the principles of sovereignty and self-determination and existing frontiers. There have been several follow-up conferences, and there is now a permanent organization called the Conference on Security and Co-operation in Europe (CSCE). ▷ **détente**

Henderson, Arthur (1863–1935)
British politician. Several times Chairman of the **Labour Party** (1908–10, 1914–17 and 1931–2), he was elected an MP in 1903, served in the coalition cabinets (1915–17), and became Home Secretary (1924) and Foreign Secretary (1929–31) in the first Labour governments. He was President of the World Disarmament Conference in 1932, won the Nobel Peace Prize in 1934, and also helped to establish the **League of Nations**. ▷ **MacDonald, Ramsay**

Heng Samrin (1934–)

Cambodian (Kampuchean) politician. He served as a political commissar and commander in **Pol Pot**'s **Khmer Rouge** (1976–8) but, alienated by his brutal policies, led an abortive coup against him, then fled to Vietnam. Here he established the Kampuchean People's Revolutionary Party (KPRP) and became head of the new Vietnamese-installed government in Cambodia in 1979. He has since remained in *de facto* control of Cambodia but, following Vietnam's withdrawal of its troops in 1989, his influence began to wane.

Henlein, Konrad (1898–1945)

Sudeten German politician. A bank clerk and then gym teacher, he was the leader from 1935 onwards in the agitation and conspiracy that led, in 1938, to Germany's seizure of Sudetenland from Czechoslovakia, and in 1939 to the institution of its Protectorate of Bohemia and Moravia and the dissolution of Czechoslovakia. Gauleiter of Sudetenland (1938–9) and Civil Commissioner for the Protectorate from 1939 to 1945, he committed suicide when in US hands.

Hepburn, Mitchell Frederick (1896–1953)

Canadian politician. A farmer who came to power as the Liberal Premier of Ontario (1934–42) with the promise of a 'swing to the left' and a fight in favour of the 'dispossesed and oppressed', he soon began to fight the CIO, which was asked in to help organize the General Motors plant at Oshawa in 1937, branding them as 'foreign agitators' and communists. After Mackenzie **King** refused to send in the **Mounties**, Hepburn organized his own anti-labour force, nicknamed 'Hepburn's Hussars' or the 'Sons of Mitch's' and attacked the federal government for its 'cowardice'. Although the strikers won company recognition, Hepburn gained increased electoral support, winning 75 per cent of the seats in the subsequent election. Hepburn continued his feud with the federal administration of Mackenzie King over both provincial rights (wrecking the 1941 conference on the recommendations of the **Rowell–Sirois Commission**) and its war policies, but this fight ruined his party and destroyed his health. Resigning from office in 1942, he lost his seat in the election of 1945 in which the **Liberal Party** was decimated. ▷ **AFL–CIO**

Herero Revolt (1907)

A resistance movement by Bantu-speaking peoples in Namibia, crushed by the Germans with great brutality. They participated in the struggle for Namibian independence against South African rule.

Hermansson, Steingrímur (1928–)

Icelandic politician. He trained as an electrical engineer in the USA, returning to pursue an industrial career. He became Director of Iceland's

National Research Council (1957–78) and then made the transition into politics, becoming Chairman of the Progressive Party (PP) in 1979. He became a minister in 1978 and then Prime Minister, heading a PP–Independence Party (IP) coalition (1983–7) after which he accepted the Foreign Affairs portfolio in the government of Thorsteinn Pálsson. He became Prime Minister again in 1988.

Herriot, Edouard (1872–1957)

French politician. Mayor of Lyons from 1905 until his death, he became Minister of Transport during **World War I**. A radical, he was three times Premier (1924–5, 1926 (for two days) and 1932), and was on several occasions President of the Chamber of Deputies. In 1942 he became a prisoner of the Nazis. After the war he was President of the National Assembly (1947–53). ▷ **Nazi Party; World War II**

Hertzog, J(ames) B(arry) M(unnik) (1866–1942)

South African politician. He was a Boer general (1899–1902), and in 1910 became Minister of Justice in the first Union government. In 1913 he founded the Nationalist Party, advocating complete South African independence. As Premier, in coalition with Labour (1924–9), and with **Smuts** in a United Party (1933–9), he pursued a legislative programme which destroyed the African franchise, created job reservation for Whites, and also tightened land segregation. He renounced his earlier secessionism, but at the outbreak of **World War II** declared for neutrality, was defeated, and in 1940 retired.

Herzl, Theodor (1869–1904)

Hungarian Zionist leader. He moved to Vienna at the age of 18, where he trained as a lawyer and pursued a career as a journalist and author. In Paris as a newspaper correspondent (1891–5), he covered the **Dreyfus** trial in 1894 and was deeply affected by its anti-Semitism. In 1895 he published *Der Judenstaat* (The Jewish State), in which he argued that the Jews should have their own state, which would receive Jews from those parts of the world where they experienced rejection or persecution. In 1897, in Basel, he convened the First Zionist Congress, which declared its goal to be the founding of a national Jewish home in Palestine and established the **World Zionist Organization** to that end. Herzl spent his remaining years strengthening this organization and seeking support for its aims from influential European leaders, and succeeded in moulding it into an efficient institution. While not original in his ideals, Herzl's efforts have rendered his name inseparable from the emergence of political **Zionism** in the modern period. ▷ **Ben-Gurion, David**

Heseltine, Michael (Ray Dibdin) (1933–)
British politician. He built up a publishing business before becoming a Conservative MP in 1966. After holding junior posts in Transport (1970), Environment (1970–2), and Aerospace and Shipping (1972–4), he was appointed Secretary of State for the Environment (1979–83), and then Defence Secretary (1983–6). He resigned from the government in dramatic fashion by walking out of a cabinet meeting over the issue of the takeover of Westland helicopters. His challenge to Margaret **Thatcher**'s leadership of the **Conservative Party** directly led to her resignation (Nov 1990) but he was defeated by John **Major** in the election to succeed her. He became Secretary of State for the Environment (1990–2) and Secretary of State for Trade and Industry (1992–).

Hess, (Walter Richard) Rudolf (1894–1987)
German Nazi politician, **Hitler**'s deputy as party leader. Educated at Godesberg, he fought in **World War I**, then studied at Munich. He joined the **Nazi Party** in 1920, and became Hitler's close friend and (in 1934) deputy. In 1941, on the eve of Germany's attack on the USSR, he flew alone to Scotland to plead the cause of a negotiated Anglo-German peace. He was temporarily imprisoned in the Tower of London, then placed under psychiatric care near Aldershot. At the **Nuremberg Trials** (1946) he was sentenced to life imprisonment, and remained in Spandau prison, Berlin (after 1966, as the only prisoner), until his death. ▷ **World War II**

Heuss, Theodor (1884–1963)
West German politician and President. Educated at Munich and Berlin, he became editor of the political magazine *Hilfe* (1905–12), professor at the Berlin College of Political Science (1920–33), and an MP (1924–8 and 1930–2). A prolific author and journalist, he wrote two books denouncing **Hitler**, and when the latter came to power in 1933, he was dismissed from his chair and his books publicly burnt. In 1946 he became a founder member of the Free Democratic Party (**FDP**), and helped to draft the new federal constitution. He was the first President of the Federal Republic of Gemany (1949–59).

Heydrich, Reinhard (1904–42)
Prominent Nazi functionary and Deputy-Chief of the **Gestapo**. As a youth, he joined the **Freikorps** ('Volunteer Corps'), and was later a naval sub-lieutenant; in 1931 he had to quit the navy and entered the **SS**, rising to be second-in-command of the secret police, and charged with pacifying occupied territories. In 1941 he was made protector of Bohemia and Moravia, but the following year was killed by Czech assassins parachuted in from the UK. In the murderous reprisals, Lidice village was razed and every man put to death.

Higgins, Henry Bournes (1851–1929)
Irish-born Australian politician and judge. His family emigrated to Melbourne in 1870 and he went on to become a successful lawyer, entering the Victorian assembly in 1894. As a supporter of Irish **Home Rule**, and opposing both the terms of **federation** and Australian participation in the **Boer War**, he lost his seat in the Victorian elections of 1900, although he remained popular with the Labor movement. In 1901 he entered Commonwealth politics as a Liberal, but became Attorney-General in the brief Labor administration of 1904. In 1906 he was appointed to the High Court, and in 1907 became President of the Commonwealth Conciliation and Arbitration Court. A firm believer in state intervention in industrial relations, he had, with Charles Kingston, been responsible for the conciliation and arbitration provisions of the constitution. As President of the Arbitration Court he made the **Harvester Judgement** which established the principle of the minimum wage. He fought for the Commonwealth's right to arbitrate in the High Court, and resigned in protest against the interference of Prime Minister **Hughes** in 1921. By then arbitration had become an integral part of the Australian industrial system.

Hijaz Railway
The railway, running between Damascus and Medina, which was built between 1901 and 1908, when the area was under Ottoman domination. The construction and subsequent operation of the railway was the province of a subdepartment of government later to become the Hijaz Railway Ministry. Financed by popular subscription and grants from the central treasury, the railway was constructed with German technical assistance. Its strategic importance to the Turkish military effort in the Hijaz during **World War I** made it an immediate target after the proclamation of the **Arab Revolt** by Sharif **Husayn ibn 'Ali** of Mecca in 1916. The Amir, Faysal, and British officers (among whom was T E **Lawrence**) successfully destroyed the railway as an effective transport system and were thus able to wrest control of Mecca and Jedda from the Ottomans, at the same time as isolating those Ottomans then in the Yemen. ▷ **Faysal I**

Hillery, Patrick (John) (1923–)
Irish politician. Following his election as an MP (1951), he held ministerial posts in Education (1959–65), then Industry and Commerce (1965–6), and Labour (1966–9), then became Foreign Minister (1969–72). Before becoming President of the Irish Republic (1976–90), he served as the **EEC** Commissioner for Social Affairs (1973–6).

Himmler, Heinrich (1900–45)
German Nazi politician and Chief of Police. He joined the **Nazi Party** in 1925, and in 1929 was made head of the **SS**, which he developed from

Hitler's personal bodyguard into a powerful party weapon. In 1933 he commanded the Bavarian political police and in 1934 took over the secret police (**Gestapo**) in **Prussia**. Chief of Police from 1936, he later initiated the systematic liquidation of Jews. In 1943 he became Minister of the Interior, and in 1944 Commander-in-Chief of the home forces. He was captured by the Allies, and committed suicide at Lüneburg. ▷ **Holocaust; World War II**

Hindenburg, Paul (Ludwig Hans Anton von Beneckendorff und) von (1847–1934)

German general and President (1925–34). Educated at Wahlstatt and Berlin, he fought in the **Franco-Prussian War** (1870–1), rose to the rank of general (1903), and retired in 1911. Recalled at the outbreak of **World War I**, he won victories over the Russians (1914–15), and later directed the creation of strategic fortifications on the Western Front (the Hindenburg Line). A national hero, he became the second President of the German Republic in 1925 despite his known anti-republican views. He was re-elected in 1932 to block **Hitler**'s candidacy, but in 1933 appointed Hitler as Chancellor.

Hindu Mahasabha

An Indian socio-political organization concerned with advancing Hindu nationalism. It started in Punjab in 1907 and claimed that the Congress and its concern for Hindu-Muslim unity would endanger Hindus. Within the Mahasabha, there was a divide between those who sought social reforms and those who were orthodox. The organization expanded under the leadership of **Lajpat Rai** and **Malaviya** who kept it linked with the **Congress**. Under Savarkar, it broke completely with the Congress in 1937 and strengthened links with the **RSS**. Its members included Nathuram Godse, M K **Gandhi**'s assassin. Mahasabha electoral support declined after 1952 as its Hindu nationalist themes were pre-empted by the Jan Sangh.

Hirohito (1901–89)

Emperor of Japan (1926/89). The 124th emperor in direct descent, his reign was marked by rapid militarization and the aggressive wars against China (1931–2 and 1937–45) and Britain and the USA (1941–5). The latter ended with the dropping of atomic bombs on **Hiroshima** and Nagasaki. Under US occupation, Hirohito in 1946 renounced his mythical divinity and most of his powers, and became a democratic constitutional monarch. ▷ **Akihito; World War II**

Hiroshima, Atomic Bombing of (6 Aug 1945)

Hiroshima, the capital of Hiroshima prefecture, South Honshu Island, Japan, was chosen as the target for Little Boy, the first atomic bomb ever dropped, because of its importance as a centre of military and supply bases, shipyards and industrial plants. Approximately 150 000 people were killed or wounded as a result, and 75 per cent of the city's buildings were destroyed or severely damaged.

Hirota Koki (1878–1948)

Japanese diplomat and politician. He had close links with the ultra-nationalist **Genyosha** and served in diplomatic posts in China, Britain, the USA and the USSR before becoming Foreign Minister in various non-party cabinets (1933–4 and 1934–6). He championed an assertive foreign policy to protect Japan's interests in China, and in 1935 laid down principles to guide Sino-Japanese relations: the formation of a Japan-China-Manchuria economic bloc, suppression of all anti-Japanese activities in China, and the creation of a Sino-Japanese front against **communism**. As Prime Minister (1936–7), he increased the military budget and signed the Anti-Comintern Pact with Germany and Italy, thus alienating Japan even further from the Anglo-Saxon powers. Appointed Foreign Minister again (1937–9), Hirota supported Japan's full-scale invasion of China in 1937. After the war, he was tried as a Class A war criminal and executed in 1948, the only civilian to be so sentenced.

Hiss, Alger (1904–)

US civil servant. He reached high office as a State Department official, then stood trial twice (1949, 1950) on a charge of perjury, having denied before a Congressional Un-American Activities Committee that in 1938 he had passed secret state documents to Whittaker Chambers, an agent for an international communist spy ring. The case roused great controversy, but he was convicted at his second trial, and sentenced to five years' imprisonment. He did not return to public life after his release. The justice of his conviction continues to be disputed. ▷ **HUAC; McCarthy, Joseph**

Histadrut

Israeli Zionist labour organization, formed in 1920, incorporated into the International Confederation of Free Trade Unions. Comprising both industrial and agricultural workers, its remit nonetheless includes activities beyond those normally associated with trade unions. *Histadrut* is involved in marketing and distribution, banking, building programmes, irrigation, healthcare, education and entertainment, as well as in traditional negotiations on working conditions and wages. Of considerable economic importance, Histadrut is run by an elected executive whose leaders have had strong ties with the **Mapai Party**. ▷ **Jewish Labour Movement in Palestine; World Zionist Organization**

Hitler, Adolf (1889–1945)

German dictator and leader of the **Nazi Party**. The son of a minor customs official, he was educated at Linz and Steyr, attended art school in Munich, but failed to pass into the Vienna Academy. He lived on his family subventions in Vienna (1904–13), yet inhabited hostels and did a variety of menial jobs. In 1913 he emigrated to Munich, where he found employment as a draughtsman. In 1914 he served in a Bavarian regiment, became a corporal, was decorated, and was wounded in the last stages of **World War I**. In 1919 he joined a small political party which in 1920 he renamed as the National Socialist German Workers' Party. In 1923, with other extreme right-wing factions, he attempted to overthrow the Bavarian government as a prelude to a 'March on Berlin' in imitation of **Mussolini**'s 'March on Rome', but was imprisoned for nine months in Landsberg jail, during which time he dictated to Rudolf **Hess** his political testament, *Mein Kampf* (1925, My Struggle). He expanded his party greatly in the late 1920s, won important parliamentary election victories in 1930 and 1932 and though he was unsuccessful in the presidential elections of 1932 against **Hindenburg**, he was made Chancellor in 1933. He then suspended the constitution, silenced all opposition, exploited successfully the burning of the **Reichstag** building, and brought the **Nazi Party** to power, having dozens of his opponents within his own party and the **SA** murdered by his bodyguard, the **SS**, in the **Night of the Long Knives** (1934). He openly rearmed the country (1935), established the Rome–Berlin 'axis' with Mussolini (1936) and pursued an aggressive foreign policy which culminated in **World War II** (3 Sep 1939). His domestic policy traded off social and economic improvements for political dictatorship enforced by the Secret State Police (**Gestapo**). His government established concentration camps for political opponents and Jews, over 6 million of whom were murdered in the course of World War II. With his early war successes, he increasingly ignored the advice of military experts and wantonly extended the war with his long-desired invasion of the USSR in 1941. The tide turned in 1942 after the defeats at **El Alamein** and **Stalingrad**. He miraculously survived the explosion of the bomb placed at his feet by Colonel **Stauffenberg** (July 1944), and purged the army of all suspects. When Germany was invaded, he retired to his *Bunker*, an air-raid shelter under the Chancellory building in Berlin. All available evidence suggests that Hitler and his wife committed suicide and had their bodies cremated (30 Apr 1945).

Hitler Youth (*Hitler-Jugend*)

The organization, set up by Adolf **Hitler** in 1933, designed to inculcate Nazi principles in German youths. By 1935, membership accounted for almost 60 per cent of German boys. It became (1 July 1936) a state agency that all young 'Aryan' Germans were expected to join. On his tenth birthday, after various investigations (especially for 'racial purity'), a German boy would enter the *Deutsches Jungvolk* ('German Young

People'). At 13, he was eligible to join the Hitler Youth, in which he remained until the age of 18, living an austere life, dominated by Nazi theory, generally with minimun parental guidance. When he was 18, he became a member of the Nazi Party, serving in the state labour service and the armed forces until at least the age of 21. A parallel organization, the *Bund Deutscher Mädel* ('League of German Girls'), trained girls for domestic duties and motherhood.

Hizbullah (Hizbollah)

The umbrella organization in south Beirut of militant Shiite Muslims with Iranian links; the name means 'Party of God'. They came to world attention after the TWA hijacking in Cairo in 1985, and the subsequent taking of hostages. ▷ **Shiites**

Hlinka, Andrei (1864–1938)

Slovak priest and politician. As a young man he was attracted by the political stance of the Slovak National Party and by the concern for the peasants of the Magyar Populist Party. In 1905 he established the Slovak Populists Party as a compromise, but he was soon being harassed by the Hungarian authorities. In 1918 he supported the creation of Czechoslovakia but he was subsequently disappointed with centralist rule from Prague and his own non-involvement in governing his countrymen. In the 1920s and 1930s he built up his party and secured some political concessions from Prague. But in the middle of 1938 he used the opportunity of **Benes**'s discomfiture to demand autonomy for Slovakia. However, he died in Aug and left **Tiso** to develop a treasonable relationship with Germany.

HNP (*Herstigte Nasionale Party*, 'Reconstituted National Party')

Founded in 1969 by dissidents from the **National Party**, the HNP seeks to preserve **apartheid** undiluted, the Afrikaans language, and a public policy based upon Calvinist principles. It allied with the Conservative Party in the late 1980s to embarrass the Nationalist Party in individual constituencies, which it occasionally defeats.

Ho Chi Minh (1892–1969)

Vietnamese politician, born Nguyen That Thanh. From 1912 he visited London and the USA, and lived in France from 1918, where he was a founder member of the Communist Party. From 1922 he was often in China and then Moscow. He led the **Viet Minh** independence movement from 1941, and directed the successful military operation against the French (1946–54). Prime Minister (1954–5) and President (1954–69) of North Vietnam, he was the leading force in the war between North and South Vietnam during the 1960s. ▷ **Vietnam War**

Hoare–Laval Pact

An agreement concluded in 1935 by the British Foreign Secretary Samuel Hoare and the French Prime Minister Pierre **Laval** aimed at the settlement of a dispute between Italy and Abyssinia. By this pact, large parts of Abyssinia were ceded to Italy. A public outcry against the pact led to its repudiation by Britain and to Hoare's resignation.

Hodza, Milau (1878–1944)

Slovak politician. A Lutheran, he worked with Catholics such as **Hlinka** before **World War I** in order to secure some kind of autonomy for Slovakia. He hoped for improvement within Austria-Hungary but failing that, he favoured a Czech-Slovak solution, which is what came in 1918. He never abandoned his Slovak sentiments, though he became mostly a convinced Czechoslovak and was appointed Czechoslovak Premier in 1935. The strain of dealing with **Hitler** and **Henlein** from 1937 through 1938 put his loyalties to test, and there is evidence that he was talking out of turn both to the Germans and to disloyal Slovaks at the height of the pre-Munich crisis. In the final days before the **Munich Agreement** he was dropped from the premiership, and even abroad during **World War II** his political contribution was slight.

Hohenzollern Dynasty

The German ruling dynasty of Brandenburg-Prussia (1415–1918) and Imperial Germany (1871–1918). **World War I** ruined Hohenzollern militarism, and forced the abdication of the last Emperor, **William II** (1918).

Holkeri, Harri (1937–)

Finnish politician. A political activist in his teens, he joined the youth league of the centrist National Coalition Party in 1959 and was its Information, Research and National Secretary between 1962 and 1971. Holkeri was elected to Helsinki City Council in 1969, entered Parliament the following year and was Prime Minister from 1987 to 1991.

Holocaust

The attempt by Nazi Germany to destroy systematically European Jews. From the inception of the Nazi regime in 1933 Jews were deprived of civil rights, persecuted, physically attacked, imprisoned, pressurized to emigrate, and murdered. With the gradual conquest of Europe by Germany, the death toll increased, and a meeting at Wannsee (Jan 1942) made plans for the so-called 'final solution'. Jews were herded into concentration camps, slave labour camps, and extermination camps. By the end of **World War II** in 1945, more than 6 million Jews had been murdered out of a total Jewish population of 8 million in those countries occupied by the Nazis. Of these the largest number, 3 million, were from Poland. Other minorities (gypsies, various religious sects, homosexuals) and millions of Soviet prisoners were also subject to Nazi atrocities, but the major genocide was against the Jewish people. ▷ **Babi Yar; concentration camp; Nazi Party**

Holt, Harold Edward (1908–67)
Australian politician. He entered the House of Representatives in 1935, becoming Deputy Leader of the **Liberal Party of Australia** (1956), and Leader and Prime Minister, when Robert **Menzies** retired (1966). During the **Vietnam War** he strongly supported the USA with the slogan 'all the way with LBJ'. He died in office while swimming at Portsea, near Melbourne.

Holyoake, Sir Keith Jacka (1904–83)
New Zealand politician. A successful farmer who represented New Zealand's agricultural industry overseas, he sat in the House of Representatives as its youngest member (1932–8). Re-elected in 1943, he became Deputy Leader of the National Party in 1947, Deputy Prime Minister in 1949 and, briefly, Party Leader and Prime Minister in 1957. He was Prime Minister (1960–72) and Governor-General of New Zealand (1977–80).

Home Guard
A home defence militia, raised during the summer of 1940, when the German armies seemed poised to complete the conquest of Western Europe by invading Great Britain. At first called the Local Defence Volunteers, the name was changed at Prime Minister Winston **Churchill**'s urging to the more evocative title of 'Home Guard'. The force was finally stood down in 1945. ▷ **World War II**

Home of the Hirsel, Baron (formerly, **Sir Alec Douglas-Home)**
(1903–)
British politician. He became a Conservative MP in 1931 and was Neville **Chamberlain**'s Secretary during the negotiations with **Hitler** and beyond (1937–40). He was Minister of State at the Scottish Office (1951–5), succeeded to the peerage as 14th Earl of Home (1951), was Commonwealth Relations Secretary (1955–60), and Foreign Secretary (1960–3). After **Macmillan**'s resignation, he surprisingly emerged from the process of consultation as Leader of the **Conservative Party** and, thus, Premier (1963–4). He made history by renouncing his peerage and fighting a by-election, during which, although Premier, he was technically a member of neither House. After the 1964 defeat by the **Labour Party**, he was Leader of the Opposition until replaced in 1965 by Edward **Heath**, in whose 1970–4 government he was Foreign Secretary. In 1974 he was made a life peer.

Home Rule

The handing down of certain legislative powers and administrative functions, previously exercised by a higher authority, to an elected body within a geographically defined area; usually put forward as an alternative to separatism. In British history, it has usually been applied to policies for Ireland, as with Gladstone in the 1880s and 1890s. It was also illustrated by the government of Northern Ireland (1922–72) when **Stormont**, the Northern Ireland parliament, was abolished. Since the early 1970s in the UK, for political movements such as the **Scottish National Party** and Irish republicans, home rule has tended to become synonymous with separatism. ▷ **IRA; Plaid Cymru**

Honecker, Erich (1912–)

East German politician. Active in the communist youth movement from an early age, he was involved in underground resistance to **Hitler**, and was imprisoned for 10 years. Released by Soviet forces, he became the first Chairman of the Free German Youth in the German Democratic Republic (1946–55). He first entered the Politburo in 1958, oversaw the building of the **Berlin Wall** in 1961 and was elected party chief in 1971, becoming Head of State from 1976 to 1989. Although prepared to deal with the West, he maintained a tight grip on East Germany. He was dismissed as a consequence of the anti-communist revolution. Manslaughter charges, instigated against him for the deaths of those fleeing East Germany, who fell victim to his regime's 'shoot-to-kill' policy at her borders, were dropped in Jan 1993, after it was revealed that he was suffering from terminal illness. ▷ **Germany, East; Revolution of 1989**

Hong Kong

A country divided into Hong Kong Island, Kowloon and New Territories, with a mainly Chinese population. Under British rule from 1842, it was occupied by the Japanese in World War II. In 1997 Britain's 99-year lease of the New Territories will expire, whereupon, under the Sino-British Declaration initialled in 1984, Hong Kong will be restored to China in July. China has designated Hong Kong a special administrative region from 1997, and has stated it will allow regional independence in domestic affairs. Hong Kong will stay a freeport and separate customs zone. Foreign markets will be retained, and the Hong Kong dollar will remain as official currency. However, anxiety about the colony's political future grew in 1989 in the aftermath of the shootings in Tiananmen Square, Beijing (Peking), followed by controversy over the UK's refusal to guarantee British residents a home in Britain, should conditions in Hong Kong prove unacceptable to them.

Hooks, Benjamin Lawson (1925–)

US civil rights leader. A minister and lawyer, he was appointed by President **Nixon** to the Federal Communications Commission (FCC) in

1972 and became the first black American to serve there. After leaving the FCC in 1977, he took over the leadership of the **NAACP**.

Hoover, Herbert C(lark) (1874–1964)
US politician and 31st President. During **World War I** he was associated with food and relief efforts in Europe. In 1921 he became Secretary of Commerce. As President (1929–33), his belief in spontaneous economic recovery made him reluctant to provide massive federal assistance for the unemployed after the stock market crash of 1929. This unpopular position led to his defeat by Franklin D **Roosevelt** in 1932. Following **World War II**, he assisted **Truman** with the various US European economic-relief programs. ▷ **Great Depression; Republican Party**

Hoover, J Edgar (1895–1972)
US public official. Director of the FBI, his length of service, from 1924 until his death (because President Lyndon B **Johnson** exempted him from civil-service retirement regulations) has been interpreted both as a tribute to his national importance in the fight against crime and as a recognition that he had learnt too much about the politicians. In the early days, his force was at a disadvantage in dealing with the gangsters of **Prohibition**, but with the **Lindbergh** kidnapping case the FBI's powers were considerably strengthened. His selection and training of the 'G-Men' created an effective and efficient organization. The application of modern scientific techniques enabled him to develop counter-espionage methods of value not only during **World War II** and the **Cold War**, but also in operations against the **Mafia** and the **Ku Klux Klan**. Very sensitive to criticisms of the FBI, Hoover responded angrily to the strictures contained in the Warren Commission's report on the assassination of President **Kennedy**, but he then used the urban riots of the 1960s with great political skill to increase the Bureau's powers and funding. A fanatical anti-communist, he saw much **civil rights** protest in this light and flagrantly abused his powers in some investigations of the civil rights and anti-**Vietnam War** movements (notably that of Martin Luther **King**) .

Hopkins, Harry Lloyd (1890–1946)
US administrator. He was federal emergency relief administrator in the 1933 **Great Depression**, became Secretary of Commerce (1938–40), and supervised the Lend-Lease programme in 1941. A close friend of Franklin D **Roosevelt**, he undertook several important missions to Russia, Britain, and other countries during **World War II**. ▷ **Lend-Lease Agreement; New Deal**

Hore-Belisha (of Devonport), (Isaac) Leslie Hore-Belisha, 1st Baron (1893–1957)

British barrister and politician. He became a London journalist, and a Liberal MP (1923). In 1934, as Minister of Transport, he gave his name to the 'Belisha' beacons, drafted a new highway code, and inaugurated driving tests for motorists. As Secretary of State for War (1937–40) he carried out several army reforms, and introduced conscription in 1939. He received a peerage in 1954. ▷ **Liberal Party** (UK)

Horrocks, Sir Brian (Gwynne) (1895–1985)

British general. He joined the army in 1914, and served in France and Russia. In 1942 he commanded the 9th Armoured Division and then the 13th and 10th Corps in North Africa, where he helped to defeat **Rommel**. Wounded at Tunis, he headed the 30th Corps during the Allied invasion (1944). Horrocks was well known as a military journalist and broadcaster. ▷ **North African Campaign; World War II**

Horthy, Miklós Nagybányai (1868–1957)

Hungarian sailor, politician and regent (1920/44). He became commander of the Austro-Hungarian fleet in 1918, and was then Minister of War in the counter-revolutionary 'white' government in 1919, opposing and suppressing Béla **Kun**'s communist regime in 1920. He became regent, presiding over a resolutely conservative, authoritarian system. In 1937 he became politically more active and in **World War II** he supported the Axis Powers until Hungary was overrun by the Germans in 1944. He was imprisoned by the Germans, but released by the Allies in 1945. He lived thereafter in Portugal, where he died.

Hot Autumn of 1969

The term (in Italian, *Autunno caldo*) applied to the period of workers' sit-ins and strikes in Italy that represented the climax of student and worker demonstrations and agitation, begun in 1967.

Houphouet-Boigny, Felix (1905–93)

Ivorien politician. The son of a chief, he was educated in Cote d'Ivoire and at Dakar, and was a medical assistant and planter before turning to politics. He was President of the Syndicat Agricole Africain in 1944 and a founder of the Parti Democratique de la Cote d'Ivoire (PDCI). Elected to the French Constituent Assembly (1945–6) and then National Assembly (1946–58), he held a series of ministerial posts. He became Prime Minister of Cote d'Ivoire in 1959 and President, at independence, in 1960. His paternalistic rule, which also combined close relations with France and support for capitalist enterprises, saw Cote d'Ivoire initially develop more successfully than most other West African countries, but economic decline and profligacy, especially the building of a palace and cathedral at Yamoussoukro, reduced his popularity.

Howe, Clarence Decatur (1886–1960)
Canadian businessman and politician. In 1936 he was appointed Minister of Transport in the Liberal government of Mackenzie **King** and played a major role in establishing Trans-Canada Airlines (later Air Canada). He proved to be a superb administrator during **World War II** as director of the Wartime Prices and Trade Board and Minister for Munitions and Supply. Faced with the refusal by private companies to produce synthetic rubber, he set up the Polymer Corporation as a crown company. Its success, both financial and in research and development, enabled the government to refuse its competitors' demands to close it down. Although he always had little patience for politics and politicians, Howe became Minister of Reconstruction in **St Laurent**'s administration in 1951, when the Defence Production Act gave him such wide economic powers that he became known as the 'Minister of Everything'. However, his management of the Trans-Canada Pipeline project, which he rammed through parliament in 1956 over outspoken opposition and charges that he had sold out the public interest to private American companies, marked the beginning of the end of more than 20 years of Liberal federal government and allowed the Conservatives a platform of reform on which they won the 1957 election. ▷ **Liberal Party** (Canada)

Howe, Sir (Richard Edward) Geoffrey (1926–)
British politician. He became a Conservative MP in 1964. Knighted in 1970, he became Solicitor-General (1970–2), Minister for Trade and Consumer Affairs (1972–4), Chancellor of the Exchequer (1979–83), and then Foreign Secretary (1983–9). A loyal supporter of Margaret **Thatcher**, in 1989 he was made Deputy Prime Minister, Lord President of the Council, and Leader of the House of Commons, but resigned from the government (Nov 1990) because of Thatcher's hostility towards European Monetary Union. His resignation speech set in train the events which led to the Premier's resignation. ▷ **Conservative Party** (UK)

Hoxha, Enver (1908–85)
Albanian politician. Born into a middle-class Muslim family, he joined the French Communist Party while he was living in France (1930–6). Returning home during **World War II**, he joined the Albanian Labour Party (Puna), becoming provisional Secretary-General in 1941. With Mehmet **Shehu**, he was a leader of the Albanian National Liberation Movement which began in 1942 under the direction of the Yugoslav partisans of **Tito**, and he became Chief Political Commissar of the National Liberation Army. In 1946, after Albania was declared a People's Republic, Hoxha held office as Prime Minister, Foreign Minister and

Minister of Defence until 1954 when, as First Secretary of the Albanian Communist Party, he preferred to rule through the party. He presided over the most doctrinaire and rigid of post-war communist governments. A Stalinist, he broke with Yugoslavia (1948), then the USSR (1960) and finally China (1978), denouncing them as revisionists and imperialists. With each turn in foreign policy, he eliminated his rivals and opponents but the late purge (1981–2) and the mysterious suicide of Shehu (1981) show he never succeeded in entirely destroying his critics. ▷ **Alia, Ramiz; Xoxe, Koci**

Hoyte, (Hugh) Desmond (1929–)
Guyanese politician. After studies at London University and the Middle Temple, he taught in a boys' school in Grenada (1955–7) and then practised as a lawyer in Guyana. He joined the socialist People's National Congress (PNC) Party and in 1968, two years after Guyana achieved full independence, was elected to the National Assembly. He held a number of ministerial posts before becoming Prime Minister under Forbes **Burnham**, and after Burnham's death, President (1985–92).

Hrushevsky, Mikhail S (1866–1934)
Ukrainian writer and political thinker. Russian-born and trained as a historian, he was appointed Professor of Ukrainian History in the University of Lvov, Galicia, in 1894, at a time of intensifying Russian nationalism. Since Galicia was then ruled by Austria, he was in a position to take up the Ukrainian case. He founded the Ukrainian National Democratic Party in exile, and he wrote extensively in Ukrainian which he helped to transform from a language of the peasantry to a medium for culture and for politics. He was able to return to Kiev in the **Duma** period, without however having much impact, but in 1917–18 he was among the founders of the short-lived Ukrainian Republic.

Hu Hanmin (Hu Han-min) (1879–1936)
Chinese politician. An early leader of the Chinese Nationalist Party, he was a founder-member of the Alliance Society created (1905) in Tokyo by **Sun Yat-sen**, from which the Party later developed. After Sun's death (1925) he lost influence, and broke with **Chiang Kai-shek** in 1931. He was imprisoned briefly for his opposition, and thereafter played little part in politics until his death. ▷ **Guomindang**

Hu Yaobang (Hu Yao-pang) (1915–89)
Chinese politician. Born into a poor peasant family in Hunan province, he joined the Red Army in 1929 and took part in the **Long March**. He held a number of posts under **Deng Xiaoping** before becoming Head of the Communist Youth League (1952–67). During the **Cultural Revolution** he was purged as a 'capitalist roader' and 'rusticated'; briefly rehabilitated

(1975–6), he did not return to high office until 1978, when, through his patron Deng, he joined the Communist Party's Politburo. From Head of the Secretariat, he was promoted to Party Leader in 1981, but dismissed in 1987 for his relaxed handling of a wave of student unrest. Popularly revered as a liberal reformer, his death triggered an unprecedented wave of pro-democracy demonstrations.

Hua Guofeng (Hua Kuo-feng) (c.1920–)
Chinese politician. He was Vice-Governor of Hunan (1958–67), but came under attack during the **Cultural Revolution**. A member of the Central Committee of the Party from 1969 and of the Politburo from 1973, he became Deputy Prime Minister, Minister of Public Security (1975–6), and was made Prime Minister (1976–80) and Chairman of the Central Committee. Under him, China adopted a more pragmatic domestic and foreign policy, with emphasis on industrial and educational expansion, and closer relations with Western and Third World countries. He resigned as Chairman in 1981. ▷ **Mao Zedong**

HUAC (House Committee on Un-American Activities)
A committee of the House of Representatives, it became a permanent committee in 1938 under the chairmanship of Democrat Martin Dies, with the purpose of investigating subversive activities. After the Republicans took control of the House of Representatives in 1946, the committee's focus became largely anti-communist. In the 1950s, when it became associated with Republican Senator Joseph **McCarthy**, it targeted alleged communists in the theatre, the movie industry, Hollywood, government and the trades. HUAC was notorious for basing its charges on loose gossip and for bullying witnesses. The committee was dissolved in 1975.

Huai-hai, Battle of (1958–9)
A crucial battle of the **Chinese Civil War** (1946–9) between the Communists and Nationalists. By the summer of 1948, communist armies already controlled Manchuria and much of the north China countryside. In order to open the way to the Yangzi River in central China, **Mao Zedong** launched a mass offensive (Oct 1948) against the Nationalist-held railway junction of Xuzhou (Hsuchow), which fell in Dec 1948. By the time the Battle of Huai-hai ended (Jan 1949), the Nationalists had lost 200 000 men; thereafter they were unable to prevent rapid communist advances throughout central and southern China.

Huggins, Godfrey Martin, 1st Viscount Malvern of Rhodesia and Bexley (1893–1971)
Rhodesian politician. Born in England, he emigrated to Southern Rhodesia in 1911 as a doctor but was soon drawn into politics, being elected

at the first election after internal self-government. He was catapulted into the premiership of Southern Rhodesia in 1933, a post he held until his elevation to the premiership of the Central African Federation, of which he was one of the chief architects. He retired in 1956. Although the Central African Federation proved short-lived and Huggins' readiness to respond to nationalist pressures was too limited, he established a liberal base in Southern Rhodesia where class was deemed more significant than race. The combined forces of African nationalism and white reaction squeezed such liberals into positions of no power in the 1960s, but the development of the state which Zimbabwe's politicians inherited owes a great deal to Huggins' leadership in difficult economic conditions in the 1930s, 1940s and 1950s.

Hughes, Charles Evans (1862–1948)
US politician and jurist. Elected Governor of New York State (1907) after exposing huge frauds in the insurance industry, he served as an Associate Justice of the Supreme Court (1910–16). He resigned to run as the Republican candidate in the presidential election of 1916, when he narrowly lost to Woodrow **Wilson**. He was appointed Secretary of State in 1921 by President Warren **Harding**, and served until 1925.

Hughes, William M(orris) (1864–1952)
British-born Australian politician and Prime Minister (1915–23). Hughes emigrated to Australia in 1884. He entered the New South Wales Legislature in 1894 and federal politics in 1901. He was Attorney-General (1908–9, 1910–13 and 1914–15), succeeding Fisher as Labor Leader and Prime Minister in 1915. A long-standing supporter of compulsory military service, he returned from a visit to Britain in 1916 to campaign for conscription. The referendum was lost, but Hughes and his followers were expelled from the **Australian Labor Party**. He formed the Nationalist Party in 1917, retained office and represented Australia at the **Paris Peace Conference** of 1919. After the election of 1922, the Country Party held the balance of power and forced his retirement in favour of S M Bruce (1923). He engineered the overthrow of the Bruce–Page government in 1929 for which he was expelled from the Nationalist Party. Involved in the foundation of the United Australia Party, he held various offices during the 1930s and was briefly party leader in 1941. He remained in parliament until his death in 1952. ▷ **National Party of Australia**

Hukbalahap (Huk)
Filipino peasant movement, concentrated in central Luzon. The term in fact refers to two related organizations: the People's Anti-Japanese Army, which was the most prominent of the indigenous resistance groups during the Japanese occupation of the Philippines; and the People's Liberation Army, which mounted a rising (the Huk Rebellion) against the newly-

independent Filipino Republic from late 1946. The origins of the rebellion lay in the severe deterioration of agrarian relations in central Luzon from the 1930s, arising from the increasingly harsh treatment of tenant farmers by the big landowners, many of whom had collaborated with the Japanese during the war years. The Communist Party of the Philippines was sometimes aligned with, and occasionally provided leadership within, the Huks. However, the rebellion remained essentially a rural one. By 1953 it had been broken, by a combination of effective military operations and changes in government policy which appeared to offer an alleviation of rural grievances.

Hull, Cordell (1871–1955)
US politician. He became Secretary of State under **Roosevelt** in 1933, and served for the longest term in that office until he retired in 1944, having attended most of the great war conferences. He was a strong advocate of maximum aid to the Allies. He helped to organize the **UN**, for which he received the Nobel Peace Prize in 1945.

Humphrey, Hubert Horatio (1911–78)
US politician. He became Mayor of Minneapolis in 1945, and was elected Senator in 1948. He built up a strong reputation as a liberal, particularly on the **civil rights** issue, but, as Vice-President from 1965 under Lyndon B **Johnson**, alienated many of his supporters by defending the policy of continuing the **Vietnam War**. Although he won the Democratic presidential nomination in 1968, a substantial minority of Democrats opposed him, and he narrowly lost the election to Richard **Nixon**. He then returned to the Senate. ▷ **Democratic Party**

Hundred Flowers Campaign (1956–7)
A campaign in China which encouraged freedom of expression, under the slogan 'Let a hundred flowers bloom and a hundred schools of thought contend', in art and literature as well as political debate. By June 1957 a clampdown was imposed on the violent criticism of the Communist Party, and an anti-rightist campaign was launched.

Hungarian Uprising (Oct–Nov 1956)
National insurrection centred on Budapest following the denunciation of **Stalin** at the 20th Congress of the Soviet Communist Party for his oppressive rule. Rioting students and workers pulled down statues of Stalin and demanded radical reform. When the new Prime Minister, Imre **Nagy**, announced plans for Hungary's withdrawal from the **Warsaw Pact**, among other things, Soviet troops and tanks crushed the uprising. Many were killed, thousands fled abroad, and Nagy was executed. Reform was set back for more than a decade.

Hungary

A republic formed after World War I, which had been part of the dual monarchy of Austria and Hungary since 1867. However a communist revolt introduced a new regime in 1919. A monarchical constitution was restored in 1920, but in 1949 a new republic under communist government was formed. Soviet forces crushed an uprising in 1956. In 1989 pressure for political change was led from within the Communist Party. The same year Hungary was declared a democratic state and in 1990 multiparty elections were held.

Hurd, Douglas (Richard) (1930–)

British politician. He followed a career in the Diplomatic Corps (1952–66) before moving to work in the Conservative Research Department (1966–70). A Conservative MP from 1974, he was Northern Ireland Secretary (1984–5), Home Secretary (1985–9), and Foreign Secretary from 1989. He was an unsuccessful candidate for the **Conservative Party** leadership (Nov 1990). ▷ **Thatcher, Margaret**

Husák, Gustáv (1913–)

Czechoslovak politician. He trained as a lawyer, joined the Communist Party in 1939 and became a member of the resistance movement during **World War II**. After the war he was a parliamentary deputy and Party official and became Minister of Agriculture in 1948–9 before being imprisoned, as an alleged Slovak bourgeois nationalist, in 1951. Rehabilitated in 1960, he worked at the Academy of Sciences (1963–8) until he became First Secretary of the Slovak Communist Party and Deputy Premier during the **Prague Spring**. After the 1968 Soviet invasion, of which he approved, he replaced Alexander **Dubček** as General-Secretary of the entire Czechoslovak Communist Party in 1969. His task was to restore public order, 'cleanse' the Party and introduce a new federal constitution. He became state President in 1975 and, pursuing a policy of minimal economic reform, remained the dominant figure in Czechoslovakia until his retirement from the general-secretaryship, under pressure, in 1987. He was finally replaced as state President by Václav **Havel** in Dec 1989 in the course of the so-called **Velvet Revolution**.

Husayn ibn 'Ali (1856–1931)

Sharif of Mecca (1908/16) and King of the Hijaz (1916/24). The founder of the modern Arab Hashimite Dynasty, when **World War I** began and the British tried to persuade him to rise up against the Turks, he negotiated with Sir Henry McMahon, British High Commissioner in Egypt, and proposed that Britain should accept as independent an area that included the present states of Syria, Lebanon, Iraq, Jordan and the Arabian Peninsula, except for Aden. McMahon accepted most of his demands but the British were making other agreements which conflicted with the promises made to Husayn, such as the **Sykes–Picot Agreement** with France (May 1916). Husayn began his revolt in June 1916, soon captured Mecca and in 1917 moved out of the Hijaz and supported Allenby as he advanced into Palestine. At the end of the war, he was frustrated and bitter, as the Allies recognized him only as King of the Hijaz and he was driven from there after a conflict (1919–24) with 'Abd al-'Aziz ibn Sa'ud. His sons, Faysal and Abdullah, became respectively King of Iraq and of Transjordan, but Husayn felt betrayed by Britain and France, who had left only Arabia as a truly independent Arab area. ▷ **Abdullah ibn Husayn; Arab Revolt; Faysal I; Husayn–McMahon Correspondence**

Husayn–McMahon Correspondence

The notorious correspondence between Sharif **Husayn ibn 'Ali** of Mecca and Sir Henry McMahon, the British High Commissioner in Egypt, initiated in 1915. It resulted in Husayn's becoming convinced that Britain supported the emancipation of the Arabs from Ottoman rule and the establishment of a Greater Arab Kingdom in the Arabian Peninsula and parts of the Fertile Crescent. This conviction derived from an assurance dispatched by McMahon in Oct 1915 that Britain was 'prepared to recognize and support the independence of the Arabs' in accordance with Husayn's demands, subject to three reservations. Despite these reservations (which concerned those parts of the Levant 'west of the districts of Damascus, Homs, Hama and Aleppo' as not being wholly Arab, an exclusion with regard to British interests in lower Iraq, and an allusion to the 'interests of her (Britain's) ally France'), this correspondence was (and remains) a major source of irritation amongst the Arabs where their relations with Britain are concerned. It undoubtedly played a decisive part in encouraging the 1916 **Arab Revolt**, and the conflict between the tenor of the correspondence with the **Sykes–Picot Agreement**, coupled with the absence of any specific mention in the correspondence of the status of Palestine (despite McMahon's much later avowal that he had always thought of Palestine as being excluded from the territories promised to the Arabs), has done nothing to promote cordial relations between Britain and the Arabs.

Hussein (ibn Talal) (1935–)

King of Jordan (1952/). Educated in Alexandria, and at Harrow and Sandhurst in England, he steered a middle course in the face of the political upheavals inside and outside his country, favouring the Western powers, particularly Britain, and pacifying Arab nationalism. After the 1967 war with Israel, the **PLO** (Palestine Liberation Organization) made increasingly frequent raids into Israel from Jordan; their power developed to such an extent that he ordered the Jordanian army to move against them and, after a short civil war (1970), the PLO leadership fled abroad. His decision to cut links with the West Bank (1988) prompted the PLO to establish a government in exile. He has been married four times; his second wife was an Englishwoman, by whom he had an heir, Abdullah, in 1962.

Hussein, Saddam (1937–)
Iraqi soldier and President. He joined the Arab Baath Socialist Party in 1957, and was sentenced to death in 1959 for the attempted execution of General Abd al-Krim **Qassim**, but escaped to Egypt. He played a prominent part in the 1968 revolution, and became Vice-President of the Revolutionary Command Council in 1969. On the retirement of his colleague President al-**Bakr**, he became sole President (1979–). His attack on Iran in 1980, to gain control of the Strait of Hormuz, led to a war of attrition which ended in 1988. His invasion of **Kuwait** in Aug 1990 led to the 1991 **Gulf War**, but by Feb of that year he had been defeated by an Allied Force backed by the **UN**. However, he defied UN ceasefire resolutions imposed on Iraq and made further raids on Iran in 1993. ▷ **Iran–Iraq War**

Huysmans, Camille (1871–1968)
Belgian politician. After studying at Liège University, he became a teacher (1893–7). He subsequently worked as a journalist and trade unionist, and was a socialist MP from 1910 to 1965. Active in the Second International, and also in the **Flemish Movement**, Huysmans was especially concerned that Dutch be made the language of instruction at Ghent University. He was involved in municipal politics in Antwerp (of which he was Mayor, 1933–40 and 1944–6) and in Brussels; he held several national cabinet posts and from 1946 to 1947 was Prime Minister. His party dropped him in 1965 (when he was in his nineties); he set up his own socialist group but was not elected.

I

Ibárruri (Gómez), Dolores ('La Pasionaria') (1895–1989)

Spanish communist orator and politician. Born into a Catholic mining family in the Basque country, she became a member of the Central Committee of the Spanish Communist Party (1930), served as Spanish delegate to the Third International (1933 and 1935), and was elected Deputy to the Spanish Cortes (1936). With the outbreak of the **Spanish Civil War** (1936), she became the Republic's most emotional and effective propagandist. After the war she took refuge in the USSR, becoming Secretary-General (1942–60) and then (1960) President of the Spanish Communist Party in exile. In 1977 she returned to Spain as Communist Deputy for Asturias.

Ibbetson, Denzil (1847–1948)

British Lieutenant-Governor of Punjab. Educated at Cambridge, Ibbetson entered the Indian Civil Service in 1870 and was posted to Punjab. During his career, he held various posts among which were the posts of the Superintendent of Census, Financial Commissioner, and Secretary to the Government of India in the Department of Revenue and Agriculture. He was also a retired member of the Viceroy's Executive Council, India. Ibbetson published the census Report of Punjab in 1883 and the Gazetteer of Punjab in 1883–5.

Ibn Saud (Ibn Abd al-Rahman al-Saud) (1880–1953)

First King of Saudi Arabia (1932/53). Seeking exile with his family in 1890, he was brought up in Kuwait. In 1901 he succeeded his father, and set out to reconquer the family domains from the Rashidi rulers, an aim which he achieved with British recognition in 1927. He changed his title from Sultan of Nejd to King of Hijaz and Najd in 1927, and in 1932 to King of Saudi Arabia. After the discovery of oil (1938), he granted substantial concessions to US oil companies. He died in Ta'if, Saudi Arabia. His son, Saud (1902–69) had been Prime Minister for three months when he succeeded his father in 1953. In 1964 he was peacefully deposed by the Council of Ministers, and his brother, Faisal (1904–75), became king, as well as remaining Prime Minister and Minister of Foreign Affairs.

Iceland

An island state lying south-east of Greenland and west of Norway. It was an independent kingdom with the same sovereign as Denmark from

1918 to 1944, when it became an independent republic. Extension of the fishing limit around Iceland in 1958 and 1975 precipitated the 'Cod War' disputes with the UK.

Ichikawa Fusaye (1893–1981)
Japanese politician and feminist. Starting her working life as a teacher, she then became involved in politics and feminism, helping to found the New Women's Association (c.1920) which successfully fought for women's right to attend political meetings. During her time in the USA (1921–4) she was impressed by the US suffrage movement, and in 1924 formed the Women's Suffrage League in Japan. Following **World War II** she became head of the New Japan Women's League, which secured the vote for women in 1945, and went on to fight for their wider rights. She campaigned against legalized prostitution and served in the Japanese Diet (1952–71), where she continued to press for an end to bureaucratic corruption. After defeat in 1971 she was triumphantly returned to parliament in 1975 and 1980.

Ikeda Hayato (1900–65)
Japanese politician and economic expert. Educated in Kyoto, he became Finance Minister (1949) of the Liberal-Democratic (Conservative) Party, and introduced an 'income doubling policy' of economic growth and higher living standards. As Prime Minister (1960–4), he was a supporter of the US-Japan Security Treaty (1960), and developed a low-key style in international relations during the post-war recovery period.

ILGWU (International Ladies Garment Workers Union)
US labour organization. Founded in 1900, it saw conflict in its early years as different ethnic and political groups and skilled and unskilled workers vied for control. Massive strikes in 1909–11 in New York led to a settlement with dress manufacturers that included the 'Protocol of Peace'. Negotiated under the aegis of Louis D **Brandeis**, the protocol offered improved wages and working conditions in exchange for a ban on strikes and lock-outs and imposed impartial arbitration as a means of ending disputes. By the 1920s, the presence of a strong communist faction had caused the union's fortunes to decline, but David Dubinsky's election as President in 1932, coupled with **New Deal** legislation favourable to labour, helped it regain strength. Membership continued to grow at a rapid pace until the 1960s, but later fell with the gradual decline of the labour unions. The ILGWU's advanced social welfare programs, which included such benefits as medical and disability insurance and unemployment compensation, provided a model for other unions.

Iliescu, Ion (1930–)

Romanian politician. He joined the Communist Youth Union in 1944 and the Communist Party in 1953, and from 1949 to 1960 served on its Central Committee. In 1965 he began a three-year term as Head of Party Propaganda, and as a member of the Central Committee again from 1968 held office as First Secretary and Youth Minister (1967–71), and First Secretary of Jassy County (1974–9). In 1984 he withdrew from office but, in the wake of the 1989 revolution and the execution of Nicolae **Ceauşescu**, he returned to politics, becoming President of the National Salvation Front (Dec 1989) and, two months later, of its successor, the Provisional Council for National Unity. In May 1990 he was elected President and resigned his party posts. Discontent with the economic situation resulted in protests against his government in late 1990 and early 1991.

Ilinden Uprising (St Elijah's Day Revolt) (2 Aug 1903)

VMRO, hoping to provoke the Great Powers to intervene, organized a rebellion among the peoples of Macedonia against Ottoman rule. The uprising was badly planned, its leader, Gotse Delchev, was captured and executed before it began and the Great Powers avoided involvement. The Ottoman authorities' brutal suppression of the revolt did, however, prompt Emperor **Franz Josef** and Tsar **Nicholas II** to force the Ottoman government to pay compensation and to allow foreign advisers into Macedonia. ▷ **Macedonians**

Ilyushin, Sergei Vladimirovich (1894–1977)

Soviet aircraft designer. Born of a peasant family in the Vologda region, he found his way to the military Aviation Academy in Moscow and by about 1930 was already working on new aeroplane designs. These were used to equip the wartime and post-war Soviet air force and increasingly to provide aircraft for Aeroflot, the Soviet civilian airline.

Imam Ahmad (d.1962)

Imam Ahmad of the Yemen succeeded his father the Imam Yahya who was assassinated in 1948, and ruled the country until his death in 1962, when with the backing particularly of Egypt, the Yemen Arab Republic (YAR) was proclaimed. A protracted civil war ensued with Egyptian troops being sucked into what was for them a particularly undesirable conflict, insofar as the so-called 'royalists', who supported Ahmad's son, the Imam Muhammad al-Badr and were backed by the Sa'udis (who naturally had no wish to see a left of centre republican regime on their back doorstep), were familiar with the mountainous terrain of the country, a terrain which was totally alien to the Egyptian forces sent to support the Republican cause.

Immigration Legislation (USA)

Throughout the colonial period and the 19c, for the mixture of ideological and economic reasons symbolized by the Statue of Liberty (1886), immigration to the USA was actively encouraged rather than controlled; and it was regulated by local authorities at the ports of entry rather than by the federal government, whose sole requirement before the American Civil War was for enumeration (1819). During the late 19c and early 20c Congress took control of immigration, established the reception centre on **Ellis Island** (1892), and began to exclude various socially undesirable categories such as prostitutes, convicts, lunatics, and sufferers from tuberculosis. Although the entry of Asians was severely restricted by the Chinese Exclusion Act (1882, passed in response to Californian fears of the 'Yellow Peril') and the 'Gentlemen's Agreement' with Japan (1907), all this legislation still left an essentially open door to Europeans. However, the massive influx from 1880 to 1910 (almost 18 million in total) aroused fears for the future character of US society, stimulated **Nativism** and fuelled an increasingly effective immigration restriction movement. The Dillingham Commission (1911) compared the 'new' migrants from Southern and Eastern Europe very unfavourably with the 'old' migrants from the north and west, and recommended control by literacy tests with limits set in proportion to the size of national groups already within the country. These recommendations were followed in the xenophobia of **World War I** and its aftermath. In 1921 an annual ceiling of 385 000 p.a. was established with national quotas based on the 1910 census, thus bringing to an end an era in the social evolution of the USA. Restrictions were then tightened with the Johnson–Reed Act (1924), shifting the quota base back to the census of 1890 and so limiting the entry from South-East Europe even further; and the Oriental Exclusion Act entirely ended immigration from Asia. Further amendments in 1927 lowered the ceiling to about 150 000 p.a. and moved the quota base to 1920. Since **World War II** immigration policy has been progressively liberalized with measures allowing entry to displaced persons and refugees (1948, 1950, 1953, 1957, 1960, 1962, 1980), while the quota system itself was extended to all countries by the McCarran–Walter Act (1952), which also eliminated race as a disqualification for entry and so reversed the exclusion of Asians. A more fundamental revision took place with the Immigration Act of 1965, which replaced the national quotas with a first-come, first-served and a family preference system, together with a hemispheric distinction (totals of 120 000 for the Western Hemisphere, and 170 000 elsewhere with a limit of 20 000 for each country). These distinctions were removed in 1976 and 1978 to give a worldwide total of 290 000, a single country limit of 20 000, and a consistent family reunification system. However, since the 1920s, alongside the official immigration restriction policies has existed the problem of illegal immigration, particularly from Mexico since the ending of the bracero programme (which from 1942 to 1964 regulated the flow of temporary seasonal labour). By the middle of the 1980s there were probably 3–5 million illegal immigrants in the USA, and political pressure from the Hispanic and Irish communities in particular led to the passage of the 1986 Immigration Reform and Control Act which granted an amnesty to those resident since 1982 (about 2.5 million) and prohibited the employment of 'undocumented aliens', as illegal immigrants now became known. The Immigration Act of 1990 raised the overall total of admissions to 700 000 p.a., and its provisions for skill-based and diversity visas represented a significant attempt to alter the overwhelmingly Latin-American and Asian profile of the previous 25 years' immigration, by once again attracting Europeans. The USA remains, as it has done so for the past 200 years, the major immigrant-receiving nation in the world.

impeachment

A legal process for removing public officials from office. Originating in medieval England, the process was revived in that country in the 17c, when the Rump Parliament voted to bring Charles I to trial, resulting in his conviction and beheading. In the USA, the Constitution provides that the House of Representatives may move to impeach for 'high crimes and misdemeanors'. The case is then tried by the Senate, where a two-thirds majority is required for conviction. It is generally agreed that impeachment is a cumbersome method because of the problem of defining unacceptable behaviour and crimes. The move to impeach President Richard **Nixon** in 1974 did, however, have the effect of forcing his resignation. Earlier, the impeachment proceedings against President Andrew Johnson in 1867, which were politically inspired, resulted in his acquittal by the Senate.

Imperial Conferences

The consultative arrangements devised in 1907 by which the British and Dominion governments met on a regular basis. A permanent secretariat was established and meetings at four-year intervals were organized. The Canadian Prime Minister, Sir Wilfred **Laurier**, was suspicious of both the title and its implications, but he wished to challenge the London government's right to decide the foreign policy of the empire as a whole and thereby commit Canada without proper consultation. The 1911 conference provided the first occasion for at least some briefing by the imperial government when Sir Edward Grey gave the Prime Ministers a cagey description of the European situation. By 1926 the conference at last accepted the principle that the dominions were independent nations. The **Balfour Declaration** recommended a new constitutional framework for the Empire in which the dominions became 'autonomous communities within the **British Empire**, equal in status' but still 'united by a common allegiance to the crown', and this was embodied in the Statute of **Westminster**. However, there were limits to the British government's readiness to see the dominions as equal partners. At the 1930 conference it refused to consider the Canadian Prime Minister R B **Bennett**'s plea for imperial preferential tariffs. By 1944, however, the Imperial Conference had become a genuine means by which the Prime Ministers discussed problems and suggested mutually acceptable solutions.

Imperial Rule Assistance Association (IRAA)
An umbrella organization created in Japan (Oct 1940) to promote a New Order whereby all interests in society would be united behind mobilization for war and the national interest. Launched by the Prime Minister Fumimaro **Konoe** in the summer of 1940, the IRAA was originally intended to be the nucleus of a mass-based reformist party that would absorb all existing political parties and occupational groups, thereby challenging the political, bureaucratic and economic elites. It was supported by army officers who wanted to see a controlled economy as well as intellectuals attracted to models of European Fascism. In practice, however, the IRAA soon came under the control of the bureaucracy (in particular the Home Ministry) and became merely an instrument of government control. Although political parties were formally abolished, former party elites continued to exercise leadership in the Diet, while business elites were able to obstruct all attempts to impose total state control of the economy.

Imperial Way Faction (*Kodo-ha*)
Japanese army faction in the 1930s which stressed the importance of the samurai spirit and mystic devotion to the emperor. The faction comprised ultra-nationalist junior officers who denounced corruption amongst political and business elites (who were seen as insensitive to the economic hardships of the people as a result of the Great Depression) and advocated direct action to sweep away the civilian establishment and achieve national renovation in preparation for what they saw as an inevitable war with the USSR. In Feb 1936 the faction attempted a coup in Tokyo but it was suppressed by the army senior command.

Imrédy, Béla (1891–1946)
Hungarian financier and politician. He was Director of the national bank from 1932 to 1935 and thereafter its President. Between 1932 and 1935 he was also Minister of Finance, and from May 1938 to Feb 1939 Prime Minister. Internally he supported authoritarian rule and externally he supported **Hitler**'s policies, particularly after the **Munich Agreement** in Sep 1938. During the Nazi occupation 1944–5 he acted as Minister of Economic Affairs. After the war he was executed as a war criminal.

Independent Labour Party (ILP)
British political party formed in 1893 with the objective of sending working men to parliament. It was socialist in aim, but wished to gain the support of working people whether they were socialist or not. One of its

leading figures was Keir **Hardie**. Many of its leaders played a major part in founding the Labour Representation Committee (1900), which became the **Labour Party** in 1906. It was affiliated to the Labour Party but put up its own candidates, and was disaffiliated in 1932. It continued to have a few members of parliament up to 1950. ▷ **socialism**

Independent Republican Party

French political party. Those members of the CNI (*Centre national des independants*, 'National Centre of Independents') who continued to support de **Gaulle** after 1962 and who formed a new party in 1966, led by **Giscard d'Estaing**. At first little more than a weak adjunct to the Gaullist Party, it emerged as an equal partner with its leader's election as President in 1973, and became one of the two main right-wing parties. In 1978 it was incorporated in the UDF (*Union pour la démocratie française* ('Union for French Democracy'), an electoral coalition, with various small centre groups. Often referred to as Giscardiens, after their leading figure. ▷ **Gaullists; Independents** (France)

Independents (France)

French political party, officially known as the CNI (*Centre national des indépendants*, 'National Centre of Independents' or 'Independents'. Organized in 1948, the party was the successor to the pre-**World War II** parties known collectively by the name *Modérés* ('**Moderates**'). In 1951 it incorporated the *Parti paysan* ('Peasant Party'), and in 1952 many former **Gaullists**. It was led by Antoine Pinay and supported de **Gaulle** in 1958, but its opposition to his Algerian policy led to its collapse in 1962. A small faction, led by **Giscard d'Estaing**, remained loyal to de Gaulle's government, and resurrected the party as the **Independent Republican Party** in 1966.

India

A federal republic in south-east Asia, where a movement for independence from Britain took place in the late 19c. The Government of India Act in 1919 allowed the election of Indian ministers to share power with appointed British governors. A further Act in 1935 allowed the election of independent provincial governments. Passive resistance campaigns led by Mahatma **Gandhi** began in the 1920s. Independence was granted in 1948, on the condition that a Muslim state be established (**Pakistan**). Indian states were later reorganized on a linguistic basis. Pakistan and India warred over disputed territory in Kashmir and Jammu in 1948. There was Hindu–Muslim hostility, notably in 1978, and further India–Pakistan conflict in 1965 and 1971. Separatist movements continue, especially relating to Sikh interests in the Punjab; the suppression of the militant Sikh movement in 1984 led to the assassination of Indira **Gandhi**. Rajiv **Gandhi**, leader of the Congress (I) Party, was assassinated in 1991 during the general election. Increasing tension resulted in inter-communal violence and the declaration in 1993 of a national state of emergency. ▷ **Government of India Acts**

India, Partition of (1947)

Under the Indian Independence Act of July 1947, the formerly British-ruled Indian sub-continent was partitioned on 14–15 Aug into two independent countries, a predominantly Hindu India and a predominantly Muslim Pakistan. There was a lot of communal violence at this time which had started in the spring of 1947. Many Muslims migrated from India to Pakistan and many Hindus from Pakistan to India, resulting in a refugee population of some 6 000 000 Muslims (in Pakistan) and 4 500 000 Sikhs and Hindus (on the Indian side of the border). In places there was a total collapse of law and order, before, during and after the partition. The violence which accompanied the migration resulted in what is believed to have been near to a million deaths — although the official total was 180 000. All princely states in the Indian subcontinent were left to choose their own fate but were advised to integrate with either India or Pakistan according to the religious affiliations of their peoples and their geographical positions. The state of Kashmir, however, remains in dispute.

Indian National Congress

A broad-based political organization, it was founded in 1885 and became a nationwide political party in 1920. It spearheaded the nationalist movement for independence from Britain under the leadership of charismatic figures such as M K **Gandhi** and Jawaharlal **Nehru**. An uneasy alliance of left and right, business and rural interests, it has been the dominant political party in India since 1947. Exceptions to its rule occurred in the periods 1977–80, when the Janata Party ruled, and 1989–91, when India was ruled by the Janata Dal and Janata Dal (S). ▷ **Non-Cooperation Movement; Quit India Movement**

indirect rule

A form of colonial rule especially characteristic of British rule in Africa during the inter-war years. In general terms it involved the use of existing political structures, leaders, and local organs of authority. Thus local political elites enjoyed considerable autonomy, although they still had to keep in accord with the interests of the colonial power. It was adopted on grounds of its cheapness and to allow for independent cultural development, but was increasingly criticized for its failure to introduce a modernizing role into colonial administration, and was gradually given up after 1945.

Indo-Pakistan Wars (1947–9, 1965 and 1971)

The conflict between Hindus and Muslims that first led to partition at Independence in 1947 and the creation of **India** and **Pakistan**, has been kept alive since for a number of reasons, including, most obviously, resentment at the bloodshed which accompanied partition and the ineptitude with which the boundary between the two countries was delineated by the British in the months before their departure. Roughly drawn, the boundary often divided families, villages and communities and has been a cause of dispute ever since. The fate of various nominally still independent Princely states had also not been decided at the time of partition. Owing to their loyalty to the British, there had been a reluctance to force them into joining either of the new nations and in Kashmir, on the border between India and Pakistan, the Raja, Hari Singh, was in a dilemma since, although himself a Hindu, the majority of his population were Muslim. An uprising in the west of the country decided the matter for him, forcing him to turn to India for help, which was afforded only on the condition that Kashmir joined the Indian union. This decision, made without consulting the population, was contested by Pakistan, which supported the insurgents against the Indian army, the fighting in Kashmir only being brought to an end in 1949 after the **UN** arranged a ceasefire, pending a plebiscite to decide the fate of the territory. This plebiscite was never held, and fighting broke out between India and Pakistan again in 1965, a ceasefire being brokered by the Soviet Premier, Alexei Kosygin, after an arms embargo was imposed by the USA and USSR. In 1971 a third war was occasioned by the uprising in East Pakistan that led to the foundation of the independent state of Bangladesh. This time it was India that intervened in support of Sheikh Mujibur Rahman and the Awami League; fighting also occurred on the western frontier between India and Pakistan, and in Kashmir. On this occasion the superior size of the Indian army outmatched the Pakistanis and an uneasy peace has persisted ever since. In the 1980s the rearming of Pakistan by the USA following the Soviet invasion of Afghanistan, accelerated the arms race between the two countries, both sides acquiring the capacity to manufacture nuclear weapons (the first test explosion of an Indian bomb occurring in 1974). The foundation of the South Asian Association for Regional Cooperation in 1986 (comprising India, Pakistan, Bangladesh, Bhutan, Nepal and Sri Lanka) has helped to relieve tension in subsequent years. ▷ **India, Partition of; Princely States, Indian**

Indo-Sri Lankan Peace Accord (1987)

The agreement signed by Rajiv **Gandhi**, then Prime Minister of India, and J R **Jayawardene**, the President of Sri Lanka. The Accord was Gandhi's attempt to impose a solution to Sri Lanka's Tamil secessionist problem, but collapsed due to a lack of support from all sections of Sri Lankan society. Troops from the Indian Peacekeeping Force (IPKF) were quickly embroiled in conflict with the militants of the **LTTE**, while

Jayawardene's government was threatened by violent protests led by the **JVP**.

Indochina

The term, as currently used, refers to the present-day states of Vietnam, Laos and Cambodia. French Indochina, the Indochinese Union, was established in 1887, and comprised the protectorates of Cambodia, Laos, Tonkin and Annam, together with the colony of Cochinchina. French Indochina as a political unit ceased to exist in 1954, following the conclusion of the Geneva Agreements and the withdrawal of the French.

Indonesia

The world's largest island group, situated in South-East Asia. It was occupied by **Japan** in **World War II** and gained independence in 1945, under Dr **Sukarno**. The 1945 constitution established a 1 000-member People's Consultative Assembly. The federal system was replaced by unified control in 1950. The expulsion of Dutch citizens led to a breakdown of the economy, causing hardship and unrest. Sukarno's rule became increasingly authoritarian and was opposed by the Communist Party. A military coup was staged in 1966. East Timor became the 27th province of Indonesia in 1976 but the United Nations refuses to recognize Indonesian sovereignty in East Timor and continues to regard it as a Portuguese colony. Protesters for independence were massacred by the Indonesian army in Dili, the East Timor capital, in 1991, provoking international condemnation.

Industrial Workers of the World (IWW)

US radical labour organization movement, whose members were known as Wobblies. An offshoot of the Western Federation of Miners, it was founded in 1905 by a group who opposed the craft unionism of the AFL and proposed instead a union of both skilled and unskilled workers. The movement was soon splintered because of the radical ideology of its leader, 'Big Bill' **Haywood**, who called for the destruction of capitalism and the formation of a new society and maintained that employers' violence must be met in kind. He was less interested in negotiation than in striking and sabotage. Lack of organization and funds meant that the IWW had few successes in industrial conflicts although its membership reached a peak of at least 60 000. It declined rapidly after the Red Scare of 1919. ▷ **AFL–CIO**

Inkatha Freedom Party

A loose political organization based in Zululand and answerable to Chief Gatsha **Buthelezi** which in the 1970s and 1980s offered an opposition voice to **apartheid** but then became the vehicle for Zulu nationalism and a sometimes violent antagonist to the **ANC** (African National Congress).

It received clandestine support from the police and probably government sources as well. It eventually participated in the 1994 elections, with the ANC.

Inönü, Ismet (1884–1973)
Turkish soldier and politician. He fought in **World War I**, then became **Atatürk**'s Chief-of-Staff in the war against the Greeks (1919–22), defeating them twice at Inönü. As the first Premier of the new republic (1923–37), he introduced many political reforms, and was elected President in 1938 on Atatürk's death. From 1950 he was Leader of the Opposition, and held office as Premier again from 1960 to 1965, when he resigned.

Inouye, Daniel (1924–)
US Senator. He was Assistant Public Prosecutor in Honolulu (1953–4) before going into private practice. He became US Senator from Hawaii in 1963, and served on the Senate Watergate Committee investigating the scandal that led to Richard **Nixon**'s resignation. He was later made chairman of the Senate committee investigating the **Iran–Contra Affair** in 1986.

integralismo
A Brazilian fascist movement of the 1930s. Its supporters were noted for their green shirts and aggressive street actions. The Brazilian Integralists Party, led by Plinio Salgado, was suppressed after a vain attack on the presidential Catete Palace in Rio de Janeiro (10 May 1938). The party had been used as a tool by Getúlio fi**Vargas** against liberals and the communist-led *Aliança Nacional Libertadora* (ANL) headed by Luís Carlos Prestes, a leading *tenente* in the struggle against the old republic.

Intensive Development (post-1953)
The term used by Soviet-style economists to describe the second stage of growth following initial industrialization, itself entitled **Extensive Development**. After **Stalin**'s death Nikita **Khrushchev** and later Leonid **Brezhnev** tried to diversify the economy of the USSR by expounding the production of consumer durables and introducing new materials and technologies. Other communist countries followed suit. Largely because of too much central planning, the communist world lagged behind the West, a fact which sapped confidence in the regimes and contributed to their downfall in the period 1989–91.

INF (Intermediate Nuclear Force) Treaty
A treaty signed (Dec 1987) in Washington by US President Ronald **Reagan**, and Soviet General-Secretary Mikhail **Gorbachev**, involving the elimination of 1 286 missiles from Europe and Asia, and over 2 000 warheads. It was noted for its inclusion of the most comprehensive,

stringent and intrusive verification procedures ever seen in an arms control treaty, including short notice on-site verification, and was a major break in the arms race and a step forward in arms control generally, leading to later agreements in both the nuclear and conventional fields.

International

An abbreviation originally of International Working Men's Association, the name given to successive organizations attempting to establish international co-operative mechanisms for socialist, communist and revolutionary groups. The Second International was formed in Paris in 1889, but it largely collapsed in 1914 as socialist parties took sides in **World War I**. The Third International (**Comintern**) was founded by **Lenin** in Moscow in 1919 and represented mainly communist parties. It became in effect a tool of **Stalin**'s foreign policy until he abolished it in 1943 during **World War II**. There was a brief attempt in the 1930s by **Trotsky** to launch a Fourth International, which came into existence in Périgny in France in 1938 but remained merely an umbrella for miscellaneous left-wing groups of no particular importance. ▷ **communism**

International Brigades

In the **Spanish Civil War**, foreign volunteer forces recruited by the **Comintern** and by individual communist parties to assist the Spanish Republic. Almost 60 000 volunteers, mostly workers, fought in Spain between Oct 1936 and the brigades' withdrawal in Oct 1938, playing a particularly important role in the defence of Madrid.

Iorga, Nicolae (1871–1940/1)

Romanian politician and historian. As editor (1903–6) of 'The Sower' (*Sămănătorul*), he advocated conservative and patriotic values. Active in political life, he was elected to the Romanian parliament (1907) and founded the National Democrat Party. As Prime Minister and Minister of Education (1931–2), he supported **Charles II** of Romania. With the establishment of the **Antonescu** regime, he was one of several leading figures in Romanian political and cultural life who were murdered in the years 1940–1.

IPLA (Irish People's Liberation Army)

An offshoot of the Irish National Liberation Army (itself an **IRA** breakaway group) that once had left-wing pretensions, but which in the 1980s became identified once more with drug-dealing — an activity forbidden to IRA supporters and punishable by execution.

Iqbal, Sir Mohammed (1875–1938)

Indian poet and philosopher. He was educated at Lahore, Cambridge (where he read law and philosophy) and Munich. On his return to India, he achieved fame through his poetry, whose compelling mysticism and nationalism caused him to be regarded almost as a prophet by Muslims. His efforts to establish a separate Muslim state eventually led to the formation of Pakistan. He was knighted in 1923, and died at Lahore, Punjab.

IRA (Irish Republican Army)

An anti-British paramilitary guerrilla force established in 1919 by Irish nationalists to combat British forces in Ireland. It opposed the Anglo-Irish Treaty of 1921 because Ireland was a dominion and the six counties of the North of Ireland were part of the UK, but it was suppressed by the Irish government in the 1922 rising, banned by Eamon **De Valera** in 1936 and remained largely inactive until the late 1960s. In 1969, a major split in its ranks led to the formation of the Provisional IRA alongside the Official IRA, and a serious schism between the two sides in the early 1970s. The Official IRA has been virtually inactive since 1972, and generally supports political action to achieve Irish unity. The Provisionals have become the dominant republican force, responsible for shootings and bombings in Northern Ireland, Britain, and Western Europe. Targets have mainly been security and military personnel and establishments, although there have been many sectarian killings and attempts to disrupt civilian life. ▷ **Sinn Féin**

Iran, formerly **Persia** (to 1935)

A republic in south-west Asia, which was ruled by Arabs, Turks and Mongols until the Sasavid Dynasty in the 16c–18c and the Qajar Dynasty in the 19c–20c. A military coup in 1921 led to independence under **Reza Shah Pahlavi** in 1925. Protests against the Shah's regime in the 1970s led to a revolution in 1978, the exile of the Shah, and the proclamation of an Islamic Republic under Ayatollah **Khomeini** in 1979. The US embassy in Tehran was occupied in 1979–81. The **Iran–Iraq War** took place from 1980 until 1988.

Iran, Anglo-Soviet Invasion of (Aug 1941)

Suspicions that Reza Shah was sympathetic to the Germans in **World War II** led to the Anglo-Soviet invasion of Iran in Aug 1941, although it is possible that a desire to protect oil supplies among other things was as much of a motive for the invasion on the British side as any inklings of pro-German leanings in the Shah. The invasion and subsequent occupation forced the abdication of Reza Shah in favour of his son, Muhammad Reza, and the presence of the Soviets allowed a brief reappearance of the Tudeh Party. The country was subjected to Anglo-Soviet military occupation until 1946.

Iran–Contra Affair (1986)

A major US political scandal. It grew out of the **Reagan** administration's efforts to obtain the release of US hostages held in Lebanon by groups friendly to Iran by secretly supplying arms to Iran's strongly anti-American government. **National Security Council** officials (notably, Colonel Oliver North) had been involved in the diversion of the proceeds of the arms sales to Iran to Nicaragua, to support the anti-government Contra rebels, even though Congress had banned the supplying of arms to the Contras. Congressional hearings in 1987 centred on the legality of the arms-for-hostages deal and on whether Colonel North had acted on his own as the Administration claimed, or whether top government officials, including President Reagan himself, were involved. The issues have not been satisfactorily resolved.

Iran Hostage Crisis (1979–81)

On 4 Nov 1979 the US Embassy in Tehran, Iran, was seized by a mob and its staff of 52 were taken hostage. The action was approved by the Ayatollah Khomeini who, like many Iranians, hated Americans for the role of the **CIA** in the overthrow of the Mossadegh government (1953) and for their training of Shah Muhammad Reza Pahlavi's secret police. The price demanded for the release of the hostages was the return of the Shah and all his wealth. Neither **UN** appeals nor President Jimmy **Carter**'s move to freeze all Iranian assets induced Iran to release the hostages. In 1980, an attempted helicopter rescue operation using US marines, failed, causing the Carter administration great political embarrassment. The crisis preoccupied Carter during his last months in office and may well have been the single most important factor in his defeat by Ronald **Reagan** in the 1980 election. After 444 days of captivity, the hostages were released on the day President Reagan was inaugurated, and Iranian assets were unfrozen.

Iran–Iraq War (1980–8)

Although the 1975 peace agreement with Iran ended Iraq's Kurdish revolt, Iraq still wanted a readjustment of its borders with Iran. After the Islamic Revolution in Iran, the Iranians accused Baghdad of fomenting demands for autonomy by the Arabs of Iran's Khuzestan province. In addition, Iraq feared Iranian provocation of its own 60 per cent Shiite population. After some border fighting in 1980, Iraqi forces advanced into Iran (22 Sep). By the time a peace was agreed (1988), the war had cost about half a million lives on both sides, and represented a serious threat to shipping in the Gulf. Iraq accepted Iran's terms in Aug 1990.
▷ **Kurds; Shiites**

Iranian Revolution

The 1979 revolution in Iran which deposed the Shah (15 Jan) and led to the triumphant return (1 Feb) from his French exile of the Ayatollah

Khomeini. Khomeini appointed Dr Mehdi Bazargan as Prime Minister (1979–80), although real power was to remain with Khomeini's 15-man Islamic Revolutionary Council. Revolutionary forces took control of the country, and Khomeini announced the establishment of the Islamic Republic.

Iraq

A republic in south-west Asia, which was part of the Ottoman Empire from the 16c until **World War I**. Captured by British forces in 1916, it became a British-mandated territory in 1921. It gained independence under the Hashemite Dynasty in 1932. The monarchy was replaced by military rule in 1958. Since the 1960s, Kurdish nationalists in the north-east have been fighting to establish a separate state. Iraq's invasion of Iran in 1980 led to the **Iran–Iraq War**, which lasted until 1988. Its invasion of Kuwait in 1990 led to **UN** sanctions, the **Gulf War** (1991), and Iraqi withdrawal. Tension in the area remained, Iraqi attacks on Kurdish settlements and Shiite refugees continued, and UN sanctions remained in place.

Irgun (Zvai Leumi)

The terrorist organization operating in Palestine during the **British Mandate** and seeking the establishment of a Jewish state. Formed in 1931 after disagreement with the **Haganah** and reconstituted in 1937, it accepted **Jabotinsky**'s ideology and engaged in armed conflict with Arabs and the British. Led by Menachem **Begin** from 1943, Irgun bombed Jerusalem's **King David Hotel** in 1946, hanged two British sergeants in 1947 in response to the execution of its members, and attacked the Arab village of Deir Yassin in 1948. Condemned for this by the **Jewish Agency**, the Irgun became the nucleus of the right-wing Herut Party in Israel after 1948.

Irish Free State

A form of **Home Rule**, established by the Anglo-Irish Treaty (Dec 1921). Accordingly, 26 counties (excluding the six of Northern Ireland) became a Dominion under the British crown. The treaty was ratified by a small majority in the **Dáil Eireann** and power was transferred from Westminster (Mar 1922). Republicans, led by **De Valera**, refused to accept the authority of the crown and civil war (1922–3) ensued. The name 'Irish Free State' was retained until Dominion status was dismantled with the new constitution of 1937. ▷ **Collins, Michael; Eire; Griffith, Arthur**

Irish National Liberation Army (INLA)

The military wing of the **Irish Republican Socialist Party**, a small paramilitary group which commits few terrorist attacks, but is noted for the ruthless nature of those it does carry out. Probably created by former members of the Official **IRA** disenchanted with the 1972 ceasefire, it was responsible for the killing of the Conservative MP Airey Neave (Mar 1979). Its impact lessened with internal feuds in the 1980s.

Irish Republic or Ireland (Irish Éire)

A republic which was formerly united with Britain (by the Act of Union, 1801). Two Home Rule Bills were introduced by Gladstone (1886, 1893) and a third Home Rule Bill, passed in 1914, never came into effect because of World War I. In 1916 there was an armed rebellion against British rule. A republic was proclaimed by Sinn Féin in 1919. A partition proposed by Britain in 1920 was largely ignored by the Irish Republic. A treaty signed in 1921 gave Ireland dominion status, subject to the right of Northern Ireland to opt out. This right was exercised, and a frontier was agreed in 1925. The southern republic was renamed Éire in 1937, and all constitutional links between the Irish Republic and the UK were severed by 1948. In 1949 it left the Commonwealth. The Irish Republic has been a member of the EC since 1973.

Irish Republican Socialist Party

A political party formed in 1974 largely as a breakaway group from the official **Sinn Féin**, which disagreed with its political strategy and the ceasefire. Its most prominent member was Bernadette McAliskey. It was involved in a feud with the Official **IRA** in the 1970s, and subsequently moved closer to the Provisional Sinn Féin. ▷ **Irish National Liberation Army**

Iron Curtain

A term formerly used to describe the separation of certain East European countries from the rest of Europe by the **Cold War** and in particular the political and military domination of the USSR. It was first used by Nazi Propaganda Minister **Goebbels** in 1943, and became widely known after Winston **Churchill** used it in a speech in 1946.

Iron Guard

The name commonly applied to the Legion of the Archangel Michael, a movement with a fascist ideology which in the 1930s, under the leadership of Corneliu Zelea **Codreanu**, established a mass following in Romania. Founded in 1927, the Legion was at first a quasi-religious organization encouraging moral regeneration. Chauvinist and anti-Semitic, it founded its military section, the Iron Guard, to combat the communists. First dissolved by the Romanian government in 1933, it operated under a front, 'All for the Fatherland'. In 1938 the Guard was again disbanded and Codreanu shot. Ion **Antonescu** established links with the Guard and its new leader, Horia Sima, but in 1941 the movement was crushed with German support. ▷ **Charles II** of Romania

Ironside, William Edmund, 1st Baron (1880–1959)

British field marshal. He served as a secret agent disguised as a railwayman in the **Boer Wars**, held several staff appointments in **World War I**, and commanded the Archangel expedition against the **Bolsheviks** (1918). He was Chief of the Imperial General Staff at the outbreak of **World War II**, and placed in command of the Home Defence Forces (1940). The 'Ironsides', fast light-armoured vehicles, were named after him. He was made a peer in 1941.

Isaacs, Sir Isaac Alfred (1855–1948)

Australian jurist and politician, the son of a Jewish tailor. He became a barrister and, as Attorney-General for Victoria, helped prepare the federal constitution (1897–9). He sat in the federal parliament (1901–6), was a justice of the High Court (1906–30), and Chief Justice (1930–1). From 1931 to 1936 he was Governor-General, the first Australian to hold that office.

Isa ibn Sulman (1932–)

Ruler of Bahrain (1971/). Despite encouragement from Britain to maintain a federal connection with Arab Emirates further down the Persian Gulf, he declared his island's full independence in 1971; in this he adopted much the same attitude as the ruler of Qatar, Khalifa ibn Ahmad al-Thani. He has also made a show of attempting a democratic approach to government, but after little more than a year dissolved the elected assembly and full powers reverted to the Shaykh and his family.

Ishibashi Tanzan (1884–1973)

Japanese politician. In the 1930s he was an economic journalist and vociferous critic of the militarists. He joined the Liberal Party (*Nihon Jiyuto*) after the war and served as Finance Minister in 1946. In 1951 Ishibashi became head of **MITI**, a powerful government ministry created in 1949 to promote economic development. He served briefly as Prime Minister for two months in 1956 before illness forced him to retire. Ishibashi was a keen supporter of the **normalization** of relations between Japan and communist China during the 1950s and 1960s.

Ishiwara Kanji (1889–1949)

Japanese army officer. He graduated from the prestigious Army War College in 1918 and lectured there 1925–8. Influenced by the apocalyptic doctrines of the Japanese medieval Buddhist monk, Nichiren, Ishiwara believed in the inevitability of a final conflict between East and West, as represented by Japan and the USA. To prepare for this conflict, he maintained that Japan needed to harness resources in East Asia (especially Manchuria). After 1929, as an operations officer attached to the Japanese army (**Guandong Army**) that protected Japan's interests in south Manchuria and along the South Manchuria railway, Ishiwara helped plan the campaign in 1931 (without reference to the civilian government in Tokyo) that resulted in the transformation of Manchuria into the Japanese puppet-state of **Manzhuguo**. On his return to Japan (1932), his abrasiveness and independent way of thinking brought him into conflict with his military superiors. In 1937, especially, he criticized Japan's invasion of China, fearing that a long drawn-out war of attrition would sabotage Japan's efforts in building a national defence state. He was forced out of the army in 1941.

Israel

A state in the Middle East. When the Zionist movement was founded by Theodor Herzl at the end of the 19c thousands of Jews returned to **Palestine**, which was then part of the Ottoman Empire. Britain was given a League of Nations mandate to govern Palestine and establish a Jewish national home there in 1922. Nazi persecution of Jews in the 1930s greatly increased Jewish immigration. The British evacuated Palestine, and Israel proclaimed independence in 1948. Invasion by Arab nations resulted in an armistice in 1949. The **Six-Day War** in 1967 brought Israeli control of the **Gaza Strip**, the Sinai Peninsula as far as the Suez Canal, the **West Bank** of the River Jordan including the east sector of Jerusalem, and the Golan Heights in **Syria**. The Camp David conference between Egypt and Israel took place in 1978. Israel withdrew from Sinai in 1979 and invaded **Lebanon**, forcing the **PLO** to leave Beirut in 1982–5. Renewed tension began in 1988, with the uprising of Arabs in occupied territories (the *Intifada*). A peace agreement between Israel and the PLO, signed in 1993, set out the introduction of limited self-rule for the Palestinians in the Gaza Strip and Jericho, with plans for the cities of the West Bank to follow suit.

Istria

The peninsula at the north end of the Adriatic, divided between the republics of **Slovenia** and **Croatia**. By the 15c, Istria was divided between the Austrian Habsburgs and the Republic of Venice, with the latter holding about three-quarters of the area. After **Napoleon I** took Venice in 1797, the French included the whole peninsula in the Illyrian Provinces (1809–13). Austrian forces took Istria in 1813 and Habsburg possession was confirmed at the Congress of Vienna (1814–15). In 1921 it was annexed by **Mussolini**'s Italy and the fascist government tried to suppress all expression of Slovene and Croatian national identity. After **World War II**, in 1947, it was formally ceded to the Socialist Federal Republic of Yugoslavia and was divided between the Republics of Croatia and Slovenia. ▷ **Habsburg Dynasty**

Itagaki Seishiro (1885–1948)

Japanese army officer. Along with **Ishiwara Kanji**, he was a key player in the Japanese military conquest of Manchuria. He became Army Minister in 1937 and then Chief of General Staff of the China Expeditionary Army in 1939. After **World War II** he was tried as a war criminal and executed.

Italian Social Movement (*Movimento Sociale Italiano*)

The post-war Italian neo-fascist movement that stands on the extreme right of Italian parliamentary politics. It is a fringe party which has never received more than 10 per cent of the national vote. However, it remains strong in some regions such as the Alto-Adige, where it is seen as defending the interests of the Italian-speaking population against the privileged German population and their *Südtiroler Volkspartei*. Its most able leader was Giorgio Almirante (1915–88).

Italy

A republic in southern Europe, which fought alongside the Allies in **World War I**. The Fascist movement brought **Mussolini** to power in 1922. His policies led to the conquest of **Abyssinia** (1935–6) and **Albania** (1939), but his alliance with **Hitler** in **World War II** led to the end of the Italian Empire. Political instability has resulted in over 45 governments in power since the formation of the republic. Growing disillusionment with the political parties following a series of corruption scandals in the early 1990s led to voting reforms. In the 1994 elections the right-wing Forza Italia party won the most seats and formed a government by enlisting support from more right-wing parties, causing fears in Europe about a resurgence of the extreme right.

Ito Hirobumi (1838–1909)

Japanese politician. He was Premier (1885–8, 1892–6, 1898 and 1900–1). Ito visited Europe and the USA on several occasions, drafted the **Meiji Constitution** (1889), and played a major role in abolishing Japanese feudalism and building up the modern state. He was assassinated at Harbin by a supporter of Korean independence.

Ivanov, Nikolai Veniaminovich (1952–)

Russian lawyer. He was the junior partner of **Gdlyan** in proving corruption in high places during the last years of Leonid **Brezhnev**'s dictatorial rule. He helped Gdlyan in the 'Uzbek affair' and then in attacking senior Muscovite communists. With Gdlyan, he attracted bothofficial disapproval and popular encouragement.

Ivashko, Vladimir Antonovich (1932–)

Ukrainian politician. He became First Secretary of the Ukrainian Communist Party in 1989 and Deputy General-Secretary of the Soviet Communist Party in 1990, only to see the party as a whole dissolved a year later. He was engineer, lecturer and, more particularly, party official who rose to the top quickly when the hardline and aging **Shcherbitsky** died and Mikhail **Gorbachev** seized the reform opportunity. He certainly outpointed Yegor **Ligachev**, but he was not particularly liberal and in any case did not have long to make an impact on a conservative USSR.

J

Jabotinsky, Vladimir (1880–1940)

Jewish writer and Zionist, born in Odessa. Realizing that **World War I** would spell the end of the **Ottoman Empire**, Jabotinsky and others persuaded the British government to allow Jewish involvement in the fight for Palestine. The result was a Jewish transport unit which fought in the **Gallipoli Campaign** but was disbanded in 1916. However, Jabotinsky was instrumental in convincing the British to sanction the more substantial Jewish Legion which took recruits from Britain, North America and, towards the end of the war, Jews from Palestine. Thereafter, the Legion became the basis for the **Haganah**. Unlike that of others, Jabotinsky's **Zionism** was right-wing and hostile to socialism. This led him to found in 1925 the Zionist Revisionist Movement, later renamed the New Zionist Organization. With growing resistance to Jewish immigration to Palestine under the **British Mandate**, Jabotinsky supported terrorist activities by the **Irgun**.

Jackson, Jesse (1941–)

US **civil rights** leader and minister. As Martin Luther **King**'s lieutenant, he established a strong branch of the **SCLC** in Chicago. In 1967 he initiated Operation Breadbasket, which aimed to create jobs by attracting business investment in black enterprises in the cities. In 1971 he became the executive director of Operation PUSH (People United To Serve Humanity), these two projects helped get him national attention, and in 1983 he became a candidate for the Democratic presidential nomination. His 'Rainbow Coalition' attracted a good deal of media attention, but without an organized political base, he had little chance of success. He was the first black American to mount a serious campaign for the office. He was a candidate again in 1987, but was again unsuccessful in gaining the nomination.

Jagan, Cheddi (1918–)

Guyanese socialist politician and writer. With **Burnham**, he led the nationalist People's Progressive Party (PPP) in demanding self-government in the early 1950s. The Jagan–Burnham alliance won the 1953 election but the Governor, accusing Jagan of 'communist' policies, suspended the constitution, dismissed Jagan and his cabinet and called in British troops. He came to power with the PPP again in 1957, but an austerity budget and Jagan's desire to hasten the end of imperial rule led to racial rioting and a long general strike in Georgetown only ended by further British military intervention (1961–4). In the 1964 election, based on a British-devised proportional representation constitution, Burnham's **People's National Congress** was victorious, and Jagan became the leader of the official opposition. He became President after the 1992 election.

Jakeš, Miloš (1922–)

Czechoslovak politician. Originally an electrical engineer, he joined the Communist Party of Czechoslovakia in 1945 and studied at the Higher Party School in Moscow (1955–8). He supported the Soviet invasion of Czechoslovakia in 1968 and later, as head of the Party's Central Control Commission, oversaw the purge of reformist personnel. He became a member of the Central Committee in 1977 and of the Politburo in 1981, and in Dec 1987 replaced Gustáv **Husák** as Party leader. Although enjoying close personal relations with the Soviet leader, Mikhail **Gorbachev**, he emerged as a cautious reformer who made it clear that restructuring (*prestavba*) in Czechoslovakia would be a slow and limited process. He was forced to step down as CCP leader in Nov 1989, following a series of pro-democracy rallies.

Jamaat-i Islami Party

The party founded in 1941 by Maulana Abu'l Ala Maududi, to voice his opposition to the **Muslim League**'s demands for Pakistan, which he regarded as not properly Islamic and liable to encourage Hindu nationalism. Following the Partition of India in 1947, Maududi moved to Pakistan and the party became a persistent critic of the government. Banned in 1953 for fomenting trouble over the Ahmadiyyas, it later staged a comeback. An Indian succesor party, established in 1948, was banned by the Indian government in 1992 following the Ayodhya disturbances.
▷ **India, Partition of**

Jamaica Labour Party (JLP)

One of the two major political parties which have shared power in Jamaica since independence in 1962. **Bustamante**'s JLP, founded in 1943, grew out of his Industrial Trade Union while its rival, the People's National Party (PNP), was the creation of Norman **Manley** in 1938. The PNP dominated politics from 1957 to 1962, but Bustamante won the election of that year and the JLP retained power until 1972 under Bustamante, Sangster and Shearer. The PNP returned to power in 1972 under Michael **Manley** but Manley's socialist policies, his troubles with the IMF and his inability to stimulate the economy saw the return of the JLP under Edward Seaga in 1980. However, the JLP's reliance on capitalism fared no better in creating economic stability and Manley and the PNP were returned in the 1989 election.

James, C(yril) L(ionel) R(obert) (1901–89)
Trinidadian writer, lecturer, political activist and cricket enthusiast. James's aim was the freedom of the black race through **Marxism** and revolution. For his Trotskyite writings he was deported from the USA, while in Trinidad his former pupil, Eric **Williams**, the Prime Minister, put him under house arrest. His most influential book was *The Black Jacobins: Toussaint L'Ouverture and the San Domingo Revolution* (1938).

Jan Sangh
'The Hindu People's Party' was the Major Hindu Nationalist political party until the rise of the BJP (Bharatiya Janata Party). It was formed in 1951 by Syama Prassad Mookerjee and leaders of the **RSS** (*Rashtriya Swayamsevak Sangh*), a militant Hindu cultural organization, in order to promote and represent Hindu political interests more effectively in government. It was most specifically designed to offer a national alternative to the secularist Congress Party of Jawaharlal **Nehru**, from which Mookerjee himself had resigned in 1947. The Jan Sangh's support came primarily from the merchant and middle classes of the north Indian states. It is considered by its detractors to be a communal anti-Muslim political party with fascistic inclinations. This charge its members have always denied, although it has consistently demanded the maintenance of traditional Hindu institutions, replacement of English by Hindi as the sole official language of India, and has opposed concessions to Muslims. These, it has argued, are legitimate and appropriate policies in a predominantly Hindu society. On economic issues, it supported liberalization. The Jan Sangh merged into the Janata Party which ruled India under the ledadership of Morarji **Desai** in 1977–9, but broke away in the early 1980s to emerge as the BJP, the main opposition party since 1991.
▷ **Hindu Mahasabha**

Janata Dal
A minority Indian political party, led by Prime Minister V P Singh, which governed India with the support of the BJP and CPIM during the period Dec 1989–Oct 1990. A faction of the Janata Dal, the Janata Dal (S), then held power, with Chandra Shekhar as Prime Minister, with the support of the much larger Congress (I) Party.

Japanese Communist Party (JCP; ***Nihon Kyosanto*****)**
Formed in July 1922 as a branch of the **Comintern**, it was to remain a small and illegal organization until 1945. Severe government repression in the late 1920s and in the 1930s resulted in many members being imprisoned. With Japan's defeat in 1945 and the ensuing US occupation, the JCP was legalized and played a leading role in the workers' movement of the late 1940s. In the 1946 elections the party garnered 2.1 million votes, obtaining five seats in the lower house. The suppression of the left-

wing movement that coincided with the outbreak of the **Korean War** in 1950 forced the JCP underground and some of its members resorted to terrorist tactics. After the mid-1950s, under the leadership of Miyamoto Kenji, the JCP adopted a gradualist approach and regained parliamentary ground. In 1980 the party won 29 lower house seats with nearly 10 per cent of the popular vote. Communist-backed candidates were also elected mayors of several cities. The JCP remains one of Japan's largest political parties in terms of active membership and has increasingly adopted a nationalist orientation.

Japanese Socialist Party (JSP; *Nihon Shakaito*)
Japan's largest opposition party. Socialism was introduced to Japan at the end of the 19c and the country's first socialist party was formed in 1901, but was banned by the government two days later. Although several anti-communist 'proletarian' parties did emerge during the 1920s and contested Diet elections, they were all banned in the 1930s, except for the Socialist Masses Party (*Shakai Taishuto*), which supported the aggressive nationalism of the Japanese militarists. The present-day JSP was formed in Nov 1945, winning a plurality of seats in the 1947 elections for the lower house. The party then led a coalition government (1947–8) under **Katayama** Tetsu, the only time the JSP had been in power before economic crisis and internal rivalries led to its downfall. The party has been plagued by a left-right division; in 1951–5 it split over the 1951 Security Treaty with the USA, while in 1959 a right-wing faction bolted to form the Democratic Socialist Party. Despite losing public support in the 1960s and 1970s, the JSP remained the largest opposition party, and championed neutralism and a non-nuclear defence policy. After 1986, under the leadership of **Doi Takako**, the JSP gained additional public support, making important gains in the 1989 and 1990 elections. The party suffered a set-back in 1991 local elections, however, and Doi was replaced by Masashi Ishibashi. The party is now known as the Social Democratic Party of Japan.

Japan
An island state off the east coast of Asia. It annexed Korea in 1910, occupied Manchuria in 1931–2, and entered **World War II** with a surprise attack on the US fleet at **Pearl Harbor**, Hawaii, in 1941. In 1941–2 Japan occupied British and Dutch possessions in South-East Asia, but was pushed back during 1943–5. Atomic bombs were dropped on **Hiroshima** and **Nagasaki** in 1945 which led to the Japanese surrender. Japan was then occupied by Allied troops commanded by General **MacArthur**. The occupation ended in 1952 but Japan and the USA continued to have a close relationship, despite anti-American demonstrations in the 1960s by some militant groups. Economic growth during the 1960s continued, to provide prosperity and trade surpluses into the 1990s.

Jarring, Gunnar (1907–)

Swedish diplomat. He was appointed a special representative to the **UN**, with responsibilities for the Middle East, in late 1965. However, despite many visits to the Middle East in the period 1967–9, he was unable to generate any real enthusiasm amongst either Israelis or Arabs in his attempts to gain acceptance of UN Resolution 242, aimed at a Middle Eastern settlement, with the Israeli return of territories occupied in the wake of the June War of 1967. After the civil war in Jordan in late 1970, he was again involved in trying to broker a peace settlement in the area.

Jarrow March (Oct 1936)

A march to London by unemployed workers in the Durham shipbuilding and mining town, to put the unemployed case. Jarrow was among the towns worst affected by the Depression, and the march took place at a time when the economy was recovering in much of the rest of the country. It alerted the more prosperous South and Midlands to the intractable problems of depressed areas.

Jaruzelski, Wojciech Witold (1923–)

Polish general and President. He took part in the Soviet liberation of Poland from German occupation in 1944–5. Afterwards he rose to become Chief of the General Staff in 1965, Minister of Defence in 1968, a full member of the Politburo in 1971, and First Secretary of the Communist Party and Prime Minister in 1981. In Dec of that year, in order to end the power of the mass free trade union, **Solidarity**; to prevent the break-up of **communism** in Poland and to obviate Soviet intervention; and, at the same time, to promote moderate economic reform, he introduced martial law, which he only partially lifted a year later. His many attempts to find a middle way proved unsuccessful and in 1988 he had to negotiate a reform package with Solidarity. The communists lost power in the consequent elections that year, and Jaruzelski became a token president until Lech **Wałesa** was ready to run for election himself in 1990. Although a sad figure at the end, he did not entirely fail. It was probably largely due to him that the USSR did not invade Poland in 1981 and that the eventual transfer of power was essentially peaceful.

Jaszi, Oszkar (1875–1957)

Hungarian politician and scholar. Before **World War I** he held an appointment at the Ministry of Agriculture, but he was to radical in his views to progress far in administration or in politics. He was close to the Social Democrats in opposing vestiges of feudalism and in supporting minority rights against the prevailing policy of Magyarization; but in 1914 he founded his own Radical Party. After the war he tried to woo the minority peoples, but in the wake of the peace settlement this proved unpopular with the Magyars. In 1919 he left for the USA where he wrote extensively on Central Europe.

Jaurès, (Auguste Marie Joseph) Jean (1859–1914)
French political leader, writer and orator. He lectured on philosophy at Toulouse, then became a moderate republican deputy in 1885. Defeated in 1889, he returned to parliament as a socialist; defeated again in 1898, he campaigned on behalf on **Dreyfus**, and founded the *parti socialiste français* ('French Socialist Party'), which, unlike its rival the *parti socialiste de France* ('Socialist Party of France'), led by Jules **Guesde**, supported Dreyfus and ministerial participation. Jaurès was persuaded to drop the latter policy as the price to pay for unification of the two factions in the United Socialist Party, known officially as the SFIO (*section française de l'Internationale ouvrière*, 'French Section of the Workers' International') in 1905, but he retained much influence in parliament until his assassination in 1914. He helped to found the socialist newspaper *'Humanité* (1904), and wrote in it frequently; the need to avert a war between the Great Powers was a major theme. ▷ **Socialist Party** (France)

Jawara, Alhaji Sir Dawda Kairabi (1924–)
Gambian politician. Educated at a Muslim primary school, Methodist Boys' GS Bathurst and Achimota College (Ghana), he continued his veterinary studies at Glasgow and Edinburgh Universities. He returned to the Gambia as a veterinary officer (1954–60), before entering politics as leader of the People's Progressive Party, becoming Minister of Education (1960–2) and Prime Minister at independence in 1963. On Gambia becoming a republic in 1970 he became President. He was re-elected in 1972, 1977, 1983 and 1987, despite an abortive coup against him in 1981, which was put down by Senegalese troups and paved the way for the creation of the short-lived confederation of **Senegambia**.

Jayatilaka, Sir Baron (1868–1944)
Ceylonese lawyer and government official. Representative of the Ceylon government in India. Educated in Colombo and Oxford, Jayatilaka became an advocate at the Supreme Court of Ceylon in 1913. He was a member of the Legislative Council of Ceylon from 1924 to 1931. He held during his career the posts of the Vice-Chairman of the Board of Ministers, the Leader of the State Council, and the Minister of Home Affairs, Ceylon. Jayatilaka also revised and edited a number of old Sinhalese works.

Jayawardene, J(unius) R(ichard) (1906–)
Sri Lankan politician. After studying law in Colombo, he became a member of the State Council (1943) and the House of Representatives (1947). Honorary Secretary of the Ceylon National Congress (1940–7),

he went on to hold office as Minister of Finance (1947–53), Vice-President of the **UNP** (United National Party) and Deputy Leader of the Opposition (1960–5). As Leader of the Opposition after the 1970 election defeat, he rebuilt the UNP's organization and led it to a landslide victory in 1977, when he became Prime Minister. The following year he became the country's first Executive President under a new constitution and he won a second term of office in 1982. In 1988 he retired and was succeeded by his Prime Minister, Ranasinghe **Premadasa**. His period as head of state was marked by his pro-Western 'open economy' policies and by deteriorating relations between the **Sinhala** and **Tamil** communities, culminating in the 1987 **Indo-Sri Lankan Peace Accord** and the second **JVP** (People's Liberation Front) insurrection of 1987–9.

Jellicoe, John Rushworth, 1st Earl (1859–1935)
British admiral. He became Third Sea Lord (1908), and was Commander-in-Chief, Grand Fleet at the outbreak of **World War I**. His main engagement was the inconclusive Battle of **Jutland** (1916), for which at the time he was much criticized. Promoted First Sea Lord, he organized the defences against German submarines, and was made Admiral of the Fleet (1919). He later became Governor of New Zealand (1920–4). He was created an earl in 1925.

Jenkins, Roy (Harris), Baron (1920–)
British politician. He became a Labour MP in 1948, and was Minister of Aviation (1964–5), Home Secretary (1965–7), Chancellor of the Exchequer (1967–70), Deputy Leader of the **Labour Party** in opposition (1970–2) and again Home Secretary (1974–6). He resigned as an MP in 1976 to take up the presidency of the European Commission (1977–81). Upon his return to Britain, he co-founded the **Social Democratic Party** (1981), and became its first leader, standing down after the 1983 election in favour of David **Owen**. Defeated in the 1987 election, he was given a life peerage and also became Chancellor of Oxford University.
▷ **Liberal Party** (UK)

Jewish Agency
The executive body of the **World Zionist Organization**, established in 1922 as the Jewish Agency for Palestine. The shorter title was adopted in 1929 and, until 1948, the Jewish Agency regulated the **Yishuv**'s relations with world Jewry and the British authorities. The latter recognized its oversight of Jewish affairs in Palestine and its role as negotiator for the Zionist position. Although many of its functions passed to the Israeli government after 1948, the Agency continued to be involved in immigration and agricultural settlement, as well as in education abroad. With headquarters in Jerusalem and New York, the Agency was reconstituted

in 1971 to take account of relations with non-Zionists. ▷ **Balfour Declaration**

Jewish Labour Movement in Palestine
Labour was an issue which preoccupied many Jewish settlers in Palestine in the late 19c and early 20c, including David **Ben-Gurion**. This stemmed from Zionist-socialist critiques of the situation of Russian and European Jewry, who were experiencing both emancipation and anti-Semitism. Their aim was to create a Jewish homeland to whose economy Jews themselves would contribute through a complete range of occupations. Numerous trade unions and political parties resulted in the early 1900s. Most of the unions combined in 1920 to form the **Histadrut**, while **Mapai** became the main socialist party of the **Yishuv** and, after 1948, the State of Israel. ▷ **Aliyah; Zionism**

Jewish National Fund
The fund established (Dec 1901) by the **World Zionist Organization**, with the aim of buying land in Palestine. Although initially based in Vienna, its headquarters were in Jerusalem by 1922. The fund spent most of its first 45 years acquiring land in Palestine for Jewish settlement, so that by 1947 it possessed 234 000 acres. It operated leases of 49 years to its lessees, based on Leviticus 25:10, 23–4. Since Israeli independence in 1948, the Fund has concentrated on land improvement, irrigation and afforestation. Supported by worldwide Jewish contributions, it is headed by a board of directors. ▷ **British Mandate; Jewish Agency**

Jiang Jing'guo (Chiang Ching-kuo) (1910–88)
Taiwanese politician. The son of **Chiang Kai-shek**, he studied in the USSR during the early 1930s, returning to China with a Russian wife in 1937 at the time of the Japanese invasion. After the defeat of Japan in 1945 he held a number of government posts before fleeing with his father and the defeated **Guomindang** forces to Taiwan in 1949. He became Defence Minister (1965–72), and was Prime Minister from 1972 to 1978. He succeeded to the post of Guomindang leader on his father's death (1975) and became state President in 1978. Under his stewardship, Taiwan's post-war 'economic miracle' continued, but in the political sphere there was repression. During the closing years of his life, with his health failing, he instituted a progressive programme of political liberalization and democratization, which was continued by his successor, **Lee Teng-hui**.

Jiang Qing (Chiang Ch'ing) (1914–91)
Chinese politician. She trained in drama and literature, and then became an actress in Shanghai. In 1936 she went to Yenan to study Marxist-Leninist theory, met **Mao Zedong** and became his third wife in 1939. She

was attached to the Ministry of Culture (1950–4), and in the 1960s began her attacks on bourgeois influences in the arts and literature. One of the leaders of the **Cultural Revolution**, she was elected to the Politburo (1969), but after Mao's death (1976) was arrested with three others — the **Gang of Four** — imprisoned, expelled from the Communist Party and tried in 1980. She was sentenced to death, but the sentence was later suspended.

Jiang Zemin (Chiang Tse-min) (1926–)
Chinese politician. The son-in-law of former President **Li Xian'nian**, after university he began a career as an electrical engineer and trained in the USSR. He was Commercial Counsellor at the Chinese Embassy in Moscow (1950–6) and during the 1960s and 1970s held a number of posts in the heavy and power industry ministries. Elected to the Chinese Communist Party (CCP)'s Central Committee in 1982, he was appointed Mayor of Shanghai in 1985. Here he gained a reputation as a cautious reformer, loyal to the party line. He was inducted into the CCP's Politburo in 1987 and in June 1989, following the **Tiananmen Square** massacre and the dismissal of **Zhao Ziyang**, was elected Party Leader. Fluent in English and Russian, Jiang has, as a compromise figure, pledged to maintain China's 'open door' economic strategy.

Jiangxi (Kiangsi) Soviet
The most important rural base area under the control of the Chinese Communist Party (CCP) between 1930 and 1934. It had its origins in **Mao Zedong**'s decision to abandon the cities and create a peasant-based Red Army controlling the countryside. Emphasis henceforth was on 'protracted revolution' in which liberated rural base areas would eventually surround the cities. Mao began (Feb 1930) organizing a rural soviet in the southern province of Jiangxi, which was to become the most important of several such soviets established in this region with control over an estimated 3 million inhabitants. In Nov 1931 the First National Congress of the Chinese Soviet Republic formally established a soviet government under Mao. After 1932, however, when the Moscow-trained urban party leadership came to Jiangxi, Mao lost influence. His flexible attitude towards rich peasants was condemned, while his guerrilla tactics were replaced by a strategy of conventional warfare to confront the series of encirclement campaigns launched against the soviet by **Chiang Kai-shek**'s Nationalist armies. By the end of 1933, the Jiangxi soviet had to be abandoned and the communists embarked on the **Long March** that would take them to the far north-west of China.

jihad
Literally meaning 'striving' in Arabic, the term is often used with the specific sense of struggling against enemies of Islam in 'holy war'. According to the Quran, Muslims have a duty to oppose those who reject Islam,

by armed struggle if necessary, and *jihad* has been invoked to justify both the expansion and defence of Islam.

Jim Crow Laws
A term used to characterize US state laws passed from the 1890s onwards, to segregate blacks from whites in the south in schools, public transport, housing, and other areas. They were gradually abolished from the mid-20c, largely because of the **civil rights** movement, which led to Supreme Court decisions and changes in Federal policies. ▷ **Plessey v Ferguson**

Jinggangshan (Ching-Kang shan)
The mountain stronghold on the border between the central Chinese provinces of Hunan and Jiangxi where **Mao Zedong** took the survivors of his armed force that had participated in one of the abortive **Autumn Harvest Uprisings** in 1927. During the ensuing year, Mao began the task of building a Red Army recruiting from amongst vagrants and bandits, as well as agricultural labourers and poor peasants. Mao also carried out a radical land redistribution policy, although he later adopted a more flexible policy towards rich peasants. He was forced to abandon Jinggangshan in 1928, following repeated Nationalist attacks and moved to south-east Jiangxi where he was to create the first rural soviet.

Jinnah, Muhammad Ali (1876–1948)
Indian Muslim politician and founder of Pakistan. Educated in Bombay and London, he was called to the Bar in 1897, and practised in Bombay. He became a member of the **Indian National Congress** (1906) and the **Muslim League** (1913), and supported Hindu–Muslim unity until 1930, when he resigned from the Congress following disagreement over the demands attached to M K **Gandhi**'s programme of **civil disobedience**. His advocacy of a separate state for Muslims led to the creation of Pakistan in 1947, and he became its first Governor-General. ▷ **Muslim League**

Jodl, Alfred (1890–1946)
German general and Nazi collaborator. An artillery subaltern in **World War I**, he became **Hitler**'s close associate. General of Artillery in 1940, he was the planning genius of the German High Command and Hitler's chief adviser. He was found guilty of war crimes at the **Nuremberg Trials** (1946), and executed. ▷ **World War II**

Joffre, Joseph Jacques Césaire (1852–1931)
French general. He joined the army in 1870, and rose to be French Chief-of-Staff (1914) and Commander-in-Chief (1915), carrying out a policy of attrition against the German invaders of France. He retired as Commander-in-Chief and was made Marshal of France (1916). ▷ **World War I**

John, Patrick (1937–)

Dominican politician. In the period before full independence he served in the government of Chief Minister Edward LeBlanc, and succeeded him in 1974. On independence in 1978 he became the country's first Prime Minister. His increasingly authoritarian style of government led to the loss of his assembly seat in 1980 and his replacement as Prime Minister by Eugenia **Charles**. The following year he was arrested for alleged complicity in a plot to overthrow Charles but was acquitted of the charge. A subsequent trial, in 1985, found him guilty and he was given a 12-year prison sentence.

John Paul II (Karol Jozef Wojtyla) (1920–)

Polish Pope (1978/). The first non-Italian pope in 456 years, he was educated and ordained in Kraków in 1946, received further education in Rome and Lublin, and became Professor of Moral Theology at Lublin and Kraków. Archbishop and Metropolitan of Kraków (1964–78), he was created cardinal in 1967. Noted for his energy and analytical ability, his pontificate has seen many foreign visits, in which he has preached to huge audiences. In 1981 he survived an assassination attempt, when he was shot and wounded in St Peter's Square by a Turkish national, Mehmet Ali Agca, possibly at Bulgarian instigation. A champion of economic justice and an outspoken defender of the Church in communist countries, he has been uncompromising on moral issues. In the 1980s his visits to Poland and his meetings with Mikhail **Gorbachev** were of great assistance to **Solidarity** in promoting Polish independence, achieved in 1989.

Johnson, Lyndon B(aines) ('LBJ') (1908–73)

US politician and 36th President. Educated at Southwest Texas State Teachers College, he was a teacher and congressman's secretary before becoming a Democratic member of the House of Representatives in 1937. He became a Senator in 1949, and later an effective Democratic majority leader (1954). Vice-President under John F **Kennedy** in 1961, he assumed the presidency after Kennedy's assassination, and was elected to the office in 1964 with the biggest majority ever obtained in a presidential election up until that time. His administration (1963–9) passed the Civil Rights Act of 1964 and the **Voting Rights Act** of 1965, and his **Great Society** programme to reduce poverty, eliminate racial discrimination, provide medical care, and improve education. However, the escalation of the **Vietnam War** led to large-scale marches and protests and to his growing unpopularity, and he decided not to seek re-election in 1968. ▷ **Civil Rights Acts; Democratic Party**

Jonathan, Chief (Joseph) Lebua (1914–)

Lesotho chief and politician. Educated in mission schools before working in South African mines and then in local government in Basutoland, he entered politics in 1952. He joined the Basutoland National Council in 1956 and in 1959 founded the Basutoland National Party, which favoured a free enterprise economy and cordial relations with South Africa. He was elected to the Legco in 1960 and became Prime Minister in 1965 but he suspended the Constitution in 1970. Parliamentary government was restored in 1973 and elections held regularly until 1985, when they were cancelled. Chief Jonathan was overthrown in a military coup (Jan 1986).

Jordan

A kingdom in the Middle East, which was part of the Turkish Empire from the 16c until during World War I. Its area was divided into **Palestine** (west of the River Jordan) and Transjordan (east of the River Jordan), both administered by Britain. Transjordan gained independence in 1946 and the British mandate over Palestine ended in 1948, with the newly-created **Israel** fighting to control the **West Bank** area. An armistice in 1949 left Jordan in control of the West Bank. The West and East Banks united within Jordan in 1951, but Israel seized the West Bank during the **Six-Day War** in 1967. Civil war followed attempts by the Jordanian army to expel Palestinian guerrillas from the West Bank in 1970–1. An amnesty was declared in 1973, and Jordanian claims to the West Bank were ceded to the Palestine Liberation Organization in 1974. Legal and administrative links with the West Bank were cut in 1988, prompting the **PLO** to establish a government in exile. A ban on political parties was ended in 1991.

Jordan, Vernon E, Jr (1935–)

US civil rights leader. After earning a law degree from Harvard University (1960), he became a field secretary for the **NAACP**, and in 1970 director of the United Negro College Fund. He was President of the National Urban League (1972–81), and became an influential voice in politics for black concerns.

Joørgensen, Anker (1922–)

Danish politician. He worked his way up through the organizations of the Danish labour movement and has been a member of the Danish parliament (**Folketinget**) since 1964. From 1973 to 1987 he was leader of Denmark's **Social Democratic Party** and was Prime Minister in 1972–3 and again in 1975–82. Since 1982 he has been chairman of the Danish delegation in the Nordic Council.

Jouhaux, Léon (1879–1954)

French trade-union leader. He became General-Secretary of the CGT (*Confédération générale du travail*, 'General Confederation of Labour') in 1909, remaining until 1947. Originally an advocate of revolutionary syndicalism, he soon adopted a more moderate position, supporting the

French government during **World War I**, and rejecting **communism** in 1920. Nevertheless, he supported the reunification of the trade union movement in 1936, which rapidly led to commmunist domination of the CGT under his ineffective presidency. In Dec 1947 this led to his resignation from the CGT, and to his becoming President of the anti-communist trade-union federation (CGT-FO).

Joyce, William ('Lord Haw-Haw') (1906–46)
British traitor. As a child, he lived in Ireland and in 1922 his family emigrated to England. In 1937, he founded the fanatical British National Socialist Party, and fled to Germany before war broke out. Throughout **World War II**, he broadcast from Radio Hamburg propaganda against Britain, gaining his byname from his upper-class drawl. He was captured by the British at Flensburg, and was tried and executed in London.

Juan Carlos I (1938–)
King of Spain (1975/). The son of Don Juan de Borbón y Battenberg, Count of Barcelona, and the grandson of Spain's last ruling monarch, **Alfonso XIII**, he was educated in Switzerland, and from 1948, by agreement between his father and General **Franco**, in Spain. He earned commissions in the army, navy, and air force, and studied at the University of Madrid before marrying (1962) Princess Sophia of Greece. In 1969 Franco named him as his eventual successor, and he was proclaimed King on Franco's death in 1975. Instead of upholding the Franco dictatorship (as had been intended), he decisively presided over Spain's democratization, helping to defeat a military coup (1981) and assuming the role of a constitutional monarch.

Jugnauth, Sir Aneerood (1930–)
Mauritian politician. After qualifying as a barrister in London (1954), he returned to Mauritius and was elected to the Legco in 1963. In 1970 he helped found the socialist Mauritius Militant Movement, but broke from it to form his own Mauritius Socialist Party. He became Prime Minister (June 1982) in a coalition government, altered the name of his party to Mauritius Socialist Movement and retained leadership of the coalition after elections in 1983 and 1984.

Juin, Alphonse Pierre (1888–1967)
French soldier. He passed out top of his class, which included Charles de **Gaulle**, at the Saint-Cyr military academy, fought in **World War I**; as divisional commander in the 1st French Army he was captured by the Germans in 1940, but was later released (June 1941). He became Military Governor of Morocco. After the Allied invasion of Tunisia, he changed sides, helped to defeat von Arnim's Afrika Corps remnants and distinguished himself in the subsequent Italian campaign. He was resident-

general in Morocco (1947–51) and served in senior **NATO** commands. He broke with de Gaulle in 1960 over his Algerian policy, and retired. ▷ **World War II**

Juliana (Louise Emma Marie Wilhelmina) (1909–)
Queen of the Netherlands (1948/80). The daughter of Queen **Wilhelmina** and Prince Hendrik, she was educated at Leiden University and became a lawyer. In 1937 she married Prince **Bernhard Leopold**; they have four daughters. On the German invasion of Holland (1940), Juliana escaped to Britain and later resided in Canada. She returned to Holland in 1945, and became Queen on the abdication of her mother in 1948. In 1980 she herself abdicated in favour of her eldest daughter, **Beatrix**, and once more took the title of Princess.

July Days (16–20 July 1917)
Largely spontaneous anti-government demonstrations in Petrograd in Russia, marking growing popular dissatisfaction with the Provisional Government's record since the beginning of the Revolution. Demonstrators demanded that Russia withdraw from **World War I**, the actual overthrow of the Provisional Government, and the transfer of 'All power to the soviets'. **Lenin** initially opposed the demonstrations, judging the time for a proletarian–socialist revolution to be premature, but he eventually gave half-hearted support. Despite several hundred deaths, nothing was achieved except a slight swing to the Right within the Provisional Government. Lenin was more convinced than ever of the need for a highly-organized revolutionary party and carefully-directed revolution of the kind he had advocated since first establishing the **Bolsheviks**. ▷ **April Theses; February Revolution; October Revolution**

Jumblatt, Kemal (1919–77)
Lebanese politician and hereditary Druze chieftain. He founded the Progressive Socialist Party in 1949, held several Cabinet posts (1961–4) and was Minister of the Interior (1969–70). The Syrian intervention on the side of the Christians in 1976 was a response to the increasing power of his authority in partnership with the Palestinians. He was assassinated in an ambush outside the village of Baaklu in the Chouf Mountains. His son **Walid**, became leader of the Druze after his death.

junta
An administrative council, especially in Italy and Spain. The term is now commonly applied to a military leadership who have taken control of a country, particularly in Latin America.

justicialismo

This was the populist doctrine, lying midway between **capitalism** and **communism**, espoused by the followers of Juan Domingo **Perón** between 1946 and 1970. It was a combination of creole nationalism, support for the *descamisados* ('shirtless masses'), and the massive extension of state power into every aspect of Argentine social and economic life. It also entailed government controls over employment and social security provision. Industrial and trading corporations were designed to maintain the descamisados as passive support to Perón, while destroying opposition groups, whether the Church, British investors or trade unions. After he was ousted in 1955, *justicialismo* became the official doctrine of the Peronists. ▷ **Peronism**

Jutland, Battle of (31 May–1 June 1916)

A sea battle of **World War I** (and the first major challenge to British naval supremacy since the Battle of Trafalgar in 1805), in which Admiral **Jellicoe** led the British Grand Fleet from Scapa Flow and intercepted the German High Seas Fleet of the west coast of Jutland, Denmark. Though the battle itself was inconclusive, German naval chiefs withdrew their fleet to port, and turned to unrestricted submarine warfare as a means of challenging British command of the sea.

JVP (*Janata Vimukti Peramuna*, 'People's Liberation Front')

Left-wing Sri Lankan political group, founded in the late 1960s by Rohan Wijeweera and other left-wing activists from the small group of Sri Lankan Maoists. In 1971 Wijeweera was detained just before the JVP launched an insurrection against the government of Sirimavo **Bandaranaike**. After a brief period of legality in the late 1970s, the party was again proscribed after the 1983 anti-Tamil riots, but re-emerged to lead the opposition to the 1987 **Indo-Sri Lankan Peace Accord**. Between 1987 and 1989 a huge number of people died in the JVP's clash with the government's security forces, which eventually ended with the capture and killing of Wijeweera.

K

Kabaka Yekka

Literally 'the King Alone', this was a neo-traditionalist movement in Buganda organized round allegiance to, and support of, the *Kabaka* (or 'King') of Buganda in the 1960s. It disintegrated when the Kabaka was forced into exile in 1966.

Kadalie, Clements (c.1895–1951)

Nyasaland (Malawian) trade union leader. A migrant, he founded in 1919 the Industrial and Commercial Workers' Union of South Africa, the first large-scale trade union for black people. Kadalie started the union in the Cape, where he led a series of dock strikes. By 1923, it had become a mass movement reaching a peak of membership of 86 000 in 1928. However, it declined rapidly from 1929 onwards and was defunct by 1933, failing because Kadalie led it into political action, split it into moderate and radical factions, expelled the Communists and forced the creation of a separate organization in Natal. It never secured a large membership among the workforce of the Rand gold mines and failed to gain international recognition.

Kádár, János (1912–89)

Hungarian politician. He joined the illegal Communist Party in 1931, and was arrested several times. He became a member of its Central Committee (1942) and of the Politburo (1945). As Minister of the Interior from 1948 to 1951, he organized the trial of László **Rajk**, but he was arrested and imprisoned for his anti-Stalinist views (1951–4). When the anti-Soviet **Hungarian Uprising** broke out in 1956, he was a member of the 'national' government of Imre **Nagy**, but he then formed a puppet government which invited measured Soviet intervention and helped to suppress the uprising. He resigned in 1958, becoming Prime Minister again in 1961. His long reign as Party Secretary ended in 1988, and during that time he did manage to introduce elements of reform into the Hungarian economy. However, by the mid-1980s he had become comparatively conservative, and reform petered out, to the immediate advantage of Hungarian **communism**. ▷ **Stalin, Joseph**

Kadets (1905–18)

The short name for the Russian Constitutional Democratic Party that was established in the Russian **Revolution of 1905** to represent liberal non-Marxist interests. The main plank in their programme was their demand for a constituent assembly completely to reform Russia's political structure. This was unacceptable to **Nicholas II**; and even though they were the largest group in the first **Duma**, their numbers dropped in the succeeding three, which were in any case powerless assemblies. Eventually in 1917 they participated in the **Russian Provisional Government**, with Pavel **Miliukov** as Foreign Minister, but they were already falling behind popular cries for change. When the **Russian Constituent Assembly** was finally elected in Nov, they had a mere 15 out of 703 representatives. When it was disbanded in Jan 1918, they were declared illegal.

Kaganovich, Lazar Moiseyevich (1893–1991)
Soviet politician. He joined the Communist Party in 1911 and, after participating actively in the 1917 **Russian Revolution**, became First Secretary of the Ukrainian Party in 1925. In 1928 he moved to the secretariat of the All-Union Party and in 1930 became a full member of the **Politburo**, as well as serving for five years as First Secretary of the Moscow Party. He played a prominent role in the brutal, forced collectivization programme in the early 1930s, and in the great purges of 1936–8. He also served as Commissar for Railways and was responsible for building the Moscow metro. A close ally of **Stalin**, he survived the latter's death in 1953 but, having fallen foul of Nikita **Khrushchev** and participated in the **Anti-Party Plot**, was dismissed in 1957, being posted to a managerial position in a Siberian cement works. He retired into obscurity in Moscow, to die just as the USSR was about to collapse.

Kagawa Toyohiko (1888–1960)
Japanese social reformer and evangelist. A convert to Christianity, he was educated at the Presbyterian College in Tokyo, and Princeton Theological Seminary in the USA. Returning to Japan, he became an evangelist and social worker in the slums of Kobe. He became a leader in the Japanese labour movement, helping to found the Federation of Labour (1918), Farmers' Union (1921), as well as establish agricultural collectives. In 1928 he founded the Anti-War League and after **World War II** was a leader in the women's suffrage movement, and helped with the process of democratization.

Kalashnikov, Mikhail Timofeevich (1919–)
Soviet military designer. He invented the famous Soviet rifle also used extensively by foreign armies and international terrorists. Born of peasant stock in the Altai area, he joined the army in 1938. Seriously wounded in 1941, he began experimenting with what was to be the AK 7.62 assault rifle taken into Soviet service in 1949. Other versions were produced later.

Kalinin, Mikhail Ivanovich (1875–1946)
Soviet politician. He was the formal head of state after the 1917 Revolution and during the years of **Stalin**'s dictatorship (1919–46). A peasant and metal-worker, he entered politics as a champion of the peasant class, and won great popularity. He became President of the Soviet Central Executive Committee (1919–38), and of the Presidium of the Supreme Soviet (1938–46). A member of the **Politburo** from 1926 onwards, he was an influential figure; but he was sufficiently pliable to survive the purges in the late 1930s and to die a natural death.

Kallay, Miklos (1887–1976)
Hungarian politician. A big landowner, he became lord lieutenant of Szabolcs county. To the right in politics, he was Minister of Agriculture from 1932 to 1935. During **World War II** he served as Prime Minister (Mar 1942–Mar 1944). Initially he cooperated with Germany but after the Battle of **Stalingrad** he tried to make a separate settlement with the Allies, only to be imprisoned in Nov 1944 in Mauxhaussen concentration camp. He subsequently settled in the USA.

Kamenev, Lev Borisovich (1883–1936)
Soviet politician. He was an active revolutionary throughout Russia and abroad from 1901 onwards, associating with **Lenin**, **Trotsky** and **Stalin**, and was exiled to Siberia in 1915. Liberated after the **February Revolution**, he was active as a Bolshevik throughout 1917, became the first Chairman of the Central Executive Committee of the All Russian Congress of Soviets and subsequently held various Party, government and diplomatic appointments. Expelled from the Party as a Trotskyist in 1927, he was readmitted the next year but again expelled in 1932. The same happened in 1933–4. He was finally executed for allegedly conspiring against **Stalin**. Like many others falsely accused, he was rehabilitated in 1988 during the **Gorbachev** years.

kamikaze
A Japanese term (literally, 'divine wind') identifying the volunteer suicide pilots of the Japanese Imperial Navy, who guided their explosive-packed aircraft onto enemy ships in **World War II**. They emerged in the last year of the Pacific War, when Allied forces were closing on the Japanese homeland.

Kang Sheng (1899–1975)
Chinese politician. He studied Soviet security and intelligence techniques in Moscow during the early 1930s. He was a prominent member of the Chinese Communist Party during the 1960s, and exercised considerable behind-the-scenes influence in his capacity as Head of Party Security. During the **Cultural Revolution** he was associated with the radical left

group led by **Mao Zedong**'s wife, **Jiang Qing**. Since Mao's death in 1976, Kang's role in the persecution of party members and intellectuals during the Cultural Revolution has been condemned.

Kapp Putsch (Mar 1920)
An unsuccessful coup by **Freikorps** units against the **SPD**-dominated German government, led by extreme right-wing politicians and a small number of army commanders. Scheduled reductions in the size of Germany's armed forces under the terms of the Treaty of **Versailles** led one of the affected commanders, von Lüttwitz, to order forces loyal to him to seize **Berlin** and force a change in policy. The government fled rather than comply, leading to the creation of a rebel government under Wolfgang Kapp, a civil servant, which lasted three days. He was toppled by a general strike organized by the **ADGB** and by passive resistance from the Civil Service and the national bank. Significant was the failure of the army to oppose the coup, even if it did not actively support it.

Kapwepwe, Simon (1922–89)
Zambian nationalist leader and politician. Educated in mission schools before becoming a teacher, he helped found the Northern Rhodesian African National Congress in 1946. After a period of study in India, he returned to be Treasurer and then helped form the breakaway United National Independence Party (**UNIP**) of which he became Treasurer 1960–7. After holding several ministerial posts in the early days of independence, including the vice-presidency, he resigned from UNIP to form his own party, the United Progress Party, in 1971 in order to oppose Kenneth **Kaunda**. The party was banned in 1972, when Zambia became a one-party state and Kapwepwe was detained. He rejoined UNIP in 1977.

Karageorgević, Paul (1893–1976)
Prince Regent of Yugoslavia (1934/41). The son of Arsen and brother of King **Peter I Karageorgević**, he became regent for King **Peter II** of Yugoslavia after the assassination of the latter's father, **Alexander I**. Although he upheld the constitution of the previous dictatorial regime, his regency marked the beginning of a more relaxed period in the government of Yugoslavia. He worked closely with **Stojadinović** and his right-wing party, the Yugoslav Radical Union (1935–9), and with **Cvetković** and **Maček** played a leading role in bringing about the **Sporazum** (1939). In foreign affairs he developed relations with Germany and Italy so that at the outbreak of **World War II** Yugoslavia, although officially neutral, was in the Axis camp. After signing the Tripartite Pact with **Hitler** and Benito **Mussolini**, the regency was overthrown in a coup led by General Dušan Simović (Mar 1941). He left Yugoslavia for Kenya and later settled in Paris.

Karakhan Manifesto (25 July 1919)

A declaration issued by the Soviet Assistant Foreign Commissar, Leo Karakhan, renouncing all former Tsarist rights and privileges in China. A similar declaration had been issued the year before by the Foreign Commissar, G V Chicherin. Although the Soviet government in 1920 insisted that such a declaration had not implied handing over the **Chinese Eastern Railway** without compensation (it remained, in fact, under Soviet control until 1935, when it was sold to Japan), the Karakhan Manifesto had a profound effect on young Chinese radicals, convincing them that the new Soviet state was the only foreign country willing to treat China as an equal.

Karamanlis, Constantine (1907–)

Greek politician. A lawyer, he was elected to parliament in 1935, became Minister of Public Works (1952), then in 1955 succeeded Alexander **Papagos** as Prime Minister and reconstituted the right-wing Greek Rally as the National Radical Union. Confronting the Cyprus dispute and sensitive to US and **NATO** anxiety over the activities of **EOKA**, in 1959 he signed a treaty with the Greek and Turkish Cypriot communities whereby Cyprus would become an independent republic in the British **Commonwealth of Nations**. After his party's election defeat in 1963, he left politics and lived abroad. He returned to become Prime Minister again in 1974, when he supervised the restoration of civilian rule after the collapse of the Colonels' dictatorship (1967–74) led by Georgios **Papadopoulos**. He served as President from 1980 to 1985, and was re-elected in 1990.

Karami, Rashid (d.1987)

Lebanese politician. The son of Abd al-Hamid Karami, he succeeded to the leadership, albeit disputed, of the Muslims in the Tripoli area of Lebanon while still a young man. In the 1950s Karami established himself, along with Sa'ib Salam, as a politician with pro-**Nasser** sympathies, and became a member of the newly-formed National Front, which constituted a concentration of all Camille **Chamoun**'s opponents. After Chamoun's departure following the disturbances of 1958, and Chehab's assumption of the presidency, Karami formed a predominantly National Front cabinet. A subsequent Christian strike drove home the fact that some Phalange and pro-Christian elements would have to be included and, accordingly, a new and more representative cabinet was formed. During the civil war in the 1970s, Karami was himself called upon to become Prime Minister. He was confronted with the problem of trying to ensure stability while, on the one hand, negotiating with the President to bring an end to the fighting and, on the other hand, having to recognize that, in the environs of Tripoli, Tony Franjiyeh's ultra-Right Zghorta Liberation Army was at daggers drawn with his own supporters. Much later Karami, who must be regarded as amongst those Lebanese politicians who strove to save the country, headed the coalition government formed by President Amin **Gemayel** in 1984. Karami was assassinated in 1987.

Kardelj, Edvard (1910–79)
Yugoslav (Slovene) politician. A schoolteacher, he joined the Communist Party and was among the many imprisoned during the dictatorship of **Alexander I**. He lived in the USSR and joined **Tito** as a partisan during **World War II**, becoming Vice-President of **AVNOJ** and in 1946 Foreign, and Deputy Prime Minister. With **Djilas** he went to Moscow in 1948 to face **Stalin**'s criticism of Yugoslavia's independent foreign policy and stood firm with Tito in demonstrating that Yugoslavia would not become merely a Soviet satellite. He was the prominent theoretician of Tito's post-war regime, drawing up the federal constitution and leading the search for a **Marxism** purified of all Stalinist accretions.

Karl XVI Gustaf (1946–)
King of Sweden (1973/). As his father had died in an air accident in 1947, he became Crown Prince from the time of the accession of his grandfather, King **Gustav VI Adolf**, in 1950. A new constitution, which reduced the king to a purely ceremonial head of state, was approved by the Swedish Parliament just before his accession. In 1976 he married Silvia Sommerlath, the daughter of a West German businessman. They had two daughters, Victoria and Madeleine, and a son, Carl Philip.

Karmal, Babrak (1929–)
Afghan politician. The son of an army officer. Educated at Kabul University, where he studied law and political science, he was imprisoned for anti-government activity during the early 1950s. In 1965 he formed the Khalq ('Masses') Party and, in 1967, the breakaway Parcham ('Banner') Party. These two groups merged in 1977 to form the banned People's Democratic Party of Afghanistan (PDPA), with Karmal as deputy leader. After briefly holding office as President and Prime Minister in 1978, he was forced into exile in Eastern Europe, returning in 1979, after the Soviet military invasion, to become head of state. Karmal's rule was fiercely opposed by the Mujahidin guerrillas and in 1986 he was replaced as president and PDPA leader by Najibullah Ahmadzai.

Karolyi, Mihalyi, Count (1875–1955)
Hungarian politician. In 1901 he classified himself a liberal, but from 1906 an independent. Despite his aristocratic background he struggled for democratic reforms, and during **World War I** he opposed the alliance with Germany. In 1918 he was briefly Prime Minister, and President from Jan to July 1919. His well-known willingness to accommodate the subject nationalities won him the wrath of most of his fellow Magyars

and he was forced into exile. Before and during **World War II** he won an international reputation as a champion of democratic Hungary, and he served as Ambassador in Paris (1947–9). With the triumph of **communism**, he was once more compelled to flee abroad.

Karume, Sheikh Abeid (1905–72)
Zanzibari politician. A sailor, he became active in local politics in the 1940s, was elected a town councillor in 1954 and helped found the Afro-Shirazi Party in 1957. Following the 1964 coup which deposed the Sultan of Zanzibar, he became President of the Revolutionary Council. When Zanzibar united with Tanganyika in 1964 to form Tanzania, he became Vice-President, but his expressed opposition to democratic changes made him enemies and he was assassinated in 1972.

Kasavubu, Joseph (1910–69)
Zairean politician. Educated locally in a seminary, he worked as a teacher and civil servant in the Belgian colonial administration before entering politics. He was Mayor of Leopoldville in 1957 and, supported by the **UN** in his struggle for power against Patrice **Lumumba**, became President of the Republic of the Congo in 1960. In the ensuing civil war he first defeated **Mobutu**'s challenge and recaptured the presidency, but was later deposed by Mobutu, whom he had appointed as Commander-in-Chief.

Kashmir Problem
In 1947, at the time of the partition of India, Kashmir was a largely Muslim-populated state with a Hindu king. In Oct 1947 there was an uprising of Muslims in western Kashmir, supported from across the border in Pakistan. Kashmir appealed to India, which sent troops in exchange for the accession of the kingdom to the Indian Union. After fighting had continued for several months, the **UN** intervened in 1949, establishing along the cease-fire line a provisional demarcation line, which left most of Kashmir with India. India and Pakistan fought a second war over Kashmir in 1965, with a truce being agreed at Tashkent the following year. After the 1971 **Bangladesh War**, both countries accepted, under the terms of the 1972 Simla Agreement, that the Kashmir problem ought to be settled bilaterally. Subsequent years have witnessed further turmoil in Kashmir, with some Kashmiris demanding an independent nation.

Katayama Tetsu
Japanese politician. A Christian socialist, he helped form the Socialist People's Party (*Shakai Minshuto*) in 1926, one of a number of 'proletarian parties' founded during the 1920s. In 1945 Katayama emerged as the leader of the newly-created **Japan Socialist Party**, which achieved a plurality of votes in the first elections held under the 1947 Peace Constitution. He headed a coalition government in 1947–8, the country's first

and, to date, only socialist Prime Minister. Katayama's government created a new Ministry of Labour, enacted the Anti-Monopoly Law, and presided over the dissolution of the *zaibatsu,* the pre-war financial combines. The government became increasingly unpopular, however, when economic crisis forced it to impose price and wage controls. After his resignation in 1948, Katayama became identified with the party's right wing. In 1960 he joined a breakaway group that formed the moderate Democratic Socialist Party, which, unlike the larger Socialist Party, supported the 1951 Security Treaty with the USA.

Kato Takaaki (Komei) (1860–1926)
Japanese politician. He initially worked for the firm of Mitsubishi, marrying the daughter of its founder, Yataro Iwasaki. He studied in England (1883–5) and was to remain an enthusiastic Anglophile throughout his life. As Minister to Britain (1894–1900), he supported the idea of an **Anglo-Japanese Alliance**. Elected to the Diet in 1902 he joined a political party, the *Doshikai* (Constitutional Association of Friends) in 1913, soon becoming its leader. While Foreign Minister (1914–16) Kato attempted to follow a policy free from the interference of the **genro**. He engineered Japan's entrance into **World War I** on the side of the Allies in 1914 as a means of expanding Japan's influence in China. As leader of the moderately progressive **Kenseikai**, which became the largest single party in the 1924 elections, Kato became Prime Minister (1924–6). During his premiership, universal manhood suffrage was enacted (1925), but attempts to reform the upper house (House of Peers) failed. In order to placate conservative critics, Kato's government also enacted the Peace Preservation Law (1925) to restrict left-wing thought. He died in office. ▷ **Peace Preservation Laws**

Katyn Massacre (May 1940)
A massacre of more than 10 000 Polish army officers in the Katyn forest near Smolensk, Belorussia. The officers were shot and buried, and their mass graves were discovered by German occupying forces in 1943. Soviet authorities persistently denied responsibility for the massacre, blaming it on the Germans. In 1989 the Soviet–Polish Historical Commission (set up in 1987 to establish the truth) reported that the crime was most probably committed by the Soviet security service (NKVD). This was later confirmed by the Soviet authorities. ▷ **World War II**

Kaunda, Kenneth (David) (1924–)
Zambian nationalist leader and politician. Educated in mission schools and Munali Secondary School, he became a teacher and welfare officer before entering politics and becoming Secretary-General of the (Northern Rhodesian) African National Congress (**ANC**) in 1953, breaking away from it to form the Zambian African National Congress in 1958. After

a spell in prison as a result of his nationalist activities, he replaced Mainza Chona as leader of the United National Independence Party (**UNIP**) in 1960 and, after UNIP won elections in 1961, he was made Minister of Local Government and Social Welfare (1962–3) in the first black African government and then, on independence in 1964, he became President. A close friend of Julius **Nyerere**, he espoused a version of African socialism called humanism, made UNIP the sole legitimate party and oversaw a steady decline in the country's economic position and political liberalism. Forced by the democratic movement elsewhere in the world and internal pressures, he called an election in 1991 and was defeated.

Kautsky, Karl Johann (1854–1938)
German socialist leader. In 1883 he founded and edited *Die Neue Zeit*. A disciple of Karl Marx, he wrote a study of Marxist economic theory (1887), and of Sir Thomas More and his *Utopia* (1888). He also wrote against Bolshevism in *Die Diktatur des Proleteriats* (1918, trans 1931).
▷ **Marxism**

Kawakami Hajime (1879–1946)
Japanese economist. He played a significant role in popularizing Marxism in Japan after 1918. As Professor of Economics at Kyoto University (1908–28), Kawakami placed most emphasis on the moral aspects of Marxism, and drew the public's attention to the poverty-stricken conditions of Japanese workers and tenant farmers. He was forced to resign his university post in 1928 as part of the government's campaign against left-wing thought. After an unsuccessful attempt to run for the Diet in 1930, he joined the **Japanese Communist Party** (1933). He was arrested shortly afterwards and imprisoned until 1937.

Kawawa, Rashidi Mfaume (1929–)
Tanzanian trade unionist, nationalist leader and politician. From an early age he was involved in labour politics, becoming President of the Tanganyika African Civil Servants' Association. He joined the Tanganyika African Association (1951–6) and was a founder member, and later Secretary-General and President, of the Tanganyika Federation of Labour. From 1957 he was a member of the Tanganyika Legislative Council and, when Julius **Nyerere** resigned as Prime Minister (1962), Kawawa briefly replaced him. He became first Vice-President (1962–4) and was re-elected after the amalgamation of Tanganyika and Zanzibar until 1972, when he was once again appointed Prime Minister. As a result of his overly zealous commitment to the **TANU** Guidelines set forth in the **Arusha Declaration**, he was demoted to Minister of Defence and National Service in 1977, but returned to the office of President in 1980. He lost status in government when **Mwinyi** replaced Nyerere, but he was

re-elected almost unanimously as Secretary-General of **CCM** in the 1987 Congress.

Keating, Paul (1944–)
Australian politician. He began his career as a trade union official, before being elected as a Labour member to the House of Representatives in 1969. In 1975 he was minister for Northern Australia, and in the Labour administration of 1983 he was appointed treasurer. He became Prime Minister in 1991, succeeding Bob **Hawke**. Although widely unpopular at his appointment, his commitment to establishing Australia as a republic and his sensitivity to difficult issues such as Aboriginal land rights, tax increases and immigration won him much support.

Keita, Modibo (1915–77)
Mali politician. Educated at William Ponty School, Dakar, he helped to found the **Rassemblement Democratique Africaine** in 1946 and was elected to the territorial assembly in 1948. He was a deputy in the French Assembly (1956–9) before becoming President of the Mali Federation (1959–60) and President of Mali (1960–8). A radical who looked to **Nkrumah** for leadership, he was overthrown by the military in 1968 and was imprisoned until his death.

Keitel, Wilhelm (1882–1946)
German field marshal and Nazi collaborator. He joined the army in 1901, and became an artillery staff officer in **World War I**. An ardent Nazi and close associate of **Hitler**, he was made Chief of the Supreme Command of the Armed Forces (1938). In 1940 he signed the Compiègne armistice with France, and in 1945 was one of the German signatories of surrender in Berlin. He was convicted of war crimes at the **Nuremberg Trials**, and executed. ▷ **Nazi Party; World War II**

Kekkonen, Urho Kaleva (1900–86)
Finnish politician. After studying law at Helsinki University and fighting against the **Bolsheviks** in 1918, he entered the Finnish parliament as an Agrarian Party deputy, holding ministerial office in 1936–9 and 1944. He was Prime Minister on four occasions in the early 1950s before being elected President (1956), in succession to Juo **Paasikivi**. Although Kekkonen had always been hostile to Stalinist Russia, as President he encouraged a policy of cautious friendship with the USSR. At the same time his strict neutrality ensured that he retained the confidence of his Scandinavian neighbours. He supported Finland's membership of the European Free Trade Association (1961) and in 1975 was host to the 35-nation European Security Conference in Helsinki. Five years later he accepted a Lenin peace prize. His popularity in Finland led to the passage

of special legislation enabling him to remain in office until 1984, but his health gave way and he resigned in 1981. ▷ **Stalinism**

Kellogg–Briand Pact (27 Aug 1928)
A proposal made by French Foreign Minister Aristide **Briand** to US Secretary of State Frank B Kellogg that the two countries should sign a pact renouncing war as an instrument of national policy. At Kellogg's suggestion, a Paris conference in 1928 formally condemned recourse to war, and the pact was subsequently signed by 65 states (the Pact of Paris). However, no provision was made for the punishment of aggressors. ▷ **Paris, Pact of**

Kennan, George Frost (1904–)
US diplomat and historian. After graduating from Princeton in 1925 he joined the US foreign service. During **World War II** he served in diplomatic posts in Berlin, Lisbon and Moscow, and in 1947 was appointed director of policy planning by Secretary of State George C **Marshall**. He advocated the policy of 'containment' of the USSR by political, economic and diplomatic means, which was adopted by Secretaries of State Dean **Acheson**, and John Foster **Dulles**. Kennan subsequently served as US Ambassador in Moscow (1952–3) and Yugoslavia (1961–3). From 1956 to 1974, as Professor of History at the Institute for Advanced Study at Princeton, he revised his strategic views and called for US 'disengagement' from Europe.

Kennedy, Edward Moore (1932–)
US politician. The younger brother of John F **Kennedy** and Robert F **Kennedy**, he was educated at Harvard and the University of Virginia, he was called to the Bar in 1959, and elected a Democratic Senator in 1962. In 1969 he became the youngest ever majority whip in the US Senate, where he has established a notable record on advancing liberal issues. But his involvement the same year in a car accident at Chappaquidick, in which a companion (Mary Jo Kopechne) was drowned, dogged his subsequent political career. In 1979, he was an unsuccessful candidate for the presidency; the nomination went to Jimmy **Carter**, who became President in 1980.

Kennedy, John F(itzgerald) (1917–63)
US politician and 35th President. Educated at Harvard, he joined the US navy in 1941 and became a torpedo boat commander in the Pacific. Elected to the House of Representative as a Democrat in 1947, he became Senator from Massachusetts in 1952 and President in 1960. He was the first Catholic, and the youngest person, to be elected President. His domestic policies called for a 'new frontier' in social legislation, involving a federal desegregation policy in education, and **civil rights** reform.

Although criticized for his handling of the **Bay of Pigs**, he later displayed firmness and moderation in foreign policy. In 1962 he induced the USSR to withdraw its missiles from Cuba, and he achieved a partial nuclear test ban treaty with the Soviets the following year. On 22 Nov 1963, he was assassinated by rifle fire while being driven in an open car through Dallas, Texas. The alleged assassin, Lee Harvey Oswald, was himself shot and killed two days later, during a jail transfer. ▷ **Cuban Missile Crisis; Democratic Party; Kennedy, Robert Francis**

Kennedy, Joseph Patrick (1888–1969)
US businessman and diplomat. The grandson of an Irish Catholic immigrant, he was educated at Harvard. During the 1930s, as a strong supporter of **Roosevelt** and the '**New Deal**', he was rewarded with minor administrative posts, and the ambassadorship to Great Britain (1937–40). He had political ambitions for his sons, and placed his large fortune at their disposal for that purpose. The eldest, Joseph Patrick (1915–44), was killed in a flying accident while on naval service in **World War II**. The others achieved international political fame. ▷ **Kennedy, Edward Moore; Kennedy, John F; Kennedy, Robert Francis**

Kennedy, Robert Francis (1925–68)
US politician. Educated at Harvard and the University of Virginia, he served in the US navy during **World War II**, was admitted to the Bar (1951), and became a member of the staff of the Senate Select Committee on Improper Activities (1957–60). He managed the presidential campaign of his brother, John F **Kennedy**, and as his Attorney-General (1961–4) and closest advisor, actively sought to enforce laws that guaranteed blacks **civil rights**. In 1964 he was elected Senator for New York. On 5 June 1968, he was shot after winning the Californian primary election, and died the following day. His assassin, Sirhan Sirhan, was later convicted of murder.

Kenseikai
The Japanese political party (literally, 'Constitutional Association') formed in 1916 by **Kato** Takaaki, calling for moderate reform and constitutional government. In 1924 the *Kenseikai* became the majority party in the Diet and joined with other parties to bring down a genro-chosen non-party cabinet. Kato then became Prime Minister of a Kenseikai-dominated coalition government (1924–6). This government promoted international cooperation, normalized relations with the USSR, reduced the number of army divisions and enacted universal manhood suffrage. In 1927 the Kenseikai fell from power and shortly thereafter became the *Rikken Minseito* ('Constitutional Democratic Party').

Kenya
A republic in East Africa, which was under British control as the East African Protectorate from 1895. A British colony was established in 1920. An independence movement led to the **Mau Mau** rebellion in 1952–60, and independence was gained in 1963. In 1991 a multiparty system was legalized. In 1992 there was unrest in many areas, leading to the Rift Valley being regarded as a War Zone.

Kenyatta, Jomo (Kamau Ngengi) (1891–1978)
Kenyan nationalist and politician. Educated by Scots missionaries, he joined the Young Kikuyu Association in 1922 and politics thereafter dominated his life. He edited the Kikuyu Central Association's news-sheet, *Mwigwithania*, and played a major role in representing progressive black Kenyan opinion in the 1930s, visiting London on more than one occasion to lobby government. He visited the USSR several times and got to know most of the anti-colonial lobby in the UK, where he worked throughout **World War II**. He attended the famous Fifth Pan-Africanist Conference at Manchester (1945) and, on his return, to Kenya in 1946, he was elected President of the Kenyan African Union, becoming the country's major spokesman for the anticolonial movement. On the outbreak of the **Mau Mau** uprising and the subsequent emergency, he was tried, found guilty on what later proved to be perjured evidence and was detained until 1961. Chosen in absentia to be President of the Kenyan African National Union in 1960, he was elected in 1962 to the Legco and then, after the independence elections, became Prime Minister in 1963 and President when Kenya became a republic in 1964. A remarkable mixture of Kikuyu nationalist, pragmatic politician and father-figure (he was known as *Mzee* or 'old man'), he surprised observers by leading Kenya into a period of economic growth and unexpected tribal harmony.

Kerekou, Mathieu Ahmed (1933–)
Benin soldier and politician. The son of a soldier, he joined the colonial army, being trained in France whose army he served. He joined the Dahomey army at independence in 1961, rising to command it in 1966. He took part in the 1967 coup which overthrew President Soglo but returned to the army, while remaining Vice-President of the Military Revolutionary Council (CNR). In 1972 he led a further coup, establishing a National Council of Revolution and espousing 'scientific socialism'. He renamed Dahomey Benin and began to return the country to democracy, being first elected to the presidency in 1980 and re-elected in 1984 and 1989. He dissolved the CNR and finally resigned from the army in 1987 as a gesture of his commitment to democracy.

Kerensky, Alexander Fyodorovich (1881–1970)
Russian socialist. He studied law in St Petersburg and made a name for himself as counsel for the defence in Tsarist times in several leading

political trials. He was a critical but reasonable member of the Third and Fourth Dumas. In the 1917 **Russian Revolution** he became Minister of Justice in Mar, Minister of War in May, and Prime Minister in July in the Provisional Government. Though crushing **Kornilov**'s military revolt in Aug, he found it increasingly difficult to put through moderate reforms in a deteriorating political situation, and in Oct was swept away by the **Bolsheviks**, and fled to France. In 1940 he went to Australia and in 1946 to the USA, writing several books on the Revolution. He died in New York City. He was a talented, well-meaning politician, possibly too superficial and flamboyant to deal with a turbulent society and dedicated revolutionaries. ▷ **Mensheviks; October Revolution**

Kesselring, Albert (1885–1960)

German air commander and field marshal in **World War II**. He led the **Luftwaffe** attacks on France and (unsuccessfully) on Britain. In 1943 he was made Commander-in-Chief in Italy, and in 1945 in the West. Condemned to death as a war criminal in 1947, he had his sentence commuted to life imprisonment, but was released in 1952. ▷ **Nazi Party**

KGB (*Komitet Gosudarstvennoy Bezopasnosti*, 'Committee for State Security')

From 1953 to 1991 one of the Soviet Union's two secret police organizations with joint responsibility for internal and external order and security and espionage. Its tasks included the surveillance of key members of the Communist Party, the administration, and the military; the monitoring and regulation of dissidents and the population at large; and espionage and subversion abroad.

Khalid, ibn Abdul Aziz (1913–82)

King of Saudi Arabia (1975/82). The fourth son of the founder of the Saudi Dynasty, he ascended the throne after the assassination of his brother, Faisal. His caution and moderation served as a stabilizing factor in the Middle East: Khalid's personal influence was seen in the halting of the Lebanese Civil War (1975–6), and in his country's disagreement with the other members of OPEC over oil price increases. He died at Ta'if, Saudi Arabia.

Khama, Sir Seretse (1921–80)

Botswana Chief and politician. Educated Fort Hare College and London, where he trained as a lawyer. The heir to the chieftainship of the Ngwato, he only inherited the title in 1963. He was banned by the colonial authorities from returning to Bechuanaland because of his marriage to a white woman. When he was permitted to return as a private citizen in 1956, he founded the Bechuanaland Democratic Party, won a seat to Legco in 1965 and became President of the Republic of Botswana from its independence in 1966 to his death in 1980. Plagued by health problems, he nevertheless managed to steer Botswana with great skill along a democratic path in the shadow of South Africa.

Khilafat Movement

A protest campaign by Indian Muslims (1919–24) against British policy towards the Sultan of Turkey, who was also Caliph of Islam. It joined forces with the **Non-Cooperation Movement** for Indian independence. However, it was weakened by the Turks' own deposition of the Sultan (1923) and the abolition of the Caliphate (1924).

Khmer Rouge

A Cambodian communist guerrilla force which opposed the right-wing government that deposed Prince **Sihanouk** in 1970 and the subsequent US invasion of eastern Cambodia. After gaining control of the country in 1975, its government, led by **Pol Pot**, set about a drastic transformation of 'Democratic Kampuchea', involving the mass forced evacuation from the towns to the countryside, the creation of agricultural cooperatives, and the execution of thousands of 'bourgeois elements'. In late 1978, Vietnam invaded Cambodia, and the Khmer Rouge were ousted, retiring to the Thai-Cambodian border region. Following the Vietnamese withdrawal from Cambodia in 1989, they mounted a major offensive, especially in the western and southern provinces. In 1991 they agreed to a ceasefire and signed a peace agreement with the other factions in Cambodia. However, they refused to accept the authority of the UN peacekeeping force UNTAC, and fighting continued throughout 1992. Following their exclusion from the government which was formed after the general election (May 1993), the Khmer Rouge continued their guerrilla attacks (especially against the Vietnamese population in Cambodia), and in Aug 1993 government forces launched a major military offensive against them. Pol Pot is still regarded as the overall leader; other senior personnel include the deputy leader Ieng Sary (1930–), guerrilla commander Son Sen (1930–), and the leader of Khmer Rouge delegations at international conferences seeking a settlement of Cambodia's political future, Khieu Samphan (1931–).

Khomeini, Ayatollah Ruhollah (1900–89)

Iranian religious and political leader. A Shiite Muslim who was bitterly opposed to the pro-Western regime of Shah Mohammad Reza Pahlavi, he was exiled to Turkey and Iraq in 1964, and from Iraq to France in 1978. He returned to Iran amid great popular acclaim in 1979 after the collapse of the Shah's government and became virtual head of state. Under his leadership, Iran underwent a turbulent 'Islamic Revolution' in which a return was made to the strict observance of Muslim principles and traditions. In 1979, a new Islamic constitution was sanctioned, into which was incorporated his leadership concept of the *Vilayet-i faqih*

(Trusteeship of the Jurisconsult). This supreme religious and political position was recognized as belonging to Khomeini, as was the title *Rabhar* (Leader). In 1989 he provoked international controversy by publicly commanding, through the issue of a fatwa, the killing of Salman **Rushdie**, author of the novel *The Satanic Verses*.

Khrushchev, Nikita Sergeevich (1894–1971)
Soviet politician. Coming from a poor background and with little education but a sharp intellect, he joined the Communist Party in 1918, fought in the **Russian Civil War** and rose rapidly in the Party organization through working with **Kaganovich** and **Stalin**. In 1939 he was made a full member of the **Politburo** and of the Presidium of the Supreme Soviet. During **World War II** he served as a senior political officer on the Ukrainian front. In 1953, on the death of Stalin, he became First Secretary of the **Communist Party of the Soviet Union**, though his position was not secure until 1955. In 1956, at the 20th Party Congress, he denounced **Stalinism** and the 'personality cult' in a well-known secret speech that fundamentally altered the course of Soviet history. Among the events of his administration were the 1956 Poznan Riots that he quietened down, and the **Hungarian Uprising** that he crushed, and the failed attempt to install missiles in Cuba (1962). The latter and his inability fundamentally to improve the Soviet economy led to his being deposed in 1964 and replaced by Leonid **Brezhnev** and Alexei **Kosygin**. He died in retirement in Moscow. ▷ **Cuban Missile Crisis**

Kiesinger, Kurt Georg (1904–)
West German politician. Educated at Berlin and Tübingen, he then practised as a lawyer (1935–40), and served during **World War II** at the Foreign Office on radio propaganda. Interned after the war until 1947, he was exonerated of Nazi crimes. In 1949 he became a member of the **Bundestag**, and succeeded **Erhard** as Chancellor (1966). A Christian Democrat and long a convinced supporter of **Adenauer**'s plans for European unity, he formed with Willy **Brandt** a government combining the Christian Democratic Union (**CDU**) and the Social Democrats (**SPD**). He was Chancellor from 1966 to 1969, when, following election defeat, he was succeeded by Brandt.

Kikuyu Central Association (KCA)
A society founded in Kenya in 1922 under the leadership of Harry Thuku. Jomo **Kenyatta**, the future nationalist leader and President of Kenya, became Secretary-General of the KCA, which became the basis of African politics in the British colony. It took up African grievances such as the European occupation of Kikuyu lands in the 'White Highlands' and the missionary campaign to abolish female circumcision. It established the Kikuyu leadership of nationalism in Kenya, but was banned

during **World War II**. The Kenya African Union emerged as its successor in 1944.

Kim Chong-il (1942–)
North Korean politician. The eldest son and chosen heir of the North Korean communist leader **Kim Il-sung**, he was born in the USSR where his mother had retreated from the Korean anti-Japanese guerrilla base in Manchuria. Kim Chong-il has played a leading part in ideological and propaganda work, helping to create the cult that surrounds his father. In 1980 he became First Secretary of the Party's Central Committee. Since 1982, frequently referred to as the 'dear leader', he has been virtual heir-apparent.

Kim Dae Jung (1924–)
South Korean politician. A Roman Catholic, he was imprisoned by communist troops during the **Korean War**. He challenged General **Park** for the presidency in 1971 and was later imprisoned (1976–8 and 1980–2) for alleged 'anti-government activities'. He lived in exile in the USA (1982–5) and on his return successfully spearheaded an opposition campaign for democratization. Although popular among blue-collar workers and fellow Chollans, Kim is distrusted by the business and military elite and in the 1987 presidential election was defeated by the government nominee, **Roh Tae Woo**.

Kim Il Sung (Kim Song-ju) (1912-)
North Korean soldier and politician. He founded the Korean People's Revolutionary Army in 1932, and led a long struggle against the Japanese. He proclaimed the Republic in 1948, and has been effective head of state ever since. He was re-elected President in 1982, having named his son, **Kim Chong-il**, as his eventual political successor.

Kim Yong-sam (1927–)
South Korean politician. After election to the National Assembly in 1954, he was a founder member of the opposition New Democratic Party (NDP), becoming its President in 1974. His opposition to the **Park** regime resulted in his being banned from all political activity. In 1983 he staged a 23-day pro-democracy hunger strike and in 1985 his political ban was formally lifted. In that year he helped form the New Korea Democratic Party (NKDP) and in 1987 the centrist Reunification Democratic Party (RDP). In his 1987 bid for the presidency he came second, behind the governing party's candidate, **Roh Tae Woo**. In 1990 he merged the RDP with the ruling party to form the new Democratic Liberal Party (DLP).

Kimberley, Siege of (1899–1900)

One of the three sieges of the second Boer War, in which Boer forces attempted to pen up their British opponents and secure control of vital lines of communication. The siege lasted from the middle of Oct 1899 until Feb 1900, when the town was relieved by General **French**. ▷ **Boer Wars**

King, Martin Luther (1929–68)

US civil rights leader. The son of a Baptist minister, he studied at Morehouse College and Boston University, set up his first ministry in Montgomery, Alabama. In 1957 he helped found the **SCLC** (Southern Christian Leadership Conference) as a base for coordinating efforts in the struggle for racial equality. Embracing M K **Gandhi**'s message of achieving change through non-violent resistance, he mobilized the black community to challenge segregation laws in the South through non-violent marches and demonstrations, boycotts and freedom rides, and broadened support for the 1964 Civil Rights Act. His voter registration drive in Alabama, culminating in the Selma march, led to the passage of the Voting Rights Act in 1965. In 1968, he was assassinated in Memphis, Tennessee, by James Earl Ray. ▷ **civil rights movement**

King, William Lyon Mackenzie (1874–1950)

Canadian politician. He studied law at Toronto, and became an MP (1908), Minister of Labour (1909–11), **Liberal Party** leader (1919), and Prime Minister (1921–6, 1926–30 and 1935–48). His great ability to find common ground among differing political views made a major contribution to the Liberal domination of national politics for a whole generation, and his view that the dominions should be autonomous communities within the **British Empire** resulted in the Statute of **Westminster** (1931). He resigned from office in 1948. ▷ **Compulsory Service Act; Rowell–Sirois Commission**

King–Crane Commission

The commission, composed of two US members, Henry King and Charles Crane, which carried out its work in June, July and Aug 1919. Its remit — to ascertain local reactions to the proposed Middle Eastern mandatory arrangements — resulted in their reporting opposition to separation from Palestine and to the proposal for a French mandate in Syria. The commission also found that the Zionist programme for Palestine could not, at least in its extreme form, be reconciled with the **Balfour Declaration** in which the rights of the non-Jewish population of Palestine were enshrined. The Commission's report was published in 1922 and its findings were all but disregarded.

King David Hotel, Bombing of the (22 July 1946)
The attack by the **Irgun** on a wing of the King David Hotel in Jerusalem, the headquarters of British rule in Palestine. It took place as part of a wider campaign by the Irgun and others in response to opposition from the British Labour government to Jewish immigration into Palestine. ▷ **British Mandate; Jewish Agency; Zionism**

Kinnock, Neil (Gordon) (1942–)
British politician. He became a Labour MP in 1970, joined the **Labour Party**'s National Executive Committee (1978), and was chief opposition spokesman on education (1979–83). He was elected Party Leader in 1983, following Michael **Foot**. During the 1980s he reorganized the party and led successsful attacks on its left-wing influence and on **Militant Tendency**. He resigned the Labour Party leadership in 1992, following his defeat by John **Major** in the general election of Apr 1992.

Kirk, Norman Eric (1923–74)
New Zealand politician. While working as an engine-driver, he joined the Labour Party and became involved in local, then national politics, becoming President of the party in 1964. He entered parliament in 1957, was Leader of the Opposition (1965–72) and became Prime Minister in 1972, at a time when his country's economy was in difficulties. Forced by Britain's entry into the **EEC** and the USA's disengagement in Asia, he sought a more independent regional role for New Zealand, opposed French nuclear testing in the Pacific and sent ships into the test area. He died in office.

Kirov, Sergey Mironovich (1886–1934)
Russian revolutionary and politician. In and out of prison from 1905 onwards, he played an active part in the **October Revolution** and **Russian Civil War**, and during the 1920s held a number of leading provincial Party posts. He had been elected a full member of the Central Committee by 1923, and in 1934 he became a full member of the **Politburo** at the 17th Party Congress and was elected as a secretary of the Central Committee. Later that year he was assassinated at his Leningrad headquarters, possibly at the instigation of **Stalin**, who then used his death as the pretext for a widespread campaign of reprisals. ▷ **Bolsheviks; Bukharin, Nikolai Ivanovich; communism; Trotsky, Leon**

Kisan Sabhas
'Peasant associations' in India. The first All-India Kisan Congress of Apr 1936 brought together regional groups which had developed during the **civil disobedience** movement of 1930–4. After the second congress (Dec 1936), relations between the Congress and the Kisan Sabha movement were strained; after the Sabha's demands for radical agrarian reform

became very insistent, Congress forbade (1938) its members from joining any Sabhas. During **World War II**, the Sabha came increasingly under communist control and went underground soon after independence. It reemerged as part of the Communist Party of India in 1952, but its strength varied regionally.

Kishi Nobusuke (1896–1991)

Japanese politician. The brother of Eisaku **Sato**, he took the name of Kishi when he was adopted into his uncle's family. He entered the Ministry of Agriculture and Commerce (1920) and during the interwar years was identified as one of the 'new bureaucrats' (*shinkanryo*), who championed more extensive economic planning. While he served in the Japanese puppet-state of **Manzhuguo** (1936–9), Kishi worked closely with the military in developing heavy industry. On returning to Japan, he became a vice-minister of Commerce and Industry, helping to place the economy on a war footing. He then served in the wartime cabinet of Hideki **Tojo**. After the war, he was imprisoned by the US occupation authorities but was released in 1948. Kishi was one of the architects, in 1955, of the Liberal Democratic Party (LDP), formed when the two major conservative parties merged. A controversial Prime Minister (1957–60), he ensured ratification of the renewed Security Treaty with the USA (1960) in the face of an opposition boycott in the Diet and massive public demonstrations. He resigned shortly afterwards, but remained influential within the LDP.

Kissinger, Henry Alfred (1923–)

US political scientist and politician. His family emigrated from Germany to the USA in 1938, to escape the Nazi persecution of Jews. He was educated at Harvard, served in **World War II**, and subsequently joined the Harvard faculty. He became President Richard **Nixon**'s adviser on national security affairs in 1969, was the main US figure in the negotiations to end the **Vietnam War**, and became Secretary of State in 1973, serving under Nixon and **Ford**. His 'shuttle diplomacy' during the Arab–Israeli War of 1973 helped bring about a cease-fire, and resulted in a notable improvement in Israeli–Egyptian relations. He left public office in 1977.

Kita Ikki (1883–1937)

Japanese national socialist. A promoter of a Japanese-led Pan-Asianism, in 1919 he wrote *An Outline Plan for the Reorganization of Japan* in which he argued that a radical reordering of Japanese society was required in order for Japan to take her rightful place as leader of Asia. He called for a military coup that would sweep away the constitution and civilian political establishment and establish direct rule under the Emperor. Kita also advocated nationalization of industry, confiscation of all excess wealth and land reform. His ideas influenced the radical army officers of the **Imperial Way Faction**. When they staged an abortive coup in 1936, Kita was arrested as an accomplice and executed.

Kitchener (of Khartoum and of Broome), (Horatio) Herbert, 1st Earl (1850–1916)
British field marshal and statesman. He joined the Royal Engineers in 1871, and served in Palestine (1874), Cyprus (1878), and the Sudan (1883). By the final rout of the Khalifa at Omdurman (1898), he won back the Sudan for Egypt, and was made a peer. Successively Chief-of-Staff and Commander-in-Chief in South Africa (1900–2), he brought the Boer War to an end, and was made viscount. He then became Commander-in-Chief in India (1902–9), Consul-General in Egypt (1911), and Secretary for War (1914), for which he organized manpower on a vast scale ('Kitchener armies'). He was lost with HMS *Hampshire*, mined off the Orkney Islands. ▷ **Boer Wars; World War I**

KKE (*Kommunistikon Komma Ellados*, 'Communist Party of Greece')
Founded in 1918 as the Socialist Workers' Party of Greece by Greek socialists, the character of the KKE changed after 1924 as Moscow-trained communists started to 'bolshevize' and take control of the party. The most 'westernized' of Greek political parties, at least a quarter of its support came from the urban middle classes as well as industrial workers and peasants, but particularly among refugees from Anatolia after the **Graeco-Turkish War**. In the 1926 election, the KKE gained 10 seats in parliament, although total party membership did not exceed 2000. In 1936, the KKE's plans for a general strike on 5 Aug were foiled when the **Metaxas** regime arrested all leading members on the preceding day — a black day, still not forgotten, in the history of Greek communism. Until 1939 the KKE was incapable of action, with its members in prison or having been released after signing 'declarations' denouncing the party. The government infiltrated and manipulated the party so that, in 1940, there were no less than three central committees. During **World War II** the KKE was the dominant force behind the **EAM** (National Liberation Front); it tried to seize power during the German occupation, and again in Dec 1944 after the German withdrawal and during the **Greek Civil War**.

Klaras, Athanasios ▷ **Veloukhiotis, Aris**

Kleist, Ewald von (1881–1954)
German military commander. He joined the army in 1900 and served as a cavalry officer during **World War I**. During **World War II** he commanded an armoured group in the French campaign (1940) and from 1942 to Mar 1944 commanded an army group on the Russian front.

Promoted field marshal in 1943, he was later dismissed by **Hitler** and was subsequently taken prisoner by the Allies. He died in captivity in the USSR.

Kobayashi Takaji (1903–33)
Japanese revolutionary. A literary activist and prominent leader of the proletarian literature movement in the late 1920s, he participated in strikes while his short stories and novellas (all censored or banned outright until after 1945) championed the heroic struggle of the working class against oppression and exploitation. Forced to go underground after 1929, Kobayashi was eventually arrested, tortured, and executed in 1933.

Kohl, Helmut (1930–)
German politician. Educated in Frankfurt and Heidelberg, he became a lawyer, and joined the **Christian Democrats**. In 1976 he moved to Bonn as a member of the Federal Parliament, became leader of the opposition, and his party's candidate for the chancellorship. After the collapse of the **Schmidt** coalition in 1982, Kohl was installed as interim Chancellor (1982–), and in the elections of 1983 he formed a government which has since adopted a central course between political extremes. Following the **Revolution of 1989** in East **Germany**, Kohl played a decisive part in ensuring the integration of the former communist state within the Federal Republic of Germany.

Koht, Halvdan (1873–1965)
Norwegian politician and historian. He was a professor of history at Oslo University from 1910 to 1935, when he became Foreign Minister under the Labour government (1935–40). A prolific writer on Norwegian history and literature, he was also a highly controversial figure in Norwegian political life. Koht was strongly criticized for his failure to anticipate the German invasion of Norway (Apr 1940) and was replaced as Foreign Minister in the government-in-exile by Trygve **Lie**. ▷ **Norway, German Invasion of**

Koivisto, Mauno (1925–)
Finnish politician. A Social Democrat, he served as Minister of Finance in 1966–7 and Prime Minister in 1968–70 and 1979–81. As Governor of the Bank of Finland after 1968 (retaining office while serving as Prime Minister, with another politician serving as acting governor), he presided over a period of tight monetary policy which helped to consolidate the country's economic growth. President from 1982, he had a more relaxed political style than his predecessor, Urho **Kekkonen**, although he maintained the latter's policy of close cooperation with the USSR until its demise in 1991.

Kokovstov, Vladimir N (1853–1943)
Russian politician. He had two spells as Finance Minister before becoming Prime Minister following **Stolypin**'s assassination in 1911. He was good at reducing budget expenditure and resisting right-wing corruption, at raising French loans and giving sound advice to **Nicholas II**. However, he exercised little power and was replaced in 1914 by someone more conservative and compliant.

Kokutai
A Japanese term, meaning 'national essence', used to denote the country's unique polity, in particular the role of an unbroken imperial line descended from the gods. From the 1890s onwards, the idea of Japan as a family-state in which the close relationship between the Emperor and his subjects was likened to that of a father and his children increasingly took hold. During the 1920s and 1930s, protection of the *kokutai* was used as justification for the suppression of dissident thought. With the dismantling of the Emperor-centred state after **World War II**, the term was no longer used and it has little meaning in today's Japan.

Kolchak, Alexander Vasilievich (1874–1920)
Russian naval commander. In **World War I** he was in command of the Black Sea fleet. After the **Russian Revolution** of 1917, he went to Omsk as War Minister in an anti-Bolshevik government. He cleared Siberia in co-operation with **Denikin** and other leaders of the White Army, styling himself latterly 'supreme ruler of Russia'. In 1919 Omsk fell to the **Bolsheviks**; Kolchak was betrayed, and shot.

Kollontai, Alexandra Mikhailovna (1872–1952)
Russian feminist and revolutionary. The world's first female ambassador, she was born in St Petersburg into an upper-class family, but rejected her privileged upbringing and became interested in socialism. Married to an army officer, she nevertheless joined the Russian Social Democratic Party and, for her revolutionary behaviour and the radical views she expressed at the First All-Russian Congress of Women, was exiled to Germany in 1908. In 1915 she travelled widely in the USA, begging the nation not to join **World War I**, and urging the acceptance of socialism. In 1917, following the **Russian Revolution**, she returned to Russia, becoming Commissar for Social Welfare. In this post she agitated for reforms, including collective childcare and easier divorce proceedings. Partly because her private liaisons and aggressive feminist advocacy shocked the Party, she was appointed Minister to Norway, Mexico and Sweden, becoming ambassador in 1943. She played a vital part in negotiating the termination of the **Continuation War** (1944).

Komeito

The 'Clean Government' Party of Japan, which achieved the power of veto over the traditional ruling Social Democratic Party by winning 20 seats in the Upper House in the 1989 elections, following revelations about government corruption. *Komeito* is an offshoot of *Soka Gakkai*, a born-again Buddhist cult founded in 1930 but based on the teachings of a 13c holy man. In **World War II**, Soka Gakkai's leader was jailed by Japan's thought police and starved to death. The organization was unbanned in 1964 and formed Komeito as its political wing, but six years later the party broke its secular links to broaden its appeal.

Komorowski, Tadeusz Bór (1895–1966)

Polish soldier. As 'General Bór' he led the heroic but unsuccessful Warsaw rising against the occupying Germans in 1944, and settled in England after **World War II**.

Komsomol

The All-Union Leninist Communist League of Youth, founded in 1918, incorporating the majority of persons between the ages of 14 and 28. Its purpose being the socialization of youth in the thought and ways of the **Communist Party of the Soviet Union**, it served as a recruiting ground for Party membership until 1991.

Koniev, Ivan Stepanovich (1897–1973)

Soviet military commander. Born into a peasant family, he was drafted into the Tsarist army in 1916, and joined the **Red Army** and the Communist Party in 1918. For some time he was a political commissar, but after graduating from the Frunze Military Academy in 1934 he held various commands, including in the Far East, before the USSR was drawn into **World War II**. In the years 1941–5 he served with great distinction on several sections of the Western front. Made Marshal of the USSR in 1944, he was Commander-in-Chief, Ground Forces in 1946–50, First Deputy Minister of Defence, and, in 1956–60, Commander-in-Chief of the **Warsaw Pact** forces, which he built into an effective fighting force. ▷ **Russian Civil War**

Konoe Fumimaro (1891–1945)

Japanese politician. From an aristocratic family, he inherited the title of prince from his father. Konoe was a prominent member of the Upper House (House of Peers), before becoming Prime Minister for the first time in 1937. He favoured the growth of Japanese influence in Asia, criticizing what he felt was an Anglo-American attempt to preserve the status quo. During his first term as Premier (1937–9) he led Japan into full-scale war with China in an attempt to create a New Order in East Asia. During his second term (1940–1), Japan's relations with the USA worsened, especially after his government signed a military alliance with the Axis powers (Tripartite Pact) in Sep 1940. He resigned when his offer of a summit meeting with President **Roosevelt** was rebuffed. Although Konoe was a member of the first post-war government (1945), he was indicted as a war criminal by the US occupation authorities. He committed suicide on the day he was to turn himself in for confinement and trial.

Korean War (1950–3)
A war between communist and non-communist forces in Korea, which had been partitioned along the 38th parallel in 1945 with Soviet forces occupying the north and US forces the south. Two governments were established in 1948. The communist North invaded the South in 1950 after a series of border clashes, and the **UN** asked member states to intervene. Troops from 15 nations, commanded by General **MacArthur**, drove the invaders back to the Chinese frontier. China then entered the war and, together with the North Koreans, occupied Seoul. The UN forces counter-attacked, and recaptured all territory south of the 38th parallel. MacArthur wished to advance further, and was removed from command. An armistice was signed in 1953.

Kornilov, Lavr Georgevich (1870–1918)
Russian general. With previous intelligence and diplomatic experience, he was a divisional commander in **World War I**, tried to turn the tide against the Germans by an offensive in June 1917 and, in Aug 1917, marched on St Petersburg, in an attempt to set up a military directorate. He was forced to surrender by **Kerensky**, but subsequently escaped. Kornilov then organized a Cossack force against the **Bolsheviks**, but fell in battle. ▷ **Kornilov Affair**

Kornilov Affair (1917)
A military attempt to prevent the **Bolsheviks** coming to power. The failure of the **Brusilov Offensive** in July 1917 greatly weakened the **Russian Provisional Government**. **Kerensky** appointed the adventurous General **Kornilov** as Commander-in-Chief, but he apparently succumbed to right-wing influence and in Aug attempted a military coup by sending cavalry to Petrograd. He failed and simply increased support for the Bolsheviks.

Korošec, Anton (1872–1940)
Slovene politician. He studied theology at Maribor and was ordained priest, taking a leading role in the Slovene People's Party before **World War I**. An advocate of **trialism**, he became President of the coalition of **South Slav** members in the Austrian parliament (1917) and President of the National Council of Slovenes, Croats and Serbs in Zagreb (Oct 1918). After the creation of the Kingdom of Serbs, Croats and Slovenes (later

Yugoslavia), he served as Vice-Premier (1919). Conservative and opportunistic, he continued to represent the interests of the Slovenes and was the only non-Serb inter-war Prime Minister and Minister of the Interior (July 1928–Jan 1929). During the dictatorship of **Alexander I**, he was interned on the island of Hvar (1933) but was released during the regency to serve again as Minister of the Interior (1935–8).

Kosice Programme (Apr 1945)

The political programme on which post-1945 Czechoslovakia was based. It consisted of a compromise between 'Westernizers' and communists, the pre-war ministries who had accompanied **Beneš** to exile in London and Klement **Gottwald** and his colleagues coming home from Moscow. It was based on the hope that good East–West relations would continue after the war; and while it excluded some parties and concentrated on socializing the economy, it stipulated free elections and did not contemplate collectivizing agriculture. However, Kosice in Slovakia was liberated by the **Red Army** and when the **Cold War** got under way, the compromise was abandoned in 1948 to fit the objectives of **communism**.

Kosovo

The region of southern Serbia, bounded by Montenegro, Albania and Macedonia. The heart of medieval Serbia, it encompasses many sites of religious significance for the Serbs as well as the scene of their defeat by the Ottoman Turks (1389). Settled by **Albanians** as well as Serbs, it has long been the cause of friction between the two nations. In the 19c it was the centre of the Albanian national revival, but was granted to Serbia when the first Albanian state was established (1913). In **World War II** it was included within Albania by the Italian fascists and its future was a contentious issue between Albanian resistance movements (79 per cent of the population is Albanian). Returned to Yugoslavia in 1945, it became an autonomous province within the Socialist Federal Republic of Serbia, with Albanian and Serbian as its official languages. In 1981 Albanian students led demands for the establishment of Kosovo as the seventh Yugoslav republic and the ensuing riots led to the declaration of a state of emergency. The province's autonomous status was effectively removed by Serbia in 1990. In 1992 ethnic Albanians held parliamentary and presidential elections which were declared invalid by the Serbs. ▷ **Balli Kombëtar; LNC; Milošević, Slobodan**

Kostov, Traicho (?1897–1949)

Bulgarian politician. He studied law and joined the Bulgarian Communist Party (BCP) in 1920. He was tortured and imprisoned under the regime of **Boris III**, and left a cripple. During **World War II**, a 'home' rather than a 'Moscow' communist, he served in the post-war **Fatherland Front** government as Secretary of the Central Committee of the BCP (1944–8), Deputy

Prime Minister (1946–9) and Minister for Electrification (1947–9). After criticizing the terms of economic deals with the USSR, he was summoned with the Yugoslavs **Kardelj** and **Djilas** to justify himself before **Stalin** (1948). In 1949 he was tried on charges of wartime collaboration with the police and the British and plotting to assassinate Georgi **Dimitrov**. He was executed in Dec 1949, a victim of Stalin's purges of 'home communists' and 'Titoists'. However, he was posthumously rehabilitated and decorated (1956). ▷ **Tito; Velchev, Damian**

Kosygin, Alexei Nikolaievich (1904–80)
Soviet politician. A textile-worker by training, he owed his advancement in the 1930s to the vacancies resulting from **Stalin**'s purges. Elected to the Supreme Soviet (1938), he held a variety of political industrial posts, and became a member of the Central Committee in 1939 and of the **Politburo** in 1948. He had a chequered career in the post-**World War II** period, falling in and out with both Stalin and Nikita **Khrushchev**. It was only really when, in 1964, he succeeded the latter as Chairman of the Council of Ministers (or Prime Minister) that he could attempt serious, if decentralizing, reforms. However, he was blocked in the late 1960s by the Party machine and the caution of Leonid **Brezhnev**. He soldiered on until 1980, when he resigned because of ill health, and he died soon after, having failed to rescue the economy from over-centralization and -planning.

Kountche, Seyni (1931–87)
Niger soldier and politician. Trained in France, he served with the French army in Indochina and Algeria. He joined the Niger army at independence in 1961, undertaking further military training in France before becoming Chief of Staff in 1973. He led the military coup against Hamani **Diori** in 1974 and established a military government. However, he set about restoring the country's economy and a return to civilian rule, but died in Paris while undergoing surgery.

Kozlov, Frol Romanovich (1908–65)
Soviet politician. Graduating in 1936 from what later became the Leningrad Polytechnic, he held Communist Party functions in various parts of the country before returning to Leningrad in 1949 to work his way up to be First Secretary there. In 1957 he became a member of the **Politburo** in the wake of the **Anti-Party Plot**. Thereafter he held two brief ministerial posts before becoming Second Secretary to Nikita **Khrushchev** in the Soviet party as a whole. As such he tried to restrain Khrushchev's reforms in the interests of conservative forces and was reputed to be behind an unsuccessful coup in 1963, but that year he suffered a stroke and had to leave the field to Leonid **Brezhnev**.

KPD (*Kommunistische Partei Deutschlands*, 'Communist Party of Germany')
German political party. Founded at New Year 1919, the KPD was, initially, a coalition of left-wing Social Democrats within the Spartacus League (Spartakus Bund) and various anarcho-syndicalist groupings which opposed the **Weimar Republic**. At first an independent-minded party led by Rosa **Luxemburg** and Karl **Liebknecht**, the KPD later came increasingly under Russian control and became virulently hostile to the **SPD** by the mid-1920s. Cooperation with the SPD, which it branded 'Social Fascist', or with other republican parties to defend the Weimar Republic during the early 1930s was therefore out of the question. Its relationship with the **Nazi Party**, however, although highly violent, became more and more equivocal. When the organization was banned by the Nazis (Mar 1933), many members left politics or even switched to the Nazi Party or **SA**, but a minority put up sustained if low-level passive resistance to the end of the Third **Reich**. After **World War II**, the revived KPD in eastern Germany forced the SPD there into a merger to form the **SED**, the ruling party of the German Democratic Republic. Soon afterwards it was banned in the Federal Republic. During Weimar, the KPD failed to gain a significant foothold in the trade-union and working-class cultural movement and towards the end of Weimar relied on the unemployed and marginalized working-class groups for its growing, if minority, support. ▷ **communism; Spartacists**

Krag, Jens Otto (1914–78)
Danish politician. He was Minister of Foreign Affairs (1958–62), when he became Leader of Denmark's **Social Democratic Party**, which he led until 1972. During this time he had two periods as Prime Minister (1962–8 and 1971–2). In 1972 he led Denmark into the Common Market, but after the EEC referendum (Oct 1972), which showed 63.3 per cent of the votes in favour of membership and 36.7 per cent against, he surprisingly decided to resign and was succeeded by Anker **Joørgensen**.

Kramar, Karel (1860–1937)
Czechoslovak politician. He almost became a professor, but took up politics in the 1890s as a member of the Young Czech Party that wished to improve the lot of all Slavs within Austria-Hungary. He was also pro-Russian, and at the beginning of **World War I** he tried to float a scheme that would make Bohemia and Moravia a kingdom with a Russian prince. He was accordingly imprisoned by the Austrian authorities for much of the war but emerged at the end as provisional Prime Minister in **Masaryk**'s government. He was then very active, pressing the Czechoslovak case during the **Versailles** peace conference. However, in the middle of 1919, he lost his place in the government as too conservative for the majority. Although he remained in parliament, his influence waned; he had been overtaken by history.

Krasin, Leonid Borisovich (1870–1926)

Soviet politician, diplomat and engineer. Expelled from St Petersburg Technological Institute in 1888 for radical political activity, he graduated from Kharkov Technological Institute in 1900 and continued thereafter to be both practising engineer and occasional revolutionary activist. He took part in the negotiations leading up to the Treaty of **Brest-Litovsk** in 1918; and as Commissar for Foreign Trade (1920–6), he was deeply involved in most of the negotiations leading to the **normalization** of Soviet relations with other European states. Increasingly pragmatic in his approach, he died shortly after being appointed Ambassador to Britain.

Kreisau Circle (*Kreisauer Kreis*)

A German anti-Nazi resistance group founded by Count Helmuth von Moltke in 1940, which met on his estate at Kreisau. The Circle drafted a Christian–conservative political programme for post-war Germany. Von Moltke was arrested in Jan 1944 after which most of his colleagues attached themselves to von **Stauffenberg**'s group which tried, unsuccessfully, to kill **Hitler** in July 1944.

Kreisky, Bruno (1911–90)

Austrian politician. Educated at Vienna University, he joined the Social Democratic Party of **Austria (SPÖ)** as a young man and was imprisoned for his political activities from 1935 until he escaped to Sweden in 1938. He returned to Austria and served in the Foreign Service (1946–51) and the Prime Minister's office (1951–3). He was increasingly active in party politics and in 1970 became Chancellor in a minority SPÖ government. He steadily increased his majority in subsequent elections but in 1983, when that majority disappeared, he refused to serve in a coalition and resigned.

Kremlinology

The once essential art of deducing by 'reading between the lines' from various, often indirect, sources what was happening in Soviet politics. The need arose from the 'monolithic unity' presented by Soviet leaders to their own people and the outside world, hiding their conflicts and divisions through strict control of the media. Under Mikhail **Gorbachev**, **glasnost** lessened the need for Kremlinology to the point where the supply of information became as abundant as elsewhere.

Kriegel, Frantisek (1908–79)

Czechoslovak politician. Active in the Communist Party from the 1930s, a doctor by training, he practised his profession in both the **Spanish Civil War** and **Chinese Civil War** from 1936 through to 1945. He subsequently held a series of party and government appointments and acted as health adviser in Cuba in the years 1960–3. In 1968 he played an important role as chairman of the National Front and he was abducted to Moscow along with Alexander **Dubček** and others after the invasion. The Soviet authorities initially refused to release him, and he never signed the protocol that was extracted in Moscow; that and his subsequent outspokenness lost him all his positions and privileges.

Krishna Menon, Vengalil Krishnan (1896–1974)
Indian politician. He was educated at the Presidency College, Madras, and at London University. He came to Britain in 1924 and became a history teacher and a London barrister. In 1929 he became Secretary of the India League and the mouthpiece of Indian nationalism in Britain. When India became a Dominion in 1947 he became India's High Commissioner in London. In 1952 he became leader of the Indian delegation to the **UN**, bringing Jawaharlal **Nehru**'s influence to bear on international problems as leader of the Asian 'uncommitted' and 'neutralist' bloc. During the first 1956 **Suez Crisis** on the nationalization of the Canal he formulated a plan to deal with it. As Defence Minister (1957–62) he came into conflict at the UN with Britain over Kashmir. He was Minister of Defence Production for a short time in 1962.

Kristallnacht (Reichskristallnacht) (9–10 Nov 1938)
A pogrom against the Jews in National Socialist Germany unleashed by the **SA** and **Nazi Party** members following a provocative speech by Joseph **Goebbels**. The ostensible reason was the murder in Paris of a German official by a Polish Jew. The result was the massive destruction of Jewish property in Germany, the death of 91 Jews, and subsequently heightened pressure on Jews to emigrate from the country combined with the further isolation and persecution of those remaining.

Krofta, Kamil (1876–1945)
Czechoslovak historian and diplomat. A professor at Charles University in Prague, he entered diplomatic service as Ambassador to the Vatican (1920–2), and then held postings in Vienna and Berlin. He became Deputy Foreign Minister in 1927 and Foreign Minister in 1936. It was not easy to follow **Beneš** or even to serve him when he was elected President, but Krofta proved both able and loyal in the pre-Munich struggle to preserve Czechoslovakia. He was imprisoned in a **concentration camp** during **World War II** and died just after he was set free.

Kronstadt Rebellion (Mar 1921)
An uprising of sailors from the Baltic fleet stationed at Kronstadt in the Gulf of Finland. Protesting against the dictatorial Bolshevik policy of 'war communism', the mutineers demanded political and economic reforms under the slogan of 'free soviets', and established a revolutionary

commune on the orders of **Lenin**. The rising was crushed by **Red Army** units after fierce fighting and heavy losses on both sides. But at the 10th Communist Party Congress in the same month, Lenin was sensitive enough to introduce his '**New Economic Policy**', which at least improved the material conditions of the Soviet people. ▷ **Bolsheviks**

Kruchina, Nikolai Yefimovich (1928–91)
Soviet politician. Graduating as an agronomist in 1952, he was a **Komsomol** official from then until 1962 when he was transferred to the Communist Party proper. From 1978 to 1983 he was second-in-command of the agricultural section of the Central Committee and came into close contact with Mikhail **Gorbachev**. He was then made chief administrator of party affairs, a post that gave considerable financial responsibility. Suddenly in 1991, as the **August Coup** crumbled, he committed suicide, suggesting corruption as well as disloyalty among Gorbachev's former lieutenants.

Krupskaya, Nadezhda Konstantinova (1869–1939)
Russian revolutionary, and wife and widow of **Lenin**. A Marxist activist before she met Lenin in 1894, she was sentenced to exile about the same time as he was and allowed to join him in Siberia in 1898 on condition that they got married. Thereafter they were inseparable, and Krupskaya acted as his agent, organizer and fellow-thinker in both Europe and Russia. She disliked the political limelight and, following the Bolshevik **Russian Revolution**, she was mainly active in promoting education and the status of women. As Lenin's widow she at first opposed **Stalin** but subsequently supported some of his policies, and was accordingly exploited. She left a rather brief *Reminiscences of Lenin*. ▷ **Bolsheviks**

Kryuchkov, Vladimir Alexandrovich (1924–)
Soviet lawyer, diplomat and secret policeman. Born and educated in Volgagrad (Stalingrad), he immediately threw himself into local Communist Party work. However, in 1954 he was recruited into the diplomatic service and became Third Secretary in Budapest, where Yuri **Andropov** was serving as ambassador. Thereafter he went everywhere with Andropov, to the Central Committee as a sector head in 1957 and to the **KGB** in a similar posting in 1967. From 1974 to 1988 he was deputy chairman, mainly responsible for foreign intelligence; but in 1988, under Mikhail **Gorbachev**, he became Chairman. Obviously expected to support reform, he was brought into the **Politburo** in 1989 and transferred to the presidential council in 1990. But in 1991, disenchanted or ambitious, he helped organize the attempted **August Coup** that led to his own imprisonment and Boris **Yeltsin**'s advancement.

Ku Klux Klan
US white supremacist organization. The first klan was founded after the American Civil War to oppose Reconstruction and the new rights being granted to blacks. The members, disguised in white robes and hoods, engaged in whippings, lynchings, and cross burnings to terrorize blacks and their sympathizers in the rural areas of the South. The Klan declined in influence after federal laws were passed against it, but was re-established after **World War I**. This times its influence was felt far beyond the South, and its targets were enlarged to include Catholics, foreigners, and Jews as well as blacks. It declined during the 1930s, but was revived by the fear of **communism** in the 1950s. In the 1960s, its violent opposition to the **civil rights movement** led to a federal government crackdown, and the prosecution of key members. Subsequently the Klan moved toward working through traditional political channels in order to further its agenda.

Kubitschek (de Oliveira), Juscelino (1902–76)
Brazilian politician. The grandson of a Czech immigrant, he studied medicine in Belo Horizonte, Minas Gerais, and went on to become Mayor of the city (1940–5). He was elected to Congress by the PSD (*Partido Social Democrático*) in 1945 and was Governor of Minas Gerais in 1951–5. As President (1956–61), his ambitious *Programa de Metas* ('Programme of Goals') emphasized transportation, energy, manufacturing and the building of Brasília, rather than social measures, and was the blueprint for subsequent programmes during military rule. The political necessity for high GDP growth-rates hampered effective counter-inflationary policies and the achievement of a modus vivendi with international creditors, bequeathing massive problems to subsequent **Quadros/Goulart** and **Castelo Branco** administrations. He was a candidate for the presidency in 1965 when he was exiled by Castelo Branco.

Kučan, Milan (1941–)
Slovenian politician. During the late 1980s, Kučan as the communist President of Slovenia, resisted pressure from Belgrade to stifle the emergence of opposition parties in his republic, long the most liberal in the Yugoslav federation. In 1990, after the Slovenes held the first free elections anywhere in Yugoslavia since **World War II**, he was re-elected as non-Party President of Slovenia. He declared Slovenia's secession from the Yugoslav Federation on 25 July 1991. With the backing of Serbia's President, Slobodan **Milošević**, Yugoslav Federal army units attacked Slovenia, but Milošević was obliged to withdraw and to accept Slovenia's independence.

Kulikov, Viktor Georgevich (1921–)
Soviet commander. He rose to be Chief of Staff of a tank brigade during **World War II**, then worked his way up until in 1969 he became the

commander of Soviet forces in Germany. His subsequent promotion was even quicker: Chief of the General Staff and first Deputy Defence Minister in 1971; and Commander-in-Chief of the **Warsaw Pact** and Marshal of the USSR in 1977. He was therefore deeply involved in Leonid **Brezhnev**'s military build-up and opposed Mikhail **Gorbachev**'s cutbacks. He was relieved of his appointment in 1989 not long before the disbandment of the Warsaw Pact, the two events obviously being connected.

Kun, Béla (1886–1939)
Hungarian political leader and revolutionary. He was a journalist and social democrat, who was conscripted into the Austro-Hungarian army and became a prisoner of war in Russia in 1916. In 1917 he sympathized with the **Bolsheviks**, and in 1918 founded the Hungarian Communist Party. In Mar 1919 he organized a communist revolution in Budapest and set up a Soviet republic which followed **Károlyi**'s post-**World War I** government. His policy of nationalization and other socialist measures failed, however, to gain popular support, and he was forced to flee for his life in Aug of that year. After escaping to Vienna, he returned to Russia where, in 1921, he became a member of the Executive Committee of the **Comintern**. He then fell victim to the Stalinist purges of the late 1930s. ▷ **Stalin, Joseph**

Kunaev, Dimmukhamed Akhmedovich (1912–)
Kazakh politician. A metallurgist by occupation and communist by inclination, he worked his way up the Kazakh party ladder in the 1940s and 1950s, coming into close contact with Leonid **Brezhnev** and being made First Secretary in 1960. He was demoted by Nikita **Khrushchev** in 1962, but reappointed in 1964 by Brezhnev who also brought him into full membership of the **Politburo**. This gave Brezhnev support and the Politburo a nationality following; inevitably it meant his dismissal by Mikhail **Gorbachev** in 1986. His ousting led to riots in Alma Ata but these were countered by charges of extensive corruption.

Kung, H H (Kong Xiangxi/K'ung Hsiang-hsi) (1881–1967)
Chinese politician and banker. He came from a family of traditional bankers and received a missionary education in China before studying in the USA (1901–7). Through marriage, Kung developed close ties with **Sun Yat-sen** and **Chiang Kai-shek** (their wives were sisters), joining the **Guomindang** in 1924 and becoming Minister of Industry and Commerce of the new Nationalist government in 1928. As Governor of the Bank of China and Minister of Finance (1933–44), Kung attempted to increase the government's financial control of the modern sector. Through control of the four major banks, the government floated more bond issues to finance its military projects. Kung's abandonment of the silver standard in favour of a managed paper currency in 1935 was to lead ultimately to

hyperinflation in the 1940s. During the war against Japan, Kung was instrumental in obtaining US loans and was China's representative at the **UN** Bretton Woods Conference (1944). He moved to the USA permanently in 1948.

Kurds

A nationalistic West Iranian-speaking ethnic group settled in neighbouring mountainous areas of Anatolia, Iraq, Iran and Turkey (including some in Syria and Armenia), an area which they themselves call Kurdistan. They were originally pastoral nomads with some agriculture, but the creation of national boundaries after **World War I** restricted their seasonal migrations, and most are now urbanized. They have been Sunni Muslims since the 7c. They are politically oppressed in Turkey, and have suffered religious persecution in Iran, especially after the Iranian Revolution of 1979. In Iraq, the Kurds' failure to achieve autonomous status for Kurdistan during the 1970s resulted in hostilities between Kurds and government forces. After the allied victory over Iraq in Kuwait in Feb 1991, the Kurds revolted against the government but were suppressed. Following continued Iraqi attacks on the Kurdish population in northern Iraq, the **UN** created a security zone there to protect them. In July 1992, Kurds in northern Iraq formed their first government, which was not acknowledged by central government in Baghdad.

Kuril Islands, Dispute over the

A territorial dispute between the USSR and Japan over ownership of the southern group of Kuril Islands. During the 18c Russia began settling the northern and central Kurils, while the Tokugawa Shogunate laid claim to the southern islands, an arrangement that was formalized by the Treaty of Shimoda (7 Feb 1855). With the Treaty of St Petersburg (7 May 1875), Russia surrendered its claim to the northern and central Kurils (in return for which, Japan gave up her claims to Sakhalin Island), and the islands were then administered by Japan as part of Hokkaido (1875–1945). The Kurils were occupied by Soviet forces shortly after the USSR declared war on Japan (9 Aug 1945) and were formally declared Soviet territory. Since Japan insisted on the return of the southern Kurils (Kunashiri, Etorofu, Shikotan, Habomai islands), which it regards as inalienable Japanese territory (and are referred to as the Northern Territories), a Soviet–Japanese peace treaty was never signed, although relations were normalized in 1955. Even with the dismantling of the USSR in 1991, the dispute remains unresolved.

Kut al-Amara, Battles of (28 Sep 1915 and 29 Apr 1916) and Siege of (1915–16)

Kut al-Amara, on the west bank of the Tigris, some 100 miles from Baghdad, was taken first by the British under Major-General Charles

Townshend in Sep 1915. Townshend later over-reached himself and was forced to fall back on Kut al-Amara, having suffered a reverse near the site of the ancient Ctesiphon. The Turks laid siege to Kut in Dec 1915 and, despite attempts to relieve Kut by British forces in Iraq, Townshend was forced to ask for terms. Townshend's proposals for terms were refused by the Turks and he surrendered, having first obtained a guarantee for his troops, in 1916.

Kuusinen, Otto Vilgelmovich (1881–1964)
Finnish-born Soviet politician. An active Bolshevik in both the 1905 and 1917 Russian Revolutions, he founded the Finnish Communist Party in 1918, but emigrated to Moscow when it was outlawed in 1930. He had already been working there as Secretary of the **Comintern** Executive Committee, a function he performed until 1939. He was then briefly Chairman of the Presidium of the so-called Karelo-Finnish Republic, which won him membership of the Soviet Party's Central Committee. A survivor, he was selected by Nikita **Khrushchev** in 1957 to be a member of the **Politburo** in the aftermath of the **Anti-Party Plot**. However, he died before it could be known how he would fare with Leonid **Brezhnev**.

Kuwait
An independent state at the head of the Arabian Gulf. Britain became responsible for Kuwait's foreign affairs in 1899. It became a British protectorate in 1914 and gained full independence in 1961. The invasion and annexation by Iraq in Aug 1990 led to the **Gulf War** in Jan–Feb 1991, with severe damage to Kuwait City and the infrastructure of the country. The Kuwait government went into exile in Saudi Arabia until the country was liberated in 1991. Major post-war problems included large-scale refugee emigration, the burning of oil wells by Iraq (all capped by Nov 1991), and the pollution of Gulf waters by oil. In 1992 the port of Umm Quasr and part of an oilfield were passed to Kuwait when the boundary between Iraq and Kuwait was moved by 600m.

Kuyper, Abraham (1837–1920)
Dutch theologian and politician. As a clergyman, founder of the Free University of Amsterdam (1880), member of the Dutch parliament and Prime Minister (1900–5), Kuyper sought to develop a Christian world-view of society. He founded and edited two newspapers and wrote numerous books, few of which have been translated into English, apart from *Lectures on Calvinism* (1898), *Principles of Sacred Theology* (1898), and *The Work of the Holy Spirit* (1900). His theology of common grace, the kingdom of God, and the 'sphere-sovereignty' of the Church and other social institutions, offer a Calvinistic version of Social Christianity. In the Netherlands he is remembered as the emancipator of the orthodox Calvinists and as the founder of the **Anti-Revolutionary Party**.

Kuznetsov, Vasili Vasilevich (1901–90)
Soviet politician. He joined the Communist Party in 1927, and so managed to steer clear of trouble that in 1952 he became a member of the **Politburo**. Although he held various second-level political posts, he achieved little. Mikhail **Gorbachev** took the first opportunity to get rid of him in 1986 in order to free the system and make room for new blood.

KwaZulu
A former national state or non-independent Black homeland in Natal province, eastern South Africa. Situated close to the Indian Ocean between the Transkei and Durban, it was granted self-governing status in 1971. It became defunct in May 1994, following the first all-race elections in South Africa. ▷ **apartheid**

L

La Follette, Robert Marion, Snr (1855–1925)

US politician. Three times Progressive Governor of Wisconsin, he began his political career by winning election as a district attorney after exposing corruption in the local Republican Party **machine**. From 1885 to 1891, he served in the US House of Representatives. As Governor of Wisconsin, he reformed the primary election process and the civil service, made the railroad commission stronger and introduced measures for workers' compensation and the conservation of natural resources. His widely publicized and imitated reforms became knowns as the 'Wisconsin Idea'. He would have been the **Progressive Party** presidential candidate in 1912 but for the re-entry into politics of ex-President Theodore **Roosevelt**; in 1924 he became the nominee; although he failed in his presidential bid, he received nearly 5 million votes.

La Guardia, Fiorello Henry (1882–1947)

US politician. He became Deputy Attorney-General (1915–17) and served seven terms in the House of Representatives as a Republican (1917–21 and 1923–33). Three times mayor of New York City (1934–46), he was a popular and effective leader who initiated broad reforms in public services, fought corruption, and undertook a major rebuilding program. New York's La Guardia Airport is named after him. ▷ **Republican Party**

La Rocque, François, Colonel, Count of (1886–1946)

French regular army officer. He resigned from the army in 1928 to enter business; in 1931 he became leader of the Ligue des **Croix de Feu** which expanded its membership very rapidly under him. In 1936 he became leader of the *Parti social français* ('French Social Party') which replaced the *Croix de Feu*. During **World War II** he supported the **Resistance Movement**.

Labour Party (UK)

A British socialist/social democratic political party, originally formed in 1900 as the Labour Representation Committee to represent trade unions and socialist societies as a distinct group in parliament. In 1906, 26 MPs were elected, and the name changed to the Labour Party. In 1922 it overtook the Liberals as the main opposition party, and the first minority Labour government was elected in 1924, lasting 11 months. The first majority Labour government under Clement **Attlee** (1945–51) established the welfare state and carried out a significant nationalization programme. Since then Labour have been in office 1964–70 and 1974–9. The breakaway **Social Democratic Party** of the 1980s hurt the party's electoral chances throughout that decade. Outside parliament, the annual conference and the National Executive Committee share policymaking, though their influence is greater in opposition. The leader and deputy leader are elected annually when in opposition by an electoral college composed of trade unions, constituency parties, and the parliamentary Labour Party. The British Labour Party has been little influenced by **Marxism**, unlike the corresponding parties in Europe. ▷ **socialism**

Lacoste, Robert (1898–1989)

French socialist politician. He began his career as a civil servant, becoming a trade-union official. In **World War II** he began the first trade-union Resistance group. In 1944 he was Minister of Industrial Production, and was Minister for Industry and Commerce in 1946–7 and again in 1948. From 1956 to 1958 he was resident minister in Algeria, and was accused of allowing the military authorities to use torture and other ruthless measures against the rebels. He was Senator for the Dordogne (1971–80). ▷ **Resistance Movement**

Ladysmith, Siege of (1899–1900)

One of the three sieges of the second Boer War in which Boer forces attempted to pen up their British opponents, and around which many of the actions of the war took place. An attempt to relieve the town was frustrated at the Battle of **Spion Kop** (Jan 1900), but General Sir Redvers Buller (1839–1908) succeeded in raising the siege on 28 Feb 1900. ▷ **Boer Wars; Kimberley, Siege of; Mafeking, Siege of**

Lafontaine, Oskar (1943–)

West German politician. Educated at Bonn University, he became leader of the Saar regional branch of the Social Democratic Party (**SPD**) in 1977 and served as Mayor of Saarbrücken (1976–85). He gained a reputation for radicalism and was variously dubbed 'Red Oskar' and the 'Ayatollah of the **Saarland**'. He began to mellow, however, after his election as Minister-President of the **Saarland** state parliament in 1985. In 1987 he was appointed a deputy chairman of the SPD's federal organization and served as the SPD's unsuccessful chancellor-candidate in the 1990 **Bundestag** elections after surviving an assassination attempt.

Lajpat Rai, Lala (1865–1928)

Indian politician and writer. He was a follower of the Arya Samaj and when, in 1893, it split, he and Hans Raj led the moderate 'college faction' which concentrated on building up a chain of 'Dayanand Anglo-Vedic colleges'. At the same time, Lajpat Rai developed a somewhat sporadic interest in Congress politics, as well as a more sustained involvement in **Swadeshi** enterprises. In the two articles published (1901) in the *Kayastha Samachar*, Lajpat Rai advocated technical education and industrial self-help and criticized the Congress as being a gathering of English-educated elites. He also argued that Congress should openly and boldly base itself on the Hindus alone. He led the wave of so-called extremist nationalism in Punjab between 1904 and 1907. The Congress split in the Surat session in 1907 and Lala Lajpat Rai formed the famous 'extremist' trio of Lal, Pal and Bal, with Tilak and Bipin Chandra Pal. Deported on charges of instigating the peasants, he led the **Non-Cooperation Movement** in Punjab in 1921.

Lampião (Virgulino Ferreira da Silva) (d.1938)
Brazilian bandit. Dubbed the 'King of the Cangaçeiros', he began his career in 1921. His fame rested on the size of his band, some 40–50 men on routine raids, who attacked large properties and even interior cities within the states of north-eastern Brazil. His brother's savage attack on Sousa (Paraíba) in 1924 and his equivocal role in combatting the Prestes Column (a group of young soldiers, led by Luís Carlos Prestes, which were in conflict with the federal government under President Washington Luís from 1926 to 1928) stimulated the growth of federal rule in the interior, limiting the control previously exercised by **coroneis**. Nevertheless, he was regarded as a popular hero in the country at large, and was the subject of a vast popular literature. ▷ **cangaço; coronelismo**

Lancaster House
The London venue for various conferences preparing the way for independence in several parts of the British empire. It is most noted for the 1961 conference, which paved the way to Kenyan independence and the 1989 conference in which the British Foreign Secretary, Lord Carrington, managed to forge agreement for an independence constitution for Zimbabwe and procedures to end the civil war in that country.

Land
A constituent 'state' in the German (and also the Austrian) federation. The majority of the Federal (West) German *Länder* (the plural form of the word) were set up by the Allied occupation authorities before the Federation (**Bund**) was created. Most *Land* constitutions are strongly plebiscitary in nature and envisage the democratization of broad aspects of society. The Länder enjoy sovereign rights in defined fields and are further strengthened in German constitutional life by the fact that the upper house of the Federal Parliament (the **Bundesrat**) consists of nominees of the Land governments. However, in practice the *Bund* has con-

siderable influence over the shape of legislation at Land level. ▷ **Basic Law; Germany, West**

Land Acts, Irish

A succession of British Acts passed in 1870, 1881, 1903, and 1909 with the objective first of giving tenants greater security and compensation for improvements, and later of enabling tenants to buy the estates they farmed. The Acts also aimed at reducing nationalist grievances and agitation.

Landdrost

Full-time officials and magistrates of the Dutch East India Company in South Africa who administered the interior regions of the colony. They were normally strangers to their areas, and were assisted by a secretary, a messenger and a number of soldiers. They managed all legal matters, border conflicts and wars and frequently came into conflict with the Boer citizens of their districts.

Landtag

Literally 'state diet' or 'parliament', this term describes the parliament of German (and Austrian) states (*Länder*). ▷ **Basic Law; Bund; Germany, West; Land**

Lange, David Russell (1942–)

New Zealand politician. After studying law at Auckland University and qualifying as a solicitor and barrister, he worked as a crusading lawyer for the underprivileged in Auckland. Elected to the House of Representatives in 1977, he became Deputy Leader of the Labour Party in 1979 and Leader in 1983. He won a decisive victory in the 1984 general election on a non-nuclear defence policy, which he immediately put into effect, despite criticism from other Western countries, particularly the USA. Re-elected in 1987, he resigned the premiership in 1989, following bouts of ill health and disagreements within his party.

Lansbury, George (1859–1940)

British politician. Active as a radical since boyhood, he became a convinced socialist in 1890 and a Labour MP in 1910, resigning in 1912 to stand in support of women's suffrage. He was defeated and not re-elected until 1922. He founded and edited the *Daily Herald* (1912–22), and became Commissioner of Works (1929) and Leader of the **Labour Party** (1931–5). ▷ **MacDonald, Ramsay; socialism**

Lansing–Ishii Agreement (2 Nov 1917)

The name given to the exchange of diplomatic notes between the Japanese ambassador to the USA, Ishii Kikujiro, and US Secretary of State,

Robert Lansing, which agreed on a set of principles concerning policy towards China. The agreement helped soothe tensions between the two countries at a time when the USA was becoming increasingly critical of Japan's attempts to enhance its influence in China. Respect for China's territorial integrity and commitment to the Open Door policy (ie that all powers should have equal economic opportunities in China) were confirmed; at the same time, the USA recognized that Japan had special interests in China because of 'territorial propinquity'. The agreement was superseded by the Washington Treaties of 1921–2, which committed all the powers to respect China's independence.

Laos

A landlocked country on the Indochinese Peninsula, which became a French protectorate in 1893. It was occupied by the Japanese in **World War II**. Independence from France was gained in 1949. In 1953 civil war broke out between the Lao government, supported by the USA, and the communist-led Patriotic Front (Pathet Lao), supported by North Vietnam. It lasted until 1975, when a communist republic was established.

Lapointe, Ernest (1876–1941)

Canadian politician. As a Liberal with rouge tendencies, he was very critical of the **Borden–Meighen** stand against the **Winnipeg General Strike**. In 1921 he was appointed to a minor position in the Mackenzie **King** administration, but it was as an adviser on French-Canadian affairs and attitudes that the Prime Minister valued him. In 1924 he became Minister of Justice. Like King, he believed the unity of the country was the foremost issue and therefore put his concern for social reform to one side (accepting, for instance, the notorious anti-communist **Padlock Act** in Quebec). Although he opposed conscription, he played an important role in generating support within Quebec for Canada's participation in **World War II**, and when Maurice **Duplessis** challenged the **War Measures Act**, Lapointe's threat to resign was an effective contribution to the return of a more amenable provincial administration. ▷ **Liberal Party** (Canada)

Lapua Movement

A semi-fascist political movement which originated in the Finnish town of Lapua in 1929. Composed mainly of small farmers who were influenced by Lutheran pietism and who were fiercely both nationalist and anti-communist, the movement agitated for the suppression of the Finnish Communist Party (which had been formally illegal in Finland since 1919). Its pressure on parliament and acts of violence led to the banning of the Communist Party's front organizations in Oct 1930. The Lapua Movement was itself declared illegal in 1932 following an abortive armed uprising against the government. However, during its short period of existence Lapua was one of the most significant manifestations of right-wing extremism in inter-war Europe. ▷ **Communist Party** (Finland)

Largo Caballero, Francisco (1869–1946)
Spanish trade union and socialist leader. Secretary-General of the **UGT** from 1918 to 1936, his corporativist aspirations led him to collaborate with the dictatorship of **Primo de Rivera** of 1923–30. As Minister of Labour (1931–3) under the Second Republic, he altered the exploitative economic and social relations of rural Spain. From 1934 to 1935 he was the leader of the socialists' increasingly revolutionary left wing as the Right reversed the reforms of 1931–3. His revolutionary stance contributed significantly to the polarization of the Republic in 1936. Appointed Prime Minister (Sep 1936) after the **Spanish Civil War** broke out, he proved a conservative and rigid war leader, curtailing the social revolution and re-establishing state authority. He was nonetheless ousted by the communists in May 1937 for opposing the suppression of the **CNT** and **POUM**. First detained in exile by the **Vichy** French and then, in Feb 1943, by the **Gestapo**, he was liberated from a **concentration camp** in Apr 1945. ▷ **Republic, Second** (Spain)

Lari Massacre (26 Mar 1953)
A notorious incident during the 'Mau Mau' emergency in Kenya in which over 100 Kikuyu of the loyal chief Luka were killed by insurgents of the secret society. As with the assassination of the senior chief, Waruhiu, in the previous year, the massacre revealed the extent to which the emergency was in one of its aspects a Kikuyu civil war.

Lateran Pacts (Feb 1929)
The name given to agreements, between the Italian fascist state and the papacy, reached after negotiations between **Mussolini** and Pius XI's Secretary of State, Cardinal Gaspari. The pacts brought an end to the Church–state conflict which had been raging in Italy since the Risorgimento. By them, Italy recognized the sovereignty of the Vatican city, gave substantial compensation to the papacy for the loss of its territories during the Risorgimento, and guaranteed religious education at all levels of state schooling. In return, the Church recognized the Italian state for the first time. The pacts were confirmed in the constitution of 1948.

Lattre de Tassigny, Jean de (1889–1952)
French soldier. He commanded an infantry battalion in **World War I**, and in 1940 he commanded the 14th Division; he was then sent by the **Vichy** government to command in Tunisia. He was recalled for sympathy with the Allies and arrested in 1942. He escaped from Riom prison via North Africa to London in 1943. As commander of the French 1st Army he took a brilliant part in the Allied liberation of France (1944–5), signing

the German surrender. He was responsible for the reorganization of the French Army and was appointed Commander-in-Chief of Western Union Land Forces under **Montgomery** in 1948. In 1950 as Commander-in-Chief in French Indo-China, for a time he turned the tide against the Vietminh rebels. He was posthumously made a Marshal of France in 1952. ▷ **Riom Trial**

Latvia
A republic in north-east Europe, which was incorporated into Russia in 1721. It became an independent state in 1918, but was proclaimed a Soviet Socialist Republic in 1940. Germany occupied it during **World War II**. A new Latvian nationalist movement grew up in the 1980s and in 1990 independence talks began with the Soviet Union, resulting in a declaration of independence in 1991.

Laurier, Sir Wilfrid (1841–1919)
Canadian politician. He became a lawyer, a journalist, and a member of the Quebec Legislative Assembly. He entered federal politics in 1874, and became Minister of Inland Revenue (1877), leader of the **Liberal Party** (1887–1919), and the first French-Canadian and Roman Catholic to be Prime Minister of Canada (1896–1911). A firm supporter of self-government for Canada, in his home policy he was an advocate of compromise and free trade with the USA. ▷ **Imperial Conferences**

Lausanne, Treaty of (1923)
After the Graeco-Turkish war, it replaced the Treaty of Sèvres and granted considerable concessions to the Turks, freeing them from paying the reparations imposed on them as a defeated power at the end of **World War I**. The Turks retained their lands in Anatolia and Thrace, while Greece lost most of its major war gains: Eastern Thrace, the Smyrna region and the Imvros and Tenedos islands. The Turkish minister **Inönü** and the Greek Eleuthérios **Venizélos** agreed to the exchange of populations which led to the uprooting of 380 000 Turks from Greece and 1.3 million Greeks from Anatolia. The treaty also confirmed the British annexation of Cyprus.

Lausanne Conference (1932)
The conference held between the Allied powers and Germany to discuss the question of German reparation payments, which had been suspended by the moratorium imposed by the unilateral decision of US President Herbert **Hoover** in 1931, after the onset of the Great Depression. A final reparation payment by Germany was agreed, but the Lausanne convention was never ratified, and no more payments were actually made.

Laval, Pierre (1883–1945)
French politician. He became a lawyer, Deputy (1914), and Senator (1926), before serving as Premier (1931–2, 1935–6). From a position on the extreme left of the **Socialist Party**, he moved rightwards during the 1920s and 1930s, and in the **Vichy** government was **Pétain**'s deputy (1940). He was removed from office in Dec 1940 but restored with much greater power in Apr 1942. Again Prime Minister in 1942–4, he openly collaborated with the Germans. Fleeing after the liberation to Germany and Spain, he was brought back, charged with treason, and executed in Paris. ▷ **World War II**

Lavrentev, Mikhail Alexevich (1900–80)
Soviet mathematician. He held several influential academic appointments in both Moscow and Kiev, and during and after **World War II** came into close contact with Nikita **Khrushchev**. He was a full member of the Soviet Academy of Sciences from 1946, a deputy in the Supreme Soviet from 1958, and a candidate member of the Central Committee from 1961. This enabled him to build Akademgorodok, or Academic City, in Novosibirsk, designed to educate generations of superbrains and promote outstanding research. His creation partly achieved its purpose but it also helped to expand the intellectual frustration that built up under Leonid **Brezhnev**.

Law, (Andrew) Bonar (1858–1923)
British politician. He was an iron merchant in Glasgow, became a Unionist MP in 1900, and in 1911 succeeded **Balfour** as Unionist leader. He acted as Colonial Secretary (1915–16), a member of the war cabinet, Chancellor of the Exchequer (1916–18), Lord Privy Seal (1919), and from 1916 Leader of the House of Commons. He retired in 1921 through ill health, but returned to serve as Premier for several months in 1922–3.

Lawrence, T(homas) E(dward) ('Lawrence of Arabia') (1888–1935)
British soldier and author. Before **World War I** he travelled in the Middle East, studying Crusader castles and participating in the excavation of Carchemish. In 1914 he joined military intelligence and was sent to Cairo, where he became a member of the Arab Bureau. In 1916 he was appointed the British liaison officer to the **Arab Revolt**, led by **Faysal**, the son of Sharif **Husayn ibn 'Ali** of Mecca, and was present at the taking of Aqaba (1917) and of Damascus (1918). He was an adviser to Faisal at the **Paris Peace Conference** and a member of the Middle East Department at the Colonial Office (1921). His account of the Arab Revolt, *Seven Pillars of Wisdom*, abridged by himself as *Revolt in the Desert*, became one of the classics of war literature. His exploits received so much publicity that he became a legendary figure, and so he attempted to escape his fame by enlisting in the ranks of the RAF (1922) as J H Ross, in the Royal Tank

Corps (1923) as T E Shaw, and again in the RAF in 1925. He retired in 1935 and was killed in a motorcycling accident the same year.

Lawson, Nigel (1932–)
British politician. He spent some time working for various newspapers and also for television (1956–72), and during this time edited the *Spectator* (1966–70). Elected to parliament in 1974, when the Conservatives returned to office he became Financial Secretary to the Treasury (1979–81), Energy Secretary (1981–3), and Chancellor of the Exchequer (1983–9). During his time at the Exchequer, Britain saw lower direct taxes, but high interest rates and record trade deficits. ▷ **Conservative Party** (UK)

Le Clerc (de Hauteclocque), Jacques Philippe (1902–47)
French soldier. After fighting in 1940, he joined the **Free French** forces under de **Gaulle** in England. He became military commander in French Equatorial Africa, and led a force across the desert to join the British 8th Army, in 1942. He commanded the French 2nd Armoured Division in Normandy, and received the surrender of Paris in 1944. ▷ **Normandy Campaign; World War II**

Le Duc Tho (Phan Dinh Khai) (1911–90)
Vietnamese politician. He joined the Indo-Chinese Communist Party in 1929 and was exiled to the penal island of Con Dia by the French in 1930. Released in 1937, he became head of the Nam Dinh revolutionary movement, but was re-arrested and imprisoned (1939–44). After **World War II**, he worked for the Communist Party of Vietnam (CPV), entering its Politburo in 1955. As leader of the Vietnamese delegation to the Paris Conference on Indo-China (1968–73), he was awarded the 1973 Nobel Peace Prize, jointly with Henry **Kissinger**, but he declined to accept it. He retired from the Politburo in 1986.

Le Pen, Jean-Marie (1928–)
French politician. The son of a Breton fisherman, he served in the 1950s as a paratrooper in Indochina and Algeria. In 1956 he was elected as a right-wing Poujadist Deputy. During the 1960s he had connections with the extremist **OAS** (*Organisation Armée Secrète*), before forming the National Front in 1972. This party, with its extreme right-wing policies, emerged as a new 'fifth force' in French politics, winning 10 per cent of the national vote in the 1986 Assembly elections. A controversial figure and noted demagogue, he unsuccessfully contested the presidency in 1988.

League of Nations
A former international organization whose constitution was drafted at the **Paris Peace Conference** in 1919 and incorporated into the Treaty of

Versailles. The main aims were to preserve international peace and security by the prevention or speedy settlement of disputes and the promotion of disarmament. With its headquarters in Geneva, the League operated through a Council, which met several times a year, and an annual Assembly. Its original members included the victorious Allies of **World War I**, except for the USA, which refused to join, and most of the neutral nations. Germany joined in 1926, and the USSR in 1934, but Germany and Japan withdrew in 1933, and Italy in 1936. Although the League succeeded in settling some minor disputes, it became increasingly ineffective in the later 1930s, when it failed to stop major acts of aggression by Japan, Italy, and Germany. In 1946 it transferred its functions to the **UN**. ▷ **Wilson, Thomas Woodrow**

Learn from the PLA Campaign (1963–4)

A political campaign in China which began within the **People's Liberation Army** (PLA), aiming to stress the importance of service to the Communist Party and commitment to socialist ideals. A key aspect of the campaign was to elevate the position of **Mao Zedong** and his thought at a time when his influence within the party had waned following the disasters of the **Great Leap Forward**. With the active support of **Lin Biao**, appointed by Mao in 1959 as Defence Minister and head of the PLA, a compilation of Mao's sayings (*Quotations from Chairman Mao*, known as the 'Little Red Book') was studied and memorized throughout the PLA, thereby initiating the cult of Mao that was to attain grotesque proportions during the **Cultural Revolution**. By the end of 1963, Mao was calling upon the entire country to 'learn from the PLA', implying that it was the army rather than the party that incarnated the spirit of self-sacrifice and dedication to collective values. The campaign marked the beginning of the PLA's increasing involvement in politics (army personnel were assigned to work in various government organizations) and Mao's attack on the party hierarchy.

Lebanon

A republic on the east coast of the Mediterranean Sea. In 1920, following the collapse of the Ottoman Empire after **World War I**, it was created under French mandate as the State of Greater Lebanon, based upon Maronite Christian Jabal Lubnan. The Muslim coastal regions were incorporated in this new state despite great opposition. It became a constitutional republic in 1926 and gained independence in 1941. Palestinian resistance units were established in Lebanon by the late 1960s, despite government opposition. Palestinian raids into Israel were followed by Israeli reprisals. Several militia groups developed in the mid-1970s, notably the Shiite Muslim Afwaj al-Muqawama al-Lubnaniya (AMAL) and the Muslim Lebanese National Movement (LNM). Palestinian firepower was used to back up the political struggle of the LNM against the Maronite Christian and Sunni Muslim establishment. Muslim and Christian differences grew more intense and from 1975 Lebanon was beset by civil disorder as rival political and religious factions sought to gain control. Palestinian commandos joined the predominantly leftist Muslim side. The Syrian-dominated Arab Deterrent Force (ADF) was created to prevent Palestinian fighters gaining control. In 1976, Palestinian forces moved from Beirut to south Lebanon where the ADF was unable to deploy. West Beirut, also outside government control, was the scene of frequent conflict between opposing militia groups. Meanwhile, Christian militias, backed by Israel, sought to regain control in east Beirut and areas to the north. Following Palestinian terrorist attacks, Israel invaded south Lebanon in 1978 and 1982. The Israeli siege of Palestinian and Syrian forces in Beirut led to the withdrawal of Palestinian forces in 1982. Unilateral withdrawal of Israeli forces brought clashes between the Druze (backed by Syria) and the Christian Lebanese militia. A ceasefire was announced in late 1982 but was broken many times. International efforts to achieve a political settlement were unsuccessful. In the mid-1980s rival groups began taking foreigners as hostages. Syrian troops entered Beirut in 1988 in an attempt to restore order. In the early 1990s the foreign hostages were gradually released, the Lebanese army extended government control, and government elections took place. Plans were made to rebuild the economy.

Lebensraum

An expansionist concept (literally, 'living space') developed by the Nazis (especially **Hitler**) from the early 1920s onwards, which planned to extend German control far into the USSR to provide land for colonization. Hitler argued that Germany was over-populated, and needed more agriculturally productive land to guarantee future food supplies for an expanded German population. The alleged inferiority of East European peoples was used to justify this, parallels being made with European/British colonialism in America and Australia. ▷ **Nazi Party; World War II**

Lebowa

A former national state or non-independent Black homeland in northern Transvaal province, north-east South Africa. Situated north-east of Pretoria, it was granted self-governing status in 1972. It ceased to exist in May 1994 following the first all-race elections in South Africa. ▷ **apartheid**

Lebrun, Albert (1871–1950)

French politician and President (1932–40). He became a Deputy in 1900, was Minister for the Colonies (1911–14), for Blockade and Liberated Regions (1917–19), Senator (1920), and President of the Senate (1931). The last President of the Third Republic, he surrendered his powers to **Pétain** in 1940. ▷ **Republic, Third** (France)

Leburton, Edmond (1915–)

Belgian politician. He studied at Liège University and in 1946 became a MP for the **Belgian Socialist Party**. From 1954 to 1971 he held numerous cabinet posts with economic and social portfolios; in 1973–4 he was Prime Minister.

Lee (of Asheridge), Jennie, Baroness (1904–88)

British politician. The daughter of a Scottish miner, she made her own way in socialist politics, becoming the youngest elected woman MP (1929–31). She married Aneurin **Bevan** in 1934. Re-elected to parliament in 1945, she became Minister for the Arts (1967–70), and was given the task of establishing the Open University. She retired from the House of Commons in 1970 to be made a life peer. ▷ **Labour Party** (UK); **socialism**

Lee Kuan Yew (1923–)

Singaporean politician, born into a wealthy Chinese family. He studied law at Cambridge and qualified as a barrister in London before returning to Singapore in 1951 to practise. He founded the moderate, anti-communist People's Action Party (PAP) in 1954, and entered the Singapore Legislative Assembly in 1955. He became the country's first Prime Minister in 1959, a position he held until 1990. He acquired a formidable reputation for probity and industry, and oversaw the implementation of a successful programme of economic development. His son, Brigadier-General Lee Hsien Loong (1952–), is viewed as a possible successor in the longer term.

Lee Teng-hui (1923–)

Taiwanese politician. Educated at universities in the USA and Japan, he taught economics at the National Taiwan University before becoming Mayor of Taipei in 1979. A member of the ruling **Guomindang** and a protégé of **Jiang Jing'guo**, he became Vice-President of Taiwan in 1984 and state President and Guomindang leader on Jiang's death in 1988. The country's first island-born leader, he is a reforming technocrat who has significantly accelerated the pace of liberalization and 'Taiwanization'.

Left-Republicans

Spanish political parties. In the 1920s two new Republican parties emerged in reaction against the old-style populism and patronage politics of Alejandro **Lerroux**'s **Radical Republican Party**: Republican Action in 1925 and the Radical–Socialist Party in 1929. They aimed to provide the Republican movement with a more progressive and modern content, their most coherent and articulate representative being Manuel **Azaña**. Under the Second Republic, the Left-Republicans dominated the liberal reformist administrations of 1931–3, but were devastated in the general election of Nov 1933. They were nonetheless central to the creation of the Popular Front coalition which won the election of Feb 1936. However, the Left-Republicans' vacillatory leadership during the spring and summer of 1936 not only contributed to the polarization of the political climate, but also was critical in the conversion of the military rising of July 1936 into a civil war. ▷ **Republic, Second** (Spain); **Spanish Civil War**

Lega Lombarda
The main party of the *Lega Nord*, a coalition of north Italian political parties seeking autonomy from Rome, which has become an increasingly potent political force in the early 1990s. Its appeal is based on traditional *campanilismo* (intense particularism) and north–south hostility (which have been exacerbated by anxieties over immigration, both from the south and from outside Italy) and on the premise that politicians in Rome are too ready to tax the prosperous north to provide for the backward and endemically criminal south. Under the leadership of Umberto Bossi, the Lega Nord won over 50 seats in the 1992 general election.

Lena Goldfields Strike (1912)
A landmark on the road to the unrest that led to the **Russian Revolution** (1917). In the British-owned goldfields about 5 000 workers protested against poor living conditions in the difficult climate of Eastern Siberia; their complaints were ignored. When they went on strike, troops opened fire and killed over 200. The **Duma**, the public and foreign observers were equally distressed. Improvements were promised but did not materialize. The number of strikes then increased year by year down to the outbreak of **World War I**.

Lenart, Jozef (1923–)
Slovak politician. He fought in the **Slovak uprising**, then gained industrial experience in the Bata shoe concern. He rose quite suddenly to the premiership in 1963 while Czechoslovakia experienced industrial stagnation; and as a pragmatic reformer he achieved important results in the next few years. However, discontent increased with the **Novotný** regime and Lenart found himself turning away from reform. When the **Prague Spring** eventually broke through in 1968 he lost the premiership.

Lend-Lease Agreement (1941)
The arrangement by which the USA lent or leased war supplies and arms to Britain and other Allies during **World War II**. It was a measure in which President **Roosevelt** took a close personal interest. The Lend–Lease Act was passed by Congress in Mar 1941, when British reserves were almost exhausted. By the time the agreement terminated in 1945, the allies had received about £5 000 million worth of materials.

Lenin, Vladimir Ilyich (V I Ulyanov) (1870–1924)
Russian Marxist revolutionary and political leader. He was educated at the Universities of Kazan and St Petersburg, where he graduated in law. From 1895 to 1897 he was in prison and from 1897 to 1900 he was exiled to Siberia for participating in underground revolutionary activities; there he used his time to study and write extensively about **Marxism**. At the Second Congress of the Russian Social Democratic Labour Party (1903) he caused the split between what came to be called the Bolshevik and Menshevik factions. Apart from the frustrating period of the Russian **Revolution of 1905**, he spent the entire period until 1917 abroad, developing and publicizing his political views. Following the **February Revolution** in 1917, he returned to Petrograd from Zurich, and urged the early seizure of power by the proletariat under the slogan 'All Power to the Soviets'. In Oct 1917 he initiated the Bolshevik revolution and became head of the first Soviet government. He made peace with Germany at **Brest-Litovsk** in order to concentrate on defeating the Whites in the ensuing **Russian Civil War** (1918–21) and then changed tactics again by switching from a ruthless centralized policy of 'war communism' to the **New Economic Policy**, which his critics in the Party saw as a 'compromise with capitalism' and a retreat from strictly socialist planning. On his death, his body was embalmed and placed in a mausoleum in Red Square until Jan 1994 when it was removed and buried in St Petersburg. In 1924 Petrograd (formerly St Petersburg) was renamed Leningrad in his honour. Much was subsequently done in his name by **Stalin** and others, some of which he would not have approved of. But the nature of the USSR and the reasons for its final collapse in 1991 owed much to him; and it was not altogether surprising that the citizens of Leningrad voted for their city to resume the name of St Petersburg. ▷ **April Theses; Bolsheviks; Mensheviks; October Revolution; Russian Revolution**

Leningrad, Siege of (1941–4)
One of the more heroic incidents in Soviet and world history. The Soviet Union's second city, formerly Tsarist Russia's capital, **St Petersburg**, was besieged for 28 months and lost over a third of its population from the fighting or from starvation. It received less help than it might have from **Stalin** though it played a large part in the defeat of **Hitler**; it survived largely on the will of its people. Memories of the siege influenced many Leningraders to object to the reversion to the former name, St Petersburg, in 1991.

Lenshina, Alice
The leader of a millenarian movement, the Lumpa Church, which from 1964 led opposition to the newly independent regime in Zambia. The church and its followers represented the split between urban politics and rural aspirations, between modernizers and traditionalists. Lenshina's

church became a major focus of opposition to the regime of Kenneth **Kaunda**.

Leopold III (1901–83)
King of the Belgians (1934/51). The son of **Albert I**, in 1926 he married **Astrid** of Sweden, and after her death Liliane Baels in 1941. On his own authority he ordered the capitulation of the Belgian Army to the Germans (1940), thus opening the way to Dunkirk. He then remained a prisoner in his own palace at Laeken until 1944, and afterwards in Austria. After returning to Belgium in 1945, he was forced to abdicate in 1951 in favour of his son, **Baudouin I**. ▷ **World War II**

Lerroux, Alejandro (1864–1949)
Spanish politician and journalist. During the first decade of the 20c he was the highly innovative and audacious populist leader of Barcelona. In forging a new basis for collaboration between the working class and republicanism, he formed the first modern party in Spain. Mythologized by his fiery anticlerical demagogy, the charismatic Lerroux was known as the 'Emperor of the Parallel' (a working-class thoroughfare). After he founded the **Radical Republican Party** in 1908, he became increasingly conservative, even offering in 1923 to become the civilian figurehead of **Primo de Rivera**'s dictatorship. Although he also dedicated more and more time to his own varied business interests, Lerroux retained an extraordinary hold over his party. During the Second Republic, he led the Radicals as the principal source of opposition to the progressive Republican–Socialist coalition of 1931–3, having left the government in Dec 1931. He was crucial to the formation of the alliance with the non-Republican Right, which ruled Spain from Nov 1933 to Oct 1935 and which polarized the regime to an unprecedented degree. During this period he headed five administrations before falling from power through a bribery scandal. Despite backing the Nationalists during the **Spanish Civil War**, he was prevented from returning to Spain from his exile in Portugal until 1947, because of his earlier involvement with freemasonry. ▷ **Republic, Second** (Spain)

Lesage, Jean (1912–80)
Canadian politician. He became the Liberal Premier of Quebec in 1960, carried into power on a wave of nationalist fervour, although the Liberals won only 50 out of the 95 seats. He then introduced the **Quiet Revolution** against corruption, the Catholic Church's involvement in lay issues such as education, welfare and health, and against the economic domination of the USA and of anglophone Canadians in Quebec. His demands for a more active governmental role in the province, because of its special situation within the Confederation, began to cause unease among other Canadian provinces, especially when he asked for an increased share of

tax revenue. In 1966 his government was defeated by the **Union Nationale**. He remained leader of the Provincial Party until his retirement in 1970.
▷ **Liberal Party** (Canada)

Lettow-Vorbeck, General Paul Emil von (1870–1964)
Prussian officer. He commanded the German forces in East Africa in **World War I**. These forces, largely composed of black troops recruited from warlike peoples in Tanganyika, were expanded and reorganized by him and raided the Uganda railway early in the war. He failed to hold the Kilimanjaro area, where most German settlers were located, and fell back to the Tanganyika Central Railway. In 1916 the railway was captured by forces led by General Smuts and he moved south to the Rufiji. He subsequently invaded Portuguese East Africa and Northern Rhodesia and surrendered after the Armistice at Abercorn (now Mbala, Zambia) on 25 Nov 1918.

Lévesque, René (1922–87)
Canadian politician. He founded the **Parti Québecois** in 1968 after **Lesage**'s defeat and the refusal of the **Liberal Party** to become more nationalist. By uniting the majority of francophones who wished greater autonomy for Quebec and those who wanted complete political independence for the province, he won a stunning victory in 1976, with 41 per cent of the vote. He then introduced electoral and labour reforms, pressed hard for the completion of the huge Quebec Hydro scheme and initiated legislation to place foreign-owned and other corporations under public ownership. More controversial were Bill 101, which legislated for a unilingual province, and a referendum law on the question of Quebec's future. With the other provinces refusing to commit themselves to economic relationships with Quebec, and with Prime Minister Pierre **Trudeau**'s full involvement in the campaign, the Quebeckers voted against secession. Lévesque then began to demand enhanced provincial powers, along with Alberta's Premier Peter **Lougheed**. In 1981 Quebec became increasingly isolated, with Lévesque refusing to endorse Trudeau's constitutional reforms which challenged not only Bill 101 but also Lévesque's demand for compensation from Ottawa if the province opted out of federal socio-economic programmes. The party became deeply divided over the secession issue, but in 1985 Lévesque maintained his leadership with a 75 per cent vote.

Lewis, John L (1880–1969)
US labour leader. Born the son of a Welsh coalminer, he grew up to hold the presidency of the Union of United Mineworkers from 1920 to 1960. When its membership was reduced by the **Great Depression** to 150 000 in 1933, fearing a communist takeover, Lewis led a vigorous recruitment drive which increased the membership to 500 000. When, in 1935, he was

unsuccessful in his attempts to change the AFL's traditional exclusion of industrial workers, he reacted by founding the Committee for Industrial Organizations, which became the CIO after its expulsion from the AFL in 1938. He took the coal miners out on several strikes during **World War II**, and his fiery personality and stubborn drive led to clashes with Presidents Franklin D **Roosevelt** and Harry S **Truman**. Although he swung the vote of organized labour behind Roosevelt in 1936, he reverted to his original Republicanism in 1940, and was a member of the isolationist **America First Committee**. ▷ **AFL–CIO**

Leyte Gulf, Battle of (1944)
A battle during **World War II**, when the Japanese fleet converged on the US 3rd and 7th Fleets protecting Allied landings on Leyte in the central Philippines. The Japanese suffered irreplaceable losses of 300 000 tonnes of combat ships, compared to US losses of 37 000 tonnes. The way was opened for further US gains in the Philippines and on islands nearer Japan.

Li Dazhao (Li Ta-chao) (1888–1927)
Chinese revolutionary. One of the founders of the Chinese Communist Party, whose interpretation of Marxism as applied to China had a profound influence on **Mao Zedong**. Appointed Head Librarian of Beijing University and Professor of History (1918), he had the young Mao as a library assistant, and founded one of the first of the communist study circles which in 1921 were to form the Communist Party. In 1927, when the Manchurian military leader, Zhang Zuolin (Chang Tso-lin), then occupying Beijing, raided the Soviet Embassy, Li was captured and executed.

Li Lisan (Li Li-san) (1900–67)
Chinese politician. Chinese Communist Party leader and effective head of the Party (1928–30), he enforced what has since become known as the 'Li Lisan line', in which the Party's weak and undeveloped military forces were used in futile attempts to capture cities. His authoritarian methods alienated his fellow leaders. He was demoted in 1930, and lived in the USSR until 1945. Thereafter, he was employed by the Chinese Communist Party in various minor roles.

Li Peng (1928–)
Chinese politician. He was the son of the radical communist writer, Li Shouxun, who was executed by the **Guomindang** in 1930. Adopted by **Zhou Enlai** on his mother's death (1939), he trained as a hydro-electric engineer and was appointed Minister of the Electric Power Industry in 1981. He became a vice-premier in 1983, was elevated to the Politburo in 1985 and made Prime Minister in 1987. As a cautious, orthodox

reformer, he sought to retain firm control of the economy and favoured improved relations with the USSR. In 1989 he took a strong line in facing down the student-led, pro-democracy movement, becoming in the process a popularly reviled figure.

Li Shizeng (Li Shih-tseng) (1881–1973)
Chinese anarchist, educator and prominent member of the **Guomindang**. From an influential official family, Li went to France in 1902 to study. While there he became attracted to anarchism and founded a journal, *Xin Shiji* ('New Century'). This not only called for the overthrow of the **Qing Dynasty** but also condemned Confucian social institutions, such as the family, for stifling the individual and entrenching sexual inequality. As an enthusiastic Francophile, Li organized a work-study programme for Chinese students in France (1919–21). He championed work-study as part of his vision to create a harmonious and cooperative society, in which class divisions would be dissolved through education and the integration of intellectual and manual labour. Ironically, many work-study students later became prominent members of the **Chinese Communist Party**. Li's hostility to **communism** and his close personal ties with **Sun Yat-sen** and **Chiang Kai-shek** drew him into the Guomindang and he became a member of the party's supervisory committee in 1924. In the 1950s he was a policy adviser to Chiang Kai-shek's regime in Taiwan.

Li Xian'nian (Li Hsien-nien) (1909–92)
Chinese politician. Born into a poor peasant family in Hubei province, he worked as a carpenter before serving with the **Guomindang** forces (1926–7). After joining the Chinese Communist Party (CCP) in 1927 he established the Oyuwan Soviet (People's Republic) in Hubei, participated in the **Long March** and was a military commander in the war against Japan and in the Chinese Civil War. He was inducted into the CCP Politburo and secretariat in 1956 and 1958, but fell out of favour during the **Cultural Revolution**. He was rehabilitated, as Finance Minister, by **Zhou Enlai** in 1973, and later served as state President in the 'administration' of **Deng Xiaoping** (1983–8).

Li Yuanhong (Li Yuan-hung) (1864–1928)
Chinese militarist. As the commander of the army division in central China whose mutiny (Oct 1911) against the **Qing Dynasty** signalled the collapse of the monarchy and creation of a republic, Li served briefly and reluctantly as the overall leader of the revolutionary army. He failed to curb the growing influence of the northern (Beiyang) militarists during his two terms as President of the Chinese Republic (1916–17 and 1922–3) and was a virtual figurehead.

Liang Qichao (Liang Ch'i-ch'ao) (1873–1929)
Chinese reformer and intellectual. He was a student and follower of Kang Youwei, with whom he served during the Hundred Days of Reform (1898). He escaped to Japan, thereafter devoting himself to journalism, through which he became the most influential political writer of his generation. Liang returned to China in 1912, and was influential in creating the Progressive Party, which supported **Yuan Shikai** in the hope of maintaining national unity. However, the violence and corruption prevalent under Yuan led him to despair of the possibility of democracy in China, and he retired from politics to study Buddhism.

Liao Zhongkai (Liao Chung-k'ai) (1878–1925)
Chinese politician. Born into an overseas Chinese family in the USA, he studied in Japan before becoming the **Guomindang**'s leading financial expert after 1912. Associated with its left wing, he supported the United Front with the communists in 1923, advocating a planned economy along socialist lines. In 1924 he played an important role in setting up both the workers and peasant departments under Guomindang auspices as part of its new strategy of mass mobilization. As the leading Guomindang representative at the Whampoa Military Academy, Liao also laid the basis for the political commissar system that was to be used throughout the National Revolutionary Army. He aroused opposition from right-wing members of the Guomindang who opposed the United Front, and who may have been involved in his assassination.

Liaquat Ali Khan (1895–1951)
Pakistani politician. After leaving Oxford he became a member of the Inner Temple. He joined the **Muslim League** in 1923, and became Prime Minister of Pakistan in 1947. He was assassinated in 1951.

Liberal Democratic Party (LDP; *Jiyu minshuto*)
The conservative party that has ruled continuously in Japan since its formation (Nov 1955). It was created by the merger of the two principal conservative parties established after 1945. The party gained the support of business groups because of its commitment to economic growth, the free enterprise system and traditional values, while its policy of subsidizing domestic rice production proved popular with the farmers. Until the late 1960s, the party won every Diet election with substantial margins (although never achieving the $\frac{2}{3}$ majority required for any revision of the 1947 **Peace Constitution** which some LDP members desired). From the 1970s, however, its popularity dipped and its share of the popular vote has never exceeded 50 per cent. The fragmentation of the opposition, though, has ensured the LDP's position as the majority party. In reality, the LDP is a collection of various factions whose leaders rotate as LDP President (and hence Prime Minister since the LDP is the permanent

governing party) on renewable two-year terms. The interests of the factions have to be catered for in the allocation of cabinet posts and decision-making is often a long drawn-out process because of the need to ensure consensus. Recent bribery scandals and the growing importance of money politics, whereby factions expend huge sums of money to get their candidates elected, have tarnished the LDP's reputation and in 1989 the party lost its majority in the Upper House.

Liberal Party (Australia)

Australia's largest conservative party, formed by R G **Menzies** in 1944–5 from existing conservative groups. It built up a mass following in the late 1940s, and was victorious in 1949. It governed from 1949 to 1972 and again from 1975 to 1983, sometimes in coalition with the Country/National Party. As the major anti-Labor grouping in Australian politics, the party is the descendant of **Deakin**'s Liberal Party in the early years of **federation**, W M **Hughes**'s Nationalist Party (1917) and the United Australia Party (1931). Organized through branches in federal and state electorates, the party stands for individual liberty, private enterprise and economic competition, law and order, the family, and state rights. Out of office since 1983, the party lost its fourth successive general election in 1990. ▷ **National Party of Australia**

Liberal Party (Canada)

This party's origins lie in the early 1840s and 1850s. After initial lack of cohesion, it came to power in 1873 under Alexander Mackenzie, but lost the 1878 election. Sir Wilfrid **Laurier** led the party to success in 1896, but it was severely damaged by the defection of Clifford **Sifton** and Henri **Bourassa**, and joined the union government of R L **Borden** to bring in conscription during **World War I**. After Laurier's death, W L Mackenzie **King** led the party back into office in 1921, and kept it in power until 1930, and from 1935 until his retirement in 1948. His successor, Louis **Saint Laurent**, was unable to maintain this unity and the party was defeated in 1957. Lester **Pearson** led the party back into minority government in 1963, but it was not until Pierre **Trudeau** took the leadership that the party was successful in re-establishing itself nationally.

Liberal Party (Sweden)

Formed in 1900 to fight for parliamentary government and an extension of the franchise, it is the oldest of Sweden's modern political parties. It formed an administration for the first time in 1905 under Karl Staaff. Divided in 1924 over the question of prohibition, it was reunited in 1934. Under its leader Ola Ullsten, it participated in the non-socialist government formed in 1976 and, when this collapsed in 1978, Ullsten was briefly Prime Minister at the head of a minority administration.

Liberal Party (UK)
One of the two major political parties in the UK in the 19c and early 20c. It developed from the aristocratic Whig Party in the middle years of the 19c when, especially under Gladstone's leadership, it appealed to the rapidly growing urban middle classes, to skilled working men and to religious nonconformists. Many of its landowning supporters and also radical imperialists were alienated by Gladstone's Irish **Home Rule** policy from the mid-1880s. Based on values of economic freedom and, from the late 19c, social justice, the last Liberal government enacted in the decade before **World War I** many important social reforms which anticipated the Welfare State. Internal splits and the challenge of a reorganized **Labour Party** weakened it from 1918 onwards and by the end of the 1920s the Liberals were clearly a minority third party on the centre-left of British politics, a position they have not been able to escape despite revivals in the 1970s and alliance with the **Social Democratic Party** in the 1980s. The party became known as the Liberal Democrats after the decision to merge with the Social Democrats in 1987. ▷ **Conservative Party** (UK); **Tories**

liberation theology
A style of theology originating in Latin America in the 1960s, and later becoming popular in many developing countries. Accepting a Marxist analysis of society, it stresses the role and mission of the Church to the poor and oppressed in society, of which Christ is understood as liberator. Its sympathy for revolutionary movements led to clashes with established secular and religious authorities.

Liberman, Yevsesi Grigorevich (1897–1983)
Soviet economist. Born and educated in Kharkov, he spent all his working life practising there as an academic economist. In 1962 he published an article in *Pravda* entitled 'Plan, Profit, Bonuses', which in a mild way advocated something of a market mechanism. Though far short of Mikhail **Gorbachev**'s ideas, this was the basis for the reforms introduced by **Kosygin** in 1965 but undermined by the **Brezhnev** hardliners after the **Prague Spring** in 1968.

'Liberty, Equality, Fraternity'
The motto of the French Republic; adopted in June 1793, it remained the official slogan of the state until the Bourbon Restoration (1814). It was re-adopted during the Second Republic (1848–51), and has remained the national slogan from 1875 to the present day, except during the German Occupation (1940–4). ▷ **French Revolution**

Libya

A north African state which was under Turkish rule from the 16c until the Italians gained control in 1911. It was named Libya by the Italians in 1934. It witnessed heavy fighting during World War II, followed by British and French control, until in 1951 it became the independent Kingdom of Libya. A military coup established a republic under Muammar **Gaddafi** in 1969 and the country was governed by a Revolutionary Command Council. Foreign military installations were closed down in the early 1970s. Government policy since the revolution has been based on the promotion of Arab unity and the furtherance of Islam. Relations with other countries have been strained by controversial activities, including the alleged organization of international terrorism. Diplomatic relations were severed by the UK after a policewoman was killed by a shot fired from the Libyan People's Bureau at protesters in St James's Square, London, in 1984. Tripoli and Benghazi were bombed by the US Air Force in response to alleged terrorist activity in 1986. Two Libyan fighter planes were shot down by aircraft operating with the US Navy off the North African coast in 1989. Sanctions were imposed against Libya in 1992 following its refusal to extradite two Lockerbie bomb suspects for trial.

Lidice, Destruction of (1942)

A Nazi-German act of savage revenge on innocent Czech villagers. In late May resistance fighters fatally wounded Reinhard **Heydrich**, the **Gestapo** officer who was in charge of the **Bohemian Protectorate**. Heydrich had a nasty reputation, but that was quickly overshadowed by actions to avenge his death. The worst of these was in June when, as an example, the village of Lidice was destroyed, its almost 200 males shot, its 200 females sent off to Ravensbruck **concentration camp**, and its 100 children dispersed, many to their deaths. However, the tragedy was to stiffen the Czech resistance and convince the Allies of the need to expel the Germans from Czechoslovakia after the war.

Lie, Trygve Haldvan (1896–1968)

Norwegian lawyer. After becoming an MP, he was appointed Minister of Justice and of Shipping before fleeing to Britain with other members of the Norwegian Government in 1940, where he acted as Foreign Minister until the end of **World War II**. In 1946 he was elected **UN** Secretary-General, but resigned in 1952. He served as Minister for Industry (1963–4) and for Commerce and Shipping until his death.

Liebknecht, Karl (1871–1919)

German barrister and politician. The son of Wilhelm **Liebknecht**, he was a member of the **Reichstag** (1912–16). During **World War I** he was imprisoned as an independent, anti-militarist, social democrat. He was a founder member with Rosa **Luxemburg** of the German Communist Party (**KPD**) in 1918–19 and led an unsuccessful revolt in Berlin, the 'Spartacus Rising', in Jan 1919, during which he and Rosa Luxemburg were killed by army officers. ▷ **Spartacists**

Ligachev, Yegor Kuzmich (1920–)
Soviet politician. After graduating as an engineer in 1943, he worked in the Urals region before joining the Communist Party in 1944. From then until 1961 he worked in his native Novosibirsk as an official first of **Komsomol** and then of the local Party. As Party Chief of the new 'science city' of Akademgorodok, he gained a reputation as an austere opponent of corruption. He was brought to Moscow by Nikita **Khrushchev** in 1961 but, after the latter was ousted in 1964, he was sent to Tomsk, where he was regional party boss for 18 years. However, he became a full member of the Central Committee in 1976, and in 1983 he was promoted to the Secretariat by Yuri **Andropov**, becoming Ideology Secretary in 1984. With the accession to power of Mikhail **Gorbachev** in 1985, he was brought into the **Politburo**. He initially served as Gorbachev's deputy, but they became estranged over the issue of reform and, in 1988, he was demoted to the position of Agriculture Secretary. As Gorbachev became more radical, he became more conservative, and in 1990 he was expelled from the Central Committee as well as the Politburo. He remained an anti-reform critic even after the USSR collapsed.

Likud
The coalition of right-wing political parties in Israel, named *Likud Liberalim Leumi* in full ('National Union of Liberals'). Formed in 1973 in opposition to the Israel Labour Party, it governed Israel from 1977 to 1990 under Menachem **Begin** and Yitzhak **Shamir**. The coalition was composed mainly of the Herut Party and Liberal Party. The former was constructed in 1948 out of the **Irgun** and **Haganah**, while the latter was created in 1961. To maintain a working majority, Likud has sometimes negotiated the support of small parties, which have been influential beyond their size as a result. ▷ **Mapai Party**

Limann, Hilla (1934–)
Ghanaian diplomat and politician. He was educated in Ghana and then at the LSE and the Sorbonne, where he earned a doctorate. He was a teacher before joining the Ghanaian diplomatic service as Head of Chancery at Lome (1968–71). Limann then served his country at many international gatherings while being his country's counsellor at its permanent mission to the **UN** in Geneva (1971–5) and senior officer Ministry of Foreign Affairs (1975–9). In 1979 he was chosen to lead the People's National Party and was its successful presidential candidate in the 1979

elections, becoming President until his removal from office (31 Dec 1981) as a result of a military coup led by Flt-Lt Jerry **Rawlings**.

Lin Biao (Lin Piao) (1907–71)
Chinese military leader. He was one of the leaders of the Chinese Communist Party and a Marshal of the Red Army. Lin became Minister of Defence in 1959, and in 1968 replaced the disgraced **Liu Shaoqi** as heir-apparent to **Mao Zedong**. He was one of the promoters of the **Cultural Revolution**, and appears to have been a patron of extreme left-wing factions. In 1971, after a political struggle, he was killed in a plane crash in Mongolia, apparently in the course of an attempt to seek refuge in the USSR.

Lindbergh, Charles Augustus (1902–74)
US aeronaut. His 1927 flight from New York to Paris, taking $33\frac{1}{2}$ hours in his monoplane, *Spirit of St Louis*, won him a prize of US$25 000 for the first solo transatlantic flight and instant fame. To this was added national sympathy when his son was abducted and murdered in 1932. In 1940 he became a member of the isolationist America First Committee, and his popularity was seriously damaged in 1941 because of his suggestion to negotiate a settlement with **Hitler**'s Germany.

Linlithgow, Victor Alexander John Hope, 2nd Marquess of (1887–1952)
British politician. He served during **World War I** on the Western Front. He was Chairman of the Royal Commission on Agriculture in India (1926–8) and was also a member of the Select Committee on Indian Constitutional Reform. In 1936 he became Viceroy of India, in succession to Lord Willingdon, and held the post until 1943, thus becoming the longest holder of that office. In 1939, he declared war against Germany before consulting the Indian political parties; the Congress Party was offended by this step, and provincial Congress ministries resigned in protest. Although he suppressed opposition to British rule in India during **World War II**, under him provincial autonomy functioned smoothly. He was responsible for jailing the Congress leaders of the **Quit India Movement** in 1942–3.

Lister, Enrique (1907–)
Spanish Communist leader and general. During the **Spanish Civil War** he became commander of the Republic's famous Fifth Regiment. Exiled in the USSR, he fought with the Soviet army in **World War II**, reaching the rank of general. A member of the Spanish Politburo from 1946, he was expelled in 1970. In 1973 he founded the stalinist Spanish Workers' Communist Party (PCOE), and returned to Spain in 1977, where his party made little impact.

Listone

The Italian word (literally, 'big list') used to describe the fascist-approved candidates put forward by **Mussolini** when contesting the Apr 1924 Italian elections. It included not only members of the **Fascist Party** but also nationalists, right-wing liberals (including **Orlando**, **Salandra** and De Nicola) and even a few **Popolari**. Indeed, of the 374 victorious candidates on the *Listone* under two-thirds were genuine fascists. The Listone was remarkably successful, bringing Mussolini a comfortable parliamentary majority.

Lithuania

A republic in north-east Europe, where intensive Russification led to revolts in 1905 and 1917. It was occupied by Germany in both World Wars. Proclaimed a republic in 1918, it was annexed by the USSR in 1940. The growth of a nationalist movement in the 1980s led to its declaration of independence in 1990.

Little Entente

A system of alliances between Czechoslovakia and Yugoslavia (1920), Czechoslovakia and Romania (1921), and Yugoslavia and Romania (1921), consolidated into a single treaty signed in Belgrade in 1929. The alliances aimed to maintain post-1919 boundaries in central Europe, and prevent a Habsburg restoration.

Litvinov, Maxim Maximovich (1876–1951)

Soviet revolutionary and diplomat. He was an early critic of Tsarist rule and joined the Social Democratic Party in 1898. He was soon exiled abroad and joined the Bolshevik faction after 1903. Having lived in Britain for over a decade, he was appointed Bolshevik Ambassador in London (1917–18), and held various roving commissions before becoming Deputy Commissar (1921), then Commissar (1930) for Foreign Affairs. Until **Stalin** dismissed him in the spring of 1939, he was the chief architect of improved relations between the USSR and the West in the face of **Hitler**. He did not return to favour until after Hitler's attack in 1941, when he became Ambassador to the USA (1941), and Vice-Minister of Foreign Affairs (1942–6). A strong advocate of co-operation between the USSR and the West even at the onset of the **Cold War**, he died in Moscow. ▷ **Bolsheviks; Litvinov Protocol**

Litvinov Protocol (1929)

The term used to describe Soviet attempts to improve security by working with Western proposals. Maxim **Litvinov**, Soviet Deputy Foreign Commissar, had been attempting to normalize relations with neighbouring states and to secure guarantees against Germany. When the US Secretary of State, Frank B Kellogg, proposed the renunciation of war as the core of a new international treaty (**Kellogg–Briand Pact**), Litvinov managed to persuade the USSR's Western neighbours to adhere to his protocol, also renouncing war, as a kind of Eastern alliance against Germany.

Liu Shaoqi (Liu Shao-ch'i) (1898–1969)
Chinese politician. A leading figure in the Chinese communist revolution, he was educated in the USSR, returned to China in 1922 and became a communist trade-union organizer. In 1939 he joined **Mao Zedong** at Yan'an, where he emerged as the chief party theorist on questions of organization. In 1943 he became Party Secretary, and succeeded Mao in 1959. After the **Cultural Revolution**, the extreme left made Liu their principal target, and in 1968 he was stripped of all his posts and dismissed from the party. ▷ **Great Leap Forward**

Ljotić, Dimitrije (1891–1945)
Serbian lawyer. He held a few minor offices under King **Alexander I** then, during **World War II**, working for the collaborationist government of General Milan **Nedić**, he led the Serbian fascist movement, Zbor, and its youth movement, the White Eagle. Serb-nationalist in ideology, Zbor aspired to the creation of a corporate regime on the model of **Mussolini**'s Italy. Ljotić was killed while trying to escape from Yugoslavia at the end of the war.

Lliga
Catalan regionalist party. Originally founded in 1901 as the *Lliga Regionalista*, it became the principal representative of the Catalan bourgeoisie. It was instrumental in the creation of the Mancomunitat, a limited form of autonomous government, in 1913. However, the *Lliga*'s principal aim was to establish the Catalan bourgeoisie as the ruling class within Spain. The general strike of 1917 led the Lliga to withdraw into an alliance with the central government, thereby gravely undermining the opposition to the monarchy. The party split in 1922. Rebuilt by Francesc **Cambó** under the Second Republic as the *Lliga Catalana*, it was overshadowed throughout the regime by the *Esquerra* (Catalan Left). ▷ **Republic, Second** (Spain)

Lloyd-George (of Dwyfor), David, 1st Earl (1863–1945)
British politician. Born of Welsh parentage, he became a solicitor, and in 1890, as a strong supporter of **Home Rule**, a Liberal MP for Caernarvon Boroughs (a seat he was to hold for 55 years). He was President of the Board of Trade (1905–8), and Chancellor of the Exchequer (1905–15). His 'people's budget' of 1909–10 was rejected by the House of Lords, and led to a constitutional crisis and the Parliament Act of 1911, which removed the Lords' power of veto. He became Minister of Munitions (1915), Secretary for War (1916), and superseded **Asquith** as coalition

Prime Minister (1916–22), carrying on a forceful war policy. After **World War I**, he continued as head of a coalition government dominated by Conservatives. He negotiated with **Sinn Féin**, and conceded the **Irish Free State** (1921) — a measure which precipitated his downfall. His energies could not sufficiently revive the fortunes of a divided **Liberal Party** and, following the 1931 general election, he led a 'family' group of Independent Liberal MPs. He was made an earl in 1945. ▷ **Boer Wars; New Deal**

LNC (*Lufta Nacional Çlirimtare*, 'National Liberation War')

Dominated from its inception by the communists, this Albanian movement also included members from other political parties. Closely supervised by the Yugoslav resistance, it was forced by **Tito** to abandon any hope of acquiring **Kosovo**, and reached an agreement with the other Albanian resistance group, **Balli Kombëtar**. In May 1944, following the Yugoslav example of **AVNOJ**, the LNC met at Permët and founded an Anti-Fascist Council of National Liberation with Enver **Hoxha** as leader. When the regime in Tirana collapsed, following the withdrawal of German forces (Nov 1944), the LNC quickly established its authority, trying and executing members of the former government and eliminating all opposition to the establishment of a communist regime. Renamed the Democratic Front, in Dec 1945 it alone fielded candidates in the elections and in Jan 1946 it declared Albania a people's republic.

Locarno Pact (Oct 1925)

The international agreement, held at Locarno, Italy, guaranteeing the post-1919 frontiers between France, Belgium and Germany, and the demilitarization of the Rhineland. The treaty was guaranteed by Italy and Britain as well as signed by the three states directly concerned, France, Germany and Belgium. At the same time, Germany agreed to arbitration conventions with France, Belgium, Poland and Czechoslovakia, and France signed treaties of mutual guarantee with Poland and Czechoslovakia.

Lockheed Scandal

A political scandal in Japan that revealed the close links between the **Liberal Democratic Party** (LDP) and business interests. It broke in 1976, when Kakuei **Tanaka** (who had resigned as Prime Minister in 1974 amidst allegations of shady financial dealings) was named during US Senate hearings into the bribery of foreign officials by US multinationals. The American Lockheed Aircraft Corporation was alleged to have paid Tanaka, as Prime Minister, 500 million yen to ensure the purchase of its planes by a Japanese civil airline. Subsequent investigations in Japan highlighted the extent of bribes and kickbacks involved, and several businessmen and politicians, including Tanaka, were prosecuted. In 1983 Tanaka was sentenced to four years in prison but was released on bail pending appeal; the case has dragged on since then. Significantly, however, Tanaka remained a Diet member and his faction continued to be influential within the LDP during the 1980s.

Lok Dal

The Lok Dal, an agrarian-based political party, started as the Bharatiya Lok Dal (BLD) in 1969 under the leadership of Charan **Singh**. Its supporters belonged mainly to the so-called backward or middle-status peasant castes. The BLD merged into the Janata Party towards the end of the **Emergency**. The Janata government collapsed in 1979 when the BLD reemerged as the **Lok Dal**, ruling India briefly with Charan Singh as Prime Minister. Upon Charan Singh's death in 1987, the party split into two and his son, Ajit Singh, presided over one faction. The two factions merged into the Janata Dal, which ruled briefly from 1989, but soon parted company in 1990 when the Janata Dal government fell.

Lomé Convention

A series of agreements, named after the capital of Togo where the first Convention was signed, between the European Communities and a number of developing nations in Africa, the Caribbean and the Pacific (ACP). It came into force on 1 Apr 1976 and was intended to provide preferential trading arrangements for the ACP countries within the Common Market. The fourth agreement, intended to last 10 years, began in Mar 1990.

London, Treaties of (1913 and 1915)

By the 1913 treaty at the end of the **Balkan Wars**, Ottoman possessions in Europe were reduced to the area around Constantinople, while Crete was ceded to Greece and Bulgaria gained Adrianople. The 1915 treaty secured Italian entry into **World War I** on the side of the Allies and promised the Italians the South Tyrol, Trentino, Gorizia, Gradisca, **Trieste**, **Istria**, part of **Dalmatia**, Saseno and Vlorë in Albania, as well as continued possession of the **Dodecanese** Islands and a share in the Turkish and German colonies.

Long, Huey Pierce (1893–1935)

US politician. Flamboyant, astute and ambitious, he used the grievances of poor whites and his record as Public Service Commissioner to win the governorship of Louisiana, and then (1928–31) proceeded to build one of the most effective political machines in the history of US politics. His programme of extensive public spending on roads, educational institutions and hospitals not only reformed and developed Louisiana's public services, but also mitigated the impact of the Depression upon the state. Although a ruthless manipulator of the state legislature and judiciary, Long refused to use race as a political issue. Aiming at a national audience, he developed the 'Share Our Wealth' plan for income redistribution.

A Democratic US Senator from 1931, by 1935 he claimed to have a following of 7.5 million for the plan. Initially supportive of the **New Deal** and President Franklin D **Roosevelt**, he became a vehement critic of the president and planned to run against him as a third-party candidate in 1936. However, he was widely feared and reviled as a potential dictator, and was assassinated in Sep 1935.

Long March (1934–5)
The long trek in China, covering over 5 000 miles, made by approximately 100 000 communists under **Mao Zedong** to reach their base in Shaanxi from the **Jiangxi Soviet**, which had been encircled by nationalist government troops.

Lopes, Francisco Higino Craveiro (1894–1964)
Portuguese politician. Born into a distinguished military family, Lopes was educated at the Military School in Lisbon and fought in the expeditionary force in Mozambique in **World War I**. As a full colonel, in 1942 he entered negotiations for cooperation with the Allies and was responsible for the modernization of the Portuguese air force. In 1944 he entered parliament, in 1949 was promoted to general, and was President of Portugal from 1951 to 1958.

Lopéz Rodó, Laureano (1920–)
Spanish politician, academic and lawyer. He was the most influential **Opus Dei** technocrat to serve in a **Franco** government. As Secretary-General of the Presidency and Commissar of the Plan of Development, he formed part of the Opus Dei group which undertook the economic modernization of Spain from the late 1950s onwards. An intimate ally of Admiral **Carrero Blanco**, he became one of Franco's closest associates, being the dominant minister in the cabinet from 1965 to 1973. He was also Minister of Foreign Affairs (1973–4) and Ambassador to Austria (1974–7). He played an important role in persuading Franco to accept the candidacy of **Juan Carlos I** as heir to the throne. After Franco's death, he joined the *Alianza Popular* on its foundation in 1976, being elected as a deputy for Barcelona in 1977. He left the party in 1979.

Lords, House of
The non-elected house of the UK legislature. Its membership, currently c.1 200, includes hereditary peers and life peers (including judicial members — the *Lords of Appeal in Ordinary*); also the two archbishops and certain bishops of the Church of England. The House can no longer veto, though it can delay, bills passed by the House of Commons, with the exception of a bill to prolong the duration of a parliament. Its functions are mainly deliberative, its authority based on the expertise of its mem-

bership. The House of Lords also constitutes the most senior court in the UK. Appeals heard by the House are confined to matters of law.

LTTE (Liberation Tigers of Tamil Eelam)
Also known simply as the 'Tigers', the Sri Lankan secessionist group which has been fighting to establish a separate Tamil state (Eelam) in the north and east of the country. The group was founded in Jaffna in the mid-1970s and gradually grew in size and effectiveness, particularly after the anti-Tamil violence of the early 1980s. A reluctant partner to the **Indo-Sri Lankan Peace Accord** overseen by Rajiv **Gandhi**, it soon found itself fighting the Indian Peacekeeping Force (IPKF) and it was widely believed to have been responsible for Gandhi's assassination in Tamil Nadu in 1991.

Lubbers, Rudolf Franz Marie (1939–)
Dutch politician. After graduating from Erasmus University, Rotterdam, he joined the family engineering business of Lubbers Hollandia. He made rapid progress after entering politics, becoming Minister of Economic Affairs in 1973 and, in 1982, at the age of 43, Prime Minister, leading a **Christian Democratic Appeal** (CDA) coalition.

Ludendorff, Erich von (1865–1937)
German general. He and **Hindenburg** defeated the Russians at the Battle of Tannenberg (1914). In 1916 he became Chief of Staff under Hindenburg and conducted the 1918 spring offensives on the Western Front. In 1923 he was a leader in the unsuccessful **Hitler** putsch at Munich, but was acquitted of treason. He became involved with the **Nazi Party**, but from 1925 led a minority party of his own. ▷ **World War I**

Luftwaffe
The correct name for the German Air Force, re-established in 1935 under **Goering**, in contravention of the Treaty of **Versailles**. Dominant in the early years of German victory in **World War II**, the *Luftwaffe* suffered production shortfalls and poor central leadership which led to defeat in the Battle of Britain. It had all but ceased to exist by 1945, having lost some 100 000 aircraft. The Federal Republic of Germany's air force, also known as the *Luftwaffe*, was re-established in 1956, and today is a critical element in **NATO**, operating over 600 combat aircraft. ▷ **Britain, Battle of**

Lugard, Frederick John Dealtry, Baron Lugard (1858–1945)
British soldier and colonial administrator. Appointed Commissioner in the Nigerian hinterland by Joseph **Chamberlain** (1897), he kept a French challenge at bay and kept the peace. Britain having declared a protectorate over Northern and Southern Nigeria, Lugard was high com-

missioner for the North (1900–7), and established administrative paternalistic control with minimal force. He was Governor of Hong Kong from 1907, helping to establish its University in 1911. He returned to Nigeria as Governor of the two protectorates, becoming Governor-General (1914–19) on their amalgamation. His principle was one of use of existing tribal institutions as the infrastructure for British rule.

Lukács, György (1885–1971)
Hungarian Marxist philosopher, critic and politician. From a wealthy Jewish family, he studied in Budapest, Berlin and Heidelberg. He published two important early works on literary criticism, *Soul and Form* (1910) and *The Theory of the Novel* (1916). In 1918 he joined the Hungarian Communist Party, but after the defeat of the uprising in 1919 he lived abroad in Vienna (1919–29) and Moscow (1930–44). He returned to Hungary after **World War II** as Professor at Budapest; he came in for political criticism in the early 1950s and, more or less inevitably, joined **Nagy**'s short-lived revolutionary government in 1956 as Minister of Culture. After the Russian suppression he was briefly deported and interned but returned to Budapest in 1957. His major book on Marxism, *History and Class Consciousness* (1923), was repudiated as heretical by the Russian Communist Party and in the 1950s, in abject public confession, by Lukács himself. His situation and influence grew in the 1960s as his works were published.

Lukyanov, Anatoli Ivanovich (1930–)
Soviet lawyer, bureaucrat and political conspirator. Born in Smolensk and educated in Moscow, he held a series of legal positions within the Soviet and the party. A moderate reformer, he began to rise very quickly first with Yuri **Andropov** and then with Mikhail **Gorbachev**. In 1989 he was elected deputy chairman under Gorbachev's chairmanship of the new Supreme Soviet, and in 1990, when Gorbachev was elevated to the presidency, then Luykanov in turn became chairman. In 1991 it was to save his vision of the USSR that he participated in the **August Coup** to oust Gorbachev; but he achieved quite the opposite of what he wanted and landed in prison.

Lula (Luis Inácio Lula da Silva) (1944–)
Brazilian labour leader. He came to national prominence as leader of the Metalworker's Union of São Bernardo, a São Paulo industrial zone housing key industries, especially in motor vehicles. Forced by the military regime's labour legislation to concentrate on local issues, Lula led strikes in the Saab-Scania plant in May 1978 and 1979 involving 500 000 workers and making the employers concede higher wages through direct negotiations rather than via government-led labour courts. In Oct 1979 he founded the PT (*Partido dos Trabalhadores*), to achieve representation

for workers in Congress; it has drawn support from a range of traditional radical movements and the left wing of the Church. Elected to Congress in 1986, he narrowly defeated Leonel **Brizola** as the candidate for the Left against Fernando **Collor de Mello** in the 1989 presidential race.

Lumumba, Patrice (Hemery) (1925–61)
Congolese (Zairois) politician. Educated at mission schools, both Catholic and Protestant, he was a post office clerk and then director of a brewery. He helped form the *Mouvement National Congolais* in 1958 to challenge Belgian rule and, when the Congo was granted independence, he was made its first Prime Minister (1960). A major symbolic figure in the African history of the period, he sought a unified Congo and opposed the secession of Katanga under Moise **Tshombe**. He was arrested by his own army in Sep 1960, handed over to the Katangese and murdered. His name, however, remains significant as the embodiment of African nationalism and the opponent of balkanization manipulated by ex-colonial countries and their allies.

Lunacharsky, Anatoli Vasilevich (1875–1933)
Russian philosopher and revolutionary. As a student and writer he dabbled in Marxism. He was imprisoned several times for his political activities and spent much time associating with émigrés in Western Europe. In 1917 he offered his services to **Lenin** who made him in effect the Minister of Education, a function he performed none too well down to 1929 when he took up a somewhat similar party port. He died on his way to becoming ambassador to Spain, a cultural adornment who was perhaps fortunate not to have to face the purges of the 1930s.

Luns, Joseph Marie Antoine Hubert (1911–)
Dutch politician. After studying law, he joined the Dutch diplomatic service (1940–52). In 1952 he became Minister without Portfolio for the Dutch **Catholic People's Party**, and from then on was inextricably bound up with Dutch foreign affairs. For the whole of the period 1957–71 he was Foreign Minister, and from 1971 to 1984 he was Secretary-General of **NATO**. He was integrally involved in the formation and consolidation of the European Communities, and was a central figure in international relations during the days of the **Cold War**.

Lupescu, Magda (1902–)
Mistress and second wife of King **Charles II** of Romania. Her Jewish descent as much as her dissolute behaviour earned her the disapproval of Romanian society, itself notorious for its profligacy. Because of the scandal surrounding their affair, Charles renounced his claim to the throne and when he returned to Romania in 1930 it was on condition that she remained abroad. When she also returned and took up residence

in the palace, the Prime Minister, Iuliu **Maniu**, resigned. Upon her marriage in 1947 to Charles, she took the name Princess Elena and lived in exile with the former king.

Lusitania, Sinking of the (May 1915)
A Cunard passenger liner torpedoed by a German submarine off the Irish Coast while in transit from New York to Liverpool, with 128 Americans among those lost. The German government had announced (Feb 1915) that any passenger ship caught within a designated war zone around the British Isles would be sunk without warning. President Woodrow **Wilson** declared he would hold Germany accountable for such deaths in the future. Although the German authorities argued that the *Lusitania* was carrying war munitions for the Allies, they did eventually make **reparations**. However, any US sympathy toward Germany up to this point disappeared, and many called for a declaration of war.

Luther, Hans (1879–1962)
German politician. After an early career in local government, Luther entered national government in 1922. He served in various cabinets and, as Finance Minister, succeeded in re-establishing a stable German currency (the *Rentenmark*) after the Great Inflation of 1923. He became Chancellor in Jan 1925 at the head of the centre-right coalition which concluded the Treaty of Locarno with the Allies. He resigned in 1926, but served as President of the National Bank between 1930 and Mar 1933 and then as Ambassador to Washington until 1937. He held various public and academic offices in the Federal Republic and published a number of books. ▷ **Locarno Pact**

Luthuli, Albert (John Mvumbi) (1898–1967)
South African nationalist. He qualified as a teacher and taught for 15 years before succeeding to the chieftainship of Groutville, the community in Natal in which he had been raised, in 1935. He joined the **ANC** (African National Congress) in 1946, became President of the Natal branch and led a campaign of passive resistance against **apartheid**, for which he was deposed from his chieftainship by the South African government. He became President of the ANC in 1952, reflecting the 'colour-blind' traditions of the party, but was repeatedly 'banned', and was imprisoned (1956–7). He was awarded the Nobel Peace Prize in 1960.

Luwum, Janani (1922–77)
Ugandan bishop. The son of a Christian, he became a teacher and was converted in 1948. He was ordained into the Anglican Church and, despite his evangelicanism which disturbed more conventional Christians in Uganda, he became a theological college principal, Bishop of Northern Uganda and was then elected Archbishop of Uganda in 1974. He spoke

out fearlessly against the atrocities committed during Idi **Amin**'s period of rule, as a result of which he was murdered. So concerned was the Amin government that a memorial service for him was forbidden.

Luxembourg

An independent constitutional monarchy in north-west Europe which was recognized as a neutral independent state in 1867. Occupied by Germany in both World Wars, it joined the Benelux economic union in 1948, and abandoned neutrality on joining NATO in 1949.

Luxemburg, Rosa (1871–1919)

German social democrat. She emigrated to Zurich in 1889, where she studied law and political economy, and subsequently became a German citizen in 1895. A radical, she and the German politician, Karl **Liebknecht**, formed the Spartacus League (1916), which later became the German Communist Party (**KPD**, 1919). She was arrested and murdered during the 'Spartacus Rising' in Berlin. ▷ **Marxism; Spartacists**

Lynch, Jack (John) (1917–)

Irish politician. Following a career in the Department of Justice (1936), he was called to the Bar (1945). Elected an MP in 1948, he held ministerial posts in Lands (1951), the Gaeltacht (1957), Education (1957–9), Industry and Commerce (1959–65) and Finance (1965–6), before becoming Prime Minister (1966–73 and 1977–9). Perceived as a strong supporter of the Catholic minority in Ulster, he drew criticism from both Ulster and mainland Britain. In 1979 he resigned both as Prime Minister and from the leadership of **Fianna Fáil**. He retired from politics in 1981. ▷ **Haughey, Charles**

Lyons, Joseph Aloysius (1879–1939)

Australian politician. He became a teacher, entering politics in 1909 as Labor member in the Tasmanian House of Assembly. He held the posts of Treasurer, Minister of Education and Railways (1914–16), and was Premier (1923–8). Then in the federal parliament (1929–39), he was in turn Postmaster-General and acting Treasurer. Lyons favoured balanced budgets and reduced public expenditure to meet the Depression and when these were rejected, left the **Australian Labor Party** to found the **United Australia Party**; he became Prime Minister (1932/9) after the election of Dec 1931.

Lysenko, Trofim Denisovich (1898–1976)

Soviet agronomist. He first became famous in 1929 for 'vernalization', making possible the spring sowing of winter wheat, a technique of beating nature which appealed to **Stalin** and, later, Nikita **Khrushchev**. He began to produce attractive theories to transform agricultural production, he discredited genetics and had geneticists imprisoned or shot, and he dominated the scene as President of the Soviet Academy of Agricultural Sciences (1938–56 and 1961–2). Although an investigation in 1965 proved his innovations useless, he continued to exert some influence until his death.

M

M'ba, Leon (1902–67)
Gabon politician. Educated in Catholic schools, he was in turn accountant, journalist and administrator. He was elected for the **Rassemblement Democratique Africaine** to the Gabon Assembly in 1952 and, in the French tradition, used the mayoral position (of Libreville) to enhance his political ambitions. He was Head of Government (1957–60) and President from Gabon's independence until his death in 1967.

Macao, Portuguese Settlement of
The settlement in the Pearl River Delta on the southern coast of China acquired by Portugal in 1557. Until the 19c, Macao was a flourishing trade centre, but the silting of its harbour and increasing competition from Hong Kong led to its decline. With the overthrow of the **Salazar** dictatorship in Portugal in 1975 and the new government's commitment to decolonization, China exercised more influence in the colony. In 1987 it was agreed that Macao be formally returned to Chinese control in 1999 under the same arrangements applying to the British return of Hong Kong to China in 1997 (ie that the capitalist system should remain in place).

MacArthur, Douglas (1880–1964)
US general. Educated at the US Military Academy at West Point, he joined the US army, and in **World War I** served with distinction in France. In 1941 he became commanding general of the US armed forces in the Far East, and, after losing the Philippines, from Australia directed the recapture of the south-west Pacific (1942–5). He formally accepted the Japanese surrender, and commanded the occupation of Japan (1945–51). In 1950 he led the UN forces in the **Korean War**, defeating the North Korean Army, but was relieved of command when he tried to continue the war against China.

MacDonald, (James) Ramsay (1866–1937)
British politician. He had little formal education, worked as a clerk, then joined the **Independent Labour Party** in 1894, eventually becoming its leader (1911–14 and 1922–31). He became an MP in 1906, and was Prime Minister and Foreign Secretary of the first British Labour government (1924). Prime Minister again (1929–31 and 1931–5), he met the financial crisis of 1931 by forming a largely Conservative 'National' government,

most of his party opposing, and reconstructed it the same year after a general election. Defeated by Shinwell in the 1935 general election, he returned to parliament in 1936, and became Lord President. He died on his way to South America. ▷ **Labour Party** (UK)

Macedonia

A region in north Greece. It forms part of the ancient country of Macedonia which was divided between Serbia, Bulgaria and Greece after the Balkan Wars of 1912–13.

Macedonia, in full **Former Yugoslav Republic of Macedonia**

A republic in southern Europe. It was incorporated into Serbia after the Balkan Wars. Independence was declared in 1991 and in 1992–3 **UN** and US peacekeeping forces arrived to maintain borders and prevent the conflict in Bosnia spreading to Macedonia.

Macedonians

The nation inhabiting the area of ancient Macedonia and speaking a Slav language closer to Bulgarian than Serbo-Croat. Through the centuries many tribes and nations have settled in Macedonia and its ethnic composition is accordingly complex; the French *macédoine* is a synonym for 'medley' or 'mixture'. At the end of the 19c, a Macedonian nationalist movement emerged, its members insisting that the Macedonians were neither Bulgars nor Serbs, but a distinct Slav nation with its own language; this was a claim which the neighbouring Serbs, Bulgars and **Greeks**, nations all bent on territorial expansion, were determined to discount. ▷ **Ilinden Uprising; South Slavs; VMRO**

Maček, Vladko (1879–1964)

Croatian politician. A doctor of law, he served in the Austrian Army during **World War I**. As a member of the Croatian Peasant Party, he was imprisoned in 1924 with its leader, Stephen **Radić**, becoming party leader himself in 1928. Again imprisoned in 1933, on charges of treason, he was released the following year under the regency of Prince Paul Karageorgević. In 1939 he signed the **Sporazum** with **Cvetković**, thus securing Croatian participation in government, and became Vice-President of Yugoslavia, continuing in this position under General Dušan Simović who seized power in a coup (27 Mar 1941). He refused **Ribbentrop**'s offer of assistance in creating an independent **Croatia** and at first urged the Croats to support the **Ustaša** regime of **Pavelić**. He retired from political life shortly afterwards and was interned on his farm until the end of **World War II** when he went into exile in France and the USA.

Machel, Samora Moises (1933–86)
Mozambique nationalist leader and politician. He trained as a medial assistant before joining **Frelimo** in 1963, soon becoming active in the guerrilla war against the Portuguese colonial power. Commander-in-Chief in 1966, he succeded **Mondlane** on the latter's assassination in 1969 and was President of Mozambique from its independence in 1975 until his death in an air crash. Avowedly a Marxist, his success at politicizing the peasantry in northern Mozambique during the liberation war led him to believe in the dominant role of the party but, after the flight of white Portuguese in 1974 and the economic failure of his policies, he became more pragmatic, turning to the West for assistance, advising **Mugabe** to temper principle with prudence, and began establishing more harmonious relations with South Africa.

machine ▷ **political machine**

Macía, Francisco (1859–1933)
Catalan leader. The leader and founder, in 1922, of *Estat Català*, the Catalan nationalist party, he was a central figure in the Catalan struggle to achieve autonomy. After **Primo de Rivera**'s dictatorship collapsed, Macía forged a coalition of the Catalan Republican Party and his own *Estat Català*, creating the Republican Left of Catalonia. He was the first President of Catalonia under the autonomy statute of 1932 granted by the Second Republic. His Republican Left was defeated in the elections of 1933 and Macía died a few weeks later. ▷ **Catalan Autonomy Statutes; Republic, Second** (Spain)

Maclean, Donald (Duart) (1913–83)
British double agent. He studied at Cambridge at the same time as **Burgess** and **Philby**, and was similarly influenced by **communism**. He joined the diplomatic service in 1935, served in Paris, Washington (1944–8), and Cairo (1948–50), and from 1944 acted as a Soviet agent. He became head of the American Department of the Foreign Office, but by 1951 was a suspected traitor, and in May of that year, after Philby's warning, disappeared with Burgess to the USSR. He died in Moscow.

Macmillan, (Maurice) Harold, 1st Earl of Stockton (1894–1986)
British politician. He became a Conservative MP in 1924. He was Minister of Housing (1951–4) and Defence (1954–5), Foreign Secretary (1955), Chancellor of the Exchequer (1955–7), and succeeded **Eden** as Premier (1957–63). He became popular and respected during a period of economic boom, earning the sobriquet 'Supermac'. He was re-elected in 1959. After several political setbacks, and a major scandal (the **Profumo** Affair), he resigned through ill health in 1963, and left the House of

Commons in 1964. He became Chancellor of Oxford University in 1960, and an earl in 1984. ▷ **Conservative Party** (UK)

Madariaga y Rojo, Salvador de (1886–1978)
Spanish diplomat and writer. Educated in Madrid and Paris, he became a journalist in London (1916–21), a member of the **League of Nations** secretariat (1922–7), Professor of Spanish Studies at Oxford (1928–31), and Spanish Ambassador to the USA (1931) and France (1932–4). During 1934 he was briefly Minister of Education and Justice under the Spanish Second Republic. An opponent of the **Franco** regime, he was in exile from 1936 to 1976. The author of many historical works, especially on Spain and Spanish-America, he died at Locarno, Switzerland. ▷ **Republic, Second** (Spain)

Madero, Francisco Indalécio (1873–1913)
Mexican revolutionary and politician. The son of a wealthy landowner, groomed in Paris and educated in the USA, he was no social revolutionary, although he greatly improved the *peons*' condition on his own estates. He unsuccessfully opposed Porfirio **Díaz**'s local candidates in 1904, and in 1908, when Díaz was quoted as saying that he would not seek another term, Madero took the dictator at his word and launched his own presidential campaign. A spiritualist, vegetarian, and practitioner of homoeopathic medicine, he was an unlikely challenger, and at first was not taken seriously. But his popularity grew rapidly and Díaz turned to repression, imprisoning Madero and many of his supporters. He escaped to the USA, from where he directed a military campaign. His supporters, including **Villa**, captured Ciudad Juárez, where he established his capital (May 1911), and the dictatorship crumbled. Once elected President (Oct 1911), Madero's moderate political reform programme pleased no one and he faced a succession of revolts by Emiliano **Zapata** and others demanding land reform, as well as by supporters of the old dictatorship. On the night of 23 Feb 1913, he and his Vice-President were murdered following a military coup led by General Victoriano Huerta, planned with the assistance of US ambassador Henry L Wilson. ▷ **peon**

Madiun Rebellion (Sep–Oct 1948)
A rebellion by major elements in the Indonesian Communist Party (**Partai Komunis Indonesia**, PKI) against the Indonesian government, at a time when the peoples of Indonesia were still engaged in their violent post-war struggle to prevent the restoration of Dutch colonial rule. The rebellion was primarily driven by deep disagreements with other forces in Indonesia over the ways in which the struggle with the Dutch should be pursued and over the aims of the revolution. It was fiercely crushed by government forces, with much loss of life. In launching the rebellion against the government, the PKI provoked the charge, long-sustained, of

treachery against the revolution. The defeat of the communists, however, opened the way for stronger US support for the Indonesian government, which was crucial in effecting the final Dutch withdrawal in 1949–50.

Mafeking, Siege of (Oct 1899–May 1900)

The most celebrated siege of the second Boer War, during which Colonel Robert **Baden-Powell** and a detachment of British troops were besieged by the Boers. The news of their relief aroused public hysteria in Britain, the celebrations being known as 'mafficking'. The truth about the siege was rather different from the heroic action depicted by the British press. It is now known that the White garrison survived in reasonable comfort as the result of appropriating the rations of the Blacks, who were faced either with starvation or with running the gauntlet of the Boers by escaping from the town. ▷ **Boer Wars; Kimberley, Siege of; Ladysmith, Siege of**

Mafia (also known as **'the Mob'**, **'Cosa Nostra'**, **'the Syndicate'** or, in Chicago, **'the Outfit'**)

US development of the Sicilian Mafia. Evolving in the early 20c with the migration to the USA of Neapolitans, Calabrians and Sicilians, who took with them their state-suspicious structures of authority and clientage, a series of gangland wars ended with a 1931 'peace treaty' which established its modern structure. The Mafia has flourished because it satisfied demands for alcohol during **Prohibition**, and for narcotics and gambling since. The infiltration of some labour unions has also enabled the organization to benefit from extortion. While the code of *merta* ('silence') has protected it during repeated investigations, these have shown that some officials, at all levels of government, have been controlled by Mafia, which now consists of at least 24 families, each led by a *capo* ('head').

Maginot Line

French defensive fortifications stretching from Longwy to the Swiss border, named after André Maginot (1877–1932), French Minister of Defence (1924–31). The line was constructed (1929–34) to act as protection against German invasion, but Belgium refused to extend it along her frontier with Germany. The German attack of 1940 through the Low Countries largely by-passed the Maginot Line, whose name became synonymous with passive defence and defeatism. ▷ **World War II**

Mahathir bin Mohamad (1925–)

Malaysian politician. He practised as a doctor (1957–64) before being elected to the House of Representatives as a United Malays' National Organization (UMNO) candidate. He won the support of UMNO's radical youth wing through his advocacy of 'affirmative action' in favour of *bumiputras* (ethnic Malays). Following sharp attacks on the then Prime

Minister, Tunku **Abdul Rahman**, in the wake of the 1969 race riots, he was expelled from UMNO. He was, however, subsequently readmitted and, after holding several ministerial posts, was appointed UMNO Leader and Prime Minister in 1981. He immediately launched a 'look east' economic policy, which sought to emulate East Asian industrialization. Despite severe divisions within UMNO, he has seen off all challengers and led the ruling alliance to successive electoral victories.

Maichew (Mai Ceu), Battle of (31 Mar 1936)
The decisive battle of the Italian invasion of Abyssinia, in which the Emperor **Haile Selassie** was defeated and the Italian commander, Marshal Badoglio, prepared for the final advance on Addis Ababa. The Emperor decided that, instead of withdrawal, he would attack the Italian camp at Maichew with forces which consisted of the Imperial Guard and large numbers of Galla under feudal chiefs. The Italians had forewarning of the attack, harried the Ethiopians with air power, and were able to repulse the Ethiopian forces with superior artillery. It became Selassie's last despairing gesture before he fled into exile and the Italians were able to complete their conquest. Ethiopian resistance passed from the traditional leaders to the guerrilla Patriots.

Maji Maji (1905)
A rising against German rule which took place in southern Tanganyika. People from a variety of ethnic backgrounds rose against harsh tax exactions and compulsory cotton growing. Priests and messengers moved from village to village urging people to rise and claiming that they had a medicine which would turn bullets into water or *maji*. German administration broke down for several months, but the rising was put down with great brutality causing a famine, in which a million people died, and a major ecological disaster in the region.

Major, John (1943–)
British politician. He had a career in banking before becoming a Conservative MP in 1976. He rose to become Chief Secretary to the Treasury, was unexpectedly made Foreign Secretary in Margaret **Thatcher**'s cabinet reshuffle in 1989, and soon after replaced Nigel **Lawson** as Chancellor of the Exchequer. He won the leadership contest following Thatcher's resignation, and became Prime Minister (1990–). ▷ **Conservative Party (UK)**

Makarios III (Mihail Khristodoulou Mouskos) (1913–77)
Cypriot political and religious leader. He was ordained priest in 1946, elected Bishop of Kition in 1948, and Archbishop and Primate of the Orthodox Church of Cyprus in 1950. He reorganized the **enosis** (union) movement, was arrested and detained in 1956, but returned to a tumultu-

ous welcome in 1959 to become chief Greek–Cypriot minister in the new Graeco-Turkish provisional government. Later that year he was elected President (1960–74 and 1974–7).

Malan, Daniel F(rançois) (1874–1959)
South African politician. Educated at Stellenbosch and Utrecht Universities, in 1905 he joined the ministry of the Dutch Reformed Church but in 1915 left to become editor of Die Burger, the Nationalist newspaper. Elected an MP in 1918, he held the portfolios of Interior, Education and Public Health by 1924. He helped reform the **National Party** with Hertzog and became leader of the Opposition to Smuts's United Party. He led the National Party to its decisive electoral victory in 1948 and oversaw the initial implementation of the policy of **apartheid**. He retired in 1954.

Malaviya, Madan Mohan (1861–1946)
Indian politician and journalist. A nationalist, he joined the Congress in 1886 and was a prominent member of the Uttar Pradesh Legislative Council and the Central Legislature. Mainly concerned with the furtherance of Hindu interests, Malaviya campaigned for the use of Hindi and was the dominant force in the creation of the Benares Hindu University in 1916. He was an important member of the **Hindu Mahasabha**, from which he broke away in 1928, although he remained the chief Hindu spokesman within Congress. He opposed the Communal Award of 1932, which created separate electorates representing different religious and social groups, and left the Congress to form a new party to fight the award, which he regarded as 'communal'. ▷ **communalism**

Malawi
A republic in South-East Africa. Claimed as the British Protectorate of Nyasaland in 1891, it was established as a British colony in 1907. In the 1950s it joined with North and South Rhodesia to form the Federation of Rhodesia and Nyasaland. It gained independence in 1964 and became a republic in 1966. As a result of international pressure and growing unrest within the country a referendum was held in 1993 in which the population voted for a multiparty system.

Malawi Congress Party (MCP)
Founded in 1959, this party grew out of the Nyasaland African National Congress. It is the only legal party in Malawi and has, as its Life President, Hastings Kamuzu **Banda**.

Malayan Emergency (1948)
The name given to the insurrection led by the Malayan Communist Party (MCP) against British rule, and the campaign to crush that insurrection,

in post-war Malaya. Following growing MCP violence, including the murder of European estate managers, on 18 June 1948 the British administration declared a state of emergency throughout Malaya. In the early years of the insurrection, the MCP achieved a number of notable successes, including the assassination of the High Commissioner, Sir Henry Gurney, in Oct 1951. However, by the mid-1950s, through a combination of fierce military measures, substantial resettlement of the Chinese rural population (which had provided much of the MCP's support) and the introduction of political initiatives that clearly would soon take Malaya to independence, the insurrection was broken, although, officially, it did not end until 31 July 1960.

Malaysia

An independent federation of states in South-East Asia, comprising 11 states and a federal territory in Peninsular Malaysia, and the eastern states of Sabah and Sarawak on the island of Borneo. British protection, which extended over Perak, Selangor, Negeri Sembilan and Pahang, was constituted into the Federated Malay States in 1895. Protection treaties with several other states (Unfederated Malay States) were agreed in 1885–1930. They were occupied by Japan in **World War II**, following which Sarawak became a British colony, Singapore became a separate colony, the colony of North Borneo was formed, and the Malay Union was established, uniting the Malay states and the Straits Settlements of Malacca and Penang. The Federation of Malaya was created in 1948 and independence was gained in 1957. The constitutional monarchy of Malaysia came into existence in 1963. Singapore withdrew from the Federation in 1965.

Malcolm X (1925–65)

US militant black activist, who became the most effective spokesman for **Black Power**. Born Malcolm Little, he took the name 'X' to symbolize the stolen identities of the generations of black slaves. After an adolescence of violence, narcotics and petty crime, he came under the influence of Elijah **Muhammad** while in prison for burglary and after his release in 1952 became Muhammad's chief disciple within the **Black Muslims**, greatly expanding the organization's following. In 1963 Malcolm was suspended from the Nation of Islam after disagreements with Muhammad and gained the deep hatred of the leader's loyal followers. Malcolm founded the Organization for Afro-American unity, dedicated to the alliance of American blacks and other non-white peoples. In the last year of his life, following a pilgrimage to Mecca, Malcolm announced his conversion to orthodox Islam and put forward the belief in the possible brotherhood between blacks and whites. Malcolm's extreme stance and the inflammatory nature of his oratory had scared many whites, appealed to many northern blacks in the urban ghettos, and had been met with criticism by moderate civil rights leaders who deplored his violent message. In 1965

Malcolm was the victim of Black Muslim assassins who retaliated against the man they viewed as a traitor.

Malenkov, Giorgiy Maximilianovich (1902–88)
Soviet politician. He joined the **Red Army** in 1919 and the Communist Party in 1920, and by 1925 he was a Central Committee official. He was very closely involved in the collectivization of agriculture and the purges of the 1930s under **Stalin**. Malenkov became a member of the Central Committee in 1939 and of the **Politburo** in 1946; he became Deputy Premier in the same year, succeeding Stalin as Party General-Secretary and Premier in 1953. However, he was very quickly forced out of his Party post and, under pressure from Nikita **Khrushchev**, in 1955 he resigned as Premier, admitting responsibility for the failure of Soviet agricultural policy. Having participated in the so-called **Anti-Party Plot** in 1957, he was sent by Khrushchev to Kazakhstan as manager of a hydroelectric plant. He died an obscure pensioner in Moscow. ▷ **communism**

Malik, Jakub Alexandrovich (1906–80)
Soviet politician. Having been educated and having practised as an economist in the Ukraine until 1935, he studied at the Diplomatic Institute in Moscow from then until 1937, when he entered the Foreign Service. Said to be one of **Stalin**'s favourite 'juniors', he was ambassador to Japan from 1943 to 1945 and Deputy Foreign Minister with particular responsibility for Far Eastern affairs in 1946–53. From 1948 to 1952 he was also Soviet spokesman at the **UN**, succeeding Andrei **Gromyko**. Ambassador to Britain in 1953–60, from 1960 he was again Deputy Foreign Minister, serving a second term as Ambassador to the UN in 1968 to 1976.

Malinovsky, Rodion Yakovlevich (1898–1967)
Soviet general. He was a corporal in **World War I**, when, after the Russian collapse, he escaped via Siberia and Singapore to fight in a Russian brigade in France. He joined the **Red Army** in 1919 after the **Russian Revolution**, built up experience as a military adviser and instructor, and was major-general at the time of the Nazi invasion in 1941. He commanded the forces which freed Rostov, Kharkov and the Dnieper basin and led the Russian advance on Budapest and into Austria (1943–5). When Russia declared war on Japan, he took a leading part in the Manchurian campaign and after **World War II** he held important commands in the Far East. In Oct 1957 he succeeded **Zhukov** as Nikita **Khrushchev**'s Minister of Defence and remained in that post under Brezhnev until his death. He therefore bore considerable responsibility for the great Soviet build-up of the 1960s.

Malraux, André (Georges) (1901–76)
French politician and novelist. He studied oriental languages and spent much time in China, where he worked for the **Guomindang** and was active in the 1927 revolution. He also fought in the **Spanish Civil War**, and in **World War II** escaped from a prison camp to join the French Resistance. He was Minister of Information in de **Gaulle**'s government (1945–6) and Minister of Cultural Affairs (1960–9). He is known for his novels, notably *La Condition humaine* (1933), winner of the Prix Goncourt, and *L'Espoir* (1937). ▷ **Resistance Movement** (France)

Malta
An archipelago republic in the central Mediterranean Sea. It became a British Crown Colony in 1815 and formed an important strategic base in both World Wars. In 1942 Malta was awarded the George Cross for its resistance to heavy air attacks. It achieved independence in 1964, and became a republic in 1974. The British Military Facilities agreement expired in 1979.

Man, Hendrik de (1885–1953)
Belgian politician. He took a doctorate at Leipzig University in economic history, and was appointed to a Chair at Frankfurt University in 1929. In 1933 he was forced to leave Germany, and entered active politics in his native Belgium. He rejected Marxism, and developed his own socialist theory, laid out in his Labour Plan (*Plan du Travail*) of 1934. This non-revolutionary socialism, working with the bourgeoisie and using the democratic state as the instrument of socialism, was highly influential in Europe in the 1930s. De Man served as a cabinet minister (1935–8), and was chairman of the **Belgian Socialist Party** from 1939. When the Germans invaded, he entered into collaboration with the New Order, and dissolved his Socialist Party. He escaped to Switzerland in 1942, where he died in a traffic accident; in Belgium he was convicted in absentia in 1945.

Manchuria
A former region of north-east China. A mountainous area, sparsely populated by nomadic tribes, this was the home of the Manchus, who overthrew the Ming Dynasty to become the last Chinese emperors as the **Qing Dynasty**. Rich in natural resources (timber, coal, iron, magnesite, oil, uranium and gold), Manchuria came under Russian military control in 1900. Captured by Japan in 1932, it became part of the puppet-state of **Manzhuguo**, until Russian control was reasserted in 1945. Chinese sovereignty was recognized in 1950, but the border area with Russia remains a continuing focus of political tension. ▷ **Puyi**

Mandal Commissions

The name commonly given to the Backward Classes Commission, appointed by India's Janata government in 1978 (under President Morarji **Desai**) to examine the position of the former 'untouchable' castes and other low status groups within Indian society. The Commission, under Janata Party member Bindeshwari Prasad Mandal, was asked to report on the effectiveness of the measures taken since independence (1947) to end discrimination against the so-called 'backward classes' and to recommend means by which anti-discriminatory policies could be improved. Following a national survey, the report was published in Dec 1980, but later the same year the Congress Party, under Indira **Gandhi**, was returned to power, and its proposals were never implemented. Viewed by some, particularly on the political right, as a divisive political initiative, Mandal himself resigned from the Janata Party soon after publication of the report. However, after the defeat of the Congress Party in Dec 1989, the Commission's proposals were revived by the new Prime Minister, V P Singh, in an attempt to boost the popularity of his minority government. Subsequent attempts to increase the reservation of student places in higher education and appointments in the government service for members of the backward classes proved highly controversial, provoking widespread rioting and unrest in the towns and cities of northern India. The agitation was led mostly by students and younger members of high-caste groups, who adopted the self-immolation as a means of protest. The widespread outrage this provoked, together with the controversy over attempts by Hindu fundamentalist groups, backed by the Janata Party, to demolish a Muslim shrine at Ayodhya in northern India to make way for the construction of a Hindu temple on the site, led ultimately to the collapse of V P Singh's government, following a motion of no-confidence in the Indian parliament (Nov 1990). In practice, the Commission's proposals would have proved of little benefit to the untouchables; nor did they pose much of a threat to the upper castes. However, the implementation of the recommendations caused widespread opposition amongst the increasingly desperate, unemployed, educated youth of north India, a discontent that persists. After the restoration of the Congress Party to power (May 1991), new proposals were discussed for the modification of positive discrimination, placing more emphasis on economic rather than social disadvantage and thus avoiding the issue of **caste**.

mandates

A system under which former territories of the German and Ottoman empires were to be governed by the victorious powers of **World War I** under international supervision. The mandates were granted by the **League of Nations**, and annual reports had to be submitted to its Permanent Mandates Commission. Britain and France acquired mandates in the Middle East (Palestine, Iraq, Transjordan, Syria, Lebanon) and

Africa (Tanganyika, Togo, Cameroon) while Belgium acquired Rwanda Urundi, South Africa acquired South-West Africa, and Australia and New Zealand acquired New Guinea and Western Samoa. The functions of the Commission were later taken over by the Trusteeship Council of the **UN**.

Mandela, Nelson Rohlihlahla (1918–)

South African nationalist leader. Educated at Fort Hare College (1938–40), he practised law in Johannesburg before joining the **ANC** (African National Congress) in 1944 and founding the Congress Youth League. For the next 20 years he was at the forefront of black opposition to **apartheid**, being 'banned' (1956–61) and sentenced to life imprisonment in 1964 for his leadership of the ANC. He spent most of the next 25 years in prison on Robben Island; in the 1980s there was a co-ordinated international campaign for his release, and he was finally set free, on President F W **De Klerk**'s orders, on 11 Feb 1990. He was elected Deputy President of the ANC by the party in exile (Apr 1990) and in July 1991, in Durban, at the party's first congress inside South Africa for a quarter of a century, he was elected President. He separated from his wife Winnie Mandela (1934/6–) in 1992. In 1993 he was jointly awarded the Nobel Peace Prize with F W De Klerk, and following the first all-race elections in South Africa in May 1994, he became the first black President of South Africa.

Mandelstam, Osip (1891–1938)

Russian poet. Born of Jewish parents in Warsaw, he was brought up in St Petersburg. His early success with *Kamen* (1913, Stone), *Tristia* (1922, Sad Things), and *Stikhotvorenia 1921–25* (1928, Poems) was followed by suspicion and arrest (1934) by the Soviet authorities. His death was reported from Siberia in 1938. His *Sobranie sochineny* (Collected Works) were published in three volumes (1964–71). His wife, Nadezhda, wrote their story in *Hope Against Hope* (1970).

Manhattan Project

The codename for the most secret scientific operation of **World War II**, the development of the atomic bomb, undertaken successfully in the USA from 1942 onwards. The project culminated in the detonation of the first atomic weapon near Alamogordo, New Mexico (16 July 1945).

Maniu, Iuliu (1873–1953)

Romanian politician. The leader of the National Party, he directed the provisional government in Transylvania which proclaimed union with Romania (Dec 1918). Later, as leader of the National Peasant Party, he

:rved as Prime Minister and tried to carry out agrarian reform (1928–0) but resigned from office when King **Charles II** of Romania introduced is mistress, Magda **Lupescu**, into the Romanian court. He was again 'rime Minister (1932–3) and his electoral alliance with the **Iron Guard** vas an expediency aimed at curbing the King's power (1937). He played major role in the coup (Aug 1944) and was a minister without portfolio n General Sănătescu's national government which declared war on Germany. The post-war communist regime, in a move intended to destroy he Peasant Party, had him arrested, accused of conspiring with US ntelligence agents. He received a life sentence (1947) and died in prison.

Manley, Michael Norman (1923–)
Jamaican politician. The son of Norman **Manley**, he was educated in Jamaica, served in the Royal Canadian Air Force in **World War II**, and then studied at the London School of Economics (1945–9). He worked as a journalist in Britain before returning to Jamaica, where he became a leader of the National Workers' Union in the 1950s, sat in the Senate (1962–7) and was then elected to the House of Representatives. In 1969 he became Leader of the People's National Party (PNP) and, in 1972, Prime Minister. He embarked on a radical, socialist programme, cooling relations with the USA and forming links with Cuba, and despite rising unemployment was re-elected in 1976. He was decisively defeated in 1980 and 1983, but returned to power in 1989 with a much more moderate policy stance.

Manley, Norman Washington (1893–1969)
Jamaican politician. A Rhodes scholar at Oxford, he was called to the Bar and then became a respected QC. In 1938 he won fame by successfully defending his cousin, and political opponent, Alexander **Bustamante**, who was then an active trade unionist, on a charge of sedition. In the same year Manley founded the People's National Party (PNP) and in 1955, seven years before Jamaica achieved full independence, became Chief Minister. He handed over leadership of the PNP to his son, Michael **Manley**, in 1969.

Mannerheim, Carl Gustav Emil, Baron (1867–1951)
Finnish soldier and politician. When Finland declared her independence (1918), he became Supreme Commander and Regent. Defeated in the presidential election of 1919, he retired into private life, but returned as Commander-in-Chief against the Russians in the **Russo-Finnish War** of 1939–40. He continued to command the Finnish forces until 1944, when he became President of the Finnish Republic until 1946. He died at Lausanne, Switzerland. ▷ **World War II**

Mannix, Daniel (1864–1963)
Irish-born Australian Catholic archbishop. He was appointed Coadjutor Archbishop of Melbourne in 1912 and Archbishop in 1917, and campaigned strongly for the rights of Catholics in Australian society, especially state aid for church schools. After the **Easter Rising** in Ireland (1916) he became an outspoken supporter of Irish **Home Rule**, and opposed **Hughes** demands for conscription in 1916–17. His position verged on a populist identification with the working classes, with whom he enjoyed an immense prestige which he never lost; the social establishment demanded his deportation. In 1920, returning to Europe, he was fêted in the USA, but refused entry to Ireland by the British government. His social views involved a hostility to capitalism that for many years made him close to the **Australian Labor Party**, but increasingly he came to regard **communism** as the greater threat, and he supported the **Democratic Labor Party** after the Labor Party split of the mid-1950s. His involvement with the Catholic laity and combative nature made him a powerful force in Australian society and politics for half a century.

Manstein, Fritz Erich von (1887–1973)
German soldier. At the outset of **World War II** he became Chief of Staff to **Rundstedt** in the Polish campaign and later in France, where he was the architect of **Hitler**'s **Blitzkrieg** invasion plan. In 1941 he was given command of an army corps on the Eastern Front and though not trained in armoured warfare handled his panzers with great resource in the Crimea. After the disaster of **Stalingrad**, he contrived to extricate the right wing in sufficient strength to stage a successful counter-attack at Kharkov, though he failed to relieve **Paulus**'s 6th Army. After being captured in 1945 he was imprisoned as a war criminal but released in 1953. A strong advocate of fluid defence for preventing the enemy from exploiting an advantage, he embodied his theories and an account of his military career in his *Lost victories* (trans 1959).

Manuel II (1889–1932)
King of Portugal (1908/10). On the assassination of his father, King Charles (Carlos) I, and Crown Prince Luis, on 1 Feb 1908, he became king, but was forced to abdicate at the revolution of 3 Oct 1910. He subsequently settled in England.

Manzhuguo (Manchukuo)
A Japanese puppet-state established in 1932 in Manchuria, which Japanese forces had invaded in 1931. Henry **Puyi**, the last Qing Emperor, was its nominal head. The regime ended with the defeat of Japan in 1945.
▷ **Qing Dynasty; Sino-Japanese War**

Mao Dun (1896–1981)
Chinese writer. Born Shen Yanbing, he was educated at Beijing University, and became one of the foremost left-wing intellectuals and writers in China, adopting the pseudonym Mao Dun. In 1926 he joined the Northern Expedition as a propagandist, but had to go underground in Shanghai as a communist activist. In 1930 he helped to organize the influential League of Left-Wing Writers. After the communists came to power in 1949, he was China's first Minister of Culture (1949–65), and was founder-editor of the literary journal, *People's Literature* (1949–53). During the **Cultural Revolution** he was kept under house arrest in Beijing (1966–78).

Mao Zedong (Mao Tse-tung) (1893–1976)
Chinese political leader. He was the leading theorist of the Chinese communist revolution which won national power in China in 1949. The son of a farmer, at the age of 12 he sought an education in Changsha, where he was introduced to Western ideas. After graduating from a teachers' training college there, he went to Beijing, where he came under the influence of **Li Dazhao**. He took a leading part in the **May Fourth Movement**, then became a Marxist and a founding member of the Chinese Communist Party (CCP) (1921). During the first United Front with the Nationalist Party, he concentrated on political work among the peasants of his native province, and advocated a rural revolution, creating the **Jiangxi Soviet**. After the break with the Nationalists in 1927, the communists were driven from the cities, and with the assistance of **Zhu De**, he evolved the guerrilla tactics of the 'people's war'. In 1934 the nationalist government was at last able to destroy the Jiangxi Soviet, and in the subsequent **Long March** the communist forces retreated to Shaanxi to set up a new base. When in 1936, under the increasing threat of Japanese invasion, the nationalists renewed their alliance with the communists, Mao restored and vastly increased the political and military power of his party. His claim to share in the government led to civil war; the regime of **Chiang Kai-shek** was ousted from the Chinese mainland; and the new People's Republic of China was proclaimed (1 Oct 1949) with Mao as both Chairman of the CCP and President of the Republic. He followed the Soviet model of economic development and social change until 1958, then launched his **Great Leap Forward**, which encouraged the establishment of rural industry and the use of surplus rural labour to create a new infrastructure for agriculture. The failure of the Great Leap lost him most of his influence, but by 1965, with China's armed forces securely in the hands of his ally, **Lin Biao**, he launched a **Cultural Revolution**, and the Great Leap strategy was revived (though with new caution) when the left wing was victorious in the ensuing political struggles (1965–71). He died in Beijing after a prolonged illness, which may well have weakened his judgement during his last years. A strong reaction set in against the excessive collectivism and egalitarianism which had emerged, but his

anti-Stalinist emphasis on rural industry and on local initiative was retained and strengthened by his successors. ▷ **communism; Maoism**

Maoism

Specifically, the thought of **Mao Zedong**, and more broadly a revolutionary ideology based on Marxism–Leninism and adapted to Chinese conditions. Maoism shifted the focus of revolutionary struggle from the urban workers or proletariat to the countryside and the peasantry. There were three main elements: strict Leninist principles of organization; Chinese tradition; and armed struggle as a form of revolutionary activity. Mao gained political power in 1949 through a peasant army, his slogan being 'Political power grows through the barrel of a gun'. While there were attempts to take account of the views of the masses, the Chinese Communist Party was organized along strict centralist, hierarchical lines, and increasingly became a vehicle for a personal dictatorship. In domestic terms, Mao pursued a radical and far-reaching attempt to transform traditional Chinese society and its economy, using thought reform, indoctrination and the psychological transformation of the masses. Maoism was regarded in the 1960s at the height of the **Cultural Revolution** as a highly radical form of Marxism–Leninism that was distinct from the bureaucratic repression of the USSR, and had a strong appeal among the New Left. Since his death, his use of the masses for political purposes, his economic reforms and his conception of political power have been increasingly criticized inside and outside China as seriously misguided and too rigid.

Mapai Party

Acronym for the Hebrew *mifleget poalei eretz yisrael* ('Party of the Workers of the Land of Israel'). A political party created in 1930 from two already existing parties by David **Ben-Gurion** among others, Mapai aimed to establish a national Jewish homeland in Palestine built on socialist principles and became the main party in the **Yishuv**. During **World War II**, Mapai opposed British policy in Palestine but supported the war against the Nazis; after 1948 it maintained a dominant position within Israeli politics. Mapai combined with two other socialist parties in 1968 to form the Israel Labour Party (Heb. *mifleget ha-avodah ha-yisraelit*), which remained in power until 1977. ▷ **Jewish Agency; Likud**

Maquiladoras

A Spanish term used in Mexico (literally, 'assembly') signifying foreign-owned industrial assembly plants built on the US border, in order to take advantage of lower wage rates and less onerous labour legislation in Mexico. The growth of *maquiladora* industries was most rapid in the

1960s as both the US and Mexican authorities sought to limit the flight of the *braceros* to California and Texas, while major multinational manufacturing firms sought to take advantage of tax-breaks conceded under Mexican legislation designed to stimulate industrial growth and exports. Their effective contribution to Mexican growth is hotly debated, while their existence is also unpopular with US labour unions.

Maquis

The local name given to the dense scrub in Corsica; adopted in German-occupied France by groups of young men who hid in the hills and forests to escape forced labour in Germany. Organized into Resistance groups, they led the national rising against the Germans on and after **D-Day**. ▷ **Resistance Movement** (France); **World War II**

March, Juan (1884–1962)

Spanish business magnate. If Barcelona was the nexus of his financial empire, Mallorca (where he was born) became his own personal fiefdom. Imprisoned for fraud by the Second Republic, he retaliated by aiding the military rebellions of 1932 and July 1936. During the **Spanish Civil War** he was a key backer of the Nationalists. He died the richest person in modern Spain, allegedly the seventh in the world. ▷ **Republic, Second** (Spain)

March First Movement (1919)

A non-violent protest in Korea led by religious groups (both Buddhist and Christian) in response to the failure of the Paris Peace Conference to grant Korean independence from Japan (Korea had been a colony since 1910). The timing of the demonstration coincided with funeral ceremonies for the former Korean king, Kojong (1864/1907). Mourners signed a declaration of independence amidst rumours that Kojong had been poisoned for having refused to sign a statement supporting permanent unity with Japan. Japanese troops responded with violence and hundreds of Koreans were killed (553 according to Japanese figures at the time; 7 189 according to later Korean figures). Colonial control was relaxed for a time during the 1920s by party governments in Japan anxious to atone for the incident, but with the emergence of military-led cabinets in the 1930s Japanese policy in Korea once more became oppressive.

March on Rome (Oct 1922)

The largely symbolic march on the Italian capital by several thousand fascists. Although **Mussolini** subsequently liked to portray the event as a glorious seizure of power, he had already successfully negotiated and bullied his way into office before his supporters actually arrived in the capital. He did not reach Rome himself until he was already certain of success in his bid for power and had been invited to form a government by **Victor Emmanuel III**.

Marchais, Georges (1920–)

French communist politician, the son of a miner. A former metalworker, he joined the French **Communist Party** (PCF) in 1947, becoming its General-Secretary in 1972. Under his leadership the PCF pledged its commitment to the 'transition to socialism' by democratic means, and joined the **Socialist Party** (PS) in a new 'Union of the Left'. This union was, however, severed by Marchais in 1977 and the party returned to an orthodox 'Moscow line', although PCF ministers participated in the **Mitterrand** government (1981–4). He unsuccessfully contested the 1981 presidential election.

Marchand, Jean Baptiste (1863–1934)

French soldier and explorer. He explored the White Nile, and caused a Franco-British crisis by hoisting the tricolour at Fashoda in 1898. As a general he distinguished himself in **World War I**.

Marchenko, Anatoli Tikhonovich (1938–86)

Soviet dissident. One of the small group of prominent Soviet dissidents whose continuing courage did much to bring down the communist system. A young worker and writer, he was first imprisoned in 1960 for attempting to travel abroad and spent 18 of his remaining 26 years in jails or camps for championing his rights. He wrote the first detailed account of Buzhnev labour camp in *My Testimony* in 1968, and died in prison on hunger strike but in suspicious circumstances.

Marco Polo Bridge Incident (7 July 1937)

A clash between Chinese and Japanese troops near the Marco Polo Bridge, south-west of Beijing, that was to lead to full-scale war between China and Japan (1937–45). Exercising their right under the Boxer Protocol (1901), which allowed foreign troops to be stationed in the vicinity of Beijing, Japanese soldiers were engaged in manoeuvres when skirmishes with local Chinese forces took place. Although a local ceasefire was arranged (11 July 1937), the Japanese Prime Minister, **Konoe**, announced plans to mobilize five divisions for north China. The head of the Chinese Nationalist government, **Chiang Kai-shek**, reversing the appeasement policy he had followed regarding persistent Japanese attempts to remove north China from Chinese central government control, responded by reinforcing Chinese forces. Chiang's unyielding stand was prompted by the anti-Japanese united front agreement he had been compelled to sign in 1936 with the communists. On 29 July 1937

Japanese troops attacked and occupied Beijing, signalling the start of the war between the two countries.

Marcos, Ferdinand (Edralin) (1917–89)
Filipino politician and President (1965–86). He trained as a lawyer, and as a politician obtained considerable US support as an anti-communist. His regime as President was marked by increasing repression, misuse of foreign financial aid, and political violence (notably, the assassination of Benigno **Aquino** in 1983). He declared martial law in 1972. Overthrown in 1986 by a popular revolt led by Corazon **Aquino**, he went into exile in Hawaii, where he and his wife, Imelda, fought against demands from US courts investigating charges of financial mismanagement and massive corruption. He died in Honolulu.

Margai, Albert Michael (1910–80)
Sierra Leone politician. The son of a trader and the brother of Sir Milton **Margai**, he was educated in Roman Catholic schools before becoming a nurse and pharmacist. He studied law in London (1944–7) and was elected a member of Legco in 1951, when he was appointed Minister of Education, Welfare and Local Government. A member of the Sierra Leone People's Party from 1951–8, he helped found the People's National Party and became Minister of Finance at independence. When his brother died, he succeeded him as party leader and Prime Minister (1964–7). Following the military coup led by Siaka **Stevens** in 1967, he went into exile in London.

Margai, Milton A S (1895–1964)
Sierra Leone nationalist leader and politician. The elder brother of Sir Albert **Margai**, he was educated in Roman Catholic mission schools, Fourah Bay College and in the UK, where he qualified as a doctor. Appointed a member of the Protectorate Assembly in 1940, he was elected to Legco in 1951, when he helped found the Sierra Leone People's Party and played a major role in pressing for independence. He was Chief Minister (1954–8) and, on independence, Prime Minister until his death in 1964.

Margrethe II (1940–)
Queen of Denmark (1972/). The daughter of **Frederick IX**, whom she succeeded, she is an archaeologist, and was educated at the universities of Copenhagen, Aarhus and Cambridge, the Sorbonne, Paris, and the London School of Economics. In 1967 she married a French diplomat, Count Henri de Laborde de Monpezat, now Prince Henrik of Denmark. Their children are the heir-apparent, Prince Frederik André Henrik Christian, and Prince Joachim Holger Valdemar Christian.

Markievicz, Constance (Georgine), Countess (1868–1927)
Irish nationalist. The daughter of Sir Henry Gore-Booth of County Sligo, she married the Polish count, Casimir Markievicz. She fought in the **Easter Rising** (1916), and was sentenced to death but reprieved. Elected the first British woman MP in 1918, she did not take her seat, but was a member of the **Dáil Eireann** from 1923.

Marković, Ante (1924–)
Yugoslav politician. He joined the Communist Youth Movement in Yugoslavia in 1940 and fought in **Tito**'s partisans, becoming a member of the Communist League of Yugoslavia in 1943. He was a member of the Central Committee of the League of Communists of Croatia (1982–6). As Prime Minister of the Socialist Federal Republic of Croatia, he introduced a programme of economic reform. A member of the Central Committee of the League of Communists of Yugoslavia since 1986, he succeeded Branko Mikulić as Prime Minister of Yugoslavia (Mar 1989). A liberal and pro-Western, he was hailed as 'man of the year' by the popular Croatian magazine *Danas* (1990). After six months of civil war between the Serbs and Croats, he announced his resignation as Prime Minister of Yugoslavia (Dec 1991).

Marne, Battle of the (1914)
A battle early in **World War I**, in which General **Joffre**'s French armies and the **British Expeditionary Force** halted German forces which had crossed the Marne and were approaching Paris, thus ending German hopes of a swift victory. The German line withdrew across the River Aisne, dug in, and occupied much the same positions until 1918.

Marryshow, Albert (1885–1958)
Grenadian champion of a federation of the British West Indies. In 1913 he founded a newspaper, *The West Indian*, which campaigned for greater West Indian unity and for an extension of the franchise, based on his belief that the 'People's Parliament' should be founded on universal adult suffrage. Marryshow lived long enough to sit in the Federation of the **West Indies**, for which he had so long struggled, but not long enough to see it dissolved four years later.

Marshall, George Catlett (1880–1959)
US general and politician. Educated at the Virginia Military Institute, he became Chief-of-Staff (1939–45), and directed the US Army throughout **World War II**. After two years in China as special representative of President **Truman**, he became Secretary of State (1947–9), originating the **Marshall Plan** for the post-war reconstruction of Europe, and Secretary of Defense (1950–1). He retired (Sep 1951) after nearly 50 years of

military and civilian service, and was awarded the Nobel Peace Prize in 1953.

Marshall, Thurgood (1908–93)
US jurist. Associate justice of the US Supreme Court and civil rights advocate. Educated at Lincoln and Howard universities, he joined the legal staff of the National Association for the Advancement of Colored People, and argued many important civil rights cases. He served as a judge of the US Court of Appeals (1961–5), and as Solicitor-General of the United States (1965–7), before becoming the first black Associate Justice of the US Supreme Court, a post he held until his retirement in 1991. ▷ **civil rights**

Marshall Plan
The popular name for the European Recovery Program, a scheme for large-scale, medium-term US aid to war-ravaged Europe, announced in 1947 by US Secretary of State, George Marshall. 'Marshall Aid' was rejected by the USSR and the Eastern bloc, but during the period 1948–50 it materially assisted Western Europe's economic revival.

Martens, Wilfried (1936–)
Belgian politician. Educated at Louvain University, he was adviser to two governments, in 1965 and 1966, before becoming Minister for Community Problems in 1968. He was President of the Dutch-speaking Social Christian Party (CVP) from 1972 to 1979, when be became Prime Minister at the head of a coalition. He continued in office, apart from a brief break in 1981, heading no fewer than six coalition governments.

Martínez Barrio, Diego (1883–1962)
Spanish politician. Under the Second Republic he was Minister of Communications (Apr–Dec 1931) and caretaker Prime Minister (Oct–Dec 1933). A leading freemason, he was national Grand Master from 1931 to 1934. His opposition to the alliance with the non-Republican Right led him to split with the **Radical Republican Party** in May 1934, taking up to a quarter of the party with him. After the Popular Front victory of Feb 1936, he was elected President of the Cortes and, on the outbreak of the military rising of July 1936, tried to form a government of conciliation. A man of immense integrity and reserve, he was President of the republic in exile until his death. ▷ **Republic, Second** (Spain)

Marx, Wilhelm (1863–1946)
German politician. A member of the **Centre Party**, Marx pursued a varied legal and political career before serving in the National (constituent) Assembly (1919–20) and as Chairman of the Centre Party (1922–8). He served as Chancellor between Nov 1923 and Jan 1925 at the head

of a centre-right coalition which renegotiated Germany's **reparations** obligations with the Allies (**Dawes Plan**). In Mar 1925 he was, as the republican candidate, narrowly defeated by **Hindenburg** in the presidential elections. After this he held further ministerial posts, including that of Chancellor (Jan 1927–May 1928). He withdrew from public life in 1932.

Marxism

The body of social and political thought informed by the writings of Karl Marx. It is essentially a critical analysis of capitalist society contending that such societies are subject to crises which create the conditions for proletarian revolutions and the transformation to socialism. Much of Marx's writing, especially *Das Kapital*, was concerned with the economic dynamics of capitalist societies, seeing the state as an instrument of class rule supporting private capital and suppressing the masses. Because of private capital's need to earn profits or extract surplus value, wages have to be kept to a subsistence minimum. This produces economic contradictions, because it restricts the purchasing power of workers to consume the goods produced. Capitalism is, therefore, inherently unstable, being subect to crises of booms and slumps. Marx's view was that these crises would become increasingly worse, and eventually lead to revolution, whereby the working class would seize the state and establish a dictatorship of the proletariat, productive power would be in public hands, and class differences would disappear (socialism). This classless society would eventually lead to the withering away of the state, producing a communist society. Marxism has tried to popularize and extend this kind of analysis to contemporary conditions. In particular, Western Marxism has examined the impact of state intervention in smoothing out the crises of capitalism and establishing a legitimacy for the existing capitalist order through its control over education and the media. In non-industrialized societies Marxism has been adapted to account for revolution in countries where there is no extensive development of capitalism, in contrast to Marx's view of history. It is generally recognized that his writings regarding the transformation to, and the nature of, socialism lacked detail. Consequently, Marxism has adopted a wide range of interpretations. ▷ **capitalism; communism; Marxism-Leninism; socialism**

Marxism-Leninism

A distinct variant of Marxism formulated by **Lenin** who, prior to the Bolshevik Revolution, argued for direct rule by the proletariat, defined as workers and poor peasants, and in the circumstances of Russia after 1905 advocated direct democracy through the soviets (councils). In practice, the Bolshevik Revolution did not produce a democratic republic, but gave a 'leading and directing' role to the Communist Party, seen as the vanguard of a working class which had insufficient political consciousness to forge a revolution; such a well-organized and disciplined party, operating according to the principles of democratic centralism, would be able to exploit the revolutionary situation and create a new socialist society. Leninist principles of a revolutionary vanguard became the central tenet of nearly all communist parties. They were organized according to the idea of democratic centralism that afforded the leadership, on the grounds of its revolutionary insight, the right to dictate party policy, to select party officials from above, and to discipline dissenting party members. In addition, Lenin modified Marx's theory of historical materialism, contending that revolutionary opportunities should be seized when they arose, without waiting for the social and economic crisis of bourgeois capitalism leading to proletarian revolution. He also developed a theory of imperialism which held that it was the last stage of a decaying capitalism. This was used to justify revolution in feudal Russia, because it was an imperial power, and subsequently to justify communist intervention in underdeveloped countries as part of the struggle between socialism and imperialism. Serious doubts were cast upon Lenin's views by the many failures of the socialism they led to and eventually by the collapse of the USSR in 1991. ▷ **Maoism; Russian Revolution**

Masaryk, Jan (1886–1948)

Czechoslovak diplomat and politician. The son of Tómaš **Masaryk**, after a youth of travelling and developing a variety of skills, he entered the diplomatic service in 1918, and from 1925 to 1938 was Czechoslovak envoy in London. There, his fluent English and personal charm won him many friends, but proved inadequate to prevent Chamberlain imposing the Munich Agreement on his country. He became a popular broadcaster during the war. In July 1941 he was appointed Foreign Minister of the Czechoslovak government in exile, returning with President **Beneš** to Prague in 1945 and remaining in office in the hope of bridging the growing gap between East and West in the developing **Cold War**. On 10 Mar 1948, following the Communist takeover of power in Czechoslovakia, his body was found beneath the open window of the Foreign Ministry in Prague, and it is generally believed that he killed himself in protest at the Stalinization of his homeland. ▷ **Stalin, Joseph**

Masire, Quett Ketumile Joni (1925–)

Botswanan journalist and politician. A journalist, he was Director of African Echo in 1958 before, with Sir Seretse **Khama**, founding the Botswana Democratic Party in 1962, whose Secretary-General he became. Deputy Prime Minister in 1965, he was Minister of Finance in 1966 and Vice-President 1966–80, taking over the presidency on Sir Seretse Khama's death in 1980.

Massey, Charles Vincent (1887–1967)

Canadian politician and diplomat. In 1952 he became the first native-born Governor-General. In 1925 Mackenzie **King** invited him to join his cabinet but he failed to win a seat in 1926 and he was appointed instead as Canada's first minister to the USA. He was chairman of the 1949 Royal Commission on National Development in the Arts, Letters and the Sciences which inquired into the federal cultural agencies, such as the Canadian Broadcasting Corporation, the National Film Board, the National Gallery and the National Research Council. Its report, submitted in 1951, suggested that a Canadian Council for the 'Encouragement of the Arts, Letters, Humanities and Social Sciences be established' and that Canada's cultural institutions be supported in order to limit US influence.

Mata Hari (Margaretha Gertruida Zelle) (1876–1917)

Alleged Dutch spy. She became a dancer in France (1903), had many lovers, several in high military and governmental positions (on both sides during and before **World War I**) and, found guilty of espionage for the Germans, was shot in Paris.

Matsuoka Yosuke (1880–1946)

Japanese diplomat and politician. After studying in the USA, Matsuoka joined the diplomatic service (1904) and attended the Paris Peace Conference (1919) as a member of the Japanese delegation. As Vice-President, and later President, of the South Manchuria Railway, he supported the expansion of Japan's interests in Manchuria. Matsuoka led the withdrawal of the Japanese delegation from the **League of Nations** in 1933 in response to the league's adoption of the Lytton Commission report, which had criticized the actions of the Japanese military in Manchuria. As Foreign Minister (1940–1), Matsuoka sought to strengthen Japan's position in the Far East and counter US hostility to its war in China by concluding the Tripartite Pact with Germany and Italy (27 Sep 1940) and signing a neutrality pact with the USSR (13 Apr 1941). Matsuoka's grand scheme ultimately failed; **Hitler**'s invasion of the USSR brought the latter into the allied camp, while US hostility to Japan's war in China (1937–45) merely intensified. In 1946 he was indicted as a class-A war criminal, but died before the trial was concluded.

Matteotti, Giacomo (1885–1924)

Italian politician. As a talented young deputy, belonging to Filippo **Turati**'s moderate Socialist Unity Party, Matteotti bravely and openly denounced the corruption and intimidation practised by the **Fascist Party** in the 1924 elections, only to be murdered by thugs acting on the orders of **Mussolini**. The murder resulted in widespread hostility and disgust towards Mussolini and a wave of anti-fascist feeling, which briefly threatened to bring an end to his rule.

Mau Mau

The phrase used by the colonial authorities for the uprising in Kenya, largely among the Kikuyu, which caused a state of emergency in the early 1950s. Its aims were anti-colonial and anti-settler (especially in the formerly Kikuyu 'White Highlands'), rather than self-consciously nationalist, and much of its violence was directed against fellow Kikuyu who were thought to be collaborating with the colonial authorities. But the disruption it caused hastened the transition to independence. However, very few of those who fought for Mau Mau benefited materially from the transfer of power.

Maududi, Maulana Abu'l Ala (1903–79)

Muslim revivalist thinker and founder of the **Jamaat-i Islami Party**. Beginning as a journalist, he became known as an opponent of both Pakistani and Indian nationalism. After India gained its independence, he was several times imprisoned by the Pakistan government.

Maura, Antonio (1853–1925)

Spanish politician. As the leader of a regenerationist movement within the Conservative Party, he sought a revolution from above. Autocratic and clerical, he was, however, unable to implement his nebulous ideas because of opposition from both Right and Left. In 1903 he tried, as Prime Minister, to replace *caciquismo* with an indirect, corporate franchise, but was dismissed the following year by King **Alfonso XIII**. His second period in office was from 1907 to 1909; he fell from power after the **Tragic Week**, a popular revolt in Barcelona against conscription. Four years later, he organized a proto-fascist party. Appointed Premier again in 1913, he hoped to become the 'iron surgeon' of the national government, but the Cabinet fell that same year. He headed a further two governments in 1919 and 1921–2.

Mauritius

A small island nation in the Indian Ocean, including c.20 surrounding islets, and the dependencies of Rodrigues Island, the Agalega Islands, and the Cargados Carajos Islands (St Brandon Islands). Formerly owned by France, it was ceded to Britain and governed jointly with the Seychelles as a single colony from 1814 to 1903. It became an independent sovereign state within the Commonwealth in 1968 and an independent republic in 1992. The sovereignty of Tromelin Island is in dispute between France and Mauritius.

Mauroy, Pierre (1928–)
French politician. He was a teacher before becoming involved with trade unionism and socialist politics, and was prominent in the creation of a new French **Socialist Party** in 1971. He became Mayor of Lille in 1973, and was elected to the National Assembly the same year. A close ally of **Mitterrand**, Mauroy acted as his spokesman during the socialists' successful election campaign. He was Prime Minister from 1981 to 1984.

Maurras, Charles (1868–1952)
French royalist journalist and political theorist. He was early influenced by the ideas of Auguste Comte. By 1894 he was established as an avant-garde journalist and a proponent of monarchism. From 1908, in the newspaper *Action française*, his articles wielded a powerful influence on the youth of the country. In 1936 he was imprisoned for violent attacks on the government. At the fall of France (1940), he supported the **Vichy** government, and in 1945 was sentenced to life imprisonment, but released on medical grounds in 1952. ▷ **collaboration** (France); **World War II**

Max, Adolphe (1869–1939)
Belgian politician and patriot. First a journalist, then an accountant, he became Burgomaster of Brussels in 1909. When the German troops approached Brussels in Aug 1914, he boldly drove to meet them and opened negotiations. He defended the rights of the Belgian population against the invaders, and in Sep was imprisoned by the Germans, later refusing an offer of freedom on condition that he went to Switzerland and desisted from anti-German agitation. In Nov 1918 he returned to Belgium, was elected to the House of Representatives, and became a minister of state.

May Fourth Movement (1919)
A student demonstration in Beijing which crystallized the political and cultural aspirations of those who struggled for a new China. Originally a protest against the Japanese takeover of Germany's rights in Shandong (agreed by the Western powers at the Versailles Peace Conference), the movement spread nationwide, rallying students and intellectuals across a broad political spectrum. ▷ **Versailles, Treaty of**

May Thirtieth Movement (1925)
The large-scale anti-imperialist demonstrations in China which resulted in increased membership for both the **Chinese Communist Party** and the **Guomindang**. On this day, a crowd of workers and students in Shanghai protesting against the earlier killing of a Chinese worker in a Japanese textile mill was fired upon by the British-led International settlement police force. The incident, during which 13 died and many more were injured, led to nationwide strikes and boycotts. The most significant of

these was the 15-month boycott against the British colony of Hong Kong following the killing of 52 demonstrators by British and French troops in Canton (23 June 1925). The movement clearly revealed the strength of opposition to foreign privilege in China. The powers, adapting to the new situation, began discussions in 1925 on the return to China of tariff autonomy.

Mayakovsky, Vladimir Vladimirovich (1893–1930)
Russian poet. He began writing at an early age, and was regarded as the leader of the Futurist school. Involved in underground activity before the **Russian Revolution** (1917) and deeply committed to its success, he emerged as the propaganda mouthpiece of the Communist Party but also wrote satirical plays. Travelling abroad frequently in the 1920s, he became critical of the regime and eventually committed suicide in Moscow.

Mboya, Tom (Thomas Joseph) (1930–69)
Kenyan trade unionist and politician. Educated at Catholic mission schools and Ruskin College, Oxford, he was an employee of the Nairobi City Council when he became Treasurer of the Kenyan African Union in 1953. He was elected Secretary-General of the Kenyan Federation of Labour in 1955 and a member of Legco in 1957. Mboya was a founder member, and Secretary-General (1960–9) of the Kenyan African National Union (KANU). His reformist instincts brought him into conflict with his fellow Luo, Oginga **Odinga**, but he eventually won out, forcing Odinga out of KANU after the party's conference at Limuru (1966), thus binding himself closer to Jomo **Kenyatta**. He was Minister of Labour (1962–3), Minister of Justice and Constitutional Affairs (1963–4), and Minister for Economic Planning and Development (1964–9) when his essentially Fabian philosophy established the 'free enterprise with state regulation' economic system which Kenya epitomizes. He was assassinated in 1969.

McCarthy, Joseph Raymond (1909–57)
US politician. Educated at Marquette University, Milwaukee, he became a circuit judge in 1939, and after war service was elected Senator in 1946. He achieved fame for his unsubstantiated accusations in the early 1950s that communists had infiltrated the State Department, and in 1953 became chairman of the Senate permanent subcommittee on investigations. By hectoring cross-examination and damaging innuendo he arraigned many innocent citizens and officials, overreaching himself when he came into direct conflict with the army. This kind of anti-communist witchhunt became known as 'McCarthyism'. His power diminished after he was formally condemned by the Senate in 1954. ▷ **Fifth Amendment; HUAC**

McKinley, William (1843–1901)
US politician and 25th President. He served in the American Civil War, then became a lawyer. As a Republican, he was elected to the US House of Representatives in 1877, and in 1892 was elected Governor of Ohio, despite his name being identified with the unpopular high protective tariff carried in the McKinley Tariff Act of 1890. During the presidential election of 1896 he secured a large majority as an advocate of the gold standard. His term as President (1897–1901) saw the outbreak of the Spanish–American War (1898), which culminated in the acquisition of Cuba and the Philippines. He was re-elected in 1900, but his second term ended when he was shot by an anarchist in Buffalo, New York. ▷ **Republican Party**

McNamara, Robert Strange (1916–)
US politician and businessman. After service in the air force (1943–6), he worked his way up in the Ford Motor Company to the office of President by 1960. A Democrat, in 1960 he joined the J F **Kennedy** administration as Secretary of Defence, being particularly involved in the **Vietnam War**. He resigned in 1967 to become President of the World Bank (a post he held until 1981). In the 1980s he emerged as a critic of the nuclear arms race. ▷ **Democratic Party**

Médici, Emílio Garrastazú (1905–90)
Brazilian military dictator. A career military officer, he was Chief-of-Staff to Artur da Costa e Silva in the late 1950s, Military Academy Commander in 1964 and Head of the SNI (National Information Service, the military intelligence operation attached to the presidency) during Costa's government. Nominated President by the military junta in 1969, he governed until 1974, using a military-technocratic team to balance repression and rapid economic growth. He manipulated elections and liquidated guerrillas in major cities as well as Araguaía in Goías and Pará, at the cost of creating an almost autonomous security apparatus, and stimulated settlement of Amazonia.

Medvedev, Roy Alexandrovich (1925–)
Soviet historian, dissident and politician. Although remaining a Marxist, he was highly critical of **Stalin** and other communist leaders. In 1968 he was expelled from the Communist Party and denied employment in academic bodies. However, he continued writing as a private individual; for example he published his best book *Let History Judge* in 1971. In this way he helped to sustain ideological criticism of Leonid **Brezhnev**'s dictatorship. Under Mikhail **Gorbachev** he was able to enter politics. He was readmitted to the party and elected to the Congress and the Supreme Soviet in 1989. His twin brother, Zhores **Medvedev**, also suffered as a critic of Brezhnev.

Medvedev, Zhores Alexandrovich (1925–)
Soviet geneticist and dissident. Like his twin brother, Roy **Medvedev**, he became an opponent of the communist system through his scientific studies. As a reputable geneticist, he was particularly critical of the damage **Lysenko** had done with political support. In 1970 he was confined to a psychiatric hospital but was released as a result of protests from abroad. On visiting Britain in 1973, he was deprived of his Soviet citizenship and he stayed on working as a genontological researcher. His publications include *The Rise and Fall of Lysenko*, helping to set the Soviet scientific record straight.

Meech Lake Accord (1987)
Canadian constitutional amendment, which recognized French-speaking Quebec as a 'distinct society', in response to the province's demands for special status within the confederation. The agreement was concluded in 1987 but did not receive enough support from the English-speaking provinces to be ratified. The failure of the Accord intensified Quebec separatism and also fuelled resentment among the native Inuit and Indians at their own lack of representation. The Charlottetown Agreement, balancing concessions for greater autonomy for Quebec and the Inuit and Indian populations with other consitutional reforms aimed at the Western provinces, was put to a referendum on 26 Oct 1992. This was defeated by 54.4 per cent to 44.6 per cent.

Meighen, Arthur (1874–1960)
Canadian lawyer and politician. A Conservative, in 1913 he became Solicitor-General in Robert **Borden**'s Union government and was the architect of much of its strategy during **World War I**: railway nationalization, conscription and the deeply-resented Wartime Elections Act. It was Meighen who also orchestrated the government's draconian response to the **Winnipeg General Strike** (1919), insisting that organized labour was revolutionary. Both the Immigration Act and the criminal code were amended so that strike leaders would face either deportation or long prison sentences. In 1920 Meighen succeeded Borden as Prime Minister and his high tariff policy was a major factor in the defeat of the Conservative Party in 1921. He became Prime Minister again in 1925 but when the Progressives deserted him, the Governor-General allowed him to dissolve parliament, a mechanism which had not been afforded to Mackenzie **King** in a similar situation. King won the election by promising to prevent such imperial intervention. Meighen then resigned as Conservative leader a few months later, and was replaced by R B **Bennett**. In 1940 the Conservatives invited him to lead the party again but he failed to win a seat and retired from politics.

Meiji Emperor (Mutsuhito) (1852–1912)
Emperor of Japan (1867/1912). He became the symbol of Japan's modernization. He is commemorated by the Meiji Shrine and the Meiji Memorial Picture Gallery, Tokyo, and a large mausoleum at Momoyama, near Kyoto.

Meir, Golda (1898–1978)
Israeli politician. Born in Kiev, she emigrated with her family to Milwaukee, USA, when she was eight. She married in 1917 and settled in Palestine in 1921. She was Israeli Ambassador to the USSR (1948–9), Minister of Labour (1949–56), and Foreign Minister (1956–66). As Prime Minister (1969–74), her efforts for peace in the Middle East were halted by the fourth Arab–Israeli War (1973). ▷ **Arab–Israeli Wars; Mapai Party**

Menderes, Adnan (1899–1961)
Turkish politician. Though educated for the law, he became a farmer, and entered politics in 1932, at first in opposition, then with the party in power under Kemal **Atatürk**. In 1945 he was one of the leaders of the new Democratic Party and became Prime Minister when it came to power (1950). He was deposed (1960) in an army coup, put on trial, and hanged at Imrali.

Mendès-France, Pierre (1907–82)
French politician. He entered parliament in 1932 as a member of the **Radical Party**, in 1941 escaping to join the **Free French** forces in England. He was Minister for National Economy under de **Gaulle** in 1945. As Prime Minister (1954–5), he ended the war in Indo-China, but his government was defeated on its North African policy. A firm critic of de Gaulle, he lost his seat in the 1958 election.

Menem, Carlos Saul (1935–)
Argentine politician. While training for the legal profession, he became politically active in the Peronist (Justice Party) movement, founding the Youth Group in 1955. In 1963 he was elected President of the party in La Rioja and in the same year unsuccessfully contested the governorship of the province, eventually being elected in 1983 and re-elected in 1987. In 1989 he defeated the Radical Union Party (UCR) candidate and became President of Argentina. A highly pragmatic ruler, he rapidly jettisoned inflammatory rhetoric to move towards discussion of the Falklands/Malvinas issue, and to begin an ambitious privatization policy.

Mengistu, Haile Mariam (1941–)
Ethiopian soldier and politician. He trained at Guenet Military Academy and took part in the attempted coup against Emperor **Haile Selassie** in 1960, but was not put on trial. He was a member of the Armed Forces Co-

ordinating Committee (**Dergue**) which helped overthrow Heile Selassie in 1974. He manipulated himself into the chairmanship of the Dergue and became undisputed leader and Head of State in 1977. Allying himself with the USSR and modelling himself upon Cuba's **Castro**, he sought a socialist transformation for Ethiopia, while retaining its territorial borders intact. Mismanagement, drought and internal war weakened his hold on the country and he fled from Addis Ababa on 21 May 1991, travelling to Zimbabwe where he was offered political asylum.

Mensheviks

In Russian literally 'minority-ites', the members of the moderate faction of the Marxist Russian Social Democratic Labour Party, led by J Martov, which split with **Lenin**, who engineered a false majority for his supporters (hence called **Bolsheviks** or 'majority-ites') at the Party's Second Congress in 1903. The Mensheviks particularly opposed Lenin's policy of organizing a small disciplined party dedicated to promoting and provoking revolution. In 1917 some Mensheviks joined the Provisional Government; but from 1918 onwards they were subject to increasing persecution, their leaders forced abroad in 1921 and many one-time members put on trial in 1930–1. ▷ **Russian Revolution**

Menzies, Robert Gordon (1894–1978)

Australian politician. He practised as a barrister, entering the Victoria parliament in 1928. In 1934, he moved to federal politics as member for Kooyang. He was Attorney-General (1935–9), Prime Minister (1939–41), and Leader of the Opposition (1943–9), during which time he rebuilt the conservative elements in Australian politics from the disintegrating **United Australia Party** into the formidable **Liberal Party of Australia**. Successful in the 1949 election, he became Prime Minister, an office he held for 16 years, until his retirement in 1966. Old-fashioned in his regard for British traditions, Menzies was also strongly anti-communist and supported US involvement in the Pacific. He led Australia into SEATO, the **ANZUS** pact and actively supported the USA in the **Vietnam War**. He shrewdly exploited the **Australian Labor Party**'s divisions over **communism** in the 1950s, but failed in his attempt to ban the Australian Communist Party. The 'Menzies Era' was one of economic growth and prosperity which made Australia briefly 'the lucky country'. In 1956 he headed the Five Nations Committee which sought to come to a settlement with Gamal Abd al-**Nasser** on the question of the **Suez Crisis**.

Mesopotamia Campaign

This campaign in **World War I** represented an effort by the British to safeguard both the route to India and the newly discovered oilfields of Persia. The Ottomans had declared for the German interest in the war and it was thus essential, for the realization of the above two aims, that

British arms prevail in Iraq. After the catastrophe of **Kut al-Amara** earlier in the war, a regrouped British offensive under General Maude took Kut early in 1917 and entered Baghdad in Mar of the same year. Further operations on the River Euphrates and the River Tigris as far as Mosul resulted in a complete British occupation of Mesopotamia.

Metaxas, Ioannis (1870–1941)
Greek general and dictator. He fought against the Turks in 1897, studied military science in Germany, and in 1913 became Chief of the General Staff. On the fall of King **Constantine I** in 1917 he fled to Italy, but returned with him in 1921. In 1935 he became Deputy Prime Minister, and as Premier in 1936 established a fascist dictatorship. He led the resistance to the Italian invasion of Greece in 1940. He remained in office until his death, which, it was rumoured, was brought about by posion administered by agents of **Hitler**.

Mexico
A federal republic in the south of North America. Formerly a Spanish dependency, it became a federal republic in 1823. The French attempted to establish a monarchy, but in 1876 Porfirio Díaz led a revolt and established an autocratic rule which lasted until 1910. The gulf between rich and poor caused continuing discontent amongst the workers, many of whom relied on the land. In the 1930s land reforms were carried out by President **Cárdenas**. The discovery of oil led to a new prosperity, but government borrowing led to a massive foreign debt.

Michael (1921–)
King of Romania (1927/30 and 1940/7). The son of **Charles II** of Romania, he first succeeded to the throne on the death of his grandfather, **Ferdinand**, his father having renounced his own claims in 1925. In 1930 he was supplanted by Charles, but was again made king in 1940 when the Germans gained control of Romania. In 1944 he played a considerable part in the overthrow of the dictatorship of Ion **Antonescu**. He announced the acceptance of the Allied peace terms, and declared war on Germany. His attempts after the war to establish a broader system of government were foiled by the progressive communization of Romania. In 1947 he was forced to abdicate and has since lived in exile.

Michurin, Ivan Vladimirovich (1855–1935)
Soviet agronomist. In 1875 he started improving fruit varieties by stock-scion grafting on his plot in Kozlov. It was **Lenin** who drew attention to him in 1920, and **Stalin** then exploited him as an example of what could be done through collectivization. He never developed any theories, but after his death **Lysenko** claimed to be his scientific heir and managed in

this way to raise his own respectability. In 1932 Kozlov, in the Soviet manner, was renamed Michurinsk.

Midway, Battle of (1942)
US naval victory. Admiral Chester **Nimitz**, forewarned of Japanese intentions by the breaking of their naval codes, reinforced Midway Island and forced the Japanese to withdraw with the loss of four aircraft carriers. This was the first battle in which the use of aircraft enabled engagement beyond visual range, and together with the Battle of the **Coral Sea**, saved Australia and Hawaii and stemmed the Japanese push into the Central Pacific.

Mihailović, Draža (1893–1946)
Serbian soldier. He rose to the rank of colonel in the Yugoslav Army, and in 1941 remained in Yugoslavia after the German occupation, forming groups (**Chetniks**) to wage guerrilla warfare. He later allied himself with the Germans and then with the Italians to fight the communists. He was executed in Belgrade by the **Tito** government for collaboration. ▷ **World War II**

Mikolajczyk, Stanislaw (1901–67)
Polish politician. He was born the son of an émigré miner in Westphalia and, returning to independent Poland at the end of **World War I**, he soon entered politics and became leader of the Peasant Party (1931–9). From 1940 to 1943 he held office in the exiled Polish government in London and, following the death of General **Sikorski**, became Prime Minister (1943–4). After the German defeat, he became Deputy Premier in the new coalition government in Warsaw, promoted by the USSR and accepted by the Western Allies. With a large peasant following, he hoped to resist a total takeover by the pro-Soviet communists. However, following rigged elections in 1947 he had no alternative but to flee to the West, where he settled in the USA.

Mikoyan, Anastas Ivanovich (1895–1970)
Soviet politician. Educated in a seminary, he became a Bolshevik in 1915 and was active in the Caucasusu. A candidate member of the Central Committee from 1922 and of the **Politburo** from 1926, he supported **Stalin** against **Trotsky** in the 1920s and survived the former's purges in the 1930s. He held various ministerial posts connected with trade, doing much to improve Soviet standards of living and introducing several ideas from the West. Mikoyan survived Stalin and allied with Nikita **Khrushchev**. He was Vice-Chairman of the Council of Ministers (1955–64) and President of the Presidium of the Supreme Soviet (1964–5). An extremely versatile politician, he helped Khrushchev survive the **Anti-**

Party Plot in 1957, and in 1962 persuaded Fidel **Castro** to accept the withdrawal of Soviet missiles from Cuba.

Militant Tendency

A British political group which came to prominence in the 1980s. Ostensibly, *Militant* is a newspaper published by **Labour Party** members espousing Marxist positions. In practice, critics have argued, the newspaper is a front for a 'party within a party', a separate organization of revolutionary Trotskyists who have entered the Labour Party (entryism) to use its organizational base for its own political ends. They claim that Militant is a cover for the Revolutionary Socialist League, the original British section of the Fourth International. In the 1980s, its supporters infiltrated a number of local Labour parties and the Young Socialists (its youth wing). Fearing the adverse electoral publicity resulting from Militant activities, the Labour Party moved to expel members of Militant on the grounds that they were members of a separate political party, which is against the party's constitution. Many of those expelled took the party to court, but their cases were not upheld. Since then, Militant's influence has declined.

Military Service Act (1917)

Canadian conscription legislation. It was introduced because Canada's voluntary militia had been unable to fulfil the commitment to provide four full divisions on the Western Front. Robert Laird **Borden**'s Minister for Militia, Sir Sam Hughes, had deterred many French-Canadians from volunteering by his Ulster Protestant prejudices. The Act was particularly unpopular in Quebec, where many believed they were being asked to fight for the empire, while being denied equal rights at home. With **World War II** the government tried to maintain a policy of 'no conscription' to ensure national unity, despite continuous pressure from the English-speaking provinces, especially after the fall of France. In response **King** held a referendum which showed that although 80 per cent of the English-speaking population wished to free the government from its pledge, 72 per cent of French-Canadians were against doing so. King therefore retained the policy and sacked his Defence Minister when he was advised that there were not enough volunteers to maintain the Canadian commitment after the Normandy landings in 1944. But with the failure of the policy to enlist home defence draftees, King was forced to reintroduce conscription. Protestation from French-Canadians, both among civilians and in the forces, was fierce, while one French-Canadian minister resigned from the government and 34 Quebec Liberals voted against it in a vote of confidence. Even so, King managed to survive the election of 1945, albeit with a reduced majority.

Miliukov, Pavel Nikolaevich (1849–1943)
Russian historian and politician. As a professor of history in Moscow he wrote extensively on the condition of the people and was almost inevitably drawn into criticizing the Tsarist regime. During the Russian **Revolution of 1905** he campaigned for the establishment of a constituent assembly. In the dumas that followed he led the Constitutional Democrats or **Kadets**, whose aim remained the eventual establishment of a constituent assembly. That became the official policy of the **Russian Provisional Government** in 1917 in which Miliukov was Minister of Foreign Affairs. Unfortunately his wish that Russia should continue the war cost him his job in May and helped to undermine the government that might have made his assembly a reality. It was easy for **Lenin** to dismiss the one and only **Russian Constituent Assembly** in Jan 1918.

Millerand, Alexandre (1859–1943)
French politician. He entered parliament (1885) and was Minister of Commerce (1899–1902), the first socialist to hold ministerial office. However, in 1905 he refused to join the SFIO and moved towards the Right, holding office as Minister of Works (1909–10) and of War (1912–13 and 1914–15), when he resigned on complaints of deficiency of supplies. His chief critic, **Clemenceau**, later appointed him *commissaire général* in Alsace–Lorraine (1919). As Prime Minister (1920), he formed a right-wing coalition (**Bloc national**) and gave support to the Poles during the Russian invasion of 1920. He became President in 1920 and resigned in 1924 in face of opposition from the **Cartel des gauches** under **Herriot**. He later entered the Senate. ▷ **Socialist Party** (France)

Milner (of St James's and Cape Town), Alfred, 1st Viscount (1854–1925)
British politician and colonial administrator. He was appointed Governor of the Cape and High Commissioner in South Africa (1897). There he became convinced that the British position was endangered by the South African Republic (Transvaal), and set about the political rationalization of the region through the **Boer Wars**. He hoped to encourage sufficient English-speaking immigration to outnumber the Boers in a South African dominion. He additionally became Governor of the Transvaal and Orange River Colony in 1901, but was forced to resign in 1905 as a result of irregularities over Chinese labour he had introduced for the Rand gold mines. He was Secretary for War (1916–19) and Colonial Secretary (1919–21), and died in Kent, England.

Milorg
Abbreviated form of *Milit*ær Organisasjonen, the secret resistance force formed in Norway following the German invasion of the country in Apr 1940. ▷ **Norway, German Invasion of**

Milošević, Slobodan (1941–)
Serbian politician. He joined the Communist League in 1959 while a student. In 1966 he entered government service as an economic adviser to the Mayor of Belgrade and later held senior posts in the Yugoslav federal banks and gas industry (1969–83). Appointed President of the Serbian League of Communists in 1984, he became President of Serbia in 1988. Both a Serbian nationalist and a hardline Communist Party leader in the pre-**perestroika** mould, he withdrew the status of Kosovo and Vojvodina as autonomous provinces within the Republic of Serbia. He remained in power after the multi-party elections held in Serbia in 1990. The crisis in Yugoslavia gathered pace in 1991, when Milošević at first refused to accept a Croat, Stipe Mesić, as President of Yugoslavia, and when it was revealed that he had appropriated £875-worth of Yugoslav federal reserves to buttress the Serbian economy. Bitterly opposed to the break-up of Yugoslavia, after Slovenia and Croatia declared their independence in June 1991, he agitated for the Yugoslav federal army to be sent into Slovenia and Croatia and later, in Apr 1992, into Bosnia-Herzegovina. An unrepentant champion of a 'Greater Serbia', he has done nothing to prevent the fighting in Bosnia led by avowedly 'independent' Serbian militias bent on joining the greater part of the newly-independent Republic of Bosnia to the Republic of Serbia and eliminating all non-Serb residents through 'ethnic cleansing'. ▷ **Kučan, Milan; Tudjman, Franjo**

Milyutin, Vladimir Petrovich (1884–1937)
Russian economist. Menshevik, turned Bolshevik, turned practical economist, he joined the Russian Social Democratic Party in 1903 when only 19; but by 1917 he was as well schooled in prisons as in splits in the party. He tended to waver in his politics which may have turned him to economics, a discipline in which the communists were short of specialists. He held various posts, including Commissar for Agriculture (1919–22) and vice-chairman of Gosplan (1929–37). ▷ **Bolsheviks; Mensheviks**

Mindszenty, József (1892–1975)
Roman Catholic Primate of Hungary. He became a priest in 1915, Archbishop of Esztergom and Primate in 1945, and Cardinal in 1946. He then acquired international fame in 1948 when he was charged with treason by the communist government in Budapest. He was sentenced to life imprisonment the following year, but in 1955 was released on condition that he did not leave Hungary. At the end of the **Hungarian Uprising** in 1956 he was granted asylum in the US legation, where he remained as a voluntary prisoner until 1971, when conditions in Hungary eased and he was allowed to go abroad. He spent his last years in a Hungarian religious community in Vienna.

Minobe Tatsukichi (1873–1948)
Japanese constitutional scholar. A member of the House of Peers (Upper House of the Diet), he was accused by the military in 1935 of *lèse-majesté* for his views on the Emperor. A supporter of party cabinets and democratic constitutionalism, Minobe asserted that the Emperor was an 'organ' of the state, a notion that was seen as an attack on the sacred nature of the imperial institution. Amidst growing calls during the 1930s by both the military and civilian ultra-nationalists for the elimination of 'dangerous thoughts', Minobe was forced to resign from the House of Peers and many of his works were banned.

Minto, Gilbert John Elliot-Murray-Kynynmound, 4th Earl of (1845–1914)
British colonial administrator. After serving in the Scots Guards (1867–70) and working as a journalist in Spain and Turkey (1874–7), he fought in the second Afghan War (1879) before going to Canada. As Governor-General (1898–1905) he was an intermediary between the Prime Minister, Wilfrid **Laurier**, and Joseph Chamberlain, the British Colonial Secretary. As Viceroy of India (1905–10), in succession to Lord Curzon, he found an associate in John Morley, the radical Secretary of State. Both were convinced that something must be done to associate articulate Indian opinion more closely with the government. The two men, though different in their origins and natures, made an effective team. Among the problems tackled by Minto and Morley were the securing of better representation of important Indian interests and the enlargement of the powers of the existing legislative councils. The Indian Councils Act, the core of what is generally known as the **Morley–Minto Reforms**, became law in 1909. As a result of a campaign by a Muslim delegation for representation of Muslim interests through special constituencies this law introduced the principle of communal representation. Six special Muslim constituencies of land-holders were created for the Imperial Legislative Council, and others in some other provinces. This measure is considered as the official germ of Pakistan.

Mishima Yukio (Hiraoka Kimitake) (1925–70)
Japanese writer. He passionately believed in the chivalrous traditions of Imperial Japan, became expert in the martial arts, and in 1968 founded the Shield Society, a group of a hundred youths dedicated to a revival of **bushido**, the samurai knightly code of honour. The most extreme expression of his elitist right-wing views was in an essay *Sun and Steel* (1970); in the same year he committed suicide by performing hara-kiri after a carefully-staged token attempt to rouse the nation to a return to pre-war nationalist ideals.

Mitbestimmung
As early as 1848, German working-class organizations had demanded their rights of *Mitbestimmung*, or co-determination, in the workplace.

However, effective employee rights of co-determination (as against mere consultation) have only come into being with the establishment of the Federal Republic. The 1952 Factory Constitution Law (or *Betriebsverfassungsgesetz*) allowed co-determination in social matters, but similar rights across a broad range of company affairs was introduced in the iron, steel and coal industries at that time and universally in larger firms in 1976. Elected workers' and staff representatives sit on the upper board (*Aufsichtsrat*) of German companies where they enjoy equal rights with shareholders' representatives in defined key areas. Co-determination is not unrestricted in Germany, but the contemporary system is regarded by the trade unions and the **SPD** as an important element of the democratic order.

Mitchell, James Fitzallen (1931–)
St Vincent and the Grenadines politician. He trained and worked as an agronomist (1958–65) and then bought and managed a hotel in Bequia, St Vincent. He entered politics through the St Vincent Labour Party (SVLP) and in the pre-independence period served as Minister of Trade (1967–72). He was then Premier (1972–4), heading the People's Political Party (PPP). In 1975 he founded the New Democratic Party (NDP) and, as its leader, became Prime Minister in 1984, achieving re-election in 1989.

MITI (Ministry of International Trade and Industry)
The powerful Japanese government ministry created in 1949 to formulate and implement trade and industrial policy. The initial aim was to provide unified control over industrial recovery and export growth so as to end dependence on US aid. Until the mid-1960s MITI exercised total control over imports and exports, and allocated imported technology, investment funds and resources to those sectors (coal, steel, shipbuilding) deemed crucial for industrial growth. After the mid-1960s, in response to foreign accusations of protectionism, MITI relaxed its controls and began to liberalize foreign trade, although it continued to exercise influence over the economy through informal 'administrative guidance', encouraging rationalization of industry (such as mergers) and recommending loans for chosen institutions. As a key component of the 'economic bureaucracy', MITI has played a crucial role in Japan's post-war recovery and its attainment of economic superpower status. On retirement, many of its officials become executives of leading private corporations, illustrating the close ties that exist between government and business.

Mitsotakis, Costas (Constantine) (1918–)
Greek politician. Leader of the New Liberals, a party on the centre-right founded in 1977 which claims to be the successor to the Liberal Party of his uncle, Eleuthérios **Venizélos**. Since 1990 he has served as Prime Min-

ister and Minister for the Aegean in the government of Constantine **Karamanlis**.

Mitterrand, François (Maurice Marie) (1916–)
French politician. Having served in the French Army (1939–40) and been taken prisoner, he escaped from capture and was active in the **Resistance Movement**. Elected a Deputy in 1946, and at once appointed a cabinet minister, he continued to hold office frequently for the rest of the Fourth Republic; he belonged to none of the major parties, but was a member of a tiny faction, the UDSR (*Union démocratique et socialiste de la Résistance*, 'Democratic and Socialist Union of the Resistance'). In 1958 he was a stubborn opponent of de **Gaulle**, and of the new constitution, which he characterized as being semi-fascist, in a book entitled *Le Coup d'Etat permanent* (1964). He worked assiduously to unify the left, standing unsuccessfully as the left-wing candidate in the 1965 presidential elections. After the collapse of the Left in 1968, and its very poor showing in the 1969 presidential elections, in which he was not a candidate, he achieved this aim in 1971 when the SFIO (**Socialist Party**) merged with various left-wing groups, including Mitterrand's own, to form the new Socialist Party of which he was at once elected leader. This was followed by agreement with the French Communist Party on a common programme (1972). Although this was later denounced by the communists, the two parties remained close allies. After he was elected President in 1981, a coalition government that included communists was formed (1981–4), which embarked on a major programme of nationalization and job creation; in 1983 this produced economic crisis, and had to be abandoned. The right won the parliamentary elections of 1986, opening a period of 'cohabitation', in which his powers as President were restricted, but Mitterrand won the presidential elections of 1988, and managed to achieve in the parliamentary elections of the same year an assembly with no overall majority, but in which it was possible to form left-wing cabinets, thus restoring his political authority. ▷ **Republic, Fourth** (France)

Mlada Bosna
The revolutionary organization (literally, 'Young Bosnia') opposed to **trialism** and to the Austrian annexation of Bosnia (1908). Its members were drawn from the Bosnian–Serb intelligentsia.

Mlynar, Zdenek (1930–)
Czechoslovak politician. Coming of age in communist Czechoslovakia, educated in law in Moscow in the last years of **Stalin** and the first years of **Khrushchev**, and then observing the slow stagnation of the **Novotný** years in Czechoslovakia, he became a reformer through disillusionment. However, during the period of the **Prague Spring**, when he became a secretary of the purged Communist Party Central Committee, he made

a major contribution to Alexander **Dubček**'s action programme and was one of the leaders abducted to Moscow following the Soviet invasion. Released with the others, he quickly lost his party function and eventually, when he signed **Charter 77**, he lost his employment and went abroad.

Mobutu, Sese Seko Kuku Ngbendu Wa Za Banga (Joseph Desire) (1930–)

Zairean soldier and politician. After army training and a period of study in Brussels, he joined the Belgian Force Publique in 1949. By 1956 he was a colonel. He joined Patrice **Lumumba**'s Mouvement National Congolais in 1958 and was Chief of Staff in 1960 at the time of independence. The indecisiveness of government in Leopoldville led him to take over the government to deal with the problem of Katanga's secession but he handed power back to civilians within five months. After the 1963–5 civil war, he intervened again, this time permanently. He renamed the country Zaire in place of the Belgian Congo and imposed a degree of stability on to the country which had hitherto been unknown. Backed by US money and the power of the army, his regime has become increasingly corrupt and unpopular.

Moderate Unity Party (Sweden)

The name adopted in 1969 by the party of Swedish Conservatives, previously called 'The Right', whose origins can be traced back to 1904. It last formed an administration in 1928–30 under Arvid Lindman, but has participated in non-socialist coalitions since **World War II**. In the person of Carl Bildt it provided a prime minister for the administration formed in 1991.

Moderates (*Modérés*)

French political grouping. The name applied for most of the Third Republic to the more conservative part of the republicans, as opposed to the radicals and socialists. Originally known as the Opportunists, and then as the Progressists, between 1900 and 1940 they were usually known as the Moderate Republicans, or simply as the Moderates. They were organized in two factions: the *Alliance démocratique* ('Democratic Alliance'), more to the Left, and the *Fédération républicaine* ('Republican Federation'), more to the Right. The heirs to this tradition were the **Independents** (1948–62) and then (since 1966) the **Independent Republican Party**. ▷ **Republic, Third** (France)

Moeller van den Bruck, Arthur (1876–1925)

German writer. A radical right-winger, he was strongly opposed to Weimar's parliamentary order and toyed with Bolshevik as well as right-wing and racist ideas. In 1923 he published *The Third Reich* whose title was subsequently adopted by the National Socialists to describe the successor state to the **Weimar Republic**. ▷ **Bolsheviks; Nazi Party; Reich**

Mohamed, Murtala Ramal (1937–76)
Nigerian soldier. A Muslim Hausa from Northern Nigeria, he trained at Sandhurst and the Royal School of Signals before returning to Nigeria and then serving in the **UN** Congo operations in 1960. He commanded the Nigerian 2nd Battalion at the start of the Biafran War and was made federal Commissioner of Communications in 1974. When General **Gowon** was deposed in 1975, he became Head of State, but he was himself assassinated in an unsuccessful uprising on 13 Feb 1976.

Mohammed Nadir Shah (c.1880–1933)
King of Afghanistan (1929/33). The brother of Dost Muhammad, as Commander-in-Chief to **Amanullah Khan** (ruler and later King of Afghanistan from 1926) he played a prominent role in the third of the **Afghan Wars** against Britain (1919), which secured the country's full independence in 1922. He subsequently fell into disfavour and was forced to live in exile in France. In 1929, with British diplomatic support, he returned to Kabul and seized the throne, immediately embarking on a programme of economic and social modernization. These reforms, however, alienated the Muslim clergy and in 1933 he was assassinated. He was succeeded by his son, Mohammed **Zahir Shah**.

Moi, Daniel T arap (1924–)
Kenyan politician. Educated in local schools he was a primary school, and unqualified, teacher (1946–56). He entered Legco in 1957 and then was elected for the Baringo constituency which he represented 1963–78. Chairman of the Kenyan African Democratic Union (KADU) 1960–1, he was Minister of Education in the coalition pre-independence government 1960–1 and, after KADU had merged with the Kenyan African National Union (KANU), he was made Minister of Home Affairs (1964–7). He became Vice-President of Kenya in 1967 and succeeded Jomo **Kenyatta** on the latter's death in 1978. He has shifted the ethnic balance of central politics away from the Kikuyu towards the Kalenjin peoples of the Rift Valley and has cracked down hard on dissidents and opponents, reducing the already limited opportunities for meaningful political participation available to Kenyans. Despite an attempted coup in Aug 1982 he has remained in power.

Mollet, Guy Alcide (1905–75)
French socialist politician. A schoolteacher and member of the **Socialist Party**. In 1946 he became Mayor of Arras, a Deputy in the National Assembly, Secretary-General of the Socialist Party and a cabinet minister in the Léon **Blum** government. He survived the international crisis over

the Anglo-French intervention in Suez (Nov), but fell from office in May 1957. In 1959 he was elected a Senator, remaining leader of the SFIO until its absorption into the new Socialist Party in 1971, which ended his political influence.

Molotov (Skriabin), Vyacheslav Mikhailovich (1890–1986)
Soviet politician. Of middle-class origin and a student at Kazan University, he became a Bolshevik in 1906 and was close to **Lenin** and **Stalin** during the **Russian Revolution** in 1917. He subsequently acted as Stalin's right-hand man, first in domestic politics and, from 1939 onwards, as Foreign Minister, in foreign affairs. Holding office until 1949, he negotiated the Nazi–Soviet Pact with Ribbentrop and was then Stalin's chief adviser at the **Tehran Conference** and **Yalta Conference**, and was present at the founding of the **UN** (1945). After **World War II**, he emerged as the uncompromising champion of Soviet ambition; his *nyet* ('no') at meetings of the UN became a byword, and helped to foster the **Cold War**. He was less in favour in Stalin's last years, but became Foreign Minister again in 1953 until he was forced out by Nikita **Khrushchev** in 1956. He was then a leading figure in the failed **Anti-Party Plot** in 1957, but was gracefully allowed to occupy two further official posts before retiring in 1962. ▷ **Bolsheviks; communism; German–Soviet Pact**

Molotov Cocktail (1939–40)
A bottle filled with petrol, kerosene and tar used by Finnish soldiers as an anti-tank weapon during the Russo-Finnish War with the USSR. Originally the fuse was a rag ignited with a match, but eventually ampules of sulphuric acid were used. With little armour themselves the Finns used their Molotov Cocktails with devastating effect. The name 'Molotov' was that of the Soviet Foreign Minister. ▷ **Molotov (Skriabin), Vyacheslav Mikhailovich**

Momoh, Joseph Saidu (1937–)
Sierra Leone soldier and politician. Educated in secondary school in Freetown and military academies in Ghana, Britain and Nigeria, he was commissioned into the Sierra Leone army in 1963. He was a battalion commander by 1968 and was appointed a minister of state in 1975. When Siaka **Stevens** announced his retirement in 1985, Momoh, who had been hand-picked to be Stevens's successor, was endorsed by the country's only political party, the All People's Congress, as the sole presidential candidate. Having won the election, he has sought to distance himself from his predecessor's policies in an attempt to restrain corruption and reform the economy.

Monash, Sir John (1865–1931)
Australian soldier. He practised as a civil engineer and also held a commission in the Australian Citizen Force (1887), rising to command the 13th Infantry Brigade by 1913. He commanded the 4th Australian Infantry Brigade at Gallipoli (1914–15), the 3rd Australian Division in France (1916), and the Australian Corps as Lieutenant-General (1918). Recognized as one of the outstanding generals of **World War I**, he was noted for the meticulous preparation and planning of his operations. After the war, he was chairman of the Victorian State Electricity Commission. ▷ **Gallipoli Campaign**

Mondlane, Eduardo (1920–69)
Mozambiquan nationalist leader. Educated in mission schools, he furthered his training at Fort Hare College and Lisbon University and developed into a respected sociologist with research posts in the USA and with the **UN**. He returned to Mozambique in 1961 to form **Frelimo** and launched the guerrilla war against Portuguese colonialism in 1964. He was murdered by a parcel bomb in Dar es Salaam.

Monnet, Jean (1888–1979)
French political economist and diplomat. He introduced in 1947 the Monnet Plan for the modernization of French industry. He was President of the European Coal and Steel High Authority (1952–5), and of the Action Committee for the United States of Europe (1956–75). ▷ **EEC**

Monseny, Federica (1905–)
Spanish anarchist writer and leader. She fought for women's rights within both the **CNT** and the **FAI**. Monseny strongly supported anarchist participation in the Popular Front elections of Feb 1936. She became Minister of Public Health in the Republican government of Sep 1936–May 1937 — the first woman in Spain to achieve a ministerial portfolio. Exiled to France in 1939, she remained active in anarchist circles, returning to Spain in 1975.

Montagu–Chelmsford Reforms
After a report (Apr 1918) by the Secretary of State for India, E S Montagu, and the Viceroy, Lord Chelmsford, the British agreed the 1919 Government of India Act. Promising progressive moves towards Indian self-government within the British Empire, it provided as a first step enlarged electorates, and partial provincial autonomy whereby responsibility for certain aspects of government was transferred to elected Indian ministers; at the centre a bicameral legislature comprising a Council of State and a Legislative Assembly with increased powers. The number of Indians on the central executive council was also enlarged; the Indian government gained a larger degree of independence from the control of

Whitehall. It was rejected by many Indians, and its promise of future progress was resisted by some British Conservatives, but a further step was taken, with full provincial autonomy under Indian control, in 1935. ▷ **Government of India Acts**

Montenegro

One of the two constituent republics of Yugoslavia. It was an independent monarchy until incorporated into Serbia in 1918, and in 1946 it became a republic of Yugoslavia. It sided with Serbia in the 1991 conflict with Slovenia and Croatia. Montenegrins voted to remain part of the Yugoslav federation in 1992.

Montgomery (of Alamein), Bernard Law, 1st Viscount (1887–1976)

British field marshal. Commissioned into the Royal Warwickshire Regiment (1908), in **World War II** he gained renown as arguably the best British field commander since Wellington. A controversial and outspoken figure, he was nevertheless a 'soldier's general', able to establish a remarkable rapport with his troops. He commanded the 8th Army in North Africa, and defeated **Rommel** at the Battle of **El Alamein** (1942). He played a key role in the invasion of Sicily and Italy (1943), and was appointed Commander-in-Chief, Ground Forces, for the Allied **Normandy Campaign** (1944). On his insistence, the invasion frontage was widened, and more troops were committed to the initial assault. Criticized for slow progress after **D-Day**, he uncharacteristically agreed to the badly-planned airborne landings at Arnhem (Sep 1944), which resulted in the only defeat of his military career. In 1945, German forces in north-western Germany, Holland, and Denmark surrendered to him on Lüneberg Heath. Appointed field marshal (1944) and viscount (1946), he served successively as Chief of the Imperial General Staff (1946–8) and Deputy Supreme Commander of **NATO** forces in Europe (1951–8). ▷ **North African Campaign**

Montoire sur Loir

A village in central France, where **Laval**, and two days later **Pétain**, met **Hitler** (22–4 Oct 1940) to define the policy of Franco-German **collaboration**.

Montoneros

Argentine urban guerrillas claiming allegiance to **Peronism** and (from 1970) staging terrorist actions against the military regime then in power. Repudiated by Juan Domingo **Perón** himself (1974), the Montoneros renewed their attacks on the regime installed in 1976, meeting with severe repression. Their activities encouraged the Argentine military to embark on the 'Dirty War' against the urban guerrillas, culminating in the Malvinas (Falklands) imbroglio.

Montreux Convention (1936)
This agreement revised the terms of the Treaty of **Lausanne** (1923) and allowed Turkey to remilitarize the Straits. Turkey was given absolute control of the waterway and could regulate the passage of warships through it in times of conflict, and in peacetime if it felt threatened. These generous concessions are explained by Britain's desire to prevent Turkey allying itself with **Hitler**.

Moonje, Balakrishna Shivaram (1872–1948)
Indian nationalist. A reputed eye surgeon who joined the Indian freedom struggle. He studied at Hislop College, Nagpur and at Grant Medical College, Bombay. He attended the Bombay Congress session and adopted **Tilak** as his guru. He subsequently gave up his medical practice to enter politics. He worked for the **Swadeshi** boycott and took a prominent part in the Home Rule Movement. He was elected President of the Central Legislature in 1926, but resigned the post at the call of Congress. He represented **Hindu Mahasabha** on the joint parliamentary committee and in 1937 formed a Hindu Military Education Society and started the Bhonsle Military School. He wrote a new Manusmriti which was never published. He received the popular title Dharmavira for his religious activities and was nicknamed Field Marshal Moonje for his military qualities.

Moral Majority
A US pressure group founded in 1979 which campaigns for the election of morally conservative politicians and for changes in public policy in such areas as abortion, homosexuality, and school prayers. It is associated with Christian fundamentalists who in the 1980s played a prominent role in US politics.

Morley–Minto Reforms
The popular name given to the 1909 Indian Councils Act. They broadened the basis of Indian Government, allowed Indians to sit on the Imperial Legislative Council, introduced direct elections for non-official seats in provincial legislative councils, and granted separate or communal electorates to minorities. They were not intended to progress to full parliaments, and were soon criticized for holding up administration, dividing Muslims and Hindus, and failing to appease Indian opinion.

Moro, Aldo (1916–78)
Italian politician. A leading figure in the **Christian Democrats**, he served twice as Prime Minister (1963–8 and 1974–6) and was Foreign Minister (1970–2). During the 1970s he was one of the DC moderates who sought to cooperate with **Berlinguer**. He was one of several important figures to die at the hands of the **Red Brigades**.

Morocco
A kingdom in North Africa. Following European interest in the regio throughout the 19c, the Treaty of Fez established Spanish Morocc (capital Tétouan) and French Morocco (capital Rabat). The inter national zone of Tangier was created in 1923 and the protectorates gaine independence in 1956. Former Spanish Sahara (Western Sahara) cam under the joint control of Spain, Morocco and Mauritania in 1975 an became the responsibility of Morocco in 1979, but there is an inde pendence movement in the region and Moroccan sovereignty is no recognized universally.

Morrison (of Lambeth), Herbert Stanley, 1st Baron (1888–1965)
British politician. Largely self-educated, he helped to found the London **Labour Party** of which he became Secretary (1915). First elected an MP in 1923, he was Minister of Transport (1929–31), Minister of Supply (1940), and Home Secretary (1940–5). He served in the war cabinet from 1942, and became a powerful post-war figure, acting as Deputy Prime Minister (1945–51), but was defeated by **Gaitskell** for the leadership of the Labour Party in 1955. He was made a life peer in 1959.

Mosaddeq, Mohammad (1880–1967)
Iranian politician. He held office in Iran in the 1920s, returned to politics in 1944, and directed his attack on the Anglo-Iranian Oil Co, which, by his Oil Nationalization Act of 1951 (in which year he became prime minister), he claimed to have expropriated. His government was overthrown by a royalist uprising in 1953, and he was imprisoned. He was released in 1956.

Mosaic Theory of Ethnicity
Canadian social theory. The concept emerged in the 1920s to describe the pluralism of Canadian society. The analogy facilitated the description of each racial group, its status and influence within the whole society as well as its cultural and institutional contributions to the nation. In 1965 John Porter suggested the refinement of a vertical mosaic, with status and prestige indicated by layers, so that some ethnic groups were heavily represented in the upper strata whilst others, without power, remained in the lower strata. He believed the idea of the mosaic (as opposed to that of the melting pot) impeded social mobility, and thus encouraged the persistence of conservative traits within Canadian society.

Mościcki, Ignacy (1867–1946)
Polish politician and scientist. Opposed to Tsarist rule as a young man, he spent many years in Switzerland, where he became a chemist. He later returned to Poland, where he was Professor of Chemistry at Lvov (1912–26). In 1926, as part of his coup d'état, Józef **Piłsudski** made him

President of Poland, a respectable figure hiding a virtual dictatorship. In 1939 he fled to Romania and then retired to Switzerland, where he died.

Moshoeshoe II (Constantine Bereng Seciso) (1938–)
King of Lesotho (1960/). Educated at Roma College, Ampleforth and Corpus Christi College, Oxford, he was installed as Paramount Chief of the Basotho in 1960 and then proclaimed King when Lesotho became independent in 1966. His political involvement resulted in his being twice placed under house arrest and in 1970 he spent eight months of exile in Holland. He returned on the understanding that he would behave as a constitutional monarch. He remained King after the military coup in Jan 1986, but was exiled (Mar 1990) to England and did not take up Major-General Lekhanya's invitation to return to Lesotho. In Nov 1990 his eldest son succeeded to the throne as King Letsie II.

Mosley, Sir Oswald (Ernald), 6th Baronet (1896–1980)
British politician. He was successively a Conservative, Independent and Labour MP, and a member of the 1929 Labour government. He resigned from the **Labour Party**, and founded, first, the New Party (1931), and then, following a visit to Italy, the British Union of Fascists, of which he became leader, and which is remembered for its anti-Semitic violence in the East End of London and its support for **Hitler**. Detained under the Defence Regulations during **World War II**, he founded another racialist party, the **Union Movement**, in 1948. He died in Orsay, near Paris, where he mainly lived after the war. ▷ **Blackshirts**

Motlana, Nthato (1925–)
South African doctor and politician. Educated at Kilnerton High School and Fort Hare College where he came into contact with the **ANC** (African National Congress) Youth league, he qualified as a doctor at the University of the Witwatersrand. Involved in establishing a network of ANC branches on the Witwatersrand, he was banned in 1953 for five years. By the mid-1970s he had became a leading figure in Soweto and played a major role in the 1976 uprising, helping to establish the Soweto Committee of Ten, which developed into the Soweto Civil Association, of which he is Chairman. One of the few figures to have lived in the townships and retained the respect of ordinary citizens, he became an articulate spokesman for black interests in the 1980s while the ANC was still banned.

Mountbatten (of Burma), Louis (Francis Albert Victor Nicholas), 1st Earl (1900–79)
British Admiral of the Fleet and statesman. He was the younger son of Prince Louis of Battenberg (later Louis Mountbatten, Marquess of Milford Haven) and Princess Victoria of Hesse, the granddaughter of Queen

Victoria. Having joined the Royal Navy in 1916, in **World War II** he became chief of **Combined Operations Command** (1942), and played a key role in preparations for **D-Day**. In 1943 he was appointed Supreme Commander, South-East Asia, where he defeated the Japanese offensive into India (1944), and worked closely with **Slim** to reconquer Burma (1945). He received the Japanese surrender at Singapore, and in 1947 was sworn in as last Viceroy of India prior to independence. Created an earl in 1947, he returned to the Admiralty, and became First Sea Lord (1954) and Chief of the Defence Staff (1959). Retiring in 1965, he remained in the public eye, and was assassinated by Irish terrorists while fishing near his summer home in the Irish Republic.

Mounties (The Royal Canadian Mounted Police)

The force was founded as the Royal North-West Mounted Police in 1873 by Lt Col George Arthur French who was the first commissioner, recruited mainly from the British Army and retaining its red jackets and pillbox hats. Organized on strictly military lines, the Mounties established tight control over the new territories as compared with law enforcement in the American West. Policing was only one of their many roles in the North West until 1953, when the Department of Northern Affairs took over most of their civic duties. In the other provinces the Mounties were amalgamated with the federal Dominion Police in 1920 and became the Royal Canadian Mounted Police. In 1928 Saskatchewan became the first province to contract the RCMP to provide a police force, followed by Alberta and other provinces in the later decades. Ontario and Quebec have not followed their example.

Moyne Commission (1940)

A royal commission of the British government set up after the **Disturbances** to investigate the social and economic conditions prevailing in the British West Indies. Headed by the Lord Moyne, its members toured the British Caribbean colonies (1938–9) and its recommendations were made public in 1940, although because of its critical nature, the full report was not published until 1945. It attributed social discontent to the current appalling socio-economic conditions and recommended the creation of an imperially-financed Colonial Development and Welfare Fund to encourage spending on health, education and housing projects. The Commission also supported the growth of trade unions, but was ambivalent towards constitutional progress.

Moynihan, Daniel Patrick (1927–)

US politician. Educated at the City College of New York and Tufts University, he taught at Syracuse, Harvard, and the Massachusetts Institute of Technology. He served in the administrations of Presidents **Johnson** and **Nixon**, acquiring notoriety as the author of *The Negro Family:*

The Case for National Action (1965). He became Ambassador to India (1973–4), and won a seat in the US Senate as a Democrat from New York in 1976. ▷ **Democratic Party**

Mozambique

A republic in south-east Africa. Settled by the Portuguese in the 15c, Mozambique acquired separate colonial status as Portuguese East Africa in the late 19c and became an overseas province of Portugal in 1951. An independence movement formed in 1962, the *Frente de Libertação de Moçambique* (FRELIMO), with armed resistance to colonial rule. The country gained independence in 1975, but civil war continued. The first peace talks took place in 1990, and a ceasefire took effect in 1992 as the first stage of a peace agreement. The country suffered severe drought in 1992.

MPLA (*Movimento Popular de Libertação de Angola*)

Formed in 1975, under the leadership of Agostinho **Neto**, by the merger of several nationalist groups, the organization faced opposition from **UNITA** and **FNLA** which could not be defused through negotiation. After the ensuing civil war, the MPLA with its Cuban and Soviet allies formed the government in Angola, but was faced with a continuing insurrection from UNITA with its South African and US allies. With neither side being able to prevail, negotiations took place and a cease fire was agreed in Estoril, Portugal, in May 1991.

MRP (*Mouvement républicain populaire*, 'Popular Republican Movement')

French political party, founded in 1944 by a group of Catholics, led by **Bidault**, who were active in the **Resistance Movement**. It was heir to the tradition of Christian democracy that had found expression before **World War II** in the *Parti démocrate populaire* ('Popular Democratic Party'), founded in 1924. It won nearly a quarter of the vote in 1945–6, and was one of the three pillars of the coalition government (Tripartism) 1945–7. However, its support declined rapidly, being halved in the 1951 elections. It supported Charles de **Gaulle** in 1958, but was divided by his Algerian policy, as some of its leaders, notably Bidault, opposed Algerian independence. Other members of the MRP objected to de Gaulle's opposition to European integration, and it withdrew from the government in 1962. Its electoral support continued to decline, and it merged in a new political formation, the *Centre démocrate* ('Democratic Centre') in 1963.

Mubarak, Hosni (c.1928–)

Egyptian politician. A former pilot and flying instructor who rose to become Commander of the Egyptian Air Force, he was Vice-President under Anwar **Sadat** from 1975 until the latter's assassination in 1981. The only candidate for the presidency, Mubarak pledged to continue

Sadat's domestic and international policies, including firm treatment of Muslim extremists and the peace process with Israel.

muckrakers

A derogatory term coined in 1906 by President Theodore **Roosevelt** for crusading journalists, authors, and critics whose accounts of social evils were attracting widespread attention. Among the most important were Ida M Tarbell (1857–1944), Lincoln Steffens (1866–1936), Ray Stannard Baker (1870–1946) and Upton Sinclair (1878–1968).

Mudros Armistice (30 Oct 1918)

The armistice which took the Ottomans out of **World War I**, signed at Mudros, a harbour on the Aegean island of Lemnos. The principal participants were Huseyn Rauf Bey, the Ottoman Navy Minister, and Vice-Admiral Calthorpe, commander of the British forces in the Aegean, representing the Entente. The armistice provided for an immediate end to hostilities, demobilization of the Ottoman land forces, surrender of the Ottoman fleet, the withdrawal of Ottoman troops from certain specified territories, and the breaking of all contact with the Austro-Hungarian and German empires. This break in relations was to be accompanied by the expulsion of all nationals of the two Powers' name. The agreement also covered the opening of the Dardanelles and Bosphorus, the stationing of appropriate personnel in strategic positions and access to all Ottoman naval and military facilities. Despite the theoretically provisional nature of the armistice, the British handling of it left suspicions of British intent in the minds of both the French and the Turks. Calthorpe had been ordered by the British government to exclude the French from the talks, and the British approach to enforcing the terms of the armistice, particularly regarding demobilization and the surrender of important positions, led the Turks to suspect that the British intention was no less than a piecemeal dismemberment of what remained of the **Ottoman Empire** in Thrace and Anatolia. Although the Nationalists were able successfully to oppose some of the armistice provisions, the British handling of the matter did little for future relations between the two countries.

Mugabe, Robert (Gabriel) (1924–)

Zimbabwean nationalist leader and politician. Educated in Catholic missions schools and Fort Hare College, he was a teacher successively in Southern Rhodesia, Northern Rhodesia and Ghana before returning to Southern Rhodesia in 1960 as Publicity Secretary to the National Democratic Party. He was Deputy Secretary-General of **ZAPU** in 1961 before being detained and then imprisoned, but co-founded **ZANU** in 1963. He was detained again (1964–74) during which period he replaced Ndabaningi **Sithole** as President of ZANU and qualified as a lawyer. Released in 1974, he went to Mozambique to oversee the guerrilla war against the white regime. United uncomfortably with Joshua **Nkomo**'s ZAPU in the **Patriotic Front**, Mugabe essentially retained his independence and, to the surprise of many, led ZANU (PF) as his party was called to a decisive victory in 1980 and hence became Prime Minister in the first Zimbabwe independence government. In Dec 1987 he became executive President but his radical views, both on the virtues of socialism and the one-party state, have not prevailed.

Muhammad, Elijah (1897–1975)
US black leader. Born Elijah Poole, he moved to Detroit from Georgia in 1923, where eight years later he came into contact with Wali Farad, the founder of the **Black Muslims**. In 1934, Muhammad became the leader of the movement as 'Messenger of Allah'. During **World War II** he was arrested and imprisoned for discouraging his followers from registering for the draft. After his release he initiated a period of fast expansion for the Black Muslims. ▷ **Malcolm X**

Mujahidin
Muslim guerrillas (literally, 'holy warriors') who resisted the Soviet occupation of Afghanistan after the invasion (Dec 1979). Based in Iran and Pakistan, they formed various armed bands united by their common aim of defeating the invaders, and the conflict was proclaimed a **jihad** ('holy war'). The Russians withdrew from Afghanistan in 1989, and the Mujahidin subsequently experienced much internal dissent over their role in the country's future.

Mujibur Rahman (Sheikh Mujib) (1920–75)
Bangladesh politician. Born in Tungipana, into a landowning family, he was educated in Calcutta and Dacca University, from which he was expelled for political activities. In 1949 he co-founded the **Awami League**, campaigning for autonomy for East Pakistan (Bangladesh), became its leader in 1953, and led it to electoral victory in 1970. In 1972, after the civil war between East and West Pakistan, he became Prime Minister of newly independent Bangladesh. He introduced a socialist economic programme but became increasingly intolerant of opposition, establishing a one-party state. In Aug 1975 he and his wife were assassinated in a military coup.

Mukhitdinov, Nuritdin Akramovich (1917–)
Soldier and apparatchik, the first central Asian to achieve prominence in Soviet politics. Having fought during **World War II**, he rose to be First Secretary of the Communist Party in Uzbekistan in 1955. Nikita **Khrushchev** then made him a candidate member of the **Politburo** in 1956 and a full member in 1957, essentially to boost his own support, but also to

secure backing from beyond the Slav states. But he failed to measure up and was dismissed in 1961.

Muldoon, Robert David (1921–92)
New Zealand politician. He served as an infantryman in **World War II** before becoming an accountant. He was elected to parliament in 1960 as an MP for the New Zealand National Party, was Minister of Finance (1967–72) and briefly Prime Minister (1972) when the government was defeated. He became Party Leader and Leader of the Opposition (1974) and was Prime Minister (1975–84). He resigned the party leadership in 1984, and became shadow Foreign Affairs Spokesman (1986–92).

Mulroney, (Martin) Brian (1939–)
Canadian politician. The son of an Irish immigrant, he studied law and then practised as a labour lawyer in Montreal, while becoming increasingly active in the Progressive Conservative Party. In 1976 he failed to wrest the party leadership from Joe **Clark** and returned to business as President of a US-owned iron-ore company. In 1983 he replaced Clark and in 1984 became Prime Minister, with a landslide victory over the Liberals. He initiated a number of radical measures, including the **Meech Lake Accords**, settling disputes between the provinces and the centre, and negotiating a free-trade agreement with the USA. Decisively re-elected in 1988, he resigned abruptly from office in 1993. ▷ **Constitution Act of 1982**

Munich Agreement (29 Sep 1938)
One of the more infamous acts in history that has come to stand for a betrayal for the worst of reasons and with the worst of consequences. After a long period of pressurizing Czechoslovakia to make whatever concessions its Sudeten German subjects demanded, the Prime Ministers of Britain and France, **Chamberlain** and **Daladier**, sat down with the two fascist dictators of Italy and Germany, **Mussolini** and **Hitler**, and, in the absence of **Beneš**, they agreed to its virtual dismemberment, allegedly in the interest of European peace. But the peace Chamberlain and Daladier bought at the price of Czechoslovakia only encouraged Hitler and Mussolini and, a year later, they had to go to war in worse circumstances for the sake of Poland.

Munich Putsch (1923)
The abortive attempt by **Hitler** to overthrow the state government of Bavaria, as a prelude to the March on Berlin and the establishment of the Nazi regime in Germany. It was supported by General **Ludendorff**, but badly planned, and it disintegrated in the face of firm Bavarian police action. Hitler was tried for treason, and sentenced to five years' imprisonment. ▷ **Nazi Party**

Muñoz Marín, Luis (1898–1989)
Puerto Rican politician and architect of the modern state. Son of the nationalist, Muñoz Rivera, and educated in the USA, he took up the cause of the peasant in 1938 and founded the Popular Democratic Party which took power in that year. Muñoz, with the aid of the last US Governor, Guy Rexford Tugwell, introduced social reforms and industrialization and was the creator of 'Operation Bootstrap'. He was elected Governor himself in 1948 and held the post until his retirement (1960). Previously a supporter of Puerto Rican independence, in 1950 he devised the status of commonwealth (associated free statehood) for the island in its relationship with the USA.

Museveni, Yoweri Kaguta (1944–)
Ugandan revolutionary leader and politician. A graduate of Dar es Salaam University, he was Assistant Secretary for Research in President Obote's office until Idi **Amin**'s coup of 1971. He returned to Dar es Salaam as an exile and headed the Front for National Salvation against Amin while teaching at the Cooperative College, Moshi. He led the attack on Mbarar, with Tanzanian troops, and participated at the forefront of the fighting which drove Amin from power. Museveni became Minister of Defence in the governments of Yusof Lulu and Godfrey Binaisa (1979–80) but he fell out with Obote on the latter's return to power. When the Tanzanian troops left in 1982 a virtual civil war ensued until 1986, when Museveni's forces prevailed and Obote once again fled the country. Museveni has since attempted to follow a policy of national reconciliation.

Muslim Brotherhood
An Islamic movement, founded in Egypt in 1928 by an Egyptian schoolteacher, Hasan al-**Banna**. Its original goal was the reform of Islamic society by elimination of Western influences and other decadent accretions. Subsequently, it became more radical, and its goal of a theocratic Islamic state found support in many other Sunni countries. ▷ **Sunnis**

Muslim League
Founded in 1906 by politicized Muslims, many of whom were active in the Muhammadan Educational Conference established by Sayyid Ahmed Khan, the league saw itself as the spokesman for all Muslims in British India. By the 1930s, it had begun to articulate a Muslim nationalism expressed through the concept of Pakistan, a separate Muslim state. In 1927 the league split over the question of the Simon Commission. Muslim fear of a Hindu self government led to the reorganization of the league under Muhammad Ali **Jinnah** in 1934. The search for a positive programme led the league in two directions. The first was that of safeguards:

Muslims welcomed federation as it gave provinces greater freedom and thus tended to safeguard Muslims in their majority areas. They sought to reduce the scope of the centre as much as possible. The second direction was towards autonomy in the Muslim majority areas. In 1930 Iqbal suggested the union of the Frontier Province, Baluchistan, Sind, and Kashmir as a Muslim state within a federation. Choudhari Rahmat Ali Khan developed the concept of a separate Muslim state at Cambridge and invented the term Pakistan in 1933. The ideology of Iqbal and the vision of Rahmat ali Khan were turned into a practical programme by Jinnah, the future President of Pakistan, and the Muslim League was the dominant party in Pakistan after 1947. ▷ **India, Partition of**

Mussert, Antoon Adriaan (1894–1946)
Dutch politician. He made his early career as a hydraulic engineer in Dutch government service, but under the influence of fascism and Nazism he founded the **National Socialist Movement** (*Nationaal Socialistische Beweging*, NSB), the main Dutch fascist party. During the German occupation of the Netherlands he collaborated fully, and was given the title of 'Leader of the Dutch People'; however he had little real power. After the war he was captured, sentenced to death and executed by firing squad.

Mussolini, Benito (1883–1945)
Italian politician. The son of a blacksmith and a schoolteacher, he fled Italy in 1902 to avoid military service. In 1904 he returned to Italy as editor of the socialist newspaper *Avanti!*, but resigned in 1914 because of his refusal to support Italian neutrality. He was wounded while serving on the front and began to edit his own nationalist paper, *Il Popolo d'Italia*. In Mar 1919 Mussolini established the fascist movement, borrowing ideas from Gabriele **D'Annunzio** and the 'futurists'; in Oct 1921 he converted this into the **Fascist Party**. Profiting from the economic and political instability of post-war Italy and the support of para-military **squadristi** and local **ras**, as well as a readiness to ally with politicians of differing ideologies, he was able first to take control of a number of provincial cities and then present himself as the only man capable of restoring order to a country that seemed to be slipping ever more rapidly into political chaos. In Oct 1922 he was asked by **Victor Emmanuel III** to form a government and the following month assumed dictatorial powers. His rule came under serious threat only once after the ill-judged murder of **Matteotti** (1924) and during the course of the mid-1920s he was able to consolidate power. Using a mixture of intimidation, patronage and propaganda, he was able to turn Italy into a totalitarian state by 1929. Despite his early aggression over **Corfu** and his fierce nationalism, his foreign policy was not marked by overt expansionism or aggression until the mid-1930s. However, in 1935 he launched the Conquest of **Abyssinia** which was followed by large-scale intervention in the **Spanish Civil War**

on the side of **Franco**. During this period he moved increasingly towards cooperation with **Hitler**, which culminated in the Pact of **Steel** and eventually in the invasion of France in 1940. In 1939 Mussolini annexed Albania but (Oct 1940) failed to seize Greece. The arrival of German troops to assist in the conquest of Greece signalled the beginning of his dependence on Hitler, and henceforth his actions were dictated largely by the needs of Berlin. Dissatisfaction with this policy and a realization of the likely victory of the Allies persuaded many of his **gerarchi** to oppose him, and at a meeting of the **Fascist Grand Council** (25 July 1943) it became clear that he had lost the support of most of his closest associates. The following day he was arrested after being summoned by **Victor Emmanuel III**, but was subsequently rescued by German paratroopers. In Sep 1943 he was established at the head of the puppet Republic of **Salò** in German-occupied northern Italy but was no more than an impotent quisling. On 28 Apr 1945 he was captured by partisans and shot while trying to flee Italy. ▷ **Duce**

Mutesa II ('King Freddie') (1924–69)
Kabaka or King of Buganda (1939/53 and 1955/66). Mutesa was educated in England and was an honorary captain in the Grenadier Guards. He succeeded as Kabaka during **World War II** and set about safeguarding the position of his kingdom within Uganda, even attempting to lead it to separate independence. At the centre of several controversies relating to the independence and post-colonial politics of Uganda, Mutesa was exiled (1953–5) by the Governor, Sir Andrew Cohen, for opposing British plans for unitary decolonization. On independence, he was briefly President of Uganda with Milton Obote as his Prime Minister, but in 1966 Obote overthrew him in a coup. Mutesa escaped to London, where he died.

mutilated victory
The term (in Italian, *vittoria mutilata*) coined originally by Gabriele **D'Annunzio** to describe the consequences of Italy's treatment by its allies after **World War I**. Italy, having been brought into war by promises of extensive territorial and colonial gains, suffered among the greatest human and material losses of any of the Western states. However, the Italian delegates at the Paris Peace Conference were virtually ignored by those of Britain, France and the USA. While most of the territory promised by the Treaty of **London** (1915) was handed over, Italian claims for colonies and mandates were disregarded (doubly offensive given the readiness to allow Australia and South Africa control of mandated territory) and the Dalmatian littoral was given to Yugoslavia. This not entirely unfounded sense of being cheated played a large part in stimulating aggressive nationalist sentiment which helped contribute to the growth of **fascism**.

Muzorewa, Abel (Tendekayi) (1925–)

Zimbabwean cleric and politician. Educated in Methodist schools in Southern Rhodesia and at theological college in the USA, he was ordained in 1963 and became a bishop of the United Methodist Church in Southern Rhodesia in 1968. Founder President of the **African National Council** in 1971, he failed to hold together the differing elements of the nationalist movement and chose the path of an 'internal settlement' rather than guerrilla war. After the ANC won the first universal suffrage election in 1979, he was Prime Minister of 'Zimbabwe–Rhodesia' for a few months before the 1980 election swept Robert **Mugabe** into power.

MVSN (*Milizia Volontaria per la Sicurezza Nazionale*)

The fascist militia set up in Jan 1923 by **Mussolini**. Recruited mainly from ex-**squadristi**, paid out of state funds and answerable only to Mussolini himself, the militia was established primarily to keep the fascist movement under the **Duce**'s own control. By organizing the members of the fascist squads, Mussolini was able to prevent powerful **ras** from mustering their own private armies and to prevent also the worst excesses of *squadrismo*, so fostering his image as the one man able to keep order. However, the MVSN served little real military or policing purpose.

Mwinyi, (Ndugu) Ali Hassan (1925–)

Tanzanian politician. Having trained as a teacher, he taught in Zanzibar (1954–61) before going to the UK to study for two years. On his return, he joined the Zanzibari Ministry of Education and then the Zanzibar State Trading Corporation. In 1969 he became a Minister of State in the Office of President Julius **Nyerere** and thereafter Minister of Health and Home Affairs, Minister of Natural Resources and Tourism, and Minister of State in the Vice-President's Office. In Apr 1984 he was elected President of Zanzibar and in Oct 1985 he succeeded Nyerere as President of Tanzania. Since then, he has attempted to loosen the state's control over the country's economy while retaining a faith in the single party, the **CCM**.

My Lai incident (Mar 1968)

The massacre of several hundred unarmed inhabitants of the South Vietnamese village of My Lai by US troops, an incident exposed by *Life* magazine photos in 1969. The officer responsible, Lieutenant Calley, was court-martialled in 1970–1. ▷ **Vietnam War**

N

NAACP (National Association for the Advancement of Colored People)
US civil rights organization established in 1910. This biracial association developed from the National Negro Committee Conference, held in 1909 in the aftermath of riots in Springfield, Illinois, in which eight people had died. Though Booker T **Washington** refused to join the association, its founding members included Jane **Addams**, William Monroe Trotter and W E B **Du Bois**, who became editor of its magazine, *Crisis*. The NAACP's aim was to 'make 11 000 000 Americans physically free from peonage, mentally free from ignorance, politically free from disenfranchisement and socially free from insult', through educating public opinion, lobbying for legislative reform and sponsoring court action. Its first major success came in 1915 when the Supreme Court ruled the grandfather clause (a device used in the South to keep blacks from voting) to be unconstitutional, and a series of victories over aspects of segregation culminated in **Brown v Board of Education of Topeka, Kansas** (1954). The membership of the movement grew from 6 000 in 1914 to 500 000 in the early 1990s.

Nagano Osami (1880–1947)
Japanese naval officer. Educated at the Naval Academy, Etajima, he studied law at Harvard and was naval attaché in Washington (1920–3). Promoted rear-admiral in 1928, he was superintendent of the Naval Academy (1928–9). As head of the Japanese delegation to the 2nd London Naval Conference (1935–6), he advocated the expansion of Japanese naval power. He was Navy Minister (1936–7), Commander-in-Chief Combined Fleet (1937), and Chief of Naval General Staff (1941–4). He planned and ordered the Japanese attack on **Pearl Harbor** (Dec 1941) and died while on trial for war crimes.

Nagasaki
The capital of Nagasaki prefecture, western Kyushu, Japan, it was the target for the second atomic bomb of **World War II** (9 Aug 1945) which killed or injured c.75 000 people and destroyed over a third of the city.

Nagy, Imre (1896–1958)
Hungarian politician. Born into a poor peasant family, he came into contact with Bolshevism as a prisoner in Russia in **World War I** and, after returning to Hungary, he held a minor post in the Béla **Kun** revolutionary government in 1919. He fled to the USSR for two years, but returned to

participate in the illegal Hungarian communist movement until 1929, when he again had to flee. Returning with the **Red Army** in 1944, he held various ministerial posts in a chequered career until he became Prime Minister. As a moderate he was ousted in 1955 and brought back during the **Hungarian Uprising** the following year. His decision to declare Hungary neutral and to appeal to the **UN** for help provoked Soviet suppression of the uprising. He was displaced by János **Kádár** and executed in 1958. What was regarded as his martyrdom was avenged with the overthrow of the communists in 1989. ▷ **Russian Revolution**

Nahayan, Sheikh Zayed bin Sultan al- (1918–)
Amir of Abu Dhabi. He was governor of the eastern province of Abu Dhabi, one of seven Trucial States on the southern shores of the Persian Gulf and the Gulf of Oman, which were under British protection, until in 1969 he deposed his brother, Sheikh Shakhbut, and became Amir. When the States decided to federate as the United Arab Emirates in 1971 he became President of its Supreme Council. He was unanimously re-elected in 1986.

Nahhas, Mustafa al- (1879–1965)
Egyptian politician. He was the leader of the Wafd Party in Egypt in 1923 and Premier in 1928, 1930 and 1950. In addition, al-Nahhas acted as regent for King Farouk in his early years and, despite their being dismissed by Farouq in 1938, the Wafd were brought back in 1941 at Britain's behest. The damage done to the reputation of the Wafd by their cooperation with the British was irreparable. Although al-Nahhas became Premier again in 1950 after the Wafd's victory in the elections, and despite his endeavours to regain credibility for the Wafd by giving the party an anti-British bias, they were again dismissed by Farouk in 1952. Al-Nahhas then left the political stage, charged with but not tried for corruption and in the same year (1952) King Farouk was deposed by General Neguib on behalf of the **Free Officers**. The Wafd Party was dissolved in 1953.

Naicker, E V Ramaswami (1879–1973)
Indian social reformer. A fiery anti-Brahmin crusader, he was responsible for reorganizing the Justice Party, a rival of the **Indian National Congress**, into the *Dravid Munnetra Kazagam* (DMK), an exclusively Tamil party. He began his public career as an exponent of social equality and became a crusader against 'untouchability' — the synonym for the range of prejudices (particularly acute in the south of India) which were directed against low-caste members of Indian society. He was elected Chairman of Erode Municipal Council and joined the Congress in the 1910s. Naicker participated in the **Non-Cooperation Movement** and courted arrest in 1922. In 1925 he launched the Self Respect Movement and, in 1933, led

his first anti-Hindu march. He was elected President of the Justice Party in 1938 and reorganized it into the DMK in 1944. He denounced Hinduism, the **caste** system and child marriage, and opposed the imposition of Hindi, the northern language, on the population of southern India, the 'Dravidians'. ▷ **Untouchables**

Naidu, Sarojini (1879–1949)
Indian feminist, politician and poet. Educated at Madras, London and Cambridge, she became known as 'the Nightingale of India' as the author of three volumes of lyric verse between 1905 and 1915. She lectured widely on feminism and campaigned for the abolition of purdah, and in 1925 became the first President of M K **Gandhi**'s **Indian National Congress**. She was imprisoned several times for **civil disobedience**, and took a leading part in the negotiations that led to her country's independence in 1947, when she was appointed Governor of the United Provinces, now Uttar Pradesh.

Najibullah, Major General (1947–)
Afghan politician. He became active in the Moscow-inspired People's Democratic Party of Afghanistan (PDPA) in the mid-1960s, and was twice imprisoned for his political activities. After King Mohammed **Zahir Shah** was deposed in a military coup and abdicated (1973), he rose rapidly in the party hierarchy, and as a member of the PDPA's Central Committee, played a key role in the negotiations that led to the 1978 Treaty of Friendship with the USSR that served as a pretext for the Russian invasion the following year, when he was made Information Minister. He was admitted to the Afghan Politburo in 1981, and became President in 1987. Strong guerrilla resistance by the members of the National Islamic Front continued, and insistence by the Russian army, in the wake of continued attacks by Pakistani **Mujahidin** guerrillas on the Kabul-Soviet border, that Najibullah's regime should continue to be funded despite the USSR's own economic difficulties was a factor in the resignation in Dec 1990 of Foreign Minister Eduard **Shevardnadze**. In 1991, the **UN** renewed its call for elections in mujaheddin-controlled territories with a view to replacing Najibullah's regime with a democratically-elected Government. Najibullah finally resigned, handing over power to a coalition of Mujahidin leaders in May 1992.

Nakasone Yasuhiro (1918–)
Japanese politician. Educated at Tokyo University, he was a junior naval officer in **World War II**, and entered the Ministry of Home Affairs in 1945. Elected to the Diet at the age of 29 for the Liberal-Democratic (Conservative) Party, he held a range of ministerial posts from 1959 to 1982. As Prime Minister (1982–8), he supported the renewal of the

US–Japan Security Treaty, and maintained close relations with US President Ronald **Reagan**.

Namboodripad, E M S (1909–)

Indian politician. Hailing from Kerala, he was educated in Victoria College, Palghat, and St Thomas College, Trichur. He was Chief Minister of Kerala in 1957–9 and again in 1967–9. Acting General-Secretary of the Communist Party in 1962–3, he became its Secretary-General in 1978 and went on to hold the post of Secretary-General of the Communist (Marxist) Party of India (CPM). He has also written on various Indian political and economic issues. ▷ **Communist Parties of India**

Namibia, formerly **South-West Africa**

A republic in south-west Africa. A German protectorate since 1884, Namibia was mandated to South Africa by the League of Nations in 1920. The UN assumed direct responsibility in 1966, changing the name to Namibia in 1968, and recognizing the South-West Africa People's Organization (**SWAPO**) as representative of the Namibian people. South Africa however continued to administer the area as South-West Africa. SWAPO commenced guerrilla activities in 1966, and bases were established in south Angola, involving Cuban troops in the 1970s. An interim administration was installed by South Africa in 1985 and the country gained full independence in 1990. In 1993 agreement was reached with South Africa that the Walvis Bay area would be governed by Namibia.

Nansen, Fridtjof (1861–1930)

Norwegian explorer, scientist and statesman. Educated at Oslo and Naples, in 1882 he travelled into the Arctic regions, and in 1888 made an east–west journey across Greenland. His greatest scheme was to reach the North Pole by letting his specially built ship, the *Fram*, get frozen into the ice north of Siberia and drift with a current setting towards Greenland. During the union crisis with Sweden (1905) he was one of the leading spokesmen for Norwegian independence and Norway's unofficial representative in Britain. In 1906–8 he was the first ambassador of independent Norway in London and played an active part in the negotiations leading to the Norwegian integrity treaty of 1907. During **World War I** he headed a trade delegation to the USA which led to a war trade agreement in Apr 1918. As Norway's first delegate to the **League of Nations** (1920), Nansen became deeply engaged in post-war relief work. He was appointed League Commissioner for Refugees, and thousands of displaced persons were issued with special 'Nansen passports'. In 1921 he organized relief for the victims of famine in Russia, saving 1.5–2 million people from death by starvation. In 1922 he was awarded the Nobel Peace Prize in recognition of his relief efforts.

Narayan, Jaiprakash ('JP') (1902–79)
Indian freedom fighter and politician. He was educated in a village primary school and abandoned his studies in 1921 to join the **Non-Cooperation Movement**. He went to the USA on a scholarship and obtained a masters degree from the University of Ohio. Influenced by Marxist ideas, he joined the communist movement. He however accepted **Nehru**'s offer to take charge of the Labour Department in Congress, joined the **civil disobedience** movement after the failure of the M K **Gandhi**–Irwin talks and was jailed. One of the founders of the Congress Socialist Party in 1934, he advocated the abolition of the zamindari system and the nationalization of heavy industries. The author of a number of books and booklets on social, political and economic problems, he took an active part in the **Quit India Movement** of 1942, but gave up politics after India gained independence and joined the **Bhoodan** movement of Vinoba **Bhave**. Later, he was closely involved in the protest movement against the Chinese policy on Tibet and also toured the tribal areas of Nagaland in an attempt to bring about a rapprochement between the rebel Nagas and the government of India. He organized famine relief for the affected people of Bihar in 1967 and persuaded several dacoits of Madhya Pradesh to surrender their arms in 1972. He led the movement for restoration of democracy and liberties after the imposition of the 'emergency' by Indira **Gandhi** in 1975, for which he was arrested. Released in 1977, he led the Janata Party to victory in the general election of that year.

Narodna Obrana
Literally 'National Defence', this term refers to the Serbian nationalist society which was founded after the annexation of Bosnia-Herzegovina by Austria (1908).

Nash, Sir Walter (1882–1968)
British-born New Zealand politician. Nash went to New Zealand in 1909. From 1919 to 1960 he served on the national executive of the New Zealand Labour Party, encouraging the adoption of a moderate reform programme in the Christian socialist tradition. A member of parliament from 1929, he held numerous ministerial appointments from 1935 onwards and in **World War II** was Deputy Prime Minister to Peter **Fraser**, although from 1942 to 1944 he headed a special mission to the USA. He was Prime Minister (1957–60), retiring from the party leadership in 1963.

Nasriddimova, Yadgar Sadykovna (1920–)
Soviet bureaucrat and politician. Born in Uzbekistan and educated in the Tashkent Institute of Railway Engineering, she rose through various party and government offices eventually to become chairman of the Soviet of Nationalities in Moscow (1970–4). Her corruption was such,

however, that she had to be demoted to a ministry in 1974; it was not until 1988 that she could be removed from the party itself.

Nasser, Gamal Abd al- (1918–70)
Egyptian politician. An army officer, he became dissatisfied with the corruption of the regime of King **Farouk**, and was involved in the military coup of 1952. He became Prime Minister (1954–6) and then President (1956–70), deposing his fellow officer, General Mohammed **Neguib**. During his term of office, he nationalized the Suez Canal, which led to Israel's invasion of Sinai, and the intervention of Anglo-French forces. He aimed to build a North African Arab empire, and in 1958 created a federation with Syria, the **United Arab Republic**, from which Syria withdrew in 1961. After the Arab–Israeli **Six-Day War** (1967), heavy losses on the Arab side led to his resignation, but he was persuaded to stay on, and died while still in office in Cairo.

National American Woman Suffrage Association (NAWSA)
A US feminist organization. Founded in 1890, it united the National Woman Suffrage Association (for which the suffrage was only one cause amongst others) with the American Woman Suffrage Association (for which the suffrage was the only cause). Elizabeth Cady Stanton was President of the new organization for the first two years, followed by Susan B Anthony until 1900. By 1912, under the leadership of Carrie Chapman **Catt**, the movement had become increasingly staid in contrast with the more militant National Women's Party organized by Alice **Paul**. Nevertheless its policy of intense lobbying was instrumental in achieving passage of the 19th Amendment, giving women the vote, which was finally ratified in June 1919, and went into effect in Aug 1920.

National Front (NF)
A strongly nationalist political party in Britain which centres its political programme on opposition to immigration, and calls for the repatriation of ethnic minorities even if they were born in the UK. The party was created in 1960 by the merger of the White Defence League and the National Labour Party, and in its early years was a small neo-Nazi grouping. In the mid- and late 1970s it had some minor impact in elections and its membership grew. It tried to develop a more respectable face and recruited some members from the right of the **Conservative Party** to widen its base beyond hardline neo-fascists. Its political appeal declined with the election of a Conservative government in 1979.

National Labor Relations Act (Wagner Act) (1935)
US labour legislation. Instigated and steered through Congress by Senator Robert **Wagner**, the act sought to find an effective means of guaranteeing the right of collective bargaining. It established a National Labor

Relations Board with legal powers to ensure compliance by employers, especially in allowing employees to elect their own bargaining agent without fear of discrimination. It also prohibited company unions and opened the way for a huge expansion in union membership. ▷ **Lewis, John L; Taft–Hartley Act; United Automobile Workers**

National Party (NP)

A party formed in South Africa, in 1912, to reflect the Boer (Afrikaner) interest. Over the years it absorbed smaller parties like the Afrikaner Party and developed an explicit programme of Afrikaner advancement and separation of the races. It gained power in 1948 and pursued a policy of apartheid until 1991. Under the leadership of F W **De Klerk** from 1989, the party began to orchestrate the transfer of power from whites to a more democratic political base. In May 1994, in the first all-race elections to be held in South Africa, the National Party was defeated by the **ANC**, led by Nelson **Mandela**.

National Party of Australia

The third largest party in Australia, it grew out of the Australian Country Party formed in 1920. Renamed the National Country Party in 1975, it took its present title in 1982, but except in Queensland it remains sectional in both its support and its policies. Socially conservative, favouring low tariffs and support for agriculture, it has generally acted in coalition with the major anti-Labor grouping of the time, most notably the **Liberal Party of Australia** (1949–72). Only in Queensland, where the National Party title was adopted in 1974, has the party been able to rule in its own right.

National Revolution (1940)

In France, the name given by the supporters of **Pétain** and the **Vichy** regime to the abolition of the Third Republic; it symbolized their political programme, also epitomized in the national motto, *Travail, Famille, Patrie* ('Work, Family, Fatherland'), that was imposed in place of the republican **'Liberty, Equality, Fraternity'**. ▷ **collaboration** (France); **Republic, Third** (France); **World War II**

National Security Council (NSC)

A body created by Congress in 1947 to advise the US President on the integration of domestic, foreign, and military policies relating to national security. It was designed to achieve effective coordination between the military services and other government agencies and departments, and is composed of the President, Vice-President, Secretary of State, and Secretary of Defence. The Chairman of the Joint Chiefs of Staff and the Director of Central Intelligence are advisers.

National Socialist Movement (*Nationaal Socialistische Beweging*, NSB)

Dutch fascist party. Founded in 1931 by A A **Mussert** and C van Geelkerken (1901–76), the party attracted some support in the Netherlands in the 1930s, achieving 8 per cent of the votes in the local elections of 1935. During the German occupation of **World War II** there were 87 000 members, but the German authorities gave the leaders of the NSB very little real power. After the war the NSB members were widely persecuted, interned, tried and imprisoned; several of the leaders, such as Mussert, were executed.

National Urban League

US civil rights organization. Founded in 1911 by professional blacks and progressive whites, it aimed to provide for rural blacks arriving in Northern cities the same services as those provided to white arrivals by settlement houses and charities. The definition of its aims demonstrates the influence of Booker T **Washington**: 'to promote, encourage, assist and engage in any and all kinds of work for improving the industrial, economic, social and spiritual condition among Negroes'.

Nativism

US anti-immigrant attitude, generally expressed by native-born white Protestants. From the early 19c, a major focus of anti-immigrant feeling was directed toward Irish Catholics who were accused by nativists of bringing the papacy into US politics. Nativist antagonism was also extended to other immigrant groups. Nativism began to diminish in importance as the slavery issue became a dominant American concern. With the renewal of immigration in the late 19c and early 20c, nativist sentiment resurfaced and contributed largely to the passage of the Immigration Act of 1924, which eventually brought a sharp curtailment to immigration by establishing immigration quotas.

NATO (North Atlantic Treaty Organization)

An organization established by a treaty signed in 1949 by Belgium, Canada, Denmark, France, Iceland, Italy, Luxembourg, the Netherlands, Norway, Portugal, the UK, and the USA; Greece and Turkey acceded in 1952, West Germany in 1955, and Spain in 1982. NATO is a permanent military alliance established to defend Western Europe against Soviet aggression. The treaty commits the members to treat an armed attack on one of them as an attack on all of them, and for all to assist the country attacked by such actions as are deemed necessary. The alliance forces are based on contributions from the member countries' armed services and operate under a multi-national command. The remit includes the deployment of nuclear, as well as conventional, weapons. Its institutions include a Council, an International Secretariat, the Supreme Headquarters Allied Powers, Europe (SHAPE), and various committees to formulate common policies. In the 1970s and 1980s, NATO policy of a first-strike nuclear attack to fend off a Soviet conventional attack became controversial in Western Europe, where many thought it increased the possibility of nuclear war. In 1966 France under Charles de **Gaulle** withdrew all its forces from NATO command, but it remains a member. After the 1989 changes in E Europe, a NATO summit in London (July 1990) began the process of redefining NATO's military and political goals. ▷ **nuclear weapons**

Naxalites

An extremist group which broke away from the Communist Party of India in 1969, with the aim of forming a truly revolutionary Marxist-Leninist party; their name derived from the 1967 Naxalbari revolts in west Bengal. Influenced and approved by the Chinese Communist Party, their intention was to seize power by violent means, rather than through parliamentary channels. In the early 1970s the group was involved in political violence, including murder, in a number of Indian states. Most members were subsequently arrested, and what had been a serious threat to law and order removed.

Nazarbaev, Nursultan Abishevich (1940–)

Kazakhstan politician. He was elected President of his state in 1991. Originally a metal worker, he turned to party duties in 1969 and rose steadily in the 1970s and dramatically in the 1980s. By 1984 he was Chairman of the Kazakhstan Council of Ministers, and by 1989 he had been selected as First Secretary of the Kazakh Communist Party. In 1990 he was chosen for the Soviet **Politburo** and became President of the Kazakh Supreme Soviet. As elected President of Kazakhstan in 1991 he took his republic out of the USSR but kept it in the new Commonwealth of Independent States (CIS).

Nazi Party (NSDAP)

A German political party which originated as the German Worker's Party (DAP), founded in 1919 as a patriotic working-man's party to protest against the German surrender of 1918 and the Treaty of **Versailles**, and renamed the *Nationalsozialistische Deutsche Arbeiterpartei* ('National Socialist German Worker's Party', NSDAP or Nazi Party) in 1920. Adolf **Hitler** became the party's leader the following year. Its ideology was a blend of imperialist nationalism, racism, **socialism** and more traditional ideas. Nazi ideology maintained that the world was divided into a hierarchy of races: Aryans, of whom Germans were the purest example, were the supreme culture-bearing race, while the Jews were the lowest. It was also contended that the Jews were intent on world conquest through infesting the Aryan race. This set of ideas was set out by Hitler in *Mein Kampf* (1925), although public opinion forced the

NSDAP to play down this theme until after 1933. It was not until the 1930s, with the onset of economic crisis, that the Nazi Party gained a position of significant support: in 1932 with 37.3 per cent of the vote it became the largest party in the **Reichstag**. Support came from people of all backgrounds, although its electorate was strongly Protestant and its membership young. In 1933 Hitler was appointed Chancellor in a coalition government, a position from which he was able to build up a personal dictatorship, through legal measures, terror, and propaganda. Once in power, the Nazis ruthlessly crushed opposition, initiated a vigorous job-creation programme, from 1935 engaged in extensive rearmament, and in the late 1930s invaded **Austria** and the **Sudetenland** (1938), and Bohemia-Moravia and Memel (1939) as a strategic and economic prerequisite for the conquest of Eastern Europe to obtain land (**Lebensraum**) for the 'master race'. During **World War II**, Nazi policies included slave labour, plunder, and mass extermination, leading to the **Nuremberg Trials** of 1946. Nazism as a political ideology is now viewed as a terrifying combination of populism and technocracy with inhumanity, Social-Darwinistic imperialism, and almost nihilistic amorality. ▷ **Anschluss; Holocaust**

Nazi–Soviet Pact ▷ **German–Soviet Pact**

Ne Win (1911–)

Burmese politician. He was an active anti-British nationalist in the 1930s. In **World War II** he became Chief of Staff in the collaborationist army after the Japanese invasion of Burma, but joined the Allied forces later in the war. He held senior military and cabinet posts after Burma's independence (1948), before becoming caretaker Prime Minister (1958–60). In 1962, following a military coup, he ruled the country as chairman of the revolutionary council and became state President in 1974. After leaving this office in 1981, he continued to dominate political affairs as chairman of the ruling Burma Socialist Programme Party (BSPP). He followed an isolationist foreign policy and a unique domestic 'Burmese Way to Socialism' programme, a blend of **Marxism**, Buddhism and Burmese nationalism. In 1988, with economic conditions rapidly deteriorating and riots in Rangoon, he was forced to step down as BSPP leader although he remained a formidably powerful political figure.

Nedić, Milan (1877–1946)

Serbian politician and soldier. Chief of Staff and Minister of War during the 1930s, he collaborated with the German occupation during **World War II** and was President of the puppet government in Belgrade from 1941 to 1944. At the end of the war, he was imprisoned and committed suicide. ▷ **Ljotić, Dimitrije**

Negrín (López), Juan (1892–1956)
Spanish politician. He studied medicine in Germany, and became Professor of Physiology at the University of Madrid (1923–31). As a moderate Socialist, he was a parliamentary deputy throughout the Second Republic (1931–6). During the **Spanish Civil War** he served as Finance Minister (1936–7) and Prime Minister (1937–9), and for a time was also Defence Minister. As Premier he adopted a pro-Soviet, pro-communist but anti-revolutionary position, aimed at winning the Western democracies' support for the Republic, but his 'Thirteen Points' (1938) failed to impress Britain and France. In 1939, shortly before the end of the war, he was overthrown by an anti-communist coup. He died in exile in France. ▷ **Republic, Second** (Spain)

Neguib, Mohammed (1901–)
Egyptian leader. As general of an army division in 1952 he carried out a coup d'état in Cairo which banished King **Farouk I** and initiated the 'Egyptian Revolution'. Taking first the offices of Commander-in-Chief and Prime Minister, he abolished the monarchy in 1953 and became President of the republic. He was deposed in 1954 and succeeded by Colonel Gamal Abd al-**Nasser**.

Nehru, Jawaharlal ('Pandit') (1889–1964)
Indian politician. Educated at Harrow and Cambridge, he became a lawyer, and served in the Allahabad High Court. He joined the Indian Congress Committee (1918), became an admirer and follower, if sometimes a critic, of M K **Gandhi**, and was imprisoned several times by the British. In 1929 he was elected President of the **Indian National Congress**. From 1947 to 1964 he was India's first Prime Minister and Minister of External Affairs, following a policy of neutrality during the **Cold War**. He introduced a policy of industrialization, reorganized the states on a linguistic basis, and brought the dispute with Pakistan over Kashmir to a peaceful, though not final, solution.

Nehru, Motilal (1861–1931)
Indian nationalist leader, lawyer and journalist. The father of Jawaharlal **Nehru**, he became a follower of M K **Gandhi** in 1919, founded the *Independent* of Allahabad and became the first President of the reconstructed **Indian National Congress**. In the 1920s he co-headed the **Swaraj** Party (with Chittaranjan **Das**) in which members of the Congress entered the legislatures, and wrote a report as a basis for Indian constitutional development and to solve the political differences between Hindus and Muslims. The report was not, however, acceptable to members of the All-India **Muslim League**, led by Muhammad Ali **Jinnah**.

Nejedly, Zdenek (1878–1962)
Czechoslovak communist ideologue. A professor of music in the Charles University, Prague, from before **World War I**, he joined the Communist Party during the depression in 1929 and emigrated to Moscow with other leaders during **World War II**. In subsequent National Front governments down to 1953 he held ministerial posts, usually education; and in 1952 he became chairman of the Academy of Sciences. A man of many words but simple thoughts, he restricted the education of a whole generation of Czechoslovaks to narrow Marxist ideas; however, he was very popular with sympathizers abroad.

Nelken, Margarita (1896–1968)
Spanish politician and feminist. The daughter of German Jews, she was born in Madrid but did not achieve Spanish nationality until 1931. During her early years she was a painter, exhibiting her works in Paris and Vienna as well as Spain, but following a severe eye-illness dedicated herself to literary criticism. She was also active on behalf of women's rights, publishing *The Social Condition of Women* (1922), as well as being involved in land reform movements in Estremadura and Andalucia. Under the Second Republic (1931–6) Nelken was successful in all three general elections as a deputy for the Socialist Party (**PSOE**). She agitated for land reform, was active in the national arbitration boards, and formed part of the National Committee of Women against War and Fascism. Her impatience with the parliamentary process led her to become one of the most radical Socialist deputies. During the **Spanish Civil War** (1936–9) she led various campaigns for the mobilization of women. In 1937 Margarita Nelken entered the Communist Party (**PCE**). After the war, she was exiled in Paris, Moscow and finally Mexico, where she died. ▷ **Republic, Second** (Spain)

Nenni, Pietro (1891–1980)
Italian politician. As editor of the socialist paper *Avanti!* he was exiled by the fascists in 1926, and served as a political commissar for the International Brigades during the **Spanish Civil War**. He became Secretary-General of the Italian Socialist Party (PSI) in 1944, Vice-Premier in the **De Gasperi** coalition (1945–6) and Foreign Minister (1946–7). In 1963–8 he once again served as Vice-Premier in the four-party left-centre coalition headed by Aldo **Moro**. In Dec 1968 he accepted the post of Foreign Minister but resigned in July 1969.

Netherlands, sometimes known as **Holland**
A maritime kingdom in north-west Europe. After a brief period of French control as the Batavian Republic in the early 18c the country was united with Belgium in 1813 as the Kingdom of the United Netherlands, but Belgium broke away to form a separate kingdom in 1830. Holland

remained neutral in World War I, but there was strong Dutch resistance to German occupation during World War II. The country joined with Belgium and Luxembourg to form the Benelux economic union in 1948. There was conflict over independence of Dutch colonies in South-East Asia (such as the expulsion of Dutch citizens from Indonesia) in the late 1940s.

Neto, Antonio Agostinho (1922–79)
Angolan nationalist and politician. The son of a methodist missionary, he was educated in a methodist school in Luanda before studying medicine in Portuguese universities. He returned to Angola to work in the colonial medical service and joined the **MPLA**. He was imprisoned several times (1952–62) but escaped from the Cape Verde Islands to Zaire where he soon became President of the MPLA and its leader in the guerrilla war against Portuguese colonialism. His close ties with **Castro** gave him both Cuban and Soviet backing and this assistance enabled him to prevail in the civil war which followed the Portuguese retreat from Angola. He became the first President of Angola in 1974, holding the post until his death.

Neuilly, Treaty of (27 Nov 1919)
This agreement dictated the terms to be paid by Bulgaria as a defeated power at the end of **World War I**. Bulgaria surrendered to Greece the gains it had made in Western Thrace after the **Balkan Wars** and ceded to Serbia four regions of strategic significance. The Bulgarians were also to pay an indemnity of $450 million, about a quarter of the national wealth, and a great quantity of their livestock. The size of the Bulgarian Army, police force and border guard was greatly reduced. ▷ **Boris III; Stamboliski, Alexander; Thrace**

Neutrality Acts
A series of US acts passed in the 1930s which aimed to prevent the USA becoming involved in the escalating European conflict. The 1935 Act authorized a temporary embargo on arms shipments to all belligerents; the 1936 Act outlawed loans or credits to belligerents; and the 1937 Act forbade munitions shipments to either side in the **Spanish Civil War**. By the time of the attack on Pearl Harbor, the bans had been lifted and the neutral course had been abandoned.

Neves, Tancredo de Almeida (1910–85)
Brazilian politician. He was a local politician in the 1930s and became a federal deputy for the **PSD** in the 1950s. Justice Minister under Getúlio **Vargas** in 1953–4, he was Head of the Banco do Brasil under **Kubitschek (de Oliveira)** (1956–8) and first Prime Minister and Justice Minister under João **Goulart**. Neves was a master of conciliação, both as architect of the

1961 compromise, which allowed President Goulart to assume office under a 'parliamentary regime', and the referendum of Jan 1963, which restored traditional powers to the President. His inability to cobble together cross-party support for moderate policies was a leading factor in the coup of 1964. A man of moderate centrist views, he managed to gain the confidence of conservative groups in the 1970s for the transition to civilian rule. As **PMDB** Governor of Minas Gerais (1982–4), he articulated the 'Democratic Alliance' which won the presidential nomination in 1985, with José **Sarney (Costa)** as running-mate. Overtaken by illness a few hours before he was to take office, he remained the 'President who never was'.

New Deal (Canada)
The name given to the legislation influenced by US President **Roosevelt**'s New Deal, passed in 1935 by the Conservative administration of R B **Bennett**, after the failure of more orthodox measures to solve the problems of the Depression. It established a social insurance plan, maximum hours and minimum wages, a marketing board for natural products, and farm credit provisions. This programme and the fears of several Conservative supporters that the government would involve itself in economic planning and price-fixing led to a split in the party and the formation of the Reconstruction Party, which let in the Liberals under Mackenzie **King** with a landslide victory in the 1935 elections. Bennett's New Deal measures were declared unconstitutional in 1937, but they served as a basis for the **Liberal Party** programme after constitutional amendment. ▷ **New Deal** (USA); **Price Spreads Commission; Stevens, Harry H**

New Deal (USA)
The administration and policies of US President Franklin D **Roosevelt**, who pledged a 'new deal' for the country during the campaign of 1932. He embarked on active state economic involvement to combat the **Great Depression**, setting the tone in a hectic 'first hundred days'. Although some early legislation was invalidated by the Supreme Court, the New Deal left a lasting impact on US government, economy and society, not least by the effective creation of the modern institution of the presidency. Major specific initiatives included the National Recovery Act (1933), the Tennessee Valley Authority (1933), the Agricultural Adjustment Act (1933), the National Youth Administration (1935), the **National Labor Relations Act** or Wagner Act (1935) and the Social Security Act (1935). The 'first New Deal' (1933–4), concerned primarily with restarting and stabilizing the economy, is sometimes distinguished from the 'second New Deal' (1935), aimed at social reform. Although Roosevelt was triumphantly re-elected in 1936 (losing only two states), his reform programme slowed considerably after his failure to reorganize the Supreme Court (1937), growing opposition to government spending and taxes,

and the worsening situation in Europe, which increasingly directed Roosevelt's attention to foreign affairs.

New Democratic Party (NDP)

Canadian political party. It was established in 1961 by the merger of the **CCF** and the **CLC**. Whilst it did not attract much support in the Atlantic provinces, it presented a much wider appeal to the urban electorate of British Columbia, Saskatchewan, Ontario and Manitoba. Under the leadership of T C (Tommy) Douglas the party won 19 seats in the federal elections of 1962, while in 1969 it was elected into government in Manitoba. In the early 1970s a group of Trotskyites, the 'Waffle' group, seized power until they were expelled from the party in 1972. Later that year the NDP managed to win 30 seats in the federal elections and was able to keep the Liberals in power, giving its support in return for policies of economic nationalism. By the 1980s the NDP had become more centrist because the Liberals had taken over its characteristic policies. In 1984, however, under the leadership of Ed Broadbent the party was still able to muster 19 per cent of the vote and 30 seats in the legislature. The greatest contribution of the NDP to Canadian political life has been to present the country with an alternative to the major parties and exert a constant pressure from the left, which has ensured that social issues retained political importance.

New Economic Policy (NEP)

A partly experimental economic system introduced by **Lenin** in the USSR in 1921. Its main objective was to help the country recover from the ravages of the **Russian Civil War** and the diseconomies of the policy of 'war communism'; but it also emerged from a dispute about the best way to organize economic development in the new society. The system privatized some small-scale business, decentralized major parts of industry and encouraged foreign investment. **Stalin** abandoned it in 1928 after Lenin's death and as part of his battle with **Trotsky**. He forged ahead instead with the collectivization of agriculture and forced industrialization.

New Fourth Army Incident (4 Jan 1941)

The military clash in central China between the communist New Fourth Army and Nationalist forces that effectively ended the second of the **United Fronts** forged in 1937 to counter Japanese aggression. The New Fourth Army had been created (1937) from communist remnants in south China and had been allowed to operate south of the Yangzi River against the Japanese. Tension grew, however, as the army expanded its operations north of the Yangzi, leading to frequent clashes with Nationalist troops. **Chiang Kai-shek**, fearing an expansion of communist influence, ordered an attack on the headquarters force of the New Fourth Army at

Maolin (Anhui province) in Jan 1941 as it was evacuating the region in accordance with an agreement reached the previous year. Most of the force was annihilated and the New Fourth Army was dissolved. This, together with Chiang's economic blockade of the communists' principal base in the north-west, signified the end of any cooperation between the communists and nationalists for the remainder of the Russo-Japanese War.

New Freedom

The political programme on which US President Woodrow **Wilson** was elected in 1912. It was directed against the acceptance of large-scale enterprise by his opponent, Theodore **Roosevelt**, and was intended to return the spirit of free enterprise to the market-place, restoring an open society which would benefit individual entrepreneurs, immigrant minorities and women. The chief architect of Wilson's central argument that trusts and monopolies should be broken up by the federal government was Louis **Brandeis**, but the domestic record of Wilson's administration showed a very partial adherence to these principles. ▷ **New Nationalism**

New Frontier

The administration and policies of US President John F **Kennedy** (1961–3). The programme was characterized by a high international profile and a liberal domestic stance. ▷ **Peace Corps**

New Guard

In Australian history, an extreme right-wing organization formed in New South Wales in 1932 by Eric Campbell, which claimed 100 000 members by 1933. Its principal achievement was the disruption of the official opening of Sydney Harbour Bridge (1932). In some respects a fascist organization, the Guard was defunct by 1935.

New Left

A neo-Marxist movement which espoused a more libertarian form of socialism compared to orthodox Marxism. In part, it was inspired by the earlier writings of Marx, which were essentially humanistic, and the ideas of Italian politician Antonio Gramsci (1891–1937) regarding the importance of ideological hegemony. It also drew on dialectical sociology and radical forms of existentialism. It is, however, difficult to pinpoint any central ideas specific to the New Left. The movement had some influence in the 1960s, particularly in student politics and in opposition to the **Vietnam War**, but it never became an effectively organized political force. Its importance in the 1980s declined, and it gave way in part to the **New Right**.

New Liberal Club (*Shin Jiyu Kurabu*)

The Japanese political party formed in 1976 when six members of the ruling **Liberal Democratic Party** (LDP) broke away to form their own party in protest against government corruption. Although only ever gaining a handful of parliamentary seats, the New Liberal Club formally entered into a coalition with the LDP following the 1983 elections in which the LDP had fallen short of a majority (the only time the LDP has entered a coalition with another party). The LDP's renewed parliamentary strength after 1983, plus the fact that New Liberal Club members always tended to support government policy, made the party's existence increasingly redundant. It was quietly disbanded in 1985 and its members rejoined the ranks of the LDP.

New Nationalism

The US political programme outlined by ex-President Theodore **Roosevelt** in a speech at Osawatomie, Kansas in Aug 1910, and on which he campaigned as the **Progressive Party**'s candidate in the election of 1912. Roosevelt advocated such policies as graduated income and inheritance taxes, compensation for employee accident, closer supervision of female and child labour, and more effective corporate regulation. Greatly influenced by Herbert Croly's *The Promise of American Life*, the programme was essentially a call for government intervention to achieve social justice, and it later influenced such **New Deal** brain trusters as Raymond Moley.
▷ **New Freedom**

New Right

A wide-ranging ideological movement associated with the revival of conservatism in the 1970s and 1980s, particularly in the UK and USA. Its ideas are most prominently connected with classical liberal economic theory from the 19c. It is strongly in favour of state withdrawal from ownership, and intervention in the economy in favour of a free-enterprise system. There is also a strong moral conservatism — an emphasis on respect for authority, combined with a strong expression of patriotism and support for the idea of the family. Politically, the New Right adopts an aggressive style which places weight on pursuing convictions rather than on generating a consensus. In the USA in the 1980s it has been associated with the emergence of Christian fundamentalism (eg the **Moral Majority**).

New Zealand

An independent state comprising a group of islands in the Pacific Ocean south-west of Australia. The Cook Islands and Niue are New Zealand self-governing territories and Tokelau and the Ross Dependency are New Zealand non-self-governing territories. Outbreaks of war between European immigrants and Maoris occurred in 1860–70. A dependency of New South Wales until 1841, it became the Dominion of New Zealand in 1907 and gained independence within the Commonwealth in 1947.

Nghe-An/Ha-Tinh Uprisings (1930–1)
A fierce revolt against French colonial rule, which took place in the northern **Annam** provinces of Nghe-An and Ha-Tinh. The precise causes of the revolt are a matter of considerable scholarly dispute but important elements would include the markedly harsh agricultural conditions of that region, the burden of colonial taxation, social disintegration and the organizational skills of the **Indochina** Communist Party. For a short period the rebels were able to seize power. However, French repression, including the bombing of demonstrations from the air, broke the revolt. Approximately 2 000 Vietnamese were killed.

Ngo Dinh Diem (1901–63)
Vietnamese political leader. He became Prime Minister of the State of Vietnam in June 1954. This was the territory south of the 'temporary' demarcation line, established at the 1954 Geneva Conference. Ngo Dinh Diem quickly consolidated his position, securing the abdication of **Bao Dai** and suppressing the political-religious sects. He allied himself strongly with the USA, which saw in him a tool by which the reunification of Vietnam, under the communists, might be prevented. However, by the beginning of the 1960s, Ngo Dinh Diem's internal position was weakening, largely because his encouragement of Catholic interests greatly angered the Buddhist majority. His violent treatment of Buddhist protest lost him US support. Ngo Dinh Diem was assassinated on 2 Nov 1963, in the course of a military coup that had, at the very least, tacit US approval.

Nguyen Van Thieu (1923–)
Vietnamese army officer and political leader. His military career began in the late 1940s and by 1963 he was Chief of Staff of the Armed Forces of the Republic of Vietnam (South Vietnam), becoming Minister of Defence and Deputy Premier in the following year. In 1965 he became Head of State. Under a new, American-style presidential constitution, he was President from 1967 until the collapse of the Saigon regime in 1975. During those years, his relationship with the USA, and with American public opinion, was central to his survival. He was roundly condemned in the West for his authoritarian, commonly corrupt, methods; he, in turn, felt betrayed by the US withdrawal from Vietnam, agreed with his northern enemies in Paris in early 1973. With the communist victory in 1975, he went into exile, first in Taiwan and then in the UK.

Niagara Movement

US **civil rights** movement. Founded in 1905 by W E B **Du Bois** and others to resist the public acceptance of segregation advocated by Booker T **Washington**, and to agitate for 'every single right that belongs to a freeborn American, political and social'. The movement was superseded by the establishment of the **NAACP**.

Nicaragua

The largest of the Central American republics south of Mexico. It gained independence from Spanish rule in the early 19c. The plains of east Nicaragua, the Mosquito Coast, remained largely undeveloped under British protection until 1860. Dictatorship rule under Anastasio Somoza began in 1938, but the Sandinista National Liberation Front seized power in 1979 and established a socialist junta of national reconstruction. Under the 1987 constitution, a President and a 96-member national Constituent Assembly are elected for six-year terms. The former supporters of the Somoza government (the Contras), based in Honduras and supported by the USA, carried out guerrilla activities against the junta from 1979. A ceasefire and disarmament were agreed in 1990 but unrest continued.

Nicholas II (1868–1918)

Last Emperor of Russia (1895/1917). He was the son of Alexander III. In foreign affairs his reign was marked by a switch from co-operation with Austria and Germany to an alliance with France, an *entente* with Britain, the disastrous **Russo-Japanese War** (1904–5) and, eventually, involvement in **World War I**. Inadequate industrialization and insufficient social change helped precipitate the Russian **Revolution of 1905**. His failure to concede any real power to the assembly or **Duma** instituted in 1906 and also his incompetence as commander of the army against the Central Powers in turn helped to precipitate the 1917 **Russian Revolution** that led to his immediate abdication and to the murder of himself and his family by Red Guards at Ekaterinburg in 1918.

Niemöller, Martin (1892–1984)

German theologian and resistance figure. After serving as a **U-boat** commander in **World War I**, Niemöller entered the Lutheran Church and held various positions, most notably as Pastor in Berlin-Dahlem from 1931. He was a prominent member of the anti-Nazi **Confessing Church** for which he was arrested in 1937 and sent to Sachsenhausen and **Dachau** concentration camps. Freed in 1945, he resumed his church career and adopted outspoken views on current affairs, most notably on German reunification and nuclear disarmament. ▷ **concentration camp**

Nigeria
A republic in West Africa. A British colony was established at Lagos in 1861 and protectorates of North and South Nigeria, created in 1900, were amalgamated as the Colony and Protectorate of Nigeria in 1914. It became a federation in 1954, gained independence in 1960 and was declared a federal republic in 1963. In 1966 a military coup took place and the eastern area formed the Republic of Biafra in 1967. Civil war ensued and Biafra surrendered in 1970. Military coups followed in 1983 and 1985. Although military rule ended in 1993 with power being transferred to a Transitional Council, the military re-established control later in the year.

Night of the Long Knives (30 June–1 July 1934)
The event which took place in Germany when the **SS**, on **Hitler**'s orders, murdered **Röhm** and other leaders of the **SA** (Stormtroopers). The aim was to crush the political power of the SA, reassure the German establishment which was worried by SA excesses and settle old political scores. It has been estimated that up to 150 of Hitler's political opponents and rivals were killed, including von **Schleicher**, the former Chancellor.

Nikolaevna, Klavdiya Ivanovna (1893–1944)
Russian and Soviet women's rights activist. Born in St Petersburg, a bookbinder by trade, she was early involved in revolutionary activities and frequently arrested from 1908 onwards. After 1917 she organized women's groups in St Petersburg and in 1924 she was appointed head of *zhenotdel*, the Communist Party's women's section. In 1926 she was dismissed for supporting **Zinoviev** but survived to hold various lower rank appointments until her death.

Nimeri, Gaafar Mohamed al- (1930–)
Sudanese soldier and politician. Educated at Sudan Military College in Khartoum, he joined the army, and continued his training in Egypt, where he became a disciple of Gamal Abd al-**Nasser**. In 1969, with the rank of colonel, he led the military coup which removed the civilian government and established a Revolutionary Command Council (RCC). In 1971, under a new constitution, he became President. Although twice re-elected, by the 1980s his regional policies and his attempts to impose strict Islamic law had made his regime unpopular and in 1985, while visiting the USA, he himself was deposed by an army colleague, General Swar al-Dahab.

Nimitz, Chester William (1885–1966)
US admiral. He trained at the US Naval Academy, served mainly in submarines, and by 1938 had become rear-admiral. Chief of the Bureau of Navigation during 1939–41, he then commanded the US Pacific Fleet,

is conduct of naval operations contributing significantly to the defeat of apan. He was made Fleet Admiral (1944) and Chief of Naval Operations 1945–7). ▷ **World War II**

Iishio Suehiro (1891–1981)
apanese labour leader and politician. A moderate trade union leader in he 1920s, Nishio was first elected to the Diet in 1928 as a member of the *Shakai Minshuto* (Social Masses Party), a proletarian party founded in 1926 that subsequently supported the military cabinets of the 1930s. He oined the **Japan Socialist Party** (JSP) in 1945 and was a member of Tetsu **Katayama**'s socialist cabinet in 1947. Condemning the party's left-wing bias, in particular its opposition to Japan's security treaty with the USA, Nishio left the JSP in 1959 to form the Democratic Socialist Party, of which he remained Chairman until 1967.

Nitti, Francesco Saverio (1868–1953)
Italian politician and professor. A deputy of radical and socialist sympathies from 1904, he grew closer to **Giolitti** in whose 1911–14 government he served as Minister of Agriculture and Industry. After **Caporetto**, he became **Orlando**'s Finance Minister, before replacing him as Prime Minister (1919). A victim of fascist attacks on account of his consistent and outspoken attacks on **Mussolini**, he went into self-imposed exile but returned to Italy after the war and remained active in politics until his death.

Nixon, Richard M(ilhous) (1913–94)
US politician and 37th President. He became a lawyer, then served in the US Navy. A Republican, he was elected to the House of Representatives in 1946, where he played a prominent role in **HUAC**. He became Senator in 1950 and Vice-President under **Eisenhower** for two terms (1952–9). He lost the 1960 presidential election to John F **Kennedy** but won in 1968. As president he sought to bring an end to the Vietnam War, but did so only after the US invasion of Cambodia and Laos and the heaviest US bombing of North Vietnam of the entire conflict. He had diplomatic successes with China and the USSR. In his domestic policy he reversed many of the social programmes that had come out of the previous Democratic administrations. He resigned under the threat of impeachment after several leading members of his staff had been found guilty of involvement in the **Watergate** affair, and because he was personally implicated in the cover-up. He was given a full pardon by President Gerald **Ford**.

Nkomati Accord
Essentially this was a non-aggression treaty, signed between Mozambique and South Africa in 1984, in which the former agreed not to support the

ANC (African National Congress) militarily and the latter agreed not to support **RENAMO** militarily. In practice, the superior power of South Africa meant that the agreement was implemented unilaterally.

Nkomo, Joshua (Mqabuko Nyongolo) (1917–)
Zimbabwean nationalist and politician. Educated in Natal and at Fort Hare College, where he joined the **ANC** (African National Congress), he returned to Bulawayo as a social worker and became General-Secretary of the Rhodesian Railway African Employees Association in 1951. Elected Chairman of the (Southern Rhodesian) African National Congress in 1951, he became its President in 1957, leaving the country for exile in 1959. When the ANC was banned, he became President of its successor, the National Democratic Party, but that, too, was banned. He then helped form the Zimbabwe African People's Union **(ZAPU)** of which he became President. His non-confrontationist tactics and tendency to spend time outside Rhodesia led to a more radical group breaking away to form the Zimbabwe African National Union (**ZANU**). ZANU and ZAPU, with different international patrons and separate military wings, competed for the representation of African opinion but were persuaded to unite to form the **Patriotic Front** in 1976. ZAPU, however, was increasingly an Ndebele party and in the 1980 elections won only 20 seats. Nkomo, who still saw himself as the father of Zimbabwean nationalism, was disappointed to be offered only the post of Minister of Home Affairs, from which he was dismissed in 1981. Violence in Matabeleland encouraged him into a period of further exile, but he returned and agreed to integrate his party into ZANU, a union ratified in Apr 1988. He became Vice-President of the new party and was one of three senior members in the President's office forming in effect a 'super cabinet'.

Nkrumah, Kwame (1909–71)
Ghanaian politician. Educated in a Catholic primary school and Achimota College, he then went to Lincoln and Pennsylvania Universities in the USA. He studied law in London (1945–7) and was Co-Chairman of the famous Fifth Pan-African Congress held in Manchester in 1945. He returned to the Gold Coast as Secretary-General of the **United Gold Coast Convention**, but broke with it to form the **Convention People's Party (CPP)** in 1949. Imprisoned briefly (he was elected to Legco while in prison), he became leader of government business (1951), Prime Minister (1952–7) and continued in that post on independence until Ghana became a republic in 1960, when he became President. A radical Pan-Africanist, for which he was widely admired throughout much of the continent, he created considerable opposition within Ghana, most of which was repressed; ultimately, however, the military intervened while he was abroad, symbolically on a visit to Beijing. He spent his years of exile in Guinea, where Sekou **Toure** gave him the status of co-head of state. He died in Bucharest.

Nkumbula, Harry M (1916–83)
Zambian nationalist. Educated in local schools, he became a teacher before studying at Makerere College and the London School of Economics (1946–50). He was elected President of the Northern Rhodesian African National Congress (1951) and he was imprisoned briefly for his political activities. His support for a moderate independence constitution cost him the support of **Kaunda**, who left the **ANC** to form **UNIP**. He was a member of the pre-independence coalition government but was leader of the opposition during the first Republic, being restricted for a while in 1970. With the one-party state Second Republic, he joined UNIP in 1973 but remained outside politics in his last years.

Noli, Fan S (1882–1965)
Albanian bishop and politician. Born into an Orthodox family in Thrace, he was educated in Greece and taught at a Greek school in Egypt, where he first encountered the Albanian national movement. After studying law at Harvard, he was ordained a priest and became a bishop in the Albanian Orthodox Church (1908). In 1920 he returned to Albania to represent the American Albanians at the National Assembly held in Lushnjë. Left-wing and known as the 'Red Bishop', he was Foreign Minister in the 1921 Popular Party regime, but he criticized the conservative policies of King **Zog** and went on to form his own opposition party. After Zog fled (1924), Noli formed a government and tried to establish constitutional rule. He introduced agrarian reforms, tried to minimize Italian influence in Albania and made steps towards recognizing the Soviet regime. However, his government collapsed after only seven months, when Zog invaded the country. In 1930 he retired from political life and resumed his religious duties in the USA. ▷ **William of Wied**

Nomenklatura (post-1930)
A list of official positions in the Communist Party of the USSR, and in Soviet government at most levels, and of people suited to fill them, predominantly communist. It was originally intended to identify good candidates in a developing society, but it was gradually abused first to support dictatorship and then to create and perpetuate an elite. By 1985 a corrupt system had paradoxically made reform essential in party and state and at the same time difficult to implement, as Mikhail **Gorbachev** found to his cost.

Nomonhan Incident (May–Sep 1939)
A military clash between Japanese and Soviet troops on the border between north-west Manchuria and Outer Mongolia. When the Japanese **Guandong Army** engaged in hostilities with Mongolian troops on the border at Nomonhan, Soviet troops intervened under the terms of a mutual defence treaty with Outer Mongolia. A full-scale border war

ensued involving the use of aircraft and armoured divisions. Soviet mechanized units under Georgii **Zhukov** inflicted a heavy defeat on the Japanese forces (17 450 dead or missing). Japan's humiliation at Nomonhan convinced Tokyo that war with the USSR (which the Guandong Army had consistently advocated) was to be avoided, and led to the signing of the Japan–USSR Neutrality Pact in 1941.

Non-Aligned Movement

A movement of states in the early years of the **Cold War** which positively espoused the cause of not taking sides in the major division within world politics between the USA and the USSR. Non-alignment was different from neutralism in that it was associated with moves to mediate between the **superpowers**, and aimed to make a direct contribution to the achievement of peace. It was particularly associated with countries like India and statesmen like Nehru. Attempts by Mediterranean, African and Asian countries in the 1960s to give renewed impetus to the movement were badly shaken by continuing superpower hostility. However, conferences were still being held in the 1980s.

Non-Cooperation Movement

A nationalist campaign (1919–22) led by M K **Gandhi** and Congress in protest against the **Amritsar Massacre** and the Montagu-Chelmsford Reforms, and to force the British to grant Indian independence. Locally, it took up many issues, and was linked, especially by Gandhi, with the **Khilafat Movement**. The movement marked M K **Gandhi**'s rise to pre-eminence in the Congress. It involved the boycott of Government institutions and foreign goods, and was abandoned when the protest became violent.

non-violent resistance

The use of non-violent means to resist occupation by a foreign power or other political purposes. It can involve an appeal to wider world opinion, as well as various forms of peaceful political reistance, such as general strikes and **civil disobedience**. Damage to property is not necessarily ruled out. Non-violent resistance is most famously associated with M K **Gandhi**'s resistance to British rule in India, and was popular with the civil rights movements of the 1960s.

Noriega, Manuel (Antonio) (1939–)

Panamanian military leader. The ruling force behind the presidents of Panama in the period 1983–9, he had been recruited by the CIA in the late 1960s and supported by the US government until 1987. Alleging his involvement in drug trafficking, the US authorities ordered his arrest in 1989: 13 000 US troops invaded Panama to support the 12 000 already there. He surrendered in Jan 1990 after taking refuge for 10 days in the Vatican nunciature, and was taken to the USA for trial.

normalization

A term used to describe the restoration of previously ostensibly friendly relations between states or other political organizations after a period of tension or conflict. It was more specifically applied to what was frankly the reimposition of Soviet-style **communism** on those East European socialist states, such as Czechoslovakia in 1968, that had attempted to modify Soviet forms to suit their own conditions. ▷ **détente**

Normandy Campaign (1944)

A **World War II** campaign which began on **D-Day** (6 June 1944). Allied forces under the command of General **Eisenhower** began the liberation of Western Europe from Germany by landing on the Normandy coast between the Orne River and St Marcouf. Artificial harbours were constructed along a strip of beach so that armoured vehicles and heavy guns could be unloaded. Heavy fighting ensued for three weeks, before Allied troops captured Cherbourg (27 June). Tanks broke through the German defences, and Paris was liberated (25 Aug), followed by the liberation of Brussels (2 Sep), and the crossing of the German frontier (12 Sep).

North African Campaign (1940–3)

A campaign fought during **World War II** between Allied and Axis troops. After an initial Italian invasion of Egypt, Italian forces were driven back deep into Libya, and **Rommel** was sent to North Africa with the specially trained Afrika Corps to stem a further Italian retreat. The British were driven back to the Egyptian border, though they defended Tobruk. They counter-attacked late in 1941, and fighting continued the following year, with Rommel once more gaining the initiative. In Oct, British troops under **Montgomery** defeated Rommel at the Battle of **El Alamein**, and drove the German troops W once more. In Feb 1943, the Germans attacked US troops in Tunisia, were driven back, and finally 250 000 Axis troops, half of them German, were caught in a pincer movement by Allied forces advancing from the east and west. ▷ **Axis Powers**

North Korea

A socialist state in East Asia, in the northern half of the Korean Peninsula, separated from South Korea by a demilitarized zone of 487 square miles (1 262 square kilometres). After centuries of Chinese dominion, the Korean Peninsula was formally annexed by Japan in 1895. With the downfall of the Japanese in 1945, it was occupied by Soviet troops from the north and US troops from the south, with a demarcation along latitude 38°N. The North Koreans, under the leadership of Kim Il Sung, invaded the South in 1950. The Security Council of the UN authorized the sending of troops, who were led by General **MacArthur**. Reunification talks in 1980 were broken off by North Korea, but in 1990 there were summit talks with South Korea. Tension heightened in the early 1990s with fears about North Korea's secret development of nuclear weapons.

Northern Expedition (1926–8)

The military expedition undertaken by the Chinese Nationalists (**Guomindang**) and their communist allies to defeat provincial warlords and reunify the country. Under the command of **Chiang Kai-shek**, the National Revolutionary Army marched northwards from south China (July 1926) and had reached the Yangzi River (central China) by early 1927. At this point the left wing of the Guomindang, with the support of the communists, established its own government at Wuhan, while the right wing under Chiang Kai-shek, after taking Shanghai (Apr 1927), embarked on a campaign of terror against communists and their labour supporters. By June 1927 the left-wing Guomindang government had collapsed, effectively ending the United Front between Nationalists and communists. Chiang then proceeded northwards, capturing Beijing (1928). Although a Nationalist government was formally proclaimed (with the capital at Nanjing), Chiang's control over the country was tenuous. Most warlords had simply enrolled under the Nationalist banner and continued to exercise control of their own armies. Furthermore, although the communists' urban base had been destroyed during the Northern Expedition they developed rural bases after 1928 that were ultimately to engulf the entire country.

Northern Ireland

A constituent division of the United Kingdom of Great Britain and Northern Ireland, traditionally divided into six counties. In 1920 a Northern Irish parliament was established, with a House of Commons and a Senate. The population is predominantly Protestant, generally supporting political union with Great Britain, but many of the Roman Catholic minority look for union with the Republic of Ireland. Violent conflict between the two communities broke out in 1969, leading to the establishment of a British army peace-keeping force, but sectarian murders and bombings continued both within and outside the province and as a result of these disturbances the parliament was abolished in 1973. Administrative powers are now vested in the UK Secretary of State for Northern Ireland. A 78-member Assembly was formed in 1973 and replaced by a Constitutional Convention in 1975; although the Assembly reformed in 1982, Nationalist members did not take their seats. Under the 1985 Anglo-Irish agreement, the Republic of Ireland was given a consultative role in the government of Northern Ireland. All the Northern Ireland MPs in the British Parliament resigned in protest the following year, and the agreement continued to attract controversy in the late 1980s. Direct negotiations between the political parties took place in

Belfast in 1991, and further talks were held in 1992 but were inconclusive. The 'troubles' continue in the province, together with terrorist activity in mainland Britain.

Norway

A kingdom in north-west Europe, occupying the western part of the Scandinavian peninsula. After annexation by Sweden in the early 19c, growing nationalism among Norwegians resulted in independence in 1905. The country declared itself neutral in both World Wars, but was occupied by Germany in 1940–4.

Norway, German Invasion of (8–9 Apr 1940)

A daring seaborne operation, undertaken in defiance of British naval superiority, which was carried out as a preliminary to the German invasion of France and in order to protect Germany's supply of iron ore from northern Sweden. It brought all major Norwegian cities, including Oslo, Bergen, Trondheim and Narvik under German control within a single night. Refusing to capitulate or to hand over authority to **Quisling**, the Norwegian government and King **Haakon VII** maintained a resistance to the Germans which lasted, with British and French support, until June 1940. ▷ **World War II**

Notting Hill Riots (1958)

A series of violent demonstrations in north-west London. Directed at non-white immigrants living there, they brought immigration into the British political arena for the first time.

Novotný, Antonín (1904–75)

Czechoslovak politician. He became a communist at the age of 17 and held various party jobs in the years before **World War II**. Arrested in 1941, he survived four years in a Nazi concentration camp. After his release, he rose rapidly in the Czechoslovak Communist Party, becoming Regional Secretary in Prague in 1945 and a member of the Central Committee in 1946. He played a leading part in the communist takeover of the Czechoslovak government in 1948. Novotný became all-powerful First Secretary of the Party in 1953 and from 1958 to 1968 he was also President of the republic. He was essentially a Soviet-style communist so much committed to central planning and the needs of heavy industry that by 1961 there was an economic recession. His unpopularity forced him to make token concessions from 1962 onwards, especially in the hope of placating the Slovaks, but these empty gestures failed to satisfy his critics within the Party. He was therefore forced out, and succeeded as First Secretary by, the reformist Slovak, Alexander **Dubček**, in Jan 1968, and was also forced to resign the presidency two months later. However, his negative and protracted tenure of office lost the Czechoslovak reform movement more time than it could make up in the course of the **Prague Spring**. ▷ **Stalinism**

NPD (*Nationaldemokratische Partei Deutschlands*, 'National Democratic Party of Germany')

German political party. Founded in 1964 through the amalgamation of extreme right-wing splinter parties, notably the German Reich Party (DRP) and German Party (DP), the NPD became increasingly radical, especially under von Thadden's leadership from 1967. In its internal structure, politics and membership the NPD showed some disturbing parallels with the **Nazi Party**, but although it gained seats temporarily in various **Land** (state) parliaments, it failed to enter the **Bundestag** and by the mid-1970s had, to all intents and purposes, collapsed.

Nu, U (1907–)

Burmese politician and Prime Minister (1948–56, 1957–8 and 1960–2). He became a teacher, and in 1934 came to prominence through the student political movement. Imprisoned by the British for sedition (1940), he was released by the Japanese and served in Ba Maw's puppet administration. In 1946 he became President of the Burmese Constituent Assembly, and the first Prime Minister of the independent Union of Burma (1948). He was overthrown by a military coup in 1962, and imprisoned, but released in 1966. He then lived abroad, organizing resistance to the military regime, but returned to Burma in 1980 to become a Buddhist monk.

Nuclear Non-Proliferation Treaty (NPT)

A treaty signed in 1968 by the USA, the USSR, the UK and an open-ended list of over 100 other countries. It sought to limit the spread of nuclear weapons, those possessing them agreeing not to transfer the capability to produce them, and those not possessing them agreeing not to acquire the capability. Recent reductions in US and Russian nuclear stockpiles appear to have reinforced the Treaty, but a number of other states are thought to be close to producing their own nuclear arms.

nuclear weapons

Bomb, missile or other weapon of mass destruction deriving its destructive force from the energy released during nuclear fission or nuclear fusion. According to their size and the means of delivery, they may be classified as tactical short-range weapons (for use on the battlefield), theatre medium-range weapons (for use against deep military targets), or strategic long-range weapons (for use against enemy cities and command centres). ▷ **Nuclear Non-Proliferation Treaty**

Nujoma, Sam Daniel (1929–)

Namibian nationalist. Educated at a Finnish missionary school in Windhoek, he was a railway worker and clerk until entering politics as the co-founder of the South West Africa People's Organization (**SWAPO**). He was exiled in 1960, set up a provisional headquarters in Dar es Salaam and led SWAPO's armed struggle from 1966 until 1989 when he returned to Namibia for the pre-independence elections, which his party won. He became the first President of Namibia in Mar 1990.

Nuremberg Laws (1935)

Two racial laws promulgated in Nuremberg at a **Reichstag** meeting held during the **Nazi Party** Congress of that year. The first deprived of German citizenship those not of 'German or related blood'; the second made marriage or extra-marital relations illegal between Germans and Jews. Following on earlier arbitrary terror, the laws were the first formal steps in the process of separating off Jews and other 'non-Aryans' in Nazi Germany.

Nuremberg Trials

Proceedings held by the Allies at Nuremberg after **World War II** to try Nazi war criminals, following a decision made in 1943. An International Military Tribunal was set up in Aug 1945, and sat from Nov 1945 until Oct 1946. Twenty-one Nazis were tried in person, including **Goering** and **Ribbentrop** (who were sentenced to death), and **Hess** (who was given life imprisonment). ▷ **Nazi Party**

Nyerere, Julius (Kambarage) (1922–)

Tanzanian nationalist leader and politician. While working as a schoolteacher, he became President of the Tanganyika African Association (1953). He left the profession to co-found (1954) the Tanganyika African National Union, of which he became President, and led the movement to independence. After a brief spell as a nominated member of Legco (from which he resigned), Nyerere was elected (1958) in his own right, becoming Chief Minister (1960–1) and, on independence, Prime Minister. He resigned from the post to reorganize the party and returned to central politics as President, negotiating the union of Tanganyika and Zanzibar in 1964. His idealism, reflected in the **Arusha Declaration**, dominated Tanzania's public policy and the country's reputation abroad. He resigned the presidency in 1985, but retained the presidency of the party until 1987.

O

OAPEC (Organization of Arab Petroleum Exporting Countries)
An organization formed under the umbrella of the Organization of Petroleum Exporting Countries (OPEC) in 1968 by Saudi Arabia, Kuwait, and Libya, with its headquarters in Kuwait. By 1972 all the Arab oil producers had joined. ▷ **OPEC**

OAS (*Organisation Armée Secrète*, 'Secret Army Organization')
The clandestine organization of French Algerians, led by rebel army generals Jouhaud and Raoul **Salan**, active (1960–2) in resisting Algerian independence. It caused considerable violence in Algeria and metropolitan France until thrown into rapid decline by the Franco-Algerian cease-fire (Mar 1962), Salan's capture (Apr 1962) and Algerian independence (July 1962). ▷ **Algerian War of Independence; FLN**

Obasanjo, Olusegun (1937–)
Nigerian soldier and politician. Educated at Abeokuta Baptist High School and Mons Officers' School, he joined the Nigerian army in 1958, training in both the UK and India, specializing in engineering. He served with the Nigerian unit in the **UN** Congo (Zaire) operations and was military commander of the federal forces during the **Biafran War** (1967–70). He was made Federal Commissioner of Works and Housing (1975) as well as Chief of Staff. After the short interim military rule led by Murtala Mohammed, he became Head of State (1976–9) overseeing the transfer back to civilian rule. Since then, he has played an important role on the international stage, especially within the Commonwealth, and as founder and leader of the African Leadership Forum.

Obote, (Apollo) Milton (1924–)
Ugandan politician. Educated in mission schools and Makerere College, he worked in Kenya (1950–5), being a founder member of the Kenyan African Union. He kept his political links with his home country and was a member of the Uganda National Congress (1952–60), being elected to Legco in 1957. He helped form the Uganda People's Congress in 1960, became its leader and then leader of the opposition during the Kiwanuka government of 1961–2. The 1962 elections resulted in a coalition between Obote's UPC and the neo-traditionalist **Kabaka Yekka** and he became Prime Minister. When fundamental differences between himself and the Kabaka could not be mediated, he staged a coup in 1966, deposing

the Kabaka and establishing himself as Executive President. In 1971, however, his government was overthrown in a military coup, led by Idi **Amin**. He went into exile in Tanzania and returned to Uganda with the Tanzanian army in 1979, regaining the presidency after elections in 1980. But he was once more overthrown by the military (July 1985) and went into exile again, this time in Zambia.

O'Connor, Sandra Day (1930–)
US lawyer and jurist. She studied at Stanford, and after practising law she entered Arizona politics as a Republican, becoming majority leader in the state Senate before moving to the state bench. In 1981 President **Reagan** named her to the US Supreme Court. She was confirmed, becoming the first woman in that position. ▷ **Republican Party**

October Crisis (1970)
Terrorist crisis in Quebec. After the arrest of Pierre Vallière and Charles Gagnon, the **Front de Libération du Québec (FLQ)** changed its tactics from bombing to kidnapping. One plan was foiled, but on 5 Oct the group kidnapped the British Trade Commissioner in Quebec, James Cross. A ransom of C$500 000 was demanded, along with the release of a number of 'political prisoners'. There was to be no police pursuit, transport out of the country was to be provided for the gang and the FLQ manifesto was to be broadcast on radio and television. The last two demands were accepted, and the Attorney-General of Quebec promised to support parole for a number of 'political prisoners'. Cross was not released, however, and on 10 Oct the Minister of Labour and Immigration, Pierre Laporte, was also kidnapped. Three days later students began a campaign of rallies and sit-ins, and the **Parti Québecois** began to put pressure on Premier Robert **Bourassa** to form an emergency coalition government. Instead, he brought in the army to back up the police and the **War Measures Act** was implemented to round up FLQ sympathizers. Although over 450 were arrested, only 20 were convicted in the 62 cases brought. Protest against the Act died down after Laporte's murder on 17 Oct. Cross was discovered and his release obtained after safe passage to Cuba was guaranteed to the kidnappers. Later that month the murderers of Laporte were apprehended and imprisoned.

October Manifesto (17 Oct 1905)
The proclamation issued by **Nicholas II** at the height of the Russian **Revolution of 1905**, promising the Russians freedom of speech and assembly and the election of a legislative body. This took the steam out of the opposition. But gradually the freedoms were ignored, while the dumas that were elected were increasingly unrepresentative and powerless. This breach of promise was one of many factors decreasing Tsarism's chances of survival.

October Revolution (1917)

The overthrow of the Russian Provisional Government by Bolshevik-led armed workers (Red Guards), soldiers and sailors (25–6 Oct 1917 old style; 7–8 Nov new style). The revolution was organized by the Military Revolutionary Committee of the Petrograd Soviet, but was based on **Lenin**'s tactical exploitation of the Provisional Government's failure to provide effective leadership in a rapidly escalating crisis. The members of the government were arrested and it was replaced by the Soviet of People's Commissars (*Sovnarkom*), chaired by Lenin. This first Soviet government then proceeded to totally reorganize the economy and polity of Russia on lines that lasted for over 70 years. ▷ **April Theses; Bolsheviks; February Revolution; July Days**

October War (1973)

This war, which followed the launching of a surprise attack by Egypt and Syria on Israel on the Jewish Day of Atonement (*Yom Kippur*), gave the Arabs an important lift in morale as a result of some initial success. The Israeli counter-attack could not, however be contained by the Egyptian and Syrian forces, and the USA was persuaded by the Saudis to get Israel to cease her military activities pending mediation by the **UN**. The importance of the war from the Egyptian point of view was that it went some way to salving the national pride which had taken a severe pounding in the **Six Day War** (June 1967).

Octobrists (1905–18)

The short name for the Union of 17 Oct, those Russian liberals who, in contrast with the **Kadets**, accepted the Tsar's **October Manifesto** in 1905 as a basis on which to achieve moderate reform. Their numbers were greatest in the third and fourth dumas for which the franchise was most biased, but they still achieved little. In 1911 their leader, Alexander **Guchkov**, was elected Duma President but could not even exercise influence upon **Nicholas II**. Although Guchkov was Minister of War in the **Russian Provisional Government** of 1917, they were even more out of touch than the Kadets with the changing public mood and had virtually no representation in the **Russian Constituent Assembly** in 1918.

Oder–Neisse Line

The new Polish–German border, drawn by the **World War II** Allies in a series of conferences and negotiations in 1944–5, and involving the transfer to Poland of a sizeable area of the Third Reich. The decision was partly based on historical arguments but also facilitated the transfer of territory in the east of Poland claimed by the USSR. A source of contention between the Federal Republic of Germany on the one hand and the German Democratic Republic and Poland on the other, the border was finally recognized by the Federal Republic in 1970 and by the reunited Germany in 1990.

Odinga, (Zaramogi) Oginga (Ajuma) (1911–94)
Kenyan nationalist and politician. Educated at Alliance High School and Makerere College, he was a schoolteacher when he became active in local Luo politics. He was elected to Legco in 1957 and was Vice-President of **KANU** (1960–6), during which period he pressed unflinchingly for independence, his apparent extremism being contrasted with the moderation of **Mboya**. He was Minister of Home Affairs (1963–4) and then Vice-President (1964–6). At the Limuru Party Conference in 1966, Mboya managed to remove Odinga from positions of authority and he soon resigned to form the Kenya People's Union. He was re-elected on the KPU ticket in the Little General Election of 1966 and provided a charismatic figure round which dissidents might congregate. Consequently, the party was soon banned and Odinga spent some of the next 25 years in and out of detention.

Ogarkov, Nikolai Vasilevich (1917–94)
Soviet military adviser and politician. Son of a peasant, he joined the **Red Army** in 1938 and rose through wartime experience and subsequent commands to become First Deputy Chief of the General Staff in 1968 and full member of the Communist Party Central Committee in 1971. From 1977 to 1984 he was Chief of Staff and Deputy Defence Minister. For over a decade he helped to strengthen and expand the Soviet forces. But his advocacy of further improving conventional forces met opposition even from Leonid **Brezhnev** and certainly from Yuri **Andropov**. His removal in 1984 got rid of an obstacle to East-West arms control talks.

Ohira Masayoshi (1910–80)
Japanese politician. A Finance Ministry bureaucrat, Ohira was first elected to the Diet in 1952 and later went on to serve as Foreign Minister and Finance Minister in **Liberal Democratic Party (LDP)** cabinets of the 1970s. He became LDP President (and Prime Minister) in 1978 under new party election rules that aimed to give a greater role to the party rank and file in the constituencies. During his premiership, Ohira hosted the 1979 Tokyo economic summit of developed countries. Following a no-confidence vote against him in 1980, when rival LDP factions joined the opposition, Ohira dissolved the Diet. He died 10 days before new elections, but the LDP won handsome majorities in both houses.

Ojukwu, Chukwenmeka Odumegwu (1933–)
Nigerian soldier and politician. Educated in church schools in Lagos, Epsom College and Lincoln College, Oxford, he joined the Nigerian Army in 1957. After attending military college in England, he served

with the Nigerian force in the **UN** Congo (Zaire) operations and was named Military Governor of the mainly Ibo-speaking Eastern Region of Nigeria after the military coup of Jan 1966. He proclaimed the Eastern Region the independent Republic of Biafra in May 1967, thus precipitating the **Biafran War**, and for three years acted as Head of Government and Supreme Commander. When his forces were finally defeated in 1970, he fled to the Ivory Coast.

Okawa Shumei (1886–1957)
Japanese ultranationalist. He was involved in several right-wing plots against the civilian government. A fierce critic of Western colonialism in Asia, Okawa founded societies to protect the **Kokutai** ('national essence') and promote renovation of the state. Unlike Ikki **Kita**, Okawa was willing to work with military and bureaucratic elites, and lectured to the Army Academy on the need for Asian unity and struggle against the West. He was imprisoned in 1932 for his participation in an abortive military coup but was released in 1934. Okawa was indicted by allied authorities as a class-A war criminal in 1945 (the only person to be so indicted who was not a military or government figure). Judged to be insane, however, Okawa was never brought to trial.

Olav V (1903–91)
King of Norway (1957/91). A keen sportsman and Olympic gold medallist, Crown Prince Olav escaped from Oslo with his father, King **Haakon VII**, following the German invasion in Apr 1940, accompanying him into exile in Britain (June 1940). He participated actively in the war effort and from 1944 to 1945 served as chief of the Norwegian armed forces. He succeeded his father as king in 1957, but performed a mainly ceremonial role as monarch. ▷ **Norway, German Invasion of**

Olympio, Sylvanus (1902–63)
Togolese politician. Educated at the London School of Economics, he returned to Africa as District Manager of the United Africa Company. He was President of the Togolese Assembly in 1946 and then led the country's government from 1958 to 1960 when, on independence, he became President. He was killed on 13 Jan 1963 in a military coup.

Onassis, Jacqueline Kennedy (1929–94)
US wife of President **Kennedy**. Born Jacqueline Lee Bouvier, she married John F Kennedy in 1953, and as First Lady from 1960 she became internationally renowned for her fashionable elegance. Following Kennedy's assassination in 1963 she moved with their two children to New York City (1964). In 1968 she married Greek tycoon Aristotle Onassis (1906–75). After his death she returned to New York City, where she worked as an editor in a publishing house. She died in her New York home.

O'Neill (of the Maine), Terence (Marne), Baron (1914–90)
Ulster politician. He served in the Irish Guards during **World War II**. A member of the Northern Ireland parliament (1946–70), he held junior posts before becoming Minister for Home Affairs (1956), Finance (1956–63), and then Prime Minister (1963–9). A supporter of closer cross-border links with the Irish Republic, he angered many Unionists. Following a general election in 1969, dissension in the Unionist Party increased, and he resigned the premiership soon after. Made a life peer in 1970, he continued to speak out on Northern Ireland issues. ▷ **Democratic Unionist Party**

OPEC (Organization of Petroleum Exporting Countries)
An international economic organization set up in 1960 with its headquarters in Vienna; the longest-surviving major cartel. It consists of 13 oil-producing countries: the founder members were Iran, Iraq, Kuwait, Saudi Arabia, and Venezuela; and they have since been joined by Algeria, Ecuador, Gabon, Indonesia, Libya, Nigeria, Qatar, and the United Arab Emirates (formerly Abu Dhabi). Its purpose is to co-ordinate the petroleum policy of members to protect their interests, especially in relation to the fixing of prices for crude oil and the quantities to be produced.

Open Door Policy
US foreign policy towards China, formulated in response to the weakness of the later **Qing Dynasty**. Announced in Mar 1900 by Secretary of State John Hay, the Open Door policy sought to preserve Chinese integrity and US trade rights by opposing the development of spheres of influence dominated by Britain, Germany, Russia, France, Italy and Japan.

Opus Dei
Established in Spain in 1928 by an Aragonese priest, José María Escrivá, Opus Dei (literally, 'the Work of God') is a lay order within the Catholic Church which has sought secular power through the recruitment of leading professionals. With its ultra-conservative theology and its severe subjugation of women, the sodality has moved in the opposite direction to most other orders within the church. Under the **Franco** regime Opus Dei, dubbed 'the Holy Mafia', rose rapidly to a position of considerable power. It orchestrated Spain's economic modernization from the late 1950s on and remained the major force within the government until 1973. The three ministers involved in the most notorious scandal of the Franco regime, the Matesa affair of 1969, were all Opus Dei members. Elsewhere, Opus has been linked to numerous dictatorial regimes in Latin America, often in collaboration with the **CIA**. Under Pope John Paul II, Opus Dei has become the most powerful order in the Roman Catholic Church. Its extreme secretiveness, its unique semi-autonomous status, and its colossal

wealth have combined to produce what is, in effect, a church within the church.

Ordzhonikidze, Gregori Konstantinovich (1886–1937)
Georgian politician. The son of a small landowner, he had already joined the **Bolsheviks** before graduating as a director at Tiflis in 1905. Between then and 1917 he was in and out of prison and in and out of Russia for his revolutionary activities. In 1920–1 he helped establish Soviet rule in Georgia and Armenia; and by 1930 he was a **Politburo** member and chairman of the council for Soviet economy. However, as friends and relatives were shot in **Stalin**'s purges, he lost heart and took his own life.

Organic Acts
Statutes of the US Congress which laid down the relationship of Puerto Rico to the USA between 1900 and 1950. The First Organic Act of 1900 (the Foraker Act) effectively made Puerto Rico a US dependency in that supreme power was vested in the US governor and a nominated executive council. The Second Organic Act of 1916 (the Jones Act) conferred universal male suffrage and made Puerto Ricans citizens of the USA. The Public Law Act of 1950 allowed the new Commonwealth (a status devised by **Muñoz Marín** to draft its own constitution.

Organization of African Unity (OAU)
An organization founded in 1963 by representatives of 32 African governments meeting in Addis Ababa, which reflected the views of the moderate leaders, such as **Nyerere**, rather than radicals such as **Nkrumah**. By protecting territorial integrity, the organization accepted the artificial boundaries bequeathed by the colonial powers and preserved individual self-interest over continental political and economic unity. It remained, however, the main forum for the African continent to express its political views and, through its Liberation Committee in Dar es Salaam, assisted the decolonization of southern Africa. It has had some success at mediation, but its lack of sanctions has resulted in its inability to solve problems where major African powers disagree.

Organization of American States (OAS)
A regional agency established in 1948 to coordinate the work of a variety of inter-American departments recognized within the terms of the United Nations Charter. The organization was formed to promote peace, economic cooperation, and social advancement in the Western hemisphere. Its central organ, the General Secretariat, is housed in Washington DC, and consists of one representative from each member country. Thirty-one countries within the Americas are members. ▷ **Pan-American Union; UN**

Organization of Central American States
An agency established in 1951 by Costa Rica, El Salvador, Guatemala, Honduras, and Nicaragua (Panama refused to join) to promote economic, social, and cultural cooperation. In 1965 this was extended to include political and educational cooperation. The Organization has also been involved in legal reform.

Orlando, Vittorio Emanuele (1860–1952)
Italian politician. Professor of Law at Palermo University, he was elected to parliament in 1897. He served as Minister of Education, before becoming Minister of Justice in 1916. At the height of the **Caporetto** crisis he became Prime Minister, remaining in office until June 1919. His inability to force Woodrow **Wilson** and **Clemenceau** to honour the terms of the Treaty of **London** (1915) at the Paris peace talks, coupled with post-war economic dislocation and growing political violence, brought about his downfall. He made little attempt to resist **Mussolini** and appeared on the fascist **Listone** in the Apr 1924 election. He belatedly adopted a more openly anti-fascist stance in 1925. After **World War II** he became a Senator.

Ortega (Saavedra), Daniel (1945–)
Nicaraguan military leader. Educated in Managua, he became active in his teens in the resistance movement against the **Somoza** regime, and in 1963 joined the Sandinista National Liberation Front (FSLN), which had been founded in 1960. He became National Director of the FSLN in 1966, was imprisoned for seven years for urban guerrilla bank raids, and then, in 1979, played a major part in the overthrow of Anastasio Somoza. A junta led by Ortega established a provisional government, and in 1985 he became President, but US-backed counter-revolutionary forces, the 'Contras', threatened his government's stability. By 1989, however, there were encouraging signs of peace being achieved. He surprisingly lost the 1990 general election to Violeta Chamorro, and supervised the peaceful handover of power.

Oscar II (1829–1907)
King of Sweden (1872/1907) and of Norway (1872/1905). He was the younger son of Oscar I and brother of Charles XV, whom he succeeded. A vigorous, intelligent and highly cultured man, his foreign policy was marked by admiration of the new German Empire of Otto von **Bismarck**. His reign saw growing tension between his Norwegian and Swedish subjects until in 1905 he was compelled to surrender the crown of Norway to Prince Carl of Denmark, elected King of Norway as **Haakon VII**. The sacrifice saddened the last years of Oscar's life. He was married to Sofia of Nassau, by whom he had four sons, of whom **Gustav V** succeeded him as King.

Ostpolitik

The policy initiated in West Germany in the 1960s as part of the process of détente to normalize relations with communist countries which recognized the German Democratic Republic (GDR) and with the GDR itself. It led to treaties with Poland and the USSR, the recognition of the Polish border (the **Oder–Neisse Line**) and, most significantly, the recognition of the GDR. Largely masterminded by Willy **Brandt**, the policy sought to prevent, and even reverse, the deepening schism between the Federal Republic and GDR and had the broader aim of generally improving relations between West and East. It culminated in German reunification in 1990. ▷ **Germany, East; Germany, West**

Oswald, Lee Harvey (1939–63)

US alleged assassin of President John F **Kennedy**. A Marxist and former US marine, he lived for a time in the USSR (1959–62). On 24 Nov 1963, during a jail transfer two days after the assassination, he was killed in Dallas by nightclub owner Jack **Ruby**.

Ottawa Conferences (1894, 1932)

British **Imperial Conferences**. The main topic in 1894 was the development of communications between the individual units of the **British Empire**. Underlying the conference was a realization that the nature of imperial relationships had altered and that a new way of dealing with them had to be found. A major evolution was evident by 1932 in the agreements at the Ottawa economic conference held between Britain and its dominions at the height of the world depression. The conference negotiated a limited amount of imperial preference following the adoption of a new protective tariff by the British government earlier that year.

Ottoman Empire

A Muslim empire founded c.1300 by Sultan Osman I, and originating in Asia Minor. Following the 'golden age' of Suleyman I, 'the Magnificent', the empire began a protracted decline. During the 19c and early 20c, Ottoman power was eroded by the ambitions of Russia and Austria in south-east Europe, the ambitions of France, Britain, and Italy in North Africa, the emergence of the Balkan nations, and internal loss of authority. It joined the Central Powers in 1914, and collapsed with their defeat in 1918. ▷ **Young Turks**

ÖVP (*Österreichische Volkspartei*, 'Austrian People's Party')

Austrian political party. Founded in 1945, the ÖVP represented the key Christian (Catholic) political groupings of inter-war **Austria** and identifies with contemporary European Christian Democracy. It has played a major role in Austrian government (1945–70, 1986–) sometimes in coalition with the **SPÖ**, but in 1986–7 became embroiled in the controversy surrounding Kurt **Waldheim**'s candidacy for the Austrian presidency.

OVRA
In Italy, the name given to **Mussolini**'s secret police force. Never really an integral part of the **Fascist Party** machinery, the OVRA was little more than a slightly expanded version of the old secret branch of the Ministry of the Interior police.

Owen, David (Anthony Llewellyn) (1938–)
British politician. He trained in medicine, then became an MP (1966) and Under-Secretary to the Navy (1968). He was Secretary for Health (1974–6), and Foreign Secretary (1977–9). One of the so-called 'Gang of Four' who formed the **Social Democratic Party** (SDP) in 1981, he succeeded Roy **Jenkins** as its leader in 1983. Following the Alliance's disappointing result in the 1987 general election, he opposed Liberal leader David **Steel** over the question of the merger of the two parties. In 1988, after the SDP voted to accept merger, Owen led the smaller section of the party to a brief independent existence. He retired from parliament in 1992 and went on to become, along with Cyrus Vance, a peace-broker in the troubles that erupted after the disintegration of Yugoslavia.

Ozaki Yukio (1859–1954)
Japanese politician. A journalist before he turned to politics, Ozaki participated in the formation of the *Rikken Kaishinto* (Constitutional Reform Party) in 1882 and was elected to the first Diet in 1890 (he was to be elected a further 24 times). Ozaki remained a consistent advocate of party government and expansion of the suffrage. Outspoken, he maintained an independent stance even during **World War II**, criticizing the dictatorial style of Prime Minister Hideki **Tojo**. He retired from politics in 1953.

Özal, Turgut (1927–93)
Turkish politician. Educated at Istanbul Technical University, he entered government service and in 1967 became Under-Secretary for State Planning. From 1971 he worked for the World Bank, in 1979 joined the office of Prime Minister Bülent **Ecevit**, and in 1980 was Deputy to Prime Minister Bülent Ulusu, within the military regime of Kenan Evren. When political pluralism returned in 1983, Ozal founded the Islamic, right-of-centre Motherland Party (ANAP, *Anavatan Partisi*) and led it to a narrow, but clear victory in the elections of that year. In the 1987 general election he retained his majority, and in 1989 became Turkey's first civilian President for 30 years.

P

Paardeberg, Battle of (1900)

The first major British victory of the second Boer War, following the relief of the Siege of **Kimberley**. The Boers abandoned the position they had held at Magersfontein, and moved east to defend Bloemfontein. Their defeat at Paardeberg opened the way for the full-scale attack on the Orange Free State and the Transvaal, and the taking of the Boer cities. ▷ **Boer Wars**

Paasikivi, Juo Kusti (1870–1956)

Finnish politician. He became Conservative Prime Minister after the civil war in 1918. He recognized the need for friendly relations with Russia, and took part in all Finnish–Soviet negotiations. He sought to avoid war in Sep 1939, conducted the armistice negotiations and became Prime Minister again in 1944. He succeeded Carl Gustav **Mannerheim** as President (1946–56). ▷ **Continuation War; Russo-Finnish War**

Paderewski, Ignacy (Jan) (1860–1941)

Polish pianist, composer, and patriot. He studied in Warsaw, becoming a professor in the Conservatoire (1878), and a virtuoso pianist, appearing throughout Europe and the USA. During **World War I** he used his popularity abroad to argue the case, particularly in the USA, for Poland regaining its independence, and in 1919 he became for a time Prime Minister of Poland in order to establish a sense of political unity. But he soon retired from politics, lived in Switzerland, and resumed concert work. He was elected President of Poland's provisional parliament abroad in 1940, though poor health prevented him pursuing an active role. He died in New York City.

Padlock Act (1937)

Canadian anti-communist legislation. Enacted by the **Duplessis Union Nationale** administration of Quebec, it authorized the closure of any premises which was suspected of producing communist propaganda. Since the term 'communist' was not properly defined, the government was able to hinder the growth of the **CCF** and also to use it against trade unions. The law was declared unconstitutional by the Supreme Court in 1957.

Padmore, George (1902–59)
Trinidadian international revolutionary and Pan-Africanist. He spent most of his life campaigning against colonialism in Africa and preaching African **socialism** and unity; his memory is revered in West Africa.

Page, Sir Earle Christmas Grafton (1880–1961)
Australian politician. He practised medicine and sat in the federal parliament from 1919 until his death. He became Leader of the Country Party in 1921 and Deputy Prime Minister and Treasurer in the Bruce–Page coalition government of 1923–9. He was Deputy Prime Minister (1934–9) and briefly Prime Minister in 1939. In 1941 he became Australian minister in London, representing Australia on war cabinet committees. Minister of Health in 1949, he retired to the backbenches in 1956. ▷ **National Party of Australia**

Pahlavi, Mohammad Reza (1919–80)
Shah of Persia (1941/79). He succeeded on the abdication of his father, Reza Shah, in 1941. His reign was for many years marked by social reforms and a movement away from the old-fashioned despotic concept of the monarchy, but during the later 1970s the economic situation deteriorated, social inequalities worsened, and protest at Western-style 'decadence' grew among the religious fundamentalists. After several attempts at parliamentary reform the Shah, having lost control of the situation, left the country, and a revolutionary government was formed under Ayatollah **Khomeini**. The ex-Shah having been admitted to the USA for medical treatment, the Iranian government seized the US embassy in Tehran and held many of its staff hostage for over a year, demanding his return to Iran. He made his final residence in Egypt at the invitation of President Anwar **Sadat** and died there.

Paisley, Rev Ian (Richard Kyle) (1926–)
Northern Ireland militant Protestant clergyman and politician. An ordained minister since 1946, he formed his own Church (the Free Presbyterian Church of Ulster) in 1951, and from the 1960s became deeply involved in Ulster politics. He founded the Protestant **Democratic Unionist Party** and stood as its MP for four years until 1974, since when he has been the Democratic Unionist MP for North Antrim. He has been a member of the European Parliament since 1979. A rousing orator, he is strongly in favour of maintaining the Union with Britain, and fiercely opposed to the **IRA**, Roman Catholicism, and the unification of Ireland.

Pakistan
An Asian state, situated between the Hindu Kush mountain range in the north and the Arabian Sea in the south. After British colonial rule during the 19c, Pakistan separated from India to form a state for the Muslim

minority in 1947, consisting of West Pakistan (Baluchistan, North-West Frontier, West Punjab, Sind) and East Pakistan (East Bengal), physically separated by 1 000 miles (1 600 kilometres). Pakistan occupied Jammu and Kashmir in 1949 (these territory gains, disputed with India, were the cause of wars in 1965 and 1971). Pakistan was proclaimed an Islamic republic in 1956, but the differences between East and West Pakistan developed into civil war in 1971, resulting in East Pakistan becoming an independent state, Bangladesh. A military coup by General Zia ul-Haq in 1977 was accompanied in 1979 by the execution of former Prime Minister **Bhutto**, despite international appeals for clemency. In 1991 there was increased violence within the country, particularly in Sind, and several changes of government took place amid allegations of corruption in the early 1990s.

Pal, Bipin Chandra (1858–1932)

Indian nationalist and freedom fighter. Though born into an orthodox Zamindar family in Sylhet (in present-day Bangladesh), he opposed traditional orthodoxy and religious practices. He entered politics in 1877 and his association with the great reformist Brahmo Samaj leader, Keshab Chandra Sen, drew him into this movement in 1880. He was also greatly influenced by B G **Tilak, Lala Lajpat Rai** and Aurobindo **Ghosh**. In 1898 he went to England on a scholarship for theological studies and, on his return, launched a weekly journal, *Young India* (1902), through which he championed the complete freedom of India. He campaigned for the boycott of British goods and also advocated a policy of passive resistance and non-cooperation. A member of the famous Congress trio 'Lal, Pal and Bal', he spent the years 1908–11 in England, where he worked for India's freedom and published *Swaraj*. In the later stages of the freedom movement, he withdrew from political life, although he continued to write on national matters. ▷ **Lajpat Rai, Lala; Non-Cooperation Movement; Swaraj**

Palach, Jan (1948–69)

Czech philosophy student. As a protest against the invasion of Czechoslovakia by **Warsaw Pact** forces (Aug 1968) and its subsequent '**normalization**', he burnt himself to death in Wenceslas Square in Prague in Jan 1969. He became a hero and symbol of hope, and was mourned by thousands. Huge popular demonstrations marking the 20th anniversary of his death were held in Prague in 1989.

Palestine

A region bordering the east Mediterranean, historically settled by Philistines then Israelites. During the 20c it has been disputed by Jewish and Arab interests. Palestine was viewed by the Jews as the 'Promised Land', but it also contains Islamic holy sites associated with Muhammed. After

World War I a mandate was granted to the UK by the **UN** to administer the territory (1920–48). The **Balfour Declaration** supported the establishment of a Jewish homeland. After World War II the UN recommended that there should be separate Jewish and Arab states in Palestine. The State of Israel came into being in 1948 and was immediately invaded by its Arab neighbours. The Israelis were victorious, and gained more land than had been allotted by the UN. Over 700 000 Arab refugees left the Israeli-occupied areas. The **PLO** was recognized by the Arab League in 1974 as the official voice of Palestinian Arabs. ▷ **Jordan**

Palme, (Sven) Olof (1927–86)
Swedish politician. He graduated in law from the University of Stockholm in 1951 and became private secretary to the Social Democratic Prime Minister, Tage **Erlander** in 1954. He was elected to parliament four years later and was appointed minister without portfolio in 1963. He succeeded Erlander as Prime Minister on the latter's resignation in 1969. Palme lost power in 1976, but returned at the head of a minority government in 1982. He was shot dead by an unknown assailant in the centre of Stockholm after a visit to the cinema with his wife. His leadership of the Social Democratic Labour Party saw a leftward swing in its policies, and he was an outspoken critic of US policy in the **Vietnam War**.

Pan-Africanist Congress (PAC)
A South African political party and offshoot of the **ANC** (African National Congress), the PAC was formed in 1959 as a movement rejecting the multi-racial assumptions of the ANC as well as its communist and Soviet links. It was banned in 1960 and its leaders went into exile, organizing opposition to the **apartheid** regime in South Africa from Zambia. The ban was lifted in 1990, and it remains a smaller, but perhaps more closely knit, party than the ANC, despite its leadership problems in the years of exile.

Pan-American Union
An organization founded in 1890 (and first called the International Bureau for American Republics) to foster political and economic cooperation among American states, and to draw North and South America closer together. Until **World War II** the Union concluded many agreements covering trade, migration, and neutrality zones around their coasts, despite fears among many members of domination by the USA. In 1948 it became part of the wider Organization of American States (OAS), and now forms its permanent administrative and advisory machinery. It has four departments: economic and social affairs; international law; cultural affairs; and administrative services.

Pan-Arabism

The belief that Arabs should unite to form one nation had its origins in the Arab nationalist movement before **World War I**. With the collapse of the **Ottoman Empire** in that war and the foundation of separate Arab states after it, the belief in a single Arab nation declined. It was revived in the late 1930s when the Palestinian Arabs, revolting against Jewish colonization and British rule, appealed to Arabs everywhere for support. Egypt took up pan-Arabism as a means of asserting Egyptian leadership in the Middle East. In 1945 the Arab League was formed with its headquarters in Cairo, but it foundered in 1948 as it was unable to prevent the formation of the state of Israel. In the 1950s the cause of Arab unity was taken up by Gamal Abd al-**Nasser** in Egypt and by the Ba'ath Party in Syria, in order to oppose Israel and domination by foreign powers. There was a short-lived union of Syria and Egypt (1958–61) but the rivalries of Egypt, Syria and Iraq prevented Arab unification. With the defeat of Arab states by Israel in the 1967 war, Nasser's leadership was discredited and the idea of pan-Arabism lost its appeal.

Panama Canal

A canal bisecting the Isthmus of Panama and linking the Atlantic and Pacific Oceans. It is 51 miles (82 kilometres) long, 490 feet (150 metres) wide in most places; built by the US Corps of Engineers (1904–14). In 1979, US control of the Panama Canal Zone (5 miles/8 kilometres of land flanking the canal on either side) passed to the Republic of Panama, which has guaranteed the neutrality of the waterway itself when control of the canal is passed to it in 2000.

Panchayati Raj

A form of local self government in rural India initially put forward by M K **Gandhi**. It advocated rule by village councils and other rural local bodies. It was promoted by the central government as a matter of national policy from 1957 to 1963, when the state governments were pressured to adopt some form of democratic decentralization and to involve the people down to the village level directly in the planning process. By the mid-1960s, however, support for Panchayati Raj had declined, even in its stronghold of Maharashtra and Gujarat. In 1977, the Janata government began to reopen the question of the importance and relevance of Panchayati Raj institutions, an issue which has since become important in the national political debate.

Pandit, Vijaya Lakshmi (1900–)

Indian politician and diplomat. The sister of Jawaharlal **Nehru**, she was the leader of the Indian **UN** delegation (1946–8 and 1952–3), and also held several ambassadorial posts (1947–51). In 1953 she became the first woman president of the UN General Assembly and from 1954 to 1961 she was Indian High Commissioner in London.

Pankhurst, Emmeline (1858–1928)
British suffragette. In 1905 she organized the Women's Social and Political Union, and fought for women's suffrage by violent means, on several occasions being arrested and going on hunger strike. After the outbreak of **World War I**, she worked instead for the industrial mobilization of women. Of her daughters and fellow workers, Dame Christabel turned later to preaching Christ's Second Coming; and Sylvia diverged to pacificism, internationalism, and Labour politics. ▷ **suffragettes**

Papadopoulos, George (1919–)
Greek soldier and politician. He underwent army training in the Middle East and fought in Albania against the Italians before the German occupation of Greece in **World War II**. A member of the resistance during the occupation, he then rejoined the army, reaching the rank of colonel. In 1967 he led a coup against the government of King **Constantine II** and established a virtual military dictatorship. In 1973, following the abolition of the monarchy, he became President under a new republican constitution, but before the year was out he was himself ousted in another military coup. In 1974 he was arrested, tried for high treason and convicted, but his death sentence was commuted.

Papagos, Alexandros (1883–1956)
Greek soldier and politician. After a brilliant military career involving service in the **Balkan Wars** (1912–13) and the Greek invasion of Turkey (1919–22), he was made Minister of War in 1935 and Chief of Staff the following year. In 1940, as Commander-in-Chief, he repelled the Italian attack on Greece, pushing the enemy forces back into Albania. Less successful against a German attack in Apr 1941, he was captured and taken as a hostage to Germany. After his release at the end of **World War II**, he led the campaign in Greece against the communist guerrillas. He was made field marshal in 1949, but resigned as Commander-in-Chief two years later in order to concentrate on a political role. He formed a new political party, the Greek Rally, and was Prime Minister of an exclusively Greek Rally government from 1952 until his death in 1955.

Papandreou, Andreas George (1919–)
Greek politician. The son of George **Papandreou**, before entering active politics he had an impressive academic career, holding professorial posts at universities in the USA and Canada. He became a US citizen in 1944, but returned to Greece as Director of the Centre for Economic Research in Athens (1961–4) and Economic Adviser to the Bank of Greece, and

resumed his Greek citizenship. His political activities led to imprisonment and exile after the military coup led by **Papadopoulos** in 1967. He returned to Greece in 1974 and threw himself wholeheartedly into national politics, founding the Pan-Hellenic Liberation Movement, which later became **PASOK** (the Pan-Hellenic Socialist Movement). He was leader of the opposition from 1977 and in 1981 became Greece's first socialist Prime Minister. Re-elected in 1985, in 1988 a heart operation and news of his impending divorce, following his association with a young former air stewardess, created speculation about his future. The 1989 general election produced no clear result and, after unsuccessful attempts to form a new government, he resigned and was succeeded by Tzannis Tzannetakis.

Papandreou, George (1888–1968)
Greek politician. A lawyer by training, he moved into politics in the early 1920s. The monarchy had been temporarily removed in 1923 and reinstated by the army in 1925 but Papandreou, a left-of-centre republican, held office in several administrations including the brief period when the monarchy was temporarily removed (1923–5) and in the following decade. In 1942 he escaped from Greece during the German occupation and returned in 1944 to head a coalition government, but, suspected by the army because of his socialist credentials, remained in office for only a few weeks. He remained an important political figure, founding the Centre Union Party (1961), and returning as Prime Minister (1963 and 1964–5). A disagreement with the young King **Constantine II** in 1965 led to his resignation, and in 1967, when a coup established a military regime, he was placed under house arrest. His son, Andreas **Papandreou**, was to carry forward his political beliefs.

Papen, Franz von (1879–1969)
German politician and Nazi collaborator. He was military attaché in Mexico and Washington, Chief of Staff with a Turkish army, and in 1921 joined the **Centre Party**. He was Chancellor (1932), playing a major part in undermining the **Weimar Republic**, **Hitler**'s Vice-Chancellor (1933–4), and Ambassador to **Austria** (1936–8) and Turkey (1939–44). Taken prisoner in 1945, he was acquitted at the **Nuremberg Trials**.

Papua New Guinea
An independent island group in the south-west Pacific Ocean, comprising the eastern half of the island of New Guinea, the Bismarck and Louisiade Archipelagos, the Trobriand and D'Entrecasteaux Islands, and other offlying groups. The British proclaimed a protectorate in south-east New Guinea in 1884, while some of the islands came under a German protectorate in 1884 and German New Guinea was established in the north-east in 1899. The German colony was annexed by Australia in **World War I**, and after the war, in 1920, Australia was mandated to govern

both British and German areas. The two regions combined in 1949 as the United Nations Trust Territory of Papua and New Guinea, which gained independence within the Commonwealth in 1975. Since 1989 there has been fighting between separatists and government forces on the island of Bougainville.

Paraguay

A landlocked country in central South America. After gaining independence from Spain in the early 19c, Paraguay lost over half its population in the War of the Triple Alliance against Brazil, Argentina, and Uruguay between 1864 and 1870. The disputed territory was regained in 1935 after the three-year **Chaco War** with Bolivia, but the country was torn by civil war in 1947. General Alfredo **Stroessner** seized power in 1954 and was appointed President, but was compelled to stand down following a coup in 1989.

parentela

A term used in Brazil meaning ‘extended family’, including all relatives (*parentes*) by blood, marriage and ritual, generally living in a number of households. Colloquially, the term is understood as a plethora of obedient kin, and elite *parentelas* have crucial national significance. The practice of endogamous marriage conserved patrimony (especially on *fazendas*) within the family group by preventing the dividing-up of property among legitimate heirs entailed by inheritance laws. *Patria potestas* — the authority of the head of the household — denied wives the right to alienate landed property without their husband’s consent. By no means limited to the elite, parentelas explain the preponderance of **coronelismo** throughout Brazil, especially in the north-east.

Paris, Treaty of (10 Feb 1947)

This treaty exacted indemnities from nations allied with Germany during **World War II**. Italy was obliged to surrender the Dodecanese Islands to Greece.

Paris Pacts (1954)

A series of amendments and protocols to the Treaty of Brussels and the Brussels Treaty Organization. Italy and the Federal Republic of Germany became members of what became known as the Western European Union. Germany agreed not to manufacture atomic, bacteriological, or chemical weapons, thus clearing the way for its rearmament and membership of **NATO**.

Paris Peace Conference (1919–20)

A meeting of 32 ‘allied and associated powers’ who met in Paris to draw up a peace settlement after **World War I**. Five treaties were concluded:

with Germany (Treaty of **Versailles**, 1919), Austria (Treaty of **St Germain**, 1919), Hungary (Treaty of **Trianon**, 1920), Bulgaria (Treaty of **Neuilly**, 1919) and Turkey (Treaties of Sèvres, 1920, and **Lausanne**, 1923).

Paris Peace Conference (1946–7)

Meetings of the five members of the Council of Foreign Ministers, representing the main **World War II** Allies (USA, Russia, UK, France and China), and delegates from 16 other nations involved against the **Axis Powers**. It drew up peace treaties with Bulgaria, Finland, Hungary, Romania and Italy. Despite repeated divisions, agreement was finally reached and the treaties signed in the spring of 1947.

Park Chung-hee (1917–79)

South Korean soldier and politician. Educated at a Japanese military academy, he fought with the Japanese forces during **World War II**. Park joined the South Korean army in 1946, becoming a major general by 1961, when he ousted the civilian government of Chang Myon in a bloodless coup. He formed the Democratic Republican Party (DRP) and was elected State President in Dec 1963. He embarked on an ambitious, and remarkably successful, programme of export-led industrial development, based on strategic government planning and financial support, which attained 'miracle' annual growth rates of 10–20 per cent during the 1960s and 1970s. However, he ruled in an austere and authoritarian manner, imposing martial law (Oct 1972) and introducing restrictive 'emergency measures' (May 1975). In Oct 1979, during a brief economic downturn, he was assassinated by the head of the Korean Central Intelligence Service.

Parks, Rosa Lee (1913–)

US civil rights protester. Her action as a black woman who refused to give up her seat to a white man on a bus in Montgomery, Alabama, led in 1955 to the Montgomery bus boycott by the black community. The boycott led to the Supreme Court decision in 1956 that declared bus segregation unconstitutional. Parks became an inspiration to other blacks and a symbol of the nonviolent protest advocated by the civil rights movement. ▷ **civil rights movement**

Parri, Ferruccio (1890–1982)

Italian politician. Imprisoned for helping Fillipo **Turati** to escape from fascist Italy, he was one of the founders of the **Party of Action**. Briefly Prime Minister in 1945, he remained a constant champion of left-wing cooperation and solidarity throughout the 1950s and 1960s.

Partai Komunis Indonesia (PKI)

The Indonesian Communist Party. The mid-1910s saw the establishment of a small social-democratic movement in the Netherlands East Indies, entirely Dutch in its membership. By the beginning of the 1920s, the movement had evolved into a communist organization and the membership had become predominantly Indonesian. It took the name 'Partai Komunis Indonesia' in 1924. In 1926–7 the PKI launched an ill-planned rebellion against the Dutch, and was fiercely crushed, re-emerging as a major political force in 1945, as the Indonesian rebellion against the post-war return of the Dutch got underway. In 1948 elements within the PKI launched a rebellion at Madiun against the republican government. This rebellion was also quelled, leaving the PKI open to the charge that it had threatened the revolution. The PKI rose again in the late 1950s and early 1960s, developing as a very powerful political force in **Sukarno**'s 'Guided Democracy'. But its power was broken in 1965–6 when, in the aftermath of an attempted coup, hundreds of thousands of PKI members and sympathizers were slaughtered.

Parti Québecois

Canadian political party. Formed by **Lévesque** after the **Liberal Party** under **Lesage** was defeated in 1966, essentially for refusing to be more nationalistic. The party members (or *Péquistes*) gained support from all classes and from organized labour as well as from the business community. The major aim of the party has been to attain sovereignty-association for Quebec, that is parity of status with the federal government. The pressure for this, however, has had to be balanced against the wish of the majority of Québecois to remain within Canada. As a result, the parliamentary party lost the support of its more radical *indépendentistes* in 1984.

Party Cadres (post-1920)

Highly trained, dedicated communist or communist-model party functionaries whose task was to win and maintain support for policies decided from above and to ensure absolute party loyalty. **Stalin** developed the idea during his rise to power in the 1920s and was fond of saying that 'cadres decide everything'. They became somewhat less important in the more sophisticated society of the 1970s and 1980s.

Party of Action (*Partito d'Azione*)

The underground Italian anti-fascist movement founded in July 1942, formed of a broad coalition of left-wing liberals, republicans and radicals, most of whom came from the educated and professional classes. The *Azionisti* remained outside both the 'United Freedom Front' established by **Bonomi** and its successor, the **Committee of National Liberation**. They were, however, actively involved in the creation of local CLNs (**Com-**

mittees of National Liberation) and fiercely supported the **Committee for the Liberation of Upper Italy**: in Nov 1944 they published an open letter to other anti-fascist parties urging the strengthening of both as instruments of popular democracy. The Action Party played a key role in the anti-German risings in the north of Italy in Apr 1944, but was too radical and idealistic to win substantial electoral support after the end of the war. Among the most prominent Azionisti was Ferruccio **Parri**.

Party of Labour (*Partij van de Arbeid*, PvdA)
Dutch political party, founded in 1946 to replace the Social Democratic Workers Party (*Sociaal-Democratische Arbeiders Partij*, SDAP), founded in 1894 in Amsterdam. The SDAP was originally a Marxist socialist party, although there were always debates between Marxists and revisionists. In 1918 the Marxists, led by P J **Troelstra**, launched an abortive coup attempt. Thereafter, the labour unions gained a greater role in the party; in the 1930s the Dutch socialists fully embraced the Plan Socialism of Hendrik de **Man**. In 1939 the socialists first joined the government. After **World War II**, in 1946, in an attempt to create a broad left party, the PvdA was formed to replace the SDAP, and indeed a number of liberals and confessionals joined for a short time; however in the long run there was little change. The PvdA, as the second most popular party, joined the Catholics (the largest) in a long spell of coalitions after the war (1945–58); after another stint of government (1965–6), the party underwent considerable radicalization, with the emergence of a New Left movement. In 1973 the socialists again formed a government with the confessionals, but it fell because of internal strife in 1977; in the ensuing election Labour increased its vote, but was unable to find any coalition partners. It spent the 1980s out of office, but returned to power in 1989 (again with the confessionals), by then reformed along social-democratic lines.

pasdaran
A name applied since 1979 to the revolutionary guards of the Islamic Republic of Iran. ▷ **Iranian Revolution**

Pašić, Nikola (c.1846–1926)
Serbian politician. Condemned to death in 1883 for his part in the plot against King Milan, he survived on the accession of King Peter to be Prime Minister of Serbia (five times, from 1891) and later of Yugoslavia (1921–4 and 1924–6), which he helped to found.

PASOK (*Panellinion Socialistikou Kinema*, 'Panhellenic Socialist Movement')
Established in 1974 under the leadership of Andreas **Papandreou**, its original programme was based on socialization, decentralization and worker self-management. In foreign policy it advocates neutrality: it

opposed Greece's entry into the EEC (1979); it remains hostile to **NATO**; and is opposed to the establishment of US military bases in Greece.

Passchendaele, Battle of (31 July–10 Nov 1917)
The third battle of Ypres during **World War I**; a British offensive which was continued despite no hope of a breakthrough to the Belgian ports, the original objective. It was notable for appallingly muddy conditions, minimal gains, and British casualties of at least 300 000. In the final action, Canadians captured the village of Passchendaele, six miles north-east of Ypres.

Pasternak, Boris Leonidovich (1890–1960)
Russian poet, translator and novelist. Before and after the 1917 **Russian Revolution** he established his reputation as a poet. It was because of political pressure during the **Stalin** years that he became the official translator into Russian of several major authors, such as Shakespeare, Verlaine, and Goethe. His major work, *Dr Zhivago* (completed in 1956), caused a political furore and was banned in the USSR, but was an international success after its publication in Italy in 1957. Expelled by the Soviet Writers' Union, he was compelled to refuse the Nobel Prize for Literature in 1958. *Dr Zhivago* was finally published in the USSR in 1988, a clear indication of how Mikhail **Gorbachev** had changed official attitudes.

Patel, Vallabhbhai Jhaverbhai ('Sardar') (1875–1950)
Indian politician and lawyer. A Gujarati peasant leader, described as M K **Gandhi**'s right-hand man, he was Deputy Prime Minister and first Minister of Home Affairs in independent India. By background a staunch Hindu, conservative and broadly identified with the interests of the business community, he was a lawyer by training and began his political career after being elected as a municipal councillor in Ahmadabad (1917). Soon after, he joined the Gujarat Sabha, a political body of great assistance to M K **Gandhi** during his political campaigns. Patel distinguished himself during India's independence struggle by his leading role in the Kheda peasants' **Satyagraha** (1918) and the Bardoli Satyagraha (1928), both launched in opposition to the colonial government's attempts to raise the land tax on peasant farmers. Following the successful conclusion of these campaigns, he was given the honorific title, Sardar ('Leader') by Gandhi. He joined the Salt Satyagraha of 1930, the individual **civil disobedience** movement of 1940–1 and the **Quit India Movement** of 1942, following each of which he spent long periods in prison. A great party organizer, he was also, along with Jawaharlal **Nehru**, a key negotiator on behalf of the **Indian National Congress** during the talks leading to the transfer of power from the British in 1947. As Deputy Prime Minister of Independent India, Patel assumed responsibility for the Indian States

as well as Home Affairs and Information and Broadcasting, and was responsible for persuading, or coercing, the nominally independent Indian Princely States into joining the Indian Union soon after independence. In tackling these and many other problems of post-Partition India, he acted with a thoroughness and ruthless efficiency that has caused him to be greatly admired, both as a statesman and politician, by subsequent generations.

Pathet Lao

Laotian nationalist movement (literally, 'Land of Lao') founded in 1950. In alliance with the **Viet Minh** of North Vietnam, it employed armed resistance to French rule in Indochina. After the country's civil war, the movement (officially renamed the Lao People's Liberation Army in Oct 1965), took part in the coalition government set up in 1974; early the following year it assumed effective control of the country. In Dec 1975 it abolished the monarchy in Vientiane and made its leader, Prince **Souphanouvong**, President of the newly proclaimed Lao People's Democratic Republic.

Patriotic Front (PF)

A Zimbabwean movement formed by the merging of the Zimbabwe African National Union (**ZANU**), led by Robert **Mugabe**, and the Zimbabwe African People's Union (**ZAPU**), led by Joshua **Nkomo**, in 1976. It was intended to unite the major exiled nationalist movements in a concerted opposition, both political and military, to Ian **Smith**'s white minority regime. In the elections held under the Lancaster House Agreement in 1980 the PF won an overwhelming victory. In the post-independence period, however, the Front broke up when Nkomo, whose principal power base was among the Ndebele people in Matabeleland, and Mugabe, who represented the majority Shona people, became estranged. Later (1988) they were reconciled as moves were made to create a one-party state.

Patton, George (Smith) (1885–1945)

US general. Known as 'Old Blood and Guts', Patton trained at the US Military Academy at West Point and became one of the most daring and flamboyant US combat commanders in **World War II**. An excellent strategist and proponent of mobile tank warfare, he played a key role in the Allied invasion of North Africa (1942–3), led the US 7th Army in its assault on Sicily (1943), commanded the 3rd Army in the invasion of France, and contained the German counteroffensive in the Ardennes (1944). He was fatally injured in a motor accident near Mannheim, and died at Heidelberg. ▷ **Bulge, Battle of the; Normandy Campaign**

Pauker, Ana (1893–1960)
Romanian politician. The daughter of a Moldavian rabbi, she joined the Social Democrat Party in 1915 and took part in revolutionary movements in Romania (1917–18). She married Marcel Pauker (1920) and with him joined the Communist Party, becoming a member of the Central Committee in 1922. She was arrested in 1925, but escaped to the USSR where she worked for **Comintern**. She returned to Romania in 1934 and was again arrested. A 'Moscow communist' who spent **World War II** in the USSR, she returned home after the overthrow of Ion **Antonescu** (Sep 1944). Summoned to Moscow with **Gheorgiu-Dej** (Jan 1945), she was instructed by **Stalin** to establish a government under the control of the National Democratic Front, the communist front in Romania. She entered the Foreign Ministry in 1947 and took part in organizing the collectivization of all land. With Stalin's consent, she was relieved of her offices in 1952.

Paul I (1901–64)
King of Greece (1947/64). In 1922 he served with the Greek Navy against the Turks; but in 1924, when a republic was proclaimed, went into exile. In 1935 he returned to Greece as Crown Prince. In **World War II** he served with the Greek general staff in the Albanian campaign, and was in exile in London (1941–6). His reign covered the latter half of the **Greek Civil War** and its difficult aftermath; during the early 1960s his personal role, and that of his wife Queen Frederika, became sources of bitter political controversy.

Paul, Alice (1885–1977)
US feminist. Involved with the British suffragette movement while living in England, on her return to the USA (1912) she became the leader of the **National American Woman Suffrage Association** (NAWSA) congressional committee and organized a march of several thousand women in Washington (1913). Although her tactics generated much publicity, they proved too militant for most members of NAWSA and she left the organization to found the National Women's Party. After the Nineteenth Amendment (1920) gave women the right to vote, she turned her efforts to working for other women's rights. ▷ **Pankhurst, Emmeline; suffragettes**

Paulus, Friedrich (1890–1957)
German field marshal and tank specialist. He capitulated to the Soviets with the remnants of his army at the siege of Stalingrad in 1943. Released from captivity in 1953, he became a lecturer on military affairs under the East German government. ▷ **Stalingrad, Battle of; World War II**

Pavel, Josef (1908–73)

Czechoslovak soldier, politician and reformer. Joining the Communi Party in the depression in 1929, he studied with the **Comintern** in Mosco in 1935–7, fought in the **Spanish Civil War** in 1937–8 and in the West 1939–45. He then rose to be commander of the people's militia that ga their backing to the **February Revolution** (1948) and acted as deputy t the Minister of the Interior until his arrest (1950). Because of his servic in the West he was viewed as suspect by the puppets who did **Stalin'** dirty work in Prague and was sentenced to 25 years in prison. Release in 1955, he did little until he became Minister of the Interior during th **Prague Spring**. His attempt to make the political police reponsible wo him enemies and soon after the Soviet invasion he was dismissed. Experiences such as his were one of the ingredients that made for the revulsio against **communism** expressed in Europe in 1989.

Pavelić, Ante (1889–1959)

Croatian fascist leader. A member of the extreme nationalist wing of the Croatian Party of (State) Right, he left Yugoslavia for Italy where, with Benito **Mussolini**'s support, he organized the **Ustaša**, the Croatian fascist movement. Chosen by Mussolini to run the puppet government of the Independent State of **Croatia** (1941–5), he instituted a reign of terror. At the end of the war, he escaped with the retreating German Army and settled in Argentina.

Paz Estenssoro, Víctor (1907–)

Bolivian revolutionary and politician. He was the founder of the left-wing *Movimiento Nacionalista Revolucionario* (MNR, National Revolutionary Movement) in 1941, going on to become its principal leader. Following the 1952 revolution, he served as President (1952–6) and held office again from 1960 to 1964, when he was ousted by a military coup. He went into exile in Peru, returning to Bolivia in 1971 as an adviser to the government of President Hugo Banzer Suárez. He failed to win election in 1979, but in 1985, after no candidate managed to achieve a majority, Congress elected him President. His main achievement in office (1985–9) was to reduce the raging inflation which had crippled Bolivia's economy.

PCE (*Partido Comunista Español*, 'Spanish Communist Party')

Established in 1920, the PCE was of little significance in the 1920s. Under the Second Republic of 1931–6 it played a minor role in the Asturias rising of Oct 1934 and, as part of the Popular Front coalition, won a total of 16 parliamentary seats in the Feb 1936 general election. However, once the **Spanish Civil War** broke out, the PCE soon became the dominant force in the Republic. This was because the USSR, in the absence of support from Britain and France, was the Republic's principal backer. The Communists opposed all other tendencies within the Republican camp, partly in order to meet the needs of **Stalin**'s foreign policy, and partly because of its authoritarian nature. This policy culminated in the May Days of 1937 when the **CNT** and **POUM** were defeated by the Communists. Under the **Franco** dictatorship (1939–75) the PCE emerged as the leading opposition force, due in great measure to the **CCOO (Comisiones Obreras)**. After Franco, the party failed to capitalize on its widespread support during the last years of the regime, despite having evolved from neo-Stalinism to, in 1978, Eurocommunism. Having won 23 seats in the 1979 election, it was reduced to a mere four in 1982. The PCE subsequently split into various factions, the official party forming the backbone of the *Izquierda Unida* (United Left) coalition. In the general election of 1986 the PCE won seven seats. ▷ **Republic, Second** (Spain)

PCI (*Partito Communista Italiano*, 'Italian Community Party')

Established in 1921 after the split in socialist ranks which followed the decision of the majority to join the Third International, the party was driven underground during the fascist regime. However, at the end of **World War II** it emerged as the most active force in the resistance, dominating the partisan struggle against the Germans and the Republic of **Salò**. Under the leadership of **Togliatti**, it initially sought to work together with the other anti-fascist parties but found itself increasingly at loggerheads with the **Christian Democrat Party**. It remained, however, consistently the second-biggest party in parliament, reaching its pinnacle under the leadership of **Berlinguer** during the 1970s. In the course of the 1980s it declined, losing direction completely with the collapse of Eastern European **communism** after 1989. It has since changed its name to *Partito Democratico della Sinistra*, with a more militant splinter group calling itself *Rifondazione Communista*. Both performed poorly in the Apr 1992 elections.

PDS (*Partido Democrático Social*)

The heir to a long tradition of Brazilian conservatism, the immediate progenitor of this party was the UDN (*União Democrático Nacional*) formed in 1945 to challenge the power of Getúlio **Vargas**, and it is arguably the descendant of the Spanish Empire's Liberal Party (1831–89). The UDN had conspired with the army to break the natural majority achieved by the PDS and PTB (*Partido Trabalhista Brasileiro*), which were both Vargas's creations, in the 1950s; it supported **Castelo Branco** in 1964 and in 1965 united with a conservative PDS faction to form the ARENA (*Aliança Renovadora Nacional*) Party. The Figueiredo government's attempt (1979–85) to reshuffle political groupings to divide the opposition created the PDS, in turn, as the successor to ARENA. The PDS became notorious as the personal vehicle for wealthy beneficiaries of the military regime, such as Paulo Salim Maluf, whose bid for the presidency divided the party in 1985, forcing a major faction to form the

PFL (*Partido do Frente Liberal*). Ostracized during the mid-1980s, the PDS forms part of the coalition upon which President Collor has based his government.

Peace Constitution (1947)

The name given to the post-**World War II** Japanese constitution that replaced the authoritarian Meiji Constitution (1889). Based on the draft imposed (Feb 1946) on the Japanese cabinet by US occupation authorities, the constitution attributed sovereignty to the people rather than the Emperor, who was now to be considered merely as a symbol of state. (In Jan 1946 **Hirohito** had renounced his divinity.) In contrast to the 1889 Constitution, an elected bicameral Diet, to which cabinets were collectively responsible, was to be the sole law-making organ of the state; furthermore, the lower house (House of Representatives) clearly had precedence over the upper house (House of Councillors) since it could override any veto by the upper house by repassing a disputed bill by a two-thirds majority. Prime ministers were to be chosen by the Diet (and hence the majority party), thus enshrining the principle of party government so fiercely opposed by governing elites in the pre-war period, while most cabinet ministers had to be both civilian and members of the Diet. The constitution also provided for an extensive guarantee of civil rights and freedoms (including women's suffrage), which could not be limited by law. The most controversial aspect of the constitution was Article 9 (Peace Clause), which renounced war as a sovereign right of the nation and provided for permanent disarmament. Subsequent interpretations of this article, however, led to the creation of the Self-Defence Forces, an army in all but name to be used solely for defence of the homeland. The constitution could be amended by a two-thirds majority of both houses followed by approval from a majority of voters. It was formally promulgated by Emperor Hirohito on 3 Nov 1946 and came into effect on 3 May 1947. The constitution has never been amended.

Peace Corps

A corp of volunteers created during the Kennedy Administration in 1961 to assist and educate people in developing countries. By 1966, volunteers numbered more than 10 000 in 52 countries. The programme concentrates on education, health, agriculture, and public works and emphasizes self-sufficiency. ▷ **Kennedy, John F**

Peace Preservation Laws

The repressive legislation in pre-**World War II** Japan that sought to clamp down on all strands of dissident thought. The first Peace Preservation Law was passed in 1887 to restrict the activities of the Freedom and People's Rights Movement, and led to the arrest and internal exile of many activists calling for the election of a national assembly. The Peace

Preservation Law of 1925 outlawed any association calling for an alteration of the **Kokutai** ('national essence') or denying the system of private property. Although the law was applied to both rightists and leftists, it was primarily used to detain suspected communists, of whom 66 000 were arrested between 1928 and 1941. The law was repealed in Oct 1945.

Pearl Harbor

US naval base on the island of Oahu, Hawaii. On 7 Dec 1941, the bombing of the base by the Japanese, before any declaration of war, brought the USA into **World War II**. Nineteen US ships were sunk or disabled in the surprise attack, and over 2 000 lives were lost.

Pearse, Patrick (Pádraic) Henry (1879–1916)

Irish writer, educationist, and nationalist. A barrister, he was a leader of the Gaelic League, and editor of its journal. Having commanded the insurgents in the **Easter Rising** (1916), he was proclaimed President of the Provisional Government. After the revolt had been quelled, he was court-martialled and shot, along with his brother, William.

Pearson, Lester Bowles (1897–1972)

Canadian politician. Educated in Toronto and at Oxford, he was leader of the Canadian delegation to the **UN**, becoming President of the General Assembly in 1952–3. Secretary of State for External Affairs (1948–57), his efforts to resolve the Suez Crisis were rewarded with the Nobel peace prize in 1957. As prime minister (1963–8), he introduced a comprehensive pension plan, socialized medicine and sought solutions to the growing separatist feeling in Quebec. ▷ **Bilingualism and Biculturalism, Royal Commission on**

Peel Commission

The report of this commission (issued 7 July 1937) is famous (or notorious) for being the first formal recommendation of the partition of Palestine into separate states, Arab and Jewish, with the retention by the British of a corridor to the Mediterranean. Serious rioting by the Arabs, directed against the Jews, had led Stanley **Baldwin**, the British Prime Minister, to appoint a royal commission to enquire into the working of the British mandate under the leadership of Earl Peel. Despite the commission's evident recognition that there was an intractable problem in Palestine (a situation which had been foreseen by Henry King and Charles Crane nearly two decades before) and their earnest endeavour to find a solution of some sort, the commission's recommendations found favour with only some Arabs and Zionists, and was rejected by the British House of Lords. ▷ **King–Crane Commission**

Pelikan, Jiri (1923–)

Czechoslovak student politician and media reformer. An underground member of the Communist Party in **World War II**, he was President of the Czechoslovak Students Union in 1948 and became President of the International Union of Students for the period 1953–63. He then switched to another political appointment as Director of Czechoslovak state television. In the course of the **Prague Spring** this brought him into the forefront of the reform movement, for the opening of television had an important impact within Czechoslovakia and abroad. But after the events of Aug 1968, he had to leave the country, much to the detriment of Czech broadcasting for some 20 years.

Pelshe, Arvid Yanovich (1899–1983)

Latvian politician. He joined the **Bolsheviks** in 1915, participated in the Petrograd Soviet in 1917, and failed with others to establish **communism** in Latvia in 1919. He then drifted through various jobs until the USSR seized Latvia in 1941. From then on he rose within the Latvian Communist Party. By 1959 he was its First Secretary; in 1966 he was called to the **Politburo** in Moscow of which he was still a member when he died at the age of 84. He acquired a reputation as illiberal but corrupt, which did little to endear his fellow Latvians to communism.

PEMEX (*Petróleos Mexicanos*)

One of the largest state-owned corporations in Latin America, and a virtual state within a state in Mexico, the oil company was created in 1938 by President Lázaro **Cárdenas**. He seized the assets of foreign (mainly British) multinationals as a result of the failure to implement the wage rates decreed by the 1917 Constitution's *junta de arbitraje y conciliación*, invoked by Cárdenas to rule on labour practices; the companies received compensation in Mexican bonds. PEMEX was charged with the management, regulation and production of oil found on Mexican soil. A logical outcome of the Criollo nationalism enshrined in the constitution, PEMEX was free from other ministries; only after the 1982 debt crisis was its autonomy curtailed.

Peng Dehuai (Peng Te-huai) (1898–1974)

Chinese communist general. He fought in the **Sino-Japanese War** (1937–45), became second-in-command to **Zhu De**, and led the Chinese 'volunteer' forces in the **Korean War**.

Peng Pai (P'eng P'ai) (1896–1929)

Chinese rural revolutionary. From a landlord family, Peng studied in Japan before joining the **Chinese Communist Party** and organizing rural tenants in his home district of Haifeng in the southern province of Guangdong. In 1923 he succeeded in establishing a peasants' association, which campaigned for lower rents, led anti-landlord boycotts, and organized welfare activities. When the association was crushed by a local warlord in 1924 Peng fled to the **Guomindang** base at Canton, where he became Secretary of the Peasants' Bureau and Director of the Peasant Movement Training Institute. By 1925 Peng had helped form the Guangdong Provincial Peasant Association, which claimed 200 000 members. During the **Northern Expedition** (1926–8) Peng returned again to his home district and organized China's first rural soviet. In the wake of **Chiang Kai-shek**'s counter-revolution against the communists, however, Peng's soviet was crushed in 1928. Peng was captured and executed by the Guomindang the following year.

Peng Zhen (P'eng Chen) (1902–)
Chinese politician. A leading member of the **Chinese Communist Party** and Mayor of Beijing (1951–66), he was the first high-ranking party member to be purged during the **Cultural Revolution**. Accused by **Mao Zedong** of protecting party intellectuals who had been critical of the policies of his **Great Leap Forward**, he disappeared from public view in 1966 and was not rehabilitated until 1979, three years after Mao's death. He was reappointed to the party's Central Committee and became known as a hardliner opposed to **Deng Xiaoping**'s free market reforms. Peng retired in 1987.

Peniakoff, Vladimir ('Popski') (1897–1951)
Belgian soldier and author. Born in Belgium of Russian parentage, he was educated in England. He joined the British army and from 1940 to 1942 served with the Long Range Desert Group and the Libyan Arab Force. In Oct 1942, with the sanction of the army, he formed his own force, Popski's Private Army, which carried out spectacular raids behind the German lines. He rose to the rank of lieutenant-colonel and was decorated for bravery by Britain, France and Belgium.

People's Liberation Army (PLA)
The Chinese army, numbering over 3 million troops. It is a significant political as well as military force, although in recent years its political role has been somewhat reduced. ▷ **Cultural Revolution**

People's National Congress (PNC)
A major political party in Guyana, which provided the government from 1964 to 1992. Founded in 1955 by **Burnham** as a breakaway African party after a split in **Jagan**'s People's Progressive Party, it took Guyana to independence in 1966 and generally implemented socialist policies. It retained power under the leadership of Desmond **Hoyte** until the election in 1992, when it was defeated by the People's Progressive Party.

People's National Movement

The major political party in Trinidad, which provided the government of that state from its inception in 1956 until 1986. The personal party of Eric **Williams**, its founder, until his death in 1981, its rivals, the People's Democratic Party of Bhadase Maraj and the Democratic Labour Party of Dr Rudranath Capildeo, never mounted an effective challenge to its monopoly of power. In 1986 it was ousted by the National Alliance for Reconstruction led by Arthur Robinson, but returned to power in the election of 1991.

Péquistes

Members of the **Parti Québecois**.

Peres, Shimon (1923–)

Israeli politician. He emigrated with his family from Poland to Palestine as a child in 1934, and was raised on a kibbutz, but received most of his education in the USA, studying at New York and Harvard Universities. In 1948 he became Head of Naval Services in the new state of Israel, and later Director-General of the Defence Ministry (1953–9). In 1959 he was elected to the Knesset. He was Minister of Defence (1974–7), and in 1977 became Chairman of the Labour Party and leader of the opposition until 1984, when he entered into a unique power-sharing agreement with the leader of the **Likud** Party, Yitzhak **Shamir**. Under this agreement, Peres was Prime Minister from 1984 to 1986, when Shamir took over. After the inconclusive 1988 general election, Peres eventually rejoined Shamir in a new coalition. ▷ **Mapai Party**

perestroika

The process of 'reconstructing' the Soviet economy and society through a programme of reforms gradually introduced after 1985 by General-Secretary Mikhail **Gorbachev**. These reforms, meant to be consistent with the ideals of the Bolshevik Revolution, were directed at relaxing control over the economy, reducing the power of the bureaucracy and eliminating its corruption, and in due course democratizing the **Communist Party of the Soviet Union** itself. Unfortunately from Gorbachev's point of view, they exposed the failings of the previous regime without removing enough of them, and actually worsened the state of the Soviet economy. Challenged first by the conservatives and then by the radicals, Gorbachev was swept from power in Dec 1991, his reconstruction still incomplete. ▷ **Bolsheviks; glasnost**

Pérez de Cuellar, Javier (1920–)

Peruvian diplomat. After graduating from Lima University, he embarked on a career in the Peruvian diplomatic service and represented his country at the first **UN** assembly in 1946. He succeeded the openly ambitious

Kurt **Waldheim** as UN Secretary-General in 1982, his quiet, modest approach contrasting sharply with that of his predecessor. His patient diplomacy secured notable achievements, particularly in his second term, including a ceasefire in the **Iran–Iraq War** and the achievement of independence for Namibia. His work enhanced not only his own reputation but that of the UN as well. He was succeeded as Secretary-General in 1992 by Boutros Boutros-Ghali.

Perkins, Frances (1882–1965)
US politician. She was the first woman to hold cabinet rank, as Secretary of Labor (1933–45) in President Franklin D **Roosevelt**'s cabinet. This appointment recognized her reputation as a social reformer, especially concerned with child labour and factory legislation. In 1945 she resigned from President Harry S **Truman**'s cabinet, became a member of the Civil Service Commission (1946–52). Her memoir, *The Roosevelt I Knew* (1946), was the first, and in many ways remains one of the best, recollections of the **New Deal**.

Permanent Revolution (post-1918)
Trotsky's adaptation of Marxism and Bolshevism in Russia in the wake of **World War I**. When communist revolutions did not materialize in Germany and other advanced countries, Trotsky pronounced that Marxist revolution was a continuous process and ought to be supported everywhere in the world, including in backward countries. This contrasted with **Lenin**'s and **Stalin**'s adoption of **Socialism in One Country**, Russia, and exacerbated the quarrel that led to his exile and death. ▷ **Bolsheviks**

Perón, Evita (Maria Eva Duarte) (1919–52)
Argentine political figure. The second wife of Juan **Perón**, she was a radio and screen actress before her marriage in 1945. She became a powerful political influence and a mainstay of the Perón government. Idolized by the poor, after her death in Buenos Aires, support for her husband waned. Her body was stolen, taken to Europe, and kept in secret until 1976.

Perón, Isabelita (María Estrela Martínez Cartas) (1931–)
Argentine political figure. A dancer, she became the third wife of Juan **Perón** in 1961. She lived with him in Spain until his return to Argentina as President in 1973, when she was made Vice-President. She took over the presidency on his death in 1974, but her inadequacy in office led to a military coup in 1976. She was imprisoned for five years, and on her release settled in Madrid.

Perón, Juan (Domingo) (1895–1974)
Argentine soldier and President. He took a leading part in the army coup of 1943, gained widespread support through his social reforms, and became President (1946–55). He derived immense popularity by cultivating the support of the urban working and middle classes of Buenos Aires, expanding government expenditure in the wake of an export boom. He was deposed and exiled in 1955 when the boom burst, having antagonized the Church, the armed forces and many of his former Labour supporters. He resumed the presidency in triumph in 1973, and won an overwhelming electoral victory, but died the following year. ▷ **Perón, Evita; Perón, Isabelita; Peronism**

Peronism
A heterogeneous Argentine political movement formed in 1945–6 to support the successful presidential candidacy of Juan **Perón** and his government thereafter. The movement later underwent division, some left-wing Peronists forming the **Montoneros** guerrilla group, but it survived Perón's death (1974). Despite continued internal disputes, the party made a good showing in the congressional elections of 1986. The ideology of Peronism (formally labelled Justicialism (**justicialismo**) in 1949) has proved difficult to describe, and can perhaps best be viewed as a unique amalgam of nationalism and social democracy, strongly coloured by loyalty to the memory of Perón.

Pershing, John Joseph ('Black Jack') (1860–1948)
US general. He trained at the US Military Academy at West Point, and served in several Indian Wars (1886–91), in the Spanish–American War (1898), in the Philippines (1899–1903), in the **Russo-Japanese War** (1904–5), and in Mexico (1916). In 1917 he commanded the American Expeditionary Forces in Europe, and after the war became Chief of Staff (1921–4). His book *My Experiences in the World War* (1931) won a Pulitzer Prize. ▷ **World War I**

Peru
A republic on the west coast of South America. Its gold and silver mines made Peru the principal source of Spanish power in South America, until independence was declared in 1821. There were frequent border disputes in the 19c (eg the War of the Pacific in 1879–83), and clashes between Ecuador and Peru continued in recent decades. In recent years governments have changed swiftly as a result of several military coups, and drug-related violence and terrorist activities have led to large areas being placed under a state of emergency. The constitution was suspended in 1992 to allow the President absolute power to implement reform and deal with terrorism. In 1993 the constitution was reinstated, with plans to hold a referendum on a new constitution.

Pétain, (Henri) Philippe (1856–1951)
French soldier and politician. During **World War I** he became a national hero for his defence of **Verdun** (1916), and was made Commander-in-Chief (1917) and Marshal of France (1918). When France collapsed in 1940, the National Assembly voted him full powers to negotiate the armistice with Germany and Italy, and made him Chief of State, with his government at **Vichy**. His aim to unite France under the slogan 'Work, Family and Country', and keep it out of the war, involved active **collaboration** with Germany. After the liberation, he was tried in the French courts, his death sentence for treason being commuted to life imprisonment on the Ile d'Yeu, where he died. His role remains controversial, and some still regard him as a patriot rather than a traitor. ▷ **French State; World War II**

Peter I Karageorgević (1844–1921)
King of Serbia (1903/18) and King of the Serbs, Croats and Slovenes (1918/21). The son of Prince Alexander Karageorgević, he fought in the French Army in the Franco-Prussian War (1870–1), and was elected King of Serbia by the Serbian parliament in 1903. In **World War I** he accompanied his army into exile in Greece in 1916. He returned to Belgrade in 1918 and was proclaimed titular King of the Serbs, Croats and Slovenes until his death, although his second son, Alexander (later **Alexander I Karageorgević**), was regent.

Peter II (1923–70)
King of Yugoslavia (1934/45). The son of **Alexander I Karageorgević**, he was at school in England when his father was assassinated in 1934. His uncle, Prince Paul **Karageorgević** was regent until 1941 when he was ousted by pro-Allied army officers, who declared King Peter of age and the latter assumed sovereignty. The subsequent German attack on Yugoslavia forced the King to go into exile within three weeks. He set up a government in exile in London, but lost his throne when Yugoslavia became a republic in 1945. From then on the ex-king lived mainly in California.

Petkov, Nikola (1893–1947)
Bulgarian politician. The son of Prime Minister Dimitŭr Petkov, he studied law in Paris and was later attached to the embassy there. He remained in exile in France after the military coup which overthrew **Stamboliski** (June 1923) until 1931, when he returned to Bulgaria and led the left-wing Pladne group of the Bulgarian Agrarian National Union. During **World War II** he worked with the **Fatherland Front** and was interned (1942–4). He was a minister without portfolio in the Provisional Government (Sep 1944–July 1945) and then edited the *National Agrarian Banner* (1945–7), leading the pro-Western opposition to full communist

rule. After the 1946 elections, he attacked Georgi **Dimitrov** as a Soviet puppet. Dimitrov waited until the USA had ratified the Bulgarian peace agreement (June 1947) before executing Petkov after a farcical show trial.

Petrokov, Nikolai Yakovlevich (1937–)
Soviet reform economist. A brilliant graduate of Moscow University in 1959, he joined the party and became the Deputy Director of the Institute of Mathematical Economics in 1965. He joined Mikhail **Gorbachev**'s team of advisers in 1985 and was appointed personal assistant in 1990. But in the autumn of that year he failed to persuade him to adopt serious economic reforms, which proved to be part of Gorbachev's undoing.

Petrov Affair
The defection by Soviet Embassy Third Secretary, Vladimir M Petrov, in Canberra (Apr 1954); he was granted political asylum by the Australian government. The Soviet government tried to fly Petrov's wife back to Moscow, but the aircraft was intercepted at Darwin, and she too was granted asylum. Later the Petrovs revealed they had been spying in Australia, and in one of their documents they implicated two members of the staff of Dr H V **Evatt**, the federal leader of the **Australian Labor Party** opposition. Evatt defended his staff before a Royal Commission (1954–5), but it refused to clear them. The affair exacerbated the split in the Labor Party over **communism** during the 1950s. ▷ **Democratic Labor Party**

Phalange Party
The *Phalanges Libanaises* (Arabic, *kata'ib*) were founded in Lebanon in 1936 by Pierre **Gemayel**, a young Maronite Christian, to counteract the provocative activities of Muslim elements seeking union with Syria. Originally a Christian youth movement, the Phalanges Libanaises then crystallized into a political party under the leadership of Gemayel, adding yet another factor to the Lebanese political equation. This factor was to have a destabilizing influence some four decades later when the Phalange aimed at the eradication of the **PLO** (Palestine Liberation Organization) in Lebanon. Gemayel himself played a leading part in the Lebanese politics of the 1960s and led the Phalange militia in the 1975–6 civil war. Gemayel's son, Amin, subsequently became leader of the Maronite Christians and was able to gain support also from the Sunni Muslims. President of Lebanon from 1982 to 1988, Amin **Gemayel** was no friend of extremists as his relations with Shiite factions and the more headstrong elements of the Phalanges bear witness.

Phan Boi Chau (1867–1940)
Vietnamese nationalist. Together with **Phan Chau Trinh**, he dominated the anti-colonial movement in Vietnam in the early 20c. Born into a

Confucian scholar family, he was in essence a Confucian revolutionary. In 1905 he went to Japan where, working under the supervision of the exiled Liang Ch'i-ch'ao, he wrote a history of Vietnam's loss of independence to the French, copies of which were then smuggled back to Vietnam. In 1912, now in China, he was involved with other Vietnamese in the establishment of the 'Revival Society' (*Quang Phuc Hoi*) which sought to bring about a democratic republic in Vietnam. Forces were raised which launched, from South China, poorly-organized attacks on French units (1915). In 1925, Phan Boi Chau was arrested by French agents in Shanghai and returned to Vietnam. Brought before the Criminal Commission (Nov 1925), he was sentenced to life imprisonment. The ensuing widespread public outcry led to his release and he spent the rest of his life, in gently guarded retirement, at Hue.

Phan Chau Trinh (1871–1926)
Vietnamese nationalist. Along with **Phan Boi Chau**, he was a leading figure in the anti-colonial movement in Vietnam in the early 20c. In contrast to Phan Boi Chau's commitment to a revolutionary monarchism, Phan Chau Trinh advocated Western-style republicanism. Between 1911 and 1925 he was in France, spending some of that time in prison. From France he launched strong attacks on the Vietnamese monarchy. Phan Chau Trinh's funeral in 1926 was held in Saigon, provoking unprecedented mass demonstrations and student strikes. This heralded a new phase in the anti-colonial struggle in Vietnam, one that would involve greater popular participation.

Phibunsongkhram (1897–1964)
Thai military and political leader. Of humble origin, Phibun was educated at the Thai Military Academy and then, on a government scholarship, at the French Artillery School. In France he came into contact with a group of Thai students who were disaffected with the absolute monarchy in Bangkok and became involved in the coup which brought down the absolute regime (24 June 1932). Phibun gathered increasing authority in the first constitutional governments, becoming Prime Minister in 1938. During that premiership, he cultivated a close relationship with Japan, in late 1941 agreeing to allow Japanese forces to pass through his country in order to attack the British in Burma and Malaya. However, when the war turned against Japan, Phibun fell from office (July 1944). He returned as Prime Minister in 1947, this time aligning Thailand closely with the USA. Phibun remained in office until Sep 1957, when he was overthrown in a Sarit Thanarat coup. He died in exile in Japan.

Philby, Kim (Harold Adrian Russell) (1912–88)
British double agent. He was educated at Cambridge, where, like **Burgess**, **Maclean** and **Blunt**, he became a communist. Already recruited as a

Soviet agent, he was employed by the British Secret Intelligence Service (MI6), from 1944 to 1946 as head of anti-communist counter-espionage. He was First Secretary of the British Embassy in Washington, working in liaison with the **CIA** (1949–51), and from 1956 worked in Beirut as a journalist. In 1963 he disappeared to the USSR, where he was granted citizenship.

Philippines

A republic consisting of an archipelago of more than 7 100 islands and islets, north-east of Borneo and south of Taiwan. After the Spanish–American War of 1898 Spain surrendered its colonial interests in the Philippines to the USA, and the region became a self-governing Commonwealth in 1935. It was occupied by the Japanese during **World War II** and liberated by US troops in 1945. The independent republic was set up in 1946. During the period 1945–53 the communist-dominated Huk rebellion was suppressed, but the Muslim separatist movement in the south continued. Ferdinand **Marcos** established his dictatorship in 1965, and political unrest resulted in martial law from 1972 to 1981. The exiled political leader Benigno **Aquino** was assassinated on his return to Manila in 1983. A coup headed by his widow, Cory **Aquino**, in 1985 ended the 20-year rule of President Marcos. Although a new constitution was formed in 1987, several attempted coups followed and political unrest continued.

Pichon, Stéphen Jean Marie (1857–1933)

French politician and journalist. He served on **Clemenceau**'s newspaper *La Justice* before entering the Chamber of Deputies in 1885. Becoming a diplomat, he served in Port-au-Prince, San Domingo, Rio de Janeiro, Beijing and Tunis; he represented the powers in negotiations with China during the Boxer Rebellion. He was Minister of Foreign Affairs twice (1906–11, 1917–20), after which he joined *Le Petit Journal* as its political editor. He was always seen as Clemenceau's protégé, and abandoned control of foreign policy to him in 1917–20.

PIDE (*Policia Internacional de Defensa do Estado*, 'International Police for State Defence')

Portuguese secret police. With the establishment in 1933 of the PVDE ('Police of Vigilance and State Defence'), the secret police in Portugal became the most feared institution of the **Estado Novo** under **Salazar**. The Salazar dictatorship, in common with other authoritarian regimes, created an unscrupulous secret police force to safeguard its interests. In the 1930s the PVDE drew on the police state techniques of Nazi Germany and Fascist Italy. The creation of a nationwide network of spies and informers effectively banned the discussion of politics in public for almost half a century. In 1945 the secret police was renamed the International

Police for State Defence (PIDE). With even greater powers than those of its predecessor, the PIDE lasted until the end of the Salazar era, reaching the height of its influence during the 1960s. Not only did it have a leading role in the colonial war being fought in Portuguese Africa (launching vicious dirty tricks campaigns), but it also dealt a devastating blow to the opposition through the murder of General **Delgado** in 1965. The PIDE was undoubtedly the most loathed of all the state institutions of the Salazar dictatorship. In 1969 it was rechristened the General Directorate of Security (DGS) and its powers were curtailed.

Pieck, Wilhelm (1876–1960)
East German politician. The son of a labourer, he initially worked as a carpenter and was active from an early age in socialist politics. In 1915 he helped found the Spartacus League and in 1918–19 the German Communist Party (**KPD**), leading the unsuccessful 'Spartacus Uprising' in Berlin in 1919. During the **Weimar Republic**, Pieck was elected as a communist to the **Reichstag** in 1928, but was forced into exile in 1933 when **Hitler** came to power. He fled to Moscow where he became, in 1935, Secretary of the **Comintern**. In 1945 he returned to Berlin in the wake of the **Red Army** and created, in 1946, the dominant Socialist Unity Party (**SED**) out of the former KPD and Social Democratic Party (**SPD**). From 1949 he served as President of the German Democratic Republic, the post being abolished on his death.

Pierlot, Hubert (1883–1963)
Belgian politician. After training and practising as a lawyer, he became a senator in 1926. He served as Minister for Internal Affairs (1934–5) and Agriculture (1936–8), and formed a government in Apr 1939. After the surrender of the Belgian forces in June 1940, he led the government in exile in London, leaving King **Leopold III**, who had decided to stay with the army. His negative attitude to the King continued during his post-war government (1944–5), but his **Christian People's Party** in general supported the King, so he retired from public life in 1945.

Pig War (1906–11)
The name given to the period of 'economic warfare' between the Habsburg government and Serbia. In 1905 Serbia and Bulgaria had agreed to closer economic ties which would lead to eventual economic union. To force Serbia to break this agreement, the government in Vienna banned the import of all Serbian livestock (chiefly pigs) into the Habsburg Empire. The embargo, combined with the annexation of Bosnia and Herzegovina (1908), caused Austro-Serb relations to deteriorate yet further and drove Serbia closer to France and Russia.

Piłsudski, Józef (1867–1935)

Polish marshal and politician. Born near Vilna in Russian Poland, he was educated at the University of Kharkov. Imprisoned several times by the tsarist authorities for his activities in the cause of Polish independence, he was the founder and leader of the Polish Socialist Party (1892). He formed a band of troops which fought on the side of Austria against Russia for part of **World War I** but in 1917 he was imprisoned in Germany. Freed the following year, he was in a good position to declare Poland's independence and to become head of state and commander-in-chief. Still anti-Russian, he was not unhappy to lead his country in the Polish-Soviet War in 1920–1 and to emerge with considerable territorial gains. In 1922 he was pushed out of power by more moderate politicians, but in 1926 he organized a coup d'état to become Prime Minister, Minister of War and leader of an authoritarian, right-wing nationalist regime until his death.

Pimen, Patriarch (1910–90)

Russian Orthodox patriarch. Ordained a priest in 1932, he spent the later **Stalin** years in jail. However, in Nikita **Khrushchev**'s time, in 1957, he was consecrated a bishop and in Leonid **Brezhnev**'s time, in 1971, became the Patriarch. He supported Soviet peace initiatives and was a member of the World Peace Committee. Finally, in 1988, he met Mikhail **Gorbachev** and secured his permission to celebrate the millennium of Christianity in Russia.

Pindling, Sir Lynden Oscar (1930–)

Bahamanian politician. Educated in the Bahamas and at London University, he practised as a lawyer before becoming centrally involved in politics, eventually as Leader of the Progressive Liberal Party (PLP). He became Prime Minister in 1969 and led his country to full independence, within the **Commonwealth of Nations**, in 1973. The PLP, under Pindling, was re-elected in 1977, 1982 and 1987.

Pinochet (Ugarte), Augusto (1915–)

Chilean dictator. A career army officer, he led the military coup overthrowing the government of Salvador **Allende** (1973), establishing himself at the head of the ensuing military regime. In 1980 he enacted a constitution giving himself an eight-year presidential term (1981–9). A plebiscite held in 1988 rejected his continuation as president beyond 1990. Free elections were held in 1990 and the Christian Democrat Patricio Aylwin was installed as President.

Pintasilgo, Maria de Lurdes (1930–)

Portuguese politician. From 1970 to 1974 she was the Chairwoman of the National Committee on the status of women. After the 1974 revolution she was made Minister for Social Affairs, legislating above all on women's rights. In 1976–9 she was Ambassador to UNESCO, and from 1979 to 1980 acted as caretaker Prime Minister. She has also written widely on international affairs and women's issues.

Pittsburgh Agreement (1918)
The agreement between **Masaryk**, the future President of Czechoslovakia, and Czech and Slovak immigrants to the USA, setting out the possible lines of a Czechoslovak constitution. As leader of the exiles struggling to win support from the Allied Powers in **World War I**, Masaryk wanted the immigrants' backing and promised the Slovaks that, to ensure the autonomy of Slovakia, it might be possible to create a federal state. When a unitary state emerged, the Slovaks in the USA felt betrayed and, particularly in the 1930s, worked hard to secure the separation of Slovakia that transpired in 1939 when **Hitler** occupied the Czech Lands and set up a puppet Slovakia.

Plaatje, Sol T (1876–1932)
South African journalist, politician and literary figure. One of the founders of black nationalism, he first worked as a Post Office messenger and later a magistrates' court interpreter in Kimberley. He was in the town throughout the siege during the Boer War and kept a lively diary of those events. After the war he founded and edited newspapers, wrote books (including *Native Life in South Africa*), translated Shakespeare into his native tongue, Tswana, and was one of the founders of the South African Native National Congress, later the **ANC** (African National Congress).

Plaid Cymru
The Welsh National Party, founded in 1925, with the aim of achieving independence for Wales. It stands for election throughout Wales, but finds support mainly in the north of the country. It had one MP following the 1987 general election, and has never had more than three.

Plastiras, Nikolaos (1883–1953)
Greek politician. A Republican close to **Venizélos**, he organized the 1922 coup d'état following the humiliation of the Greek army by Kemal **Atatürk** in Asia Minor. Determined to be seen to punish those responsible for the debacle, he contrived the execution of six politicians and military commanders, charging them with treason. After the Republicans' election defeat (1933), he organized another coup which failed and fled with Venizélos to France. Remaining in exile during **World War II**, he was recognized as nominal leader of **EDES**. In 1945, during the regency of **Damaskinos**, he replaced George **Papandreou** as Prime Minister. After the **Greek Civil War**, he led the National Progressive Union (EPEK) and

was again Prime Minister in one of the many coalition governments during 1951.

Platt Amendment (1902)
Appendage to the Cuban independence constitution after the Spanish–American War (1898) which gave the USA the right to 'intervene for the preservation of Cuban independence'. Such interventions took place in 1906, 1912 and 1920 and, while the Platt Amendment was annulled in 1934, the USA's lease of the naval base at Guantanamo Bay was retained. The Reciprocal Trade Treaty of 1903 continued to allow the USA to dominate the Cuban economy, particularly under the **Batista** administration. The **Castro** revolution of 1959 can be seen as a response to that alien control while the US response (the **Bay of Pigs** invasion of 1961) was another manifestation of the rights claimed under the Platt Amendment.

Plessy v Ferguson (1896)
US Supreme Court decision that opened the way to racial segregation under the **US Constitution** by upholding the concept of 'separate but equal'. Homer Plessy was appealing against his conviction for refusing to leave a railroad car reserved for whites. The court ruled that if the facilities offered blacks were equal to those for whites, there was no infringement of the **Fourteenth Amendment**. Justice John M Harlan dissented with the prescient warning that the ruling was 'inconsistent with civil freedom' and would support prejudice. The decision came to underpin the whole structure of segregation in the Southern states during the first half of the 20c, eventually being overturned by **Brown v Board of Education** (1954).

PLO (Palestine Liberation Organization)
An organization that consists of several of the Palestinian groups opposed to Israel. Its chairman is Yasser **Arafat**, leader of the largest constituent group, al-Fatah. Founded in 1964, its charter denied the right of Israel to exist and called for Palestine to be liberated by armed conflict. In 1974 the Arab Summit in Rabat, Morocco, recognized the PLO as the sole legitimate representative of the Palestinian people. In 1982 its forces in Lebanon were attacked and expelled by Israel, with the support of the US Reagan administration; many US servicemen and diplomats in Lebanon were killed as a result. Secret talks in Norway (1991–3) between the Israeli Prime Minister Yitzhak **Rabin** and the PLO led to the agreements signed in Washington, DC (1993) and Cairo (1994) by Rabin and Arafat on mutual recognition and limited self-rule in the **Gaza Strip** and West Bank town of Jericho.

Plojhar, Josef (1902–81)
Czechoslovak politician. A member of the People's Party and an active Catholic priest, he agreed to support the communists in their takeover of power in 1948 and be a member of the new National Front government. He became Minister of Health and remained such until 1968 when the reformers removed him. Archbishop **Beran** banned him from preaching, but his clerical collar gave his government some degree of respectability in foreign parts.

PMDB (*Partido do Movimento Democrático Brasileiro*, 'Brazilian Democratic Movement Party')
The political party created in Brazil (1979) by opposition groups in response to the military government's attempts to dissolve the two-party system created in the aftermath of the 1964 military coup. This system pitted ARENA (*Aliança da Renovação Nacional*), heir to the conservative and golpista UDN (*União Democrática Nacional*) and conservative **PSD**, against the MDB (*Movimento Democrático Brasileiro*), itself the successor to **Vargas**' PSD (pro-**Kubitschek (de Oliveira)**) and the pro-**Goulart** PTB (*Partido Trabalhista Brasileiro*). By 1979, the strength of the PMDB in the cities and industrial zones of Brazil meant that it could outflank the Figueiredo government. Although the regime did succeed in dividing the PMDB between adherents to **Brizola**'s PDT, a rump PTB, **Lula**'s PT (*Partido dos Trabalhadores*) and Tancredo **Neves**' *Partido Popular*, the PMDB gained decisive victories in 1982. It provided the platform for Neves' presidential campaign in 1984–5, and was an uneasy supporter of **Sarney (Costa)** in the gubernatorial contest of 1986. Its identification with Sarney, and the 'old politics' lost it the presidential campaign of 1989 to Fernando **Collor de Mello**.

PNV (*Partido Nacionalista Vasco*, 'Basque Nationalist Party')
Founded in 1895, the PNV (or *Eusko Alderdi Jeltzalea* in Basque), was the first political party to defend Basque nationalism. Under the Second Republic of 1931–6 it was the leading party in Basque politics, though it never had a majority. With the outbreak of the **Spanish Civil War** (July 1936), the PNV backed the Republic in exchange for an autonomy statute, which was passed in Oct 1936. Under the dynamic leadership of José Antonio **Aguirre**, the PNV gained control of the autonomous government. During the Basque government's exile of 1939–75 the PNV provided most of its leadership. From 1977 to 1984 the PNV was again the leading force in the Basque country, but splits in the 1980s reduced its share of the Basque vote to 22 per cent in 1987. ▷ **Basque Autonomy Statutes; Republic, Second** (Spain)

Podgorny, Nikolai Viktorovich (1903–83)
Soviet politician. Born in the Ukraine, the son of a foundry worker, he worked in the sugar industry and in due course held managerial,

educational and ministerial posts connected with food. In 1930 he joined the Communist Party, and after **World War II** took a leading role in the economic reconstruction of the liberated Ukraine. He held various senior posts (1950–65), becoming a full member of the **Politburo** in 1960. Following the dismissal of Nikita **Khrushchev** (1964), he became Chairman of the Presidium and therefore titular head of state in 1965. He was relieved of this office in 1977 and replaced by Leonid **Brezhnev**, partly because his performance was lacklustre, but mainly because Brezhnev wanted to be head of state as well as General-Secretary of the Party. ▷ **communism**

Poincaré, Raymond (Nicolas Landry) (1860–1934)
French politician. He studied law, became a Deputy (1887) and Senator (1903), and held office as Minister of Public Instruction (1893 and 1895), of Finance (1894–5 and 1906), and of Foreign Affairs (1912–13, 1922–3). Elected Prime Minister (1912–13) and President (1913–20), he sought to play a more directive role than previous incumbents. He had some success at first, especially in foreign affairs, but when **Clemenceau** became Prime Minister in 1917, he found himself sidelined, and was unable to influence decisions at the post-war peace conference. As Prime Minister once again (1922–4) he sought to enforce the terms of the Treaty of **Versailles** (notably the payment of reparations) against a recalcitrant Germany by occupying the Ruhr (1923–4). Although Germany was thus forced to negotiate, Poincaré had by then been defeated in the 1924 elections, and his successor as Prime Minister, **Herriot**, bowing to British and US pressure, conceded much of what Poincaré had hoped to achieve. He was brought back to power (1926–9), as Prime Minister and Finance Minister, to deal with a financial crisis; he stabilized the franc, inaugurating a brief period of prosperity before France succumbed to the **Great Depression**.

Pol Pot (Saloth Sar) (1926–)
Kampuchean (Cambodian) politician. After working on a rubber plantation in his early teens, he joined the anti-French resistance movement during the early 1940s, becoming a member of the Indo-Chinese Communist Party and Cambodian Communist Party in 1946. During the 1960s and early 1970s he led the communist **Khmer Rouge** in guerrilla warfare against the governments of Prince **Sihanouk** and then Lieutenant General Lon Nol. After the destruction of the Lon Nol regime in 1975, he became Prime Minister. He proceeded brutally to introduce an extreme regime which resulted in the loss of perhaps more than 2 500 000 lives. The regime was overthrown by Vietnamese troops in Jan 1979 and Pol Pot took to the resistance struggle once more. Despite announcing his retirement as the Khmer Rouge military leader in Aug 1985, he remained an influential and feared figure within the movement.

Poland

A republic in central Europe. Poland became a semi-independent state following the 1815 Congress of Vienna, and was incorporated into the Russian Empire; it became a fully independent state after **World War I**. Germany invaded Poland in 1939, precipitating **World War II**, and partition of Poland between Germany and the USSR took place in the same year. There was a major Polish resistance movement, and a government in exile during World War II. A People's Democracy was established under Soviet influence in 1944 and by 1947 Communists controlled the Government. In the late 1970s the independent trade union Solidarity began to gain popularity and political power, and from 1981 to 1983 Solidarity leaders were detained and a state of martial law was imposed. The worsening economic situation meant continuing unrest in the 1980s, resulting in loss of support for the Communist government and major success for **Solidarity** in the 1989 elections. The subsequent transition to a market economy was accompanied by popular discontent and political difficulties.

Polisario

Properly, the Popular Front for the Liberation of Saguia el-Hamra and Rio de Oro, this is a movement of tribesmen from what is now called Western Sahara, which aims at resisting the attempts of King **Hassan II** of Morocco to absorb these areas into Morocco itself. This move on the part of Hassan followed Spain's granting of independence to the region (its former colony), and the division of the region between Morocco and Mauretania. Hostilities in 1975 and Polisario's establishment (1976) of a 'government-in-exile' of the so-called Sahrawi Arab Democratic Republic (SADR) was the prelude to Mauritania's renouncing the portion of the former Spanish Sahara it had shared with Morocco. Polisario guerrillas put up armed resistance from bases in Algeria, where they were supplied with arms by both Algeria and Libya, thereby provoking a Moroccan response which included the building of defensive works on the 'borders'. In 1988 the **UN** proposed a referendum to enable the indigenous population to choose between the area becoming an independent state under Polisario or becoming part of Morocco.

Politburo

The Political Bureau of the Central Committee of the **Communist Party of the Soviet Union**; at various times, known as the Presidium. It was the highest organ of the Party, and, therefore, of the entire Soviet political system. Formally elected by the Central Committee, there were latterly about 15 members plus about seven candidate members who had no votes; in practice, though, membership was decided by the Politburo itself under the General-Secretary, who presided over it. Its functions might be compared to those of a cabinet, though its authority varied over the years. It was seldom questioned by the Party Congress or even by the Central Committee; in turn, it could only question the General-Secretary at times of crisis. Most other communist parties adopted the Soviet model.

political machine

A term used to describe the US urban political organization developed in the late 19c in response to the constitutional decentralization of local politics intersecting with the flood of immigration into Northern cities such as New York, Philadelphia and Boston at a time of very rapid physical growth. Hierarchically structured from the city level, down through the ward to the precinct, the machine depended on the ability of the 'boss' to respond to the individual needs of constituents who voted at his direction in return, thus allowing him to control nominations and to discipline office holders. Developed by both parties and sizable ethnic groups, political machines have been characterized by endemic corruption and inefficiency, and many contemporary observers regard them as a degradation of democratic politics.

Polyansky, Dmitri Stepanovich (1917–)

Ukrainian politician. Of peasant stock, he graduated in agriculture in Kharkov in 1939 and immediately became a Communist Party functionary. However, in 1958 his career blossomed when Nikita **Khrushchev** made him chairman of the Russian Council of Ministers. In 1960 he became a member of the **Politburo**. Even under Leonid **Brezhnev** he held several other ministerial posts, but in 1976 he was dropped from all but ambassadorial appointments as he was no longer in favour.

polycentrism

A political term, first used by the Italian Communist Party (**PCI**) leader, Palmiro **Togliatti** after the 20th Congress of the Soviet Communist Party in Feb 1956 to describe and support the growing independence of other communist parties from the Soviet party after the **Stalin** era. The trend was forced on Yugoslavia when it was expelled from the **Cominform** in 1948; it became more difficult to believe in after the Soviet suppression of the **Hungarian Uprising** in Oct 1956; but it reasserted itself in the late 1950s and early 1960s. It was no longer used after the Soviet invasion of Czechoslovakia in 1968. ▷ **Marxism-Leninism; Stalinism**

Pompidou, Georges (Jean Raymond) (1911–74)

French politician. He trained as an administrator, joined Charles de **Gaulle**'s staff in 1944, and held various government posts from 1946. He helped to draft the constitution for the Fifth Republic (1959) and negotiate a settlement in Algeria (1961) and in the student-worker revolt of 1968. Prime Minister from 1962 to 1968, he was elected President, as the socialist candidate, after de Gaulle's resignation in 1969, and died in office. ▷ **Republic, Fifth** (France)

Ponomarev, Boris Nikolaevich (1905–)
Soviet ideologue. He joined the Communist Party at 14, and at 21 became an official propagandist. His subsequent appointments included spells at the **Comintern** and at the Institute of Marxisim-Leninism. In 1955 he became director of the international department of the Central Committee and was only moved when Mikhail **Gorbachev** came to power in 1985. Throughout 30 years he was a conservative influence, asserting the ideological aspects of foreign policy.

Popieluszko, Jerzy (Alfons) (1947–84)
Polish priest. Serving in several Warsaw parishes after ordination, and inspired by the faith of his compatriot, St Maximilian Kolbe, he became an outspoken supporter of the **Solidarity** trade union, especially when it was banned in 1981 with the introduction of martial law. His sermons at 'Masses for the Country' regularly held in St Stanisław Kostka church were widely acclaimed. He ignored harassment and resisted official moves to have him silenced, but was kidnapped and murdered by the secret police in Oct 1984 more than a year after the lifting of martial law. It was probably this tragedy more than any other event that, in a profoundly Catholic country, spelt the eventual demise of the Communist Party. His grave and his church became a place of national pilgrimage.

Popolari
Members of the Italian Popular Party (*Partito Popolare Italiano*) which briefly emerged as a major force in Italian politics in the period between **World War I** and the fascist seizure of power. It appealed basically to the Catholic voter and helped undermine the traditional liberal parties which could no longer guarantee Catholic support simply by promising not to introduce anticlerical measures. It ceased to exist under **fascism**, but many of its leaders subsequently played a part in the formation of the **Christian Democrat Party**.

Popov, Gavril Kharitonovich (1936–)
Soviet economist and politician. Of Greek ethnic background, he graduated in economics in Moscow and joined the Communist Party in 1959. He was appointed Dean of the Faculty of Economics in 1971 and, with official backing, proceeded to introduce management studies. He blossomed on Mikhail **Gorbachev**'s accession to power. In 1989 he was elected to the Congress of Deputies and in 1990 became Mayor of Moscow. A fierce critic of the slow pace of change, he left the party in 1990 to survive Gorbachev's downfall in 1991.

Popular Front

A strategy of the communist movement begun in the 1930s as a means of fostering collaboration among left and centre parties to oppose the rise of right-wing movements and regimes, most obviously fascist ones. There were Popular Front governments in France, Spain, and Chile. The strategy virtually died with the signing of the **German–Soviet Pact** (1939), but re-emerged after **Hitler** had invaded the USSR.

Portsmouth, Treaty of (5 Sep 1905)

The treaty, signed in Portsmouth, New Hampshire (USA), which concluded the **Russo-Japanese War**. Japan acquired south Sakhalin from Russia as well as the Russian leasehold in south Manchuria (Liaodong Peninsula) and the Russian-built South Manchuria Railway. Japan's predominant position in Korea was also confirmed, enabling Tokyo to declare a protectorate over Korea and then to annex it as a formal colony (1910). The Japanese demand for an indemnity, however, was abandoned when Russia adamantly refused, a compromise that provoked angry public demonstrations in Tokyo. This treaty marked the beginning of Japanese expansion on the Chinese mainland, which was increasingly to arouse the suspicion of the USA.

Portugal

A country in south-west Europe on the west side of the Iberian peninsula. The Portuguese monarchy was overthrown and a republic established in 1910. A period of dictatorship under Dr **Salazar** followed from 1932 to 1968, but a military coup in 1974 was followed by 10 years of political unrest under 15 governments. Portugal joined the **EC** in 1985.

Potemkin (1905)

The Russian warship immortalized in Sergei Eisenstein's 1926 film for mutinying in the course of the Russian **Revolution of 1905**. The crew put to sea and resisted the attempts of loyal ships to capture them but eventually surrendered to the Romanian authorities. There were subsequent mutinies in the naval bases of Kronstadt and Sevastopol. Tsar **Nicholas II** rode out the revolution, but disaffection in his forces was an ominous sign of what was to unseat him in 1917.

Potsdam Conference (17 July–2 Aug 1945)

The last of the great **World War II** strategic conferences, following the **Tehran Conference** and **Yalta Conference**. During this period Winston **Churchill** (and later Clement **Attlee**), **Stalin** and **Truman** met to discuss the post-war settlement in Europe. Soviet power in Eastern Europe was recognized *de facto*, and it was agreed that Poland's western frontier should run along the **Oder–Neisse Line**. The decision was also made to divide Germany into four occupation zones. The political differences which began to emerge between the USA and the USSR could be said to have marked the start of the **Cold War**.

Poujade, Pierre (1920–)
French right-wing political leader. A small shopkeeper in a tiny town, in 1951 he was elected a member of the Saint Cére municipal council, and in 1954 he organized his Poujadist movement (union for the defence of tradesmen and artisans) as a protest against the French tax system. His party had successes in the 1956 elections to the National Assembly, but disappeared in 1958. Jean-Marie **Le Pen**, leader of the National Front, was first elected as a Poujadist Deputy in 1956.

POUM (*Partido Obrero de Unificación Marxista*, 'Workers' Marxist Unification Party')
Independent Spanish Marxist party. The POUM, founded in Sep 1935, never had a mass following, but its outstanding thinkers led it to exert considerable influence. Its leading figures were the Marxist theoreticians Joaquín Maurín, the originator of the *Alianza Obrera* ('United Workers' Front'), and Andreu Nin. The POUM's defence of a revolutionary war effort and general independence during the **Spanish Civil War** resulted in its persecution by the Communist Party (**PCE**) in the May Days of 1937. It was vigorously repressed thereafter until the end of the war.

Powell, Adam Clayton (1908–72)
US clergyman and politician. Pastor of the Abyssinian Baptist Church in Harlem, he was a charismatic community leader. In 1941 he was elected as a Democrat to the City Council of New York and the following year he founded the People's Voice. Elected to the US House of Representatives in 1945, he was chairman of the House Committee on Education and Labor from 1951, though persistent absenteeism did inhibit his effectiveness. It was Powell who first used the phrase '**Black Power**' (at Howard University in 1966), and who acted as convenor of the first National Conference on Black Power. In 1967 he was expelled from the US House of Representatives for misusing public funds and for unbecoming conduct. Re-elected in 1968, he had the satisfaction of a Supreme Court ruling in favour of his appeal against expulsion, but he lost his seat in 1970.

Powell, (John) Enoch (1912–)
British politician. He was Professor of Greek at Sydney (1937–9), and became a Conservative MP in 1950. He held several junior posts before he became Minister of Health (1960–3). His outspoken attitude on the issues of non-white immigration and racial integration came to national attention in 1968, and as a consequence of this he was dismissed from

the shadow cabinet. He was elected as an Ulster Unionist MP in Oct 1974, losing his seat in 1987. ▷ **Conservative Party** (UK)

PP (*Partido Popular*)
Spanish conservative party. Founded in 1976 as *Alianza Popular* (AP, 'Popular Alliance') and headed by 'the magnificent seven', all former Francoists under the leadership of Manuel **Fraga Iribarne**. The party defended laissez-faire capitalism alongside more traditional Spanish conservative values. In the 1977 election AP won only 16 seats, but in 1982 it came second to the Socialist Party with a quarter of the vote cast. In 1989 the party was renamed *Partido Popular*, with Manuel Fraga stepping down as leader the following year.

Prague
The industrial and commercial capital of the Czech Republic, an important trading centre since the 10c. It became capital of the newly-created Czechoslovakia in 1918 and was occupied by **Warsaw Pact** troops in 1968.

Prague Spring (1968)
The name given to the events associated with the attempt made to reform **communism** in Czechoslovakia and to create instead what Alexander **Dubček** called '**Socialism with a Human Face**'. The action programme anticipated many of Mikhail **Gorbachev**'s subsequent reforms in the USSR and attracted widespread popular support. But the thought that Czechoslovakia might develop a political system with several parties in which the communists could be defeated at the polls and themselves divided on Czech/Slovak ethnic grounds did not occur to Leonid **Brezhnev**, who saw his control over Eastern Europe and within the USSR itself threatened. Hence the Soviet invasion in Aug, the Dubček Doctrine, and the removal of Dubček and his colleagues who had not had quite enough time to dispose of conservative opposition. The whole area lost a great opportunity.

Prajadhipok (1893–1941)
The 7th King of the **Chakri Dynasty** of Thailand, and the last absolute monarch in that line. He was educated in England, at Eton and the Woolwich Military Academy. Prajadhipok ascended the throne in 1925. His apparent instincts for political reform were smothered by an older generation of ministers and advisers. In June 1932 the absolute monarchy was overthrown in a bloodless coup. Prajadhipok remained as a constitutional monarch until Mar 1935, when he abdicated. He then lived in England until his death.

Prasad, Rajendra (1884–1963)
Indian politician. Having been active in Bihari politics, he left legal practice to become a supporter of M K **Gandhi**, helped found the *Searchlight* newspaper, and was President of the **Indian National Congress** on several occasions between 1934 and 1948. In 1946 he was made Minister for Food and Agriculture, and was India's first President (1950–62). He died at Patna.

Prat de la Riba, Enric (1870–1917)
Catalan nationalist and conservative theorist of the Catalan bourgeoisie. A founder in 1901 of the *Lliga Regionalista* (which sought autonomy within the Spanish state), he was Secretary of the party. His ideas on autonomy contributed to the creation of a regional government, the Mancomunitat, in 1914. He served as President of the Mancomunitat until his death, undertaking numerous projects to strengthen Catalan culture. ▷ **Lliga**

Prchlik, Václav (1922–)
Czechoslovak general and politician. He joined the forces and the Communist Party at the end of **World War II**, rose through various official appointments to be political administrator of the army from 1955 to 1968, and in Jan 1968 apparently foiled an attempt by some of his colleagues to suppress the reform movement before it began. During 1968 he began a purge of the top security services and prepared to transfer the political responsibility for them from the party to parliament. After the Soviet invasion in Aug, which he was prepared to resist, he was dismissed, and fear of the secret police returned to Czechoslovakia.

Prem Tinsulanonda, General (1920–)
Thai soldier. Educated at the Chulachomklao Royal Military Academy, Bangkok, he entered the army as a sub-lieutenant in 1941 and rose to become Commander-General of the 2nd Army Area in 1974, and assistant Commander-in-Chief of the Royal Thai Army in 1977. During the administration of General Kriangsak Chomanam (1977–80) he served as deputy Minister of the Interior and, from 1979, as Defence Minister. He was appointed Prime Minister (Mar 1980). Prem then formally relinquished his army office and established a series of civilian coalition governments. He withstood coup attempts in Apr 1981 and Sep 1985, and ruled in a cautious manner, retaining the confidence of key business and military leaders. Under his stewardship, 'newly industrializing' Thailand achieved annual growth rates in excess of 9 per cent. He retired, on 'personal grounds', in July 1988.

Premadasa, Ranasinghe (1924–93)

Sri Lankan politician. The first Sri Lankan head of government to have emerged from the urban working classes rather than the traditional elite families, he began his political career attached to the Ceylon Labour Party. He formed a temperance group dedicated to moral uplift, then joined the **UNP** (United National Party) in 1950 and became Deputy Mayor of the Colombo municipal council (1955). Elected to Sri Lanka's parliament in 1960, he served, successively, as UNP Chief Whip (1965–8 and 1970–7), the Minister of Local Government (1968–70) and Leader of the House (1977–8), before becoming Prime Minister, under President **Jayawardene**, in 1978. During 10 years as Prime Minister, Premadasa implemented a popular housebuilding and poverty alleviation programme, which provided the basis for his election as President (Dec 1988). He was assassinated in Colombo on 1 May 1993.

Prempeh (d.1931)

Last King of the **Ashanti** (1888/96). He was deposed by the British, imprisoned at Elmina, and exiled to the Seychelles. He was allowed to return in 1924, with chief's rank from 1926.

Preobrazhensky, Yevgeni Alexandrovich (1886–1937)

Soviet economist. The son of a priest in the Urals, he developed revolutionary tendencies quite early in life. After the 1917 **Russian Revolution** he spent some time in his home territory, but mainly he was active in Moscow, drafting, amongst other things, the 1919 party programmes. He associated with **Trotsky** and **Bukharin** and joined with the latter in publishing the *ABC of Communism*, thereby incurring **Stalin**'s anger. He died in prison in 1937. His writings have now attracted renewed interest.

PRI (*Partido Revolucionario Institucional*)

Mexican political party, previously known as the PRN (*Partido Revolucionario Nacional*, National Revolutionary Party) and the PRM (*Partido de la Revolución Mexicana*, Mexican Revolutionary Party). Founded by Plutarco **Calles** in 1929, in the wake of the Mexican Revolution (1910–20), as an instrument for change through the achievement of unified and dictatorial centralism, the party has dominated Mexican political life ever since. The PRN was a coalition of local military chiefs, officeholders and CROM, the largest labour organization, and owed its strength to Calles' steady erosion of the autonomy of the states. **Cárdenas**, Calles' successor, created the succeeding PRM by replacing regional chiefs with military, labour, peasant and popular groups: labour and peasant organizations were seen as an effective counterpoise to the military, while the resolution of conflict lay in the hands of the President. By the time the PRM became the PRI (in 1945, under Avila Camacho), the military sector had been disbanded, other interest groups had been included and the state organization strengthened. The party's political monopoly remained unchallenged until the late 1970s when opposition parties began to win congressional seats; the 1988 elections saw the PRI's first-ever loss of Senate seats, and in 1989 the PRI state governorship monopoly was broken for the first time.

Pribičević, Svetozar (1875–1936)
Serbian politician. Head of the Serbian Independent Party, which represented the Serbs within the Habsburg Empire, during **World War I** he advocated union with Serbia to form a South Slav state. Soon disillusioned with the organization of the Kingdom of Serbs, Croats and Slovenes (later Yugoslavia) under the arch-Serbian nationalists, Nikola **Pašić** and King **Alexander I**, in 1919 he led the Democratic Party, a breakaway group from the Serbian Radical Party. He was Minister of Education (1921–2). After 1927 he advocated the reorganization of the Kingdom of Yugoslavia as a federation. He was imprisoned during the royal dictatorship but was released to seek medical treatment in Czechoslovakia, where he died. ▷ **Korošec, Anton; Maček, Vladko; Radić, Stjepan**

Price, George (1919–)
Belize politician. Educated in Belize City and the USA, he was elected to the Belize City Council in 1947 and in 1950 founded the People's United Party (PUP), a left-of-centre grouping which grew out of the People's Committee, a smaller group calling for the independence of Belize. Partial self-government was achieved in 1954 and Price became Prime Minister, continuing to lead his country until it achieved full independence in 1981. In 1984 PUP's 30 years of uninterrupted rule ended when the general election was won by the United Democratic Party (UDP), led by Manuel Esquivel, but Price unexpectedly returned to power in 1989.

Price Spreads Commission (1934)
Canadian governmental inquiry. Instituted by the Ministry of Trade and Commerce to investigate the retail trade, the Commission found that retailers, especially the large department and chain stores, made their employees work very long hours for very low wages. Premier R B **Bennett** went public with its findings, condemning employers for their exploitation. His radio addresses on 'the state of the times' upset many of his conservative adherents, but Bennett insisted on the reforms, such as the Wages and Hours Bill and Unemployment Insurance, which had been suggested by the commission. Employers who broke the new laws were to be punished as criminals, not civil offenders. It was the controversy over the commission that led Harry H **Stevens** to resign from the cabinet to lead the Reconstruction Party of disaffected conservatives in the 1935 election. ▷ **New Deal** (Canada)

Pridi Phanomyong (1900–83)
Thai politician. Trained as a lawyer, notably in France in the 1920s, Pridi was a leading civilian figure in the coup group which overthrew the absolute monarchy in June 1932. He was then a prominent, but also highly controversial, government minister for much of the rest of the 1930s. In 1933 he drafted a National Economic Plan. This radical initiative, widely seen as communist, created a storm in Bangkok and forced Pridi into brief exile in France. During the Japanese occupation (1941–5) Pridi acted as Regent for the absent King Ananda but also, towards the end of that period, as a clandestine leader of the anti-Japanese 'Seri Thai' movement, codename 'Ruth'. He was briefly Prime Minister in 1946. However, he remained a highly controversial figure in Thai politics. He left Thailand for exile in 1949, never to return, but living first in China and then, from 1970, in France.

Prieto, Indalecio (1883–1962)
Spanish socialist leader. He served under the Second Republic first as Minister of Finance in 1931 and then as an innovative Minister of Public Works from 1931–3. The outstanding parliamentary orator of the Socialist Party, Prieto was also the leader of its moderate wing. He was unable to take up the premiership in May 1936 because of the opposition of **Largo Caballero**, the leader of the party's left wing. Such a move may have thwarted the military rising of July 1936 which led to civil war. During the **Spanish Civil War**, he proved a defeatist Minister of the Navy and Air Force (Sep 1936–May 1937) and Minister of Defence (May 1937–Apr 1938). He was forced to resign because of his opposition to the Communist Party. After the war, he tried to unite the socialists with the Republicans and even the monarchists in an effort to overthrow the **Franco** regime. ▷ **Republic, Second** (Spain)

Primo de Rivera, José Antonio (1903–36)
Spanish fascist leader. The son of the dictator, General Miguel **Primo de Rivera**, he was an aristocratic playboy turned charismatic political leader. He founded the **Falange Española**, a totalitarian and nationalistic movement, in Oct 1933. After the Falange fused with the *Juntas de Ofensiva Nacional Sindicalista* (JONS) in Feb 1934, he was elected leader. Detained in Mar 1936 by the Popular Front, he supported the rising of July 1936 against the Republic. He was shot on 20 Nov 1936 in Alicante jail. The cult of 'the absent one' became a central myth of the **Franco** regime.

Primo de Rivera (y Orbaneja), Miguel (1870–1930)
Spanish dictator. He served in Cuba, the Philippines, and Morocco, and in 1923 led a military coup, inaugurating a dictatorship which lasted until 1930. During 1928–9 he lost the support of the army, the ruling class, and the King, **Alfonso XIII**, and in 1930 gave up power. He died in Paris.

His son, José Antonio **Primo de Rivera** founded the Spanish Fascist Party, **Falange Española**, in 1933, and was executed by the Republicans in 1936. ▷ **fascism; Spanish Civil War**

Princely States, Indian

Before the colonial period, India was composed of various independent kingdoms, with only the north of the country being dominated by the Mughal Empire. With the slow collapse of this empire, many of its constituent parts broke off to become effectively independent states (such as Hyderabad). With the rise of British colonial rule, many of these newly emergent successor states, as well as others with much longer histories, succeeded in maintaining their independence by entering into treaties with the British, who propped up the Indian aristocracy wherever possible, provided they were willing to serve as loyal collaborators. The rewards for this loyalty were sumptuous, giving many rulers fabulous wealth which, combined with a lack of real power, earned them a reputation for decadence. On independence in 1947, the government of Independent India and Pakistan saw the Indian princes as a relic of colonial rule and had little use for them. Some, such as Hyderabad, Kashmir and Junagadh, made a bid for independence, but all were sooner or later annexed. Some ex-rulers went on to enjoy successful political careers but, following the abolition of aristocracy and all its privileges by Indira **Gandhi** in 1971, the majority sank into obscurity. ▷ **Communalism; India, Partition of**

Princip, Gavrilo (1895–1918)

Serbian nationalist and revolutionary. He was a member of the secret Serbian terrorist organization known as the **Black Hand**, dedicated to the achievement of independence for the South Slav peoples from the Austro-Hungarian Empire. He and a group of young zealots assassinated **Francis Ferdinand**, Archduke of Austria, and his wife Sophie on a visit to Sarajevo (28 June 1914). The murder precipitated **World War I**, after Austria declared war on Serbia (28 July 1914). Princip died in an Austrian prison.

Priscillian (c.340–385)

Bishop of Ávila. He was excommunicated by a synod at Saragossa in 380, then tolerated, but ultimately executed (the first case of capital punishment for heresy in the history of the Church). His doctrine, said to have been brought to Spain from Egypt, contained Gnostic and Manichean elements, and was based on dualism. The Priscillianists were ascetics, eschewed marriage and animal food, and were said to hold strict truth obligatory only between themselves.

Profumo, John (Dennis) (1915–)

British politician. He became a Conservative MP in 1940, and held several government posts before becoming Secretary of State for War in 1960. He resigned in 1963 after admitting that he had been guilty of a grave misdemeanour in deceiving the House of Commons about the nature of his relationship with Christine Keeler, who was at the time also involved with a Soviet diplomat. He later sought anonymity in social and charitable services. ▷ **Conservative Party** (UK)

Progressive Party (Canada)

The political party established in 1920 with the support of the farming community, it fought the 1921 federal election on a platform of lower tariffs and a reciprocity agreement with the USA. When it won 65 seats it became the second largest group in the Commons, to the surprise of the country. Its leader, T A **Crerar**, chose not to make the party the official opposition and over the next few years Mackenzie **King** was able to cut away the farmers' support, so that by 1926 the party had all but disappeared.

Progressive Party (USA) (1912–16, 1924, and 1948)

US political parties. The name was used by three separate third-party political initiatives. The first, essentially a breakaway from the Republican Party, centred on former President Theodore **Roosevelt**, who was its presidential candidate in 1912. The second developed in 1924 from midwestern farmer and labour discontent. Its presidential candidate, Senator Robert **La Follette** of Wisconsin, won 4 million votes. In the 1948 election, Democrats opposed to President Harry S **Truman**'s cold war policy ran Henry A Wallace, who received only 1 million popular votes. ▷ **Bull Moose; New Nationalism; Republican Party**

Prohibition (1920–33)

An attempt to forbid the manufacture, transportation and sale of all alcoholic drinks in the USA, authorized by the 18th Amendment to the **US Constitution** (1919). Building on 19c temperance movements and the powerful lobbying of the Anti-Saloon League, Congress passed the national legislation as a wartime emergency measure. Its enforcement, through the Volstead Act, gave rise to one of the great political controversies of the 1920s, and led to various 'bootlegging' operations that created new opportunities for organized crime. It also gained celebrity for J Edgar **Hoover** and his 'G-Men'. It was repealed in 1933 by the 21st Amendment. ▷ **Capone, Al**

Protocols of the Elders of Zion

A fraudulent document, originally printed in Russia (1903) and much translated, ostensibly reporting discussions among Jewish elders of plans to subvert Christian civilization and erect a world Zionist state. Exposed as forgeries in *The Times* (1921), the 'Protocols' have nevertheless been, and remain, a staple of right-wing, anti-Semitic propaganda. ▷ **Zionism**

Prussia

A North European state, originally centred in the East Baltic region as a duchy created by the Teutonic Knights, but later owing suzerainty to Poland. Inherited by the German House of Brandenburg in the early 17c, Brandenburg-Prussia was consolidated and expanded, and Polish sovereignty thrown off, by **Frederick William, the 'Great Elector'**. Within the federated German Empire (1871–1918) it was dominant, and within the **Weimar Republic** (1919–33) it retained considerable autonomy and influence. As a legal entity, Prussia ceased to exist with the post-1945 division of Germany and the establishment of a revised East German–Polish frontier. ▷ **Franco-Prussian War; Frederick William III; German Confederation; North German Confederation**

PSD (*Partido Social Democrático*)

The Brazilian party, formed in 1945, as a coalition of rural *coroneis* and urban leaders, including industrialists who had benefited substantially from the rule of **Vargas**, yet could not readily support his own PTB (*Partido Trabalhista Brasileiro*, Brazilian Labour Party). The PSD effectively retained control of Vargas' political machine in 1945, electing Eurico Gaspar Dutra as President, and receiving nearly 43 per cent of the vote. The party's 'natural alliance' with the PTB came to the fore during the 1950 presidential election, when the bulk of its leaders supported Vargas rather than its 'own' candidate. The blend of populist politics espoused by the PTB and the **coronelismo** of the countryside provided a powerful base for **Kubitschek (de Oliveira)**'s *Programa de Metas*, but foundered under the weak leadership of João **Goulart**. Much of the PSD merged with the ARENA party after 1965, inexorably delivering the rural vote to the military government.

PSOE (*Partido Socialista Obrero Español*, 'Spanish Socialist Workers' Party')

Spanish political party, founded in 1879, which established itself slowly, limited both by organizational rigidity and theoretical shortcomings. Although the party proclaimed a revolutionary rhetoric, it remained wedded to reformist practices, even to the extent of collaborating with the dictatorship of Miguel **Primo de Rivera** (1923–30). Under the Second Republic of 1931–6 the PSOE was the leading political force on the Left, forming the backbone of the reformist Republican–Socialist administrations of 1931–3. However, the reversal of reform after the electoral victory of the Right in Nov 1933 rapidly radicalized the PSOE, culminating in the Asturian rising of Oct 1934. The insurrection's defeat divided the party between the 'revolutionary' stance of **Largo Caballero** and the moderate Indalecio **Prieto**. After the **Spanish Civil War** broke out, Largo Caballero was made Premier in Sep 1936, but in May 1937 he was ousted by the Communists to be replaced by Juan **Negrín**, a socialist who supported communist policies. In Apr 1938, Negrín removed Indalecio Prieto, the last obstacle to communist domination. As the Republic plunged to defeat, the PSOE collapsed and during **Franco**'s dictatorship PSOE opposition was negligible. However, it played an important role during the transition to democracy. Moreover, in 1982 the PSOE won an overall majority in the general election, repeating its success in 1986. The PSOE in power has done much to modernize Spain and raise its international profile, though it has proved intolerant of dissent, lost the support of the trade unions, and been discredited by corruption scandals. ▷ **Republic, Second** (Spain)

Public Against Violence (1989)

The Slovak offshoot and equivalent of Czech **Civic Forum** that united most of the anti-communist groups in Slovakia in Nov 1989 to help bring down the Czechoslovak communist government. There was no bloodshed and the 'party' won more seats than any other in the June 1990 election. But it subsequently split on the issue of relations with the Czech Lands. Even Jan Carnogursky, Slovak Prime Minister and leader of the rump 'party', had inevitably to talk in nationalist terms.

Puyi (P'u-yi) (1906–67)

Last Emperor of China (1908/12) and the first of Manzhuguo (1934/5). This was the personal name of Hsuan T'ung. Emperor at the age of two, after the **Chinese Revolution** (1911) he was given a pension and a summer palace. Known in the West as Henry Puyi, in 1932 he was called from private life by the Japanese to be provincial dictator of Manzhuguo, under the name of **Kang Teh**. Taken prisoner by the Russians in 1945, he was tried in China as a war criminal (1950), pardoned (1959) and became a private citizen. The story of his life was made into a film, *The Last Emperor*, in 1988.

Q

Qaboos bin Said (1940–   )
Sultan of Oman (1970/   ). The son of Sa'id bin Taimur, he is the 14th descendant of the ruling dynasty of the Albusaid family. Educated in England, where he was trained at Sandhurst, the Royal Military Academy, he disagreed with the conservative views of his father and in 1970 overthrew him in a bloodless coup and assumed the sultanship. He proceeded to pursue more liberal and expansionist policies, while maintaining an international position of strict non-alignment.

Qajar Dynasty
A Turcoman tribe which furnished Persia with a dynasty which ruled from 795 to 1924. The absolute nature of Qajar rule, coupled with the affectation of ostentatious luxury on the part of some Qajar Shahs, led to many disturbances, and this coupled with foreign interference led to difficulties with the religious hierarchy. A coup d'état in the early 1920s at the instigation of **Reza Khan** led in due course to the deposition of the last Qajar ruler, Ahmad Shah, and the coronation of Reza as Reza Shah Pahlavi.

Qassim, Abd al-Krim (1914–63)
Iraqi soldier and revolutionary. The son of a carpenter, he joined the army and by 1955 had risen to the rank of brigadier. In 1958 he led the coup which resulted in the overthrow of the monarchy and the deaths of King **Faisal II**, his uncle Prince Abdul Ilah, and the pro-Western Prime Minister, General Nuri al-**Sa'id**. Qassim suspended the constitution and established a left-wing military regime with himself as prime minister and head of state, but soon found himself increasingly isolated in the Arab world. He survived one assassination attempt, but failed to crush a Kurdish rebellion (1961–3) and was killed in a coup led by Colonel Salem Aref, who reinstated constitutional government.

Qing Dynasty (1644–1911)
The last dynasty of imperial China, it was founded by the Manchus following their conquest of China in 1644. The dynasty entered a period of decline in the 19c as China fell more and more under the domination of the European powers but did not finally collapse until the **Chinese Revolution** in 1911, when China became a republic.

Quadros, Jânio da Silva (1917–92)
Brazilian politician. Trained as a teacher, he was elected to the municipal council of São Paulo in 1947. He was a masterful campaigner and orator, with a unique personal style: as the 'man of destiny', he won election to the São Paulo State Assembly, Prefecture and Governorship between 1951 and 1955. He began preparing for the presidential race in 1960, as the only hope of the UDN (*União Democrático Nacional*), mobilizing popular support in the process. He defeated his **PSD** opponents and assumed the presidency in 1961, determined to overcome the economic crisis bequeathed by **Kubitschek (de Oliveira)**. This he did by exercising near-dictatorial prerogatives to temper crisis economic measures with a strongly nationalist foreign policy. He incurred the wrath of Congress and the far right, led by Carlos Lacerda, and resigned (25 Aug 1961), pitching the country into crisis. Banned from political life in 1965, he returned to politics in 1985 as Prefect of São Paulo, failing in another bid for the presidency in 1989.

Queipo de Llano, Gonzalo, Marquis of Queipo de Llano y Sevilla (1875–1951)
Spanish soldier. After military service in Cuba and Morocco, he was promoted to the rank of major-general in the Republican army, but went over to the rebel side at the beginning of the **Spanish Civil War**. In July 1936 he led the forces which captured Seville, and became Commander-in-Chief of the Southern army. In his many propaganda broadcasts from Seville, he drew on General Emilio Mola's phrase '**fifth column**', as used to describe the rebel supporters inside Madrid, who were expected to add their strength to that of the four columns attacking from outside. In Apr 1950 he was given the title of marquis.

Quiet Revolution (1960–6)
Quebec reform programme. Pursued by Jean **Lesage**'s Liberal government of Quebec with the slogan, *Il faut que ça change* ('Things must change'), it sought to counteract the influence of the Catholic Church in civic spheres such as education and promoted state activism to 'decolonize' Quebec's economy from the influence of American and English-speaking institutions. It also began to participate in the federal/provincial shared-cost programmes, though previously shunned by **Duplessis** and the **Union Nationale**, to provide the range of social services available elsewhere in Canada. However, the resulting huge increases in the size of the provincial civil service and the tax burden gave the **Union Nationale** a platform for their return to power under Daniel Johnson. ▷ **Liberal Party** (Canada)

Quisling, Vidkun (Abraham Lauritz Jonsson) (1887-1945)
Norwegian fascist leader. He embarked on a military career, graduating from military academy with high honours in 1911, and went on to serve

as a military attaché in Russia and Finland (1918–21) and to work with Fridtjof **Nansen** as a relief administrator in the USSR (1922–6). Quisling entered politics in 1929 and was Minister of Defence in 1931–2. In May 1933 he founded a new party, *Nasjonal Samling* ('National Union') in imitation of the German National Socialist Party. However, the party met with little electoral success and disintegrated after 1936. He then turned to Germany and in Dec 1939 made contact with the Nazi leader, Alfred Rosenberg, and the head of the German navy, Admiral **Raeder**, as well as with **Hitler** himself. Following the German invasion of Norway (Apr 1940), Quisling declared himself head of a government but won no support and was forced to step down six days later. It was from this point onward that his name became synonymous with 'traitor'. The German occupation authorities reluctantly allowed Quisling to head a puppet government from May 1942. At the end of **World War II** he was arrested and put on trial, and executed by firing squad on 24 Oct 1945.

▷ **Fascism; Norway, German Invasion of**

Quit India Movement

A campaign launched (Aug 1942) by the **Indian National Congress** calling for immediate independence from Britain, and threatening mass non-violent struggle if its demands were not met. M K **Gandhi** and other Congress leaders were arrested, and the movement was suppressed, though not without difficulty. It was described by the Viceroy, Lord Linlithgow, as 'by far the most serious rebellion since that of 1857': 57 army battalions had to be used to help restore order and there were more than 1 000 deaths. It contributed significantly to the eventual decision by Britain to withdraw from India soon after the end of **World War II**.

Quwwatli, Shukri al- (1891–1967)

He was early a member of the Young Arab Association, which was founded in Paris but later moved to Syria. This group aimed originally to free Arabs from Turkish rule, while at the same time discouraging the Western powers from interfering in Arab affairs. Al-Quwwatli went on to become a leader of the National Bloc in Syria, which distinguished itself by winning the first elections permitted by the French (1943). However, despite a declaration of independence in 1944, full independence was not achieved until 1946. Al-Quwwatli had a resurgence of political influence when he returned to power after the election of 1955, but this only lasted until the following year, when the government fell. He was President in 1958 and, with Gamal Abd al-**Nasser**, proclaimed the short-lived **United Arab Republic** (effectively the creation of Salah al-Din **Bitar** of the Syrian Ba'th party).

R

Rabin, Itzhak (1922–)
Israeli soldier and politician. After studies at a school of agriculture, he embarked on an army career, completing his training in Britain. He fought in the 'War of Independence' (1948–9) and represented the Israeli Defence Forces (IDF) at the armistice in Rhodes. In the IDF he rose to become Chief-of-Staff in 1964, heading the armed forces during the successful **Six-Day War** of 1967. After serving as Ambassador to the USA (1968–73), he moved decisively into the political arena, becoming Labour Party leader and Prime Minister (1974–7) and Defence Minister from 1984. In Feb 1992 he again became Chairman of the Labour Party, and in July 1992 was elected Prime Minister in a new coalition government. In 1993 and 1994 he and Yasser **Arafat** signed peace agreements by which Israel agreed to withdraw from Jericho and the **Gaza Strip**. ▷ **Arab-Israeli Wars; Mapai Party**

Rabuka, Sitiveni (1948–)
Fijian soldier and politician. He completed his army training at Sandhurst Military College in England, and then served with a **UN** peacekeeping force in the Lebanon, before returning to Fiji with the rank of colonel. When the 1987 elections produced an Indian-dominated coalition government, he engineered a coup that deposed the Prime Minister, Kamisese Mara, and established his own provisional administration. In Dec 1987, he declared the country a republic and reinstated Mara as Premier, while retaining control of the security forces and of internal affairs.

Radek, Karl Berngardovich (1885–1939)
Russian revolutionary and politician. Educated in Kraków and Bern and left-wing in his views, he became a journalist in Germany and Switzerland. He was active in Petrograd following the Bolshevik Revolution and participated obliquely in the unsuccessful German revolution. Returning to the USSR, he became a leading member of the Communist International, but lost standing with his growing distrust of extremist tactics. He was charged as a supporter of **Trotsky**, and expelled from the Party (1927–9). He was readmitted after recanting, but in 1937 he was a victim of one of **Stalin**'s show trials, being sentenced to 10 years in prison, where he is believed to have been murdered by fellow-prisoners two years later. ▷ **Bolsheviks; communism; Russian Revolution**

Radhakrishnan, Sarvepalli (1888–1975)
Indian philosopher and politician. Educated in Madras, he taught at Mysore and Calcutta Universities, and became Professor of Eastern Religions and Ethics at Oxford (1936–52). In 1946 he was chief Indian delegate to UNESCO, becoming its Chairman in 1949. A member of the Indian Assembly in 1947, he was Indian Ambassador to the USSR (1949), Vice-President of India (1952–62) and President (1962–7). He was knighted in 1931.

Radić, Stjepan (1871–1928)
Croatian politician. An admirer of the Czech leader, Thomas **Masaryk**, he and his brother, Antun, founded the Croat People's Peasant Party (HPSS, *Hrvatska Pučka Seljačka Stranka*) in 1904. A member of the National Council which represented the South Slavs of the Habsburg monarchy in the months before the creation of the Kingdom of Serbs, Croats and Slovenes (Dec 1918), he was deeply suspicious of the motives of Nikola **Pašić** and of the Serbs in general. After unification, he and the HPSS maintained their vehement opposition to the new Belgrade-based government. Imprisoned in Mar 1919, on his release (Dec 1920) he sought foreign support for an autonomous Croatian republic. He visited Moscow (1924) and affiliated the HPSS with the Communist Peasant International. The Belgrade government charged him with cooperation with **Comintern** and imprisoned him and the other HPSS leaders until 1925 when, in an apparent volte-face, he accepted the constitution and agreed to cooperate with the Serbian Radical Party. He alternately sat and withdrew from the Belgrade parliament until 1928, when he and his nephew, Pavle Radić, were shot by a Montenegrin deputy during a parliamentary sitting. His death shortly afterwards brought an end to any semblance of Croat-Serb cooperation and precipitated the establishment of the royal dictatorship. ▷ **Alexander I; Korošec, Anton; Maček, Vladko; Pribičević, Svetozar**

Radical Party (Argentina)
Formed as the Radical Civic Union (*Unión Cívica Radical*) in 1891, it commanded wide support in the early 20c, remaining a leading Argentine party thereafter, though at times divided into two separate branches. The party gained its great strength from the support of the lower middle classes in Buenos Aires, and from the ability of the first **Yrigoyen** administration (1916–22) to secure their loyalty against the lower classes. Radicals won the Argentine presidency in 1916, 1922, 1928, 1958, 1963 and 1983.

Radical Party (France)
Political party founded in 1901. Radicalism as a political tendency came into existence around 1840, and after 1870 the term designated the left-

wing faction of the republicans, as opposed to the Opportunists, or **Moderates**. However, an organized political party only appeared in 1901, with the title *Parti républicain radical et radical-socialiste* ('Republican Radical and Radical-Socialist Party'). It at once became the largest political party in France, and had representatives in office throughout the remaining years of the Third Republic. Its most important leaders were **Caillaux**, **Herriot**, and **Daladier**. Paradoxically **Clemenceau**, the most important representative of the radical tendency before 1901, was never close to the organized party. It was always loosely organized and undisciplined, and was discredited by the collapse of the Third Republic. It was revived after **World War II**, but was much reduced in strength; its most important leader in that period was **Mendès-France**, Prime Minister in 1954. After 1958 it faded even more, and was eventually absorbed in other political formations. ▷ **Republic, Third** (France)

Radical Republican Party (*Partido Republicano Radical*)

Spanish political party. Founded in 1908, the Radical Party soon moved away from its revolutionary working class origins in Barcelona to become a federation of largely middle class regional parties centred on the charismatic figure of the populist leader Alejandro **Lerroux**. By the advent of the Second Republic, the Radical Party was not only the most historic Republican party, but also the largest. It had also become staunchly conservative. From 1931 to 1933 it was the most formidable source of opposition to the reforms of the progressive Republican-Socialist administrations under Manuel **Azaña**. From 1933 to 1935, the Radical Party was the principal element in a succession of right-wing coalition governments formed in alliance with the non-Republican Right (resulting in a major internal party split in May 1934), which overturned the reforms of the first two years and thereby polarized the Republic to an unprecedented degree. The resulting breakdown of the regime culminated in the **Spanish Civil War** of 1936–9. ▷ **Republic, Second** (Spain)

Raeder, Erich (1876–1960)

German grand admiral. He joined the navy in 1894, and became a Chief of Staff during **World War I**. In 1928 he was made Commander-in-Chief of the navy, a Grand Admiral in 1939, and in 1943 head of an anti-invasion force. At the **Nuremberg Trials** (1946), he was sentenced to life imprisonment, but released in 1955. ▷ **World War II**

Rafsanjani, Ali Akbar (1934–)

Iranian cleric and political leader. He trained as a mullah under Ayatollah Ruholla **Khomeini** at the holy city of Qom, from 1950. His friendship with Khomeini led him into opposition against Shah Mohammad Reza **Pahlavi** and brief imprisonment in 1963. During the 1970s he became wealthy through the construction business in Tehran, but continued to keep in close touch with the exiled Khomeini. Following the 'Islamic Revolution' of 1979–80 he became Speaker of the Iranian parliament (Majlis), emerging as an influential and pragmatic power-broker between fundamentalist and technocrat factions within the ruling Islamic Republican Party (which he helped to found), playing a key role in securing an end to the Gulf War (1980–8). In Aug 1989, soon after the death of Ayatollah Khomeini, Rafsanjani became State President and 'de facto' national leader.

Rajagopalachari, Chakravarti (1878–1972)
Indian political leader. The first Governor-General of free India, he was educated at Central College, Bangalore, and Presidency and Law Colleges, Madras. He joined the Bar in 1900 and practised until 1919 at Salem. Rajagopalachari joined the non-cooperation and **Satyagraha** movements and was elected Congress General-Secretary in 1921–2. He was a member of the Congress Working Committee in 1922–42, 1946–7 and 1951–4. Prime Minister of Madras from 1937 to 1939, he was a member of the interim government in 1946–7, Governor of West Bengal in 1947–8, acting Governor-General of India (Nov 1947), and Governor-General from June 1948 to Jan 1950. He was Chief Minister of Madras between 1952 and 1954 and founded the **Swatantra Party** in 1959. ▷ **Non-Cooperation Movement**

Rajk, László (1908–49)
Hungarian politician. An early convert to **communism**, he was expelled from Budapest University for his political activities and became a building worker. Leader of the left-wing faction of his union, he organized an important building workers' strike in 1935 but then deemed it wise to go abroad. He was Party Secretary to the Hungarian battalion of the **International Brigades** during the **Spanish Civil War** but was eventually imprisoned in France. He returned to Hungary in 1941 to become a secretary to the Communist Party Central Committee, but he was first interned by the Hungarians and then imprisoned by the Germans. He rose rapidly after 1945, becoming a full member of the Central Committee, Minister of the Interior, then Foreign Minister. In 1949 he was arrested and tried on trumped-up charges during the Stalinist purges and, like many others who had first-hand experience of the West, was executed. In 1955 he was rehabilitated, but his fate had much to do with undermining **communism** in Hungary. ▷ **Stalinism**

Rakosi, Matyas (1892–1971)
Hungarian politician. He was already active in the labour movement before **World War I**. Conscripted in 1914, he spent most of the war years as a prisoner in Russia and moved further to the Left, joining the Hungarian Communist Party on his return home. He was commander

of the Red Guard in Béla **Kun**'s Soviet Republic in 1919 and then fled to the USSR where he became Secretary of the Communist International. Returning to Hungary in 1924, he spent the years 1925–40 in prison until he was released to return to Moscow. He led the Hungarian communist émigrés there and came back to Budapest in 1945 as their General-Secretary. Rakosi was then responsible for many of the changes introduced and was deeply implicated in the Stalinist purges. He was much criticized after **Stalin**'s death, but in 1955 he attempted to reinstate Stalinist practices, thus helping to provoke the 1956 **Hungarian Uprising**. He was then removed from office and, in 1962, expelled from the party.
▷ **Stalinism**

Ramaphosa, Matamela Cyril (1952–)
South African trade unionist. He became Chairman of the all-black South African Students' Organization in 1974. After 11 months of detention in 1974–5, he became an articled clerk in Johannesburg and was active in the **BPC** (Black People's Convention). He was detained again in 1976 but, after graduating from the University of South Africa with a law degree in 1981, he joined CUSA as an adviser in its legal department. He became General-Secretary of the National Union of Mineworkers in 1982 and led (Sep 1984) the first legal strike by black mineworkers. He brought the NUM into COSATU (Congress of South African Trade Unions) and was elected Secretary-General of the **ANC** in July 1991 at the party's congress held in Durban.

Ramgoolam, Sir Seewoosagur (1906–86)
Mauritian doctor and politician. Educated in Mauritius and London University, he practised as a doctor before becoming a member of Legco (1940–48) and then the Executive Council (1948–58). He was Ministerial Secretary to the Treasury (1958–60), then Minister of Finance (1961–5), and also Prime Minister (1965–80). After retirement, he was Governor-General of Mauritius from 1984 until his death.

Ramphal, Shridath Surrendranath ('Sonny') (1928–)
Guyanan and Commonwealth lawyer and diplomat. After studying law in London, he was called to the bar in 1951. He returned to the West Indies, and from 1952 held increasingly responsible posts in Guyana and the West Indies before becoming Guyana's Foreign Minister and Attorney-General in 1972, and Justice Minister in 1973. During much of this time he sat in the Guyanan National Assembly. From 1975 to 1989 he was Secretary-General of the Commonwealth.

Randolph, A Philip (1889–1979)
US labour organizer, socialist and civil rights activist. Initially a supporter of Marcus **Garvey**, he opposed the idea of economic separatism

in his journal, *The Messenger*. In 1925 he organized the Brotherhood of Sleeping Car Porters, the first black union to gain major successes, such as recognition by the Pullman Company. In 1941 he organized a march on Washington to demand equal employment opportunities for blacks in the defence industries, and racial desegregation in the armed forces. The march was called off after President Franklin D **Roosevelt** established the **Fair Employment Practices Committee**, but the tactic was revived during the civil rights movement of the 1960s, when he became the director of the March on Washington for Jobs and Freedom (Aug 28, 1963).

Rankin, Jeannette (1880–1973)
US feminist and pacifist, the first female member of Congress. Educated at Montana University and the New York School of Philanthropy, she went on to work as a social worker in Seattle (1909), where she became involved in the fight for women's rights. In 1914 she was appointed Legislative Secretary of the **National American Woman Suffrage Association**, and in 1916 entered the House of Representatives as a Republican, the first woman to do so. During her terms there (1917–19 and 1941–3) she consistently voted against US participation in both world wars, promoted women's welfare and rights, and was instrumental in the adoption of the first bill granting married women independent citizenship. Continuing to campaign for women's issues throughout her career, she worked for the National Council for the Prevention of War from 1928 to 1939, and led the Jeannette Rankin March (1968) in which 5 000 women gathered on Capitol Hill, Washington, to protest against the **Vietnam War**.

Ranković, Aleksander (1909–)
Yugoslav politician. He joined the Communist Party in 1928 and was imprisoned during the dictatorship of King **Alexander I Karageorgević**. During **World War II** he fought with **Tito** and the partisans and in 1945 became Director of the secret police, overseeing the ruthless elimination of all opposition to communist rule. He was also Minister of the Interior (1946–53) and Vice-President of Yugoslavia (1963). After 'bugging' Tito's home, he was accused of abusing his authority and was forced to resign (July 1966).

Rapacki, Adam (1909–70)
Polish politician. He studied in France and Italy, then became a soldier in the Polish army. Following the German invasion of Poland at the beginning of **World War II**, he was captured and held in various prisoner-of-war camps until 1945. A communist from 1948, he was Minister for Higher Education (1950–6) before being appointed Foreign Minister. He was removed from this post in 1968 for failing to support anti-Semitic

legislation. He is particularly noted for a speech (the Rapacki Plan) delivered to the **UN** General Assembly in Oct 1957, in which he called for the establishment of a nuclear-free zone in central Europe. The zone, which would include Poland, Czechoslovakia, the German Democratic Republic and the German Federal Republic, would contain neither 'stockpiled' nuclear weapons nor the means to manufacture them; the implementation of the Plan would be supervised by both NATO and **Warsaw Pact** states. However, despite approval by **Khrushchev**, the Plan was rejected by Britain, West Germany and the USA, who believed it would work only to their disadvantage because the countries of the Soviet-bloc possessed larger numbers of troops and conventional weapons.

Rapallo, Treaty of (12 Nov 1920)
The treaty of friendship and neutrality bringing together a defeated Germany and an ostracized Russia. It recognized Istria as Italian and Rijeka (**Fiume**) as a free city; it also made provision for future economic accords and stressed a mutual obligation to uphold the Treaties of Trianon and St Germain. The countries both gained diplomatically and economically. Their military cooperation was of particular benefit to the USSR, whose communist revolution was never seriously challenged thereafter: Allied intervention in Russia finally ended the same year. It was a triumph for the conciliatory policy of **Chicherin**, then Foreign Minister, and was echoed in the **German–Soviet Pact** of 1939.

Rapallo, Treaty of (16 Apr 1922)
The treaty signed by Germany and the Russian Federation during the World Economic Conference in Genoa. German fears of an agreement between the Western Allies and the USSR on German **reparations** payments and a Russian desire to escape economic and diplomatic isolation led to this agreement which, first, saw both parties renounce all claims arising from **World War I** and, second, saw economic and trade links established on a 'most favoured nation' basis. The treaty was extended to the whole of the USSR and was a significant blow against the post-**World War I** settlement. German–Soviet military and diplomatic cooperation subsequently became more extensive.

ras
Derived from the Arabic word for 'head', used in Abyssinia to denote a feudal warlord, this term was adopted and used in Italy to describe local fascist bosses in the 1920s. Amongst the *ras* numbered many figures who were to play a key role in the development of the **Fascist Party**, such as **Farinacci**, Italo **Balbo** and Dino **Grandi**. After attaining power in 1922, however, **Mussolini** felt it essential to check the power of the ras and to control the excesses of the **squadristi**, both because his position was

threatened by other charismatic fascist leaders and because he needed to prove that he could restore order to an Italy scarred by political violence. Some ras consequently fell victim to purges, while others were brought within the establishment and given important jobs in the party and government.

Rasin, Alois (1867–1923)
Czechoslovak politician. He took part in a famous student riot in 1893 and became involved in serious radical politics in the later 1890s. Rasin was imprisoned during **World War I** and was then the first Finance Minister of the new Czechoslovak Republic. His tight monetary policies were, however, unpopular with particular groups and he was assassinated in 1923. Despite his unpopularity, it was Rasin who had set the new state on its feet economically, both domestically and internationally.

Rasputin, Grigoriy (1871–1916)
Russian peasant and self-styled religious 'elder' (*starets*). A member of the schismatic sect of *Khlysty* (flagellants), he was introduced into the royal household, where he soon gained the confidence of Tsar Nicholas II and the Empress, Alexandra, by his apparent ability to control through hypnosis the bleeding of the haemophiliac heir to the throne, Tsarevich Alexei. He was also a notorious lecher and drunkard, and created a public scandal through the combination of his sexual and alcoholic excesses, and his political influence in securing the appointment and dismissal of government ministers. His influence was particularly baneful during **World War I**, especially when the Tsar was away from St Petersburg commanding his army; it helped destroy cooperation between the Tsar and the **Duma** that might have won the war and prevented the 1917 **Russian Revolution**. He was murdered by a clique of aristocrats, led by Prince Felix Yusupov, a distant relative of the Tsar.

Rassemblement Démocratique Africaine (RDA)
Established in 1944, the RDA was a cross-national political party with branches in most parts of the French African empire, which sent members to the National Assembly in Paris. Its major figure was Felix **Houphouet-Boigny**.

Rassemblement Wallon (RW)
Belgian political party of Walloon (French-speaking southern Belgian) nationalist/separatists. Formed in 1968 from a number of small Walloon groupings in reaction to increasing **Flemish Movement** activity, it elected 14 MPs in 1971, and took part in the government coalition in 1974–7. The Francophone wing of the liberals joined the RW in 1976 to form the *Parti des Reformées et des Libertés Wallones*, which gained only four seats in the 1978 election.

Rastafarianism

A religious movement from Jamaica, followed by c.1 million people. It largely derives from the Old Testament and the thought of Jamaican political activist Marcus **Garvey**, who advocated a return to Africa as a way to solve the problems of black oppression. When **Haile Selassie I** was crowned Emperor of Ethiopia in 1930, he came to be viewed as the Messiah, with Ethiopia seen as the promised land. Rastafarians follow strict taboos governing what they may eat (eg no pork, milk, coffee); ganja (marijuana) is held to be a sacrament; they usually wear their hair in long dreadlocks; and they cultivate a distinctive form of speech.

Ratsiraka, Didier (1936–)

Malagasy naval officer and politician. Educated in Madagascar and then at naval college in France, he served in the Navy (1963–70) before becoming military attaché in Paris (1970–2). A coup brought him to the centre of power in 1972, when he became Minister of Foreign Affairs and then, in 1975, President of the Supreme Revolutionary Council. He established a political party, the Advanced Guard of the Malagasy Revolution, and won elections in 1983 and 1989, although dissent remained high.

Rau, Johannes (1931–)

West German politician. He began his career as a salesman for a church publishing company before being attracted to politics as a follower of Gustav **Heinemann**. He joined the Social Democratic Party (**SPD**) and was elected to the parliament of his home state, North Rhine-Westphalia, the country's most populous, in 1958. He served as chairman of the SPD's parliamentary group (1967–70), and as Minister of Science and Research in the state parliament (1970–8) before becoming its Minister-President in 1978. His successful record as state leader, his moderate policy outlook, and his optimistic and youthful personality persuaded the SPD to elect him federal party deputy chairman in 1982 and chancellor-candidate for the 1987 **Bundestag** election. However, the party was heavily defeated, and since this setback he has concentrated on his work as state Premier.

Rawlings, Jerry (John) (1947–)

Ghanaian soldier and politician. Educated at Achimota College and the University of Ghana, he joined the air force. He led an unsuccessful coup in 1979, was imprisoned and then escaped to mount a successful one later the same year. He headed the Armed Forces Revolutionary Council, returning power to an elected government, led by Hilla **Limann**, in that year, when he retired from the air force. However, he re-entered the political scene in Dec 1982 when he led another successful coup and has remained head of government since then, despite attempts to overthrow him in 1983 (twice) and 1987.

Reagan, Ronald (Wilson) (1911–)

US politician and 40th President. He began his career as a radio sports announcer, then went to Hollywood in 1937, where he acted in more than 50 films, and served as President of the Screen Actors Guild (1947–52 and 1959). Originally a Democrat and supporter of liberal causes, he became actively involved in politics as a union leader and increasingly anti-communist. He registered as a Republican in 1962. Governor of California for two terms (1967–75), he campaigned unsuccessfully for the Republican presidential nomination in 1968 and 1976. He was elected President in 1980, defeating Jimmy **Carter**, and, with George **Bush** as his running mate, won a second term in 1984. Reagan's popularity enabled him to make sweeping changes in social and economic policy, including cuts in social services, the deregulation of many industries, and a tax cut that mainly benefited the wealthy. His foreign policy was dominated by a strong anti-communist stand, which led to a massive increase in defence spending and the introduction of the Strategic Defence Initiative (**SDI**), or 'Star Wars'. During his second term, when his attitude toward the USSR became less confrontational, largely as a result of President Mikhail **Gorbachev**'s policy of **perestroika**, he reached a major accord on nuclear arms reduction. The **Iran–Contra Affair** (Irangate) tarnished the reputation of his administration in its last two years. Instead of the balanced budget Reagan had sought, 'Reaganomics' left behind a huge federal deficit.

Red Army

The Red Army of Workers and Peasants (RKKA, *Raboche Krest'yanskaya Krasnaya Armiya*), the official name of the army of the USSR from 1918 to 1945. It was built around the original Bolshevik Red Guards from 1917, but was the most important land force engaged in the defeat of Nazi Germany in the period 1941–5. The epithet 'Red' gave it a political connotation which it never lost, even when 'Red' was changed to 'Soviet' in 1946. ▷ **Bolsheviks**

Red Brigades (*Brigate Rosse*, **BR**)

An Italian left-wing terrorist organization founded in 1970 by Alberto Franceschini, Renato Curcio and Margherita Cagol. Its early years were marked by little real violence, but by 1974 the organization had hardened. The BR was at its most active in the period 1976–80, its energies directed at the killing and kidnapping of judges, politicians, businessmen and journalists. Lack of public sympathy and a more efficiently coordinated anti-terrorist campaign (based on using former BR members as informers) led to widespread arrests and a virtual end to its activities by the early 1980s. ▷ **Moro, Aldo**

Red Front (*Roter Frontkampferbund*, **RFB**)
German paramilitary league. This organization was founded by the Communist Party (**KPD**) in July 1924 as a counter-weight to the monarchist **Stahlhelm** and the republican **Reichsbanner Schwarz-Rot-Gold**. Its membership grew to 100 000, but it was banned by the authorities in May 1929 after bloody disturbances between it and the police in Berlin. It nonetheless continued to operate and was involved in violent confrontations with the Nazi **SA** in the early 1930s. After **Hitler**'s takeover it ceased to function effectively and some of its members deserted to the SA.

Red Guards
Young radical Maoist activists (mostly students) who spread the **Cultural Revolution** across China, destroying whatever was 'old', and rebelling against all 'reactionary' authority. The first Red Guards were a group formed in Qinghua University in Beijing on whom **Mao Zedong** bestowed his blessing (18 Aug 1966) at a mass rally in the capital. ▷ **Maoism**

Redondo, Nicolás (c.1927–)
Spanish trade union leader. He helped revive the Spanish Socialist Party (the **PSOE**) in the late 1960s and early 1970s. Redondo was arrested 13 times during the period 1951–73, but in 1971 he became the leader of the **UGT**. In 1974 he was effectively offered the leadership of the PSOE, but turned it down. From 1984, he was increasingly critical of the socialist government, breaking with it in 1988. In the same year he organized Spain's first general strike since 1934.

rehabilitation
The (usually posthumous) restoration to Party favour, and even membership, of communists who had been purged under a previous leadership. It was most prominently applied to Soviet communist leaders executed under **Stalin**, but was also a common practice in Eastern Europe. It was noticeable, however, that it usually remained selective; not all the innocents were rehabilitated. ▷ **communism**

Rehnquist, William H(ubbs) (1924–)
US jurist. Educated at the Universities of Stanford and Harvard, he became a law clerk to Justice Robert H Jackson on the US Supreme Court before entering private practice. He served as Assistant Attorney-General from 1968 to 1971, became head of the Office of Legal Counsel of the Justice Department, and challenged many laws protecting the rights of defendants, such as Miranda v Arizona, giving him the repu-

tation of a protector of law enforcement. In 1971, he was named Associate Justice of the Supreme Court by President Richard **Nixon**. He was chosen by President Ronald **Reagan** in 1986 to succeed Warren E **Burger** as Chief Justice of the Supreme Court, a controversial nomination due to his history of extremely conservative opinions. As Chief Justice, he has presided over a Supreme Court that has followed a conservative trend away from the more liberal Warren Court.

Reich

The term used to describe the German Empire and the German national state between 1918 and 1945. The Holy Roman Empire was regarded as the First Reich, and unified Germany after 1870 was referred to as the Second Reich (*Kaiserreich*). After 1933, the enlarged Germany envisaged in **Hitler**'s plans was known as the Third Reich. The term is no longer used.

Reichsbanner Schwarz-Rot-Gold

German paramilitary league (literally, 'National Flag Black-Red-Gold'). Founded in Feb 1924, the republican *Reichsbanner* sought to provide a counter-attraction to the monarchist leagues for Weimar military veterans and youth. Organized by the **DDP**, **Centre Party** and **SPD**, but dominated by the last, its membership exceeded 3.5 million by 1932, although with just 400 000 activists. It fought the Nazi **SA** and, occasionally, the communist **Red Front** and monarchist **Stahlhelm** on the streets during the early 1930s, but was ineffective against the dismantling of republican democracy and **Hitler**'s eventual takeover. It dissolved itself in Mar 1933.

Reichstag

Literally 'imperial diet', the term refers to three German political institutions: (1) The lower, elected house of the German parliament (1871–1918). Seen by Bismarck as a symbolic concession to national and liberal sentiment, the *Reichstag*, although elected by universal male suffrage, possessed very limited functions in Imperial Germany where power rested primarily with the crown and the Emperor's ministers. However, it could block legislation and budgets and, as parties seeking an extension of parliamentary power gained a majority in the Reichstag, in 1912 a constitutional crisis, delayed by **World War I**, developed. (2) The lower, elected house of the German parliament (1920–33). In this period (the **Weimar Republic**), governments were formed by dominant coalitions in the Reichstag, but political polarization and the growing strength of anti-republican parties (**Nazi Party**, **KPD**) necessitated the conduct of government under Article 48 of the constitution (presidential emergency powers) from 1930 to 1933. (3) An assembly dominated by the Nazi Party in the Third **Reich**, 1933–45. **Hitler** periodically addressed the

Reichstag, but real power had passed to Hitler, his ministers and to party officials.

Reichstag Fire (27 Feb 1933)

The deliberate burning down of Germany's parliament building, shortly after the Nazi accession to power. A deranged Dutch ex-communist, van der Lubbe, was accused of arson and executed. The new Nazi government, insisting that the act was evidence of a wider communist conspiracy, used the situation to ban and suppress the German Communist Party (**KPD**). Communist conspiracy was certainly not behind the fire; nor were the Nazis themselves, though it was long believed to be so. It is now agreed that, however convenient the fire may have been to the regime, van der Lubbe acted alone. ▷ **Nazi Party**

Reichswehr

Literally 'national defence', this is the term used to describe the armed forces of Germany in the period 1919–35. Consisting of 100 000 soldiers and 15 000 sailors, the Reichswehr was a professional force with junior ranks serving 12 years and officers 25 years. Relations between the Reichswehr and the republic were equivocal. The officers were opposed to any open, violent challenge to the state, but secretly supported anti-republican paramilitary leagues in Germany and undertook secret rearmament in collaboration with the USSR. Allegedly 'above politics', senior *Reichswehr* officers such as **Groener** and **Schleicher** were active in late Weimar government affairs and did much indirectly to pave the way for **Hitler**'s takeover. In 1935, with rearmament, the Reichswehr, by now bound by oath of personal loyalty to Hitler, was reorganized as the **Wehrmacht**.

Reid, Sir George Houstoun (1845–1918)

British-born Australian politician. A strong supporter of free trade, in 1880 he was elected to the Legislative Assembly of New South Wales, and in 1891 succeeded Sir Henry **Parkes** as Leader of the Opposition, becoming Premier of the state from 1894 to 1899. A cautious supporter of **federation**, he moved to the first federal parliament in 1901, still representing his old constituency, and became Leader of the Opposition in the House of Representatives. He was Prime Minister of Australia (1904–5) and retired from politics in 1908. In 1909 he was appointed Australia's first High Commissioner to London, a post he held with distinction until 1916. He then took up the seat for Hanover Square in the British House of Commons, which he held until his death.

RENAMO (*Resistencia Nacional Mozambicana*)

An armed movement set up in 1976, first with Rhodesian and later with South African support, to oppose the **Frelimo** government of Mozambique. Although lacking a clear political aim, it has managed to disrupt Mozambique's economy and transport system and was responsible for pressurizing the government into signing the **Nkomati Accord**.

René, France-Albert (1935–)

Seychelles politician. Educated locally, and in Switzerland and at King's College, London, he was called to the bar in 1957. He returned to the Seychelles and entered politics, founding the socialist Seychelles People's United Party in 1964, which he led. A member of the National Assembly since 1965, he formed a coalition at independence in 1976 with his opponent James Mancham (who became President) while Rene became Prime Minister. When Mancham was abroad in 1977, René staged a coup, created a one-party state and made himself Executive President.

Renner, Karl (1870–1950)

Austrian politician. He trained as a lawyer, joined the Austrian Social Democratic Party (**SPÖ**), and became the first Chancellor of the Austrian Republic (1918–20). Imprisoned as a socialist leader, following the brief civil war (Feb 1934), he was Chancellor again (1945) after **World War II**, and first President of the new republic (1945–50).

reparations

Payments imposed on the powers defeated in war to cover the costs incurred by the victors. For example, they were levied by the Allies on Germany at the end of **World War I**, though the final sum of £6 000 million plus interest was not fixed until Apr 1921. The Dawes (1924) and Young (1929) Plans revised the payment schedule and reduced the scale of the payments, which were finally abandoned after 1932, because of the Depression.

Republic, First (Portugal) (1910–26)

The transition from the oligarchical rule of the monarchy to the pluralistic democracy of the new regime produced acute political instability because of a weak party system enhanced by the 1911 Constitution. The reforms of the Republic largely benefited the urban lower middle classes, its main constituency, spurning the aspirations of the urban working class, women, and the rural peasants and labourers. For example, the labourers' strike in Alentejo of 1911–12 was brutally suppressed. Political uncertainty, a lack of resources, and the exclusivity of the Republicans all combined to prevent change. Military discontent and Republican divisions resulted in a conservative dictatorship, Jan–May 1915. Back in power, the Republican politicians entered **World War I** in 1916 on the side of the Allies. Rocketing prices, food shortages, and heavy losses in France led to the coup under Bernardino Sidonio Pais (5 Dec 1917); this young charismatic man became the first Republican dictator of the 20c.

The so-called New Republic was a forerunner of the authoritarian and corporatist state created by **Salazar** in the 1930s. Unable to secure his power-based and thrown into crisis by the Allied victory of Nov 1918, Sidónio Pais was assassinated in Lisbon on 14 Dec 1918. From 1918 to 1926 the Republic was more unstable than ever. In 1919 there were four governments and in 1920, nine. Civil war broke out in northern Portugal, the economy collapsed and violence mounted. Several Republican politicians were murdered, including Antonio Machado Santos, the leading figure of the 1910 revolution. The failure to maintain public order and protect living standards, and the political strangehold of the PRP (preventing the emergence of other parties), alienated many of the Republic's own supporters. Though the internecine party warfare seemed remote, it reflected wider economic conflicts. The progressive governments of Dec 1923–July 1925 further consolidated the rapidly growing forces of counter-revolution. A marked swing to the Right took place in the 1920s. Following the abortive coups of Apr and July 1925, the Republic was finally overthrown by the military rising of 28 May 1926.

Republic, Second (Spain) (1931–6)

Spain's first democratic regime in nearly 60 years was established (14 Apr 1931) amidst great popular expectation following the disastrous policies of the monarchy. The Left-Republican–Socialist administrations of 1931–3 under Manuel **Azaña** made the most determined effort yet to transform Spain from a reactionary and backward society into a modern and progressive 'European' state. The failure of reform was partly due to the lack of unity and expertise within the governmental coalition, but more so to a scarcity of resources and the world depression. Above all, reform proceeded slowly because of the hostility of the traditional ruling classes to meaningful change, especially the landowners. The course of the Republic was fundamentally altered by the general election of Nov–Dec 1933. A parliamentary alliance was formed between the **Radical Republican Party** and the Catholic **CEDA**. The Centre-Right administrations of Dec 1933 to Oct 1935 moved steadily to the Right while demolishing the reforms of the first two years. This led to a major Radical schism (May 1934) and to mounting socio-economic conflict. The entry of three members of the proto-fascist CEDA into the government (4 Oct 1934) resulted in a Socialist general strike, a declaration of Catalan independence, and an armed rising in Asturias. The brutal repression of the Oct protest polarized the Republic to an unprecedented extent. As the CEDA gained more and more power at the expense of the Radicals throughout 1935, so the previously divided Left rallied to the banner of the Popular Front. In the general election of Feb 1936 the Popular Front won a narrow victory. The political climate became increasingly volatile as the weak Left-Republican governments, now bereft of Socialist support, proved unable to impose themselves. The military rising of 17–18 July 1936 resulted in a civil war that lasted until Apr 1939. The origins of the **Spanish Civil War** were overwhelmingly domestic in nature, embracing not one but several conflicts, ranging from social and political tensions to religious and regional ones.

Republic, Fourth (France)
The regime established unofficially in France in 1944 on the country's liberation; it was, however, only legally confirmed by the referendum of 13 Oct 1946, which approved the new constitution by a small majority. The republic was brought down by the Algerian crisis of 13 May 1958, which led, first, to de **Gaulle** being voted into office as the last Prime Minister of the Fourth Republic and, second, to its replacement by the Fifth Republic on 5 Oct 1958. ▷ **Republic, Fifth** (France)

Republic, Fifth (France)
The regime established in France by the referendum of 28 Sep 1958, approving the new constitution embodying the political ideas of de **Gaulle**.

Republic, Third (France)
The regime established in France on 4 Sep 1870, which lasted until the National Assembly voted full powers to **Pétain** on 10 July 1940; it remains by far the longest French regime since 1789.

Republican Party
US political party. It was formed in 1854 by Northern anti-slavery factions of the existing Whig and Democratic Parties who opposed the Fugitive Slave Act (1850) and the Kansas-Nebraska Act (1854). With the exception of four terms, the Republicans held the presidency from the end of the American Civil War until the **Great Depression**, which set the stage for the election of Franklin Delano **Roosevelt** in 1932 and 20 years of Democratic Presidents. Although the Republicans had espoused isolationism before **World War II**, they won the 1952 presidential election with the popular war hero Dwight D **Eisenhower**. The next 40 years saw a series of split governments on the national level, with the Republicans often winning the presidency while the Democrats held majorities in Congress. The **Watergate** scandal, which led to the first resignation of an American president, Richard M **Nixon**, was a black mark for the party, but it regained the presidency with the election of Ronald **Reagan** in 1980 and held it for the next 12 years through George **Bush**'s one-term administration. The party has traditionally been identified with big business rather than with labour, and favoured states' rights, limited government regulation, free market economic policies, and (in the **Cold War** period that followed World War II) a strong military and firm anticommunistic stance. It has generally had the support of voters of high socioeconomic status and of white Anglo-Saxons rather than of

ethnic minorities; however, Ronald Reagan managed to broaden the party's historical base, drawing in many so-called Reagan Democrats, who were disillusioned with the policies of Democratic President Jimmy **Carter**, and including right-wing conservatives and religious fundamentalist groups as well. ▷ **Progressive Party**

Resistance Movement (Belgium, *Weerstand*)

Clandestine opposition to the German occupation of Belgium during **World War II**, which took on serious proportions after the severe winter of 1940–1. Aid was provided to escaped prisoners of war and to Allied airmen, and there was also a lively underground press. Alongside there were sabotage and guerrilla groups, ranging from right-wing nationalist to communist; the largest was the Independence Front, with its own armed units (Patriotic Militias). The government in exile in London provided financial help; the Belgian resistance made an important contribution to the country's liberation in 1944.

Resistance Movement (France)

There was very little active resistance for the first two years of the German occupation during **World War II**, but it developed rapidly from the summer of 1942. A great number of different organizations existed, covering the whole range of political opinion from Left to Right, although after the German invasion of the USSR communist recruitment was especially high. De **Gaulle** sought to coordinate the different groups from London and then, after the Allied invasion of North Africa, from Algiers; his delegate, Jean Moulin, was able to bring them all together in the *Conseil national de la résistance* ('National Council of the Resistance') before being murdered by the Germans. As well as guerrilla warfare against the occupying forces, there was a large political dimension to the Resistance, and elaborate and idealistic programmmes were drawn up; only some of these found any embodiment after 1944. ▷ **World War II**

Resistance Movement (Netherlands, *Het Verzet*)

Also known as the 'Illegality' and the 'Underground', most Dutch resistance to the German occupation during **World War II** was clandestine. Only a few strikes, notably on the railways from Sep 1944, and limited actions by individual students, doctors and churchmen in particular, were public displays of resistance. The underground resistance was active, however, especially in producing and distributing newspapers, and looking after the several hundred thousand people, many of them Jewish, trying to evade the German authorities. Help was also provided for Allied airmen, and espionage work was carried out, though not always with success. Finance was provided by the National Support Fund (*Nationaal Steunfonds*). ▷ **Englandspiel; Frank, Anne; Resistance Movement** (Belgium); **Resistance Movement** (France)

Restitution Agreement (Sep 1952)

The settlement reached between representatives of the State of Israel and Chancellor **Adenauer** of the Federal Republic of Germany. Signed in Luxembourg, the agreement committed Germany to make material reparations to Israel, deemed to represent the Jewish people, and to another Jewish body representing the Diaspora, for persecutions suffered by the Jews under the Third Reich. As a result, and despite some opposition in both Israel and Germany, large sums of money were paid out to Israel and to individual survivors of **World War II** in subsequent years. ▷ **Holocaust; Israel, State of**

Restoration System (1875–1923)

Spanish political system. The rotation in power of the two dynastic parties — the Liberal-Conservatives and the Liberals — through an institutionalized form of electoral corruption. Election results were fixed by the Minister of the Interior through the local party bosses (or *caciques*). This was known as the *turno pacifico* ('peaceful rotation'). Although it quelled the interventionism of the army and brought a measure of political stability, it effectively excluded the non-monarchical opposition from the political process. The system was dismantled by the dictatorship of **Primo de Rivera** in 1923, though the caciques continued to exercise considerable influence under the Second Republic. ▷ **Republic, Second** (Spain)

Revolution of 1905

A series of nationwide strikes, demonstrations, and mutinies in Russia, given added stimulus by the massacre by soldiers of workers demonstrating peacefully in St Petersburg on what came to be called 'Bloody Sunday' (9 Jan 1905 new style). Faced with continuing popular unrest, Tsar **Nicholas II** was forced to make some marginal concessions, including the legalization of most political parties, and qualified elections to a form of national assembly — the **Duma**. ▷ **Russian Revolution**

Revolution of 1918 (Germany)

In the hour of Germany's defeat in **World War I**, attempts to preserve the monarchy failed in the face of growing civil disorder. On 9 Nov a republic was declared by the **SPD** leader **Scheidemann** and a provisional government of majority and independent socialists formed. Although the Workers' and Soldiers' Councils, which were established spontaneously at this time, bore a superficial resemblance to the Russian soviets, the former supported the principle of parliamentary government in Dec 1918 and a National Assembly met in Weimar on 19 Jan 1919 to draft a constitution. Controversy has raged over how far the Social Democrats were wise to restrict major socio-economic change and changes in non-parliamentary institutions (army, Civil Service, judiciary) at this point, as well as relying on monarchist and right-radical military forces to restrain the radical left. The survival of many monarchist institutions and grandees was subsequently to weaken the **Weimar Republic**.

Revolution of 1989 (Germany)

Once the Soviet government under Mikhail **Gorbachev** had declared it would not intervene in the affairs of its Eastern European allies, the future of East **Germany** (German Democratic Republic) was in doubt. Militarily dependent on the USSR and economically dependent on the Federal Republic of Germany and the USSR, East Germany's economy and society were wracked by increasing difficulties. During the summer of 1989, East German tourists in Hungary spilled across the recently demilitarized border into Austria and also invaded Federal German embassies in Prague and Warsaw. As East Germany's population haemorrhaged, widespread civil unrest broke out within the country and culminated in the storming of the **Berlin Wall** on 9 Nov. The communist regime collapsed and unification with the Federal Republic of **Germany** followed in 1990.

Revolutions of 1848–9 (Italy)

The series of insurrections that broke out in the mid-19c in all the states of the Italian Peninsula against a backdrop of similar disturbances in France, the Habsburg Empire and the German Confederation. A growing distaste for Austrian rule in the Kingdom of Lombardy-Venetia and for Habsburg hegemony elsewhere in the peninsula combined with incipient liberalism and nationalism, and separatist and economic grievances to stimulate protest and revolt. The granting of concessions by many rulers simply served to encourage greater demands from the populace and briefly most Italian states fell under some form of constitutional or republican control. However, regional and ideological differences, the fear of the propertied classes of radical social change and the re-establishment of conservative governments in Paris and Vienna led to the suppression of revolt and the restoration of the old order in almost every state: only in the Kingdom of Sardinia was there any significant change, the Statuto granted by Charles Albert being retained as the basis for constitutional government.

Rexism

Belgian fascist political movement, founded by Léon **Degrelle**, and named after his publishing firm. Rexism grew out of right-wing Roman Catholic circles in Walloon (French-speaking) Belgium in the 1930s. In 1936 the Rex Party contested the national elections, and gained several seats in both chambers. During the late 1930s the party became increasing fascist and authoritarian, and during **World War II** collaborated fully with the Nazi occupation forces. By 1944 it had lost all its support.

Reynaud, Paul (1878–1966)
French politician. Elected a Deputy in 1919, he sat as an independent on the centre right, frequently holding office, notably as Finance Minister (1930 and 1938–40) and Colonial Minister (1931–2). During his second term as Finance Minister he instigated a remarkable recovery from the economic crisis in which France found herself after the **Popular Front** experiment. He was influenced by de **Gaulle**'s advocacy of armoured warfare, and opposed appeasement. His appointment as Prime Minister (Mar 1940) was seen as a move towards a more vigorous prosecution of the war, but he had achieved little before the German onslaught led to his fall, and replacement by **Pétain**, who asked for an armistice, which Reynaud had refused to do. He was imprisoned by the Germans during the war, re-entering politics after 1944, but without regaining his former influence. ▷ **Independents; World War II**

Reynolds, Albert (1932–)
Irish politician. His early career was as an entrepreneur in the entertainment and food-manufacturing industries. He became **Fianna Fáil** MP for Longford-West Meath (1977) and was Minister for Industry and Commerce (1987–9) and Finance (1989–91). Dismissed after an unsuccessful challenge to Charles **Haughey** (1991), he nevertheless won the party leadership by a large majority after Haughey's resignation (Feb 1992), becoming Prime Minister the same year.

Reza Shah Pahlevi (1877–1944)
Shah of Iran (1925/41). In 1921 the then Reza Khan, as Commander of the Cossack Brigade in Persia, brought down the ruling Qajar Dynasty by encouraging the last Qajar, Shah Ahmad, to leave the country and by establishing a new government. In the ensuing four years, Reza Khan wooed the Persian religious establishment to such effect that he was able to boast their support for his government at the beginning of 1925 and be crowned Shah in Dec of the same year. He paid scant attention, however, to the susceptibilities of this same religious establishment after his assumption of full power. Amongst other things, he set about the secularization of religious law and began harking back to Iran's imperial past with his adoption of Pahlavi (the name of the language of Persia prior to Islam) as his family name, rather than recognizing the Islamic orientation of the country as a whole; both actions augured ill for the future. Reza Shah himself was however able to deprive the religious leaders of much of their former influence, an influence they only began to regain after Reza's abdication and exile in 1941 when the British and Russians occupied the country (renamed Iran in 1935) during **World War II**. He was succeeded by his son, Muhammad Reza.

Rhee, Syngman (1875–1965)

Korean politician. Imprisoned (1897–1904) for his part in an independence campaign, he later went to the USA, returning to Japanese-annexed Korea in 1910. After the unsuccessful rising of 1919, he became President of the exiled Korean Provisional Government. On Japan's surrender (1945) he returned to become the first elected President of South Korea (1948). Re-elected for a fourth term (1960), he was obliged to resign after only one month, following major riots and the resignation of his cabinet. He died, in exile, in Honolulu.

Rhineland

German territory largely to the west of the River Rhine demilitarized and occupied by the victorious Allies from 10 Jan 1920. Governed by an Inter-Allied High Commission based in Koblenz, a customs frontier was established between the Rhineland and the rest of Germany. French attempts to establish a separate Rhine Republic failed and the occupation forces withdrew between 1926 and 1930. In Mar 1936 **Hitler** violated the area's demilitarized status (Treaty of **Versailles**, **Locarno Pact**) when troops were ordered back into the territory.

Rhodes, Cecil (John) (1853–1902)

South African politician. After studying in Oxford, he entered the Cape House of Assembly, securing Bechuanaland as a protectorate (1885) and the charter for the British South Africa Company (1889), whose territory was later to be named after him, as Rhodesia. In 1890 he became Prime Minister of Cape Colony, but was forced to resign in 1896 because of complications arising from the **Jameson Raid**. He was a conspicuous figure during the Boer War of 1899–1902, when he organized the defences during the Siege of **Kimberley**. He died at Muizenberg, Cape Colony, and in his will founded scholarships at Oxford for Americans, Germans, and colonials ('Rhodes scholars'). ▷ **Boer Wars**

Rhodesia Crisis

The series of events that began with the declaration by Prime Minister Ian **Smith** of a Unilateral Declaration of Independence (11 Nov 1965), following the Rhodesian Government's failure to agree with successive British Administrations on a constitutional independence settlement that ensured the continuance of white supremacy. The British Government was successful in gaining **UN** support for sanctions while ruling out the use of force and, in 1966 and 1968, Smith engaged with Prime Minister Harold **Wilson** in (ultimately unsuccessful) attempts to resolve the crisis. An agreement was reached with Edward **Heath**'s Conservative Government in 1971, but was ruled out after an independent fact-finding mission determined that it would be unacceptable to the black majority. The growing influence of the **ANC** (African National Congress), and the withdrawal of the Portuguese from Angola and Mozambique, served to remind Smith of his isolationism, and in 1977 he announced that he was willing to enter into new talks on a one-man, one-vote basis, and released nationalist leaders Ndabaningi **Sithole** and Joshua **Nkomo** as a sign of good faith. However, they initially refused to participate in negotiations, and the escalation of terrorist activities continued unabated despite Smith having attained in 1978 an internal settlement, thus providing for multiracial government, with the moderate Sithole and Bishop Abel **Muzorewa.** The return of a Conservative Government in 1979 provided the springboard for fresh talks and a new settlement, leading to elections in 1980 that were won by the former Marxist guerrilla leader, Robert **Mugabe**.

Rhodesian Front (RF)

The Rhodesian political party formed in 1962 to oppose the relatively liberal United Federal Party, with Winston Field as its leader. Ian **Smith** replaced him in a putsch in 1964 and led Rhodesia to its **UDI** (Unilateral Declaration of Independence). The RF, which gained a majority of seats in the 1962 general election, made a clean sweep of all contested seats thereafter and sought to preserve white political and economic dominance in the country. In 1977, however, under pressure of civil war and outside influence, it accepted the principle of universal adult suffrage and attempted to devise an 'internal settlement'. At independence in 1980, it changed its name to Republican Front and soon afterwards to Conservative Alliance of Zimbabwe.

Ribbentrop, Joachim von (1893–1946)

German Nazi politician. He became a member of the **Nazi Party** in 1932, and as **Hitler**'s adviser in foreign affairs, was responsible in 1935 for the Anglo-German naval pact. He became Ambassador to Britain (1936) and Foreign Minister (1938–45). Captured by the British in 1945, he was condemned and executed at the **Nuremberg Trials**. ▷ **World War II**

Rickover, Hyman George (1900–86)

Russian-born US naval engineering officer. He graduated from the US Naval Academy in 1922, and in 1929 received a master's degree in electrical engineering from Columbia University. He led the team that adapted nuclear reactors as a means of ship-propulsion and developed the world's first nuclear submarine, the USS *Nautilus*, launched in 1954.

Ridgway, Matthew B(unker) (1895–1993)

US general. Educated at the US Military Academy at West Point, he commanded the 82nd Airborne Division in Sicily (1943), and Normandy (1944). He commanded the 18th Airborne Corps in the North-West Europe campaign (1944–5) and the US 8th Army in **UN** operations in

Korea (1950). He succeeded Douglas **MacArthur** in command of US and UN forces (1951), and was supreme allied commander Europe in succession to **Eisenhower** (1952–3), and Army Chief of Staff (1953). He received the Presidential Medal of Freedom in 1986.

Rio de Janeiro Treaty (1947)
The Inter-American Treaty of Reciprocal Assistance, signed in Rio, which enshrines principles of hemispheric defence laid down during **World War II**, especially a US-Brazilian alliance. It provides for certain types of mutual assistance in the case of an armed attack on any American state from outside the region and for mutual consultation in the event of any aggression between them or warlike action affecting territories situated outside them. It was the first permanent collective defence treaty signed by the USA and has remained the cornerstone of its military commitment to Latin America and the institutional basis for its hegemony. It has been applied on 16 occasions since 1948, in all cases to long-standing inter-American disputes, and to incidents within the Caribbean and Central American regions. It was not, however, invoked during the Falklands/Malvinas conflict. Directed mainly against Cuba, Latin American diplomats have argued that it has disguised, but not modified, the extent of US hegemony in Latin America. Since the breakup of the USSR, its purpose has become more questionable. ▷ **Falklands War**

Riom Trial (1942)
The trial by the **Vichy** regime of General **Gamelin** and the leading figures of France's pre-war governments, notably **Blum** and **Daladier**, held responsible for the defeat of 1940; it was abandoned when it proved embarrassing for the military and for many who were in positions of authority under Vichy, but the defendants remained imprisoned, and were later handed over to the Germans. ▷ **World War II**

Ripka, Hubert (1895–1958)
Czechoslovak journalist and politician. Prominent in the National Socialist Party (totally different from **Hitler**'s of the same name), he was given a place in **Beneš**'s government in exile during **World War II**. Returning to Czechoslovakia in 1945, he became Minister of Foreign Trade until Feb 1948 when he joined the group of democratic politicians who tried to force an election by resigning. Since they constituted a minority, the **February Revolution** went the other way. Ripka found himself, like others, forced once again to flee abroad.

Rishon Massacre (Mar 1991)
The murder, at a labour market in Rishon le Zion, of seven Arab workmen from the **Gaza Strip** by a 22-year-old Israeli, Ami Popper, served to

refocus political attention on the conditions of Palestinians under Israeli occupation after the distraction of the 1991 Gulf War.

Roberts (of Kandahar, Pretoria, and Waterford), Frederick Sleigh Roberts, 1st Earl (1832–1914)
British field marshal. He took an active part in the **Indian Uprising** of 1857–8, for which he was decorated with the Victoria Cross in 1858. He became Commander-in-Chief in India (1885–93), and served as Supreme Commander in South Africa during the Boer War, relieving the Siege of **Kimberley** (1900). He was created earl in 1901, and died while visiting troops in the field in France. ▷ **Afghan Wars; Boer Wars**

Robinson, Arthur Napoleon (Ray) (1926–)
Trinidad and Tobago politician. Educated in Trinidad and at Oxford, he qualified as a barrister. On his return to the West Indies, he became politically active and in 1967, on independence, was Deputy Leader of the moderate-centrist People's National Movement (PNM). In 1984, with other colleagues, he broke away to form a left-of-centre coalition which became the National Alliance for Reconstruction (NAR), and which in the 1986 general election swept the PNM from power, making Robinson Prime Minister. Wounded in the Aug 1990 attempted coup, he fought another election in Dec 1991, but he and the NAR were ousted by a rejuvenated PNM under Patrick Manning.

Robinson, Mary (1944–)
Irish politician. She trained as a lawyer and was Professor of Law at Trinity College, Dublin, from 1969. She was a member of the Irish Senate (1969–89) and participated in numerous legal associations in the European Community (**EC**). She became an activist on many social issues, including women's and single-parents' rights and the decriminalization of homosexuality. Nominated by the Labour Party, from which she had resigned in 1985 over the **Anglo-Irish Agreement**, she unexpectedly defeated the **Fianna Fáil** candidate Brian Lenihan in the presidential elections of Nov 1990.

Roca–Runciman Pact (May 1933)
A commercial treaty between Britain and Argentina, referred to by the names of the chief negotiators, Vice-President Julio Argentino Roca (Argentina) and Walter Runciman (Britain). The pact guaranteed Argentina a share of the British meat market in return for various economic concessions. Nevertheless, the debates over the pact weakened the *Concordancia* or 'coalition' government of General Augustín Justo, which was faced with a vigorous nationalist campaign.

Rocard, Michel (1930–)
French politician. He trained at the Ecole National d'Administration, where he was a classmate of Jacques **Chirac**, and in 1967 became leader of the Unified Socialist Party (PSU). He joined the Socialist Party (PS) in 1973, emerging as leader of its moderate social democratic wing, and unsuccessfully challenged François **Mitterrand** for the party's presidential nomination in 1981. After serving as Minister of Planning and Regional Development (1981–3) and Agriculture (1983–5) in the ensuing Mitterrand administration, he resigned in Apr 1985 in opposition to the government's expedient introduction of proportional representation. In May 1988, however, as part of a strategy termed the 'opening to the centre', he was appointed Prime Minister by President Mitterrand. He was replaced as Prime Minister by Mme Edith Cresson in 1991. ▷ **Socialist Party**

Rodney, Walter (1942–80)
Guyanese historian and politician. Formerly Professor of African History at the University of Dar es Salaam, Rodney provoked a riot when he was deported from Jamaica in 1968 for his supposed connections with **Black Power**. Although debarred from holding the history chair at the University of Guyana, he returned to his homeland and founded the Working People's Alliance which was antipathetic to the policies of **Burnham**'s ruling **People's National Congress**. The author of *How Europe Underdeveloped Africa* (1972), he was killed by a bomb in mysterious circumstances in Guyana.

Roe v Wade (1973)
US Supreme Court decision legalizing abortion. It struck down state laws which prohibited abortion within the first three months of pregnancy on the grounds that the right to privacy, which included the right to have an abortion, was protected by due process.

Roh Tae Woo (1932–)
South Korean politician. He was educated at the Korean Military Academy (1951–5), where he was a classmate of a future president, **Chun Doo-hwan**. He fought briefly in the **Korean War** and was a battalion commander during the **Vietnam War**. He became commanding general of the Capital Security Command (1979), from which position he helped General Chun seize power in the coup of 1979–80. He retired from the army in 1981 and successively served, under President Chun, as Minister for National Security and Foreign Affairs (1981–2) and for Home Affairs (from 1982). He was elected Chairman of the ruling Democratic Justice Party in 1985 and in 1987, following serious popular disturbances, drew up a political reform package which restored democracy to the country. He was elected President in 1987.

Röhm, Ernst (1887–1934)
German soldier, Nazi politician and paramilitary leader. He became an early supporter of **Hitler** and played a vital role in fostering good relations between the **Nazi Party** and the Bavarian authorities up until Nov 1923. The organizer and commander of the **SA** or stormtroopers ('Brownshirts') during the mid-1920s and from 1931 to 1934, his plans to pursue policies independently of the NSDAP and his wish to supplant the traditional army, led to his execution on Hitler's orders, in Munich. ▷ **Night of the Long Knives**

Rojo, Vicente (1894–1966)
Spanish soldier. The most brilliant strategist on the Republican side during the **Spanish Civil War**. He organized the remarkable defence of Madrid in Nov 1936 as well as the Jarama and Guadalajara campaigns of 1937. Having been made Chief of the General Staff in May 1937, he not only reorganized the Popular Army, but planned the offensives of Brunete, Teruel, and the Ebro. He returned to Spain from exile in 1957 and lived under virtual house arrest until his death in 1966.

Rokossovsky, Konstantin Konstantinovich (1896–1968)
Russian soldier. Born in Warsaw of a Polish father and a Russian mother, he served in **World War I** in the tsarist army and joined the Red Guards in 1917. He served in the Red Army cavalry during the **Russian Civil War** and after, but was lucky to survive imprisonment during the **Stalin** purges. In **World War II** he was one of the defenders of Moscow, played a leading part in the Battle of **Stalingrad** (1942–3), recaptured Orel and Warsaw, and led the Russian race for Berlin. In 1944 he was promoted Marshal of the USSR and then served as Commander-in-Chief of Soviet forces in Poland (1945–9). In 1949 he was appointed Polish Minister of Defence as Stalin's man in Warsaw, a post he was made to resign in 1956 during the anti-Soviet unrest in Poland, as part of the bargain under which **Gomułka** became Premier, with greater control over Polish domestic affairs in return for supporting Soviet foreign policy. Rokossovsky then became a Deputy Minister of Defence of the USSR from 1956 to 1962, apart from a brief period in a military command in Transcaucasia.

Romania
A republic in south-east Europe, on the Balkan Peninsula and the lower Danube. Romania was formed in 1862 after the unification of Wallachia and Moldavia, and a monarchy was created in 1866. The country joined the Allies in **World War I**, and united with Transylvania, Bessarabia, and Bucovina in 1918. In **World War II**, however, Romania supported Germany, and Soviet forces occupied the country in 1944; after the war territories were lost to Russia, Hungary and Bulgaria. The monarchy was abolished and a People's Republic declared in 1947, and in 1965

Romania became a Socialist Republic. From the 1960s onwards it became increasingly independent of the USSR, with relationships being forged with China and several Western countries. The leading political force at this time was the Romanian Communist Party, led by dictator Nicolae **Ceauşescu**, but in 1989 violent repression of protest, resulting in the deaths of thousands of demonstrators, sparked a popular uprising and the overthrow of the Ceauşescu regime. A provisional government led by previously imprisoned dissidents promised free elections in 1990, but unrest and demonstrations continued. In 1991 the country became a multiparty democracy, with a President as head of state.

Romanov, Grigori Vasilevich (1923–)
Soviet politician. The son of a Novgorod peasant, he educated himself as a shipbuilding engineer at night classes and by correspondence. It was 1955 before he agreed to be a party functionary, but by 1970 he was in charge of the Leningrad party as First Secretary and by 1976 in the **Politburo**. Yuri **Andropov** made him a secretary of the Central Committee in 1983, a jumping-off platform for the general secretaryship, but he lacked Mikhail **Gorbachev**'s skill and commitment to change and was simply brushed aside for the party succession in 1985.

Romanov Dynasty
The second (and last) Russian royal dynasty (1613–1917). The Romanovs ruled as virtually absolute autocrats, allowing no constitutional or legal checks on their political power. Even when **Nicholas II** conceded the establishment of a national assembly or **Duma** in 1905, he allowed it little power in practice. The dynasty ended with Nicholas II's abdication in Feb 1917, and his execution by Bolshevik guards in July 1918. ▷ **February Revolution; Nicholas I; Revolution of 1905; Russian Revolution**

Rommel, Erwin (Johannes Eugen) (1891–1944)
German field marshal and Nazi sympathizer. Educated at Tübingen, he fought in **World War I** and taught at Dresden Military Academy. He commanded **Hitler**'s headquarters guard during the early occupations, and led a Panzer division during the 1940 invasion of France. He then commanded the **Afrika Corps**, where he achieved major successes. Eventually driven into retreat by a strongly reinforced 8th Army, the 'Desert Fox' was withdrawn, a sick man, from North Africa, and appointed to an Army Corps command in France. Returning home wounded in 1944, he condoned the plot against Hitler's life. After its failure and his implication in it, he committed suicide at Herrlingen. ▷ **El Alamein, Battle of; World War II**

Roosevelt, (Anna) Eleanor (1884–1962)
US humanitarian and diplomat. The niece of Theodore **Roosevelt** and wife of Franklin D **Roosevelt**, she became active in politics during her husband's illness from polio and proved herself invaluable to him as an adviser on social issues when he became President. In 1941 she became Assistant Director of the Office of Civilian Defence and after her husband's death in 1945 extended the scope of her activities, becoming a US delegate to the UN Assembly (1945–53, 1961), chairman of the UN Human Rights Commission (1946–51), and US representative to the General Assembly (1946–52).

Roosevelt, Franklin D(elano) ('FDR') (1882–1945)
US politician and 32nd President. The fifth cousin of Theodore **Roosevelt**. He became a lawyer (1907), a New York State Senator (1910–13), and Assistant Secretary of the Navy (1913–20), and was Democratic candidate for the vice-presidency in 1920. Stricken with polio in 1921, he recovered partial use of his legs and went on to become Governor of New York (1929–33). During his first 'hundred days' as President (1933–45), he bombarded the economic crises with his **New Deal** for national recovery (1933), and became the only President to be re-elected three times. At the outbreak of **World War II** he strove to avoid US involvement and instead provided economic resources to the Allies in the form of a 'lend-lease' agreement, but Japan's attack on **Pearl Harbor** (1941) left him no choice and the US entered the war. He met with **Churchill** and **Stalin** at the **Tehran Conference** (1943) and **Yalta Conference** (1945) to formulate post-war plans, including the **UN**, but died three weeks before the German surrender. Throughout his presidency, his wife, Eleanor **Roosevelt**, was active in human rights and after his death became the US delegate to the **UN**.

Roosevelt Corollary (1904)
Amendment to the Monroe Doctrine enunciated by Theodore **Roosevelt** which stated that the USA had a duty to prevent political instability and financial mismanagement in the countries of its Caribbean 'backyard'. In its crudest form it was a justification for Roosevelt's 'big stick' and **Taft**'s 'dollar diplomacy' policies, and sanctioned US military intervention in Haiti (1915–34) and the Dominican Republic (1916–24). Such interference was theoretically reversed by F D **Roosevelt**'s 'good neighbour' policy of 1934 but this has not precluded further overt and covert interventions in Guatemala (1954), Cuba (1961), Dominican Republic (1965), Nicaragua (1979–87), Grenada (1983) and Panama (1989).

Rose-Innes, Sir James (1855–1942)
South African judge. Educated at the University of the Cape of Good Hope, he became Attorney-General (1890–93 and 1900–02), and then

Judge President (later Chief Justice) of the Supreme Court of the Transvaal (1902–10), Judge of Appeal (1910–14), and Chief Justice of the Union of South Africa (1914–27). He advocated a liberal policy towards the Africans and, as head of a strong bench, was probably the greatest of all South African judges. His opinions are notable for their clarity and their willingness to rely on both the English and Roman-Dutch traditions in South African law.

Rosenberg, Alfred (1893–1946)
German Nazi ideologue. A fervent advocate of national socialism, he joined the **Nazi Party** in 1920, edited Nazi journals, for a time (1933) directed the party's foreign policy, and in 1934 was given control of its cultural and political education policy. In his *The Myth of the 20th Century* (1930) he expounded the extreme Nazi doctrines which he later put into practice in eastern Europe, for which crime he was hanged at Nuremberg in 1946. ▷ **Nuremberg Trials**

Rosenberg Affair (1953)
US treason trial. Julius and Ethel Rosenberg were found guilty, like Klaus Fuchs in Britain, of passing atomic bomb secrets to the USSR. The worth of the information they had passed to the Russians was dubious and the sentence of death passed by Judge Irving Kaufman was more a measure of US fears of **communism** and the anger felt at betrayal than a judicial decision. The Rosenbergs' prison letters aroused great sympathy in Europe, and their execution compounded the fears aroused by McCarthyism. ▷ **McCarthy, Joseph**

'Rosie the Riveter'
US epithet. The generic name given to US women employed in defence production during **World War II**. By 1944, over 50 per cent of workers in aircraft manufacture and shipbuilding were women and the number of married women in work had increased from around 15 per cent to almost 25 per cent. Their level of performance, in jobs for which they had previously been considered unsuitable, was so high that attitudes towards women in work were permanently altered.

Round Table Conferences (1930–2)
A series of meetings in London between British government and Indian representatives to discuss the future constitution of India. It was prompted by the Simon Commission Report (1930) on the working of the 1919 Government of India Act. It helped in the formulation of the 1935 Government of India Act. ▷ **Government of India Acts; Montagu–Chelmsford Reforms**

Rowell–Sirois Commission (1940)

Canadian Royal Commission on national economic problems. Appointed by Mackenzie **King** in 1937, the commission was chaired by N W Rowell and, after his resignation in 1938, by J N Sirois. Its remit was to find a way by which the Dominion government, after R B **Bennett**'s New Deal had been declared unconstitutional, could administer federal aid without infringing provincial rights. The commission's report analysed regional economic inequalities in depth and recommended a fundamental revision in the balance of federal and provincial powers. In particular it suggested that the Dominion should take over responsibility for social services (the major area of provincial expenditure), while in return the provinces should cease to levy income taxes and succession duties. A federal-provincial conference called to discuss the report in 1941 was torpedoed by the hostility of Ontario, Quebec and British Columbia (while Alberta had already boycotted the Commission itself), but in 1946 new revenue sharing proposals were accepted by all the provinces except Ontario, which acceded in 1950, and Quebec, which made its own agreement in 1954.

Rowlatt Act (1919)

Passed by the British colonial government, the Anarchical and Revolutionary Crimes Act, popularly known by the name of its author, Sir Sidney Rowlatt, made the suspension of civil liberties during wartime by the Defence of India Act of 1915 a permanent feature of India's peacetime constitution. The Act aroused opposition amongst Indian nationalist politicians and caused M K **Gandhi** to organize the first all-India **Satyagraha**, an initially peaceful protest involving strikes, demonstrations and the deliberate courting of arrest, in opposition to the measure. Popular support was widespread, partly because of economic distress but also due to anger amongst the Muslim community at the proposed post-war division of the empire of the Ottoman Sultan, Khalifa, the protector of Islam's holy places in the Middle East and the organization and involvement of India's Sikh community as part of a general movement of religious revivalism in India at this time. Unfortunately, the Satyagraha was accompanied by violent incidents, some of them committed by Ghadrites, which led to the imposition of martial law in the Punjab and the infamous Amritsar Massacre. Shocked at this outcome, Gandhi called the Satyagraha a 'Himalayan blunder', but the real blunder was committed by the British, as clumsy attempts to cover up the massacre and to absolve those involved from responsibility convinced many moderate and reformist Indian politicians (including Gandhi himself) of the impossibility of Indians ever securing justice under colonial rule.

Roy Manabendra Nath (Narendranath Bhattacharya) (1887–1954)

Indian political leader. Involved with terrorist groups against British rule, he was sent in 1915 to request aid from the Germans in Batavia.

His mission having failed, he arrived in San Francisco in 1916, where he changed his name. He then went to Mexico, where he helped to found the Mexican Communist Party, and to Moscow, where he became a member of the Executive Committee of the **Comintern**, and founded the Communist Party of India in Tashkent (1920). He broke with the Comintern in 1929 but was arrested and imprisoned on his return to India. After independence, he abandoned **communism**.

RSS (*Rashtriya Swayamsevak Sangh*, 'National Self-Service Society')
A militant Hindu cultural organization, founded in Nagpur in the 1930s by K B Hedgewar with help from B S **Moonje**, organized into cells, whose members practise martial arts, and which promotes an exclusively Hindu definition of the Indian nation. By 1940 its membership numbered 100 000 under the leadership of Golwalkar. The **Jan Sangh**, a political party which was originally an offshoot of the RSS, is now an independent political party but the RSS provides the Jan Sangh with the most vigorous canvassers at election time. ▷ **Hindu Mahasabha**

Ruby, Jack (1911–64)
US assassin of Lee Harvey **Oswald**. He shot Oswald at close range two days after the assassination of President **Kennedy**. A nightclub owner, Ruby was reputedly also a small-town gangster with Mafia links, who claimed to be avenging Jacqueline Kennedy.

Rundstedt, (Karl Rudolf) Gerd von (1875–1953)
German field marshal. He served in **World War I**, and in the early 1930s became Military Commander of Berlin. In 1939 he directed the attacks on Poland and France. Checked in the Ukraine in 1941, he was relieved of his command, but in 1942 was given a new command in France. He was recalled after the success of the 1944 Allied invasion, but returned to direct the Ardennes offensive. War crimes proceedings against him were dropped on the grounds of his ill health. ▷ **World War II**

Rushdie, (Ahmad) Salman (1947–)
British writer. Born in Bombay in India of Muslim parents, he was educated there and in England, at Rugby and Cambridge. He became widely known after the publication of his second novel, *Midnight's Children* (1981). *The Satanic Verses* (1988) caused worldwide controversy because of its treatment of Islam from a secular point of view, and in Feb 1989 he was forced to go into hiding because of a sentence of death passed on him by Ayatollah **Khomeini** of Iran.

Russian Civil War
A war which took place in Russia following the 1917 **October Revolution**. Anti-Bolshevik forces (Whites) led mostly by tsarist generals mounted a

series of military and political campaigns against the new Soviet regime, supported by the intervention of Allied troops with the support of the governments of Britain, France, the USA, and Japan. They were opposed by the Soviet **Red Army**, created by **Trotsky**, which successfully fought back against them between 1918 and 1922. There were five main theatres of war: the Caucasus and southern Russia; the Ukraine; the Baltic provinces; the Far North; and Siberia. After the end of **World War I**, the military justification for intervention disappeared and the Allied governments eventually lost heart. The Red Army, which increasingly enjoyed more popular support than the Whites, gradually defeated the counter-revolutionary forces on all fronts, and established Soviet military and political power throughout the whole of Russia and its borderlands, with the exception of Poland, Finland, and the Baltic states, which received their independence. Among the legacies of the war was continuing Soviet–Western mutual suspicion, and the inclusion within the USSR of peoples such as the Ukrainians, Armenians and Georgians, who had tried to regain their independence, which had been lost to Tsarist Russia. ▷ **Bolsheviks; Czechoslovak Legion; Russian Revolution; White Russians**

Russian Constituent Assembly (1918)

Russia's first-ever, genuinely representative, constitution-making body. One reason for the **February Revolution** (1917) was Tsar **Nicholas II**'s autocratic government. What emerged was the **Russian Provisional Government**, which was to hold power until a more democratic system could be decided upon by a representative constituent assembly. This was elected (Nov 1917) on the basis of proportional representation. The Socialist Revolutionaries gained over half of the seats (380 out of 703); the **Bolsheviks** less than a quarter (168). **Lenin** still let the Assembly meet in Jan 1918 in the half-hearted hope that it would legitimize his new government. When it refused on the first day, he dissolved it on the second, thus ending all democratic experimentation for the next 70 years.

Russian Orthodox Church

A Church originating in missionary activity on the part of the see of Constantinople and in political interest on the part of Kiev Rus in the 10c. In 988 Prince Vladimir declared Christianity the official faith; in the 14c Moscow became the see of the metropolitan; and in the 15c the Church effectively declared itself autonomous. In 1721 Peter I, 'the Great' engineered a Spiritual Regulation that virtually brought the Patriarch and the church under the tsar's control right until 1917. Subsequently the church was separated from the state and suffered considerable persecution. Gaining some recognition as a result of its support for **Stalin** during the Great Patriotic War (1941–5), it was still largely controlled by government agencies. In the mid-20c there was some revival of interest in the church on the part of the intelligentsia, conscious of the role it formerly played in Russian art and culture. The contemporary Russian

Church retains its former doctrine and liturgy, but since **Gorbachev**'s time and the collapse of **communism** it has become more popular, not least among young people.

Russian Provisional Government (1917)
The government that was supposed to rule Russia until the **Russian Constituent Assembly** could produce a legitimate alternative, although its interim approach to revolutionary events flawed it from the start. It discussed minor issues, rather than making the big decisions that were required. It also lacked military power, was constantly opposed by the **Soviets**, and was too slow to move from modest liberal to reasonable centrist. In the end, it was swept away by **Lenin** and his **Bolsheviks**.

Russian Revolution (1917)
The revolution which overthrew the Russian imperial regime and brought to power the first communist government. Mass demonstrations of discontented and revolutionary workers and soldiers in Petrograd led to the abdication of **Nicholas II** in Feb 1917. There followed a period of power-sharing between a liberal-minded provisional government and the more socialist Petrograd Soviet, known as 'dual power'. **Lenin**'s **Bolsheviks** soon refused to collaborate, and in Oct led an insurgency of armed workers, soldiers and sailors, removing the provisional government, seizing political power and establishing the first Soviet government. This very quickly shaped the revolution to its own Leninist/Stalinist prescription. ▷ **April Theses; February Revolution; July Days; Mensheviks; October Revolution; tsar**

Russo-Finnish War (Winter War) (1939–40)
The war between the USSR and Finland during the winter of 1939–40. Soviet forces invaded Finland in order to secure Finnish territory from which to defend Leningrad against a possible German attack. In spite of courageous and damaging Finnish resistance and early Russian bungling and because of lack of support from Britain and France, Finland capitulated (Mar 1940) and was forced to cede valuable territory to the USSR. ▷ **Continuation Wars; World War II**

Russo-Japanese War (1904–5)
The war between an expanding Russian Empire and a modernizing Japan over rival territorial claims and imperial ambitions in northern China. Tsar **Nicholas II** and most of his ministers were keen on a war that they expected to win and that they hoped would divert attention from internal unrest, but it turned out to be a series of military and naval disasters for Russia; it had little popular support, and was marked by ineffectual command and political confusion. The war ended in Japanese victory

with the Treaty of **Portsmouth** (1905). It also precipitated the Russian **Revolution of 1905**.

Ruthenia, Emergence and Disappearance of (1918–45)

An ethnically mixed area of about half a million people, moved through four countries' control in a quarter of a century. In 1918 Ruthenia was part of Austria-Hungary but was summarily transferred to the new Czechoslovakia. Between Sep 1938 and Mar 1939 it hovered uncertainly on the brink of independence, which it enjoyed for a few days, before it passed to Hungary. In 1945 it was transferred to the Ukraine, part of the USSR. Its population was 60 per cent Ruthenian, related to Ukrainians, but it had Slovak and Hungarian minorities (and Polish). It was neither Catholic nor Orthodox, but Greek Catholic (Uniate). Small and divided, its fate was decided by crude power politics. Post-1991, it provided some of the internal drive towards the separation of the Ukraine from Russia.

Rwanda

A landlocked republic in central Africa. Established as a German protectorate in 1899, Rwanda was mandated along with Burundi to Belgium as the Territory of Ruanda-Urundi in 1919. After **World War II** it became a United Nations Trust Territory administered by Belgium. Unrest in 1959 led to a Hutu revolt and the overthrow of Tutsi rule. Rwanda gained its independence in 1962, and after a military coup in 1973 civilian rule was only re-established in 1980. Further fighting took place in 1990 and a new constitution took effect in 1991. A peace accord was signed in 1993, but following the death of the Hutu President in an air crash in 1994, fighting between the mainly Tutsi rebels and the Hutu government forces resulted in an estimated 200 000–500 000 deaths and the flight of hundreds of thousands of refugees to Burundi and Tanzania.

Ryan, Claude (1925–)

Canadian politician. Replacing Robert **Bourassa** as the Quebec **Liberal Party** leader after the defeat of 1976, he was largely responsible, with Jean **Chrêtien**, for the successful campaign against secession in **Lévesque**'s referendum of 1980. However, his own suggestions for a decentralized federation with a Federal Council serving as a provincially-based watchdog were not favourably received by anglophones and he resigned the Liberal leadership after defeat by the **Parti Québecois** in the elections of 1981. He has remained a Minister of the National Assembly, and following the Liberal victory in 1985, he was named minister of education in the Bourassa government.

Rykov, Alexei Ivanovich (1881–1938)

Russian revolutionary and Communist Party and government official. Born in Saratov into a poor peasant family, he was educated at Kazan

University and soon became involved in social democratic politics, being arrested, imprisoned and exiled several times. In mid-1917 he was elected to the Moscow Soviet and helped to organize the Bolshevik Revolution there, becoming People's Commissar for Internal Affairs in the first Soviet government. He held a number of senior government posts (1919–36), and was also a member of the **Politburo** (1919–29). But in 1928, together with **Bukharin** and Tomsky, he led the 'right opposition' to **Stalin**'s economic policies and had to give up his Party positions. In 1937 he was arrested for alleged anti-Party activities, and was shot the following year. He was among other prominent victims of Stalin's purges rehabilitated during the **Gorbachev** era. ▷ **Bolsheviks; February Revolution**

Ryzhkov, Nikolai Ivanovich (1929–)
Soviet politician. A Russian born in the Donetsk region in the Ukraine, he worked as a miner before studying engineering in Sverdlovsk. He then worked his way up from welding foreman in a heavy machine building plant to head of the giant Uralmash engineering conglomerate, the largest industrial enterprise in the USSR. A member of the Communist Party since 1956, he was brought to Moscow in 1975 to work as First Deputy Minister for Heavy Transport and Machine Building. Four years later, he became First Deputy Chairman of Gosplan, and in 1982 was inducted into the Party Secretariat by Yuri **Andropov**, as Head of Economic Affairs. He was made a member of the **Politburo** by Mikhail **Gorbachev** in Apr 1985 and became Prime Minister in Sep 1985, with the task of restructuring the Soviet planning process on the quasi-autonomous Uralmash model. He was not particularly successful in introducing economic change, and living standards declined. In the reform debate that followed in the autumn of 1990, Ryzhkov produced a very modest scheme compared with Stanislav **Shatalin**'s radical plan. Gorbachev opted for a middle course and Ryzhkov was relieved of his post.

S

SA (*Sturmabteilung*, 'Storm Division')

German paramilitary league. Founded in 1921, the SA (sometimes dubbed the Brownshirts by virtue of its uniform) served as the paramilitary arm of the **Nazi Party**. In its early years it vied with the Nazi Party for supremacy within the movement and its leader, Ernst **Röhm**, envisaged a military rising against the **Weimar Republic**. However, the failure of **Hitler**'s **Munich Putsch** in Nov 1923 persuaded the latter to seek power through electoral means. The SA was subordinated to the Nazi Party in which role it gave excellent service as a proselytizer, propaganda vehicle, defence league and terrorist organization. Following Hitler's takeover, its 400 000, largely working-class, members were joined by over 2 million recruits, often blue-collar unemployed. Their impatience with Hitler's relative caution in political matters resulted in mounting lawlessness, which their leaders, still resenting their subordination to the party, did too little to control. Furthermore, Röhm openly aspired to replace the fi**Reichswehr** by the SA and carry the revolution further. All these factors combined to trigger the purging of the SA in mid-1934. After this it played a minor role in the Third **Reich**.

Saarland

Territory in south-west Germany, now a **Land** of the Federal Republic. A heavily industrialized region on the north-eastern border of France, the Treaty of **Versailles** placed the Saarland under a **League of Nations** administration and economically at France's disposal. The referendum scheduled for Jan 1935 to decide on the territory's ultimate future witnessed an overwhelming vote for, and a return to Germany. After **World War II** the region was again detached from Germany, being constituted as an autonomous territory under French occupation, but the referendum of Jan 1957 saw the Saarland return to Germany.

Sabra

Palestinian refugee camp on the outskirts of Beirut, Lebanon, created following the evacuation of Palestinians from the city after the June 1982 Israeli attack. It was the scene of a massacre of Palestinians by Christian Phalangists in Sep 1983.

Sacco and Vanzetti Affair (1921–7)

US political cause célèbre. Nicola Sacco and Bartolomeo Vanzetti were arrested in 1920, during the Red Scare, for a post office robbery and murder in South Braintree, Massachusetts. During the trial, the prosecutor was allowed to deliver inflammatory anti-communist speeches by the judge, who privately called the two defendants 'those anarchist bastards'. Their conviction and sentence to death therefore caused an uproar throughout the world. In response Governor Fuller of Massachusetts appointed a committee to examine the case. It found that, although the trial judge had been in grave breach of official decorum, justice had been done. The two men died in the electric chair in 1927. Debate on the case continues.

Sadat, Anwar el- (1918–81)
Egyptian politician. He trained for the army in Cairo, and in 1952 was a member of the coup which deposed King **Farouk**. After becoming President (1970), he temporarily assumed the post of Prime Minister (1973–4), after which he sought settlement of the conflict with Israel. He met Menachem **Begin**, the Israeli Premier, in Jerusalem (1977) and at Camp David, USA (1978), in which year he and Begin were jointly awarded the Nobel Peace Prize. Following criticism by other Arab statesmen and hard-line Muslims, he was assassinated while still in office in Cairo by extremists. ▷ **Arab–Israeli Wars**

Sa'id, Nuri al- (1888–1958)
Iraqi politician. After military training at the Istanbul Staff College for the Turkish army, he fled to Egypt when his Pan-Arab activities became suspect, taking an active part in the **Arab Revolt** in which he served under T E **Lawrence** and the Amir, **Faysal**. He followed Faysal to Iraq, where he was active in the establishment of the Iraqi army. In 1921 he became Iraq's first Chief of the General Staff and a year later Defence Minister. From 1930 onwards he held office as Prime Minister several times. Very pro-British and anti-communist in his sympathies, he fell foul of the Left and, in particular, those with pro-**Nasser** leanings. He was captured at the time of Abd al-Krim **Qassim**'s coup d'état in 1958, and killed.

Saint Laurent, Louis Stephen (1882–1973)
Canadian lawyer and politician. In 1914 he became Law Professor at Laval University and was appointed counsel to the **Rowell–Sirois Commission** between 1937 and 1940. In 1941 Mackenzie **King** appointed him Minister of Justice and, unlike other Quebec Liberals, he supported King on conscription in 1944, for which he was made Secretary of State for External Affairs in 1946. King's own choice as his successor, Saint Laurent became prime minister in 1948, and enacted such social programmes as the extension of the old-age pension scheme and hospital insurance. Under his leadership the Liberals were re-elected in 1949 and again, with a huge majority, in 1953; but he was defeated by the Conservatives under **Diefenbaker** in 1958. ▷ **Liberal Party** (Canada)

Sakharov, Andrei (1921–89)

Russian physicist and dissident. In 1948 he joined the nuclear weapons research group, and played a critical role in developing the Soviet hydrogen bomb. He received many honours and was elected a full member of the Academy of Sciences in 1953 at a very early age. While still supporting the USSR's possession of nuclear arms, he began opposing nuclear testing in the late 1950s because of the harmful effects of fall-out, thereafter supporting East–West co-operation and human rights, and in 1975 he was awarded the Nobel Peace Prize. All of this brought him criticism and harassment at home and, exiled to Gorky in 1980 as a leading dissident, he lived under poor conditions until he was restored to favour, somewhat reluctantly, by Mikhail **Gorbachev** in 1987. He was elected to the Congress of People's Deputies in 1989 as a representative of the Academy and was active within it until the day he died of a heart attack. His contribution to the promotion of political tolerance in the USSR and the relaxation of East–West tension was almost unmatched. ▷ **civil rights**

Salan, Raoul (1899–1984)

French general. From 1956 he was Commander-in-Chief of the French army in Algeria. In 1958 he played an important part in the crisis that brought Charles de **Gaulle** back to power, and was appointed by him as delegate of the government in Algeria, with full powers. An opponent of Algerian independence, he was brought back to France in 1959, and retired in 1960. In 1961 he joined in an attempted putsch led by General Challe. When this failed, he went underground in Algeria, and launched the **OAS** (*Organisation Armée Secrète*), using terrorist methods in its struggle against de Gaulle's Algerian policy. He was arrested in 1962, condemned to life imprisonment, but later amnestied.

Salandra, Antonio (1853–1931)

Italian politician and university professor. Elected a deputy in 1886, Salandra was a right-wing liberal who held various ministerial posts in the Pelloux and **Sonnino** governments. After 1910, he tried to become the focus for moderate and conservative forces, becoming Prime Minister in 1914. Together with Sidney Sonnino he was responsible for Italy's entry into **World War I**, deciding to back France and Britain against Italy's former allies, Austria and Germany, feeling such a policy would bring greater territorial gains. He was replaced as Prime Minister in 1916, but formed part of the delegation to the Paris Peace Conference. He refused to form a government in Oct 1922 and made little effort to oppose **Mussolini**, actually being on the fascist **Listone** in the Apr 1924 elections. After the murder of **Matteotti**, Salandra withdrew his support from the fascists.

Salazar, António de Oliveira (1889–1970)

Portuguese dictator. From the conservative, devout smallholding peasantry of the north, Salazar's seminary education allowed this reserved and studious individual to become a lecturer in economics at Coimbra, the university of the elite. He was active in a Catholic lay group and stood as a parliamentary candidate under the First Republic on three occasions. His economic expertise led to his ascendancy under the military dictatorship of General **Carmona** (1926–32). During the early 1930s he laid the foundations of the **Estado Novo** which he would dominate as dictator for over 35 years. The authoritarian and supposedly corporatist Salazarist state was underpinned by the army and the feared security police, the **PIDE**. Salazar's retrogressive economic policies made Portugal the poorest country in Europe (in 1960 per capita income was lower than that of Turkey), while greatly enhancing the wealth of its opulent oligarchy. Indeed, Salazar's economic failure made Portugal determined not to give up its African colonies. Yet it was the revolt of the army against the war in Africa against the independence movements (1961–74) that led to the downfall of the regime after his death. Although he fell from power in 1968 through ill health, he died in 1970 still thinking that he was dictator. ▷ **Republic, First** (Portugal)

Saleh, Ali Abdullah (1942–)

North Yemeni soldier and politician. A colonel in the army of the Yemen Arab Republic, he took part in the 1974 coup when Colonel Ibrahim al-Hamadi seized power, with rumours that the monarchy was to be restored. Hamadi was assassinated in 1977 and Colonel Hussein al-Ghashmi took over, only to be killed by a South Yemen terrorist bomb in 1978. Against this background of death and violence Saleh became President. Under his leadership, the war with South Yemen was ended and the two countries agreed to eventual reunion. He was re-elected in 1983 and 1988.

Salò, Republic of

The fascist 'Italian Social Republic' established in the north of Italy under German protection in autumn 1943, with **Mussolini** as its puppet ruler. The republic had no single administrative centre, different ministries being located in different towns eg Public Works in Venice, Finance in Brescia, Propaganda at Salò. It is from the last that it derived its usual name, a reflection of the fact that it was little more than a propaganda exercise, real power being located not in Italy but in Germany.

SALT (Strategic Arms Limitation Talks)

The name given to two rounds of talks held between the USA and USSR to limit their nuclear weapons arsenals and slow down the arms race. The first began in Helsinki in 1969, designed to place a numerical limit on intercontinental nuclear weapons. An agreement (SALT I) was reached in 1972. SALT II talks began that same year, and agreement was reached in 1979. There developed, however, a hardening of attitudes in the West towards the USSR, brought on in large part by the Soviet refusal to allow on-site verification. Once the USSR invaded Afghanistan, US Senate ratification of SALT II was doomed. Both countries, nevertheless, initially kept to the limitations established in the agreement. The arms situation was ultimately transformed by the **Reagan–Gorbachev** arms reduction accord, the revolutions of 1989 and the break-up of the USSR in 1991.

samizdat

From the Russian *sam*, 'self' and *izdatelstvo*, 'publishing', the term refers to privately-circulated editions of books and pamphlets not authorized for publication by the state censorship in the former USSR, and usually reproduced laboriously in typescript. The habit caught on in Poland and other communist countries, and helped to mould critical public opinion.

Samsonov, Alexander (1859–1914)

Russian general. He was in charge of a force in the **Russo-Japanese War** (1904–5). In **World War I** he commanded the army which, in order to take pressure off Russia's French ally, was given the task of invading East Prussia in Aug 1914, but was decisively defeated by **Hindenburg** at the Battle of **Tannenberg** (26–31 Aug). His shame and losses were so great — 100 000 prisoners — and his awareness that the last Battle of Tannenberg (Grunwald) in 1410 had been a huge Russian victory over the Teutonic Knights so strong, that he committed suicide.

Samuel, Herbert (Louis), 1st Viscount (1870–1963)

British politician and philosopher. Educated at Oxford, he became an MP in 1902, and held various offices, including Postmaster-General (1910–14 and 1915–16), Home Secretary (1916 and 1931–2), and High Commissioner for Palestine (1920–5), where he pursued a policy of trying to establish a multi-national commonwealth to include the Jews. He was Leader of the **Liberal Party** in the Commons (1931–5), and later Liberal Leader in the Lords (1944–55). He was created a viscount in 1937.

San Francisco, Treaty of (8 Sep 1951)

The treaty which brought to an end the war between Japan and the 48 other signatory nations. Those other signatories were the nations which had declared war on Japan (with the exceptions of the USSR, the Republic of China (Taiwan) and the People's Republic of China) and those nations which had been created since the Japanese surrender in 1945 in territories which had been occupied by Japan. The San Francisco Treaty brought to an end the post-war occupation of Japan, and marked the restoration of Japan to the community of nations.

San Remo, Conference of (Apr 1920)
This conference, attended by representatives of Britain, France and Italy, reached agreement on the Middle East settlement after **World War I**. The agreement covered the peace treaty with Turkey (eventually signed in Sèvres, Aug 1920), and the eventual independence of the Middle Eastern states. However, it also granted interim mandates to Britain over Iraq and Palestine, and to France over Syria and Lebanon (as had earlier been formulated in principle by the **Sykes–Picot Agreement**). Japan, Greece and Belgium were also party to the Conference, but not the USA or USSR.

Sandino, Augusto César (1895–1934)
Nicaraguan revolutionary. From the mountains of northern Nicaragua, he led guerrilla resistance to US occupation forces after 1926. His success in evading the US forces and the Nicaraguan National Guard generated sympathy for his cause, as well as a significant degree of anti-American feeling. After the withdrawal of the US Marines (Jan 1933), Anastasio **Somoza**, Chief of the National Guard, arranged a meeting with him, apparently to discuss peace. It transpired, however, that this was a ruse: Sandino was murdered, on Somoza's orders, near Managua. The Nicaraguan revolutionary government of 1979–90 (later known as the *Sandinistas*) took him as their principal hero.

Sanger, Margaret Louise (1883–1966)
US social reformer and founder of the birth control movement. Educated at Claverack College, she became a trained nurse, and married William Sanger in 1902. Appalled by the tragedies she encountered as a nurse, in 1914 she published a radical feminist magazine, *The Woman Rebel*, with advice on contraception, and two years later founded the first American birth-control clinic, in Brooklyn, New York, for which she was imprisoned. After later completing a world tour, she founded the American Birth Control League in 1921. Divorced in 1920, she married J Noah H Slee in 1922.

Sanguinetti, Julio María (1936–)
Uruguayan politician. A member of the long-established, progressive Colorado Party (PC), which had its origins in the civil war of 1836, he was elected to the assembly in 1962, and then headed the Ministry of Labour and Industry, and then Education and Culture (1969–73). The oppressive regime of Juan Maria Bordaberry (1972–6) was forcibly removed, and military rule imposed before democratic government was restored in 1985. The 1966 constitution was, with some modifications,

restored, and Sanguinetti was elected President. He took office in 1986, leading a government of National Accord. Sanguinetti's major achievement was the restoration of democracy and human and civil rights. However, the means by which he brought this about — a general amnesty to the military, rather than criminal trials — weakened his popular support. He lost the presidency, in 1989, to Luis Alberto Lacalle of the Blanco Party.

Sanjurjo, José (1872–1936)

Spanish soldier. As director of the **Civil Guard** he played an important role in the establishment of the Second Republic in 1931 by refusing to place his forces at the service of the King, **Alfonso XIII**. Nevertheless, he led an abortive monarchist rising against the new regime in 1932. Sentenced to life imprisonment, he was amnestied by the right-wing government of **Lerroux** in 1934. Popular in the army for his down-to-earth style, he accepted the leadership of the Nationalist rising of 17–18 July 1936 against the Republic, only to die on 20 July 1936 in an air crash. ▷ **Republic, Second** (Spain)

Sankara, Thomas (1950–87)

Burkina Faso soldier and politician. He joined the army in Ouagadougou in 1969 and attended the French Parachute Training Centre (1971–4) where he began to acquire radical political ideas. As a minister in Saye Zerbo's government, he increasingly came to believe in the need for a genuinely popular revolution to expunge the consequences of French colonialism. Leading a coup in 1983, he became Prime Minister and Head of State and introduced a wide range of progressive policies which made him enemies. Despite his great symbolic popularity among young radicals (outside Burkina Faso as much as inside the country), he was shot during a coup led by his close associate, Blaise **Compaore**, on 15 Oct 1987.

Sapru, Tej Bahadur (1875–1949)

Indian political leader and lawyer. He studied law and practised as a lawyer in Allahabad. Entered politics in 1907 as a moderate, joined Annie Besant's Home Rule League Movement (1917) and became a member of Lord Reading's Executive Council in 1921. As a member of the government of India, Sapru took the initiative to remove restrictions on the press following the Press Act 1910, and to withdraw the Criminal Law Amendment Act, 1910. He represented India at the Imperial Conference London in 1923 and after M K **Gandhi**'s conviction and imprisonment, resigned from the Executive Council in 1923. At the Round Table Conference in London in 1930, he reiterated the demand for provincial autonomy with responsibility to the legislature at the centre. He was member of the Privy Council in 1934 and was in favour of a new constitution under the Government of India Act in 1935. As a leader of the Non-Parties Conference at Allahabad in 1942, Sapru demanded that Winston **Churchill** declare India's position equal to that of dominions. He was the first President of the Indian Council of World Affairs (1943), a position which he held until his death. He was a Persian and Urdu scholar, with a keen judicial mind free of religious and communal prejudices — one of the greatest statesmen of the Indian freedom movement. ▷ **communalism**

Sarajevo

The capital of Bosnia-Herzegovina republic, lying on the River Miljacka. Sarajevo was governed by Austria from 1878 to 1918. It was the scene of the assassination of Archduke **Francis Ferdinand** and his wife (1914), which precipitated **World War I**. After the war it became known as a cultural and educational centre, but it was besieged and attacked frequently in the early 1990s in the fighting following the break up of Yugoslavia. A devastating mortar attack on the market in 1994 aroused world opinion and led to a ceasefire in the area.

Sarekat Islam

The first mass political movement in the Netherlands East Indies (Indonesia), indeed the only mass movement in the colony prior to 1945. Sarekat Islam (Islamic Union) was founded in 1912 by a prominent batik merchant from Surakarta, Hadji Samanhudi, to protect the economic interests of batik traders at a time of increasing organization within the Chinese commmercial community. However, the movement soon moved beyond this narrow aim, attracting a wide range of frequently disparate elements. Indeed, at one time or another during its brief history, virtually every persuasion within the Indies population had come within it, and the membership had grown to more than 2 million in 1919. That figure may mean little. Only a few tens of thousands were in any sense formal members while far more than 2 million were swept along by the movement. At the close of the 1910s, socialist elements achieved a growing influence within Sarekat Islam, provoking a major split with the Muslim wing. In 1921 the Indies Communist Party (PKI) was forced out of the central organization. However, by the late 1920s Sarekat Islam had largely faded into inactivity. ▷ **Partai Komunis Indonesia**

Sarit Thanarat (1908–63)

Thai military and political leader. Educated at the Royal Thai Military Academy, Sarit first saw combat during the suppression of the 1933 royalist Boworadet rebellion. Following distinguished service during the Pacific War, in the post-war years Sarit played an increasingly important role in military politics. He became Commander-in-Chief of the army in 1954, supreme commander of the armed forces in 1957. In Sep the same year, he staged a coup against Phibun. He became Prime Minister in 1958. Sarit ruled in a highly authoritarian manner, dealing harshly with all dissent. He was fiercely anti-communist. However, during his premiership, considerable attention was also given to improvement in the country's infrastructure and the development of the economy. He died in office, leaving behind a great fortune; most of it was confiscated by the government which succeeded him.

Sarney (Costa), José (1930–)
Brazilian politician. A follower of the UDN Bossa Nova (nationalist) group in the early 1950s, he became ARENA (National Renewal Alliance) Governor of Maranhão in 1965 under **Castelo Branco**. A prominent Senator during the 1970s, he led the Social Democratic Party (PDS) under Figueiredo. Running-mate to Tancredo **Neves** in 1985 on a breakaway ticket, he became President on Neves' sudden death. Saddled with the latter's commitments, but without either the backing or skill to carry them through himself, he drifted from crisis to crisis. His attempt to retain the executive during the 1987–8 Constituent Congress succeeded, but at enormous political and economic cost. He was succeeded in 1990 by Fernando **Collor de Mello**.

Sassou-Nguesso, Denis (1943–)
Congolese soldier and politician. After completing his secondary education in the Congo Republic, he joined the army and trained in Algeria and France. An active member of the radical Parti Congolais du Travail (PCT), he was appointed Minister of Defence in 1975 and survived the military coup of 18 Mar 1977 in which President N'Gouabi was assassinated. In 1979, under popular pressure, power was transferred to the PCT and Sassou-Nguesso became President later in the year. Since then, he has moved politically towards the centre, rebuilding links with France and establishing more harmonious relations with the USA.

Sastri, V S Srinivasa (1869–1946)
Indian politician. Greatly influenced by Annie Besant, C P Ramaswami Aiyar and Gokhale, he was the Secretary of the Madras session of Congress (1908). He took an active part in drawing up the Lucknow Pact between the Congress and **Muslim League**, which demanded 'responsive government for India', and was opposed to M K **Gandhi**'s policy of non-violence and non-cooperation. Elected to the Madras Council in 1913, he became a member of the Imperial Legislative Council in 1915 and of the Council of State in 1921. Sastri was a member of the delegation to South Africa which led to the Cape Town agreement, committing the South African government to shelve its Class Area Bill to segregate Indians. He also struggled for the cause of Indians living in Kenya and British East Africa and was President of the Servants of India Society

for some years. In 1945, he strongly opposed Muhammad Ali **Jinnah**'s two-nation theory. ▷ **Non-Cooperation Movement**

Sato Eisaku (1901–75)
Japanese politician. The younger brother of Nobusuke **Kishi**, he was an official in the Ministry of Railways before **World War II**, and was first elected to the Diet in 1949. Indicted for corruption in 1954, he was released in 1956 before completion of his trial as part of a general amnesty celebrating Japan's entry into the **UN**. During Sato's premiership (1964–72), relations with South Korea were normalized (1965) and US-held Okinawa was returned to Japan (1972). Although the 1960 security treaty with the USA was automatically extended in 1970, a dispute over Japanese textile exports and President Richard **Nixon**'s **normalization** of relations with China without consulting Japan soured US-Japan relations during the last years of Sato's premiership. It is widely believed that Sato's three non-nuclear principles (non-manufacture, non-possession and non-introduction into Japan of nuclear weapons) earned him the Nobel Peace Prize in 1974.

Satyagraha
Literally 'truth-force', the term refers to M K **Gandhi**'s philosophy of non-violent resistance to evil. It was conceived in South Africa in response to laws discriminating against Asians (1906), and used in campaigns against British rule in India. The approach involved fasting, economic boycotts, hand-spinning, and hand-weaving.

Saudi Arabia
An Arabic kingdom comprising about four fifths of the Arabian Peninsula. The land is famed as the birthplace of Islam with the holy cities of Mecca, Medina and Jedda. The modern state was founded by Ibn Saud who, by 1932, had united the four tribal provinces of Hejaz in the north-west, Asir in the south-west, Najd in the centre, and Al Hasa in the east. Oil was discovered in the 1930s and Saudi Arabia is now the world's leading oil exporter; its oil reserves account for about a quarter of the world's known supply.

Savage, Michael Joseph (1872–1940)
Australian-born New Zealand politician. In 1907 he emigrated to New Zealand, where he became a moderate trade unionist. He later moved into politics, and helped to found the Labour Party in 1916. He was elected to parliament in 1919 and in 1933 became leader of the New Zealand Labour Party. By cultivating the support of rural interests he secured a win for his party in the Nov 1935 general election, thus becoming the country's first Labour Prime Minister. His popularity grew and

he was re-elected in 1938 but died in office two years later, to be succeeded by Peter **Fraser**.

Savimbi, Jonas Malheiro (1934–)
Angolan soldier and nationalist. Educated in Angola and at Lausanne University, he returned to Zambia and became a leader of the Popular Union of Angola, being Foreign Minister of the Angolan government-in-exile (1962–4). After a period with the **FNLA**, he broke away to form **UNITA** and fought against the Portuguese until independence. Unable to agree with the leaders of the **MPLA** and the FNLA, he continued the struggle against the MPLA from bases in the south of Angola, supported by South Africa and the USA. A man of considerable charisma, he stood for a democratic and capitalist Angola, but his associations with South Africa and the USA made him a pariah in third world circles. However, the strength of his position and diplomatic bargaining by the USA led to a series of meetings designed to end the civil war and remove the Cubans from Angola. Agreement for a cease-fire and democratic elections was finally achieved in Estoril in 1991.

Savornin Lohman, Alexander Frederik de (1837–1924)
Dutch Protestant politician. From 1879 to 1921 he sat in the Second Chamber, initially as a member of the Calvinist **Anti-Revolutionary Party** (ARP). In 1884–95 he was also Professor of Law at the Calvinist Free University in Amsterdam. He was the leader of the more conservative tendency within the ARP, and as such objected to A **Kuyper**'s schism from the Dutch Reformed Church in 1886, and his democratic politics; Savornin Lohman therefore led a splinter group away from the ARP in 1894, calling itself the Free Anti-Revolutionary Party, which in 1908 became the **Christian Historical Union**.

Saxe-Coburg-Gotha
The name of the British royal family, 1901–17. King **Edward VII** inherited it from his father, Prince Albert, the second son of the Duke of Saxe-Coburg-Gotha. The obviously Germanic name was abandoned during **World War I** as a means of asserting the 'Englishness' of royalty and playing down the extent of its German blood. ▷ **Windsor, House of**

Saya San Rebellion (1930–1)
A major anti-colonial uprising in Burma, named after its leader, Saya San. In inspiring rebellion, Saya San utilized both modern political organization at the local level and the millenarian expectations of folk belief, casting himself as the *Setkya-min*, the avenging king in Burman legend. However, the rebellion also took its strength from harsh economic conditions in the rural areas, as the world depression struck Burma, and the burden of colonial taxation borne by the peasantry. In the course of the

rebellion, some 3 000 were killed or wounded. A further 350 were executed for their part in the rebellion, including Saya San himself.

SBZ (*Sowjetische Besatzungs zone*, 'Soviet Zone of Occupation')
The territories in central Germany, between the western and Polish-occupied zones, which, in 1949, became the German Democratic Republic (East **Germany**, GDR). For many years thereafter the territory continued to be described by official and other sources in Federal (West) **Germany** as the SBZ so as to question the GDR's legitimacy.

Schacht, (Horace Greely) Hjalmar (1877–1970)
German financier. In 1923 he became President of the Reichsbank, and founded a new currency which ended the inflation of the mark. He was Minister of Economics (1934–7), but in 1939 was dismissed from his bank office for disagreeing with **Hitler** over rearmament expenditure. Involvement with the resistance led to his internment. He was acquitted of war crimes at the **Nuremberg Trials**. In 1953 he set up his own bank in Düsseldorf. ▷ **Nazi Party**

Scheduled Castes and Tribes
Initially defined by the Government of India Act of 1919 and later by that of 1935, the schedule included all the castes and tribes in India considered by the British to be either of too inferior a social standing in the Indian caste system or too economically backward to be capable of exercising a vote and having a say in local government. Ostensibly, the scheduling of these groups was intended to protect them from exploitation and discrimination, but by insisting that the so-called 'untouchable' castes and those living in India's tribal areas should be represented by officials, the schedule also provided a convenient pretext for packing provincial councils with British nominees. On Independence, the Indian government adopted a universal adult franchise and the scheduled castes and tribes were temporarily forgotten. Soon, however, the government realized that, to carry out its commitment to abolish all social discrimination, it would need to adopt measures of positive discrimination and would have need of a convenient definition of those so disadvantaged. A proportion of all government posts and university and college places was therefore reserved for those from the tribal communities and 'backward' castes, and the 'schedule' of the 1930s was revived. The list of scheduled castes has expanded in accordance with political expediency. In 1991 the attempts to implement further increases in reservation, in line with the recommendations of the controversial 1980 Mandal Commission, led to widespread rioting in northern India and helped to bring down the minority Janata Dal government under V P Singh. ▷ **communalism; Government of India Acts; Janata Dal**

Scheel, Walter (1919–)
West German politician. After serving in the **Luftwaffe** in **World War II** he went into business, joined the Free Democratic Party (**FDP**), and was elected to the **Bundestag** in 1953. He was Minister for Economic Cooperation (1961–6) and Foreign Minister (1969–74), and in 1970, as part of the **Ostpolitik**, negotiated treaties with the USSR and Poland. Scheel was President of West Germany from 1974 to 1979. ▷ **Germany, West**

Scheidemann, Philipp (1865–1939)
German political leader. A leading member of the Social Democratic Party (**SPD**), he proclaimed the German Republic in Nov 1918. He was Minister of Finance and Colonies in the Provisional Government of 1918, and first Chancellor of the republic in 1919. He resigned rather than sign the Treaty of **Versailles**.

Schiller, Karl (1911–)
German economist and politician. A distinguished academic career, latterly at the University of Hamburg, was complemented from 1949 by a growing involvement as an **SPD** member in municipal and national politics. In 1966 he became Economics Minister in the **CDU**/SPD coalition, retained the post in the SPD/**FDP** coalition (1969–72) and also served as Finance Minister (1971–2) before resigning from the government. He is credited with Germany's economic recovery from the 1966 recession and with introducing a Keynesian style of economic management to Germany.

Schleicher, Kurt von (1882–1934)
German soldier and politician. He was on the general staff during **World War I**. Politically active behind the scenes during **Brüning**'s chancellorship, he became Minister of War in von **Papen**'s government of 1932, then succeeding him as Chancellor. However, his failure to obtain either a parliamentary majority or emergency powers provided the preconditions for **Hitler**'s appointment as Chancellor in 1933. Schleicher and his wife were murdered by the Nazis in mid-1934 on a trumped-up charge of treason. ▷ **Night of the Long Knives**

Schlüter, Poul Holmskov (1929–)
Danish politician. After studying at Aarhus and Copenhagen Universities, he qualified as a barrister and Supreme Court attorney but was politically active at an early age, becoming leader of the youth movement of the Conservative People's Party (KF) in 1944. He became its national leader in 1951 and in 1952 a member of the Executive Committee of the KF. He was elected to parliament (**Folketinget**) in 1964 and 10 years later became Chairman of the KF (Conservative People's Party), and in 1982

Prime Minister, heading a centre-right coalition which survived the 1987 election but was reconstituted, with support from one of the minor centre parties, *Det Radikale Venstre*, in 1988. Since the election in Dec 1990 the coalition has consisted of only two parties: Schlüter's Conservative Party and the Danish Liberal Party, *Venstre*, led by the Foreign Minister, Uffe Elleman-Jensen.

Schmidt, Helmut (Heinrich Waldemar) (1918–)
West German politician. After service in **World War II**, he studied at Hamburg, joined the Social Democratic Party in 1946, and became a member of the **Bundestag** in 1953. He was Minister of Defence (1969–72) and of Finance (1972–4), in which role he created a firm basis for Germany's continued economic growth. He succeeded Willy **Brandt** as Chancellor in 1974, describing his aim as the 'political unification of Europe in partnership with the United States'. In 1982 his **SPD**/**FDP** coalition collapsed, to be replaced by a **CDU**/FDP administration. ▷ **Germany, West; Kohl, Helmut**

Schools Question (Belgium)
The extended political conflict between the supporters of neutral state education and of Roman Catholic schools, dominating the third quarter of the 19c, and also the 1950s. The French revolutionary period had removed the traditional monopoly held by the Catholic Church over education; during the union with the northern Netherlands (1815–30) King William I insisted that education be regulated by the state, which became one of the contributory causes of the Belgian Revolution. The liberals held sway in Belgian politics around the middle of the 19c, and much of their anti-clericalism was manifested in Education Acts which progressively reduced the influence of the Church in primary education. During the years 1878–84 more anti-Catholic provisions in education brought the Schools Question to a head; at the elections of 1884 the liberals were soundly beaten and the Catholics, embarking on 30 years of uninterrupted power, reversed the legislation. After **World War II** the battleground switched to secondary education, and in 1954–8 education dominated Belgian politics once more. In 1958 the Schools Pact was signed, by which the three major parties (Catholics, socialists and liberals) agreed to a free choice of education at secondary level, with largely equivalent state funding.

Schools Question (Netherlands)
The extended political conflict surrounding Calvinist and Roman Catholic attempts to gain equal status for confessional education, especially in terms of state funding. In Napoleonic times primary education had been made a state monopoly; from the 1820s both Catholics and Calvinists began to raise objections to this, for example by means of petitions.

The issue dominated Dutch domestic politics from 1850 to 1917: the confessionals objected to the 'neutral' religious content of state education, and so set up their own schools, demanding state funds to run them. In 1889, during the first confessional government in the Netherlands, an Act was introduced giving partial subsidy to 'free' or non-state schools. During the government of 1901–5 led by A **Kuyper** there were more laws increasing subsidies to religious schools; in 1917 a great compromise was struck, granting universal male suffrage, and financial equality to 'free' and state education: the constitution was amended accordingly. Since the pacification of 1917 the heat has left the debate, but education continued to be a highly divisive issue in the Netherlands in the interbellum and after **World War II**.

Schumacher, Kurt Ernst Karl (1895–1952)
German politician. He studied law and political science at the universities of Leipzig and Berlin, and from 1930 to 1933 was a member of the **Reichstag** and of the executive of the Social Democratic parliamentary group. An outspoken opponent of National Socialism, he spent 10 years from 1933 in Nazi concentration camps, where he showed outstanding courage. He became in 1946 Chairman of the Social Democratic Party (**SPD**) and of the parliamentary group of the **Bundestag**, Bonn. He strongly opposed **Adenauer**'s policy of integration with Western Europe at the expense of reunification.

Schuman, Robert (1886–1963)
French politician. He was a popular Christian Democrat Deputy (1919–40) and then (1945–62) one of the leaders of the **MRP** ('Popular Republican Movement'). After holding office as Prime Minister (1947–8), he remained Foreign Minister (1948–53), during which time he carried through the Schuman Plan (1950) for pooling the coal and steel resources of Western Europe, the predecessor of the European Economic Community. He was Minister of Justice (1955–6) after which he concentrated on the European movement, becoming President of the **EEC** assembly (1958–60). ▷ **EC**

Schuschnigg, Kurt von (1897–1977)
Austrian politician. He served in **World War I**, practised law, was elected a Christian Socialist Deputy (1927), and became Minister of Justice (1932) and of Education (1933). He was Chancellor of Austria from 1934 to 1938. His attempt to prevent **Hitler** occupying **Austria** led to his imprisonment until 1945. He then lived in the USA, where he became Professor of Political Science at St Louis (1948–67).

Schwimmer, Rosika (1877–1948)
Hungarian feminist and pacifist. As a journalist she was active in the Hungarian women's movement, and was a co-founder of a feminist-pacifist group. She became Vice-President of the Women's International League for Peace and Freedom, and in 1918–19 was Hungarian minister to Switzerland. In 1920, fleeing from the country's anti-Semitic leadership, she emigrated to the USA, but was refused citizenship since, as a pacifist, she could not promise to fight should war break out. For the rest of her life she continued to campaign for pacifism and before the outbreak of **World War II** was outspoken in her criticism of growing European Fascism.

SCLC (Southern Christian Leadership Conference)
US **civil rights** organization. Formed in 1957 by Martin Luther **King** and other ministers to pursue racial integration, primarily in the South, through non-violent protest. As ministers they were natural leaders in their communities, able to explain their aims in terms of the Christian creed, and in a rhetoric which their people understood. An unsuccessful campaign in Albany, Georgia, in 1961, demonstrated the need for careful planning and preparation. In later campaigns the movement sought to develop a 'creative tension', inciting whites to overreact, attracting the media, and forcing the federal government to intervene. The success of this strategy was seen in Birmingham and Selma. However it did not succeed in Chicago where blacks lacked unity, the issues were far more complicated and white opposition was far more skilful. After the death of Martin Luther King, the organization lost much of its moral authority, though it still remained an important platform for leaders such as Ralph Abernathy and, later, Jesse **Jackson**.

Scotland
The northern constituent part of the United Kingdom, comprising all the mainland north of the border that runs from the Solway Firth to Berwick-upon-Tweed, and the island groups of the Outer and Inner Hebrides, Orkney and Shetland. The crowns of Scotland and England were united in 1603 and the two parliaments were subsequently united under the Act of Union in 1707. Scotland has a separate legal and educational system, and other institutions which are distinct from those of England or Wales. Nationalist feeling grew in the 1960s and 11 Scottish Nationalist MPs were returned in the 1974 General Election. A proposal for devolution failed in a referendum in 1979; although a majority voted in favour, they formed only 32% of the electorate, rather than the 40% required. The issue of devolved power or independence for Scotland continued to be an important political issue in the country.

Scottish National Party (SNP)

A political party formed in 1928 as the National Party of Scotland, which merged with the Scottish Party in 1934. It first won a seat at a by-election in 1945. Its greatest success was in the 1974 general election, when it took nearly a third of Scottish votes and won 11 seats. Led by Alex Salmond (1955–) since 1990, it won three seats in the 1992 general election. Its principal policy aim is independence for Scotland from the UK. ▷ **Home Rule**

SDI (Strategic Defense Initiative)

The proposal first made by President **Reagan** in 1983 (dubbed by the press 'Star Wars') that the USA should develop the technologies for a defensive layered 'shield' of weapons based primarily in space, able to shoot down incoming ballistic missiles. SDI has remained controversial because it seemed to overthrow the principle of 'mutual assured destruction' on which the idea of deterrence rested. Also the technologies it would need to perfect, such as directed energy, as well as being extremely difficult to achieve, might ultimately be used for offensive as well as defensive purposes.

Securities and Exchange Commission (SEC)

A body set up in 1934 in the USA during the **Great Depression** to regulate and control the issue of shares by corporations. It ensures that statements about the stocks being sold are accurate, and generally regulates the way US stock markets operate.

SED (*Sozialistische Einheitspartei Deutschlands*, 'Socialist Unity Party of Germany')

East German political party. Formed in East **Germany** in 1946 out of the **KPD** and a somewhat unwilling **SPD**, the SED became the Marxist-Leninist party of government in East Germany. Led initially by Wilhelm **Pieck** and Otto Grotewohl, it then saw Walter **Ulbricht** become General-Secretary in 1950 (1963 renamed First Secretary) and Erich **Honecker** replace him in 1971 (1976 renamed General-Secretary). The SED claimed its moral authority as the German proponent of Soviet-style socialism, but despite a membership of over 2 million in 1987, its style of government was never popular. Following the **Revolution of 1989**, the SED reconstituted itself as the PDS (Party of Democratic Socialism), but only enjoys limited support. ▷ **Marxism**

Seeckt, Hans von (1866–1936)

German army officer. After serving with merit as a staff officer in **World War I**, Seeckt acted as military expert to the German delegation at the Treaty of **Versailles** before becoming Army Chief of Staff in 1920. His equivocal attitude to the republic saw him uphold order with emergency powers during the troubles of late 1923 and early 1924, but also saw him fail to act decisively against far-right conspirators (**Kapp Putsch**, 1920). Eventually this equivocation forced his resignation in 1926. As Chief of Staff he had been a strong advocate of military cooperation with the USSR, not least to undermine Poland. He sat in the **Reichstag** (1930–2), and functioned briefly thereafter as a military adviser in China.

segregation

The cultural, political, and typically geographical separation imposed by one racial or ethnic group over another. The term is most often applied to the subjugation of blacks by a politically dominant white elite, particularly through **apartheid** (literally 'separateness') in South Africa, and in the southern states of the USA c.1900–60. Segregation of blacks has been most apparent in housing, public facilities and transportation, and education. ▷ **civil rights; Jim Crow Laws**

Seguí, Salvador (1887–1923)

Spanish anarcho-syndicalist. He took part in the **Tragic Week** of 1909 and had to flee the repression afterwards. Having participated in the foundation of the **CNT** in 1910, he became President of the Federation of Construction Workers of Barcelona in 1914. Seguí was the architect of the Pact of Saragossa (1916) with the Socialist trade union movement, the **UGT**, which led the two movements to pressure the government jointly in the fight against inflation and unemployment. Indeed, he believed that common action against capitalism required cooperation not only with the Socialists, but also with groups beyond the organized working class. Consequently, in 1917 he participated in the general strike committee, even though the CNT was not officially part of the Republican-Socialist coalition. After **World War I**, the down-to-earth Seguí was the CNT's most prominent figure, and in 1919 almost single-handedly persuaded it to accept the agreement reached in the La Canadiense strike, only to be undermined by the revolutionary anarchists. On 10 Mar 1923 Seguí, despite his moderation, was assassinated in Barcelona by the employers. His 'libertarian possibilism' maintained that the working class should not renounce politics in order to achieve its ends, and his untimely death robbed the Spanish anarcho-syndicalists not just of an outstanding organizer, but of their most gifted figure.

Seipel, Ignaz (1876–1932)

Austrian politician. After an early career as a theologian, Seipel played a leading role in Austrian politics from 1918 until his death. A member of the Christian Social Party, he served on the Constituent Assembly (1919–20) and as the Federal Chancellor (1922–4, 1926–9). Throughout the period he was a determined opponent of Social Democracy and gradually came to question the efficacy of democracy as such. His foreign policy achievements included the Geneva Protocol (1922) which obtained foreign credit and stabilized the Austrian economy, but at the cost of economic deflation and social suffering.

Seiyukai

Literally, 'Association of Political Friends', the leading political party in Japan between 1900 and 1940. Created by **Ito Hirobumi** in 1900 as a pro-government party in the Diet, the *Seiyukai* attracted the support of bureaucrats and landowners. Under the leadership of **Hara Kei** after 1914, the Seiyukai became the largest single party in the Diet. In 1918 Hara became Prime Minister of a Seiyukai-dominated cabinet, the first time a government had been formed from the majority party in the Diet. Despite high hopes, his government (1918–21) proved to be conservative on issues of political and social reform. The Seiyukai supported the military cabinets of the 1930s and advocated a hardline policy in China. The party was dissolved in 1940 as part of a government attempt to bring all political parties under the umbrella of the **Imperial Rule Assistance Association**.

Senanayake, Don Stephen (1884–1952)

Sri Lankan politician. Born in Colombo, he was educated there and then worked on his father's rubber estate. Entering the Legislative Council in 1922, he founded the co-operative society movement in 1923, and was elected to the State Council in 1931 where he was Minister of Agriculture for 15 years. Following independence, he was Sri Lanka's first Prime Minister (1947–52), and also held the posts of Minister of Defence and External Affairs. He died after falling from his horse in Colombo.

Sendero Luminoso

Literally 'Shining Path', the name refers to a Maoist rural guerrilla movement of uncompromisingly revolutionary character, operating in the Peruvian central Andes (though capable, also, of mounting terrorist actions in cities) during the 1980s and 1990s. Its leader, Abimael Guzman, was captured in Sep 1992 and sentenced to life imprisonment.

Senegambia, Confederation of

An association between The Gambia and Senegal, begun in 1982, designed to integrate military, economic, communications, and foreign policies, and to establish joint institutions, while preserving independence and sovereignty. It proved to be of limited value and was ended by mutual agreement in 1989.

Senghor, Leopold Sedar (1906–)

Senegalese poet and politician. Educated in Roman Catholic schools in Dakar, he went to the University of Paris and, after graduation, taught in France itself (1935–9). He joined the French army at the outbreak of war and was a prisoner (1940–2). A member of the Resistance (1942–4), he was a member of the French Constituent Assembly in 1945 and was Deputy for Senegal in the French Assembly (1948–58), during which period he was a university lecturer. He was one of the founders of *Presence Africaine* in 1947 and wrote widely in that, and other intellectual magazines, establishing himself as a major poet and an exponent of the philosophy of negritude. He formed the *Union Progressiste Senegalaise* in 1958 and, as its leader, became President of Senegal on the country's independence in 1960. He retained cordial links with France and, although nominally a socialist, espoused a mixed economy. In 1981 he retired from politics.

Separation of Church and State (France) (1905)

The conflict between the Church and the French Republic had been renewed as a result of the **Dreyfus** Affair (1898–9) and the Law on Associations (1901), which was used to dissolve the religious orders. **Combes**'s government (1902–4) opened a conflict with the papacy which led to the law of 1905 abrogating the Concordat (1801), ending the position of the Catholic Church as an established Church, financially supported and to some extent controlled by the state. The separation was at first fought bitterly by the Church, but the mollifying policies of **Briand**, Minister of Religious Worship in the **Clemenceau** government (1906–9), reduced the confrontation, and in a short time the new regime proved acceptable to both sides. ▷ **Republic, Third** (France)

Séparatisme

French-Canadian independence movement. It has played a significant role in Canadian politics since the 1960s. Some groups such as the **Front de Libération de Québec (FLQ)** were prepared to resort to the sort of violence which resulted in the **October Crisis**. One of the largest groups was the *Rassemblement Démocratique pour l'Indépendence* which was important in the defeat of **Lesage**, and became even stronger after the defeat of the **Parti Québecois** by the Liberals in 1985. Initially the federal government responded by attempting to remedy French-Canadian dissatisfactions through such initiatives as the **Royal Commission on Bilingualism and Biculturalism**. As Prime Minister, Pierre **Trudeau** reasserted the tradition of tolerant Canadianism for which **Laurier** had stood, in the hope that the province might be prevented from becoming racist and introverted. As a Québecois Liberal, his own success controverted the image of disadvantage that the separatist groups attempted to convey.

Serbia

A constituent republic of Yugoslavia. Formerly a kingdom of the Balkan Peninsula, it was incorporated into Yugoslavia in 1918 and was established as a constituent republic in 1946. The provinces of Kosovo and Vojvodina were autonomous until 1990 when they each lost their autonomous status to Serbia. Serb minority populations are substantial in Croatia and Bosnia-Herzegovina and civil war between the ethnic groups followed their declarations of independence from Yugoslavia.

Sergei (1876–1944)
Russian Orthodox religious leader. Already a bishop in 1901, he managed to survive the **Russian Revolution** (1917) and the subsequent campaigns against religion. In 1925 he became Patriarch by default when Patriarch **Tikhon** died, and in 1927 made a declaration of loyalty to the state which allowed something of Orthodoxy to continue. During **World War II**, **Stalin** sought his support in defence of the country and allowed him to call a council in 1943 at which he was finally properly elected.

Seyss-Inquart, Artur von (1892–1946)
Austrian politician. He practised as a lawyer in Vienna and saw much of **Schuschnigg**. When the latter became Chancellor in 1938, he took office under him, informing **Hitler** of every detail of Schuschnigg's life, in the hope of becoming Nazi leader in **Austria** after the **Anschluss**. Instead, he was appointed Commissioner for the Netherlands in 1940. In 1945 he was captured by the Canadians, tried at the **Nuremberg Trials** and executed for war crimes.

Sforza, Carlo (1872–1952)
Italian diplomat and politician. As Foreign Minister (1920–1), he negotiated the **Rapallo** Treaty. In 1922 he was made Ambassador to Paris, but resigned on **Mussolini**'s seizure of power and chose to live in exile. After the fall of Mussolini, he returned to Italy and was a member of the first democratic governments. As Foreign Minister (1947–51), he backed European unity and Italian membership of **NATO**.

Shagari, Alhaji Shehu Usman Aliyu (1925–)
Nigerian politician. Educated in Northern Nigeria, he became a schoolmaster, then was elected as a member of the Federal Parliament (1954–8). He was Minister of Economic Development (1959–60), Minister of Establishments (1960–2), Minister of Internal Affairs (1962–5) and Minister of Works (1965–6). After the 1966 coup, he was both State Commissioner for Education in Sokoto province and Federal Commissioner for Economic Development and Reconstruction (1968–70) and then Commissioner for Finance (1971–5). He was a member of the Constituent Assembly which drew up the Constitution for the Second Republic and was the successful presidential candidate for the National Party of Nigeria in 1979. He was President of Nigeria from 1979 until 1983, when he was overthrown in a military coup.

Shalaev, Stepan Alexevich (1929–)
Soviet trade union leader. He spent his early years working in the timber industry, became a manager and then, in 1963, changed occupations to become a trade union official. Yet his function remained that of running the workforce. So in 1980 he could become Minister of the Timber Industry and two years later was chairman of the whole trade union movement. This kind of dual role could not survive the reform period, and in 1990 he was pushed out.

Shamir, Yitzhak (1915–)
Israeli politician. Born in Poland, he studied law at Warsaw University and, after emigrating to Palestine, at the Hebrew University of Jerusalem. In his twenties he became a founder member of the **Stern Gang**, the Zionist terrorist group which carried out anti-British attacks on strategic targets and personnel in Palestine. He was arrested by the British (1941) and exiled to Eritrea in 1946, but given asylum in France. He returned to the new State of Israel in 1948 but spent the next 20 years on the fringe of politics, immersing himself in business interests. He entered the Knesset in 1973, becoming its Speaker (1977–80). He was Foreign Minister (1980–3), before taking over the leadership of the right-wing **Likud** Party from Menachem **Begin**, and becoming Prime Minister (1983). From 1984, he shared power in an uneasy coalition with the Israel Labour Party. In 1990 the 'national unity' government collapsed, and in June 1992 Likud was defeated in the general election by the Labour Party, led by Itzhak **Rabin**. ▷ **Mapai Party**

Shaposhnikov, Boris Mikhailovich (1882–1945)
Russian officer and Soviet marshal. Once he went over to the **Bolsheviks** after 1917, he rose rapidly through the ranks until in 1928 he became Chief of Staff. He was commandant of the Frunze Military Academy (1932–7) and was promoted to be Chief of the General Staff (1937–40 and 1941–2). His role was particularly important in the wake of **Stalin**'s army purge. During **World War II** his subservience to Stalin made him less valuable than several other commanders.

Sharett, Moshe (1894–1965)
Israeli politician. Born in the Ukraine, he settled in Palestine in 1906. Sharett served in the Turkish Army during **World War I**, after which he studied at the London School of Economics. Returning to Palestine, he was prominent in the **Jewish Agency** in the 1930s and 1940s, and was arrested by the British authorities along with other Jewish leaders in 1946. Sharett was Israel's first Foreign Minister, and was then Prime Minister (1954–5). From 1960 he headed the executive of the **World Zionist Organization** and the Jewish Agency, spending his remaining years engaged in Zionist work. ▷ **Ben-Gurion, David; Zionism**

Sharon, Ariel (1928–)

Israeli general and politician. Prominent in the War of Independence (1948) and Sinai Campaign (1956), he became a major general shortly before the **Six-Day War** of 1967, during which he recaptured the Milta Pass in the Sinai Peninsula. Leaving the army (July 1973), he was recalled to fight in the **Yom Kippur War**. That year he helped to form **Likud** and was voted into the Knesset. As Defence Minister (1981–3) under Menachem **Begin**, Sharon planned Israel's invasion of Lebanon in 1982.

Sharpeville

An African township outside Johannesburg in South Africa. It was here, on 21 Mar 1960, that the police opened fire on a crowd demonstrating against laws restricting non-white movements and requiring non-Whites to carry indentification cards (the so-called pass laws), killing 69 people and wounding 180 others. It led to the banning of both the **ANC** and the PAC and remained a symbolic day for all Black nationalists in South Africa as a mark of their determination for self-rule and white intransigence. ▷ **Pan-Africanist Congress**

Shastri, Lal (Bahadur) (1904–66)

Indian politician. He joined the independence movement at the age of 16, and was often imprisoned by the British. He excelled as a Congress Party official, and in **Nehru**'s Cabinet became Minister of Transport (1957), Commerce (1958), and Home Affairs (1960). He succeeded Nehru as Prime Minister (1964–6), but died of a heart attack in Tashkent, USSR, the day after signing a 'no war' agreement with Pakistan. ▷ **Indian National Congress**

Shatalin, Stanislav Sergeievich (1934–)

Soviet economist. In 1989 he was appointed Secretary of the Economics Division of the Academy of Sciences and in 1990 he was made a member of Mikhail **Gorbachev**'s new presidential council. He acquired particular fame in the autumn of 1990 when he proposed a very radical economic reform, the '500-days plan', as an alternative to **Ryzhkov**'s more conservative one. Gorbachev promised to amalgamate the two but retreated before his right-wingers, in this way undermining both the cause of **perestroika** and his own position.

Shcharansky, Natan (Anatoli Borisovich) (1948–)

Soviet dissident. A brilliant mathematician who was disillusioned with Soviet society, in 1973 he applied for a visa to emigrate to Israel. This was repeatedly refused, prompting him to become increasingly active in the Soviet dissident movement. In 1976 he joined Yuri Orlov's Helsinki Watch Group, a body formed to monitor Soviet human rights violations, and in 1977 was sentenced to 13 years in a labour colony for allegedly spying on behalf of the **CIA**. He was freed from confinement in Feb 1986 as part of an East–West 'spy' exchange and joined his wife, Avital, in Israel, where he assumed the name Natan. In 1989 he was nominated as Israeli Ambassador to the **UN**.

Shchelokov, Nikolai Anisimovich (1910–84)
Soviet politician. A Ukrainian metallurgist, he had close associations with Leonid **Brezhnev** in party work based in Dnepropetrovsk, as political officers in the army during **World War II**, and subsequently in party work in Moldavia. In 1966 Brezhnev brought him to Moscow to become Minister of Internal Affairs (and Central Committee member from 1968). He utilized his position to help himself and his friends to have an easy life: his corruption became notorious. In 1983 Yuri **Andropov** dismissed him immediately on entering office; a year later he killed himself before charges could be brought against him.

Shcherbitsky, Vladimir Vasilevich (1918–90)
Ukrainian politician. A chemical engineer and wartime soldier, after 1945 he climbed up the Communist Party bureaucratic ladder until, by 1971, he was a member of the **Politburo** and, by 1972, First Secretary for the Ukraine. He silenced both dissidence and nationalism, and in dealing with the latter he was also of help to Mikhail **Gorbachev**. He was typical of the obstacles facing **perestroika**, paying it lip-service, but resisting it by all possible means. He was the last of the old guard, and Gorbachev was only able to get rid of him a few months before his death.

Shehu, Mehmet (1913–81)
Albanian politician. Born into a prosperous Muslim family, he studied at the American school in Tirana and later at an Italian military college, from which he was expelled for communist activities. He fought with the communists in the **Spanish Civil War** and returned to Albania to fight in the resistance during **World War II**. After the war, he studied at the military academy in Moscow (1945–6) and returned to Albania to become Chief of Staff in the Albanian army. With the ascendancy of the pro-Yugoslav faction within the Albanian Communist Party, he was expelled from party meetings but after the purges which followed Yugoslavia's expulsion from Cominform (June 1948), Shehu was readmitted and replaced **Xoxe** as Minister of the Interior. He resumed his position as Chief of Staff and in 1954 became Prime Minister. He survived successive purges but it is a matter of speculation whether his suicide in 1981 was entirely voluntary. ▷ **Hoxha, Enver**

Shelest, Petr Yefimovich (1908–)
Ukrainian politician. A poor peasant, he became a Communist Party official and won Nikita **Khrushchev**'s patronage. By 1957 he was First

Secretary in Kiev, by 1963 First Secretary in the Ukraine, and by 1964 a Central Committee member. In 1968, under Leonid **Brezhnev**, he took an interventionist approach in the Czechoslovak crisis. However, he tended to be soft on Ukrainian nationalism and lost Brezhnev's backing in 1972. In any case Brezhnev had his own more subservient candidate, **Shcherbitsky**.

Shepilov, Dmitri Trofimovich (1905–)

Soviet politician. Educated at Moscow University, from 1926 to 1931 he was a public prosecutor in Siberia and later became a lecturer in political economy. During **World War I** he was a political commissar in the Ukraine, where he came into contact with Nikita **Khrushchev**, and in 1945 he joined the Central Committee Secretariat. In 1952 he became chief editor of *Pravda*; in 1954 a member of the Supreme Soviet; and in 1956 Foreign Minister. But, disillusioned with Khrushchev, he participated in the **Anti-Party Plot** in 1957, was 'purged' by the Party leadership and banished to a distant teaching post.

Shevardnadze, Eduard Amvrosievich (1928–)

Soviet politician. Having studied history at the Kutaisi Institute of Education, he joined the Communist Party in 1948, and rose rapidly through the Komsomol youth league to the party apparatus during the 1950s and to the Georgian Ministry of the Interior in 1964 as minister. There from 1965 to 1972, he gained a reputation as a stern opponent of corruption, including that on the part of Mahavanadze, the Georgian Party Secretary. For his courage, he became Georgian Party Secretary himself in 1972 and introduced imaginative agricultural experiments. In 1978 he was brought into the **Politburo** as a candidate member and, having enjoyed longstanding connections with Mikhail **Gorbachev**, was promoted to full Politburo status and appointed Foreign Minister in 1985, contrasting starkly with his dour predecessor, Andrei **Gromyko**. He rapidly overhauled the Soviet foreign policy machine and, alongside Gorbachev, was responsible for the Soviet contribution to the ending of the **Cold War**. He was also a powerful influence for political reform inside the USSR and over the winter of 1990–1 constantly warned Gorbachev against the danger of a coup. In 1992 he returned to Georgia in the midst of a virtual civil war and, eventually becoming President of the newly independent state, took on himself the task of making it stable.

Shidehara Kijuro (1872–1951)

Japanese politician. From a wealthy landlord family who had close links (through marriage) with the Mitsubishi financial combine, Shidehara was ambassador to the USA and a delegate to the Washington Conference (1921–2) before becoming Foreign Minister in the reforming **Kenseikai** government of 1924–6, and again in 1929–31. He adopted a policy of cooperation with the Western powers in China and aroused the ire of ultra-nationalists when he supported the 1930 London Naval Treaty, which placed restrictions on Japan's naval build-up. He served as the second post-war Prime Minister in 1945–6 (because of his pro-Western reputation), seeing as his main task the preservation of the emperor system. This may have been behind Shidehara's suggestion that a disarmament clause (the eventual Article 9) be included in the 1947 **Peace Constitution**. Shidehara was defeated in Japan's first post-war election in Apr 1946.

Shigemitsu Mamoru (1887–1957)
Japanese diplomat and politician. During the 1930s, as vice-Foreign Minister, Shigemitsu was associated with the Asia faction of diplomats, who favoured an aggressive and independent foreign policy in China rather than working with the West. As Ambassador to the USSR (1936) and Britain (1938), however, he also cautioned against war with the USA and opposed the alliance with **Hitler**'s Germany in 1940. He served as Foreign Minister in 1943–5, trying unsuccessfully during the last year of **World War II** to involve the USSR as a mediator to bring about an early peace. Convicted as a war criminal in 1946, Shigemitsu served four years of a seven-year sentence before being released in 1950. He was Foreign Minister again in the cabinet of Ichiro **Hatoyama** (1954–6), helping to normalize relations with the USSR in 1956.

Shiites
Members of an Islamic religious movement prominent in Iran and Iraq. After the murder of **'Ali**, the son-in-law and nephew of the Prophet **Muhammad**, his followers continued to support his claim to the Muslim caliphate and became known as *Shi'at 'Ali* ('partisans of 'Ali'), usually anglicized as Shiites. They believe that 'Ali and his followers were both temporal rulers and imams. Today about 99 per cent of Iranians and 60 per cent of Iraqis are Shiites. The most important group is the 'Twelver' Shiites, who believe that there were twelve imams — 'Ali and his descendants — after the Prophet Muhammad, and that the twelfth did not die, but disappeared, and one day will return to bring justice to the world. Since the 16c, Twelver Shiism has been Iran's state religion.

Shipov, Dimitri N (1851–1920)
Russian political philanthropist. Chairman of the board of the **Semstvo** in St Petersburg, he organized a meeting of his fellow chairmen in the summer of 1896 to exchange views and present them to the Tsar. They encountered many official obstacles but held to their view that consultation was essential. Some became more radical and formed the Union of Liberation in 1903 to seek full representative government. In 1905

they went on to form the **Kadets**. But Shipov split to join **Guchkov** in establishing the **Octobrists** who were altogether less radical.

Shmelev, Nikolai Petrovich (1936–)
Soviet academic reformer and politician. An economist graduate of Moscow University, he had a short period in the 1960s in the propaganda section of the Central Committee. But he spent most of his career from the time of Nikita **Khrushchev** to that of Mikhail **Gorbachev** between three of the major institutes of the Soviet Academy, latterly having the opportunity to influence people in high places with his liberal ideas. From 1989 to 1991 he was a member of the Soviet Congress of Deputies.

show trials
Originally a series of political trials held in Moscow in the late 1930s under **Stalin**'s direct control. Because of what happened, the term came to refer to any political trial where the accused under pressure made public confessions of their alleged crimes, although their guilt would not have been established in any normal court. The process was an attempt to obscure personal vendettas and to justify political repression by demonstrating the use of apparently proper and just judicial procedures in dealing with so-called enemies of the state. ▷ **Stalinism**

Sidi Muhammad ben Yusuf (1911–61)
Sultan of Morocco (1927/61). A member of the Alouite Dynasty, he exercised both spiritual and temporal power; privately supporting the nationalist Istaqlal Party, he constantly obstructed French hegemony. Tribal hostility to him gave the French the chance to depose him in 1953, but he was restored in 1955, and when Morocco attained independence in 1957 he became King Mohammed V. He died suddenly after a minor operation and was succeeded by his eldest son, Prince Moulay Hassan, who had already emerged as the spokesman of chauvinistic Moroccan youth. His eldest daughter, Princess Lalla Ayesha, repudiated the yashmak and became a leader of the women's emancipation movement.

Siegfried Line
A fortified defensive line on Germany's western border with Belgium and France, known in German as the *Westwall* or 'Western Wall'. Built from 1936, to a large degree with conscripted labour, the Westwall turned out to be of limited military significance upon the Allied invasion of Germany (1944–5). ▷ **World War II**

Sifton, Sir Clifford (1861–1929)
Canadian politician. As Minister of the Interior he established a very effective immigration policy which drew large numbers of Ukrainians and Doukhobors to the north-west. He broke with the Liberal govern-

ment first in 1905, when he resigned over the restoration of separate schools in the north-west; and again when his defection over reciprocity helped the Conservatives to win the election of 1911. ▷ **Liberal Party (Canada)**

Sihanouk, Prince Norodom (1922–)
Cambodian (Kampuchean) politician. Educated in Vietnam and Paris, he became King of Cambodia in 1941. He negotiated the country's independence from France (1949–53), before abdicating in 1955 in favour of his father, so as to become an elected leader under the new constitution. As Prime Minister and then, from 1960 after his father's death, also as head of state, he steered a neutralist course during the **Vietnam War**. In 1970 he was deposed in a right-wing military coup led by the US-backed Lieutenant-General Lon Nol. Fleeing to Peking (Beijing), he formed a joint resistance front with **Pol Pot**, which overthrew Lon Nol in Apr 1975. Prince Sihanouk was reappointed head of state, but a year later was ousted by the **Khmer Rouge** leadership. In 1982, while living in North Korea, he became head of a broad-based Democratic Kampuchea (Cambodia) government-in-exile, which aimed to overthrow the Vietnamese-installed regime in Cambodia. Following the Vietnamese troop withdrawal in 1989, he has been involved in the attempts to negotiate a settlement of the country's civil war.

Sik, Ota (1919–)
Czechoslovak economist and politician. Imprisoned in a concentration camp during **World War II**, he joined the Communist Party in 1945. His main claim to fame was then as an economist, becoming Director of the Institute of Economics of the Academy of Sciences in 1962. This put him at the heart of the minor economic reform in the early 1960s and of the major political reform in 1968. He became a member of the Central Committee and a deputy premier. Not all of his ideas would necessarily have prospered, but he and they were swept away by the Soviet invasion in Aug; he then found it wiser to go abroad.

Sikandar Hayat Khan (1892–1942)
Indian politician. He came from a rich, landed family and after matriculating from school in Aligarh, entered University College, London to study medicine, but returned after two years. In **World War I** he offered his services to the British government. He was appointed an honorary recruiting officer and was granted a commission. During the third of the **Afghan Wars** he acted as a company commander (1919). He was elected to the Punjab legislative council in 1921, and was appointed chairman of Punjab Reforms Committee to work with the Simon Commission. He was knighted in 1933 and was appointed Governor of Reserve Bank in 1935. He was made Chief Minister of Punjab at the start of **World War II**

and held this office until 1942. During this time he launched rural reconstruction programmes, extended irrigation facilities, laid new roads, and established and strengthened panchayats. In his lifetime, the **Muslim League** could not get hold on the Punjab province. After his death Punjab plunged into political turmoil.

Sikorski, Władysław (Eugeniusz) (1881–1943)
Polish general and politician. Educated at Kraków and Lvov, he fought in the Russian-Polish War (1920–1), became Commander-in-Chief (1921), and Premier (1922–3). After **Piłsudski**'s coup (1926) he retired and wrote military history in Paris. He returned to Poland in 1938, but on being refused a command, fled to France, becoming Commander of the Free Polish forces and from 1940 Premier of the Polish government in exile in London. He was killed in an air crash at Gibraltar.

Simeon (1937–)
King of Bulgaria (1943/6). The son of **Boris III** and Tsaritsa Giovanna, he was proclaimed King on 28 Aug 1943 but was never crowned. Since he was too young to rule, Prince Kiril, together with the former Prime Minister, Bogdan Filov, and the former War Minister, General Nikola Mikhov, formed a council of regents. In Dec 1944 the **Fatherland Front** regime put the regents on trial and secured their execution. After the plebiscite (Sep 1946), Bulgaria was declared a People's Republic and Simeon went with his mother to Spain, where he still lives as a businessman.

Simmonds, Kennedy Alphonse (1936–)
St Christopher-Nevis politician and physician. He practised medicine in the USA and Caribbean before entering politics and founding (1965) the People's Action Movement (PAM) as a centre-right alternative to the Labour Party. After a series of unsuccessful elections, in 1980 Simmonds and PAM won enough seats in the Assembly to form a coalition government with the Nevis Reformation Party (NRP) and he became Prime Minister. Full independence was achieved in 1983 and Simmonds' coalition was re-elected in 1984. In the 1989 election, Simmonds and his party were again victorious.

Simon (of Stackpole Elidor), John (Allsebrook), 1st Viscount (1873–1954)
British politician and lawyer. A Liberal, he entered parliament in 1906, and was knighted in 1910. He was Attorney-General (1913–15) and Home Secretary (1915–16), before resigning from the cabinet for his opposition to conscription. Deserting the Liberals to form the Liberal National Party, he supported Ramsay **MacDonald**'s coalition governments and became Foreign Secretary (1931–5), Home Secretary in the Conservative government (1935–7), Chancellor of the Exchequer

(1937–40), and Lord Chancellor in Winston **Churchill**'s war-time coalition (1940–5). Created viscount in 1940. ▷ **Liberal Party** (UK)

Sinai Campaign (1956)

This campaign, which can be seen as forming a prelude to the Suez Crisis, took Israeli armour to the Suez Canal. Terrorist raids from Gaza in 1955 were put forward as the reason for Israel's move into the **Gaza Strip**, which caused the Egyptians to close the Gulf of Aqaba. Egypt consulted on a joint military response with Syria and Jordan, but secret talks between Britain, France and Israel (so effectively secret that it appears that not even the British Ambassador in Cairo knew of them) resulted in an Israeli attack on the Sinai Peninsula on 29 Oct 1956. By 5 Nov, when the **UN** imposed a ceasefire, the Israelis under the leadership of Moshe **Dayan** had occupied Sinai and reached the Suez Canal.

Singapore

A republic at the southern tip of the Malay Peninsula, South-East Asia, consisting of the island of Singapore and about 50 adjacent islets. Singapore became a British Crown Colony in 1867 but was occupied by the Japanese in wartime from 1942 until 1945. Self-government was established in 1959, and the area became part of the Federation of Malaya from 1963 until its establishment as an independent state in 1965.

Singh, Charan (1902–87)

Indian politician. Born into a poor peasant family in Meerut District, Uttar Pradesh, he obtained a law degree in 1925. He started practising law in Ghaziabad, and soon became involved in the freedom movement. He courted arrest in the Salt **Satyagraha** in 1932. In 1929 he joined the Congress, and was elected to the Uttar Pradesh Legislative Assembly in 1937, going on to represent his constituency for 40 years until 1977, when he was elected for the Lok Sabha. He joined both the **Non-Cooperation Movement** and **Quit India Movement** in 1940. He was Chief Minister of Uttar Pradesh twice, and in 1969 formed the ministry of *Bharatiya Kranti Dal* (BKD). Charan Singh's *Bharatiya Lok Dal* revolted against Morarji **Desai**'s 28-month-old Janata government and he was sworn in as the fifth prime minister of India in July 1979. He served in this capacity until Congress won the general elections in 1980.

Singh, V(ishwanath) P(ratap) (1931–)

Indian politician. The son of an influential Raja in Uttar Pradesh, he was educated at Pune and Allahabad Universities and was elected (1971) to the Lok Sabha (federal parliament) as a representative of the Congress (I) Party. During the administrations of Indira **Gandhi** and Rajiv **Gandhi**, he served as Minister of Commerce (1976–7 and 1983), Chief Minister of Uttar Pradesh (1980–2), Minister of Finance (1984–6) and Minister of

Defence (1986–7), instigating a zealous anti-corruption drive in the finance and defence posts. In 1987 he was ousted from the government and Congress (I) when he unearthed the 'Bofors Scandal', which involved the payment of alleged arms deal 'kickbacks' to senior officials closely connected to Rajiv Gandhi. Respected for his probity and sense of principle, as head of the broad-based Janata Dal coalition he emerged as the most popular opposition politician in India. He was elected Prime Minister in 1990.

Sinhala

A language of North Indian origin. The speakers of the language, the Sinhala or Sinhalese, form the largest group in the population of Sri Lanka and have dominated the country's politics since independence in 1948. Most Sinhala people are Buddhists and modern Buddhist nationalists believe that the Buddha himself entrusted the care of the island to the Sinhala people as custodians of his teaching. The election of S W R D **Bandaranaike** in 1956, with a promise to make Sinhala the sole language of used in government led to opposition from the country's predominantly Hindu Tamil minority, which has continued ever since.

Sinn Féin

Irish political party (literally, 'Ourselves Alone') which developed during the period 1905–8 under the direction of Arthur **Griffith** in support of Irish independence from Britain. By the end of **World War I** it had become the main Irish nationalist party. It formed a separate assembly from the UK parliament, and succeeded in creating the **Irish Free State** (1922). Following the Anglo-Irish Treaty (1921), it split to form the two main Irish parties, and in 1970 it split again into official and provisional wings. It has remained active in Northern Ireland, and has close contacts with the **IRA**. ▷ **Fianna Fáil; Fine Gael**

Sino-Japanese War (1937–45)

The war proper broke out in 1937 with the Japanese invasion of Tianjin (Tientsin) and Beijing, but this was only the ultimate phase of Japan's territorial designs on China. Manchuria had already been occupied (1931) and the puppet-state of **Manzhuguo** created in 1932. Nanjing was invaded in Dec 1937, and most of northern China was soon under Japanese control. From Dec 1941, US intervention became the major factor in the Pacific War, which ended with Japan's surrender in 1945. ▷ **United Fronts; World War II**

Sino-Soviet Dispute (1960–89)

The period of extreme tension between the USSR and China, even leading to border war in 1969. **Stalin** had been a half-hearted supporter of the Chinese Communist Party down to 1953; Nikita **Khrushchev** had subsequently been more generous; but both had been patronizing. **Mao Zedong** objected to being treated as inferior, and he had developed his own somewhat different brand of **communism**. Ideological sparring led to Khrushchev withdrawing all Soviet assistance and advisers in 1960. Behind the border dispute also lay serious territorial differences. The situation only improved after **Deng Xiaoping** launched China on an outward-looking reform programme in 1978 and Mikhail **Gorbachev** started his revolutionary upheaval in 1985. Their meeting in Beijing in 1989 signalled the end of the dispute, though internal developments in both countries have since renewed the strain.

Siroky, Viliam (1902–71)
Czechoslovak politician. As a young Slovak railway worker, he helped create the Communist Party in Bratislava in 1921 and by 1935 he was both a secretary of the Central Committee and a communist member of parliament. His experiences in **World War II** included imprisonment in Slovakia and service in Moscow. Siroky's subsequent rise made him Deputy Prime Minister (1945–53), Foreign Minister (1950–3), following the executed **Clementis**, and Prime Minister (1953–63), in succession to **Zapotocky**. He survived the purges, but his bureaucratic credentials were inadequate to cope with the transitional needs of the late 1950s/early 1960s and he was dropped in favour of another Slovak, **Lenart**, whose supposed reform credentials achieved little more.

Sisulu, Walter Max Ulyate (1912–)
South African nationalist. After working as a labourer in Johannesburg and then running his own real estate agency, he joined the **ANC** in 1940, becoming Treasurer of the Youth League in 1944. A leader of the Programme of Action in 1949, he was elected Secretary-General of the ANC in the same year. He resigned his post in 1954 because of banning orders, but continued to work underground. Sisulu was captured in 1963 and found guilty of treason, being sentenced in 1964 to life imprisonment. He was released in 1989 and took responsibility for the party's internal organization after its legalization in 1990.

Sithole, Ndabaningi (1920–)
Zimbabwean cleric and politician. He worked as a teacher (1941–53) before going to the USA to study theology (1953–6) and was ordained a congregational minister in 1958. He wrote *African Nationalism* in 1959, when he was also President of the African Teachers' Union. Sithole was Treasurer of the National Democratic Party in 1960 and, after it was banned, formed with Joshua **Nkomo** the Zimbabwe African People's Union (**ZAPU**), from which he split in 1963 and formed the Zimbabwe African National Union (**ZANU**). Imprisoned by the RF government from 1964 to 1975, during which time the leadership of ZANU was

wrested from him by Robert **Mugabe**, he went into exile in Zambia in 1975, forming his own faction of the **African National Council**. He negotiated with Ian **Smith** and was a member of the Executive Council of the transitional government in Rhodesia-Zimbabwe (1978–80). Although he was elected to the first post-independence parliament, he ceased thereafter to play a major role in politics.

Six-Day War (5–10 June 1967)
Arab–Israeli war. In May 1967 President Gamal Abd al-**Nasser** of Egypt blocked the Tiran Straits to Israeli shipping and massed troops in the Sinai Peninsula, while King Hussein allowed Iraqi forces into Jordan. Taking preemptive action, Israel paralysed the Egyptian air force and then, responding to Jordanian and Syrian attacks, captured East Jerusalem, the West bank, Golan Heights and Sinai. Israel's unexpected victory was achieved in six days. Afterwards, Arab states refused to negotiate peace with Israel which has therefore held on to the so-called 'occupied territories', except Sinai which was returned to Egypt after the peace agreement of 1979. ▷ **Arab–Israeli Wars; Israel, State of; Sharon, Ariel; West Bank**

Skobtsova, Maria (1891–1945)
Russian Orthodox nun. She early identified herself with the Social Revolutionaries when a student in St Petersburg, where she was the first woman to enrol at the Ecclesiastical Academy. Bolshevik excesses having disillusioned her, she was among those who escaped to France. She began work with the Russian Orthodox Student Christian Movement which administered also to refugees, and in 1932, despite having had two divorces, became a nun. Unconventional and radical, she worked among society's cast-offs whom she fed and housed. Nazi measures against the Jews in wartime Paris provided a new challenge. She was arrested and sent to Ravensbrück concentration camp in 1943, where she brought Christian light and hope despite appalling conditions. She was gassed on the eve of Easter, 1945, reportedly going voluntarily 'in order to help her companions to die'.

Slánský, Rudolf (1901–52)
Czechoslovak politician. Born in Moravia, an intellectual, he joined the Communist Party when it was founded in 1921 and, in 1929, became one of Klement **Gottwald**'s chief aides in revolutionizing or 'bolshevizing' it. He spent much of **World War II** in Moscow but in 1944 was flown in to assist the Slovak uprising. From 1945 to 1951 he held the most important party post as Secretary-General, masterminding much of what produced and followed the **February Revolution** in 1948. However, he was arrested, then executed during the purges, a victim of **Stalin**'s dislike of independent-minded communists, especially Jewish intellectuals. It was little

comfort to the majority of his countrymen that he suffered the self-same fate he had imposed on others.

SLFP (Sri Lanka Freedom Party)

Left-of-centre Sri Lankan political party formed by S W R D **Bandaranaike** after his departure from the **UNP** in 1951. The SLFP formed the largest party in government in 1956–9, 1960–5 and 1970–7. Each time, the party achieved power as leader of a coalition formed with smaller left-wing parties, and each time the coalition was undermined by internal friction and gradual defections to the opposition. The leadership of the party has been dominated by Bandaranaike, his widow, Sirimavo **Bandaranaike**, and their children and close relatives.

Slim (of Yarralumia and of Bishopston), William (Joseph), 1st Viscount (1891–1970)

British field marshal. He served during **World War I** in the **Gallipoli Campaign** and in Mesopotamia. In **World War II**, his greatest achievement was to lead his reorganized forces, the famous 14th 'forgotten' army, to victory over the Japanese in Burma. He was Chief of the Imperial General Staff (1948–52) and a highly successful Governor-General of Australia (1953–60). Knighted in 1944, he became a viscount in 1960.

Slovak Republic (1939–45)

The supposedly independent republic carved out of Czechoslovakia by Slovak nationalists on **Hitler**'s instructions. Many Slovaks had genuine complaints: the Czechs had established a centralized state in 1918, were less devoutly Catholic and economically better off. However, those who led the new republic (such as **Tiso** and **Tuka**) soon lost popularity as the Germans exploited the Slovak economy and expected Slovaks to fight in the hated Russian front. Resistance produced the **Slovak Uprising** in 1944. Although it was put down by the Germans, their presence and brutality simply recruited more volunteers to fight against them and Tiso. Little was done after 1945 to meet legitimate Slovak aspirations, but in Jan 1993 Slovakia finally regained its independence.

Slovak Uprising (Sep–Oct 1944)

A rising against **Tiso**, President of the **Slovak Republic**, and his German masters. The rebels comprised partisans, civilians, Allied helpers and insurgent regiments from the Slovak army. Their aim was to free eastern Slovakia as the **Red Army** advanced and to block German reinforcements. For two months they held a large area around Banska Bystrice. But the Germans moved quickly, the Russians slowly, and there were divided counsels. Despite great heroism, the rising was put down. Many fighters escaped to the mountains; inevitably the civilians suffered. The Slovaks gained little except an important historical memory.

Slovenia, Republic of

A mountainous republic in central Europe, part of the Austro-Hungarian Empire until 1918 when it joined with Croatia, Montenegro, Serbia and Bosnia-Herzegovina to form the Kingdom of Serbs, Croats and Slovenes. This union was renamed Yugoslavia in 1929 and became a people's republic in 1946. In June 1991, Milan **Kučan** declared the Republic's independence from the Yugoslav Federation. The Yugoslav National Army invaded but, after the so-called 'Ten-Day War', Serbia's President, Slobodan **Milošević**, acknowledged Slovenia's independence in the vain hope that he could arrest the secession of the Republics of Croatia and Bosnia.

Slovo, Joe (1926–)

South African nationalist. Born in Lithuania, he emigrated to South Africa in 1935, where he worked as a clerk before volunteering for service in **World War II**. After joining the South African Communist Party (SACP), he qualified as a lawyer and defended many figures in political trials. He married Ruth First, daughter of the SACP Treasurer, and was a founding member of the Congress of Democrats in 1953. Charged in the treason trial of 1961, he nevertheless escaped the country in 1963 working for the **ANC** and SACP abroad. In 1985 he became Chief of Staff of **Umkhonto we Sizwe** but resigned to become Chairman of the SACP. He returned to South Africa after the legalization of the SACP and was a major figure in the negotiations between the nationalist parties and the government.

Smeral, Bohumir (1880–1941)

Czechoslovak politician. A lawyer, he joined the Social Democratic Party in 1897 and was editing its paper by 1906. During **World War I** he was slow to join the struggle for Czechoslovak independence, and following the 1917 **Russian Revolution** his loyalty swung increasingly towards the left. In 1921 he helped found the Communist Party and became very active in Czechoslovak politics in the 1920s. In the 1930s he was also very active in the **Comintern**, which involved much travelling. Although he fled to Moscow in 1938 and died there, he was never a Stalinist, preserving some traces of his social democratic moderation. ▷ **Stalinism**

Smirnov, Georgi Lukich (1922–)

Soviet communist ideologue. Of Cossack stock with a long career in the Communist Party bureaucracy, he became adviser to Mikhail **Gorbachev** in 1985 and Director of the Institute of Marxism-Leninism in 1987. In both positions he attempted to modify Brezhnevite orthodoxy; he was still trying, with only moderate success, when the party was closed down in 1991.

Smith, Alfred Emanuel (1873–1944)
US politician. He rose from newsboy to be Governor of New York State (1919–20 and 1923–8) with an impresive record of liberal reform. 'Al' Smith was beaten as Democratic candidate for the US presidency in 1928, and later became an opponent of President Franklin D **Roosevelt**'s **New Deal**.

Smith, Ian (Douglas) (1919–)
Rhodesian politician and farmer. Educated at Chaplin High School and Rhodes University, he served with the Royal Airforce in **World War II** before returning to his farm. He was elected a member of the Southern Rhodesian Legislative Assembly in 1948 for the United Party and then, for the United Federal Party (UFP), to the Federal Parliament in 1953, becoming Chief Whip. He broke with the UFP, ostensibly on the question of Britain's failure to grant independence to the white minority-ruled states of central Africa, and helped found the **Rhodesian Front** in 1962. He replaced Winston Field as leader after a putsch and was Prime Minister from 1964 to 1978, when he became a member of the Executive Council of the transitional government in Zimbabwe-Rhodesia. A cautious and secretive man, he declared **UDI** (Unilateral Declaration of Independence) in 1965, negotiated without success with successive British governments and was immensely popular with his white voters. He was elected to the post-independence parliament and remained a vigorous opponent of Robert **Mugabe** and his government.

Smith, John (1938–94)
Scottish politician. He was called to the Scottish bar in 1967 and made a QC in 1983. He entered the House of Commons, representing Lanarkshire North, in 1970 and from 1983 Monklands East. He served in the administrations of Harold **Wilson** and James **Callaghan**, becoming trade secretary in 1978. From 1979 to 1992 he was front bench opposition spokesman on trade, energy, employment and economic affairs, one of Labour's most respected politicians. After the Labour election defeat of 1992 and the subsequent resignation of Neil **Kinnock**, he emerged as the leader of the party. His political career had been threatened by a heart attack in 1988, and although he appeared to have made a complete recovery and returned to the front bench in 1989, a second heart attack proved fatal. His death was a great and unexpected blow to his party.

Smrkovsky, Josef (1911–74)
Czechoslovak politician. A baker's assistant, he joined the Communist Party in 1933 and was active in the resistance during **World War II**. He was one of the leaders of the Prague rising in 1945 and held a series of party and government posts until, in 1951, he was imprisoned during the Stalinist purges. It was 1963 before he was rehabilitated and 1966 before

he was readmitted to the party. In 1967–8 he was a prime mover in the reforms and became a popular chairman of parliament. His very moderation made him a Soviet target; and like Alexander **Dubček** himself he was taken to Moscow in Aug 1968 and then removed from power at the first opportunity the following year.

Smuts, Jan (Christian) (1870–1950)
South African general and politician. Educated at the University of Cambridge, England, he became a lawyer, fought in the second Boer War (1899–1902), and entered the House of Assembly in 1907. He held several Cabinet posts, led campaigns against the Germans in south-west Africa and Tanganyika, was a member of the Imperial War Cabinet in **World War I**, and succeeded Louis **Botha** as Prime Minister (1919–24). He was a significant figure at Versailles, and was instrumental in the founding of the **League of Nations**. As Minister of Justice under **Hertzog**, his coalition with the Nationalists in 1934 produced the United Party; he was Premier again from 1939 to 1948. ▷ **Boer Wars**

Snamek, Jan (1870–1956)
Czechoslovak politician. Born and educated in Moravia, he was variously a priest, professor of theology and papal negotiator, and helped found Christian democracy in the late 1890s. A deputy from 1907, he supported **Masaryk** during **World War I** and, as leader of the Populist Party in the interwar period, held several ministerial appointments. During **World War II** he was Prime Minister in **Beneš**'s government-in-exile in London, and Deputy Prime Minister (1945–8) in the National Front government. Usually a moderate, he nevertheless joined those resigning in 1948 and precipitating the **February Revolution**. The middle road had not been easy and it became impossible under **communism**.

Soares, Mario Alberto Nobre Lopez (1924–)
Portuguese politician. Educated at Lisbon University and in the Faculty of Law at the Sorbonne, Paris, he was politically active in the democratic socialist movement from his early twenties and was imprisoned for his activities on 12 occasions. In 1968 he was deported by **Salazar** to São Tomé, returning to Europe in 1970 and living in exile in Paris until 1974 when he returned to co-found the Social Democratic Party (PSD). In the same year he was elected to the Assembly and was soon brought into the government. He was Prime Minister (1976–8 and 1983–5), and then in 1986 was elected Portugal's first civilian President for 60 years.

Sobbuza II (1899–1982)
King of Swaziland. Educated at Lovedale College, he was installed as Paramount Chief or Ngwenyama of the Swazi people in 1921. He was Head of State when Swaziland became independent in 1968, but in 1973

he assumed full executive and legislative powers and introduced a new Constitution in 1978 which re-established traditional authorities, rather than universal suffrage, as the basis of legitimate authority.

Sobchak, Anatoli Alexandrovich (1937–)
Russian politician. A talented law graduate who became Dean of the Faculty of Law in Leningrad (now St Petersburg), long before turning to politics. In the **Gorbachev** period he became critical of many past communist practices and was chosen in 1989 as a member of both the Congress of Deputies and the Supreme Soviet, where he demonstrated his investigative and debating skills. In May 1990 he was elected Mayor of St Petersburg and in July abandoned the Communist Party to become both locally and nationally one of the driving forces for serious reform.

Sobukwe, Robert (1924–77)
South African nationalist leader. Educated at mission schools and Fort Hare College, he was President of the Students' Representative Council in 1949 and a member of the **ANC** Youth League. He was dismissed from his teacher's post in 1952 because of his participation in the Defiance Campaign, but taught for the next seven years at Fort Hare College. He helped found the **Pan-Africanist Congress** (PAC) in 1959 and was elected its President. He was banned in 1960 and then imprisoned until 1969 when he was released, but restricted to Kimberley where he died in 1977.

Social and Liberal Democratic Party (SLDP) ▷ **Liberal Party** (UK)

Social Credit Party
Canadian political party. The monetary theory known as social credit (regarded as nonsense by most economists) was developed by a British engineer, Major Clifford H Douglas, during the early 1930s. It held that government should issue payments (social credits) to everyone, in order to balance consumers' buying power with agricultural and manufacturing productivity. It attracted the attention of an Albertan radio-evangelist, William Aberhardt, who spread the doctrine to the depression-hit prairie farmers. In the provincial election of 1935, the Social Credit Party came to power. The federal government, however, disallowed its attempts to implement its policies, and in a short time the party became just another free enterprise neo-conservative political party. As such, it retained power and had cleared the province's debts by the mid-1950s. In 1952 it also defeated the Liberal–Conservative coalition in British Columbia, and throughout the 1950s it grew in federal strength. By 1962 **Diefenbaker** required its support to maintain his fragile hold on power, but in 1979 it contributed to a Conservative defeat when Joe **Clark** refused to bargain for its support in a vote of confidence. By the 1980s, however, the party had all but disappeared. ▷ **Créditistes**

Social Democratic Party (SDP)

UK political party formed in 1981 by a 'gang of four', comprising David **Owen**, Shirley **Williams**, Roy **Jenkins**, and Bill Rogers. They broke away from the **Labour Party** primarily over disagreements on policy and the degree of influence exerted on party policy by the trade unions. Although espousing socialist principles, the party was a moderate centrist one. The SDP formed an electoral pact with the Liberals in 1981, but despite some early electoral successes failed to break the two-party 'mould' of British politics. It merged with the **Liberal Party** in 1988 becoming the **Social and Liberal Democratic Party**, although a rump, led by David Owen, continued in existence as the SDP until 1990.

Social Democratic Party (Denmark)

Founded in 1871 and represented in the Danish parliament, **Folketinget**, for the first time in 1884. After the general election in 1924, the Social Democrats became the largest party in parliament and formed their first government, with Thorvald **Stauning** as Premier. The party has remained Denmark's largest. During the interwar period the party, under Stauning's leadership, moved away from the socialist idea of a class struggle. Instead, it became the party's ambition to create a welfare state for all social groups through democratic, parliamentary reforms. This ambition was fulfilled during the post-war period under the party leaders Hedtoft, Hansen, Kampmann and **Krag**, all of whom were also prime ministers. After 1973, when the Danish economy was hit by recession, the party, led by Jørgensen (1972–87) and Auken (1987–92), became the chief defender of the welfare system, since 1982 as the main opposition party. In 1992 Poul Nyrup Rasmussen was elected the new party leader.

Social Democratic Party (Finland)

Founded in 1899, the party adopted a revolutionary, Marxist programme. It collaborated with Russian socialists against the Tsarist regime but was also committed to achieving Finland's independence from the Russian Empire. By 1916 it had won an absolute majority in the Finnish parliament, but was taken by surprise by the 1917 **Russian Revolution**. Despite its collaboration with the bourgeois parties, the SDP's radicalism alarmed its partners in government, who achieved a parliamentary majority in the elections of Oct 1917. At this point, the SDP was urged by the new Bolshevik regime in Russia and by its own working-class supporters to seize power in its own right. The workers took control of the country through a revolutionary general strike, but the party leadership hesitated. When the bourgeois parties gave in to their demands for reform, the SDP called off the strike and a bourgeois government was formed. In Jan 1918 the Social Democrats declared this government deposed and set up a provisional workers' government. Civil war followed, in which the Reds were supported by the **Bolsheviks** and the Whites by the Germans. The Reds were defeated (Apr 1918) and much of the leadership went into exile in Russia; in Aug 1918 they formed the Finnish Communist Party. The SDP in Finland was suppressed after the civil war but was revived, largely through the efforts of Väinö **Tanner**, in late 1918. Although the SDP retained the loyalties of the majority of the working class, an important minority was attracted to the communist-influenced Finnish Socialist Workers' Party, formed in 1920. Tanner formed a minority government, with the support of the Swedish People's Party, in 1926–7, but lost the leadership of the SDP for four years. SDP support grew steadily in the 1930s despite the attempt by the **Lapua Movement** to repeat against the SDP the success of its anti-communist agitation. Excluded from office in 1936 by the opposition of President Svinhufvud, the Social Democrats formed a stable, broad-based coalition with the Agrarians and the Progressives following Svinhufvud's defeat in the presidential election of 1937, and were in government throughout Finland's two disastrous wars with the USSR in 1939–40 and 1941–4. A minority of the party opposed the war and linked up with the Communist Party when the latter was legalized after Finland's defeat, forming part of the communists' parliamentary organization, the Finnish People's Democratic League (SKDL). Tanner regained control of the SDP in Nov 1944 but was imprisoned as a war criminal (1946–9). Throughout the 1950s the party was weakened by internal struggles and was under the shadow of Soviet suspicion, heightened by the re-election of Tanner as Party Chairman in 1957. A major realignment of Finnish politics occurred in 1966; from this point onwards, the majority of Finnish governments were coalitions of Social Democrats, SKDL and the Centre Party, usually with a Social Democrat as Prime Minister. The 1980s saw a strong revival of the Finnish Conservative Party (which had also been the object of Soviet mistrust), but the SDP remained the largest party. In 1982 a Social Democrat, Mauno **Koivisto**, was elected President. ▷ **Communist Party** (Finland)

Social Democratic Party (Sweden)

The party was founded in Stockholm in 1889. Under the leadership of Hjalmar **Branting**, who became its first parliamentary representative in 1896, it came to adopt a reformist programme and was the largest party in the directly-elected chamber of the parliament by 1915. Social Democratic ministers sat in a coalition government with the Liberals in 1917, and Branting headed purely Social Democrat administrations in 1920–5. Under Per Albin **Hansson**, Tage **Erlander** and Sven Olof **Palme** the Social Democrats enjoyed continuous power from 1932 to 1976 (except for a brief break in 1936) either alone or in coalition with the Agrarians, but only rarely have they enjoyed an overall majority.

Social Gospel

An early 20c movement in the USA concerned with the application of Christian principles to the social and political order in the service of the

Kingdom of God. Among its most prominent leaders were Washington Gladden (1836–1918), Walter Rauschenbusch (1861–1918), and Shailer Matthews (1863–1941).

social market economy (*soziale Marktwirtschaft*)
Otherwise known as neo-liberalism, the social market economy was adopted first in the western zones of Germany (1948) and then by the Federal Republic (1949). Its guiding principle is that economic stability should be achieved through market forces, although the state is accorded a role in ensuring the smooth operation of a competitive market and in providing social security and welfare benefits in as far as they did not flout market principles. In the 1950s the **CDU** government and its Economics Minister, **Erhard**, were staunch proponents of the social market economy and credited it with Federal Germany's 'economic miracle' (**Wirtschaftswunder**) and by the end of the 1950s all major German parties accepted the principle of a market economy. In practice, however, there had always been and there continue to be deviations from this principle in areas such as competition policy, social policy and labour policy.

socialism
A wide-ranging political doctrine which first emerged in Europe during industrialization in the 18c. Most socialists would agree that social and economic relationships play a major part in determining human possibilities, and that the unequal ownership of property under **capitalism** creates an unequal and conflictive society. The removal of private property or some means of counterbalancing its power, it is held, will produce a more equal society where individuals enjoy greater freedom and are able to realize their potential more fully. A socialist society will thus be more co-operative and fraternal. Possibly the major division within socialism is between those who believe that to bring it about revolution is necessary, and those who believe change can be achieved through reforms within the confines of democratic politics. There are also differences as to how far capitalist production needs to be eradicated to bring about a socialist society.

Socialism in One Country (post-1918)
The slogan epitomizing Soviet policy after the **Russian Revolution**. **Lenin** forced the events of late 1917 on the basis that a few workers and a mass of poor peasants constituted a genuine 'working class'. However, he still expected communist revolutions in more advanced industrial countries. When these did not materialize, he and **Stalin** opted for a policy of building socialism within formerly Tsarist Russia, using their 'working class' to build the industry that the country needed to have a genuine proletariat. What resulted was not socialism, but a personal dictatorship

within a forcibly industrialized country. The USSR also developed a very defensive foreign policy.

Socialism with a Human Face (1968)
The description applied to the reform **communism** proposed by Alexander **Dubček** in Czechoslovakia in 1968. It included genuine elections, an end to censorship, and freedom of assembly and travel. The threat this seemed to pose to communist parties everywhere provoked the Soviet invasion in Aug of the same year and the end of reform. Ironically, Mikhail **Gorbachev** adopted a somewhat similar but more radical approach which helped to destroy his party.

Socialist Party (France)
Officially known (1905–71) as the SFIO (*section française de l'Internationale ouvrière*, 'French Section of the Workers' International'). Organized socialist parties emerged from 1879, but were for 20 years only tiny sects, divided among themselves, usually known by the name of their leaders, as Guesdists, Broussists, Allemanistes, etc, with very little representation in parliament. By 1901, two main parties had emerged, the *parti socialiste de France* ('Socialist Party of France') under **Guesde**, more dogmatically Marxist, and the *parti socialiste français* ('French Socialist Party') under **Jaurès**, more prepared to work within the existing system, and supporting the entry of a socialist, **Millerand**, into the cabinet. Under pressure from the Second International (the umbrella organization, created in 1889, in which all recognized Socialist parties of the world are represented) they united in 1905, accepting in theory the intransigent Marxism of Guesde, but in reality more influenced by Jaurès. Nevertheless the policy of refusing to accept office in 'bourgeois' cabinets was accepted, and maintained until 1936, except for **World War I**, leading to defection from the party of many of its Deputies who had ministerial ambitions. The majority of the party agreed to support the government in 1914 *Union Sacrée* ('Sacred Union'), but as the war continued, a growing minority turned to opposition. This split foreshadowed the division of 1920 between socialists and communists. The majority of party members voted to join the Third International, and founded a new party. The leading figures in the Socialist Party after 1920 were Léon **Blum**, the leader of the parliamentary group, and Paul Faure, the General-Secretary of the party. In opposition for most of the inter-war period, the socialists overtook the radicals as the main party of the left in 1936, allowing Blum to form a coalition government, the **Popular Front** (1936–7, 1938). The party was divided over support for **Pétain** in 1940, but emerged in 1945 as one of three large parties that ruled France (1946–7) in a coalition (Tripartism). In 1947 the communists were excluded from that coalition, and the division of the left between socialists and commmunists reduced the political influence of both parties for over 30 years. By 1971 the SFIO, which had been led by Guy **Mollet** since 1946,

appeared almost moribund; it combined in that year with other small parties and was renamed the *parti socialiste* ('Socialist Party') with François **Mitterrand** as leader. In 1981 it achieved the feat of winning a majority of seats in parliament, something very rarely achieved in France by a single party, although the majority was lost in 1986. ▷ **socialism**

Socialist Revolutionary (SR) Party

A neo-populist revolutionary party in Russia, founded in 1902 and led by Victor Chernov (1873–1952). The SR's radical agrarian programme envisaged the uncompensated redistribution and 'socialization' of the land among a communally organized peasantry. Their 'fighting detachments' carried out a number of spectacular political assassinations between 1902 and 1918. In 1917 Chernov was Minister of Agriculture in the Provisional Government. ▷ **Russian Revolution**

Sokolov, Sergei Leonidovich (1911–)

Soviet military commander. He rose rapidly during **World War II** and was subsequently given a series of staff posts. In 1965 he became Commander of the Leningrad district and in 1967 Deputy Defence Minister. He was long retired when he was chosen to succeed **Ustinov** as Defence Minister in 1984. This represented a downgrading of the army, a process that was completed when dismissal came in 1987 because of the forces' failure to intercept a German light plane that landed provocatively in Red Square.

Sokolovski, Vasili Danilovich (1897–1968)

Soviet marshal. He was already a staff officer by 1921 and led several assaults against Germany in **World War II**, aiding the capture of Berlin. From 1945 to 1949 he was head of the Soviet military administration in Germany and was held responsible for the failure of the **Berlin blockade**. Yet he became a deputy defence minister for the years 1949–60 and Chief of the General Staff for the period 1952–60. He wrote standard studies of Soviet military strategy.

Solidarity

An organization established in Poland (Sep 1980) as the National Committee of Solidarity (*solidarność*) to co-ordinate the activities of the emerging independent trade union following protracted industrial unrest, notably in the Lenin shipyard in Gdańsk. Its first President was Lech **Wałesa** (later to become President of Poland). It organized a number of strikes in early 1981 for improved wages and conditions, and became a force for major political reform. It attempted to seek reconciliation with the Polish government through proposing a council for national consensus, but suffered continuous harassment and was rendered largely ineffective by the declaration of martial law (Dec 1981) and by being made illegal. It remained underground, but came back into the political arena in mid-1988. Following its successes in the 1989 elections, Solidarity entered into a coalition government with the communists, with one of its members (Tadeusz Mazowiecki) eventually becoming Prime Minister.

Solzhenitsyn, Alexander Isayevich (1918–)

Russian writer. Educated at Rostov in mathematics and physics, he fought in **World War II**, and was imprisoned (1945–53) for unfavourable comment on **Stalin**'s conduct of the war. On his release, he became a teacher, and started to write. His first novel, *Odin den iz zhizni Ivana Denisovicha* (1962, One Day in the Life of Ivan Denisovich), set in a prison camp, was acclaimed both in the USSR and the West; but his subsequent denunciation of Soviet censorship led to the banning of his later, semi-autobiographical novels, *Rakovy korpus* (1968, Cancer Ward) and *V kruge pervom* (1968, The First Circle). He was expelled from the Soviet Writers' Union in 1969, and awarded the Nobel Prize for Literature in 1970 (received in 1974). His later books include *Arkhipelag Gulag* (1973–8, The Gulag Archipelago), a factual account of the Stalinist terror, for which he was arrested and exiled (1974). He now lives in the USA.

Somalia

A north-eastern African republic. The opening of the Suez Canal in 1869 brought Italian, French and British interests to this Muslim area, and after **World War II** Somalia was formed by the amalgamation of Italian and British protectorates. It gained independence in 1960 and since then there has been territorial conflict with Ethiopia (which has a large Somali population). There was a military coup in 1969, followed by a new constitution adopted in 1979, introducing a single-party state. In 1991 President **Barre** was overthrown by the USC (United Somali Congress) guerillas and a new constitution was implemented. The north-east region seceded as the Somaliland Republic. In the early 1990s the population faced starvation largely as a result of such civil war, and **UN** troops secured routes for relief convoys carrying food aid. The UN forces completed their withdrawal after the signing of a peace agreement in March 1994.

Somme, Battle of the (1 July–19 Nov 1916)

A major **World War I** British offensive against German troops in north-western France which developed into the bloodiest battle in world history, with more than a million casualties. It was launched by British Commander-in-Chief, Douglas **Haig**. When the attack was abandoned, the Allies had advanced 10 miles from previous positions. The battle formed part of the war of attrition on the Western Front.

Somoza (García), Anastasio (1896–1956)
Nicaraguan dictator. The son of a wealthy coffee planter, he was educated in Nicaragua and the USA. As Chief of the National Guard (Nicaragua's army), he established himself in supreme power in the early 1930s. With army backing, he deposed President Juan Bautista Sacasa, replacing him at the beginning of 1937. Exiling most of his political opponents and amassing a huge personal fortune, he retained power until his assassination. His sons, Luis Somoza Debayle (1923–67) and Anastasio Somoza Debayle (1925–80), continued dynastic control of Nicaragua until the 1979 revolution.

Song Jiaoren (Sung Chiao-jen) (1882–1913)
Chinese revolutionary and champion of parliamentary government. He was a leading member of **Sun Yat-sen**'s revolutionary anti-Manchu organization, the *Tongmenghui* ('Alliance League'), before 1911, helping to set up a branch in central China. Following the establishment of the republic in 1912, the Tongmenghui was transformed into a political party, the **Guomindang** (Nationalist Party). Song became its principal spokesman in the elections of Dec 1912, carrying out a vigorous Western-style electioneering campaign calling for a figurehead presidency, a responsible cabinet system and local autonomy. The Guomindang won the elections and Song was widely tipped to become Prime Minister. Song's programme, however, was a direct challenge to the hegemonic ambitions of the president, **Yuan Shikai**. On his way to Beijing, in Mar 1913, Song was assassinated at Shanghai railway station by Yuan's henchmen.

Song Qingling (Soong Ch'ing-ling) (1892–1981)
Chinese politician. The wife of the Chinese revolutionary leader, **Sun Yat-sen**, she played an increasingly active political role after his death (1925) and became associated with the left wing of the **Guomindang**. After a Christian education in the USA, she became Sun Yat-sen's English-language secretary (1913) and married him in 1914. She was elected to the Central Executive Committee of the Guomindang (1926) and was a member of the left-wing Guomindang government established at Wuhan in 1927 in opposition to **Chiang Kai-shek**. (Ironically her younger sister, Meiling, married Chiang Kai-shek in 1927.) After the collapse of the Wuhan government, Song Qingling had two years in the USSR (1927–9). During the 1930s she was a prominent member of the China League for Civil Rights, which was constantly harrassed by Chiang Kai-shek's government. She stayed on in China following the victory of the Chinese communists (1949), becoming one of three non-communist vice-chairpersons of the People's Republic. As the widow of Sun Yat-sen, of whom the communists claimed to be the legitimate heirs, she was accorded much respect by the Chinese Communist Party, although her presence in the new government remained an honorary one.

Song Ziwen (Sung Tzu-wen/Soong, T V) (1894–1971)
Chinese financier and politician. His sister, **Song Qingling**, married **Sun Yat-sen**, and through this Song became closely associated with the **Guomindang**. He provided the financial stability which made possible the 1926 **Northern Expedition** that reunited China under the Nationalists. A second sister, Meiling, married **Chiang Kai-shek** in 1927. Song served as Finance Minister of the new government until 1931, and was Foreign Minister from 1942 to 1945. When the Nationalist government was overthrown in 1949, he moved to the USA, where he died.

Sonnino, Giorgio Sidney (1847–1922)
Italian diplomat and politician. He entered parliament in 1880 and occupied various ministerial posts, including Treasury Minister (1894–6). He was twice Prime Minister (1906 and 1909–10), and as Foreign Minister was responsible with **Salandra** for bringing Italy into **World War I** on the side of the Allies. He remained Foreign Minister throughout the war and was part of the Italian delegation to the post-war conference in Paris.

Sorsa, (Taisto) Kalevi (1930–)
Finnish politician. After graduating from Tampere University, he worked in publishing and with the **UN** in the Ministry of Education. In 1969 he became Secretary-General of the Social Democratic Party and went on to become its President in 1975. He was elected to the Eduskunta in 1970, and served two terms as Foreign Minister between 1977 and 1987. When the SPP formed a government with the conservative National Coalition Party in 1987, he became Deputy Prime Minister.

Souphanouvong, Prince (1902–)
Lao prince and politician. On graduating as a civil engineer in 1937, he worked under the French administration in Vietnam. Following the capitulation of the Japanese in Aug 1945, he was returned to Laos, with the assistance of **Ho Chi Minh**, to assist in the liberation of his country from the French. He was badly wounded when his forces were routed by the French in Mar 1946. In the early 1950s he became head of a Vietnamese front organization (later known as the **Pathet Lao**), accompanying the Vietnamese invasion of Laos in 1953–4. Souphanouvong entered the government in 1957, but his strongly pro-Vietnamese, communist ties inevitably caused great tensions and he was imprisoned in 1959–60. In the 1960s it proved impossible to secure an integrated government in Laos, which consequently was driven apart by civil war, and Souphanouvong and the Pathet Lao left for the hills. The communist victory in Vietnam in 1975 brought the Pathet Lao to power in Laos and Souphanouvong became President of the Lao People's Democratic Republic, in effect a Vietnamese colony; a position he held until 1986. ▷ **Vietnam War**

South Africa

A republic in the S of the African continent, formerly divided into the four provinces of Cape, Natal, Orange Free State, and Transvaal. The discovery of diamonds (1866) and then of gold (1886) led to rivalry between the British and the Boer settlers, which resulted in the South African Wars of 1880–1 and 1899–1902. In 1910 Transvaal, Natal, Orange Free State and Cape Province were united to form the Union of South Africa, a dominion of the British Empire. This became a sovereign state within the Commonwealth in 1931 and subsequently an independent republic in 1961. Botswana and Lesotho obtained independence in 1966 and Swaziland in 1968. South Africa granted independence to Transkei in 1976, Bophuthatswana in 1977, Venda in 1979 and Ciskei in 1981, but these were not recognized internationally. From 1948 onwards, when the introduction of the **apartheid** policy resulted in the development of separate political institutions for different racial groups, politics in South Africa was dominated by the treatment of the non-white majority. Africans were considered permanent citizens of the 'homelands' to which each tribal group was assigned, and were given no representation in parliament. Continuing racial violence and strikes led to the declaration of a state of emergency in 1986, while several countries imposed economic and cultural sanctions (especially in the field of sport) in protest at the apartheid system. Under the government of President **de Klerk** progressive dismantling of apartheid took place from 1990, but negotiations towards a non-racial democracy were hampered by continuing violent clashes. In 1994 the first all-race elections saw Nelson **Mandela**, leader of the **ANC**, elected President.

South Africa Act (1909)

The act of the British parliament which created the Union of South Africa, with dominion status, in 1910. After the Boer War, the Liberal government which came to power in 1905 moved rapidly to restore responsible self-government to the Transvaal (1906) and the Orange Free State (1907). A series of constitutional conventions then set about federating the two Boer territories with the British colonies of the Cape and Natal. In the event, a union constitution was agreed upon, with the parliamentary capital in Cape Town, the administrative capital in Pretoria and the major law courts in Bloemfontein. The Union constitution ensured that the **Afrikaners** would remain the dominant political force in South Africa. It was hailed as a colonial triumph for **Asquith**'s government in keeping South Africa within the British Empire and ultimately ensuring its participation in two world wars. However, the British failed to establish black political rights or protect the franchise enjoyed by limited numbers of Africans at the Cape. It led not to a liberalizing of the South African system, as the British had hoped, but to white supremacist rule and **apartheid**. ▷ **Boer Wars**

South Korea, official name **Republic of Korea**

A republic in East Asia occupying the southern half of the Korean peninsula. Ruled by the Yi dynasty from 1392 to 1910, the country was recognized as independent by China in 1895. It was annexed by Japan in 1910 and in 1945 the country was entered by Russia (from the north) and the USA (from the south) to enforce the Japanese surrender, dividing the country by the 38th parallel of latitude. North Korean forces invaded the South in 1950, and **UN** forces assisted South Korea in stopping the advance in 1950–3. A military coup followed in 1961 and **Park Chung-hee** was assassinated in 1979. Summit talks with North Korea in 1990 were inconclusive, and tensions rose when North Korea refused to allow inspection of its nuclear facilities.

South Slavs

The Slavs began to establish themselves as farmers in the Balkans in the first decades of the 6c and eventually covered the entire peninsula. In the 7c a second wave of invaders, including the Croats and Serbs, who were Slavs, and the Turkic Bulgars, who assimilated to the earlier Slav settlers, entered the Balkans and established the first South Slavic states, Bulgaria, Croatia and Serbia. During the 15–17c, Croat, Slovene and Serb scholars became conscious of their common Slav ancestry and referred to themselves as Illyrians or simply Slavs, in addition to their more specific national name. In the 19c, under the influence of romantic nationalism, this Slav consciousness grew and gave rise to various movements for South Slav unification which led to the creation of the Kingdom of Serbs, Croats and Slovenes (later Yugoslavia) at the end of **World War I**. ▷ **Bosnia and Herzegovina; Carinthia; Carniola; Dalmatia; Istria; Macedonians; Slovenia; Yugoslavs**

South-East Asia Treaty Organization (SEATO)

An organization founded in 1954 to secure South-East Asia against communist ‘aggression’. The eight signatories to the treaty were Australia, France, New Zealand, Pakistan, the Philippines, Thailand, UK, and USA. SEATO’s headquarters was in Bangkok. It was phased out in the mid-1970s.

Southern African Development Coordination Conference (SADCC)

An association of 10 states (Angola, Botswana, Lesotho, Malawi, Mozambique, Namibia, Swaziland, Tanzania, Zambia and Zimbabwe) with its headquarters in Gaberone. Its first meeting was held in Arusha in 1979 and its Lusaka Declaration (Apr 1980) set forth a commitment to a peaceful transition to majority rule in Zimbabwe and opposition to **apartheid** in South Africa. Intended to help limit members’ dependence on South Africa, it is based upon sectoral coordination and acts as a conduit for international aid to the region.

soviet

Originally, a workers' council established in Russia after the 1905 revolution. They re-appeared as workers' and soldiers' councils, important instruments of the 1917 revolution. Members of soviets are now elected by popular vote, and lower soviets cannot control higher ones. The highest is the Supreme Soviet, the legislative body of the USSR.

Soviet–Chinese Friendship Treaty (1950)

The treaty bringing together the longest-established communist power and the most important new one, and settling some of their differences. **Stalin** had been less helpful to **Mao Zedong** than most had expected, but he now promised him protection against Japan and gave him $300 million in aid. However, he did not offer protection against the USA, and kept him waiting for 10 weeks in the middle of a Moscow winter to give him in fact less aid than Poland. On the other hand he did agree to abandon Soviet positions within China. Relations prospered for a few years but gradually deteriorated into the **Sino-Soviet dispute**.

Soweto Riots (Apr 1976)

The student disturbances which took place in the Transvaal African township of Soweto, when several hundred people were killed resisting the teaching of Afrikaans in schools. The township (whose name derives from *So*uth *We*st *To*wnship) has remained a source of tension and violence in South Africa. ▷ **apartheid**

Spaak, Paul Henri (1899–1972)

Belgian politician. He became Belgium's first socialist Premier (1938–9) and was Foreign Minister with the government-in-exile during **World War II**. In 1945 he was chairman of the first General Assembly of the **UN**. After his later periods as Premier (1946 and 1947–9), he was again Foreign Minister (1954–7 and 1961–8), in which role he became one of the founding fathers of the **EEC**. Secretary-General of **NATO** in 1957–61, he was sometimes known as 'Mr Europe'.

Spain

A country in south-west Europe, occupying four fifths of the Iberian Peninsula, and including the Canary Islands, Balearic Islands, and several islands off the coast of North Africa as well as the Presidios of Ceuta and Melilla in northern Morocco. War with the USA in 1898 led to the loss of Cuba, Puerto Rico and those Pacific possessions remaining from the declined Spanish Empire of the 16c and 17c. A dictatorship under Primo de Rivera (1923–30) was followed by the exile of the king and the establishment of the Second Republic in 1931. The military revolt headed by General **Franco** in 1936 led to civil war and the establishment of a Fascist dictatorship. Prince Juan Carlos of Bourbon, nominated by

Franco in 1969 to succeed him, acceded to the throne in 1975 and a democratic constitution was implemented in 1978. In 1981 an attempted military coup failed. The Basque separatist movement, **ETA**, has carried out a number of terrorist attacks.

Spanish Civil War (1936–9)

The conflict between supporters and opponents of the Spanish Second Republic (1931–6). The 'Republicans' included moderates, socialists, communists, and Catalan and Basque regionalists and anarchists. The 'Nationalist' insurgents included monarchists, Carlists, conservative Catholics, and fascist Falangists. The armed forces were divided. Both sides attracted foreign assistance: the Republic from the USSR and the **International Brigades**; the Nationalists from fascist Italy and Nazi Germany. The Nationalist victory was due to the balance of foreign aid; to 'non-intervention' on the part of the Western democracies; and to greater internal unity, achieved under the leadership of General **Franco**. The war took the course of a slow Nationalist advance. The Nationalists initially (July 1936) seized much of north-west Spain and part of the south-west, then (autumn 1936) advanced upon but failed to capture Madrid. They captured Malaga (Mar 1937) and the north coast (Mar–Oct 1937); advanced to the Mediterranean, cutting Republican Spain in two (Apr 1938); overran Catalonia (Dec 1938–Feb 1939); and finally occupied Madrid and south-east Spain (Mar 1939). ▷ **Basques; Carlism; Falange Española; fascism; Republic, Second** (Spain)

Spartacists

A left-wing revolutionary faction (the *Spartakusbund*), formed by Rosa **Luxemburg** and Karl **Liebknecht** in 1917, which advocated ending **World War I** and worked for a German socialist revolution. Initially part of the Independent **SPD**, it formed the core of the German Communist Party (**KPD**) when the latter was founded in 1919. Luxemburg and Liebknecht were murdered in disturbances during the German revolution in early 1919. ▷ **Revolution of 1918** (Germany)

SPD (*Sozialdemokratische Partei Deutschlands*, 'Social Democratic Party of Germany')

German political party. In 1875 the two main workers' parties in Germany (Association of German Workers, Social Democratic Workers' Party) merged to form the SAP (Socialist Workers' Party). Despite severe persecution by the Bismarckian state, the party steadily gained support and because of this persecution its politics became increasingly Marxist and revolutionary in tone. In 1890 the SAP was renamed the SPD and in 1891 formally adopted a Marxist ideology (the Erfurt Programme). However, the more pragmatic stance of the trade unions and the increasing involvement of south German Social Democrats in public affairs encouraged the growth of 'revisionism' within the party, as advocated by Eduard **Bernstein**. By 1914 the SPD had over 1 million members and the support of 34.8 per cent of voters and although it split in 1917 on whether to tolerate the war effort, the majority SPD played the pre-eminent role in the founding of the **Weimar Republic** (1918–19). During the Weimar Republic the SPD pursued a reformist policy which found little favour either among political conservatives or the radicals of other parties. Banned by **Hitler** in 1933, the SPD was refounded in 1945 and in 1959, at Bad Godesberg, formally abandoned its Marxist ideology and committed itself to achieving reforms in the existing social order. In 1966 it entered government in coalition with the **CDU/CSU** and from 1969 to 1982 governed in coalition with the **FDP** when it achieved noteworthy successes in foreign policy (**Ostpolitik**) and domestic policy (**Mitbestimmung**). Current membership is around 900 000. ▷ **Godesberg Programme; Marxism**

Special Operations Executive (SOE)
An organization set up with British war cabinet approval in July 1940 in response to Winston **Churchill**'s directive to 'set Europe ablaze'; it later also operated in the Far East. It promoted and coordinated resistance activity in enemy-occupied territory until the end of **World War II**. ▷ **FFI; Free French; Maquis; Resistance Movement** (France)

Speer, Albert (1905–81)
German Nazi official. An architect by training, he joined the **Nazi Party** in 1931 and became **Hitler**'s chief architect (1934) and Minister of Armaments (1942). Always more concerned with technology and administration than ideology, he openly opposed Hitler in the final months of **World War II**, and was the only Nazi leader at the **Nuremberg Trials** to admit responsibility for the regime's actions. He was imprisoned for 20 years in Spandau, Berlin, and after his release in 1966 became a writer.

Spiegel Affair (Oct–Nov 1962)
A political scandal in the Federal Republic of **Germany**. Following the publication of an article in the periodical *Der Spiegel* on 10 Oct 1962, which questioned the efficacy of West German defence policy, the authorities reacted by arresting its publisher (Rudolf Augstein) and several journalists. Augstein was charged with treason and *Der Spiegel* in effect subjected to censorship. However, a vigorous public reaction and opposition from **SPD** and **FDP** members of parliament revealed government complicity in the affair, in particular by Franz-Josef **Strauss**, the Minister of Defence. The government backed down, delivering a setback to Strauss's wider political ambitions, undermining the authority of the Chancellor, **Adenauer**, but consolidating individual and press freedoms and wider democratic values in post-war Germany.

Spínola, António de (1910–)

Portuguese general and politician. From a well-to-do landed family which was a pillar of the Establishment, he fought on the side of **Franco** during the **Spanish Civil War** and was sent to Nazi Germany for training. A teetotaller and non-smoker, Spínola's trade-marks were his monocle, riding crop and African cane. As Governor-General of Guinea-Bissau (1968–73) he endeavoured to halt the independence movement through a combination of welfare and community projects (designed to win over the local population) and the latest counter-insurgency methods. Though he believed the war was militarily unwinnable, he returned to Portugal a war hero. After the bloodless coup of 25 Apr 1974 toppled the remnants of the **Salazar** regime, the conservative Spínola became President as a compromise candidate. He proved a limited and naive politician. Moreover, he clashed gravely with the Armed Forces Movement (MFA) over the granting of independence (July 1974) to Angola, Mozambique and Guinea. The ensuing power struggle led to his resignation (30 Sep 1974). After staging an unsuccessful coup attempt (Mar 1975), he fled into exile. He returned the following year, but played no further part in events.

Spion Kop, Battle of (1900)

A battle of the second Boer War which was part of the British attempt to relieve the Siege of **Ladysmith**, a town in Natal besieged by the Boers since Oct 1899. British forces attempted to take a hill a few miles from the town, and although they were close to success at one stage, the Boers succeeded in beating them off. There were 1 500 British casualties, and together with the reverse at Vaal Krantz in the same week, it continued the succession of defeats which the British suffered during the early months of the war. ▷ **Boer Wars**

SPÖ (*Sozialistische Partei Österreichs*, 'Socialist Party of Austria')

Austrian political party. Founded in 1889, the SPÖ functioned as a democratic Marxist party which attracted substantial support before 1914 and held power between 1919 and 1920 at the birth of the Austrian Republic. In opposition thereafter, it was opposed by the right with increasing stridency and crushed in 1934 when it tried to resist by force the institution of crypto-fascist constitutional measures. Refounded in 1945, the SPÖ has held office in **Austria** for much of the inter-war period, either alone or in coalition. In 1978 it eschewed **Marxism**, instead supporting the democratization of society at all levels and the furtherance of workers' co-determination in the private sector.

Sporazum (1939)

The agreement reached on the eve of **World War II** between the Yugoslav government led by Dragiša **Cvetković** and the Croatian Peasant Party (HSS) led by Vladko **Maček**. The Croats agreed to cooperate with the

Belgrade government in return for a large measure of self-government. The internal administration of Yugoslavia was reorganized to include Dalmatia, Slavonia and parts of Bosnia Herzegovina within Croatia, and a Croatian assembly met at Zagreb to regulate Croatian domestic affairs.
▷ **Subašić, Ivan**

squadristi

The term applied to members of the fascist para-military movement that developed in Italy in the period after 1919. *Squadrismo* was often no more than a manifestation of political thuggery and intimidation, often directed against members of left-wing groups, strikers and ethnic minorities. However, in some cases, particularly in rural areas, it represented an understandable reaction to intimidation by similar left-wing groups. Local 'squad' leaders came to be known as **ras**. After **Mussolini**'s seizure of power, he tried to reduce the threat to order posed by these militant supporters of **fascism**, channelling them with considerable success into the **MVSN**.

Sri Lanka, formerly **Ceylon**

An island state in the Indian Ocean. Ceylon became a British colony in 1802, and the whole island united for the first time in 1815. Tamil labourers were brought in from southern India during colonial rule, to work on coffee and tea plantations. Ceylon was given Dominion status in 1948 and became an independent republic in 1972. In the early 1980s Tamil separatists began warring against government forces for control of Tamil majority areas; the fighting was confined mainly to the Jaffna Peninsula.

Srobar, Vavro (1867–1950)

Slovak politician. As a medical student in Prague he was greatly influenced by **Masaryk**, and in 1898 he established a journal for Slovak youth that developed the idea of collaboration with the Czech National Movement. During and just after **World War I** he was able to give effect to the idea in the establishment of the Czechoslovak state. He did the same during and just after **World War II** to get Czechoslovakia reestablished. On both occasions, other Slovak attitudes were pushed aside.

SS (*Schutz staffel*, 'protective squad')

A Nazi organization founded in 1925 as **Hitler**'s personal bodyguard. From 1929 it was transformed and expanded by **Himmler** into an élite force. Within the Third **Reich** it became an independent organization, controlling the police forces, and responsible for concentration camps and racial policy. It formed its own armed detachments, which after 1939 became the *Waffen* ('armed') SS. During **World War II** it became an alternative army, an autonomous power within the Third Reich, and the principal agent of racial extermination policy. ▷ **Nazi Party**

St Germain, Treaty of (10 Sep 1919)
The treaty between the Allied victor powers and **Austria**, signed unwillingly by the latter, which defined the limits of the rump Austrian state, confirmed its separation from Hungary, and in effect blocked the desired union of German Austria with Germany. ▷ **World War I**

Stabilization Plan (1959)
The economic autarky sought since 1939 by the **Franco** regime by means of a heavily protected command economy had failed so signally by the late 1950s that the country was on the verge of bankruptcy. The Stabilization Plan of 1959 was the cornerstone of the regime's programme of capitalist modernization. This dramatic change in policy was engineered above all by Mariano Navarro Rubio (Minister of Finance, 1957–65) and Alberto Ullastres (Minister of Commerce, 1957–65), both prominent members of **Opus Dei**. Although the regime's switch to laissez-faire capitalism proved economically successful, the short-term social cost was extremely high. However, the economic modernization of Spain did more than anything else to undermine the political foundations of the Franco dictatorship.

Stack, Lee (d.1924)
British soldier. He was Sirdar (British Commander-in-Chief of the Egyptian Army) in 1924, at a time when a combination of the first Wafdist government in Egypt and the first Labour government in Britain was resulting in a certain amount of British sympathy being shown for Egyptian nationalist aspirations. Unfortunately for both sides, when Sa‘d **Zaghlul** came to London for negotiations his demands were well beyond what the British government was prepared to concede. The upshot was increased hostility to the British in Egypt and particularly to the rank and status of the Sirdar. Stack was murdered in Cairo in late 1924 to some extent as a result of this. The subsequent ultimatum presented to Egypt by the British, although certainly not strong enough for the British expatriates in Egypt, was sufficient to jolt the Egyptian government. This, coupled with the complicity in a number of political murders with which certain Wafdists were charged, was enough to bring down the Wafdist government.

Stefanik, Milan Rastislav (1880–1919)
Hero of the Slovak National Movement. Born in Slovakia and educated in Prague, he migrated to Paris in 1904 and became a French citizen in 1910. An astronomer, then civil servant, he volunteered for the French air force in 1914 and was appointed general in 1918. He also worked

with **Masaryk** and **Beneš** as a representative of the Slovaks. A spokesman at the **Versailles** peace conference in 1919, his words carried great weight with the French and with his own Slovaks. In 1919 he was killed in an air crash while travelling back to Slovakia.

Stahlberg, Kaarlo Juho (1865–1952)
Finnish politician. Having established his reputation as Professor of Law at Helsinki University, as well as a judge and a member of the Finnish Diet, in 1919 he drafted Finland's constitution and served as the republic's first president until 1925. Kidnapped by members of a pro-Fascist movement in 1930, he was narrowly defeated in the elections of 1931 and 1937.

Stahlhelm Bund der Frontsoldaten
German paramilitary league (literally, 'Steel Helmet League of Front-line Soldiers'). This monarchist paramilitary veterans' association was founded in Nov 1918 to resist radical left-wing unrest. It then quickly became the main focus of anti-republican paramilitary activity in the **Weimar Republic**, propagating extreme nationalist and racist views, and did much thereby to undermine the democratic parliamentary order. Its political links to the **DNVP**, which formed a coalition with the **Nazi Party** in Jan 1933, allowed the *Stahlhelm* a minor role in **Hitler**'s consolidation of power after which its members were either absorbed into the **SA** (1933) or eventually saw their units disbanded (1935).

Stakhanov, Alexei Grigorievich (1906–77)
Russian coalminer. He started an incentive scheme (1935) for exceptional output and efficiency by individual steel workers, coalminers, etc. Such prize workers were called Stakhanovites.

Stakhanovism
An economic system in the USSR designed to raise productivity through incentives. It was named after the first worker to receive an award, coalminer Alexei Grigorievich **Stakhanov**, who in 1935 reorganized his team's workload to achieve major gains in production. The movement lasted only until 1939.

Stalin, Joseph (Iosif Vissarionovich Dzhugashvili) (1879–1953)
Georgian Marxist revolutionary and virtual dictator of the USSR. The son of a cobbler and ex-serf, he was educated at Tiflis Orthodox Theological Seminary, from which he was expelled in 1899. After joining a Georgian Social Democratic organization (1898), he became active in the revolutionary underground, and was twice exiled to Siberia (1902 and 1913). As a leading Bolshevik he played an active role in the **October Revolution**, and became People's Commissar for Nationalities in the first

Soviet government and a member of the Communist Party **Politburo**. In 1922 he became General-Secretary of the Party Central Committee, a post he held until his death, and also occupied other key positions which enabled him to build up enormous personal power in the party and government apparatus. After **Lenin**'s death (1924) he pursued a policy of building 'socialism in one country', and gradually isolated and disgraced his political rivals, notably Leon **Trotsky**. In 1928 he launched the campaign for the collectivization of agriculture during which millions of peasants perished, and the first five-year plan for the forced industrialization of the economy. Between 1934 and 1938 he inaugurated a massive purge of the party, government, armed forces, and intelligentsia in which millions of so-called 'enemies of the people' were imprisoned, exiled, or shot. In 1939 he signed the Non-Aggression Pact with **Hitler** which bought the USSR two years respite from involvement in **World War II**. After the German invasion (1941), the USSR became a member of the Grand Alliance, and Stalin, as war leader, assumed the title of Generalissimus. He took part in the **Tehran Conference**, **Yalta Conference** and **Potsdam Conference** which with other factors resulted in Soviet military and political control over the liberated countries of postwar Eastern and central Europe. From 1945 until his death he resumed his repressive measures at home, and conducted foreign policies which contributed to the **Cold War** between the USSR and the West. He was posthumously denounced by Nikita **Khrushchev** at the 20th Party Congress (1956) for crimes against the party and for building a 'cult of personality'. Under Mikhail **Gorbachev** many of Stalin's victims were rehabilitated, and the whole phenomenon of '**Stalinism**' officially condemned by the Soviet authorities. ▷ **Bolsheviks; Russian Revolution**

Stalingrad, Battle of (1942–3)
One of the great battles of **World War II**, fought between Nazi German and Soviet troops in and around Stalingrad (now Volgograd) on the River Volga during the winter of 1942–3. After savage fighting, which cost 70 000 German lives, the German 6th army surrendered (Feb 1943), yielding 91 000 prisoners of war to the Russians. The battle is regarded as a major turning-point in the Allied victory over Germany.

Stalinism
A label used pejoratively outside (and ultimately inside) the USSR to refer to the nature of the Soviet regime during the period 1929–53. It referred to a monolithic system, tightly disciplined and bureaucratic, with the party hierarchy having a monopoly of political and economic power. It also encompassed the total subservience of society and culture to political ends, the suppression of political opponents and total disregard of human rights, and especially the promotion of an individual above the party. ▷ **communism; Stalin, Joseph**

Stamboliski, Alexander (1879–1923)
Bulgarian politician. A staunch republican, in 1906 he took over the leading role in the Bulgarian Agrarian National Union (BANU). During **World War I**, he was imprisoned by the pro-German King **Ferdinand I** for his outspoken support of the Allies. In 1918 he led a march on Sofia and forced the King to abdicate, briefly declaring a republic. After the 1919 elections, he became Prime Minister and represented defeated Bulgaria at the **Paris Peace Conference**. He established an authoritarian regime, organizing the anti-communist Orange Guard, undermining the position of the urban middle class and introducing a programme of radical reform designed to turn Bulgaria into a model agricultural state. Abroad, he tried to improve Bulgaria's international position, joining the **League of Nations** and attempting to mend relations with Yugoslavia. The military and the parties of the centre and right united against him while the Communist Party and **VMRO** agitated against his policies. In 1923 he was overthrown in a military coup and was tortured and decapitated by members of VMRO. ▷ **Tsankov, Alexander**

Stanfield, Robert Lorne (1914–)
Canadian politician. In 1967 he took over the leadership of the Conservative Party from John **Diefenbaker** after a bitter fight. He sought French-Canadian support by proposing to accept bilingualism and special conditions for Quebec, but in doing so, he lost the support of many anglophone Conservatives. A successful Premier of Nova Scotia, he failed to project himself in national politics and in 1976 was replaced by Joe **Clark**.

Starace, Achille (1889–1945)
Italian politician. An interventionist in 1914 and a Bersaglieri officer in **World War I**, Starace was one of the most energetic of the **Fascist Party** (PNF) bosses in the immediate post-war era, dominating the PNF in both the Veneto and Venezia-Tridentina. Party Vice-Secretary (1921–2 and 1926–31), and Secretary (1931–9), he was most renowned for his profound stupidity and was a constant butt of popular jokes. In May 1941 he was made head of the **MVSN**, but was imprisoned under the Republic of **Salò** for insufficient attachment to the regime. He was captured and executed by partisans in Milan.

START (Strategic Arms Reduction Talks)
Discussions held between the USA and the USSR, beginning in 1982–3 after President Ronald **Reagan** came to power and resuming after Mikhail **Gorbachev** became General-Secretary in 1985. They were concerned with a reduction in the number of long-range missiles and their nuclear warheads and were complicated partly by issues of mutual distrust and partly by the need to deal also with other types of weapons. Agreements were

reached on the abolition of intermediate-range nuclear missiles in 198' (the INF Treaty) and on conventional forces in Europe in 1990 (the CFI Treaty). The way was then open for President George **Bush** to agree th(START I Treaty with President Gorbachev in July 1991 and the STARI II Treaty with President Boris **Yeltsin** in Jan 1993. Roughly speaking, the two powers agreed to cut their long-range nuclear capability by two-thirds within 10 years.

States Reorganization Act (1956)

The process of linguistic reorganization of states in India was a prolonged and divisive one and raised fundamental questions of centre–state relations. The first step occurred in the aftermath of a major movement in the Andhra region of the former province of Madras. This led to the appointment of the States Reorganization Commission which published its report in 1955. Following the States Reorganization Act, the boundaries of the southern states were reorganized in closer conformity with traditional linguistic regions. The bifurcation of Bombay province into the present states of Gujarat and Maharashtra followed in 1960. In 1966, Punjab was reorganized and its several parts distributed among three units: Punjab, the new state of Haryana, and Himachal Pradesh. Several new states have also been carved out in response to tribal demands in the north-eastern region of the country from time to time. Presently India has 25 states and seven union territories.

states' rights

A US constitutional doctrine based on the Tenth Amendment that the separate states enjoy areas of self-control which cannot be breached by the federal government. Debate has surrounded the interpretation of this Doctrine. At issue are the concepts of the implied power of the federal government and the extent or limitations of that power. The doctrine has been applied inconsistently and to support opposing points of view. It was adopted by white Southerners between Reconstruction and the **civil rights** movement, and amounted to a code term for white supremacy.

Stauffenberg, Claus, Count von (1907–44)

German soldier. Initially welcoming the advent to power of **Hitler**, he quickly became alienated by Nazi brutality. He was a colonel on the German general staff in 1944, and placed the bomb in the unsuccessful attempt to assassinate Hitler at Rastenburg (20 July 1944). He was shot the following day. ▷ **Nazi Party; World War II**

Stauning, Thorvald (1873–1942)

Danish politician. He became a member of the Danish parliament, the **Folketinget** (1906), leader of the Danish Social Democratic Party (1910) and Scandinavia's very first Social Democratic minister in 1916. After the general election of 1924, he became Premier of Denmark's first Social Democratic government. The longest-serving Danish Premier of the 20c (1924–6 and 1929–42), one of the achievements of the parliamentary reform policies of the Stauning administration was the social reform bill of May 1933 based upon the principle of the needy citizen's right to public support. In the general election of 1935, fought by the Social Democrats under the slogan 'Stauning or Chaos', the party's popularity reached its peak when 46 per cent of the electorate voted for it. Stauning's reform policy was interrupted (Apr 1940) with the German occupation of Denmark, but he continued as Premier of a national coalition government. He died on 3 May 1942 and his funeral became a manifestation of popular and national solidarity. ▷ **Denmark, German Invasion of**

Steel, Sir David (Martin Scott) (1938–)

British politician. He became an MP in 1965, sponsored a controversial Bill to reform the laws on abortion (1966–7), and was active in the anti-**apartheid** movement. He became Liberal Chief Whip (1970–5), before succeeding Jeremy Thorpe as Liberal Party leader (1976–88). In 1981 he led the party into an alliance with the **Social Democratic Party**. Following successful merger negotiations between the two parties (1987–8), he was the last leader of the Liberal Party. He remains active in politics both as an MP and party spokesman.

Steel, Pact of (28 May 1939)

An offensive alliance concluded between fascist Italy and Nazi Germany and based on the earlier Rome–Berlin Axis. It committed either power to join the other should it become involved in hostilities.

Steinem, Gloria (1934–)

US feminist and writer. A journalist and activist in the 1960s, she emerged as a leading figure in the women's movement. She co-founded *New York* magazine in 1968, was a co-founder of Women's Action Alliance in 1971, and was a founder of the feminist *Ms Magazine*.

Stepinac, Aloysius (1898–1960)

Yugoslav prelate and cardinal, and Primate of Hungary. He was imprisoned by **Tito** (1946–51) for alleged wartime collaboration and, with failing health, was released but lived the remainder of his life under house arrest.

Stern Gang

Palestinian covert organization formed under Avraham Stern in 1940 after disagreement with the **Irgun** over a cease-fire with the British during **World War II**. Conflict between the Stern Gang and the British climaxed in 1942, when British forces sought and killed members of the group, including Stern himself. Thereafter, his followers adopted the name *Lohamei Herut Yisrael* ('Fighters for Israel's Freedom'), but others dubbed them the Stern Gang/Group. Their aim was to attack British installations and personnel in Palestine in the struggle for a Jewish state. Although collaborating with the **Haganah** and Irgun during 1945, many found the Stern Gang unnecessarily brutal. After 1948 the group was disbanded. ▷ **British Mandate**

Stevens, Harry H (1878–1973)
Canadian politician. A member of **Meighen**'s Conservative administrations in 1921 and 1926, he was Minister of Trade and Commerce in **Bennett**'s government from 1930. In 1934 he became chairman of the **Price Spreads Commission**, and after the controversy surrounding its recommendations, he resigned to found the Reconstruction Party. He was its only successful candidate in the 1935 election, and returned to the Conservative Party in 1939.

Stevens, Siaka Probyn (1905–88)
Sierra Leone politician. Educated in Freetown, he was a railwayman and miner, founding the Mineworkers Union in 1943. Appointed a representative in the Protectorate Assembly, he then went to study at Ruskin College, Oxford in 1945. On his return, he helped found the Sierra Leone People's Party (APC) in 1951. The APC won the 1967 general election but the result was disputed by the army and Stevens withdrew from the premiership. In 1968 an army revolt brought him back and in 1971 he became President. He established a one-party state and remained in power until his retirement at the age of 80.

Stevenson, Adlai Ewing (1900–65)
US politician. Educated at Princeton, he became a lawyer, took part in several European missions for the State Department (1943–5), and was elected Governor of Illinois (1948) as a Democrat. He helped to found the **UN** (1946), ran twice against **Eisenhower** as a notably liberal presidential candidate (1952 and 1956), and was the US ambassador to the UN in 1961–5.

Stimson, Henry L (1867–1950)
US politician. Appointed a US District Attorney in New York by President Theodore **Roosevelt**, he made his reputation in anti-trust actions. In 1911 he became Secretary of War in President **Taft**'s administration and modernized the army in which, as an artillery colonel, he fought in France in 1917. President Calvin **Coolidge** sent him to Nicaragua to negotiate an end to the civil war, and then to the Philippines as Governor-General. He became Secretary of State in President Herbert **Hoover**'s cabinet, and was the chief negotiator for the USA at the London Naval Conference

(1930). At the 1932 Geneva Conference on arms limitation, he issued the 'Stimson Doctrine', condemning the Japanese occupation of Manchuria. Recalled as Secretary of War (1940) by President Franklin D **Roosevelt**, his experience made him a formidable influence on wartime policy, and (fearing that an invasion would be too costly in Allied lives) his advice was crucial in President Harry S **Truman**'s decision to use the atom bomb against Japan.

Stojadinović, Milan (1888–1961)
Serbian politician and economist. After studying law at Belgrade University, he began his career in finance, becoming a minister in the Serbian Treasury (1914), Director of the English bank in Belgrade (1919) and Finance Minister in successive Yugoslav governments (1922–35). As head of the Yugoslav Radical Union, he was Prime Minister and Foreign Minister (1935–9). He led Yugoslavia away from the **Little Entente** and **Balkan Entente** towards the Axis camp, but his consent to Italian domination in Albania lost him the support of the regent, Prince Paul Karageorgević, and he was dismissed. Interned by the **Cvetković–Maček** government (1939), he made his way to the British at Athens, who deported him to Mauritius and held him there until 1948. He then went to Argentina, where he worked as an economist and journalist. ▷ **Ljotić, Dimitrije**

Stolypin, Peter Arkadevich (1862–1911)
Russian politician. After service in the Ministry of the Interior (from 1884) he became Governor of Saratov province (1903–6), where he ruthlessly put down local peasant uprisings and helped to suppress the revolutionary upheavals of 1905. As Premier (1906–11), he introduced a series of agrarian reforms, which had only limited success. In 1907 he suspended the second **Duma**, and arbitrarily limited the franchise. He was assassinated in Kiev. ▷ **Nicholas II; Revolution of 1905**

Stormont
A suburb of east Belfast and site of a castle which housed the seat of government in Northern Ireland from 1921 to 1972. The Northern Ireland parliament, created by the Government of Ireland Act 1920, comprised a Senate and a House of Commons, both dominated by Protestants. It had jurisdiction over domestic affairs in the province until suspended by the Northern Ireland (Temporary Provisions) Act, 1972 which established direct rule from Westminster. ▷ **Bloody Sunday** (1972); **Ulster 'Troubles'**

Straits of Tiran, Closure of the (22 May 1967)
The Straits of Tiran, which control entry to the Red Sea from the Gulf of Aqaba, were closed in May 1967 by the Egyptian President Gamal

'Abd al-**Nasser** operating from the vantage point of Sharm al-Shaykh which commands the western side of the straits. The closure of the straits, whereby the Israeli port of Eilat was effectively cut off from the sea, was seen by Israel as direct provocation and may be regarded as in part at least as the casus belli of the June War of 1967 between Israel and the Arabs which resulted in the Israeli occupation of Golan, the **West Bank**, the Old City of Jerusalem, the **Gaza Strip**, and Sinai as far as the Suez Canal.

Straits Settlements
The name given to the former British crown colony which consisted of Singapore, Malacca, the Dindings, Penang, and Province Wellesley. Singapore became a separate city state in 1965; the remaining components are now part of Malaysia.

Strauss, Franz-Josef (1915–88)
West German politician. He served in the German Army during **World War II** and in 1945 joined the **CDU**'s Bavarian-based sister party, the Christian Social Union (**CSU**), being elected to the **Bundestag** (federal parliament) in 1949. He became leader of the CSU in 1961 and held a succession of ministerial posts. His career was seriously blighted when, for security purposes, he authorized a raid on the offices of the journal *Der Spiegel*, leading to his sacking as Minister of Defence in 1962. Throughout the 1970s he vigorously opposed the **Ostpolitik** initiative of the Willy **Brandt** and Helmut **Schmidt** administrations. In 1980 he sought election as Federal Chancellor for the CDU and CSU alliance, but was heavily defeated. Nevertheless, from 1978 he had success as State Premier of Bavaria, using this base to wield significant influence within the **Bundesrat** (federal upper house) and, from 1982, in the coalition government headed by Chancellor **Kohl**. ▷ **Spiegel Affair**

Streicher, Julius (1885–1946)
German Nazi journalist and politician. He was associated with **Hitler** in the early days of Nazism, taking part in the 1923 putsch. A ruthless persecutor of the Jews, he incited anti-Semitism through the newspaper *Der Stürmer*, which he founded and edited and also served as Nazi *Gauleiter* (Party Regional Leader) for Nuremberg–Franconia. He was hanged at Nuremberg as a war criminal. ▷ **Gau; Nazi Party; Nuremberg Trials**

Stresa, Conference of (11–14 Apr 1935)
Following **Hitler**'s declaration of German rearmament (16 Mar 1935), the Italian, French and British governments condemned the move at a meeting in Stresa. They guaranteed Austria's independence and agreed on future cooperation (Stresa Front). The Front was quickly undermined

by the Anglo-German Naval Treaty (18 June 1935) and Italy's invasion of Abyssinia and intervention in the **Spanish Civil War**.

Stresemann, Gustav (1878–1929)
German politician. Entering the **Reichstag** in 1907 as a National Liberal, he became leader of the party, and later founded and led its successor, the German People's Party. He was Chancellor of the new German Republic in 1923, then Minister of Foreign Affairs (1923–9). He pursued a revisionist policy through the medium of diplomacy, helped to negotiate the **Locarno Pact** (1925), and secured the entry of Germany into the **League of Nations** (1926). He shared the Nobel Peace Prize for 1926. ▷ **Weimar Republic**

Strijdom, Johannes Gerhardus (1893–1958)
South African politician. Educated at Stellenbosch and Pretoria Universities, he was first a farmer and then a lawyer. Elected to parliament in 1929, he became the major spokesman for the least flexible members of the **National Party** (NP) but was nonetheless made Minister of Lands and Irrigation when the NP came to power in 1948. He was chosen to succeed **Malan** as leader and so became Prime Minister in 1954. He saw one of his cherished objectives achieved, namely **apartheid**, but died before South Africa became a republic.

Stroessner, Alfredo (1912–)
Paraguayan dictator. The son of a German immigrant, he took up a military career, fighting in the **Chaco War** (1932–5). He became President in 1954 after leading an army coup which deposed Federico Chávez. He was re-elected at regular intervals (having had the constitution modified to allow this) but was forced to stand down after a military coup in 1989, led by Andres Rodríguez.

Strougal, Lubomir (1924–)
Czechoslovak politician. A lawyer who entered the Communist Party bureaucracy in 1955 and government office in 1959. In 1961 he took over the Ministry of the Interior at a sensitive time, managing to correct some of its worst excesses before reverting to a Central Committee function in 1965. His reputation was sufficient to make him a deputy prime minister in 1968, but he was a half-hearted supporter of the **Prague Spring**. In Aug he took the **Husák** line of ostensibly trying to save something through working with the Soviet authorities. He was Prime Minister (1970–87) and was regarded as the man who might yet reinvigorate the reform movement; he never did.

Struve, Peter Bergardovich (1870–1944)
Russian political economist. The grandson of Friedrich Struve, he was a leading Marxist and wrote *Critical Observations on the Problem of Russia's Economic Development* (1894), which **Lenin** attacked for its 'revisionism'. He edited several political magazines with Liberal tendencies, was professor at the St Petersburg Polytechnic (1907–17) and was closely connected with the 'White' movement in South Russia after the **Russian Revolution**. After 1925 he lived in exile in Belgrade and Paris, where he died during the Nazi occupation. His principal work is *Economy and Price* (1913–16).

Suárez, Adolfo (1932–)
Spanish politician. He was a high-ranking Francoist bureaucrat who owed much to his good looks, great charm and single-minded ambition. Appointed Prime Minister in Mar 1976, Suárez carried out a swift transition from the **Franco** dictatorship to democracy, the elections of June 1977 proving a personal triumph. Backed by the newly established centrist party, the **UCD**, he undertook the creation of the new democratic state. Having embodied consensual change in the Constitution of 1978, Suárez triumphed again in the general election of 1979. However, economic and regional problems, divisions within both the government and UCD, as well as his own secretiveness and authoritarian style, led to his resignation in Jan 1981. The following year he founded the CDS ('Democratic and Social Centre Party'), which has won little support. The most important politician of the transition, Suárez helped establish democracy in Spain through pragmatism and conciliation.

Subašić, Ivan (1882–1955)
Croatian politician. A leading member of the Croatian Peasant Party (HSS) between the two World Wars, he became *ban* (governor) of **Croatia** after the 1939 **Sporazum** between **Cvetković** and **Maček**. During **World War II**, he served in the Yugoslav government-in-exile in London and, as its Prime Minister, met **Tito** on the British-occupied island of Vis where he agreed to recognize **AVNOJ** as the only political authority within Yugoslavia (June 1944). In accordance with the provisions of the Vis agreement, in Mar 1945 he and two colleagues from the London-based regime joined Tito's Provisional Government, but he resigned as Foreign Minister six months later and was under house arrest until after the communist victory in the Nov 1945 elections. Obliged to retire from public life, he settled in Croatia.

Sudan People's Liberation Movement
The proclamation of an Islamic state in the Sudan by Numayri in 1977, led to unrest in the south which found its expression in the emergence of the Sudan People's Liberation Movement. This movement initially

represented a political refusal to accept the dictates of the government in Khartum but subsequently moved to armed rebellion under Colonel John **Garang**.

Sudetenland

Mountainous territory on Polish–Czech border. After **World War I**, the name applied to the parts of Bohemia and Moravia occupied by German-speaking people that were incorporated into Czechoslovakia. The region was occupied by Germany after the **Munich Agreement** in 1938, and restored to Czechoslovakia in 1945 when the German-speaking population was expelled. ▷ **World War II**

Suez Canal

A canal connecting the Mediterranean and Red seas in north-east Egypt, passing through Lake Timsah and the Great and Little Bitter Lakes. Built by Ferdinand de Lesseps between 1859 and 1869, under the 1882 Convention it is open to vessels of any nation except in wartime. The canal was controlled by the British from 1882 until 1956, when it was nationalized by Egypt. It was blocked by Egypt during the war with Israel in 1967 and re-opened in 1975.

Suez Crisis (1956)

A political crisis focused on the Suez Canal. Intensive rearmament by Egypt, the Egyptian nationalization of the Suez Canal, and the establishment of a unified command with Jordan and Syria aimed at surrounding and eliminating Israel, led in Oct to a pre-emptive strike by Israel in Sinai. Following this attack, the UK and France asked both sides to withdraw from the Canal Zone and agree to temporary occupation. When this was rejected by Egypt, the British and French invaded, but had to withdraw following diplomatic action by the USA and USSR. Israel was also forced to relinquish the Sinai Peninsula. There have been many allegations of collusion between Israel, France, and the UK. ▷ **Arab–Israeli Wars; Eden, Anthony; Nasser, Gamal Abd al-**

suffragettes

Those women who identified with and were members of the late 19c movement to secure voting rights for women. The vote was 'won' after the end of **World War I** (1918), though it was limited to those women of 30 years of age or over. There were many men and women opponents of female suffrage, and in England it was not until 1928 that women over 21 achieved the right to vote. ▷ **Pankhurst, Emmeline**

Suharto, Thojib N J (1921–)

Indonesian soldier and statesman. Educated for service in the Dutch colonial army, he was given a command in the Japanese-sponsored

Indonesian army in 1943 and played an important role in the revolutionary struggle against the Dutch. He became a major political figure during the crises of 1965 and 1966, and assumed full executive power in 1967, ordering the mass arrest and internment of alleged communists. He became President in 1968, thereafter being re-elected every five years. Suharto's virtual dictatorship under the 'New Order' saw an improvement in Indonesia's relations with her neighbours in South-East Asia, the republic's return to membership of the **UN**, and considerable economic advance, sustained in large part by buoyant oil revenues.

Suhrawardy, Husein Shaheed (1893–1963)
Pakistani politician. Born in East Bengal, he was educated at Oxford University in England. In 1921 he became a member of the Bengal Assembly. He was Pakistan's Minister of Law (1954–5) and Prime Minister (1956–7).

Sukarno, Ahmed (1902–70)
Indonesian statesman and first President of Indonesia (1945–66). He formed the Indonesia National Party (PNI) in 1927, was imprisoned by the Dutch in Bandung (1929–31), and lived in forced exile until 1942, when he emerged as a major nationalist leader during the Japanese occupation. He became President when Indonesia was declared independent in 1945 and was a crucial unifying figure during the subsequent struggle against the Dutch. His popularity waned as the country suffered increasing internal chaos and poverty in the late 1950s and 1960s, while his governments laid themselves open to charges of corruption and extremism. An abortive coup (1965) led to massive violence and a takeover by the army, Sukarno's powers gradually devolving to General Suharto. Sukarno finally retired in 1968.

Sulh, Taqi al-Din al- (1909–88)
Lebanese Sunni politician. He was a fervent campaigner on behalf of the Arab peoples against any form of foreign interference in their affairs. Initially focusing on the way in which the Ottoman Turks had kept the Arab peoples in subjection, when the problems of Ottoman dominion had receded, he turned his attentions to the French and British. A moderate who aimed at reconciliation between Christians and Muslims in Lebanon, Taqi al-Din, together with his brother Kazim, maintained that, although the Lebanese people were part of the great Arab nation, the regional peculiarities of Lebanon made the country's independence an essential concomitant of its peaceful development. Politically active throughout his life, he played a prominent role in the late 1960s and early 1970s, and was Prime Minister in 1973–4.

Sultan-Galiev, Mivza Said (1892–1939)
Tatar intellectual and politician. He attempted to synthesize Islam and **communism**. He joined the **Bolsheviks** in 1917 in his native Kazan and soon had an official post. **Stalin** welcomed him on to the commissariat of nationalities in 1920 as one of the few non-Russians and then had him arrested in 1923 for his dissident Islamic views. Freed, he continued to preach communism as a means of liberating his fellow non-Russian Muslims. However, he was rearrested in 1929 and disappeared. His name has been much revered among Muslims ever since.

Sun Yat-sen (Sun Zhongshan/Sun Yixian) (1866–1925)
Chinese politician. The founder and early leader of China's Nationalist Party, the **Guomindang**, he first trained as a doctor in Hawaii and Hong Kong. Alarmed by the weakness and decay of China, he founded the Society for the Revival of China, and sprang to fame when, on a visit to London, he was kidnapped by the Chinese legation, and released through the intervention of the Foreign Office. He then helped to organize risings in southern China. He returned to China after the 1911 Wuhan rising, realized that he would not be widely acceptable as President, and voluntarily handed over the office to **Yuan Shikai**. After the assassination of his follower, **Song Jiaoren**, civil war ensued (1913), and he set up a separate government at Guangzhou (Canton). He died in Beijing, widely accepted as the true leader of the nation. ▷ **Lenin**

Sunnis
Members of an Islamic religious movement representing 'orthodoxy' in Islam, comprising about 80 per cent of all Muslims. They recognize the first four caliphs as 'rightly-guided' (*rashidun*), and base their *sunnah* (the 'path' of the Prophet Muhammad) upon the Quran and the *hadith* or 'traditions' of the Prophet. They are organized into four legal schools which all enjoy equal standing. The other major Islamic group is made up of **Shiites**.

superpowers
The description applied during the **Cold War** period to the USA and the USSR, the two nations with economic and military resources far exceeding those of other powers. With the collapse of the USSR in 1991, it is sometimes argued that there is only one superpower left. But arguments concerning gross national product and real or potential military strength suggest that China, Japan and the European Community might merit the description if still in use.

Supilo, Frano (1870–1917)
Croatian politician. A Croat from **Dalmatia**, during **World War I** he worked closely with Ante **Trumbić**, co-founding with him the Social

Democrat Party. Supilo helped to found the **Yugoslav Committee** which, from its base in London, tried to win Allied support for South Slav unification. ▷ **South Slavs; Yugoslavs**

Suslov, Mikhail Andreevich (1902–82)
Soviet politician. He joined the Communist Party in 1921, and was a member of the Central Committee from 1941 until his death. An ideologist of the Stalinist school, he became a ruthless and strongly doctrinaire administrator. Very different from Nikita **Khrushchev** in temperament and political outlook, he opposed Khrushchev's 'de-Stalinization' measures, economic reforms, and foreign policy, and was instrumental in unseating him in 1964. ▷ **Stalinism**

Suzman, Helen (1917–)
South African politician. Educated at Parktown Convent and Witwatersrand University, she lectured part-time at the University (1944–52) but became deeply concerned by the rightward shift of the **National Party** (NP); she joined the opposition United Party and was elected to parliament in 1953. Closely involved with the South African Institute of Race Relations in the 1970s, she was often a solitary voice against the NP's policy of **apartheid** in parliament. A formidable debater, Suzman earned the respect of opponents of apartheid and received the **UN** Human Rights Award in 1978. She retired from parliament in 1989 after 36 uninterrupted years of service.

Suzuki Zenko (1911–)
Japanese politician. He was elected in 1947 to the lower house of the Diet as a Socialist party deputy, but moved to the Liberal Party in 1949 and then, on its formation in 1955, to the conservative **Liberal Democratic Party (LDP)**. During the 1960s and 1970s he held a series of ministerial and party posts, including Post and Telecommunications (1960–4), Chief Cabinet Secretary (1964–5), Health and Welfare (1965–8) and Agriculture, Forestry and Fisheries (1976–80). Following the death of his patron, Masayoshi **Ohira**, he succeeded to the dual positions of LDP President and Prime Minister in 1980. His premiership was marred by factional strife within the LDP, deteriorating relations with the USA and opposition to his defence policy. He stepped down in 1982, but remained an influential LDP faction leader.

Svehla, Antonin (1873–1933)
Czechoslovak politician. Born near Prague, he was active in the Agrarian Party from its foundation in 1899, establishing its newspaper in 1906 and chairing its executive committee from 1909 until his death in 1933. Halfway through **World War I** he threw his weight behind **Masaryk**'s drive for complete independence. As Minister of the Interior (1918–20), he

protected the new state against threats from the revolutionary left. As Prime Minister for most of the period 1922–9, he gave it economic prosperity and social stability, based on a combination of middle-of-the-road agrarian and socialist interests.

Sverdlov, Yakov Mikhailovich (1885–1919)
Bolshevik politician. Born and brought up in Nizhni Novgorod, he embraced socialism early and was arrested for the first time when he was 17 years old. Between 1902 and 1907 he was often in prison or in exile. In 1917 he rose rapidly to become Chairman of the Central Executive Committee, running both the party and the country while others fought their military and political battles. However, in 1919 he died suddenly, leaving a serious gap at the top which was never really filled.

Svestka, Oldrich (1922–)
Czechoslovak editor and politician. A journalist, he joined the Communist Party in 1945 and became one of the editors of its daily *Rudé Právo*. In 1958 he became editor-in-chief, and in 1962 he became a member of the Central Committee, and so held an influential political position. In 1968 he was admitted to the presidium of the party, but his allegiance to the **Prague Spring** was only formal. With **Bil'ak** and others he welcomed the Soviet invasion, and by 1975 he was once more editor-in-chief of *Rudé Právo*, but it disappeared with the party in 1990.

Svoboda, Ludwik (1895–1979)
Czechoslovak soldier and politician. He fought with the Czechoslovak Legion in Russia in 1917 before becoming a professional soldier. After escaping from Czechoslovakia in 1939 he became commanding general of the Czechoslovak army corps attached to the **Red Army** in 1943, and helped to liberate Kosiče, Brno and Prague in 1944 to 1945. In 1948 he joined the Communist Party and was Minister of Defence until 1950. From 1952 to 1963 he lived in obscurity, mistrusted by the Stalinists; but, with Nikita **Khrushchev**'s backing, he was subsequently brought forward as a 'safe' patriotic father-figure and, in 1968, he succeeded the discredited Antonín **Novotný** as President. He gave loyal support to the abortive reforms of Alexander **Dubček** and, after the hostile Soviet intervention in 1968, he travelled to Moscow to seek relaxation of the repressive measures imposed on the Czechoslovaks. He remained in office until 1975, when failing health forced his retirement.

Swadeshi
A Hindi term meaning 'of one's own country', this was a slogan used as part of an Indian campaign of boycotting foreign-made goods, initiated in protest against the partition of Bengal into two separate administrative divisions by the British in 1905, in defiance of Indian public opinion. The

policy was viewed as an attempt to perpetuate British rule by dividing the Indian population, particularly the Muslims of East Bengal from the Hindus of West Bengal. Advocates of *swadeshi* urged the Indian people to wear *khadi* or home-made country-cloth, amongst other things. The first example of mass opposition to British rule, the campaign led eventually to the abandonment of the partition of Bengal in 1911. ▷ **Bengal, Partition of**

SWAPO (South West Africa People's Organization)

Founded in 1958 as the Ovambo People's Organization, SWAPO became the main nationalist movement for South-West Africa (Namibia) and organized the guerrilla war against the South African administration of the country. Based initially in Tanzania and then Zambia, the guerrilla movement established bases in Angola in the 1970s and became embroiled in the general conflict involving South Africa, **UNITA**, and the **MPLA** government in Luanda with its Cuban and Soviet support. Recognized by the **Organization of African Unity (OAU)**, and later by the world community, as the authentic voice of Namibian aspirations, an international agreement was reached in Geneva in 1988 which linked Namibia's independence with Cuban withdrawal from Angola and the cessation of South African support for UNITA. In the ensuing 1989 election, SWAPO won over half the votes and a majority of seats and formed the first independent government.

Swaraj

A Hindi term meaning 'self-government' or 'home rule'. It was used by Indian nationalists to describe independence from British rule.

Swatantra Party

The only authentic Indian political party of the traditional Right, as the term would be understood in Europe. It was a coalition of big urban business and rural aristocratic and landlord elements in which the later were dominant. The Swatantra Party was formed on an all-India basis in 1959 and was of consequence nationally only in three general elections: 1962, 1967 and 1972. In 1967, it succeeded in winning 44 seats in the Lok Sabha (the lower house of Parliament), emerging as the second largest party in the House after Congress. During its heyday, the Swatantra Party was the leading party of the Right offering a full scale critique of the Congress policies of centralized planning, nationalization of industries, agrarian reform, and nonalignment.

Sweden

A kingdom in Northern Europe, occupying the east side of the Scandinavian Peninsula. The former union with Norway was dissolved in

1905. Sweden has been a neutral country since 1814. It has been ruled by the Social Democrats for most of the time since 1932.

Sykes–Picot Agreement (1916)

A secret agreement concluded in this year by diplomat Sir Mark Sykes (for Britain) and Georges Picot (for France) partitioning the **Ottoman Empire** after the war. France was to be the dominant power in Syria and Lebanon, and Britain in Transjordan, Iraq, and northern Palestine. The rest of Palestine was to be under international control, and an Arab state was to be established.

syndicalism

A revolutionary socialist doctrine that emphasized workers taking power by seizing the factories in which they worked; developed in the 1890s, and common in France, Italy, and Spain in the early 20c. The state was to be replaced by worker-controlled units of production. Often a general strike was advocated as part of the strategy. By 1914 it had lost its political force. The name, deriving from *syndicat* (French, 'trade union'), has also been applied to various non-revolutionary doctrines supporting worker control.

Syria

A republic in the Middle East. Part of the Ottoman Empire from 1517, Syria enjoyed a brief period of independence in 1920 before being made a French mandate. Mandatory rule ended when Syria gained independence in 1946. It merged with Egypt and Yemen to form the United Arab Republic in 1958 but re-established itself as an independent state under its present name in 1961. The Golan Heights region was seized by Israel in 1967. After the outbreak of civil war in Lebanon in 1975 Syrian troops were sent to restore order, and Syrian soldiers were part of the international coalition force which opposed Iraq in the Gulf War. Syria also took part in the Middle East peace talks in 1992 which gave rise to hopes of agreement being reached with Israel.

Szabo, Ervin (1877–1918)

Hungarian intellectual. A lawyer by training and a librarian by occupation, he was very active in shaping socialist ideas from 1899 onwards. After a few years he switched from support for the Social Democratic Party to syndicalism. He translated Marx and Engels and wrote extensively about Marxism. He left behind a circle of young critics of bureaucracy, opportunism and militarism.

Szalasi, Ferenc (1897–1946)

Hungarian soldier and politician. A major on the general staff, he joined a secret racist group in 1930, and in 1933 published his *Plan for the*

Building of the Hungarian State, which became the ideological handbook for Hungarian pacifism. Retired from military service in 1935, he formed the first of a series of fascist parties culminating in the **Arrow Cross** in 1940. Under Nazi pressure he became Prime Minister in 1944 and instituted a racist reign of terror. In 1946 he was executed as a war criminal.

T

Tacna-Arica Question

A prolonged diplomatic dispute between Peru and Chile concerning sovereignty over Tacna and Arica provinces, occupied by Chile in the War of the Pacific. It was finally resolved in 1929 by the award of Tacna to Peru and Arica to Chile.

Taft, Robert Alphonso (1889–1953)

US politician. The son of President William **Taft**, he studied law at Yale and Harvard and in 1917 became counsellor to the American Food Administration in Europe under **Hoover**. A conservative Republican, he was elected to the Senate from Ohio in 1938, and co-sponsored the **Taft–Hartley Act** (1947) directed against the power of the trade unions and the 'closed shop'. A prominent isolationist, he was Republican leader from 1939 to 1953, failing three times (1940, 1948 and 1952) to secure the Republican nomination for the presidency.

Taft–Hartley Act (1947)

US labour legislation. It outlawed 'unfair' labour practices such as the closed shop, and demanded that unions supply financial reports and curtail their political activities. It also gave the US government the power to postpone major strikes endangering national health or safety for a cooling-off period of 80 days. The National Management Relations Act, its official name, was passed over President Truman's veto by the first Republican-controlled Congress in almost 20 years to limit the power of the **National Labor Relations Act** (the 'Wagner Act') of 1935, which the Republicans believed had shifted the balance between employers and workers far too much in favour of the unions.

Taif Accord (1898)

When Amin **Gemayel** left office as President of Lebanon in Sep 1988, the country found itself without a government. Michel Awn, then Commander-in-Chief of the Lebanese army and a Maronite Christian, took over the presidential palace and went on to attack Syrian forces in Beirut. In response to the crisis, the **Arab League**, represented by King Fahd of Saudi Arabia and King Hasan of Morocco, together with President Chadli of Algeria, proposed a peace plan (Oct 1989) and the Lebanese members of parliament gathered in Taif in Saudi Arabia. The Taif Accord was the result of their talks on the reduction of Maronite Christian domination in government. The essence of the agreement was that the cabinet and the National Assembly, to whom the President would be subject, would be equally divided between Christian and Muslim members. Not surprisingly, this proposal was criticized by both Druze and Shi'a, and rejected by Awn.

Taisho Emperor (Yoshihito) (1879–1926)
Emperor of Japan (1912/26). The only son of the **Meiji Emperor (Mutsuhito)**, he was proclaimed Crown Prince in 1889 and succeeded his father on the imperial throne in 1912. His 14-year reign saw the emergence of Japan as a world great power. Unlike his father, however, he took little part in active politics, for his mental health gave way in 1921. In the last five years of his life, Crown Prince **Hirohito** was regent.

Taiwan, formerly **Formosa**
An island republic consisting of Taiwan Island and several smaller islands. The island was ceded to Japan by the Manchus in 1895 and returned to China in 1945. The Nationalist government was moved here in 1949, and in 1991 Taiwan officially recognized the People's Republic of China for the first time in over 40 years.

Takeshita Noboru (1924–)
Japanese politician, The son of an affluent sake brewer, he trained as a kamikaze pilot during **World War II**. After university and a brief career as a schoolteacher, he was elected to the House of Representatives as a **Liberal Democratic Party (LDP)** deputy in 1958, rising to become Chief Cabinet Secretary (1971–2) to Prime Minister **Sato** and Minister of Finance (1982–6) under Prime Minister **Nakasone**. Formerly a member of the powerful 'Tanaka faction', he founded his own faction, the largest within the party, in 1987, and three months later was elected LDP President and Prime Minister. Although regarded as a cautious, consensual politician, he pushed through important tax reforms. His administration was undermined by the uncovering of the Recruit-Cosmos insider share dealing scandal, which, though dating back to 1986, forced the resignation of senior government ministers, including, eventually, Takeshita himself (June 1989).

Talat Pasha, Mahmud (1872–1921)
Initially a civil servant, he was a supporter of the liberal Young Turks movement along with Enver Pasha who had been a military attaché in Berlin. An associate of Enver, who as Minister of War was regarded as having been largely responsible for bringing Turkey into the Great War on the German side, Talat was excluded from the peace negotiations after the conclusion of the Mudros Armistice in Oct 1918 and fled to Germany. He was assassinated by an Armenian in Berlin.

Tambo, Oliver (1917–93)
South African politician. The son of a peasant farmer, he went to Johannesburg to attend a school set up by the Community of the Resurrection, where he came under the influence of Trevor Huddleston. Having graduated from Fort Hare College, he embarked upon a teaching diploma but was expelled for political activity. He joined the **ANC** Youth League in 1944, rising to be a member of the ANC executive (1949), Secretary-General (1955), and Deputy President (1959). He then went into exile and was President of ANC in exile from 1977. He returned to South Africa in 1989 as titular leader of the party, but gave up this position at the meeting of the party in exile in 1990.

Tamil
A Dravidian language originally found in South India and Sri Lanka. The term 'Tamil' also refers to the speakers of the language, most of whom live in the South Indian state of Tamil Nadu, although there are substantial Tamil populations in Sri Lanka, where some have been agitating for secession from the state dominated by the Sinhala majority, and Malaysia. Nationalist political aspirations have been promoted by Tamil parties like the DMK in India as well as the militant LTTE in Sri Lanka.

Tammany Hall
US **political machine** of the Democratic Party in New York City and State. It was originally a club (the Society of Tammany) founded in 1789, and in the late 19c and early 20c became notorious for its political corruption. Its power declined in the 1932 election, and although revived for a short time, it has ceased to exist as a political power in New York politics.

Tanaka Giichi (1864–1929)
Japanese militarist and politician. A member of the Choshu clique, Tanaka served in both the **Sino-Japanese War** (1894–5) and the **Russo-Japanese War** (1904–5) and became a vigorous supporter of army expansion. He became leader of the **Seiyukai** in 1925 (signalling that party's close association with the military) and Prime Minister in 1927. During his premiership (1927–9) thousands of suspected communists were arrested under the **Peace Preservation Laws**. Tanaka also initiated the policy of direct Japanese military intervention in China when he sanctioned three expeditions (1927–8) to east China (Shandong province), ostensibly to protect Japanese residents in the wake of **Chiang Kai-shek**'s **Northern Expedition**.

Tanaka Kakuei (1918–)
Japanese politician. After training as a civil engineer and establishing a successful building contracting business, he was elected to Japan's House of Representatives in 1947. He rose swiftly within the dominant **Liberal Democratic Party (LDP)**, becoming Minister of Finance (1962–5), Party Secretary-General (1965–7) and Minister of International Trade and Industry (1971–2), before serving as LDP President and Prime Minister (1972–4). He was arrested in 1976, while he was Prime Minister, on charges of accepting bribes as part of the **Lockheed Scandal**, and eventually in 1983 was found guilty and sentenced to four years' imprisonment. He had resigned from the LDP in 1976, becoming an independent deputy, but remained an influential, behind-the-scenes, faction leader. His appeal against the 1983 verdict was rejected by the High Court in 1987, but a further appeal was lodged.

Tangier
A seaport in Nord-Ouest province, north Morocco, occupying an important strategic position at the entrance to the Mediterranean Sea. It was established in 1923 as an international zone, governed by Britain, France, Spain and Italy, and was occupied by the Spanish during **World War II**. International administration was removed in 1956, and Tangiers became a part of Morocco in 1959. In 1962 its free port status was restored.

Tannenberg, Battle of (26–30 Aug 1914)
A **World War I** battle between Russian and German forces. The Russian army under General Alexander **Samsonov** was completely routed; 100 000 prisoners of war were taken, and Samsonov himself committed suicide. German nationalists claimed the victory as revenge for the defeat of the Teutonic Knights by Russian, Polish and Lithuanian forces at the first Battle of Tannenberg (Grunwald) in 1410.

Tanner, Väinö (1881–1966)
Finnish politician. A controversial figure in Finnish politics, Tanner emerged as leader of the **Social Democratic Party** after the end of the civil war in 1918. Tanner distanced the party from the radical Left in order to cooperate with the Centre, a policy which enabled the Social Democrats to participate in a majority government in 1937. He was identified by the USSR as one of those who had blocked a peaceful outcome to the negotiations which resulted in the **Russo-Finnish War** (1939–40). Tanner earned further Soviet hostility through his role in government, first as Foreign Minister and later, during the **Continuation War** of 1941–4, as Minister of Finance. In 1946 he was one of eight Finnish war leaders who were tried and convicted as war criminals. Following his release from prison in 1949 Tanner returned to parliament and in 1957 was re-elected Leader of the Social Democratic Party.

Tanganyika African National Union (TANU)

This party, founded in 1954, grew out of the Tanganyika African Association and was the dominant party in Tanganyika during the period leading to independence. Under the leadership of Julius **Nyerere**, it became first de facto the only party in the country and then, in 1966, de jure the only party. Noted for the internal competition it provided at election time and for its unique brand of socialist ideology, laid out in the **Arusha Declaration**, the party merged in 1977 with the Afro-Shirazi Party of Zanzibar to form **CCM** (Chama Cha Mapinduzi).

Tanzania

An East African republic. After exploration of the African interior by German missionaries and British explorers in the mid-19c, Zanzibar became a British protectorate in 1890 and German East Africa was established in 1891. British mandatory rule was established over Tanganyika in 1919, but in 1961 Tanganyika became the first East African country to gain independence and become a member of the Commonwealth, becoming a republic the following year. Zanzibar was given independence as a constitutional monarchy with the Sultan as head of state, and when the Sultan was overthrown in 1964 an Act of Union between Zanzibar and Tanganyika led to the formation of the United Republic of Tanzania. A multiparty system was approved in 1992. The country suffered from severe drought in several areas in 1992.

Tardieu, André (1876–1945)

French politician. A well-known journalist before 1914, he was a Deputy (1914–24 and 1926–36), High Commissioner in the USA (1917–18), and one of **Clemenceau**'s chief advisers during the negotiation of the peace treaties. His political position was right of centre; he was Minister of Public Works (1926–8), Prime Minister (1929–30), Minister of the Interior (1928–30), of Agriculture (1931–2), and of Foreign Affairs during his own second term as Prime Minister (1932), thus clearly being the dominant figure throughout the 1928–32 parliament. During that time, he practised what he called a 'prosperity policy', providing government assistance for the modernization of agriculture and industry, the electrification of rural areas, etc, and put through measures to abolish fees in state secondary schools and to improve social insurance. The victory of the left in the 1932 elections put him in opposition, but after the crisis of Feb 1934 he was brought back to office in the **Doumergue** cabinet with the task of producing proposals for constitutional reform. When it became evident that they were not going to be adopted, he left active politics to defend his plans for a stronger executive power in books and articles.

Teamsters' Union (International Brotherhood of Teamsters, Chauffeurs, Warehousemen and Helpers of America)
The largest US labour union, with over 1.5 million members. Founded in 1903, it was expelled from the **AFL–CIO** in 1957 for corruption, but was reaffiliated in 1987.

Teapot Dome Scandal (1923)
US political scandal. One of several in the administration of President Warren G **Harding**, it involved the lease of naval oil reserves at Teapot Dome (Wyoming) and Elk Hills (California) by the Secretary of the Interior, Albert B Fall. He allowed no competition to the bids of Harry F Sinclair (Mammoth Oil) and Edward Doheny (Pan-American Petroleum), who had both lent him considerable sums of money. A Senate investigation uncovered the scandal and Fall was eventually sentenced to prison for one year and fined US$100 000. Sinclair and Doheny were cleared of bribery charges, although Sinclair did serve nine months in jail for contempt of the Senate. In 1927 the Supreme Court found that neither of the leases was valid and the oilfields were returned to the government.

Tehran Conference (28 Nov–1 Dec 1943)
The first inter-allied conference of **World War II**, attended by **Stalin**, **Roosevelt** and Winston **Churchill**. The subjects discussed were the coordination of Allied landings in France with the Soviet offensive against Germany, Russian entry in the war against Japan, and the establishment of a post-war international organization. Failure to agree on the future government of Poland foreshadowed the start of the **Cold War**.

Teleki, Count Paul (1879–1941)
Hungarian politician. He became Professor of Geography at the Budapest University in 1919 and, combining politics with an academic career, was in the same year appointed Foreign Minister and, from 1920 to 1921, Premier. The founder of the Christian National League and chief of Hungary's boy scouts, he was Minister of Education in 1938 and again Premier in 1939. He was fully aware of the German threat to his country, but all measures to avert it, including a pact with Yugoslavia, were unavailing through lack of support. When Germany marched against Yugoslavia through Hungary, he took his own life.

Telengana Disturbances
Telengana, in northern Hyderabad, India, was the scene of the most widespread, violent and long-lived peasant insurrection in South Asia in the 20c. (It was also possibly one of the largest communist-led insurrections seen in all Asia (outside China and Vietnam) in modern times.) Beginning in 1946, at its height, the movement against the Nizam, the pro-British ruler of the independent princely state of Hyderabad, covered

3 000 villages spread over 16 000 square miles. A peasant army was established, and communes set up in the villages under communist control which, among other things, raised agricultural wages and redistributed waste lands to the poor. Unwilling to come to terms even after the granting of independence from Britain and the formal incorporation of Hyderabad into the Union of India, central government troops were sent to the area in Sep 1948, although the movement was not finally suppressed until 1951. Nonetheless, a guerrilla movement is still active in the hills and communist MPs are regularly elected to the Lok Sabha (or Parliament) in Delhi. Since the **States Reorganization Act** of 1956, Hyderabad has been part of the modern Telugu-speaking state of Andhra Pradesh, and Telengana has seen continuing protest movements against immigration to the region and the alleged control of the Andhra state by what are said to be politicians and business interests originating in the north.

temperance movement

An organized response to the social disruption caused by the alcoholism so widespread in the 18c and 19c. Temperance societies were started first in the USA, then in Britain and Scandinavia. The original aim was to moderate drinking, but prohibition became the goal. Federal prohibition became a reality in the USA in 1919, but was impossible to enforce and was repealed in 1933.

tenentismo

Deriving from the Portuguese *tenente* ('lieutenant'), this term originally referred to the generation of young Brazilian army officers who graduated from the military school in Realengo after 1919. Trained by the 'indigenous mission' of officers who had been seconded to the Imperial German Army before **World War I**, they emerged to general service highly critical of both superior officers and the regime they served. As a result, they took leading roles in the 1922 Copacabana Revolt, the Revolt of São Paulo, the Prestes Column and Revolution of 1930. Many continued in politics until the 1960s. Such men included Luís Carlos Prestes (leader of the Communists), Eduardo Gomes (éminence grise of the UDN), Cordeiro de Farias (the major support for **Castelo Branco**), Jaurêz Távora and Jurací de Maghalâes, and were the progenitors of the military regime of 1964–85.

Tet Offensive (Jan–Feb 1968)

A campaign in the **Vietnam War**. On 30 Jan 1968, the Buddhist 'Tet' holiday, the Viet Cong launched an attack against US bases and more than 100 South Vietnamese towns (which had been considered safe from guerrilla attack), the targets including the US Embassy in Saigon and the city of Hue. There were heavy casualties, including large numbers of civilians. US public opinion was shocked by the scale of death and destruction, and support for the war declined rapidly. The offensive proved to be a turning-point in the war: on 31 Mar 1968, President Lyndon B **Johnson** announced an end to escalation and a new readiness to negotiate.

Thailand, formerly **Siam**

A kingdom in South-East Asia, the only country in South and South-East Asia to have escaped colonization by a European power. It was occupied by the Japanese during **World War II** and was ruled by a military-controlled government for most of the time after 1945. Mass demonstrations in 1992 resulted in the fall of this government and led to a reduction in the power of the military.

Thakurdas, Purshottamdas (1879–1961)

Indian industrialist and social reformer. He joined the family cotton business and started rooting out evil practices in the cotton industry. At the age of 28, the 'Cotton King of Bombay' was elected Vice-President of the Indian Merchants Chamber, Bombay. A founding member of the Federation of Indian Chambers of Commerce and Industry (FICCI), he went on to become its President. He was a member of the Retrenchment Committee (1922) and served on the Royal Commission on Indian Finance, Currency and Practice (1925), where he fought for a better exchange-rate for the Indian rupee. He was appointed Sheriff of Bombay in 1920. Secretary of the Gujarat Famine Relief Fund in 1911, he also made generous contributions to schemes involving education and self-help. It was thanks to his initiative that the Indenture Act was abolished.

Thalmann, Ernst (1886–1944)

German politician. After joining the **SPD** in 1903, Thalmann switched to the **KPD** in 1920, joining its Central Committee in 1921. Convener of the KPD from 1925, he was heavily reliant on the **Comintern** in Moscow for his authority and steered the party increasingly along lines acceptable to the USSR. Arrested by the National Socialists in 1933, he was shot in **Buchenwald** concentration camp in 1944. ▷ **Nazi Party**

Thani, Khalifa ibn Hamad al- (1932–)

Shaykh and Prime Minister of Qatar. The oil-rich Persian Gulf state of Qatar entered into treaty relations with Britain in 1916, having earlier been under Ottoman control. As with the Trucial States (now the United Arab Emirates), it was arranged that the foreign affairs of Qatar would be conducted by the British in return for naval protection, while internal affairs should be regulated by the state itself (and thus by extension the Al-Thani family). The discovery of oil made Qatar extremely wealthy and the state became fully independent in 1971.

Thant, U (1909–74)
Burmese diplomat. He was a teacher who became a civil servant when Burma became independent in 1948; he became Burma's **UN** representative in 1957. As Secretary-General of the UN (1962–71), he played a major diplomatic role during the **Cuban Missile Crisis**. He also formulated a plan to end the Congolese Civil War (1962) and mobilized a UN peace-keeping force in Cyprus (1964). He died in New York City. The return of his body to Burma provoked major anti-government demonstrations.

Thatcher, Margaret (Hilda) (1925–)
British politician. Elected to parliament in 1959, and after holding junior office, she became Minister of Education (1970–4). In 1975 she replaced Edward **Heath** as Leader of the **Conservative Party** to become the first woman party leader in British politics. Under her leadership, the Conservative Party moved towards a more 'right-wing' position, and British politics and society became more polarized than at any other time since **World War II**. Her government (1979–90) privatized several nationalized industries and utilities, made professional services, such as healthcare and education, more responsive to market forces, and reduced the role of local government as a provider of services. Her election for a third term of office in 1987 was aided, as in 1983, by divisions in the **Labour Party** and a more equal division of votes between the opposition parties than had hitherto been usual. She became the longest serving 20c Prime Minister in 1988 but her popularity waned and her anti-European statements caused damaging division within the Conservative Party. She resigned soon after failing to win a sufficiently large majority in the Conservative leadership contest of Nov 1990, and retired from her parliamentary seat of Finchley in 1992.

thirty-eighth parallel
The boundary line proposed for the partition of Korea at the Potsdam Conference in 1945, after the defeat of Japan (who had annexed Korea in 1910). In 1948 the Democratic People's Republic of North Korea was proclaimed (but not recognized by the Western powers). Since the **Korean War**, the 38th parallel again forms the line of division between North and South Korea.

Thorez, Maurice (1900–64)
French politician. Having worked briefly as a coalminer, he joined the **Communist Party** in 1920; he was made General-Secretary in 1930, when the earlier generation of leaders fell foul of **Stalin**, and remained in undisputed command of a highly disciplined party until his death. He was one of the creators of the **Popular Front**, thus bringing the party out of the political wilderness, although communists tended not to join in

the Popular Front governments. He survived the difficult period of the **German–Soviet Pact** (1939–41) by deserting from the French Army into which he had been conscripted and fleeing to the USSR. He was amnestied, and returned to France in 1944, becoming Deputy Prime Minister in the cabinet of the socialist Ramadier (Nov 1946–May 1947). After the exclusion of the party from office he led it through its most Stalinist period, adopting a position of unwavering support for the USSR on all questions until 1956, when he refused to accept Nikita **Khrushchev**'s denunciation of Stalin.

Tiananmen Square

The largest public square in the world, covering 40 hectares and lying before the gate to the Imperial Palace in central Beijing. It was here that the People's Republic was proclaimed in Oct 1949. In June 1989, it was the scene of mass protests by students and others against the Chinese government. The demonstrations were crushed by troops of the Chinese Army, leaving an undisclosed number of people dead.

Tibet

An autonomous region in south-west China. Tibet was dominated by Buddhist lamas from the 7c until the departure of the Dalai Lama into exile in 1959. It was controlled by the Manchus in the 18c. Chinese rule was restored in 1951, and full control was asserted after a revolt in 1959. Most monasteries and temples are now closed or officially declared historical monuments, but many people still worship daily. There are thought to be fewer than 1 000 lamas in Tibet, compared to almost 110 000 monks in 2 500 monasteries prior to 1959.

Tikhon (1865–1925)

Patriarch of the Russian Orthodox Church. He was the first to have to face up to the new communist regime. A bishop by 1898, he had few crises to face until he became patriarch in 1918. His first approach was to condemn the new Soviet state; but before his death he called on the faithful to show it political loyalty. Neither policy was to prove successful, and his *de facto* successor, **Sergei**, faced the same problem.

Tikhonov, Nikolai Alexandrovich (1905–)

Soviet politician. He began his career as an assistant locomotive driver, before training in the late 1920s at the Dnepropetrovsk Metallurgical Institute, where he met Leonid **Brezhnev**, then a Communist Party (CPSU) organizer. Tikhonov worked for two decades in the ferrous metallurgy industry, before being made Deputy Minister for the Iron and Steel Industry (1955–7), Deputy Chairman of Gosplan (1963–5) and Deputy Chairman of the Council of Ministers (1965–80). He was inducted into the CPSU **Politburo** as a full member by party leader

Brezhnev in 1979 and appointed Prime Minister in 1980, a post which he held until 1985. A cautious, centralist Brezhnevite, his period as state Premier was characterized by progressive economic stagnation.

Tilak, Bal Gangadhar (1856–1920)
Militant Indian nationalist, scholar, and philosopher. After teaching mathematics, he became owner and editor of two weekly newspapers. A member of the so-called 'extremist' wing within the **Indian National Congress**, he was twice imprisoned by the British for his nationalist activities. He helped found the Home Rule League in 1914, and died in Bombay.

Timoshenko, Semyon Konstantinovich (1895–1970)
Russian general. He joined the Tsarist army in 1915, and in the **Russian Revolution** took part in the defence of Tsaritsyn. In 1940 he smashed Finnish resistance during the **Russo-Finnish War**, then commanded in the Ukraine, but failed to stop the German advance (1942). He also served as People's Commissar of Defence, improving the system of army training. He retired in 1960. ▷ **World War II**

Tindemans, Leo (1922–)
Belgian politician. He studied economics and social sciences at Antwerp, Ghent and Leuven universities; in 1958 became Secretary to the **Christian People's Party** (CVP). In 1961 he entered parliament for Antwerp. From 1968 he regularly held cabinet posts, and led the government from 1974 to 1978. In 1979 he became chairman of the CVP, and is particularly known for his role in the European Community.

Tirpitz, Alfred (Friedrich) von (1849–1930)
German admiral. He joined the Prussian Navy in 1865, was ennobled in 1900, and rose to be Lord High Admiral (1911). As Secretary of State for the Imperial Navy (1897–1916), he raised a fleet to challenge British supremacy of the seas, and acted as its commander (1914–16). He advocated unrestricted submarine warfare, and resigned when this policy was, initially, opposed in government circles (to be implemented later, on 1 Feb 1917); he later sat in the **Reichstag**. ▷ **World War I**

Tiso, Jozef (1887–1947)
Slovak priest and politician. Like many other Slovak priests he was attracted to politics by Catholic and ethnic feelings against the Czechs in the united state established in 1918. In 1938 he succeeded **Hlinka** as leader of the Populist Party and began talks with **Henlein**, the Sudeten leader, whose objective was to enable **Hitler** to destroy Czechoslovakia. Following the **Munich Agreement**, ably assisted by **Durcansky**, he conspired with Hitler and in Mar 1939 obeyed the order to declare Slovakia inde-

pendent, leaving Czechs to Hitler's mercy in the **Bohemian Protectorate**. As President of the new Slovakia he eventually, in 1944, invited the Germans in to suppress the patriotic **Slovak uprising**. In 1947 he was tried and executed in Bratislava. The Slovak-Czech relationship had been little improved by his efforts.

Tito (Josip Broz) (1892–1980)

Yugoslav politician. He served with the Austro-Hungarian army in **World War I**, was taken prisoner by the Russians, and became a communist. He was imprisoned for conspiring against the regime in Yugoslavia (1928–9), and became Secretary of the Communist Party in 1937. In 1941 he organized partisan forces against the Axis conquerors, and after the war became the country's first communist Prime Minister (1945), consolidating his position with the presidency (1953–80). He broke with **Stalin** and the Cominform in 1948, developing Yugoslavia's independent style of **communism** ('Titoism'), and played a leading role in the association of nonaligned countries. ▷ **Axis Powers; Chetniks**

Titulescu, Nicolae (1883–1941)

Romanian politician. At the end of **World War I**, he was one of the Romanian representatives at the peace negotiations in Paris and later signed the Treaty of **Trianon** (1920). He worked at the Romanian embassy in London (1922–6 and 1928–32), returning to Romania to serve as Foreign Minister (1927 and 1932–6). He negotiated Romania's membership of the **Little Entente** and the **Balkan Entente** and courted the support of France and the USSR. He was dismissed by **Charles II** of Romania in 1936.

Tobruk, Battles of (1941–2)

A key city in Libya, Tobruk was taken from the Italians in Jan 1941 by Wavell, then in command of the Eighth Army. The arrival, however, in Libya of **Rommel** with his Afrika Corps in Mar of the same year saw the British withdrawing eastward. The subsequent siege of Tobruk, which was garrisoned largely by Australian troops, lasted for some eight months until the garrison was able to break out. Auchinleck, who was now in command of the Eighth Army and whom they managed to join, mounted a major offensive which was to extend British control over Cyrenaica as far as Benghazi bringing back Tobruk with it. But Rommel's counter-offensive towards Egypt meant that Tobruk was again placed under siege, this time falling in June 1942. In the event, Auchinleck was able to check Rommel's advance at the first Battle of **El Alamein** and it was the successful western drive of Montgomery which finally recaptured Tobruk in Nov 1942.

Todd, Sir (Reginald Stephen) Garfield (1908–92)

Rhodesian politician. Born in New Zealand, he was educated there and in South Africa. Having come to Southern Rhodesia in 1934 as a missionary, he was elected to the Legislative Assembly (1946) and then to the leadership of the United Rhodesia Party (1953) which made him Prime Minister of Southern Rhodesia. He was removed from the leadership by an internal putsch because of his liberalism and he helped form the overtly liberal Central African Party in 1959. After the party's failure in 1962, he returned to farming but remained the spokesman for white liberalism in the country, as a result of which he was restricted by the **Rhodesian Front (RF)** government under Ian **Smith** (1965–6 and 1972–6). A close friend and ally of Joshua **Nkomo**, he supported the latter in the 1980 elections.

Togliatti, Palmiro (1893–1964)

Italian politician. A member of the Italian Socialist Party in 1914, he was one of the founders of the Italian Communist Party (**PCI**) in 1921. Forced to flee Italy by the fascists in 1926, he organized the activities of the party from abroad and was part of the **Comintern** secretariat in charge of communists fighting in the **Spanish Civil War**. In Mar 1944 he returned to Italy, played a key part in the coalition governments that controlled Italy until 1947 and was instrumental in stressing the need to avoid insurrectionary attempts. Until his death (while visiting Nikita **Khrushchev** in Yalta), he was Party Secretary, presiding over the PCI's development from a relatively small group of militants into the largest communist organization in the West. ▷ **Berlinguer, Enrico**

Togo

A republic in West Africa, formerly part of the Kingdom of Togoland. It was a German protectorate from 1884 to 1914, and a mandate of the League of Nations in 1922 divided it between France (French Togo) and Britain (part of British Gold Coast). These became trusteeships of the United Nations in 1946, and French Togo became an autonomous republic within the French Union in 1956. British Togoland voted to join the Gold Coast (Ghana) in 1957 while French Togo gained independence in 1960. Military coups took place in 1963 and 1967, followed by a return to civilian rule in 1980. There was an unstable period in the early 1990s as the country began to move towards democracy.

Tojo Hideki (1885–1948)

Japanese general and politician. He attended military college, became military attaché in Germany (1919), served in **Manchuria** as Chief of Staff (1937–40), and during **World War II** was Minister of War (1940–1) and Prime Minister (1941–4). Arrested in 1945, he attempted to commit suicide, but was hanged as a war criminal in Tokyo.

Tolbert, William Richard (1913–80)
Liberian politician. Educated at Liberia College in Monrovia, he was a civil servant (1935–43) before becoming a member of the House of Representatives for the True Whig Party (1943–51). Vice-President from 1951 to 1971, he became President in 1971 and remained in this post until he was assassinated in a military coup on 12 Apr 1980.

Tombalbaye, N'Garta (François) (1918–75)
Chadian politician. Educated locally, he was a teacher before becoming a trades union organizer. He then helped organize the **Rassemblement Démocratique Africaine (RDA)** in Chad in 1947 and was elected to the territorial assembly (1953). He rose to be Prime Minister in 1959 and then President on Chad's independence in 1962. He remained in this position until the military coup of 13 Apr 1975, during which he was killed.

Tomsky, Mikhail Pavlovich (1880–1937)
Soviet trade unionist. Born into a poor working-class family in St Petersburg, he organized factory strikes from his mid-teens. From 1909 to 1917 he was either in prison or in exile. He returned to trade union activity in Moscow in 1917, and by 1919 was Chairman of the Central Council of Trade Unions and by 1922 a full-blown member of the **Politburo**. In these capacities he destroyed the unions in the Western sense and made them vehicles for party and government control. In the period 1928–30 he changed his stance and defended workers' rights. He was thereupon dismissed and committed suicide in protest against **Stalin**'s purges.

Tories (UK)
The British political party which emerged in 1679–80 as the group opposed to the exclusion of James, Duke of York, from succession to the throne. The name was taken from 17c Irish outlaws who plundered and killed English settlers. Toryism developed into Conservatism under Peel, but survived as a nickname for the Conservatives. ▷ **Conservative Party** (UK)

Touré, Ahmed Sékou (1922–84)
Guinean politician. Educated in Quran schools and at Conakry (1936–40), he turned to trade union activity and attended the *Conféderation Générale des Travailleurs* (**CGT**) Congress in Paris in 1947, after which he was imprisoned for a brief period. He was a founder member of the **Rassemblement Démocratique Africaine (RDA)** in 1946 and became its Secretary-General in 1952, as well as Secretary-General of the local CGT branch. He was a member of the Territorial Assembly from 1953, Mayor of Conakry in 1955 and then Deputy in the French National Assembly

in 1956. In 1958 he organized an overwhelming 'non' vote to de **Gaulle**'s referendum on self-government within a French Community. Guinea was granted its independence at once, the French removing as much of their possessions as possible. He was President from 1958 to 1984, and retained his uncompromisingly radical views of domestic and foreign politics. He survived several attempts, supported by outside powers, to overthrow him. Soon after his death, the military did take control.

Tours, Congress of (25–30 Dec 1920)
The Congress of the **Socialist Party** (SFIO) at which the majority of members decided to join the Third International, and thus to create a new party, the **Communist Party** (SFIC). His impassioned oratory against this decision made Léon **Blum** the most influential figure among those who decided to stay with the 'old firm', the Socialist Party. The subsequent general election (1924) revealed that the majority of socialist voters agreed, and the Communist Party had little support until the **Popular Front** period (1934–6).

Trade Unions (Belgium)
As one of the first industrialized nations, with strong mining and heavy industrial sectors in Wallonia and Ghent, Belgian socialism developed early, having a radical syndicalist trade-union movement as one of the moving forces. In 1898 the various socialist organizations joined a Syndical Committee, which in 1938 became the Belgian Labour League, and after **World War II** the General Belgian Labour League (*Algemeen Belgisch Vakverbond*; *Fédération Générale du Travail de Belgique*). The Catholics were much slower to adopt organizations exclusively for workers, but after the papal encyclical *Rerum Novarum* in 1891 work started, and in 1904 the General Secretariat for Christian Professional Organizations was set up, which, after several changes, in 1923 became the General Christian Labour League (*Algemeen Christelijk Vakverbond*; *Confédération des Syndicats Chrétiens*). The importance of heavy industry to the Belgian economy has always meant that the more radical socialist Belgian trade unions have had a strong political influence, albeit sometimes rather negative, eg in the strikes of the 1880s; in the 20c both branches have been integrated into Belgian political culture and the power-sharing mechanism of Belgian society.

Tragic Week, The (July 1909)
Spanish popular protest. The Tragic Week (*La Semana Tragica*) took place when a public demonstration in Barcelona against the conscription of soldiers for the war in Morocco developed into a violent popular protest with the widespread burning of churches and convents. This was largely a spontaneous backlash against the oppressive and anti-regionalist policies of the monarchy (with the church being seized on as

the most visible manifestation of the ancien regime), though the inflammatory anticlerical propaganda of the **Radical Republican Party** had done much to create the volatile climate of opinion. The Tragic Week was a turning-point in the history of modern Spain because it brought the Republican and Socialist movements together, which eventually culminated in the establishment of the Second Republic in 1931. ▷ **Republic, Second** (Spain)

Transkei

Formerly, an independent black homeland in south-east South Africa, the traditional territory of the Xhosa people. Transkei achieved self-government status in 1963 and was granted independence by South Africa in 1976. It was re-incorporated into South Africa after the election in 1994.

Transvaal

A province in South Africa. It was settled by the Boers after the Great Trek of 1831 and its independence, gained in 1852, was recognized by Britain. It became known as the South African Republic until annexed by Britain in 1877, but the Boer rebellion of 1880–1 led to the restoration of the republic. Transvaal was annexed as a British colony in 1900 and granted self-government in 1906; it joined the Union of South Africa in 1910.

Trenchard (of Wolfeton), Hugh Montague, 1st Viscount (1873–1956)

British marshal of the RAF. He joined the army in 1893, served in India, South Africa, and West Africa, and developed an interest in aviation. He commanded the Royal Flying Corps in **World War I**, helped to establish the RAF (1918), and became the first Chief of Air Staff (1918–29). As Commissioner of the London Metropolitan Police (1931–5), he founded the police college at Hendon. He became a peer in 1930.

Treurnicht, Andries Petrus (1921–93)

South African politician. He studied at the Universities of Cape Town and Stellenbosch and was a minister in the Dutch Reformed Church from 1946 until his election as a **National Party** representative in 1971. Elected Transvaal provincial leader in 1978, he held several cabinet posts under P W **Botha**, gaining a reputation as an unreconstructed supporter of **apartheid**. He opposed even Botha's partial liberalization of the regime and was forced to leave the party with 15 colleagues in 1982. He formed a new party, the **Conservative Party of South Africa**, which pressed for a return to traditional apartheid values and effective partitioning of the country. Following the 1989 general election his party took over from the moderate Progressive Federal Party as the official opposition within arliament. He was defeated in a whites-only referendum on political eform in Mar 1992.

rianon, Treaty of (1920)

The treaty agreed between the new state of Hungary and the Allies of **World War I**, which reduced the territory of Hungary to about a third of its pre-war size. Romania received almost all that it had hoped to gain by entering the war, acquiring Transylvania with its mixed Romanian and Magyar population, Bessarabia, Crişana and **Bukovina** with part of the Banat, the rest of which was ceded to the Kingdom of Serbs, Croats and Slovenes (later Yugoslavia). Czechoslovakia also benefited from the treaty, gaining areas of mixed Czech and Magyar population.

Trieste, Free Territory of

This Adriatic port, at the north-west junction of the Istrian Peninsula, was promised to Italy in the Treaty of **London** (1915). In the inter-war years it was the subject of dispute between Italy and Yugoslavia and, following **World War II**, it was established as the 'Free Territory of Trieste', with the northern zone administered by the USA and Britain and the southern zone under Yugoslav control (1946). In 1954 the status of Trieste was revised and the northern zone was returned to Italy.

Tripartite Declaration (May 1950)

This represented an attempt by Britain, France and the USA to limit arms supplies to Israel and the Arab states in the wake of the emergence of the state of Israel, in the hope that this would ensure some stability for the area. Arms supplies were to be conditional on non-aggression, and the signatories to the Declaration undertook to take action both within and outside the framework of the **UN** in cases of frontier violation. Closer French relations with Israel subjected the Declaration to some strain, and with the Soviet arms deal with Gamal Abd al-**Nasser**'s Egypt in 1955 it became a dead letter.

Triple Entente

A series of agreements between Britain and France (1904) and Britain and Russia (1907) initially to resolve outstanding colonial differences. It aligned Britain to France and Russia, who had concluded a military alliance in 1893–4. In 1914, the Triple Entente became a military alliance.

Tripolitania

Region of North Africa, lying between Tunis and Cyrenaica; former province of western Libya; under Turkish control from the 16c until 1911; under Italian control until 1943; British control until 1952.

Tripolitanian War (1911–12)

The war between Italy and Turkey, in which Italian forces invaded an occupied the Turkish province of Tripolitania (present-day Libya) t gain useful ports and to prevent an extension of French influence i North Africa. After the declaration of war (Sep 1911), the initial invasio went smoothly but the Italians were surprised to discover that the loca Arab population did not welcome them as liberators from Turkish rule The Italians therefore found themselves fighting not only the Turkisl Army, but also Arab tribesmen. **Giolitti**'s response was to try to pu pressure on the Turks elsewhere, and, in May 1912, 13 Turkish Aegean islands were seized. The outbreak of the Balkan war (Oct 1912) obliged Turkey to concentrate on resisting the threat from Bulgaria, Serbia, Montenegro and Greece, and so peace negotiations were begun with Italy, leading to the surrender of both Tripolitania and neighbouring Cyrenaica. Although the Italians were able to claim a considerable victory, the war brought them little real advantage: the colony was of little economic value and until the early 1930s required a constant and expensive military presence to combat a hostile native population.

Troelstra, Pieter Jelles (1860–1930)

Dutch politician. Trained as a lawyer, he disagreed with the anarchist tendencies of F **Domela Nieuwenhuis**, and helped set up the Social Democratic Workers' Party (SDAP) in 1894. From 1897 onwards he sat in parliament, and led the socialist group there. Often caught between the extreme left and the moderates, he never held a government post, but managed to keep the Dutch socialists together in their most turbulent period. In 1918 he tried to stage a coup, announcing the revolution in parliament, but support was insufficient and the effort collapsed; he remained an MP until 1925. ▷ **Party of Labour**

Trotsky, Leon (Lev Davidovich Bronstein) (1879–1940)

Russian revolutionary. Educated in Odessa, in 1898 he was arrested as a Marxist and exiled to Siberia. He escaped in 1902, joined **Lenin** in London, and in the abortive **Revolution of 1905** was President of the St Petersburg Soviet. He then worked as a revolutionary journalist in the West, returning to Russia in 1917, when he joined the **Bolsheviks** and played a major role in the **October Revolution**. In the **Russian Civil War** he was Commissar for War, and created the **Red Army**. After Lenin's death (1924) his influence began to decline; he was ousted from the Party by **Stalin**, who opposed his theory of 'permanent revolution', exiled to Central Asia (1927), and expelled from the USSR (1929). He continued to agitate as an exile, and was sentenced to death *in absentia* by a Soviet court in 1937. He finally found asylum in Mexico, where he was assassinated by one of Stalin's agents. ▷ **Russian Revolution; Trotskyism**

Trotskyism

A development of Marxist thought by Leon **Trotsky**. Essentially a theory of permanent revolution, Trotskyism stressed the internationalism of socialism, avoided coexistence, and encouraged revolutionary movements abroad; this conflicted with **Stalin**'s ideas of 'socialism in one country'. Trotskyism has since inspired other extreme left-wing revolutionary movements but they are factionally divided, and have little support outside some Western capitalist states. ▷ **communism; Marxism–Leninism; Stalinism**

Trudeau, Pierre (Elliott) (1919–)

Canadian politician. Educated at Montreal, Harvard, and London, he became a lawyer, helped to found the political magazine, *Cité Libre* (1950), and was Professor of Law at the University of Montreal (1961–5). Elected a Liberal MP in 1965, he became Minister of Justice (1967) and an outspoken critic of Québecois **séparatisme**. His term of office as Prime Minister (1968–79 and 1980–4) saw the **October Crisis** (1970) in Quebec, the introduction of the Official Languages Act, federalist victory during the Quebec Referendum (1980), and the introduction of the **Constitution Act of 1982**. He resigned as leader of the **Liberal Party** and from public life in 1984.

Trujillo (Molina), Rafael Leonidas (1891–1961)

Dominican Republic dictator. He was dictator of the Dominican Republic from 1930 until his assassination in Santo Domingo, a city he had renamed Ciudad Trujillo. Born in San Cristóbal, Dominican Republic, he rose to prominence as commander of the police. His regime was both highly repressive and highly corrupt.

Truman, Harry S (1884–1972)

US politician and 33rd President. He fought in **World War I**, was a presiding judge in the Jackson County Court in Missouri (1926–34), was elected to the US Senate as a Democrat in 1934 and became chairman of a senate committee investigating defence spending. He became Vice-President (1944) and, on Franklin D **Roosevelt**'s death (Apr 1945), President. He was re-elected in 1948 in a surprise victory over Thomas E Dewey. As president (1945–53) he ordered the dropping of the first atomic bomb on Japan in Aug 1945, which led to Japan's surrender. Following **World War II**, he established a 'containment' policy against the USSR, developed the **Marshall Plan** to rebuild Europe and created **NATO** (1949). He authorized the sending of US troops to South Korea in 1950, and promoted the Four-Point Programme that gave military and economic aid to countries threatened by communist interference. He established the CIA (1947) and ordered the **Berlin Airlift** (1948–9). At home, he introduced his '**Fair Deal**' programme of economic reform. ▷ **Democratic Party**

Trumbić, Ante (1864–1938)
Croatian politician. A proponent of **trialism**, with Frano **Supilo** he founded the Croatian Social Democrat Party in 1895. During **World War I** he was a founder and President of the **Yugoslav Committee**, helping to formulate the Declaration of **Corfu** in which the Committee and the Serbian government agreed to cooperate in establishing a South Slav state (July 1917). He was Minister for Foreign Affairs in the post-1918 Provisional Government but became disillusioned with the Serb nationalist programme of Nikola **Pašić** and **Alexander I** and retired from political life in 1921.

Trusteeship
A system developed by the **UN** after 1945 for the international supervision of colonial territories that had been removed from the German and Ottoman empires at the end of **World War I**. These territories had been supervised originally under the mandates commission of the **League of Nations** and mandates in the Middle East, Africa and the South Pacific were held by Britain, France, South Africa, Australia and New Zealand. Only South Africa refused to hand over South-West Africa (now Namibia) to the UN, leading to the long-running dispute over the independence of that territory. The British Palestine mandate became the setting for Arab/Jewish conflict and the British were forced to hand it over to the UN in 1948. The trusteeship system, in internationalizing key areas of colonial rule, has been seen as pressing forward decolonization.

Tsankov, Alexander (1879–1959)
Bulgarian politician. He became Prime Minister in 1923 after the military coup which overthrew **Stamboliski**. Drawing his support from a coalition of parties called the Democratic Concord, his government tried to eliminate **VMRO** and the Bulgarian Communist Party. In Jan 1926 he was replaced by Andrei Liapchev.

Tshombe, Moise Kapenda (1919–69)
Congolese politician. Educated in mission schools, he was a businessman who helped to found the Confederation des Associations du Katanga in 1957. When Belgium granted the Congo independence in 1960, he declared the copper-rich province of Katanga independent and became its President. On the request of **Lumumba**, **UN** troops were called in to reintegrate the province and Tshombe was forced into exile in 1963; he returned again in 1964, supported by some of the mining interests and white settlers of Katanga. Forced into exile again after **Mobutu**'s 1966 coup, Tshombe was kidnapped in 1967 and taken to Algeria, where he

died. A talented conservative, he became the representation of neo-colonialism's ugly face in the mythology of African nationalism throughout the continent.

Tsiranana, Philibert (1912–)

Madagascar politician. Educated on the island and in France, he organized the Social Democratic Party, on whose ticket he was elected a member of the Representative Assembly in 1956, as well as the French National Assembly in 1957. He was Deputy President of Madagascar in 1958 and President in the following year. He remained in the post until being overthrown in a military coup in 1972.

Tsouderos, Emmanuel (1882–1956)

Greek politician. A banker from Crete, he was a republican and follower of Eleuthérios **Venizélos**. In Apr 1940, after the suicide of Alexander Koryzis, he became Prime Minister and fled with King **George II** after Greece's surrender to Germany. He continued as Prime Minister in the Greek government-in-exile but, following the mutinies in the Greek Army and Navy in Egypt (Apr 1944), he was succeeded briefly by Sofoklis **Venizélos** and then by George **Papandreou**.

Tsushima, Battle of (27 May 1905)

Admiral Togo's crushing victory over the Russian Baltic fleet, in the Tsushima Straits, during the **Russo-Japanese War**. It is remarkable for being the only instance in world history of a decisive engagement between all-gun iron-clad ships. The battle gave the Japanese naval supremacy and dashed Russian hopes of achieving a land victory.

Tubman, William V S (1895–1971)

Liberian politician. Educated in a methodist seminary, he was a teacher, lawyer and Methodist preacher. Tubman was elected for the True Whig Party, which protected the interests of the Americo-Liberian elite, and became a member of the Liberian Senate in 1922. In 1937 he was appointed Deputy President of the Supreme Court and, in 1944, was chosen as President of Liberia, a post he retained until his death.

Tudeh

The Communist Party of Iran, founded in 1920. It had the varying fortunes to be expected of a communist party in a primarily Islamic state and despite its temporary demise in 1930, it had its heyday with the Soviet intervention in Northern Iran during **World War II**. It helped, with the USSR, in the founding of the Kurdish Republic of Mahabad which lasted about a year, but was itself again outlawed in 1946. Surfacing yet again to support the left wing leader Mosaddeq in the early fifties, the Tudah Party was once more banned, this time by Shah Muhammad Reza.

Tudjman, Franjo (1922–)

Croatian politician and historian. He served in the partisan army led by **Tito** and in 1945 became the youngest general in the Yugoslav Federal Army. In 1972 he was imprisoned during the purge of the Croatian nationalist movement and in 1981 was again sentenced to three years' imprisonment in the first major political trial since Tito's death. A professor of modern history at the Faculty of Political Science at Zagreb, he became Chairman of the History of the Workers' Movement of Croatia. Following the elections in Apr 1990, as leader of the right-wing Croatian Democratic Union, he became President of Croatia. He declared the Republic of Croatia's independence from the Yugoslav federation (25 June 1992), but the republic soon found itself engaged in a brutal war against the Yugoslav Federal Army, which occupied eastern Slavonia, besieged and destroyed Vukovar and shelled cities and towns, including Dubrovnik, on the Dalmatian coast. While international recognition of the independence of the Republic of Croatia followed in Dec 1991 and spring 1992, over a third of the republic still remained beyond the reach of Tudjman's government in Zagreb. He was re-elected as President of Croatia in Sep 1992.

Tuka, Vojtech (1880–1946)

Slovak politician. Of Magyar parentage and pro-Hungarian orientation, he was a member of **Hlinka**'s Slovak Populist Party during the 1920s and encouraged it to be more assertive in demanding Slovak autonomy. But in 1929 he was proved to be a Hungarian agent and was imprisoned, to the serious embarrassment of Hlinka and the whole party. In 1939 he reappeared as Deputy Prime Minister and then as Prime and Foreign Minister in the puppet government of **Tiso**. In 1946 he was condemned to death.

Tukhachevsky, Mikhail Nikolaevich (1893–1937)

Soviet military leader. From 1926 he was Chief-of Staff of the **Red Army**, which he was influential in transforming from a peasant army into a modern, mechanized force. His vigour and independence made him suspect to **Stalin**, and in 1937 he was executed, an early victim of the great purge which decimated the Red Army's officer corps.

Tunisia

A North African republic. It became a French protectorate in 1883 until gaining independence in 1956. The monarchy was then abolished and a republic was declared in 1957. The tough economic policies of Hedi Nouira, prime minister from 1970 to 1980, led to much unrest. Unemployment and poverty continued to cause problems. A military coup in 1987 deposed President **Bourguiba**.

Tupamaros

Uruguayan urban guerrillas belonging to the *Movimiento de Liberación Nacional* (National Liberation Movement). The movement was founded by Raúl Sendic, a labour organizer, in 1963 and was named after the 18c Peruvian Indian rebel, Tupac Amaru. The organization was suppressed by the military-controlled government of 1972–85, and since then has been re-created as a legitimate political party.

Tupolev, Andrei Nikolaevich (1888–1972)

Soviet military and civilian aircraft designer. The son of a lawyer and product of Moscow Higher Technical School, he was already working in a Moscow aircraft factory in the pre-revolutionary period. In the 1920s and 1930s he designed several bombers of world class, and even when imprisoned on false accusations of treason in 1937 he combined designing and was therefore released in 1943. Subsequently he worked on everything down to the supersonic passenger plane, becoming the best-known international name in the business and keeping the Soviet air force at least on a par with the American.

Turati, Filippo (1857–1932)

Italian politician. In 1892 he helped to found the party that three years later was to become the Italian Socialist Party (**PSI**). He was elected deputy in 1896 and remained one until he fled the country in 1926. In 1898 he was condemned to 12 years' imprisonment for his part in protests in Milan, but was released the following year. He refused to participate in **Giolitti**'s governments, but was always on the moderate wing of the socialist movement. He opposed the **Tripolitanian War** and Italian intervention in 1915. In the aftermath of **World War I** and the Bolshevik Revolution, Turati found it hard to check the increasing radicalism of the PSI; he left the party when it joined the Third International (1919) and founded the Socialist Unity Party. With the assertion of fascist power, he fled Italy for France, where he died.

Turkey

A republic lying partly in Europe and partly in Asia. The Turkish empire was at its peak in the 16c under Sulaiman the Magnificent, but in the 17c the Turks were pressed back by Russian and Austrian armies. In the 19c Turkey was regarded by Britain as a bulwark against Russian expansion but, following alleged Armenian massacres, Britain abandoned its support of Turkey. The Young Turks seized power in 1908 and became embroiled in the Balkan War (1912–13). Turkey allied with Germany during **World War I**. The Republic of Turkey was founded in 1923 following the Young Turk Revolution led by Kemal **Atatürk**, who introduced a policy of westernization and economic development. Turkey was neutral throughout most of **World War II**, before siding with the Allies. Military coups took place in 1960 and 1980 and relations with Greece were strained during this period, leading to an invasion of Cyprus in 1974 and on-going Turkish control of the north part of the island. The south-east of Turkey has been under martial law since the mid-1980s as a result of fierce fighting between Kurds in the area and government forces.

Tutu, Desmond Mpilo (1931–)

South African cleric. Educated in mission schools and at Pretoria Bantu Normal College, he studied at St Peter's Theological College and King's College, London. He was ordained a deacon in the Anglican Church in 1960 and held a variety of church positions in England, South Africa and Lesotho, including lecturing at the Federal Theological Seminary in Cape Province (1967–9), the University of Botswana, Lesotho and Swaziland (1970–2). He returned from England to South Africa in 1975 as Dean of Johannesburg, from where he went to be Bishop of Lesotho. As Secretary-General of the South African Council of Churches from 1978 to 1985, he spoke out strongly from the relative safety of his church position against the extremes of **apartheid** and was awarded the Nobel Peace Prize in 1984. He was elected Bishop of Johannesburg in 1985 and Archbishop of Cape Town in 1986. A critic of the apartheid system, he nonetheless also criticized violence in the townships.

Tvardovsky, Alexander Trifonovich (1910–71)

Soviet poet, editor and **samizdat** publisher. Writing during and after **World War I**, he was editor of *Novy Mir* in the years 1958–70 when he exposed the excesses of **Stalinism**; for example, he secured the publication of Alexander **Solzhenitsyn**'s *One Day in the Life of Ivan Denisovich*. His task became increasingly difficult following Leonid **Brezhnev**'s rise to power in 1964, hence his resort to underground publication. However, he had laid the foundations for the **Gorbachev** years of open debate.

Twenty-One Demands

A series of demands presented by Japan to China in 1915, which included: the recognition of Japanese control of **Manchuria**, Shandong, Inner Mongolia, south-eastern China and the Yangzi Valley; the imposition of Japanese advisers in the Chinese administration; and the compulsory purchase of 50 per cent of its munitions from Japan. President **Yuan Shikai** accepted them as the basis of a treaty, but the resulting popular patriotic protest movement gave impetus to the rise of Chinese nationalism.

U

U-2 Incident (1960)

On 1 May 1960 a US U-2 spy plane was brought down over Sverdlovsk in the USSR. After US denials, Premier Nikita **Khrushchev** produced the pilot, Francis Gary Powers, and his photographs of military installations. President **Eisenhower** justified the flights as essential for US national security. Khrushchev took advantage of the situation at the scheduled Paris Summit Meeting a few days later, when he withdrew Eisenhower's invitation to visit the USSR and demanded that he condemn the flights. The President's refusal allowed Khrushchev to walk out of the summit and to blame the USA for its failure.

U-boat

An abbreviation of the German *Unterseeboot* ('submarine'). The German Navy launched large-scale submarine offensives in both world wars, and each time the U-boats came close to victory.

UCD (*Unión Central Democrática*, 'Central Democratic Union') (1977–82)

A coalition of liberal, regional, Christian and social democratic groups under the leadership of Adolfo **Suárez** which formed a political party after its success in the 1977 Spanish general election. Having formed the minority governments of 1977–82, numerous schisms and defections, caused by struggles over the party apparatus and ideological differences, led to the Union's rout in the 1982 election and its disbandment shortly thereafter. However, although it had failed as a party, the UCD had succeeded in transforming Spain from a dictatorship into a democracy.

UDI (Unilateral Declaration of Independence) (11 Nov 1965)

The declaration by Ian **Smith**'s Rhodesia Front government which attempted to maintain white supremacy in Southern Rhodesia (Zimbabwe). After the dissolution of the Central African Federation at the end of 1963, Nyasaland and Northern Rhodesia achieved independence as Malawi and Zambia. The British government then expected that Southern Rhodesia would also pursue unimpeded progress to black majority rule, but the white settlers attempted to maintain their dominance of the economy and politics of the territory. Harold **Wilson**'s British Labour government declined to use force against them, but imposed sanctions. Because of South Africa's initial support of Rhodesia, these took some time to take effect, but the Smith regime was ultimately defeated by guerrilla incursions from Zambia and Mozambique and by economic collapse. Zimbabwe achieved its independence in 1980.

Uganda

An East African republic. Much of the land of present Uganda was granted to the British East Africa Company in 1888, and the Kingdom of Buganda became a British protectorate in 1893. Further territory was included by 1903, and the country gained independence in 1962. Dr Milton **Obote** assumed all powers in 1966 until a successful coup was led by General Idi **Amin** Dada in 1971. Once in power, Amin expelled all Asian residents who were not Ugandan citizens. In reaction to this repressive regime, Tanzanian troops and Ugandan exiles marched on Kampala, overthrowing the government in 1979. A further coup took place in 1985. In 1993 the government instituted a policy of returning property to Asians who had been expelled by Amin.

UGT (*Unión General de Trabajadores*, 'General Union of Workers')

Spanish socialist trade union movement. The UGT grew extremely slowly after its foundation in 1888, not achieving a national presence until the Second Republic of 1931–6. Throughout this period it was distinguished by its rigid centralism, ideological confusion, and practical moderation. The pragmatism of the UGT was shown above all by its collaboration with the dictatorship of Miguel **Primo de Rivera** (1923–30) in an effort to reshape the trade unions along corporatist lines. Under the Second Republic the UGT grew spectacularly, especially among the landless day labourers. The failure of reform led to demands for action from an increasingly militant rank and file, culminating in the agricultural strike of June 1934 and the general strike and rising of Oct 1934. The defeat of these protests and their savage repression led the UGT to adopt a revolutionary line in 1935, though it still backed the Popular Front in the general election of Feb 1936. Once the Popular Front came to power, the UGT's rural section, frustrated by the lack of reform, encouraged landless labourers to take the law into their own hands, thereby polarizing the political climate further. During the **Spanish Civil War** the UGT lost more and more influence to the **PCE** and by the end of the war it had been torn apart by internal divisions. Like the **PSOE**, it played an extremely limited role in the opposition to the **Franco** regime. With the restoration of democracy in Spain in 1977, the UGT was re-established. By 1982 it had become the largest trade union body in Spain, but it fell out with the socialist government in 1988 over its modernization programme. ▷ **Republic, Second** (Spain)

Ulbricht, Walter (1893–1973)

East German politician. At first a cabinetmaker, he entered politics in 1912, and in 1928 became communist Deputy for Potsdam. He left

Germany on **Hitler**'s rise in 1933, spending most of his exile in the USSR. In 1945 he returned as head of the German Communist Party (**KPD**), and became Deputy Premier of the German Democratic Republic and General-Secretary of the Socialist Unity Party (**SED**) in 1950. He was largely responsible for the 'sovietization' of East **Germany**, and had the **Berlin Wall** built in 1961. ▷ **communism**

Ulster

A province in the Irish Republic, comprising the counties of Cavan, Donegal, and Monaghan. The name is commonly used to refer to Northern Ireland. Ulster was a former kingdom, and one of the four traditional provinces of Ireland, divided into 9 counties in the 16c. Following refusal by the Protestant counties of Ulster to accept the new Irish Free State, the province was divided in 1921 between Northern Ireland and the Irish Republic.

Ulster 'Troubles'

The name conventionally given to violence in Northern Ireland from 1968. They originated in conflict between Catholics and Protestants over civil rights and perceived discrimation against the Catholic minority in the Province. The promise of reforms by the Ulster Premier Terence O'Neill lost him the confidence of loyalists in his Unionist Party and he resigned in 1969. Reforms implemented by his successor, James Chichester-Clark, provoked rioting between Protestants and Catholics and an increase in the specific acts of sectarian violence. The British Army was sent to maintain peace in 1969 but continuing violence resulted in the imposition of internment without trial for Catholics only under Brian Faulkner's administration. Anti-British Army feeling among the Catholics and mainland **IRA** attacks increased markedly after the **Bloody Sunday** demonstrations (30 Jan 1972) and direct rule was imposed in Mar. In Dec 1973, the British, Ulster and Irish governments signed the power-sharing Sunningdale Agreement, providing for representation in the Province's government of both the Catholic and Protestant populations, but continued Protestant Unionist resistance to the agreement led to the collapse of the **Stormont** executive in May 1974. Since then Ulster has been ruled directly from Westminster and sectarian killings have continued. The IRA has from time to time concentrated its attention on England with bombings and assassinations of prominent Conservative politicians, such as Airey Neave in 1979 and Ian Gow in 1990. Political initiatives to find a solution to an apparently intractable problem have been frustrated.

Umberto II (1904–83)

King of Italy (May/June 1946). Made *de facto* Regent ('Lieutenant-General of the Realm') by his father, **Victor Emmanuel III**, in June 1944, he ascended the throne on the latter's abdication in 1946, at a time when the monarchy had become widely unpopular. In a referendum later the same year 12 718 641 Italians voted in favour of a republic and 10 718 502 for the retention of the monarchy, most support for the latter stance being located in the south. Victor Emmanuel was forced to leave Italy, setting up residence in Portugal as the self-styled Count Di Sarre.

Umkhonto we Sizwe

The military wing (literally, 'Spear of the Nation') of the **ANC** (African National Congress), which was established when the party was banned. Its main bases were in Angola and its Chief of Staff in the 1980s was Joe **Slovo**. It has provided a number of the new generation of leaders in the ANC.

UN (United Nations Organisation)

An organization formed to maintain world peace and foster international cooperation, formally established on 24 Oct 1945 with 51 founder countries. The UN Charter, which was drafted during the war by the USA, UK and USSR, remains virtually unaltered despite the growth in membership and activities. There are six 'principal organs'. The **General Assembly** is the plenary body which controls much of the UN's work, supervises the subsidiary organs, sets priorities, and debates major issues of international affairs. The 15-member Security Council is dominated by the five permanent members (China, France, UK, USSR and USA) who each have the power of veto over any resolutions; the remaining 10 are elected for two-year periods. The primary role of the Council is to maintain international peace and security; its decisions, unlike those of the General Assembly, are binding on all other members. It is empowered to order mandatory sanctions, call for ceasefires, and establish peacekeeping forces (these forces were awarded the Nobel Peace Prize in 1988). The use of the veto has prevented it from intervening in a number of disputes, such as Vietnam. The **Secretariat**, under the Secretary-General, employs some 16 000 at the UN's headquarters in New York City and 50 000 worldwide. The staff are answerable only to the UN, not national governments, and are engaged in considerable diplomatic work. The Secretary-General is often a significant person in international diplomacy and is able to take independent initiatives. The International Court of Justice consists of 15 judges appointed by the Council and the Assembly. As only states can bring issues before it, its jurisdiction depends on the consent of the states who are a party to a dispute. It also offers advisory opinions to various organs of the UN. The Economic and Social Council is elected by the General Assembly; it supervises the work of various committees, commissions, and expert bodies in the economic and social area, and co-ordinates the work of UN specialized agencies. The Trusteeship Council oversees the transition of Trust territories to self-government. In addition to the organs established under the Charter, there is a range of subsidiary agencies, many with their own constitutions and membership, and some pre-dating the UN. The main agencies are the Food and Agriculture Organization, the Intergovernmental Maritime Consultative Organization, the International Atomic Energy Authority, the International Bank for Reconstruction and Development ('World Bank'), the International Civil Aviation Organization, the International Development Association, the International Finance Corporation, the International Fund for Agricultural Development, the International Labour Organization, the International Monetary Fund, the United Nations Educational, Scientific and Cultural Organization, the Universal Postal Union, the International Telecommunication Union, the World Meteorological Organization, and the World Health Organization. The UN has presently 160 members. It is generally seen as a forum where states pursue their national interest, rather than as an institution of world government, but it is not without considerable impact.

Unidad Popular

Literally 'Popular Unity', this was a coalition of six left-wing political parties in Chile (Communists, Socialists, Radicals, and three minor groups) formed to support the presidential candidacy and government (1970–3) of Salvador **Allende**.

Union Movement

A party formed by Sir Oswald **Mosley** in 1948 as a successor to his New Party (1931) and the British Union of Fascists (1932). It put up a handful of candidates during the period 1959–66, but failed to secure a significant number of votes. The party's main platform was opposition to immigration, but it also included a call to unite Europe into a vast market to buy from and sell to Africa. Mosley gave up the leadership in 1966, and the movement went into decline, dying out by the end of the 1960s. ▷ **Blackshirts**

Union Nationale

French Canadian political party. It was formed by a coalition of the Conservatives and *Action Libérale Nationale* to fight the 1935 provincial elections in Quebec. Its failure to win led to an amalgamation under Maurice **Duplessis**. With the support of the rural and small-business sector, it won an easy victory in 1936 on a platform of political, social and economic reform. In practice, this turned out to be anti-radicalism and pro-corporatism. In 1939 it was defeated after the intervention of Quebec Liberals in the federal government, but it returned to power in 1944 after accusing them of betraying nationalist rights, and it was to emphasize nationalist leanings thereafter. Duplessis maintained a very personal control of the party until his death in 1959, following which the party lost the 1960 election. In 1966 it regained power under Daniel

Johnson, but he died in 1968 and very soon the **Parti Québecois** had seized the nationalist mantle. The *Union Nationale* lost the 1970 election and its upport declined precipitously.

Union of Liberation (1903)
A loose alliance of Russian liberals coming together to advocate some form of representative government. They included the former Marxist, Peter **Struve**; but predominantly they were well-to-do zemstvo activists annoyed at **Nicholas II**'s incompetence and continued refusal to meet them. As the Russian **Revolution of 1905** developed, they split: **Shipov** and **Guchkov** to form the moderate **Octobrists**, and **Miliukov** and Muromtsev the more far-seeking **Cadets**. The Union represented an important transitory stage in Russian politics.

UNIP (United National Independence Party)
Formed in 1959 with Kenneth **Kaunda** as its leader, UNIP was the strongest party in the last years of Northern Rhodesian colonial rule and provided the first independence government of Zambia. It became the only legal party in 1972, but in 1991, after pressure from the international community and widespread signs of dissatisfaction within the country, multiparty elections were held and UNIP was convincingly defeated.

UNITA (*União Naçional para a Independência Total de Angola*, 'National Union for the Total Independence of Angola')
An Angolan nationalist party, founded in 1966 by Jonas Savimbi. Its support was based in south-eastern Angola and, even after Angola gained independence from Portugal in 1975, it waged a guerrilla war against the **MPLA** government, receiving backing from the USA and South Africa. When the civil war seemed to have reached an inconclusive position of stalemate, after long and difficult negotiations, UNITA and the MPLA agreed upon a ceasefire in Estoril in early 1991.

United Arab Emirates, formerly **Trucial States**
A federation comprising seven internally self-governing emirates, in the eastern central Arabian Peninsula. A peace treaty with Britain was signed by rulers of the Trucial States in 1820, and the new state formed by six emirates was established in 1971. Ras al Khaimah joined in 1972.

United Arab Republic (UAR)
The short-lived union between Egypt and Syria proclaimed in 1958. Gamal Abd al-**Nasser** was elected as head of state and the union generated considerable euphoria in both countries. Syria seceded however in late 1961, although Egypt retained the name until 1971 when it adopted the name Arab Republic of Egypt (ARE).

United Australia Party

Australian political party formed in 1931 from the Nationalist Party and dissident Australian Labor Party members under the former Labor minister, Joseph **Lyons**. Although the party governed through the 1930s (in coalition with the Country Party after 1934), it was never stable, and merged into the **Liberal Party of Australia** (1944–5).

United Automobile Workers (UAW)

US labour union. Originally formed by the AFL under the aegis of the NRA, an attempt to impose a president on the UAW led to a revolt in the spring of 1936, when the members elected their own leader, Homer Martin, and enrolled in the CIO. The UAW had to operate in an industry dominated by three aggressively anti-union companies, General Motors, Chrysler and Ford. However, by Dec 1936 the union had become strong enough to demand official recognition from General Motors. This was refused, despite the Wagner Act, so an official strike began in Jan 1937, the workers sitting in rather than walking out. The employers brought in the police, who used tear gas, but ineffectually. Michigan Governor Frank Murphy refused to use the state militia to remove the strikers and demanded negotiations between the employers and John L **Lewis**, President of the CIO. Backed also by President Franklin D **Roosevelt**, these discussions led to the UAW being recognized by General Motors, who also promised not to discriminate against union workers. Later that year, the same tactic was used to gain recognition from Chrysler. ▷ **AFL–CIO**

United Fronts

Two political movements in China, which promoted cooperation between the **Chinese Communist Party** (CCP) and **Guomindang**. In the first, begun in 1924, to promote the defeat of regional militarists and reunify the country, **Sun Yat-sen** agreed to members of the Communist Party joining the Guomindang as individuals, while still retaining CCP membership, in exchange for Soviet military and organizational aid. The alliance relied heavily on Sun's personal prestige, however, and after his death (1925) friction developed between the right wing of the Guomindang and the communists, culminating in Mar 1926 when **Chiang Kai-shek**, commander of the Guomindang army, expelled communists from senior positions within the organization. After the success of Chiang's Northern Expedition, he initiated (Apr 1927) a purge of all communists in areas under his control; the alliance was subsequently officially dissolved (July 1927). In Dec 1936, the **Xi'an Incident** ended with an anti-Japanese alliance between the two parties and, after the outbreak of the **Sino-Japanese War** in 1937, the Communist Party initiated the second United Front. Clashes between Guomindang and Communist forces made it an uneasy alliance from the start, and by 1941 it had virtually disintegrated, although efforts were made to revive it in 1943.

United Gold Coast Convention (UGCC)

The political party founded in 1947, which was led originally by Dr J B Danquah. It was the first organization to seek self-government within a short time frame. For a while its General-Secretary was Nkwame **Nkrumah**, but he broke away to form the more radical CPP (**Convention People's Party**) and defeated the UGCC in the 1951 elections, after which the latter was dissolved.

United Mine Workers of America (UMW)

US labour union. Formed in 1890 by an amalgamation of mining unions within the AFL and the Knights of Labor. After unexpectedly successful strikes in 1897 and 1900, and the election in 1898 of a vigorous young president, John Mitchell, the union consolidated its position in 1902 with a strike in the anthracite fields. When it demanded recognition, an increase in wages and shorter hours, the coalfield operators responded aggressively and lost public sympathy when violence broke out. President Theodore **Roosevelt** saw the conflict as of national economic importance, and the intransigence of the operators led him to force arbitration. This established an important precedent for government intervention in the future. Under the leadership of John L **Lewis** (1920–60) the union became part of the CIO, which merged with the AFL in 1957. Its membership, which was as high as 500 000 in the 1930s, declined steeply in the latter half of the 20c, along with the decline of the labour movement itself. ▷ **AFL–CIO**

United Nations Organisation ▷ **UN**

UNP (United National Party)

Sri Lankan political party. A right-of-centre alliance, it was originally formed out of the disbanded Ceylon National Congress at independence in 1948. The UNP held power from then until 1956, when it was defeated by a coalition headed by S W R D **Bandaranaike**'s **SLFP**. It only enjoyed one sustained period of government in the next 20 years, under the leadership of Dudley Senanayake from 1965 to 1970, but after J R **Jayawardene**'s landslide victory of 1977 it won all subsequent elections, not least because of weakness and division among the opposition parties.

untouchables ▷ **caste**

Uruguay

A republic in eastern South America. Uruguay gained independence from Spanish Brazil in 1828. Political unrest was caused by Tupamaro guerrillas in the late 1960s and early 1970s, leading to military rule until 1985.

US Constitution

The US Constitution embodies the concepts on which the US system of government is based. The law of the land since 1789, it establishes a federal republic, balancing the power of the states and that of the federal government. In the federal government, power is divided among three independent branches: legislative, executive and judicial. The constitutional document comprises a short preamble followed by seven articles which include: the organization, powers and procedures of the legislative branch (Congress); the powers of the President and executive; the powers of the judiciary, including the Supreme Court; the rights of the states; and procedures for amending the Constitution. The articles are followed by 26 amendments, the first 10 of which are known as the **Bill of Rights** (although later amendments also deal with **civil rights** issues). The others cover such matters as the election, death or removal of the President, and eligibility to stand for election to Congress.

Ustaša

The name (meaning 'uprising') of the Croatian fascist movement which was organized in the 1930s by Ante **Pavelić** and supported by **Mussolini**'s Italy, and Hungary. Its right-wing nationalist ideology was an extension of the politics of Ante Starčević's Croatian Party of (State) Right. A terrorist organization, it carried out the assassination of the Yugoslav King, **Alexander I**. During **World War II** it upheld the regime of Pavelić in **Croatia** and brutally massacred many thousands of Serbs, Jews, gypsies, communists and non-Ustaša Croats.

Ustinov, Dmitri Fedorovich (1908–84)

Russian politician and Soviet marshal. Born into a working-class family, he acquired a technical eduation in his twenties, and by 1938 he was manager of an arms factory in Leningrad. In 1941 he was appointed as People's Commissar for Armaments; from then until 1976, when he became Minister of Defence, his primary function was to develop the arms industry. He gave it a civilian element and secured it an unfair share of the Soviet budget. He also helped find it an outlet by supporting the invasion of Afghanistan in 1979. His death removed from the ministry and the **Politburo** a fierce opponent of Mikhail **Gorbachev**'s campaign to reduce expenditure on the military.

V

Vaal Kraantz Reverse (5–8 Feb 1900)

An incident in the Boer War in which the British general Sir Redvers Buller attacked Boers on a ridge of kopjes a few miles east of Spion Kop in an attempt to relieve Ladysmith. He was forced to withdraw and the British commander-in-chief, Roberts, was given authority to dismiss Sir 'Reverses' Buller.

Vafiadis, Markos (1906–92)

Greek politician. Like many other Greeks driven from Anatolia in 1923, he found work in the Greek tobacco industry. He joined the **KKE** (Communist Party of Greece) in 1928 and was frequently imprisoned during the 1930s for his communist activities. In 1941 he escaped from the island where he was being held and went to Macedonia where he became Captain of the **ELAS** 10th Division operating there. During the **Greek Civil War** (1944–9), he led the Democratic Army of Greece which was founded by the KKE (Oct 1946). He organized communist bases in the villages and was one of those responsible for the abduction and forced enrolment in the army of many Greek youths and girls. Often at variance with the KKE leadership, he fled to Albania in 1949 after the KKE made a clumsy attempt on his life. He was expelled from the KKE the following year and was condemned for never having been 'a real communist'. ▷ **Lausanne, Treaty of; Zachariadis, Nikos**

Vandervelde, Emile (1866–1938)

Belgian politician. Having studied law, he joined parliament as a socialist in 1894 and became the leader of the **Belgian Socialist Party**. He repeatedly held cabinet posts from 1916 to 1937, and was also a noted theorist in revisionist Marxism. He published widely and was chairman of the Second International from 1900.

Vanunu, Mordechai (1948–)

Israeli nuclear technician. A relatively junior member of the technical staff developing Israel's nuclear arsenal, Vanunu's disillusionment with the duplicity of his country's government, which had always claimed that it would not be the first Middle East country to acquire atomic weapons, led him to resign his post in 1986, and later that year the *Sunday Times* published an interview with Vanunu in which he revealed that Israel had already stockpiled up to 200 atomic bombs at an underground factory in the Negev Desert. In Sep of that year, he was abducted at Rome airport by agents of Mossad, the Israeli secret service, and returned to Jerusalem. After a secret trial, Vanunu was found guilty of treason and sentenced to life imprisonment in solitary confinement. ▷ **Israel, State of**

Vargas, Getúlio (Dornelles) (1883–1954)
Brazilian politician. After serving in the army and training as a lawyer, he was elected a Federal deputy in 1923. He was Minister of Finance under Washington Luís Pereira de Souza and headed the Liberal Alliance ticket for the presidency in 1930. Defeated in the polls, he won the support of significant military force to govern with the army from 1930–45. A man who stood aloof from party politics, he sought a conciliação based upon support from the army, major industrial groups in Sao Paulo and Minas Gerais to achieve a more centralized state. Ousted in 1945 by the army, he returned as constitutional President in 1951. Four years later, in the face of mounting opposition from the right wing, he committed suicide. He created two political parties, the **PSD** and PTB, but his political heirs were Leonel **Brizola** and João **Goulart**.

Varotnikov, Vitali Ivanovich (1926–)
Soviet politician. He began work as a fitter in 1942, joined the Communist Party in 1947, and started to climb the bureaucratic and political ladder in his native Voronezh and Kubyshev. In 1975 he was brought to Moscow to become Deputy Chairman of the Russian Ministerial Council, but quickly clashed with Leonid **Brezhnev** and was sent to Cuba as ambassador in 1979. Yuri **Andropov** brought him back as Chairman in 1938, and Mikhail **Gorbachev** then made him Chairman of the Presidium of the Supreme Soviet in 1988. Not quite able, however, to accept full-blooded reform, he was dropped in 1990.

Vasilevski, Alexander Mikhailovich (1895–1977)
Soviet marshal. An ensign in the Tsarist army in 1915, he joined the **Red Army** in 1919 and served in the war with Poland. He subsequently demonstrated great skill in staff work. By 1940 he was Deputy Chief of the General Staff, and in 1942 he was confirmed as Chief. Along with **Zhukov** he planned the **Stalingrad** counter-offensive; he went on to liberate White Russia and take Konigsberg. In 1945 he directed the rapid defeat of the Japanese in the Far East. After **World War II** he supervised the reorganization of the Soviet forces, eventually serving as Deputy Defence Minister in 1953–6. In 1959 he retired from active service, disenchanted with Nikita **Khrushchev**'s military doctrine.

Vatican Council

The second Vatican Council (1962–5), called by John XXIII, was aimed at renewing religious life and bringing the belief, structure and the discipline of the Church up to date.

Velchev, Damian (1883–1954)

Bulgarian politician. A member of the Military League, in 1934 he led the military coup supported by **Zveno**. In the 1944 government of the **Fatherland Front**, he became Minister of War but lost his position in 1946 during the communist purge and was sent to Switzerland as the Bulgarian representative. ▷ **Dimitrov, Georgi; Kostov, Traicho; Petkov, Nikola**

Veloukhiotis, Aris (1905–45)

Greek resistance leader. He led **ELAS** resistance bands in Greece during **World War II**, took part in the settlement of Greek refugees from Asia Minor (1922) and joined the Greek Communist Party (1924). Under the dictatorship of Ioannis **Metaxas** he was interned (1936–9), but was released after retracting his communist beliefs. After the German occupation of Greece (Apr 1941), he received orders in Mar 1942 from **EAM**, the communist-led National Liberation Front, to form guerrilla bands. Committed to the establishment of a communist regime, he organized communist-led self-administration in the liberated regions, oversaw the brutal coercion of the local population and waged war against the other resistance organizations. He attacked **EKKA** (May 1943) and launched a campaign against **EDES**, led by his cousin, Napoleon **Zervas** (Oct 1943). He condemned the EAM leaders for their compliance with the Allies and the Greek government-in-exile at the Lebanon Conference (May 1944) and at Varkiza (Feb 1945). For the sake of party unity, he formally agreed to the demobilization of ELAS, but withdrew with sections of his followers to the mountains. At its Apr 1945 plenum, the Greek Communist Party, now led by Nikos **Zachariadis**, condemned Veloukhiotis who eventually committed suicide.

Velvet Revolution (1989)

The sudden, almost bloodless, process by which the communist regime in Czechoslovakia collapsed. Ever since the **Prague Spring** was blighted in 1968 by the Soviet invasion, **communism** had been tolerated but lacked popularity. Its mainstay remained the USSR with local military and police assistance. As Mikhail **Gorbachev** tolerated change elsewhere in Eastern Europe, the public in Czechoslovakia saw their opportunity. On 17 Nov a crowd of 50 000 in Wenceslas Square was attacked by the police, but for the last time. The crowds grew, Miloš **Jakeš** resigned on 24 Nov, and Václav **Havel** became the new President on 30 Dec.

Venezuela

The most northerly country in South America. After frequent revolts against Spanish colonial rule in the region the independence movement under Bolívar led to the establishment of the State of Gran Colombia (Colombia, Ecuador, Venezuela) in 1821. Venezuela became an independent republic in 1830. There were two unsuccessful attempted coups in 1992.

Venizélos, Eleuthérios (Kyriakos) (1864–1936)

Greek politician. As Prime Minister (1910–15) after the 1909 military coup, he restored law and order, promoted the Balkan League against Turkey and Bulgaria (1912–13), extended Greek territory and enacted land reform. His sympathies with France and Britain in **World War I** clashed with those of King **Constantine I** and led him to establish a rival government (1917–20), forcing the King's abdication. During the 1920s and early 1930s, he was leader of the anti-royalist political faction. In 1935 he came out of retirement to support a military revolt staged by his sympathizers, but after its failure he fled to Paris, where he died.

Venizélos, Sofoklis (1894–1964)

Greek politician. The son of Eleuthérios **Venizélos**, in 1944 he was briefly Prime Minister of the Greek government-in-exile, resigning in favour of George **Papandreou**. In the elections of Mar 1946 he led the National Political Union with Papandreou and Panayiotis Kanellopoulos. After the **Greek Civil War** (1944–9), in the elections of Mar 1950, as leader of the Liberal Party he joined the coalition government with the National Progressive Centre Union and Papandreou's Democratic Socialist Party, becoming Prime Minister later that year.

Verdinaso

Belgian fascist political party, founded in 1931 by Joris Van Severen (1894–1940). The name is a shortened form of the League of Low Countries National Solidarists (*Verbond van Dietsch-Nationaal Solidaristen*). The party was influenced by French and Italian right-wing politics, and opposed parliamentary processes and all forms of liberalism and socialism; it never achieved a large membership. Originally heavily supportive of the **Flemish Movement**, Van Severen later championed a neo-Burgundian nationalist ideal; at the outbreak of **World War II** he was executed by French forces (20 May 1940), and Verdinaso rapidly disappeared.

Verdun, Battle of (1916)

A battle in **World War I**. The German army chose to attack a salient in the French line at this point because it was thought that its symbolic value would force the French to defend it to the bitter end. This did happen but, in spite of huge losses on both sides, Verdun did not fall. General **Pétain**, the French commander for most of the battle, earned his reputation at Verdun.

Vereeniging, Peace of (1902)
The peace treaty which ended the Boer War, signed at Pretoria. The Boers won three important concessions: an amnesty for those who had risen in revolt within the Cape Colony; a promise that the British would deny the franchise to Africans until after the Boer republics were returned to representative government; and additional financial support for reconstruction. The Peace ensured that there would be no significant change in the political relationship of Whites and Blacks in South Africa. ▷ **Boer Wars**

Versailles, Treaty of (1919)
A peace treaty drawn up between Germany and the Allied powers at Paris. Of the 434 articles, the most controversial was article 231 assigning to Germany and her allies responsibility for causing **World War I**, and establishing liability for reparation payments. Germany lost all overseas colonies, and considerable territory to Poland in the East. The **Rhineland** was demilitarized and to be occupied by Allied troops for up to 15 years, and German armed forces were strictly limited. ▷ **Paris Peace Conference**

Vichy
The informal name of the French political regime between 1940 and 1945; officially the **French State** (*Etat français*). Established at the spa town of Vichy following Germany's defeat of France (1940), its head of state was Marshal Philippe **Pétain** and its other dominant political figure Pierre **Laval**, Prime Minister from 1942. Although a client regime of Germany, Vichy at first succeeded in maintaining a degree of autonomy. ▷ **collaboration; Riom Trial; World War II**

Victor Emmanuel III (1869–1947)
King of Italy (1900/46). He came to the throne after the assassination of his father, Umberto I. After Italy's entrance into **World War I**, he took an active part in the campaign, appointing his uncle, the Duke of Aosta, as Regent. With the arrival of peace, he took little active part in politics. In 1922, however, faced with **Mussolini**'s bid to seize power he refused to declare a state of emergency, which would have enabled the army to crush the fascist movement. Instead, when **Salandra** declined to form a government, he asked Mussolini to do so, opening the way for the creation of the fascist regime. Among suggested motives for Victor Emmanuel's ready capitulation to the fascists are his fear that the alternative to Mussolini might have been a socialist revolution, anxieties about the loyalty of the army and rumours that the Duke of Aosta

was planning to depose him. Mussolini's regime effectively deprived the monarchy of its powers, but it did make Victor Emmanuel Emperor of Ethiopia (1936) and King of Albania (1939). Eventually, however, the King was to play a part in toppling the **Duce**: on 24 July 1943, the **Fascist Grand Council**, disillusioned by the progress of the war and dissatisfied with Mussolini's gutless readiness to accept orders from **Hitler**, begged Victor Emmanuel to assume power. On 25 July, Mussolini was summoned by the King and dismissed; shortly afterwards, with Mussolini under arrest, Victor Emmanuel invited General **Badoglio** to form a government. However, he was irredeemably tarnished by his association with **fascism** and did little in the final stages of the war to improve his or his dynasty's popularity. In May 1946, in a last effort to save the monarchy, he abdicated in favour of his son, **Umberto II**. He died in exile in Egypt.

Vieira, Joao Bernardo (1939–)

Guinea-Bissau politician. He joined the Party for the Independence of Portuguese Guinea and Cape Verde (PAIGC) in 1960, and in 1964 became a member of the political bureau during the war for independence from Portugal. After independence in 1974, he served in the government of Luiz **Cabral**, but in 1980 led the coup which deposed him. In 1984 constitutional changes combined the roles of head of state and head of government, making Vieira Executive President.

Vienna Award (1st) (2 Nov 1938)

The alteration of the Czechoslovak-Hungarian frontier following the **Munich Agreement**. **Hitler**'s success against Czechoslovakia encouraged other predators, and Hungary laid claim to **Ruthenia** and part of Slovakia. **Ribbentrop** and **Ciano** acted as arbitrators, although Hitler was still not sure what he wanted to happen to Ruthenia. But the Vienna Award gave Hungary a fertile slice of Slovakia with almost a million inhabitants, just over half of whom were, admittedly, Hungarian. Most of the area was restored to Czechoslovakia in 1945.

Vienna Award (2nd) (29 Aug 1940)

The alteration of the Hungarian-Romanian frontier following the **German–Soviet Pact**. When **Stalin** moved his forces into **Bessarabia** (July 1940) in accordance with the terms of his pact with **Hitler**, Hungary saw its opportunity to reclaim Transylvania, which had been lost to Romania at the end of **World War I**. Hitler was anxious to weaken Romania to his own advantage but not to encourage Hungary (or **Mussolini**) excessively. Eventually **Ribbentrop** and **Ciano** again acted as arbitrators. This 2nd Vienna Award gave Hungary two-thirds of Transylvania. Most of this area, too, was restored to Romania in 1945.

Viet Cong or **Vietcong** ('Vietnamese communists')

The name commonly given in the 1960s to the communist forces that fought the South Vietnamese government during the **Vietnam War**.

Viet Minh or **Vietminh**

The abbreviation of **Vietnam Doc Lap Dong Minh** ('League for the Independence of Vietnam'), a politico-military organization formed by **Ho Chi Minh** in 1941. It included nationalists and communists, and aimed at liberating Vietnam from the Japanese and then gaining independence from France. In 1945, on the Japanese surrender, it formed a government following the dropping of the bombs on Hiroshima and Nagasaki, in Hanoi. Its army defeated the French at Dien Bien Phu in 1954. ▷ **Vietnam War**

Vietnam

An independent socialist state in Indo-China. In 1887 the region formed the French Indo-Chinese Union with Cambodia and Laos. It was occupied by the Japanese in **World War II** and following the war the communist Viet Minh League, led by **Ho Chi Minh**, was formed, but was not recognized by France. The Indo-Chinese War, 1946–54, resulted in French withdrawal from Indo-China. In 1954 an armistice divided the country between the communist 'Democratic Republic' in the north and the 'State' of Vietnam in the south. Attacks on US bases led to US intervention on the side of South Vietnam in 1965. The US withdrew in 1973 and Saigon fell in 1975; with the defeat of South Vietnam nearly 200 000 Vietnamese fled the country. In 1976 the country was reunified as the Socialist Republic of Vietnam in 1976. Large numbers of refugees tried to find homes in the West in the late 1970s, and the Chinese invasion of Vietnam in 1979 greatly increased the number attempting to leave the country by sea. These 'Boat People' have presented non-communist countries with a continuing immigration problem. Market reforms are being implemented under Communist Party rule.

Vietnam War (1964–75)

A war between communist North Vietnam and non-communist South Vietnam which broadened to include the USA. It was preceded by the Indo-China War (1946–54) between France and the Viet Minh, which ended with the defeat of the French at Dien Bien Phu. The Geneva Conference left North Vietnam under the rule of Ho Chi Minh, while the South was ruled first by the Emperor Bao Dai and then by Ngo Dinh Diem. Elections were planned to choose a single government for all of Vietnam, but when they failed to take place, fighting was renewed. From 1961, in an attempt to stop the spread of **communism**, the USA increased its aid to South Vietnam and the number of its 'military advisors'. In 1964 following a North Vietnamese attack on US ships, President Lyndon

Johnson ordered retaliatory bombing of North Vietnam. Although the US Congress never declared war officially, it passed the **Gulf of Tonkin Resolution** which authorized US forces in South-East Asia to repel any armed attack and to prevent further aggression. US bombing of North Vietnam was continued, and in 1965 the USA stepped up its troop commitment substantially. By 1968 over 500 000 US soldiers were involved in the war. As the conflict dragged on, victory against the elusive communist guerrilla forces seemed unattainable. Opposition to the war within the USA badly divided the country, and pressure mounted to bring the conflict to an end. In 1968 peace negotiations were begun in Paris, and in 1973 a ceasefire agreement was signed. Hostilities did not end until two years later when North Vietnam's victory was completed with the capture of Saigon (renamed Ho Chi Minh City).

Villa, Pancho (Francisco) (1877–1923)
Mexican revolutionary. The son of a field labourer, he followed a variety of modest occupations until he joined **Madero**'s uprising against **Diáz** (1911) and the Mexican Revolution made him famous as a military commander. In a fierce struggle for control of the revolution, he and **Zapata** were defeated (1915) by Venustiano **Carranza**, with whom Villa had earlier allied himself against the dictatorship of General Victoriano Huerta. Both Villa and Zapata withdrew to strongholds in north and central Mexico, from where they continued to direct guerrilla warfare. In 1916 Villa was responsible for the shooting of a number of US citizens in the town of Santa Isabel, as well as an attack on the city of Columbus, New Mexico, which precipitated the sending of a US punitive force by President Woodrow **Wilson**. The troops failed to capture Villa and he continued to oppose Carranza's regime until the latter's death (1920), when he laid down his arms and was pardoned. He was murdered at his hacienda in Chihuahua.

Vimy Ridge
An escarpment five miles north-east of Arras (Pas-de-Calais), and a strongly held part of the German defence line on the Western Front in **World War I**. It was successfully stormed during the Battle of Arras by the Canadian Corps of the British 1st Army (1917). This feat of arms had great symbolic significance in establishing Canada's identity as an independent nation.

Violencia, La
The name given in Colombia to the undeclared civil war between Conservatives and Liberals, at its most intense between 1948 and 1955. The period was marked by numerous atrocities, especially in the countryside. Deaths attributable to the conflict probably exceeded 200 000.

Vittorio Veneto, Battle of (Oct 1918)
The major victory for the Italians and their allies under General **Diaz** over Austrian forces at the end of **World War I**.

Vlasov, Andrei Andreevich (1900–46)
Soviet general. During **World War II** he distinguished himself defending his country until he was captured during 1942 when he emerged as the leader of a Russian group intending to overthrow **Stalin**. It was only subsequently in 1944 that he was allowed to raise two divisions to serve on the Russian front. In 1945 he surrendered to the Americans who handed him over to the Soviet authorities, who tried and hanged him in 1946. He was seen as a traitor to his country, but later revelations concerning Stalin and the more recent collapse of **communism** have caused some observers to question that judgement.

VMRO (*Vnutrašnja Makedonska Revolucionarska Organizacija*, 'Internal Macedonian Revolutionary Organization')
Founded in Salonica in 1893, the organization's goal was 'Macedonia for the Macedonians'. The failure of the **Ilinden Uprising** of 1903, however, divided its membership: the federalists wanted autonomy within a Balkan federation; the centralists wanted annexation to Bulgaria. After the **Balkan Wars** and **World War I**, when Macedonia was divided, VMRO, with Italian and Hungarian backing, waged a terrorist campaign from Bulgaria against the Yugoslav government. It kidnapped, tortured and murdered **Stamboliski** after he signed the Treaty of Niš (1923) and was involved in the assassination of King **Alexander I** of Yugoslavia (1934). ▷ **Macedonians; Tsankov, Alexander**

Vogel, Hans-Jochen (1926–)
West German politician, successor to Helmut **Schmidt** as leader of the Social Democratic Party (**SPD**). A former Minister of Housing and Town Planning (1972–4) and Minister of Justice (1974–81), he also served briefly as governing Mayor of West Berlin (1981). ▷ **Germany, West**

Vojvodina
Literally 'duchy', the name refers to the region bounded by Hungary, Croatian Slavonia and the River Danube, with its chief town at Novi Sad. Settled by the Slavs (6–7c) and by the Magyars (9–10c), it fell to the Turks in 1526. By the Treaties of Karlowitz (1699) and Passarowitz (1718), it came under the rule of Vienna. Under the Habsburgs, its fertile plains were settled by Germans, Slovaks, Hungarians, Ruthenians and Romanians. In Nov 1918, at the end of **World War I**, the National Assembly of the Vojvodina voted to join the Kingdom of Serbs, **Croats** and Slovenes (later Yugoslavia). Occupied by the Germans (Apr 1941), it was divided between the Nazi-collaborating governments of Hungary

and the Independent State of **Croatia**. In 1945 it became an autonomous unit within the republic of **Serbia** in the Socialist Federal Republic of Yugoslavia, but lost this autonomous status to Serbia in 1990.

Volstead, Andrew John (1860–1947)
US politician. A lawyer, he entered Congress for the Republicans in 1903 and is best remembered as the author of the 1919 Volstead Act, which prohibited the manufacture, transportation and sale of alcoholic beverages. The purpose of the legislation, which remained in force until 1933, was to placate the influential temperance movement, and to divert grain to food production in the wake of **World War I**. In fact, prohibition proved impossible to enforce effectively, and did little other than to create enormous profits for bootleggers and speakeasies, and to provide Hollywood with the inspiration for countless gangster movies.

Voroshilov, Kliment Yefremovich (1881–1969)
Soviet Marshal and politician. He joined the Russian Social Democratic Labour Party in 1903, but political agitation soon brought about his exile to Siberia, where he remained a fugitive until 1914. He played a military rather than a political role in the 1917 **Russian Revolution**, and as Commissar for Defence (1925–40) was responsible for the modernization of the **Red Army**. He was removed from office after the failure to prevent the German siege of Leningrad, but stayed active in the party, and after **Stalin**'s death became head of state (1953–60). ▷ **World War II**

Vorrink, Jacobus Jan (1891–1955)
Dutch politician. Beginning as a schoolteacher, he joined the Socialist Party (SDAP) in 1918, and was highly active in the socialist youth movements, eventually becoming Party Chairman in 1934. He sat in the First Chamber of parliament from 1935 to 1946, and was a member of the Second Chamber (1946–54). Despite having spent the period 1943–5 in a **concentration camp**, after **World War II** a press campaign accused him of having harboured fascist sympathies; perhaps this was the reason that he never held a cabinet post. ▷ **Party of Labour**

Vorster, John (Balthazar Johannes Vorster) (1915–83)
South African politician. Educated at Stellenbosch University, he became a lawyer and was a leader of the extreme Afrikaner group, Ossewa Brandwag, in **World War II**, as a result of which he was interned for the duration of the war. He was elected to parliament for the **National Party** in 1953 and was Minister of Justice (1961–5) before becoming Prime Minister (1966–78) and, for a brief moment, President. He was largely responsible for the imposition of the repressive **apartheid** laws and did not hesitate to employ state power to protect white interests. However,

he was implicated in the 'Muldergate' scandal in which government funds had been misappropriated and was forced to resign.

Voting Rights Act (1965)
US suffrage legislation. The law prohibited all means by which the segregationist Southern states had been able to prevent blacks from registering to vote. The Attorney-General was empowered to dispatch federal registrars anywhere that local officials were obstructing registration of blacks; the act was so effective that 250 000 new black voters had been able to register before the end of the year.

Voznesenksy, Nikolai Alexeevich (1903–50)
Soviet economist. Educated after the **Russian Revolution** (1917) in the Institute of Red Professors, he lectured there until in 1935 **Zhdanov** recruited him as a planning assistant. He then became Chairman of the State Planning Bureau (1938–49), with one short interval in 1941–2 when Giorgiy **Malenkov** was in the ascendant. He managed both the war-time economy and the post-war recovery, but **Stalin** had him arrested in 1949 and executed in 1950, seemingly because of the Zhdanov connection.

Vranitzky, Franz (1937–)
Austrian politician. Educated at what is now the University of Commerce, Vienna, he embarked on a career in banking and in 1970 became adviser on economic and financial policy to the Minister of Finance. After holding senior appointments in the banking world he became Minister of Finance himself in 1984 and two years later succeeded Fred Sinowatz as Federal Chancellor.

Vyshinsky, Andrei Yanuaryevich (1883–1954)
Russian jurist and politician. He studied law at Moscow, joined the Communist Party in 1920, and became Professor of Criminal Law and then Attorney-General (1923–5). He was the public prosecutor at the state trials (1936–8) which removed **Stalin**'s rivals, and later became the Soviet delegate to the **UN** (1945–9 and 1953–4), and Foreign Minister (1949–53).

W

Wacha Dinshaw Edulji (1844–1936)
Indian politician. A member of the Bombay Legislative Council and the Imperial Legislative Council, he worked in close association with Dadabhai Naoroji and Ferozshah Mehta for the peaceful development of his country through social reform, education and participation in politics. A founder-member of the Congress, he was its President in 1901. He criticized the British government's economic and financial policies and freely expressed his nation's viewpoint before the Welby Commission in London.

Wafd Party
The name of the Egyptian nationalist party which sent a delegation under the nationalist leader Sa'd **Zaghlul** to the British High Commissioner in 1919; the word means 'delegation'. The 'New Wafd' became Egypt's official opposition party in 1984, but was replaced as such in 1987 by an alliance headed by the **Muslim Brotherhood**.

Wahhabis
An Islamic movement which derives from Muhammad ibn Abd al-Wahhab, a religious reformer from Uyayna near Riyadh, and Muhammad ibn Saud, the ancestor of the present rulers of Saudi Arabia. The alliance was to lead to the unification in the 18c of most of the peninsula under the Saudi banner. The modern reunification of the kingdom was carried out (1902–32) by King Abd al-Aziz, otherwise known as 'Ibn Saud'. Arabs call the followers of Abd al-Wahhab *muwahhidun* or 'unitarians' rather than *Wahhabis*, which is an anglicism. The movement maintains that legal decisions must be based exclusively on the Quran and the *Sunna*. The original Wahhabis banned music, dancing, poetry, silk, gold, and jewellery, and in the 20c, the *ikhwan* ('brotherhood') have attacked the telephone, radio and television as innovations not sanctioned by God.

Waldheim, Kurt (1918–)
Austrian politician. He entered the Austrian foreign service (1945) and became Minister and subsequently Ambassador to Canada (1955–60), Director of Political Affairs at the Ministry (1960–4), Austrian representative at the **UN** (1964–8 and 1970–1), Foreign Minister (1968–70), and then UN Secretary-General (1972–81). His presidential candidature

was controversial, because of well-substantiated claims that he had lied about his wartime activities, and been involved in anti-Jewish and other atrocities in the Balkans. He denied the allegations and, despite international pressure, continued with his campaign, winning the presidency in 1986. ▷ **Austria, Republic of**

Wales

A principality and western constituent part of the United Kingdom. Wales was politically united with England in the Act of Union in 1535 but there is still a sizeable movement for independence; the political nationalist movement (Plaid Cymru) returned its first MP in 1966. In the 1979 referendum, however, only 11.9% voted for devolution.

Wałesa, Lech (1943–)

Polish trade unionist. A former Gdansk shipyard worker, he became the leader of the independent trade union, **Solidarity**, which in 1980 openly challenged the Polish government's economic and social policies. He held negotiations with the leading figures in the Communist Party and had tacit but strong support from the Roman Catholic Church, but was detained by the authorities when martial law was declared in 1981. He was released in 1982, and was awarded the Nobel Peace Prize in 1983. Despite restrictions imposed on him, he continued to be a prominent figure in Polish politics, and was mainly responsible for the success of the negotiations which led to Solidarity effectively forming the first Polish non-Communist government in Sep 1989. This not only transformed the course of events in Poland but was an important contributory factor in the whole East European revolution in the winter of 1989–90. Wałesa became President in Dec 1990.

Wallenberg, Raoul (1912–?47)

Swedish diplomat. He was a member of a prominent Swedish business family. In 1944 he was sent to Hungary under the auspices of the American War Refugee Board to attempt to rescue the 700 000 Jews put at risk by the German occupation of the country. With the help of special passports and warnings to the occupying power of post-war retribution, he managed to save over 100 000 Hungarian Jews. He was arrested by the Russians when they marched into Budapest in 1945, and disappeared. In spite of Russian claims that he died in 1947 as their prisoner, rumours continued to circulate that he was alive even in the 1970s.

Walloon Movement

Belgian political movement, formed largely in reaction to the progress made by the **Flemish Movement**. Ever since Flemish rights were claimed in the early 19c, Walloon (southern Belgian, French-speaking) counter-claims have been lodged; since the early 20c there have been Walloon congresses each year in Liège. The movement has often been rather negative, perhaps because of the decline of Wallonia in economic and demographic terms in relation to Flanders in the 20c. After **World War II** a National Walloon Congress spoke out for such things as federalism, Walloon independence, or even annexation of Wallonia by France. In 1961 the Popular Walloon Movement was founded, agitating for the federal solution. In 1968 all the various Walloon organizations came together in the **Rassemblement Wallon**; its power to win seats had declined by the late 1970s. The movement's contribution to Belgian politics has been to accelerate the country's federalization.

Wandervogel

German and Austrian youth movement. Founded in Germany in 1901 and **Austria** in 1909, this movement asserted youthful values in society and an affinity with nature. Organized hikes, rural trysts and a search for adventure attracted a significant membership to the various *Wandervogel* associations. These continued to function during the **Weimar Republic**, but were closed by the **Nazi Party** in 1933, with members being transferred to the Hitler Youth.

Wang Jingwei (Wang Ching-wei) (1883–1944)

Chinese politician. An associate of the revolutionary and Nationalist leader **Sun Yat-sen**, he studied in Japan, where he joined Sun's revolutionary party, and from 1917 became his personal assistant. In 1927 he was appointed head of the new **Guomindang** government at Wuhan, and in 1932 became the party's President, with his main rival for control of the Guomindang, **Chiang Kai-shek**, in charge of the military. In 1938, after the outbreak of war with Japan, Wang offered to cooperate with the Japanese, and in 1940 he became head of a puppet regime ruling the occupied areas.

War Measures Act (1914)

Canadian statute. Enacted in the first weeks of **World War I**, it gave the federal government extraordinary powers. It could bypass the normal legislative process, suspend habeas corpus and deport without trial. It also included emergency economic regulations. Under the Act, immigrants from Germany and Austria-Hungary were forced to carry special identity cards and to register at regular intervals, while 8 300 aliens were interned in special camps. During **World War II** 6 414 orders were made under the War Measures Act; and it was still in force in 1945 when a defector from the USSR, Igor Gouzenko, informed on a Soviet spy ring in Canada. The findings of a Royal Commission led to the arrest, under the Act, of the single communist MP, a prominent scientist and members of the civil and military service. In 1970 the Act was again invoked to deal with the **October Crisis** in Quebec.

War Powers Act (1973)
US legislation requiring that Congress be consulted before the President dispatch US forces into battle, and that Congress approve any continuance of war beyond 60 days. Public confidence in the executive branch had been greatly diminished after the **Vietnam War** and **Watergate** and, like the **Freedom of Information Act**, this act aimed to limit its power.

warlords
Chinese provincial military rulers who engaged in a bitter power struggle and civil war after the death of President **Yuan Shikai** in 1916. They were eventually subdued by the 1926–8 **Northern Expedition** of **Chiang Kai-shek**.

Warren, Earl (1891–1974)
US jurist. He attended the University of California law school and was admitted to the bar. An active Republican, he became Governor of California (1943–53) and made an unsuccessful run for the vice-presidency in 1948. He became Chief Justice of the US Supreme Court in 1953. The Warren Court (1953–69) was active and influential, notably in the areas of civil rights and individual liberties. It was responsible for the landmark decision in **Brown v Board of Education of Topeka, Kansas** (1954), which outlawed school segregation, and for Miranda v Arizona (1966), which ruled that criminal suspects be informed of their rights before being questioned by the police. Warren was chairman of the federal commission (the Warren Commission) that investigated the assassination of President John F **Kennedy**.

Warsaw Pact
The shorthand name for the East European Mutual Assistance Treaty signed in Warsaw in 1955 by Albania, Bulgaria, Czechoslovakia, East Germany, Hungary, Poland, Romania and the USSR. Albania withdrew in 1968. The pact established a unified military command for the armed forces of all the signatories who were committed to giving immediate assistance to one another in the event of an attack in Europe. It was a Soviet bloc response, in part, to the formation of **NATO** by the West. But it also had a political purpose, as was demonstrated when it was used in Czechoslovakia to restore communism, allegedly endangered by the **Prague Spring** in 1968. In the wake of the East European revolution in the winter of 1989–90, the pact effectively disintegrated before it was officially terminated in 1991.

Washington, Booker Taliaferro (1856–1915)
US black leader and educationist. He was born a slave in Franklin County, Virginia. After emancipation (1865), he was educated at Hampton Institute, Virginia, and Washington DC, then became a

teacher, writer, and speaker on black problems and the importance of education and vocational training. In 1881 he was appointed principal of the newly-opened Tuskegee Institute, Alabama, and built it into a major centre of black education. The foremost black leader in the late 19c, he encouraged blacks to focus on economic equality rather than fight for social or political equality. He was strongly criticized by W E B **Du Bois**, and his policies were repudiated by the **civil rights** movement. He is the author of *Up From Slavery* (1901).

Watergate (1972–4)
US political scandal. It led to the first resignation of a President in US history (Richard **Nixon**, in office 1968–74). The actual 'Watergate' is a hotel and office complex in Washington, DC, where the **Democratic Party** had its headquarters. During the presidential campaign of 1972, a team of burglars was caught inside Democratic headquarters, and their connections were traced to the White House and to the Committee to Re-elect the President. Investigations by the *Washington Post*, a grand jury and two special prosecutors revealed that high officials who were very close to Nixon were implicated, and that Nixon himself was aware of illegal measures to cover up that implication. A number of officials were eventually imprisoned. Nixon himself left office when it became clear that he was likely to be impeached and removed. ▷ **Iran–Contra Affair**

Wavell, Archibald Percival, 1st Earl (1883–1950)
British field marshal. He served in South Africa and India, became **Allenby**'s Chief-of-Staff in Palestine, and in 1939 he was given the Middle East Command. He defeated the Italians in North Africa, but failed against **Rommel**, and in 1941 was transferred to India, where he became Viceroy (1943). He was made field marshal and viscount (1943), earl (1947), Constable of the Tower (1948), and Lord-Lieutenant of London (1949). ▷ **World War II**

Webb, Sidney (James) (1859–1947) and
(Martha) Beatrice (1858–1943)
British social reformers, historians, and economists, married in 1892. Sidney became a lawyer, and joined the **Fabian Society**, where he wrote many powerful tracts. Beatrice interested herself in the social problems of the time. After their marriage they were committed to advancing the causes of **socialism** and trade unionism, publishing their classic *History of Trade Unionism* (1894), *English Local Government* (1906–29, 9 vols), and other works. They also started the *New Statesman* (1913). Sidney became an MP (1922), President of the Board of Trade (1924), Dominions and Colonial Secretary (1929–30), and Colonial Secretary (1930–1), and was created a baron in 1929.

Wehrmacht

Literally 'defence force', this is the term used to describe the German armed forces during the period 1935–45. Recruited by conscription, the *Wehrmacht* constituted the military strength of the National Socialist state and conducted the victorious **Blitzkrieg** campaigns of the period 1939–41. However, from 1938 the *Waffen-SS* ('Armed' **SS**) was developed as a parallel, Nazi army which, in the closing months of the war, came to overshadow the Wehrmacht. The members of the Wehrmacht were bound to **Hitler** by a personal oath of loyalty and its commanders generally carried out Hitler's orders willingly, although individuals, such as those involved in the July 1944 plot against him, did offer resistance. ▷ **Nazi Party**

Wei Jingsheng (Wei Ching-sheng) (1949–)

Chinese political prisoner. A Red Guard during the **Cultural Revolution**, Wei served in the **People's Liberation Army** during the early 1970s before becoming an electrician at Beijing Zoo. During the **Democracy Wall Movement** (1978–9) he called for greater democracy (what he called the 'fifth modernization') and became the editor of an outspoken unofficial journal. He was arrested in Mar 1979 and brought to trial six months later on charges of divulging state secrets to foreigners and spreading counter-revolutionary propaganda. He was sentenced to 15 years in prison.

Weil, Simone (1909–43)

French philosophical writer and mystic. She taught philosophy in several schools, interspersing this with periods of manual labour to experience the working-class life. In 1936 she served in the republican forces in the **Spanish Civil War**. In 1941 she settled in Marseilles, where she developed a deep mystical feeling for the Catholic faith, yet a profound reluctance to join an organized religion. She escaped to the USA in 1942 and worked for the **Free French** in London, before her death at Ashford, Kent. Her posthumously published works include *La Pesanteur et la Grâce* ('Gravity and Grace') and *Attente de Dieu* ('Waiting for God').

Weimar Republic

The name by which the German Federal Republic of 1918–33 is known. In 1919 a National Constituent Assembly met at Weimar, on the River Elbe, and drew up a constitution for the new republic. The government moved from Weimar to Berlin in 1920. In 1933, two months after becoming Chancellor, **Hitler** passed an Enabling Act suspending the Weimar constitution.

Weisse Rose

The German anti-Nazi resistance group (literally, 'White Rose'), centred on Professor Kurt Huber and the students Hans and Sophie Scholl of Munich University. From autumn 1942 until their arrest on 18 Feb 1943 the group pursued a leafleting campaign in which they called for resistance against a morally-bankrupt National Socialism. Arrested by the **Gestapo**, the Scholls were executed on 22 Feb 1943 and Huber on 13 July 1943.

Weizmann, Chaim (Azriel) (1874–1952)

Israeli politician. Born in Russia, he studied in Germany and Switzerland, then lectured on chemistry at Geneva and Manchester. He helped to secure the **Balfour Declaration** of 1917, and became President of the **World Zionist Organization** (1920–30 and 1935–46), and of the **Jewish Agency** (from 1929). He played a major role in the establishment of the state of Israel (1948), and was its first President (1949–52). ▷ **Zionism**

Weizsäcker, Richard Freiherr, Baron von (1920–)

West German politician, the son of a baron-diplomat who was tried at Nuremberg. He was educated at Berlin, Oxford, Grenoble and Göttingen universities, studying history and law. During **World War II** he served in the **Wehrmacht**. After the war he worked as a professional lawyer and was active in the German Protestant Church, becoming President of its congress (1964–70). A member of the conservative Christian Democratic Union (**CDU**) since 1954, he served as a Deputy in the **Bundestag** from 1969, as CDU Deputy Chairman (1972–9) and, from 1981, as a successful Mayor of West Berlin, before being elected federal President in May 1984. He was re-elected in May 1989. ▷ **Germany, West**

Welensky, Roland (Roy) (1907–92)

Rhodesian politician. Born in Bulawayo, he was educated in local schools and then started work on the railways at the age of 14. He became leader of the Railway Workers' Union in Northern Rhodesia in 1933, by which time he had also been heavyweight boxing champion (1926–8). Elected to the Northern Rhodesia Legco in 1938, he founded the Northern Rhodesia Labour Party in 1941 and was appointed Director of Manpower by the Governor. He became Chairman of the unofficial opposition in 1946. A strong supporter of the proposed Federation of Rhodesia and Nyasaland, he was elected to its first parliament. Welensky was appointed Minister of Transport and Development in 1953, to which he soon added the portfolios of Communications and Posts. Promoted to Deputy Prime Minister in 1955, he succeeded Sir Godfrey **Huggins** (Lord Malvern) as Prime Minister in 1956, which post he held until the Federation's demise at the end of 1963. Although considered a doughty champion of white rule, he was strongly opposed to Southern Rhodesia's

UDI and tried, unsuccessfully, to return to politics as an opponent of Ian **Smith**. He retired to a smallholding near Salisbury (Harare).

Weltpolitik

A concept (literally, 'world policy') widely promoted in post-Bismarckian Imperial Germany and taken to mean the acquisition of new colonies, a greater German share in international trade and parity with the other major powers, especially Britain. The creation of a large, high-seas battle fleet by **Tirpitz** was seen as essential to the realization of these aims, but this attempt led in turn to a costly and ultimately futile arms race with Britain. *Weltpolitik* was further seen as a means of diverting public attention from the steadily growing constitutional tensions within Germany, but its limited success led to failure in this regard. The resulting crises in domestic and foreign policy led to calls for war from sections of the establishment from 1912 onwards.

West Bank

The region of the Middle East west of the River Jordan and the Dead Sea. Administered by Jordan (1949–67), the area was seized by Israel in the **Six-Day War**. Because of Arab refusal to negotiate peace terms, Israel retained it, administered it as the district of Judea-Samaria and allowed Jewish settlement. The West Bank includes Old (East) Jerusalem, as well as Bethlehem, Jericho, Hebron and Nablus, and was a focus of territorial aspirations by the **PLO** (Palestine Liberation Organization). It was the scene of the *intifada* ('uprising') against the Israelis between 1988 and 1993, resulting in numerous deaths and the intermittent closure of schools and shops. Palestinian sources claimed that Israeli troops had killed many Palestinians in their attempts to control the uprising. In 1993, Israel reached agreement with the PLO on the implementation of limited Palestinian self-rule, but in 1994 talks faltered following attacks on a mosque in Hebron and a reprisal attack by Hamas in Afula in northern Israel. ▷ **Arab–Israeli Wars; Israel, State of; Zionism**

West Indies, Federation of the (1958–62)

Ill-fated union of the British West Indies devised at the Montego Bay Conference (Sep 1947). Damaged from the outset by the failure of Guyana, Belize, the Bahamas and the British Virgin Islands to join, the federation was further weakened by disputes. These ranged from the powers of the federal government, taxation and the constitutional backwardness of the union relative to constitutional progress in Jamaica, Trinidad and Barbados, to the under-representation in the federal parliament of these states, given their contribution in population and finance. As it was, the West Indian Federal Labour Party led by Grantley **Adams** relied on small island support to maintain its majority over the Democratic Labour Party of **Bustamante**; when the latter withdrew Jamaica from the federation (1961) and **Williams** took out Trinidad (1962), the union collapsed and was dissolved.

Western Sahara

A disputed north-west African territory administered by Morocco. This area was claimed as a protectorate by Spain in 1884 and partitioned by Morocco and Mauritania after its Spanish status ended in 1975. In 1979 Mauritania withdrew. The independence movement, *Frente Polisario*, has named it the Saharan Arab Democratic Republic and has set up a 'government in exile', and Saharan guerrillas operate from within Algeria.

Westminster, Statute of (1931)

Legislation which clarified that Dominions in the **British Empire** were autonomous communities and effectively independent, though owing common allegiance to the crown. The statute closely followed the formulation made by Arthur **Balfour** in the 1920s about the relationship of the Dominions to Britain and it also established a free association of members in the '**Commonwealth of Nations**'.

Weygand, Maxime (1867–1965)

French soldier. As Chief of Staff to **Foch** (1914–23), he rendered great services in **World War I**. He was High Commissioner in Syria (1923–4), and appointed Chief of Staff (1930), and then designated Commander-in-Chief in a future war (1931). Retired in 1935, he was recalled and sent to command in Syria in 1939. In May 1940, in the middle of the battle, he was recalled to replace **Gamelin** as Commander-in-Chief, but arrived too late to do much more than recommend an armistice. The **Vichy** government sent him as its delegate to North Africa, but he was recalled in response to German pressure and imprisoned in Germany until the end of **World War II**. In 1948 he was brought before the High Court for his role in 1940, but the case was dropped.

White Australia Policy

The unofficial national policy of Australia from 1901 until the late 1960s, designed to exclude non-European migrants; it was particularly aimed at Asians and Pacific Islanders. It also assumed the decline and ultimate extinction of the native **Aboriginals**. The policy enjoyed general support, including that of the trade-union movement to protect union wage rates. In the late 1960s, the policy was progressively dismantled, and race was replaced as a basis for admission by other, largely economic, criteria. ▷ **Dictation Test**

White Russians

The name collectively given to counter-revolutionary forces led by ex-tsarist officers, which fought unsuccessfully against the Bolshevik **Red Army** during the **Russian Civil War** (1918–22). The Whites were supported by the military intervention of British, American, French, and Japanese troops; when these withdrew, White resistance to the Red Army collapsed. ▷ **Bolsheviks**

Whitehead, Edgar (1905–71)

Southern Rhodesian politician. Born in England, he emigrated to Southern Rhodesia in 1928 and, after two years in the civil service, went into farming. He was elected to the legislative assembly in 1939 and, after war service, became the country's High Commissioner in London (1945–6) before being called back as Minister of Finance (1946–53). After a further period of farming, he was asked to be the Central African Federation's representative in the USA, from where he was recalled again, this time to be Prime Minister. His term of office introduced several liberalizing measures but, lacking charisma and facing a more avowedly racist opposition in the **Rhodesian Front**, he lost office in the 1962 elections and retired, yet again, to his farm.

Whitlam, (Edward) Gough (1916–)

Australian politician. A lawyer, he entered politics in 1952 and led the **Australian Labor Party** (1967–77), forming the first Labor government since 1949. His administration (1972–5) was notable for its radicalism, ending conscription and withdrawing Australian troops from the **Vietnam War**, recognizing communist China, relaxing the restrictions on non-white immigrants, abolishing university fees and creating Medibank (the state-funded healthcare system). He was controversially dismissed by the Governor-General in 1975, after the Senate had blocked his money bills, and lost the subsequent election. He retired from politics in 1977 and in 1983 became Australian Ambassador to Unesco in Paris.

Wilhelm, Crown Prince of Germany and Prussia (1882–1951)

After serving as an army field commander during **World War I**, he sought exile in the Netherlands on 13 Nov 1918 and renounced his claims to the German and Prussian thrones in Dec. He returned to Germany in 1923 and despite identifying with monarchist groups and, for a time, with the **Nazi Party**, he played a limited role in political life. ▷ **Prussia**

Wilhelmina (Helena Pauline Maria) (1880–1962)

Queen of the Netherlands (1890/1948). She succeeded her father William III at the age of 10, her mother acting as Regent until 1898. In 1901 she married Duke Henry of Mecklenburg-Schwerin. An upholder of constitutional monarchy, she especially won the admiration of her people during **World War II**. Though compelled to seek refuge in Britain, she steadfastly encouraged Dutch **resistance** to the German occupation. In 1948 she abdicated in favour of her daughter **Juliana**, and assumed the title of Princess of the Netherlands.

'Wilhelmus'

The Dutch national anthem. It was originally a song of the Beggars (irregulars in the early part of the Eighty Years War of the Dutch against Spain), composed c.1570 by an admiring follower of William I, Prince of Orange. The melody is derived from a French army marching song. In 1932 it became the official Dutch anthem, emphasizing the bond between Dutch nationalistic feeling and the House of Orange-Nassau.

Wilkins, Roy (1901–81)

US civil rights leader. He began working for the NAACP in 1931, and became its executive director (1965–77). Throughout his career he fought to end segregation, rejecting the concept of separate development for blacks and opposing the black nationalism of both Marcus **Garvey** and the **Black Power** movement. Because of his insistence on using constitutional means to effect change, he fell out of favour in the 1960s with the more militant civil rights leaders.

William II (1859–1941)

German Emperor and King of **Prussia** (1888/1918). He was the eldest son of Frederick (II) and Victoria (the daughter of Britain's Queen Victoria), and grandson of William I. He dismissed Bismarck (1890), and began a long period of personal rule, later displaying a bellicose attitude in international affairs. He and his government pledged full support to Austria-Hungary after the assassination of the Archduke **Francis Ferdinand** at Sarajevo (1914), thereby setting Europe on the road to war. During **World War I** he became a mere figurehead, and when the German armies collapsed, and US President Woodrow **Wilson** refused to negotiate while he remained in power, he abdicated and fled to the Netherlands, living as a country gentleman until his death.

William of Wied (1876–1945)

Prince of Albania (7 Mar/3 Sep 1914). He arrived in newly-independent Albania in Mar 1914, as a 35-year-old captain in the German Army, with 75 million francs for financing the government. Seeing him as an Austrian protégé, the Italian government intrigued against him. He never gained control of the country which was split into factions and, after losing the support of the Emperor **Franz Josef**, he left Albania in 1914. Fan **Noli**'s verdict upon him was that 'he can be criticized only for being unable to perform miracles'. ▷ **Albanians**

Williams, Eric (1911–81)
Trinidadian politician and historian. Williams was Prime Minister of Trinidad and Tobago for 30 years. In 1956 he founded the PNM and, as Chief Minister, took Trinidad into the Federation of the **West Indies** (1958), insisting on a powerful centralized government. When that failed to materialize, Williams took Trinidad out of the union and obtained independence (1962) with the slogan 'Discipline, Production and Tolerance'. Thanks to a favourable economic situation and PNM expenditure on public works and social services, Williams's popularity soared until 1970, when an economic downturn and his increasing authoritarianism led to **Black Power** violence. Saddened by the materialism his own policies had helped to create, Williams committed suicide in 1981.

Williams, Shirley (Vivien Teresa) (1930–)
British politician. A former journalist, and Secretary of the Fabian Society (1960–4), she became a Labour MP in 1964. After many junior positions, she was Secretary of State for Prices and Consumer Protection (1974–6), and for Education and Science (1976–9). She lost her seat in 1979, became a co-founder of the Social Democratic Party in 1981, and the Party's first elected MP later that year. She lost her seat in the 1983 general election, but remained as the SDP's President (1982–7). She supported the merger between the SDP and the Liberal Party. ▷ **Labour Party** (UK); **Liberal Party** (UK); **Social Democratic Party**

Williams Thesis
Revolutionary argument postulated by Eric **Williams** in *Capitalism and Slavery* (1944) that British emancipation was more the consequence of 'laissez-faire' self-interest than imperial altruism. The idea that the abolition of the slave trade and slavery was simply the result of the high-minded idealism of the Abolitionists had been set in historical truth by books such as Reginald Coupland's *The British Anti-Slavery Movement* (1933); Williams argued cogently that while slavery and the slave trade had provided the necessary capital to finance the Industrial Revolution in England, by the beginning of the 19c the British West Indies sugar plantocracy with its expensive production, captive, monopolistic market and inefficient labour force had become an obstacle to a booming industrial society and its metropolitan, free-trading entrepreneurs.

Wilson, Arnold (1884–1940)
British administrator. Having carried out surveying work in southern Persia as a young Indian Army officer, he was appointed, by the British, to the commission charged with looking into the Ottoman–Persian Shatt al-Arab frontier dispute in 1913. He was a member of Cox's civil administration in 1915–16 and became (mid-1918) Acting Civil Commissioner,

on Cox's departure to Tehran. Wilson's administration, although generally fair and efficient, was distinctly unsympathetic towards local, and particularly nationalist, aims. After **World War I**, he urged opposition both to the Anglo-French Declaration and to the notion of an Iraq run by a prince from the Sharifian family. His government appeared increasingly intolerant, giving rise to Iraqi fears that they had merely exchanged a Turkish master for a British, and that their political aspirations would be thwarted; this helped to bring about the insurrection of 1920. Later that year, Cox returned to Iraq, relieving Wilson of the task of carrying out the proposed constitutional programme for the country. He went on to become an MP, was arrested early in **World War II** because of alleged fascist sympathies and was killed in action, having volunteered as a rear-gunner in the RAF.

Wilson, Sir Henry Hughes (1864–1922)
British field marshal. He joined the Rifle Brigade in 1884, and served in Burma (1884–7) and South Africa (1899–1901). As Director of Military Operations at the War Office (1910–14), he elaborated plans for the rapid support of France in the event of war with Germany. By the end of **World War I**, he was Chief of the Imperial General Staff. Promoted field marshal and created a baronet (1919), he resigned from the army in 1922, and became an MP. His implacable opposition to the leaders of **Sinn Féin** led to his assassination on the doorstep of his London home.

Wilson, (Thomas) Woodrow (1856–1924)
US politician and 28th President. He practised law in Atlanta, later became a university professor and, in 1902, President of Princeton University. He served as Democratic Governor of New Jersey (1911–13), and was elected President in 1912, running against Theodore **Roosevelt** and William Taft, and served two terms (1913–21). His 'New Freedom' program, establishing equality and opportunity for all men, created the Federal Reserve Board and the Clayton Anti-Trust Act (1914), which accorded many rights to labor unions. Wilson tried to keep the USA out of **World War I** but was compelled to enter the war in Apr 1917 to make the world 'safe for democracy'. He laid out his peace plan proposal in the **Fourteen Points**, and actively championed the idea of forming a **League of Nations**, which was part of the Treaty of **Versailles**. When the Senate rejected the treaty, his idealistic vision of world peace was shattered. In 1919 he was awarded the Nobel Peace Prize, but thereafter his health declined severely, and he never recovered.

Wilson (of Rievaulx), (James) Harold, Baron (1916–)
British politician. He became a lecturer in economics at Oxford in 1937. An MP in 1945, he was President of the Board of Trade (1947–51), and the principal opposition spokesman on Economic Affairs. An able and

hard-hitting debater, in 1963 he succeeded **Gaitskell** as Leader of the **Labour Party**, then he became Prime Minister (1964–70). His economic plans were badly affected by balance of payments crises, leading to severe restrictive measures and devaluation (1967). He was also faced with the problem of Rhodesian independence, opposition to Britain's proposed entry into the Common Market, and an increasing conflict between the two wings of the Labour Party. Following his third general election victory, he resigned suddenly as Prime Minister and Labour leader in 1976. Knighted in 1976, he became a life peer in 1983. ▷ **EC; EEC; Rhodesia Crisis**

Wilson (of Libya and of Stowlangtoft), Henry Maitland, 1st Baron (1881–1964)
British field marshal. He fought in South Africa and in **World War I**, and at the outbreak of **World War II** was appointed Commander of British troops in Egypt. Having led the first British advance in Libya (1940–1) and the unsuccessful Greek campaign (1941), he became Commander-in-Chief Middle East (1943) and Supreme Allied Commander in the Mediterranean theatre (1944). Wilson headed the British Joint Staff Mission in Washington (1945–7), and was raised to the peerage in 1946.

Windsor, House of
The name of the British royal family since 1917. This unequivocally English name resulted from a declaration by **George V**, a member of the House of **Saxe-Coburg-Gotha**. It was felt that a Germanic surname for the British monarchy was inappropriate during a war against Germany.

Wingate, Orde (Charles) (1903–44)
British general. He was commissioned in 1922, and served in the Sudan (1928–33) and Palestine (1936–9), where he helped create a Jewish defence force. In the Burma theatre (1942) he organized the Chindits — specially trained jungle-fighters who were supplied by air, and thrust far behind the enemy lines. He was killed in a plane crash in Burma. ▷ **World War II**

Winnipeg General Strike (1919)
One of the most significant Canadian strikes, it began when the employers in the building and metal trades refused to negotiate a collective bargaining procedure or to raise wages. After two weeks, the Winnipeg Trades and Labour Council voted to strike in sympathy. Fearing, like business leaders, that unionization would damage industrial profitability, the federal government immediately intervened. Despite the strikers' non-violence, specials were brought in to replace the city police force. A peaceful march was broken up, one spectator killed and 30 injured. The strike came to an end; its leaders jailed for sedition and the premier's promise of a Royal Commission. It did, however, politicize the issues,

and in Manitoba's provincial elections of 1920 four of the jailed strike leaders were elected as socialists. The following year J S **Woodsworth** became the first socialist member of the federal House of Commons, as a representative from Winnipeg. ▷ **Meighen, Arthur**

Winter Palace, Storming of (1917)
A symbolic victory for the Bolshevik revolutionaries. The Tsar's residence had become the headquarters of the **Russian Provisional Government**. With the Neva River on one side, and an open square on the other, it could have been defended. However, before the attack began on the night of 7 Nov (25 Oct old style) **Kerensky**, the Prime Minister, had already fled, and those left to face the attacking soldiers, sailors and workers' red guards were mainly young cadets and a women's battalion. An easy triumph subsequently made good political theatre. The Winter Palace is now the Hermitage Museum, one of the richest storehouses of art and artefacts in the world. ▷ **Bolsheviks**

Wirth, Josef (1879–1956)
German politician. After an early teaching career, Wirth entered politics in Baden as a member of the **Centre Party** (1913) and national politics as a member of the **Reichstag** (1914). National Finance Minister after **World War I**, he became Chancellor in May 1921. As such he headed a minority coalition of the republican parties (Centre, **SPD**, **DDP**) which tried to fulfil Allied **reparations** demands so as to demonstrate their excessiveness. He resigned in Nov 1922, held further ministerial posts between 1929 and 1931 and then sought exile in Switzerland (1933) when **Hitler** took power. He returned to Germany in 1948, where he advocated a policy of German neutrality.

Wirtschaftswunder
Literally 'economic miracle', this is the term given to Federal Germany's rapid economic recovery from the devastation of **World War II**. Rapid growth from 1948 onward appeared to confirm the efficacy of the **social market economy** and helped to legitimize the democratic-parliamentary order.

Wittelsbach
The premier Bavarian family, the Wittelsbachs provided successive dukes and kings for Bavaria from medieval times until the early 20c. They still have a disputed claim to the Spanish throne.

Wolseley, Garnet Joseph, 1st Viscount (1833–1913)
British field marshal. He joined the army in 1852, and served in the Burmese War (1852–3), the Crimean War (where he lost an eye), the Indian Uprising (1857–8), and the Chinese War (1860). He put down the

Red River Rebellion (1870) in Canada, and commanded in the Ashanti War (1873). After other posts in India, Cyprus, South Africa and Egypt, he led the attempted rescue of General Gordon at Khartoum. He became a baron (1882) and, after the Sudan campaign (1884–5), a viscount. As army Commander-in-Chief (1895–1901), he carried out several reforms, and mobilized forces for the Boer War (1899–1902). ▷ **Boer Wars**

Woodsworth, James Shaver (1874–1942)
Canadian social worker, Methodist minister and politician. Having emerged as the country's conscience following the **Winnipeg General Strike** and the federal elections of 1921, his social work in the cities showed him that his church's complicity with capitalist society compromised any capacity for reform. He then turned to politics, but in 1917 lost his job in provincial government for criticizing conscription. He also resigned his ministry as a protest against the Church's support for the war. Arrested for sedition (as an editor of the Winnipeg strikers' bulletin), although not convicted, the resulting publicity helped to spread his reputation as a spokesman for the disadvantaged. Well-informed also on the problems of the prairie farmers, he was a founder and President of the **CCF**. In 1926 he and A A Heaps were able to take advantage of the government's tiny majority: while **Meighen** refused to negotiate with them, Mackenzie **King** promised to introduce an Old Age Pensions Act and rescind the 1919 amendments to the Immigration Act and the Criminal Code. Woodsworth argued that both parties were corrupt and that it was his duty to use his parliamentary position to promote the cause of socialism. Although it took 10 years to repeal the 1919 amendments, the Old Age Pensions Act was passed in 1927. Winning his last election in 1940, Woodsworth was the one MP who voted against Canada's involvement in **World War II**, and his speech of conscience was heard in respectful silence.

Works Projects Administration (WPA) (1935–43)
A US federal agency established under President Franklin D **Roosevelt** to combat unemployment during the **Great Depression**. Originally called the **Works Progress Administration**, it built transportation facilities, parks and buildings. Some 8 500 000 people were employed during its history, including artists and writers as well as manual workers. ▷ **New Deal**

World War I (1914–18)
A war whose origins lay in the increasingly aggressive foreign policies as pursued by Austria-Hungary, Russia and, most significantly, Germany. The assassination of the heir to the Habsburg throne, **Francis Ferdinand**, at Sarajevo in Bosnia (28 June 1914), triggered the war which soon involved most European states following Austria's declaration of war on Serbia (28 July). Russia mobilized in support of Serbia (29–30 July); and

Germany declared war on Russia (1 Aug), and on France (3 Aug). The German invasion of neutral Belgium (4 Aug) brought the British into the war on the French side. Japan joined Britain, France and Russia under the terms of an agreement with Britain (1902, 1911), and Italy joined the Allies in May 1915. Turkey allied with Germany (Nov 1914), and they were joined by Bulgaria (Oct 1915). Military campaigning centred on France, Belgium and, later, Italy in Western Europe, and on Poland, western Russia and the Balkans in Eastern Europe. The French Army prevented the Germans from executing the **Schlieffen** Plan and then, with the **British Expeditionary Force**, at the first Battle of Ypres, from reaching the Channel ports. By the end of 1914, a static defence line had been established from the Belgian coast to Switzerland. The Allies attempted to break the stalemate by the **Gallipoli Campaign** aimed at re-supplying Russia and knocking out Turkey (Apr 1915–Jan 1916), but failed. On the eastern and south-eastern fronts, the **Central Powers** occupied Russian Poland and most of Lithuania, and Serbia was invaded. After staunch resistance, Serbia, Albania and, latterly, Romania were overrun. For three years, an Allied army was involved in a Macedonian campaign, and there was also fighting in Mesopotamia against Turkey. Naval competition had played a crucial role in heightening tension before 1914, but in the event, the great battle fleets of Germany and Britain did not play an important part in the war. The only significant naval encounter, at Jutland in 1916, proved indecisive. The Allies organized a large offensive for the Western Front in 1916, but were forestalled by the Germans, who attacked France at Verdun (Feb–July). To relieve the situation, the Battle of the Somme was launched, but proved indecisive. The Germans then unleashed unrestricted submarine warfare (Jan 1917) to cripple Britain economically before the USA could come to her aid. The USA declared war on Germany (2 Apr 1917) when British food stocks were perilously low, and the German submarine menace was finally overcome by the use of convoys. Tanks were used effectively by the Allies at the Battle of Cambrai (1916). By 1917, the Russian armies were broken and revolution broke out in St Petersburg and Moscow. In late 1917 **Lenin**'s Bolshevik government sued for peace and in Mar 1918 Germany and her allies imposed the punitive peace of Brest-Litovsk on the USSR (annulled after Germany's defeat). Following this, in the spring of 1918, the Germans launched a major attack in the west, but after several months of success were driven back, with the USA providing an increasing number of much-needed troops. By Sep, the German Army was in full retreat, and signified its intention to sue for peace on the basis of President **Wilson**'s **Fourteen Points**. By Nov, when the armistice was signed, the Allies had recaptured western Belgium and nearly all French territory. Military victories in Palestine and Mesopotamia resulted in a Turkish armistice (31 Oct 1918); Italian victories and a northward advance by Franco-British forces finished Austria-Hungary (and Bulgaria). Estimated combatant war losses were: British Empire, just under 1 million: France, nearly 1.4 million; Italy, nearly $\frac{1}{2}$ million; Russia, 1.7 million; USA,

115 000; Germany 1.8 million; Austria-Hungary 1.2 million, and Turkey 325 000. About double these numbers were wounded. ▷ **ANZAC; Marne, Battle of the; Paris Peace Conference; Passchendaele, Battle of; reparations; Somme, Battle of the; Triple Entente; Verdun, Battle of; Versailles, Treaty of; Vimy Ridge, Battle of**

World War II (1939–45)
A war whose origins lay in three different conflicts which merged after 1941: **Hitler**'s desire for European expansion and perhaps even world domination; Japan's struggle against China; and a resulting conflict between Japanese ambitions and US interests in the Pacific. The origins of the war in Europe lay in German unwillingness to accept the frontiers laid down in 1919 by the Treaty of **Versailles** and the National Socialists' hegemonial foreign policy. After the German invasion of rump Bohemia-Moravia (Mar 1939), Britain and France pledged support to Poland. Germany concluded an alliance with the USSR (Aug 1939), and then invaded Poland (1 Sep). Britain and France declared war on Germany (3 Sep), but could not prevent Poland from being overrun in four weeks. For six months there was a period of 'phoney war', when little fighting took place, but the Germans then occupied Norway and Denmark (Apr 1940), and Belgium and Holland were invaded (10 May), followed immediately by the invasion of France. A combination of German tank warfare and air power brought about the surrender of Holland in four days, Belgium in three weeks, and France in seven weeks. Italy declared war on France and Britain in the final stages of this campaign. There followed the Battle of Britain, in which Germany tried to win air supremacy over Britain, but failed. As a result, German attempts to force Britain to come to terms came to nothing, not least because of Winston **Churchill**'s uncompromising stance. Germany launched submarine (**U-boat**) attacks against British supply routes, but then moved east and invaded Greece and Yugoslavia (Apr 1941) and, following an Italian military fiasco there, Greece. British military efforts were concentrated against Italy in the Mediterranean and North Africa. After early reverses for Italy, **Rommel** was sent to North Africa with the German **Afrika Corps** to reinforce Italian military strength, and fiercely-contested campaigning continued here for three years until Allied troops finally ejected German and Italian forces in mid-1943, invaded Sicily and then Italy itself, and forced Italy to make a separate peace (3 Sep 1943). In June 1941, in line with Hitler's longheld hostility to the USSR, and in his quest for **Lebensraum**, Germany invaded her ally Russia along a 2 000 mile front, and German armies advanced in three formations: to the outskirts of Leningrad in the north, towards Moscow in the centre, and to the Volga River in the south. After spectacular early successes, the Germans were held up by bitter Soviet resistance, and by heavy winter snows and Arctic temperatures, for which they were completely unprepared. From Nov 1942 they were gradually driven back, suffering decisive reverses at **Sta-**

lingrad (winter 1942–3) and Kursk (May 1943). Leningrad was under siege for nearly 2½ years (until Jan 1944), and about a third of its population died from starvation and disease. The Germans were finally driven out of the USSR (Aug 1944). A second front was launched against Germany by the Allies (June 1944), through the invasion of Normandy, and Paris was liberated (25 Aug). Despite German use of flying bombs and rockets against Allied bases, the Allies advanced into Germany (Feb 1945) and linked with the Russians on the River Elbe (28 Apr). The Germans surrendered unconditionally at Rheims (7 May 1945). In the Far East, Japan's desire for expansion, combined with a US threat of economic sanctions against her, led to her attack on **Pearl Harbor** and other British and US bases (7 Dec 1941), and the USA declared war against Japan the next day. In reply Japan's allies, Germany and Italy, declared war on the USA (11 Dec). Within four months, Japan controlled South-East Asia and Burma. Not until June 1942 did naval victories in the Pacific stem the advance, and Japanese troops defended their positions grimly. Bitter fighting continued until 1945, when, with Japan on the retreat, the USA dropped two atomic bombs on Hiroshima and Nagasaki (6 and 9 Aug). Japan then surrendered 14 Aug. Casualty figures are not easy to obtain accurately, but approximately 3 million Russians were killed in action, 3 million died as prisoners of war, 8 million people died in occupied Russia, and about 3 million in unoccupied Russia. Germany suffered 3¼ million military casualties, around 6 million total casualties, and lost a million prisoners of war. Japan suffered just over 2 million military casualties and just over ¼ million civilian deaths. France lost a total of ½ million dead, and Britain and her Commonwealth just over 600 000. The USA suffered just over 300 000 casualties. It is also estimated that in the course of the German occupation of a large part of Europe, about 6 million Jews were murdered in extermination and labour camps, along with a million or more other victims. ▷ **Anschluss; appeasement; Atlantic, Battle of the; Atlantic Charter; Blitzkrieg; Britain, Battle of; Bulge, Battle of the; Casablanca Conference; D-Day; Desert Rats; El Alamein, Battle of; Free French; Gestapo; Holocaust; kamikaze; Lend-Lease Agreement; Maginot Line; Munich Agreement; Normandy Campaign; North African Campaign; Nuremberg Trials; Paris Peace Conference; Potsdam Conference; Special Operations Executive; SS; Yalta Conference**

World Zionist Organization

The political institution established under the leadership of Theodor **Herzl**, its first President, at the First Zionist Congress, held in Basel (29–31 Aug 1897). The goal of the organization was the establishment of a national home for world Jewry in Palestine. For this purpose, the first Zionist bank and the **Jewish National Fund** were also formed. With time, the World Zionist Organization opened offices all around the world and, in the years before his death, Herzl shaped it into an efficient and effective political institution. ▷ **Zionism**

Wörner, Manfred (1934–)
West German politician. He studied law at the universities of Heidelberg, Paris and Munich, then joined the conservative Christian Democratic Union (**CDU**) and was elected to the **Bundestag** (federal parliament) in 1965. Establishing himself as a specialist in strategic issues, he was appointed Defence Minister in 1982 by Chancellor **Kohl** and then oversaw the controversial deployment of US Cruise and Pershing-II nuclear missiles in West **Germany**, an extension of military service from 15 to 18 months to compensate for a declining birthrate, and, in 1984, the dismissal of General Gunter Kiessling, for alleged, though subsequently disproven, homosexual contacts. Wörner succeeded Lord **Carrington** as Secretary-General of **NATO** in 1988.

Wounded Knee (29 Dec 1890)
The site in South Dakota (USA) of the final defeat of the Sioux. The 'battle' was in fact a massacre of men, women, and children by US troops, finally suppressing The Ghost Dance cult inspired by the visions of the Paiute Indian religious leader Wovoka. In 1973, members of the American Indian Movement occupied the site to protest at the conditions of Native Americans. Two people were killed in the ensuing seige by **FBI** agents and federal marshals.

Wrangel, Pyotr Nikolaievich, Baron (1878–1928)
Russian army officer. He entered military service in 1904 and commanded a cavalry corps during **World War I**. In the **Russian Civil War**, he commanded cavalry divisions and the Volunteer Army in the Ukraine, and in 1920 became Commander-in-Chief of the White armies in the south. After the **Red Army** victory, he fled to Turkey with the remnants of his troops. He died in Brussels, and was buried in Belgrade.

Wu Peifu (Wu P'ei-fu) (1874–1939)
Chinese warlord. A major figure in the warlord struggles of China (1916–27). He joined the **Beiyang Army**, newly created by **Yuan Shikai**, and rose rapidly in its ranks. After Yuan's death (1916), when **Duan Qirui** sought to reunite China by force and in dependence on Japan, Wu and other northern generals refused Duan's orders. In the civil war which followed, he was unable to sustain his government of national unity (1923). He died in Japanese-occupied Beijing.

Wyszynski, Stepan (1901–81)
Polish cardinal. Educated at Włocławek and Lublin, he was ordained in 1924, and became Bishop of Lublin (1946), Archbishop of Warsaw and

Gniezno (1948), and a cardinal (1952). Following his indictment of the communist campaign against the Church, he was imprisoned (1953). Freed in 1956, he agreed to a reconciliation between Church and state under the **Gomułka** regime, but relations remained uneasy.

Xi'an Incident (12–25 Dec 1936)
The incident during which the **Guomindang** leader, **Chiang Kai-shek**, was kidnapped and held hostage in Xi'an by some of his own troops, under the 'Young Marshal', Zhang Xueliang (Chang Hsueh-liang). The hostage-taking was designed to force Chiang Kai-shek into acceding to demands for an alliance between the Guomindang and the Communists against the Japanese, who had occupied Manchuria in 1931. He was released, after 13 days, thanks to intervention by the Communist leader, **Zhou Enlai** (further to urging by **Stalin**). Chiang Kai-shek made a verbal agreement to review Guomindang policy, and the second of the **United Fronts** followed.

Xoxe, Koci (d.1949)
Albanian politician. A member of the Communist Party, and a wartime protégé of the Yugoslav partisan leader, **Tito**, he was Minister of the Interior in the post-war government, presiding over the trials of 'war criminals' which consolidated the position of Enver **Hoxha**. As a supporter of Albania's ties with Yugoslavia, his position weakened after Yugoslavia was expelled from Cominform and Hoxha moved closer to **Stalin**. From being second only to Hoxha in importance, he was demoted, then tried for treason and executed in 1949, a victim of Stalin's purge of 'Titoists'.

Y

Yaba Higher College

A college founded in Lagos, Nigeria in 1934 by the British Governor General, Sir Donald Cameron, with the intention of training Africans for administrative work. By **World War II** it offered some degree courses.

Yagoda, Genrikh Grigorevich (1891–1938)

Soviet police chief. A shadowy figure of Jewish origin, he became number two in the **OGPU** (or secret police) in 1924 and head of its successor, the **NKVD**, in 1934. He was **Stalin**'s agent in the great purges that started in that year. Yagoda was dismissed as inefficient in 1936 and brought before a firing squad in 1937. His successor, **Yezhov**, was a much nastier figure.

Yahya Khan, Agha Muhammad (1917–80)

Pakistani soldier. The son of a Pathan police superintendent, he was educated at Punjab University and the Indian Military Academy, Dehra Dun. He was commissioned in 1938, fought with the British Eighth Army during **World War II** and afterwards rose to become Chief of the Army General Staff (1957–62). He supported General **Ayub Khan**'s successful coup in 1958, became Army Commander-in-Chief in 1966 and, in 1969, with popular unrest mounting, replaced Ayub Khan as military ruler. In 1980 he sanctioned the nation's first national elections based on universal suffrage, but his mishandling of the Bangladesh separatist issue led to civil war and the dismemberment of the republic in 1971. After defeat by India in the **Bangladesh War**, Yahya Khan resigned and was sentenced to five years' house arrest.

Yakovlev, Alexander Nikolaevich (1923–)

Soviet party official and intellectual. Born into a simple peasant family in the Yaroslavl area, he first became an **apparatchik** after being invalided out of the army and by 1953 had been called to Moscow where, with the exception of four years of academic leave, he spent the period down to 1973 servicing the Central Committee of the Communist Party. He was then exiled as Ambassador to Canada for a decade for offending communist hardliners. It was on Mikhail **Gorbachev**'s advice that he was brought back to the Central Committee to assist with ideological work and by 1987 he was a full member of the **Politburo**. Although previously anti-American he did much to give body to Gorbachev's new thinking on home and foreign affairs. He was eventually more reformist than

Gorbachev but still did everything possible to rescue him politically after the attempted **August Coup** in 1991.

Yalta Conference (4–11 Feb 1945)

A meeting at Yalta, in the Crimea, during **World War II**, between Winston **Churchill**, **Stalin** and **Roosevelt**. Among matters agreed were the disarmament and partition of Germany, the Russo-Polish frontier, the establishment of the **UN**, and the composition of the Polish government. In a secret protocol it was also agreed that Russia would declare war on Japan after the war with Germany ended. ▷ **Curzon Line**

Yamagata Aritomo (1838–1922)

Japanese soldier and politician. Made commanding officer of the Kiheitai in 1863, he went on to become Vice-Minister of War (1871) and then Army Minister, issuing in 1878 the 'Admonition to the Military', which emphasized the traditional virtues of bravery and loyalty to the **Meiji Emperor**, in an attempt to counteract the trend of liberalization. As Chief of Staff, he was the driving force behind the promulgation of the 1882 Imperial Rescript to Soldiers and Sailors and 1890 Imperial Rescript on Education. He was Home Minister (1883–9) and was Japan's first Prime Minister (1889–1 and 1898–1900). His modernization of the military system led to Japanese victories in the **Sino-Japanese War** (1894–5) and **Russo-Japanese War** (1904–5), for which he was made Prince (*Koshaku*), and the emergence of Japan as a significant force in world politics. From 1903 he alternated with Ito Hirobumi as President of the Privy Council; after the latter's death (1909), he was the dominant senior statesman, with the backing of the military and bureaucracy. His downfall came about in 1921 when he interfered in the marriage of the Crown Prince; he was publicly censured and died in disgrace the following year.

Yamamoto Isoroku (1884–1943)

Japanese naval officer. Educated at the Naval Academy, Etajima, he was wounded in the Battle of Tsushima in the **Russo-Japanese War** (1904–5). He studied at Harvard (1917–19), serving thereafter as a language officer (1919–21) and as naval attaché at the Japanese embassy in the USA (1926–2). He became Chief of the Aviation Department of the Japanese navy in 1935, and was vice-Navy Minister from 1936 to 1939. Opposed to the Japanese entry into **World War II**, Yamamoto was nevertheless made Admiral (1940) and Commander-in-Chief Combined Fleet (1939–43). A great strategist, it was he who planned and directed the attack on **Pearl Harbor** in Dec 1941. His forces were defeated at the Battle of **Midway** (June 1942), and he was killed when his plane was shot down over the Solomon Islands.

Yamani, Sheikh Ahmed Zaki (1930–)
Saudi Arabian politician. Educated in Cairo, New York and Harvard, he worked as a lawyer before entering politics. Yamani has been Minister of Petroleum and Mineral Resources since 1962, and an important and 'moderate' member of **OPEC** (the Organization of Petroleum-Exporting Countries).

Yamashita Tomoyuki (1885–1946)
Japanese soldier. After serving in the **Russo-Japanese War**, **World War I** and **Sino-Japanese War**, he commanded the Japanese 25th Army which overran Malaya and captured Singapore (15 Feb 1942). He then took over the Philippines campaign, capturing Bataan and Corregidor. Still in charge when General **MacArthur** turned the tables in 1944–5, he was captured and hanged in Manila for atrocities perpetrated by his troops.

Yameogo, Maurice (1921–)
Burkina Faso politician. Educated in Upper Volta (now Burkina Faso), he was a civil servant and trade unionist before turning to politics and being elected to the Territorial Assembly in 1946. He was Vice-President of the Upper Volta section of the Confédération Français du Travailleurs Chrétiens and was active within the **Rassemblement Démocratique Africaine (RDA)**. Founder of the Mouvement Démocratique Voltaique, he was Minister of Agriculture (1957–8), Minister of the Interior (1958) and President (1958–66), before being toppled by a military coup on 4 Jan 1966 led by Lt-Col Sangoule Lamizana. He was imprisoned until 1970, when he went into exile in the Ivory Coast.

Yanaev, Gennadi Ivanovich (1937–)
Soviet lawyer and politician. He made his career in the **Communist Party of the Soviet Union** as a **Komsomol** official and union **apparatchik**. That he had some genuine popularity was proved in 1989, when he was elected by the unions to the **congress of deputies**. In 1990 his promotion was unbelievably fast: Chairman of the trade unions, a **Politburo** member, and Soviet Vice-President. In all these positions he attempted to steer a middle course between reform and reaction; but in 1991 he opted for reaction, whether of his own free will or under pressure. His leadership of the attempted coup was so disastrous as to suggest that neither his heart nor his mind was in it. He was arrested with the others from the '**junta**'.

Yang Shangkun (Yang Shang-k'un) (1907–)
Chinese politician. The son of a wealthy Sichuan province landlord, he joined the Chinese Communist Party (CCP) in 1926 and studied in Moscow (1927–30). He took part in the **Long March** and the liberation war (1937–49), and became an alternate member of the CCP's secretariat

in 1956, but during the **Cultural Revolution** was purged for alleged 'revisionism'. He was subsequently rehabilitated in 1978 and in 1982 inducted into the CCP's Politburo and Military Affairs Commission. A year later he became a vice-chairman of the state Central Military Commission and in 1988 was elected state President. Viewed as a trusted supporter of **Deng Xiaoping**, he has strong personal ties with senior military leaders and in June 1989 it was 27th Army troops, loyal to him, who carried out the brutal massacre of pro-democracy students in **Tiananmen Square**, Beijing.

Yazov, Dmitri Timofeevich (1923–)
Soviet marshal. Of peasant stock from Omsk, he fought in **World War II** as an officer. He subsequently rose through various junior and senior commands, went through the General Staff Academy in 1967, and in 1984 became commander of the important Far East military district. In 1987 Mikhail **Gorbachev** appointed him Deputy Minister, then Minister of Defence to bring the army into line with his reforms. However, Yazov supported only limited changes and was particularly unpopular with radical deputies. In Aug 1991 he felt that reform had proceeded to the point of endangering the army, but in the event his men would not obey him and fire on the crown. When the attempted **August Coup** failed, he was arrested.

Yegarov, Alexander Ilich (1883–1939)
Soviet marshal. Of relatively humble origins in Samova, he was a colonel in the Tsarist army by 1917. He then threw in his lot with the **Bolsheviks** and rose rapidly in the course of the **Russian Civil War** during which he came into close contact with **Stalin**. By 1935 he was Chief of the General Staff and in 1937 he succeeded the executed **Tukhachevsky** as Deputy Defence Minister, only to be shot himself two years later. The loss of his fighting experience and his organizational talent was sorely felt.

Yeltsin, Boris Nikolaevich (1931–)
Soviet politician. He joined the **Communist Party of the Soviet Union** in 1961 and was appointed First Secretary of the Sverdlovsk region in 1976. He became a full member of the Central Committee in 1981 and was made its Secretary by Mikhail **Gorbachev** in 1985 for a few months, before being appointed Moscow Party Chief, replacing the disgraced Viktor Grishin. Yeltsin, a blunt-talking, hands-on reformer, rapidly set about renovating the corrupt 'Moscow machine' and was elected a candidate member of the **Politburo** in 1986, but in 1987–8, after he had bluntly criticized party conservatives at two meetings of the Central Committee for sabotaging political and economic reform, he was downgraded to a lowly administrative post. No longer in the Politburo, he returned to public attention in 1989 by being elected to the new Congress

of People's Deputies and becoming an outspoken critic of Gorbachev's failings. In May 1990 he was elected President of the Russian Federation and achieved even greater fame. But his moment of triumph came in Aug 1991, when he took the open stand that foiled the anti-Gorbachev coup and in Dec effectively put an end to both Gorbachev and the USSR. ▷ **August Coup**

Yemen

A republic in the south of the Arabian Peninsula. Yemen was part of the Ottoman Empire from the 16c until 1918, when the Hamid al-Din Dynasty took power until the revolution in 1962. Fighting between royalists and republicans continued until 1967, when the republican regime was recognized, but border clashes with South Yemen continued in the 1970s. The fishing port of Aden in South Yemen was occupied by Britain in 1839. South Yemen formed part of the Federation of South Arabia in 1963. It was overrun by the National Liberation Front, British troops withdrew, and a republic was proclaimed in 1967 but border disputes with Oman and North Yemen continued in the 1970s. The Yemen Arabic Republic (North Yemen) and The People's Democratic Republic of Yemen (South Yemen) formally united in 1990 as the Republic of Yemen.

Yevtushenko, Yevgeny (Alexandrovich) (1933–)

Soviet poet. His early poetry, such as *The Third Snow* (1955), made him a spokesman for the young post-**Stalin** generation. His long narrative poem *Stantsiya Zima* (1956, Zima Junction), considering issues raised by the death of Stalin, prompted criticism, as did his *Babi Yar* (1962) which attacked anti-Semitism. In 1960 he began to travel abroad to give readings of his poetry. ▷ **Babi Yar**

Yezhov, Nikolai Ivanovich (1894–1939)

Soviet police chief. He first emerged in 1933 as a member of a small group charged by **Stalin** with the task of purging the Communist Party of undesirable elements, essentially those opposed to him. In 1936 he succeeded **Yagoda** as head of the NKVD (secret police) and turned the confined purges into mass terror. The bloodletting took on the title, the *Yezhovshchina*. Succeeded by **Beria** in 1938, he too disappeared for ever in 1939.

Yi Dynasty (1392–1910)

The dynasty which ruled Korea under the official dynastic name of *Choson* ('morning serenity'). Founded by Yi Song-gye (1335–92), a prominent general under the preceding Koryo Dynasty (918–1392), the Yi Dynasty provided Korea with a long period of political and social stability until the incursions of Japan and the Western powers in the late 19c and its annexation as a Japanese colony in 1910. The Yi rulers were assisted by a centralized bureaucracy recruited through competitive civil service examinations on the Chinese pattern. Until the late 19c, the Yi maintained Korea's traditional tributary relationship with China.

Yishuv
The Hebrew term (literally, 'settlement') used to describe the Jewish community living in Palestine before 1948. It was also used for the declaration of the State of Israel in that year. ▷ **Balfour Declaration; Israel, State of; Jewish Agency**

Yogyakarta (Jogjakarta)
A court city and sultanate in Java. In the early 20c Yogyakarta became an important centre for the emerging nationalist and religious reformist movements. During the war against the Dutch for independence, following the Japanese surrender in 1945, the Indonesian Republic government resided in Yogyakarta.

Yom Kippur War (1973)
the hostilities that broke out towards the end of Golda **Meir**'s last term as Israeli Premier, when an attack on the State of Israel by Egypt and Syria coincided with Yom Kippur, the holiest day in the Jewish calendar. A cease-fire was reached after three weeks of fighting in which there were heavy losses on both sides. ▷ **Arab–Israeli Wars**

Yonai Mitsumasa (1880–1948)
Japanese naval officer and politician. Born of samurai descent, he was educated at the Naval Academy, Etajima and served in Russia (1915–17). He was Commander of the Imperial Fleet (1936–7), Navy Minister (1937–9 and 1944–5), and was briefly Prime Minister in 1940.

Yoshida Shigeru (1878–1967)
Japanese politician. Educated at Tokyo Imperial University, he served as a diplomat in several capitals. Vice-Foreign Minister (1928–30), in 1930–2 he was Ambassador to Italy and in 1936–8, after the army had blocked his appointment as Foreign Minister, he was Ambassador in London. As a fervent advocate of Japanese surrender, he was imprisoned (June 1945) for this view in the closing stages of **World War II**. He was released (Sep 1945) under the US occupation and was appointed Foreign Minister. After **Hatoyama**'s removal by the US authorities from public office, he stepped into his shoes as leader of the Liberal Party. As Prime Minister (1946–7 and 1949–54), he was instrumental in the socio-economic development of post-war Japan and in fostering relations with the West. In 1954, Hatoyama (who had been rehabilitated in 1951) forced him out of office and, when the **Liberal Democratic Party** was formed (1955), with Hatoyama as its leader, Yoshida withdrew from politics.

Youlou, Abbe Fulbert (1917–72)

Congo politician. Educated in Catholic seminaries and ordained a priest in 1946, he became Mayor of Brazzaville in 1957 and formed a moderate party to oppose the local socialists. He was elected to the territorial assembly in 1957 and was, in turn, Minister of Agriculture (1957–8), Prime Minister (1958–9) and President of the Congo Republic (1959–63), before being forced into exile in Spain as the result of popular opposition within the country.

Young, Whitney M, Jr (1921–71)

US civil rights leader. Born in Kentucky, he was a graduate in social work from the University of Minnesota. Executive director of the National Urban League from 1961 until his death, some of his social welfare proposals were incorporated into President **Johnson**'s anti-poverty programmes.

Young Turks

The modernizing and westernizing reformers in the early 20c **Ottoman Empire**. With the support of disaffected army elements under **Enver Pasha**, they rebelled against Sultan **Abd ul-Hamid II** in 1908, and deposed him (1909). The Young Turk revolution helped precipitate Austria-Hungary's occupation of Bosnia-Herzegovina (1908), the somewhat similar Greek officers' revolt of 1909, the Italian attack on Libya (1911), and the **Balkan Wars** (1912–13).

Ypres, Battle of (Oct–Nov 1914)

In **World War I** the halting of a German offensive to outflank the **British Expeditionary Force**. It left Ypres (Belgium) and its salient dominated on three sides by German-occupied heights.

Ypres, Battle of (Apr–May 1915)

A series of German attacks, using poison gas (chlorine) for the first time in warfare. It forced the British to shorten their defence line in the Ypres salient.

Yrigoyen, Hipólito (1852–1933)

Argentine politician. A lawyer and teacher, he was the principal leader of the **Radical Party** (*Unión Cívica Radical*) from 1896. He mounted a successful attack on the dominant conservative governments of the time, ushering in a period of Radical dominance. Yrigoyen was President in 1916–22, during which term he maintained Argentine neutrality in **World War I**, and again in 1928–30. His second presidential term was ended by a military coup, precipitated by the country's prevailing economic depression and Yrigoyen's growing senility and weakening grasp on national affairs.

Yuan Shih-k'ai ▷ Yuan Shikai

Yuan Shikai (Yuan Shih-k'ai) (1859–1916)
Chinese politician and soldier. He was careful to remain neutral during the **Boxer Rising**, from which he thus emerged with his army intact and with the gratitude of the foreign powers. On the death of his patron, the Empress Dowager **Cixi** (1908), he was removed from influence, but recalled after the successful **Chinese Revolution** of 1911. As the first President of the Republic (1912–16), he lost support by procuring the murder of the parliamentary leader of the **Guomindang** and making war on them, accepting Japan's **Twenty-One Demands**, and proclaiming himself Emperor (1915). Forced to abdicate, the humiliation may have hastened his death. ▷ **Hundred Days of Reform; Qing Dynasty**

Yugoslav Committee
Established during **World War I** (Apr 1915) in Paris by, among others, Ivan **Meštrović**, Ante **Trumbić** and Frano **Supilo**, the Yugoslav Committee held that the **South Slavs** were entitled to their own state on the principles of national right and self-determination. Claiming to represent the interests of the South Slavs in the Habsburg Monarchy, it moved to London where it campaigned to win the support of the Allies for the political unification of the South Slavs. By the Declaration of **Corfu**, it agreed to cooperate with the Serbian government in establishing a South Slav state (July 1917). At the end of **World War I**, the National Council of **Slovenes**, Croats and Serbs in Zagreb authorized the Yugoslav Committee to act as its representative in international negotiations. After the Serbian regent, Alexander Karageorgević, accepted the Council's proposals (1 Dec 1918), the South Slavs were united for the first time within the Kingdom of Serbs, Croats and Slovenes (later Yugoslavia). ▷ **Yugoslavs**

Yugoslavia
A federal republic in the Balkan peninsula of south-east Europe, consisting since 1992 of the republics of Serbia and Montenegro. Serbs, **Croats**, and Slovenes united under one monarch in 1918 and the region was renamed Yugoslavia in 1929. Yugoslavia was occupied by Germany during **World War II**, and a Federal People's Republic was established at the end of the war in 1945. Following a break with the Soviet Union in 1948, the country followed an independent form of communism and a general policy of nonalignment. At the end of the 1980s political disagreement between the federal republics increased, and in 1989 Slovenia declared its sovereignty and its strong opposition to the Communist Party. In an attempt to preserve Yugoslavian unity the Government announced plans to allow a multiparty system with direct elections, but ethnic unrest in Serbia and Croatia placed further strains on the federal

system. Croatia and Slovenia ceded from Yugoslavia in 1991 and Bosnia-Herzegovina in 1992, followed by Macedonia which declared its independence in 1992. Since 1991 there has been prolonged civil war and atrocities between ethnic factions in Bosnia-Herzegovina, forcing economic sanctions by the **UN**. A new Federal Republic of Yugoslavia consisting of Serbia and Montenegro was declared in Apr 1992 but is unrecognized by the United Nations. In 1992 rigorous sanctions were imposed upon Yugoslavia, regarded as a supply route and ally for the Serbian forces in Bosnia-Herzegovina.

Yugoslavs

Literally the 'South Slavs', this was the collective name for the members of several different nations which formed part of Yugoslavia from 1929 to 1991. While the Serbs, **Croats**, Slovenes, Bosnian Muslims and Macedonians are all South Slavs, Yugoslavia had many non-Slav inhabitants including the Hungarians in the **Vojvodina** and the Albanians in Kosovo. At the end of **World War I**, the South Slavs of the former Habsburg Monarchy, the Croats, Slovenes and some Serbs were joined to the Serbs of the Kingdom of Serbia and Montenegro within a new independent state, the Kingdom of Serbs, Croats and Slovenes, later renamed the Kingdom of Yugoslavia (1929). During **World War II**, Yugoslavia capitulated to the Axis forces and puppet governments were established in Zagreb and Belgrade. The resentment which had built up during the inter-war years among different nations within Yugoslavia combined with longstanding national rivalries to erupt in a 'civil war' of brutal reprisals; the only semblance of 'Yugoslav' unity remained in the communist-led partisan army which waged a brave and effective tactical campaign against the occupying Axis forces. After the war, **Tito**'s version of **communism** promised to neutralize old national rivalries and to unite the nations of Yugoslavia in pursuit of a common future. While Yugoslavia was reorganized as a federation of six republics and two autonomous provinces, each of which was based around a core nation, the different nationalisms were strictly repressed and the expression of national identities stifled. Uneven economic development among the republics, however, continued to fuel resentment among the nations. After Tito's death, nationalisms resurfaced and Yugoslavia fell into political and economic decline. When the President of Bosnia and Herzegovina, Alia Izetbegović, declared his republic's secession in Mar 1992, international recognition again followed, but the Yugoslav National Army and nationalist militia groups fought to divide the republic on ethnic lines, plunging the civilian population into a brutal war. ▷ **AVNOJ; Bosnia and Herzegovina; Chetniks; Dalmatia; Istria; Macedonia; Ustaša**

Z

Zachariadis, Nikos (1903–73)

Greek political leader. The son of a tobacco worker, he was one of the many Greeks who were forced to leave Anatolia in 1923 after the **Graeco-Turkish War** and who became communists. He was Secretary-General of the **KKE** (Communist Party of Greece) from 1931 to 1941. Imprisoned during **World War II** in **Dachau** concentration camp, he lived to return home in 1945 to direct communist opposition to the British-backed Greek government and resumed his post as Secretary-General of the KKE. Believing that the communists would achieve their victory in the towns, he quickly came into conflict with Markos **Vafiadis**, who was based in the country, and succeeded Vafiadis as commander of the Democratic Army in 1949. ▷ **Lausanne, Treaty of**

Zaghlul, Sa'd (c.1857–1927)

Egyptian politician and lawyer. Effectively the founder of the Egyptian **Wafd Party**, he headed a campaign to change the political position of Egypt, leading the delegation (*wafd*) of Egyptians who petitioned Britain for an end to the protectorate. This petition failed and, as a result, he was banished to Malta (1919). Anti-British riots followed and he was released, later achieving the desired recognition of independence for Egypt. After varying fortunes, during the course of which he was once more arrested and banished, Zaghlul eventually led his Wafd Party to success in Egypt's first election. By 1924 Zaghlul had become Egypt's first Prime Minister; a modern campaign conducted during the first Wafd government meant, however, that despite the success once more of the Wafdists in the 1926 election, the British refused to accept Zaghlul as Prime Minister. He was allowed, though, to become President of the Chamber, a cabinet containing six members of the Wafd, three Liberals and an independent, with the cabinet as a whole headed by the Liberal leader. Zaghlul, however, relinquished office shortly afterwards.

Zahir Shah, Mohammed (1914–)

King of Afghanistan (1933/73). Educated in Kabul and Paris, he was Assistant Minister for National Defence and Education Minister before succeeding to the throne in 1933 after the assassination of his father, Nadir Shah. His reign was characterized by a concern to preserve neutrality and promote gradual modernization. He became a constitutional monarch in 1964, but, in 1973, while in Italy receiving medical treatment, was overthrown in a republican coup led by his cousin, General Daud Khan, in the wake of a three-year famine. Since then he has lived in exile in Rome and remains a popular symbol of national unity for moderate Afghan opposition groups.

Zahle, Carl Theodore (1866–1946)
Danish politician. After studying law, he became a member of the Danish parliament, **Folketinget**. In Jan 1905, he and seven other members were expelled from the then leading Danish political party, *Venstrereformpartiet* ('Left Reform Party'), because they advocated a reduction in Denmark's defence expenditure. In response to the expulsion, Zahle in May 1905 became one of the founding members of a new centre party, *Det Radikale Venstre* ('The Radical Left'), which was to develop into a major middle-ground force of Danish pre-war and inter-war politics. It was a socially committed, non-socialist party that wanted Denmark declared 'lastingly neutral' and the working-class party, *Socialdemokratiet*, drawn into the democratic process. The party's core electorate was made up of the unusual alliance of smallholders, schoolteachers and Copenhagen academics. As early as Oct 1909, Det Radikale Venstre formed its first, shortlived government, with Zahle as Premier. After the general election in 1913, he headed a much stronger government which, supported by the Social Democrats, secured the Danish policy of neutrality during **World War I**. After the war, there was in financial and nationalistic circles a growing dissatisfaction with Zahle's government which resulted in his being dismissed by the Danish King, **Christian X**, on 29 Mar 1920, causing the so-called Easter Crisis.

Zaire, formerly **Congo Free State** (1885–1908), **Belgian Congo** (1908–60), **Democratic Republic of the Congo** (1960–71)
A central African republic. Belgian claims to the area were recognized in 1895 at the Berlin Conference, and the Congo Free State became a Belgian colony in 1908, renamed the Belgian Congo. It gained independence in 1960, but the mineral-rich Katanga (later Shaba) province also claimed independence, leading to civil war. The UN peace-keeping force maintained a presence until 1964. The country was renamed Zaire in 1971, but there was further conflict in 1977–8. Power struggles in the early 1990s coupled with ethnic unrest in Shaba, Kivu and Kasai provinces in 1993 resulted in many deaths.

Zalygin, Sergei Pavlovich (1913–)
Soviet fiction writer. Born in the Bashkin autonomous region, he spent much of his life in Siberia. He came into his own under Mikhail **Gorbachev**, being one of the main campaigners against the project to reverse the Siberian rivers. In 1986 he became Chief Editor of *Novy Mir* and

was responsible for securing the publication of Solzhenitsyn's previously banned works.

Zambia, formerly **Northern Rhodesia**

A republic in southern Africa. David Livingstone's discovery of the Victoria Falls in 1855 brought European influence to the area, and it was administered by the British South Africa Company under Rhodes during the latter half of the 19c, with Northern and Southern Rhodesia declared a British sphere of influence in 1888. Northern Rhodesia took its name in 1911 and became a British protectorate in 1924. Massive copper deposits were discovered there in the late 1920s. It joined with Southern Rhodesia and Nyasaland as the Federation of Rhodesia and Nyasaland in 1953, but the Federation dissolved in 1963. The country gained independence in 1964 and the first multiparty elections since independence were held in 1991. An unsuccessful coup attempt was made in 1993.

Zamyatin, Evgeny Ivanovich (1884–1937)

Russian novelist and short-story writer. He was exiled in 1905 after joining the Bolshevik Party, and again in 1911, but on each occasion soon returned to Russia. In 1921 he was a founder member of the Modernist group, the Serapion Brothers, and was briefly imprisoned by the Soviets in 1922. In 1932 he travelled to Paris, where he remained until his death. He is best known for the novel *My* (1920, We). ▷ **Bolsheviks**

ZANU (Zimbabwe African National Union)

The party which was formed in 1963, under the leadership of Ndabaningi **Sithole**, as a breakaway from **ZAPU** in opposition to ZAPU's strategy. The party split again, as a result of which Robert **Mugabe** became leader. Banned from Southern Rhodesia, the party relocated to Mozambique and became, through its military wing, the Zimbabwe African National Liberation Army (ZANLA), the most effective guerrilla movement. Associated with ZAPU in 1976 to form the Patriotic Front, it nevertheless fought the 1980 elections separately as ZANU (PF) and won 57 of the 80 seats available to black voters. It has been the dominant party since then, increasing its majorities at both subsequent general elections. In 1988, after long discussions, it absorbed **Nkomo**'s wing of the **Patriotic Front**.

Zapata, Emiliano (1879–1919)

Mexican revolutionary. The son of a mestizo peasant, he became a sharecropper and local peasant leader. After the onset of the Mexican Revolution, he occupied estates by force and mounted a programme for the return of land in the areas he controlled to the native Indians. He initially supported Francisco **Madero** and, with a small force of men was largely responsible for toppling the dictatorship of Porfirio **Díaz**. Along with Pancho **Villa**, he subsequently fought the **Carranza** government. Meanwhile, he continued to implement agrarian reforms in the southern area under his control, creating impartial commissions responsible for land distribution and setting up the Rural Loan Bank. He was eventually lured to his death at the Chinameca hacienda in Morelos.

Zapotocky, Antonin (1884–1957)
Czechoslovak trade unionist and politician. A stonemason from Kladno, he was active in the socialist youth movement from 1900 and in the Socialist Party from 1907. In 1920 he was a major organizer of an unsuccessful general strike, and in 1921 helped found the Communist Party. Imprisoned during **World War II**, he emerged in 1945 to become the President of the revolutionary trade-union organization that played a key role in seizing power in 1948. He was appointed Prime Minister and succeeded to the presidency when Klement **Gottwald** died unexpectedly in 1953. His responsibility for the purges was probably less than Gottwald's, but despite the moderation of old age, he lost much of the opportunity to make amends.

ZAPU (Zimbabwe African People's Union)
Founded in 1961 with Joshua **Nkomo** as its leader, in the 1960s it was the most popular party in Southern Rhodesia, espousing the end to white minority rule. It was banned in 1964 and moved to Zambia where it organized, through its military wing, the Zimbabwe Independent People's Revolutionary Army (ZIPRA), guerrilla attacks within Southern Rhodesia. It reassociated itself with **ZANU** to form the Patriotic Front (**PF**) in 1976, but fought the independence elections in 1980 independently from its partner, although under the Patriotic Front label. It became effectively an Ndebele Party and finally fused with **ZANU (PF)** on 1988.

Zaslavskaya, Tatyana Ivanovna (1927–)
Soviet economist, sociologist and political reformer. Born into an academic family in Kiev, she was educated and researched in economics in Moscow until in 1963 she joined **Aganbegyan** in Novosibirsk and turned her attention to sociology. In the early 1980s she came into contact with Mikhail **Gorbachev** through her writings on the countryside and at the same time earned herself a reputation for criticism of Soviet life. In 1988 she returned to Moscow to head a centre devoted to the study of public opinion and became in effect a most influential member of Gorbachev's reform team, including the Congress of Deputies.

Zaydis
A moderate Shiite grouping who take their name from Zayd, son of the fourth Imam, 'Ali Zayn al-Abidin. 'Ali's son, Muhammad al-Baqir, is the traditionally accepted fifth Imam of both the Seveners (Isma'ilis) and

the Twelvers (Ithna ashariyya). Of a more militant disposition than his elder brother, Muhammad, Zayd attracted his own following. In modern times most Zaydis are to be found in the Yemen. Under Turkish rule from 1517 to 1918, the Zaydi Imam Yahya was established as ruler of the Yemen as a kingdom, principally with support from the British in Aden. Assassinated in 1948, Yahya was succeeded by his son, Ahmad, who ruled until 1962. Despite the subsequent proclamation of Yemen as a republic, discontent having been principally fomented by Gamal Abd al-**Nasser**'s Egypt, the religious basis of the Yemen continues to be principally Zaydi, with pockets of Isma'ilism principally in the Jabal Haraz.

Zeeland, Paul van (1893–1973)
Belgian politician. He studied law and political science at Leuven (Louvain) University, where he held a chair from 1928 to 1963. He first became cabinet minister (without portfolio) in 1934, and in 1935–7 was Prime Minister and Minister of Foreign Affairs. Having spent **World War II** in England, he became Minister of Foreign Affairs (1949–54), and was intensively involved in the moves towards European union during those years.

Zenkl, Peter (1884–1975)
Czechoslovak politician. Born in Tabor and educated in Prague, he was a relatiely late entrant to politics. He was elected to the city council in 1923 as a National Socialist (Czechoslovak-style, totally different from **Nazi Party**) and became Mayor in 1937. He became a government minister just before the **Munich Agreement** and remained one for a few more months. He was then imprisoned in **Buchenwald** concentration camp. In 1945 he resumed as Mayor but became a deputy prime minister in the National Front government in 1946. In 1948 he was one of those who resigned to provoke a fresh election and instead gave the communists an excuse for their **February Revolution**. He died in exile.

Zervas, Napoleon (1891–1957)
Greek resistance leader. In 1926 with General Kondylis he led a coup against the military dictatorship of General Pangalos (1925–6). During **World War II** he was the leader in Greece of the non-communist resistance movement **EDES**, the National Republican Greek League. At the end of the war he bitterly opposed the communists in their attempts to seize power. ▷ **EAM; EKKA; ELAS; Plastiras, Nikolaos**

Zhang Guotao (Chang Kuo-t'ao) (1897–1979)
Chinese politician. As a student he played a part in the **May Fourth Movement** of 1919, and in 1921, as a founding member, joined the new Chinese Communist Party. He rose to prominence as a labour leader and played a leading role in the Nanchang Mutiny (1927). He opposed the

elevation of **Mao Zedong** as Leader of the Party, but his army was destroyed by Muslim forces in the north-west. He defected to the **Guomindang** in 1938. When the Chinese Communist Party won national power in 1949, he moved to Hong Kong.

Zhao Ziyang (Chao Tzu-yang) (1918–)
Chinese politician. He joined the Communist Youth League (1932) and worked underground as a Chinese Communist Party (CCP) official during the liberation war (1937–49). Zhao rose to prominence implementing land reform in Guangdong, becoming the province's CCP First Secretary in 1964. As a supporter of the reforms of **Liu Shaoqi**, he was dismissed during the **Cultural Revolution**, paraded through Canton in a dunce's cap and sent to Nei Monggol. However, enjoying the support of **Zhou Enlai**, he was rehabilitated (1973) and appointed Party First Secretary of China's largest province, Sichuan (1975). Here he introduced radical and successful market-orientated rural reforms, which attracted the eye of **Deng Xiaoping**, leading to his induction into the CCP Politburo as a full member in 1979 and his appointment as Prime Minister a year later. As Premier, he oversaw the implementation of a radical new 'market socialist' and 'open door' economic programme, and in 1987 replaced the disgraced **Hu Yaobang** as CCP General-Secretary, relinquishing his position as Premier. However, in June 1989, like his predecessor, he was controversially dismissed for his allegedly overly liberal handling of the **Tiananmen Square** pro-democracy demonstrations.

Zhdanov, Andrei Alexandrovich (1896–1948)
Soviet politician. A school inspector's son, he joined the **Bolsheviks** in 1915 and took part in the 1917 **Russian Revolution** and the **Russian Civil War**. He then rose through the Communist Party bureaucracy until in 1934 he became Secretary of the Central Committee and in 1939 was appointed to the **Politburo**. He performed a prominent role in the defence of **Leningrad** from 1941 to 1944, and subsequently assumed responsibility for ideological purity, bitterly attacking the West and its alleged imitators in the USSR.

Zhivkov, Todor (1911–)
Bulgarian politician. A Communist Party member since 1932, in **World War II** he fought in the resistance movement that in 1944 overthrew the pro-German Sofia regime. He was made Party Secretary in 1954 and Prime Minister in 1962 and, as Chairman of the Council of State from 1981, he was effectively the republic's President. In 1989 Zhivkov was replaced by Petur Mladenov as leader of the Bulgarian Communist Party, and in 1990 he was indicted on charges of 'especially gross embezzlement'. When his trial began in Feb 1991, he pleaded not guilty, complaining that the trial was 'a farce'.

Zhou Enlai (Chou En-lai) (1898–1976)
Chinese politician. One of the leaders of the Chinese Communist Party (CCP), he was Prime Minister of the Chinese People's Republic from its inception (1949) until his death. After pursuing his studies in Japan, he returned to China after the 1919 **May Fourth Movement**. Imprisoned in 1920 as an agitator, on his release he spent four years in Europe, where he dedicated himself to the communist cause. In 1927, under the first of the **United Fronts**) he organized the revolt in Shanghai for the **Guomindang**; he became a member of the CCP Politburo later the same year. In 1932 he was appointed to succeed **Mao Zedong** as Political Commissar of the Red Army, but after 1935, following Mao's elevation, he served him faithfully, becoming the Party's chief negotiator and diplomat. As Prime Minister (1949–76) and Minister of Foreign Affairs (1949–58) he vastly increased China's international influence. Perhaps his greatest triumph of mediation was in the **Cultural Revolution** in China, when he worked to preserve national unity and the survival of government against the forces of anarchy. ▷ **Chiang Kai-shek; Comintern; communism; Xi'an Incident**

Zhu De (Chu Teh) (1886–1976)
Chinese soldier. He was one of the founders of the Chinese Red Army and was closely associated throughout his later career with **Mao Zedong**. Zhu took part in the Nanchang Mutiny (1927) and his defeated troops joined with those of Mao to found the **Jiangxi Soviet**. There, he and Mao evolved the idea of 'people's war', beating off attacks by **Chiang Kai-shek**'s vastly superior **Guomindang** forces until finally driven out in 1934. The Red Army then undertook the **Long March**, in which Zhu De was the leading commander. During the **Sino-Japanese War** (1937–45), he was in charge of the **Eighth Route Army**. After the Japanese surrender and the renewal of civil war in China (1946), Zhu was Supreme Commander of the renamed **People's Liberation Army**, which expelled the Nationalists from mainland China. He was Chairman of the Standing Committee of the National People's Congress from 1959. 'Purged' at the beginning of the **Cultural Revolution**, he was rehabilitated in 1967.

Zhukov, Giorgiy Konstantinovich (1896–1974)
Soviet marshal. He joined the **Red Army** in 1918, commanded Soviet tanks in Outer Mongolia (1939), and became army Chief-of-Staff (1941). He lifted the siege of Moscow, and in 1943 his counter-offensive was successful at the Battle of **Stalingrad**. In 1944–5 he captured Warsaw, conquered Berlin, and accepted the German surrender. After the war he was Commander of the Russian zone of Germany, and became Minister of Defence (1955), but was dismissed by Nikita **Khrushchev** in 1957. ▷ **World War II**

Zia, Begum Khaleda

Bangladeshi politician. The widow of General **Ziaur Rahman** who was President of Bangladesh from 1977 until his assassination in 1981, she became leader of the Bangladesh Nationalist Party (BNP) in 1982. In 1990, when President Hussain Muhammad **Ershad** was forced to resign, elections were called. The BNP's main contestant was the **Awami League** led by Sheikh Hasina Wajed; in the event, the latter only gained 30 per cent of the seats and in 1991 Begum Zia became the first woman prime minister of Bangladesh.

Zia ul-Haq, Muhammad (1924–88)

Pakistani general and President. He served in Burma, Malaya, and Indonesia in **World War II**, and in the wars with India (1965, 1971), rising rapidly to become general and Army Chief-of-Staff (1976). He led a bloodless coup in 1977, was President (1978–88), imposed martial law, banned political activity, and introduced an Islamic code of law. Despite international protest, he sanctioned the hanging of former President **Bhutto** in 1979. He was killed in an air crash near Bahawalpur.

Ziaur Rahman (1935–81)

Bangladeshi soldier and President. He played an important part in the emergence of the state of Bangladesh. Appointed Chief of Army Staff after the assassination of Mujibur Rahman (1975), he became the dominant figure within the military. President from 1977 to 1981, his government was of a military character, even after the presidential election of 1978 which confirmed his position. He survived many attempted coups, but was finally assassinated in Dhaka.

Zimbabwe, formerly **Southern Rhodesia**

A landlocked republic in southern Africa. Southern Rhodesia came under British influence in the 1880s as the British South Africa Company, under Cecil Rhodes, began exploitation of the rich mineral resources of the area. The region was divided into Northern and Southern Rhodesia in 1911, and Southern Rhodesia became a self-governing British colony in 1923. Northern and Southern Rhodesia and Nyasaland formed a multiracial federation in 1953, but Nyasaland and Northern Rhodesia gained independence in 1963. Opposition to the independence of Southern Rhodesia under African rule resulted in a Unilateral Declaration of Independence (UDI) by the White-dominated government in 1965, but economic sanctions and internal guerrilla activity forced the government to negotiate with the main African groups. Power eventually transferred to the African majority, and the country gained independence as Zimbabwe in 1980. Government plans for land distribution announced in 1992 caused unrest among white farmers.

Zimmermann, Arthur (1864–1940)

German politician. After diplomatic service in China, he directed from 1904 the eastern division of the German Foreign Office and was Foreign Secretary (Nov 1916–Aug 1917). In Jan 1917 he sent the famous 'Zimmermann telegram' to the German minister in Mexico with the terms of an alliance between Mexico and Germany, by which Mexico was to attack the USA with German and Japanese assistance in return for the US states of New Mexico, Texas and Arizona. This telegram finally brought the hesitant US government into the war against Germany. ▷ **World War I**

Zinoviev, Grigoriy Yevseyevich (1883–1936)

Russian revolutionary and politician. Educated at Berne University, in 1924 he was made a member of the ruling **Politburo**, but because of opposition to **Stalin**'s policies was expelled from the **Communist Party of the Soviet Union** (1926). Reinstated in 1928, he was again expelled in 1932, and in 1935 was arrested after the assassination of Kirov. Charged with organizing terrorist activities, he was executed following the first of Stalin's Great Purge trials in Moscow. The so-called **Zinoviev Letter** urging British Communists to incite revolution in Britain contributed to the downfall of the Labour government in the 1924 general elections. ▷ **Bolsheviks; Lenin; October Revolution**

Zionism

The movement which sought to recover for the Jewish people its historic Palestinian homeland (the *Eretz Israel*) after centuries of dispersion. The modern movement arose in the late 19c with plans for Jewish colonization of Palestine, and under Theodor **Herzl** also developed a political programme to obtain sovereign state rights over the territory. Gaining support after **World War I**, its objectives were supported by the British **Balfour Declaration** in 1917, as long as rights for non-Jews in Palestine were not impaired. After **World War II**, the establishment of the Jewish state in 1948 received **UN** support. Zionism is still active, as a movement encouraging diaspora Jews to immigrate to and take an interest in the Jewish state. ▷ **Aliyah; Israel, State of**

Zog I (1895–1961)

King of Albania (1928/39). Educated in Istanbul, he became leader of the Nationalist Party, and formed a republican government in 1922. Forced into exile in 1924, he returned with the assistance of Yugoslavia, and became President (1925–8), proclaiming himself King in 1928. After Albania was overrun by the Italians (1939), he fled to Britain, and later lived in Egypt and France. He formally abdicated in 1946, and died in France.

Zulu Kingdom

The Zulu kingdom was formed in the early 19c, when Shaka, building on the military achievements of his predecessor, Dingiswayo, welded the northern **Nguni** into an expansive and highly militarized state. His troops became a formidable fighting force, dispersing many of the other peoples of southern Africa far afield; however, they were defeated by the Boers and British, and much of their territory annexed. They have retained a strong self-identity, and are organized politically into the modern **Inkatha Freedom Party** under their leader Chief Gatsha **Buthelezi**. Their territory, greatly contracted, became one of the 'Homelands' of modern South Africa. ▷ **Afrikaners; KwaZulu**

Zveno

Literally 'the Link', this is the name given to the Bulgarian civilian organization, formed in 1927 under the leadership of Colonel Kimon Georgiev, which aimed at the modernization of Bulgaria through the development of technology and industry. The government of Colonel Damian **Velchev**, who had come to power in the 1934 military coup, implemented the Zveno programme and depended on the support of its members. During **World War II**, members of Zveno joined the communist-backed **Fatherland Front** and Georgiev became Prime Minister in the new Bulgarian government organized by the Front (Sep 1944). In 1946, when Zveno became the target of the communists, Georgiev was demoted in stages as the Soviet-backed Georgi **Dimitrov** established himself in power.

Zulu kingdom

Zulu kingdom [illegible]
[illegible]
[illegible]
[illegible]
[illegible]
Boers and much of their [illegible]
[illegible]
[illegible] in KwaZulu/Natal. Their [illegible]
[illegible]
[illegible]

Zveno

[illegible]
[illegible]
[illegible]
[illegible]
[illegible]
[illegible] programme and [illegible]
[illegible] During World War [illegible]
[illegible]
[illegible]
[illegible] when Zveno [illegible]
[illegible]
[illegible]